THE PAPERS OF ULYSSES S. GRANT

THE PAPERS OF

ULYSSES S. GRANT

Volume 15: May 1–December 31, 1865

Edited by John Y. Simon

ASSOCIATE EDITOR

David L. Wilson

EDITORIAL ASSISTANT

Sue E. Dotson

SOUTHERN ILLINOIS UNIVERSITY PRESS

CARBONDALE AND EDWARDSVILLE

Library of Congress Cataloging in Publication Data (Revised)

Grant, Ulysses Simpson, Pres. U.S., 1822–1885.
    The papers of Ulysses S. Grant.

    Prepared under the auspices of the Ulysses S. Grant Association.
    Bibliographical footnotes.
    CONTENTS: v. 1. 1837–1861—v. 2. April–September 1861.
—v. 3. October 1, 1861–January 7, 1862.—v. 4. January 8–March 31,
1862.—v. 5. April 1–August 31, 1862.—v. 6. September 1–December
8, 1862.—v. 7. December 9, 1862–March 31, 1863.—v. 8.
April 1–July 6, 1863.—v. 9. July 7–December 31, 1863.—v. 10.
January 1–May 31, 1864.—v. 11. June 1–August 15, 1864.—v. 12.
August 16–November 15, 1864.—v. 13. November 16, 1864–February 20, 1865.—v. 14. February 21–April 30, 1865.—v. 15. May 1–
December 31, 1865.
    1. Grant, Ulysses Simpson, Pres. U.S., 1822–1885. 2. United
States—History—Civil War, 1861–1865—Campaigns and battles
—Sources. 3. United States—Politics and government—1869–1877
—Sources. 4. Presidents—United States—Biography. 5. Generals—
United States—Biography. I. Simon, John Y., ed. II. Wilson, David
L. 1943–. III. Ulysses S. Grant Association.
E660.G756 1967   973.8′2′0924   67–10725
ISBN 0–8093–1466–5 (v. 15)

To Edith Grant Griffiths

Contents

Introduction

===

ON MAY 1, 1865, Lieutenant General Ulysses S. Grant was in Washington attempting to put an end to the Civil War. Two sizable Confederate armies surrendered during May: one under Lieutenant General Richard Taylor, commanding the Department of Alabama, Mississippi, and East Louisiana, the other under Lieutenant General Edmund Kirby Smith, commanding the Trans-Mississippi Department, the second only after the grand reviews in Washington of the largest U.S. armies. In the meantime, federal troops captured Confederate President Jefferson Davis and the remnants of his government. On May 29, President Andrew Johnson issued an amnesty proclamation affecting all participants in the "rebellion" with exceptions for wealthy and prominent rebels, and these were eligible for clemency which Johnson promised would be "liberally extended." Grant joined in these sentiments, believing that amnesty for Robert E. Lee "would have the best possible effect towards restoring good feeling and peace in the South." Despite Grant's urging, Lee remained one of the few rejected applicants.

As overall commander, Grant faced the problems of mustering out the volunteer forces and reorganizing the regular army for peacetime duties. He could not reduce the army to prewar size because he needed to retain troops in the South to maintain order and to protect the rights of freedmen. Concurrently, he sent a large military force to the Mexican border to put pressure on the government of Emperor Maximilian, installed as a puppet of Napoleon III of France, who had gambled on taking advantage of American disunion to build an empire in North

America. French rule could be eliminated, Grant observed sarcastically, "by observing the same sort of neutrality that has been observed towards us for the past four years." Other troops maintained an Indian frontier, where, Grant suggested, "the Indians require as much protection from the whites as the whites do from the Indians."

While Grant retained major military responsibilities, his trusted subordinates Major General Philip H. Sheridan in New Orleans and Major General William T. Sherman in St. Louis maintained surveillance and administration while the Grant family enjoyed both domestic reunion and opportunities to travel. Grant originally intended to establish a home in Philadelphia and commute to Washington but soon reunited the family in Georgetown. Throughout the North people sought visits from the Grants, and an extensive series of journeys took them up the East Coast into Canada, then to Galena for a few weeks in the new house given them by grateful townspeople. Near the close of the year, Grant inspected the South for Johnson, submitting a report in December, completing a busy year filled with matters great and small.

At the close of the Civil War, an officer could fill as many as four ranks simultaneously. For example, James Harrison Wilson, a captain and brevet colonel in the regular army, served as brigadier and brevet major general of volunteers. When mustered out of volunteer service, officers like Wilson reverted to their regular ranks without brevet unless especially assigned. Many still used volunteer or brevet rank in correspondence. Accordingly, confusion about rank bedeviled both army and public from the close of the war through the death of Lieutenant Colonel and Brevet Major General George A. Custer in 1876. A flood of letters concerning military personnel crossed the desk of the general in chief.

In order to ensure the completion of these volumes within reasonable limits of time and length, we have applied somewhat more stringent selection standards to incoming correspondence. After the war, numerous officers and their friends wrote directly to Grant or to his staff officers concerning promotions, by brevet or otherwise, and sought retention in the regular army. Others wrote concerning personal claims and issues involved in routine military administration. During Grant's absences from Washington, staff officers attended to routine matters of military housekeeping that might otherwise have received Grant's attention. In cases where Grant's involvement in the subject appeared to be minimal as evidenced by a brief endorsement penned by him or a member of his staff, no involvement by Grant could be demonstrated, or the subject did not shed much light on either Grant or his times, we have excluded some incoming correspondence with regret tempered by an intention to provide it for later scholarship through a microform supplement. Correspondence concerning military operations of the Civil War, the role of the army in Reconstruction, on the Mexican border, and on the western frontier is included even when Grant's involvement is minimal, and Grant himself dealt frequently enough with personnel and military administration so that material printed will provide an indication of what is omitted. More stringent selection standards largely affect the calendared items, and henceforth these volumes will continue to provide a comprehensive edition of substantive writings by Grant himself and thorough coverage of important incoming correspondence on subjects military, political, personal, or otherwise significant.

We are indebted to Sara Dunlap Jackson for assistance in searching the National Archives; to Harriet F. Simon for proofreading; and to Jane Cole and David Woodard, graduate students at Southern Illinois University, for research assistance.

Financial support for the period during which this volume was prepared came from Southern Illinois University, the National Endowment for the Humanities, and the National Historical Publications and Records Commission.

JOHN Y. SIMON

August 17, 1987

Editorial Procedure

===

1. Editorial Insertions

A.   Words or letters in roman type within brackets represent editorial reconstruction of parts of manuscripts torn, mutilated, or illegible.

B.   [. . .] or [— — —] within brackets represent lost material which cannot be reconstructed. The number of dots represents the approximate number of lost letters; dashes represent lost words.

C.   Words in *italic* type within brackets represent material such as dates which were not part of the original manuscript.

D.   Other material crossed out is indicated by ~~cancelled type~~.

E.   Material raised in manuscript, as "4th," has been brought in line, as "4th."

2. Symbols Used to Describe Manuscripts

AD	Autograph Document
ADS	Autograph Document Signed
ADf	Autograph Draft
ADfS	Autograph Draft Signed
AES	Autograph Endorsement Signed
AL	Autograph Letter
ALS	Autograph Letter Signed
ANS	Autograph Note Signed

D	Document
DS	Document Signed
Df	Draft
DfS	Draft Signed
ES	Endorsement Signed
LS	Letter Signed

3. *Military Terms and Abbreviations*

Act.	Acting
Adjt.	Adjutant
AG	Adjutant General
AGO	Adjutant General's Office
Art.	Artillery
Asst.	Assistant
Bvt.	Brevet
Brig.	Brigadier
Capt.	Captain
Cav.	Cavalry
Col.	Colonel
Co.	Company
C.S.A.	Confederate States of America
Dept.	Department
Div.	Division
Gen.	General
Hd. Qrs.	Headquarters
Inf.	Infantry
Lt.	Lieutenant
Maj.	Major
Q. M.	Quartermaster
Regt.	Regiment or regimental
Sgt.	Sergeant
USMA	United States Military Academy, West Point, N.Y.
Vols.	Volunteers

4. *Short Titles and Abbreviations*

ABPC	*American Book-Prices Current* (New York, 1895–)

CG   *Congressional Globe* Numbers following represent the Congress, session, and page.

J. G. Cramer   Jesse Grant Cramer, ed., *Letters of Ulysses S. Grant to his Father and his Youngest Sister, 1857–78* (New York and London, 1912)

DAB   *Dictionary of American Biography* (New York, 1928–36)

Garland   Hamlin Garland, *Ulysses S. Grant: His Life and Character* (New York, 1898)

HED   *House Executive Documents*
HMD   *House Miscellaneous Documents*
HRC   *House Reports of Committees* Numbers following *HED, HMD,* or *HRC* represent the number of the Congress, the session, and the document.

Ill. AG Report   J. N. Reece, ed., *Report of the Adjutant General of the State of Illinois* (Springfield, 1900)

Johnson, Papers   LeRoy P. Graf and Ralph W. Haskins, eds., *The Papers of Andrew Johnson* (Knoxville, 1967–)

Lewis   Lloyd Lewis, *Captain Sam Grant* (Boston, 1950)
Lincoln, Works   Roy P. Basler, Marion Dolores Pratt, and Lloyd A. Dunlap, eds.,*The Collected Works of Abraham Lincoln* (New Brunswick, 1953–55)

Memoirs   *Personal Memoirs of U. S. Grant* (New York, 1885–86)

O.R.   *The War of the Rebellion: A Compilation of the Official Records of the Union and Confederate Armies* (Washington, 1880–1901)

O.R. (Navy)   *Official Records of the Union and Confederate Navies in the War of the Rebellion* (Washington, 1894–1927) Roman numerals following *O.R.* or *O.R.* (Navy) represent the series and the volume.

PUSG   John Y. Simon, ed., *The Papers of Ulysses S. Grant* (Carbondale and Edwardsville, 1967–)

Richardson   Albert D. Richardson, *A Personal History of Ulysses S. Grant* (Hartford, Conn., 1868)

SED   *Senate Executive Documents*
SMD   *Senate Miscellaneous Documents*
SRC   *Senate Reports of Committees* Numbers following

SED, *SMD*, or *SRC* represent the number of the Congress, the session, and the document.

USGA Newsletter   *Ulysses S. Grant Association Newsletter*

Young   John Russell Young, *Around the World with General Grant* (New York, 1879)

5. *Location Symbols*

CLU   University of California at Los Angeles, Los Angeles, Calif.

CoHi   Colorado State Historical Society, Denver, Colo.

CSmH   Henry E. Huntington Library, San Marino, Calif.

CSt   Stanford University, Stanford, Calif.

CtY   Yale University, New Haven, Conn.

CU-B   Bancroft Library, University of California, Berkeley, Calif.

DLC   Library of Congress, Washington, D.C. Numbers following DLC-USG represent the series and volume of military records in the USG papers.

DNA   National Archives, Washington, D.C. Additional numbers identify record groups.

IaHA   Iowa State Department of History and Archives, Des Moines, Iowa.

I-ar   Illinois State Archives, Springfield, Ill.

IC   Chicago Public Library, Chicago, Ill.

ICarbS   Southern Illinois University, Carbondale, Ill.

ICHi   Chicago Historical Society, Chicago, Ill.

ICN   Newberry Library, Chicago, Ill.

ICU   University of Chicago, Chicago, Ill.

IHi   Illinois State Historical Library, Springfield, Ill.

In   Indiana State Library, Indianapolis, Ind.

InFtwL   Lincoln National Life Foundation, Fort Wayne, Ind.

InHi   Indiana Historical Society, Indianapolis, Ind.

InNd   University of Notre Dame, Notre Dame, Ind.

InU   Indiana University, Bloomington, Ind.

KHi   Kansas State Historical Society, Topeka, Kan.

MdAN   United States Naval Academy Museum, Annapolis, Md.

MeB	Bowdoin College, Brunswick, Me.
MH	Harvard University, Cambridge, Mass.
MHi	Massachusetts Historical Society, Boston, Mass.
MiD	Detroit Public Library, Detroit, Mich.
MiU-C	William L. Clements Library, University of Michigan, Ann Arbor, Mich.
MoSHi	Missouri Historical Society, St. Louis, Mo.
NHi	New-York Historical Society, New York, N.Y.
NIC	Cornell University, Ithaca, N.Y.
NjP	Princeton University, Princeton, N.J.
NjR	Rutgers University, New Brunswick, N.J.
NN	New York Public Library, New York, N.Y.
NNP	Pierpont Morgan Library, New York, N.Y.
NRU	University of Rochester, Rochester, N.Y.
OClWHi	Western Reserve Historical Society, Cleveland, Ohio.
OFH	Rutherford B. Hayes Library, Fremont, Ohio.
OHi	Ohio Historical Society, Columbus, Ohio.
OrHi	Oregon Historical Society, Portland, Ore.
PCarlA	U.S. Army Military History Institute, Carlisle Barracks, Pa.
PHi	Historical Society of Pennsylvania, Philadelphia, Pa.
PPRF	Rosenbach Foundation, Philadelphia, Pa.
RPB	Brown University, Providence, R.I.
TxHR	Rice University, Houston, Tex.
USG 3	Maj. Gen. Ulysses S. Grant 3rd, Clinton, N.Y.
USMA	United States Military Academy Library, West Point, N.Y.
ViHi	Virginia Historical Society, Richmond, Va.
ViU	University of Virginia, Charlottesville, Va.
WHi	State Historical Society of Wisconsin, Madison, Wis.
Wy-Ar	Wyoming State Archives and Historical Department, Cheyenne, Wyo.
WyU	University of Wyoming, Laramie, Wyo.

Chronology

═══

MAY 1. USG at hd. qrs. in Washington, D.C.

MAY 2. USG at Burlington, N.J.

MAY 3–5. USG at his Philadelphia home.

MAY 4. C.S.A. Gen. Richard Taylor surrendered troops in the Dept. of Ala., Miss., and East La. on the same terms given at Appomattox.

MAY 4. Abraham Lincoln buried at Springfield, Ill.

MAY 6. USG asserted that Robert E. Lee should be granted amnesty.

MAY 7. USG ordered the arrest of Robert M. T. Hunter and John A. Campbell. The following day he ordered the arrest of Zebulon B. Vance.

MAY 9. USG informed Julia Dent Grant that he could not leave Washington for Philadelphia because of the press of business.

MAY 10. C.S.A. President Jefferson Davis captured in Ga. by forces commanded by Bvt. Maj. Gen. James H. Wilson, and President Andrew Johnson issued a proclamation declaring that armed resistance had practically ended.

MAY 12. USG testified before the military commission trying the conspirators in the assassination of Lincoln.

MAY 14–15. USG, ill at Philadelphia, distressed by his inability to return to hd. qrs. "knowing the almost absolute necessity of my presence in Washington . . ."

MAY 17. USG assigned Maj. Gen. Philip H. Sheridan to command Tex. and La. to arrange for final surrender of C.S.A. forces and to prepare to exert pressure on the French in Mexico.

MAY 18.　USG testified before the Joint Committee on the Conduct of the War, praising Secretary of War Edwin M. Stanton for his wartime support.

MAY 18.　USG favored allowing former C.S.A. soldiers to return to their homes in northern states and also suggested that they be allowed to join the U.S. Army. He wanted to release military prisoners quickly so that they could get home in time to plant crops.

MAY 18.　USG directed Maj. Gen. Edward R. S. Canby to send a substantial military force to the Rio Grande to be commanded by Sheridan and also arranged to send the 25th Army Corps from Va. to Tex.

MAY 18.　USG accepted Maj. Gen. Henry W. Halleck's offer to use his home in Georgetown, D.C.

MAY 21.　USG instructed Maj. Gen. Frederick Steele concerning his role in the expedition to Tex. and directed Maj. Gen. George H. Thomas to send the 4th Army Corps from Tenn. to Tex.

MAY 22.　USG directed Steele to prevent the Ala. legislature from meeting.

MAY 22.　Johnson removed trade restrictions with the South excluding Tex.

MAY 23.　USG attended the grand review of the Army of the Potomac and the following day attended the review of Maj. Gen. William T. Sherman's army.

MAY 26.　The C.S.A. Army of Trans-Mississippi surrendered, the last significant force to do so.

MAY 28–29.　USG directed Canby and Maj. Gen. John M. Schofield to expedite cotton shipments to the North.

MAY 29.　Johnson issued an Amnesty Proclamation.

MAY 31.　USG recommended the gradual release of all C.S.A. prisoners captured in battle and also the release of all civilian prisoners.

JUNE 2.　USG issued General Orders No. 108 praising soldiers of the U.S.

JUNE 2.　USG suggested reorganization of army commands; Johnson issued the order on June 27.

JUNE 2.　USG recommended that free trade with the South be opened, renewing his application on June 19.

JUNE 8.   USG visited West Point.

JUNE 10–12.   USG attended a Chicago fair to benefit disabled soldiers and sailors.

JUNE 15.   USG approved Indian policies of Maj. Gen. John Pope and sent reinforcements to Ark.

JUNE 15.   USG instructed Sheridan to demand that the French return all C.S.A. arms and munitions taken into Mexico. USG had originally wanted Sheridan to take the arms by force if necessary, but Secretary of State William H. Seward secured modification of USG's instructions.

JUNE 16–20.   USG protected Lee from prosecution for treason.

JUNE 19.   USG advised Johnson to pursue an aggressive policy against the French in Mexico.

JUNE 20.   USG began writing his report of operations during the last year of the Civil War, completing his draft around July 16. The report was published in Dec.

JUNE 23.   Johnson terminated the blockade of the South.

JUNE 23–25.   USG at Philadelphia.

JULY 1.   USG directed Sheridan to prepare for "active service."

JULY 3–5.   USG traveled to Albany, N.Y., to attend a July 4 celebration.

JULY 7.   Four of the eight persons convicted of conspiring to assassinate Lincoln executed at Washington.

JULY 10.   USG reported that two-thirds of the vol. army had been mustered out and recommended that most vol. gens. also be mustered out.

JULY 13.   USG directed Sheridan to go to the Rio Grande to report on affairs.

JULY 15.   USG advised Johnson to send a U.S. commander to Mexico to fight against the French.

JULY 17.   USG directed Thomas and Maj. Gen. George G. Meade to reduce to a minimum the troops occupying the South.

JULY 20.   USG recommended naming Bvt. Col. Ely S. Parker to a commission to negotiate with Indian tribes.

JULY 24.   USG left Washington for an extended summer tour.

JULY 25–27.   USG, at West Point, arranged for Schofield to go to Mexico to command troops. Seward, however, diverted Schofield to France to represent U.S. military views to the French.

JULY 27–28. USG at Saratoga, N.Y.

JULY 29–AUG. 1. USG at Boston, then traveled through Maine.

AUG. 5–11. USG visited Canada at the invitation of British Maj. Gen. Charles Hastings Doyle. While in Montreal, Aug. 8, he requested amnesty for Montrose A. Pallen and Daniel M. Frost, both former residents of St. Louis.

AUG. 9. USG at Niagara Falls.

AUG. 12–14. USG at Detroit.

AUG. 13. USG instructed Sheridan to keep up pressure along the Rio Grande frontier.

AUG. 16–18. USG at Chicago.

AUG. 18. USG welcomed home to Galena by an enormous crowd and presented a house by leading citizens.

AUG. 19. USG recommended that paroled prisoners be allowed to leave the U.S. not to return without permission.

AUG. 23. USG at Dubuque, Iowa.

AUG. 24–28. USG on excursion to St. Paul, Minn.

SEPT. 4. USG at Milwaukee.

SEPT. 5. USG attended fair in Chicago.

SEPT. 6. USG directed Sheridan to reduce his forces to a minimum except in Tex.

SEPT. 8. USG informed Johnson of his conviction that "nonintervention in Mexican affairs will lead to an expensive and bloody war . . ."

SEPT. 10. USG arranged to meet with Sherman in St. Louis.

SEPT. 12. USG at Springfield, Ill.

SEPT. 13–22. USG at St. Louis.

SEPT. 23–OCT. 2. USG at Cincinnati making side trips to Covington, Ky., Indianapolis, Ind., and Batavia, Bethel, and Georgetown, Ohio.

OCT. 3. USG at Columbus, Ohio.

OCT. 4. USG at Pittsburgh, Pa.

OCT. 6. USG returned to Washington.

OCT. 14. USG reinforced Pope.

OCT. 18. USG sent staff officer to Ky. to investigate political affairs.

OCT. 20. USG made suggestions to Stanton concerning reorganization of the U.S. Army, making additional recommendations on Nov. 3.

Nov. 3. USG arranged to rent his Philadelphia house after purchasing a house in Washington.

Nov. 6. USG defended the U.S. Army against French accusations of unneutral behavior along the Rio Grande.

Nov. 7. USG recommended amnesty for James Longstreet.

Nov. 10. USG supported survey of the Isthmus of Panama to locate the best route to construct an American-controlled canal.

Nov. 13. USG directed Halleck, commanding U.S. troops in Calif., to revoke an order preventing arms and munitions from passing into Mexico.

Nov. 13–21. USG in New York City attended a reception in his honor at the Fifth Avenue Hotel on Nov. 20.

Nov. 26. USG instructed Maj. Gen. Edward O. C. Ord to prevent Irish nationalists, Fenians, from invading Canada.

Nov. 27–Dec. 11. At Johnson's request, USG made a tour of the South, stopping at Richmond, Raleigh, Wilmington, Charleston, Hilton Head, Savannah, Augusta, Atlanta, and returning via Knoxville and Lynchburg.

Dec. 16. USG arranged for Matías Romero, Mexican minister, to communicate with his forces using the U.S. military telegraph.

Dec. 18. USG reported to Johnson on his Southern tour.

Dec. 18. The Thirteenth Amendment to the U.S. Constitution, abolishing slavery, declared in effect.

Dec. 18. USG submitted recommendations to the House of Representatives concerning the reorganization of the U.S. Army.

Dec. 30. USG ordered Meade and Sheridan to reduce further remaining vol. forces.

The Papers of Ulysses S. Grant
May 1–December 31, 1865

To Brig. Gen. Lorenzo Thomas

———

Washington May 1st 1865

THE ADJUTANT GENERAL OF THE ARMY
WASHINGTON D, C,

In compliance with G, O, No, 244 War Dept, series of 1863, I have the honor to report the following named Officers as comprising my Staff, and on duty with me as such during the Month of April

Brevet Maj, Gen, Jno A, Rawlins Chief of Staff

Brevet Col, T. S. Bowers Asst, Adjt, Genl,

Brevet Brig Gen, C. B. Comstock Aid de Camp on Special duty with Gen Canby until Apr 25th/65

Brevet Col, O, E, Babcock Aid-de-Camp

Brevet Col, Horace Porter Aid-de-Camp

Brevet Col, F, F, Dent Aid-de-Camp Brig, Gen, Ap'l 5th and assigned to duty in Richmond

Brevet Maj, Gen, S, Williams Asst, Insp Genl,

Brevet Col, Adam Badeau Military Secretary

Brevet Col, E. S. Parker Military Secretary

Major Geo, K, Leet Asst, Adjt, Genl,

Brevet Major P, T, Hudson Aid-de-Camp[1]

Captain H, C, Robinette Aid-de-Camp Brevetted Maj, April 9th 1865[2]

Captain Robt T, Lincoln Asst, Adjt, Gen,

Lieut, Wm M, Dunn Jr, Actg Aid-de-Camp Promoted Capt, & A, A, G, Ap'l 9th 1865

Lieut, D, E, Porter Actg-Aid-d-Camp Brevetted Capt, Ap'l 9th
      1865
Capt, Amos Webster Asst, Qr, Mr, Brevetted Maj, Apl, 9th 1865
                              Very Respectfully
                              Your obt svt
                              U. S. GRANT
                              Lieut, Genl,

Copies, DLC-USG, V, 46, 76, 108; DNA, RG 108, Letters Sent.

1. On May 1, 1865, Bvt. Col. Theodore S. Bowers wrote to Brig. Gen. Lorenzo Thomas. "Please announce in Order of this date, if practicable, Capt. Peter. T. Hudson A. D. C. as A. D. C. on the Staff of the Lieut General with the rank of Lieut. Colonel vice Lieut Col F. T. Dent promoted Brig. Genl." LS, *ibid.*, RG 94, Letters Received, 434A 1865. See *O.R.*, I, xlvi, part 3, 1057.

2. On March 14, USG telegraphed to Bvt. Brig. Gen. James A. Hardie. "Please inform me if a vacancy has occured in the 1st Inf.y which promotes Capt. Robinette A. D. C. to a Captaincy in the line. If so I wish to have him ordered to his company and his Staff appointment cancelled." ALS (telegram sent), Kohns Collection, NN; telegram received (at 5:00 P.M.), DNA, RG 94, ACP, G74 CB 1865. On the same day, Hardie telegraphed to USG. "There is no vacancy in the first Infantry which will promote Robinett to be Captain—He is senior first lieutenant in his regiment however." ALS (telegram sent), *ibid.*, RG 107, Telegrams Collected (Bound). On May 3, Bowers wrote to Thomas. "The Adjutant General of the Army Will please issue a special order releiving the following named officers from duty on the staff of the Lieut Gen Commanding and order them to report to their respective commands for duty: 1st Lieut H. C. Robinette, 1st Infantry, U S A. Capt and Brevet Major and AdC of Vols. 1st Lieut and Brevet Captain David E Porter Comp "E" 1st Regt Artillery, U S A." LS, *ibid.*, RG 94, ACP, C299 CB 1865.

To Maj. Gen. Lewis Wallace

Washington, D. C., May 1st *1864* 5. [*7:20* P.M.]
MAJ GEN. WALLACE
BALTIMORE MD

Direct that no recruits, substitutes or men returning to their regiments be sent to Wilmington [o]r Morehead City except for the 10th and 23d corps and that none be sent to City Point except for the 24th and 25th corps. Retain all others in camp at Baltimore for further orders

U. S. GRANT
Lt Gen

Telegram sent, DNA, RG 107, Telegrams Collected (Bound); telegram received (press), *ibid.* On May 1, 1865, Bvt. Col. Theodore S. Bowers wrote to Maj. Gen. Christopher C. Augur an almost identical message concerning the sending of troops to New Berne, N. C. LS, *ibid.*, RG 94, War Records Office, Washington. See *O.R.*, I, xlvii, part 3, 412. On the same day, Bvt. Maj. Gen. Montgomery C. Meigs wrote to USG. "Twenty-three hundred and fifty-two Substitutes and Soldiers, it appears from reports received at this Office, have been forwarded from Baltimore to City Point between the 26th & 29th April, both inclusive. As it is understood that the troops are about to be withdrawn, I respectfully call attention to this and suggest that it may be possible to avoid this Expenditure for the future." LS, DNA, RG 108, Letters Received.

Also on May 1, D. Sullivan, Baltimore, telegraphed to USG. "My Son Joseph Sullivan was with Genl. Lees Army, besides his Parole he has taken the Oath of Allegiance—He is ordered to leave here today at one (1) oclock, Please send me an order to prevent it" Telegram received, *ibid.*, Telegrams Received; copy, DLC-USG, V, 54. At 2:00 P.M., USG telegraphed to Maj. Gen. Lewis Wallace, and at 3:30 P.M. to Sullivan. "Why has Joseph Sullivan been [or]dered to leave after having taken the oath of allegiance? Rescind the orders and let all returned prisoners who take the oath voluntarily remain." "~~Your dispatch answered~~ Answer to your dispatch sent to Gn Wallace." ALS (telegrams sent), DNA, RG 107, Telegrams Collected (Bound); telegrams sent, *ibid.*; telegram received (1), *ibid.* (Press). At 6:45 P.M., Wallace telegraphed to USG. "Col. Woolley reports that one of his Assistants directed Sullivan to go North under the old order relating to deserters and refugees. This was a mistake. ~~Sin~~ My general directions ~~have are~~ were not to send off any body who has taken the oath of allegiance since Lee's surrender, until instructions are recieved from Secretary Stanton upon the questions, whether persons within the meaning of Attorney Gen. Speed's opinion ~~were to be~~ could be permitted to take the oath, and what effect the taking it would have upon the question of residence. In case those who ~~had~~ have taken the oath have the means and desire to leave, they ~~are~~ have been permitted to do so. ~~As to~~ As it is uncertain what order you desire me to rescind, cant I run up tonight, get your views exactly, and return on the morning train?" ALS (telegram sent), *ibid.*, Telegrams Collected (Unbound); *ibid.*, RG 393, Middle Dept. and 8th Army Corps, Telegrams Sent (Press); telegram received (at 7:00 P.M.), *ibid.*, RG 107, Telegrams Collected (Bound); *ibid.*, RG 108, Telegrams Received.

To Edwin M. Stanton

Burlington N. J.
10 p m May 2d 1865

HON E. M STANTON
SECY OF WAR

After leaving you last evening I had so many papers to examine that it escaped my memory to order Gen. Hancock to send a brigade ~~of~~ to Dover Del. Will you please direct it?

I would recommend that orders be given at once to muster out of service all the cavalry, whose term of service will expire before the first of September, with the view of getting clear of all that cannot be mounted with present stock of horses; also to consolidate what will be left—Two 2 regiments of Kilpatricks cavalry were ordered to turn over their horses, and to come to Alexandria by water. I would recommend mustering them out as soon as they arrive. I would also suggest that orders be given to the Quarter Master General to advertise and sell all horses and mules on hand not fit for immediate issue—

U S GRANT
Lt Gen

Telegram received (at 11:30 P.M.), DNA, RG 107, Telegrams Collected (Bound); copies, *ibid.*, RG 108, Letters Sent; DLC-USG, V, 46, 76, 108. *O.R.*, I, xlvi, part 3, 1066. See *ibid.*, p. 1090.

To Maj. Gen. Henry W. Halleck

From Philadelphia midnight May 4th *1865*

MAJ GEN H W HALLECK
RICHMOND VA

I gave Gen Hancock several days ago, verbal directions to treat all men in arms in Virginia as you propose to notify them you will do.

I wish you would have efforts made to arrest Smith, Hunter,[1]

Letcher[2] and all other particularly obnoxious political leaders in the state. I would advise offering a reward of five thousand dollars for Moseby if he is still in the state

U S GRANT

Lt Genl

Telegram received (on May 5, 1865, 11:00 A.M.), DNA, RG 107, Telegrams Collected (Bound); copies, *ibid.*, RG 108, Letters Sent; DLC-USG, V, 46, 76, 108. *O.R.*, I, xlvi, part 3, 1082. On May 4, 1:00 P.M., Maj. Gen. Henry W. Halleck telegraphed to USG. "Genl Meade has arrived here & the 2d & 5th corps will probably start from Manchester to-morrow. A squadron of cavalry sent to Lynchburg report that that city is held by about a thousand of Moseby's guerrillas & that parties are conscripting horses & arms in the country under orders of Gov. Smith. I have directed Genl Sheridan to send out a brigade of cavalry to capture them if possible & bring them in. Wheaton's Division of 6th corps has been ordered from Danille back to Burkesville. I propose to soon issue an order that all armed men in Va who do not surrender by a certain date shall be held as outlaws & robbers." ALS (telegram sent), DNA, RG 107, Telegrams Collected (Unbound); telegram received (at 4:30 P.M.), *ibid.*, Telegrams Collected (Bound); (at 11:00 P.M. in Philadelphia) *ibid.*, RG 108, Telegrams Received. *O.R.*, I, xlvi, part 3, 1081–82.

On May 5, 4:00 P.M., Halleck telegraphed to USG. "I ordered the arrest of Smith when I first arrived. I think he has gone to South Carolina. I have ordered Genl Schofield to endeavour to catch him. I have also ordered the arrest of Letcher. Hunter is said to be quietly at his home, advising all who visit him to support the union cause. His hostility to Davis did much to make him (Davis) unpopular in Va. Considering these, and the fact that President Lincoln advised against disturbing Mr. Hunter at this time, I would prefer not to arrest him unless specially ordered to do so. All classes are applying to take the amnesty oath, and those excluded from its benefit are nevertheless taking it and filing petitions for pardon. It would be unfortunate to check, by unnecessary arrests, this general desire for amnesty. Many of Genl Lee's officers have come forward to take the oath, and it is reported that even Lee himself is considering the propriety of doing so and of petitioning the President for pardon. Should he do so this, the whole population with few exceptions will follow his example." ALS (telegram sent), DNA, RG 107, Telegrams Collected (Unbound); telegram received (at 7:00 P.M.), *ibid.*, Telegrams Collected (Bound); *ibid.*, RG 108, Telegrams Received. *O.R.*, II, viii, 534.

On May 4, 2:30 P.M., Halleck telegraphed to USG. "Genl Rosser has offered to collect his command & surrender them at Staunton. I have ordered a regiment of cavalry there to recieve their arms & paroles. On its return it will be stationed at Gordonsville to preserve order & repress any incipient guerrillas. To supply it the Rail road should be reopened to that place. The company can do this in a few days, if permitted to purchase iron at the Tredegar workes. I shall direct the officer in charge to sell them what is required for that purpose, the money or obligation to pay, being held subject to the disposal of the government. By rendering these companies slight assistance to be paid for hereafter, I think these roads can be repaired & put in operation by them much cheaper than by the government. This of course will not affect the question of confiscating the stock of rebel stockholders." ALS (telegram sent), DNA, RG 107, Telegrams Collected (Unbound); telegram received (at 7:00 P.M.), *ibid.*, Telegrams Collected (Bound); *ibid.*, RG 108, Telegrams Received. *O.R.*, I, xlvi, part 3, 1082. At midnight, USG, Philadelphia, telegraphed to Secretary of War Edwin M. Stanton. "I think Hallecks notion of allowing railroads companies to rebuild their roads in Virginia the best to pursue. If you concur, will you please so telegraph." Telegram received (on May 5, 11:00 A.M.), DNA, RG 107, Telegrams Collected (Bound); copies, *ibid.*, RG 108, Letters Sent; DLC-USG, V, 46, 76, 108. *O.R.*, I, xlvi, part 3, 1081. See *ibid.*, p. 1091.

On May 3, Halleck had telegraphed to USG. "Would it not be well to repair the Petersburg & Weldon Road as far South as possible so as to meet Genl Sherman with supplies   it is reported to be in good order south of Stoney Creek" Telegram received (at 5:30 P.M.), DNA, RG 107, Telegrams Collected (Bound); (at 5:25 P.M.) *ibid.*, RG 108, Telegrams Received; copy, DLC-USG, V, 54. *O.R.*, I, xlvi, part 3, 1073; *ibid.*, I, xlvii, part 3, 380. On May 4, 10:00 A.M., USG, Philadelphia, telegraphed to Halleck. "There will be no need of repairing the Weldon road to supply Sherman. There would not be time to repair it out one days march from Petersburg before his troops will be up. Having no ammunition to haul they will find no difficulty in hauling supplies for the whole march" Telegram received (at 11:30 A.M.), DNA, RG 107, Telegrams Collected (Bound); copies, *ibid.*, RG 108, Letters Sent; DLC-USG, V, 46, 76, 108. *O.R.*, I, xlvi, part 3, 1081; *ibid.*, I, xlvii, part 3, 387.

On May 6, Governor Francis H. Peirpoint of Va. wrote to Stanton requesting that the U.S. rebuild trestle bridges. ALS, DNA, RG 107, Letters Received, V195 1865. On May 8, USG endorsed this letter. "I would not recommend Govt. to expend any money on the repairs of roads in the states which have been in rebellion except where it is necessary to do so to supply garrisons that must be kept up in the interior. I would recommend however that loyal stock holders of Southern roads be allowed every facility for repairing and running their roads at the earlyest possible day, under restrictions that will preclude the possibility of disloyal stock holders receiving any of the benefits accruing." AES, *ibid.*

1. On May 7, 9:00 P.M., USG telegraphed to Halleck. "Arrest R. M. T. Hunter and John A. Campbell and hold them prisoners in Richmond for further orders. They will be kept in prison. By order of the President" ALS (telegram sent), *ibid.*, Telegrams Collected (Bound); telegram sent, *ibid.*; copies, *ibid.*, RG 108, Letters Sent; DLC-USG, V, 46, 76, 108. *O.R.*, I, xlvi, part 3, 1106. On July 5, Robert M. T. Hunter, Fort Pulaski, wrote to USG. "You perhaps will be a little surprised at this letter asking you to interfere in my behalf. But from what I have seen & heard of you I believe you to be possessed of a kindly and magnanimous nature & I know that such persons value power and influence because of the good which it enables them to do. I have been now confined for about two months. I have taken the oath and applied not only for amnesty & pardon but for leave to go home on parole as has been allowed to Gov Brown to Mr Trenholm & I hear to Gov. Smith. If I was arrested under the idea that I would throw obstructions in the way of peace & the establishment of the Government policy it was a great a mistake. At the time of my arrest I was counselling the people to take the oath & submit & conform to the Government policy—I think you know that my disposition was pacific when I went down to the conference at Hampton Roads. That President Lincoln thought so is proved by the

fact that he ordered me to be sent for when he was in Richmond and expressed
the opinion that I would do what I could to aid him in reconstructing society &
Government in Virginia. That he was not mistaken in this expectation is well
known to my friends—But for the unhappy crime which ~~his pl~~ destroyed his life
~~he~~ I should have had no trouble which at least is my opinion—I write now to beg
that you will aid me to obtain a pardon & amnesty or at least permission to return
home on parole. I have been confined now for two months and this is no light
thing to a man of my age. I desire to return not to mingle in politics but to devote myself to the pursuits of private life—My desires are all for peace & a quiet
life for the remnant of my days. As a proof that I too would be glad to gratify
you if it were in my power I may I hope without impropriety refer to the fact
that upon our being informed by Col Mulford on our return from Old Point that
Col Dent was a prisoner, Judge Campbell the assistant Secty of War interfered
immediately and ordered his release. I mention this not by way of claiming it as
a favor confered but merely as evidence of a kindly disposition on our parts. I
will only add that if you will aid me in this matter you will confer on me an obligation which I shall never forget." ALS, DNA, RG 94, Amnesty Papers, Va.
On July 11, USG endorsed this letter. "Respectfully refered to the Atty. Gn. of
the United States. I have no special recommendation in this case further than
my conviction that all prisoners who are not to be tried should be released on
parole or otherwise as soon as some general plan for such releases can be agreed
upon." AES, *ibid.*

On May 8, Stanton wrote to USG. "The President directs that Z. B. Vance,
who has been claiming to act as Governor of North Carolina, be immediately
arrested, and sent under close guard to Washington. You will please issue orders
to carry this direction into effect." LS, *ibid.*, RG 108, Letters Received. At 11:00
P.M., USG telegraphed to Maj. Gen. John M. Schofield. "By direction of the
President you will at once arrest Zebulon B. Vance, late Rebel Governor of
North Carolina, and send him to Washington under close guard. Please acknowledge receipt of this order." Telegrams sent (2), *ibid.*, RG 107, Telegrams Col-
lected (Bound); telegram received, *ibid.*, Telegrams Collected (Unbound).
O.R., I, xlvii, part 3, 440. On May 9, 4:00 P.M., Schofield, Raleigh, telegraphed
to USG. "Your order to arrest the rebel Governor Vance is received and will be
executed at once" Telegram received (at 10:45 P.M.), DNA, RG 107, Telegrams
Collected (Bound); (2) *ibid.*, Telegrams Collected (Unbound); *ibid.*, RG 108,
Telegrams Received; copies, *ibid.*, RG 393, Dept. of N. C. and Army of the
Ohio, Telegrams Sent; DLC-USG, V, 54; DLC-John M. Schofield. *O.R.*, I, xlvii,
part 3, 450.

On May 12, 11:00 A.M., Schofield telegraphed to USG. "The rebel Governor
of South Carolina is at Spartansburg and can be arrested if it is desired." Telegram received (at 1:30 P.M.), DNA, RG 107, Telegrams Collected (Bound);
(2) *ibid.*, Telegrams Collected (Unbound); *ibid.*, RG 108, Telegrams Received;
copies, *ibid.*, RG 393, Dept. of N. C. and Army of the Ohio, Telegrams Sent;
DLC-USG, V, 54; DLC-John M. Schofield. *O.R.*, I, xlvii, part 3, 481. At 7:00
P.M., USG telegraphed to Schofield. "Arrest the Governor of S. C. if you can.
Hold him at New Berne or Wilmington for further orders." ALS (telegram sent),
DNA, RG 107, Telegrams Collected (Bound); telegram sent, *ibid.*; telegram
received (at 9:00 P.M.), *ibid.*, RG 393, Dept. of N. C. and Army of the Ohio,
Telegrams Received. *O.R.*, I, xlvii, part 3, 481. See *ibid.*, pp. 560–61, 565–66,
579, 588.

2. John Letcher, who had served as governor of Va. for four calendar years (1860–63), was arrested on May 20, 1865, and imprisoned in Washington, D. C., until July. F. N. Boney, *John Letcher of Virginia* (University, Ala., 1966), pp. 217–21.

To Maj. Gen. George H. Thomas

Philadelphia May 5th 1865 [*3:00* P.M.]

MAJ, GEN, G, H, THOMAS
NASHVILLE TENN

There is no use attempting to rebuild the road to Atlanta   A much cheaper and earlier way for supplying the Country where Gen, Wilson is can be found from the Sea, coast,   It may not be necessary for us to keep troops in the Interior

U. S. GRANT
Lieut, Gen,

Telegram, copies, DLC-USG, V, 46, 76, 108; DNA, RG 108, Letters Sent; *ibid.*, RG 393, Dept. of the Cumberland, Telegrams Received. *O.R.*, I, xlix, part 2, 613. On May 4, 1865, 10:00 P.M., Maj. Gen. George H. Thomas had telegraphed to USG. "Do you think it advisable to repair the R R to Atlanta. It may prove useful in holding control over the country" Telegram received (on May 5, 1:00 A.M.), DNA, RG 107, Telegrams Collected (Bound); (at Philadelphia, May 5, 10:00 A.M.) *ibid.*, RG 108, Telegrams Received; copies, *ibid.*, RG 393, Dept. of the Cumberland, Telegrams Sent; DLC-USG, V, 54. *O.R.*, I, xlix, part 2, 597. On May 1, Adna Anderson, Nashville, telegraphed to Bvt. Brig. Gen. Daniel C. McCallum. "The Construction Corps is now repairing the Railroad between Knoxville & Bristol & are within about twenty five (25) miles of the Virginia line,   If the railroad is not to be opened through to Lynchburg I can have most of the Construction Corps discharged at once. Please advise me" Telegram received (on May 2, 4:05 A.M.), DNA, RG 108, Telegrams Received; copy, DLC-USG, V, 54. *O.R.*, I, xlix, part 2, 549. On May 2, Bvt. Maj. Gen. Montgomery C. Meigs endorsed this telegram. "Respectfully referred to Lt Gen Grant with recommendation that all expenditure for repair or extension of repair of the Virginia & Tennessee Road Eastward be stopped by telegraphic order to Major Gen Thomas Commanding." AES, DNA, RG 108, Telegrams Received. *O.R.*, I, xlix, part 2, 549. On May 3, 12:30 P.M., Brig. Gen. John A. Rawlins telegraphed to USG, "Burlington or Philadelphia." "The Railroad between Knoxville and Bristol is finished to within twenty five miles of the Virginia State line. Shall the work be continued. Gen. Meigs recommends its discontinuance." Telegrams sent (2), DNA, RG 107, Telegrams Collected (Bound); telegram received, *ibid.*, RG 108, Telegrams Received. *O.R.*, I, xlix, part 2, 580. At 7:30 P.M., USG, Philadelphia, telegraphed to Rawlins. "Your telegram of 12 30 P M received   please order the work stopped" Telegram sent, DNA, RG 108, Telegrams Received; telegram received (at 8:40 P.M.), *ibid.*; *ibid.*, RG 107, Telegrams Collected (Bound). *O.R.*, I, xlix, part 2, 581. On the same day, Thomas telegraphed to USG. "Do you design opening the East Tenn. & Virginia R R through to Lynchburg or shall repairs be discontinued from this date? The road is completed to Jonesboro East. Tenn." Telegram received (at 8:00 P.M.), DNA, RG 107, Telegrams Collected (Bound); (at 7:50 P.M.) *ibid.*, RG 108, Telegrams Received; copies, *ibid.*, RG 393, Dept. of the Cumberland, Telegrams Sent; DLC-USG, V, 54. *O.R.*, I, xlix, part 2, 581. On May 4, 9:50 A.M., Rawlins telegraphed to Thomas. "You will order all work on the railroad between Knoxville and Bristol discontinued." Telegrams sent (2), DNA, RG 107, Telegrams Collected (Bound); copies, *ibid.*, RG 108, Letters Sent; DLC-USG, V, 46, 76, 108. Printed as received at 9:50 A.M. in *O.R.*, I, xlix, part 2, 597. On the same day, Rawlins wrote to Meigs. "I have the honor to inform you that Maj, Gen, George H, Thomas Commanding Department of the Cumberland has this day been ordered by telegraph to discontinue all work on the Knoxville and Bristol Railroad" Copies, DLC-USG, V, 46, 76, 108; DNA, RG 108, Letters Sent. On the same day, Thomas telegraphed to Rawlins. "Telegraphic order to discontinue to repairs on E T & Va R R recd and instructions issued accordingly" Telegram received (at 7:00 P.M.), *ibid.*, RG 107, Telegrams Collected (Bound); (at 6:45 P.M.) *ibid.*, RG 108, Telegrams Received; copies, *ibid.*, RG 393, Dept. of the Cumberland, Telegrams Sent; DLC-USG, V, 54. Printed as sent at noon in *O.R.*, I, xlix, part 2, 597.

To Maj. Gen. Henry W. Halleck

Washington May 6th 1865 [*1:00* P.M.]

MAJ. GN. HALLECK, ~~W~~RICHMOND VA.

Since receipt of your dispatch of of 3d I think it will be advisable to leave Hunter alone for the present.[1]

Although it would meet with opposition in the North to allow Lee the benefit of Amnesty I think it would have the best possible effect towards restoring good feeling and peace in the South to have him come in. All the people except a few political leaders South will accept what ever he does as right and will be guided to a great extent by his example.

U. S. GRANT
Lt. Gn.

ALS (telegram sent), USMA; telegram sent, DNA, RG 107, Telegrams Collected (Bound); copies, *ibid.*, RG 108, Letters Sent; DLC-USG, V, 46, 76, 108. *O.R.*, II, viii, 535–36.

1. See telegram to Maj. Gen. Henry W. Halleck, May 4, 1865, note 1.

To Maj. Gen. William T. Sherman

Hd Qrs. Armies of the U. States
Washington D. C, May 6th 1865

DEAR GENERAL,

Your letters to Rawlins and myself,[1] written but the day after my departure from Raleigh, have but just reached. I answered immediately but concluded not to mail to Petersburg thinking it doubtful whether, now that it is so late, it would reach you before you will be starting back. I will not furnish copies, of your letters to the Sec. of War and ask the publication of them until I see you.

I do not know how to answer your dispatch asking whether you should submit to Hallecks insult contained in a dispatch published in the New York Herald of the 28th.[2] I never saw that dispatch except as published in the papers. I question whether it was not an answer, in Hallecks style, to directions from the Sec. of War giving him instructions to do as he did. I do not know this to be the case although I have spoken to Mr. Stanton on the subject.

Your correspondence with Johnston has not yet been published. I have been absent from the City four or five days and returning to day and finding this to be so I requested its publication. It is promised for to-morrow.

Although I did not agree with you in the advisability of adopting your agreement with Johnston, of the 18th of Apl. yet it mayde no change in my estimate of the services you have rendered or of the services you can still render, and will, on all proper occasions. I know very well it is a difference of opinion which time alone will decide who was right.

Yours Truly
U. S. GRANT
Lt. Gn.

MAJ. GN. W. T. SHERMAN
COMD.G MIL. DIV. OF THE MISS.

ALS, DLC-William T. Sherman. *O.R.*, I, xlvii, part 3, 410.
On May 2, 1865, Maj. Gen. William T. Sherman, "In Savannah River,"

wrote to USG. "Capt Hosea is here with despatches for you and me from Genl Wilson at Macon. I have sent to him copies of the Terms of surrender made by Gen Johnston with copies of my orders 65. and 66., which devolved on him the parolling the prisoners there I have also sent him orders to destroy the Guns muskets and munitions that he cannot carry away and to move his command back to the neighborhood of Decatur Alabama, to report to me or Genl Thomas. Yesterday I sent up to Augusta the captured River Boat Jeff Davis loaded with sugar, coffee, bread & clothing for Gen Wilson which can go out to him by cars. By her I sent a small detachmt of 40 men, all she can carry to open communication with him and to occupy the Arsenal until relieved by a Brigade which Genl Gilmore will send up under command of Genl Molyneux. Another Boat the Amazon, loaded at Hilton Head will follow to day to Augusta so that Wilson should have in less than a week supplies to enable him to make his return march in all May. In Savannah the most admirable order is preserved, and I saw many People from the Interior who were overjoyed at the fact that the war is over, and all accept the acknowledged fact that slavery is forever dead. But as was to be expected an undefined fear exists because no one can give any clue to the form which their civil affairs may take. I have cautioned Gen Gilmore on this matter so that the administration can proceed in their own way to substitute some form of civil Government. I will go into Charleston tomorrow and thence return to Morehead City to confer with Gen Schofield by telegraph and when assured that all things are proceeding well in North Carolina will go to Richmond to meet my army which will begin to arrive there about the 12th inst. I should like to have orders meet me there. Inas much as the command of the Depts of the South & North Carolina were conferred on me to facilitate my operations in the Field, and as these are concluded, I shall abstain from exercising further command, except on the four Corps marching from Raleigh for Richmond." ALS, DNA, RG 94, Letters Received, 1006M 1865. *O.R.*, I, xlvii, part 3, 371–72. On May 14, USG endorsed this letter. "Respectfully forwarded to the Secretary of War" ES, DNA, RG 94, Letters Received, 1006M 1865.

1. On April 28, Sherman, Raleigh, wrote to USG. "Since you left me yesterday I have seen the New York Times of the 24, containing a Budet of Military News authenticated by the signature of the Secretary of War, which is grouped in such a way as to give very erroneous impressions. It embrases a Copy of the basis of agreemt between myself & Gen Johnston and myself of April 18 with Commentaries which it will be time enough to discuss two or three years hence, after the Governmt has experimented a little more in the machinery by which Power reaches the scattered People of the vast area of Country Known as the south; but in the meantime I do think howev that my Rank, if not past services, entitled me at least to the respect of Keeping secret what was Known to none but the Cabinet, until further inquiry could have been had made instead of giving publicity to documents I never saw, and drawing inferences wide of the Truth. I never saw or had furnished me a copy of President Lincolns despatch to you of the 3rd of March until after the agreemt nor did Mr Stanton or any human being ever convey to me its substance or any thing like it. But on the Contrary I had seen Gen Weitzells invitation to the Virginia Legislature made in Mr Lincoln's very presence and had failed to discover any other official hint of a Plan of reconstruction, or any ideas calculated to allay the fears of the People of the South, after the destruction of their armies and civil authorities would leave

them without any Governmt at all. We should not drive a People into anarchy,
and it is simply impossible for our Military Power to reach all the recesses of
their Unhappy Country. I confess I did not wish to ~~drive~~ break Gen Johnstons
Army into ~~fragments of roving~~ bands of armed men, roving about without purpose and capable only of infinite mischief. But you saw on your arrival that I
had my army so disposed, that his escape was only possible in a disorganized
shape: and as you did not choose to direct military operations in this quarter, I
infer you were satisfied ~~of~~ with the military situation. At all events the instant I
learned what was proper enough, the disapproval of the President, I acted in
such a manner as to compel the surrender of Gen Johnstons whole army on the
same terms you prescribed to Genl Lees Army when you had it surrounded and
in your absolute Power. Mr Stanton in stating that my orders to General Stoneman were likely to result in the escape of 'Mr Davis to Mexico or Europe' is in
deep error. Stoneman was not at Saulsbury then, but had gone back to 'Statesville'—Davis was supposed to be between us and therefore Stoneman was ~~going
straight from~~ beyond him. By turning towards me he was approaching Davis,
and had he joined me as ordered I ~~then~~ would have had a mounted force greatly
needed for that and other purposes. But even now I dont Know that Mr Stanton
wants Davis caught, and as my official papers deemed sacred are hastily published to the world it will be imprudent for me to state what has been done in
that respect. As the Editor of the Times has (it may be) logically and fairly
drawn from this singular document the conclusion that I am insubordinate I can
only deny the intention. I have never in my life questioned or disobeyed an order,
though many and many a time have I risked my life, my health and reputation
in obeying orders or even hints to execute plans and purposes not to my liking.
It is not fair to withhold from me plans and Policy, if any there be, and expect me
to guess at them. For facts and events appear quite different from different stand
Points. For four years I have been in Camp dealing with soldiers, and I can assure you—that the conclusion at which the Cabinet arrived with such singular
unanimity differs from mine. I conferred freely with the best officers in this
army as to the points involved in this controversy and strange to say they were
singularly unanimous in the other conclusion, and they will learn with pain and
amazement that I am deemed insubordinate & wanting in common sense, that I,
who in the complications of last year ~~cut the Gordian Knot in which our State
Affairs seemed entangled~~ worked day and night, summer and winter for the
Cause and the administration, and who ~~haves~~ brought an army of seventy thousand men in magnificent condition across a country deemed impassible, and placed
it just where it was wanted almost on the day appointed have brought discredit
on our Governmt. I do not wish to boast of this but I do say that it entitled me
to the courtesy of being consulted before publishing to the World a proposition
~~left open~~ rightfully submitted to higher authority for ~~the~~ proper adjudication,
and then accompanied by ~~such~~ other statements ~~as~~ which invited the Press to be
let loose upon me. It is true that non-combatants, men who sleep in comfort &
security whilst we watch on the distant Lines are better able to judge than we
poor soldiers, who rarely see a newspaper, hardly can hear from our families, or
stop long enough to get our Pay. I envy not the task of reconstruction, and am
delighted that the Secretary has relieved me of it. As you did not undertake to
assume the managemt of the affairs of this army I infer that on personal inspection your mind arrived at a different conclusion from that of the Secretary of
War. I will therefore go on and execute your orders to their conclusion, and when

done will with intense satisfaction leave to the Civil Authorities the execution of the task of which they seem to me so jealous. But as an honest man and soldier I invite them to follow my path, for they may see some things, and hear some things that may disturb their Philosophy. . . . P. S. As Mr Stantons singular paper has been published, I demand that this also be made public, though I am in no manner responsible to the ~~Public~~ Press, but to the Laws, and my proper superiors." ALS, *ibid.*, 1055M 1865. *O.R.*, I, xlvii, part 3, 334–35. On May 27, USG endorsed this letter. "Respectfully forwarded to the Secretary of War. This is the letter of Maj Gen Sherman, referred to in my note of the 19th inst., asking permission to withdraw the one addressed by him to Gen Rawlins, Chief of Staff, and forwarded by mistake to the War Department. This has not been before transmitted." ES, DNA, RG 94, Letters Received, 1055M 1865. *O.R.*, I, xlvii, part 3, 336. Secretary of War Edwin M. Stanton endorsed this letter. "Received May 27. 1 Oclock p m. Referred to the Adjt. General for publication" AES, DNA, RG 94, Letters Received, 1055M 1865. *O.R.*, I, xlvii, part 3, 336.

On April 29, 3:00 A.M., Sherman, Goldsboro, wrote to Brig. Gen. John A. Rawlins. "I worked all day at Raleigh and am now here en route to Charleston where I will instruct Gilmore to send in Georgia to Augusta to open communication with Wilson at Macon. I wish you would have the enclosed letter copied carefully and send a copy to Mr. Stanton, and say to him I want it published. The tone of all the papers of the 24th is taken up from the compilation of the War Dept. of the 22nd which is untrue, unfair and unkind to me, and I will say undeserved. There has been at no time any trouble about Joe Johnston's Army. It fell and became powerless when Lee was defeated, but its dispersion when the country was already full of Lee's men, would have made North Carolina a Pandemonium. I desired to avoid that condition of things. The South is broken and ruined and appeals to our pity. To ride the people down with persecutions and military exactions would be like slashing away at the crew of a sinking ship—I will fight as long as the enemy shows fight, but when he gives up and asks quarter I cannot go further. This state of things appeals to our better nature, and it was an outrage to torture my forbearance into the shape the Secretary has done. He has either misconceived this whole case, or he is not the man I supposed him. If he wants to hunt down Jeff Davis or the Politicians who have instigated Civil War let him use sheriffs, bailiffs and Catch Thieves, and not hint that I should march heavy columns of Infantry hundreds of miles on a fools errand. The idea of Jeff Davis runnig about the Country with tons of Gold is ridiculous—I doubt not he is a beggar and who will say that if we catch him, ~~that~~ he will be punished. The very men who now howl the loudest will be the first to intercede. But all this is beneath the dignity of the occasion and I for one will not stoop to it. We must if possible save our Country from Anarchy   I doubt not efforts will be made to sow dissension betwn Grant & myself on a false supposition that we have political aspirations, or after Killing me off by libels he will next be assailed. I can Keep away from Washgtn and I confide in his good sense to save him from the influences that will surround him there. I have no hesitation in pronouncing Mr Stantons compilatn of Apl 22, a gross outrage on me which I will resent in time. he knew I had never seen or heard of that Dispatch to Gnl Grant, till he sent it to me a few days ago, by Gen Grant himself, and the deduction from Stonemans order is exactly the reverse of the fact & truth, as an inspection of the map will show—Davis was supposed to be cached somewhere about Greensboro, & Stoneman was at Statesville to the West of Greensboro, and I could not communicate with him, because Johnston had more Cavalry than I. by getting him to me at Chapell Hill I would have had superior cavalry and on the renewal of hostilities I could have broken up Hampton, Butler and Wheeler and pursued Davis. But even Grant would not say that we had any interest to hunt up Davis. Look at the hunt after Booth with a hundred thousand dollars Reward—at your very Capital and in a friendly country, what would be the chances after Davis with all the Carolinas and Georgia to hide in. I will be with Gillmore for four or five days—he will be reinforced by two Brigades from here, and can occupy Augusta and Orangeburg,—I can then return to Morehead City, whence I can learn how Schofield progresses at Greensboro, when I will go to Petersburg to meet my marching columsns which ought to reach Richmond about the 12th or 14th. Thence I will report for orders. If the Northern papers take up as they will the lead Stanton has given, I will be obliged if you will send a copy of my letter to Gen. Grant and this to John Sherman, who will vindicate me. I cannot neglect current business and events. If however Gen. Grant thinks I have been outwitted by Joe Johnston, or that I have made concession to the Rebels, to save them from Anarchy, and us the needless expense of military occupation I will take good care not to embarrass him" ALS (facsimile—incomplete), Parke-Bernet sale, Nov. 14, 1978, no. 553; copies, DNA, RG 108, Letters Received; DLC-Edwin M. Stanton. *O.R.*, I, xlvii, part 3, 345–46. On May 15, USG endorsed this letter. "Respectfully forwarded to the Secretary of War for his information." Copy, DLC-Edwin M. Stanton. *O.R.*, I, xlvii, part 3, 346. Stanton also endorsed this letter. "Recd May 17th and Referred back to General Grant with permission to General Sherman to publish if he chooses to do so" AES, CtY. *O.R.*, I, xlvii, part 3, 346.

On May 19, USG wrote to Stanton. "I would respectfully request the return of the letter of Gen. Sherman to Gen. Rawlins, of the 29th ult. which was sent to the War Dept. through mistake. It enclosed a letter to me which sherman requested might be forwarded and publication asked." ALS, DLC-Edwin M. Stanton. *O.R.*, I, xlvii, part 3, 530. At 8:30 P.M., Stanton wrote to USG. "The letter of General Sherman to General Rawlins, dated Goldsboro', April 29, 3 A. M., and referred to me by your endorsement dated May 15th, is herewith returned, as requested by your note of this evening, received at 7.35. P. M. General Sherman's letter, forwarded by you, was received by me on the afternoon of the 17th, and permission to General Sherman to publish it endorsed thereon, of which you were informed the same evening; and when you expressed your wish to withdraw it, as having been sent to the Department through mistake, I desired time for consideration. As your request is now repeated, I return the letter, with assent to its publication, directing a copy to be retained on the files of the Department, so that General Sherman may have any benefit it can afford him. The letter which you mention as having been enclosed to you has not been received at this Department, and I do not understand from your letter that it was transmitted." LS, DNA, RG 108, Letters Received. *O.R.*, I, xlvii, part 3, 530.

2. On May 4, 9:00 P.M., Sherman, Morehead City, N. C., telegraphed to USG. "Just arrived from Savannah—All well in that quarter. Sent two boats with stores for Gen. Wilson up to Augusta. Gen. Gilmore will occupy Augusta and Orangeburg. The two brigades from here have sailed for Savannah. Have you any reason why I should longer submit to the insult contained in Gen. Hallecks dispatch in the New York papers of the twenty eighth. I will come to City Point in a few days Answer me there." Telegram received (on May 5, 10:30 A.M.),

DNA, RG 107, Telegrams Collected (Bound); (4—two misdated April 4) *ibid.*, Telegrams Collected (Unbound); (at Philadelphia) *ibid.*, RG 108, Telegrams Received; copy, DLC-USG, V, 54. *O.R.*, I, xlvii, part 3, 387–88.

To Maj. Gen. George H. Thomas

Washington May 6th/65 [*1:00* P.M.]

MAJ. GEN. THOMAS, NASHVILLE TENN.

Paroled prisoners surrendered by Lee & Johnston, and others entering into the same arrangement, will be allowed to return to their homes if within any of the states which Seceded. If belonging to other states they must take the oath of Allegiance first under the decission of the Attorney Gen.

Prisoners captured in battle are not to be allowed paroles nor the privilege of discharge in any way except on authority of the War Dept.

U. S. GRANT
Lt. Gn

ALS (facsimile telegram sent), Madigan Collection, NN; Thomas F. Madigan, Inc., *Autograph Letters Manuscripts and Historical Documents* (New York, 1935), p. 57; telegram sent (at 2:00 P.M.), DNA, RG 107, Telegrams Collected (Bound); copies, *ibid.*, RG 108, Letters Sent; *ibid.*, RG 393, Dept. of the Cumberland, Telegrams Received; DLC-USG, V, 46, 76, 108. *O.R.*, II, viii, 536.

On May 5, 1865, Maj. Gen. George H. Thomas telegraphed to USG. "The following despatches recd at these Head Quarters yesterday are forwarded for your information. Ashville N C May first via Greenville May second (2) Eighteen sixty five (1865) five (5) P m MAJ G M BASCOM A A G I have just recd a despatch from Col Palmer dated at Mooreville thirty seven (37) miles from Yorkville on the Road from Rutherfordton to Yorkville April twenty ninth (29) Eighteen sixty five (1865) acknowledging the receipt of General Stonemans dispatch of April twenty seventh (27)—He had heard of the surrender of Johnstons Army on the twenty sixth (26) but says it was reported that Hamptons Cavy was not included in the surrender and that they will try to make their way out of the country He states that a chaplain just from yorkville in whose statements he places Entire reliance says that Jeff Davis with Escort debrills division two Brigades of Cavalry left Yorkville the morning of the twenty Eighth (28) taking the unionville road They had a number of wagons reported to be loaded with specie. other accounts say ~~they~~ that the specie left Charlotte on the 15th ultimo in Eleven (11) wagons for Blackstock with a guard of two hundred (200) Infantry Col Palmer informant saw the secys Breckenridge and Benjamin and says Dehrills command was admirably mounted Col Palmer thinks Jeff

Davis and Party will go Either through Lawrenceville or Abbeville Probably the former to Bealton, Anderson & across the River to Karnsville Georgia & then across through or north of Atlanta to avoid wilsons Cavy   Col Palmer states that Debrills command numbers from fifteen hundred to twenty five hundred & that it is possible they will be joined by Dukes and Fergusons Commands. Col Palmer has moved his Brigade by the way of Island ford Broad River and Greenville to Pendleton S C & has given the necessary directions to Col Brown to Enable him to join his Command   Colonel Palmer states that if able to communicate with my force it ~~It~~ will ~~be~~ probably be by way of ~~Rohoen~~ Robins Gap   He thinks Ashville too far north Of the head Qurs of the Infantry and suggests that the Gap from Hickory Nut Gap to Saluda Gap included be blockaded and that the Gaps west ~~If~~ if any, be held by the Infantry—the reason given for blockading the first mentioned gaps to wit—To Enable a few men to pick up any stragglers from Johnstons Army who might become gucrrillas I deem ~~it~~ insufficient & shall not adopt. Col Kirk ~~i~~Informs me that the large number of the Guerrillas remaining in this Country are now on the road leading from this place to Waynesville Webster and Franklin   He states that the Country is rich in products of all kinds & will furnish all supplies for the men and animals of his command. ~~f~~For the double purpose of Exterminating guerrillas & opening Communication with the Cavalry I have decided to send the two (2) N C Regts over this route with instructions to hold Robins gap and the Gaps adjacent East & West   The Colored Regt will remain at Ashville until I can receive further instructions from the Maj Gen Comdg the Dist   Very Respectfully (signed) DAVIS TILLSON Br Gen Knoxville May ~~fourteenth~~ fourth Eighteen hundred sixty five twelve thirty P M MAJ GEN THOMAS   The following dispatch May second (2) just recd from Gen Tillson   Three (3) deserters from Johnsons army have just come in and state Positively they saw Jeff Davis and Party pass through Charolotte Wednesday April twenty sixth   He had a train of wagons which was guarded by Debrills Command of which Fergusons Brigade formed a part—they state that whole force did not exceed one thousand 1000—D TILSON Brig Genl'. From other sources I learn that Davis passed through Concord north of Charlotte on the twenty fourth 24 through Yorkville south of Charlotte on the 28th—at his rate of travel he aught today to be on or near the Savannah River, & if he has not yet crossed my Cavalry, now under under Col Palmer very energetic & capable officer, ought to be up with him—Davis has promised to every man on their arrival in Mexico four hundred 400 dollars in gold. Davis himself is riding in an ambulance. Every man splendidly mounted, but Debrills whole command is very much scattered & discouraged. (Signed) GEO STONEMAN Maj Genl'   The following was also recd today   'Ressaca Ga May second 2   Eighteen hundred sixty five 1865   BRIG GEN H M JUDAH Comdg U S forces Resacca Georgia— GENL—I hereby surrender myself & the Confederate forces under my command to you upon the terms under which Genl Lee C S A surrendered to Lt Genl U S Grant U S A—a copy of which is appended hereto—Very Respy your obt. servt W H WOFFORD Brig Gen.'   'Decatur Ala May fourth 4 Eighteen sixty five 1865—BRIG GEN A D WHIPPLE A A G. Meade refuses to surrender his guerrillas north of the River on Paint Rock. Your order will be carried out & they will at once be proceeded against as outlaws. Signed R S GRANGER B Genl'   'Decatur May fourth 4 1865   BRIG GENL W D WHIPPLE A A G. I have just returned from Fletchers Ferry—I had an interview with Col Patterson who accepts the terms of Surrender: ~~h~~He requires time to Collect his force: will Surrender all troops under his command when he can get them together & requests time for this purpose. Will get Roddy & hope to bring him in with all that is left of his command—Signed R S GRANGER Brig Genl' 'Decatur Ala may 4th 1865. 1 P M—BRIG GENL W D WHIPPLE A A G. Col Norwood from South side of River sends communication offering to surrender on terms of Lee—Officers sent to receive the surrender. R S GRANGER Brig Genl'. 'Eastport Miss May 3d 1865. 1 P M via Johnsonville May 4th MAJ GEN GEO H THOMAS COMDG. The following despatch has just been received by flag of truce—'South Western Tele- graph Co Baldwin Miss May 2d 1865 Telegraph from Garnesville Ala May 1st 1865 TO COL S McCALLAUGH. The following dispatch is received Which you will observe & send copy by flag of truce to Genl Hatch Commanding U S forces at Eastport—By order of Lt Gen Forrest—'Meridian Apl 30th 1865. LT GEN FORREST—Lt Genl Taylor directs me to inform you as follows—that he has arranged with Gen Canby for cessation of hostilities until resumed in forty eight 48 hours notice by either party. No new movement or changes from disposition of troops to be made until such notice—Notify immediately all subordinate Com- manders that scouting outside our lines will cease. Details of the arrangements will be published in orders. Send reliable officers under flag of truce to find Genl *Crofxton* and ~~address~~ advise him of it—also of that between Genls Johnson & Sherman both of which are made with a view ~~of~~ to a final settlement of difficulties under these arrangements Genl *Crofxton* cannot leave unless back to his former lines in Tennessee Valley nor forage on the Country after the receipt of this in- formation: By terms of Genl Shermans agreement, his supplies must be paid for— Signed E SARGENT Lt Col & A A G.' (Signed) J. P STRANGE A A G. Very Respy—EDWARD HATCH Brig Genl.' 'Eastport Miss May 3d 1865 via Johnson- ville May 4th 1865 MAJ GEN G. H. THOMAS COMDG ~~the~~ The following despath just been recd per flag of truce South western Telegraph Co Baldwin May 2. 1865, Telegram from Macon May 1st 1865. TO COL ROBT McCALLOCH, A truce has been agreed upon between Genls Canby & Taylor for the final settle- ment of terms, ~~a~~All scouting beyond the lines must cease, Send copy of this by flag of truce to Federal Comdr (signed) F. C. ARMSTRONG Brig Genl Very Respy EDWD HATCH Brig Genl Eastport Miss May 3, 1865 One P M via John- sonville May 4, 1865 MAJ GEN G, H, THOMAS COMDG, A Citizen direct from Taylors Hd Qrs at Meridian arrived here yesterday He states that the Rebels were expecting to cross the Miss but found river too strongly guarded I shall await orders from you in regard to the truce as stated in the dispatches sent today. Vy Respy signed EDWARD HATCH Brig Gen Immediately upon receipt of the foregoing telegrams from Gen Hatch I forwarded by telegraph the procla- mation of May 3rd offering reword for Jeff Davis and others to Maj Genl Stone- man, Maj Gen Stedman, Br Gen R. S. Granger, Br Gen Hatch Eastport Miss & Maj Gen Washburn Memphis Tenn with the further instructions to make every ~~eff~~ exertion to intercept & capture Davis. ~~w~~When last heard from he was ap- parently endeavoring to pass across the Country to the north of Atlanta so as to avoid Wilsons Cavalry and the forces at Dalton, Decatur in north Ala, & at East- port & Memphis. He may attempt to cross between Memphis & Vicksburg, ~~I~~if he can reach the Mississippi. Genl Hatch will send a copy of this dispatch & procla- mation under flag to Genl Crofxton together with a copy ~~with~~ of the terms of surrender of Lee & Johnston for Gen Croxtons information & guidance. Genl Croxton will disgregard the stipulations of the first terms between Sherman & Johnston and require all organized confederate forces in his front to surrender upon the same terms allowed to Lee by Lieut Gen Grant. He will remain some where about Elkton Ala or Columbus Miss ~~He~~ as he may elect after the receipt of this order if he can find ~~substance~~ subsistance & forage, & scout the Country thoroughly north & south for a distance of fifty (50) miles each way for the purpose of intercepting & arresting Jeff Davis. He will report as soon as possible to these Hd Qrs by way of Eastport or Decatur whichever place may be most convenient . . . The following telegram was also forwarded to Gen Hatch yesterday—Hd Qrs Dept Cumberland Nashville May 4. 65. BRIG GEN HATCH Eastport Miss Inform Gen F. C. Armstrong that the agreement between Lieut Gen Taylor & Maj Gen Canby only effects them and their troops but my troops will not be trammelled in their movements by such arrangements but will be required to obey such orders for a continuance of operations as in my judgement may seem proper & necessary and as Gen Forrest has caused a copy of the agreement between Gen Canby & Gen Taylor to be sent with a notice to Gen Croxton that he cannot under said agreement move his command except to leave the territory of Alabama, I shall expect and require of him that a copy of this be forwarded to Gen Croxton without delay (signed) G. H. THOMAS. Maj Gen Comdg,' I am in hopes now that every precaution has been taken to insure the capture of Davis Should he attempt to cross to the north of the Mississippi River" Telegram received (at 7:00 P.M.), DNA, RG 107, Telegrams Collected (Bound); *ibid.,* RG 108, Telegrams Received; copies, *ibid.,* RG 393, Dept. of the Cumberland, Telegrams Sent; DLC-USG, V, 54. *O.R.,* I, xlix, part 2, 555–56, 569, 589, 590, 592, 605, 607, 608, 613–14.

On May 6, 1:30 P.M., Brig. Gen. John A. Rawlins telegraphed to Thomas. "Please send such Cavalry as you can spare, not exceeding a full brigade to Maj. Gen. John Pope, Com'd'g Military Division of Missouri." Telegrams sent (2— one marked as sent at 4:00 P.M.), DNA, RG 107, Telegrams Collected (Bound); copies, *ibid.,* RG 108, Letters Sent; *ibid.,* RG 393, Dept. of the Cumberland, Telegrams Received; DLC-USG, V, 46, 76, 108. *O.R.,* I, xlviii, part 2, 332; (printed as sent at 4:00 P.M.) *ibid.,* I, xlix, part 2, 627. At 10:30 P.M., Thomas telegraphed to Rawlins. "I can send a brigade of Hatch's division to Gen Pope, but it will be dismounted, All of my mounted cavalry is with Gen Wilson— Hatchs division is at Eastport," Telegram received (at 11:10 P.M.), DNA, RG 107, Telegrams Collected (Bound); *ibid.,* RG 108, Telegrams Received; copy, DLC-USG, V, 54. *O.R.,* I, xlix, part 2, 628.

On May 7, Thomas telegraphed to USG. "I forward the following telegrams just recd. for your information. Telegraphic communication can be opened in a few days with Mobile also with Montgomery & Selma if you deem it advisable, I learn from Lt Haywood that Gen Wilson Captured eighty thousand bales cotton in Macon & then besides as much if not more in the hands of Citizens. I have directed him if it becomes necessary to leave Macon before the Cotton can be sent off to leave a responsible officer and a small guard to protect the Cotton from robbers & to make the Citizens of Macon responsible for its safety. ~~fFrom eCitronell Ala~~ May 4.th MAJ GEN G H THOMAS Lieut Gen Taylor has this day surrendered to me with the forces under his command on substantially the same terms as those accepted by Genl Lee, There are no confederate troops immediately south of the Tennessee River, in consequence of the scarcity of supplies in that region & I recommend that for the present no troops be sent there except to garrison Corinth & Tuscumbia which are the present terminea of the Mobile & Ohio & the Memphis & Charleston Railroad, I request today the commanding officer at Memphis to prepare to garrison Grenada Miss as soon as Genl Taylor apprises him that the present garrison is ready to be relieved. Be pleased to establish telegraph communication with Corinth as soon as possible (signed) E. R. S. CANBY Maj Gen' From Eastport 6th MAJ GEN THOMAS The officer in command of flag of truce reports that Maj Gens Steele is at Selma Ala, federal gunboats run up the river to that point (Signed) EDWARD HATCH Brig Genl" Telegram received (on May 8, 2:20 A.M.), DNA, RG 107, Telegrams Collected (Bound); *ibid.*, RG 108, Telegrams Received; copy, DLC-USG, V, 54. *O.R.*, I, xlix, part 2, 610, 636, 646.

On May 9, Thomas telegraphed to USG. "Maj Gen Canby Telegraphs me from Mobile May 2d received to day—'Lieut Gen Taylor surrendered ~~last~~ on the terms proposed to [hi]m I will meet him at Citronville on the 4th inst and will arrange with him that the troops & property [w]ithin your command be surrendered to Officers designated by you.'—I have already directed Gen Granger at Decatur to receive [the] surrender of Roddy & all others near Decatur, Gen Hatch to receive the surrender of troops and property in North East Mississippi, and Gen Washburne the troops and property in North West Miss" Telegram received (on May 10, 1:30 A.M.), DNA, RG 107, Telegrams Collected (Bound); *ibid.*, RG 108, Telegrams Received; copies, *ibid.*, RG 393, Dept. of the Cumberland, Telegrams Sent; DLC-USG, V, 54. *O.R.*, I, xlix, part 2, 678.

To Maj. Gen. Gouverneur K. Warren

Washington, May 6th 1865.

MAJ. GEN. G. K. WARREN.

GENERAL,

Your note requesting authority to publish your application for an investigation of the grounds upon which you were relieved from the command of the 5th Army Corps or to have the investigation, is received.

It is impossible at this time to give the Court and witnesses necessary for the investigation, but I see nothing in your application which I see objectionable to have published.

Very respectfully
Your obt. Svt.
U. S. GRANT.

Copy, DLC-Henry J. Hunt. *O.R.*, I, xlvi, part 3, 1103.

On April 7, 1865, Maj. Gen. Gouverneur K. Warren, Petersburg, telegraphed to Bvt. Maj. Gen. Alexander S. Webb. "Genl Hartsuff has relieved me of the command along the line you assigned me as far west as Sutherland Station Genl Wilcox begins at that point & has acted under the orders of Genl Parke. I

have virtually no command except a cavalry picket under Col Sanders. No order
states what troops are under my command. what do you wish done with the
troops under Genl Benham and of the dismounted Cavalry. Night before last
Genl. Rawlins told me to await instructions from Genl Grant which I have since
been doing" Telegram received, DNA, RG 108, Letters Received. *O.R.*, I, xlvi,
part 3, 636. On April 8, Maj. Gen. George G. Meade endorsed this telegram.
"Respectfully referred to the Lt. Genl—Comdg—The command given to Maj-
Genl Warren was under the instructions of the Lt Genl—Comdg—The change of
position of troops, has caused the command no longer to exist—further instructions as to the disposition of Maj. Genl. Warren are asked." AES, DNA, RG
108, Letters Received. *O.R.*, I, xlvi, part 3, 636.

On April 9, Warren telegraphed to Brig. Gen. John A. Rawlins. "The order
of Maj Genl Sheridan taking from me the Command of my Corps on the Evening of the first (1) April after the Victory was won assigns no cause & leaves
me open to the inference now finding expression in the public prints & which
are ein Every way to my prejudice I am unconscious of having done any thing
improper or unbecoming to my position or the Character of a soldier or neglecting any order or duty I therefore respectfully request a full investigation of the
matter as soon as the exigiciences of the service will admit I make this application now while awaiting Orders which I deem the most appropriate time but I
do not intend by it nor desire to press the matter upon the Consideration of the
Lieut Genl until he can give it his attention without interfering with more important duties the Consideration already shown me in immediately assigning
me another Command on the 2d last gives me the assurance he will not deem it
an intrusion to solicit an opportunity to Vindicate the honor & reputation of a
faithful soldier of the Union who waits in silence an unmerited injury till such
time as his superior shall be ready to give him a hearing" Telegram received,
DNA, RG 94, Letters Received, 925W 1866. *O.R.*, I, xlvi, part 3, 679. On April
22, Warren wrote to Bvt. Col. Theodore S. Bowers. "I beg leave to forward you
a copy of a communication addressed to Hd Qurs armies of the U. S. on the 9th.
inst with the request to be permitted to publish the same. This will relieve me
and my friends from an unpleasant relation to the public; will answer many
letters daily received; and will prevent my silence being an injury to me. I can
then patiently await the investigation that I do not doubt will in due time be
accorded me" ALS, DNA, RG 94, Letters Received, 925W 1866. *O.R.*, I, xlvi,
part 3, 896. See telegram to Maj. Gen. George G. Meade, April 18, 1865.

On May 1, 1:00 P.M., Meade telegraphed to USG. "Permit me if you have
not already acted to call your attention to the case of Gen Warren" Telegram
received (at 5:00 P.M.), DNA, RG 107, Telegrams Collected (Bound); *ibid.*,
RG 108, Telegrams Received; copy, DLC-USG, V, 54. *O.R.*, I, xlvi, part 3, 1055.
At 7:00 P.M., USG telegraphed to Meade. "I have this day ordered Maj. Gen.
G. K. Warren to report to me in person for orders." Telegrams sent (2—marked
as sent at 9:10 P.M.), DNA, RG 107, Telegrams Collected (Bound); telegram
received (at 9:40 P.M.), *ibid.*, Telegrams Collected (Unbound). *O.R.*, I, xlvi,
part 3, 1056. On the same day, Bowers wrote to the AG. "Please publish an
order releiving Maj Gen N. J. T. Dana from command of the Department of the
Mississippi, and assign Maj Gen. G. K. Warren U. S. Vols. to the command of
that Dept. On being releived Gen Dana will proceed to his place of residence and
from there report to the Adjt. General of the Army for orders." LS, DNA, RG
94, Letters Received, 438A 1865. See *O.R.*, I, xlvi, part 3, 1056, 1069.

To Jesse Root Grant

May 6th *1865*

Dear Father,

I have ordered a Sixty days furlough for Saml A. Tearne. He can be discharged at any time after his return home. It will take probably three weeks for my directions to reach him and he return.

I have just returned from Phila leaving Mr. Cramer there. He can discribe our new house to you when he returns.

My health is good but I find so much to do that I can scarsely keep up with public business let alone answering all the private letters I receive. My going to Phila and spending half my time there as I hope to do will give me some leasure. I attend to public business there by telegraph and avoid numerous calls taking up much time, or hope to do so.

My kind regards to all at home. I hope to hear of mothers entire recovery soon.

Ulyses

ALS, PPRF.

To Edwin M. Stanton

Washington D. C, May 7th *1865*

Sir:

I would respectfully recommend the revocation of the order prohibiting officers who have purchased public horses taking them out of the Dept. where purchased. In all cases where officers take horses home they should be required to have a Quartermasters Certificate showing that they purchased and paid for the horses taken with them and Govt. should not furnish transportation beyond the point where the officer is to be mustered out of service.

Very respectfully
your obt. svt.
U. S. Grant
Lt. Gen

ALS, DNA, RG 94, Letters Received, 464A 1865. Although the letter is unaddressed, Secretary of War Edwin M. Stanton endorsed it. "Approved   The
Adjt General will prepare an order in accordance" AES, *ibid*. On May 7, 1865,
USG again wrote to Stanton. "I would respectfully suggest that orders be given
the Q. M. Gen. to issue at once all public animals fit for service and advertise all
others for immediate sale. Sales should take place where the animals are and in
small lots." ALS (facsimile), Sotheby's Sale No. 5504, Oct. 29, 1986, no. 59.

On May 9, Bvt. Maj. Gen. Montgomery C. Meigs endorsed a letter of the
same day from Bvt. Brig. Gen. James A. Ekin. "Respectfully referred to Lt
Gen Grant—and recommendation that the cavalry horses which can be re-
cuperated in 60 days be retained as if a considerable cavalry force is kept in
service these horses will be needed to keep it mounted. The sales at Giesboro do
not produce as much as those in the interior & it is recommended that discretion
be left with the chief of the 1st Division of this office as to the places for sale
of the animals to be disposed of—" AES, DNA, RG 92, Miscellaneous Letters
Sent (Press).

To Julia Dent Grant

———

May 7th *1865*

Dear Julia,

I did not write yesterday but telegraphed twice[1] which answered every purpose, particularly as I had nothing to write. I
find a great deal to do here and will yet for a few weeks. I will probably be back on Wednesday[2] or Thursday next taking Bowers with
me. I think on that occation I shall run over to West Point for one
day. I want to see all my old professors again and as they are always absent from about the 20th of June until the 1st of Sept. I
will not have an aportunity of doing so at the time I propose taking you and the children there.

Love and kisses for you and the children.

Ulys.

ALS, DLC-USG.

1. On May 6, 1865, USG twice telegraphed to Julia Dent Grant. "Ask
Mr. Cramer what regiment Geo. Griffith belongs to." ALS (telegram sent),
Wayde Chrismer, Bel Air, Md.   "Tell Jane her husband was released from
prison to-day." AL (telegram sent, signature clipped), DNA, RG 107, Telegrams Collected (Unbound). On May 9, Maj. George K. Leet wrote a letter
received at hd. qrs., Middle Dept. "Directs a furlough be granted to G R.

Griffith Co. G 36th Ohio Vols for 60 days." *Ibid.*, RG 393, Middle Dept. and 8th
Army Corps, Register of Letters Received.
 2. May 10.

To Edwin M. Stanton

Head. Qrs. Armies. of the U. States.
Washington. D. C. May. 8th 1865.

HON. E. M. STANTON
SEC. OF WAR,

SIR I would respectfully recommend Robert McClermont. for
an appointment in the regular army of the United-states. He is an
old soldier, having served in the Mexican War, in the Regiment
of which I was then a Lieutenant. In this War he enlisted early
as a Private. He has served since with credit as a Private, Sergeant
and Lieutenant.

I give this letter now, as a recommdation for McClermont.
when the reorganization of the regular army takes place, as I anticipate it will soon after the meeting of next Congress, and I hope
no Citizen appointments will be made except from persons. who
have served faithfully and with credit in this War, and who have
Military recommendations.

Very respectfully
Your Ob't. Serv't.
U. S. GRANT
Lt. Gen

LS, DNA, RG 94, ACP, M1330 CB 1865.
 On April 3, 1864, USG wrote to Maj. Gen. Nathaniel P. Banks. "Allow me
to call your attention to Robert. McClermont of company "B" Scotts 900 11th
N. Y. Cavalry recently ordered to Texas. I am Satisfied from information in my
possession that he is a good Soldier and a competent and worthy man who deserves promotion. May I hope he will receive it at your hands." Copy, *ibid.*
 On Feb. 15, 1865, USG wrote to Secretary of War Edwin M. Stanton. "I
would respectfully recommend 2nd. Lieut. Robt. Mc Clermont 11th. New York
Cavalry for a Lieutenantcy in the Regular Cavalry. Mc Clermont served in the
4th. Infantry, to which I formerly belonged in the Mexican War; in this War he
volunteered early as a private and has served in that capacity, a Quartermaster
Sergeant and Lieutenant with credit ever since. His appointment in the regular

army I believe would secure to the service a valuable officer and would reward past services." Copy, *ibid*.

On July 19, USG wrote to Stanton. "I would respectfully recommend 1st Lt. Robt. McClermont for the appointment of Lieu't. Col. or Colonel of a Colored Regiment if such vacancy exists. Lt McClermont is an Old Soldier having served in the Mexican War in the same regiment with myself and through this war as a volunteer. His acquirements are such as to enable him to pass any required examination I think and he has good recommendations otherwise." Copy, *ibid*.

On Dec. 18, USG wrote to Col. Henry K. Craig, president of a board examining candidates for officers, U.S. Colored Troops. "I would respectfully ask that the recommendation of Robt McClermont, late of the 11th N. Y. Cavalry, and who served faithfully throughout the whole rebellion, beside having served in the Mexican War with credit, be taken up by your board and favorably concidered. Lt. McClermont's recommendations were approved by me. If not before your board I would request that this be regarded as a recommendation" ALS, *ibid*.

USG signed a petition dated Jan. 13, 1866, also signed by thirty-one members of Congress, to President Andrew Johnson requesting an appointment in the U.S. Army for Robert McClermont. DS, *ibid*. McClermont was appointed 1st lt., 4th Cav., as of Jan. 30. On April 25, USG wrote to Bvt. Maj. Gen. Joseph B. Kiddoo. "This will introduce you to Lieu't McClermont of the 4th U. S. Cavalry, who has just been ordered to report to you for duty in the 'Freedman's Bureau'. McClermont is an old soldier of the regiment to which I belonged in the old service, and a man I think to be trusted and relied upon. In the distribution of offices I hope you will be able to give him a place where he can be of service and at the same time live pleasantly." Copy, *ibid*.

On Jan. 13, 1868, eight U.S. representatives and two U.S. senators from N. Y. signed a petition to USG asking that McClermont be appointed bvt. lt. col. DS, *ibid*. On Jan. 16, USG endorsed this petition. "Respectfully forwarded, disapproved." ES, *ibid*.

On May 14, 1873, McClermont, Fort Concho, Tex., wrote to USG. "I have the honor to recall your attention to a subject discussed by us in March 1867. viz: My right as a Captain in the U. S. Army to rank as such from July 28th 1866. I having been appointed on the 22d of January 1867. to fill an Original vacancy in the 41st Reg't. U. S. Infty: As a multiplicity of business may prevent your giving attention to such Law-Points, I respectfully request that you would lay the subject before the United-states Attorny General for his Decision, as to whether an Original vacancy in the U. S. Army when filled—*at any time* should not rank from date of the Act of Congress creating such vacancy as well as those vacancies which were filled at an earlier date—than mine. Circumstances have occurred recently which make it important to me to have it settled, particularly if in my favor." ALS, *ibid*.

To Maj. Gen. William T. Sherman

(Cipher)   Washington May 9th/65 [1:30 P.M.]
MAJ. GN. W. T. SHERMAN, FT. MONROE

Your dispatches of yesterday received. I know of no order which changes your command in any particular. Gen. Wilson is in telegraphic communication with Washington whilst you have not been consequently instructions have been sent him direct.

U. S. GRANT
Lt. Gn.

ALS (telegram sent), DNA, RG 107, Telegrams Collected (Bound); telegram sent, *ibid.*; telegram received, *ibid.*, Telegrams Collected (Unbound). *O.R.*, I, xlvii, part 3, 445; *ibid.*, I, xlix, part 2, 678. On May 8, 1865, Maj. Gen. William T. Sherman, Fort Monroe, twice telegraphed to USG, the second time at midnight. "Am just arrived. All well with Schofield—Expect to reach City Point tomorrow and receive my orders from you. Did you get my despatch from Morehead City. Am informed that Gn Slocum will march from Richmond on the 10th, I expect to join and march with the Right wing with which my horses are." ALS (telegram sent), Haskell Collection, MiU-C; telegram received (on May 9, 9:30 A.M.), DNA, RG 107, Telegrams Collected (Bound). *O.R.*, I, xlvii, part 3, 434. "I have full dispatches from Wilson of the 6th—One boat has arrived at Augusta all right. He is after Jeff Davis who cannot escape save in disguise. He is reported in Georgia escorted by about Seventy officers as a special body-guard and about 3000 Cavalry. Does the Secretary of War's news-paper order take Wilson from my command or shall I continue to order him—If I have proven incompetent to manage my own command let me know it" Telegram received (on May 9, 10:00 A.M.), DNA, RG 107, Telegrams Collected (Bound); *ibid.*, RG 108, Telegrams Received; copy, DLC-USG, V, 54. *O.R.*, I, xlvii, part 3, 434; *ibid.*, I, xlix, part 2, 662.

On May 9, Sherman, first at City Point, then at Manchester, Va., twice telegraphed to USG, first at 12:30 P.M. "I have the honor to report my arrival at City Point pursuant to your orders and my army is reported by Genl Easton Qr Master to be at Manchester opposite Richmond—I have as yet seen no order for me to come on to Alexandria although that was contemplated by you at Raleigh—Will you please telegraph me orders at Manchester where I will forthwith join the army—I have nothing from you since you left Raleigh" Telegram received (at 6:35 P.M.), DNA, RG 107, Telegrams Collected (Bound); *ibid.*, RG 108, Telegrams Received; copy, DLC-USG, V, 54. *O.R.*, I, xlvii, part 3, 446. "I have found my army at manchester opposite Richmond & await your orders—Gen Wilson telegraphs through Gen Schofield for hay and forage for twenty thousand animeals to be sent up the savannah River to Augusta. under secretary Stantons newspaper order taking Wilson substantially from my command I wish you would give the order necessary for the case." Telegram received (at 8:15 P.M.), DNA, RG 92, Letters Received from Hd. Qrs.; *ibid.*, RG 107, Telegrams Collected (Bound); *ibid.*, Telegrams Collected (Unbound); *ibid.*, RG 108, Telegrams Received; copy, DLC-USG, V, 54. *O.R.*, I, xlvii, part 3, 446; *ibid.*, I, xlix, part 2, 678. On May 10, USG endorsed a telegram received. "Respectfully refered to the Q. M. G. with directions that he send the forage called for in this dispatch." AES, DNA, RG 92, Letters Received from Hd. Qrs. *O.R.*, I, xlix, part 2, 678.

On May 7, Maj. Gen. Edward R. S. Canby telegraphed to Maj. Gen. George H. Thomas and USG transmitting telegrams of April 13 and 17 from Bvt. Maj. Gen. James H. Wilson to Canby reporting the capture of Montgomery, Ala., and Columbus, Ga. Telegram received, DNA, RG 107, Telegrams Collected (Bound); copy, *ibid.*, RG 393, Dept. of the Cumberland, Telegrams Received. The enclosures are in *O.R.*, I, xlix, part 2, 347, 383. On May 11, 8:00 P.M., Thomas telegraphed to USG transmitting a telegram of May 6, 6.00 P.M., from Wilson to Thomas. Telegram received (on May 12, 4:10 A.M.), DNA, RG 107, Telegrams Collected (Bound); *ibid.*, RG 108, Telegrams Received; copy, DLC-USG, V, 54. The Wilson telegram is dated May 7 in *O.R.*, I, xlix, part 2, 648–49. On May 11, Thomas telegraphed to USG. "I forward the following telegram just recd from Major General stoneman for your information   from Knoxville Eleventh (11) TO BR GEN W D WHIPPLE—Despatch from Gen Palmer Athens Georgia dated May sixth (6) Eighteen sixty five (65)   The substance of the dispatch is that Genl Palmer with the Cavalry Div succeeded in crossing the Savannah river at Hattans Ford north of Pontoon bridge at Petersburg mouth of Broad River Ga where Davis Breckenridge most of the Cabinet Gov Harris & a large number of gents crossed the same river. The party with Davis finding that Palmer had got in advance of them cutting them off from the Miss broke up into small detachments   are scattered over the country. it is supposed the specie or paortion of it was distributed among the officers & men or secreted. Breckenridge with about five hundred 500 men had gone towards Macon. It is said to surrender at that point   Dibbrell with a large portion of the Cavalry is still back on Savannah River waiting to surrender. Davis when last heard from had left Washn by RR with a small party for Atlanta but finding Palmer had cut the Road at Union Point he went south west on horseback. He has a small party of about thirty five (35) men with him and is travelling incognito. The men he started south with are scattered over the Country and a large number them have been Captured and informally paroled. Prisoners state that the Treasure before it crossed Savannah River was contained in one hundred boxes filled with gold and sixty (60) Kegs filled with silver. Palmer has Communicated with Wilsons Cavy giving him all the information he has & hopes to prevent Davis from getting West of the Miss as his forces are well distributed. guarding all fords & main roads   (signed) GEO STONEMAN—MGen." Telegram received (on May 12, 5:30 P.M.), DNA, RG 107, Telegrams Collected (Bound); *ibid.*, RG 108, Telegrams Received; copies (dated May 12), *ibid.*, RG 393, Dept. of the Cumberland, Telegrams Sent; DLC-USG, V, 54. *O.R.*, I, xlix, part 2, 717; (incomplete—dated May 12) *ibid.*, p. 731. On May 12, 4:00 P.M., Sherman, Concord Church, Va., telegraphed to USG transmitting a telegram of May 10, 3:00 P.M., from Wilson, Macon, to Sherman. Telegram received (at 8:50 P.M.), DNA, RG 107, Telegrams Collected (Bound); (2—incomplete) *ibid.*, Telegrams Collected (Unbound); *ibid.*, RG 108, Telegrams Received; copy, DLC-USG, V, 54. *O.R.*, I, xlix, part 2, 702–3, 731.

On May 12, 11:00 A.M., Wilson twice telegraphed to Secretary of War Edwin M. Stanton, sending copies to USG and Thomas. "I have the honor to report that at daylight of the 10th inst Col. Pritchard Comdg 4th Mich. Cavy. Captured Jeff Davis and family with Regan Post Mr. Genl Col. Harrison Private Secretary, Col. Johnson ADC, Col Morris, Col Lubbick, Lt Hathaway & others. Col Prittchard surprised their camp at Irwinville in Irwin Co. Ga. 75 miles south east of this place. They will be here tomorrow night and will be forwarded under strong guard without delay. I will send further particulars atonce." Telegrams received (2—on May 13, 10:00 P.M.), DNA, RG 107, Telegrams Collected (Bound); *ibid.*, Telegrams Collected (Unbound); *ibid.*, RG 108, Telegrams Received; copies, DLC-USG, V, 54; DLC-James H. Wilson. *O.R.*, I, xlix, part 2, 732–33. "Following dispatch announcing capture of Jeff Davis has just been handed me by Col Minty Com'd'g 2d Division—'HdQrs 4th Mich cavy Cumberlandville Ga   May 11th 1865   To CAPT T, W, SCOTT A. G. 2d Div—SIR:—I have the honor to report that at daylight, yesterday, at Irwinville I surprised and captured Jeff Davis and family, together with his wife, sisters and brother, his Post Master Genl Regan, his Private Secretary Col Harrison, Col Johnston ADC, on Davis staff, Col Morris Lubbick, Lt Hathaway, also several important names, and train of five wagons & three ambulances, making a most perfect success, had not a most painful mistake occurred by which the 4th Mich, and 1st Wis, collided, which cost us two killed, and Lt Boutelle wounded through arm in the 4th Mich, and four men wounded in the 1st Wis,   This occurred just at daylight, after we had captured the camp, by advance of the 1st Wis, not properly answering in challenge, through which they were mistaken for the enemy,   I returned to this point last night, and shall move right on to Macon without waiting orders from you, as directed, feeling that the whole object of the Expedition is accomplished—It will take me at least three days to reach Macon, as we are seventy five (75) miles out, and our stock much exhausted. I hope to reach Hawkinsville to night,   I have the honor &c   (signed) B D PRITCHARD Lt Col 4th Mich Cav'   The First Wis belongs to Lagranges Brigade of McCooks Division, and had been sent due east by Gen Croxton via Dublin,   Col Minty had distributed his command all along south bank of the Ocmulgee and Altamaha, This accounts for the collision between parts of the 1st and 2d Divisions, and shows the zeal of the command in the pursuit,   I have directed increased vigilence on part of the command in the hope of catching the other assassins,   Our dispositions are good, and so far none of the Rebel Chiefs have been able to get through,   Breckenridge's son was captured night before last eleven miles south from here—Will send further details as soon as received—" Telegram received (on May 13, 11:00 P.M.), DNA, RG 107, Telegrams Collected (Bound); *ibid.*, Telegrams Collected (Unbound); *ibid.*, RG 108, Telegrams Received; Seward Papers, NRU; copies, DLC-USG, V, 54; DLC-James H. Wilson. *O.R.*, I, xlix, part 2, 721–22, 733. On May 13, Wilson telegraphed to USG transmitting a telegram of May 4 from Canby to Wilson announcing the surrender of C.S.A. Lt. Gen. Richard Taylor. Telegram received (on May 14, 2:40 P.M.), DNA, RG 107, Telegrams Collected (Bound); (5) *ibid.*, Telegrams Collected (Unbound); *ibid.*, RG 108, Telegrams Received; copy, DLC-USG, V, 54. The enclosure is in *O.R.*, I, xlix, part 2, 599.

To Julia Dent Grant

—————

Washington May 9th *1865*

DEAR JULIA,

I could go home this evening only that the troops belonging to Sherman's & Meades Armies will begin to arrive in a few days and I must be here to give orders and directions concerning them. I have also to arrange for Texas and all the country West of the Miss. Under these circumstances I think it doubtful whether I will be home this time before Saturday night.[1] Hereafter I think I will generally be able to return about the middle of the week and remain until Monday, spending full one half of my time at home.

We are now in telegraphic communication with Wilson in Macon Ga. and in a day or two will have the whole South within telegraphic orders. What a colapse! But a short thirty-five days ago we had a defiant enemy holding the South; to-day we are telegraphing, through their own operators, and over the wires which they controled so short a time since, regarding dispositions for the capture of their pretended President and Cabinet. Management is all that is now wanted to secure complete peace.

Love and Kisses for you and the children.

ULYS.

ALS, DLC-USG.

1. May 13, 1865.

To Maj. Gen. Henry W. Halleck

—————

Washington May 10th *1865* [*3:00* P.M.]

MAJ. GEN. HALLECK, RICHMOND VA.

You need not order the arrest of Gen. Rosser unless it can be done in good faith. I was informed that he had been captured and knew that he had left Lee's Army after it had been surrendered. You may keep all of the 6th Corps until further orders except that portion that may be mustered out under general orders for reducing the Military establishment of the United-States.

U. S. GRANT

Lt. Gen.

ALS (telegram sent), DNA, RG 107, Telegrams Collected (Bound); telegram sent, *ibid.*; telegram received, *ibid.*, Telegrams Collected (Unbound). *O.R.*, I, xlvi, part 3, 1123. On May 9, 1865, 2:00 P.M., USG had telegraphed to Maj. Gen. Henry W. Halleck. "I understand Gen. Rosser has been captured. ~~If terms have not been given him which makes it improper to confine him~~ If no terms have been made with him rendering it improper to do so I wish you to send him here under guard to be tried for deserting his command after it had been surrendered." ALS (telegram sent), DNA, RG 107, Telegrams Collected (Bound); telegram sent, *ibid.*; copies, *ibid.*, RG 108, Letters Sent; DLC-USG, V, 46, 76, 108. *O.R.*, I, xlvi, part 3, 1117. On May 10, Halleck telegraphed to USG. "Genl Rosser came within our lines to arrange for the surrender of his command at Staunton. A cavalry force was sent out with him to recieve their arms and paroles. He was not captured, but surrendered himself on the terms of Lee's capitulation, and promised that his entire command should lay down their arms. Report of Guerrilla band at Lynchburg not well founded. Genl Wright reports that it will require some days to remove public property from Danville, and that a military force will be required there at present on account of the large number of disbanded rebel soldiers in the vicinity. This will cause a little delay in sending the 6th corps to Alexandria." ALS (telegram sent), DNA, RG 107, Telegrams Collected (Unbound); telegram received, *ibid.*; (at 2:30 P.M.) *ibid.*, Telegrams Collected (Bound); *ibid.*, RG 108, Telegrams Received. *O.R.*, I, xlvi, part 3, 1123.

On May 7, 10:30 A.M., Halleck telegraphed to USG. "Genl Meade's army (2 corps) passed through Richmond yesterday. Genl Slocum's army is now going into camp at Manchester. Genl Howard leaves Petersburg to day & will be in Manchester to-morrow. It will require about three days to fit them out. Genl Sherman is not expected till about the fifteenth. Shall the troops, when ready, move on to Alexandria, or await Genl Sherman's arrival here?" ALS (telegram sent), DNA, RG 107, Telegrams Collected (Unbound); telegram received, *ibid.*; (at 12:30 P.M.) *ibid.*, Telegrams Collected (Bound); *ibid.*, RG 108, Telegrams Received. *O.R.*, I, xlvi, part 3, 1106; *ibid.*, I, xlvii, part 3, 420. At 2:30 P.M., USG telegraphed to Halleck. "There is no necessity for detaining Sherman's Army for his arrival. I think however he will be in Richmond to-day or to-morrow." ALS (telegram sent), DNA, RG 107, Telegrams Collected (Bound); telegram sent, *ibid.*; copies, *ibid.*, RG 108, Letters Sent; DLC-USG, V, 46, 76, 108. *O.R.*, I, xlvi, part 3, 1106; *ibid.*, I, xlvii, part 3, 420.

On May 4, Col. John C. Kelton, Richmond, wrote to Brig. Gen. John A. Rawlins. "Several officers have reported by verbal directions from Head Quarters of the Armies of the United States to these Head Quarters enroute to Gen'l. Shermans Army. It is respectfully suggested that it would be better for officers seeking their commands in Gen'l Shermans Army to await their arrival at Alexandria, D. C. than in this city when there is so little accommodation and their expenses will be so great." LS, DNA, RG 108, Letters Received. *O.R.*, I, xlvii, part 3, 396. On May 5, Halleck telegraphed to USG. "A part of Genl Sherman's army will reach here on Monday the 8th   If Genls Easton & Beckwith are in Washington they should return here immediately." ALS (telegram sent), DNA, RG 107, Telegrams Collected (Unbound); telegram received, *ibid.*; (at 3:20 P.M.) *ibid.*, Telegrams Collected (Bound). *O.R.*, I, xlvii, part 3, 400.

On May 7, Maj. Gen. Oliver O. Howard, Petersburg, telegraphed to Bvt. Col. Theodore S. Bowers. "I have the honor to report the arrival of the Army of the Tennessee at this point. It is now encamped in the immediate vicinity of the City. I will march tomorrow and move by easy marches to Manchester where supplies await us." ALS (telegram sent), DNA, RG 107, Telegrams Collected (Unbound); telegram received (at 1:35 P.M.), *ibid.*, Telegrams Collected (Bound); *ibid.*, RG 108, Telegrams Received. *O.R.*, I, xlvii, part 3, 420. At 9:00 P.M., USG telegraphed to Howard, "Care Gen. Halleck Richmond Va." "Leave your Army for Corps commanders to bring over land and come on immediately yourself by water. Report on arrival to the Sec. of War." ALS (telegram sent), DNA, RG 107, Telegrams Collected (Bound); telegram sent, *ibid.*; copies, *ibid.*, RG 108, Letters Sent; DLC-USG, V, 46, 76, 108. *O.R.*, I, xlvii, part 3, 421. On May 10, 3:15 P.M., Howard telegraphed to USG. "Your despatch only just received. I will Conform to it at once—" ALS (telegram sent), DNA, RG 107, Telegrams Collected (Unbound); telegram received (at 8:30 P.M.), *ibid.*, Telegrams Collected (Bound); (at 8:25 P.M.) *ibid.*, RG 108, Telegrams Received. *O.R.*, I, xlvii, part 3, 455.

On May 8, 10:30 A.M., USG telegraphed to Halleck. "You may detain all the Cavalry in your Dept. placing such as you have no use for at City Point for convenience of supply. That will be as good a point as Alexandria for mustering out all whose time expires between now and October and for shipping the balance to such points as may require their services." ALS (telegram sent), DNA, RG 107, Telegrams Collected (Bound); telegram sent, *ibid.*; telegrams received (2), *ibid.*, Telegrams Collected (Unbound). *O.R.*, I, xlvi, part 3, 1110. In the telegrams received, "batteries" appeared in place of "Cavalry." On the same day, Halleck telegraphed to USG. "I presume your telegram in regard to Batteries— refers to the Commands of Gen Sheridan & Wright, but does not include Gen Sherman's army. Am I right? Please answer as Gen Slocum is preparing his Batteries to leave tomorrow." Telegram received (at 4:00 P.M.), DNA, RG 107, Telegrams Collected (Bound); (at 3:45 P.M.) *ibid.*, RG 108, Telegrams Received; copy, DLC-USG, V, 54. Printed as sent at 3:45 P.M. in *O.R.*, I, xlvi, part 3, 1110. On the same day, USG telegraphed to Halleck. "Your understanding of my dispatch is correct. I did not intend to include the Artillery of Sherman's Army." Telegrams sent (2—at 10:40 A.M., possibly on May 9), DNA, RG 107, Telegrams Collected (Bound); telegrams received (2), *ibid.*, Telegrams Collected (Unbound). *O.R.*, I, xlvi, part 3, 1111.

On May 12, Kelton telegraphed to the AG, Washington, D. C. "All the cavalry of Gen Sheridans command have left this Military Division for Washington except the Second 2 and Third 3 Brigade of the Second 2 Division Composed of the following Regiments. Fourth 4 Eighth 8 Sixteenth 16 & Twenty first (21) Penna: First 1 Maine: Second 2 N Y Mounted Rifles and Sixth 6 and Thirteenth 13 Ohio. All the Batteries of the Cavalry are at City Point except a section of Capt Millers Battery Fourth 4 U S Art'y which has gone on to join the Section in the defences of Washington." Telegram received (at 3:10 P.M.), DNA, RG 108, Telegrams Received; copy, DLC-USG, V, 54. Printed as addressed also to Bowers in *O.R.*, I, xlvi, part 3, 1138–39.

Also on May 12, Samuel H. Beckwith telegraphed to an unidentified maj. "In a cipher of 10 30 a. m. May 8th I find that the word 'battery' was used instead of 'cavalry' as written by the Lieut General in an order to Gen Halleck concerning cavalry in his Dept. The Message of Gen Halleck asking if the 'artillery' of Gen Shermans command was included was called out by this but the error was not discovered until now and I enclose a message from Col. Kelton concerning it. The mistake was occasioned by a change in the cipher operators and keys at Richmond at that time it being written at first under the impression that the same key was still being used I regret exceedingly the occurrence of so serious an error and hope it is not too late to remedy. Will you have the kindness to make the explanations" Telegram received, DNA, RG 108, Telegrams Received; copy, DLC-USG, V, 54. See telegram to Maj. Gen. Henry W. Halleck, May 24, 1865.

On May 14, Halleck telegraphed to USG. "Major Genl Wright is now here and reports everything in the southern counties as quiet as could well be expected. Genl Ord has been ordered to relieve the sixth corps, which will probably reach Richmond on its way to Alexandria about the last of this week." ALS (telegram sent), DNA, RG 107, Telegrams Collected (Unbound); telegram received, *ibid.*; (at 3:00 P.M.) *ibid.*, Telegrams Collected (Bound); *ibid.*, RG 108, Telegrams Received. *O.R.*, I, xlvi, part 3, 1149.

On May 16, Bvt. Brig. Gen. George H. Sharpe, Richmond, telegraphed to Rawlins. "Will Moseby be admitted to parole with the other officers of Rosser's command to which he belonged? The question is asked to determine the action of Moseby and some others, who would probably follow him out of the country if Hhe goes. Shall a definite answer be given, or shall it be said that he and others will learn the action of the U. S. Government after they have acknowledged its authority?" ALS (telegram sent), DNA, RG 107, Telegrams Collected (Unbound); telegram received, *ibid.*, Telegrams Collected (Bound). Printed as sent at 10:05 P.M. in *O.R.*, I, xlvi, part 3, 1158.

On May 11, 9:00 P.M., USG telegraphed to Halleck. "You may suspend the sale of public animals advertised by Gen. Ingalls until further orders. I think the condemned animals, at least a part of them, advertized will be turned over to the 'Freedmens Bureau.' for issue." ALS (telegram sent), DNA, RG 107, Telegrams Collected (Bound); telegram sent, *ibid.*; telegram received, *ibid.*, Telegrams Collected (Unbound). Printed as received on May 12 in *O.R.*, I, xlvi, part 3, 1133. For the background of this telegram, see *ibid.*

Testimony

[*May 12, 1865*]

Lieutenant General Ulysses S. Grant, a witness called for the prosecution, being duly sworn, testified as follows:

By the Judge Advocate

Q. Will you state whether you are acquainted with Jacob

Thompson, formerly Secretary of the Interior under President Buchanan's Administration?

A. I met him once. That was when the Army was lying opposite Vicksburg at what is called Milliken's Bend and Young's Point. A little boat was discovered coming up on the opposite shore, apparently surreptitiously, trying to avoid detection, and a little tug was sent out from the Navy to pick it up. When they got to it, they found a little white flag sticking out of the stern of the rowboat, and Jacob Thompson in it. They brought him to Admiral Porter's flag ship, and I was sent for, and met him. I do not recollect even the ostensible business he had. There seemed to be nothing important at all in his visit, but he pretended to be under a flag of truce, and, therefore, he had to be allowed to go back again.

Q. When was that?

A. I cannot say whether it was in January or February, 1863. It was the first flag of truce we had, though.

Q. Did he profess to be, and seem to be, in the military service of the rebels?

A. He said he had been offered a commission,—anything that he wanted; but knowing that he was not a military man, he preferred having something more like a civil appointment, and he had taken the place of an Inspector General in the rebel service.

Q. Did he then hold that position?

A. That was what he said: that he was an Inspector General or Assistant Inspector General, with the rank of Lieutenant Colonel, I think he said.

Q. The Military Department of Washington, as it is spoken of in military parlance, embraces the city of Washington, does it not, and did it not during the past year?

A. Yes, sir.

Q. And all the defences of the city?

A. Yes, sir, over on the other side of the river and Alexandria.

Q. It includes all the fortifications on both sides?

A. Yes, sir.

Q. I have in my hand a copy of your commission as Lieutenant General of the Armies of the United States bearing date the 4th day of March 1864. Will you state whether or not since that time you have continued to be in command, under that commission, of the Armies of the United States?

A. I have.

[The Judge Advocate offered in evidence, without objection, the commission of Lieutenant General Grant, dated March 4, 1864, accompanied by General Orders No. 98 M'ch 12/64, which are appended to this record marked Exhibit No. 6.]

Cross-Examined by Mr. Aiken.

Q. Are you aware that the civil courts are in operation in this city,—all of them?

A. Yes, sir.

Q. How far towards Baltimore does the Department of Washington extend?

A. I could not say exactly to what point. Any troops that belong to General Augur's command, however, that he sends out to any point would necessarily remain under his command. He commands the Department of Washington.

Q. Is any portion of the State of Maryland in the Department of Washington?

A. Oh, yes, sir. Martial law, I believe, extends to all the territory south of the railroad that comes across from Annapolis, running south to the Potomac and the Chesapeake.

Cross Examined by Mr Ewing.

Q. By virtue of what order does martial law extend south of Annapolis?

A. I never saw the order. It is just simply an understanding?.

Q. It is just an understanding?

A. Yes, sir, just an understanding that it does exist.

Q. You have never seen any order?

A. No, sir.

Q. And do not know that such an order exists?

A. No, sir, I have never seen the orders.

DNA, RG 153, MM 2251, section 7, pp. 158–63. Brackets in document. Printed in variant form in Benn Pitman, ed., *The Assassination of President Lincoln and the Trial of the Conspirators* (Cincinnati and New York, 1865), p. 37. On May 10,

1865, Bvt. Col. Henry L. Burnett, judge advocate, wrote to USG. "I have the honor to request that you will be at the court-room tomorrow at 2 o'clock p. m. as a witness in the cases now on trial before the Military Commission of which Major General Hunter is President. The Commission is holding its sessions at the Penitentiary near the Arsenal in this city." Copies (unsigned), DNA, RG 153, Letters Sent by Burnett (Press); *ibid.*, Register of Letters Sent by Burnett.

To Edwin M. Stanton

From Phila Pa May 15 *1865.*

Hon E M Stanton

I would respectfully request that the trial of Capt J B Castleman now as I understand at Indpls be deferred until I can see you in his case. It is a question with me with all the facts I now know whether it would not now be a breach of faith on the part of Govt to bring him to trial—

U S Grant
Lt Gen

Telegram received (at 1:00 P.M.), DNA, RG 107, Telegrams Collected (Bound); copy, *ibid.*, RG 94, Letters Received, 500A 1865.

On Dec. 5, 1864, C.S.A. Agent of Exchange Robert Ould wrote to USG. "I beg leave most respectfully to bring to your attention, the case of Capt. J. B. Castleman, who, a short time ago, was arrested at Sullivan, Indiana, and is now held at Camp Morton, Indianapolis, by the U. S. Authorities, under the charge of being a spy. Capt. Castleman belonged to Morgan's Command, and being separated from it, was compelled to fly to Canada for safety. He remained there until his health was recruited, and in the latter part of Sept. of this year, endeavored to make his way back to his Command. In order to do this with more facility, he put on a citizens dress, and went by the name of Clay Wilson. This, General, is a frank statement of the facts. If I did not know this to be the case, I would not say so. I assure you that whatever circumstances of suspicion may attach to Capt. Castleman, from the position in which he was found, he is an honorable gentleman, who was simply seeking to rejoin his Command. In no sense of the word was he a spy. Your own Officers and soldiers, during the progress of this war, have often been arrested under circumstances equally suspicious. In no instance has any severe penalty been visited upon them. In an attempt, some time since, to escape, more than fifty Officers were re-captured and returned to the Libby. Some of them wore the disguise of citizens, put on after they left the prison. Some had assumed names, and others had false passports. They were not even, tried as spies. We knew that the devices they employed were used for the purpose of facilitating their escape, and for no other reason. It was equally so with Capt. Castleman. I am sure the most rigid inquiry will show this to be the fact. Under these circumstances, I appeal to you that no injustice be done to a gallant gentleman, and faithful soldier. If you have any Officer or soldier now in our hands, charged with a similar offence, under circumstances even approaching those I have represented, or if hereafter, any one should be placed therein, I assure you the Confederate Authorities will, upon your suggestion, or that of any other Federal Officer, promptly put him, in every respect, upon the footing of a prisoner of war. I beg, therefore, that you will represent this case to your authorities, and that you will at an early date, inform me of their purpose." Copies, *ibid.*, RG 109, Ould Letterbook; Ould Letterbook, Archives Div., Virginia State Library, Richmond, Va. Between Dec. 12 and 14, USG endorsed this letter. "Respy. forwarded to the Sec of War. As it is one of the most natural things in the world for an escaped soldier to assume disguise, both in clothing and name, to secure his return to his own troops, I am of opinion, unless other facts can be proven against Captain Castleman, that he can be only held as a prisoner of war" Copy, DLC-USG, V, 58. On Dec. 30, Asst. Secretary of War Charles A. Dana forwarded to USG copies of opinions of Francis Lieber, Maj. Gen. Henry W. Halleck, and Judge Advocate Gen. Joseph Holt stating that a soldier captured under such conditions should be treated as a spy. ES, DNA, RG 108, Letters Received. When arrested, Capt. John B. Castleman was involved in an attempt to release C.S.A. prisoners at Camp Douglas, Chicago, and to encourage insurrection in the Midwest. See Lincoln, *Works*, VIII, 123; Jno. B. Castleman, *Active Service* (Louisville, 1917), pp. 129–88.

On March 9, 1865, Ould wrote to USG. "Capt. John B. Castleman, the Confederate Officer, who was some time since arrested in Indiana, and about whom I wrote to you on the 5th of Dec. last, was in close confinement at Camp Morton some three weeks ago. As I have released and delivered to you every prisoner who has been so confined in the South including even deserters, and those charged with being spies, will you not order the release of Capt. Castleman and have him delivered to our Authorities." Copies, DNA, RG 109, Ould Letterbook; Ould Letterbook, Virginia State Library. *O.R.*, II, viii, 368–69. On March 17, USG endorsed this letter. "Respy. referred to Brig Gen. W. Hoffman, Com. Gen of Prisoners who will cause this officer to be forwarded for exchange" Copy, DLC-USG, V, 58. On March 27, Bvt. Brig. Gen. William Hoffman endorsed this letter. "Respectfully returned to Lieut Gen'l Grant, Com'dg U. S. Army Capt Castleman, and Lieut Mumford, are confined in a tent at Camp Morton, charged with being spies, under Orders from Gen'l. Hovey. They were captured in September 1864. They will be forwarded for Exchange without delay" Copy, DNA, RG 107, Letters Received from Bureaus.

On June 1, Annie E. Martin, Louisville, wrote to USG. "Although an utter stranger to you—unknown & unheard of—in behalf of a human life in deadly peril I venture to appeal to you—With you it rests to decree his destiny, perhaps to pronounce his doom—I come to *you* then strong in the faith, that with so much greatness, goodness must be allied, & that faith confirmed by *all* that I have ever heard of you—I do not despair, for I feel that so brave a soldier *will* listen gently to a woman's earnest prayer—& tis from the bravest we may most surely hope for the precious boon of mercy—Four years ago—Kentucky was convulsed to the very centre by the fearful issues then presented to her—In a frightful civil war plainly impending over us—Kentucky had he[r] place to choose— Torn by conflicting ties—she paused & wavered—even her greatest Statesmen hesitated—On the one hand, the Government & the Union; time honored, loved & reverenced—on the other—states & people drawn most closely to her by the dearest ties of blood & kindred—While her great men lingered, her youth waiting not the dictates of Reason & of judgement rushed headlong & impetuous where *feeling* led the way—Among these last, was John Castleman, from Lexington Ky. whose life & pardon I now ask. Whatever were the merits of the cause for which he sacrificed so much. he thought it was just & righteous.—And—if he erred, I entreat you will remember that 'To err is human—to forgive Divine'—He held a commission in the once so-called Confederate Army. He was taken prisoner & succeeded in escaping to Canada—in attempting to rejoin his command. he was again captured at Cincinnati, last summer, & sentenced to be tried as a spy—After waiting some months he was sent to some point to be exchanged as a prisoner of war—no further exchanges being made, he was remanded to *a cell* at Indianapolis, to await his trial (for his life) before a military tribunal—Under the rigors of Solitary Confinement, his health is failing rapidly & we fear that Death will claim him as a victim—His mother—a very old lady & a widow, is crushed & broken under this great affliction—Now, that all is over—that all—every vestige of resistance is at an end—I beg you—give back to us this life—He is no leader—before the nation he is but an obscure individual & the life which if taken would avail the country little—if saved—would be a most precious boon to his family & friends—let me then entreat you *stay this trial*— Speak but the one noble word, that he is free & a mother's blessing & a sister's prayers will be your sure reward—Amid the laurel wreath which will encircle the Conqueror's brow—let us entwine the tender modest blossom which bespeaks his gentle acts of mercy—" ALS, *ibid.*, RG 108, Letters Received. On June 2, Richard T. Jacob, Frankfort, wrote to USG. "I enclose you a letter from Miss Annie Martin, the daughter of one of the leading citizens of Louisville Ky. in behalf of John Castleman once of the so called Confederate army. I pray you to give her letter and petition earnest thought, and if in your power and not against the interests of our beloved country pardon and restore him to the bosom of his afflicted family. I will briefly state his case. Urged on by young and hot blood but I have no doubt by honest intentions he espoused the cause of the so called Confederate Government. He was taken prisoner. From prison he made his escape to Canada. From thence he attempted to rejoin his command. In attempting this he was recaptured near Cincinnatti and Sentenced to be tried as a spy. He remained in a cell for many months when he was ordered to some point to be exchanged as a prisoner of war. After waiting several weeks, no further exchanges being made he was remanded to a solitary cell at Indianappolis to be tried for his life before a military tribunal. I am informed that his health is becoming very bad, and that unless soon pardoned he may die from the effects of confinement This young man like many others in Kentucky rashly precipitated himself into the arms of the rebellion; a rebellion utterly without cause, and which I condemn and have condemned as much as you possibly can. But the rebellion is crushed, the unity of the Country is preserved, how possibly can the life of so young and obscure a man effect any good. Its power for good would not be greater than that of the killing of a fly or worm. Though obscure he is every thing to a widowed and afflicted mother and sisters. His pardon would do good, as showing that a great and magnanimous Nation in the hour of triumph, can afford to be magnanimous and deal gently with her erring sons. I will not trouble you much more, I feel assured that if in your power that you will pardon this young man. Remember Sir, that the brightest laurel that encircles your brow amidst so many glorious ones, is the noble and magnanimous terms that you gave to an overpowered enemy under General Lee, in order to stop the further effusion of blood. Brighten those Laurels by stilling the grief of a widowed mothers heart, and changeing tears into joys upon the troubled faces of afflicted sisters. In conclusion permit me to thank you for the kinds words that you sent me by Col Mumford when I passed by City Point last January upon my return home from a forced and unjust exile, amonst those people that I had fought against, in defence of the Union. Be assured General, that I shall never forget those kind words." ALS, *ibid.*

On June 7, Castleman, Indianapolis, wrote to President Andrew Johnson. "In the Summer of the year 1862, being then less than Twenty one years of age and living near Lexington, Kentucky, I was induced to engage in the Rebellion, and joined the Rebel Army.—I continued in that service, and was arrested in Southern Indiana in the month of September 1864, and have been since that time a prisoner and held under charges for trial. In what I did I was led to believe, and at the time thought, I was doing my duty. I am now convinced that my action was wrong from the beginning, and that I have committed grievous errors. For what is past I can only express my sincere regret, and promise to strive by my future action to atone for it—by faithful efforts to discharge my duty as a citizen of the United States. With this preliminary statement, I desire now to ask that I may be permitted to take the Oath of Allegiance, and be released on such terms as may to you seem best. And if it is not possible or proper in your judgement that this should be done, I ask that I may be allowed to become a voluntary exile to some other country, for life or such shorter time, as may be deemed by you sufficient, Subject to such penalties for returning as may be imposed, and giving my obligation in such form as may be required, to observe strictly the terms of the order and to do no act of hostility in any way to the United States. I hope it will be found consistent with your views of duty and of the public interests to grant my request—" ALS, *ibid.*, RG 107, Letters Received from Bureaus. On the same day, Bvt. Maj. Gen. Alvin P. Hovey endorsed this letter. "I have no doubt that the facts will establish against Major Castleman the charge of being a spy but in consideration of his youth and family connections and his penitence would recommend that his request of becoming a voluntary exile be granted" AES, *ibid.* On June 21, USG endorsed this letter. "Respectfully forwarded to the Secretary of War, and the recommendation of Gen. Hovey that Castleman be permitted to leave the country, never to return, approved" ES, *ibid.* On June 24, Johnson endorsed this letter. "Respectfully referred to Bvt Maj. General Hovey with instructions to exercise his discretion in this matter and, if he thinks, best, to ~~comply~~ grant Castleman's request against whom proceedings will be suspended so long as he shall remain without the limits of the United States" ES, *ibid.*, RG 249, Letters Received, 1487W 1865. On June 27, Maj. Jesse W. Walker issued Special Orders No. 100, District of Ind. "In accordance with instructions from the President of the United States, dated June 24th 1865. John B. Castleman. charged with being a spy for the so called Confederate States of America, against the Government of the United States, in the late rebellion. against the United States, is released upon his parole of honor to leave the United States of America within seven days from this date, and never return to the same, and proceedings against him are suspended as long as he shall remain without the limits of the United States." DS, *ibid.*

To Brig. Gen. John A. Rawlins

From Phila' May 15 *1865*.

GEN J A RAWLINS.
CHF STAFF.

Please have two 2 rooms secured for me at the Hotel. If I feel
sufficiently well to travel I will go to Washington. Mrs Grant with
me tomorrow. I am now too unwell to set up any length of time and
cannot tell when I shall be better. Knowing the almost absolute
necessity for my presence in Washington worries me very much.

U S GRANT
Lt Gen

Telegram received (at 11:30 A.M.), DNA, RG 107, Telegrams Collected
(Bound); *ibid.*, RG 108, Telegrams Received; copy, DLC-USG, V, 54. *O.R.*, I,
xlvi, part 3, 1152. On May 14, 1865, Sunday, USG, Philadelphia, telegraphed
to Brig. Gen. John A. Rawlins. "It was my intention to have returned to Washington this evening but I find myself too unwell to do so. It is not probable that
I shall be able to go before Tuesday" Telegram received (at 6:10 P.M.), DNA,
RG 107, Telegrams Collected (Bound). *O.R.*, I, xlvi, part 3, 1149.

To Maj. Gen. John Pope

Washington, D. C. May 17th *1865* [2:00 P.M.]

MAJ GEN JNO POPE
ST LOUIS MO

I have decided to sustain your action in regard to the colonization of Missionary Indians at Red Wood. Papers indicate that
hostilities are again about breaking out in Minnesota If such is
the case you had better reinforce that country at once, If you have
not the troops to do it with, they can be furnished from Genl
Thomas command It may be the Indians require as much protection from [t]he whites as the whites do from the Indians [M]y
own experience has been that but little trouble would have ever

been had from them but for the encroachments & influence of bad
whites—

U S GRANT

Lt Genl

Telegram sent, DNA, RG 107, Telegrams Collected (Bound); telegram received (at 3:00 P.M.), *ibid.*, Telegrams Collected (Unbound). Printed as sent
at 3:00 P.M. in *O.R.*, I, xlviii, part 2, 480.

On May 8, 1865, 8:30 P.M., USG telegraphed to Maj. Gen. John Pope.
"Please report immediately your objection to friendy Sioux Indians being located at Redwing." ALS (telegram sent), DNA, RG 107, Telegrams Collected
(Bound); telegram sent, *ibid.*; telegram received (on May 9), *ibid.*, RG 94, War
Records Office, Army of the Potomac. *O.R.*, I, xlviii, part 2, 347. On May 9, 4:25
P.M., Pope telegraphed to USG. "Your telegram concerning Location of Friendly
sioux at Redwing recd & fully answered by mail today" Telegram received (at
6:30 P.M.), DNA, RG 107, Telegrams Collected (Bound); (at 6:10 P.M.)
ibid., RG 108, Telegrams Received; copies, *ibid.*, RG 393, Military Div. of the
Mo., Telegrams Sent; DLC-USG, V, 54. *O.R.*, I, xlviii, part 2, 366. On the same
day, Pope wrote to USG. "I have the honor to acknowledge the receipt this
morning of your telegram of yesterday's date, asking me to state 'my objections
to friendly Sioux Indians being located at Red Wing.' The dreadful massacres
of 1862 and the continued hostility of the great mass of the Sioux bands, has so
exasperated the people of Minnesota that I do not believe that the life of any
Indian would be safe from the frontier settlers if he came within their reach.
The attempt to bring back to their reservations and settle immediately in contact with the frontier settlement of Minnesota any Sioux Indians whatever
would, I am certain, create the profoundest anxiety and alarm and would certainly lead to hostile acts against the Indians, which being resented and revenged
would very soon plunge us again into an Indian war, if indeed such a war were
not again preceeded by extensive massacres. It is impossible for Indians and white
men to live in contact on the frontier, without continual danger of hostilities.
Surely the history of our Indian affairs for the last twenty-five years has made
this fact very plain. The massacres of 1862 and the war with Indians since have
involved nearly the entire Sioux nation. By these acts they have themselves
voluntarily forfeited all claims under former treaties and we have it now in our
power to arrange matters so that there will be comparatively little danger of
such massacres as have hitherto marked our Indian relations. I have established
a line of military posts (small posts mostly) beginning at Ft. Abercrombie on
the East and extending entirely around the frontier settlements of Minnesota to
Spirit Lake and thence across to the Missouri river at Ft. Pierre. This line of
posts is far outside of the extreme frontier settlements. I have invited all friendly
Sioux to locate in the vicinity of any of these posts, to occupy as much land as
they please and have furnished them with the means to put in crops. No white
man, except religious instructors or military officers, is permitted to go among
them. All persons duly authorised to trade with them are required to locate their
trading houses at one of the military posts and be supervised by military authority
in their trading transactions. A wide reach of country is placed between these

Indians and the frontier settlements and they are placed in that relation to the
military forces which ensures theirm protection both against white and red
rascals or enemies. I hope gradually thus to assemble most of the bands of hostile
Sioux along the chain of posts, securing them land in the neighborhood to cultivate and the wide prairie beyond for hunting grounds. Thus kept seperated from
white men and expecting nothing from the Gen. Govt. as the price of peaceful
conduct except kind treatment, I hope to keep them in peace both with whites
and Indians. I transmit enclosed my orders on this subject and would also invite
your attention to my letter to the Secretary of War—covering the whole subject
of our Indian affairs, published in the Army and Navy Gazette of April 26th
1864. Your own experience on the frontier will I am sure fully confirm all that
is therein stated. A settlement of the Sioux Indians where it is proposed to be
made by the Rev. Mr. Hinman, Missionary, again makes a nucleus in the immediate vicinity of the frontier settlements for the reassembling of nearly the
entire Sioux tribe and the recommencement of quarrels, bickerings, stealing and
outrage which will surely lead to another Indian outbreak. It is my firm belief
that by permitting this settlement to be made at Red Wing, we are simply laying
the foundation of another Indian Massacre, if indeed the Indians themselves be
not massacred in advance by the Whites. It is my purpose to keep the two races
separated by a line of soldiers and by broad extents of country. In this way I
hope to secure peace. The scheme of Rev. Mr. Hinman if carried out destroys in
my opinion all hope of securing the satisfactory result now within our reach. I
wrote to Gen. Sibley some days since informing him that although my objections
to Mr. Hinman's project were not in any manner modified, yet if the Governor
and people of Minnesota desired or would consent to such a settlement as is suggested, I would reconsider the matter. I am sure you will find the strongest opposition to this scheme, almost universally manifested by the people of Minnesota and this opposition of itself would be sufficient to bring it to naught. Both
for the sake of the Indian and the white man and for the best interests of the
Govt. I recommend that no such scheme be put into execution and no orders given
requiring me to change or greatly modify a policy which has already led to good
results and which depends upon its *permanency* for any success at all. I send
enclosed a printed letter on this subject from Hon J. K Brown of Minnesota. He
has lived in that region of country for forty years—most of the time amongst
Indians—and is the best authority on the subject that I know of." LS, DNA, RG
94, Letters Received, 2602M 1865. *O.R.*, I, xlviii, part 2, 366–67. See *ibid.*, p.
359; *ibid.*, I, xlviii, part 1, 718–20.

On May 8, Charles H. Hall, Washington, D. C., and William Welsh, Philadelphia, wrote to USG. "We respectfully present the following facts, and ask
your favourable action. By Act of Congress. app: March 3d 1863. the Secretary
of Interior gave authority (april 27. 1865), gave authority to Rev S. D. Hinman,
to locate upon a tract of land on the Minnesota River—(Gen Halleck approving
by letter)—as specified by Act of Congress 'individual Indians of the Sioux Tribe,
who remained true to the Government and exerted themselves to save the lives of
whites during the massacres of 1862'. Gen: Halleck, was particularly interested
in the case, and cheerfully aided the Missionary Mr Hinman. Major Gen John
Pope, has now instructed Gen: Sibley 'to permit no such settlement of the
Indians at the point designated, with out further orders from him, or *from
superior military authority*. Under ordinary circumstances it would be well to
take the common rule, and prove, as we think we shall do, that Gen Pope, is

laboring under some misunderstanding of the case, and has not examined the full force of the Decision of the Secretary of the Interior under the Act of Congress. But, if these people, are disappointed and delayed, for any time, even a few weeks longer, they will lose the year's crop, and be dissatisfied and burdensome—Every day is valuable to them, at this season. We request therefore—if approved by your judgement—that you, his military superior, issue the orders in the above contingency—so that, while the reasons pro and con, are being examined, this precious time may not be lost, to these faithful Indians, some of them Soldiers in the Army, and the spring crop be planted: or, failing that, that you will be good enough to Telegraph to Gen: Pope, to report his reasons for his Order—that they may be reviewed by the Secretary of the Interior—whose order he has now crossed." LS, DNA, RG 108, Letters Received. On May 10, Welsh wrote to USG. "After you left the Secretary of War this morning he received a despatch from General Halleck stating that Genl Pope had not sent any communication to him, about the obstacles he has placed in the execution of a Law as ordered by the Secretary of the Interior As the copy of that despatch reached Genl Sibley by or before the 27th ult at St Paul Minnesota it is probable that the despatch was not mailed until your telegram was received As a delay at this period of the year is fatal to the effort of the Govt to do tardy justice to the Indian, and as Genl Pope delayed to mail his letter for more than ten days after he sent a copy to Genl Sibley, and not until you asked reasons that should have been sent by telegraph, may I not beg immediate action on your part? That you might be in full possession of the facts officially, I obtained the certificate herewith from the department of the Interior. If you need information Mr Mix or Mr Whiting will furnish it, or wait upon you. Believing in Mr Lincolns motto that all should have a chance, and as delay is fatal, will you not Telegraph to Genl Sibley to withdraw all obstacles to Mr Hinmans colony of Indians in Minnesota as authorized by the Secretary of the Interior—This promptitude may save our Christian allies from ruin, and if Genl Popes reasons ever reach you and you think it best to banish them to the Desirt I will pay all the expense the Govt is put to. Excuse my seeming to add to your cares as I would prefer to relieve you I write because I return to Philada this afternoon where I must meet the Society of Friends who will rejoice to know that Genl Grant has an Indian on his Staff" ALS, *ibid.*

To Maj. Gen. Philip H. Sheridan

Washington D. C. May 17th *1865*

MAJ. GEN. P. H. SHERIDAN,
U. S. ARMY

Under the orders relieving you from the command of the Middle Mil. Div. ~~you~~ and assigning you to command West of the Miss. you will proceed without delay to the West to arrange all preliminaries for your new field of duties.

Your duty is to restore Texas, and that part of Louisiana held by the enemy, to the Union in the shortest practicable time, in a way most effectual for securing permanent peace.

To do this will be given you all the troops that can be spared by Maj. Gen. Canby, ~~he to command them~~, probably twenty-five thousand men of all arms. The troops with Maj. Gen. J. J. Reynolds in Arkansas, say twelve thousand, Reynolds to command. The 4th Army Corps, now at Nashville Tenn. awaiting orders, and the 25th Army Corps now at City Point Va. ready to embark.

I do not wish to trammel you with instructions how to do. I will state however that if Smith holds out, without even an ostensable Government to receive orders from, or to report to, he and his men are not entitled to the considerations due to an acknowledged belligerent. Theirs are the conditions of outlaws making war against the only Government having an existance over the territory where war is being waged.

You may notify the Rebel commander West of the Miss. holding intercourse with him in person, or through such officer, of the rank of Maj. Gen. as you may select, that he will be allowed to surrender all his forces on the same terms as were accorded to Lee and Johnston. If he accedes proceed to garrison the Red River as high up at least as Scrievesport; the ~~seaport~~board at Galveston, Mattagorda Bay, Corpus Christi and mouth of the Rio Grande. Place a strong force on the Rio Grande, holding it at least to opposite Camargo, and above if supplies can be procured.

In case of an active campaign, a hostile one, I think a heavy force should be put on the Rio Grande as a first preliminary. Troops for this might be started at once. The 25th Corps is now available and to it should be added a force of White troops say those now under Maj. Gn. Steele. To be clear on this last point: I think the Rio Grande should be strongly held whether the forces in Texas surrender or not and that no time should be lost in getting them there. If war is to be made, they will be in the right place: if Kirby Smith surrenders they will be on the line which is to be strongly garrisoned.

Should any force be necessary other than those designated
they can be had by calling for them at Army Hd Qrs.

> Very respectfully
> your obt. svt.
> U. S. GRANT
> Lt. Gen.

ALS, Williams College, Williamstown, Mass. *O.R.*, I, xlviii, part 2, 476.

On May 17, 1865, USG wrote to Secretary of War Edwin M. Stanton. "I
would respectfully request orders, to-night, relieving Maj. Gn. P. H. Sheridan
from command of the 'Mid. Mil. Div.' and assigning him to general command
West of the Miss. South of the Arkansas. Also for him to report to me for instructions." ALS, DLC-Edwin M. Stanton. *O.R.*, I, xlvi, part 3, 1161.

Also on May 17, Bvt. Col. Theodore S. Bowers endorsed a communication
reporting 1800 U.S. troops held as prisoners in Tex. "Respy. referred to Maj
Gen P. H. Sheridan. My agreement with Judge Ould Com of Ex. for the Confed.
authorities was that, these men were to have been and should have been released
sometime ago. Immediate steps must be taken to secure their release" Copy,
DLC-USG, V, 58.

On May 18, Brig. Gen. John A. Rawlins wrote to Brig. Gen. Amos B. Eaton,
commissary gen. "The Lieut, Genl, Comdg desires me to say that Maj, Gen,
Sheridan having been assigned to a Command South of the Arkansas River and
West of the Mississippi, he wishes you to direct Col, J. J. Harris [*Haines*] C, S. to
fill such requisitions as he may make" Copies, *ibid.*, V, 46, 76, 108; DNA, RG
108, Letters Sent. *O.R.*, I, xlviii, part 2, 488. On the same day, Rawlins wrote
to Bvt. Maj. Gen. Montgomery C. Meigs. "The Lieut, Genl, Comdg desires me
to say that Maj, Genl, Sheridan having been assigned to a Command South of the
Arkansas River and West of the Mississippi, he wishes you to direct Genl, R,
Allen Qr, Mr. to fill such requisitions as he may make" Copies, DLC-USG, V,
46, 76, 108; DNA, RG 108, Letters Sent. *O.R.*, I, xlviii, part 2, 488.

On May 20, Sheridan wrote to Bowers. "I have the honor to request that
Maj: Genl. Merritt and Maj: Genl. Custer be relieved from duty with the
Cavalry immediately after the review ordered for tuesday next, and directed to
report to me for duty without delay." LS, DNA, RG 94, Letters Received, 1212S
1865.

Testimony

> WASHINGTON, *May* 18, 1865.

Lieutenant General U. S. GRANT recalled and examined.
> By the chairman:

Question. You have been lieutenant general commanding the whole army for a year past and more?

Answer. Yes, sir.

Question. I wish to place upon our record your answer to the following question: In what manner has Mr. Stanton, Secretary of War, performed his duties in the supply of the armies and the support of the military operations under your charge?

Answer. Admirably, I think. There has been no complaint in that respect—that is, no general complaint. So far as he is concerned I do not think there has been any ground of complaint in that respect.

Question. Has there ever been any misunderstanding with regard to the conduct of the war, in any particular, between you and the Secretary of War since you have been in command?

Answer. Never any expressed to me. I never had any reason to suppose that any fault was found with anything I had done. So far as the Secretary of War and myself are concerned, he has never interfered with my duties, never thrown any obstacles in the way of any supplies I have called for. He has never dictated a course of campaign to me, and never inquired what I was going to do. He has always seemed satisfied with what I did, and has heartily cooperated with me.

Report of the Joint Committee on the Conduct of the War at the Second Session Thirty-eighth Congress (Washington, 1865), I, 524 (Army of the Potomac).
On May 9, 1865, USG wrote to U.S. Senator Benjamin F. Wade of Ohio, chairman, Committee on the Conduct of the War. "Sir I have just rec'd notice to report in person to your 'Committee' as soon as the exigency of the service will permit. I have the honor to state that any hour you may designate for to-morrow will suit me." ALS, DLC-Benjamin F. Butler. On May 16, Bvt. Brig. Gen. Edward D. Townsend, AGO, wrote to USG. "The Secretary of War directs me to communicate to you the following, extract from a letter dated the 15th instant from Hon B. F. Wade, Chairman of Committee on the Conduct of the War The Committee also request that Generals Grant and Meade be directed to appear before the Committee tomorrow (May 16th) at 11 a. m or as soon thereafter as the public service will permit.' General Meade has been informed." Copy, DNA, RG 94, Letters Sent.

To Edwin M. Stanton

———

Washington May 18th *1865*

Hon. E. M. Stanton,
Sec. of War,
Sir:

With the view of reducing expenses and breaking up numerous Hd Qrs. I would respectfully recommend that orders be issued discontinuing the 10th 23d & 24th Corps. Gen. Gibbon to report to Gen. Halleck for assignment, Gen. Cox to report to Gn. Schofield, Gen. Terry to take command of the Dept. of the South and Gn. Gilmore to report to the Adj. Gn. of the Army for orders.

> Very respectfully
> your obt. svt.
> U. S. Grant
> Lt. Gn.

ALS, DNA, RG 94, Letters Received, 1383A 1865. *O.R.*, I, xlvi, part 3, 1167.

To Edwin M. Stanton

———

Washington May 18th *1865*

Hon. E. M. Stanton,
Sec. of War,
Sir:

I return Gen. Meredith's dispatch with my view of the answer that should be given. If the Mo. rebels at Eastport are there on their way to Mo. by agreement between Canby and Taylor they should by all means be allowed to go.

For my part I do not see half the objection to having whipped rebels, bound by a solemn oath to observe the laws prevailing where they may be, and to do no act against the Government, going into loyal communities that I do to retaining in those com-

munities disloyal men, as we are doing, who are bound by no oath
and who have suffered nothing from the war.

I think it would be good policy to publish an order authorizing
so far as the gen. Govt. is concerned, all paroled prisoners claimg
homes in states which never passed the ordnance of Secession, to
go to their claimed homes. If state authority interferes the Military
will not interfere with it.

> Very respectfully
> your obt. svt.
> U. S. GRANT
> Lt. Gn.

ALS, DNA, RG 249, Letters Received. *O.R.*, I, xlix, part 2, 827. USG enclosed
a telegram of May 16, 1865, from Brig. Gen. Solomon Meredith, Paducah, Ky.,
to Secretary of War Edwin M. Stanton. "By agreement with Lieut Gen. R. Taylor C. S. A. Maj Gen Canby U. S. A has forwarded to Eastport Miss to be sent
to this place about one thousand paroled prisoners belonging to the state of Missouri I am direct[ed] by Maj Gen Thomas to telegraph you for instructions—"
Telegram received (at 5:15 P.M.), DNA, RG 249, Letters Received. *O.R.*, I,
xlix, part 2, 809.

To Edwin M. Stanton

Washington May 18th 1865

HON, E, M, STANTON
SECRETARY OF WAR
SIR

I would respectfully recommend, that the necessary orders be
issued for extending the operations of the recruiting service for
the regular Army by establishing recruiting rendezous at important
points in all the Southern States, within our lines of occupation, and
by opening branch stations at such Stations at the North not now
occupied, as may seem to offer good fields for recruiting,

Also, that Citizens of the Southern States, as well as persons
who have served in the rebel Armies, be accepted as recruits, but

all persons who have been engaged in the rebellion against the U. S. before being recieved will be required to qualify as loyal Citizens, in addition to taking the prescribed enlistment oath

Very Respectfully
Your obt svt
U. S. GRANT
Lt, Genl

Copies, DLC-USG, V, 46, 76, 108; DNA, RG 108, Letters Sent.

USG added an undated endorsement, "Approved" to a draft, dated May 19, of unnumbered AGO General Orders. "1. . . . In order to recruit the ranks of the regular regiments as soon as practicable, the Adjutant General will open recruiting stations at such points as offer a reasonable prospect of enlisting good men, including cities and towns in Southern States. 2. . . The fact of having serviceed in the rebel armies will be no bar to enlistment in the U. S. Army, but beside the oath usual oath of enlistment, the recruit will be required to take the prescribed amnesty oath. 3. . . Volunteers honorably discharged from the U. S. Service, who enlist in the regular army within ten days from date of discharge, in the regular Army will be allowed a furlough of thirty days before joining their regiments. They will be paid all pay and allowances to which they may be entitled, on being discharged from the volunteer service. 4. . . . The Adjutant General will relieve all officers of the regular army regiments serving in the volunteer Staff and in volunteer regiments, and on detached service not connected with the regular regiments, not including those who hold commissions as General Officers, officers, as soon as their services can possibly be spared, and assign them to dutiesy with their regiments, which or on Recruiting service, so as best to facilitate the efficient organization and drill, of their regiments" AES and Df, *ibid.*, RG 94, Letters Received, 546A 1865. Issued on May 28, General Orders No. 99 omitted the last phrase of section 1, all of sections 2 and 4, all marked lightly for deletion in the draft; whether marked for deletion before or after approved by USG cannot be determined. *O.R.*, I, xlvi, part 3, 1227–28.

On June 16, USG endorsed papers concerning recruiting in Richmond. "Respectfully returned to the Adjutant General Officer with the recommendation that recruiting offices for these batteries be established in Richmond and that all persons desireous of enlisting who were residents of the states that have been in rebellion, during the existence of the rebellion, or that may have been in the Military service of the rebel authorities, and who have not taken the oath prescribed in the recent amnesty proclamation of the President be required to take oath in addition to the oath usually prescribed in the case of enlistments before muster in to the service All applicants for enlistments who are excepted from the benefits of the President Amnesty Proclamation shall before muster into the service take the oath of allegiance and forward it through the recruiting officer with an application to the President for Amnesty which if granted, shall entitle them to muster into service." Copy, DLC-USG, V, 41.

To Edwin M. Stanton

Hd Qrs. Armies of the U S.

Washington May 18th 1865

Respectfully refered to the Sec. of War with recommendation that the within named prisoners be released at once and transportation ordered to their states. I hope early means may be devised for clearing our prisons as far as possible. I would recommend that all who come within the Amnesty proclamation be allowed the benefit of it. By going now they may still raise something for their subsistence for the coming year and prevent suffering next Winter. Prisoners living West of the Miss. those from states which never passed the ordnance of Secession and those from the District of Columbia might be made an exception for the present. ~~Those~~

U. S. GRANT

Lt. Gen.

AES, DNA, RG 249, Letters Received. *O.R.*, II, viii, 556. Written on a petition of forty-nine prisoners, Fort Delaware, asking release after taking an oath of allegiance. AD, DNA, RG 249, Letters Received. *O.R.*, II, viii, 556. Also on May 18, 1865, USG endorsed another list of prisoners. "Respectfully refered to the Sec. of War. I would recommend the release of the prisoners named with the exception of Gn. Page." AES, DNA, RG 249, Letters Received. Brig. Gen. Richard L. Page, born in 1807 in Va., a commander in the U.S. Navy before the Civil War, held the same rank in the C.S. Navy; while defending Fort Morgan, Mobile Bay, for the C.S. Army, he was captured on Aug. 23, 1864.

On May 16, 1865, Brig. Gen. James Barnes, Point Lookout, Md., wrote to Bvt. Brig. Gen. William Hoffman requesting that patients in the prison hospital receive transportation home after taking the oath of allegiance. *O.R.*, II, viii, 557. On May 29, USG endorsed this letter favorably. *Ibid.*, p. 558.

On May 30, seventy-three C.S.A. officers, U.S. Military Prison Hospital, Fort Delaware, petitioned USG for release and transportation home after taking the oath of allegiance. ADf, ViU. See endorsement, May 31, 1865.

To Maj. Gen. Edward R. S. Canby

(Cipher)   Washington May 18th *1865* [5:00 P.M.]

MAJ. GEN. CANBY NEW ORLEANS LA,

Your expedition against Galveston is suspended by recent orders. You will fit Steele out with a force of not less than six thousand men immediately for the Rio Grande. Send him equipped with Artillery, Ammunition for an ordinary campaign and forty days rations for the men. This force after it sails will be subject to general instructions from Gn. Sherridan. The 25th Corps will start in a few days from City Point to same destination with orders to report in Mobile Bay to Gn. Steele for further orders. Steele should be ready so that there should not be a single days delay after the arrival of 25th Corps. Hold all troops that can be spared from your command subject to the orders of Gen. Sheridan. Require your Quartermaster and Commissary to fill his requisitions with despatch.

U. S. GRANT

Lt. Gn.

ALS (telegram sent), DNA, RG 107, Telegrams Collected (Bound); telegram sent, *ibid.*; telegrams received (4—three marked as sent at 4:30 P.M., one marked as sent at 9:00 A.M.), *ibid.*, Telegrams Collected (Unbound). Printed as sent at 4:30 P.M. in *O.R.*, I, xlviii, part 2, 486–87. On May 24, 1865, 11:30 P.M., Maj. Alfred Fredberg, Mobile, telegraphed to Maj. Gen. Edward R. S. Canby. "The following telegegraph is the cipher that was received on the 20th which could not be deciphered. It has been repeated from Washington & received this evening. I shall inform Maj Genl Steele, Col, Sawtelle & Hinsdale of the contents so that they can make preliminary arrangements & await the Generals orders." Telegram received (on May 25, 1:00 P.M.), CSt. On June 7, Canby wrote to USG's hd. qrs. "I have the honor to acknowledge the receipt of copy of the telegraphic despatch of the Lieutenant-General, dated May 18th. The original was received and replied to in due course." LS, DNA, RG 108, Letters Received. No direct reply has been found.

On May 16, Canby, New Orleans, telegraphed to Brig. Gen. John A. Rawlins. "The 13 corps is now conscentrated at Mobile—Two Divisions thirteen thousand (13.000) strong and four thousand Col Infty are held in readiness for the movement against Galveston—The Head Quarters and ~~Garrards~~ Carrs Div 16th Corps are at Montgomery, furnishing the garrisons east and north of that place—~~Carrs~~ Garrards Div. is at Selma—McArthurs at Meridian garrising Gainsville, Columbus Macon and Jackson Miss.—Griersons Cavly. at Montgomery Opelika—Taledego—Union Springs and Eufaula connecting with Wilsons Cavly.—Wests Cavly. twenty four hundred (2400) is on the march from Mobile to Baton Rouge and will be in Season to cooperate with movements from Arkansas—They cannot go to Texas by water on account of the want of transportation Brashar City which on account of the Scarcity of Water transportation I intended to use as a Sub depot for the Texas expedition is under water and cannot be used. I have not yet a sufficincy of sea going ~~transportation~~ transports, but am advised today by the Quartermaster Genl that he has orderd Six (6) to report to me, This will probably make up the deficincy" ALS (telegram sent), *ibid.*, RG 107,

Telegrams Collected (Bound); telegram received (sent via Raleigh, N. C., May 21, received May 22, 3:00 P.M.), *ibid.*; *ibid.*, Telegrams Collected (Unbound); *ibid.*, RG 108, Telegrams Received. *O.R.*, I, xlviii, part 2, 456.

On May 18, 2:00 A.M., Canby, Mobile, telegraphed to Rawlins. "The Monitor 'Manhattan' and the ram 'Tennessee' are the vessels on this coast that can cope with the 'Stonewall'—To save time I have asked Adm'l Lee to send the 'Manhattan' at once to New Orleans to be fitted out for Galveston; that is, if she can be spared—There is nothing on the Georgia coast now but wooden gunboats" Telegram received (on May 24, 10:00 A.M.), DNA, RG 107, Telegrams Collected (Bound); (2) *ibid.*, Telegrams Collected (Unbound); *ibid.*, RG 108, Telegrams Received; copy, DLC-USG, V, 54. *O.R.*, I, xlviii, part 2, 487.

On May 20, 1:30 P.M., Canby telegraphed to Rawlins. "I am just advised that the requisitions for Qr Masters stores for the New Orleans depot was first reduced one half and subsequently altogether refused—This requisition embraced material for keeping the coast steamers in running order. The number of these vessels has always been inadequate to the work they have been required to perform—They are nearly all old vessels in constant need of repairs and if the materials for repairing them are not furnished the service will be greatly embarrassed—The 'present condition of the Military service' extends the line of coast service and the necessity for this service will continue for some time even if the war is not continued west of the Mississippi—May I ask that the Qr Master General be directed to supply the means of keeping the boats in order or supply their places by better boats? Six of them at least are hardly worth the cost of repairing and the risk in sending men to sea in them is greater than that of a general battle" Telegram received (on May 22, 3:00 P.M.), DNA, RG 107, Telegrams Collected (Bound); *ibid.*, RG 108, Telegrams Received; copy, DLC-USG, V, 54.

To Maj. Gen. Henry W. Halleck

(Cipher)   Washington May 18th 1865 [*3:38* P.M.]
MAJ. GN. HALLECK, RICHMOND VA.

Your very kind dispatch placing your house at Mrs. Grants disposal during her stay is rec'd. I have not seen Mrs Grant since but know she will be delighted to [ge]t out of the Hotel for the few weeks she remains here.

                                             U. S. GRANT
                                             Lt. Gn.

ALS (telegram sent), DNA, RG 107, Telegrams Collected (Bound); telegram sent, *ibid.* *O.R.*, I, xlvi, part 3, 1169. On May 17, 1865, Secretary of War Edwin M. Stanton had telegraphed to Maj. Gen. Henry W. Halleck. "General Grant is here with his wife and ~~in bad health~~ is sick. ~~For obvious reasons he ought~~ It is not safe for him to be at a hotel and he is reluctant to go into a private family.

He would go into your house for a while if agreeable to you. Will you invite him to do so while your family are absent." ALS (telegram sent), DNA, RG 107, Telegrams Collected (Bound). Printed as sent at 9:00 P.M. in *O.R.*, I, xlvi, part 3, 1162. On May 18, Halleck telegraphed to USG. "There are two servants & most of the furniture bedding &c still in the house I occupied in Georgetown I suggest that while your wife is with you you move right in & make yourself comfortable My family will not again occupuy it & I do not require the furniture here at least for the present During the hot weather you can make yourself much more comfortable there than in Washn" Telegram received (at 10:15 A.M.), DNA, RG 107, Telegrams Collected (Bound).

On May 19, Bvt. Col. Theodore S. Bowers wrote to Capt. Julius W. Mason, 5th Cav. "The Lieutenant General Commanding directs that a guard consisting of three Non-Commissioned Officers and fifteen privates be furnished daily from your Command until further orders for his quarters in Georgetown (the quarters recently occupied by by Maj, Gen, Halleck) One sentinel will be placed constantly over the Stables, one sentinel in front of the house and at night the guard around the house will be increased to four sentinels, Camp accomodations will be found on the premises for the accomodation of the guard and their horses The Officer of the day for your Command will daily report to the Assistant Adjutant General at these Headquarters for further instructions respecting the guard, . . . The Guard to be furnished from your Command will relieve the detachment of the Veteran Reserve Corps now at the quarters in Georgetown at 9, A, M, to morrow" Copies, DLC-USG, V, 46, 76, 108; DNA, RG 108, Letters Sent. *O.R.*, I, xlvi, part 3, 1176.

On May 21, 10:30 A.M., USG telegraphed to Capt. Henry W. Janes, Schuylkill Arsenal, Philadelphia. "Please put a private Watchman over my house in Phila, until I can make other arrangements, You are authorized to visit Washington this week" Copies, DLC-USG, V, 46, 76, 108; DNA, RG 108, Letters Sent.

On May 26, 2:15 P.M., USG telegraphed to Halleck. "I understand that Mrs. Halleck is expected in Washington. If you will let me know when to expect her I will be glad to meet her at the Wharf with a carriage and ~~take~~ have Mrs. Grant entertain her during her stay in the City." ALS (telegram sent), *ibid.*, RG 107, Telegrams Collected (Bound); telegram sent, *ibid.*; copy, DLC-USG, V, 76. On May 27, Halleck telegraphed to USG. "Mrs Halleck will not visit Washn till she goes north for the summer. The house will therefore remain entirely at your disposal." Telegram received (at 10:40 A.M.), DNA, RG 108, Telegrams Received; copy, DLC-USG, V, 54.

To Maj. Gen. Henry W. Halleck

(Cipher)   Washington May 18th *1865* [7:00 P.M.]
MAJ. GEN. HALLECK, RICHMOND VA.

Gen. Weitzel is directed to reduce his wagons one half and the mules he takes three fourths with the expectation of gathering in

Texas the additional animals he may want. I think the reduction of animals might be still greater. All he will want at first will be mules enough to secure about four good teams to 1000 men. The White men connected with batteries may be detached and sent here for musterout or detained if you have use for them. One gun to 1000 men will be sufficient for Weitzel to take with him.

U. S. Grant

Lt. Gen.

ALS (telegram sent), DNA, RG 107, Telegrams Collected (Bound); telegram sent, *ibid.*; copies, *ibid.*, RG 108, Letters Sent; DLC-USG, V, 46, 76, 108. Printed as received at 10:00 P.M. in *O.R.*, I, xlvi, part 3, 1169.

On May 17, 1865, Brig. Gen. John A. Rawlins wrote to Bvt. Maj. Gen. Montgomery C. Meigs. "Provide Ocean transportation with as little delay as practicable for the 25th Army Corps, numbering about 20,000 men now at City Point Virginia, together with one half of its present land transportation, say about 200 Wagons and 800 Mules, forty (40) days rations for the above number of men, and the necessary forage for the animals of the command, You will please report to Maj, Gen, Halleck at Richmond when the transportation will reach City Point" Copies, DLC-USG, V, 46, 76, 108; DNA, RG 108, Letters Sent. *O.R.*, I, xlvi, part 3, 1162.

On May 18, 10:00 A.M. and 12:40 P.M., Rawlins telegraphed to Maj. Gen. Henry W. Halleck. "The Quarter Master's Department has been directed to assemble at City Point ocean transportation for the 25th Army Corps. You will please order all officers and men of that Corps now on detached service able to travel, to be relieved, and returned to their Command, that they may move with it. The transportation will be ready within two days." Telegrams sent (2), DNA, RG 107, Telegrams Collected (Bound); telegram received, *ibid.*, Telegrams Collected (Unbound). "Please direct Maj. Gen. Weitzel, Commanding 25th Army Corps to get his Corps in readiness for embarkation at City Point immediately upon the arrival of ocean transportation. He will take with him (40) forty days rations for twenty thousand men; one-half of his land transportation, and one-fourth of his mules, with the requisite amount of forage for his animals. All surplus transportation and other public property he may have, he will turn over to the Depots at City Point." Telegrams sent (2), *ibid.*, Telegrams Collected (Bound); copies, *ibid.*, RG 108, Letters Sent; DLC-USG, V, 46, 76, 108. *O.R.*, I, xlvi, part 3, 1168.

Also on May 18, Halleck telegraphed to USG. "Your order in regard to the twenty fifth (25) Corps is recd & will be immediately Carried out. I recommend that the twenty fourth (24th) Corps as a Corps organization be discontinued & as soon as Genl Wrights Corps leaves, all Troops here be reduced to a Deptl organization It will greatly simplify returns & papers There are now too many HdQurs & staff officers—The machinery is far too complicated & extensive for the work to be done & too many 'big Indians' for a small tribe—" Telegram received (at 1:00 P.M.), DNA, RG 107, Telegrams Collected (Bound); *ibid.*, RG 108, Telegrams Received; copy, DLC-USG, V, 54. Printed as sent at 1:00 P.M. in *O.R.*, I, xlvi, part 3, 1168. On the same day, Halleck telegraphed to USG.

"There are attached to the 25th Corps several Batteries manned by white troops. Is it intended to send these with Weitzel. I understand they are very unwilling to go Gen Weitzel has plenty of Colored artillerymen without batteries Could not the guns be transferred so as to make his Command homogeneous—Moreover as the transportation of light batteries by sea is very expensive it is desirable that you indicate the amount & Kind of artillery to be taken." Telegram received (at 3:40 P.M.), DNA, RG 107, Telegrams Collected (Bound); *ibid.*, RG 108, Telegrams Received; copy, DLC-USG, V, 54. *O.R.*, I, xlvi, part 3, 1168.

On May 19, 1:00 P.M., USG telegraphed to Halleck. "Genl Weitzel will be limited in animals transported to Texas to four teams per 1000 men Two ambulance teams per thousand men. Teams for four gun batteries, and the proper number of Officers horses Any cavalry he may have will turn over their horses here, but take their horse equipments" Telegram sent, DNA, RG 107, Telegrams Collected (Bound); telegram received, *ibid.*, Telegrams Collected (Unbound). *O.R.*, I, xlvi, part 3, 1174.

On May 20, Maj. Gen. Godfrey Weitzel, City Point, telegraphed to USG. "I find a telegram to detach all my white artillery men & to man the batteries with colored artillery men. I have but one company of colored arty but have besides three (3) regular batteries. Can I not keep these batteries instead." ALS (telegram sent), DNA, RG 94, War Records Office, Dept. of Va. and N. C.; telegram received (at 10:40 P.M.), *ibid.*, RG 107, Telegrams Collected (Bound); *ibid.*, Telegrams Collected (Unbound); *ibid.*, RG 108, Telegrams Received. On May 21, 10:00 A.M., USG telegraphed to Halleck. "Gen. Weitzel reports that he has but one Company of Colored Artillerymen and wishes to take with him three Companies of Regulars now belonging to his Corps? I have no objection to his doing so. Please direct him accordingly" ALS (telegram sent), *ibid.*, RG 107, Telegrams Collected (Bound); telegram sent, *ibid.*; copies, *ibid.*, RG 108, Letters Sent; DLC-USG, V, 46, 76, 108. Variant text in *O.R.*, I, xlvi, part 3, 1185. On May 22, Weitzel telegraphed to Rawlins. "I have awaited an answer all day to my dispatch of last night about the Artillery. If the order as I received it from Gen Halleck is imperative I will have one battery of artillery & one hundred and eighty 180 horses with grooms and twelve 12 guns but not four gun batteries. I have no Colored men in the Corps that Know anything about light battery service as I Know that there is an abundance of artillery in and about new orleans I think it would be better to take my one colored battery if I cannot get the three 3 Regular batteries with me now and rely for artillery upon the Dept of the Gulf—A speedy reply to this is necessary in order that I may issue my order for Embarkation" Telegram received (at 5:30 P.M.), DNA, RG 107, Telegrams Collected (Bound); (3) *ibid.*, Telegrams Collected (Unbound); *ibid.*, RG 108, Telegrams Received; copies (misdated May 20), *ibid.*, RG 393, 25th Army Corps, Telegrams Sent; DLC-USG, V, 54. On May 22, Rawlins transmitted to Weitzel a copy of USG's telegram to Halleck. Telegrams sent (2), DNA, RG 107, Telegrams Collected (Bound); telegram received, *ibid.*, Telegrams Collected (Unbound); *ibid.*, RG 94, War Records Office, Dept. of Va. and N. C.

On May 21, USG wrote to Weitzel. "As soon as your Corps is embarked you will proceed with it to Mobile Bay, Ala., and report to Maj. Gen. Steele for further orders. In addition to rations amunition and other articles which you have received directions to take with you, you should take a fair quantity of intrenching tools." Copies, *ibid.*, RG 108, Letters Sent; DLC-USG, V, 46, 76,

108. *O.R.*, I, xlvi, part 3, 1193; *ibid.*, I, xlviii, part 2, 526. On May 22, Weitzel telegraphed to Rawlins. "I have just recd Genl Grants confidential despatch. Genl Ord has taken from me every engineer officer and soldier I had. Is it intended that I should take Engineer soldiers with me as I am ordered to take intrenching tools with me" Telegram received (on May 23, 12:45 A.M.), DNA, RG 107, Telegrams Collected (Bound); (2) *ibid.*, Telegrams Collected (Unbound); *ibid.*, RG 108, Telegrams Received; copies, *ibid.*, RG 393, 25th Army Corps, Telegrams Sent; DLC-USG, V, 54. On May 21, Weitzel telegraphed to USG. "Genl Meigs Q M Genl suggested that I take with me the fifteen hundred 1.500 Quartermaster's Employees now at City Point. Can I get the order for them?" Telegram received (at noon), DNA, RG 107, Telegrams Collected (Bound); *ibid.*, RG 108, Telegrams Received; copy, DLC-USG, V, 54. *O.R.*, I, xlvi, part 3, 1193. At 1:20 P.M., USG telegraphed to Weitzel. "I would prefer that you should take no men with you but soldiers. Any work you have to do can be done by detailed men. If not there are plenty of negroes in Texas without transporting them from here." ALS (telegram sent), DNA, RG 107, Telegrams Collected (Bound); telegram sent, *ibid.*; telegrams received (3—one marked as sent at 1:30 P.M.), *ibid.*, Telegrams Collected (Unbound); *ibid.*, RG 393, 25th Army Corps, Telegrams Received. Printed as sent at 1:30 P.M. in *O.R.*, I, xlvi, part 3, 1193. At 2:00 P.M., USG telegraphed to Weitzel. "Do you want a Division Commander? If so I will send you a good one." ALS (telegram sent), DNA, RG 107, Telegrams Collected (Bound); telegram sent, *ibid.*; telegram received, *ibid.*, RG 393, 25th Army Corps, Telegrams Received. On May 22, Weitzel telegraphed to USG. "Yes sir I do want a Division Commander" Telegram received (at 10:40 A.M.), *ibid.*, RG 107, Telegrams Collected (Bound); *ibid.*, RG 108, Telegrams Received; copies (dated May 21), *ibid.*, RG 393, 25th Army Corps, Telegrams Sent; DLC-USG, V, 54.

On May 21, Weitzel telegraphed to Rawlins. "I must apply direct for what I have repeatedly asked for through the proper channels: six AdjutantsGeneral and six Quartermasters. I respectfully request that this number of officers be ordered to report to me at once." Telegram received (at 3:00 P.M.), DNA, RG 94, Letters Received, 548A 1865; *ibid.*, RG 107, Telegrams Collected (Bound); *ibid.*, RG 108, Telegrams Received; copies, *ibid.*, RG 393, 25th Army Corps, Telegrams Sent; DLC-USG, V, 54. On May 25, USG endorsed the telegram received. "So much of the within dispatch as relates to Assistant Adjutant Generals is respectfully referred to the Adjutant General of the Army, who will supply the 25th Corps if possible. All Company officers are specially required with their companies in colored regiments, and cannot be detailed as acting Adjutants without impairing the efficiency of the troops. As this Corps is under marching orders prompt action is necessary" ES, DNA, RG 94, Letters Received, 548A 1865.

On May 23, Weitzel telegraphed to Rawlins. "The order to retain the regular batt[er]ies has been received. But Genl Ord has now ordered me to send back all the men attached to the Batteries, which again impairs their efficiency, through want of men, Can I not retain the attached men." ALS (telegram sent), *ibid.*, RG 107, Telegrams Collected (Unbound); telegram received, *ibid.*, RG 94, War Records Office, Miscellaneous War Records; (at 1:50 P.M.) *ibid.*, RG 107, Telegrams Collected (Bound); *ibid.*, RG 108, Telegrams Received. *O.R.*, I, xlvi, part 3, 1201. On May 24, 9:10 A.M., USG telegraphed to Weitzel. "You can not take with you men detailed from other commands for your Artillery. All the men properly belonging to the companies you take with you ~~will~~ you will retain. If it is necessary to have more men they can be detailed from the command where you will be serving." ALS (telegram sent), DNA, RG 107, Telegrams Collected (Bound); telegram sent, *ibid.*; telegrams received (2—one at 10:30 A.M.), *ibid.*, Telegrams Collected (Unbound); *ibid.*, RG 393, 25th Army Corps, Telegrams Received. *O.R.*, I, xlvi, part 3, 1206. On the same day, Weitzel telegraphed to Rawlins. "The despatch of Lt Genl relating to Artillery has been received" Telegram received, DNA, RG 94, War Records Office, Miscellaneous War Records; (at 2:00 P.M.) *ibid.*, RG 107, Telegrams Collected (Bound); *ibid.*, RG 108, Telegrams Received; copies, *ibid.*, RG 393, 25th Army Corps, Telegrams Sent; DLC-USG, V, 54. *O.R.*, I, xlvi, part 3, 1206.

On May 23, Weitzel telegraphed to Rawlins. "As the brigade to which the detachments of the 10th and 28th U. S. C. T. now at Point Lookout belong will be the rear guard, and as these detachments each amount to one half the regiments I request they be relieved and ordered to City Point without delay." ALS (telegram sent), DNA, RG 107, Telegrams Collected (Unbound); telegrams received (2), *ibid.*; (at 2:30 P.M.) *ibid.*, Telegrams Collected (Bound); *ibid.*, RG 108, Telegrams Received. On May 24, 7:50 P.M., Rawlins telegraphed to Weitzel. "All Regiments and men belonging to your Corps and now away from it have been ordered to join you at City Point" Telegrams sent (2—one at 7:55 P.M.), *ibid.*, RG 107, Telegrams Collected (Bound); telegrams received (2), *ibid.*, Telegrams Collected (Unbound); *ibid.*, RG 393, 25th Army Corps, Telegrams Received. *O.R.*, I, xlvi, part 3, 1206.

On May 23, Weitzel twice telegraphed to Rawlins. "Transportation has arrived up to this time for 7200 men—" ALS (telegram sent), DNA, RG 107, Telegrams Collected (Unbound); telegram received, *ibid.*; (at 11:00 A.M.) *ibid.*, Telegrams Collected (Bound); *ibid.*, RG 108, Telegrams Received. *O.R.*, I, xlvi, part 3, 1201. "The steamers to transport my Corps all report to the Depot Qr. Mr. at City Point There is a great delay in Coaling & Watering. He has orders from Gen Meigs to erect bunks in them. This is a good thing in every respect if time is not an object—The lumber Will be Valuable & useful at our point of destination but they are not yet ready to take my first Division of Infy—Does Gen Grant Know this & approve it?" ALS (telegram sent), DNA, RG 107, Telegrams Collected (Unbound); telegram received, *ibid.*, Telegrams Collected (Bound). Bvt. Col. Theodore S. Bowers endorsed the first of these telegrams. "I have notified Gen Ingalls, and requested him to give this matter his attention" AES, *ibid.*, RG 108, Telegrams Received. On May 24, Brig. Gen. Rufus Ingalls telegraphed to Weitzel. "The Lieut Gen has no particular ~~objection~~ orders to give in relation to the transports for your Command. please have them got ready as Soon as ~~poss~~ practicable in a way which will Meet your Views and let the Shipments be as rapid as the Vessels Can be got ready—" ALS (telegram sent), *ibid.*, RG 107, Telegrams Collected (Unbound); telegram received, *ibid.*

On May 27, Weitzel twice telegraphed to Rawlins. "Transportation for thirteen thousand nine hundred men has arrived up to this evening one division of nine thousand two hundred men & their Transportation has started as soon as enough arrives for the second Div it will start Then there will be left the Detached Brig of infantry and the artillery and Cavalry: I will start with the second Division of infantry and the artillery and expect to get off on Wednesday or Thursday next leaving Gen Russell to bring up the rear This is ~~isn~~ accordance with the suggestion of Gen sheridan who asked me to come with the

Bulk of my corps Is this approved" ALS (telegram sent), *ibid.*; telegram received, *ibid.*; (at 11:40 P.M.) *ibid.*, Telegrams Collected (Bound); *ibid.*, RG 108, Telegrams Received. *O.R.*, I, xlvi, part 3, 1225; *ibid.*, I, xlviii, part 2, 622–23. "The twenty second 22d U S C T now stationed at Washington City has not reported yet I understood Gen Grant to say that he would order it to report back to me ~~at~~ as Gen Augur said it was not needed there" ALS (telegram sent), DNA, RG 107, Telegrams Collected (Unbound); telegram received, *ibid.*; (at 11:45 P.M.) *ibid.*, Telegrams Collected (Bound).

On May 28, 2:10 P.M., USG telegraphed to Weitzel. "Maj. Gn. Giles Smith is ordered to report to you. Your movements are approved. Gen. Steele will probably have left Mobile before your arrival. If you find instructions there obey them, if not proceed immediately to the Mouth of the Rio-Grande and report to steele there." ALS (telegram sent), *ibid.*, Telegrams Collected (Bound); telegram sent, *ibid.*; telegrams received (2), *ibid.*, Telegrams Collected (Unbound); *ibid.*, RG 393, 25th Army Corps, Telegrams Received. *O.R.*, I, xlvi, part 3, 1230; *ibid.*, I, xlviii, part 2, 643. On the same day, Weitzel telegraphed to USG. "Your despatch is received" Telegram received (at 10:25 P.M.), DNA, RG 107, Telegrams Collected (Bound); *ibid.*, RG 108, Telegrams Received; copies, *ibid.*, RG 393, 25th Army Corps, Telegrams Sent; DLC-USG, V, 54. *O.R.*, I, xlvi, part 3, 1230; *ibid.*, I, xlviii, part 2, 643.

To Maj. Gen. Edward O. C. Ord

(Cipher)   Washington May 18th/65 [*3:00* P.M.]
MAJ. GEN. ORD, RICHMOND VA.

No one so well as Corps Commanders know ~~so well as~~ the officers under them who, by their services and qualification who are fit for the regular Army. The object is to get officers who have proven themselves qualified by their conduct in actual War. Corps and other independent commanders order the boards.

U. S. GRANT
Lt. Gn.

ALS (telegram sent), DNA, RG 107, Telegrams Collected (Bound); telegram sent, *ibid.*; telegram received, *ibid.*, RG 94, War Records Office, Dept. of Va. and N. C.; Ord Papers, CU-B. On May 18, 1865, Maj. Gen. Edward O. C. Ord telegraphed to USG. "Order No 86—fixes no plan for boards of examiners this will lead to ~~want of~~ loose examinations in some cases severe in others—Can you propose a general plan applicable to all cases with a standard to which ~~applican for~~ each grade should ~~pass~~ be found equal—Shall I order the boards or call on Genl Halleck and Genl Gibbon to do so" ALS (telegram sent), *ibid.*; telegram received (at 2:00 P.M.), DNA, RG 107, Telegrams Collected (Bound); *ibid.*, RG 108, Telegrams Received.

To Maj. Gen. John Pope

(Sipher)   Washington May 18th *1865* [*2:30* P.M.]
MAJ. GEN. POPE, ST. LOUIS MO.

Orders have been made breaking up Canby's Div. and assigning
Sheridan to general command west of the Miss. South of the Ark.
You will please direct Reynolds to ~~report~~ receive orders from Sheridan for the disposition of all troops that can be spared from Ark.
~~to to go~~ recollecting that the troops taken, with many others, are
to operate against the enemy South of him. If Reynolds can be replaced I would like him to go in command of the troops taken.

U. S. GRANT
Lt. Gn

ALS (telegram sent), DNA, RG 107, Telegrams Collected (Bound); telegram
sent, *ibid.*; telegram received (at 5:30 P.M.), *ibid.*, Telegrams Collected (Unbound). *O.R.*, I, xlviii, part 2, 492. On May 19, 1865, Maj. Gen. John Pope
telegraphed (at noon) and wrote to USG. "Your despatch concerning Sheridan
recd—Have instructed Reynolds accordingly—You may rely upon my sending
every man I can from Ark. It is proper to tell you that the troops in Ark are the
refuse of Canbys old Command—he selected the best troops for operations against
Mobile leaving in ark defensive garrison and Cav. without horses—I sent copy
of your despatch to Gen Reynolds and can replace him in ark though not easily—
For administration duties in that state he is the best man I know—I suppose you
don't wish him to go unless he desires it—Will write today on the subject"
Telegram received (at 2:30 P.M.), DNA, RG 107, Telegrams Collected (Bound);
ibid., RG 108, Telegrams Received; copies, *ibid.*, RG 393, Military Div. of the
Mo., Telegrams Sent; DLC-USG, V, 54. *O.R.*, I, xlviii, part 2, 504–5. "I have
the honor to acknowledge the receipt of your cypher dispatch of the 18th informing me that Gen. Sheridan had been assigned to the command in Texas.
You may rely upon my sending him every man I can from Arkansas and in every
way doing what is in my power to assist his operations. In this connection, I
would suggest that a considerable cavalry force, say six or eight thousand men,
be assembled at Ft. Smith to make a strong cavalry raid by way of Ft. Towson
or Doaksville into North Eastern Texas. I have plenty of supplies for this purpose already at Ft. Smith. A good cavalry commander would be needed. In connections with any operations of Sheridan, such a movement might be useful. I
have sent a copy of your dispatch to Reynolds and have asked him to notify me
immediately whether he desires to go with Sheridan. I presumed that you did
not intend him to go unless he wished it. I can of course spare him if you desire
it, but it will be difficult to replace him by an officer of equal judgement and
discretion, both of which qualities will be greatly needed in restoring order in
Arkansas. The troops Reynolds has in that State are only sufficient for defensive
purposes and were really the refuse of the troops formerly in that Dept. Gen.

Canby picked out the best, as I understand, leaving only men enough for a defensive position and leaving the Cavalry without horses. When Kirby Smith either retires into Texas, or surrenders, (one of which he must soon do) it will be necessary to occupy Marshall, in Texas, Shreveport and Alexandria, in Louisiana, and Camden, Fulton and perhaps one or two other points in Southern Arkansas merely for police purposes to keep down Guerillas, and help enforce the laws, and maintain order. I think it likely that Reynolds' troops are better for these purposes than for an actual campaign. I infer from your telegram that it is not intended to take any part of Arkansas away from this Military Division, so that eventually the troops in the Southern part of the State and the whole Administration in the State, so far as the Military Authorities are concerned, will remain with me. I understand your telegram to mean merely that all troops that can be spared from Arkansas shall be used as Gen. Sheridan directs in hostile operations against Kirby Smith. When these operations are over, the southern line of Arkansas becomes again the southern line of this Military Division. I only allude to this in view of the future, since in restoring order and quiet in Arkansas and in any view of civil administration in that State the whole State should be within one Military Command. Of this, however, you can judge hereafter. Our Indian affairs are in satisfactory condition. The small raid in Minnesota amounts to little and ought to have been intercepted and the Indians killed or captured before they reached the settlements. I really cannot see what we could do with more troops in that region, unless indeed permission could be obtained from the English Govt. to follow hostile Indians into the British possessions and then seize or punish them. I have so often reported the unfriendly conduct of British subjects north of Minnesota in these Indian hostilities and the necessity of prohibiting intercourse with them unless they cease to supply Indians with means to carry on hostilities against us and a place of safe refuge when pursued, that I think it improper to do more than refer to the matter here. In Missouri we could have entire quiet in a very short time, if only the people would consent to allow the deserters from Price's Army and the Bushwhackers to remain at peace after they surrender. All the noted Bushwhacking bands in the State nearly, have offered to surrender, but the people would shoot them whenever they could find them and thus compel them to flee the State or continue to be Bushwhackers. I am doing what I can to pacify the public mind on this subject. Col. Sprague is, I presume, on his way back from Shreveport, for which place he was about to set out when I last heard from him. I expect every hour to hear definite news of Kirby Smith's decision about surrendering." LS, DNA, RG 108, Letters Received. *O.R.*, I, xlviii, part 2, 505–6.

On May 8, 2:00 P.M., Pope had telegraphed to USG. "Col. Sprague whom I sent to Red river met Kirby Smith on suaturday last at Alexandria, The result of his mission will be Known in a couple of days." Telegram received (at 6:00 P.M.), DNA, RG 107, Telegrams Collected (Bound); *ibid.*, RG 108, Telegrams Received; copies, *ibid.*, RG 393, Military Div. of the Mo., Telegrams Sent; DLC-USG, V, 54. *O.R.*, I, xlviii, part 2, 347. On May 14, Pope wrote to USG. "I have the honor to transmit enclosed copies of dispatches received from Gen. Reynolds and Col. Sprague. I do not of course know what course Kirby Smith will adopt, but I think there is not much doubt that a campaign into Texas will be unnecessary. I presume that Kirby Smith is delaying Sprague until he receives further news of the Rebels east of the Mississippi and as every day will render it more and more clear that the rebellion and the Rebel Government are at an end, I think he will very shortly agree to the terms without the necessity of assembling an army to march against him. His men are altogether demoralized and will leave him in large numbers. Information from several sources confirms Gen. Reynolds' dispatch. Some little patience may perhaps be necessary, though I expect every moment to hear from Sprague. Unless Kirby Smith holds his army together and a campaign becomes necessary in consequence, I suppose that such points as are important in Texas can be more easily occupied from the coast. In case he accepts the terms, I will at once occupy Marshall in Texas and Shreveport and Alexandria in Louisiana. A small force may also be needed at Fulton and Camden but I will have men enough for all these purposes. A very few days will, I am sure, decide the matter. The Mississippi and its lower tributaries are very high, and at many of the usual landing places on the lower river it is now impossible to land on account of high water. Opposite Vicksburg the river is thirty miles wide. The White and Arkansas rivers and all the small streams in Arkansas are very high. From all indications there will be a great flood this year. As it is, the swamps and morasses in Arkansas are as yet impassable. Gen. Reynolds reports to me that it would be next to impossible to get ten wagons through Arkansas to Red river under present circumstances. We will be able on short notice to get every thing ready at Ft. Smith and Little Rock for a forward movement if it be necessary. I already have supplies at Ft. Smith and Ft. Gibson sufficient for the contemplated campaign. If they are not needed for that purpose, they can be readily sold to the people without any loss to the Govt. Gen. M. Jeff. Thompson surrendered with his forces. How many he has or can collect it would be difficult to say. He claims to have from five to ten thousand and his vanity will prompt him to collect as many as he can to be paroled on the 29th of this month. The terms of surrender are the same as those granted to Lee. His surrender is only important from the fact that it relieves the people of Northern Arkansas and Southern Missouri from constant alarm and apprehension and that in order to swell the dimensions of his command, he will undoubtedly persuade a great many of the disaffected and troublesome characters in that region to go in and surrender with him. Large numbers of Guerillas and Bushwhackers in Missouri are anxious to come in and surrender. The difficulty is that although the military authorities will willingly give them fair terms on condition of their surrender with all their horses, arms &c., the people of the State will not permit them to remain. The military can only protect them on condition of their living at Military posts which they cannot do and make their own living. I hope in a little while to pacify the public mind on this subject." LS, DNA, RG 108, Letters Received. Dated May 17 in *O.R.*, I, xlviii, part 2, 481–82. The enclosures are *ibid.*, pp. 322, 416–17. See *ibid.*, p. 419.

On May 17, Pope twice telegraphed to USG, the second time at 2:10 P.M. "The order requiring muster out of Cavalry whose terms expire by October first 1 will deprive me of a Considerable part of the Cavalry force now on the plains & break up Indian expedition now on foot—as this would lead to infortunate consequences I respectfully ask that the execution of this order be suspended in this Military Div until summer Campaign is over or until it Can be executed without danger or embarrassment—" "Gen Thomas has sent a brigade of Cavalry here without horses or arms I can furnish them arms from the arsenal but have no horses as purchase has been stopped by order from Washington— we need twenty five hundred (2500) horses to mount them & other Cavalry Iin Dept of Mo" Telegrams received (at 1:00 P.M. and 3:30 P.M.), DNA, RG 107,

Telegrams Collected (Bound); *ibid.*, RG 108, Telegrams Received; copies, *ibid.*, RG 393, Military Div. of the Mo., Telegrams Sent; DLC-USG, V, 54. *O.R.*, I, xlviii, part 2, 480. At 4:00 P.M., USG telegraphed to Pope. "You may suspend order for mustering out troops so far as the exigencies of service requires. Troops can be sent you soon to enable you to carry out the order." ALS (telegram sent), DNA, RG 107, Telegrams Collected (Bound); telegram sent, *ibid.*; telegram received, *ibid.*, Telegrams Collected (Unbound). *O.R.*, I, xlviii, part 2, 481. On May 18, Bvt. Brig. Gen. Cyrus B. Comstock wrote to Bvt. Maj. Gen. Montgomery C. Meigs. "The Lieut, Genl, Comdg desires that you will send at once twenty five hundred (2,500) Cavalry horses, to Maj, Gen, Pope at St, Louis and that if you are unable to do this you inform him so that other arrangements may be made" Copies, DLC-USG, V, 46, 76, 108; DNA, RG 108, Letters Sent. *O.R.*, I, xlviii, part 2, 494.

On May 19, Meigs wrote to USG. "I enclose a report from the Chief of the First Division of this office. It appears that it will require one week to collect at St. Louis the 2500 serviceable Cavalry Horses which were yesterday called for. Orders were given yesterday by telegraph to put them in motion. One thousand of them are at Lexington, Kentucky. It is desirable to know at the earliest moment to what point they are to be forwarded from St. Louis, if they are not to be all issued at that place." LS, DNA, RG 108, Letters Received. The enclosure is *ibid.* On the same day, Brig. Gen. John A. Rawlins wrote to Meigs. "The Lieutenant General desires that the two thousand five hundred Cavalry horses mentioned in your communication of this date enclosing one from Brevet Brig, Gen, Eakin be collected with as little delay as practicable at St, Louis Mo, and issued at that point under such orders respecting them as may be given by Maj, Gen, John Pope Commanding Military Division of the Missouri" Copies, DLC-USG, V, 46, 76, 108; DNA, RG 108, Letters Sent.

On May 19, 4:20 P.M., Pope telegraphed to USG. "What shall we do for horses &c for the Brigade of Cavalry general Thomas sent here" Telegram received (at 6:15 P.M.), *ibid.*, RG 107, Telegrams Collected (Bound); *ibid.*, RG 108, Telegrams Received; copies, *ibid.*, RG 393, Military Div. of the Mo., Telegrams Sent; (2) DLC-USG, V, 54. *O.R.*, I, xlviii, part 2, 505. At 8:30 P.M., Rawlins telegraphed to Pope. "The Quarter Master's Department will deliver to you at Saint Louis in about one week two thousand five hundred serviceable ~~horses~~ Cavalry horses to be issued under your orders." Telegrams sent (2), DNA, RG 107, Telegrams Collected (Bound); telegram received (on May 20), *ibid.*, Telegrams Collected (Unbound). *O.R.*, I, xlviii, part 2, 505.

On May 21, Bvt. Col. Theodore S. Bowers wrote to Maj. Gen. George Crook. "You will order the 1st Brigade 1st Cavalry Division of your Command, composed of the 1st 5th 6th & 7th Michigan Regiments to proceed at once with horse equippments and arms complete to report to Maj, Gen, John Pope at St, Louis Mo, The Quartermasters Department will furnish necessary transportation immediately" Copies, DLC-USG, V, 46, 76, 108; DNA, RG 108, Letters Sent. *O.R.*, I, xlvi, part 3, 1190; *ibid.*, I, xlviii, part 2, 526.

On May 22, 11:20 A.M. and 11:25 A.M., Pope telegraphed to USG. "I think it will be well to send two (2) more Brigades of Veteran Cavalry to St Louis in order that I may push them out to the plains to relieve the Cavalry now there which is to be discharged on account of Expiration of service on first of October, I would like to have these brigades ~~ass~~ soon as convenient & I hope they will be sent with arms & horses" "The Quarter master here has recd orders to retain twenty five hundred (2500) horses for special service of Genl Grant—I presume they are intended for the brigade of Cavalry now here Will you please give Col Eakin orders to have these horses issued to me as fast as received—I need Cavalry on plains badly" Telegrams received (at 1:00 P.M.), DNA, RG 107, Telegrams Collected (Bound); (at 12:30 P.M. and 12:35 P.M.) *ibid.*, RG 108, Telegrams Received; copies, *ibid.*, RG 393, Military Div. of the Mo., Telegrams Sent; DLC-USG, V, 54. *O.R.*, I, xlviii, part 2, 539. At 7:00 P.M., USG telegraphed to Pope. "Gen. Reynolds need not accompany the troops from Ark. He cannot probably be well replaced in that state.—The Q. M. will send you 2700 horses as fast as possible. In" ALS (telegram sent), DNA, RG 107, Telegrams Collected (Bound); telegram sent, *ibid.*; telegram received (misdated June 23, received on May 23), *ibid.*, Telegrams Collected (Unbound). *O.R.*, I, xlviii, part 2, 540.

On May 24, 9:20 A.M., USG telegraphed to Pope. "Gen. Dodge may use his Artillery to the best advantage either as mounted men or otherwise. I can send you Cavalry from here as soon as transportation can be provided." ALS (telegram sent), DNA, RG 107, Telegrams Collected (Bound); telegram sent, *ibid.*; telegram received (marked as sent at 9:30 A.M.), *ibid.*, Telegrams Collected (Unbound). Printed as sent at 9:30 A.M. in *O.R.*, I, xlviii, part 2, 582. At 11:00 P.M., USG telegraphed to Pope. "A large Brigade of Michigan Cavalry, armed and equipped for the field was shipped to you by rail to-day. Other Regiments will probably be sent you, in a few days." Telegrams sent (2), DNA, RG 107, Telegrams Collected (Bound); telegram received (at 11:50 P.M.), *ibid.*, Telegrams Collected (Unbound). *O.R.*, I, xlviii, part 2, 582. On June 2, Pope telegraphed to USG. "The Brigade of Mich Cavalry arrived today but only brought Six hundred 600 horses & some of those unfit for service." Telegram received (at 8:20 P.M.), DNA, RG 107, Telegrams Collected (Bound); *ibid.*, RG 108, Telegrams Received; copies, *ibid.*, RG 393, Military Div. of the Mo., Telegrams Sent; DLC-USG, V, 54. *O.R.*, I, xlviii, part 2, 731. On June 3, Pope telegraphed to USG. "Brigades of Michigan Cavalry needs about eighteen hundred horses. Quartermaster in charge of Cavalry Depot here has nearly that number on hand but has no order to issue them. Will you please have orders telegraphed him to issue to Michigan brigade." Telegram received (at 12:15 P.M.), DNA, RG 107, Telegrams Collected (Bound); *ibid.*, RG 108, Telegrams Received; copies, *ibid.*, RG 393, Military Div. of the Mo., Telegrams Sent; DLC-USG, V, 54. USG endorsed a telegram received to Meigs with directions to issue orders as requested. Df (unsigned and undated), DNA, RG 108, Telegrams Received.

On May 26, Maj. Gen. Joseph J. Reynolds, Little Rock, telegraphed to USG. "Can you with propriety give us any idea as to what will ultimately be done with the Volunteer troops that it is proposed now to keep in the Service? Deserving Volunteer Officers who desire to remain in the service are continually making inquiry—If they will probably be absorbed in the regular Service, they wish to remain—If not they feel that they are losing time by staying now to be mustered out, when everybody at home will have got the Start of them in business—Your telegram of May 18th to Genl Pope reached me yesterday—Very few troops can be got from this Department—I have already sent to Genl Canby & elsewhere eight thousand (8,000)—If I give up this Dep't and take with me no command, is there anything to warrant me in giving up this Dep't and going to Texas with a handful of troops?" Telegram received (on May 31, 10:00 P.M.), *ibid.*, RG 107, Telegrams Collected (Bound); *ibid.*, RG 108, Telegrams Received; copy, DLC-USG, V, 54. *O.R.*, I, xlviii, part 2, 610.

On May 27, 12:10 P.M., Pope telegraphed to USG. "Following dispatch from Reynolds just received. 'Little Rock Ark. May 26th 1865. [T]o MAJ GEN POPE. Yours of nineteenth 19 enclosing [te]llegraph from Gen Grant received yesterday. I will make an estimate for this Department & report at [o]nce what can be spared. It will not be much so far as I can see. It will be best for me to remain here—in fact with present developements [t]here is nothing for me in a change. Signed. J J REYNOLDS Maj Gen'" Telegram received (at 2:15 P.M.), DNA, RG 107, Telegrams Collected (Bound); *ibid.*, RG 108, Telegrams Received; copies, *ibid.*, RG 393, Military Div. of the Mo., Telegrams Sent; DLC-USG, V, 54. *O.R.*, I, xlviii, part 2, 610.

To Maj. Gen. John M. Schofield

Washington May 18th *1865* [*8:00* P.M.]

MAJ. GN. J. M. SCHOFIELD, RALEIGH N. C.

Until a uniform policy is adopted for reestablishing civil government in the rebellious states the Military authorities can do nothing but keep the peace. I have but just received your letter of the 10th and agree with your views.

U. S. GRANT
Lt. Gen.

ALS (telegram sent), DNA, RG 107, Telegrams Collected (Bound); telegram sent (at 8:10 P.M.), *ibid.*; telegram received, *ibid.*, Telegrams Collected (Unbound); DLC-John M. Schofield. Printed as sent at 8:10 P.M. in *O.R.*, I, xlvii, part 3, 529. On May 10, 1865, Maj. Gen. John M. Schofield wrote to USG. "I desire to submit to you my views concerning the policy that ought to be pursued in North Carolina, leaving it to your judgment, whether, or not, to submit them to the President, or Secretary of War. I am led to this mainly by a letter which I received on the 7th, from Chief Justice Chase, giving some points of the policy advocated by him, which, if adopted in this State, would, in my opinion lead to disastrous results. The points I refer to are briefly as follows, Viz:—The organization of the State government to be left to the people acting in their original sovereign capacity. In determining the right of suffrage, the old Constitution, amended in 1835, be followed in preference to the new one, which was in force at the commencement, of the rebellion—The object being to give negroes the right to vote. The first proposition is not, I think open to serious objection. With proper assistance from the Military authorities it can be successfully carried out. The second proposition is the one to which I refer as specially objectionable—And this for two reasons. First—the Constitution of the state, as it existed immediately prior to the rebellion, is still the State Constitution, and there is no power on earth, but the people of the State, that can alter it. The operations of the war have freed the slaves in this, and most other states, and doubtless slavery will be constitutionally abolished throughout the Country. But the United States cannot make a negro, nor even a white man, an elector in any State. That is a power expressly reserved, by the Constitution, to the several States. We cannot alter or amend the Constitution of North Carolina, as it now exists, without either, first altering, or else, violating the Constitution of the United States. If we hold that, by the rebellion, the States have lost their existence as States, and have been reduced to unorganized territories under the absolute sovereign authority of the United States, then, undoubtedly, we may declare that all inhabitants, White and black, shall have equal political rights, and an equal voice in the organization of a State to be admitted into the Union. But I understand President Johnson repudiates this doctrine. Hence it may be left out of the question. It appears to me beyond question that the Constitution of North Carolina is now valid and binding, as the law of the State,—and that any measures for the reörganization of the State government, must be in accordance with the provisions of that instrument. This, I am convinced is the unanimous opinion of the leading Union men of the State. My second reason for objecting to the proposition, is the absolute unfitness of the negroes, as a class, for any such responsibility. They can neither read nor write. They have no Knowledge whatever of law or government. They do not even Know the meaning of the freedom that has been given them, and are much astonished when informed that it does not mean that they are to live in idleness, and be fed by the Government. It is true they are docile, obedient, and anxious to learn—But we certainly ought to teach them something before we give them an equal voice with ourselves in government. This view is so fully recognized as correct by all who are familiar, by actual contact, with the negro character, and condition, that argument seems superfluous. I have yet to see a single one, among the many Union men, in North Carolina, who would willingly submit for a moment to the immediate elevation of the negro to political equality with the White man. They are all, or nearly all, content with the abolition of slavery. Many of them rejoice that it is done. But to raise the negro, in his present ignorant and degraded condition, to be their political equals would be, in their opinion, to enslave them. If they did not rebel against it, it would be only because rebellion would be hopeless. A government so organized would in no sense be a popular government. After careful consideration of all the questions involved I ~~can~~ am fully convinced as to the best policy to be adopted in this State, which I will submit in outline. A military governor to be appointed, who shall have command of all the troops in the State; Or the Department Commander be authorized to assume, by virtue of his command, the functions of Military governor, which naturally devolve upon him. The Military Governor to declare the Constitution, and laws, of the State in force immediately priceding the pretended act of Secession, so far as the same are not inconsistent with the Constitution, and laws, of the United States, and the War proclamations of the President, to be still in force. To make provisional appointments of Justices of the Peace, Sheriffs, and such other inferior officers as the State laws, empower the Governor to appoint, to serve until the organization of a civil government. To order an enrollment of all electors who may take the President's Amnesty Oath. As soon as this enrollment shall be completed, to call an election for delegates to a State Convention. The qualifications of voters, and Candidates, to be those prescribed by the State laws, and that they shall take the Amnesty Oath. All acts of the Convention to be submitted to the people for their ratification, or rejection, At the same time with the election of Governor and members of the Legislature, which would be ordered by the Convention. I would confidently expect a Convention, so chosen, to repudiate the doctrine of secession, abolish slavery, and fully restore the State to its practical constitutional relations to the Government of the United States. The people are now ripe for such action. They only ask to Know what the Government desires them to do, and how they are to do it. If, however, they should fail to do this, I would regard them as having violated their oaths, would dissolve the Convention, and hold the State under military government until the people should come to their senses. I would have a lawful popular government or a military government. The latter being a necessary substitute in the absence of the former. I am willing to discharge to the best of my ability any duty which may properly devolve upon me—Yet if a policy so opposed to my views as that proposed by Chief Justice Chase is to be adopted, I respectfully suggest that I am not the proper person to carry it out. If, however, after Knowing my views fully, it be desired that I execute the Presidents wishes, would it not be well for me to have a personal interview with him? in order that I may fully understand his plan, and the principles upon which it is founded." LS, DNA, RG 108, Letters Received; ADf, DLC-John M. Schofield. *O.R.*, I, xlvii, part 3, 461–63.

On May 25, Bvt. Brig. Gen. Cyrus B. Comstock wrote to Schofield. "The General wishes me to say that your letter in reference to the State of North Carolina, brought by Col, Wherry has been recieved, It was shown to the Secretary of War who as well as himself agreed with the views expressed in it H[e] was accidentally prevented from showing it to the President, but had previously had a long conversation with him on the subject, in which the President expressed ideas essentially the same as yours, No definite course has yet been adopted though there has been much discussion, and for this reason the General is as yet unable to send you instructions, He hopes that some plan will soon be settled on," Copies, DLC-USG, V, 46, 76, 108; DNA, RG 108, Letters Sent. *O.R.*, I, xlvii, part 3, 571.

To Bvt. Maj. Gen. James H. Wilson

(Cipher)   Washington May 18th 1865 [*4:30* P.M.]
MAJ. GN. J. H. WILSON, MACON GA.

You can use captured money in your hands for the purchase of supplies turning it over to the proper disbursing officer to pay out. Muster in your colored regiments. There will be no necessity for repairing the Atlanta rail-road. All your communications will be by sea.

U. S. GRANT
Lt. Gn.

ALS (telegram sent), DNA, RG 107, Telegrams Collected (Bound); telegram sent (at 5:00 P.M.), *ibid.*; telegrams received (2), *ibid.*, Telegrams Collected (Unbound). *O.R.*, I, xlix, part 2, 829. On May 21, 1865, 8:00 A.M., Bvt. Maj. Gen. James H. Wilson telegraphed to USG. "Telegram 4 30 p m 18th received. The Atlanta road is state property and has been used against Government since beginning of the war—If permitted to do so I can take possession of it and with the means at hand repair it in thirty days; in ninety days pay off all costs of repairs and make it a handsome source of revenue to the Government—Thinking that this would meet your sanction and fearing that the rivers of Georgia would fail us toward mid-summer—I have already begun repairs and constructed track north to the Chattahoochee—Am doing all of ~~my~~ the work by my own troops. With your permission to proceed I will continue operations keeping accurate accounts of expenditure so that QrMrs Dept shall be repaid at the earliest day possible—Earnings of this Railroad—being the only direct communication with the north—will be very considerable while it will benefit us and people more than anything we can do. Without it we shall have trouble to supply the Command—Shall carry out instructions at once in regard to my negro regiments" Telegram received (on May 24, 9:30 A.M.), DNA, RG 107, Telegrams Collected (Bound); *ibid.*, Telegrams Collected (Unbound); *ibid.*, RG 108, Telegrams Received; copies, *ibid.*, RG 393, Military Div. of the Miss., Cav. Corps, Telegrams Sent; DLC-USG, V, 54. *O.R.*, I, xlix, part 2, 860.

On May 14, Wilson telegraphed to Brig. Gen. John A. Rawlins. "The question of forage is becoming a very serious one for my command and unless vigorous measures are adopted at once to supply me from the north we shall suffur greatly—I have twenty thousand (20,000) horses and mules—Can get corn on line of the railroad for ten or fifteen days yet but the people have not the means for hauling it to R. R. from distance at this time of year. My Q. Mrs. are also embarrassed for the want of money Savannah river has only three and a half feet of water and falling. Ocmulgee is no better There are only two boats on former can ascend to Augusta Thomas advises grazing but I have no idea this can be done anywhere in Georgia with so large a command Chattanooga and Atlanta RR should be rebuilt at once—I can put three thousand at work on this end—The work would also be very beneficial in restoring good feeling and preventing suffering among the people I am collecting everything of value at this place and as Davis is captured can move towards North quite soon if so directed A careful and discreet officer with complete instructions from the President in regard to administration of civil affairs should be sent here at once—Steedman now at Kingston would be available—He should have a sufficint guard of Infy. to protect the public property If I am to remain here much longer I should be furnished with orders in regard to Comdr &c as soon as possible" Telegram received (misdated May 15, received 4:00 P.M.), DNA, RG 107, Telegrams Collected (Bound); (2—one marked as sent at 6:30 A.M.) *ibid.*, Telegrams Collected (Unbound); (misdated May 15) *ibid.*, RG 108, Telegrams Received; copies (marked as sent at 7:00 A.M.), *ibid.*, RG 393, Military Div. of the Miss., Cav. Corps, Telegrams Sent; (misdated May 15) DLC-USG, V, 54. *O.R.*, I, xlix, part 2, 762. On May 17, 1:00 P.M., Rawlins telegraphed to Wilson. "The Quarter Master's Department says that there is plenty of forage at Port Royal and all available means are in operation to get it to you. Maj. Thomas, Asst. Qr. Master, Department of the South leaves New York to-day with funds, and on your requisition will supply your temporary wants. Send your estimates for funds to the Quarter Master General, and funds will be forwarded you. You will remain with that part of your command that is to be left in Georgia. Gen Thomas has been so instructed. Whatever Infantry force in addition to the Cavalry ~~force~~ left with you may be required to garrison what you deem necessary points to be garrisoned, will be sent you. See that a competent officer has command of the force returned to the Tennessee river" Telegrams sent (2), DNA, RG 107, Telegrams Collected (Bound); telegram received, *ibid.*, Telegrams Collected (Unbound). *O.R.*, I, xlix, part 2, 814. On May 18, 3:00 P.M., Wilson telegraphed to Rawlins. "Telegram 1 p m yesterday received. There will be great difficulty navigating the Savannah and Ocmulgee rivers from this time forward for two reasons, scarcity of boats and lowness of water, therefore forage at Port Royal will be hard to get at—Chattahoochie to Eufalia ~~ifs~~ a good deal better stream and has in it four or five good boats.—I have telegraphed Gen Canby to send forage to Apalachicola whence I can bring it to Eufalia. In the meantime under sanction of Gen Thomas I am working on the Chattanooga and Atlanta Railroad—I have three thousand niggers and can do the work very cheaply—I regard the road as the only safe and reliable route of supplies and therefore indispensable—Have two regiments at Tallahassie, Shall I leave them there or will they be relieved by Infantry from Jacksonville after the balance of my command is concentrated and moved to the Tennessee? I can supply the remainder till railroads are open—Movements will commence at once I would respectfully suggest that an Agent of the Treasury Department be sent here for the purpose of gathering of the C. S. A cotton scattered throughout the state—" Telegram received (on May 22, 9:00 P.M.), DNA, RG 107, Telegrams Collected (Bound); *ibid.*, Telegrams Collected (Unbound); *ibid.*, RG 108, Telegrams Received; copy, DLC-USG, V, 54. *O.R.*, I, xlix, part 2, 828–29.

On May 22, 8:30 A.M., Wilson telegraphed to Rawlins. "What number shall I give to my colored regiments in mustering them in? The impression has got out among some of my troops that they are to be mustered out and is producing a bad effect. Please let me know what policy has been or will be adopted in regard to this matter. I have ten regiments of veterans which I am retaining in the state, If our old organization is to be broken up, I will organize them into one good Division" Telegram received (on May 24, 10:00 A.M.), DNA, RG 107, Telegrams Collected (Bound); (3) *ibid.*, Telegrams Collected (Unbound); *ibid.*, RG 108, Telegrams Received; copies, *ibid.*, RG 393, Military Div. of the Miss., Cav. Corps, Telegrams Sent; DLC-USG, V, 54. *O.R.*, I, xlix, part 2, 870.

On May 31, 10:00 A.M., USG telegraphed to Wilson. "Telegraph to Gen. Gilmore to know where in S. C. he will have the Cavalry which you send to him. In the mean time they can move directly towards Millen." ALS (telegram sent), DNA, RG 107, Telegrams Collected (Bound); telegram sent, *ibid.*; telegrams received (2), *ibid.*, Telegrams Collected (Unbound). *O.R.*, I, xlix, part 2, 938. See *ibid.*, pp. 970, 986.

On July 2, Maj. Gen. George H. Thomas, Nashville, telegraphed to USG. "General wilson informs me that in execution of your orders to send two thousand 2000 cavalry to south Carolina he has sent seven hundred 700 to Oranburg & general Gilmore has notified him of their arrival at that place genl. Gilmore informs genl wilson that the seven hundred 700 is enough for S., C Do you wish anything more done in the matter" Telegram received (on July 3, 10:35 A.M.), DNA, RG 107, Telegrams Collected (Bound); (misdated July 1) *ibid.*, Telegrams Collected (Unbound); *ibid.*, RG 108, Telegrams Received; copy,

DLC-USG, V, 54. *O.R.*, I, xlix, part 2, 1059. On July 3, 11:30 A.M., USG tele-graphed to Thomas. "Gen. Wilson need not send any more Cavalry to South Carolina than Gen. Gilmore thinks he will require." ALS (telegram sent), DNA, RG 107, Telegrams Collected (Bound); telegram sent, *ibid.*; telegram received, *ibid.*, Telegrams Collected (Unbound). *O.R.*, I, xlix, part 2, 1060. See *ibid.*, p. 1064.

To Edwin M. Stanton

Washington May 19th 1865,

HON, E, M, STANTON
SECRETARY OF WAR
SIR

The enclosed makes it appear that Brown of Georgia sur-rendered the Militia of that State and himself as Commander in Chief thereof to Gen, Wilson and was paroled

If this call for the meeting of the Georgia Legislature was subsequent to his parole, I suppose there can be no doubt but that he stands liable to arrest for violation of his parole, Otherwise is it not obligatory upon the Government to observe their part of the Contract, I would not advise authorizing him to go back to Georgia now under any circumstances but I do not think a paroled Officer is subject to arrest so long as he observes his parole without giving him notice first that he is absolved from further observance of it.

Very Respectfully
Your obt svt
U. S. GRANT
Lieut, Genl

Copies, DLC-USG, V, 46, 76, 108; DNA, RG 108, Letters Sent. *O.R.*, I, xlix, part 2, 836. On May 19, 1865, Secretary of War Edwin M. Stanton wrote to USG. "Governor Brown, of Georgia, was arrested for attempting to restore the rebellion by calling together an unauthorized assemblage, assuming to act as the Legislature of Georgia, without permission of the President—This I under-stand to have been subsequent to his alleged surrender. I am not advised of the terms of the surrender, or under what authority he can claim any benefit arising from it. If you have any details or report upon that point, I will thank you to send them to me." Copy, DLC-Edwin M. Stanton.

On May 20, Stanton wrote to USG. "On referring to General Wilson's despatch of May 6th, in relation to the action of Governor Brown, I find it is as follows: 'Macon, Georgia, 2 A. M. May 6th, 1865. HON. EDWIN M. STANTON, Secretary of War. Without my knowledge or consent, Governor Brown has issued a call for a meeting of the Georgia Legislature on the 22d I do not think it proper for either Governor Brown or his Legislature to exercise any influence or control, directly or indirectly, in shaping policy or opinion in regard to establishment of the relations of Georgia with the Union. I shall therefore not allow the Legislature to meet, unless so directed by the Government at Washington. I can see no necessity for conventions and public meetings in such times as these; certainly none where controlled by prominent secessionists. Please send me instructions in the case.' On the 7th of May, General Wilson was instructed to arrest Governor Brown and send him to Washington, for the act specified in the above quoted telegram. I will refer the question as to how far the parole operates to the Attorney General. It seems to me that his political action in assuming the functions of Governor are not covered by his military parole as commander-in-chief of the State militia." LS, DNA, RG 108, Letters Received. *O.R.*, I, xlix, part 2, 628, 847.

To Maj. Gen. Henry W. Halleck

(Cipher)   May 19th *1865* [*4:00* P.M.]

MAJ. GEN. HALLECK, RICHMOND VA.

Bvt. Maj. Gen. Miles is ordered to report to you for the purpose of being assigned to the Eastern District of the Dept. of Va. with Hd Qrs. at Ft. Monroe, the object being to put an officer at Ft. Monroe who will by no possibility permit the escape of the prisoners to be confined there.

U. S. GRANT
Lt. Gn.

ALS (telegram sent), DNA, RG 107, Telegrams Collected (Bound); telegram sent, *ibid.*; copies, *ibid.*, RG 108, Letters Sent; DLC-USG, V, 46, 76, 108. *O.R.*, I, xlvi, part 3, 1174. On May 19, 1865, 3:40 P.M., USG telegraphed to Maj. Gen. George G. Meade. "Order Gen. Miles to report at my Hd Qrs. without delay to receive spl. orders. He should come in to-night prepared to leave Washington at once." ALS (telegram sent), DNA, RG 107, Telegrams Collected (Bound); telegram sent, *ibid.*; telegram received, *ibid.*, Telegrams Collected (Bound). *O.R.*, I, xlvi, part 3, 1175. At 8:10 P.M., Bvt. Col. Theodore S. Bowers telegraphed to Meade. "Has Gen. Miles started for Washington to report to the Lt. Gen. as ordered this evening, and if so how long since. Gen. Grant is anxiously awaiting him. Please hurry him up if you can." ALS (telegram sent), DNA, RG 107, Telegrams Collected (Bound); telegram sent, *ibid.*; copies, *ibid.*,

RG 108, Letters Sent; DLC-USG, V, 46, 76, 108. See *O.R.*, I, xlvi, part 3, 1191–92.

To Maj. Gen. Edward O. C. Ord

Washington May 19th *1865* [*4:25* P.M.]
MAJ. GN. ORD. RICHMOND VA.

Jackson is promoted full Brig. Michie *will* have to go with the Corps. Lt. Col. [*Edward W.*] Smith can remain in the Dept. and Maj. Wheeler take his place in the Corps. [Does] Michie command troops?

U. S. GRANT
Lt. Gn.

ALS (telegram sent—marked as received by telegrapher at 4:25 P.M., sent at 7:35 P.M.), DNA, RG 107, Telegrams Collected (Bound); telegram received (at 8:00 P.M.), Ord Papers, CU-B. *O.R.*, I, xlvi, part 3, 1178. On May 19, 1865, Maj. Gen. Edward O. C. Ord telegraphed to USG. "Bvt Br Gen R H Jackson Lt Col & Inspector General Dept of Va is Commanding a Divisions 25th A Corps Shall he go south with the Corps or remain with his Dept? If made a full Br General it It would settle the question   Shall Bvt Br Gen Michie 1st Lt of Engineers and Lt Col & Inspr Gen 25th army Corps go with 25th Corps or remain here as Lt of Engineers. if made full Brigadier it would settle the question   michie & Jackson deserve the promotion   shall Lt Col Smith Adjt Gen 25th army Corps now actg a a G this Dept go with his Corps or remain here as Chief a a G. Dept. which I recommend to be done. Gen Weitzel has abl. applied for the appointment of Maj D D Wheeler as Asst Adjt Gen of his Corps and he is on duty with it" Telegram received (at 2:40 P.M.), DNA, RG 94, ACP, O82 CB 1865; *ibid.*, RG 107, Telegrams Collected (Bound); *ibid.*, RG 108, Telegrams Received; copy, DLC-USG, V, 54. *O.R.*, I, xlvi, part 3, 1177–78.

On the same day, Ord telegraphed to USG. "Michie is Chief Engineer of the Army and Dept Commands Engineers troops. I will give him a district or Division if promoted   Want him here very much. He is modest and poor   Could hardly be kept back when fighting was going on. Is only a Lieutenant of Regulars but Weitzel and I gave him Inspectorship of 25th Corps to help him support mother and sisters & his brevet of Brigadier   Weitzel has Kress of the ordnance acting Inspector Genl and can dispense with Michie who deserves the full grade as much as any one in my command" Telegram received (at 11:55 P.M.), DNA, RG 107, Telegrams Collected (Bound); *ibid.*, RG 108, Telegrams Received; copy, DLC-USG, V, 54. *O.R.*, I, xlvi, part 3, 1178.

Also on May 19, Ord telegraphed to USG. "What shall I do with the naval Brigade 13th New York Heavy—You broke it up Once   tis of no use now and as all the Steamers save one are owned by government they are wanted as transports. Should be turned in to the Quarte master Dept." ALS (telegram sent), Ord Papers, CU-B; telegram received (at 4:30 P.M.), DNA, RG 107, Telegrams Collected (Bound); *ibid.*, RG 108, Telegrams Received. *O.R.*, I, xlvi, part 3, 1178.

On May 16, Maj. Gen. Godfrey Weitzel, Camp Lincoln, Va., wrote to Bvt. Col. Theodore S. Bowers. "I have heard through several unofficial sources that the troops of my corps are charged with having committed an unusual amount of irregularities while in and about Richmond, and that these reports have reached the ears of some of the highest commanding officers in the service. As I have a telegram from my immediate commander, Maj. Gen. E. O. C. Ord, commanding Department of Virginia, that nearly all of the irregularities complained of were committed by black and white cavalry, which either did not belong to my corps, or had been with it but for a few days; as I know positively that others were committed by the convicts in soldiers' clothing, liberated by the rebels from the penitentiary at the evacuation of Richmond, and as I with my two division commanders, Bvt. Maj. Gen. A. V. Kautz and Bvt. Brig. Gen. R. H. Jackson, both officers of experience in the regular army, believe the troops of this corps to be not only as well behaved and as orderly as the average of other troops, but even more so, I respectfully request to know whether any such charge as above referred to has been either officially or unofficially made by any responsible person. The behavior of my entire corps during the last month has been most excellent. Only one complaint has been made by the people of the vicinity, and this I traced to troops that did not belong to it." *Ibid.*, p. 1160. On May 18, Ord endorsed this letter. "Respectfully forwarded. I do not consider the behavior of the colored corps from what I have heard to have been bad, considering the novelty of their position and the fact that most of their company officers had come from positions where they were unaccustomed to command, and this was perhaps the first great temptation to which their men were exposed. In the city of Richmond their conduct is spoken of as very good." *Ibid.*, pp. 1160–61.

On May 21, Ord telegraphed to USG. "I have the honor to apply for authority to discharge from the service a limited number of enlisted men to be employed as citizen clerks in the twenty fifth army corps   There is no opportunity to get men from the north   about fifty will be required" Telegram received (on May 22, 10:45 A.M.), DNA, RG 107, Telegrams Collected (Bound); *ibid.*, RG 108, Telegrams Received; copy, DLC-USG, V, 54. On May 22, 12:10 P.M., USG telegraphed to Ord. "In reply to your dispatch of yesterday I refer you to the dispatch of the Sec. of War of the 18th." ALS (telegram sent), DNA, RG 107, Telegrams Collected (Bound); telegram sent, *ibid.*; telegram received, Ord Papers, CU-B.

To Maj. Gen. William T. Sherman

Washington May 19th 1865

GENERAL

I am just in reciept of yours of this date, The orders for review was only published yesterday, or rather was only ready for circulation at that time, and was sent to you this morning

I will be glad to see you as soon as you can come to the City, can you not come in this evening or in the morning? I want to talk to you upon matters about which you feel sore. I think justly so, but which bear some explanation in behalf of those who you feel have inflicted the injury

Yours Truly

U. S. GRANT Lt, Gen,

To MAJ, GEN, W, T. SHERMAN.
U. S. ARMY COMDG &c,

Copies, DLC-USG, V, 46, 76, 108; DNA, RG 108, Letters Sent. *O.R.*, I, xlvii, part 3, 531. On May 19, 1865, Maj. Gen. William T. Sherman, "Capmp near Alexandria," wrote to Brig. Gen. John A. Rawlins. "I have the honor to report my arrival at Camp near the Washington Road, three miles north of Alexandria. All my Army should be in Camp near by today. The 15th Corps the last to leave Richmond Camped last night at the Ocoquan. I have seen the order for the review in the papers, but Col Sawyer says it is not here in official form. I am old fashioned and prefer to see orders through some other channel but if that be the new fashion so be it   I will be all ready by Wednesday though in the rough. Troops have not been paid for 8 & 10 months, and clothing may be bad, but a better set of legs & arms cannot be displayed on this Continent. Send me all orders and letters you may have for me, and let some one newspaper know that the Vandal Sherman is encamped near the Canal bridge half way between the Long Bridge & Alexandria to the West of the Road, where his friends if any can find him. Though in disgrace he is untamed and unconquered." ALS, CSmH. *O.R.*, I, xlvii, part 3, 531. On the same day, Sherman again wrote to Rawlins. "I have just received at the hands of Colonel Wm M. Wherry of General Schofields staff the enclosed communication with an abstract of the Prisoners of War surrendered and paroled at Greensboro N. C. abut the 1st of May, pursuant to the terms of the Capitulation made by General Johnston near Durham Sta on the 26 of April. The aggregate number parolled exceeds the number heretofor reported and amounts to 36,791 men." ALS, DNA, RG 94, Letters Received, 1232M 1865. *O.R.*, I, xlvii, part 3, 531–32. The enclosures are *ibid.*, pp. 481–82, 483. A footnote on p. 532 places the number of paroles at 39,012. On June 17, USG endorsed this letter. "Respectfully forwarded to the Secretary of War together with the Rolls of Officers & men of Johnstons Army" ES, DNA, RG 94, Letters Received, 1232M 1865.

On May 10, 3:00 A.M., USG telegraphed to Sherman, Richmond. "You will march your army on to Alexandria as first directed from Raleigh. I have written and telegraphed to you though not on that subject." ALS (telegram sent), *ibid.*, RG 107, Telegrams Collected (Bound); telegram sent, *ibid.*; telegram received, *ibid.*, Telegrams Collected (Unbound). *O.R.*, I, xlvii, part 3, 453. At noon, Sherman, Manchester, Va., telegraphed to USG. "Your dispatch directing me to march my Command to Alexandria just received—I have ordered the Army of Georgia to move tomorrow and the Army of Tennessee will follow next day"

Telegram received (at 3:00 P.M.), DNA, RG 107, Telegrams Collected (Bound); *ibid.*, Telegrams Collected (Unbound); *ibid.*, RG 108, Telegrams Received; copy, DLC-USG, V, 54. *O.R.*, I, xlvii, part 3, 454. On the same day, Sherman, "Camp opposite Richmond," wrote to USG. "Private & Confidential. . . . I march tomorrow at the head of my army thrugh Richmond for Alexandria, in pursuance of the orders this day received by telegraph from you. I have received no other telegram or letter from you since you left me at Raleigh. I send by Gen Howard who goes to Washington in pursuance of a telegram dated 7th but received only today my official Report of events from my last Official Report up to this date. I do think a great outrage has been enacted against me, by Mr Stanton and General Halleck. I care nought for Public opinion, that will regulate itself, but to maintain my own self respect and command on brave men I must resent a public insult. On arrival at Old Point I met a despatch from Gnl Halleck inviting me to his house in Richmond. I declined most pointedly and assigned as a reason the insult to me in his Telegram to Secretary Stanton of Apl 26. I came here via Petersburg and have gone under Canvas. Halleck had arranged to review my Army in passing Richmond. I forbad it. Yesterday I received a letter of which a Copy is enclosed. I answered that I could not reconcile its friendly substance with the public insult contained in his despatch & notified him I should march through Richmond and asked him to Keep out of sight lest he should be insulted. My officers and men feel this insult as Keenly as I do. I was in hopes to hear something from you before I got here to guide me & telegraphed with this view from Morehead City, but I have not a word from you and have acted thus on my own responsibility. I will treat Mr Stanton with like scorn & contempt unless you have reasons otherwise, for I regard my military Career as ended save & except so far as necessary to put my Army in your hands. Mr Stanton can give me no orders of himself. He may in the name of the President & these shall be obeyed to the letter, but I deny his right to Command an Army. Your orders and wishes shall be to me the Law, but I ask you to vindicate my name from the insult Conveyed in Mr Stantons despatch to Gn Dix of Apl 27 published in all the newspapers of the Land. If you do not I will. No man shall insult me with impunity, even if I am an officer of the Army. Subordination to Authority is one thing, to insult Another. No amount of retraction or pusillanimous excusing will do. Mr Stanton must publicly confess himself a Common libeller or—but I wont threaten. I will not enter Washington exscept on yours or the Presidents emphatic orders, but I do wish to stay with my army, till it ceases to exist, or till it is broken up and scattered to other duty. Then I wish to go for a time to my family and make arrangemts for the Future. Your private and official wishes when conveyed to me shall be sacred, but there can be no relation between Mr Stanton & me. He seeks your life and reputation as well as mine. Beware, but you are Cool and have been most skilful in managing such People, and I have faith you will penetrate his designs—He wants the *vast* patronage of the military Governorships of the south, and the votes of the Free Negro *loyal* citizens for political Capital, and whoever stands in his way must die. Read Hallecks letter and see how pitiful he is become. Keep *above* such influences, or you will also be a victim—See in my case how soon all past services are ignored & forgotten. Excuse this letter. Burn it, but heed my friendly counsel. The lust for Power in political Minds is the strongest passion of Life, and impels

Ambitious Men (Richard III) to deeds of Infamy." ALS, CSmH. On March 16, 1876, Sherman endorsed a copy of this letter. "I recall from the within letter the feelings of bitterness that filled my soul at that dread epoch of time. The letter must have been written hastily and in absolute confidence—a confidence in General Grant that I then felt and *still* feel. Because I sent to Washington terms that recognized the war as *over*, and promising the subjugated enemy a treatment that would have been the extreme of generosity and *wisdom*, I was denounced by the Secretary of War as a *traitor*, and my own soldiers *commanded* to disobey *my* orders; and this denunciation was spread broadcast over the world. Now, after twelve long eventful years of political acrimony, we find ourselves compelled to return to the same point of history, or else permit the enemy of that day to become the absolute masters of the country. To-day I might act with more silence, with more caution and prudence, because I am twelve years older. But these things did occur, these feelings were felt, and inspired acts which go to make up history; and the question now is not, was I right or wrong? but, did it happen? and is the record of it worth anything as an historic example?" Adam Badeau, *Military History of Ulysses S. Grant* (New York, 1868–81), III, 710.

On May 15, 1865, Sherman, Fredericksburg, Va., telegraphed to USG. "I have to report my arrival here—I left General Slocum at noon at Chancellorsville & he will Cross the 14th at Racoon Ford atnd 20th at the U S Ford tomorrow—Gen Logan is not yet in and I suspect he has found his roads badly Cut up by the troops that preceeeded us—" Telegram received (at 5:00 P.M.), DNA, RG 107, Telegrams Collected (Bound); (2) *ibid.*, Telegrams Collected (Unbound); *ibid.*, RG 108, Telegrams Received; copy, DLC-USG, V, 54. *O.R.*, I, xlvii, part 3, 499–500. On May 16, Sherman twice telegraphed to USG. "The 17th Corps ~~and~~ is now passing the bridge—The 15th will not be able to cross until tomorrow. ~~Can~~ If you design a grand review, please notify me of the date as I may want to have Mrs Sherman Come to witness it—" Telegram received (at 12:30 P.M.), DNA, RG 107, Telegrams Collected (Bound); (2) *ibid.*, Telegrams Collected (Unbound); (at 12:10 P.M.) *ibid.*, RG 108, Telegrams Received; copy, DLC-USG, V, 54. Printed as received at 12:30 P.M. in *O.R.*, I, xlvii, part 3, 507. "I will remain here all day. Have you any orders?—" Telegram received (at 12:30 P.M.), DNA, RG 107, Telegrams Collected (Bound); *ibid.*, Telegrams Collected (Unbound); (at 12:15 P.M.) *ibid.*, RG 108, Telegrams Received; copy, DLC-USG, V, 54. Printed as received at 12:15 P.M. in *O.R.*, I, xlvii, part 3, 507. At 3:00 P.M., Rawlins telegraphed to Sherman. "A review has not yet been determined on. You might send for Mrs Sherman anyhow. You will probably be here some time—There are no orders for you." Telegrams sent (2—the second at 3:40 P.M.), DNA, RG 107, Telegrams Collected (Bound); telegrams received (2), *ibid.*, Telegrams Collected (Unbound). *O.R.*, I, xlvii, part 3, 507. See *ibid.*, p. 526; *ibid.*, I, xlvi, part 3, 1171.

To Lt. Col. John Woolley

Washington, D. C. May 19th *1865* [*3:00* P.M.]

COL WOOLEY
PROVOST MARSHAL
BALTIMORE MD

Why is it that Webb a paroled soldier who has taken the [o]ath of Allegiance, is banished north? This [i]s in violation of orders. Constant complaints are made against you for banishing men who have taken the oath of allegiance much to my annoyance and consuming in addition much time.

U. S. GRANT
Lt Genl

Telegram sent (at 3:05 P.M.), DNA, RG 107, Telegrams Collected (Bound); telegram received, *ibid.*, RG 393, Middle Military Div., Telegrams Received. On May 19, 1865, Lt. Col. John Woolley telegraphed to USG. "L. L. Webb a paroled prisoner of war was discharged & went north May 6th. Your Special Order No 215. Par 9. allowing paroled Rebel officers & soldiers to Return to their former homes is dated May 8th since which time not a single one has been ordered away. Those who had been sent away by order of the General Comdg previous to your order of May 8th are constantly Returning & no action has been taken to prevent L. L. Webb from doing so. Your orders are implicitly obeyed. There was another son of Mrs Webb sent away last December for disloyalty & verry Reasonable terms were offered by the Genl Comdg for his Return and Rejected. The Webb family have annoyed every body here and at the War Department and are now annoying you." ALS (telegram sent), *ibid.*, RG 107, Telegrams Collected (Unbound); *ibid.*, RG 393, Middle Dept. and 8th Army Corps, Telegrams Sent (Press); telegram received (at 8:45 P.M.), *ibid.*, RG 107, Telegrams Collected (Bound); *ibid.*, RG 108, Telegrams Received. On the same day, Woolley telegraphed to Maj. Gen. Lewis Wallace, Washington, D. C. "Please See Gen Grant about the Webb family. They are annoying him about their son. I have answered his telegram. It is the parties who were sent away previous to his order 215, Par 9, May 8th who are annoying him. they are Returning fast. If they are Referred to me it will Relieve the Genl of the Annoyance" ALS (telegram sent), *ibid.*, RG 107, Telegrams Collected (Unbound).

On April 29, Mrs. A. P. Webb, Baltimore, wrote to USG. "As a parent (suffering in unison with hundreds of others) I assume the liberty of laying before you the case of my son—a paroled prisoner from Genl R. E. Lee's army—He returned home on the 21st of the present month (April) after being imprisoned some days on the route)—careworn and weary—impaired in health—but happy in the thought of possessing your generous parole—beleiving (as you specify) himself perfectly safe from molestation of any kind—so long as he remained, a peaceful and lawabiding citizen—Which I am proud to say—he would ever have proven himself to be—. You may then, very readily Genl, judge of the sadness and distress—into which we—(his loyal parents) a father in rapidly declining health, were plunged, when four days after his return, he was snatched from our happy little circle—and again incarcerated in a prison—where he has now been confined for nearly a week—with out any redress whatever—with the threat hanging over him, of being sent away, he knows not whither, or at what time—Were ours the only hearts crushed, and bleeding, by the rescesson of your order, and terms of surrender to Genl Lee—I should be constrained to bear it in silence and in patience—but as so many households (rejoicing like ourselves) at the return of prodigal sons—after years of absence—have been lacerated by it—I cannot but feel, Genl, judging from your noble course of late—but that you will pardon me for calling your attention to circumstances as they exist—. Most fondly hoping it may receive your early attention, amid the multifarious duties now resting upon you—. . ." ALS, *ibid.*, RG 108, Letters Received. On May 3, Bvt. Col. Theodore S. Bowers endorsed this letter. "Respectfully referred to Maj Gen. Lew. Wallace, Comdg Middle Depart't for a statement of the facts in the case of Lewis Webb, 1st Maryland Battery, Lee's Rebel Army." ES, *ibid.* On May 10, Wallace endorsed this letter to Bowers, calling attention to an endorsement of May 9 of Woolley. "*Respectfully returned to* Lt. Col Saml B. Lawrence A. A. G. with the information that *Lewis L. Webb.* the son of Mrs. A. P. Webb *has already been released and has gone north.* Mrs. A. P. Webb the mother of Lewis L Webb is as great a Rebel as there is in this city. I know her well and I know that there is not a loyal person in the city of Baltimore who will come forward and say that Mrs. Webb is loyal. She talks about 'crushed and bleeding hearts' and 'prodigal sons'. If her heart is crushed and bleeding it is because her friends the Rebils have been subjugated and have failed to destroy this Government. If her sons are 'prodigal' it is her own fault and the result of her own teachings. From my own personal knowledge it is advisable that her son Lewis remain away from this city for a time at least as there is a party in the city who threaten to kill him if he returns here." ES, *ibid.*

On May 11, 11:00 A.M., USG drafted a telegram to Wallace, then crossed out his name and redirected it to the commanding officer, Baltimore. "Relieve Col. Wooley from duty as Provost Marshal and appoint a successor." ALS (telegram sent), *ibid.*, RG 107, Telegrams Collected (Bound); telegram sent, *ibid.*; telegram received (press), *ibid.* At 8:00 P.M., USG telegraphed to the commanding officer, Baltimore. "Col. Wooley need not be replaced as Provost Marshal of Baltimore for the present." ALS (telegram sent), *ibid.*; telegram sent, *ibid.*; telegram received (press), *ibid.*

On May 22 and June 12, Wallace wrote to an unnamed col., then to Bowers. "*Personal* . . . Yesterday I recieved private information that certain parties in Baltimore were driving at Col. Woolley, Prov' Marshal, with a purpose to procure his removal for the benefit of Maj. Wiegel, his Asst Prov. The approaches of these parties are against Mr. Stanton. I feel sure Gen. Grant will not do an act of injustice to a faithful and brave soldier. If he has any doubt about Woolley's integrity, capacity, or fitness for the place, I suggest that he send an officer in whom he has confidence to inspect his office and report upon his general management of his trust. I have not the slighest fear of the result of a most rigid scrutiny. I will also suggest that Maj. Wiegel is an Asst. Adj. General, ranking as Major: that by my order he is in Woolley's office temporarily: that his present duties are hardly compatable with his commission: and that it would be no wrong to him to assign him to some General officer, who can furnish him employment. If this can be done, it will bring peace to that very important branch of my Department, the Provost Marshal's office. Please let me hear what can be done. . . . P. S. With this exception, the Mid. Dep't is running very smoothly. With Lawrence in my A. G. Office, and Woolley in the Prov'. Marshal's, I have no uneasiness." "I have the honor to call the attention of Lt. Gen. Grant to the within letters and petition of citizens of Baltimore, including Governor Swan and Mayor Chapman. The object of these parties is to procure the retention Of Lt. Col. Woolley in the Provost Marshalship Of the City and Department. As the Colonel's regiment has been consolidated, under existing orders, he will, be mustered out unless a special exception is made in his behalf. If this can be consistently done, I have no hesitation in earnestly recommending it to the General's favorable consideration. It will be very difficult for me, or for any officer who may succeed me in command of this Department, to find an officer so thoroughly possessed of the local information essential to a proper conduct of the Colonel's office. In addition to that, I call attention Col. W's satisfactory administration in the past. The petition contains the names of all the staunch and influential Union men of Baltimore." ALS and LS, *ibid.*, RG 108, Letters Received.

To Absalom H. Markland

Washington D. C. May 19th *1865*

Col. A. H. Markland
Spl. Agt. P. O. Dept.
Colonel.

I take great pleasure in presenting you the "Grimsby Saddle" which I have used in all the battles from Fort Henry, Tenn, in Feb.y 1862, to the battles about Petersburg, Va. ending in the surrender of Lee's Army at Appomattox C. H. Va. on the 9th of Apl. 1865.

I present this saddle not for any intrinsic value it possesses but as a mark of friendship and esteem after continued service with you through the Great Rebellion, our services commencing together at Cairo, Ill. in the Fall of 1861 and continuing to the present day. I hope our friendship, if not our continued services together, will continue as heretofore.

Yours Truly
U. S. Grant
Lt. Gn.

ALS (facsimile), William H. Allen, *The American Civil War Book and Grant Album* (Boston and New York, 1894), p. [35]. On the facing page is a picture of the saddle.

To Brig. Gen. Lewis B. Parsons

Washington, D C., May 20 *1865*

DEAR GENERAL.

I have long contemplated writing you and expressing my satisfaction with the manner in which you have discharged the very responsible and difficult duties of Superintendent of river and railroad transportation for the armies both in the west and east.

The position is second in importance to no other connected with the military service, and to have been appointed to it at the beginning of a war of the magnitude and duration of this one and holding it to its close, providing transportation for whole armies with all that appertains to them for thousands of miles, adjusting accounts involving millions of money and doing justice to all, never delaying for a moment any military operations dependent upon you, meriting and receiving the commendation of your superior officers and the recognition of Government, for integrity of character and for the able and efficient manner in which you have filled it—evidences an honesty of purpose, knowledge of men, business intelligence and executive ability of the highest order, and of which any man might be justly proud.

Wishing you a speedy return to health and duty,

I remain, Yours Truly

U. S. GRANT

Lt. Gen

BRIG. GEN. LEWIS B PARSONS A. Q. M.

LS, Parsons Papers, IHi. *O.R.*, I, xlvii, part 3, 539.

To Maj. Gen. Henry W. Halleck

(Cipher)   Washington May 21st/65 [*10:00* A.M.]
MAJ. GN. HALLECK, RICHMOND VA.

After carrying out the orders for discharging all men whose
time expires up to 1st of October will you require reinforcements
~~from~~ for Va.? If so retain as much of the 6th Corps as you deem
necessary and discharge there those entitled to discharge under the
orders. After Musterout all troops will be sent to their states to be
paid off.

U. S. GRANT
Lt. Gen

ALS (telegram sent), DNA, RG 107, Telegrams Collected (Bound); telegram
sent, *ibid.*; copies, *ibid.*, RG 108, Letters Sent; DLC-USG, V, 46, 76, 108.
Printed as received on May 22, 1865, 2:30 P.M., in *O.R.*, I, xlvi, part 3, 1185.
As printed, the text includes another telegram of May 21 from USG to Maj. Gen.
Henry W. Halleck. See telegram to Maj. Gen. Henry W. Halleck, May 18, 1865.

To Maj. Gen. Frederick Steele

Washington D. C. May 21st *1865*

MAJ. GN. F. STEELE,
COMD.G RIO GRANDE, EX
GENERAL,

By assignment of the President Gen. Sheridan takes general
command West of the Miss. and south of the Arkansas. It is the
intention to prossecute a vigerous campaign in that country until
the whole of Texas is reoccupied by people acknowledging allegiance to the Govt. of the United States.—Sheridan will probably
act offensively from the Red River. But it is highly important that
we should have a strong foothold upon the Rio Grande. You have
been selected to take that part of the command. In addition to the
force you take from Mobile Bay you will have the 25th Corps and
the few troops already in Southwest Texas.

Any directions you may receive from Gen. Sheridan you will obey. But in the absence of instructions from him you will proceed, without delay, to the Mouth of the Rio Grande and occupy as high up that river as your force, and means of supplying them, will admit of.—Your landing will probably have to be made at Brasos, but you will learn more fully upon that matter on your arrival.

We will have to observe a strict neutrality towards Mexico, in the *French* & *English* sense of the word. Your own good sense and knowlede of International Law, and experiance of policy pursued towards us in this war, teaches you what will be proper.

> Very respectfully
> your obt. svt.
> U. S. GRANT
> Lt. Gn.

ALS, CSt. *O.R.*, I, xlviii, part 2, 525–26.

To Maj. Gen. George H. Thomas

Washington May 21st/65 [*11:00* A.M.]
MAJ. GN. THOMAS, NASHVILLE TENN

A great part of Sherman's troops will be sent West so that you will be able to draw from them to replace the men you will loose by discharge. The 4th Corps with the other troops assigned to Sheridan will make Infantry enough for him. Cavalry is all he will be deficient in. The Cavalry horses returning from Ga. will not likely be fit for service in time to serve his purpose hence the order to send them into Ky to recruit. If you have other Cavalry that can be spared I would like to have it held in readiness and replace it with Infantry or as much of that returning from Ga. as you deem necessary.

U. S. GRANT, Lt. Gn

ALS (telegram sent), USMA; telegram sent, DNA, RG 107, Telegrams Collected (Bound); copies, *ibid.*, RG 108, Letters Sent; *ibid.*, RG 393, Dept. of the Cumberland, Telegrams Received; DLC-USG, V, 46, 76, 108. *O.R.*, I, xlix, part 2, 859. On May 21, 1865, Maj. Gen. George H. Thomas telegraphed to

USG. "All the Cavalry belonging to my command left behind in Tennessee when operations commenced in the spring was dismounted   Genl Johnson has one division at Pulaski with only a few mounted men now who are constantly occupied hunting up Guerrillas and patrolling the country to preserve quiet. Genl Hatch is in the same condition as Johnson, but I could replace him with an Infantry command, if he could get horses, as the Cavalry now in Memphis will be strong enough to patrol the North Mississippi, North Alabama and West Tennessee. But the fourth Corps & the Hatch's Cavalry should be paid before taking the field as they have received no pay for eight months." ALS (telegram sent), MH; telegram received (at 1:35 A.M.), DNA, RG 107, Telegrams Collected (Bound); *ibid.*, RG 108, Telegrams Received. *O.R.*, I, xlix, part 2, 859.

On May 19, 4:30 P.M., USG telegraphed to Thomas. "Hold the 4th Corps subject to orders from Gen. Sheridan. If you can spare other troops, especially Cavalry, hold them ready to receive orders from same quarter. You have I believe a regiment of mounted Engineers which I should like to go with Sheridan if possible to spare them." ALS (telegram sent), DNA, RG 107, Telegrams Collected (Bound); telegram sent, *ibid.*; copies, *ibid.*, RG 108, Letters Sent; DLC-USG, V, 46, 76, 108. Printed as received May 20 in *O.R.*, I, xlix, part 2, 837. On May 20, 6:00 P.M., Thomas telegraphed to USG. "Your telegram directing me to hold the fourth Corps subject to the Orders of Maj Genl Sheridan was received this a. m. I have no other troops which can be spared from this department. I have no mounted engineer troops, but an a regiment of pioneers belonging to the third division of the fourth Corps. The Cavalry ordered back from Genl Wilsons could be held subject to Genl Sheridan's orders, but in a subsequent telegram you have directed that it be distributed through Kentucky" ALS (telegram sent), MH; telegram received (at 11:30 P.M.), DNA, RG 107, Telegrams Collected (Bound); *ibid.*, RG 108, Telegrams Received. *O.R.*, I, xlix, part 2, 849.

On May 14, noon, Maj. Gen. Henry W. Halleck, Richmond, telegraphed to USG. "Would it not be well to order Genl Wilson to send Jeff Davis & party to some point on the coast & thence by steamer north? There will be disturbances if they pass through the country by land." ALS (telegram sent), DNA, RG 107, Telegrams Collected (Unbound); telegram received, *ibid.*; (at 3:00 P.M.) *ibid.*, Telegrams Collected (Bound); *ibid.*, RG 108, Telegrams Received. *O.R.*, I, xlix, part 2, 759. At 3:00 P.M., Thomas telegraphed to USG. "Gen Wilson reports to me the capture of Jeff Davis, Regan Post Master General, Col Harrison, Private Secretary, and Col Johnson A. D. C at Irwinville on the morning of the 10th   He has forwarded the prisoners to me under strong guard direct to me; I understand that Governor Brown of Georgia has also been arrested, and is on the way to this place,   To be prepared to forward the prisoners promptly & quietly I respectfully ask where it is intended that they shall be confined? I would suggest some prison north as presenting the greatest security and freedom from excitement,   I expect them at this place by wednesday next," Telegram received (on May 15, 12:20 A.M.), DNA, RG 107, Telegrams Collected (Bound); *ibid.*, RG 108, Telegrams Received; Seward Papers, NRU; copies, DNA, RG 393, Dept. of the Cumberland, Telegrams Sent; DLC-USG, V, 54. *O.R.*, I, xlix, part 2, 760. On May 15, 3:00 P.M., Thomas telegraphed to USG. "Wishing to forward Davis and party without delay and having recd no instructions to govern me I have directed that he be placed on board steamer at this place forwarded to Parkersburg Va and thence by R. R. to Washington to be turned over to the Pro. Mar Gen—This arrangement appears to me to be not only the safest but most expeditious as he will be under ample and effective guards" Telegram received (at 4:00 P.M.), DNA, RG 107, Telegrams Collected (Bound); *ibid.*, RG 108, Telegrams Received; copies, *ibid.*, RG 393, Dept. of the Cumberland, Telegrams Sent; DLC-USG, V, 54. *O.R.*, I, xlix, part 2, 774. USG endorsed the telegram received. "Gen. Thomas course approved" AE (initialed), DNA, RG 108, Telegrams Received.

On May 20, 6:00 P.M., Thomas telegraphed to USG. "I learn by telegraph from Resaca that Genl Wilson has sent Jeff Davis by way of Savannah to Washington. He first dispatched me that he was ordered from Washington I suppose, to send him direct, on the 14th Upon receiving his dispatch I telegraphed to you for orders as to how he should be forwarded, but received no answer. on the 15th I made preparations to send the prisoner by steamer under a strong guard to Parkersburg Virginia and thence in a special train to Washington and telegraphed to you what preparations I had made and asked if they were approved. I have received no answer to that telegram I am consequently led to the conclusion that Genl Wilson is considered no longer under my orders ~~but~~ I I would be glad to know if my conjectures are correct." ALS (telegram sent), MH; telegram received (at 11:40 P.M.), DNA, RG 107, Telegrams Collected (Bound); *ibid.*, RG 108, Telegrams Received. *O.R.*, I, xlix, part 2, 849. On May 21, 10:35 A.M., USG telegraphed to Thomas. "~~I~~ No orders have been made taking Wilson from you command. At the time of receiving your dispatch relative ~~by~~ to the disposition you had ordered for Jeff Davis I ~~knew~~ thought he was coming by Savannah and let the matter run until I forgot to answer it." ALS (telegram sent), DNA, RG 107, Telegrams Collected (Bound); telegram sent, *ibid.*; copies (marked as sent at 10:20 A.M.), *ibid.*, RG 108, Letters Sent; *ibid.*, RG 393, Dept. of the Cumberland, Telegrams Received; DLC-USG, V, 46, 76, 108. *O.R.*, I, xlix, part 2, 858.

On May 16, Brig. Gen. John A. Rawlins telegraphed to Thomas. "Direct Gen. Wilson to leave a force of four thousand of his command to garrison such places as he now holds and deems necessary to be garrisoned, with instructions to draw their supplies, such as they cannot get in the country, via the Savannah and Ocmulgee rivers, and to move with the remainder of his command to such point as you may designate on the Tennessee river, and by such route as you may deem most pr[ac]ticable. He should commence his movement at the earliest practicable moment. In designating the force to be left in Georgia, no Regiment whose term of service expires on or prior to the 1st day of October next should be left." LS (telegram sent), DNA, RG 107, Telegrams Collected (Bound); telegram sent, *ibid.*; copies, *ibid.*, RG 108, Letters Sent; DLC-USG, V, 46, 76, 108. Printed as sent at 11:00 A.M. in *O.R.*, I, xlix, part 2, 798. At 11:00 A.M., Rawlins transmitted a copy of this telegram to Bvt. Maj. Gen. James H. Wilson. Telegram sent, DNA, RG 107, Telegrams Collected (Bound); telegrams received (3), *ibid.*, Telegrams Collected (Unbound). On May 17, 1:35 P.M., Rawlins telegraphed to Thomas. "In transmitting to Gen. Wilson the orders telegraphed you yesterday, you will direct him to remain himself with the forces to be left in Georgia." LS (telegram sent), *ibid.*, Telegrams Collected (Bound); telegram sent, *ibid.*; copies, *ibid.*, RG 108, Letters Sent; DLC-USG, V, 46, 76, 108. *O.R.*, I, xlix, part 2, 813. On May 20, noon, USG telegraphed to Thomas. "I think it will be well for you to send all your surplus Cavalry, that returning from Wilson's command particularly into Ky. and scatter them, for the purpose of pasturing and recuperating their horses. It may also tend to keep the peace about election times." ALS (telegram sent), DNA, RG 107, Telegrams Collected (Bound); telegram sent, *ibid.*; copies, *ibid.*, RG 108, Letters Sent; DLC-USG, V, 46, 76, 108. *O.R.*, I, xlix, part 2, 848.

On May 20, Thomas telegraphed to Secretary of War Edwin M. Stanton. "Are private soldiers paroled under the convention between Gen Sherman and Gen Johnston entitled to their private horses?" Telegram received (at 8:15 P.M.), DNA, RG 108, Telegrams Received; copy, DLC-USG, V, 54. *O.R.*, I, xlix, part 2, 848. On May 21, 10:00 A.M., USG telegraphed to Thomas. "By the terms given paroled prisoners are not entitled to their private horses, but I instructed Gen. Schofiel[d] to allow them to have them." ALS (telegram sent), DNA, RG 107, Telegrams Collected (Bound); telegram sent, *ibid.*; copies, *ibid.*, RG 108, Letters Sent; DLC-USG, V, 46, 76, 108; DLC-John M. Schofield. *O.R.*, I, xlix, part 2, 858.

To Capt. Henry R. Mizner

May 21, 1865

CAPT H R MIZNER
15TH U S INFY
DEAR SIR

I am just in receipt of your letter of the 13th inst. Besides always feeling a personal interest in your welfare I ~~h~~was highly pleased with your course as Col of Volunteers except in one instance to which I attached no importance regarding it simply a difference of opinion between you and Gen Dodge as to policy to be pursued toward quiet rebels[1]—In approving of Gen Thomas endorsement which resulted in your return to your regt in the regular army I did so on the principle that commanders must be sustained even if it should work hardship upon individuals[2]—My recollection is that I afterwards approved an application to have you restored to the Colonelcy of which you had been deprived[3]—Assuring you that my friendship and confidence in you are entirely unabated

I remain
very truly
your obt servt
U S GRANT
Lt Gen

Copy, Howard Papers, MiD. The numerals "31" appear below "21" in the date-line.

1. See endorsement to Col. Henry R. Mizner, Feb. 15, 1864.
2. See letter to John Robertson, Oct. 12, 1864.
3. See *Calendar*, March 7, 1865.

To Elihu B. Washburne

Washington May 21st *1865*

HON. E. B. WASHBURN,
DEAR SIR:

I have just rec'd your letter of the 18th. It has never been my intention to give up Ill. as my home. The house in Phila was presented to me, I believe, entirely by the "Union Lague" of that City. I was not aware the project was on the way until the money for the purchase was mostly subscribed, and then I did not know the parties interesting themselves in the matter. I had selected Phila as a place for my family where the children could have good schools and be near so that I might see them whenever I had a leasure day.

It would look egotistical to make a parade in the papers about where I intend to claim as my home, but I will endeavor to be in Galena at the next election, and vote there, and declare my intention of claiming that as my home, and intention of never casting a vote elswhere without first giving notice.

I feel very grateful to the Citizens of Ill. generally, and to those of Jo Daviess Co and yourself in particular, for the uniform support I have rec'd from that quarter. Without that support it would now matter but little where I might claim a residenc[e.] I might write a letter to Mr. Stuart, Ch. of the "Christian Commission," and the most active member of the "Union League" of Phila in getting up the subscription for my house, stating what I owe to the state of Ill. and that he and his friends must not think hard of me for holding on to Galena as my home.

I will hear from you again before doing anything in this matter.—At present I am keeping house in Georgetown and have my family with me. Neither they nor I will be in Phila again, unless it be for a few days, before Fall.

> Your Truly
> U. S. GRANT
> Lt Gn.

ALS, IHi. On May 18, 1865, U.S. Representative Elihu B. Washburne, Galena, wrote to USG. "*Private* . . . You will recollect that I told you some time ago that several of your Galena friends, who regarded this city as your home, had determined very quietly, and without parade or newspaper talk, to purchase for you a homestead here. The acceptance of the house in Philadelphia, and your removal into it, together with the impudent claim set up by the Philadelphia newspapers that you have taken up your permanent residence there and become a citizen of Pennsylvania, has created great uneasiness not only among your Galena friends but the people of the State, generally. You cannot think it strange that some of us here, who expect to live here, feel a very deep interest in this matter, as well as very great pride. This town was your home and the home of your family when you entered on your military career and it was from here that you *started* into the service. Here you had friends who have stood by you in evil and good report, and when the whole country was hounding on your heels, the Galena people stood by you with unfaltering fidelity. And the County of Joe Daviess, claiming you as its citizen, honored itself by presenting you with a sword. This much in regard to our own locality. As to the State at large, you commanded an Illinois regiment; you was appointed a brigadier general, a major general and a lieutenant general, all from Illinois, and I may say all, through Illinois influances. From a State which has made the proudest and noblest record of any State in the Union—the home of Lincoln and Douglas, whose ashes now lie mingled with our soil. You will not, therefore, think strange, that the people of Illinois would feel most deeply and painfully wounded, should you now turn your back on them to become a citizen of Pennsylvania, a State to which you owe less than almost any state in the Union. Honored as I have been by a portion of the people of the State, devoted as I am to all that pertains to its honor and its glory, proud of the noble men that it has given to the country, I feel inexpressibly pained when I am told almost every day that you 'have left Illinois and gone to Philadelphia to live.' I certainly understood you to say that you did not intend to lose your residence in Illinois by accepting the house in Phila, and I think the people there, because a few gentlemen found their pleasure in presenting you a house, have no right to insist that you either expressly or impliedly agreed no longer to be a citizen of Illinois. And if ~~this~~ Illinois is to be your home, (your voting place,) why not Galena the place. You will not be able to be any where in the State much of the time, but that time could better be spent here than any where else in the State, as you and your family are better acquainted here than any other part of the State. What you want is a *legal* residence, the same as Genl Scott has at Elizabeth, N. Jersey, though he has hardly staid there at all for years.—I take it for granted you will neither expect nor desire a costly or ostentatious residence here. You will think just as much of a neat and convenient village homestead as of a palatial mansion. It will be a modest and grateful tribute of sincere personal friends, and adapted to your character, of which it may be truly said, as Napier says of the character of Sir John Moore—that it was 'more in keeping with the primitive than the luxurious age of a great nation.' Let me have a confidential line from you in this regard as soon as you can. Excuse this long letter, but I could not get at what I wanted to say in shorter limits. We are all quite well, and send kindest regards to your family." ALS, USG 3.

To Maj. Gen. George G. Meade

Washington May 22d/65 [*11:55* A.M.]

MAJ. GEN MEADE, A. P.

I would like to send Gn. Barlow to command a Div. 25th Corps. Ascertain if this will suit him. If so he should leave here on Wednsday at furthest.

U. S. GRANT
Lt. Gn

ALS (telegram sent), DNA, RG 107, Telegrams Collected (Bound); telegram sent, *ibid.*; copies (marked as sent at 11:50 A.M.), *ibid.*, RG 108, Letters Sent; DLC-USG, V, 46, 76, 108. *O.R.*, I, xlvi, part 3, 1194. On May 22, 1865, Bvt. Maj. Gen. Francis C. Barlow telegraphed to USG. "Very reluctantly & for imperative personal reasons I must decline a command which will take me so far as Texas at present—" ALS (telegram sent), CtY; telegram received (at 9:00 P.M.), DNA, RG 108, Telegrams Received. *O.R.*, I, xlvi, part 3, 1194.

At 6:10 P.M., USG telegraphed to Maj. Gen. George G. Meade. "Please direct your Eng. officer to place in the revew tomorrow a pontoon train say of four boats and two Chess wagons." ALS (telegram sent), DNA, RG 107, Telegrams Collected (Bound); telegram sent, *ibid.*; copies, *ibid.*, RG 108, Letters Sent; DLC-USG, V, 46, 76, 108.

To Maj. Gen. Frederick Steele

(Cipher)   Washington May 22d *1865* [*11:15* P.M.]

MAJ. GEN. F. STEELE,

MONTGOMERY ALA.

The ordnance of Secession being nul & void there is no necessity for a meeting of the Ala. Legislature to repeal it. There can be no meeting of men elected to office in violation of during the rebellion.

There is no objection to companies repairing rail-roads and running them subject to Military controll and ~~the~~ future action of United-States Courts as to ownership of them. All officers and employees of such roads must however before begining such repairs take the oath of Allegiance to the United-States and no benefits accruing from such roads can go to disloyal Stock-holders.

U. S. GRANT
Lt. Gn.

ALS (telegram sent), DNA, RG 107, Telegrams Collected (Bound); telegram sent, *ibid.*; telegram received (misdated May 26, received on May 26), *ibid.*, RG 393, 16th Army Corps, Letters Received. *O.R.*, I, xlix, part 2, 877.

To Maj. Gen. George H. Thomas

(Cipher) Washington May 23d/65 [*11:00* P.M.]

MAJ. GN. THOMAS, NASHVILLE
COPY FOR GN. WILSON MACON GA.

I want Gen. Wilson to remain in Ga. which state I contemplate giving him command of. He will require some Cavalry and I shall send him some Infantry from here to enable him to carry out orders for mustering out troops whose time expires before the 1st of Oct. If he can send about 5000 of his Cavalry to the Mississippi river they will be available for Gen. Sheridan. He might also send about 2000 to South Carolina. Those retained in the south should all be men whose time will not expire before the 1st of Oct. Regiments can be consolidated putting men from the same state together and those sent home to be mustered out can be attached to regiments returning North. He should move in this matter at once.

U. S. GRANT
Lt. Gn.

ALS (telegram sent), Ritzman Collection, Aurora College, Aurora, Ill.; telegram sent (marked as sent on May 24, 1865, 9:10 A.M.), DNA, RG 107, Telegrams Collected (Bound); telegram received, *ibid.*, Telegrams Collected (Unbound); *ibid.*, RG 393, Military Div. of the Miss., Cav. Corps, Telegrams Received. Printed as sent at 9:10 A.M. in *O.R.*, I, xlix, part 2, 882. On May 23, 11:00 A.M.,

Maj. Gen. George H. Thomas telegraphed to USG, sending a copy to Bvt. Maj. Gen. James H. Wilson. "Have just heard from Genl Wilson that he has received the order to leave four thousand of his command in Ga and come to Tennessee with the balance. He thinks four thousand Infantry posted at Atlanta and Macon will be ample to preserve order in Georgia. He seems to be very desirous to retain his entire Cavalry force, and in consideration of, his own personal Gallantry and ability, together with efficient condition of his command and the eminent service lately performd by this body of heroes I am disposed if it meets with your approbation to let him join General Sheridan with the three divisions he now has with him, and send him Hatch's Division as soon as Genl Pope ~~ean~~ can dispense with the Brigade ordered to report to him at St Louis under instructions from your Hd Qrs of the 6th inst—I believe I shall have a sufficient Cavly force remaining to preserve order in my Command. Should you approve of the above arrangement I respectfully suggest that Genl Wilson be directed to move to Mobile rather than in this direction if Genl Sheridan is to go to Texas as stated in the ~~papers~~ newspapers" ALS (telegram sent), MH; telegram received (at 6:00 P.M.), DNA, RG 107, Telegrams Collected (Bound); *ibid.*, Telegrams Collected (Unbound); *ibid.*, RG 108, Telegrams Received. *O.R.*, I, xlix, part 2, 882–83.

On May 29, 3:00 P.M., Wilson, Macon, Ga., telegraphed to Thomas, sending a copy to USG. "Through neglect of some one connected with the telegraph Genl Grants telegram of the 23d did not reach me until a few minutes ago. To carry out his instructions, I would respectfully suggest that Hatches Division and the Veterans of the other three, in excess of the four (4) thousand to be kept in Georgia should be got ready with as little delay as possible. This much is due to Hatch. Gen Upton has gone through to Chattanooga to carry out the instructions in regard to muster out—Please send him such further orders as may be necessary. I will communicate with him by carrier, Men whom I retain here will be mostly veterans, who have from twelve (12) to twenty four (24) months yet to serve, Shall I send the two thousand men to South Carolina, and if so, to what part? I think after making Hatches force five 5 thousand I can very well spare the two 2 thousand for that State, Will give you more details in a few days," Telegram received (on May 30, 10:45 P.M.), DNA, RG 107, Telegrams Collected (Bound); *ibid.*, RG 108, Telegrams Received; copies (misdated May 31), *ibid.*, RG 393, Dept. of the Cumberland, Telegrams Sent; DLC-USG, V, 54. *O.R.*, I, xlix, part 2, 927.

To Maj. Gen. Henry W. Halleck

(Cipher)   Washington May 24th/65 [*11:00* P.M.]
MAJ. GN. HALLECK, ~~W~~RICHMOND VA.

The batteries of the 6th Corps must either come by land or must be retained at City Point for the present. Shipping can not be had for them. The Cipher operator made a mistake in sending my first dispatch on the subject or the mistake of leaving these batteries behind would not have been made. I think the batteries had better be started over land at once and if there are any surplus teams in the Dept. of Va. they can come at the same time.

U. S. GRANT

Lt. Gen

ALS (telegram sent), DNA, RG 107, Telegrams Collected (Bound); telegram sent, *ibid.*; copies, *ibid.*, RG 108, Letters Sent; DLC-USG, V, 46, 76, 108. *O.R.*, I, xlvi, part 3, 1203.

On May 24, 1865, 9:00 A.M., USG had telegraphed to Maj. Gen. Henry W. Halleck. "I understand Gn. Wright has sent his Artillery to City Point to be transported by Water? If such is the case direct him that it must be marched over land with the balance of hims command." ALS (telegram sent), DNA, RG 107, Telegrams Collected (Bound); telegram sent (at 9:10 A.M.), *ibid.*; copies, *ibid.*, RG 108, Letters Sent; DLC-USG, V, 46, 76, 108. Printed as sent at 9:30 A.M. in *O.R.*, I, xlvi, part 3, 1202. On the same day, Halleck telegraphed to USG. "See your telegrams of May 8th and ninth (9th) for orders for sending Genl Wrights Batteries to City Point   No further orders on that subject were received by me before: Genl Wrights Corps passed through here this morning Iunderstand that they will require a Considerable number of horses to move them by land also a baggage train or a supply of forage to meet them at Fredericksburg as Genl Wrights army has passed   I shall wait your further orders about his batteries now at City Point"   Telegram received (at 1:00 P.M.), DNA, RG 107, Telegrams Collected (Bound); (at 12:30 P.M.) *ibid.*, RG 108, Telegrams Received; copy, DLC-USG, V, 54. Printed as sent at 11:55 A.M., received at 1:00 P.M., in *O.R.*, I, xlvi, part 3, 1202. Also on May 24, Chief Operator David H. Bates telegraphed to Bvt. Col. Theodore S. Bowers. "On the 8th Gen Grant teleghed to Genl Halleck 'to retain all the Cavy &c'   In arranging the telegm in cipher Mr Beckwith made it read 'retain all the batteries'   As soon as I learned of the error (on 12th) I notified Mr Caldwell at Richmond to correct it & notify Gen. Halleck of the error. Mr Beckwith at the same time made an explanation either to you or Maj. Leet. Genl Halleck's telegram of today would seem to indicate that he still understood the orders to have reference to 'batteries',   I have again directed Mr Caldwell to inform Genl Halleck of the correction, and send you this that you may know where the trouble was, and what was done on our part to rectify the error." Telegram received, DNA, RG 108, Telegrams Received; copy, DLC-USG, V, 54. *O.R.*, I, xlvi, part 3, 1203.

Also on May 24, Halleck twice telegraphed to USG. "We have here Hd Qrs Army of the James. Hd Qrs Dept of Va. Hd Qrs 24th. Corps besides numerous other Hd Qrs and staff officers without number or occupation or quarters but with wives and families & uncounted calls for quarters or commutation. I again respectfully ask that the twenty fourth 24 Corps as an organization be discontinued so that I can reduce this cumbersome, expensive & useless machinery." "The Chief of Artillery of the 25th Corps reports that the three Regular Batteries assigned have but three officers & asks that 1st Lieut Wayne Vagdes 100th New York Vols bee ordered to accompany the Brigade to Texas & retained in service" Telegrams received (at 4:00 P.M. and 9:00 P.M.), DNA, RG 107,

Telegrams Collected (Bound); *ibid.*, RG 108, Telegrams Received; copies, DLC-USG, V, 54. The first is printed as sent at 3:45 P.M. in *O.R.*, I, xlvi, part 3, 1202–3. On May 25, 2:00 P.M., USG telegraphed to Halleck. "I asked to have the 24th Corps dissolved on receipt of your first dispatch and supposed it had been done. I will reniew the request. Might not your Provost Marshal's Dept. be broken up with great relief to the City?" ALS (telegram sent), DNA, RG 107, Telegrams Collected (Bound); telegram sent, *ibid.*; copies, *ibid.*, RG 108, Letters Sent; DLC-USG, V, 46, 76, 108. *O.R.*, I, xlvi, part 3, 1209.

On the same day, Halleck telegraphed to USG. "There are several Batteries belonging to Sheridans Cavalry Corps at City Point. They are not wanted here & if you say so I will send them overland to Alexandria with Wrights Batteries." Telegram received (at 7:30 P.M.), DNA, RG 107, Telegrams Collected (Bound); *ibid.*, RG 108, Telegrams Received; copy, DLC-USG, V, 54. *O.R.*, I, xlvi, part 3, 1209. At 9:50 P.M., USG telegraphed to Halleck. "You may send all the Artillery in Va. not required there with that belonging to Wrights Corps." ALS (telegram sent), DNA, RG 107, Telegrams Collected (Bound); telegram sent, *ibid.*; copies, *ibid.*, RG 108, Letters Sent; DLC-USG, V, 46, 76, 108. Printed as sent at 10:00 P.M. in *O.R.*, I, xlvi, part 3, 1209.

On May 29, Halleck telegraphed to USG. "The artillery of Wright's & Sheridan's corps passed here yesterday. Genl Wright says the roads are in very bad condition. It is therefore probable that the artillery will require forage & provisions on reaching Fredericksburg. If the roads were good their supplies would have carried them through." ALS (telegram sent), DNA, RG 107, Telegrams Collected (Unbound); telegram received (at 1:00 P.M.), *ibid.*, Telegrams Collected (Bound); *ibid.*, RG 108, Telegrams Received. *O.R.*, I, xlvi, part 3, 1232–33.

To John J. Tallmadge

[May 25, 1865]

Your very kind invitation for me to be present at the great "Fair" to be held in Milwaukee about the last of June for the purpose of raising funds to assist in the establishment of a "Home" for soldiers disabled in our late struggle for National existence is just received. I should like very much to be with the people of Milwaukee on that interesting and patriotic occasion but foresee the impossibility of it. At present, and for weeks to come, my duties due to the country, will confine me close to Washington.

I feel the deepest interest in the enterprise you have undertaken and hope homes will be secured for every soldier who has lost the ability to make his own independent support by his devotion to country in this war.

There has been but one debt contracted in the last four years which the people of the United States cannot pay. That is the debt of gratitude due to the rank and file of our army & Navy.

Thomas F. Madigan, *Lincolniana*, [*1930*], no. 109.

To Edwin M. Stanton

———

Head Quarters, Armies of the United States,
Washington, D. C., May 27. 1865.

HONORABLE E. M. STANTON,
SECRETARY OF WAR.
SIR:

I have the honor to transmit herewith Major General W. T. Sherman's official report of the operations of his armies in the campaign of the Carolinas from April 1st 1865 to May 10th 1865; also copy of my note calling his attention to that part of his report in which he speaks of the necessity of maintaining his truce even at the expense of many lives, and giving him my views thereon, with permission to amend it, and his answer thereto.

> Very Respectfully
> Your Obedient Servant,
> U. S. GRANT,
> Lieutenant General.

Copies, DLC-USG, V, 46, 76, 108; DLC-Edwin M. Stanton; DNA, RG 108, Letters Sent. *O.R.*, I, xlvii, part 1, 41–42.

On May 9, 1865, Maj. Gen. William T. Sherman, City Point, wrote to Brig. Gen. John A. Rawlins reporting his activities since April 1 and complaining of mistreatment by Secretary of War Edwin M. Stanton and Maj. Gen. Henry W. Halleck. *Ibid.*, pp. 29–40. On May 25, Bvt. Col. Theodore S. Bowers wrote to Sherman. "Genl Grant directs me to call your attention to the part of your report in which the necessity of maintaining your truce at the expense of many lives, is spoken of. The General thinks that in making a truce the commander of an Army can control only his own Army & that the hostile General must make his own arrangements with other Armies acting against him. Whilst independent Generals acting against a common foe would naturally act in concert, the General deems that each must be the judge of his own duty & responsibility for its execution. If you should wish, the report will be returned for any change you deem best." Copies, DLC-USG, V, 46, 76, 108; DLC-William T. Sherman; DNA, RG 108, Letters Sent. *O.R.*, I, xlvii, part 1, 40. On May 26, Sherman, Washington, D. C., wrote to Bowers. "I had the honor to receive your letter of ~~March~~ May 25th, last evening and I hasten to answer. I wish to precede it by renewing the assurance of my entire confidence and respect for the President and Lt. General Grant, and that in all matters I will be most willing to shape my official and private conduct to suit their wishes. The past is beyond my control, and the matters embraced in the official report to which you refer are finished. It is but just the reasons that actuated me right or wrong should stand of record, but in all future cases, should any arise, I will respect the decision of General Grant though I think it wrong. Supposing a guard has prisoners in charge, and officers of another command should aim to rescue or Kill them, is it not clear the guard must defend the prisoners? Same of a safe-guard. So jealous is the military law to protect and maintain *Good Faith* when pledged that the law adjudges death and no alternative punishment to one who violates a safe-guard in foreign parts (see Article of War, No. 55) For murder, arson, treason and the highest military crimes the punishment perscribed by law is death or some minor punishment, but for the violation of a safe-guard death and death alone is the perscribed penalty. I instance this to illustrate how in military stipulations to an enemy, our Government commands and enforces '*Good Faith*.' In discussing this matter I would like to refer to many writers on military law, but am willing to take Halleck as the Text (see his chapter no. 27) In the very first article he prefaces that *Good Faith* should always be observed between enemies in war, because when our faith has been pledged to him, so far as the promise extends he ceases to be an enemy. He then defines the meaning of *compacts* & *conventions* and says they are made sometimes for a general or a partial suspension of hostilities for the surrender of an army &c They may be special, limited to particular places, or to particular forces, but of course can only bind the armies subject to the General who makes the truce, and coextensive only with the extent of his command. This is all I ever claimed and clearly covers the whole case. All of North Carolina was in my immediate command, with General Schofield, its Department Commander, and his army present with ~~him~~ me. I never asked the truce to have effect beyond my own *territorial* command. General Halleck himself, in his orders no. 1, defines his own limits clearly enough, viz. 'such part of North Carolina as was *not* occupied by the command of Major General Sherman.' He could not pursue and cut off Johnstons retreat towards Saulsbury and Charlotte without invading my command, and so patent was his purpose to *defy* and *violate* my truce that Mr. Stantons publication of the fact, not even yet recalled, modified ~~and~~ or explained was headed '*Shermans Truce Disregarded*' that the whole world drew but one inference. It admits of no other. I never claimed that the truce bound Generals Halleck or Canby within the sphere of *their* respective commands as defined by themselves. It was a *partial truce*, of very short duration—clearly within my limits and right, justified by events, and as in the case of prisoners in my custody, or the violation of a safeguard given by me in my own territorial limits I was bound to maintain *Good Faith* I prefer not to change my report; but again repeat that in all future cases I am willing to be governed by the interpretation of Gen. Grant, although I again invite his attention to the limits of my command, and those of Gen. Halleck at the time, and the pointed phraseology of Gen Hallecks dispatch to Mr. Stanton wherein he reports that he had ordered his Generals to pay no heed to *my orders* within the clearly defined area of my command." LS, DNA, RG 108, Letters Received. *O.R.*, I, xlvii, part 1, 40–41. On May 30, Sherman wrote to Rawlins. "I have the honor to request that the following corrections be made in my last official report dated May 9th. 1865, already forwarded viz: On page eight of the report, referring to my letter of April 18th. 1865, addressed to Major General Halleck, substitute in lieu of the words 'into his hands', the words 'at Washington', and on page twenty four, before the word 'received' (beginning line) insert the words 'must have.' At the time the report was written Major Hitchcock who bore the letter in question to Washington, was not with me, and I was under the impression that he had placed the letter in question in General Halleck's own hands on the 21st April. Having now just learned that though the letter was delivered on that day at General Halleck's former office in Washington, it arrived just after his departure for Richmond, I wish the statement to be made accordingly. But as I am satisfied for other reasons that my views as contained in that letter were made known to General Halleck before his dispatch of April 26th. was sent the inferences drawn in my report remain unchanged." Copy, DLC-Edwin M. Stanton. *O.R.*, I, xlvii, part 1, 42.

On June 7, Halleck wrote to Stanton at length refuting charges made by Sherman. LS, DNA, RG 94, Letters Received, 223J 1865. *O.R.*, I, xlvii, part 3, 634–37. On June 15, USG endorsed this letter. "Respectfully forwarded to the Secretary of War together with a copy of the telegraphic order to Maj. Gen. Halleck of date Ap. 22 '65, which copy would have been enclosed with my letter of date May 27 '65 transmitting the official report of Maj. Gen. W. T. Sherman of the operations of his armies in the campaign of the Carolinas from April 1st 1865 to May 10th 1865 had I not supposed that that part of Gen. Shermans report to which the within communication especially refers related to the new arrangment entered into between Genls Sherman and Johnston on the 25th of April, which terminated in the surrender of the latter on the 26th of April 1865" ES, DNA, RG 94, Letters Received, 223J 1865. *O.R.*, I, xlvii, part 3, 637.

To Maj. Gen. Edward R. S. Canby

(Cipher)   Washington May 27th/65 [7:00 P.M.]
MAJ. GN. CANBY, NEW ORLEANS

You may send Steele at once to the Rio Grande. I will also send the 25th Corps. The Cavalry can march as you suggest. A garrison should be got to Galveston with as little delay as possible.

U. S. GRANT
Lt. Gn.

ALS (telegram sent), DNA, RG 107, Telegrams Collected (Bound); telegram sent, *ibid.*; telegram received, *ibid.*, Telegrams Collected (Unbound). Printed as received on May 29, 1865, in *O.R.*, I, xlviii, part 2, 620; *ibid.*, I, xlix, part 2, 920. On May 31, Maj. Gen. Edward R. S. Canby telegraphed to USG. "Your telegram of the twenty seventh (27th) was received on the twenty ninth (29th) and orders were at once telegraphed to Gen. Steele, but were delayed by the bad working of the telegraph lines. He sails tomorrow morning. I will go over to Mobile tonight to see him before he leaves. I shall give him only general instructions with regard to the occupation of the country, supposing that Gen. Sheridan's orders will reach him soon after his arrival. The force for Galveston will get off, as soon as the vessels ordered by the Quartermaster General ~~get off~~ arrive. Steele's expedition will absorb everything that is seaworthy. Sabine Pass and Matagorda have been abandoned by the Rebels, and it is reported that the Texas troops have generally disbanded themselves, and gone to their homes plundering the public stores before they left. The Missouri and Arkansas troops have retained their organizations, and will protect the public property until it is finally turned over." ALS (telegram sent), DNA, RG 107, Telegrams Collected (Unbound); telegrams received (2), *ibid.*; (on June 6, 9:30 P.M.) *ibid.*, Telegrams Collected (Bound); *ibid.*, RG 108, Telegrams Received. *O.R.*, I, xlviii, part 2, 691–92.

On May 23, 3:30 A.M., Canby telegraphed to USG. "I received yesterday an application from Genl Brenk of the rebel army commanding the lines immediately west of the Miss asking for a suspension of hostilities, pending negotiations with a view to surrender. The application was refused. To day I am advised of the arrival at Baton Rouge of commissioners on the part of Kirby Smith, authorized to treat for the surrender of the rebel forces in the Trans Miss Dept. I have instructed Bowles [*Herron*] to receive and forward any proposition that may be made, but not to entertain any idea of a suspension of hostilities either general or local" Telegram received (on May 24, 3:30 P.M.), DNA, RG 107, Telegrams Collected (Bound); (2—garbled) *ibid.*, Telegrams Collected (Unbound); (2—received on May 24, 10:00 A.M. and 3:30 P.M.) *ibid.*, RG 108, Telegrams Received; copies (2), DLC-USG, V, 54. *O.R.*, I, xlviii, part 2, 558–59.

On May 24, Canby telegraphed to USG. "Gen Herron reports that the rebel Commissioners at Baton Rouge appear to be fully Empowered to act for Gen E K Smith, Genl Brent the Senior Commissioner asks for the appointment of Commissioners or a conference for the purpose of arranging details I have directed Gen Herron to notify the Commissioners that I have no authority to Entertain any question that relates to Civil matters and that any arrangement that may be made on the subject of the Commission must Conform to the conditions that Controleled the Surrender of Gen Lees Army The details corresponding with those agreed upon in the case of Gen Taylors Army with the modifications authorized by your special orders No 215. Par 9, and unless their powers warrant them in accepting these terms, it will be inexpedient to appoint Commissioners or make arrangements for a Conference, with this understanding if They still desire I will meet them at New Orleans to which place I return tonight" Telegram received (at 11:00 P.M.), DNA, RG 107, Telegrams Collected (Bound); (3) *ibid.*, Telegrams Collected (Unbound); *ibid.*, RG 108, Telegrams Received; copy, DLC-USG, V, 54. *O.R.*, I, xlviii, part 2, 579–80.

On May 25, 9:00 P.M., Canby telegraphed to USG. "I have had a conference today with Buckner, Price and Brent, commissioned by Kirby Smith to make arrangements for the surrender of the rebel forces in the trans-mississippi Department. I have explained to them that no other terms could be given than are indicated in the instructions to me of Apl. 19th, and the modifications authorized by your special order, 215, of the 9th inst, They are to give me a definite answer tonight." Telegram received (on May 26, 5:00 P.M.), DNA, RG 107, Telegrams Collected (Bound); *ibid.*, RG 108, Telegrams Received; copy, DLC-USG, V, 54. *O.R.*, I, xlviii, part 2, 591.

Also on May 25, Maj. Gen. John Pope, St. Louis, telegraphed to USG. "Following despatch from Gen Reynolds just recd   Nothing definite   I will undoubtedly hear from Sprague in a day or two—Little Rock May twenty second Eighteen sixty five (1865) CAPT J McCHELL BELL A A G   The following despatch in answer to question submitted is just recd via Pine Bluff May twenty second (1865)   To COL LOVERING   All information I have in regard to Kirby Smiths Surrender is from the twenty six men of Wests Rebel Battery who came in last Evening   The Sergt Comdg the party says that on the twelfth inst there was a conference of State men & Comdg officers at Marshall Texas   that a surrender was made at Shreveport on the fifteenth to Col Sprague—Gen Popes staff & that the Comdg officer at Pickery Mount twenty seven miles this side [o]f Shreveport where he was stationed told his men that as Kirby Smith had surrendered they must go to the military posts near their homes and give themselves up—This Sergt is an intelligent, & seems to be a reliable, man—I beleive his report Signed POWELL CLAYTON Br Gen   Very Respy   signed J J REYNOLD Maj Genl" Telegram received (at 4:10 P.M.), DNA, RG 107, Telegrams Collected (Bound); *ibid.*, RG 108, Telegrams Received; copies, *ibid.*, RG 393, Military Div. of the Mo., Telegrams Sent; DLC-USG, V, 54. *O.R.*, I, xlviii, part 2, 542, 594.

On May 26, Canby telegraphed to USG. "The arrangements for the surrender of the Confederate forces in the Trans Mississippi Department have been concluded. They include the men and material of both the Army and Navy, and the Confederate military authorities will use their influence and authority to see that public property in the hands of the civil agents of the late Rebel Government are duly surrendered to the United States authorities. I have arranged for the surrender of the troops and property within the limits of the Division of Missouri to the Commande[r] of that Division, and will ask Genl Pope to designate the Commissioners. I think it advisable, in order to prevent any possible complication on the Mexican frontier, that Steele's command should be sent to the Rio Grande, without waiting for the 25th Corps, if that should no[w] be sent. If you approve, this will be done and I can at once add four thousand (4000) colored infantry to his command. Cavalry will be needed, but it cannot be sent by sea; it may march from Berwick Bay." ALS (telegram sent), DNA, RG 107, Telegrams Collected (Unbound); telegram received (on May 27, 3:00 P.M.), *ibid.*, Telegrams Collected (Bound); *ibid.*, RG 108, Telegrams Received. *O.R.*, I, xlviii, part 2, 602–3.

Also on May 26, Pope telegraphed to USG. "Following dispatch from Genl Reynolds just recd   all rebel soldiers & guerillas in Arkansas & Missouri are rapidly surrendering even portions of Kirby Smiths army   Col Sprague will reach here today   The result of his mission I dont yet Know. Little Rock May. 24th 1865   CAPT J McC DELA [*Bell*] A A G   Since last report of surrender of detachments of rebel troops the following has come at brownsville on the 20th

Ultimo Capt Reynolds with twenty men at Pine Bluff to the twenty second Capt Mayberry with ten men & at Duvalls Bluff on the 22nd, Capt Rockburn with twenty two men (signed) J J REYNOLDS Maj Genl" Telegram received (at 1:25 P.M.), DNA, RG 107, Telegrams Collected (Bound); *ibid.*, RG 108, Telegrams Received; copies, *ibid.*, RG 393, Military Div. of the Mo., Telegrams Sent; DLC-USG, V, 54. *O.R.*, I, xlviii, part 2, 583, 608.

On May 27, 2:00 P.M., Pope telegraphed to USG. "Genl Kirby Smith has declined surrendiring on the terms granted to Genl R. E. Lee as interpreted by Attorney General Speed and by Secretary of War's orders but has transmitted propositions for surrender from himself and the Rebel governors [o]f Texas, Louisiana, Arkansas and Missouri—These propositions are [a]ccompanied by other papers of [i]nterest all of which are forwarded [to] you by todays mail— These propositions will no doubt [b]e rejected by the Government but [a]s they show to a great extent the [f]eeling and condition of things in [th]e rebel trans-Mississippi Dep't, [th]ey will be found interesting. I dont [t]hink it necessary to send their [co]ntents by telegraph as some of the [le]tters & other written statements are lengthy" Telegram received (at 5:00 P.M.), DNA, RG 107, Telegrams Collected (Bound); *ibid.*, RG 108, Telegrams Received; copies, *ibid.*, RG 393, Military Div. of the Mo., Telegrams Sent; DLC-USG, V, 54. *O.R.*, I, xlviii, part 2, 626.

On May 27, 3:30 P.M., Maj. Gen. Philip H. Sheridan, St. Louis, telegraphed to Rawlins. "I have just arrived as [so]on as I see General [P]ope & major sprague I will telegraph" Telegram received (at 7:15 P.M.), DNA, RG 108, Telegrams Received; copies, DLC-USG, V, 54; (2) DLC-Philip H. Sheridan. *O.R.*, I, xlviii, part 2, 625. At 10:00 P.M., Sheridan telegraphed to USG. "I have examined the correspondence between Gen Kirby Smith and Col Sprague of Gen Popes Staff, There does not appear to be any thing definite in it, The impression is created in my mind that a portion of the rebels mean to move towards Mexico! This is still further confirmed by Genl Pope saying that Kirby Smith was about to move to Houston—I will leave here to morrow morning and hope to have things fixed more definitely, If the enemy go towards Mexico, would it not be best to take the Fourth (4th) corps to the Rio Grande? Please telegraph me at Cairo to morrow I have ordered my Headquarters to Baton Rouge I will give directions to Gen Steele in reference to his position after reaching the mouth of the Rio Grande—" Telegram received (on May 28, 12:30 A.M.), DNA, RG 107, Telegrams Collected (Bound); *ibid.*, RG 108, Telegrams Received; copies, *ibid.*, RG 393, Military Div. of the Mo., Telegrams Sent; DLC-USG, V, 54; (2) DLC-Philip H. Sheridan. *O.R.*, I, xlviii, part 2, 625–26.

On May 31, Canby telegraphed to USG. "Gen Buckner estimates the number of troops to be paroled in the transmississippi Dept at Thirty Eight Thousand 38.000 If the number exceeds the estimate in the same proportion that it did in Taylors Command it will probably reach one hundred thousand 100.000 The Commissioners & the Staff officers to take charge of the Surrendered property went up today with the troops that are to garrison Alexandria Shreveport and Monroe La and Marshal Texas" Telegram received (on June 2, 7:00 A.M.), DNA, RG 107, Telegrams Collected (Bound); *ibid.*, RG 108, Telegrams Received; copies, *ibid.*, RG 393, Dept. of the Gulf and La., Letters Sent; DLC-USG, V, 54. *O.R.*, I, xlviii, part 2, 692.

Also on May 31, 3:12 P.M., Pope telegraphed to USG. "Following dispatch

just recd   this ends armed opposition in Arkansas   Little Rock May 30th Seven
(7) P M CAPT JAS McC BELL A A G   I report for the information of the Maj
Gen Comdg Division viz First   Brig Gen Dockery C S A who claims to be the
Senior officer of the rebel army in this Dept is on his way in person from Pine
Bluff to this place to make formal surrender of all troops left in the State   Second—The mayor of the City of Camden has requested for a force of U S troops
to occupy that place for the protection which will be done   Third   a capt Gillis
for himself & in behalf of Capts Crawford Thrasher & Harrison Comdg. Independent Companies all expected to be at Benton on Monday next for surrender
& paroled   signed J J REYNOLDS M G"   Telegram received (at 4:35 P.M.),
DNA, RG 107, Telegrams Collected (Bound); *ibid.*, RG 108, Telegrams Received; copies, *ibid.*, RG 393, Military Div. of the Mo., Telegrams Sent; DLC-
USG, V, 54. *O.R.*, I, xlviii, part 2, 683–84, 699.

To Maj. Gen. William T. Sherman

Washington May 27th 1865

DEAR GENERAL

General Augur has just been to see me on the matter of the
conduct of men and Officers of your Command since coming North
of the Potomac,   He says that a deep feeling is exibited by them,
especially when a little in liquor, on account of the difficulties between yourself and Secretary Stanton,   He has purposely avoided
arresting them for fear of leading to violence and the charge that
it is a hostility on the part of the Secretary to them and to yourself
Yesterday many of the Officers were at Willards, drinking and
discussing violently the conduct of Mr, Stanton, and occasionally
would jump on the counter and give three groans for Mr, Stanton,
then get down and take another drink,

Without giving any order in the matter, I think it will be advisable for you either to direct guards to be placed around the
Camps, and prohibit Officers and men from coming out, except
with passes from their Division Commanders or such other Officers as you may direct, or move to the South side of the river,
You can manage this without any order from me,   What we want
is to preserve quiet and decorum and without apparently making
any distinction between the different Armies

Gen, Augur says that when the men of the different Armies meet in town, if dringking, they are sure to fight, and both your Army and Meades pitch into the Veteran Reserves indiscriminately

The Army of the Potomac, being on the South side of the river, can be kept out of the City except when they come with proper passes[1]

Yours Truly

U. S. GRANT

Lieut, Genl,

MAJ, GENL, W, T, SHERMAN

COMDG MIL, DIV- OF THE MISS,

Copies, DLC-USG, V, 46, 76, 108; DNA, RG 108, Letters Sent. *O.R.*, I, xlvii, part 3, 576. On May 28, 1865, 7:00 A.M., Maj. Gen. William T. Sherman, "Camp near Finlay Hospital," wrote to USG. "I got your letter late last Evening and hastened down to see Gen Augur, but he was not in. When I saw his Officer of the day and Provost Marshal; and asked them as a favor to me, to arrest and imprison any officer or man belonging to my Command, who transgressed any orders Rules or Regulations of the Place, more Especially for acts of drunkenness, noise or rowdyism. I also went round to your office but you were not there, but I saw Colonel Bowers, & told him what I had done. I was on the Streets until midnight and assure you I never saw more order and quiet prevailing. I had also during yesterday ridden all through the Camps ~~yesterday~~, and observed no signs of riot or drunkenness, and believe I may assure you that there is no danger whatever that ~~of~~ the men we know so well, and have trusted so often, will be guilty of any acts of public impropriety. The affair at Willards Hotel was a small affair, arising from a heated discussion betwen a few officers in liquor, late at night, and unobserved save by the few who were up late. I will see that no officers presume to misbehave because of the unfortunate difference betwen the Secretary of War and myself. of that difference I can only say, that every officer and man regarded the Secretarys budget in the papers of April 24, the telegram of Genl Halleck endorsed by himself in those of the 28. and the perfect storm of accusation which followed and which he took no pains to correct as a personal insult to me. I have not yet seen a man, Soldier or Civilian, but takes the same view of it, and I could not maintain my authority over troops if I tamely submitted to personal insult: but it is none the less wrong for officers to adopt the quarrel, and I will take strong measures to prevent it. I hope the good men of the Command will have a few days in which to visit the Capitol & public grounds, to satisfy the natural curiosity, and then if the presence of so large a body of men so near washington is deemed unpleasant, I would suggest that the Armies be dissolved, and all matters of discharge be ~~devolved on~~ imposed on the Corps Commanders, who have the lawful power in the premises, and during the period of pay, & discharge & consolidation these Corps might be scattered, say one to Bladensburg, (20th), one to Relay House (14), one to 'Monocacy' 15, and one to Frederick 17th. I would much prefer this to sending them back to the South Bank of the Potomac where they are crowded in with other troops and have only choice of inferior ground for Camps. I thank you for leaving the matter of orders to my managemt, and I will put myself and command perfectly on an understanding with Genl Augur & his Garrison, and assure you that nothing offensive shall occur of any importance. Such little things as a tipsy soldier occasionally, cannot be helped, but even that shall be punished according to 'local orders'" ALS, DNA, RG 108, Letters Received. *O.R.*, I, xlvii, part 3, 581–82.

On the same day, Sherman wrote to USG. "As I am today making my ~~preparations~~ arrangements to go West, preparatory to resuming my proper duties I think it proper to state a few points on which there is misapprehension in the minds of strangers. I am not a politician, never voted but once in my Life, and never read a Political Platform. If spared I never will read a Political Platform or hold any Civil office whatsoever. I venerate the Constitution of the United States, think it as near perfection as possible, and recent events have demonstrated that it vests Governmt with all the Power necessary for self vindication and the protection to life & property of the Inhabitants. To accuse me of giving aid and Comfort to Copperheads is an insult. I do not believe in the sincerity of any able bodied man who has not fought in this War, much less in the Copperheads who opposed the War or threw obstacles in the way of its successful prosecution. My opinions on all matters are very strong, but if I am possessed properly of the views and orders of my superiors I make them my study and conform my conduct to them as though they were my own. The President has only to tell me what he wants done and I will do it. I was hurt, outraged and insulted at Mr Stanton's public arraignmt of my motives and actions, at his endorsing Gen Hallecks insulting & offensive despatch, and his studied silence when the Press accused me of all sorts of base motives, even of selling myself to Jeff Davis for Gold, of sheltering Criminals and entertaining ambitious views at the expense of my Country. I respect his office, but cannot him personally, till he undoes the injustice of the Past. I think I have soldierly instincts and feelings, but if this action of mine at all incommodes the President or endangers public harmony, all you have to do is to say so, and leave me time to seek Civil employmt and I will make room. I will serve the President of the United States not only with fidelity but with Zeal. The Governmt of the United States and its Constituted Authorities must be sustained & perpetuated, not for our good alone, but for that of rising, and coming Generations. I would like Mr Johnson to read this letter and to believe me that the Newspaper gossip of my having Presidential aspirations is absurd, and offensive to me, and I would check it if I knew how." ALS, CSmH. *O.R.*, I, xlvii, part 3, 582–83. On the same day, USG endorsed this letter. "Respectfully forwarded to the President of the United States with the request that this letter be returned after reading." AES, CSmH.

Also on May 28, Sherman wrote to Bvt. Col. Theodore S. Bowers. "I see no ~~further~~ public business that calls for my further stay at Washington. I have made my full testimony before the Committee on the Conduct of the War, as ordered and the four Corps under my Command here are in good camps and Company & Field officers are busy upon the Muster Rolls & papers needed for the payment of the troops and the discharge of such as are entitled to it under existing orders. You remember that the Commanders of Military Divisions have nothing to do with Such matters, so that my longer presence is unnecessary. I will therfore ask for orders or instructions to return to the West, say Louisville Ky or wherever the General thinks I should take post. If the Territory north of the Ohio River is to be included in the Military Divn of the Miss, I would

prefer for the Sake of Economy to reside in Cincinati. I would like to take
NewYork and Chicago in my route West, to keep appointments made by my
family before my arrival here. I will be ready to leave Washington on Wednesday." ALS, DNA, RG 108, Letters Received. *O.R.*, I, xlvii, part 3, 583.

On May 26, Bowers wrote to Sherman, Maj. Gen. George G. Meade, and
Maj. Gen. Christopher C. Augur. "Please furnish these Headquarters by 9 oclock
tomorrow morning 27th inst a complete list of all General Officers of your Command now here stating whether in Camp with their troops, if so give the location
of the camp. If they are stopping in the city, give the name of the hotel, or street
& number of the house they may be at." Copies, DLC-USG, V, 46, 76, 108; DNA,
RG 108, Letters Sent; *ibid.*, RG 393, 20th Army Corps, Hd. Qrs. Records; *ibid.*,
15th Army Corps, Letters Received. On May 27, 9:00 A.M., Sherman wrote to
Bowers. "I received late last night your communication of May 26 calling for a
detailed report of all the general officers with my army, with the location of
camps and the hotels at which any of the general officers are staying. I am stopping at Mrs. Carter's, on Capitol Hill, but have my office and staff here in camp
in the grounds of the Finley Hospital. General Slocum, commanding the Army
of Georgia, is stopping at the Metropolitan Hotel, but has his camp and headquarters staff about a mile beyond on the road passing to the north of the Finley
Hospital, Bladensburg road; the camps of the Fourteenth and Twentieth Corps
are near by, about two miles northeast of this point. Maj. Gen. John A. Logan,
commanding the Army of the Tennessee, is encamped near Silver Spring, and
his two corps are camped near him on Fourteenth street prolonged. Corps and
division commanders are camped near and with their troops. I cannot at this
moment give the exact position of each, but will send you in the course of the
day a tabular statement of all the general officers, with the position of their
camps, &c." *O.R.*, I, xlvii, part 3, 576–77. See *ibid.*, pp. 583–84.

Also on May 27, Bowers wrote to Sherman. "You will please cause all Officers and men belonging to your Armies here that come within the orders for
discharge to be immediately mustered on muster-out rolls, and sent forward to
the rendizous designated in their respective States for payment in accordance
with General Orders No, 94 Current series A. G. O. War Dept, No payment will
be made to troops to be discharged until they reach their respective States and
rendezous, Order your retained force immediately after the muster and sending
off of those to be discharged as above, to be mustered for immediate payment to
the 30th of April 1865, Direct Corps Commanders to give personal attention
and superintendence to the execution of these orders," Copies, DLC-USG, V, 46,
76, 108; DNA, RG 108, Letters Sent. *O.R.*, I, xlvii, part 3, 576.

On May 31, Bowers wrote to Sherman. "Please order your Chief Quarter
Master, General Easton to Parkersburg, West Virginia, to superintend the getting
of troops forward from that place. From there to Louisville. Kentucky water
transportation should be used as far as it is attainable, and the requisitions for
it made by telegraph upon Gen. Allen, Chief Quarter Master at Louisville. Your
Chief Commissary should also be required to go to Parkersburg and there see to
the supplying of the troops during your movement" ALS, DNA, RG 393, Dept.
of the Tenn., Unbound Material, Letters Received. *O.R.*, I, xlvii, part 3, 603–4.

1. On May 27, Bvt. Col. Orville E. Babcock wrote to Augur. "The Lieut,
Genl, Comdg directs me to inform you that he desires you will have the City well
patroled, especially at night, and arrest and send to their Quarters all Officers

below the rank of Brig, Genl, found in the City without proper passes" Copies, DLC-USG, V, 46, 76, 108; DNA, RG 108, Letters Sent. *O.R.*, I, xlvi, part 3, 1226. On May 29, Babcock wrote to Augur. "The Lieut, Gen, Comdg wishes you to close all places where Liquor is sold within the City until such time as you may deem it prudent to open them again" Copies, DLC-USG, V, 46, 76, 108; DNA, RG 108, Letters Sent.

To Maj. Gen. Edward R. S. Canby

(Cipher)   May 28th 1865 [1:30 P.M.]
MAJ. GEN. CANBY, NEW ORLEANS LA.

Ship North all captured Cotton as rapidly as possible and encourage the bringing in for sale of all private Cotton Let there be no Military interferance whatever to the sale and shipment of Cotton nor no search made to find Confederate Cotton. It is the interest of of finances to get all the Cotton to market possible and without delay.

U. S. GRANT
Lt. Gn.

ALS (telegram sent), DNA, RG 107, Telegrams Collected (Bound); telegram sent, *ibid.*; telegram received, *ibid.*, Telegrams Collected (Unbound). *O.R.*, I, xlviii, part 2, 640. On May 29, 1865, Maj. Gen. Edward R. S. Canby telegraphed to USG. "Your telegram of yesterday has just been received. aAll Captured Cotton & all questions of trade East of the Miss have already been turned over to the Tresury Dept. I have telegraphed orders to Comdrs in the interior to encourageing the bringing in of Cotton for sale, to make no search for Confederate Cotton & to offer all proper facilities for sending all Cotton forward & considerable part of the Country west of the Miss will be occupied by our troops in the Course of this week & this trade will be opened & encouraged as far as it can be without the action of the President" Telegram received (dated May 30, received at 7:00 P.M.), DNA, RG 107, Telegrams Collected (Bound); *ibid.*, RG 108, Telegrams Received; copy, DLC-USG, V, 54. Printed as sent on May 30 in *O.R.*, I, xlviii, part 2, 673.

On May 30, Canby endorsed a report concerning cotton in or near Rodney, Miss. "Respectfully transmitted to Lt. Gen. Grant, commanding Armies of the United States. There are over 200,000 bales of cotton that belonged to the late Rebel Government within the limits of the Division east of the Mississippi the greater part of which will be lost to the governmt if without the aid of this Army Under your instructions of the 28th. inst I have revoked all orders restraining the movements of this cotton." AES, DNA, RG 108, Letters Received.

To Maj. Gen. Henry W. Halleck

(Cipher) Washington May 28th/65 [7:00 P.M.]
Maj Gn. Halleck, Richmond Va

Stevens was mentioned by the Sec. of War. Is he not at Ft Monroe? Seddon had better go also. I will ask the Navy to furnish a vessel to take them.

U. S. Grant
Lt. Gn.

ALS (telegram sent), DNA, RG 107, Telegrams Collected (Bound); telegram sent, *ibid.*; copies, *ibid.*, RG 108, Letters Sent; DLC-USG, V, 46, 76, 108. *O.R.*, II, viii, 576.

On May 28, 1865, 11:30 A.M., USG telegraphed to Maj. Gen. Henry W. Halleck. "The Sec. of War directs that Stevens, Hunter and Campbell be sent to Fort Pulaski for confinement until final disposition can be made." ALS (telegram sent), DNA, RG 107, Telegrams Collected (Bound); telegram sent, *ibid.*; copies (marked as sent at 11:00 A.M.), *ibid.*, RG 108, Letters Sent; DLC-USG, V, 46, 76, 108. *O.R.*, II, viii, 576. On the same day, Halleck telegraphed to USG. "Your telegram of to day says Stevens, Hunter & Campbell. I presume Seddon is meant instead of Stevens. Will the Navy furnish a vessel for the purpose, or will the Qr. Mr. Genl send one to Fort Monroe?" ALS (telegram sent), DNA, RG 107, Telegrams Collected (Unbound); telegram received (at 2:00 P.M.), *ibid.*, Telegrams Collected (Bound); *ibid.*, RG 108, Telegrams Received. *O.R.*, II, viii, 576.

At 10:20 P.M., Halleck telegraphed to USG. "Stevens was sent to Fort Warren a week ago by direction of the Secty of War. Seddon, Hunter & Campbell will be sent to Fort Monroe to embark on any vessel the Navy or Qr. Mr. Dept may assign to transport them to Fort Pulaski. Orders should be sent to Genl Gillmore for their confinement." ALS (telegram sent), DNA, RG 107, Telegrams Collected (Unbound); telegram received (at 10:00 P.M.), *ibid.*, Telegrams Collected (Bound); *ibid.*, RG 108, Telegrams Received. *O.R.*, II, viii, 576–77.

To Maj. Gen. Philip H. Sheridan

(Cipher) Washington May 28th/65 [*11:30* A.M.]
Maj. Gn. Sheridan, St. Louis Mo. Copy for Gn. Pope.

Buckner & Price for Kirby Smith have surrendered to Gn. Canby all forces West of the Miss. I have directed Canby to push troops to the Rio Grande without awaiting the arrival of 25th Corps. Also to garrison Galveston. You had better push down the river at once and proceed to carry out the convention and garrison Texas and Louisiana as soon as it can be done.

U. S. GRANT

Lt. Gn.

ALS (telegram sent), DNA, RG 107, Telegrams Collected (Bound); telegram sent, *ibid.*; telegram received, *ibid.*, Telegrams Collected (Unbound). *O.R.*, I, xlviii, part 2, 639.

On May 28, 1865, 1:30 P.M. and 2:00 P.M., USG telegraphed to Maj. Gen. Philip H. Sheridan. "Do all you can to encourage the Shipment of Cotton from Louisiana and Texas. Let there be no Military interferance to its coming out or enquiries as to ownership. Such as may be turned over as Confederate Cotton cause to be delivered to the Treasury Dept. but do not embarass the shipments by looking up such Cotton." ALS (telegram sent), DNA, RG 107, Telegrams Collected (Bound); telegram sent, *ibid.*; copies, *ibid.*, RG 108, Letters Sent; *ibid.*, RG 393, Military Div. of the Mo., Telegrams Received; DLC-USG, V, 46, 76, 108; DLC-S. Phillips Lee. *O.R.*, I, xlviii, part 2, 639–40; *O.R.* (Navy), I, xxvii, 251. "A portion of the 25th Corps is on its way to the Rio Grande but will touch at Mobile if you wish to send orders. Send the troops placed at your disposal as you think proper. If more troops than have been ordered to the Rio Grande are required send them." ALS (telegram sent), DNA, RG 107, Telegrams Collected (Bound); telegram sent, *ibid.*; copies, *ibid.*, RG 108, Letters Sent; DLC-USG, V, 46, 76, 108; USG 3. *O.R.*, I, xlviii, part 2, 640. On May 29, Sheridan, Cairo, Ill., telegraphed to USG. "Your telegram received I will send one division from Reynolds to garrison Shreveport and will send from Canby a garrison to Alexandria I think it best to send the 4th Corps to Texas. I am well satisfied that it will be best for the public service to send it there. It is a compact corps and all at Nashville The 25th Corps will be required along the gulf coast and the 4th Corps and troops you have sent from Gen Canby can be put at points further from the coast where it is healthier. Texas has not yet suffered from the war and will require some intimidation and Mexican matters are unsettled, furthermore I am satisfied that many of the rebels will leave the United States for Mexico, so that this action may have you full approval I most respectfully request that you give orders for the 4th Corps to embark for New Orleans at once for which point I am now starting, where I will make arrangements to cross it to Texas immediately on the receipt of a notification from you at New Orleans that you have ordered the corps there. Directions will be given about Cotton at once" Telegram received (at 9:30 P.M.), DNA, RG 107, Telegrams Collected (Bound); *ibid.*, RG 108, Telegrams Received; copies, DLC-USG, V, 54; (2) DLC-Philip H. Sheridan. Printed as received at 9:50 P.M. in *O.R.*, I, xlviii, part 2, 647.

To J. Russell Jones

———

Washington May 28th *1865*

DEAR JONES,

Enclosed I send you Six hundred dollars which please credit me with on account.

I hope and expect to get out to the Fair for a day or two but shall not be there at the begining. Will advise you in time.

I have determined to present "Old Jack" to the "Fair" and have promised Mrs. Sherman that she shall have the disposal of him. So be prepared to turn the old nuisance over when called for. If he is what he was he is a splendid saddle horse but a little lazy.

Yours Truly

U. S. GRANT

ALS, MoSHi. On April 10, 1865, J. Russell Jones, Chicago, wrote to USG. "We are to have 'a big thing' here, in the way of a Sanitary Fair, Commencing 30th May, and I have been requested by Judge Bradwell to write you to know if you cant do something in the way of trophies &c   Knowing how busy you are I have written Bowers asking him if he can not detail a suitable person to collect & forward such articles as will be of interest on that occasion. The enclosed Circular will show about what we design doing. Judge Bradwell will write you on the subject, and if you can do anything for us we shall be glad—We have the news this morning of Lee's Surrender, and the City is alive with excitement. It looks now as though the end was near"   ALS, DNA, RG 393, Dept. of Va. and N. C., Letters Received.

To Edwin M. Stanton

———

Washington May 29th *1865*

HON. E. M. STANTON,

SEC. OF WAR,

SIR:

I understand that great numbers of soldiers going out of service are very desirous of retaining their Arms by paying for them. As the Govt. has now a great surplus of Arms I would suggest that an order be publishe[d] authorizing all soldiers who desire to do so to retain their Arms by paying the value to the Ordnance Dept. or by having them charged on their muster out rolls.

> Very respectfully
> your obt. svt.
> U. S. GRANT
> Lt. Gn.

ALS, DNA, RG 94, Letters Received, 550A 1865. *O.R.*, I, xlvi, part 3, 1231–32. Secretary of War Edwin M. Stanton endorsed this letter favorably to the AG. AES, DNA, RG 94, Letters Received, 550A 1865. See *O.R.*, I, xlvi, part 3, 1237.

On May 29, 1865, USG wrote to Stanton. "Owing to the great surplus of Artillery in the Army I would recommend that all the Artillery belonging to the Armies of the Potomac, Tennessee and Ga. be mutered out at once. If approved they can be started to their state Capitols at once" ALS, DNA, RG 94, Vol. Service Div., Letters Received, A1075 (VS) 1865. *O.R.*, I, xlvi, part 3, 1232. On the same day, Stanton endorsed this letter favorably to Maj. Thomas M. Vincent, AGO. AES, DNA, RG 94, Vol. Service Div., Letters Received, A1075 (VS) 1865. See *O.R.*, I, xlvi, part 3, 1233–34.

To Edwin M. Stanton

Washington May 29th *1865*

HON. E. M. STANTON,
SEC. OF WAR,
SIR:

If it is desirable to have all the rebel documents Captured in Richmond and elsewhere in the South examined and notes made of their contents for convenient reference I would respectfully recommend Brig. Gn. Alvord, who is now in the City, for the duty.

It is a duty well suited to his taste and for which I think he is eminently fitted.

> Very respectfully
> your obt. svt.
> U. S. GRANT
> Lt. Gn.

ALS, DLC-Edwin M. Stanton. On July 6, 1865, USG wrote to Secretary of War Edwin M. Stanton. "Gen. Alvord reports himself ready to commence on the duties which are to be assigned to him as soon as directed to do so. If rooms have not yet been obtained I would suggest whether Gen. Alvord might not be directed to look up suitable ones and report them to the Qr. Mr. Gn. who can then be instructed to secure them." ALS, *ibid.* On July 7, Bvt. Col. Theodore S. Bowers wrote to Brig. Gen. Benjamin Alvord. "Lieutenant General Grant directs me to say to you that the Secretary of War has informed him that the duties it was proposed to assign to you are to be performed by an officer of the Adjutant General's Department and that your services in that connection will not now be required. Gen Grant therefore directs that you proceed to your home leaving your address with the Adjutant General of the Army and there await orders." Copies, DLC-USG, V, 46, 109; DNA, RG 108, Letters Sent.

On June 14, Alvord, Rutland, Vt., wrote to Brig. Gen. John A. Rawlins offering suggestions about the placement of troops in Montana Territory. ALS, *ibid.*, Letters Received. *O.R.*, I, xlviii, part 2, 888–89.

To Edwin M. Stanton

Washington D. C, May 29th *1865*

HON. E. M. STANTON,
SEC. OF WAR,
SIR:

The bearer of this, Sgt. Fredk Sipel, 2d U. S. Infantry, is recommended as a most worthy, efficient and capable soldier for the position of Ordnance Sergeant. He has served two enlistments in the Regular Army of five years each. He lost an arm at the battle of Gettysburg and now, unless appointed an Ordnance sergeant, goes out of service a cripple. If there is a vacancy in the Ordnance Dept. I would strongly recommend that it be given to him; if not I would recommend that the Commanding Officer of his Company be ordered to re-enlist him and that his recommendation for an Ordnance Sergeancy be placed on file so that he shall receive it when a vacancy does occur.

Very respectfully
your obt. svt.
U. S. GRANT
Lt. Gn.

ALS, DNA, RG 94, ACP, 5433 1872. Secretary of War Edwin M. Stanton endorsed this letter. "Approved & referred to Adjt General to make the appointment if there be any vacancy" AES, *ibid.* On May 27, 1865, Brig. Gen. Lewis C.

Hunt, New York City, wrote to USG. "Excuse me for taking up a moment of
your time in asking you to put in a good word in behalf of the bearer Sergeant
Frederic Sifel who goes to Washington in order to push his application for an
Ordnance Sergeantcy—The Sergeant, as you will at once perceive, is a very fine
fellow, intelligent and soldierly—He has served in the 2nd Inf'y, lost his arm at
Gettysburg, and in a month will be discharged, & thrown upon the World
unless he can get the position he Seeks—He is well-fitted for that position, by
Education, character, Services, and he is about as handy with his one arm as
most men with two—He has been on duty at my Head Quarters, under my
immediate Eye, and I speak of him Knowingly. Should you feel disposed to support his application by two lines, on the strength of my assurances, it will settle
the matter I think, and Keep in the Service a well-deserving, faithful man—I
called the other day to see Mrs Grant at your house in Phil. but found no one at
home—Left my Card with Capt. McAllister, under the door.—Please give my
Kind regards to Mrs Grant.—I congratulate you on your escape in the Booth
matter—Is it not very curious how much of the *Catholic* element seems to have
been mixed up in the matter.—The only parties Known to have Expressed satisfaction at the President's murder, in this City, belong to that element, *Irish
Catholic*, a set that will in time give a heap of trouble—In haste, . . ." ALS,
ibid. On May 29, USG endorsed this letter. "Respectfully refered to the Sec.
of War with recommendation that Sgt. S̶i̶f̶e̶l̶ Frederick Sipel, 2d U. S. Inf.y be
appointed an Ordnance Sergeant in the U. S. Army." AES, *ibid.*

To Maj. Gen. John Pope

(Cipher)   Washington May 29th *1865* [*10:20* A.M.]
MAJ. GN. POPE, ST. LOUIS MO.

In addition to other regiments the 8th Ill. Cavalry has been
ordered to report to you. If not required let me know and I will have
it mustered out of service. The horses of the regiment can go to
yours if required.

U. S. GRANT
Lt Gn.

ALS (telegram sent), DNA, RG 107, Telegrams Collected (Bound); telegram
sent, *ibid.*; copies, *ibid.*, RG 108, Letters Sent; (marked as received at 2:00
P.M.) *ibid.*, RG 393, Military Div. of the Mo., Telegrams Received; DLC-USG,
V, 46, 76, 108. *O.R.*, I, xlviii, part 2, 656. See *ibid.*, I, xlvi, part 3, 1223.

On May 28, 1865, Bvt. Col. Theodore S. Bowers had written to Maj. Gen.
Christopher C. Augur. "You are hereby authorized and directed to retain the 8th
regiment of Illinois Cavalry Volunteers, The order for it to proceed to Saint
Louis is countermanded" Copies, DLC-USG, V, 46, 76, 108; DNA, RG 108,
Letters Sent. On May 31, 3:12 P.M. and 3:13 P.M., Maj. Gen. John Pope tele-

graphed to USG. "Gen Dodge reports mixed force of Texans & Indians beating up towards Arkansas River to strike Santa Fe trail There will be for some time attempts by bands of armed outlaws in the guise of indians and probably accompanied by Indians to rob the trains & coaches on overland routes—I cannot tell about Eighth Ill Cavalry until I know what troops are coming here & how many in Dept of Missouri & Arkansas will be discharged under late orders—The latter I will know in a few days Does Brigade of Mich Cavy Come here or go to Texas" "Following dispatch from Gen Dodge just received The Indians on the plains seem to be hostile and active. Ft Leavenworth May thirtieth ten twenty A M MAJ GEN POPE Do you understand from Gen Sullys dispatch the Indians he mentions as being on black Hills are there to meet him to make Peace or to fight them? ~~that~~ the direction you indicated for Gen Sully to go leaves these Indians he mentions for me to deal with Connor will ~~give~~ get off in time I want to get more troops to him if possible before he starts so that there Shall be no mistake, not only of catching the Indians but that our overland route is beyond doubt Secure—The Indians appear to be scattered all along the route in Small parties from Columbus N T to Green River and we are striking them every day—we do not find any large bodies as yet not to exceed five hundred Signed G M DODGE M G" Telegrams received (at 4:15 P.M. and 4:25 P.M.), *ibid.*, RG 107, Telegrams Collected (Bound); *ibid.*, RG 108, Telegrams Received; copies, *ibid.*, RG 393, Military Div. of the Mo., Telegrams Sent; DLC-USG, V, 54. *O.R.*, I, xlviii, part 2, 684–85, 698–99.

On June 15, Brig. Gen. John A. Rawlins wrote to the AG transmitting orders to send the 8th Ill. Cav. to St. Louis. LS, DNA, RG 94, Letters Received, 626A 1865. On June 17, 11:00 A.M., USG telegraphed to Pope. "The 8th Ill. Cavalry is ordered to report to you. If their horses, without the men, will answer your purpose you may muster the regiment out of service." ALS (telegram sent), *ibid.*, RG 107, Telegrams Collected (Bound); telegram sent, *ibid.*; telegram received (at 11:50 A.M.), *ibid.*, Telegrams Collected (Unbound). *O.R.*, I, xlviii, part 2, 911. On June 27, 3:20 P.M., Pope telegraphed to USG. "Referring to your dispatch of may twenty ninth in relation to Eighth Ills Cavalry they will be needed here—" Telegram received (at 6:30 P.M.), DNA, RG 107, Telegrams Collected (Bound); *ibid.*, RG 108, Telegrams Received; copies, *ibid.*, RG 393, Military Div. of the Mo., Telegrams Sent; DLC-USG, V, 54. *O.R.*, I, xlviii, part 2, 1007.

To Maj. Gen. John M. Schofield

(Cipher)   Washington May 29th *1865* [*12:50* P.M.]
MAJ. GN. SCHOFIELD RALEIGH N. C. COMD.G OFFICERS
AUGUSTA & SAVANNAH GA. AND GN. GILMORE, HILTON HEAD
S. C.

Give every facility and encouragement to getting to market Cotton and other Southern products. Let there be no seizures of private property or seaching to look after Confederate Cotton. The finances of the Country demand that all articles of export should be got to market as speedily as possible.

U. S. GRANT

Lt. Gn.

ALS (telegram sent), DNA, RG 107, Telegrams Collected (Bound); telegram sent, *ibid.*; telegrams received (4), *ibid.*, Telegrams Collected (Unbound); *ibid.*, RG 393, Army of the Ohio and Dept. of N. C., Telegrams Received. *O.R.*, I, xlvii, part 3, 593. On May 29, 1865, Maj. Gen. John M. Schofield telegraphed to USG. "Your despatch concerning cotton & other produce is received I Some time ago removed all military restrictions upon trade & have given every facility for carrying cotton & other products to market The only obstacles in the way are the restrictions of the treasury dept It would be a blessing to the country if the whole system could be abolished Now only one man in North Carolina is authorized to buy Cotton & he does not pay money for it It is impossible for people to get their products to market in this way—" Telegram received (at 11:00 P.M.), DNA, RG 56, Div. of Captured and Abandoned Property, Letters Received; *ibid.*, RG 107, Telegrams Collected (Bound); *ibid.*, Telegrams Collected (Unbound); copies, *ibid.*, RG 393, Army of the Ohio and Dept. of N. C., Telegrams Sent; DLC-John M. Schofield. *O.R.*, I, xlvii, part 3, 593. On May 30, 10:40 A.M., USG telegraphed to Schofield. "There is no restriction on the purchase of Cotton or other products in the South. Any one who wishes can purchase and ship; the only restriction being that all Cotton going out must pay at the Seaport where shipped one fourth. This tax is not required on other articles and I hope will be removed from Cotton." ALS (telegram sent), DNA, RG 107, Telegrams Collected (Bound); telegram sent, *ibid.*; telegram received, *ibid.*, RG 393, Army of the Ohio and Dept. of N. C., Telegrams Received. *O.R.*, I, xlvii, part 3, 602.

On May 30, Secretary of the Treasury Hugh McCulloch wrote to USG. "I enclose herewith a telegram which will, I think, remove the reported difficulties in North Carolina. If you approve, I will thank you to cause it to be transmitted by military telegraph without delay, and make such other use of it as you think proper." Copy, DNA, RG 56, Letters Sent Relating to Restricted Commercial Intercourse. On June 2, McCulloch wrote to USG. "Referring to the telegram to Mr Heaton, Special Agent of this Department in North Carolina, relative to the removal of commercial restrictions in that State, forwarded through you a few days since, I have the honor to enclose herewith copy of the reply thereto, received at this Department yesterday." Copy, *ibid.* McCulloch enclosed a copy of a telegram of May 31 from Special Agent David Heaton, Wilmington, to McCulloch. "Your dispatch in relation to Cotton rec'd Your instructions will be published over the State and strictly carried out. Treasury Agents and Custom House officers been doing all in their power to facilitate the getting out of products. Will write to you." Copy, *ibid.*

To Edwin M. Stanton

———

Washington D. C, May 30th *18645*.

HON. E. M. STANTON,
SEC. OF WAR,
SIR:

I would respectfully recommend Capt. J. W. Mason, 5th U. S. Cavalry and 1st Lieut. J. H. Kane, same regiment for promotion of one grade by brevet.

These officers belong to the Cavalry which has served at my Hd Qrs. from May last and in all the battles from the Wilderness in May 1864 to the surrender of Lee's Army in Apl. 1865 have rendered conspicuous and dangerous service.

I would suggest that their brevets should be given for gallant and meritorious services in the battles terminating in the surrender of Lee's Army on the 9th of Apl. 1865.

> Very respectfully
> your obt. svt.
> U. S. GRANT
> Lt. Gn.

ALS, DNA, RG 94, ACP, S676 CB 1865. *O.R.*, I, xlvi, part 3, 1237. See *ibid.*, p. 1066.

To Edwin M. Stanton

———

Washington D. C, May 30th *1865*

HON. E. M. STANTON,
SEC. OF WAR,
SIR:

I would respectfully recommend the appointment of Bvt. Brig. Gen. W. T. Clarke to the full rank of Brigadier General.

I am desirous of sending Gen. Clarke to Texas in command of a Division of the 25th Army Corps and as the last of that Corps is now about sailing I would respectfully ask immediate attention.

Gen. Clarke was appointed a full Brigadier General from the 26th of Jan.y 1865 but afterwards his appointment was changed to a brevet. If it can be done I would now ask to have his appointment to bear that date.

> Very respectfully
> U. S. GRANT
> Lt. Gn

ALS, DNA, RG 94, ACP, C406 CB 1865. *O.R.*, I, xlvii, part 3, 598.

On May 30, 1865, Maj. Gen. John A. Logan wrote to USG requesting the promotion of Bvt. Brig. Gen. William T. Clark; on June 1, USG endorsed this letter. "Respy. forwarded to the sec of war with the recommendation that Lt Col and Bvt Brig Genl W. F. Clarke, U S V. be appointed a full Brig Gen of Vols, to date from 26th day of January 1865. This appointment, I respectfully desire should be made" Copy, DLC-USG, V, 58.

To Edwin M. Stanton

Washington D. C, May 30th *1865*

HON. E. M. STANTON,
SEC. OF WAR,
SIR:

I would respectfully recommend the following promotions, towit: Brigadier ~~an~~ & Bvt. Maj. Gen. J. H. Wilson[1] to be full Major General, Brig. & Bvt. Maj. Gen. Chas. Griffin to be full Major General for gallantry and good conduct at the battle of Five Forks, Apl. 2d 1865.

I would also recommend that Bvt. Brig. Gn. C. H. T. Collis, Col. 114 Pa. Vols. be breveted a Maj. Gen. and Col. Geo. C. Rogers, 15th Ill. Vol. Inf.y be breveted a Brig. Gn. These two latter officers, with their regiments, go out of service.

General Emory having been recommended for full Major

General I would also recommend his promotion before leaving the service.

> Very respectfully
> your obt. svt.
> U. S. Grant
> Lt. Gn.

ALS, DNA, RG 94, ACP, G559 CB 1865. *O.R.*, I, xlvi, part 3, 1236.

1. On June 4, 1865, USG wrote to Secretary of War Edwin M. Stanton. "I would respectfully recommend the promotion of J. H. Wilson and his assignment to the command of the Dept. of Ga. For the command of the Dept. of Alabama I would recommend Bvt. Maj. Gn. Chas R. Wood." ALS, DNA, RG 94, ACP, G791 CB 1865. *O.R.*, I, xlix, part 2, 954–55. See James Harrison Wilson, *Under the Old Flag* (New York and London, 1912), II, 363.

To Maj. Gen. George H. Thomas

(Cipher)   Washington May 30th *1865* [*9:30* A.M.]
Maj. Gen. Thomas, Nashville Tenn.

Send the 4th Corps to New Orleans as soon as practicable. Separate the men whose ~~will be discha~~ time expires before the 1st of October from the Corps and if paymasters are ready to pay the ballance let them receive their money before starting.

Let there be no unavoidable delay in getting this Corps off.

> U. S. Grant
> Lt. Gn.

ALS (telegram sent), DNA, RG 107, Telegrams Collected (Bound); telegram sent, *ibid.*; telegram received, *ibid.*, RG 393, Dept. of the Cumberland, Telegrams Received. *O.R.*, I, xlix, part 2, 931. On May 30, 1865, Brig. Gen. William D. Whipple, chief of staff for Maj. Gen. George H. Thomas, telegraphed to USG. "Paymasters are busy preparing rolls for payment of fourth (4) Corps Only three and half millions required to pay portion of Corps which goes. Cannot it be hurried forward from Washington. Will the Corps transportation be sent with it" Telegrams received (2—on May 31, 5:15 A.M.), DNA, RG 107, Telegrams Collected (Bound); *ibid.*, RG 108, Telegrams Received; copy, DLC-USG, V, 54. *O.R.*, I, xlix, part 2, 931.

On May 29, 1:30 P.M., USG telegraphed to Thomas. "Have Musterout rolls prepared of all the dismounted Cavalry in your command ~~prepared~~ and report by telegraph when it is done." ALS (telegram sent), DNA, RG 107, Telegrams Collected (Bound); telegram sent, *ibid.*; telegram received, *ibid.*, RG 393, Dept. of the Cumberland, Telegrams Received.

To Edwin M. Stanton

Washington D. C, May 31st *1865*

Hon. E. M. Stanton,
Sec. of War,
Sir:

I would respectfully call attention to the case of Brig. Gn. Robt. Allen, A. Q. M. and ask that he be breveted a Major General. Gn. Allen has made no application but I am well aware of his services in this war and in the Army before the War. He has been filling a place second only to that filled by the Quartermaster General of the Army, and with very great efficiency. He is well known as an officer joining very great integrity with the greatest business capacity.

I would recommend that his brevet rank have even date with that given to General Ingalls.

> Very respectfully
> your obt. svt.
> U. S. Grant
> Lt. Gn

ALS, DNA, RG 94, ACP, 278 1875. *O.R.*, I, xlix, part 2, 937.

Endorsement

Respectfully forwarded. I think it very desirable that our p[r]isons should be emptied as rapidly as may be consistent with a due regard to public safety. I would suggest therefore a gradual release from all prisons where enlisted rebel soldiers are confined leaving the Commissioned officers to make special application. I would recom-

mend the release of all Citizen prisoners who are not charged with
Capital offences on their taking the oath of allegiance.

U. S. GRANT
Lt. Gn.

May 31st/65

AES, DNA, RG 94, Letters Received, 1656H 1865. Written on a letter of May
31, 1865, from Bvt. Brig. Gen. William Hoffman, commissary gen. of prisoners,
to USG. "To facilitate the release of prisoners of war without its being too much
hurried, and to save much labor in your office, and this one also, I would respectfully suggest that the Commanding Officers of Military Prisons be directed
to release, on their taking the oath of allegiance, fifty or more per day taking
those below the rank of General, and in alphabetical order commencing with
each letter of the alphabet, and taking of that letter in proportion to the number
of names begining with it. None to be discharged under this arrangement against
whom there are charges of any kind, and a list to be furnished daily to this
office of those discharged. There are Seventeen Military Prisons at which are
confined over 50.000 prisoners and at the rate of 50 per day, it will take near
sixty days to vacate the Prisons. There are about 5.000 officers in confinement,
all of whom might be excluded from release, except on special application, if
thought advisable. There are a number of citizens in confinement without
charges, and some against whom there are charges who have not been tried.
Inasmuch as all who have ~~not~~ been tried and sentenced to confinement during the
war, have been pardoned it would seem that the prisoners above referred to might
also be released, with perhaps a few exceptions of those awaiting trial." LS, *ibid.*
O.R., II, viii, 585. On May 30, Hoffman had written to Brig. Gen. John A.
Rawlins. "During the past day or two I have received a number of orders to
release prisoners on their taking the amnesty oath of December 8, 1863. Since
the proclamation of this morning will it not be best to release them on taking
the simple oath of allegiance?" *Ibid.*, p. 582. On the same day, Rawlins endorsed
this letter. "Respectfully returned to Brig. Gen. W. Hoffman, Commissary-
General of Prisoners. Require of those you discharge the oath of allegiance only."
Ibid. For President Andrew Johnson's Amnesty Proclamation of May 29, see
ibid., pp. 578–80. Numerous applications for the release of C.S.A. prisoners
were forwarded to Hoffman through USG's hd. qrs. during spring and summer,
1865; routine applications have been omitted from this volume.

To Maj. Gen. Henry W. Halleck

Washington May 31st 1865 [*1:00* P.M.]

MAJ. GEN. HALLECK, RICHMOND VA.

I am informed that a great many bodies have been left un-
buryed at Appomattox C. H. It is possible that some may have

been left in the same way at ~~Appomattox~~ Sailors' Creek. I think a small Cavalry force had better be sent to each place to bury any that may still be left above ground.

U. S. GRANT
Lt. Gn.

ALS (telegram sent), DNA, RG 107, Telegrams Collected (Bound); telegram sent, *ibid.*; copies, *ibid.*, RG 108, Letters Sent; *ibid.*, RG 393, Dept. of Va. and N. C., 1st Military District, Register of Letters Received; DLC-USG, V, 46, 76, 108. *O.R.*, I, xlvi, part 3, 1240. See *ibid.*, pp. 1279–80.

On May 30, 1865, 11:00 A.M., USG had telegraphed to Maj. Gen. Henry W. Halleck. "The Paymaster General complains of interferance with the pay Dept. by Gen. Ord. Instruct Gn. Ord to let the Pay Dept. make its own arrangements for the payment of discharged soldiers." ALS (telegram sent), DNA, RG 107, Telegrams Collected (Bound); telegram sent, *ibid.*; copies, *ibid.*, RG 108, Letters Sent; DLC-USG, V, 46, 76, 108.

To Maj. Gen. Philip H. Sheridan

(Cipher)   Washington May 31st *1864*5. [*9:50* A.M.]
MAJ. GN. SHERIDAN, NEW ORLEANS,

The 4th Corps has been ordered to New Orleans. There may be a few days delay in starting as it is desirable that they should be paid before starting. I send but eight teams and two ambulance teams to each One thousand men.[1] If you want more sent let me know.

U. S. GRANT
Lt. Gn.

ALS (telegram sent), DNA, RG 107, Telegrams Collected (Bound); telegram sent, *ibid.*; telegrams received (3—two marked as sent at 10:00 A.M. and addressed to Maj. Gen. James B. Steedman), *ibid.*, Telegrams Collected (Unbound). Printed as sent at 10:00 A.M. in *O.R.*, I, xlviii, part 2, 691. On June 5, 1865, Brig. Gen. James W. Forsyth, chief of staff for Maj. Gen. Philip H. Sheridan, telegraphed to Bvt. Col. Theodore S. Bowers. "Liut Gen Grants despatch dated Washington May 31st P. M. informing Gen Sheridan that the fourth (4th) Army Corps had been ordered to New Orleans only reached him today." Telegrams received (2—on June 6, 7:00 P.M.), DNA, RG 107, Telegrams Collected (Bound); *ibid.*, RG 108, Telegrams Received; copies, DLC-USG, V, 54; (2) DLC-Philip H. Sheridan. *O.R.*, I, xlviii, part 2, 775.

1. On May 31, 10:00 A.M., USG telegraphed to Maj. Gen. George H. Thomas, Nashville. "Transportation at the rate of eight teams and two Ambulance teams to one thousand men will go with the 4th Corps. More can be sent afterwards if found necessary." ALS (telegram sent), DNA, RG 107, Telegrams Collected (Bound); telegram sent, *ibid.*; copies, *ibid.*, RG 108, Letters Sent; *ibid.*, RG 393, Dept. of the Cumberland, Telegrams Received; DLC-USG, V, 46, 76, 108.

To Ellen E. Sherman

WASHINGTON, D. C., May 31st, '65.

MRS. ELLEN E. SHERMAN:

DEAR MADAM: As a slight testimonial of the interest I feel in the great Northwestern Fair, now being held in Chicago, for the benefit of sick and disabled soldiers, who have endured so much for the maintenance of our Government, permit me, through your agency, to present to this loyal and chartiable enterprise, the horse, "Jack," well known in the Western armies. I left Illinois on him in July, 1861, when commanding the 21st regiment of volunteer infantry, of that State, I rode this horse more than all others put together, from the time of leaving Springfield, on the 3d of July, 61, until called East in March 64.

On my promotion to the command of the Armies of the United States, I left "Jack in the West, latterly with J. R. Jones, United States Marshal for the Northern District of Illinois residence Chicago. Mr. Jones has been directed to deliver the horse to your order.

If I was not deceived in the purchase of "Jack," he is now eleven years old. He is a very fine saddle horse, very gentle in harness but requires whip and spur.

Hoping that the Fair will realize the full expectations of loyal people, and do credit to the great and growing Northwest, where it is being held,

I remain, very, truly your obedient servant,

U. S. GRANT,
Lieutenant General.

Galena Gazette, June 10, 1865.

On June 6, 1865, Monday, 11:10 A.M., USG telegraphed to J. Russell Jones, Chicago. "I will go by the Lake Shore road and will reach Chicago Saturday morning." ALS (telegram sent), DNA, RG 107, Telegrams Collected (Bound). Also on June 6, USG telegraphed to George W. Gage and John M. Drake, Tremont House, Chicago. "I am much obliged for your invitation to accept hospitalities of Tremont House but I had already accepted invitation from J. R. Jones to stop with him." ALS (telegram sent), *ibid.* On June 8, USG telegraphed to Jones. "I will be in Chicago Saturday morning. Please secure rooms for me." ALS (telegram sent), *ibid.* On June 9, Albert H. Bodman, Chicago city clerk, wrote to USG. "At a meeting of the Common Council of the City of Chicago, held this Evening, the following Preamble and Resolutions were unanimously adopted. I am gratified at being the vehicle of their communication to you." ALS, USG 3. The lengthy resolutions concluded: "That the *Common Council* meet at the *Tremont House* at 11½ o'clock of to-morrow, and proceed in a body to the Depot where *Gen. Grant* will arrive, and escort him to his quarters: and from thence, at the time of his own appointment, to the '*Union Hall*' of the *Sanitary Fair*; and that the public officers of the city, be, and they are hereby cordially invited to meet and unite with us in receiving the *Generalissimo of our Armies*" ADS, *ibid.*

On June 11, USG attended the Chicago fair and responded to public applause. "Gentlemen and ladies: I never made a speech myse[1]f, and therefore I will ask Governor Yates, of Illinois, to convey to you the thanks which I should fail to express." *Chicago Tribune*, June 12, 1865. Maj. Gen. William T. Sherman later said that he would make a speech if USG so requested; USG then said: "I never ask a soldier to do anything I cannot do myself." *Ibid.* On June 12, USG responded to a welcome at Bryan Hall. "*Ladies and Gentlemen:* I am not in the habit of making speeches. If I replied to every welcome the fatigue would be too great for me. I, however, thank you for the kind welcome you have given me." *Ibid.*, June 13, 1865. Also on June 12, USG responded to cheers at the Chicago Board of Trade. "Gentlemen of the Board of Trade, and citizens of Chicago: I will not be able to thank you as I would like to do, for the very kind welcome which you have given me, but I will ask my old friend Mr. Washburne to return to you the thanks I should fail to express." *Ibid.*

To Maj. Gen. Henry W. Halleck

Washington June 1st *1865* [*1:40* P.M.]

MAJ. GEN. HALLECK, RICHMOND VA.

Do you not think it advisable to relieve Gen. Patrick? The machinery kept up in his duties is represented as heavy and his kindness of heart may interfere with the proper government of the City.

U. S. GRANT
Lt. Gen.

ALS (telegram sent), DNA, RG 107, Telegrams Collected (Bound); telegram sent, *ibid.*; copies, *ibid.*, RG 108, Letters Sent; DLC-USG, V, 46, 76, 108. *O.R.*, I, xlvi, part 3, 1244. On June 2, 1865, 4:30 P.M., Maj. Gen. Henry W. Halleck telegraphed to USG. "I have urged the Governor to reorganize courts, Sheriffs, policemen, &c., in Richmond & adjacent counties as soon as possible. When this is done the Provost Marshal's organization can be dispensed with, but not before. If broken up now neither life nor property would be safe here." ALS (telegram sent), DNA, RG 107, Telegrams Collected (Unbound); telegram received (at 7:00 P.M.), *ibid.*; *ibid.*, Telegrams Collected (Bound); *ibid.*, RG 108, Telegrams Received. *O.R.*, I, xlvi, part 3, 1246. See *ibid.*, p. 1267.

To Maj. Gen. Joseph J. Reynolds

Ciphr   Washingto June 1st *18645*. [*10:00* A.M.]
MAJ. GN. J. J. REYNOLDS LITTLE ROCK ARK.

Troops will be sent to you from Sherman's Army as soon as they can be paid to enable you to carry out the order for mustering out troops. Have rolls prepared as far as practicable so there shall be no delay.

U. S. GRANT
Lt. Gn

ALS (telegram sent), DNA, RG 107, Telegrams Collected (Bound); telegram sent, *ibid.*; copies, *ibid.*, RG 108, Letters Sent; DLC-USG, V, 46, 76, 108. *O.R.*, I, xlviii, part 2, 720. On May 31, 1865, Maj. Gen. Joseph J. Reynolds telegraphed to Maj. Thomas M. Vincent, AGO. "There are now on the rolls of this Department about twenty thousand (20.000) effective men including forty five hundred (4500) colored troops—We require for the present, to garrison the depots about fourteen thousand (14000) which number can be gradually diminished—White River country requires about twenty five hundred (2.500) men—Arkansas including Rail Road and Fort Gibson about nine thousand (9.000). Camden and other points in the ~~state~~ South part of this state say Washington or Fulton about two thousand five hundred (2.500)—The terms of service of the white troops in the department expire before Sept 30th and *their muster out is suspended* until they can be replaced by other troops—This replacement is recommended and should take place at once as the fact of the existence of orders entitling them to muster out cannot be kept from the troops, and impartial treatment is essential to harmony—This Department is daily filling up with predatory bands and stragglers rendering immediate and prompt action necessary—Will send ₱ complete lists by mail—No account is herein taken of Alexandria & Shreveport which must soon be garrisoned" Telegram received, DNA, RG 107, Telegrams Collected (Bound); *ibid.*, RG 108, Telegrams Received; copy, DLC-USG, V, 54. *O.R.*, I, xlviii, part 2, 699. On June 1, Vincent endorsed the telegram received. "Respectfully submitted to Lt. Gen. U S Grant Comd'g Armies U. S.— This is in reply to the instuctions sent Maj. Gen Reynolds to muster out all white vol. troops of his command, whose terms expire prior to Oct. 1. 1865, provided his command would not be reduced thereby prejudicially to the service In case of the reductn proving prejudicial to the service, he was authorized to suspend the order *in whole, or in part,* and directed to promptly notify the Adjutent Gen, of the Army with the view of receivg further instructions" AES, DNA, RG 108, Telegrams Received. *O.R.*, I, xlviii, part 2, 699–700.

General Orders No. 108

War Department
Adjutant General's Office
Washington. D. C. June 2. 1865.

GENERAL ORDERS No. 108.

Soldiers of the Armies of the United States! By your patriotic devotion to your country in the hour of danger and alarm—your magnificent fighting, bravery and endurance—you have maintained the supremacy of the Union and the Constitution, overthrown all armed oposition to the enforcement of the Law, and of the Proclamations forever Abolishing *Slavery*, the cause and pretext of the Rebellion, and opened the way to the Rightful Authorities to restore Order and inaugerate Peace on a permanent and enduring basis on every foot of American soil.

Your Marches, Seiges, & Battles, in distance, duration, resolution and brilliancy of result, dim the lustre of the world's past military achievements, and will be the Patriot's precedent in defense of Liberty and Right in all time to come.

In obedience to your country's call, you left your Homes and Families and volunteered in its defence. Victory has crowned your valor, and secured the purpose of your patriot-hearts; and with the gratitude of your countrymen, and the highest honors a great and free nation can accord, you will soon be permitted to return to your homes and families, conscious of having discharged the highest duty of American citizens.

To achieve these glorious triumphs and secure to yourselves, your fellow-countrymen and posterity the blessings of free institutions, tens of thousand of your gallant comrades have fallen, and sealed the priceless legacy with their lives. The graves of these a grateful nation bedews with tears—honors their memories, and will ever cherish and support their stricken families.

U. S. GRANT
Lieutenant General

Copy, DNA, RG 94, Letters Received, 584A 1865; (printed) NjP. *O.R.*, I, xlvi, part 3, 1248; *ibid.*, I, xlvii, part 3, 613; *ibid.*, I, xlviii, part 2, 725–26; *ibid.*, I, xlix, part 2, 948.

Also on June 2, 1865, USG issued General Orders No. 104, directing the q. m. dept. to furnish transportation for released prisoners; General Orders No. 105, disbanding vol. light art. cos.; and General Orders No. 106, relieving surplus staff officers. *Ibid.*, II, viii, 633; *ibid.*, I, xlvi, part 3, 1247; *ibid.*, III, v, 48–49. On the same day, Maj. Gen. John A. Dix, New York City, telegraphed to USG. "Your dispatch in regard to General and Staff Officers was received at eight 8 oclock this evening. I will attend to its execution at once." Telegram received (at 10:00 P.M.), DNA, RG 107, Telegrams Collected (Bound); *ibid.*, RG 108, Telegrams Received; copy, DLC-USG, V, 54.

To Edwin M. Stanton

Washington June 2d 1865

HON. E. M. STANTON
SEC. OF WAR,
SIR:

Enclosed I send the order recommended for the reorganization of Depts. & Mil. Divisions. All the other orders spoken of by me are in the hands of the A. G: except the one for the muster-out of Gen. Palmer's Command in N. C. In that case I telegraphed to Gn.

Schofield direct ordering him to have the Muster out rolls prepared
and when ready to report the fact to the Adj. Gn.[1]

Very respectfully
your obt. svt.
U. S. GRANT
Lt. Gn.

ALS, DLC-Edwin M. Stanton. On June 5, 1865, Secretary of War Edwin M.
Stanton wrote to USG. "Your recommendation for the organization of Military
Departments and Divisions, with assignment of commands, has been submitted
to the President, who directs me to say that he desires independent commands
to be assigned to Major Genl George H. Thomas and Major Genl W. T. Sherman, suitable to their rank and services, without either being subordinate to the
other; and that he wishes General Thomas' command to embrace the States of
Kentucky—, Tennessee, Georgia, Alabama, and Florida. You will please prepare
and submit for the President's consideration a plan of organization and assignment, in accordance with his wish, above expressed." LS, DNA, RG 108, Letters
Received. On June 26, USG wrote to Stanton. "In publishing the order organizing, or defining, Military Divisions and Depts, I would have no objection to the
substitution of Gen. Foster's name for Gen. Geo. Wrights if you so desire it for
the command of the Dept. of the Columbia." ALS, *ibid.*, RG 94, Letters Received, 1386A 1865. On June 27, President Andrew Johnson issued orders reorganizing military divs. and depts. *O.R.*, I, xlvi, part 3, 1298–99. On the same
day, Brig. Gen. George Wright, Sacramento, wrote to USG. "Permit me, as your
old friend and companion in arms, to congratulate you on the successful termination of the great struggle for the preservation of the Union; and to assure you,
that no one of your old associates, feels more happy than myself, in seeing you at
the head of the Army; a position which you have so nobly won in the service of
your country during the last four years. Praying for your health, happiness and
prosperity, . . ." ALS, USG 3. Also on June 27 (or 29), Wright wrote to USG
recommending Justus Steinberger, former col., 1st Washington Territorial Vols.,
for appointment in the U.S. Army. (Dated June 29) DNA, RG 108, Register of
Letters Received; (dated June 27) Kenneth W. Rendell, Inc., *Autographs and
Manuscripts: The American Civil War*, Catalogue No. 96, [1974], p. 45. On
Nov. 23, USG endorsed this letter. "Respy. forwarded to the Sec of War." Copy,
DNA, RG 108, Register of Letters Received. Wright drowned on July 30 in the
wreck of the *Brother Jonathan* on his way to assume command of the Dept. of
the Columbia.

1. On May 31 or June 1, Maj. Gen. John M. Schofield, Raleigh, N. C., had
telegraphed to USG. "The troops in Gen Palmers Dist do not belong to any
organized Corps and they are in a bad state of inefficiency & disorganization I
think it would be best to muster them all out of service. I am Compelled to relieve
them all in order to Correct the abuses which have grown out of long Continued
post duty." Telegram received (at noon), *ibid.*, RG 107, Telegrams Collected
(Bound); *ibid.*, Telegrams Collected (Unbound); (dated both May 31 and June
1) *ibid.*, RG 108, Telegrams Received; copies, DLC-USG, V, 54; DLC-John M.
Schofield; (dated May 31) DNA, RG 393, Army of the Ohio and Dept. of N. C.,

Telegrams Sent. Dated June 1 in *O.R.*, I, xlvii, part 3, 609. On June 1, 2:30 P.M., USG telegraphed to Schofield. "You may have Musterout rolls prepared for all the troops under Gen. Palmer and when completed send them to their states for payment and discharge. Notify the Adj. Gn. when you will be ready to commence shipping them. Will you require any reinforcements to enable you to carry out all the orders for mustering out troops?" ALS (telegram sent), DNA, RG 107, Telegrams Collected (Bound); telegram sent, *ibid.*; telegram received, *ibid.*, Telegrams Collected (Unbound); *ibid.*, RG 393, Army of the Ohio and Dept. of N. C., Telegrams Received. *O.R.*, I, xlvii, part 3, 609. On the same day, Schofield telegraphed to USG. "I will have plenty of troops for this state after mustering out all that have been ordered to be mustere[d] out" ALS (telegram sent), DNA, RG 107, Telegrams Collected (Unbound); telegram received, *ibid.*; (on June 2, 9:00 A.M.) *ibid.*, Telegrams Collected (Bound); *ibid.*, RG 108, Telegrams Received. *O.R.*, I, xlvii, part 3, 609.

To Edwin M. Stanton

Washington D. C. June 2d 1865

HON. E. M. STANTON
SEC. OF WAR,
SIR:

I would respectfully suggest that orders be issued directing the Chief of Ordnance to take immediate steps to have collected all captured Ordnance & ordnance stores and all Ordnance & Ordnce stores that may be turned in to his Department collect and stored at Northern Arsenals, Charleston Arsenal, Hilton Head, Baton Rouge and Rock Island.

I would also recommend the extension of free trade in all articles, except the few enumerated as "Contraband of War," to all the States and Territories of the United States.[1]

Very respectfully
your obt. svt.
U. S. GRANT
Lt. Gn.

ALS, DNA, RG 94, Letters Received, 581A 1865. *O.R.*, I, xlvi, part 3, 1246. On June 2, 1865, USG wrote to Secretary of War Edwin M. Stanton. "I would respectfully recommend that an order be issued discontinuing the Army of Georgia, and transferring all the western troops belonging to it that are not to be discharged under existing orders, to the Army of the Tennessee." LS, DNA, RG 94, Letters Received, 637A 1865. *O.R.*, I, xlvii, part 3, 612.

1. See *ibid.*, I, xlvi, part 3, 1248. On June 19, USG wrote to Stanton. "I would respectfully recommend that the same freedom of trade be extended West of the Miss. river as is authorized East of it. If the Twenty-five per cent tax has not yet been removed from cotton shipped from Southern states I would suggest whether it would not be advisable to remove it." ALS, DNA, RG 94, Letters Received, 1384A 1865. *O.R.*, I, xlviii, part 2, 924.

To Maj. Gen. John Pope

(Cipher)   Washington June 2d *1865* [*10:00* A.M.]
MAJ. GEN. POPE, ST. LOUIS, MO.

You may authorize the issuing of Arms to all persons connected with the carrying of Government freights over the plains on proper security that the Arms will not be lost to Government.

U. S. GRANT
Lt. Gn.

Respectfully refered to the Sec. of War for approval before being dispatched.

U. S. G.

ALS (telegram sent), DNA, RG 107, Telegrams Collected (Bound); telegram sent, *ibid.*; copies, *ibid.*, RG 108, Letters Sent; DLC-USG, V, 46, 76, 108. Printed as received at 10:00 A.M. in *O.R.*, I, xlviii, part 2, 730–31. On June 2, 1865, Secretary of War Edwin M. Stanton endorsed USG's original message. "Approved." AES, DNA, RG 107, Telegrams Collected (Bound). *O.R.*, I, xlviii, part 2, 731. On May 19, Maj. Gen. Grenville M. Dodge, St. Louis, had written to Maj. Gen. John Pope. "Under orders of the War Department we have been furnishing arms, equipments &c. to State troops in active service—Under recent orders, the Chief of Ordnance does not consider himself authorized to issue as heretofore—These troops are organized in the Counties for their protection against Bushwhackers &c. they are efficient for that purpose They or the State are not able to purchase, Arms or ammunition to equip themselves. I therefore urgently request the Lt. Genl Comd'g the Army, or the War Dept. as the case may be, to order Colonel. F. D. Callender, Chief of Ordnance, to turn over to the State on requisitions approved by me, Arms, Accoutrements, and Ammunition for use of said troops, said arms, Accoutrements and ammunition to be those turned in by the M. S. M. or the U. S. Vols. that have gone out of service, we have plenty of such on hand, they are equally as good for this service as new ones, and it will not be any loss to the Government, but a great aid to us. Immediate action should be had in this as we are having great trouble from the Outlaws, Guerillas &c. and they should be put down at the start." LS, DNA, RG 94, Letters Received, 1236M 1865. *O.R.*, I, xlviii, part 2, 508–9. On May 20, Pope endorsed this letter. "respectfully referred to the Genl. in chief of the Army with the request that Genl Dodge's application be granted—I agree with him entirey as to the necessity and propriety of thus disposing of the arms turned in by the M. S. M about to be mustered out" AES, DNA, RG 94, Letters Received, 1236M 1865. On June 1, USG endorsed this letter. "Respectfully forwarded to the Secretary of War and the recommendation of Gen Dodge approved" ES, *ibid.* On June 17, Stanton endorsed this letter. "Approved" AES, *ibid.* On June 1, Dodge had telegraphed to Bvt. Col. Theodore S. Bowers. "Please give me authority to order the Chief of Ordnance to issue arms to the freighters crossing the plains carrying govt freight upon their giving proper security to return them or pay for them if lost or destroyed" Telegram received (at 10:10 P.M.), *ibid.*, RG 107, Telegrams Collected (Bound); *ibid.*, RG 108, Telegrams Received; copy, DLC-USG, V, 54. *O.R.*, I, xlviii, part 2, 721.

On June 2, Pope telegraphed to USG. "The following dispatch received and forwarded for your information—Fort Leavenworth Kansas June first—eighteen sixty five (1865). MAJ GEN JNO POPE. The detachments sent out by General Ford to scout the dry Fork Walnut Creek Smoky Hill Fork & Main republic all send in reports that they find no Indians between Arkansas & Platte River & no new signs. It is evident that the Depredations on the southern route came from Indians far south who send up small parties. The main expediti[on] are after them. (signed) G. M DODGE M G" Telegram received (at 2:30 P.M.), DNA, RG 107, Telegrams Collected (Bound); *ibid.*, RG 108, Telegrams Received; copies, *ibid.*, RG 393, Dept. of the Mo., Telegrams Sent; DLC-USG, V, 54. Incomplete in *O.R.*, I, xlviii, part 2, 722.

To Maj. Gen. Edward R. S. Canby

Washington June 3d *1865* [*1:00* P.M.]

MAJ. GEN. CANBY NEW ORLEANS,

You may turn over to rail-road companies all their roads in your Dept. except such as it may be absolutely necessary for government to run on their own account, and give them every facility for obtaining mat[e]rial for repairs, and for runing them carrying all Govt. freight at such tarriff as may be established by the Q. M. Gn. the corporations taking their chances hereafter of confiscation.

U. S. GRANT
Lt. Gn.

ALS (telegram sent), DNA, RG 107, Telegrams Collected (Bound); telegram
sent, *ibid.*; telegrams received (4), *ibid.*, Telegrams Collected (Unbound).
Printed as received on June 5, 1865, in *O.R.*, I, xlviii, part 2, 743. On June 5,
Maj. Gen. Edward R. S. Canby telegraphed to USG. "Your dispatch of the 3d
in regard to rewards [*railroads*] has been received and the necessary orders issued accordingly" Telegram received (on June 6, 6:35 P.M.), DNA, RG 107,
Telegrams Collected (Bound); *ibid.*, RG 108, Telegrams Received; copies, *ibid.*,
RG 393, Dept. of the Gulf and La., Letters Sent; DLC-USG, V, 54. *O.R.*, I,
xlviii, part 2, 775. See *ibid.*, p. 777.

To Maj. Gen. John A. Dix

Washington June 3d/65 [*11:55* A.M.]

MAJ. GN. DIX, NEW YORKS CITY.

Two regiments have been ordered to Harts Island. As soon as
they arrive musterout the Penna regiments ~~out~~ and send them to
their state to be paid off. Let the rolls be prepared at once.

U. S. GRANT
Lt. Gn

ALS (telegram sent), DNA, RG 107, Telegrams Collected (Bound); telegram
sent, *ibid.*; telegram received, *ibid.*, RG 393, Dept. of the East, Hd. Qrs., Letters
Received. *O.R.*, I, xlvi, part 3, 1252. On June 2, 1865, Maj. Gen. John A. Dix
had telegraphed to Secretary of War Edwin M. Stanton. "The 68th and 143d
Penna regiments are the only troops guarding rebel prisoners at Harts Island—
The commanding officer of Harts Island reports them as not reliable and as insubordinate to their officers—I would be glad to send them home but have no
others to replace them" Telegram received (at 9:00 P.M.), DNA, RG 108,
Telegrams Received; copy, DLC-USG, V, 54. Stanton endorsed the telegram
received. "Referred to Lt Genl Grant with request that other troops be sent to
replace the Pena troops—& that they be sent home to be mustered out" AES
(undated), DNA, RG 108, Telegrams Received.

On June 3, noon, Bvt. Col. Theodore S. Bowers telegraphed to Maj. Gen.
George G. Meade. "Please send without delay two Regiments of troops belonging to Eastern States, to Harts Island, New York, to relieve the Pennsylvania
troops now on duty there guarding prisoners of war. They will report to Maj.
Gen'l Jno. A. Dix, Com'd'g Dept. of the East. The Quartermasters Dept. will
furnish necessary transportation." ALS (telegram sent), *ibid.*, RG 107, Telegrams Collected (Bound); telegram sent, *ibid.*; copies, *ibid.*, RG 108, Letters
Sent; DLC-USG, V, 46, 76, 109. See *O.R.*, I, xlvi, part 3, 1250.

To Maj. Gen. John Pope

June 3d *1865* [*12:50* P.M.]

MAJ. GN. POPE, ST. LOUIS MO.

I do not want you to send troops out of your command unless there is a Military necessity for it. Mr. Poston[1] and others will have to avail themselves of the protection of such forces as may be traveling on the plains to reach their homes.

U. S. GRANT
Lt. Gn.

ALS (telegram sent), DNA, RG 107, Telegrams Collected (Bound); telegram sent, *ibid.*; telegram received (marked as sent at 12:40 P.M.), *ibid.*, Telegrams Collected (Unbound). *O.R.*, I, xlviii, part 2, 750. On June 3, 1865, 10:45 A.M., Maj. Gen. John Pope telegraphed to USG. "Letter of Mr Poston Delegate from Arizona asking that Regt of Cavalry be sent as escort to himself & other Territorial officers from Leavenworth to Arizona via New Mexico to be left in Arizona for service against Indians with your endorsement thereon just received—There is no trouble about going as far as Santa Fe & if additional escort is needed to that place Gen Dodge will furnish it—The Dept of New Mexico is not in this Command & I know nothing of condition of things there Do you wish me to send a Regt of Cavalry to that Dept—I have no authority otherwise to order troops out of this Division" Telegram received (at 11:45 A.M.), DNA, RG 107, Telegrams Collected (Bound); *ibid.*, RG 108, Telegrams Received; copies, *ibid.*, RG 393, Dept. of the Mo., Telegrams Sent; DLC-USG, V, 54. *O.R.*, I, xlviii, part 2, 750.

Also on June 3, 6:00 P.M., Pope telegraphed to USG. "Following dispatch from Gen Dodge is just received *By Telegraph from* Fort Leavenworth *1865. To* MAJ GEN POPE Gen Moonlight with one (1) column of cavalry and pack mules left for Powder River May 10th He reports that the Cheyennes seem to be breaking up into small parties. 200 lodges are trying to make their way south by the mountains. Troops are after that party. The Sioux except 230 lodges are on Black Hills, want to come in and treat. Little Thunder and Spotted Tail are at Laramie, do not deny that they have engaged in the troubles, say they were forced to it by Cheyennes. The Sioux all seem to be anxious to treat. Connor is evidently making every effort to carry out ~~our~~ your instructions. G. M. DODGE Maj. Genl" AES (telegram sent), DNA, RG 107, Telegrams Collected (Unbound); telegram received (at 7:35 P.M.), *ibid.*, Telegrams Collected (Bound); *ibid.*, RG 108, Telegrams Received. *O.R.*, I, xlviii, part 2, 751.

1. Charles D. Poston, born in Ky. in 1825, practiced law in Tenn. and Washington, D. C., moved to San Francisco in 1850, and went to Arizona in 1856. Fleeing from Apache Indians in 1861, he returned to Washington. Appointed superintendent of Indian Affairs when Congress organized Arizona Ter-

ritory in 1863, he became Arizona's first delegate to Congress, serving Dec. 5, 1864–March 3, 1865.

To Maj. Gen. Philip H. Sheridan

(Cipher)   Washington June 3d *1865* [*11:00* A.M.]
MAJ. GN. SHERIDAN, NEW ORLEANS LA.

It is probable a large force of Cavalry will be required in Texas. If cnough cannot be obtained in the West let me know and I will send all that is required from here. I want Custer and Merritt left in Texas for the present. The whole state should be scoured to pick up Kirby Smith's men and the Arms carried home by them.

U. S. GRANT
Lt. Gn.

ALS (telegram sent), DNA, RG 107, Telegrams Collected (Bound); telegram sent, *ibid.*; telegrams received (3), *ibid.*, Telegrams Collected (Unbound). *O.R.*, I, xlviii, part 2, 743. On June 8, 1865, 11:30 A.M., Maj. Gen. Philip H. Sheridan telegraphed to USG. "I will not require any cavalry from the East except the 8th Illinois—now I believe at St Louis. I have organized two columns of superb cavalry of 4000 men each. One is now en-route to Shreveport and will march through there to San Antoni. The other column four thousand strong will be en-route in a few days and will march from Shreveport to Houston. Cavalry cannot be transported across the gulf nor can it cross Western La. as the country is covered with water—I have countermanded the order for troops from Little Rock; The term of service of most of that command will expire in a few months— The transportation sent for it by Gen. Allen will be used for cavalry—The six steamers which the Q M. Gen promised have not yet been heard from, indeed there has been a dead-lock on movements of Troops since Steele left as every suitable transport was sent with him" Telegram received (on June 9, 5:30 A.M.), DNA, RG 107, Telegrams Collected (Bound); (at Buffalo, N. Y., June 9, 1:20 P.M.) *ibid.*, RG 108, Telegrams Received; copies, DLC-USG, V, 54; (2) DLC-Philip H. Sheridan. *O.R.*, I, xlviii, part 2, 813. See *ibid.*, pp. 775, 858, 876, 908. On June 10, 12:30 P.M., USG, Chicago, telegraphed to Sheridan. "The 8th Ills. Cavalry has not gone West but if more is required take any that is being reserved in Canby's or Thomas' Command and if necessary I can re-place it." Copies, DLC-USG, V, 46, 109; DNA, RG 108, Letters Sent. *O.R.*, I, xlviii, part 2, 839.

On June 8, Sheridan telegraphed to USG. "The following telegram has just been recd from South Pass—It is not official but I deem it correct . . . '8 a m June 8th 1865 SPECIAL TRUE DELTA—Brownsville is again in possession of the federals—Brig Gen Browne entered the town at the head of his forces at day-light on the morning of the 31st of May—The confederate forces did not await their arrival but uncerimoniously left the day before first selling their artillery to the Imperialists in Matamoras—Slates forces are scattered—he is as the head of a marauding party levying taxes upon cotton from the interior—The forces of Cortinas were hovering near Matamoras on the 22d—Mejia marched out there to drive him out—It was rumored in Brownsville on the 30th that Imperialists were driven instead—Health at Brownsville and Brazos excellent [B]usiness at Matamoras at a stand still—Steam transport Patron left Brazos at noon 3d inst. H G Agnew commands—P. S. Rushwood in Brownsville heard report that Galveston had surrendered—" Telegram received (on June 9, 12:30 P.M.), DNA, RG 107, Telegrams Collected (Bound); *ibid.*, RG 108, Telegrams Received; copies, DLC-USG, V, 54; (2) DLC-Philip H. Sheridan. *O.R.*, I, xlviii, part 2, 813–14.

On June 2, Sheridan twice telegraphed to Brig. Gen. John A. Rawlins, the second time at 10:30 A.M. "Please notify the Lt General of my arrival here this morning" "Gen Canby sent Gen Herron to Shreveport with 4000 men; I met this force at the mouth of Red River on its way up Reynolds at Little Rock was directed to send five thousand troops to the same place and Gen Allen called on to furnish the necessary boats to transport them there Nine thousand men will be used to garrison Alexandria and Shreveport—Gen Granger is in readiness with six thousand men at Mobile to sail for Galveston as soon as transportation arrives—The indications are that most of the Texas Troops have disbanded and gone home—This may have been caused by dissatisfaction with the Mil. authorities who contemplated surrendering—I will see the commissioners sent here by Gen Magruder today & perhaps may get a better idea of the condition of affairs" Telegrams received (the first on June 3, 9:25 A.M., the second at 11:30 P.M.), DNA, RG 107, Telegrams Collected (Bound); *ibid.*, RG 108, Telegrams Received; copies, DLC-USG, V, 54; DLC-Philip H. Sheridan. *O.R.*, I, xlviii, part 2, 726.

On June 4, Sheridan telegraphed to Rawlins. "I have collected within the last ten days the following information in respect to the condition of affairs in Texas. Nearly all the Texas soldiers disbanded before the surrender of Kirby Smith. They broke into the magazine, supplied themselves with powder, destroyed most all of the Confederate Government property and went to their homes. This was done in the spirit, I think, of the General Hindman's address, and to avoid surrender and parole. There has been a great deal of discussion on the subject of going to Mexico and there is an undoubted intention on the part of many to go, some are for the Imperial side and some for the Liberals, and there is a very bad element in Texas—in view of the foregoing which is unfavorable to quiet peaceful pursuits, and to the fact that I have always believed that Maximillians advent into Mexico was a part of the rebellion, I will advise that a strong force be put into Texas, and will order the 4th Army Corps there as soon as sea transportation can be prepared—Gen'l Steele is off with his command to the Rio Grande—Genl Granger will get off as soon as the transports ordered by the Quarter Master General get to Mobile—This delay on account of these transports is very bad—The 25th Army Corps has not yet reported at Mobile Bay—Orders are there awaiting it. I will collect a cavalry force here to be sent as soon as transports can be obtained—This may seem like the employment of a large force to you, but it is always best to go strong handed. The Imperialists are strengthening at Mattamoras, and according to report the Confederate property at Brownsville, including 14 pieces of Artillery, has been taken across the river—

to that place" Telegram received (on June 6, 9:00 P.M.), DNA, RG 107, Telegrams Collected (Bound); *ibid.*, RG 108, Telegrams Received; (at New York, June 7, 4:00 P.M.) *ibid.*; copies, DLC-USG, V, 54; DLC-Philip H. Sheridan. *O.R.*, I, xlviii, part 2, 767.

On June 5, Sheridan telegraphed to Rawlins. "For the information of the Lieut General I transmit the following communication—'By telegraph from South West Pass La   To Lt Col C F Christensen A A Gen   I arrived off Galveston last Wednesday and communicated with Kerby Smith—On friday afternoon he came off and after adding a short amendment to it, he signed the agreement and other arrangements for the surrender—He and his officers report that a complete disorganization of the rebel forces throughout the Department commenced about the 20th of May—The soldiers under the lead of some of their subordinate officers mutined simultaneously in all parts and plundered the Government stores, arms ammunition &c   The people seem to be anxious that more force should be sent to Gen Washburns order without delay—(signed) E F Davis Br Gen U S Vols'   A communication from Colerado at Alexandria says that the Arkansas and Missouri troops had kept together and will surrender (as per agreement with the Govt) property in their possession but that most of the other troops had gone to their homes carrying with them their arms—Every thing on wheels at Alexandria had been run to Texas—The 25th Corps has not yet reported at Mobile bay nor have the six steam transports reported yet. This delay is very annoying" Telegram received (on June 6, 8:00 P.M.), DNA, RG 107, Telegrams Collected (Bound); *ibid.*, RG 108, Telegrams Received; copies, DLC-USG, V, 54; DLC-Philip H. Sheridan. *O.R.*, I, xlviii, part 2, 775.

To Maj. Gen. John Pope

Washington June 4th *1865* [*1:30* P.M.]
Maj. Gen. Pope, St. Louis Mo.

Releive Gen. Blunt from duty and direct him to remain in St. Louis until further orders. If you have not got a suitable officer to take his place I can send one.

U. S. Grant
Lt. Gn.

ALS (telegram sent), DNA, RG 107, Telegrams Collected (Bound); telegram sent, *ibid.*; telegram received, *ibid.*, Telegrams Collected (Unbound). *O.R.*, I, xlviii, part 2, 772. On June 5, 1865, 4:50 P.M., Maj. Gen. John Pope telegraphed to USG. "Your dispatch received   I have ordered Gen Blunt to St Louis accordingly   If Reynolds wants another officer in his place he will let me know   I presume he will recommend several General officers in his Dept to be mustered out" Telegram received (at 8:30 P.M.), DNA, RG 107, Telegrams Collected (Bound);

ibid., RG 108, Telegrams Received; copies, *ibid.*, RG 393, Military Div. of the Mo., Telegrams Sent; DLC-USG, V, 54. *O.R.*, I, xlviii, part 2, 779.

Also on June 5, 11:57 A.M. and 1:05 P.M., Pope twice telegraphed to USG. "The following dispatch is transmitted for your information Fort Leavenworth June 4th To MAJ GEN JNO POPE General Conner telegraphs that Indians attack some station on Telegraph Line daily That he needs two more Regiments of Infantry and five (5) of Cavalry. Part of Cavalry are now on road—Rest will Go in few days. That his stock is poor. That he has no doubt Mormons are connected with depredations west of Mountains—That he can supply troops West of Rocky ~~of~~ Mountains with forage from Utah. If you can get two Regiments of Infantry who have over one (1) year to serve it better be done and have them shipped direct to Fort Leavenworth The trouble now mostly West of Laramie If Capt Coryell can send me five hundred more horses I would like them. Approval of Col Potters estimates arrived today signed G M DODGE Maj Genl" "The following dispatch transmitted for your insformation St Paul June third (3) Eighteen sixty five (1865) MAJ GENL POPE The Chippewa matters are not immediately dangerous & prudent action will I hope avoid conflict. further investigations will be presented and report. Near Mankata ~~n~~New discoveries of two (2) small bands of hostile Indians are reported and fresh excitement prevails—Every possible effort is being made to hunt down such obnoxious vermin It is also certain that in the vicinity of Devils Lake & Moss River Dacotah Territory about three thousand (3.000) lodges of hostile Indians are located in seperate Camps. I send papers promiscously but carefully sift and Judge the probable truth of matters just as I have done for years past when surrounded with conflicting reports The general appearance is not alarming but enough to justify caution and the need of more Cavalry and mere little howitzers. Sully moves up Missouri and other Regiments of Cavalry from this direction. Both columns to demonstrate on the divide. Will probably be sufficient. Small parties only may be troublesome Col Adams is in pursuit of a small party of Indians near ~~Abercombie~~ Abercrombie (signed) S. R CURTIS Maj Gen—" Telegrams received (the first at 5:10 P.M., the second at 6:00 P.M.), DNA, RG 107, Telegrams Collected (Bound); (the second marked as received at 5:30 P.M.) *ibid.*, RG 108, Telegrams Received; copies, *ibid.*, RG 393, Military Div. of the Mo., Telegrams Sent; DLC-USG, V, 54. *O.R.*, I, xlviii, part 2, 773, 779. The enclosure for the second (with variant text) is *ibid.*, p. 763.

To Andrew Johnson

Washington June 5th *1865*

HIS EXCELLENCY, A. JOHNSON PRESIDENT
SIR:

I have been appealed to in behalf of Capt. Chas. W. Lyman who has been pardoned out of penitentiary to say a word in his

behalf to the ennd that he may be restored to his rank in the Army
for the purpose of enabling him to resign honorably. My own impression is that the free pardon which has already been granted
does so restore him. But to avoid the delay of a decission by the
Judge Advocate General as to this point I would respectfully ask
that the order in his case be so amended as to declare this fact.

> Very respectfully
> your obt. svt.
> U. S. GRANT
> Lt. Gn.

ALS, DNA, RG 153, MM 1924. On June 5, 1865, President Andrew Johnson
endorsed this letter. "Respectfully referred to the Honorable Secretary of War.
~~who~~ The order pardoning Captain Lyman A. Q. M is hereby so amended as
to restore him to his rank in the Army so that he may resign honorably" ES, *ibid.*
Capt. Charles W. Lyman had been convicted by a court-martial on March 23
for accepting bribes from steamboat owners while in charge of transportation
at Memphis and Vicksburg during 1863 and sentenced to two years hard labor.
The court-martial record is *ibid.* On April 30, 1865, USG wrote a letter, presumably to Johnson, requesting executive clemency for Lyman. *Ibid.*, RG 94,
Register of Letters Received. On May 1, Col. William A. Nichols, AGO, wrote
to the superintendent, Ohio Penitentiary, Columbus. "The President of the
United States has pardoned Captain Charles W. Lyman, Assistant Quarter
Master, sentenced to two years hard labor, and now confined under that sentence
in the Ohio Peniten~~iten~~tiary at Columbus, and orders his release from confinement—Please report the execution of this order—" Copy, *ibid.*, Letters
Received, 429A 1865. On May 27, Lyman wrote to Secretary of War Edwin M.
Stanton. "Under what I believe to have been an unjust verdict of a General
Court Martial. I received an ignoimous sentence, I have obtained a full pardon
from the Peresident, and I beg to be informed if that pardon carries with it a
restoration to my former rank as Capt & A Q M. of Vols. I believe the effect of
the pardon is to restore me to the Army, from which I wish to resigin, If I am
mistaken I respectfuly ask that I may be so restored to the end that My resignation may be offered and excepted" ALS, *ibid.*, RG 153, MM 1924. On June 5,
Maj. Addison A. Hosmer, judge advocate, endorsed this letter. "Respectfully
returned to the Secretary of War. The pardon of *Captain Lyman*, in form announced in General Court Martial Orders, No. 213, A. G. O. May 1st. 1865,
does not operate to restore him to his rank and commission as Assistant Quarter
Master, U. S. Vols. Its effect is to relieve him from further punishment and to
remove the disabilities imposed by the sentence. His reappointment is a matter
for the discretion of the President and is not called for by any reasons growing
out of his trial. Record exhibited." ES, *ibid.* See *PUSG*, 9, 194–95.

To Edwin M. Stanton

Washington, D. C., June 6th *1865*

Hon. E. M. Stanton,
Secretary of War,
Sir:

I have the honor to recommend for promotion in the United States Army, the following named Officers of my Staff.

Captain *Cyrus B. Comstock*, Corps of Engineers U. S. A.; Lieut. Col. & A. D. C. and Bvt. Brigadier General Vols. To be *Major by Brevet*, for meritorious services in the Seige of Vicksburg; to date from July 4th 1863. To be *Lieutenant Colonel by Brevet*, for gallant conduct in the Battle of the Wilderness; to date from May 6th 1864 To be *Colonel by Brevet*, for gallant conduct in the Seige of Richmond, and especially in the attack on Fort Harrison; to date from September 29th 1864. To be *Brigadier General by Brevet*, for gallant and meritorious conduct in the assault and capture of Fort Fisher, N. C.; to date from January 15th 1865.

Major *Theodore S. Bowers*, Asst. Adjt. General U. S. A., Lieut. Colonel by assignment and Bvt. Colonel Volunteers. To be *Lieutenant Colonel by Brevet*, for gallant and meritorious services in the Seige of Richmond, and especially for gallant conduct at the storming of New Market Heights; to date from August 16th, 1864. To be *Colonel by Brevet*, for meritorious services in the Battles in front of Petersburg, Va., and in the pursuit and capture of the Army of Northern Virginia, in the Spring Campaign of 1865; to date from April 9th 1865.

Captain *O. E. Babcock*, Corps of Engineers U. S. A., Lieut. Colonel & A. D. C. and Bvt. Colonel Volunteers. To be *Major by Brevet*, for meritorious services in the defense of Knoxville, Tenn., and especially for gallant conduct in the defense of Fort Saunders; to date from November 29th 1863. To be *Lieutenant Colonel by Brevet*, for gallant conduct in the Battle of the Wilderness; to date from May 6th 1864. To be *Colonel by Brevet*, for gallant conduct in the Battles in front of Petersburg, Va., and in the pursuit and capture of the Army of Northern Virginia, in the Spring Campaign of 1865; to date from April 9th 1865.

Major *Frederick T. Dent*, 4th U. S. Infantry, Brigadier General Volunteers formerly Lieut Colonel & A. D. C. and Bvt. Colonel Vols. To be *Lieutenant Colonel by Brevet*, for gallant conduct in the Battle of the Wilderness; to date from May 6th 1864. To be *Colonel by Brevet*, for gallant conduct in the Battles in front of Petersburg, Va., and in the pursuit and capture of the Army of Northern Virginia, in the Spring Campaign of 1865; to date from April 9th 1865.

Captain *Horace Porter*, Ordnance Department U. S. A., Lieut Colonel & A. D. C. and Brevet Colonel Volunteers. To be *Major by Brevet*, for gallant conduct in the Battle of the Wilderness; to date from May 6th 1864. To be *Lieutenant Colonel by Brevet*, for gallant conduct in the Seige of Richmond, and especially in the storming of New Market Heights; to date from August 16th 1864. To be *Colonel by Brevet*, for gallant conduct in the Battles in front of Petersburg and in the pursuit and capture of the Army of Northern Virginia, in the Spring Campaign of 1865; to date from April 9th 1865.

These Officers served with distinguished zeal and ability in the Campaign of 1864 and 1865 against Richmond, from and including the Battle of the Wilderness to and including the surrender of the Rebel Army of Northern Virginia.

Brevet Brigadier General C. B. Comstock was not present at the final surrender of General Lee, but was at the time in the discharge of equally important duties, under General Canby, in the Seige and assaults of the defenses of Mobile

They have all been Brevetted in the Volunteer service but merit and deserve, for their long and valuable services, promotion in the Regular Army. I have no doubt it was the fault of my wording of my previous recommendation that they were brevetted in the Volunteer instead of the Regular service. General Comstocks Brevet was supposed to be in the Regular Army until after his confirmation was announced.

Lieut. Colonel *Seth Williams*, Asst. Adjt. General, U. S. A., Brigadier General and Bvt. Maj. General Volunteers To be *Colonel by Brevet*, for gallant conduct in the Battle of Gettysburg; to date from July 3d 1863. To be *Brigadier General by Brevet*, for gallant and meritorious services from and including the Battle of the Wilderness to and including the Battles in front of Petersburg, Va.; to date July 1st 1864.

> Very respectfully
> Your Obt. Svt.
> U. S. GRANT
> Lieut. Gen. U. S. A.

LS, DNA, RG 94, ACP, G280 CB 1865. *O.R.*, I, xlvi, part 3, 1257–58.

To Maj. Gen. John A. Dix

(Cipher)   June 6th *1865* [2:40 P.M.]
MAJ. GEN. DIX, ~~W~~NEW YORK,

Have John Mitshel,[1] formerly Editor of the Richmond Examiner, arrested and sent to Fort Monroe, Va. for confinement and trial. Make the arrangements for his immediate shipment before arrest and give this matter in charge of a discreet officer who will not let it get out that the arrest is to be made until he has his man.

> U. S. GRANT
> Lt. Gn.

ALS (telegram sent), DNA, RG 107, Telegrams Collected (Bound); telegram sent, *ibid.*; copies, *ibid.*, RG 108, Letters Sent; *ibid.*, RG 109, Union Provost Marshals' File of Papers Relating to Individual Civilians; *ibid.*, RG 393, Dept. of the East, Hd. Qrs., Letters Received; DLC-USG, V, 46, 109. *O.R.*, II, viii, 641. On June 14, 1865, Maj. Gen. John A. Dix wrote to USG. "I have the honor to report that the steamer Henry Burden has left the Battery with John Mitchell in custody of a commissioned officer, with instructions to deliver him to the Commanding Officer of Fort Monroe." ALS, DNA, RG 108, Letters Received. See *O.R.*, II, viii, 653, 725, 728, 775, 782.

On June 15, Dix wrote to USG. "*Unofficial,* . . . I wrote to you yesterday advising you that John Mitchell had just left for Fort Monroe. The arrest was made a few days later than I expected; but I could not, with the aid of the best detective I have ever had, find where he lodged. I was, therefore, obliged to take

him at the office of the Daily News at midday.—The Henry Burden had her
steam up, a carriage was in readiness at the door of the News office, and in 20
minutes after the officer entered, the steamer left the dock. The arrest has given
very general satisfaction. Only a few personal friends complain of it." ALS, NHi.

At 11:30 A.M., USG telegraphed to the commanding officer, Fort Monroe.
"John Mitchel, formerly ~~of the~~ Editor of the Richmond Examiner, is on his way
to Ft. Monroe as a prisoner. Keep him confined in a cell until further orders."
ALS (telegram sent), DNA, RG 107, Telegrams Collected (Bound); telegram
sent, *ibid.*; copies, *ibid.*, RG 108, Letters Sent; DLC-USG, V, 46, 109.

1. Irish Nationalist John Mitchel, born in Ireland in 1815, advocated rebellion against Great Britain. Convicted of treason in 1848 and sentenced to
fourteen years transportation, he escaped to the U.S. in 1853. He edited pro-
slavery newspapers in N. Y. and Tenn. before the Civil War; in 1862, he became editor of the *Richmond Enquirer*, and, in 1864, the *Richmond Examiner*.
In 1865, he moved to New York City, edited the *Daily News*, and maintained
his strong defense of the South. His imprisonment at Fort Monroe ended on
Oct. 30. See William Dillon, *Life of John Mitchel* (London, 1888), II, 213–26.

To Maj. Gen. John Pope

(Cipher)   Washington June 6th *1865* [*11:30* A.M.]
MAJ. GEN. POPE, ST. LOUIS MO.

Will you require more Cavalry after distributing the Cavalry
horses in your command to dismounted men? Two brigades are
under orders for the West but the roads are now so much used that
it may be several days before they start.

U. S. GRANT
Lt. Gn

ALS (telegram sent), DNA, RG 107, Telegrams Collected (Bound); telegram
sent, *ibid.*; telegram received, *ibid.*, Telegrams Collected (Unbound). *O.R.*, I,
xlviii, part 2, 793. On June 6, 1865, 4:35 P.M., Maj. Gen. John Pope telegraphed to USG. "I think one brigade more will answer the purpose in this
Division—One of the brigades you allude to as being under orders for the west
will be enough—Nearly all the troops now in Mississippi [*Missouri*] are mustered
out by late orders—We shall require very few in the state for the future, probably none at all by October first" Telegram received (at 6:20 P.M.), DNA,
RG 107, Telegrams Collected (Bound); (at 6:30 P.M.) *ibid.*, RG 108, Telegrams Received; copies, *ibid.*, RG 393, Military Div. of the Mo., Telegrams Sent;
DLC-USG, V, 54. *O.R.*, I, xlviii, part 2, 793.

Also on June 6, Pope telegraphed to USG. "Does the Amnesty proclamation
of the twenty ninth (29) of May change or modify special order two hundred
& fifteen (215) Par nine (9) Head Qrs of the Army   There are hundreds of

men constantly arriving here from the late rebel armies who expect to avail themselves of order two hundred fifteen (215) but who appear to be excepted by the tenth (10) Article of the Amnesty proclamation of May twenty ninth (29) An immediate decision of this question is very necessary as we are daily pressed by this class of men & it is not known exactly what to do—" Telegram received (at 5:20 P.M.), DNA, RG 107, Telegrams Collected (Bound); (at 4:35 P.M.) *ibid.*, RG 108, Telegrams Received; copies, *ibid.*, RG 393, Military Div. of the Mo., Telegrams Sent; DLC-USG, V, 54. *O.R.*, I, xlviii, part 2, 793. At 8:00 P.M., USG telegraphed to Pope. "Returning prisoners to be entitled to remain in any of the loyal States, Missouri for instance, must become loyal men; that is take the last oath presribed." ALS (telegram sent), DNA, RG 107, Telegrams Collected (Bound); telegram sent, *ibid.*; telegram received (on June 7), *ibid.*, RG 393, Dept. of the Mo., Telegrams Received. *O.R.*, I, xlviii, part 2, 793.

To Maj. Gen. Godfrey Weitzel

Washington June 6th/65 [*3:35* P.M.]

MAJ. GEN. WEITZEL, CITY POINT VA,

No Hospital ship can be furnished your command. It is not supposed that you will start with sick men and as you put in at Mobile any that become sick after starting can be left there.

U. S. GRANT
Lt. Gen.

ALS (telegram sent), DNA, RG 107, Telegrams Collected (Bound); telegram sent, *ibid.*; telegram received, *ibid.*, Telegrams Collected (Unbound); *ibid.*, RG 393, 25th Army Corps, Telegrams Received. *O.R.*, I, xlvi, part 3, 1261. On June 7, 1865, Maj. Gen. Godfrey Weitzel, Fort Monroe, telegraphed to USG. "Your dispatch concerning hospital boats received I go to sea at 12 m today" Telegram received (at 10:30 A.M.), DNA, RG 107, Telegrams Collected (Bound); (at 10:15 A.M.) *ibid.*, RG 108, Telegrams Received; copy, DLC-USG, V, 54. *O.R.*, I, xlvi, part 3, 1262.

On June 3, Weitzel, "Near City Point," had telegraphed to Brig. Gen. John A. Rawlins. "The Transports have been arriving very slowly this week and I need one more & one Hospital boat to finish the transportation of my two infantry divisions, artillery wagons and animals which is the portion of the command I intend to follow. There will then be left three thousand (3000) cavalry and three thousand (3000) infantry for which Col. Wise says he has ordered transportation from NewYork—If the two (2) vessels above mentioned arrive tomorrow I will get off on Monday—" Telegram received (at 5:00 P.M.), DNA, RG 107, Telegrams Collected (Bound); *ibid.*, Telegrams Collected (Unbound); (at 4:40 P.M.) *ibid.*, RG 108, Telegrams Received; copy, DLC-USG, V, 54. *O.R.*, I, xlvi, part 3, 1251. On June 4, Weitzel telegraphed to Rawlins. "I think a hospital Ship of the utmost importance on this expedition to provide for the sick & to carry the Med Stores The QM Genl does not wish to furnish one The Surg Genl has none Shall I go without a Hospl & take my Med Stores as freight" Telegram sent, DNA, RG 94, War Records Office, Army of the Potomac; telegram received (at 12:30 P.M.), *ibid.*, RG 107, Telegrams Collected (Bound); *ibid.*, RG 108, Telegrams Received. *O.R.*, I, xlvi, part 3, 1253.

On June 6, Weitzel, Norfolk, telegraphed to Rawlins. "I have heard nothing as yet in answer to my despatch about the hospital boat. I should like to have it settled before I go to sea. Will you please answer to Fort Monroe before 9 O'clock tomorrow morning" ALS (telegram sent), DNA, RG 107, Telegrams Collected (Unbound); telegram received, *ibid.*; (at 6:30 P.M.) *ibid.*, Telegrams Collected (Bound); (at 5:30 P.M.) *ibid.*, RG 108, Telegrams Received. *O.R.*, I, xlvi, part 3, 1260. Maj. George K. Leet endorsed the telegram received, probably to Rawlins. "Can you answer Gen. Weitzel? On Sunday The. Surg. General was requested to furnish a Hospital Boat for Gen. Ws expedition if one was available but I do not know that any reply was made by him" AES, DNA, RG 108, Telegrams Received. At 10:20 P.M., Rawlins telegraphed to Weitzel. "Your dispatch about Hospital Steamer was referred to the Surgeon General, but it is thought you will not need one as you are taking no sick with you. Transportation for Medical supplies and sufficient accommodation for those who may fall sick enroute, can be had on the transports conveying the troops and they can be transferred to hospitals where your expedition is to touch, near Mobile. You will therefore go forward without a hospital Steamer unless you receive other orders" Telegrams sent (2), *ibid.*, RG 107, Telegrams Collected (Bound); copies, *ibid.*, RG 108, Letters Sent; DLC-USG, V, 46, 109. *O.R.*, I, xlvi, part 3, 1261.

On June 3, Bvt. Maj. Gen. Montgomery C. Meigs had written to USG. "General Weitzell has applied to this office for a Hospital Ship to accompany his command—These vessels are controlled by the Medical Department. The Quartermasters Department, under existing orders, provides the Ship, pays crew & coal & owners, but has no control over the movements of the transport. I have advised the Surgeon General of Gen Weitzels wishes." ALS, DNA, RG 92, Consolidated Correspondence, Tex. Expedition. On June 9, Rawlins endorsed the letter. "Respectfully returned to the Quarter Master General. Gen. Weitzel was directed on the 6th inst. to proceed without at Hospital Steamer" ES, *ibid.*

On June 7, Meigs wrote to USG. "The Weitzel fleet is ordered to rendezvous in Mobile Bay. It may have some difficulty in filling up with fresh water which I understand it cannot approach within 25 miles. If the vessels arriving at Mobile can be telegraphed to repair to the mouth of the Mississippi and there await the collection of the whole fleet, it will be easier to supply all deficiencies of Coal and Water than if they were remain at Mobile. Unless there are controlling reasons to the contrary I suggest that this be done. As there is no Enemy to resist landing, should not the vessels proceed with all speed to their ultimate destination and avoid confinement of men on shipboard in this hot season on the Southern coast? This would shorten the voyage and diminish also the cost of the vessels by discharging them sooner." LS, *ibid.*, RG 108, Letters Received. *O.R.*, I, xlviii, part 2, 802–3.

On June 25, Bvt. Brig. Gen. Charles S. Russell, Fort Monroe and Newport News, twice telegraphed to Bvt. Col. Theodore S. Bowers. "In pursuance to instructions from Maj Gen Weitzel I have the honor to report that the last of the 25th A. C. will leave on monday the twenty sixth inst for Texas." "In accordance with instructions recd from Maj Genl Weitzel I will sail from this port on the twenty sixth inst with the balance of the 25th A. C." Telegrams received (the first at 10:35 A.M., the second at 9:25 P.M.), DNA, RG 107, Telegrams Collected (Bound); *ibid.*, RG 108, Telegrams Received; copies, DLC-USG, V, 54. The first is printed in *O.R.*, I, xlvi, part 3, 1295.

To Brig. Gen. John A. Rawlins

———

Chicago June 10th 1865 11 30 P M.

Gen J. A Rawlins
Chf of Staff
Please show the following despatch to the Secretary of War and if approved forward [it.]
Gen P. H. Sheridan
New Orleans

If the Rebels moved t[hei]r artillery & public property to Matamoras after the embargo, demand its return to you. If the demand is not complied with go and take it and all those engaged in its transfer

U. S. Grant
Lieut Genl

Telegrams received (2—on June 12, 1865, 1:00 A.M.), DNA, RG 107, Telegrams Collected (Bound); copies, *ibid.*, RG 108, Letters Sent; DLC-USG, V, 46, 109; USG 3. *O.R.*, I, xlviii, part 2, 840. See telegram to Maj. Gen. Philip H. Sheridan, June 15, 1865.

To Maj. Gen. John A. Logan

———

Chicago, Ills, June 12th 1865 [*noon*]

Maj. Gen'l Jno. A. Logan
Com'd'g Army of the Tennessee
Louisville, Kentucky.
As soon as the troops are paid, send one Brigade of Infantry to Gen'l Pope, at St. Louis, and one Division of not less than 5000

men to Gen'l Reynolds at Little Rock Arkansas. They will go
without transportation. To facilitate their going, select the Brigade
and Division at once and have them paid first.

U. S. GRANT

Lieut: Gen'l

Telegram, copies, DLC-USG, V, 46, 109; DNA, RG 108, Letters Sent. *O.R.*, I,
xlix, part 2, 987. On June 26, 1865, Maj. Gen. John A. Logan telegraphed to
Bvt. Col. Theodore S. Bowers. "I have the honor to report that the second (2d)
Division fifteenth (15) Army Corps has been sent to Arkansas & the second
(2d) brigade fourth (4) Div seventeenth (17) Army Corps to Saint Louis Mo
as directed in geGen Grants telegram of the twelfth inst" Telegram received
(on June 27, 1:00 A.M.), DNA, RG 107, Telegrams Collected (Bound); *ibid.*,
RG 108, Telegrams Received; copy, DLC-USG, V, 54. *O.R.*, I, xlix, part 2, 1037.
On July 29, 11:30 A.M., Bowers telegraphed to USG. "Gen. Reynolds, Com'd'g
Department of Arkansas, recommends the muster out of the Division of the 15th
Corps, sent him by General Logan. It numbers about Six thousand. He has no
use for it. Will have thirteen thousand without it." ALS (telegram sent), DNA,
RG 107, Telegrams Collected (Bound); telegram sent, *ibid.*; copies, *ibid.*, RG
108, Letters Sent; DLC-USG, V, 46, 109. *O.R.*, I, xlviii, part 2, 1131. On the
same day, USG, Boston, telegraphed to Bowers. "Give Gen. Reynolds, Com-
mand'g. Dept. of Arkansas, orders to muster out the Division he recommends."
Telegram received (on July 30, 11:00 A.M.), DNA, RG 94, Vol. Service Div.,
Letters Received, W2191 (VS) 1865; *ibid.*, RG 107, Telegrams Collected
(Bound); copies, *ibid.*, RG 108, Letters Sent; DLC-USG, V, 46, 54, 109. *O.R.*,
I, xlviii, part 2, 1132.

On June 9, Bvt. Brig. Gen. Edward D. Townsend, AGO, had written to
Brig. Gen. John A. Rawlins. "I am informed that the two Brigades of Cavalry
ordered to be sent to Louisville, Ky., to report to Gen. Logan, by S. O. 276, from
Hqrs. of the Army of June 3d 1865, are still here awaiting railroad transportation. Please do me the favor to inform me if it was the intention of the Lieut
General that this command should march to Louisville, sending their dismounted
men by rail or that the entire command, including horses, baggage &c., should
be sent by rail-road." LS, DNA, RG 94, Letters Received, 612A 1865. On the
same day, Rawlins endorsed this letter. "It was the intention of the Lieut. General that the entire command, Horses &c., should go by railroad. The destination however of one of the Brigades will be changed to St Louis to report to
Gen Pope." ES, *ibid.* See *O.R.*, I, xlvi, part 3, 1268–69, 1270.

On June 16, USG wrote to Secretary of War Edwin M. Stanton. "I would
respectfully recommend the Muster-out of the 110–122 & 126 regiments of
Ohio Volunteers. The times of all these regiments expire between the 1st & 10th
of October. These regiments are now here and about starting I presume for
Louisville. I would ask therefore that the order be sent to them at once so that
they may go immediately to their state rendesvous instead of to Louisville." ALS,
DNA, RG 94, Vol. Service Div., Letters Received, A1079 (VS) 1865.

To Maj. Gen. John Pope

By Telegraph from Chicago, 2.30 P. M. [*June 12*] *1865.*
To MAJ GEN POPE
I have ordered a Brigade of troops to St Louis and five thousand
Infantry to Arkansas to enable you to carry out orders for muster-
ing out troops. Will you still require Cavalry beyond what been
sent to you?

U. S. GRANT
Lt. Gen

Telegram received, DNA, RG 107, Telegrams Collected (Unbound); copies,
ibid., RG 108, Letters Sent; *ibid.*, RG 393, Military Div. of the Mo., Telegrams
Received; DLC-USG, V, 46, 109. *O.R.*, I, xlviii, part 2, 860. On June 12, 1865,
5:30 P.M., Maj. Gen. John Pope, St. Louis, telegraphed to USG. "The difficulty about the troops sent here consists in the fact that the large part of the
cavalry come without horses and many of them go out of Service in July and
August. The order requires the immediate muster out both of dismounted
cavalry and of cavalry whose term of service expires by Sept. 30th The discharge of men in Mich. Brig. only leaves two regiments the whole Brig only
brought six hundred horses, two hundred of these are unservicable. I got from
Cavalry Bureau 900 horses. the brigade needed 2300. I am discharging all
troops coming under orders for discharge except those actually in campaign on
the Plains; these could not now be replaced as they are on the march hundreds of
miles beyond the settlements—I hope Indian troubles will be settled by September
1st when all except necessary guards along overland routes and at forts in the
Indian Country can be discharged—I think if the brigade which you have ordered
here if it comes with full number of horses will be enough. The force sent to
Ark is enough to enable me to complete discharge There are no more horses
here and as I understand no expectation of any—1200 men of mich brig. have
not yet reached here, detained somewhere East—Will write you fully on this
subject" Telegram received (at Chicago, June 13), DNA, RG 108, Telegrams
Received; copies (marked as sent at 6:35 P.M.), *ibid.*, RG 393, Military Div.
of the Mo., Telegrams Sent; DLC-USG, V, 54. *O.R.*, I, xlviii, part 2, 860.

To Maj. Gen. John Pope

(Cipher)   Washington June 15th 1865 [6:30 P.M.]
MAJ. GN. POPE, ST. LOUIS MO.

Pursue the course recommended by you towards the Indians until you receive other orders. I approve of all you recommended and presume no change will be made of that policy.

U. S. GRANT
Lt. Gn.

ALS (telegram sent), DNA, RG 107, Telegrams Collected (Bound); telegram sent, *ibid.*; telegram received (on June 16), *ibid.*, Telegrams Collected (Unbound). *O.R.*, I, xlviii, part 2, 892. On June 14, 1865, Maj. Gen. John Pope wrote to USG at length about Indian affairs. LS, DNA, RG 75, Bureau of Indian Affairs, Central Office, Letters Received, Miscellaneous. *O.R.*, I, xlviii, part 2, 879–82. On May 29, Secretary of the Interior James Harlan had written to Secretary of War Edwin M. Stanton concerning lack of cooperation between civil and military authorities in Indian affairs. LS, DNA, RG 107, Letters Received from Bureaus. *O.R.*, I, xlviii, part 2, 661. On May 31, Asst. Secretary of War Charles A. Dana endorsed this letter. "Respectfully referred to Lieutenant General Grant" AES, DNA, RG 107, Letters Received from Bureaus. On June 24, USG endorsed this letter. "Respectfully returned to the Secretary of War and attention invited to the enclosed communication and its enclosures from Major General John Pope, comdg. Military Division of the Mo., to whom copies of these papers were referred for remarks; and also to copy of my dispatch to him of date June 15 1865.—The views of Gen Pope so far as they relate to Indian affairs meet with my approval." ES, *ibid.* On June 28, Stanton wrote to Harlan forwarding Pope's letter and a copy of USG's instructions to Pope. LS, *ibid.*, RG 75, Bureau of Indian Affairs, Central Office, Letters Received, Miscellaneous.

On May 26, 11:50 A.M., Pope telegraphed to USG. "Can you not send me Br Genl W. L Elliott U S V to command in Minnesota I fear there is not activity enough among the troops in that state Elliott is I think with Thomas though I am not sure" Telegram received (at 1:25 P.M.), *ibid.*, RG 107, Telegrams Collected (Bound); *ibid.*, RG 108, Telegrams Received; copies, *ibid.*, RG 393, Military Div. of the Mo., Telegrams Sent; DLC-USG, V, 54. *O.R.*, I, xlviii, part 2, 609. On June 2, 12:40 P.M., Pope telegraphed to USG. "Will you please inform me if Brig Genl W L Elliott can be sent here to Command in Minnesota? I have written you fully on the subject by mail today." Telegram received (at 3:10 P.M.), DNA, RG 107, Telegrams Collected (Bound); *ibid.*, RG 108, Telegrams Received; copies, *ibid.*, RG 393, Military Div. of the Mo., Telegrams Sent; DLC-USG, V, 54. *O.R.*, I, xlviii, part 2, 732. On the same day, Pope wrote to USG. "I have the honor to transmit enclosed, copy of a letter from Brig. Genl H. H. Sibley. Comdg: Dist of Minnesota to Major General Curtis Comd'g: Department of the Northwest and forwarded to me by the latter officer without comment—It seems difficult to know what reply to make to such communications—They exhibit a panic which I hardly know how to deal with except by asking you to send me an Officer to command in Minnesota who is not subject to such uneasiness—I telegraphed you for Brig: General W. L Elliott for that service, but any active efficient Officer, suitable for such a command will be satisfactory—General Sibley has in Minnesota. nineteen Companies of Cavalry, five companies of Infantry, and one of Artillery, numbering present for duty, according to his last Return Two thousand four hundred and ninety men—of this force one thousand eight hundred and sixty nine are Cavalry—The nearest hostile Sioux Indians in any considerable force are more than three hundred miles distant from the extreme frontier settlements of Minnesota—Small predatory parties come down towards the settlements, to steal horses and commit other hostile acts, but they ought, with such a force, always to be intercepted and cut off—The Chippewas along the upper Mississippi and Lake Superior have always been friendly and are not numerous—Such a force as this in Minnesota is unheard of in all previous time—I cannot believe that it is not abundantly sufficient, if properly posted and handled—There are many other reasons why troops are demanded on the frontier, besides fear of Indians—At all events I cannot consider it judicious to leave an Officer in command in Minnesota, who is so evidently 'stampeded,' or appears to be, with so large a force at his command.—His very apprehension will create among the people all the consequences of an actual Indian Invasion on a scale unknown to our history.—I trust you will read General Sibley' letter as it seems to me to indicate a state of mind, not encouraging to any hope of peace and quiet in Minnesota" LS, DNA, RG 108, Letters Received. *O.R.*, I, xlviii, part 2, 731–32. The enclosure is *ibid.*, p. 590. See *ibid.*, p. 909.

On May 25, Governor Stephen Miller of Minn. wrote to Stanton asking for additional troops to guard against Indians. ALS, DNA, RG 94, Letters Received, 1090M 1865. On June 10, USG endorsed this letter. "All the troops asked for by Gen. Pope have been ordered to him. I cannot at present recommend that exceptions be made in favor of the immediate muster-out of Minnesota troops, but when their station leaves them equally available with other troops for duty on the Minnesota frontier, they will be ordered there." ES, *ibid.*

On June 16, 11:20 A.M., Pope telegraphed to USG. "I earnestly request that Genl Dodge may not be removed from this command, at least until the autumn, He is thoroughly acquainted with Indian affairs on the plains, has organized the various expeditions now moving in several directions against the Indians and is so thoroughly posted on all matters relating to the troubles on the plains and in Utah that his removal for the present would be likely to throw things into confusion and be very injurious to the public interests" Telegram received (at 1:30 P.M.), *ibid.*, RG 107, Telegrams Collected (Bound); *ibid.*, RG 108, Telegrams Received; copies, *ibid.*, RG 393, Military Div. of the Mo., Telegrams Sent; DLC-USG, V, 54. *O.R.*, I, xlviii, part 2, 904–5.

To Maj. Gen. John Pope

Washington June 15th *1865* [6:30 P.M.]

MAJ. GN. POPE, ST. LOUIS MO.

I have ordered to Arkansas 5000 Infantry and to St. Louis a Brigade of Infantry and a Brigade of Cavalry to enable you to carry out orders for mustering out troops. If the troops raised from the rebel prisoners answer the purpose they may be retained.[1] New Mexico will be added to your command and I expect some additional forces will be necessary there.

U. S. GRANT
Lt. Gen.

ALS (telegram sent), DNA, RG 107, Telegrams Collected (Bound); telegram sent, *ibid.*; telegram received (on June 16, 1865, 6:30 A.M.), *ibid.*, Telegrams Collected (Unbound). *O.R.*, I, xlviii, part 2, 892. On June 15, 11:30 A.M., USG telegraphed to Maj. Gen. John Pope. "I have ordered 1000 Cavalry horses to be sent to Arkansas. You may have the 14th Kansas Cavalry remounted with these horses." ALS (telegram sent—misdated June 16), DNA, RG 107, Telegrams Collected (Bound); telegram sent (dated June 15), *ibid.*; telegram received (on June 15, 1:40 P.M.), *ibid.*, Telegrams Collected (Unbound); copies (dated June 16), *ibid.*, RG 108, Letters Sent; (dated June 15) *ibid.*, RG 393, Military Div. of the Mo., Telegrams Received; DLC-USG, V, 46, 109. On June 21, 2:40 P.M., USG telegraphed to Pope. "Retain the 14th Kansas Cavalry in service and mount it from the horses now enroute for Little Rock." ALS (telegram sent), DNA, RG 107, Telegrams Collected (Bound); telegram sent, *ibid.*; telegram received (on June 22, 9:00 A.M.), *ibid.*, Telegrams Collected (Unbound). *O.R.*, I, xlviii, part 2, 959. On June 28, 11:10 A.M., Pope telegraphed to USG. "The fourteenth regt. Kansas Cavalry brevet Brig Genl C W. Blairs regiment has been mustered out of service under instructions to Genl Reynolds from the adjt Gen U. S. A dated June fifth (5) The muster out was completed and the men enroute to their homes before receipt of your telegram of June twenty second (22d) directing its retention in the service" Telegram received (at 12:05 P.M.), DNA, RG 107, Telegrams Collected (Bound); *ibid.*, RG 108, Telegrams Received; copies, *ibid.*, RG 393, Military Div. of the Mo., Telegrams Sent; DLC-USG, V, 54. *O.R.*, I, xlviii, part 2, 1019. On July 3, Bvt. Brig. Gen. Charles W. Blair, St. Louis, telegraphed to USG. "Notwithstanding your order Genl Reynolds has mustered the 14th Kas Cavalry. What is to be done" Telegram received (at 4:50 P.M.), DNA, RG 107, Telegrams Collected (Bound); *ibid.*, RG 108, Telegrams Received; copy, DLC-USG, V, 54. On July 5, 6:30 P.M., USG telegraphed to Blair. "The 14th Kansas was mustered out before receipt of my order. It cannot be changed now." ALS (telegram sent), DNA, RG 107, Telegrams Collected (Bound); telegram sent, *ibid.*; copies (dated July 6), *ibid.*, RG 108, Letters Sent; DLC-USG, V, 46, 109. On July 7, Blair, Leavenworth, Kan., telegraphed to USG. "Your order by telegraph to retain the fourteenth (14) Kansas Cavalry was sent on the twenty first 21 of June on the third (3) of July twelve 12 days after it was started from Ft Gibson to this state for muster this looks singular the regiment is not yet mustered cannot be under General Order till it arrives an order to Gen Pope or Gen Dodge to stop the muster out & retain will yet answer the purpose revoking the preliminary steps already taken will you make the order my address at Fort Scott Kansas—" Telegram received (at 1:25 P.M.), DNA, RG 107, Telegrams Collected (Bound); *ibid.*, RG 108, Telegrams Received; copy, DLC-USG, V, 54.

On June 15, Brig. Gen. John A. Rawlins wrote to Bvt. Maj. Gen. Montgomery C. Meigs. "Please send one thousand cavalry horses from depots here to Little Rock, Arkansas, via Cairo, Illinois, to be issued under the directions of the Command'g General of the Department of Arkansas." LS, DNA, RG 92, Letters Received. On June 16, Rawlins wrote to Meigs. "In addition to the 1000 cavalry horses you were directed to send to Little Rock, Arkansas, via Cairo, Illinois, to issue under the direction of the Commanding Officer of the Department of Arkansas, please send 500 more to same destination, by same route and for same purpose." LS, *ibid.* Variant text ("via Chicago") in *O.R.*, I, xlviii, part 2, 898. See *ibid.*

1. On June 2, USG wrote to Secretary of War Edwin M. Stanton. "In addition to all orders heretofore issued for the Muster out of troops I would suggest that orders be given for the muster out of all regiments raised from prisoners of War, when their services can be spared, and as soon as they can be relieved by other troops where they can not be dispensed with at once." ALS, DNA, RG 94, Vol. Service Div., Letters Received, A1076 (VS) 1865. On June 3, Pope wrote to Bvt. Col. Theodore S. Bowers. "I have the honor to acknowledge the receipt of a dispatch from the Adjutant General of the Army directing that the regiments recruited from Rebel Prisoners and deserters be mustered out of service as soon as their places can be supplied by other troops. There are in this Division, the 1st, 2d, 3d, 4th, 5th, and four companies of the 6th, U S Vols, thus recruited. They are stationed along the Overland Routes across the Plains and at remote stations in the Indian Country, from St. Paul to the Rocky Mountains. I can not now replace them as I have no Infantry Regiments in this Division which can be spared from their present stations. The muster out of troops whose terms expire by September 30th takes from the Department of Missouri alone 8854. men, among these, five regiments now on the Plains. General Reynolds reports in detail the forces he has in Department of Arkansas, and the force he needs. Since his report General Sheridan has taken from his command, a Division of 5.000 men to garrison Shreveport, Louisiana. I transmit, enclosed, a copy of General Reynolds' report, from which it will be seen precisely how he stands in Arkansas. Of course, as time passes, the number of troops in Missouri and Arkansas can be gradually reduced. I trust that in Missouri, we will be able, in a few weeks, to get along with four or five regiments only, and by Autumn, with less still. If it is desired to muster out all these rebel regiments now on the Plains and at remote stations in the Indian Country, other regiments should be sent as soon as possible to replace them as it will take the whole summer to reach and relieve them. I am using all the troops I can get on the Plains to put down Indian Hostilities, and suppress the bands of lawless robbers and thieves which are more and more every day, begining to infest the

frontier and plunder as far as they can, trains and emigrants. We will have, for some time, much danger from this source on the Plains. The disloyal and vagrant elements set loose by the termination of the War are thronging toward the mining regions of Colorado, Idaho and Montana, and wherever they find a chance, they attack and plunder trains and mail coaches. All these outrages are, of course, laid at the door of the Indians who are themselves, sufficiently troublesome. I respectfully invite the attention of the General-in-Chief to my letters to him and previously to the Secretary of War on the subject of Indian Affairs. We need some decision of the Government as to a policy toward Indians. By throwing troops enough on to the Plains, the Indians can in a short time, be exterminated, but such cannot be the purpose of the Government. If it could be understood what policy toward Indians was determined on by the Government, we should better understand what course to pursue in the present situation of Indian troubles. The continued rush of emigration to the mines, making highways through the entire Indian Country, and attended with outrages upon the Indians which are never heard of except in acts of retaliation, makes it pretty certain that Indian hostilities will continue until the Indians are exterminated, or a more humane policy adopted such as I have several times suggested within the past three years. I hope that the General-in-Chief will find time soon to consider this question, as his long experience on the frontier, and his thorough acquaintance with the condition of the Indian Tribes, and the defects and abuses of the present Indian System, enable him to decide these questions with far better understanding of them than any other official in Washington." LS, *ibid.*, RG 108, Letters Received. *O.R.*, I, xlviii, part 2, 751–52. The enclosure is *ibid.*, p. 699.

To Maj. Gen. Philip H. Sheridan

(Cipher)   June 15th *1865* [*1:30* P.M.]

MAJ. GEN. SHERIDAN, NEW ORLEANS LA,

Demand of the commander of French forces at Matamoras the delivery to an officer of the Government of the United States the return of all Arms and other munitions of War taken to Matamoras by the rebels or obtained from them since the date of the surrender of Kirby Smith. You need not proceed to hostilities to obtain them but report the reply received for further instructions.

U. S. GRANT
Lt. Gn.

ALS (telegram sent), DNA, RG 107, Telegrams Collected (Bound); telegram sent, *ibid.*; copies, *ibid.*, RG 108, Letters Sent; DLC-USG, V, 46, 109. *O.R.*, I, xlviii, part 2, 889. See telegram to Brig. Gen. John A. Rawlins, June 10, 1865. On June 16, 1865, 3:00 P.M., Maj. Gen. Philip H. Sheridan telegraphed to

USG. "Your despatch of 3 P M June 15th has been received and will be attended to at once—I have directed Genl Steele to make a report and to hold no intercourse with the authorities at Matamoras." Telegram received (on June 17, 6:00 P.M.), DNA, RG 107, Telegrams Collected (Bound); copies (2), DLC-Philip H. Sheridan. *O.R.*, I, xlviii, part 2, 897. On July 7, Sheridan wrote to Bvt. Col. Theodore S. Bowers. "I have the honor to enclose herewith for the information of the Lieut Gen.l Comd.g copies of Major Genl Steeles demand upon the Comd.g Genl of the Imperial forces at Matamoras for 'all the artillery arms and munitions of war taken from T[e]xas to Matamoras' &c and the reply of Gen.l Mejia to said communication. A demand has also been made for all cotton. means of transportation &c which has been removed from Texas since the first surrender but no reply has yet been received." LS, DNA, RG 108, Letters Received. The enclosures are in *O.R.*, I, xlviii, part 2, 1037–38. See telegram to Maj. Gen. Philip H. Sheridan, July 1, 1865.

On June 9, Sheridan telegraphed to USG. "The following is the latest information that I have from the Rio Grande. 'Hd Qrs United States Forces Brownsville Texas May 20th Col J. S. Crosby A A Genl Dept Gulf—I have the honor to report that I moved on this place from Brazos St Iago the evening of the 2 28th inst and arrived here at daylight this morning—The Enemy evacuated the place having first delivered six pieces of Artillery, Battery wagons, forage and transportation wagons to the Mexican commander at Matamoras and Sent a large amount of cotton across the Rio Grande—We captured 500 bales of cotton and several hundred ~~bales~~ head of cattle with a few mules and horses—The Rebel forces on the Rio Grande are greatly demoralized and nearly broken up by desertion—The reports of the confinement of Genl Slaughter by his own men and subsequent release by paying them about twenty thousand Dollars is confirmed—I am informed that the Enemy is crossing cotton in considerable amounts above on the Rio Grande—I am Col &c (Signed) E. B. Brown Br Gen Vols" Telegram received (on June 10, 10:30 P.M.), DNA, RG 107, Telegrams Collected (Bound); *ibid.*, RG 108, Telegrams Received; copies, DLC-USG, V, 54; (2) DLC-Philip H. Sheridan; USG 3. Printed with the enclosure dated May 30 in *O.R.*, I, xlviii, part 2, 827–28. On June 15, Secretary of War Edwin M. Stanton wrote to USG. "I transmit herewith a copy of a letter received from the Department of State, with respect to a telegram addressed to you by Major General Sheridan on the 9th instant, which was referred to that Department. It is deemed expedient by this Department that your instructions to General Sheridan should conform to the views expressed by the Secretary of State." LS, DNA, RG 108, Letters Received. On June 12, Secretary of State William H. Seward had written to Stanton. "With reference to the telegram of the 9th instant, from Major General Sheridan to Lieutenant General Grant, which has been submitted to me, I am of the opinion that the restitution of the artillery and other public property clandestinely moved to Matamoras by the insurgents should be demanded by the proper United States commander of the French commander at that place. A similar application will be made by the Department to the French Minister here. It is not deemed advisable, however, to sanction the employment of force for the recovery of the property until the tenor of the answers to the communications referred to shall be Known here." LS, *ibid.*, RG 107, Letters Received from Bureaus.

On June 12, Sheridan telegraphed to Brig. Gen. John A. Rawlins. "The subject of transportation has given me great annoyance and been the cause of very great delay. Gen Merritt is off to Shreveport this morning and will be able to get off with his cavalry column for San Antonio in ten days—The 25th Army Corps is still enroute—Granger will get off to Galveston in day or two—I heard from Steele at Brazos Santiago—There is nothing practical in the surrender of the Texas troops of Kerby Smiths command. It looks more like a move than any thing else—Slaughter sold his artillery to the Imperialists—I have ordered Steele to make a report on the subject giving the date of the transfer—I also sent him verbal instructions to hold no intercourse with the authorities at Matamoras" Telegram received (on June 14, 12:40 P.M.), *ibid.*, RG 107, Telegrams Collected (Bound); *ibid.*, RG 108, Telegrams Received; copies, DLC-USG, V, 54; DLC-Philip H. Sheridan; USG 3. *O.R.*, I, xlviii, part 2, 858. On June 13, Sheridan telegraphed to Rawlins. "I respectfully forward the following views for the consideration of the Lieut General—I will have the following troops in Texas without the 4th A Corps, viz; Genl Merritts column of cavalry 4000 strong ordered from Shreveport to San Antonio, Gen Custars column 4000 strong ordered to Houston—Two Divisions of Grangers Corps (which after the 30th of September will number about 7000 strong)—Two divisions being under Steele on the Rio Grande and the other will be at Galveston & Houston—The 25th Army Corps numbers about 16000 and will be at Indianola Corpus Christi and Brownsville—The bulk of the corps will be at Brownsville and that vicinity—This will make a grand aggregate of 32000 men—To support a larger number of men in Texas will be very expensive and I think on due reflection that the order for the 4th Corps had better be countermanded unless our affairs are liable to become complicated with the Imperial Govt of Mexico—I do not know whether this may occur or not—My own opinion is and has been that Maximillian should leave that country and that his establishment there was a part of the rebellion—My doubt as to the intention of the Govt leads me to ask of the Lieut General the decision as to whether the 4th Corps will be sent or not—Please reply quickly as I desire to make a trip along the coast of Texas down to the Rio Grande, touching at Galveston. Indianola, Corpus Christi and other points on the coast—I shall have to remain here until I hear from you on account of the shipping of the 4th Army Corps" Telegram received (on June 14, 7:00 P.M.), DNA, RG 107, Telegrams Collected (Bound); *ibid.*, RG 108, Telegrams Received; copies, DLC-USG, V, 54; DLC-Philip H. Sheridan. *O.R.*, I, xlviii, part 2, 865–66. On June 16, 9:00 A.M., Rawlins telegraphed to Sheridan. "The 4th Army Corps is under orders for Texas, and the orders will not be changed." Telegrams sent (2), DNA, RG 107, Telegrams Collected (Bound); copies (dated June 15), *ibid.*, RG 108, Letters Sent; DLC-USG, V, 46, 109. Dated June 15 in *O.R.*, I, xlviii, part 2, 889.

On June 14, 11:30 P.M., Sheridan telegraphed to Rawlins. "I send you the following extract from a letter just received from Genl Steele—I cannot vouch for the ~~information~~ correctness of the information—'Hd Qrs United States Forces Brazos Santiago June 10th To GEN P. H. SHERIDAN Comdg Mil Div South West. (Extract) Genl The people of Texas Say that Walkers Division of rebels is in Mexico at Pedras Negras & that it is going to Sonora to join Doctor Gwinn—Yesterday I saw Doctor Cavado [*Cañedo*] a Secret Service man Sent here by Genl Canby—He goes to New Orleans today & can give you all the rumor & tell you what he Saw—When the rebels see the Presidents late proclamation I think they will declare for the Imperialists—A strong feeling of Sympathy between them has been manifested—The rebels would like to be Sure of living on the winning Side & if they could be pardoned for past offences I think they would join the Liberals believing that it is the popular Side in the United States   Very Respectfully Your Obedient Servant   signed Fredk Steele Maj Gen'"   Telegram received (on June 16, 5:00 p.m.), DNA, RG 107, Telegrams Collected (Bound); (at 11:00 p.m.) *ibid.*, RG 108, Telegrams Received; copies, DLC-USG, V, 54; DLC-Philip H. Sheridan; USG 3. *O.R.*, I, xlviii, part 2, 875–76.

On Aug. 14, Sheridan telegraphed to Rawlins. "Doctor A H Canelds [*Cañedo*] wrote me from Philadelphia July thirty first 31st   Please have him arrested and sent to me   He is without doubt a Franco-Mexico rebel spy. He was employed by Gen Canby, afterwards by myself with a man to watch him, and the foregoing character developed—" Telegram received (on Aug. 15, 1:30 p.m.), DNA, RG 107, Telegrams Collected (Bound); *ibid.*, RG 108, Telegrams Received; copies (variant text), *ibid.*, RG 94, Information File, Secret Service; DLC-USG, V, 54; DLC-Philip H. Sheridan. See *O.R.*, I, xlviii, part 2, 307–8, 414, 771.

To Edwin M. Stanton

Respectfully forwarded to the Secry of War.

In my opinion the officers and men paroled at Appomattox C. H. and since upon the same terms given to Lee, can not be tried for treason so long as they observe the terms of their parole. This is my understanding. Good faith as well as true policy dictates that we should observe the conditions of that convention. Bad faith on the part of the Governm't or a construction of that convention subjecting officers to trial for treason, would produce a feeling of insecurity in the minds of all paroled officers and men   If so disposed they might even regard such an infraction of terms, by the Government as an entire release from all obligation on their part.

I will state further that the terms granted by me met with the hearty approval of the President at the time, and of the country generally. The action of Judge Underwood[1] in Norfolk has already had an injurious effect, and I would ask that he be ordered to quash all indictments found against paroled prisoners of war, and to desist from further prosecution of them

U. S. Grant
Lieut. General

Hdqrs A U S, June 16. 65

ES, IHi. *O.R.*, I, xlvi, part 3, 1276. Written on a letter of June 13, 1865, from Robert E. Lee, Richmond, to USG. "Upon reading the Presidents proclamation of the 29th Ulto: I came to Richmond to ascertain what was proper or required of me to do; when I learned that with others, I was to be indicted for treason by the Grand Jury at Norfolk. I had supposed that the officers & men of the Army of N. Virga were by the terms of their Surrender protected by the U. S. Govt; from molestation, so long as they Conformed to its conditions. I am ready to meet any charges that may be preferred against me, & do not wish to avoid trial, but if I am Correct as to the protection granted by my parole, & am not to be prosecuted; I desire to Comply with the provisions of the Presidents proclamation & therefore enclose the required application, which I request, in that event, may be acted on" ALS, IHi. *O.R.*, I, xlvi, part 3, 1275–76. On the same day, Lee wrote to President Andrew Johnson. "Being excluded from the provisions of amnesty & pardon Contained in the proclamation of the 29th Ulto; I hereby apply for the benefits, & full restoration of all rights & privileges extended to those included in its terms. I graduated at the Mil: Academy at W. Point in June 1829. Resigned from the U. S. Army April '61. Was a General in the Confederate Army, & included in the surrender of the Army of N. Va: 9 April '65" ALS, IHi. On June 16, USG endorsed this letter. "Respectfully forwarded, through the Secretary of War, to His Excellency the President, with the earnest recommendation that, this application of Gen. R. E. Lee for amnesty and pardon may be granted him. The oath of allegiance required by the recent order of the President to accompany applications does not accompany this for the reason as I am informed by Gen. Ord, the order requiring it had not reached Richmond when this was forwarded." ES, *ibid.* Secretary of War Edwin M. Stanton noted on the docket of this letter: "Presented by Sec of War & postponed for further considerat[ion] in Cabinet" AN, *ibid.* For Lee's Amnesty Oath of Oct. 2, 1865, see Elmer Oris Parker, "Why Was Lee Not Pardoned?" *Prologue*, 2, 3 (Winter, 1970), 181. See also letter to Robert E. Lee, June 20, 1865.

U.S. District Judge John C. Underwood evidently handed down an indictment for treason against Lee on June 7. Although never pressed, authorities did not formally drop the indictment until Feb. 15, 1869; the documents, however, have since disappeared. Douglas Southall Freeman, *R. E. Lee* (New York and London, 1935), IV, 202, 381. Underwood stated in his charge to the grand jury: "To an inquiry which has been made by an officer of the Court, whether the terms of parole agreed upon with General Lee were any protection to those taking the parole, the answer is, that was a mere military arrangement, and can have no influence upon civil rights or the status of the persons interested." *Philadelphia Inquirer*, June 8, 1865. Johnson, contrary to USG's views, apparently wanted the prosecution of Lee and others to continue. Between June 16–20, USG conferred with Johnson about Lee's status and threatened to resign if Johnson persisted in the prosecution. Adam Badeau, *Grant in Peace* (Hartford, Conn., 1887), pp. 25–26; Grenville M. Dodge, *Personal Recollections of President Abraham Lincoln, General Ulysses S. Grant and General William T. Sherman* (Council Bluffs, Iowa, 1914), pp. 88–94. USG's defense of Lee prevailed, and, on June 20, Attorney Gen. James Speed instructed the U.S. district attorney, Norfolk, not to arrest any paroled officers or soldiers. J. G. Randall, *Constitutional Problems Under Lincoln* (Rev. ed., Urbana, 1951), p. 102. See also Jonathan Truman Dorris, *Pardon and Amnesty under Lincoln and Johnson* . . .

(Chapel Hill, 1953), pp. 119–34. On Dec. 25, 1868, Johnson issued a general amnesty proclamation that covered Lee, who was barred, however, from holding state or federal office by the Fourteenth Amendment.

On Aug. 26, 1867, USG endorsed papers concerning former C.S.A. Lt. Gen. Alexander P. Stewart by copying verbatim his longer endorsement of June 16, 1865, concerning Lee. ES, DNA, RG 60, Letters Received, War Dept.

1. Underwood, born in 1809 in Herkimer County, N. Y., educated at Hamilton College, studied law and moved to Clarke County, Va. He joined the Liberty Party in 1839 and eventually became a Republican. He moved to New York City and, in 1857, co-founded the American Emigrant Aid and Homestead Co., a scheme to plant antislavery settlements in western Va. He served as fifth auditor of the Treasury from 1861 until his appointment as judge of the eastern district of Va. in 1864. See Patricia Hickin, "John C. Underwood and the Antislavery Movement in Virginia, 1847–1860," *Virginia Magazine of History and Biography*, 73, 2 (April, 1965), 156–68.

To Maj. Gen. Quincy A. Gillmore

Washington June 16th *1865* [*1:30* P.M.]

MAJ. GEN. GILMORE, HILTON HEAD S. CO.

Give every facility for transporting from the interior all products going forward to market. Let rail-roads and steamers take private freight at fare remuneration to gGovt. when it does not interfere with public business. Comd.g officer at August[a] and Savannah will act upon these instructions without waiting orders from Gen. Gilmore.

U. S. GRANT
Lt. Gn.

ALS (telegram sent), DNA, RG 107, Telegrams Collected (Bound); telegram sent, *ibid.*; telegram received, *ibid.*, Telegrams Collected (Unbound). *O.R.*, I, xlvii, part 3, 649. On June 21, 1865, Maj. Gen. Quincy A. Gillmore telegraphed to USG. "Your directions of the 16th about giving facilities for getting cotton & other products to market has been anticipated   Every possible assistence is giveng in this particular" Telegram received (on June 23, 11:00 A.M.), DNA, RG 107, Telegrams Collected (Bound); *ibid.*, Telegrams Collected (Unbound); *ibid.*, RG 108, Telegrams Received; copies, *ibid.*, RG 393, Dept. of the South and S. C., Letters Sent; DLC-USG, V, 54. *O.R.*, I, xlvii, part 3, 660. On June 14, William D. W. Barnard, Augusta, Ga., had telegraphed to USG. "Govt have all transportation on this River   two steamers are now here with no down freight Genl Molineaux has every disposition to facilitate but instructions from Genl

Gillmore wont permit to let Cotton go forward on private account or for U S Cotton agent   Can you instruct Genl Molineaux to turn over down transportation to Col. Rabb [*Robb*] U S Purchasing Agent   see Rabbs dispatch this day to secy. Treasury   not much desposition at Dept Hd Qrs to facilitate operations   if transportation was needed by Military Authoriti[e]s we would not make this request   answer steamers waiting" Telegram received (on June 15, 9:00 P.M.), DNA, RG 107, Telegrams Collected (Bound); (2) *ibid.*, Telegrams Collected (Unbound); *ibid.*, RG 108, Telegrams Received; copy, DLC-USG, V, 54.

On May 9, USG had written to the commanding officer, Savannah, Ga. "The bearer of this, A. H. Powell is a citizen of Macon Ga. and as I understand from a personal and old friend of mine has been a refugee from there since a short time after the breaking out of the rebellion. On the recommendation of this friend, W. D. W. Barnard of St. Louis Mo. I give this letter asking you to afford Mr. Powell every facility for returning to Macon Ga. and for transacting all legitimate business." ALS, NNP. On the same day, USG wrote a pass. "Pass Messrs A H Powell & Agent with Horses and personal baggags to Savannah, Ga. and through to Macon." ADS, *ibid.* On Dec. 9, 1908, Adolphus H. Powell, Kensington, Md., wrote to J. P. Morgan presenting these documents to him. ALS, *ibid.* On May 21, 1865, 1:00 P.M., USG telegraphed to Bvt. Brig. Gen. Stewart Van Vliet, New York City. "I gave passes for several parties to accompany W D W Barnard to Savannah   You may authorize him to substitute other parties for those named" Telegram sent, DNA, RG 107, Telegrams Collected (Bound); copies, *ibid.*, RG 108, Letters Sent; DLC-USG, V, 46, 76, 108.

On July 15, 4:30 P.M., USG telegraphed to Gillmore. "I understand there has been undue Military interferance ~~in~~ and great corruption in transporting private freights in your Dept. Capt. Starr is reported to exercise a bad influance. ~~Private enterprise~~ Trade is to be left as free in South Carolina as in New York under existing orders." ALS (telegram sent), DNA, RG 107, Telegrams Collected (Bound); telegram sent, *ibid.*; telegram received (marked "via Beaufort 17th—"), *ibid.*, RG 393, Dept. of the South and S. C., 2nd Military District, Letters Received. On July 17 or 18, Gillmore telegraphed to USG. "Your despatch of the fifteenth 15 in reference to Capt Starr's interference with transportation of private freight, is received. The only interference that I have ever heard of is that private freight is not allowed to take precedence of Gov't freight on Gov't transports. Capt Starr is serving Dept of Georgia." Telegram received (dated July 17, received on July 20, 10:50 A.M.), *ibid.*, RG 107, Telegrams Collected (Bound); *ibid.*, RG 108, Telegrams Received; copies (dated July 18), *ibid.*, RG 393, Dept. of the South and S. C., Letters Sent; (dated July 17) DLC-USG, V, 54.

On July 20, Thursday, Barnard, New York City, telegraphed to USG. "Desiring to see you   would be pleased to know if you contemplate leaving Washington before Tuesday next." Telegram received (at 4:15 P.M.), DNA, RG 107, Telegrams Collected (Bound); *ibid.*, RG 108, Telegrams Received. On April 24, President Andrew Johnson had issued a trade permit to James J. O'Fallon, St. Louis. Copy, *ibid.*, RG 94, Letters Received, 858T 1865. On May 31, O'Fallon appointed George Schley, Augusta, as his agent. Copy, *ibid.* Barnard witnessed this document. Copy, *ibid.* On July 24, USG endorsed the permit. "The within Executive permit will be observed by all military Commanders and every facility given for its execution without hindrance or interference"

Copy, *ibid*. On Oct. 2, Schley testified that the originals of Johnson's permit and USG's endorsement were in Barnard's possession. Schley had four certified copies for use in cotton transactions. DS, *ibid*. In one transaction, Schley managed the sale of 9,778 bales of cotton to John Garsed, a Philadelphia cotton manufacturer. *Ibid*.; *ibid*., RG 107, Letters Received, T989 1865. The sellers stopped delivery after 2,680 bales had been sent to Garsed. Garsed applied to military authorities in Ga. for relief, and on Sept. 5, Maj. Gen. James B. Steedman ordered that the balance of the cotton be shipped to Garsed. Copy (printed), *ibid*. The War Dept. suspended Steedman's order, and Secretary of War Edwin M. Stanton tendered his ruling on Sept. 29. "This case has received the anxious consideration of the Secretary of War—It appears that certain cotton in the State of Georgia is claimed by Mr Garsed, on the one side, and by certain other parties, whose names are not disclosed, on the other side—both claiming under an alleged purchase from Metcalf & Company. At the instance of Garsed, the Provost Court at Augusta has undertaken to decide the questions of these conflicting claims to the ownership and possession of the property The action of the Court has been disapproved and suspended, by order of the War Department, as being an improper exercise of military authority. Mr Garsed asks that the judgment of the Provost Court be enforced by the Military Commander; and this application presents the question as to the propriety of the military authority undertaking to decide disputed claims between individuals in respect to property in which the Government has no interest. During the war, this question has been brought to the notice of the Department in various forms, by military tribunals undertaking to exercise jurisdiction over civil claims, and the existence of such authority has been denied by the Department. After the most careful consideration, I am unable to perceive any principle upon which military authority can exercise jurisdiction in such cases Its exercise would be attended with two serious evils:—1st With the u[tm]ost strictness of supervision, it would furnish occasion for the exercise of military power in many cases, and set a precedent dangerous in form; and, 2nd The Government might be subjected to a pecuniary responsibility of boundless extent, for any mistake or misconduct on the part of military officers exercising such jurisdiction. From these considerations, this Department feels compelled to abstain from any interference in respect to the disputed claims set forth in Mr Garseds application:" DS, *ibid*. Presumably in Sept., 1867, USG wrote an undated note. "Find order, if not enclosed herewith, order of the Sec. of War of 19th of Sept./65 suspending Gen Seadman's order in this case." AN, *ibid*. On Sept. 9, USG, as secretary of war *ad interim*, endorsed Stanton's decision. "This copy of order and instructions in relation to cotton transactions in Georgia are respectfully forwarded to John Garsed, Esqr. of Philadelphia. It is not seen how this Department can annul the order, or take any further action in the matter. The principles laid down therein are undoubtedly correct. The action of this Department, however, cannot be construed as a bar in any manner to recourse being had to the civil courts for redress of grievance." Copy, *ibid*. Additional information on cotton transactions in Ga. are *ibid*.; *ibid*., RG 94, Letters Received, 858T 1865.

To Maj. Gen. Philip H. Sheridan

Washington June 16th *1865*

MAJ. GEN. P. H. SHERIDAN,
COMD.G MIL. DIV. TRANS-MISS.
DEAR GENERAL,

This will introduce to you Gen. Carvajal[1] of the Liberal Army of Mexico and Governor of the State of Tamaulipas. Gen. Carvijal was educated in the United States and speaks the language perfectly. From his long services on the frontier, or Rio Grande, he can give you accurate information from that country.

I need not tell you the interest I feel in Mexican affairs for you are already informed on that subject. I know you entertain the same feelings on this subject that I do hence a mere introduction is all that is necessary. I will add however that courticies shown Gn. Carvajal will be regarded as favors to myself.

Yours Truly
U. S. GRANT
Lt. Gn.

ALS, DLC-Philip H. Sheridan.

1. José M. J. Carvajal, born in 1810, graduated from Campbellite Bethany College of Va., and fought against the U.S. during the Mexican War. Benito Juárez appointed him governor of Tamaulipas in 1864. In April, 1865, Carvajal traveled to Washington with Maj. Gen. Lewis Wallace to seek assistance for the Nationalist cause and met USG. See Robert E. and Katharine M. Morsberger, *Lew Wallace: Militant Romantic* (New York, 1980), pp. 195–98; *Personal Memoirs of P. H. Sheridan* (New York, 1888), II, 219–22; Thomas D. Schoonover, ed., *Mexican Lobby: Matías Romero in Washington, 1861–1867* (Lexington, Ky., 1986), pp. 65–66.

Endorsement

[*June 19, 1865*]

I would respectfully recommend that the benefits of Amnesty be extended to Gn. Ewell. Immediately on his capture I heard of expressions from him which I regarded as manly and favorable to us.[1] He expressed the opinion that all further resistance to the ʉUnion was criminal and that it was the duty of commanders of troops to surrender without further effusion of blood.

U. S. GRANT

Lt. Gn.

AES (undated), DNA, RG 94, Amnesty Papers, Va.; copy (dated June 19, 1865), DLC-USG, V, 58. Written on a letter of June 9 from Thomas T. Gantt, St. Louis, to Maj. Gen. William T. Sherman. ". . . Not to detain you unnecessarily, I wish to obtain your intercession in behalf of my Kinsman, Richard S. Ewell, now confined in Fort Warren—He was misguided, resigned his commission in our army took up arms in the cause of rebel Virginia, and has, as you know, fought against us. He lost a leg at the Second battle of Bull. Run. But he is now thoroughly resolved to assume, if permitted, the functions of an active union man in Virginia. . . ." ALS, DNA, RG 94, Amnesty Papers, Va. On June 16, Sherman wrote to Brig. Gen. John A. Rawlins. "I have the honor to transmit herewith a letter received from T. T. Gantt Esq. of St Louis, asking clemency to Genl Ewell of the Confederate Army. Ewell was a Class mate of mine at West Point and was then a sturdy manly fellow, but as he was full grown & embarked in the Rebel Cause I feel no desire to ask for him a treatment different from what is awarded to others in the same situation. I shall be at South Bend Indiana on the 22nd Inst to attend the School Examination of my Children. Thence shall go to Lancaster Ohio & await the orders fixing my Head Quarters. Under Existing orders the Commanders of Military Divisions will have nothing to do, as our task was during war simply to handle troops in Action, leaving to Dept Commanders all detailed work. If the Lt Genl Commdg desires me to give attention to minor matters it would be well to fix in orders the duties of the Commanders of Mil Divns & Departments to prevent conflict & confusion." ALS, *ibid.*, RG 108, Letters Received. On the same day, Richard S. Ewell, Fort Warren, Boston, Mass., wrote to President Andrew Johnson. "I have the honor to forward herewith the oath prescribed in your Proclamation of the 29th Ult—and to apply for pardon—I belong to the excepted classes as I graduated at West Point U. S. M. A. resigned an appointment in the U S. Army and when taken Prisoner on the 6th of April last held the rank of Lieut. General in the C. S. Army—This oath is the strongest proof I can give of my wish to become a loyal citizen & as far as in me lies to do my duty to the country" ALS, *ibid.*, RG 94, Amnesty Papers, Va. Secretary of War Edwin M. Stanton noted on the docket: "Presented by Sec of War & Postponed for further Consideration in Cabinet June 20." AN, *ibid.* See *O.R.*, II, viii, 582. On July 1, USG wrote to Stanton requesting permission for Ewell's wife and daughter to visit him at Fort Warren. Forest H. Sweet, List No. 103 [1950], no. 83.

1. On April 16, Ewell, Fort Warren, had written to USG. "You will appreciate, I am sure, the sentiment which prompts me to drop you these lines. Of all the misfortunes which could befall the Southern people, or any Southern man, by far the greatest, in my judgment, would be the prevalence of the idea that they could entertain any other than feelings of unqualified abhorrence and in-

dignation for the assassination of the President of the United States, and the attempt to assassinate the Sec of State. No language can adequately express the shock produced upon myself, in common with all the other general officers confined here with me, by the occurrence of this appalling crime, and by the seeming tendency in the public mind to connect the South and Southern men with it. Need we say that we are not assassins, nor the Allies of assassins, be they from the North or from the South? And that, coming as we do from most of the States of the South, we would be ashamed of our own people, were we not assured that they will reprobate this crime. Under the circumstances, I could not refrain from some expression of my feelings. I thus utter them to a Soldier who will comprehend them—The following Officers—Maj Generals Ed Johnson of Va. & Kershaw of S. C.—Brig Generals Barton, Corse, Hunton, and Jones of Va, Dubose, Semmes and H. R. Jackson of Ga—Frazer of Ala—Smith and Gordon of Tenn, Cabell of Ark, and Marmaduke of Missouri, and Commodore Tucker of Va, all heartily concur with me in what I have said—" ALS, DNA, RG 108, Letters Received. *O.R.*, I, xlvi, part 3, 787.

To Andrew Johnson

Washington D. C. June 19th *1865*

HIS EXCELLENCY, A. JOHNSON,
PRESIDENT OF THE UNITED STATES,
SIR:

The great interst which I feel in securing an honorable and permanent peace whilst we still have in sevice a force sufficient to insure it, and the danger and disgrace which, in my judgement, threatens us unless positive and early measures are taken to avert it induces me to lay my views before you in an official form.

In the first place I regard the act of attempting to establish a Monarchical Government on this continent, in Mexico, by foreign bayonetts as an act of hostility against the Government of the United States. If allowed to go on until such a government is established I see nothing before us but a long, expensive and bloody war; one in which the enemies of this country will be joined by tens of thousands of disciplined soldiers embittered against their government by the experience of the last four years.

As a justification for open resistence to the establishment of

Maximilian's Government in Mexico I would give the following reasons.

1st   The act of attempting to establish a Monarchy on this continent was an act of known hostility to the Government of the United States, was protested against at the time, and would not have been undertaken but for the great war which was raging, ~~at the time~~ and which it was supposed by all the great powers of Europe, except possibly Russia, would result in the dismemberment of the country and the overthrow of Republican institutions.

2d   Every act of ~~this~~e Empire of Maximilian has been hostile to the Government of the United States. Matamoras, and the whole Rio Grande, under his controll, has been an open port to those in rebellion against this Government. It is notorious that every article held by the rebels for export was permitted to cross the Rio Grande and from there to go unmolested to all parts of the world and they in return to receive in pay all articles, ~~and~~ Arms, Munitions of War, &c. they desired. Rebels in Arms have been allowed to take refuge on Mexican soil protected by French bayonettes. French soldiers have fired on our men from the South side of the river, in aid of the rebellion. Officers acting under the Authority of the would be Empire have receive arms, munitions and other public property from the rebels after the same had become the property of the United States. It is now reported, and I think there is no doubt of the truth of the report, that large organized and armed bodies of rebels have gone to Mexico to join the Imperialests. It is further reported, and too late we will find the report confirmed, that a contract or agreement has been entered into with Dr. Gwinn, a traitor to his country, to invite into Mexico armed immigrants for the purpose of wrenching from the rightful government of that country, states never controlled by the Imperialests.

It will not do to remain quiet and theorize that by observing a strict neutrality ~~the~~ all foreign force will be compelled to leave Mexican soil. Rebel immigrants to Mexico will go with Arms in their hands. They will not be a burden upon the State but on the contrary will become producers, always ready, when the imergency arises, to take up their Arms in defence of the cause they espouse. That their leaders will espouse the cause of the Empire, purely out of hostility to this Government I feel there is no doubt. There is a hope that the rank and file may take the opposite side if any influance is allowed to work upon their reason. But if a Neutrality is to be observed which allowes armed rebels to go to Mexico, and which keeps out all other emigrants, and which also denies to the Liberals of Mexico belligerent rights, the right to buy Arms and Munitions in foreign Markets, and to transport them through friendly territory to their homes, I see no chance for such influances to be brought to bear.

What I would propose would be a solemn protest against the establishment of a Monarchical Government in Mexico by the aid of foreign bayonettes. If the French have a just claim against Mexico I would regard them as having triumphed and would guarantee them suitable reward for their grievances. Mexico would no doubt admit their claims if it did not effect their territory or rights as a free people. The United States could take such pledges as would secure her against loss. How all this could be done with- out ~~avoiding~~ ~~without~~ bringing on an armed conflict others who have studied such matters could tell better than ~~me~~. I.

If this course cannot be agreed upon then I would recognize equal beligerent rights to both parties. I would interpose no ob- sticle to the passage into Mexico of emigrants to that country. I would allow either party to buy Arms or any thing we have to sell and interpose no obsticle to their transit.

These views have been hastily drawn up and contain but little of what might be said on the subject ~~But if the serv~~ treated of. If however it serves to bring the matter under discussion it will have accomplished all that is desired. ~~It has seemed to me proper that~~ I

ADf, USG 3. For the letter as sent, see copies, DLC-USG, V, 46, 109; DNA, RG 108, Letters Sent. *O.R.*, I, xlviii, part 2, 923–24.

To Edwin M. Stanton

———

Washington D. C. June 19 *1865*

Hon E. M. Stanton,
Sec of War,
Sir,

Enclosed I send you a letter addressed to the President on the subject of Mexican affairs, which I respectfully request to be laid before him.

The statement that French troops have fired upon our troops in aid of the rebellion, is taken from a published letter from a member of an Indiana Regiment. The statement of the sale of arms to French troops is from Gen. Steele's dispatch of the 10th of June

My time is so occupied that I have not been able to draw up the enclosed letter with the care and pains to get at the exact facts that I would like. The object however is to get this matter before the President and Cabinet in such a manner as to induce them to give the matter that study and attention its importance requires. This done, I shall feel confident that a course will be pursued creditable to the country and proper to secure our rights on this continent.

> Very respectfully
> Your obt servt
> U S. Grant
> Lt Gen

Copies, USG 3; DLC-USG, V, 46, 109; DNA, RG 108, Letters Sent. *O.R.*, I, xlviii, part 2, 922–23. See preceding letter.

To Maj. Gen. Quincy A. Gillmore

———

Washington June 19th *1865* [*11:00* A.M.]
Maj. Gen. Gilmore, Hilton Head S. C,

The troops sent to your command were intended for such distribution as you thought proper and to enable you to carry out

orders for mustering out troops. Muster out all Volunteer Light
Artillery in your Department and if you need other companies inform me and I will order regular companies from here.

U. S. GRANT

Lt. Gn

ALS (telegram sent), DNA, RG 107, Telegrams Collected (Bound); telegram
sent, *ibid.*; telegram received, *ibid.*, Telegrams Collected (Unbound). *O.R.*, I,
xlvii, part 3, 659; (misdated May 19) *ibid.*, p. 536. A copy in the hand of Bvt.
Col. Theodore S. Bowers was also sent to Maj. Gen. Quincy A. Gillmore by mail.
Copy, DNA, RG 393, Dept. of the South and S. C., 2nd Military District, Letters
Received. On June 28, 1865, Gillmore telegraphed to USG. "Your dDispatch
of June 27th directing all Volunteer Light Batteries to be mustered out is recd
In obedience to Vincent's Telegh of June 13th one (1) light battery is now on
its way to Washn & another is under orders to go there leaving But one light
battery in the Dept which I have today ordered to be mustered out—It would be
well to send me one (1) Batty of regulars" Telegrams received (4), *ibid.*, RG
107, Telegrams Collected (Unbound); (on July 1, 2:45 P.M.) *ibid.*, Telegrams
Collected (Bound); (on July 1, 1:40 P.M.) *ibid.*, RG 108, Telegrams Received;
copies, *ibid.*, RG 393, Dept. of the South and S. C., Letters Sent; DLC-USG, V,
54. *O.R.*, I, xlvii, part 3, 670–71. Gillmore may have received the mailed copy
of USG's telegram on June 27, causing some confusion on the date.

Also on June 19, 2:40 P.M., USG telegraphed to Gillmore. "The records of
the Rebel post office are said to be at the house of a Mr. Allen, Postmaster Chester
South Carolina. Send and get them and forward by special Messenger to the
Postmaster General." ALS (telegram sent), DNA, RG 107, Telegrams Collected
(Bound); telegram sent, *ibid.*; telegram received, *ibid.*, Telegrams Collected
(Unbound). *O.R.*, I, xlvii, part 3, 659. A copy in the hand of Maj. George K.
Leet was also sent to Gillmore by mail. Copy, DNA, RG 393, Dept. of the South
and S. C., 2nd Military District, Letters Received. Also at 2:40 P.M., USG tele-
graphed to Maj. Gen. John M. Schofield. "Send to Charlotte and get the Post
Office blanks which are said to be there and forward to the Postmaster General
Washington." ALS (telegram sent), *ibid.*, RG 107, Telegrams Collected (Bound);
telegram sent, *ibid.*; telegram received, *ibid.*, RG 393, Army of the Ohio and
Dept. of N. C., Telegrams Received. *O.R.*, I, xlvii, part 3, 657. On June 20,
Schofield, Raleigh, N. C., telegraphed to USG. "All post office blanks & other
property have been Collected & are now Enroute to Washington" Telegram
received (at 12:45 P.M.), DNA, RG 107, Telegrams Collected (Bound); *ibid.*,
RG 108, Telegrams Received; copies, DLC-USG, V, 54; DLC-John M. Schofield.
O.R., I, xlvii, part 3, 659.

Also on June 19, 1:00 P.M., USG telegraphed to Bvt. Maj. Gen. James H.
Wilson, Macon, Ga. "Box up and send to the Sec. of War by special Messenger
all Treasury and other public documents captured by your command." ALS
(telegram sent), DNA, RG 107, Telegrams Collected (Bound); telegram sent,
ibid.; copies, *ibid.*, RG 108, Letters Sent; *ibid.*, RG 393, Military Div. of the
Miss., Cav. Corps, Telegrams Received; DLC-USG, V, 46, 109. *O.R.*, I, xlix, part
2, 1017.

To Maj. Gen. John Pope

Washington June 19th *1865* [*noon*]

MAJ. GN. POPE, ST. LOUIS MO.

The cost of keeping the amount of cavalry called for on the Prairies is so inormous I wish you would cut down the expeditions all you can and direct that animals be grazed as far as possible.

U. S. GRANT
Lt. Gn.

ALS (telegram sent), DNA, RG 107, Telegrams Collected (Bound); telegram sent, *ibid.*; telegram received (at 3:00 P.M.), *ibid.*, Telegrams Collected (Unbound). *O.R.*, I, xlviii, part 2, 933. On June 19, 1865, 4:25 P.M., Maj. Gen. John Pope telegraphed to USG. "I will reduce cavalry expenses as far as possible & comply at once with your orders about Grazing I think the govt will find it true economy to finish this indian war this season so that it will stay finished we have troops enough now on the plains to do it & can do it now better than hereafter. if I could only get legislation or a determined resolution of the Govt to do away with the present system of Indian policy every thing would go right I have exceeded my authority already in prohibiting intercourse between Indians & indian agents & shall maintain this prohibition until otherwise ordered." Telegram received (at 8:35 P.M.), DNA, RG 107, Telegrams Collected (Bound); *ibid.*, RG 108, Telegrams Received; copies, *ibid.*, RG 393, Military Div. of the Mo., Telegrams Sent; DLC-USG, V, 54. *O.R.*, I, xlviii, part 2, 933. On June 20, 9:40 P.M., USG telegraphed to Pope. "Push out your expeditions against the Indians in your own way. The dispatch sent you a few days since was in consequence of a report of the difficulty and expense of procuring forage for so large a force as is now assembling for duty on the plains." ALS (telegram sent), DNA, RG 107, Telegrams Collected (Bound); telegram sent (on June 21, 1:10 A.M.), *ibid.*; telegram received (at 9:30 [A.M.]), *ibid.*, Telegrams Collected (Unbound). *O.R.*, I, xlviii, part 2, 946. On June 21, Pope referred to USG a letter of June 20 from Maj. Gen. Grenville M. Dodge discussing measures taken to reduce cav. expenses. Copy, DNA, RG 393, Military Div. of the Mo., Register of Letters Received. See *O.R.*, I, xlviii, part 2, 947.

On June 20, Pope wrote to USG. "I have the honor to transmit enclosed letter, with enclosures to the Hon James Harlan Secretary of the Interior. I have to request that after reading the letter to the Hon Mr Harlan you will please have it delivered into his own hands." Copy, DNA, RG 393, Military Div. of the Mo., Letters Sent. See *O.R.*, I, xlviii, part 2, 933–35.

On June 24, 3:00 P.M., Pope telegraphed to USG. "A consistant & harmonyious administration of Indian affairs within my command renders it necessary that I should see & confer in person with yourself the President & the Secy of war & the interior The settlement of Indian question will greatly simplified if a satisfactory understanding can be reached between authorities mentioned I think a full & frank conference in which I can explain my views & purposes will lead to such an undrstanding I therfore ask as a matter of great moment on this subject that I be ordered to Washington for the purpose above mentioned" Telegram received (at 6:15 P.M.), DNA, RG 107, Telegrams Collected (Bound); *ibid.*, RG 108, Telegrams Received; copies, *ibid.*, RG 393, Military Div. of the Mo., Telegrams Sent; DLC-USG, V, 54. *O.R.*, I, xlviii, part 2, 986. On June 26, 2:45 P.M., USG telegraphed to Pope. "As soon as you can properly leave your Dept. Come to Washington." ALS (telegram sent), DNA, RG 107, Telegrams Collected (Bound); telegram sent, *ibid.*; copies, *ibid.*, RG 94, Letters Received, 716A 1865; *ibid.*, RG 108, Letters Sent; *ibid.*, RG 393, Military Div. of the Mo., Telegrams Received; *ibid.*, Telegrams Sent; DLC-USG, V, 54. *O.R.*, I, xlviii, part 2, 997. At 4:00 P.M., Pope telegraphed to USG. "Did you receive my dispatch of yesterday in relation to my visiting Washington" Telegram received (on June 27, 1:15 A.M.), DNA, RG 107, Telegrams Collected (Bound); *ibid.*, RG 108, Telegrams Received; copies, *ibid.*, RG 393, Military Div. of the Mo., Telegrams Sent; DLC-USG, V, 54. On July 7, Bvt. Col. Theodore S. Bowers directed the AG to issue a special order. "The telegraphic instructions of June 26th 1865, directing Major General Pope, Commanding Military Division of Missouri, to repair to this city, are hereby confirmed, Having complied with the above instructions General Pope, will return to St Louis, Missouri, and resume his duties." Copy, DNA, RG 94, Letters Received, 716A 1865.

To Maj. Gen. Philip H. Sheridan

(Cipher). Washington D. C. June 19th *1865* [*8:30* P.M.]
MAJ. GEN. SHERIDAN, NEW ORLEANS LA.

No orders effecting policy to be pursued on the Rio Grande are to be observed except they come from the President, Sec. of War or Military Commander authorized to issue orders there. ~~This notice is given on reading an order published by the Commanding officer at Brownsville Texas seemingly acknowledging other authority~~.

U. S. GRANT
Lt. Gn.

ALS (telegram sent), DNA, RG 107, Telegrams Collected (Bound); telegram sent, *ibid.*; telegrams received (2—dated June 20, 1865), *ibid.*, Telegrams Collected (Unbound). Misdated June 18 in *O.R.*, I, xlviii, part 2, 916.

On June 15, Maj. Gen. Philip H. Sheridan wrote to Brig. Gen. John A. Rawlins. "I send you some papers in referance to an interview between Brig Gen Brown Commanding U S. Forces Brownsville Texas, and General Mejia, Commanding Matamoras. General Brown appears to be actuated by a desire for notoriety, more than the interest of the public service. I also enclose a communication from Dr Canedo Secret agent for General Canby relating to Mexican affairs and letters from General Herron on the condition of affairs at Shreveport, with a report of appointment of Commissioners to meet and confer with certain Indian chiefs at Fort Tousand including letters of instruction of Lieut General Buckner (Rebel Army) to Generals Cooper, Throckmorton & other Confederate Commissioners" LS, DNA, RG 94, Letters Received, 1514S 1865. The enclosures are *ibid*. On June 26, USG endorsed this letter. "Respectfully forwarded to the Secretary of War" ES, *ibid*.

On June 19, Sheridan telegraphed to Rawlins. "I will leave here tomorrow the 20th to make a quick trip along the coast of Texas. The information which I may gain may enable me to determine the best place to put the 4th army corps. Galveston, Indianola and Corpus Christi are or ought to be occupied by this time. Gord' Granger being the senior officer is in command of all the troops in Texas. I have had many delays in shipping troops from the delay of the 25th army corps which has come in this direction at a sails pace. The transports occupied by it will make me all right & quickly will it overtake the 4th corps. The Cavalry columns have been pushed but great delay occurred in getting them started as they were scattered and had to be collected in and fixed up, and the navigation of the Red River is very difficult, but all is well now. I will be back from Texas in seven or eight days" Telegram received (on June 20, 5:25 P.M.), *ibid*., RG 107, Telegrams Collected (Bound); *ibid*., RG 108, Telegrams Received; copies, DLC-USG, V, 54; DLC-Philip H. Sheridan. *O.R.*, I, xlviii, part 2, 924– 25. On June 28, Sheridan telegraphed to Rawlins. "I returned here this morning from a hurried trip to Texas. Galveston Houston, Columbia Indianola & Corpus Christi are now occupied by our troops and Genl Steele is advancing a force up the Rio Grande as far as Roma as soon as troops can be supplied that far up. I will send this evening or tomorrow morning all the information which I was able to obtain of the condition of affairs in Texas and along the Rio Grande" Telegram received (on June 29, 2:00 P.M.), DNA, RG 107, Telegrams Collected (Bound); *ibid*., RG 108, Telegrams Received; copies, DLC-USG, V, 54; (2) DLC-Philip H. Sheridan. *O.R.*, I, xlviii, part 2, 1014. On the same day, Sheridan telegraphed to USG. "I have just returned from a hurried trip along the coast of Texas. The following is to the best of my knowledge the condition of affairs there. The Kirby Smith and Gen. Canby surrender was for the most part a swindle on the part of Kirby Smith & Co, as all the Texas troops had disbanded or had been discharged and gone home before the commissioners were sent to Gen. Canby. Kirby Smith, Magruder, Shelby, Slaughter, Walker and others of military rank have gone to Everything on wheels artillery horses mules and c. have been run over into Mexico. Large and small bands of rebel soldiers and some citizens amounting to about two thousand have crossed the Rio Grande into Mexico. Some allege with the intention of going to Sonora. 'The Lucy Given' a small steamer was surrendered at Matagorda but was carried off and is now anchored at Bagdad on the Rio Grande. There is no doubt in my mind that the representatives of the Imperial Government along the Rio Grande have encouraged this wholesale plunder of property belonging to the U S Government and that it will only be given up when we go and take it. Gen Steele says that the French officers are very saucy and insulting to our people at Brownsville. Juarez does not appear to have any force of consequence on the Rio Grande. I cannot hear of any movements. The rebels who have gone to Mexico have their sympathies with the Imperialists and this feeling is undoubtedly reciprocated.

I will direct Gen. Steele to make a demand on the French authorities at Matamoras for a return of the property. The Lucy Given is a tangible case A Mexican
steamer loaded with cotton and flying the American flag was a few days since
between Rio Grande City and Brownsville. After the surrender eight hundred
and twenty six bales of confederate states cotton stored at Rio Grande City was
crossed into Mexico and this is only one item. There is a good deal of irritation
between French officials at Matamoras and our people and the Maximilian party
is getting nervous. My scouts report from Matamoras that seven thousand troops
are marching from the interior to that place; also that Mejia is working on the
rifle pits around Matamoras. This reported reenforcement I give for what it is
worth." Telegram received (on June 30, 5:30 A.M.), DNA, RG 107, Letters
Received from Bureaus; *ibid.*, Telegrams Collected (Bound); *ibid.*, RG 108,
Telegrams Received; copies, DLC-USG, V, 54; DLC-Nathaniel P. Banks; (2)
DLC-Philip H. Sheridan. *O.R.*, I, xlviii, part 2, 1015. On June 30, USG endorsed
this telegram. "This is respectfully refered to the President for his information.
In my judgement a demand should be made upon the Authorities of Matamoras
for all Arms and other Confederate property crossed over the Rio Grande after
the surrender with instructions to go and take them if they are not immediately
given up." AES, DNA, RG 107, Letters Received from Bureaus. *O.R.*, I, xlviii,
part 2, 1015.

To Edwin M. Stanton

Washington D. C.
June 20th 1865[1]

HON. E. M. STANTON
SEC. OF WAR,
SIR:

I have the honor, very respectfully, to submit the following report of operations of the Armies of the United States, from the
9th of March 1864, the date when the command was entrusted to
me, to present date. Accompanying this will also be found all reports of commanders, subordinate to me, received at these Head
Quarters. To these latter I refer you for all minor details of operations and battles.

From early in the War I had been impressed with the idea that
active, and continuous operations of all the troops that could be
brought into the field, regardless of season or weather, were necessary to a speedy termination of the gigantic rebellion raging in the

land. The resources of the enemy, and his numerical strength, was far inferior to ours. But as an ofset to this we had a vast territory, with a population hostile to the government, to garrison, and long lines of river and rail-road communication, tr[thr]ough territory equally hostile, to protect to secure in order that the more active Armies might be supplied.—Whilst Eastern and Western Armies were fighting independent battles, working together like a balky team where no two ever pulled together, giving Summers and Winters to almost entire inactivity, thus enabling the enemy to use to great advantage his his interior lines of communication for transporting portion of his Armies from one theatre of War to an other, and to furlough large numbers of the Armyies during these seasons of inactivity to go to their home and do the work of producing for the suport of these Armies, it was a question whether our numerical strength was not more than balanced by these [dis]advantages.

My opinion was firmly fixed long before the honor of commanding all our Armies had been confered on me that no peace could be had that would be stable, or conducive to the happiness of North or South, until the Military power of the rebellion was entirely broken. Believing us to be one people, one blood and with identical interests, I do and have felt the same interest in the welfa ultimate welfare of the South as of the North. The guilty, no matter what their offence or to what section they belong, should be punished according to their guilt. The leaders in this rebellion against the Government have been guilty of the most heinous offence known to our laws. Let them reap the reward of their offence.

Here then is the basis of all plans formed at the outset. 1st First to use the greatest number of troops practicable against the Armed force of the enemy. To prevent that enemy from using the same force, at different seasons, against first one Army and then another, and to prevent the possibility of repose for refitting and producing the necessary supplies for carrying on resistance. Second; to hammer continuously at the Armed force of the enemy, and his resources, until by mere attricion, if in no other way, there should be nothing left to him but an equal submission with the loyal section of our common country to the universal law of the land. These views have been kept constantly before me and orders given and campaigns made to carry them out. How well it has been done it is for the public, who have to mourn the loss of friends ~~who have~~ fallen in the execution, and to pay the ~~expense~~ pecuniary cost of all this, to say. All I can say is the work has been done conscienciously and to the best of my ability. It has been done in what I concieved to be the interest of the whole country, South and North.

At the date when this report begins the situation of the contending forces was about as follows. The Mississippi River was garrisoned strongly by Federal troops from St. Louis Mo. to its mouth. The line of the Arkansas was also held, thus giving us armed possession of all West of the Mississippi North of that stream. A few points in Southern Louisiana, not remote from the river, were held by us, together with a small garrison at and near the mouth of the Rio Grande. All the balance of the vast territory ~~West~~ of Arkansas, Louisiana and Texas was in the almost undisputed possession of the enemy, with an Army of probably not less than 80.000 effective men that could have been brought into the field had there been [sufficient] opposition, enough to have brought them out. ~~whilst the enemy still held his Army intact East of the Mississippi.~~ The let alone policy had demorilized this force so that probably but little more than half of this estimated ~~force~~ was ever present, in garrison, at any one time. But the one half, or 40.000 men, ~~made it necessary~~ with the scattered bands of Guerrillas through Mo. Arkansas and along the Miss, river, and disloyal character of much of the population, compelled the use of a large number of troops to keep ~~open the~~ navigation ~~of~~ open on the river, and to protect the loyal people to the West of it.

To the East of the Mississippi we held substantially with the line of the Tenn. & Holston rivers, runing Eastward to include nearly all of the state of Tennessee. South of Chattanooga a small foothold was obtained in Ga. sufficient to protect East Tenn. from incursions from the enemy's forces at Dalton Ga. West Va. was substantially within our lines. Virginia, with the exception of the Northern border, the Potomac river, a small area about the mouth of James River covered by the troops at Norfolk and Fort Monroe,

and the territory covered by the Army of the ₱Potomac, laying on
the Rapidann, was in the possession of the enemy. Along the seacoast from the mouth of James River, Va. to the mouth of the Miss.
all the ports were blockaded by our Navy. ~~Garrisons~~ Foothold had
also been obtained and Garrisons stationed at the following places.

~~Behind, or North of~~

~~All the balance of the vast territory of the South was held by
the enemy.~~

The accompanying map will show the territory held by the
contending forces, the ~~b~~Blue line indicating the Union lines, the
Red line the Rebel lines.

Behind the Union lines ~~was~~ were many bands of Guerrillas and
a large population disloyal to the Government, making it necessary
to guard every foot of road or river used in supplying our Armies.
In the South a reign of Military despotism prevailed which made
every man and boy, capable of bearing arms, a soldier and those
who could not bear Arms in the field acted as provosts for collecting
deserters and returning them to the field. This enabled the enemy
to bring almost his entire strength into the field   This, and ~~that~~ the
fact of him acting defensively, equalized the contest until it became
a question of ~~superior endurance~~ actual superiority one over the
other, or of the superior resources of the one from which to draw,
to keep up such gigantic Armies over the other, to settle the contest.
In this latter our advantages were so great that ~~that~~ I never saw any
cause for fear or dispondency except in the lukewarmness or actual
disloyalty of many of our Northern citizens. Against them a valiant
battle has been fought by the patriotic citizens who have not been
called to the field and who, in addition have borne cheerfully the
pecuniary burthens of the war. (A miserable set of politicians at
home, worse than traitors, operated on by their own cowardice, by
their opposition to the war and sympathy with the rebellion, did all
they could to insure its success and to produce dispondency among
the loyal people. They saw nothing but our own dangers and not
those of the enemy. Ever desirous of being with the wining side
they espoused the cause of *their* enemy.)

At this stage of the War ~~of~~ the enemy had concentrated the bulk of his force in two Armies, ~~One under Gen.~~ ~~J. E. Johnston, at~~ ~~and near~~ ~~Dalton Ga.~~ ~~The other under~~ commanded by their ablest and best Generals, Lee and Johnston. The former occupied the South bank of the Rapidann, extending from Mine Run Westward, and strongly ~~fortified~~ intrenched. The latter was even more strongly posted about Dalton Ga, In addition to this the enemy had a large Cavalry force under Forrest, in Northwest Mississippi, to be watched and guarded against, a conciderable force in the Shenandoah Valley and in the Western part of Va. and extreme Eastern part of Tenn. ~~a~~Also confronting the Seacoast Federal Garrisons and holding blockaded ports where we had not obtained any foothold upon the land.

~~Against~~ To carry out the principle then heretofore laid down attention was particularly directed against the two Armies under Lee and Johnston. The ~~one~~ first was regarded as defending Richmond, the capitol of the wouldbe confederacy, the latter as defending Atlanta, Ga. a place of great importance as a rail-road center and Manufacturing city. These two Armies and points then were the objective points of the campaign.

At my request Maj. Gen. W. T. Sherman was appointed to the command of the Mil. Div. of the Miss. embracing all operations and territory East of the Miss. to the Aleghenies and South to include the state of Mississippi. I ~~accompanied~~ took up my Head Quarters with the Army of the Potomac, Maj. Gn. G. G. Meade Commanding, and had general supervision of all operations in the country. The following instructions and dispatches will show the orders under which General Sherman was acting. His report gives the detail of his operations and the result shows ~~how judiciously~~ ~~this important command was bestowed~~ that confidence in him was not misplaced.

Comments upon this campaign are unnecessary. The country and the world appreciate it as one of the most difficult and best executed of which history gives any account.

Accompanying the Army of the Potomac as I did, and being within a few miles of the enemy we had to condend against, no orders were necessary further than for the first movement of the

Army. The following are the ~~orders~~ instructions given.

The movement of the Army of the Potomac commenced at an early hour on the morning of the 4th of May 1864 under the directions and orders of Gen. Meade, pursuant to the above instructions. Before night the whole Army was across the Rapidann, with a great part of its wagon train numbering more than 4000 teams. The average distance traveled by the troops that day was about twelve miles. This I regarded as a great feat and it removed from my mind the most serious apprehension I had entertained: how was so large a train to be carried through a hostile country and protected?

In co-operation with the main movements, those against Lee and Johnston, I was desirous of using to the best advantage all other troops necessarily kept in the background for the protection of our extended line between the loyal ~~and disloyal states.~~ states and the Armies operating. A very conciderable force was so held for the protection of West Virginia and along the frontier of Maryland and Pennsylvania. Whilst these troops could not be withdrawn to distant fields, without exposing the North to invasion by comparitively small bodies of the enemy, they could act directly to their front and give better protection thatn if laying idle in garrison. ~~and~~ By such use they would either compell the enemy to detach largely for the protection of his supplies and lines of communication or he would loose them. Accordingly the accompanying instructions were given to Gen. Sigel who commanded the Department embracing these troops.

Previously other instructions had been given looking to Beverly, West Va. as the starting point. Being desirous of having every thing start as near the 4th of May as possible, and the wreched state of the roads rendering it ~~necessary to~~ impossible to accumulate the necessary supplies at Beverly, in time, made a change indispensable. ~~All the report~~

All the reports I have concerning the execution of these instructions are herewith accompanying. ~~I regarded the~~

~~I regarded the operations of Gn. Sigel as a failure. and Even if the force against him was more than he could contend against his~~

~~retreat upon Harpers Ferry, and loss and distruction of public property was not managed with the skill, in my judgement, that ought to be possessed by an officer entrusted with so important a command as that of a Department. I accordingly asked and obtained his removal. Maj~~

~~Maj. Gen. D. Hunter was then~~

I did not regard the operations of Gen. Sigel as satisfactory and asked his removal from command.

Maj. Gen. Hunter was then appointed to superceed him, and [he] promptly took up the offensive.

To the point of investing Lynchburg Gn. Hunter was very successful. No doubt but the difficulty of taking with him sufficient Ordnance stores ~~through~~ over so long a march, through a hostile country, alone prevented him capturing that, to the enemy, important point. The destruction of ~~stores~~ supplies and manufacturies, important to the support of the enemy, was great. It caused Gen. Lee to detach Ewell's Corps from his main Army, but little of which, owing to Sheridans ~~Campaigns~~ battles in the Valley afterwards, ever returned to do battle for the defence of Richmond. Unfortunately the absence of Ammunition, with which to do battle, left Gen. Hunter no choise of route for his return. Coming back as he did, by the way of the Kanahwa, ~~as he~~ the use of his troops was lost for several weeks from the defence of the North.

On ~~commencing the Campaign of 1864~~ assuming command of all the armies I found that Maj. Gen. B. F. Butler, who ~~I found~~ was in command of the Dept. of Va. and North Carolina, had a force too great to stand idle ~~hol~~ merely holding the posts entrusted to him, and too small for offensive operations. To increase his movable force I directed the abandonment of Little Washington N C. and also contemplated abandoning Plymouth N. C. but unfortunately yiealded to representations of the necessity for continuing troops there. The capture by the enemy of Brig. Gn. Wessels and his entire command of about 2500 men, and much material of War, was the result.

Maj. Gen. Q. A. Gilmore had been carrying on a long, expensive and, apparently to me, hopeless siege against Charleston.

With the aid of the Navy his position, defensively, required but few troops. I accordingly ordered him to join Gen. Butler with the 10th Army Corps. This gave Gen. Butler a force to take in the field of   thousand men.

With this force I could see no good reason why Richmond ~~could~~ should not be captured or Lee compelled to detach largely for its protection. With the city in our possession, and with it all communications ~~with the South~~, southward, the Army of Northern Va. would have been compelle to retreat. The James river would have formed such an obstruction in the way that I should have confidantly hoped for its almost entire annihilation as an Army, following as I should have done with the Army of the Potomac close upon its heals.

[The army of N. Va had to be destroyed partially whilst the army doing it still covered his Capital of his country and his North, before it became safe to occupy his position south of the James]

The following are the instructions given to Gen. Butler.

Before giving these instructions I visited Gen. Butler at Fortress Monroe and in conversation pointed out the apparent importance of getting possession of Petersburg and of destroying railroad communications as far South as possible. Believing however in the practicability of Capturing Richmond, unless it was reinforced, I made that the objctive point of Gen. Butler's operations. As the Army of the Potomac was to move simultaneously with him Lee could not detach from his Army with safety, and the enemy did not have troops elswhere to bring ~~for~~ to the defence of the City ~~against~~ in time to meet a rapid movement from the mouth of James River.

Unfortunately the operations of the Army were directed against Drury's Bluff, a strongly fortified position on the James River below Richmond. This should have been passed without further notice than the detachment of a sufficient force to to meet the garrison if ~~they~~ it should come out of ~~their~~ works. This would have been necessary to cover the movement of the main Army against Richmond.

Time was lost. Beaurigard was enabled to collect the loose

forces in North & South Carolina and bring them to Richmond. ~~and compell~~ Gen. Butler was forced back, or drew back, into the forks of the rivers, between the James & the Appomattox, where he strongly entrenched; the enemy entrenching with equal strenghth in his front, thus covering his rail-roads, the city and all that was valuable to him. The Army of the James was in a bottle, strongly corked, but in a place of great security. As it required comparitively but a small force of the enemy to ~~keep~~ hold it there he, the enemy, must have felt that the Army of the James was just where he wanted it.

Sherman's movement from Chattanooga to Atlanta was prompt, skillful and brilliant. His flank movements and battles during that memorable campaign will be read in ~~the~~ future with an interest ~~unsurpassed~~ unsurpassed by anything in past history. (His own report, and the reports of his subordinate Commanders accompanying it, give all the details of that most successful Campaign).

He was dependent for the supplies of his Army upon the rail-road from Nashville to the point where he was operating. This passed the entire distance through a hostile country and had to be protected by troops over every foot of it. (Besides Guerrillas and citizens ready to break our lines of communications,) [The cavalry force of the enemy under] Forrest ~~was~~ in Northeast Mississippi, (with a large force of Cavalry) [was] evidently waiti~~ng~~[ing] for Sherman to advance far enough into the mountains of Ga. to make a retreat disastrous, to get upon this line and destroy it beyond the possibility of further use (before supplies on hand were entirely exhausted.) To provide against this danger Sherman left what he supposed a sufficient force to operate against Forrest, in Memphis. He directed Gen. Washburn, who commanded in West Tennessee, to send Brig. Gen. Sturgis in command of this force to attack him. (From some cause which I will not attempt to explain in full,) [Genl.] Sturgis was badly beatten [by an inferior force] and driven back to Memphis, a distance of more than one hundred miles, ~~and the enemy defeated.~~ [By this however] ~~T~~[t]he enemy was defeated ~~and~~ in ~~his~~ his designs upon the Nashville and Chattanooga rail-road by ~~t~~[T]he persistency with which he followed up his success.

~~This~~ exhausted him and made a season ~~of~~ for rest and repairs necessary. ~~This delay brought~~ In the mean time Major Gn. A. J. Smith, with [the troops ~~sent of Genl Sherman~~ had been sent by Genl Sherman to Genl Banks] his band of veterans, arrived at Memphis, [on their return] from the Red river, where they had done most excellent service, (in rescueing our Navy and land forces up that river from almost inevitable distruction.) Sherman ~~was~~ directed him immediately to take the offensive against Forrest. He did this with the promptness and effect which has characterized his whole Military career (in this rebellion). (Delays for preparation has been the most fruitful source of want of success we have had in this war. Against this officer that charge cannot be made.)

(Gen. Smith and his command were sent to the Red river against my ~~protest~~ judgement and with positive instructions that they should be returned to Vicksburg by the 17th of March 1864. They only reached Memphis on the   of May, just in time to repair Sturgis disaster. Had they been returned according to the instructions given they would have been with Sherman on the Atlantic Campaign The Red river failure then was the means of giving us a force with which to retrieve the disaster in Miss. the only good I can see that come out of that unfortunate and illy managed expedition.)

The Army of the Potomac crossed the Rapidann on the 4th of May with but slight opposition. Early on the 5th the advance Corps, the 5th, under Maj. Gen. G. K. Warren met the enemy, outside of his entrenchments, at Mine run. The battle raged furiously all day, the whole of the Army being brought into ~~Division by Division~~ the fight, Corps by Corps, as they could be brought ~~in~~ upon the field. Cone[s]idering the density of the forrests, and narrowness of the roads, this was done with commendable promptness by Corps Commanders, under the instructions of Gen. Meade.

~~Before going further I will st~~

Gen. Burnside, with the 9th Army Corps, was left with the bulk of his command at the crossing of the Rappahannock and Orange & Alexandria rail-road, holding the road back to Bull Run, with instructions not to move until he received notice that a crossing of the Rapidann was secured, [but] ~~To~~ move promptly as soon as that notice was received. This he was apprized of about o'clock p. m. of the 4th. By   o'clock on the 5th he was leading his corps into battle near the Wilderness Tavern, some of his corps having marched a distance of   miles, and crossed both the Rappahannock and the Rapidann. Cone[s]idering that a large proportion of his corps, probably two thirds of it, was composed of new troops, ~~that were going into their first battle~~, unaccustomed to marches, and carrying the accoutrements of a soldier, I regarded this as remarkably prompt.

Before going further with this report I will state that, commanding all the Armies of the United States as I did, I tried as ~~much~~ far as possible to leave Gen. Meade in independent command of the Army of the Potomac. My instructions for that Army were all through him, and were general in their nature, leaving all the details and the execution to him. I need only add further that the subsequent campaign proved him to be the right man in the right place.—Gen. Meade commanding always in the presence of an officer superior to him in rank, has drawn from him that public attention his zeal and ability entitled him to, and which he would have had with a more independent command.

Here insert notes of operations from the Wilderness to the James which I will forward.

My first object was to break the Military power of the rebellion, and second to capture their important strongholds. By Gen. Butler getting Richmond the latter of these objects would be accomplished in the East, and, as before stated, it would enable the accomplishment of the latter. If he failed it was my determination either by hard fighting to compell Lee to retreat or to so cripple him that he could not detach a large Army to go North and still retain enough for the defenses of Richmond. It was well understood by both Gen. Butler and Gen. Meade, before starting on the Campaign of 1864, that it was my intention to put the whole Army South of the James river in case of failure to ~~capture it~~ destroy Lee before.

During three long years the Armies of the Potomac and of Northern Va. had been confronting each other. In that time they had fought more ~~bloody~~ desperate battles probably than it ever before fell to the lot of two Armies to fight, without materially changing the vantage ground of either. The Southern press and people with more sehreudness than was displayed in the North, finding that they had faild to capture Washington, and march on to New York, as they had boasted they would, [do], assumed that they only defended their Capital and Southern territory, hence ~~Gettysburg~~ Antietam, Gettysburg, and all other battles that had been fought were failures on our part and victories for them. Their Army believed this, hence a morale which could only be overcome by desperate and continuous hard fighting. The battles of the Wilderness, of Spottsylvania, of North Anna and of Cold Harbor, bloody and terrible as they were on our side, were [were more damaging to the enemy tho his losses in men were not so great owing to the fact that we were save in the Wilderness almost invariably the attacking party and when they did attack it was in the open field] equally so to the enemy, and so crippled him as to make him [the] wary ever after of taking the offensive

These battles exibited an endurance and bravery on the part of the soldiery that could only be engendered by long training and institutions that gives to each individual a consciousness of his own manhood and equal importance ~~with~~ and rights with all others in the state. What other Nation can boast of Armies composed of such material?

The details of these battles are given in the report of Gn. Meade and the subordinate reports accompanying it. I will call attention to the fact however that in the campaign of forty-three days, from the Rapidann to the James, the Army had to be supplied from an ever shifting base, a distance of, never less than twelve, and at times twenty miles, by wagons, over narrow roads and through a densely wooded country. Concidering the lack of wharfs at each new water base, where to discharge vessels conveniently, and that ~~a train of~~ more than 4000 wagons were necessary for this, too much credit can not be given the ~~the~~ QuartersMaster' Dept. for the efficiency displayed.

Little or no difficulty was experienced in affording entire pro-

tection to the immense ~~wagon~~ train accompanying the Army. Under
the general supervision of the Chief QuarterMaster, Brig. Gn. R.
Ingalls, it was kept occupying constantly all the available roads
between the Army and the seaboard. Our Cavalry under its most
able leader, Maj. Gn. P. H. Sheridan, kept the Cavalry of the
enemy constantly on the defensive.

The Army sent to operate against Richmond having hermeti-
cally sealed itself at Bermuda Hundred the enemy was enabled to
~~send~~ bring the most, if not all, the reinforcements brought from the
South, by Beaurigard, against the Army of the Potomac, then at
Cold Harbor. In addition to this reinforcement a very cone[s]ider-
able reinforcement, probably not less than 15,000 men, was obtained by calling in the scattered troops, under Breckenridge, from
the Western part of Va. ~~As~~ The position at Bermuda Hundred was
as easy defended as it was difficult to operate from it against the
enemy. I determined therefore to bring from there all avilable
forces, leaving only sufficient to secure what had been gained. Accordingly the following instructions were given.

Maj. Gen. W. F. Smith, in command of this reinforcement, arrived at the White House with the advce of it in the —— of June.
~~He immediately sent a Staff officer to say that if he could remain
at the~~

He immediately set out to join the Army at Cold Harbor, without awaiting the arrival of the rear of his troops, and was in time
to join in the last of the assaults made at that place with the hope
of driving the enemy from his position. The enemy's position proved
too strong and too well fortified to be carried by assault.—In this
attempt our loss was heavy whilst that of the enemy, I have reason
to believe, was comparitively light. It was the only attack made
from the Rapidann to the James which did not ~~gain us substantial
advantage.~~ inflict upon the enemy losses to compensate for our own
loss. I would not be understood as saying that all ~~the att~~ previous
attacks resulted in victories to our Arms, or accomplished as much
as I had hoped from them. But they inflicted upon the enemy severe
losses which tended in the end to the complete overthrow of the
rebellion.

About this time Gn. Hunter made his appearance near Lynchburg Va. This compelled Gen. Lee to detach Ewells Corps for the
defence of that place, and to drive Gen. Hunter from the interior of
the state. This corps had been reduced by previous battles to probably ~~about one~~ not more than one half of the number it had in the
battle of the Wilderness. One of the three ~~d~~Divisions composing it
had been killed, wounded and captured, almost complete, in one
engagement at Spottsylvania C. H. and the casualties in the other
two Divisions, no doubt, made the result all that is stated, making
liberal allowances for convalescents brought from the rear to reinforce the Corps after the first battle was fought.

The enemy's position ~~having been made~~ [at Coal Harbor] was
so strongly ~~and~~ fortified that with the Chckahominy immediately
to the rear ~~precludin~~ of it, ~~with and~~ and the defences of Richmond
near ~~to it~~ by ~~precluding~~ the possibility of turning it. ~~I determined~~
was entirely precluded. I determined therefore to make no further
assaults but as speedily as possible to get to the South side of James
River, as previously intended, with the entire army.

As cone[s]iderable time was necessary to get from Washington and elsewhere the pontoons and ferry boats necessary for crossing so large a body of men over a stream more than 200 ~~feet ya~~ feet
in width, and of great debth, a number of days of comparitive quiet
was spent, after the last assault of Cold Harbor, and before commencing the last flank movement which was to place us on ~~this new~~
~~field~~ the South side of the James.

I attached so much importance to the ~~position~~ possession of
Petersburg, as a preliminary to the seige of Richmond, that I sent
back to City Point, ~~and~~ or Bermuda, ~~in advance of~~ by water, in advance of the movement of the entire Army, all the troops which had
been previously brought from there, ~~places~~ less ~~those lost in~~ casualties in battle, for the express purpose of having a force there sufficient to secure this object. This plan was not communicated in
orders because I could not foresee, with certainty, the day when
the Army of the Potomac could be placed in a position to reinforce
troops at Petersburg. I did not want to send troops there to be driven
away, as they might have been by the whole of Lee's Army falling

upon them before they could intrench. The Chickahominy, with its swamps and inextricable forrests, afforded such an obsticle to the movement of an Army, with such a train of wagons as we had, that ~~that~~ I felt by no means confidant of effecting the crossing of the James above the Mouth of the Chickahominy. Here there might be a delay of a full week in the time of reaching Petersburg, with the Army drawn so far from Richmond as to leave the enemy perfectly free to act against any exposed force. The crossings of the Chickahominy were seized however, without difficulty, and apparently by surprize to the enemy and the James River was reached at Wilcox Landing within twenty-four hours from the time of leaving Cold Harbor. This was on the 14th of June. On the following morning, after having given orders for the crossing of the 2d Army Corps at Wilcox Landing, by ~~f~~ the ferry boats which had been previously provided, and the balance of the Army by the Pontoon bridge, as soon as it could be laid, at a point a few miles lower down the river, at ———, I took a steamer for Bermuda Hundred to give the necessary orders for the capture of Petersburg. The instructions to Gen. Butler were verbal and were for him to send Gn. Smith immediately, that night, with all the troops he could ~~given~~ him without sacrificing the position he then held. I told him that I would return immediately to the Army below, ~~and~~ would hasten ~~the~~ its crossing, and would throw it forward to Petersburg, by Divisions, as rapidly as it could be done. We could reinforce our Army at Petersburg more rapidly than the enemy could bring ~~reinforcements~~ troops against us.

Gen. Smith got off as directed and confronted the enemy's pickets near Petersburg before daylight. For some reason certainly not fully justifyable ~~Gen. Smith~~ he did not get ready ~~and~~ to make his assault until near Sundown of the 16th, of the evening after his arrival. Even then the enemy had not reinforced Petersburg with a single brigade from Richmond, or the Army of Northern Va. Gen. Hancock had arrived with the advance of his Corps and the whole of it was near at hand, ready to co-operate in anything Gn. Smith might direct. The fortifications defending the city were easily carried and nothing interposed to prevent the march of our

troops immediately in to take possession. This was not done however. By the time Gn. I arrived the next day the enemy were in
force.

The after operations in trying to secure what was so nearly
gained on the 16th of June 1864 is described in the reports of Maj.
Gen. Meade, and others accompanying this.

A few days previous to the assault on Petersburg made by my
direction Gen. Butler had directed one under Gens. Gilmore and
Kautz which scarsely resulted in determining what the enemy had
either in the way of fortifications or defenders. As there was no
expectation of holding the place, if taken, it was ill advised and I
would not have permitted it had I known that in advance that it
was to be made. The tendency was to attract the attention of the
enemy to an important point for us to possess and induce him to
strengthen the weak points.

As the object to be gained was only the distruction of a bridge,
of no vital importance to the enemy, I think Gen. Gilmore was did
perfectly right in returning as soon as he ascertained that fortifications must be carried to accomplish his object. Success would
have been no compensation for the loss of life which must necessarily have ensued.

After severe fighting and successful battles about Atlanta, and
a brilliant flank movement by the right, all fully described in his
reports, Gen. Sherman succesded in the capture of that place on
the   of   .

This was a successful termination of his campaign so far as he
had written instructions I had The Army was immediately put in
camp in and about the city and all preparations made for refitting
and supplying th it for any future service. The great length of road
from Atlanta to the Cumberland river, which had to be guarded to
secure this, allowed the troops but little rest. About the   of
          Mr. Jefferson Davis appeared in Macon Ga. and made a
speach which was duly reported in the papers of the South, and
soon became known over the whole country. It disclosed the plans
of the enemy and enabled Sherman fully to meet them. He disclosed the weekness to of supposing that an Army which had been

beaten and fearfully desimated in a vain attempt at the defensive could successfully undertake the offensive against the same Army that had so often defeated it. In execution of this plan Hood, with his Army, was soon reported to the Southwest of Atlanta. Soon after by moving far to Sherman's right he sucseeded in reaching the rail-road about   and commenced moving North on it. Sherman, leaving a force to hold Atlanta, fell upon him with the remainder of his Army, and drove him to   Alabama. Seeing the constant annoiyance he would have with the roads to his rear if we attempted to hold Atlanta, Sherman proposed the abandonment and distruction of that place, with all the roads leading to it. The following ł is his letter on this subject.

It was the original design to hold Atlanta and by getting through to the seacost, with a garrison left at some point on the ~~rail-road~~ Southern rail-road leading East & West through Ga. to effectually sever the East from the West. In other words it was the design to cut the would be Confederacy in two again as it had been once cut by our gaining possession of the Mississippi River. Gn. Shermans plan virtually effected the same object. ~~and~~ It also released a great number of troops for the accomplishment of ~~its~~ that would have been required to hold Atlanta and communications with it. This course was adopted and preparations immediately commenced for the advance.

At the begining of the Campaign of 1864 it was hoped that after all opposition to the advance ~~fu~~pon Atlanta & Richmond had been overcome these two strategic points would fall into ~~the~~ our hands. The gaining these two points would be the end of the original Campaingn. A new one would then be commenced in which the objective points would depend upon the positions assumed by the enemy, and the Army at Atlanta, and the one at Richmond, would start out together a[s] they had done the 4th of May 1864. But ~~it became~~ the failure to take Richmond whilst Lee's Army was between the North Anna and the Rapidann; again the failure to capture Petersburg on the 1[6]th of June when it was easily accessible; and also again on the 30th of July, ~~at~~ the occation of the Mine explosion, ~~whilst~~ made it apparent that the fall of Richmond, whilst it was certain to occur before there would be any withdrawel of the Union Arms, would be long defered. It would not be in consonance with the idea started out upon to [of] kccp[ing] all troops actively engaged to the end of the Rebellion to keep Sherman's large and fine Army on guard duty until that event occured.

It was readily cone[s]ented to therefore that Sherman should start for the Seacoast. His coming out point could not be definitely fixed. Having to gather his subsistence as he marched through the country it was not impossible that a force inferior to his own might compell him to head for such point as he could reach instead of such as he might prefer.

The blindness of the enemy however in ignoring his movement, and sending Hood's Army, the only cone[s]iderable force he had West of Richmond, Northward, on an offensive campaign, left the whole country open and Sherman's route entirely to his own choice.—How that campaign was conducted, how little opposition was met with, and the condition of the country through which the Army passed, are all clearly set forth in Gn. Sherman's admirable report.

After the determination to start the Army from Atlanta to the Sea Coast was formed I had no desire to capture Richmond before the success of that movement was secured, unless I could get with it the greater part of the Army defending it. No move during the progress of Sherman from Atlanta to Savannah, or from Savannah to Goldsboro', was made with any expectation or desire to capture either Petersburg or Richmond. The Aim was simply to secure a better position to accomplish that end, when it might be desirable, and to cover as far as possible the enemy's Southern communications. Whilst the Army was at Savanna, or elswhere upon the Seacoast, I would have been glad to have captured Richmond if it had been feasable to do so, but at no other time during the memorable Campaigns before mentioned.

In the march from Atlanta Southward Gen. Sherman took with him a force of about 65,000 men of all Arms. This was sufficient to meet Hood's Army should he change from his threatened Northern course to meet him. It left under Gen's Thomas and Schofield, with the great numbers relived from guarding rail-roads by destroying ~~the~~ and abandoning the roads back to Dalton, a sufficient force to meet him should he continue on his threatened course. Hood, or those from whom he received his orders, persisted upon the latter alternative which seemed to me to be leading to his certain doom. At all events had I had the power to command both Armies I should not have changed those under which Hood seemed to be acting.

Hood pushed North and must have felt elated at the ease with which he reached the vicinity of Franklin, Tenn. Here he met with the first serious opposition, and, I am satisfied, the fatal blow to all his expectations.

The battle of Franklin, fought   , was an indecisive victory because, the night after the battle, the Union troops were withdrawn to Nashville, by the orders of Gen. Thomas, who was Gen. Schofields superior officer. This left the field to the enemy, not won ~~in~~ [by] battle but ~~in order~~ voluntarily abandoned so that the whole force at Gn. Thomas' command ~~could~~ might be brought against him. I am not satisfied that this withdrawel was necessary, or even the best course to pursue. But Hood's final defeat at Nashville, on the   , was so complete that it will be accepted as the part of good judgement to concentrate there for the final battle. I should have prefered seeing the Army at Franklin reinforced by everything available from Nashville, and had the pursuit of the flying columns of the enemy commenced there.

The stubborn attack of the enemy upon strongly entrench troops at Franklin, ~~and his~~ with fearful losses, and his after very weak defence of intrenchments which he was allowed to build around Nashville, show the effect of that battle [up]on the morale ~~upon~~ of Hood's Army.

But at this time troops were arriving daily at Nashville from Mo. where they were no longer needed. The withdrawel to Nashville, and delay whilst the enemy were fortifying around the city, secured the services of this additional forces

I grew very impatient over the delay ~~which took place~~ before the battle of Nashville took place, as the following dispatches sent at the time will shew,   Here insert dispatches and started West to superintend matters ~~in per~~ there in person. I was fearful Hood would cross the Cumberland and cause fearful trouble. The condition of the state of Ky. was such that I feared an enemy would raise up there, in case he crossed, more formidable than the remnant left of the Franklin beaten ~~remnant of an~~ army. Arriving at Washington City ~~however~~ I was compelled to wait over night for the train West. That night I received Gn. Thomas dispatch announcing his attack upon the enemy, and the result, so far as the battle had progressed. I was delighted. All fears and apprehensions were dispelled.

During the progress of events heretofore imperfectly narrated, the enemy, under ~~Price of the~~ General Sterling ~~p~~Price of the Rebel Army, made his appearance in Mo. His force, about 12.000 strong, mostly mounted, could not be successfully met by anything that could be concentrated against him from the limited forces then in the state. ~~Price's troops~~ This force of the enemy being drawn from Southern Arkansas however it liberated and left free for serice elsewhere a large portion of the troops we had in that state. Maj. Gn. A. J. Smith with his little band of veterans had done their work so well in Miss. after their return from the Red River expedition, that they were also free. This gave force enough to repel the invaders of Mo. and more force than ~~were~~ was ever properly used.

The following dispatches from the Chief of Staff of the Army, Maj. Gn. Halleck, and myself, will show the dispositions made to repel this invasion. The impunity with which Price was enabled to roam over the state of Mo. for a long time, and the incalculable mischief done by him will show, to Missourians at least, how ineffectually ~~they~~ these forces were used.

I will not attempt to follow the Missouri Campaign of 1864 through its progress. I have not the time nor the data to do the subject justice, and, with all the balance of my cares and responsibilities at the time I ~~was so~~ became so much dissatisfied with management there that I could think of no remedy except in a change of commanders, and might do injustice if I attempted it therefore.

Price went out of Mo. finally, carrying with him an immense

amount of plunder taken from the defensless people of the state. He was pursued, and bravely fought, by a portion of the troops left for the defence of the state. (nNone of the large number sent from Arkansas and elswhere being with them.) His plunder, and his desire to secure it, led evidently to his defeat. Price, and his Army, left the state, never to return with hostile intent, because he had staid as long as he wanted to, knowing as he did that a permanent lodgement could not be made there. The pursuit added to his disaster and expedited his marches but did not lead to them.

After the defeat of Hood at Nashville he was pursued to the Tennessee river by one Corps of Inf,y, under Maj. Gn. T. J. Wood, and a Cavalry force under Bvt. Maj. Gn. J. H. Wilson.

In this pursuit the enemy was forced to leave many pieces of Artillery and much of his transportation. It was of course demoralizing to an Army to be forced from a field of its own choosing, and pursued, but the chase being exclusively a stern one, Hood found but little difficulty in reaching the Tennessee River with the bulk of what was left of his Army, after the battles about Nashville.

About this time rains had set in heavily in Tennessee and North Alabama making it difficult to move Army transportation and Artillery. For this consideration Gen. Thomas stoped the pursuit at the Tennessee River and proposed resting and refitting his Army for a spring campaign. The following is his dispatch on the subject sent at the time.

The roads might be impracticable for active movements but rest to troops I did not regard as necessary. On the contrary the active operations of the troops from the 4th of May preceeding had fitted them for enduring physical exertion. For the The

The defense of the line of the Tenn. did not require the force which had beaten and so nearly destroyed the only armies[y] threatning it. I determined therefore to find fields of operation for the surplus troops under Gen. Thomas command, and a field too calculated to prevent what was left of the Army under Hood coming East to interpose between Sherman and his objective. I regarded this it as the peculiar province of the troops under Gen. Thomas either to destroy the Army which invaded Tennessee or to hold it from joining other Armies of the enemy. The first part of this duty was well nigh accomplished, the latter seemed impossible from the base occupied.

The Navy, under the gallant leadership of Admiral Farragut, had already secured to the occupation of United States troops the ~~possession~~ forts at the Mouth of Mobile Bay. Mobile was a point of great apparent advantage to the enemy and I believed by threatning it with a strong force the enemy would either be compelled to yieald it up or to concentrate the forces that Hood commanded for its defence. Gen. Canby commanding the Dept. of the Gulf had forces ~~enou~~ more than sufficient for holding the territory in his possession, ~~but not surplus enough~~ against all that threatened it, but not surplus sufficient for this task. This then looked to me like a field for Winter operations for a part at least of the surplus troops in North Alabama. Accordingly the following orders and instructions were given to Gens. Thomas and Canby.

The troops ordered South were got off with great promptness. But a succession of storms and bad weather in the South, rarely paralleled, delayed for weeks the expedition to Mobile Bay and left loose the greater part of the enemys force in the West, to march against Sherman, then on his march from Pocotalego and Savannah to Goldsboro.

The instructions above quoted shew that it was the forces under Maj. Gen. A. J. Smith that were sent to Mobile Bay! It will be observed that ~~they~~ these troops had scarsely found a resting place for the "soles of their feet" from the Winter of 63–4 to the time of which I now write. They went in Feb.y /6~~34~~ with Sherman to Meridian Miss. and returned to Vicksburg; thence ~~the went~~ upon the Red River expedition of which so much has been said and so little is known; thence returned to Memphis just in time to push into Miss. and retrieve our lost fortunes there; finished this in time to be sent to Mo. which was then being invaded by Price; (and I will give it as my firm conviction that they would have driven ~~him~~ Price out of the state long before he did go, and in time to have prevented much of the destruction and loss of private property, if no further instructions had been given than simply to march and find the enemy, and fight him wherever found,) thence they returned South, to Nashville just in time to take part in the battles there, and after the battles to go to North Alabama, to try to head off the enemy; thence to Mobile Bay, and after the fall of that place into the interior of the state; and, I may add, ~~they have~~ a portion of this force have now gone to Western Texas.—It would not be astonishing if it ~~would~~ should yet prove the fate of this gallant ~~men~~ band of men to establish, for ever, as a code of international law, to be observed by all Nations, the *Monroe Doctrine*.

There was still left in Tenn. a large surplus force to dispose of. Fort Fisher, N. C. had fallen into our hands, but Wilmington was still held by the enemy. Holding the entrance to the Harbor as we did the place s[eas]ed to be of importance to the enemy as an entrance for blockade runners. But with their rail-road connection with Charleston & Richmond, as well as the interior of N. C. it was a dangerous place to leave in the hands of the enemy. It afforded a good point of departure for the enemy to strike the Army commanded by Gn. Sherman in flank and rear whilst on ~~his~~ the march for Goldsboro', without the possibility of aid from our forces at the Mouth of the ~~river~~ Cape Fear river. With Wilmington in our possession the advantages were reversed. It afforded a base of supplies and reinforcements when Sherman should come opposite to it, and threatened the enemy in flank and rear should he attempt to head off our troops earl~~y~~[i]er.

This important task was confided to Gen. Schofield ~~for~~ in whose judgement and Military skill the country ~~has one of her ablest defenders~~ may well fell proud. ~~But very little~~ He, ~~and the troops~~ with the Army of the Ohio, were brought from the West for the accomplishment of this object. But little instruction was given Gn. Schofield beyond the object to be accomplished as will be seen by a perusal of the orders and dispatches given at the time.

Gen. Schofield's own report gives the details of all his operations.

~~So much has been said about the operations which led to the capture of Fort Fisher, and the origin of the great gunpowder plot which was intended to accomplish so much with such great de-~~

~~struction of rebel and traitor life that I feel it a duty to say~~ here all
~~I know on the subject.~~

Not long after getting South of the James River with the Army
of the Potomac General Butler proposed to me to blow up Charleston, Fort Sumpter, and the surrounding country generally, by the
use of gunpowder. His plan was to load a thousand ton of gunpowder on a steamer, with fuse and all fixed to explode the whole
mass s~~y~~[i]multaneously. This was to be fired by a galvanic battery
attached in some way to clockwork, which could be set so as to
insure the explosion to take place at the given time, leaving time
for those who set the Machinery opportuny to get beyond danger.
The whole was then to be run up as near the enemy's guns as possible and turned loose, with helm lashed, ~~he~~ and headed towards
the entrance to Charleston Harbor. I said but little on the subject
and that little expression of doubt as to the damage that would be
done beyond blowing up the steamer and the gunpowder aboard.
Several times after this Gen. Butler, when we would meet, would
give his theory of the effect of the explosion of large amounts of
gunpowder in the open air. He had it calculated to a nicety the
number of cubic feet of air that would be removed by the explosion
of a given amount of powder, and hence a vacuum throughout that
space that would cause all buildings, ~~within~~ casemates, and generally everything hollow, within it, to tumble in. I had no faith but
did not wish to be offensive, and had no idea of trying the experiment, hence said but little.

After this Gen. Butler sent me an ~~extr~~[act] extract from a news
paper purporting to give the effect of an accidental explosion in
England and wanted my views upon the effect. Out of
respect to Gn. Butler's position I turned this over to Lt. Col. now
Bvt. Brig. Gn. Comstock of my staff to report upon, and sent his
repl~~ys~~ to Gen. Butler. (He reported adversely to the use of powder
in the way proposed). If the can be found give here the note of
Gen. Butler, the extract refered to and Gen. Comstocks reply to it
in place of the sentence in brackets.

I thought now, if I expended further thought on the subject
atal, that this subject was exhausted and would not be brought up

again. But I found not. The Navy had been making strenuous efforts to entirely seal the Harbor of Wilmington, without effect. The nature of the outlet of Cape Fear river is such that it requires watching for a great many miles to secure this. Without possession of the land it is impossible, with all the Navy of the United States, to entirely close ~~that~~ the harbor of Wilmington against the entrance of blockade runners. The country was growing clamerous for the suppression of blockade running, and somewhat impatient with the Navy Dept. for not stopping it. As stated the only way to accomplish this was by possessing the land somewhere near the mouth of the river, and a look at the map will show that that possession would have to be North of New Inlet, or Fort Fisher. The Naval branch of our service was not only anxious to stop this clamor but were equally anxious to serve the cause and the country with those who were making it. Hence they appealed to me for co-operation. Without land forces nothing could be done. I agreed to give the necessary co-operation. Immediately commenced the assemblage in Hampton Roads of the most formidable Armada ever assembled, or consentrated, upon one given point. This necessarily attrected the attention of the enemy as well as that of the loyal North, and through the imprudence of the public press, and very likely of officers of both branches of service, the exact object of the whole expedition became a subject of common discussion in the papers both nNorth and South. The enemy prepared for it. This made me delay sending the land force, assigning one pretext and an other, the great one, not mentioned however, being that I believed after all the public notice given it would fail.

At this juncture of affairs the Hon. G. V. Fox, Asst. Sec. of the Navy, called on me, believing that the difficulty was in sparing the number of men required, and asked if I could not spare 2500 men to take and hold the point of land on which Fort Fisher stands if the Navy would take it. My reply was in the affirmative. Soon after I was in Washington City and whilst in the office of the Sec. of War, the President being present, the subject of blowing up Fort Fisher by the use of a steamer loaded with 400 tuns of gunpowder was introduced. I found that the subject had been renewed in

Washington and the Chief Engineer and the Chief of Ordnance
had both been called on to report their opinion of what would be
the effect of such explosion. I never saw their reports but understand the Chief Engineer thought about the same effect would be
produced by it that would be produced by Infantry using feathers
instead of bullets for for charging their muskets.

The Sec. of War was opposed to this useless expenditure of
public money. I replied, as near as my memory serves me, in substance, that it might prove as cheap a way as could be devised for
exploding the theory started, and it gave employment for troops
and the Navy in a direction that would give great satisfaction, and
might do some good in preventing blockade running. President
Lincoln decided to let the experiment be tried. I infered from this
that the Navy Dept. in their great anxiety to close Cape Fear river
to blockade runners, were anxious to try almost any experiment.

Preparations were at once commenced for charging this Monster Torpedo. Cone[s]iderable delay was caused by having to send
off South for a proper Steamer, in collecting the material, and in
loading the vessel. In the mean time Sherman's movements in the
South created such an call for resistence an excitement, that the
enemy called together for that purpose to resist it everything they
could spare. Every thing was taken from the defences of Wilmington, and its defences dependencies, except a little Artilley few Artil-
lerists and a class of inferior reserves, composed of old men and
children. Learning this fact I determined to make the expedition
effective without counting any thing on the explosion of the torpedo
then preparing being prepared. Accordingly Instead of 2500 men
6500 were sent, equipped with everything to carry on a siege
against fFort Fisher if a landing could be effected. Learning the
above facts I believed this force sufficient to make the expedition
against Fort Fisher effective without counting upon the monster
torpedo.

Maj. Gn. G. Weitzel was selected by me to command this expedition. Gen. Butler commanding the Army from which the troops
were taken for this enterprise, and the territory within which they
were to operate being within the limits of his Dept. Military

courticy required that all orders and instructions should go through him. They were so sent. ~~and~~ ~~b~~But Gen. Weitzel has since officially informed me that he never received them nor was he aware of them until he read Gen. Butler's official report of his Fort Fisher failure, ~~and m~~ with my endorsement thereon.

I had no idea of Gen. Butler accompanying the expedition until the evening he ~~did~~ started, and then did not dream but Gn. Weitzel had received all the instructions, and would still be allowed to command. I rather formed the idea that Gn. Butler was actuated by a desire to witness the effect of his pet *Gunpowder plot.*

After reaching Hampton Roads the expedition ~~to~~ against Fort Fisher was detained several days awaiting the loading of the powder boat. ~~It~~ The object of the expedition become known, or it was surmised, by the enemy and a Division of troops, (Hokes) was detached from Lee's Army and started South. Learning this fact I immediate concluded they were going to Wilmington. Gen. Butler was ~~at once~~ immediately informed of this and directed to start the expedition, at once, with or without the powder boat. My order seemed to have but little effect for there was still a delay after it had been given of several days.

My orders and directions in this matter have been officially reported heretofore, and laid before the public. I will however repeat them here.

The expedition ~~went to~~ got off finally on the ——— and after delays arising from consuming the supply of Water carried with them, compelling a return to Morehead City for a new supply, the result of delay at Ft. Monroe, bad weather &c. reached and effected a landing with a portion, probably not to exceed one half of it, on the   The powder boat was first exploded however; but it would seem from the notice taken of it, in the Southern papers, that the enemy were never enlightened as to the object of the explosion until they were informed by the Northern press.

The expedition returned to the James river, contrary to the instructions which had been given, reaching ~~it~~ Ft. Monroe on the

I was at Ft. Monroe when a part of the expedition from Fort Fisher arrived. Two officers, Col. now Bvt. Maj. Gn. N. R. Curtis,

and Lt.   Ross   Vt. Vol. Inf.y voluntarily reported to
me that when recalled they were nearly into the fort and could have
taken it in a few minuets, and without much if any loss. Farther,
that if they had not been recalled ~~for a~~ when they were they would
have had it.

The expedition captured and brought back with them a battalion of children the oldest of them probably not being seventeen

A few days after the return of Gn. Butler to the James River
I received a letter from Adm.l Porter informing me that he was still
off Ft. Fisher with his fleet, and expressing the conviction that
under a proper leader the place could be taken. The natural sup-
[p]osition with me was that when the troops abandoned the expedition the Navy would do so also. Finding they had not however
I wrote to Adm.l Porter to hold on and I would have an other attempt made to take the place.

This time I selected Brig. now Maj. Gn. A. H. Terry to command. The same troops that went the first time were sent back
again, with the addition of a small brigade more, numbering
about 1.400 men, and a small siege train which however it was
never found necessary to land.

This time I communicated my orders direct to the commander
of the expedition ~~It~~ As it will be seen these instructions did not
differ materially from those first given.

It will be noticed that in neither instance was there an order to
Assault Fort Fisher. That was a matter left entirely to the discretion of the commanding officer. It was enjoined however to stay,
if a landing could be effected, until Fort Fisher was reduced, claiming that to effect a landing would be a success.

This last effort proved a triumph and to the end of the Rebellion closed ~~F~~Cape Fear river against blockade runners, except to
fall into our hands.

Whilst events narrated to this time in this report were going
on, important events had transpired in the Shenandoah Valley, and
more were destined to transpire there.

The troops detached by Gen. Lee, from Cold Harbor, for the defence of Lynchburg, after fully assuring themselves of the safety of

that section of the State of Virginia from further operations of the forces under Gen. Hunter, turned Northward and threatened Maryland and the District of Columbia. General Hunter having carried his forces back through Western Va. to the Kanhawa river, and that stream and the Ohio river being low and difficult of navigation, great delay was experienced in returning his command to the defence of these places. It became necessary therefore to find other troops for the defence of the National Capitol. They were taken from the Army investing Petersburg.—For a full explanation of the information of the information under which I was then acting, and of what was done, I will here give the dispatches which passed at the time between Maj. Gn. Halleck, Chief of Staff of the Army, and myself.

It will be observed that no force was thought necessary beyond the dismounted Cavalry of the Armies about Richmond. I sent however one Division of Infantry from the 6th Army Corps, and afterwards the whole of that Corps, and two of the three Divisions of the Cavalry Corps attached to the Army of the Potomac.—It is but fare to state however that all but the first Div. of the 6th Corps sent were only sent after I had been notified of the progress the enemy were making towards Washington.

The first troops sent from the investment of Petersburg were ordered by me to Baltimore knowing that but little delay would incur in getting them to Washington if they should be wanted there, and regarding Baltimore as the better point to start from to meet the enemy. Gen. Lewis Wallace, in command at Baltimore at the time, took the force thus given him and pushed out, with commendable promptitude, to the meet the enemy on the Monocacy. His force was not sufficient to [i]nsure success, but he fought the battle nevertheless, and, although it resulted in a defeat to our arms (at least it would have to be called so disconnected from its bearing upon the defence of Washington) yet is served to delay the enemy a sufficient time to enable Gen. WH. G. Wright to reach Washington with the remaining Divisions of his Corps. From that time Washington ceased to be in danger. I gave the orders from City Point to take the offencive. The wires being down between Washington and City Point at the time made it necessary to transmit messages a part of the way by boat, and consequently took from twenty-four to thirty-six hours to get dispatches through and the return answers back. Consequently, after orders would be given information would be received showing a different state of fact from those on which they were based. Hence there was a confusion and a and contradiction of orders which must have embarassed Gen. Wright and made his pursuit of the enemy less effective that it would otherwise have been.

The enemy retired to the neighborhood of Winchester Va. whilst the Union forces concentrated on the Monocacy at the crossing of the B & O road. This left open to the enemy Western Maryland and Southern Pennsylvania. and resulted in the burning of I was afraid from where I was to give positive orders for the movement of the Army at Monocacy lest by so doing I should expose Washington. Hence on the   I determined to visit the troops defending us from a Northerly invasion and determine for myself what was best to be done. Immediately on arrival at Monocacy I determined to put the troops South of the Potomac at Harper's Ferry, near to the enemy, and then see what should be done. Gen. Hunter was holding a large amount of the rolling stock of the B. & O road with the Army t so that no difficulty was encountered in getting the troops through to Hall Town the night of my arrival. Insert name of the little town 4 miles South of Harpers Ferry. I think it is Hall town   Having become dissatisfied with the management of the Cavalry in this section, and also having ordered two Divisions of the Cavalry from the Army of the Potomac to this field, I had previously ordered Gen. Sheridan on to Washin take command of this Arm of the service. He was in Washington when I went to Monocacy. I had previously determined to place Gn. Sheridan in command of the troops actively engaged against the enemy on this field, leaving Gn. Hunter in command of the Dept. and had ordered him on for that purpose. He Gn. Sheridan was in Washington, pursuant to this at the time I visited Monocacy. Gen. Hunter expresseding a willingness however to be relieved altogether and I telegraphed for Gen. Sheridan to come on and I placed him in command of the Dept. of West Va. and as soon as I could get it effected changed his command to a Military Division embracing the Dept. of Washington, Middle Dept. and the Dept. of West Va. How well he filled this trust is now a matter of History.

All that was done after this change of commanders, all the battles fought and brilliant victories won, have been fully reported to the Dept. and laid before the public. There is one thing however connected with Gen. Sheridans command which it seems necessary that I should say. After he was placed in command the two Armies laid confronting each other between   Creek and Winchester, for a long time, nothing being done except Cavalry raiding by the enemy which inflicted on us the burning of Chambersburg, Pa, and other injury until the enquiry began to be made, "who is Sheridan"? and a distrust began to manifest itself that he was not "the right man in the right place." His Cavalry under Gen. Averill, and some of the troops of the Dept. of West Va. had not received that discipline common to most of our Armies, consequently the enemy succeeded in raids which inflicted on us much damage including the burning of Chambersburg, Pa. All the efforts of the enemy however towards the troops, Cavalry or Infantry, immediately where Gn. Sheridan could superintend in persons, proved disastrous to him, the enemy, and resulted in very conciderable captures. But the B & O. rail-road was obstructed, the use of the ——— Name of Canal to be inserted. Chesapeake & Ohio Canal was lost to us and these successes were consequently lost sight of. Th

The two Armies lay in such a position that either could bring on a battle in at any time. Defeat to us would lay open to the enemy the whole North states of Maryland and Pa. for long distances before another Army could be interposed to stop them. Under these circumstances I hesitated about allowing the initiative to be taken. Finally the use of the B & O road, and the Canal become so indispensably necessary that the risk had to be taken. Still feeling afraid to telegraph the order for an attack, without knowing the feeling more than I did, General Sheridan's feeling as to what would be the probable result, I determined to visit him and decide then what should be done. Arriving at Harpers Ferry the afternoon of

I sent word for him to meet me the following morning at Charlestown Va. I met Gen. Sheridan prepared to lay down for him a plan of battle if it was decided to attack the enemy. On meeting however he pointed out so distinctly how each Army law, what he could do the moment he was authorized, and expressed such a confidance in sucsess that I saw but two words of instruction, *go on* it, were necessary.—It was now about noon of Saturday. For the convenience of forage the teams for supplying the Army were kept at Harper's Ferry, and were there at the time, except when hawling out supplies, I asked him if he could get up his teams and supplies in time to make the attack by Teusday morning. His reply was that he could move before daylight on Monday. He was off promptly to time and I may here add the result was such that I have never deemed it necessary to visit Gen. Sheridan since before giving him orders. to do.

A succession of victories afterwards so desimated the enemy in the Valley of the Shenandoah, all duly reported to the War Dept, that I was enabled to by   to return the 6th Army Corps to the Army of the Potomac, a Division besides to the Army of the James and afterwards, to send a Division of the 19th Corps to Gen. the Dept. of the Gulf to hold Sherman's aqu new acquisitions on the Sea Coast and thus leave all the force he had taken with him free to go on with their invasion.

I have neglected to state heretofore that at the commencement of the operations of 1864 every thing that could be, without giving up territory already fought for and won, was consentrated with the Main Armies operating from Chattanooga

I have heretofore neglected to state that whilst operations were going on against the before it was determined to direct Gn. Canby to move against Mobile, and whilst it was still supposed that all the forces of the enemy could be fully employed employed where they were, without giving them the privilege of abandoning one field to consentrate against an upon another, I ordered Gen. Canby to send to the East all his spare troops. This he did by sending two Divisions of the 19th Corps. They were intended as reinforcements for the Armies around Richmond. But the advance arriving about the t in Hampton Roads about the time whilst Washington was threatened still in danger I divertet them to that field. They plaid a conspicuous part in the victories in the Shenandoah Valley.

Notwithstanding all the depletion refered to of the Army of the Cumberland there was still left in Tennessee, under Gn. Thomas, a very large Cavalry force, and especially of Cavalry still for offensive operations. In co-operation with Gen. Sherman's movement Northward from Savannah, and General Canby's effort against mMobile I directed the two expeditions, the first under Maj. Gn. Geo. Stoneman and the second under Bvt. Maj. Gen. J. H. Wilson.

The following are the instructions and dispatches that were forwarded in each case.

Owing to bad roads, extreme weather and other delays Gn. Wilson did not get off until   As Gen. Canby was delayed for the same reasons, and about the same time, these two expeditions worked about as well together, and in harmony with all other Army movents on the great theatre of War, as could be expected. Mobile fell on the very day of Gn. Lee's surrender at Appomattox C. H. Va. and Gn. Wilson captured Macon Ga. having previously taken almost every important City in Alabama and Ga. that had not been visited by other Armies, just as the first news of Johnston's surrender were received. Without these captures the rebellion may or may not have collapsed suddenly as it did. Be this as it may it was a part of the great inflictions intended to produce that result.

The delays in Gn. Stoneman's start made it necessary to change all his instructions and finally he delayed so long that I cared but little whether he got off atal or not. I know he had difficulties, besides weather, to contend against which he could not obviate. I thought by substituting equipped troops instead of those first specified the Department Commander might have got him off according to first instructions.

Gen. Stoneman succeeded in destroying the Va. & Tenn. railroad well up towards Lynchburg and the Piedmont and Danville and Charlotte, or Piedmont, road for many miles, south of Danville

I had some fears before any movement was made by the Armies investing Richmond along in the Winter that the enemy might evacuate Richmond and move to Lynchburg with the view of making a dying effort at in prolongonging the Rebellion by attempting an invasion of the North. From that point they would threaten Maryland and Pa by the way of the Valley of Va. and East Tennessee, East Ky. and Ohio by going West. In this connection Gen. Stoneman's expedition was of great service.

To guard against this a large part of the new levies coming in from the West were sent to Gen. Thomas. He was directed also to repair the rail-road East of Knoxville to the Va. line, and to concentrate supplies in Knoxville for the support of a large Army, or even to be used as a base to suplyply an Army from in case it should become necessary to make a formidable campaign towards Lynchburg.

A large part of the Eastern recruits were concentrated about Winchester either to delay an invation from that direction, or to move offensively, as might prove necessary. Incorporated here are all the directions for the distribution of new troops, supplies at Knoxville, and for preparations for movements contingent upon those of the enemy.

Previous to the expedition of Gn. Stoneman here reported ~~Gen. Stoneman~~ he had mane a very successful one to the SaltWells of Va. and the Lead ~~m~~Mines of N. C. reports of which were communicated at the time.

Before commencing the final movement of 1865 which I believed would settle the fate of Richmond, and tell materially upon the continuance of the rebellion, I thought it of the utmost importance that all communications with the City, North of James River, should be cut off. To insure this being done effectually I told ~~g~~Gen. Sheridan, verbally, that he must command the expedition for accomplishing ~~this~~ it in person. The result is known.

March 1865 found Sherman with his Veterans, reinforced by Schofields Command, occyupying Goldsboro' N. C. with his communications complete to the Sea coast, at Morehead City and Wilmington, ~~and~~ Sheridan at White House on the Pamunky, with the rail-roads and Canal North of Richmond thoroughly destroyed. After the long march made by Sheridan's Cavalry over Winter roads, a little rest was necessary for his horses before commencing new exercises, and almost every animal required reshoeing. I determined to give this rest and refitting at White House. Whilst there the enemy could not know whether it was the intention to keep him on the North side of James River or not. If he was brought to the James River for refitting I feard the enemy would evacuate Richmond before I could be prepared to make an effectual pursuit. At this time the greatest source of uneasiness ~~I experienced~~ to me was from fear that the enemy would leave his strong lines about Richmond and Petersburg before he was forced to do so.

Gen. Sherman having got his troops all quietly in camp about Goldsboro', and all his preparations for forwarding supplies to them perfected, visited me at City Point on the   of March. He stated that by the 10th of April he could be all ready to start with his Army, fully equipped and rationed for twenty days. ~~He proposed threatening Raleigh~~ The object was, if it should become necessary, to bring his command to bear against Lee's Army in co-operation with the Armies of the Potomac and the James. Gn. Sherman proposed threatening Raleigh and then by turning suddenly to the right, reach the Roanoke at Gaston or thereabouts. From there he would put himself on the Richmond & Danville rail-roads South of Burkesville. This would necessarily have sealed the fate of Richmond.—Gen. Sherman was directed to carry this plan into execution if he received no further directions in the mean time. I explained to him however of the movement I should make commencing on the 29th of March. I expected this to be successful, but if it should not prove entirely so I could cut the Cavalry loose to destroy the Danville and South side rail-roads, and thus deprive the enemy of further supplies, and also prevent the rapid concentration of Lee's and Johnston's Armies.

Instead of the 29th ~~being~~ of March being the commencement of the last ~~Cam~~ move against Richmond I regard the day Gn. Sheridan left White House as the begining. The Army was only waiting his arrival at the left to commence its movements

Some explanation may seem necessary why I moved against an Army so strongly intrenched as Lee's was, with the force which

had been so long unsuccessful in driving it from its chosen position, when the means were at hand for insuring this result beyond
a peradventure. In the first place I had spent days of anxiety lest
each morning as I arose it would be to receive the report that the
enemy had commenced a retreat the night before. I was firmly convinced that Shermans crossing the Roanoke would be the signal
for Lee to leave. With Johnston and him combined in North Carolina a long, tedious and expensive campaign, consuming most of
the Summer, might become necessary. By moving out I would put
the Army in a better position for pursuit and would at least, by the
destruction of the Danville road, retard the consentration of the
two Armies of the enemy, and cause them to abandon much ma-
teriel which ~~they~~ he might otherwise save.

There was another concideration which weighed much with
me. We have experienced in this country ~~enough~~ unfortunately to
much of sectional jealousies. ~~From the fall of Fort Donelson in
Feb.y 1862 the Western Armies had generally had the prestige of
success with them. They had opened the Miss. river to our commerce and swept around through all the Western Southern States
well nigh to the backdoor of Richmond. Should their march continue it would have it would have caused, and would rightfully have
claimed it, the evacuation of Richmond. In future years, after reconstruction is fully effected, we would, in that case, have to witness
criminations and recriminations in the Halls of Congress~~

For four years the Army of the Potomac had been contending
against the Army of Northern Va. ~~It~~ I regarded it of the greatest
importance that it should finally put down that Army. It had been
my fortune to see the Armies both in the West and the East fight
battles, and, from experience, I knew there was no difference in the
fighting qualities of either. All that is possible for man to do, in
battle, either would do.

The Western Army commenced its battles on the Miss. and
received the final surrender of the remnant of the Army they commenced against in North Carolina. The Army of the Potomac
commenced its battles on the river from which its name is derived,
and received the final surrender of its old antagonist at Appomattox

C. H. Both Armies have a proud record, and all sections can well congratulate themselves, and each other, for having done each their full share towards ~~in~~ restoring the supremicy of the law over every foot of terretory belonging to the United States. Let them hope a long peace and future harmony with that enemy whose manhood, however mistaken their, ~~their~~ cause drew forth such ~~h~~Herculean deeds of valor.

Not knowing positively ~~that the f~~ some but the effort to capture Petersburg, and Richmond, might be delayed until the forces under Gn. Sherman were brought up, my orders and instructions contemplated this contingency. I said to the commanding Generals however, and particularly impressed it on Gn. Sheridan, who by his movements must necessary be further detached from me than either of the other Army Commanders, that I expected and intended to end the contest right there and then. For this reason Gn. Sheridan was specially instructed that he was not to cut loose for the raid contemplated in orders until he received notice from me to do so. I hoped never to have to give the order.

The following are all the written instructions communicated at the time.

All the details of the performances of each Army from the time they commenced moving, to the final surrender ~~at~~ of Gen. Lee at Appomattox C. H. are fully set forth in the reports of Gens Ord, Meade and Sheridan, and their subordinate commanders. There are some points however about which I should speak.

At first it was my intention, all things promising favorable, to hold Bermuda Hundred, our intrenchments North of James river, and City Point, and with the balance of the Army cut loose and march past the right flank of the enemy. Every preparation was made for this and to carry with the moving column twelve days supplies. In moving out however it was necessary to hold every foot back to our base until it was determined to so cut loose. The first night after starting, and the next day, the rain fell in such torrents as to make it impossible to move a wheeled vehicle, Artillery or supply wagon, a single foot except as corduroy roads were laid in front of them. Before the roads had sufficiently dried to admit of

any rapid movement the army was streached from the intrenchments on Hatchers Run ~~crossing~~ to beyond, or West of, the Boyd-
ton road, near Burgiss' Mill, still leaving a Corps and one Division
loose to go beyond, or to detach, as circumstances might require.
The enemy confronted us at every ~~P~~point from Richmond to our
extreme left. If my estimate of his forces were right I concieved his
lines must be weakly held and could therefore be penetrated. If so
this would be better that to cut loose and march around the flank
of the enemy as first designed. The offensive effort of the enemy the
week before, when he Captured Fort Steadman from which he was
afterwards driven with great loss, particularly favored this. We
taking the offensive in turn, on that occation, captured much of the
enemy's intrenched picket line ~~which~~ and still held it. This threw
~~our~~ the lines occupied by the beligerents so close together at some
points that it was but a momements run from one to the other.

My idea then was to ~~turn the enemys right flank with~~ have Gn.
Sheridan turn the right flank of the enemy with his Cavalry, and
when this was done to charge upon the line between Hatchers Run
and Petersburg. A reconnois was made ~~by us~~ under the supervision
of each Corps Commander, in their respective fronts, and the best
points were selected for directing the assaulting Columns against.
Every preparation was made to carry such an order into effect,
when ever it might be given, at least two days before the order was
given. In front of the 6th Corps, Maj. Gn. H. G. Wright Commanding, promised the most favorable result. ~~and~~ It is due to that gallant officer to say that he expressed a confidance in the ability of his
command to go through the enemy's line that argued success.

The first effort of Gen. Sheridan to turn the right of the enemy,
at Five Forks, proved unsuccessful. ~~One~~ he reached that point,
but there finding the enemy's Cavalry, not far inferior to his own
~~force~~ in numbers, reinforced by 8000 Infantry, he was ~~forced~~
compelled to retire towards Dinwiddie C. H. Here Gen. Sheridan
displaid great Generalship. Instead of retreating with his whole
command, on the Main Army, to tell his story of superior forces encountered, he deploid his Cavalry, on foot, leaving only mounted
men enough to ~~lead all the balance of~~ take charge of the horses.

This compelled the enemy to deploy over a vast extent of wooded and broken territory, and made his progress slow. At this juncture he dispatched to me what had taken place and that he was dropping back slowly towards Dinwiddie. I immediately gave ~~directions~~ the following directions for the detachment of the 5th Corps to his assistance

~~It was af~~

It was after nightfall when this information was received. I immediately dispatched a Staff officer to Gen. Sheridan with information of what had been done, and the orders given, and directed him to communicate with the troops sent to his assistance, and to take command of them. The result was a splendid victory the next day, the capture of several thousand prisoners, and the turning of the enemy's right. It was again after night before I recived the news of all that had taken place on our left. Some apprehensions filled my mind lest the enemy might desert his lines during the night, and, by falling on Gen. Sheridan before assistance could reach him, drive him from his acquired position, with great loss, and open the way for retreat. To prevent this as far as possible I ordered a bombardment to be commenced at once, on the whole line from from the Appomattox to the extreme left, and to be kept up all night. Whether ~~it~~ this produced the effect desired or not I do not know. The enemy did not leave until forced to however. Another Division was immediately sent to Gen. Sheridan, ~~in addit~~ under Bvt. Maj. Gn. N. Miles, that night. Orders were given for an assault at 4th ~~a~~ a. m. the following morning. Gen. Sheridan was informed of all the orders given and directed to move boldly with the command under him directly towards Petersburg, at daylight in the morning. But at the hour of 4 a. m. the charge was made and the enemy's lines ~~a few minuets afterwards~~ penetrated by the 6th Corps and immediately afterwards followed by two Divisions of the 24th Corps. Several thousand prisoners were Captured and all left of the enemy to the ~~left~~ South of Hatcher's Run were cut off from Petersburg. These were forced to retreat Westward, and, being attacked vigerously by Gen. Sheridan, were at last forced to take refuge by crossing to the North side of the Appomattox.

The ~~troops~~ 6th & 24th Corps immediately swung to the right and closed ~~what there was~~ all of the enemy to that side of them, up in Petersburg. On reaching ~~that~~ the enemy's line surrounding Petersburg a part of 24th Corps, by a most gallant charge, captured a strong enclosed work of the enemy, the most salient and commanding point south of Petersburg, thus materially shortning the line of investment necessary for taking in the City ~~of Petersburg~~.

The following morning it was found the enemy had evacuated ~~the City~~ Petersburg during the night. Notwithstanding positive assurances from one who professed to be an Engineer belonging to the Rebel Army, and knew of what he spoke, that the enemy had taken up a new line covering the Danville road, his right resting at Amelia Court House, I believed that he was in full retreat, and would endeavor to get South. Gen. Sheridan was already pushing for the Danville road keeping near the Appomattox. I immediately ordered the balance of the Army, except the portions left for garrisoning the works North of James river, Bermuda Hundred, and City Point, to push on in the same direction. This force was divided in two Columns one pushing alon~~d~~g the South Side road to Burkesville, and the other following the road taken by Sheridan. Should the enemy halt as reported this move would take him upon his right flank, cut off his supplies and only line of retreat.

All operations connected with the pursuit are fully set forth ~~by~~ in the reports of officers commanding the different Armies.

I was at no time sanguine of capturing ~~of capturing~~ the whole of Gen. Lee's Army until after the battle of Sailor's Creek, and he had recrossed the Appomattox after that battle. I had however believed that no conciderable portion of ~~it~~ his force would get away in an organized form. ~~and f~~Feeling this I had directed Gen. Sherman to abandon the idea of moving as it was intended he should, in the absence of further instructions, but to move at once without any other objective than Johnstons Army. This is the dispatch sent to him.

Feeling, after Gen. Lee had crossed the Appomattox at the close of the battle of Sailors Creek, that ~~his~~ his only chance for escape was in dispursing his Army, I addressed him a note asking the surrender of it, believing that if he was convinced of his inability to escape and retain controll of his officers and men that he would prefer doing ~~it~~ so to having them scatter under no responsible head. The correspondence that ensued has all once been ~~given~~ officially reported but I will repeat it here.

No matter what Gen. Lee's offenses may have been against the offended dignity of the Nation, great consideration is due him for his manly course and bearing shown ~~by him~~ in ~~the~~ his surrender at Appomattox C. H. ~~Could he have been persuaded that he was to be tried for treason, and pursued~~ as a traitor, ~~the surrender never would have taken place. Gen. Lee would this day be at large and a great part of the late rebel Armies would be scattered over the South, with Arms in their hands, causing infinite trouble.~~ Gen. Lee's great influance throughout the whole South caused his example to be followed, and to-day the result is that the Armies lately under ~~him~~ his leadership are at their homes desiring peace and quiet, and their Arms are in the hands of our Ordnance officers.

~~Offences may be great but there should always be some attonement sufficient for every offence, and Some allowance should also be made for difference of education, thought and nature. Already we see among those professedly loyal throughout the great conflict happily brought to a close so differing in opinion as to what should be done in the great work of reconstruction as to endanger peace among former friends. Those who have had to fight and risk their lives have learned moderation and forgiveness. Would it not be well for all to learn to yeald enough of their individual views to the will of the Majority to preserve a long and happy peace?~~

The surrender of Gen. Lee took place at Appomattox C. H. Va. on the 9th of Apl. 1865. An army which numbered probably not less than 80,000 effective men on the 29th of March had reduced to 26.700, the number surrendered, many of whom had thrown away their arms. Previous captures had reached ~~of~~ver 20,000 men, and the loss in killed, wounded and scattered had been very large making the ~~estimated~~ here made rather under than over the enemy's force in my opinion.

My own force was   Of this number however three full
Divisions were left North of James River, one Division betwen
James river and the Appomattox and at least 10,000 men at City
Point, besides other guards for stores and trains.

The surrender of Lee's Army was followed by the surrender of
all others of the enemy in rapid succession. First come Johnston's
surrender to Gn. Sherman; then Taylor's to Canby; then we heard
of Guerrilla bands and detached forces all over the country, East
and West of the Miss. surrendering to the nearest Federal Commanders; and finally of the forces in Texas surrendering also to
Gn. Canby.

This latter surrender did not take place however until after the
capture of the President and Vice President of the would be southern Confederacy. Then the bad faith was exhibited of first disbanding most of the Army and of permitting an indiscriminate
plunder of public property by the troops. A force was also on its
way to Texas sufficient to insure an easy triumph over all the
forces commanded by Kirby Smith if he should attempt to hold
out against them.

So far as the territory of the United States is concerned the
Authority of the Government extends over every foot of it. But not
so over all the her subjects. Many thousands have taken refuge
upon the soil of a neighboring Republic, with which we are at
peace, carrying arms rightfully belonging to the United States, and
which were, by the agreement, surrendered to us it. No security is
promised to the United States in all this. Some of the very leaders
who surrendered, in person, are now with these absconding bearers
of Arms which it was their duty to see delivered to United States
Authorities.—I will submit whether it is not a duty we owe to a
weak friendly but downtroden Nation, with which we are at peace,
to send an armed force to capture these recreants who not only
threaten the very existance of that Government but the future
peace of our own!

In view of the long proclaimed *Monroe Doctrine* the very act
of attempting to establish a Monarchy on this Continent, by the

aid of foreign bayonets, was an act of hostility to the United States. The aid and comfort afforded the enemy along the Rio Grande, by these foreign troops, was little less than open War.

In this effort of France to overthrow the rightful Government of Mexico I see great danger to the peace of this country if he is allowed to continue. Let foreign bayonets be withdrawn and we will see how long the Empire, *the choice of the people*, will stand. Whilst there a large standing Army will be necessary upon our Southern frontier, to afford security to the United States. If the rightful Government is restored we will have a friendly neighbor, looking to us for example and support, and a large diminution of the force upon our frontier can be made.

> Very respectfully
> your obt. svt.
> U. S. GRANT
> Lt. Gn.

ADfS, DLC-USG, III. The docket states: "This Original Report of General U. S. Grant, was given by him to his eldest son, Colonel Frederick Dent Grant, (later Major-General, U. S. Army) at The White House, Washington D. C. 1875" AN, *ibid*.

USG probably began to draft his report on June 20, 1865, finishing on or shortly before July 16. He then turned the draft over to staff officers to add correspondence and correct any errors; USG made final revisions in Oct. Insertions in the draft by staff are bracketed. See letter to Brig. Gen. John A. Rawlins, July 16, 1865; *Indianapolis Daily Journal*, Oct. 7, 1865; Adam Badeau to Elihu B. Washburne, Oct. 20, 1865, DLC-Elihu B. Washburne.

1. A substantially expanded final report was dated July 22. LS, DNA, RG 94, War Records Office, Union Battle Reports. *O.R.*, I, xxxiv, part 1, 8–59; *ibid*., I, xxxvi, part 1, 12–63; *ibid*., I, xxxviii, part 1, 1–51; *ibid*., I, xlvi, part 1, 11–60. *Memoirs*, II, 555–632. A letterbook copy with some corrections, but without the final paragraph, is in OClWHi. The final report was made public at the opening of the 39th Congress and printed in newspapers. See *New York Times*, Dec. 6, 1865; *Philadelphia Inquirer*, Dec. 15, 1865. D. Appleton and Company published a pamphlet edition of the report in 1865 and a French translation, Librairie Militaire, Maritime et Polytechnique, appeared in Paris in 1866.

On Dec. 25, 1865, Secretary of State William H. Seward wrote to USG. "Your note of the 21st insta[nt] together with two hundred copies of your report have been received   I have in reply to inform you that, though I should have been pleased to have received the full number requested, I am very thankful for those which you were able to send" LS, Seward Collection, NRU. On Jan. 17, 1866, the U.S. Senate passed a resolution to make available to USG 500 additional copies of the report. *CG*, 39-1, 265. USG also presented autographed copies of the report to friends. For examples, see DLC-George H. Stuart; DLC-William T. Sherman; Kuntz Collection, Tulane University, New Orleans, La. USG received letters of acknowledgment from Governor John A. Andrew of Mass. (Dec. 14, 1865); Alexander T. Stewart (Dec. 20); John Sherwood (Dec. 27); James W. Beekman (Dec. 27); Henry M. Black (Dec. 28); Henry L. Kendrick (Dec. 28); Augustus Estey (Dec. 30); Henry E. Davies (Dec. 30); Albert E. Church (Jan. 1, 1866); John D. Wolfe (Jan. 2); Henry Hilton (Jan. 2); Lt. Gen. John Michel, British Army (Jan. 5); Arthur F. Kinnaird, London (Jan. 30); and James M. Henry, London (Feb. 2). ALS, USG 3.

On Dec. 7, 1865, Maj. Gen. Andrew A. Humphreys, Philadelphia, wrote to Brig. Gen. John A. Rawlins. "(personal) . . . You may recollect my taking exception to the language of Genl. Meade's Report of the closing operations of the War. I have just read Genl. Grant's Report and regret that I had not taken some official notice of Genl. Meade's since I find Genl. Grant has adopted its language. As for instance in the pursuit of Lee on the 6th ~~Augt~~ April from Amelia Sulphur Springs to Sailor's Creek where night put an end to the contest, The Second Corps *captured* on that day 13 flags, 4 guns, 1700 prisoners and over 300 wagons. The chief *captures* were made at Sailor's Creek. Genl. Grant's Report says of the 2d Corps on that day 'while the 2d & 5th Corps pressed hard after, forcing him (the enemy) *to abandon* several hundred wagons & several pieces of artillery. . . . The movements of the 2d Corps and Genl. Ord's command contributed greatly to the day's success.' This is in reference to Genl. Sheridan's '*Capturing*' 16 pieces of arty. and about 400 wagons 'and 'the *capture* of 6000 or 7000 prisoners by the cavalry & 6th Corps.' Now the 5th Corps had nothing to do with my captures, being several miles distant from the 2d Corps. The enemy did not *abandon* what I *captured—I took* them in fighting, just as Genl. Sheridan did his '*captures*'; but I perceive upon referring to Genl. Meade's report that he uses the word *abandon* respecting those *captures* of mine and that Genl. Grant derives the word from him. There are other exceptional points derived from the same source which I do not think it worth while to mention, as this will serve as a sample, indeed I hardly thought it worth while to refer to the matter, yet was not altogether satisfied to let it pass entirely unnoticed." ALS and ADf, Humphreys Collection, PHi. On Dec. 16, Maj. Gen. Winfield S. Hancock, Baltimore, wrote to Bvt. Col. Theodore S. Bowers. "In my official reports I have studiously endeavored to comply with the Regulations of the Army, which require that, in reports of battles, Brigades and Divisions should be designated by the names of their commanders; and I have always considered that commanders of larger organizations should be treated with the same consideration. Even if it is not the intention of the commander to bestow praise upon a subordinate general, it would seem to be due to him that it should be recorded that he was at least present with his command. In reading over the published report of the Lieutenant General I feel that I have great cause to complain in this respect, and that I have been injured by the omission of my name and the designation of my Corps and command on many important occasions during the great campaign of 1864. In several instances when I commanded detached troops of all arms, in addition to my own Corps, on expeditions against the enemy—having on all such occasions severe conflicts, during which I captured at different times prisoners, guns and Colors—my name is not mentioned as being the commander, and in five such instances not mentioned at all, although in some cases a subordinate part of my force is designated by its commander's name. I cite as

follows: —. . . I regret that I am compelled to consider the published report of the
Lieutenant General an injury to my troops and to myself, and one that can be
used by my enemies, should they desire to do so, with more force than anything
that could well be written by any other person on the subject of the campaigns
of our armies against Richmond. The authority of the Lieutenant General in
such matters is so great, that the omission of a commander's name in certain
connections when the rule to mention it is so general, has great weight, and is
certain to conduce to the injury of the individual whose name is omitted." LS,
DNA, RG 108, Letters Received. Hancock had already forwarded to USG copies
of correspondence between himself and Maj. William F. Smith (former maj.
gen.), U.S. Engineers, concerning the events of June 15, 1864. Copies, *ibid.*

On Jan. 25, 1866, Bvt. Maj. Gen. Nelson A. Miles wrote to Rawlins. "I
have the honor very respectfully to call your attention to the report of the Lt.
General in reference to the fight at Sutherland Station   In the report mentioned
page 69 the Lt. General says—'The enemy south of Hatchers Run retreated
westward to Sutherland Station where they were overtaken by Miles Division.
A severe engagement ensued, and lasted until both his right and left flanks were
threatened by the approah of General Sheridan who was moving from Fords
Station &c'. I would respectfully submit the following account of the fight, and
ask his attention to the reports of Generals Meade, Sheridan and Humphrey regarding it, and if the statement is deemed correct, I would respectfully request
that the troops of my Division receive credit for wining that victory, as it is
now, a casual reader would beleive that the enemy fled, not because of the troops
opposing them, but by reason of the approach of other troops. I would respectfully submit the following statement. My Division followed them ~~enemy for
several miles~~ to Sutherland Station, and on overtaking them found them occupying a ridge on the road with a line of about three fourths of a mile long, this
about 10 A. M. Two direct attacks were made to endeavour to force them from
their position, but without success. I then determined to turn their left flank,
and for this purpose I detached one brigade which moved under cover of woods
and through ravines to a position directly on their flank unobserved. During this
time the enemy were deceived by faint attacks on their right. From this point
the detached brigade charged the enemy successfully rolling up their line, at
the same time the remainder of the Division advanced routing the enemy, and
~~completely~~ driving them from the field, capturing one color two pieces of Artillery, and about six hundred prisoners. This about half past two or three in the
afternoon. The enemy were ~~pressed~~ followed about three miles. About 5 o'clock
Genl. Humphrey's with the 2nd Division approached Sutherland Station coming
up the Petersburg Road. About dark a staff officer of General Sheridans rode up,
and asked where my line was, which was the first I had seen or heard of that
command since morning   I make this statement to show that the enemy were
driven from this position by the troops of my command" ALS, *ibid.* See *PUSG*,
14, 328.

On March 5, Henry Z. Gill, Richboro, Pa., wrote to USG. "I have the honor
to report that in the copies, published by the press, of your report of the close of
the war, there are some dates given respecting the battles in N. Carolina during
March 1865, which I believe have not been correctly reported to you. I was
present at those battles, as Surgeon-in-chief 1st Div. 20. A. C. and kept notes
during the entire campaign, and at its close made the fullest report of any one
in my Department. It is only because I feel a deep interest in the war and in its

results, and know that your report will make a part of the history of that memorable campaign (though second to that of Vicksburg) that I would call attention to the dates. Permit me to give a *partial* copy of my diary of the following dates: . . ." ALS, DNA, RG 108, Letters Received.

To Edwin M. Stanton

Washington June 20 *1865*

Hon. E. M. Stanton
Secretary of War
Sir!

I have the honor to recommend the promotion of Lieutenant Colonel Jos. Stockton, 72d Regt Illinois Vols Infantry, to the rank of Brigadier General by brevet, for gallant conduct and meritorious services during the siege of Vicksburg and especially for gallantry at the battle of Franklin, Tenn., where he was severely wounded, to date November 30th 1864.

Col. Stockton is a young man of fine abilities and great personal bravery and he is justly entitled to this recognition of his services. As his regiment will soon be mustered out of service I would respectfully request that early action be taken upon this recommendation.

Very respectfully Your Obt Servt
U. S. Grant Lieut Gen.

LS, deCoppet Collection, NjP. *O.R.*, I, xlix, part 2, 1016.

To Maj. Gen. Edward R. S. Canby

Washington [*June*] 4-20th 1865 [*3:30* P.M.]
Maj. Gn. Canby, New Orleans La.

Do our forces now occupy Galveston Texas? If they do not report the moment you know it to be so occupied.

U. S. Grant
Lt. Gn.

ALS (telegram sent), DNA, RG 107, Telegrams Collected (Bound); telegram
sent (on June 21, 1865, 9:15 A.M.), *ibid.*; telegram received (on June 27, 1:20
P.M.), *ibid.*, RG 393, Dept. of the Gulf, Letters Received. *O.R.*, I, xlviii, part 2,
944. On June 27, Maj. Gen. Edward R. S. Canby telegraphed to USG. "Galveston was occupied by the army on the twentieth (20). Gen Sheridan is now here.
Your telegram of the twentieth (20) was not rcvd. until this moment" Telegram
received (on June 28, 8:25 A.M.), DNA, RG 107, Telegrams Collected (Bound);
ibid., RG 108, Telegrams Received; copies, *ibid.*, RG 393, Dept. of the Gulf
and La., Letters Sent; DLC-USG, V, 54. *O.R.*, I, xlviii, part 2, 1001.

On June 19, Secretary of State William H. Seward had written to Secretary
of War Edwin M. Stanton. "It is desirable to know if the War Department has
information from the region East of the Mississippi, including Texas, which
would warrant the President in issuing a Proclamation wholly rescinding the
blockade of ports in insurgent States. As soon as such information shall have
been received, it is deemed important that there should be no delay which can
be avoided in issuing such a Proclamation." LS, DNA, RG 107, Letters Received from Bureaus. On June 20, USG endorsed this letter. "I have no official
information that we occupy Galveston though I am so well satisfied that we do
that I would recommend the extension of free trade over all the territory of the
United States." AES, *ibid.* See letter to Edwin M. Stanton, June 2, 1865.

To Robert E. Lee

Washington June 20th 1865.

GENERAL R. E. LEE.
RICHMOND. VA,
GENERAL;

Your communications of date the 13th inst stating the steps
you had taken after reading the Presidents proclamation of the
29th ult.o with a view of complying with its provisions. When
you learned that, with others, you were to be indicted for treason
by the grand jury at Norfolk; that you had supposed the officers
and men of the Army of Northern Virginia were by the terms of
their surrender protected by the United States Government from
molestation so long as they conformed to its conditions; that you
were ready to meet any charges that might be preferred against
you and did not wish to avoid trial, but that if you were correct as
to the protection granted by your parole and were not to be prose-

cuted, you desired to avail yourself of the President's amnesty proclamation; and enclosing an application "therefor with the request that in that event it be acted on, has been received and forwarded to the Secretary of War, with the following opinion endorsed thereon by me,"

"In my opinion the officers and men paroled at Appomattox C. H., and since upon the same terms given to Lee cannot be tried for treason so long as they observe the terms of their parole. This is my understanding. Good faith as well as true policy dictates that we should observe the conditions of that convention. Bad faith on the part of the Government, or a construction of that convention subjecting the officers to trial for treason would produce a feeling of insecurity in the minds of all the paroled officers and men.

If so disposed they might even regard such an infraction of terms by the Government as an entire release from all obligations on their part."

I will state further that the terms granted by me met with the hearty approval of the President at the time, and of the country generally. The action of Judge Underwood in Norfolk, has already had an injurious effect, and I would ask that he be ordered to quash all indictments found against paroled prisoners of war, and to desist from the further prosecution of them."

This opinion I am informed is substantially the same as that entertained by the Government. I have forwarded your application for amnesty and pardon to the President with the following endorsement thereon:

"Respectfully forwarded through the Secretary of War to the President, with the earnest recommendation that this application of Gen'l R. E. Lee, for amnesty and pardon may be granted him. The oath of allegiance required by recent order of the President to accompany applications does not accompany this for the reason, as I am informed by Gen'l Ord, the order requiring it had not reached Richmond when this was forwarded."

Very respectfully
U. S. GRANT
Lieut. General

Copies, DLC-USG, V, 46, 109; DNA, RG 108, Letters Sent; ViHi. *O.R.*, I, xlvi, part 3, 1286–87. See endorsement to Edwin M. Stanton, June 16, 1865. On July 24, 1865, Bvt. Col. Adam Badeau wrote to U.S. Senator Reverdy Johnson of Md., Baltimore. "I am directed by Lieut. Gen. Grant to acknowledge the receipt of your communication of the 19th inst., asking his consent to the publication of his letter to Gen. Lee of the 20th of June last, and to state that he does not feel at liberty to authorize any public use of a paper in its nature so strictly official as that to which you allude He in fact went to the limits of what he regards as proper in furnishing Gen. Lee with a copy of his endorsement on Gen Lee's letter of June 13th to himself but considers that under the circumstances this was warranted." Copies, DLC-USG, V, 46, 109; DNA, RG 108, Letters Sent.

On July 21, 1866, George W. C. Lee, former C.S.A. maj. gen., Lexington, Va., wrote to USG. "Understanding that paroled officers are expected to confine themselves within the limits of their respective States, I have the honor to request permission for my brother, W. H. F. Lee, and myself, to proceed to Warren Co., N. C., about the 8th Augt. next, to be present at the erection of a tomb over the remains of our sister, who died at the Warren White Sulphur Springs in October 1862." ALS, USG 3.

On July 23, William Eaton, Jr., Warrenton, N. C., wrote to USG. "The ladies of Warren County have made arrangements to erect a monument over the remains of Miss Anne Lee on the 8th of August next at the White Sulphur Springs, about eleven miles from this place. They have invited her father, General Robert E Lee and his family to attend on the occasion, and learn from him that he will be present, provided you will so extend his parole so as to enable him to do so. You will have probably received, before this reaches you, an application from him for the proposed extension. Allow me, in behalf of the ladies to unite in his application, and to express the hope and the belief that indulgence to the parental affections, and sympathy for the domestic sorrows, of your illustrious competitor in arms, will induce you to grant the favor cheerfully. The history of the world proves, that brave men and great commanders have been distinguished for clemency, humanity and benevolence, and that they have rarely stained their laurels by acts, of harshness and severity towards the conquered. Miss Lee died in Oct 1862, very near to the place of the proposed monument, and her father has never yet been to the cherished spot. I am a member of the committee of arrangements, but the time is now so short that I have no opportunity of procuring the signatures of the other members." ALS, *ibid.* On July 26, Badeau wrote to Robert E. Lee. "General Grant directs me to say that he has received a letter intimating that you would like to be present at the erection of a monument over the remains of your daughter in North Carolina, in August next, and that you considered it necessary first to obtain an extension of your parole. He therefore takes the liberty of sending you the enclosed permit, although unsolicited by yourself." ADfS, *ibid.* On the same day, Maj. George K. Leet issued a revised parole. "Robert E. Lee, a paroled officer of the late Confederate Army is exempt from arrest by military authorities unless directed by the President of the United States, the Secy of War, or from these Headquarters so long as he observes the conditions of his parole. The restriction requiring paroled officers to remain at their homes is removed in this case and Mr. Robert. E. Lee will be allowed to travel unmolested throughout the United States." Copies, DLC-USG, V, 47, 60; (entered as signed by USG) DNA, RG

108, Letters Sent. Leet issued an identical document for George W. C. Lee. Copies, *ibid.* On Aug. 3, Robert E. Lee, Lexington, wrote to Badeau. "I have had the honour to receive your letter of the 26th Ulto: enclosing an extension of the limits of my parole. I am very much obliged to the Gen'l Commd the Armies of the U. States for his kind consideration. I am unable to visit North Carolina, & therefore did not think it proper to apply for the favour granted" ALS (facsimile), Adam Badeau, *Grant in Peace* (Hartford, Conn., 1887), p. [24].

On April 13, William H. F. Lee, former C.S.A. maj. gen., had written a letter received at USG's hd. qrs. asking for an extension of the limits of his parole. DNA, RG 108, Register of Letters Received. On April 16, Leet issued the requested document. Copies, DLC-USG, V, 47, 109; DNA, RG 108, Letters Sent.

To Edwin M. Stanton

Washington, June 21st 1865

Hon. E. M. Stanton,
Secretary of War
Sir!

I would respectfully recommend that the effective infantry force present of the Army of the Tennessee be reduced 12,000 or 15,000 men; that the effective infantry force present of the Army of the Potomac be reduced 18,000 men; and that the effective infantry force present of the Middle Military Division be reduced 7,000 men, by the muster out of entire organizations of veteran regiments having the shortest time to serve, including all recruits and additions to these regiments from other sources and all absentees belonging to them. The absentees thus mustered out to be an additional reduction

> Very respectfully
> Your Obed't Servant
> U. S. Grant
> Lieutenant General

LS, DNA, RG 94, Vol. Service Div., Letters Received, A1080 (VS) 1865. On June 21, 1865, Secretary of War Edwin M. Stanton endorsed this letter. "Approved & Referred back to Lt General Grant to issue the necessary orders to carry his reccommendation into effect" AES, *ibid.* On June 22, Brig. Gen. John

A. Rawlins endorsed this letter. "The Adjutant General of the Army will please issue the necessary orders to carry the within recommendation into immediate effect." ES, *ibid.*

On June 16, 11:20 A.M., USG telegraphed to Maj. Gen. John A. Logan. "Inform me what regiments you have whose time expires during the Month of October 1865." ALS (telegram sent), *ibid.*, RG 107, Telegrams Collected (Bound); telegram sent, *ibid.*; copies, *ibid.*, RG 108, Letters Sent; DLC-USG, V, 46, 109. On June 19, 4:15 P.M., Rawlins telegraphed to Logan. "With a view to a further reduction of the military force you will please forward to these Head quarters a statement showing the number of veteran regts in the Army of the Tennessee (including those that have been added to it from the Armies of Georgia and the Potomac, the effective strength present and the strength absent, with the date of original muster in and the date of remuster as veterans of each regiment. Those regiments will be mustered out who have the shortest time to serve, until the aggregate effective strength so mustered out reaches twelve thousand (12000) men" LS (telegram sent), DNA, RG 107, Telegrams Collected (Bound); telegram sent (on June 20, 8:20 A.M.), *ibid.*; telegram received (on June 20, 9:20 A.M.), *ibid.*, RG 393, Dept. of the Tenn., Unbound Materials, Letters Received. *O.R.*, I, xlix, part 2, 1015–16. A copy of this telegram, signed by Bvt. Col. Theodore S. Bowers, was also mailed to Logan. Copies, DNA, RG 108, Letters Sent; DLC-USG, V, 46, 109. On the same day, Bowers wrote similar letters to Maj. Gens. Winfield S. Hancock and George G. Meade. Copies, *ibid.* On June 22, Meade wrote to Rawlins. "In compliance with your instructions of the 19.th inst, I herewith forward a list of regiments in each corps under my command shewing the veteran & non veteran regiments—dates of entry into service & of remuster when veterans with the strength present & absent on the 20th inst.—I also enclose a list of regiments in each corps having served the longest the aggregate of enlisted men amounting 14,655—these regiments to be mustered out when so ordered." ALS, DNA, RG 108, Letters Received. The enclosed list is *ibid.* On July 1, Logan, Louisville, wrote to Rawlins. "I have the honor to acknowledge the receipt of your communication of the 19th of June, requesting a report of the Veteran Regiments of the army of the Tennessee, with the effective force present, and the number of officers and men absent; and in reply thereto would respectfully invite your attention to the enclosed plan of the organization of the Army, including all the accessions from the Armies of the Potomac and of Georgia.—In this connection I would inform you that in pursuance of orders from the General in Chief, the 2nd Division 15th Army Corps, commanded by Brigadier General Oliver, has been sent to Arkansas; and would further invite, your attention to General Orders No. 24. Current Series, from these Head Quarters, copy herewith transmitted, designating the Regiments to be Mustered out under Telegraphic instructions from the Adjt. General of the Army of date June 22nd 1865. The 2nd Division 15th A. C. and the Regiment to be mustered out under the proposed reduction of 15.000, are included in this plan of organization." LS, *ibid.* The enclosed list is *ibid.* On July 6, 12:15 P.M., USG telegraphed to Logan. "Under the last order you may muster out of service all that remains of the Army of the Tennessee remaining under your command." ALS (telegram sent), *ibid.*, RG 107, Telegrams Collected (Bound); telegram sent, *ibid.*; telegram received (misdated July 5), *ibid.*, Telegrams Collected (Unbound). *O.R.*, I, xlix, part 2, 1070; *ibid.*, III, v, 93.

To Edwin M. Stanton

———

Washington D. C. June 21st *1865*

Hon. E. M. Stanton, Sec. of War,
Sir:

I would respectfully recommend the appointment of Michael J. Cramer as Chaplain to NewPort Barracks, Covington Ky.

Mr. Cramer is a Methodist preacher, in good standing, as has been engaged as Chaplain to our hospitals during the war, or most of it. He is a brother-in-law of mine though I do not urge the appointment on that account.

> Very respectfully
> your obt. svt.
> U. S. Grant
> Lt. Gn.

ALS, DNA, RG 94, ACP, C621 CB 1864. Docketing indicates that the post of chaplain had been discontinued at Newport Barracks, Ky., in 1862, and, on June 27, 1865, Secretary of War Edwin M. Stanton directed that the position be reestablished with Michael J. Cramer as chaplain. On May 4, 1864, Cramer, Nashville, had written to President Abraham Lincoln. "No doubt, *Lieut. General U. S. Grant*, my brother-in-law, has given you my name and address, as an applicant for a Post-Chaplaincy. I would, therefore, respectfully, request Your Exellency to grant me a *Commission as a Post-Chaplain* at *Covington, Ky.*, where my family, and the family of my aged father-in-law, Mr. J. R. Grant, father of Gen. Grant, reside. There are two or three U. S. Hospitals there, supplied only with one chaplain, and he, instead of giving to the sick and dying soldiers the consolations of Religion, talks to them about Ecclesiastical Government. The soldiers are dissatisfied with him. I am a regularly ordained minister of the *Methodist Episcopal Church* in the United States of America. The testimony of Lieut. Gen. Grant to that effect, as well as to my true, unswerving loyalty to the Government of the United States of America, may be sufficient. For the last two months I have been engaged as a delegate of the U. S. Christian Commission, working among our noble soldiers in the different Hospitals and camps in and around Nashville, Tenn. And this work I have cheerfully rendered without remuneration, and an account of it have resigned the Pastorship of a flourishing church in Cincinnati, Ohio. Hoping, therefore, that your Exellency will give this application Your distinguished consideration, and grant me a Commission as Post-Chaplain at *Covington, Ky.*, . . ." ALS, *ibid.* An undated Lincoln note states: "Gen. Grant wishes Rev. Michael Cramer to be a Hospital Chaplain at Nashville Tenn." AN, *ibid.* See *PUSG*, 10, 297.

On Feb. 17, 1867, Cramer, Covington, Ky., wrote to USG's sister Virginia Grant concerning his application for a consular appointment. ALS, DNA, RG

59, Applications and Recommendations, Lincoln and Johnson. On Feb. 20, USG wrote to an unknown addressee. ". . . Mr Cramer is a highly educated man, and worthy of full confidence. He is master of three or four languages, besides being a good Latin and Greek scholar. He is a preacher who has never carried politics into the pulpit. . . ." Copy (incomplete, elipses in original), *ibid*. On the same day, President Andrew Johnson endorsed these letters. "*Respectfully referred to* the Hon the Secretary of State, who will please make this appointment. Attention is invited to the enclosed letters of Mr Cramer and Genl Grant" ES, *ibid*. Cramer was confirmed on March 2 as consul at Leipzig.

To Brig. Gen. Solomon Meredith

HEADQUARTERS ARMIES OF THE UNITED STATES,
Washington, D. C., June 21, 1865.

BRIG. GEN. S. MEREDITH,

SIR: The statement published i[n] the papers to the effect that you were relieved from command in Western Kentucky on account of sympathy with rebels is wholly false so far as I [h]ave ever heard or believe. Your administration in [t]hat command has given entire satisfaction so far as I have ever learned, to the military commanders over you, and especial satisfaction to the loyal people of [t]hat section.

It has been my desire to reliev[e] as many General and Staff Officers as can be dispe[n]sed with, without prejudice to the service, with the view of their honorable discharge, and a reduction of Government expenses. You were relieved in [t]his spirit, and not for any complaint against you.

Very respectful[l]y,
Your ob't. sv't.
U. S. GRANT, Lieut. Gen.

Indianapolis Daily Journal, Dec. 2, 1865. Solomon Meredith, born in N. C. in 1810, moved to Ind. when nineteen, was appointed col., 19th Ind., as of July 29, 1861, and brig. gen. as of Oct. 6, 1862. Meredith incorporated USG's letter in a statement of Dec. 1, 1865, Cambridge City, Ind., addressed "To the public" defending himself against allegations made by U.S. Representative George W. Julian of Ind. that he had been removed from command at Paducah because of disloyal behavior. *Ibid*. See *PUSG*, 13, 539; *ibid*., 14, 443n.

Circular

Cipher   Washington D. C. June 22nd *1865*
(CONFIDENTIAL CIRCULAR)

All Department Commanders, Commanding in States where Martial law prevails, will immediately put detectives upon the watch for gambling houses Especially "Faro" banks, and ~~on some particular night~~ at the appropriate time make a descent upon them all simultaneously, arresting all disbursing Officers of the Government, who may be found gambling in them, or visitants therein at the time, and who it can be proven had previously gambled at such places. The gambling institutions will be completely broken up, and their money and [s]tock confiscated, and the owners or proprietors [o]f such gambling institutions be made to disgorge and refund all money they may have won from United States disbursing Officers. The Officers so [t]aken will be imprisoned and tried immediately—

The same proceedings will be taken by Department Commanders in the North within their respective commands, in the cities where disbursing Officers may be located, except that instead of confiscating the money and stock of the gambling Establishments or compelling by military action the owners or proprietors of the same to disgorge or refund any moneys, they may ha[ve] won from disbursing Officers of the Governme[nt] they will be immediately reported to the Civil Authorities for their action—

This will be kept strictly confidential except so far as it may be necessary to communicate it [to] those who are to carry it into execution—

U. S. GRANT:
Lt. Gen U. S. A

Send to all Military Div. and Dept. Commander[s] in Cipher—

LS (telegram sent), DNA, RG 107, Telegrams Collected (Bound); LS (variant), *ibid.*; telegram received (on June 23), *ibid.*, RG 393, Army of the Ohio and Dept. of N. C., Telegrams Received; *ibid.*, Dept. of the Northwest, Letters Received; *ibid.*, Dept. of the Mo., Telegrams Received; Ord Papers, CU-B. *O.R.*, I, xlvi, part 3, 1289–90. On June 23, 1865, 3:00 P.M., Lt. Col. Samuel B.

Lawrence, adjt. for Maj. Gen. Lewis Wallace, telegraphed to USG. "Your order to close Gambling houses &c recd and will be promptly and discreetly executed." ALS (telegram sent), DNA, RG 107, Telegrams Collected (Unbound); telegram received (at 3:40 P.M.), *ibid.*, Telegrams Collected (Bound); *ibid.*, RG 108, Telegrams Received. On July 8, Bvt. Col. Theodore S. Bowers wrote to Wallace. "I am directed by Lieut. General Grant to respectfully acknowledge the receipt of your report of date July 5th made in pursuance of Confidential Circular of date June 22d from these Headquarters, and to say that he knows of no particular Officer or Officers in your Department to whom suspicion attaches but approves of your continuing the investigation as you propose" Copies, DLC-USG, V, 46, 109; DNA, RG 108, Letters Sent. On July 5, Lt. Col. John Woolley, provost marshal, Baltimore, had written to Maj. George H. Hooker, adjt., reporting that no U.S. disbursing officers had been discovered frequenting gambling houses, but that he was continuing the investigation. ALS, *ibid.*, RG 94, Letters Received, 1395A 1865. On July 7, Hooker endorsed this report. "Respectfully forwarded to Lieut Genl Grant Commanding U. S. Army, whose attention is invited to the enclosed reports of Col T. D. Sewall and Lieut Col Woolley, and for instructions as to what action shall be taken." AES, *ibid.* On July 13, USG endorsed this report. "Respectfully refered to the Sec. of War. Instructions have been given to prefer charges against disbursing officers known to visit gabling houses but in view of the limited number so reported to carry the orders no further." AES, *ibid.*

On July 12, Charles Merrill, military detective, Washington, D. C., wrote to Capt. John T. Potts, chief of military detectives, reporting that an officer had been observed in a gambling house. LS, *ibid.* USG endorsed this letter. "Respectfully refered to the Sec. of War. Gen Augur has been directed to proceed no further in the orders given him ~~with~~ in regard to Gambling houses, and disbursing officers visiting them, without further orders." AES (undated), *ibid.*

On June 27 or 28, Maj. Gen. Quincy A. Gillmore, Hilton Head, telegraphed to USG. "Your Confidential Circular in cipher to Mily Div & Brigade Commanders of the twenty second inst was recd last Evening" Telegrams received (2—the first on June 28, 9:20 P.M.; the second dated June 28, received on July 1, 2:05 P.M.), *ibid.*, RG 107, Telegrams Collected (Bound); (dated June 27) *ibid.*, Telegrams Collected (Unbound); (2—the first dated June 27, the second June 28) *ibid.*, RG 108, Telegrams Received; copies (dated June 27), *ibid.*, RG 393, Dept. of the South and S. C., Letters Sent; DLC-USG, V, 54; (dated June 28) *ibid.*

On June 23, noon, Maj. Gen. George H. Thomas, Nashville, telegraphed to USG. "Have received your Cipher dispatch of 8 P. M. 22nd & will give necessary instructions immediately to Department Commanders." ALS (telegram sent), DNA, RG 107, Telegrams Collected (Unbound); telegram received (at 5:40 P.M.), *ibid.*, RG 108, Telegrams Received. On July 18, Maj. Gen. George Stoneman wrote to Brig. Gen. William D. Whipple, chief of staff for Thomas, reporting that: "These papers will explain themselves, and the reasons why my directions were not complied with. . . ." LS, *ibid.*, Letters Received. The enclosures are *ibid.* On July 21, Thomas endorsed this letter. "Respectfully forwarded to the Lieutenant General in chief for his information" E (signature clipped), *ibid.*

On July 13, Col. James H. Baker, provost marshal, St. Louis, wrote to Maj. Gen. Grenville M. Dodge reporting that no disbursing officers had been observed in gambling houses although before USG's order of June 22, Capt. George May, commissary of subsistence, had been "systematically robbed at two of these gambling places." LS, *ibid.* On July 14, Dodge endorsed this letter. "Respectfully referred to Col. T. S. Bowers, A. A. G. Armies U. S. I had occasion sometime ago to seize several of the Gambling Hells. in this city. on grounds mentioned in General Grants dispatch. since then, they have been very careful. The case of Capt. May was one in which they were made to disgorge all Government funds taken from him, and he was dismissed the service, and the Houses broken up &c. These places are again running. but. as I took action once in their cases, and no more similar instances arising, I do not so interpret Gnl. Grants dispatch that I shall seize these Houses again. If that is the intention, please advise me and I will do so—and use them up." ES, *ibid.*

To Edwin M. Stanton

Washington D. C, June 22d *1865*

HON. E. M. STANTON
SEC. OF WAR,
SIR:

The enclosed is a list of officers of the Regular Army now holding Volunteer Commissions. The first Column gives their rank in the regular service, the second their Volunteer rank. I would respectfully recommend that Brevets in the Regular Army be given for gallant and meretorious service in the war just closing to bring each up to the rank designated opposite his name under the head of remarks.

My personal acquaintance with these officers does not enable me to make these recommendations from personal knowledge of the actual merits in all cases, but I have been guided by such knowledge of the service rendered by each as is at my disposal.

The fact that whilst officers in the field who have received Volunteer rank have been overlooked in confering Regular brevt rank entitles them now to an adjustment of their relative regular rank to be permanently held.

From want of personal knowledge of the service of all the officers named in these recommendations injustice may be done to some both by giving them rank inferior to their deserts and by placin~~dg~~ less deserving too high. I shall have no feeling in the matter if changes are made to correct any such error.

> Very respectfully
> your obt. svt.
> U. S GRANT
> Lt. Gn.

ALS, DNA, RG 94, ACP, G279 CB 1865. The enclosure is *ibid.* In the remarks column, USG entered the bvt. rank in the U.S. Army he believed merited for each of the 218 officers listed. He made no recommendation for seven officers: Brig. Gen. William S. Rosecrans; Cols. Daniel Butterfield, Henry B. Carrington, Lawrence P. Graham, and Israel Vogdes; Lt. Col. Samuel D. Sturgis; and Maj. Benjamin S. Roberts. All except Carrington eventually did receive bvt. promotion, Rosecrans for Stone's River. On April 22, Carrington, Indianapolis, wrote to Postmaster Gen. William Dennison requesting assignment to Calif. for reasons of health. ALS, *ibid.*, Letters Received, 1028P 1865. On May 25, Dennison favorably endorsed this letter to Secretary of War Edwin M. Stanton. AES, *ibid.* On May 31, USG endorsed this letter. "Respectfully returned. It would not be consistent with the interests of the public service to grant the within request." ES, *ibid.*

To Andrew Johnson

Respectfully refered to the President. Mr. Jas. Hewitt's wife is a cousin of mine. Owing to great wealth mostly in southern property, and being of that class of men who from being the author of their own fortunes worship money more than country, took rather a Southern view of our difficulties than a patriotic one. He was however ~~opp~~ opposed to secession and left the country early in the war and has remained absent ever sin[ce] probably to avoid taking an active par[t.] Out of three ~~sons~~ grow[n] sons one remained loyal and the other two sacrifised thei[r] lives to the cause of secession. Mr. Hewitt has therefore been severely punished. If allowed to return to the country and take the Amnesty oath I believe he will alwais be a good Citizen and loyal to the Govt.

If the authority for his return is given it will be forwarded if sent to me with this letter.

> U. S. GRANT
> Lt. Gn

June 26th/65

AES, DNA, RG 94, Amnesty Papers, Ky. On June 20, 1865, Charles H. Hewitt, Louisville, wrote to USG. "I feel assured that you will pardon this brief occupation of your time, when informed of the nature of my communication. I write to solicit your influence and aid in obtaining a pardon for my father, James Hewitt, who is now in Europe. The applications for pardons are so numerous at present, that, unless I can excite the sympathy of one so powerful as yourself, some time must elapse before my application can be answered. My family, though of different political views, speak of you with pride and affection. I have lived in Kentucky during the war, and have never forgotten my duty and loyalty to my Government. Earnestly hoping that you will grant me your immediate assistance—" ALS, *ibid*. On June 22, C. R. Atkinson, New York City, wrote to USG. "Will you oblige me as well as your friends & relations Mr James Hewitt and M O H Norton by getting a permit for them & their families to return to U. S. to pursue their ordinary business—they are prevented by the $20000 clause in the proclamation from taking its benefit   You are a Stranger to me, and I hope you will excuse this liberty   I have been associated with them for 20 years in business— I suppose you have heard of R M Hewitts death in Richmond after being exchanged   Mr Hewitt & Norton are in Europe" ALS, *ibid*. For the Hewitt family, see John Y. Simon, ed., *The Personal Memoirs of Julia Dent Grant* (New York, 1975), pp. 56, 64*n*, 138–39, 144*n*.

Circular

(Cipher)   Washington D. C. June 26th 1865 [*3:30* P.M.] Commanding officers of N. C. S. C. Ga. Ala. Florida Miss. La. & Texas are instructed whilst they are not to endanger private property by efforts to seize that heretofore claimed by the so called Confederate States will ~~protect~~ aid the officers of the Treasury Dept. in protecting and bringing to market that already in Govt. possession or which was included in the surrender of the rebel Armies.

U. S. GRANT
Lt. Gn

Forward to Commanders named.

U. S. G.

ALS (telegram sent), DNA, RG 107, Telegrams Collected (Bound); telegram sent, *ibid*.; telegrams received (2—addressed to Capt. James R. Gilmore, asst. q. m., dated "26"), *ibid*., Telegrams Collected (Unbound); *ibid*., RG 393, Dept. of the Tenn., Letters Received; *ibid*., Dept. of the South and S. C., 2nd Military District, Letters Received; *ibid*., Dept. of Ga., Letters Received; *ibid*., Dept. of the Gulf, Letters Received. *O.R.*, I, xlvii, part 3, 664; *ibid*., I, xlviii, part 2, 995;

ibid., I, xlix, part 2, 1035; (addressed to Gilmore, misdated May 26, 1865) *ibid.*, I, xlvii, part 3, 573. On June 28, Maj. Gen. George H. Thomas, Nashville, telegraphed to USG. "Your telegram of the 26th inst giving instructions to aid the Treasury Offices in collecting & bringing to market all Confederate property surrendered by the army &c has just been received. The necessary instructions will be given immediately." ALS (telegram sent), DNA, RG 107, Telegrams Collected (Unbound); telegram received (at 1:55 P.M.), *ibid.*, Telegrams Collected (Bound); *ibid.*, RG 108, Telegrams Received. *O.R.*, I, xlix, part 2, 1046.

To Edwin M. Stanton

Washington June 26th 1865.

HON. E. M. STANTON
SECRETARY OF WAR.
SIR;

I have the honor to transmit herewith a full and complete report of the battle of Belmont, Mo., fought November 7th 1861, which I would respectfully ask to have substituted in the place of my report of that action of date November 10th 1861, made to Gen. Seth Williams Assistant Adjutant General to the General in Chief.

Very Respectfully
Your Obedient Servant
U. S. GRANT
Lieut. Gen'l

Copies, DLC-USG, V, 46, 109; DNA, RG 108, Letters Sent. See *PUSG*, 3, 143–49.

To Edwin M. Stanton

Washington D. C. June 27th *1865*

HON. E. M. STANTON,
SEC. OF WAR,
SIR:

I would respectfully recommend that all the officers now at Fort Delaware be discharged on taking the oath of allegiance. All coming within the range of existing orders for the discharge of rebel prisoners have already been discharged from that place.

I would also recommend that general direction for the discharge of all remaining prisoners be given. to be executed by commanders of prisons so soon as present orders for the discharge of prisoners is carried out.

This will enable us to discharge a great many soldiers and diminish expenses materially.

> Very respectfully
> your obt. svt.
> U. S. GRANT
> Lt. Gn.

ALS, DLC-Edwin M. Stanton. *O.R.*, II, viii, 673.

On June 3, 1865, Brig. Gen. John P. Hatch wrote to Secretary of War Edwin M. Stanton asking if paroled prisoners were allowed to take the oath of allegiance. LS, DNA, RG 94, Letters Received, 821H 1865. On June 17, Bvt. Brig. Gen. William Hoffman, commissary gen. of prisoners, endorsed this letter. "Respectfully submitted to Lt. Genl U S Grant, comd'g U. S. Army." AES, *ibid.* On June 27, USG endorsed this letter. "Respectfully forwarded to the Secretary of War with recommendation that all paroled prisoners of war, who voluntarily take the oath of allegiance, be absolved from their parole and allowed all the priveleges extended to the same class of persons who are released from prisons, or who are still in the South and have never been captured." ES, *ibid.*

On June 29, Hoffman wrote five identical endorsements referring to USG cases of six paroled prisoners. AES, *ibid.*, 947H 1865. On July 5, USG endorsed these cases. "Respectfully submitted to the Secretary of War. I recommend that the status of many paroled prisoners in the Southern States and the class of cases herewith enclosed, be reached by a general order, in substance like the accompanying draft." ES, *ibid. O.R.*, II, viii, 682. The proposed general order, first approved, and then suspended by Stanton, is *ibid.*, p. 683.

To Bvt. Maj. Gen. Montgomery C. Meigs

Washington D. C. June 27th *1865*

MAJ. GN. M. C. MEIGS,
Q. M. GENERAL, U, S, A,
GENERAL,

The bearer of this, Mr. Saml Ruth,[1] is the Supt. of the Richmond & Fredericksburg rail-road. He has been friendly to the

Union throughout the rebellion and has proven his friendship by sending information from Richmond constantly of the changes and movements of the enemy. His object in visiting Washington now is to purchase rail-road material. I write this to show you that his record is right to allow him this privilege.

Yours Truly

U. S. GRANT

Lt. Gn.

ALS, DLC-Montgomery C. Meigs. See Meriwether Stuart, "Samuel Ruth and General R. E. Lee: Disloyalty and the Line of Supply to Fredericksburg, 1862–1863," *Virginia Magazine of History and Biography*, 71, 1 (Jan., 1963), 101.

1. Samuel Ruth, born in Pa. in 1818, moved to Va. in 1839 and shortly thereafter began working for the Richmond, Fredericksburg and Potomac Railroad. He became superintendent of the railroad by 1858, a position which he held throughout the Civil War. See Angus J. Johnston, II, "Disloyalty on Confederate Railroads in Virginia," *ibid.*, 63, 4 (Oct., 1955), 420–25.

On Jan. 12, 1866, Ruth and F. William E. Lohmann submitted a petition to Secretary of War Edwin M. Stanton requesting compensation for information provided by them to U.S. authorities during the war. DS, DNA, RG 107, Letters Received, 976 1873. On Jan. 1, George H. Sharpe, former asst. provost marshal, Army of the Potomac, Kingston, N. Y., had endorsed this petition. "The within named S. Ruth and F. Lohman are well known to me. While I was on the general staff of the Army of the Potomac, I knew of Mr Ruth (then & throughout the war) Genl Superintendant of the Fredg R. R. and had entire confidence in his loyalty and personal character. I had several communications with him through other agents, and always found that his information was of a high character. When the armies reached the positions below Richmond I established communications with Union people in Richmond, from whom I received regular & frequent advices, both oral and written, containing all the information that could be collected from various sources. I knew that S. Ruth and F. Lohman were among those who furnished the information to the scouts and agents sent from our Head Quarters—but I was seldom able to know from what particular source each piece of information came. Sometimes however I did know; and then to show the value of the information, the source was named by me in my reports to Col Bowers, A. A. G. Armies of the U. States, of which reports I have no copies except in a character I am at present unable to read. I know however that Mr Ruth's name occurs in those reports. Of the information referred to within, I can certify that so much thereof as is embraced in Sections 2. 3. 7. 10. 15. was received by me at the times indicated. The papers of my bureau, would probably enable me to certify to other of the information referred to herein, of which indeed I have a general recollection. There were times of course, when information forwarded to us, failed in its full transmission, but I have no doubt that throughout the war Mr Ruth and Mr Lohman were constantly endeavoring by every safe channel to send military information to the U. S. Govt. After the capture of Richmond I became acquainted with S. Ruth and F. Lohman and formed a most favourable estimate of them. I think their representations are entitled to full credence. On my recommendation they (with others) were assisted to a very limited extent, by order of Genl Grant, to relieve their present necessities, the Several amounts of which can be ascertained from Captain H. P. Clinton (then A. Q. M. Pro Mar Genl's Dept) who paid the amounts, and who is now Post Commissary at Richmond Va." AES, *ibid*. On Jan. 22, USG endorsed this petition. "In the operations against Lee's army and Richmond, from the time I took command, Bvt Brig. General (then Colonel) Geo. H. Sharpe, had charge of the Secret Service Department, or 'Bureau of Information' for the Army of the Potomac; and after our forces had crossed to the south side of the James river, up to the surrender of Lee's army, he was in charge of the same for the 'Armies operating against Richmond.' Much of the information within set forth was reported by him to me, and proved of great value to the service; and there is no question that it was obtained by Gen. Sharpe from the within named petitioners in the manner he states, and that it is but right and proper they should be liberally compensated therefor." ES, *ibid*.; (facsimile) Stuart, "Samuel Ruth and General R. E. Lee," between pp. 96–97. See *HRC*, 43-1-792; *ibid*., 44-1-823; Ruth file, Hillyer Papers, ViU.

On March 29, 1869, Ruth, Richmond, wrote to USG. "I have the honor to ask to be appointed ~~Collector~~ Assessor of Internal Revenue for the Eighth District of Virginia, and respectfully refer to the subjoined testimonials as to my fitness for the duties of the position" LS, DNA, RG 56, Internal Revenue Applications, Va., 2nd District. The enclosure is *ibid*. Three additional letters addressed to USG supporting Ruth's nomination are *ibid*. Ruth, having difficulty in securing bonding for the position, telegraphed to U.S. Marshal Alexander Sharp, probably on Dec. 20. "Please see the President & Mr Delano and get them to wait a few days more to enable me give the security" Telegram received (at 2:00 P.M.— dated "20"), *ibid*. USG endorsed this telegram. "Mr. Ruth is, no doubt, the best man we can get." AES, *ibid*. On May 27, 1870, USG nominated Ruth as collector, Internal Revenue, 2nd District of Va. LS, *ibid*., RG 46, 41st Congress, 3rd Session, Executive Nominations. *Senate Executive Journal*, XVII, 457. Ruth was confirmed as of June 7. On Dec. 2, 1871, Ruth wrote to USG. "I desire to tender herewith my resignation as Collector of Internal Revenue for the 2d Dist of Virginia to take effect upon the comfirmation of my successor, provided this is done on or before the 31st day of December 1871. as I desire my resignation to be absolute from and after that date if no confirmation of my successor should be made by the Senate by that time   Severe and protracted illness nescessitates this step,   I desire to express my heartfelt thanks for the kindness which you have ever shown me." ALS, DNA, RG 56, Internal Revenue Applications.

To Reuben E. Fenton

———

Washington D. C. June 27th *1865*

HIS EXCELLENCY, R. E. FENTON,
GOVERNOR OF NEW YORK,
SIR:

As much pleasure as it would afford me to be with the good people of Albany on the 4th of July I fear it will not be possible. The experience of the last few weeks shows me that whilst we are disbanding our Armies and there is so much to do at my "Head Quarters" I should not separate myself from it until the work is done.

I am very desirous of getting a couple of months rest this Summer, as soon as the work is done so that I can absent myself so long, and must stick close at present to accomplish this. In addition to this my Chief of Staff is now absent and will remain so until the latter end of July. When he is here I can be absent for a few days without material detriment to the service.

Hoping that your selebration will prove all that is desired, I remain,

Very Truly
your obt. svt
U. S. GRANT
Lt. Gn.

ALS, ICarbS.
On June 27, 1865, Governor Reuben E. Fenton of N. Y. telegraphed to USG. "The state expects you. I have promised that you will be here." Telegram received (at 8:35 P.M.), DNA, RG 107, Telegrams Collected (Bound). On June 28, 9:10 [A.M.], USG telegraphed to Fenton. "I do not see how it is possible for me to be with you on the 4th. I regret this very much." ALS (telegram sent), *ibid.*; telegram sent, *ibid.*

On July 1, 12:30 P.M., Saturday, USG telegraphed to Fenton. "I will leave here at 6 p. m. Monday evening and return by the boat on Teusday evening." ALS (telegram sent), *ibid.*; telegram sent, *ibid.*; copies, *ibid.*, RG 108, Letters Sent; DLC-USG, V, 46, 109. On July 2, John W. Garrett, president, Baltimore and Ohio Railroad, telegraphed to USG. "I take pleasure in arranging for yourself & party by the six (6) P M train tomorrow the 3rd" Telegram received (on July 3, 12:10 A.M.), DNA, RG 107, Telegrams Collected (Bound); *ibid.*, RG 108, Telegrams Received. On July 3, Fenton telegraphed to USG. "General

Batchelor of my Staff will meet you at N. Y   Arrangements are made for an Extra train" Telegram received (at 1:35 P.M.), *ibid.*; *ibid.*, RG 107, Telegrams Collected (Unbound); copy, DLC-USG, V, 54. USG left Washington for Albany, N. Y., on July 3, 6:00 P.M., returning to Washington late on the afternoon of July 5. For an account of USG's trip to Albany on July 4, see *New York Times*, July 6, 1865.

To Edwin M. Stanton

Washington D. C, June 28th *1865*

HON. E. M. STANTON
SEC. OF WAR,
SIR:

I understand there is great delay in carrying out orders for the Musterout of troops in hospitals throughout the ₴North arising principally from neglect of officers forwarding with sick men their discriptive rolls. In many instances the organizations to which sick men belong have been mustered out leaving no way to get at these discriptive rolls further than their record is kept in the Adj. Gens. Office.

I would recommend that a circular be sent to all hospitals directing promptness in carrying out existing orders so far as they apply to men supplied with the requisite papers to enable them to do so, and report to the Adj. General the names, regiment &c. of all men who should be mustered out but are are not supplied with discriptive rolls.

Very respectfully
your obt. svt.
U. S. GRANT
Lt. Gn.

ALS, DNA, RG 94, Letters Received, 701A 1865. *O.R.*, III, v, 60.

On July 17, Governor Richard J. Oglesby of Ill. wrote to USG. "I feel that I may safely say to you, after six weeks very patient waiting, and persuading, that it is my honest opinion, that Surgeons in Charge of Hospitals at all points are not faithfully and energetically, carrying out the Order to muster out or discharge from the service, Sick and disabled men in Hospitals, It is difficult to hurry them up, all seem to stand, all the time, on some special hindrance, Every difficulty they find in their way is magnified and hung upon, instead of being met by an earnest wish to remove and avoid it, I think they do not really wish to help these helpless men, a misery to themselves and a great expense to the country. Another cause of complaint is that, paroled or released prisoners of war reporting here to be mustered out, after unavoidably being detained at the Post for discharge, from three to six weeks, are mustered out with pay up to day of reporting to Brev Brig. Genl. Oakes, and not to the day of actual discharge. I suppose this can only be remedied by an Order from you or the War Department. Another cause of complaint urged with some vehemence, is that regiments ordered to be mustered out prior to October 1st 1865 are not, (in the Department of the Gulf, especially in Alabama) so mustered out, but are as they say, inexplicably detained. Another special cause of complaint more particularly appealing to me, is in the case of all Illinois regiments which belonged to the Army of the Tenn, but were detached and sent to Saint Lous or Leavenworth City, just before the order was issued to muster out that Army; and from the benefits of which they think they are unfairly excluded. I have thus General, called your attention to what I think are legitimate causes of complaint, and have to request that if you shall believe them well founded and entitled to relief, to grant it in such manner, as Lawyers say, ~~in such manner~~ as to you shall seem fit and proper. I am truly glad of the efforts you are making to reduce the expenses of the Nation, and to curtail and reduce the volenteer forces. I really believe that good policy would justify your recommending the prompt discharge from the service, of all white Volenteer regiments, and I hope you may see your way clear to do so at an early day—If you really require more forces than will be left, get them by new enlistments or new organizations on a known peace basis." LS, DNA, RG 108, Letters Received.

Endorsement

The services rendered by Col. Myer in organizing the Signal Corps of the Army have proved of great value to the service. I have never heard it doubted that he was the originator of the whole system, adopted with so much advantage in the Army.

Why he was displaced as Chief Signal Officer I never knew. The very fact that the Government has been allowed to use this signal without compensation to the inventor entitles Col. Myer to additional consideration. If reasons do not exist entirely unknown to me for keeping him out of the place of Chief Signal Officer I think his restoration to that place but an act of simple justice

U. S. GRANT
Lieut General.

Headqrs. A U S
June 28. 65.

ES, DNA, RG 94, ACP, 2563 1873. Written on a letter of June 28, 1865, from Maj. Albert J. Myer to President Andrew Johnson. "I respectfully request that I may be restored to my position as Signal Officer of the Army. This can be now done under the Act organizing the Signal Corps. I have been the first Signal Officer of the Army. I have originated the Signal Corps of the Army and have introduced the use of Army Signals into the Navy in time of a great war and under the gravest difficulties. From the beginning to the end of the Rebellion, no signals or equipments, and no plans for that service, other than those originated by me, have been used in our Armies or for the cooperation of our Army and Navy. The record of the service of the Signal Corps is my record. I have served the United States with my best ability and with success. I believe I am justly entitled to this position." LS, *ibid*. On the same day, Myer wrote to USG. "I am trying to have this paper strongly endorsed. I submit it to you. I think my plans have aided in this war and my experience may be useful in preparing for peace." ADfS, DLC-Albert J. Myer. On Nov. 10, 1863, Secretary of War Edwin M. Stanton had relieved Myer from duty as chief of the U.S. Signal Corps after a dispute over the role of the Signal Corps. Myer's appointment as col. and chief signal officer lapsed in the summer of 1864, and he reverted to maj. See Paul J. Scheips, "Union Signal Communications: Innovation and Conflict," *Civil War History*, 9, 4 (Dec., 1963), 410, 414–15; *PUSG*, 9, 527–28.

On Jan. 20, 1865, Myer addressed an eleven page memorial to the U.S. Senate setting forth his claim that he had been unjustly deprived of his position and asking that he be restored to duty as chief signal officer. Copy (printed), DLC-Albert J. Myer. On Feb. 14, Myer wrote to Stanton requesting vindication. Copy (printed), DNA, RG 94, ACP, 2563 1873. On Aug. 29, Johnson endorsed Myer's case. "*Respectfully referred to* Lt Gen U. S. Grant, for examination and recommendation." AES, *ibid*. On Oct. 26, USG endorsed this case. "Respectfully returned to the President of the Unite[d] States.—Unless there are reasons of which I know noth[ing] I deem A. J. Myer entitl[ed] to the position of Signal Officer of the Army and recommend it accordingly" ES, *ibid*. On Oct. 30, Johnson again endorsed this case. "Respectfully referred to the Secretary of War for report. This case was once before referred to the War Dept. for report but no report has been [r]eceived—" Copy, DLC-Albert J. Myer.

On Jan. 12 and Feb. 5, 1866, Bvt. Col. Horace Porter wrote to Myer. "I returned the other day, after an absence of more than a month, and found your letter of the 10 ult. awaiting me. This will account for any seeming neglect on my part. I spoke to the Gen. in regard to your case, He thinks no effort will be made to give you any further trouble He has promised, however, to keep an eye on you in case anything adverse should turn up. I had hoped ere this to have congratulated you in person on your triumph. I think no one outside of your own family has been more gratified at the event than myself." "I have your letter of the 20th ult. and can say to you that I have not for a moment forgotten your claims to the position mentioned. I have spoken of your case to the Gen. Several times lately, and he has expressed himself warmly in favor of your being restored to your position. The bill before Congress now proposes to have One Chief Signal Officer with rank &c of Colonel of Cavalry and that upon his recommendation the Sec. of War be allowed to detail as many officers and enlisted men as may be necessary for Signal duty. These officers and men to have the same pay, allowances &c that ~~was~~ were given them by the law reorganizing the Signal corps three years ago. You will be the General's first and only choice for the Chief of the Corps, and I hope you may succeed in obtaining it. Rest assured that I shall render you all the assistance in my power." ALS, *ibid.* On July 28, Congress restored the office of chief signal officer with "the rank, pay, and emoluments of a colonel of cavalry." *U.S. Statutes at Large*, XIV, 335–36. On July 30, Myer wrote to USG. "It is possible the President may question in reference to my appointment if urged by you, how Mr. Stanton, whose pride may be involved to my injury will pleasantly transact business with myself—There is this reply to this. As Chief Signal Officer I ought to report directly to the General Commanding the Armies of the U. S. and discharge my duties under your direction—If I do so report I have no Communication with Mr. Stanton other than through you and I need never meet him. The Course to be pursued would be for the President to appoint me and to order me to report to yourself. . . . The Ceief need now is for definitive action of some Kind which shall show why It is not for the interest of the U. S. I shall be appointed. The Paragraph of the Law of the United States organizing the Signal Corps which found that Officer of the regular Army who may be appointed in the Corps may after the rebellion be restored in the same rank and promotion as they would have had if they had not been appointed entitles me to the new position I ask your assistance to remove whatever difficulties there may be—" ADfS, DLC-Albert J. Myer. On the same day, USG wrote to Stanton. "I would respectfully recommend the appointment of Albert J. Myer to the place of Chief of the Signal Corps, as provided for by Act. of Congress. Col. Myer is the inventor of the system used both in the Army and Navy which would seem to give him a claim to the position of Chief, which he once held, and which the Senate have refused to confirm any other person to in." ALS, DNA, RG 94, ACP, 2563 1873. USG also apparently made a personal presentation to Johnson in Myer's behalf on Aug. 2. AN, DLC-Albert J. Myer. On Sept. 18, Porter wrote to Myer. ". . . Your case is still in *statu quo.* I have been very anxious to see you fully restored before this, but it seems that you are still destined to sit on the anxious bench. I spoke to the Gen. again about you this morning. If it lay in his power you would now be in the discharge of the duties which properly belong to you." ALS, *ibid.* On Oct. 25, Johnson again endorsed Myer's case. *"Respectfully referred to* the Honorable the Secretary of War. Let this appointment be made." ES, DNA, RG 94, ACP, 2563 1873. Myer was appointed col. and chief signal officer as of Oct. 30, but resumed his duties in 1867 only after USG had been appointed secretary of war *ad interim. Ibid.*

On Nov. 30, Myer wrote to USG. "I respectfully request that the within issue for the following reasons, 1st The Act organizing the Signal Corps provides a temporary organization 'during the present rebellion'. 2d All appointments and Commissions in this Corps have been held by the War Department to be of Volunteers. 3d. The law provides that 'Officers of the Army, who may be appointed in this Corps may after the rebellion, be restored to their respective regiments or Corps, and receive the same rank and promotion as if they had Continued to serve therein, The order is needed to put at rest any doubts which may be to the detriment of officers of the Army who received appointments in the Signal Corps." ALS, *ibid.* On the same day, USG wrote to Brig. Gen. Lorenzo Thomas. "The Signal Corps being a temporary organization and the law providing that 'Officers of the Army, who may be appointed in this Corps, may, after the rebellion, be restored to their respective regiments or Corps, and receive the same rank and promotion as if they had continued to serve therein,' appointments in the Signal Corps are not considered as depriving any officer of the Army of any regular Commission held by him prior to such appointment." LS, *ibid*. The text of this letter was in Myer's hand.

On Feb. 25, Myer wrote to Brig. Gen. John A. Rawlins setting forth his military history. ALS, *ibid*. On April 3, Robert Morrow, private secretary to Johnson, endorsed to USG a communication recommending Myer's appointment as bvt. brig. gen. AES, *ibid*. On April 5, USG endorsed this communication. "Respectfully forwarded to the Secretary of War" ES, *ibid*. On Nov. 23, Myer wrote to USG. "I respectfully request that my claims to brevet promotion may be considered." ALS, *ibid*. On Nov. 25, USG endorsed this letter. "Approved." AES, *ibid*. On Nov. 20, USG had appointed Myer bvt. brig. gen. as of July 28, 1866, "for distinguished services in organizing, instructing and commanding the Signal Corps of the Army," DS, *ibid*. On Nov. 27, USG endorsed this appointment. "Change this apt. to March 13th/65 and make Bvt. for services in accordance with the direction endorsed approved by the act. sec. of War." AES, *ibid*.

To Maj. Gen. William T. Sherman

Washington D. C, June 29th *1865* [2:00 P.M.]

MAJ. GN. SHERMAN, LANCASTER OHIO.

You go to St. Louis to command the Mil. Distv. of the Mo.[1] The order is out.

U. S. GRANT
Lt. Gn.

ALS (telegram sent), DNA, RG 107, Telegrams Collected (Bound); telegram sent (at 8:00 P.M.), *ibid*.; copies (dated June 28, 1865), *ibid*., RG 108, Letters Sent; DLC-USG, V, 46, 109. Dated June 29 in *O.R.*, I, xlviii, part 2, 1027. On June 30, Maj. Gen. William T. Sherman telegraphed to USG. "My assignment to St Louis is perfectly satisfactory I go to Cincinnati today & will go to Louisville & it may be to St Louis before I come back" Telegram received (at 12:55 P.M.), DNA, RG 107, Telegrams Collected (Bound); *ibid*., RG 108, Telegrams Received; copy, DLC-USG, V, 54. *O.R.*, I, xlviii, part 2, 1033. On June 25, Sherman had written to Brig. Gen. John A. Rawlins. "I arrived here yesterday after a tempestuous visit about Chicago & North Ohio, and now feel desirous to Know what is to be my next destination. I have nothing official & so far as my Record goes I could go into Kentucky & Tennessee & resume Command, but from what Genl Grant told me at Chicago, I suppose I am by him destined for St Louis: but as the War Dept may interpose it is prudent on my part to ascertain authoritatively what official orders are in Existence or Contemplation touching me. I want for Economys sake to get my office and HeadQr paraphenalia to their destination, and have written to Genl Townsend for any orders already made or determined on that will Enable me to act. I will go next Saturday July 2 to

Louisville to attend the Barbecue & Celebrations of the 4th and will probably run down to Nashville and see Thomas. I would like before starting to Know all that is proper and ask you to telegraph me by or before next Friday, sooner the better, if the new Divisions, have been determined and where my HdQrs are fixed. I can then Establish my HdQrs, make a simple order assuming command, & give some general directions for receiving Reports, when I can quietly come back to this village and spend some quiet weeks. It has been suggested to me, that I will be quietly left out in the Cold. Even if that is resolved on, I ought to Know it that I may shape my private affairs accordingly. . . . P S. Say to the General I have seen his orders to Halleck which the latter claims as the basis for his orders to Meade Sheridan & Wright to pitch into Johnston. I approve Gen Grants orders for Wright to go to Danville and Sheridan towards Greensboro, which is a different thing from Hallecks interpretation. Genl Grant did *respect* my Truce, by allowing the 48 hours notice." ALS, DNA, RG 108, Letters Received. *O.R.*, I, xlvii, part 3, 662–63.

On July 5, Sherman, Nashville, telegraphed to USG. "You promised I should have the battalion thirteenth (13) Infy that served with me so long. I find it here and Genl Thomas has always treated it as belonging to me—Shall I order it to Jefferson Barracks Missouri—Please answer to me and Genl Thomas here—I will start back for Cincinnati tomorrow night. Have not yet received the orders defining clearly my new command but expect to find them at Cincinnati" Telegram received (on July 6, 2:15 A.M.), DNA, RG 107, Telegrams Collected (Bound); *ibid.*, RG 108, Telegrams Received; copies, *ibid.*, RG 393, Military Div. of the Miss., Letters Sent; DLC-USG, V, 54. On the same day, Sherman wrote to USG. "I came down today from Louisville to see General Thomas, about some old matters and shall start back for Cincinati tomorrow and Expect to meet there the orders defining my new Command. I want to assume Command, so that Reports may be collected and an office Established for recieving & issuing orders. I find that Thomas though a Division Commander now Exercises much of the duties of a Departmt Commander which may lead to Confusion. According to instructions Halleck gave me the Commander of a Military Division had nothing to do, Except to command the troops assembled for action leaving all details to Dept Commanders. I allude to the subject lest I may be neglecting something Expected of me. Telegraphic orders came to me from Col Breck of the Secretary of War's office, about discharges, as though I was a Departmt commander. All I can do is to repeat the messages to my subordinates. You remember I spoke to you of the 1st Battalion 13 Regulars. They were left by me here, because they had lost 60 per cent in Battles, which I thought a full share. They want to go with me, and I also want them, and I find Gen Thomas has always considered them as part of my command. I ask today by telegraph for leave to order the Battalion to Jefferson Barracks. The Head Quarters are already at Camp Dennison in Ohio within the area of my new Division. I visited yesterday the camps of all the troops still remaining of my old Army, and learned from Gen Logan that all are to be mustered out forthwith. I am glad of it, for I think many of them will soon tire of the tedium of civil Life and be anxious to Enlist in the Regular Army. There are several of the Genl Officers that I want to serve all I can. I take it for granted you will take care of Logan & Hazen. I want Maj Genls Jno. M. Corse, Charles C. Walcott, and A. S Williams ⟨J. E.?⟩ retained. They are most valuable officers, and I beg you will assign them to me to be retained till the proper time for them to seek *new* Commissions in the future Army.

Corse and Walcutt have both served with me 4 years, have been wounded twice in Battle, and are most promising young Generals, No better in the Army. I would like Brig Chas Ewing to be retained. I do not Know that any of the General officers are ordered to be mustered out, but I would like to retain the services of the above, until the reorganization of the Army. As soon as I get a copy of the order defining my command I shall assume command, call for Reports &c and then complete my visit to Ohio. I take it for granted you Expect little personal service of me this year, and I will Keep as quiet as possible. No matter what you may hear, do not fail to believe me sincere in what I wrote you before I left Washington. When my name is used it is positively against my consent." ALS, DNA, RG 108, Letters Received. *O.R.*, I, xlviii, part 2, 1049–50. On July 6, Maj. Gen. George H. Thomas telegraphed to USG. "Genl Sherman would like to have the thirteenth ~~Regular~~ U S Infantry ordered to report to him at St Louis. I have no objection & will ~~ord~~ issue the necessary orders if you authorise me." ALS (telegram sent), DNA, RG 107, Telegrams Collected (Unbound); telegram received (at 6:45 P.M.), *ibid.*, Telegrams Collected (Bound); *ibid.*, RG 108, Telegrams Received. On July 7, 10:30 A.M., Bvt. Col. Theodore S. Bowers telegraphed to Thomas. "Referring to your telegram of yesterday, Lt. Gen Grant desires that you order the 13th Infantry to report to Gen Sherman at StLouis, if you can spare it." ALS (telegram sent), *ibid.*, RG 107, Telegrams Collected (Bound); telegram sent, *ibid.*; telegram received, *ibid.*, Telegrams Collected (Unbound).

On July 6, USG wrote to Secretary of War Edwin M. Stanton. "In view of operations already commenced against the Indians on the plains extending into Colorado, I would recommend that that territory be taken out of the Dept. of California and attached to the Dept. of Mo. Gen. Pope being of the opinion that the Dept. assigned to him should have Hd Qrs. at St. Louis, where all the ~~D~~depots of supplies must necessarily remain, I would suggest a change in the order to comply with his wish." ALS, *ibid.*, RG 94, Letters Received, 1047A 1865. *O.R.*, I, xlviii, part 2, 1052. On July 8, Lt. Col. Roswell M. Sawyer, St. Louis, telegraphed to Bowers. "Please telegraph me if the Territories of Colorado, Montano Utah & New Mexico ~~are~~nd the state of Iowa are included in Gen Shermans Command & in the Dept of Missouri—" Telegram received (on July 9, 10:00 A.M.), DNA, RG 107, Telegrams Collected (Bound); *ibid.*, RG 108, Telegrams Received; copies, *ibid.*, RG 393, Military Div. of the Miss., Letters Sent; DLC-USG, V, 54. On July 9, Bowers endorsed this telegram. "Will Gen. Townsend please furnish the information within required." AES, DNA, RG 108, Telegrams Received. Probably on the same day, Bvt. Brig. Gen. Edward D. Townsend endorsed this telegram. "Iowa is in Dept. of Missouri and in Genl. Sherman's Divisions. Colorado, Utah, & New Mexico are in Dept. of California—Divn of the Pacific—Montana is not mentioned in the order assigning Dept. and Divn commands; but from its locality would properly be included in Dept. of the Columbia, Divn of the Pacific—See G. O. No. 118, enclosed, herewith—" AES (undated), *ibid.* On July 13, Bowers telegraphed this information to Sawyer. ALS (telegram sent), *ibid.*, RG 107, Telegrams Collected (Bound); telegram sent, *ibid.*; copies, *ibid.*, RG 108, Letters Sent; DLC-USG, V, 46, 109. On July 14, Maj. Gen. John Pope, Pomeroy, Ohio, telegraphed to Bowers. "Please ask the General to have orders assigning Colorado to my Dept. telegraphed to St Louis also order changing my headquarters to St Louis I shall be there tomorrow or next day" Telegram received (on July 15, 11:30 A.M.), DNA, RG 107,

Telegrams Collected (Bound); *ibid.*, RG 108, Telegrams Received; copy, DLC-USG, V, 54. *O.R.*, I, xlviii, part 2, 1079. On July 15, Sherman, St. Louis, telegraphed to Bowers. "I have arrived & assumed command Genl Pope telegraphs from Pomeroy ohio that his head quarters are to be here also, & mine at Cincinnati, This change should not be made without my consent & I do not consent. What about the thirteenth 13 infantry" Telegram received (at 2:15 P.M.), DNA, RG 107, Telegrams Collected (Bound); *ibid.*, RG 108, Telegrams Received; copy, DLC-USG, V, 54. *O.R.*, I, xlviii, part 2, 1083. At 8:12 P.M., USG telegraphed to Sherman. "The 13th Inf.y is ordered to St. Louis. Your Hd Qrs. have not been changed. ₐAt Gen. Popes request I asked to have his changed to St. Louis." ALS (telegram sent), DNA, RG 107, Telegrams Collected (Bound); telegram sent, *ibid.*; copies, *ibid.*, RG 108, Letters Sent; *ibid.*, RG 393, Military Div. of the Miss., Telegrams Received; DLC-USG, V, 46, 109. *O.R.*, I, xlviii, part 2, 1083. See *ibid.*, pp. 1143–44. On Aug. 2, Pope wrote to Townsend. "By authority of the General-in-chief of the army the Head Quarters of this Dept have been transferred from FtLeavenworth to this City. I have the honor to request therefore that you will give what orders are necessary for the proper transmission of official communications from the Adjutant General's Office" ALS, DNA, RG 94, Letters Received, 1586M 1865. *O.R.*, I, xlviii, part 2, 1156. On Oct. 7, USG endorsed this letter. "I recommend that headquarters of the Department of the Missouri be fixed at StLouis by orders." ES, DNA, RG 94, Letters Received, 1586M 1865. See *O.R.*, I, xlviii, part 2, 1238.

1. On June 20, Maj. Lewis M. Dayton, adjt. for Sherman, Chicago, telegraphed to Rawlins. "Have our head quarters left Washington for the west and did the officer in charge get orders to proceed to St Louis? Please answer a₺s Genl Sherman desires the earliest possible access to the records" Telegram received (at 9:00 P.M.), DNA, RG 107, Telegrams Collected (Bound); *ibid.*, RG 108, Telegrams Received; copy, DLC-USG, V, 54. On June 21, 12:20 P.M. (sent at 1:00 P.M.), Rawlins telegraphed to Sherman. "Your Headquarters left here on Monday, in charge of Col. Sawyer, for Saint Louis." Telegrams sent (2), DNA, RG 107, Telegrams Collected (Bound); copies, *ibid.*, RG 108, Letters Sent; DLC-USG, V, 46, 109. *O.R.*, I, xlvii, part 3, 660.

To William S. Hillyer

Washington D. C. June 29th *1865*

DEAR HILLYER,

In answer to your letter urging me to be present at Saratoga on the 4th of July at the dinner to be given in honor of the old "Army of the Tenn." I wrote to you saying that I would be there. Afterwards on reflecting that it was doubtful whether I should deside upon such matters so long before hand I sent to the Post Office and withdrew the letter. I now have to state that I was obliged to write to Governor Fenton withdrawing my acceptence to be present at the Flag presentation in Albany on that day and for the same reasons will have to decline the other.

Rawlins is away which somewhat interferes with my absenting myself and the Sec. of War desires me to go to Mo. on some public business. Even this I do not think I can do.

The "Army of the Tenn." is the fi[rst] Army I ever had the honor of commanding, and, in turn, was the fi[rst] commander that Army ever had. Naturally I feel an attachment f[or] it, and have an acquaintance with it, greater than any other person can well feel.— The 4th of July is peculi[arly] a fitting day for a reunion of that gallant old army. It is the An[niver]sity of our independence and also of the most desisive blow given [the] rebellion whilst it was powerful. T[hat] blow was given by the Army of [the] Tenn.

Regreting that I can not be with you in your festivities, and wi[shing] for you a reunion equal to your highest expectations, I remain,

Your Friend
U. S. GRAN[T]
Lt. Gn.

ALS, Hillyer Papers, ViU. See *New York Times*, July 3, 1865. USG attended a July 4 celebration in Albany, N. Y., but decided not to go to Saratoga because of the press of official business. See letter to Reuben E. Fenton, June 27, 1865.

To Maj. Gen. Philip H. Sheridan

———

(Cipher)   Washington July 1st 1865. [*4:00* P.M.]
MAJ. GEN. SHERIDAN, NEW ORLEANS,

Get your troops on the Rio Grande in readiness for active service should the immergency arise. Cauttion them however against provocing hostilities.

U. S. GRANT
Lt. Gn.

Demand the return of all public property crossed to the South side of the Rio Grande since Kirby Smith's surrender and report the reply received.

U. S. GRANT
Lt. Gen.

ALS (telegram sent), DNA, RG 107, Telegrams Collected (Bound); telegram sent, *ibid.*; copies, *ibid.*, RG 108, Letters Sent; DLC-USG, V, 46, 109; USG 3. *O.R.*, I, xlviii, part 2, 1035. See telegram to Maj. Gen. Philip H. Sheridan, June 15, 1865. On June 29, 1865, Maj. Gen. Philip H. Sheridan telegraphed to Brig. Gen. John A. Rawlins. "All of the fourth corps—about 10,000 men is now here & will be embarked in a few days for Indianola Texas and will occupy San Antonio—I am in hopes that most of the articles of subsistence which will be required for the troops in Texas can be procured from the country except the small rations—Beef is very abundant and cheap—Arrangements will be made to supply the troops serving in this state with Texas beef It can be purchased there for four cents per pound—I have had some inconvenience from the anomolous condition of my command and many delays in transportation of troops but feel now 'out of the woods' I hope that this anomolous condition of my command will soon be rectified—The columns of cavalry which start from Shreveport and Alexander under Gen Merrit are perhaps the best equipped and handsomest of the war—I think Gen Merritt has already started" Telegram received (on June 30, 3:30 A.M.), DNA, RG 107, Telegrams Collected (Bound); *ibid.*, RG 108, Telegrams Received; copies, DLC-USG, V, 54; DLC-Philip H. Sheridan. *O.R.*, I, xlviii, part 2, 1024–25. On the same day, Sheridan wrote to Rawlins. "On account of the constant activity which has attended me during the last Eighteen months, and the sudden changes to which I have been subjected I have been unable to as yet to render an account of the Cavalry opperatns from Brandy Station to Petersburgh, and of the Campaign in the Shenandoah Valley—and the March from Winchester down to Peterburgh. I have all the sub reports, and the notes now in my possession, and will make out the Narrative at the first leisure I was at times seperated from this data, and the constant and exciting changes to which I was subjected must be my excuse for this neglect. I have frequently thought that the value and military points made (through my own reticence) were not fully appreciated but the constant approval and unintermitting kindness of the Lt Genl has assured me that he at least saw them—and is a sufficient recompense to me—Will you have the kindness to make my excuses to the Lt General for this which has so much of the apperance of neglect. In speaking of the unvaried kindness of Genl Grant I do not forget the deep debt I owe you for your confidence and strong support" LS, USG 3. On July 20, Sheridan wrote to Rawlins. "I have the honor to transmit herewith my report of the operations of my cavalry on the campaign from Winchester in the Shenandoah Valley to the Armies in front of Petersburg beginning February 27th and ending March 28th 1865." LS, DNA, RG 108, Letters Received. The report is in *O.R.*, I, xlvi, part 1, 474–81.

On July 1, Sheridan telegraphed to USG. "Orders have been issued declaring all slaves free. *2nd* That all arms must be given up and all public property returned. *3rd* That all acts of the Governor and Legislature of Texas since the ordinance of secession are illegitimate. *4th*. That no Home Guards or bands for self protection will be tolerated. 5th. That neighborhoods will by the possession of their property be held responsible for guerrilla warfare *6th* That all refugees may return home in safety and as well as all rebel acts have been declared illegitimate they can resume possession of their property. The state is now ready for its Provisional Governor if it is the wisdom of the President to send one. Genl Steele has been directed to make a demand for the Steamer 'Lucy Given' on the French authorities and if not given up to get her the best way he can. As soon as Genl's Merritt & Custer get to the Rio Grande the other public property will be taken whereever found. The rascality of the Rio Grande frontier is beyond solution on intermediate grounds where there is no government & a questionable Protectorate. It is due to the history of our country that this portion of the late rebellion should be crushed out in a manly way and with the power of a great nation as a contrast to this French subterfuge to assist in the attempt to ruin our country" Telegram received (on July 3, 1:00 P.M.), DNA, RG 107, Telegrams Collected (Bound); *ibid.*, RG 108, Telegrams Received; copies, DLC-USG, V, 54; (2) DLC-Philip H. Sheridan. *O.R.*, I, xlviii, part 2, 1035–36. On July 5, Secretary of State William H. Seward wrote to Secretary of War Edwin M. Stanton. "I have just read the copies which you have laid before me of Major General Sheridan's several dispatches of the 28th of June to Lieutenant General Grant of the 29th of June to Major General Rawlins, and of the 1st day of July to Lieutenant General Grant. . . . I have laid this information before the President of the United States, and taken his views thereupon. I have therefore to request that Major General Sheridan may be informed that his proceedings in demanding the restoration of the property plundered from the United States, at the hands of the French authorities in Matamoros are approved, and farther that in compliance with instructions heretofore given, no forces of the United States will make any aggressive movement within or upon the jurisdiction of Mexico in the absence of instructions to be directly issued from the War Department. Simultaneously with writing this note, the grievances complained of in the dispatches of Major General Sheridan will be brought to the notice of the Government of Mexico, the Emperor of France, and of the military authorities acting in his name within the Republic of Mexico. This Department will immediately also claim from the proper parties the restoration of the plundered property and the adoption of the measures necessary to secure the rights of the United States on the Texan frontier from aggressions to be made from any of the belligerent parties in Mexico." LS, DNA, RG 107, Letters Received from Bureaus. On July 2, Sheridan wrote to Rawlins. "I have the honor herewith to enclose for the information of the Lieutenant General Comdg, copies of my instructions to Generals Granger and Steele since the occupation of the State of Texas, also a copy of General Order No 5, Headquarters Military Division of the South West, dated June 30th 1865" LS, *ibid.*, RG 108, Letters Received. The enclosures are *ibid.* On July 3, Sheridan telegraphed to Rawlins. "The 1st Division of the 4th corps will leave here for Indianola Texas on Wednesday the 5th inst and will be pushed up to San Antonio. The whole corps will be put on the line from Victoria to San Antonio; it numbers about ten thousand (10.000) men. (The state of Texas never was in so prosperous a condition in reference to supplies as it is at present. I will I think have no difficulty in supplying all troops in the interior from the country with everything but the small rations.) I have had much chagrin at the slowness with which things move in this section on account of the anomolous condition of the commands. I have to *request* everything, which is cheerfully granted by Genl Canby, but as I have no power over the subordinate Staff Departments to drive them much delay occurs" Telegram received (on July 6, 8:30 A.M.), *ibid.*, RG 107, Telegrams Collected (Bound); *ibid.*, RG 108, Telegrams Received; copies, DLC-USG, V, 54; (2—one incomplete) DLC-Philip H. Sheridan; (incomplete) USG 3. *O.R.*, I, xlviii, part 2, 1042. On July 6, 12:00 P.M., Sheridan telegraphed to Rawlins. "Affairs on the Rio Grande frontier are getting beautifully mixed up—Cortinas has arrived and now has his Head-Quarters Six miles from Matamoras—and has driven in Mejias pickets—He also captured the Steamer Senorita and took her over to the other side of the river for safety, and she was taken down to Rio Grande City and seized by General Brown—I do not know exactly how it is as yet—Mejia replied to Genl Steeles demand for battery and other property taken across the Rio Grande that he had no authority to comply with the demand but would refer it to the Imperial Government—This is just what I expected and only confirms my former impression that the property can only be obtained when we go and take it—Genl Steele says the French Officers and Soldiers are very bitter against our people and writes me that a grandson of Marshall Ney with two thousand French Cavalry is reported approaching Matamoras and that he is very bitter and Says he is going to invade Texas—The feeling of the people in the interior of Mexico is very bitter while the natives, soldiers and all, are said to be with our Government and want to get rid of French rule—Ringgold Barracks is occupied by our troops" Telegram received (on July 8, 3:00 A.M.), DNA, RG 107, Telegrams Collected (Bound); *ibid.*, RG 108, Telegrams Received; copies, DLC-USG, V, 54; DLC-Philip H. Sheridan; (incomplete) DLC-Andrew Johnson; USG 3. *O.R.*, I, xlviii, part 2, 1053.

On July 10, Sheridan twice telegraphed to USG. "Reliable information from my own scouts at Matamoras is as follows—The French authorities are very much embarrassed—Cortinas drives in Mejias pickets at pleasure and the arrival of our heavy forces on the Rio Grand and the little irritation which I have encouraged along the river has alarmed them so much that there is a perfect exodus from Matamoras—Nearly all the people out of Matamoras are Liberals, and the majority of those within the City—The French soldiers are deserting, and there is generally a very uneasy state of affairs with the authorities—To let down a little I have empowered Gen Steele to settle little questions arising, but without any authority to settle points, for which demands have been made in accordance with your instructions—Many of the rebels who crossed near Matamoras have returned in disgust—Shelbys command, Governor ———, Clark and company crossed the Rio Grand high up—I have not yet found out where they went, but am on their track—Mejia is still at work on his fortifications around Matamoras—They are about three miles in extent and only two thousand men to fill them" Telegram received (on July 11, 11:15 P.M.), DNA, RG 107, Telegrams Collected (Bound); *ibid.*, RG 108, Telegrams Received; copies, DLC-USG, V, 54; (2) DLC-Philip H. Sheridan. *O.R.*, I, xlviii, part 2, 1067. "Genl Steele sends the following information. The French Mexicans on the Rio Grande appear to be anxious to bring on difficulties with the United States & are very bitter. Cortinas holds all the roads around Matamoras. Says he could take the place if he had ammunition. He has captured considerable of rebel cotton and broken up the thieving parties engaged in this on the upper Rio Grande. He says he will also break up the parties engaged in running over stock. He visited Genl Steele at Brownsville Has as Governor of Tamaulipas under the Liberal Government given permission for our forces to enter Mexico. Governor Mirrah of Texas & the Ex Governor & Walker, Shelby & others are at Monterey and in considerable numbers. Shelby took over an organized force. Nothing is yet known of their intentions. They are with the Imperialists without doubt, and are represented by a Matamoras paper as ten thousand (10.000) strong; this is exaggeration Genl Merritt is on his way to San Antonia" Telegram received (on July 12, 9:00 A.M.), DNA, RG 107, Telegrams Collected (Bound); *ibid.*, RG 108, Telegrams Received; Seward Papers, NRU; copies, DLC-USG, V, 54; (2) DLC-Philip H. Sheridan; USG 3. *O.R.*, I, xlviii, part 2, 1068.

Also on July 10, Sheridan wrote to Rawlins. "I have the honor to forward for the information of the Lt. Genl Comd.g, a succinct report of changes and movements of troops since my arrival here. At Cairo Ills I was notified by the Lieut Genl of the surrender of Genl Kirby Smith and the forces under his command and at once directed the movement of 5.000 troops from Little Rock to Shreveport to occupy Upper Red River and Northern Texas. On my way down the Mississippi I found that Genl Canby had sent two brigades of the 13th Corps En route for Shreveport and I met these troops at the mouth of Red River this necessitated me to countermand the order sent to Genl Reynolds the transports ordered for his troops were employed to convey Cavalry. I found also that Genl Canby had ordered the balance of the 13th Corps to embark at Mobile for the coast of Texas and that Genl. Steele was about embarking with one division; these orders of Genl Canby I did not change except in this that the order for mustering out regiments whose term of service would expire previous to Sept. 30th was countermanded and some of these regiments sent to Texas. which was a waste of transportation and I gave directions that no more of these regiments should be shipped; the military necessity for sending these regiments was not apparent and it had the appearance to me of a fear that the Corps would be consolidated and some of the General Officers mustered out, those regiments that had arrived in Texas have been ordered mustered out so that the strength of the Corps is now about Seven or Eight thousand men I recommend its consolidation as a division upon the same basis as that adopted in the Army of the Potomac. This Corps now occupies Houston, Galveston Columbia and Brennan, Texas and points on the Rio Grand from Brownsville up to Rio Grande City also Marshall Texas & Shreveport. La The 25th Army Corps came out slowly and was not very well managed, it is stationed as follows five regiments at Indianola two at Corpus Christi, one division at Brownsville under Genl Giles aA Smith and the balance at Brazos Santiago The 4th Army Corps arrived on the 24th ultimo and is now being sent to Indianola and will be pushed in from the coast and as high up as San Antonio From New Orleans. Baton Rouge. Vicksburg and Memphis. and other points two cavalry colums were organized, one at Shreveport and one at Alexandria, the one at Shreveport has marched for San Antonio the one at Alexandria will soon be ready and will go to Houston and from there to wherever it may be wanted I found the Depot at this, place entirely inadequate to supply the demand made upon it. The landing of troops on the coast of Texas was very troublesome; we have occasionally been troubled by storms; the difficulty in crossing the bar sometimes involving the necessity of lightering for a distance of twenty miles. In the organization of the Cavalry Column we were retarded by the extremely difficult navigation of Red River which could only be accomplished in day light; the absense from this Depot of horse shoes, nails &c required both time and labor to overcome but the condition of affairs is now growing more tangible Material to finish the railroad from Brazos Santiago to the Rio Grande at Clarkesville has been shipped and I propose to run it up to Brownsville it will be required and will pay for itself in a short time we have the Locomotive and rolling stock on hand for the road. The railroad from Indianola to Victoria is now being put in order by the company assisted by the military authorities The Light Houses on the coast will, I am told, be soon repaired and where they have been destroyed will be put in such a condition as to give the necessary light to assist in the navigation of this coast We have had two or three hard blows this month keeping vessels four or five days from crossing the bar at Brazos, Galveston & Indianola. The store Houses for Brazos are nearly completed and will be sent on as soon as transportation can be furnished. there has been a good deal of reluctance on the part of many of the troops to continue longer in service but no positive discontent I have worked very hard but the difficulties were unusual" LS, DNA, RG 108, Letters Received.

On July 14, Sheridan telegraphed to USG. "Genl Steele notified me yesterday evening that Maximillian has directed Mejia to give up the battery of artillery, ammunition wagons, animals, and ammunition and that it would be turned over on the 9th of this month—There is a stamped on the part of the Franco-Mexicans—Camargo has been evacuated—The garrison marched down to Matamoras with large cotton trains—This cotton is United States cotton, stolen under the auspices of the French Commandant—Genl Steele notifies me that the command of Genl Shelby which escorted the cotton agent of Texas Governors Murrah, Clark and Allen, Genl Smith, Magruder and others, had with it three pieces of artillery, forty wagon loads of Enfield rifles and a large wagon train—He has some doubt of the correctness of this report but I do not doubt it but very little myself—Cortinas has made application for his artillery which is at Brownsville (three pieces) and I have directed it to be quietly turned over to him—This was the understanding when it was left at Brownsville—Genl Steele also notifies me that they are nearly starved out in Matamoras" Telegram received (at 10:00 P.M.), *ibid.*, RG 107, Telegrams Collected (Bound); *ibid.*, RG 108, Telegrams Received; copies, DLC-USG, V, 54; DLC-Philip H. Sheridan. *O.R.*, I, xlviii, part 2, 1077.

To Maj. Gen. George H. Thomas

Washington July 3d 1865 [2:20 P.M.]

MAJ. GN. G. H. THOMAS, NASHVILLE TEN.

Gen. Wood can take his Staff with him. There is no need of sending more troops to Alabama at least not until Gen. Wood gets there and finds he will need them. We want now to discharge all troops that can be dispensed with. All the troops now in Ala. Wood will assume command of on his arrival.

U. S. GRANT
Lt. Gn

ALS (telegram sent), DNA, RG 107, Telegrams Collected (Bound); telegram sent, *ibid.*; telegram received, *ibid.*, Telegrams Collected (Unbound). *O.R.*, I, xlix, part 2, 1060. On July 1, 1865, Maj. Gen. George H. Thomas had telegraphed to USG. "Genl C. R. Woods has just reported to me in person. He desires to take with him to Alabama his old division entire   If he cannot take his Division he desires to take his staff. I have just learned from Genl Canby that there will be left in Alabama & Mississippi after the muster out of those ordered seven thousand white troops. He will make no changes in them till he learns from me what troops I have to replace them. I shall send Hatch with his Cavalry to Alabama, about three thousand. I also have about six thousand Infantry including Regulars to divide between Steedman and Woods as soon as I can learn what Steedman has at Augusta and Savannah. If the fourteenth Corps is to report to me for duty I should prefer leaving it in Kentucky for the present as the political condition of that state is ~~worse~~ more critical to-day than either Tennessee Alabama or Georgia. With judicious management I believe there will be but little trouble in restoring perfect order in the three latter named states." ALS (telegram sent), MH; telegram received (on July 3, 1:40 P.M.), DNA, RG 107, Telegrams Collected (Bound); (on July 3, 8:00 P.M.—marked "Repeated (corrected)") *ibid.*, RG 108, Telegrams Received. A variant text appears in *O.R.*, I, xlix, part 2, 1057.

To Maj. Gen. Philip H. Sheridan

July 6th *1865* [*11:20* A.M.]

MAJ. GN. P. H. SHERIDAN, NEW ORLEANS, LA.

The order has been published placing you in command of Military Division composed of Florida, Louisiana, Texas, Arkansas, Indian Territory and Mississippi. You have full authority to order and direct all Staff Depts. Relieve all Gn. and Staff officers whose services are not required and report names to the Adj. Gn.

U. S. GRANT
Lt. Gn.

ALS (telegram sent), DNA, RG 107, Telegrams Collected (Bound); telegram sent, *ibid.*; telegram received, *ibid.*, Telegrams Collected (Unbound). *O.R.*, I, xlviii, part 2, 1052. On July 7, 1865, Maj. Gen. Philip H. Sheridan telegraphed to Brig. Gen. John A. Rawlins. "Will you have the kindness to represent to the

Lieut Gen that as yet I have not been assigned to command; that for over one month I have been compelled to ask from *a Junior* for every thing that I required in consequence of that portion of Louisiana which embraces this depot being outside of my command; that in the transportation of troops to Texas and in the organization of cavalry columns to go over land I have been powerless to control subordinate Quartermasters and agents, and delays and injuries to the service have been the consequence." Telegram received (on July 8, 11:30 P.M.), DNA, RG 107, Telegrams Collected (Bound); *ibid.*, RG 108, Telegrams Received; copies, DLC-USG, V, 54; (2) DLC-Philip H. Sheridan. *O.R.*, I, xlviii, part 2, 1061. On July 9, USG endorsed this telegram. "Respectfully referred to the Sec of War with the request that the order assigning Gen. Sheridan to command of Military Div. be telegraphed to him. Much delay and embarrassment necessarily arises from want of authority to command. All the Dept. Commanders within the Mil. Div. should also receive copies of the order sent to Gen. Sheridan." Copy, DNA, RG 108, Telegrams Received. *O.R.*, I, xlviii, part 2, 1061.

On July 12, Sheridan telegraphed to Bvt. Col. Theodore S. Bowers. "Has the order for my Military Division been forwarded to me yet?" Telegram received (at 8:25 P.M.), DNA, RG 107, Telegrams Collected (Bound); *ibid.*, RG 108, Telegrams Received; copies, DLC-USG, V, 54; DLC-Philip H. Sheridan. *O.R.*, I, xlviii, part 2, 1073. On July 13, 2:15 P.M., Bowers telegraphed to Sheridan. "The order defining your Command has been sent to you by telegraph and mail" ALS (telegram sent), DNA, RG 107, Telegrams Collected (Bound); telegram sent, *ibid.*; telegram received, *ibid.*, Telegrams Collected (Unbound). *O.R.*, I, xlviii, part 2, 1075. See *ibid.*, pp. 1003–4.

To Edwin M. Stanton

Washington July 7th 1865

HON. E. M. STANTON
SECY OF WAR.
SIR;

General J. E. Johnson who had authority to go to Canada with his family declined going on account of the health of Mrs. Johnson prohibiting her traveling so far, and because his authority to go prohibited his return to the United States without authority.[1] He has made application for Amnesty and does not want to risk becoming an exile. He now asks to have his parole extended so as to authorize him to go to Maryland where his wife's relations reside.

I am in favor of so extending his parole and with your authority will so extend it.

> Very respectfully
> Your obt. Servt
> U. S. GRANT
> Lieut. Gen'l

Copies, DLC-USG, V, 46, 109; DNA, RG 108, Letters Sent. Dated July 6, 1865, in *O.R.*, I, xlvii, part 3, 675. On July 8, Bvt. Col. Theodore S. Bowers issued a permit. "By permission of the Secretary of War the parole of Joseph E.—Johnson, General in the late Rebel Army is hereby extended to permit him to return to and reside in the State of Maryland until further orders from these Headquarters. So long as he observes his parole and acts under this authority he will not be disturbed." Copies, DLC-USG, V, 46, 109; DNA, RG 108, Letters Sent. On July 11, Joseph E. Johnston wrote to President Andrew Johnson requesting amnesty. ALS, *ibid.*, RG 94, Amnesty Papers, Va.

On July 15, Asst. Secretary of the Navy Gustavus V. Fox wrote to USG. "Allan McLane of N. York. who lives some where up river writes me that Jo. Johnsons Parole has been extended to include Maryland and he regrets that it did not include N. York so that he could have taken him to his home, with his wife for the summer—His wife being McLanes Sister. Is such an extension agreeable to your views—" ALS, USG 3. Bvt. Col. Horace Porter noted on the docket. "Informed that it is perfectly agreeable to Gen Grant's views" AN, *ibid.*

1. On May 14, Johnston, Charlotte, N. C., wrote to Maj. Gen. John M. Schofield. "As soon as the terms of 'the Convention' are executed in Georgia and Florida, I wish to go to St Catherine's Springs, Canada. Will you be so kind as to inform me if I will be permitted to travel directly from Virginia to that point?" Copy, DNA, RG 107, Letters Received from Bureaus. On May 22, USG endorsed this letter. "I am very much in favor of granting Genl Johnstons request, and if authorized will telegraph the authority at once.—" Copy, *ibid.* On the same day, Secretary of War Edwin M. Stanton endorsed this letter. "Submitted to the President who directs that the permission asked by Genl Johnson be granted, with the condition that he does not return to the United States without leave of the President—" Copy, *ibid.* At 2:00 P.M., USG telegraphed to Schofield. "You may inform Gen. J. E. Johnston that he will be permitted to go to Canada, through the States as he may select, not to return to the United States without first obtaining leave to do so." ALS (telegram sent), *ibid.*, Telegrams Collected (Bound); telegram sent, *ibid.*; copies, *ibid.*, RG 108, Letters Sent; *ibid.*, RG 393, Army of the Ohio and Dept. of N. C., Telegrams Received; DLC-USG, V, 46, 76, 109; DLC-John M. Schofield. *O.R.*, I, xlvii, part 3, 560. See *ibid.*, p. 564.

To Edwin M. Stanton

Washington D. C. July 10th *1865*

HON. E. M. STANTON,
SEC. OF WAR,
SIR:

The War having been brought practically to a close, and more than two thirds of the Volunteer force of the Army having been Mustered out of service, I have the honor to report that the ~~following~~ enclosed named General officers, together with their A. A. Generals, and Aides, exsept where they belong to regiments still remaining in service, can now be dispensed with without detriment to the service.

This list can be further materially increased in a short time.

I would recommend the honorable discharge of all named from the Volunteer service, those holding commissions in the regular Army to return to their duties in it.

Very respectfully
your obt. svt.
U. S. GRANT
Lt. Gn.

ALS, DNA, RG 94, Record & Pension Office, 462080. The enclosed list is *ibid.* On Aug. 9, 1865, President Andrew Johnson endorsed this letter. "The reccommendation of Lieutenant General Grant to muster out of service the within named officers is approved and the Adjutant Generel is directed to muster them out by General Order accordingly" ES, *ibid.*

To Maj. Gen. Irvin McDowell

Washington July 10th *1865* [*1:30* P.M.]

MAJ. GN. I. McDOWELL, SANFRANCISCO

Do you need troops for Arizona? If so what number and what kind shall I be sendt?

U. S. GRANT
Lt. Gen.

ALS (telegram sent), DNA, RG 107, Telegrams Collected (Bound); telegram sent, *ibid.*; telegram received (on July 17, 12:00 P.M.), *ibid.*, RG 393, Army of the Ohio, Dept. of the Pacific, Letters Received. *O.R.*, I, l, part 2, 1277. On Aug. 11, 1865, Maj. Gen. Irvin McDowell wrote to USG. "Owing to the interruption of the telegraph line between this and the east, and, further, to my absence from head quarters on a tour of inspection beyond the Sierra Nevada to Owens River Valley, your telegram of the 10th ultimo, asking if I needed troops for Arizona and, if so, what number and kind should be sent, was not received by me till the latter part of July, since when I have been waiting, from day to day, for the telegraph to work to send an answer. But as there seems, now, no prospect of the line being in order for an indefinite time to come, I answer this by the next steamer, sending a duplicate to take its chances overland.—In the last despatches received from him, Brig. General Mason, Commanding the District of Arizona, writes as follows: 'I would respectfully request that, if possible, two additional regiments of Infantry be sent to this Territory. In the end it will be more economical. A sharp, quite active campaign against the Indians during the coming fall and winter will be all that is needed provided we have troops enough. The extent of country—[Arizona]—is so great and the number of Indians comparatively so small that they can evade the troops. Whilst we are scouting in one section they are depredating in another, but with troops enough to operate in all sections at the same time a short campaign will suffice.' I cannot agree with the General in his estimate of the short duration of hostilities in his district, though I do in the economy, in every point of view—of his having as large a force as can be used and supplied. I therefore wish two regiments of Infantry for Arizona. I can spare from the troops at the Presidio some eight companies and a company from Southern California and shall immediately order them to proceed to Arizona. Ultimately I will send four other companies from Southern California, making in all thirteen companies, all of which in a few months time will not amount to more than a regiment. For the other regiment I beg to suggest as follows: There are in New Mexico parts of the 1st and 5th Cal. Vol. Infantry, and part of the 1st Cal. Vol. Cavalry, which, it is desirable, should be drawn into Arizona where they will be nearer their homes by the time their terms of service expire. That this may be done, and at the same time, the Brig. General Commanding in New Mexico may have sufficient force to co-operate, efficiently, with the Commander in Arizona, two full regiments of Infantry or their equivalent, and two squadrons of cavalry should be sent to New Mexico, as it may be too late by the time this communication reaches you, and can be acted upon, for these troops to go from Kansas either by the Cimmeron or Roton routes, it may be necessary to send them from, or through, Texas, if that state is in a condition to admit of it. I have as yet received no reports or returns from New Mexico, and cannot write with any precision as to the number, disposition, or kind of troops in that district, and the number I have named is, therefore, a matter of conjecture, but cannot, I think, be far out of the way. In connection with this subject, I beg to ask that authority be given to consolidate the regiments of Volun Infantry in California with each other as they fall below the minimum, instead of reducing the regiments into battalions, so that some of the Colonels, who are very necessary for holding commands, may be retained." LS (2—one received Aug. 23, the other Sept. 26—brackets in original document), DNA, RG 108, Letters Received. *O.R.*, I, l, part 2, 1287.

To James Speed

Respectfully forwarded to the Atty. Gn. of the United States.
Gen. French was a classmate of mine from New Jersey. He settled
in the state of Miss. soon after resigning from the Army in 1856.
I think he is most entitled to the benefits of Amnesty, of all Northern
men that I know who entered into the rebellion. All he had was in
the South. His stock, provisions and grain the United States got
during the Vicksburg Campaign. I believe from what I heard from
Gn. J. J. Reynolds, of our service, who was in New Orleans in the
Winter of 61–2, and met French there that he had no desire, to see
the south enter into such a contest as she was then preparing for.

I would only recommend that Gn. French be among the first of
his class to receive amnesty.

U. S. GRANT
Lt. Gen.

July 11th 1865.

AES, DNA, RG 94, Amnesty Papers, Miss. Written on a letter of June 29,
1865, from Samuel G. French, Jackson, Miss., to USG. "*Private* . . . As you are
aware I resigned from the army in march 1856, and became a resident and citizen
of this state, and was engaged in planting when this state passed the ordinance
of Secession in January 1861. When Mississippi was regarded an isolated
sovereign state I was appointed, to my surprise, to the office of chief of ordnance,
which position I was induced to accept. As soon as the body politic known as
the Confederate States of America was formed I was appointed the Senior Major
of Ordnance in the regular Army. Not wishing to enter the army & being opposed to hostilities I refused this appointment. In October 1861, when I had
brought my duties as state ordnance officer nearly to a close, and had gone to
my home I was tendered the appointment of Brigadier General in the Provisional
Army of the Confederate States I was within military age—There was no alternative I had to accept this appointment or enter the service as a private
soldier. After some ten days deliberation and consultation of friends I did accept
this position, and was subsequently promoted to Maj: Genl—The right for a
state to Secede, or the doctrine of 'State sovereignty' is now forever settled by
the arbitrament of arms, and I am prepared to faithfully abide that decision,
and I have petitioned the President of the U. S. for Amnesty and pardon agree-
ably to his proclamation. I will state to you that I never had a wish to enter the
army, and never did I in any way whatever, directly or indirectly, or by friends
ask for or seek appointment, promotion, place or command, but under allegiance
to my state and country have only conscientiously performed my duty as a
citizen and as a soldier. Thus much for explanation. Now, General, as a friend
of mine I wish you to write to, or see the President and endeavor to have my

petition acted on as soon as possible—In remembrance of our former friendship, which I still cherish, I hope you will aid me in this matter. I would make a visit to the north and call and see you but the truth is, this war has swept from me at least two hundred and fifty thousand dollars worth of property, and I have now to begin the world anew finding myself pennyless. I will thank you to acknowledge the receipt of this. My address will be 'Columbus Ga'. . . . If convenient, and not inconsistent with your relations with the President I would like you to make my case as a personal favor to yourself—but of this matter you must be the judge. When you see Genl Ingalls give him my rigards." ALS, *ibid.* On June 28, French had written to President Andrew Johnson requesting amnesty. ALS, *ibid.* On June 30, French wrote to USG. "I wrote to you a few days since in regard to my petition for amnesty. I then expected to leave here, but to day the Governor instead of forwarding it my petition returned it to me with his endorsement, and I take the liberty to forward it to you. Now, General, I appeal to you as a friend, and I request that you will when you go to Washington call on the President in person with my petition,—and as a personal favor to you—have it acted on at once. That is not leave it to come up for consideration in regular order. Am I asking too much? As stated to you in my former letter the War has ruined me—I am bankrupt or I would go north and see you in person. Four times I have had *every animal* taken from my house and my family left without a team even in Winter to haul firewood. I now want to go to work and earn a livelihood for myself and family as formerly. I am sure I do not make this appeal to you in vain for a personal favor, which will relieve me from anxiety and enable me to start afresh in the world. I request that you acknowledge the receipt of this. My address will be Columbus Georgia. . . . P. S. Enclosed with this is a letter from Hon Wm Yerger to the President." ALS, *ibid.* On July 20, USG endorsed this letter. "Respectfully refered to the Atty. Gn. with attention called to previous endorsement made in the same case. Gen. French I do not think was ever a secessionest but having a large property in Miss. (All but the land Government has got,) was forced to take service. I would recommend the extension of Executive pardon to him." AES, *ibid.* Docketing indicates that French was not pardoned until Jan. 3, 1867.

To Edwin M. Stanton

———

Washington D. C. July 11th *1865*

HON. E. M. STANTON,
SEC. OF WAR,
SIR:

I would respectfully recommend the appointment, by brevet, of Col. Wm Gates (retired) to the rank of Brigadier General, for long and faithful services in the Army.[1] Col. Gates has been in the

Army near sixty years and has been retired solely, I believe, on the score of age. The brevet rank of Brig. Gen. would be but a complement well earned and I would recommend it not only to Col. Gates but to the other retired Colonals of the Army where long services are the only grounds of retirement.

> Very respectfully
> your obt. svt.
> U. S. GRANT
> Lt. Gen.

ALS, DNA, RG 94, ACP, G596 CB 1865. An enclosed list naming an additional sixteen retired cols. for appointment as bvt. brig gen. is *ibid.*

1. William Gates, born in Mass. in 1788, USMA 1806, appointed 2nd lt., 1st Art., as of March 6, 1806, served in the War of 1812, the Mexican War, and in the campaigns against the Seminole Indians. Promoted to col., 3rd Art., as of Oct. 13, 1845, he retired from active service on June 1, 1863.

To Edwin M. Stanton

Washington D C. July 12th *1865*

HON. E. M. STANTON,
SECRETARY OF WAR.
SIR:

Col. O. E. Babcock of my staff has just returned from a tour of inspection to Rock-Island, Alton and Indianapolis. He will make a written report on which I may make some recommendations for orders. He reports, however, verbally, that at each of the prisons there is considerable property which has been purchased out of prison-funds, and a large amount of funds on hand at each place.

There is now no longer any use for this property or money for the purposes for which it was obtained. It clearly belongs to Government. I would therefore recommend that an order be made requiring officers at all prisons which have been emptied to sell all property that has been purchased out of prison-fund; and at all other prisons to do the same thing as fast as they are cleared of prisoners, and to turn the money over to the proper authorities.

> Very Respectfully
> Your obedient servant
> U. S. GRANT
> Lieutenant General.

LS, DNA, RG 94, Letters Received, 760A 1865. *O.R.*, II, viii, 703–4. On June 29, 1865, Bvt. Col. Theodore S. Bowers directed the AG to issue special orders. "Lieut. Col. O. E. Babcock, A d. C., will proceed without delay to Alton, Illinois, and make an inspection of the military prison at that place. He will report in writing to these Headquarters the number of prisoners confined there, whether civil or military, stating for what offences they are confined and whether by sentence of court martial or otherwise. Upon the execution of this order he will await further instructions at Alton." Copy, DNA, RG 94, Letters Received, 687A 1865. *O.R.*, II, viii, 682. On July 3, Bvt. Col. Orville E. Babcock, Alton, Ill., telegraphed to USG. "But one Prisoner remaining here He is sick and goes Tuesday under Charge of a surgeon to St Louis—Twelve 12 were sent to Jefferson City, the rest sent to St. Louis;—prison is to be turned over to owners   One battalion of five hundred and thirty 530 men here Expecting to go to St Louis—" Telegram received (at 12:45 P.M.), DNA, RG 107, Telegrams Collected (Bound); *ibid.*, RG 108, Telegrams Received; copy, DLC-USG, V, 54. At 2:10 P.M., USG telegraphed to Babcock. "You may go to Rock Island and report condition of prison there   Then return by Indianapolis and see that prison." ALS (telegram sent), DNA, RG 107, Telegrams Collected (Bound); telegram sent, *ibid.*; copies, *ibid.*, RG 108, Letters Sent; DLC-USG, V, 46, 109. On the same day, Babcock wrote to Brig. Gen. John A. Rawlins. "I made an inspection of the Military Prison here to day, and have the honor to report the following for your information. There are no prisoners here now, all have been sent away by order of Genl Dodge to St Louis and Jefferson City, 231. Federal prisoners, 34 Citizen and 4 prisoners of war, the latter decline to take the oath. The guard five (5) companies under command of Col Kuhn are still here guarding the public property. They expect to be relieved soon, in fact a company of men have been sent from St Louis for that purpose. I examined such of the books as have not been sent to St Louis.   they show a plain record on their face, but of course I could not verrify them. The prison appears to have been kept in good police. The public property is being got in readiness for disposal—The treasurer of the Prison Fund has some $35,000.00 in his hand   The Comy of Subsistence of the Post is treasurer. All prisoners against whom no charges were forwarded were discharged some days since by direction of Lt Genl Grant through the Comy Genl of Prisoners. Col Kuhn present commander has been in command since March 10th 1865. His regiment the 144th Ill. was raised for a Prison Guard, and have some five months longer to serve. I should think it would be advisable to muster them out, and use the Veteran regiments for provost duty. The expense of a guard here will soon exceed all that can be realized from the sale of the public property   The old Prison is to be turned over to its owners— it being private property. Genl Copeland (B G), was releived from command of this place in January last and has remained here since 'awaiting orders.' " ALS, DNA, RG 108, Letters Received. *O.R.*, II, viii, 694–95. On July 7, Babcock, Rock Island, telegraphed to USG. "No prisoners in this camp last two 2 turned over from Hospital yesterday seven 7 companies of fourth (4) Regiment of Veteran Reserve Corps here now—six 6 companies under Col Johnson ordered to Spingfield one 1 company to remain to guard public property—leave for Indianapolis to day" Telegram received (at 1:00 P.M.), DNA, RG 107, Telegrams Collected (Bound); *ibid.*, RG 108, Telegrams Received; copy, DLC-USG, V, 54.

On July 13, Babcock wrote to Bowers. "I have the honor to submit the following report for the information of the Lieut Genl Comd'g. In accordance with S. O. No 343 A. G. O. War Dept June 29th 1865, and telegraph despatch of July 3rd signed by the Lieut Genl. I made an inspection of the Prison at Alton Ill on the 3rd of July. Found no inmates, all having been discharged or transferred to Jefferson City and St Louis Mo. by order of Genl Dodge Comdg Dept of Mo. I found a guard of five (5) companies of the 144th Ill Vol Inft. The old Alton Penetentiary, and the tempory barracks and Hospitals are all that require guarding. Col Kuhn comdg 144 Vol (Ill) informed me on the 4th of July that he had received orders to proceed to Springfield Ill with his regiment to be mustered out. A company having been sent from St Louis to do the necessary guard duty. I examined such of the records as remained at Alton and found them in apparent good order, but could not verify them as the prisoners had all been removed. The Prison-Fund on hand am'ts to near $35000.00 I would recommend the breaking up of this post at once. The Prison to be turned over to its owners. The public property to be sold or transferred to other depôts. I inspected the Mil Prison at Rock Island on the 6th of July. This prison is also empty. It is guarded by seven companies of Veteran Reserve Corps Six companies were under orders to proceed to Springfield Ill. The prisoners here were exchanged or released on taking the oath of allegiance. The grounds, barracks, hospitals and records all show great care and attention on the part of the Comdg Officer Col Johnson. The Prison-Fund here am'ts to $174068.15. As this Island is to be the place of deposit of a large amt of amunition, I would recommend the preservation of the buildings. The locality has the appearance of being very healthy, and would in my opinion be a fine location for a general hospital, if the establishment of such should again become necessary: I inspected the Prison at Indianapolis on the 10th of July, and found Eight (8) prisoners, one 'Citizen,' and seven 'prisoners of war' Citizen William E. Mumford, supposed to be a Lieut in the C. S. A. held as a spy, was arrested with one Maj J B Castleman on same charge. Castleman has been released on condition that he would leave the country not to return. I would recommend Mumford be released on on taking the oath of allegiance, or required to leave the country. The seven turned over as prisoners of war are held as deserters from our own army. I submit herewith a statement furnished by the Comdg officer of the Prison. I would recommend their discharge on taking the oath of allegiance, as their trial would be attended with many difficulties and great expense, and they can do no harm if released. The prison grounds, barracks and particularly the *Hospital* show great care on part of the Comdg officer Bvt Brig Genl Stevens V. R. C. The Prison-Fund am'ts to about $100,000 00 These prisoners released or transferred, the Maj Genl Comdg Dist Maj Genl Hovey, informs me that he can dispense with all but one camp at this place, which will reduce his necessary guards very much. I would recommend the immediate sale of all but one of these camps. I also found some forty (40) of the Vet R Corps prisoners in the guard house, guilty of mutiny. The Maj Genl Comdg says their guilt is clear and recommends their dishonorable discharge without pay, as an economical and judicious disposition. I am of the opinion that nearly Every temporary barrack and appendage throughout the country might be sold at once and the necessary expense of guarding be dispensed with. The discharged troops detained temporarily at specified rendézvous for payment might be supplied with *Wall* and *A* tents, which would require but small guards the tents to be kept stored whenever not occupied" ALS, DNA, RG 108, Letters Received. *O.R.*, II, viii, 704–5.

On June 13, Bowers endorsed an inspection report. "Respy. referred to Brig Gen Wm. Hoffman, Com. Gen of Prisoners for his consideration & remarks" Copy, DLC-USG, V, 58. On June 16, Bvt. Brig. Gen. William Hoffman, commissary gen. of prisoners, wrote to USG. "I have the honor to return herewith the reports of Major Davis upon the condition of the Prison Depot at Johnsons Island, Ohio, and Rock Island, Illinois with the following remarks. The report of Major Davis doubtless gives a very fair view of the state of the command at Johnsons Island. The undersigned deems the 128th Ohio, Volunteers as ample guard for the Depot, and he concurs with Maj. Davis in the belief that the other Regiment 6th V. R. may with propriety be ordered to other service, The forts were not erected on the recommendation of the undersigned and they are not now necessary for the defence of the Island. The Hospital reported by Maj Davis as recently erected was authorized by the Secy of War in Sept, last, and the barracks were ordered by Maj Genl. Hooker in Nov. The plan in use for the safe keeping and disbursements of the private funds of prisoners has been found by experience to be a very good one: Very few case have occurred where money of prisoners in the hands of the Com'dg Officer, has not been properly accounted for. To put it in the hands of a prisoner would be to place it beyond the reach of responsibility, and to require the accounts to pass through this Office, would occasion much expense and labor for a matter purely for the private benefit of prisoners of war, but with very little advantage to them. Any excess of employés or means of transportation will be dispensed with. The report of Maj Davis in regard to Rock Island is doubtless, also correct. The relief of the 108th Cold. Inf. would have been recommended ere this, but the size of the Camp is such that a small number of prisoners require nearly as many men to guard them as a large number. In view of the speedy release of all prisoners at Rock Island it is now recommended that this regiment be assigned to other duty. The remarks in reference to private funds of prisoners at Johnsons Island apply equally well to Rock-Island. Money sent to prisoners has perhaps been too often kept from them by the dishonesty of those who had the examining of their letters, but when funds are once in the hands of the Comd'g Officer there is rarely any loss, and it is believed that in the few cases where such things have unavoidably occurred, the money has been made good to the prisoners. The *Post* Fund is accounted for under the Army Regulations to the Adjt General, and not to this office. The account of the Prison Fund is rendered to this office and the amount shows that it is well administered. The weekly report made to this office of the condition of the Depot shows a better state of police than is reported by Major Davis. The Depot at Rock Island is too large to be occupied by a small number of prisoners, and for such as may remain in custody it is respectfully recommended that Fort Deleware be used in preference. If it is desirable to releive the Fort of the presence of prisoners, Camp Chase is recommended as being next most convenient, it being very central, and being divided into three prisons where officers, soldiers, and citizens may be confined separately. The barracks at Rock Island for guard and prisoners are very good, and the enclosure may be so divided, at no great cost, as to make it convenient to hold a small or large number of prisoners there. There will probably not be over 250 officers to be held after the execution of General Orders 109. I respectfully suggest that Capt Mathew H Kallock of the 108th United States Colored Troops, reported as deserted from the Naval Service, is unfit to hold a commission in the Army. I deem proper in this place, respectfully to suggest that quite extensive works having been erected on Johnsons Island It would be advisable before returning it to its owner, to decide the question as to the propriety of securing it for the location of a Naval Station for the defence of the Northern frontier." LS, DNA, RG 94, Letters Received, 887H 1865. *O.R.*, II, viii, 653–54. On June 23, Rawlins endorsed Hoffman's letter. "Respectfully forwarded to the Adjutant General with the recommendation that, as the 6th regt Veteran Reserve Corps and the 108th regt U S Col'd Troops are no longer required at Johnsons Island and Rock Island, the former regiment be disposed of as may be thought best by the Provost Marshal General and the latte[r] regiment ordered to report to Major General Thomas, Commanding Dept Cumberland. It is advised that the prisoners of war that may remain at Rock Island be transferred to Camp Chase, Ohio. It is further recommended that the attention of the chief of the colored bureau be called to the case of Capt. Kallock, 108th U S C T., and that the suggestion of Gen Hoffman respecting the establishment of a naval station at Johnsons Island be referred to the Navy Dept" ES, DNA, RG 94, Letters Received, 887H 1865.

On June 30, Hoffman wrote to USG. "I have the honor to recommend that the prisoners of war remaining in hospital at Newport News be transferred to the General Hospital at Hampton, near Fort Monroe, and that those at Elmira, Camp Chase, Camp Morton, Camp Douglas and Rock Island be transferred to the Post Hospitals at those several places to be taken charge of and accounted for by the Medical Officer in charge, Where the Post Hospital is not sufficiently large to accommodate all the sick, the Prison Hospital may be occupied. The object of this arrangement is to remove the necessity for a prison guard at these several stations. The sick prisoners, will be turned over to the Medical Officer in charge who will release them as fast as they are sufficiently, recovered, under General Orders 109. C. S. reporting such discharges to this Office," LS, *ibid.*, RG 249, Letters Received. *O.R.*, II, viii, 689. On the same day, USG endorsed this letter. "Respectfully forwarded to the Secretary of War and recommended" ES, DNA, RG 249, Letters Received. *O.R.*, II, viii, 689. See *ibid.*, p. 690. On July 5, Hoffman wrote to USG. "I have the honor to report that, except a few sick who have been transferred to the Post Hospitals, all prisoners of war have been released from the following named Military Prisons. viz. Point Lookout, Newport News, Hart Island, Elmira N. Y Camp Chase, near Columbus Ohio, Camp Morton, near Indianapolis, Indiana, Camp Douglas, near Chicago Illinois, Rock Island. Ill. and the Military Prison at Alton. Illinois, and the forces stationed at these several places as guards to the prisons may now be releived. There are now but 150 rebel officers confined at Johnsons Island, and if it is thought advisable they may be transferred to Fort Warren or Fort Deleware, by which arrangement the guard can be releived and the Island may be returned to its owners, but I would again respectfully suggest that inasmuch as there are extensive buildings and other works on the Island belonging to the Government, the Island be not given up until it is decided whether it will not be required for a Naval Depôt for which its situation in a commodious bay at the southern end of Lake Erie seems to fit it in an eminent degree." LS, DNA, RG 108, Letters Received. *O.R.*, II, viii, 700–1.

To Edwin M. Stanton

Washington D. C. July 13th *1865*

HON. E. M. STANTON,
SEC. OF WAR,
SIR:

I would respectfully recommend the following Brevt appointments in the Medical Staff of the Army; towit:

Col. Mad. Mills, Med. Inspt. Gen. to be Brig. Gn. by Bvt.

Bvt. Col. & Med. Inspt. J. N. Cuyler to be Bvt. Brig. Gn.

Lt. Col. & Med. Inspt. E. D. D. Kittoe to be Bvt. Col.

Maj. Jos. B. Brown,[1] Surgeon, to be Col. by Bvt.

Maj. Chas. Sutherland, Surgeon to be Col. by Bvt.

Asst. Surgeons S. H. Horner,[2] D. S. *Huntington*[3] & John W. Brewer[4] to be Lt. Colonels by Bvt.

> Very respectfully
> your obt. svt.
> U. S. GRANT
> Lt. Gn.

ALS, DNA, RG 94, ACP, G728 CB 1865. On July 22, 1865, Brig. Gen. Joseph K. Barnes, surgeon gen., endorsed this letter. "Respectfully returned to the Hon. Secretary of War. Major J. B. Brown has already received the brevet of Lieutenant Colonel and Colonel. Major Charles Sutherland the brevet of Lt Colonel. Assistant Surgeon D. L. Huntington, the brevet of Major upon the recommendation of the Surgeon General. As it is proposed to recommend an additional grade by brevet for the Corps of Medical Inspectors when mustered out; action upon these cases at present would be premature. There being nothing of record in this office to show that Assistant Surgeons Horner and Brewer are more entitled to brevet promotion than any other member of the Medical Corps, the appointment of Lieutenant Colonel by brevet in their cases would be unjust to others equally, or more meritorious officers, and is disapproved." ES, *ibid.* On July 7, Col. Madison Mills, medical inspector, Ithaca, N. Y., wrote to USG. "Understanding that

numbers of officers have been brevetted lately, and among them several Medical
Officers, I beg leave to request that the following be added to the list, Viz
Medical Inspector & Bvt Colonel Cuyler, Medical Inspector Lt Colonel Kittoe,
Major & Surgeon Joseph B. Brown, Major & Surgeon Charles Southerland, Assistant Surgeon S. H. Horner. Assistant Surgeon D. L. Huntington Assistant
Surgeon I. W. Brewer   Dr Cuyler is the Senior Medl Inspector of the Army,
and by his *long*, *faithful and honorable* service in the army and for the *devotion
to our cause during the late rebellion* has won the right to wear a star   Dr Kittoe
you know is a worthy man. It is not neccessary for me to speak for him. Dr Joseph
B. Brown is also a worthy man. He has been in the Asst Surgeon General's office for nearly three years past and has had much to do with the management of
the Medical Offices in the West. Drs Southerland, Horner, Huntington & Brewer
were my assistants when I was Medl Director of the Army of the Tennessee
under your command during the Vicksburg Campaign. I feel under great obligations to these gentlemen for their arduous and faithful services in the Army
of the Tennessee, and for the aid and support they gave me in reducing to order.
the discordant and undiciplined Medl material I found on joining your Army.
But for their assistance I fear I should have failed   I trust these gentlemen may
have some recognition as well as appreciation of their valuable services." Copy,
ibid., 1286 1871. On July 13, Mills wrote to USG. "A few days ago I ventured
to write you recommending for promotion by brevet several officers who had
served under me in the Vicksburg Campaign, and whose services, in my opinion,
entitled them to the compliment. I feel that they are both worthy and deserving
of the distinction—The Medical Inspector Generals Department must, by law,
cease with the rebellion, (Which it appears to me is now ended.)—~~and~~ It cannot
hold its organization much longer. Before it is dissolved I beg leave to suggest
that each officer of the Corps shall be advanced, by brevet, one grade—This, it
appears to me, will be only a fair recognition of their services, and a compliment
fully deserved by a faithful and honorable discharge of Arduous and, important
duties, in the service of their country, during the rebellion just subdued by
force of arms. I have requested Colonel Cuyler to have a list of the Inspectors
made out, with a synapsis of their services since their entry into the Corps, for
your information. You will discover that their services have been not only constant and laborous, but important to the Country and to Science—Colonel Cuyler
has had charge of the Bureau for a longer time than I have, and can give you
any information you may desire. I hope the Medical Inspecting Corps will be
complimented with the officers of the line, for services rendered—. . . P. S.
Please to ask to have Surgeon Alex: H. Hoff, brevetted two grades. You must
recollect the important services he rendered to your army on the Mississippi,
as chief of Hospital Transportation." ALS, USG 3. On Oct. 10, Mills wrote to
Brig. Gen. John A. Rawlins recommending ten medical officers for bvt. promotion.
ALS, DNA, RG 94, ACP, G526 CB 1865. On Oct. 16, USG endorsed this letter.
"Respectfully forwarded to the Secretary of War, approved. I further recom-
mend that Madison Mills, Surgeon U S A., be brevetted Brigadier General in
the Regular Army for faithful and efficient service during the war." ES, *ibid.*
On Nov. 11, Mills wrote to USG. "I have never been brevetted a Lieut. Colonel:—
I would be much pleased to have a brevet of that grade; for services at Jackson
and Champion's Hill, Mississippi, to date from the latter battle:—My brevet of
Colonel dates from 29th of November 1864, but does not specify for what it was
given. I hope to have this date changed to the surrender of Vicksburg;—July 4th

1863—If you can aid me in this matter you will place me under renewed and lasting obligations. If Colonel Cuyler and myself shall be brevetted Brigadiers, I hope the brevets will date as far back as the 13th of March 1865.—This is the date of Doctor Cranes brevet as Brigadier General, and I see no reason why he should take precedence of us: Dr Crane has been brevetted three grades, and this without having had his baggage in an Army Wagon once during the Whole War, From what I can learn the second list you were kind enough to send in at my request has been acted on: I think the first has not been: Most, if not all the officers recommended in the second list will, I have no doubt, be brevetted; But I fear the first list has fallen by the wayside. . . . P. S. Let me say one word for Medical Inspector, Lieut. Colonel Vallum:—Vallum is entitled to great credit for attaining the position he now holds. He is entirely a self made man, having risen from a Wood Engravers apprentice, and by his own unaided exertion has educated himself, and has a high standing in his profession. I now beg leave to suggest that we (you and I) throw prejudice aside and recommend him for a brevet—His reports are very thorough and show great labor and research. You know of course that in this I can only desire that justice be done a faithful officer: I have no reason to consider him my friend: on the contrary, he has been not only unjust, but unkind to me." ALS, *ibid.*, A534 CB 1865. On the same day, USG endorsed this letter. "Respectfully forwarded to the Secretary of War, with the recommendation that Dr. Mills be brevetted Lieut Colonel for battle of Champion Hills, and Colonel for Vicksburg" ES, *ibid.* On Nov. 25, USG wrote to Secretary of War Edwin M. Stanton. "I have the honor to recommend that the brevet of Lieutenant Colonel be given Surgeon Madison Mills, Brevet Colonel U. S. A., for meritorious services in the campaign and siege of Vicksburg, and that the appointment may show for what the brevet is conferred. Surgeon Mills was the most efficient medical director with me in the West, and I am particularly anxious that he should receive this recognition of his services while there." ALS, *ibid.*, 1286 1871.

On March 21, 1866, Bvt. Col. John M. Cuyler, surgeon, wrote a letter received at USG's hd. qrs. requesting that a copy of USG's letter of July 13, 1865, be forwarded to the bvt. board. *Ibid.*, RG 108, Register of Letters Received. On March 22, 1866, Maj. George K. Leet endorsed this letter. "Respy. referred to M G. W. T. Sherman, President, Brevet Board" Copy, *ibid.* On March 26, Maj. Gen. William T. Sherman returned USG's letter to Leet because the board had adjourned. *Ibid.* On April 26, Leet again endorsed this letter. "Respy. referred to B. M. G. A. J. Smith, President Staff brevet board." Copy, *ibid.* On Dec. 28, Cuyler, bvt. brig. gen., wrote to USG. "I have been informed that it was the intention of the Commanding General that the Bvts conferred upon Sugn Madison Mills and myself should date from 13th March instead of 9th April 1865 If I am correctly informed upon this subject, I respectfully ask that the date of our Bvts (Surgeon Mills & myself) be changed in conformity with the Comg General' intention" ALS, *ibid.*, RG 94, ACP, M17 CB 1867. On Dec. 30, Mills, Fort Leavenworth, wrote to USG. "Believing it was your intention that the Brevets of Brigadier General conferred on Surgeon Cuyler and myself should date March 13th 1865 I beg leave to ask if it is too late to correct the mistake; and if not too late, will you not, my dear sir, be kind enough to say a word in our favor and request that the correction be made? If I did not believe it was your intention that our Brevets should go back to 13th March, instead of 9th of April, I should not trouble you with this note." ALS, *ibid.* On Jan. 8,

1867, USG endorsed these letters. "Respectfully forwarded to the Secretary of War, with the recommendation that the date of Generals Cuyler and Mills' brevets be changed to Mar. 13. 1865." ES, *ibid.*

On Jan. 18, 1866, Bvt. Col. Charles Sutherland, surgeon, wrote a letter received at USG's hd. qrs. requesting that the date of his bvt. be changed to July 4, 1863. *Ibid.*, RG 108, Register of Letters Received. On Jan. 19, 1866, USG endorsed this letter. "Respy forwarded to the Secretary of War with the recommendation that Surgeon Sutherlands brevet promotion to a Lieut Colonelcy be so far changed as to read for meritorious services in 'the Campaign and seige of Vicksburg' insted of 'during the War' His services at Vicksburg are personally known to me to have been valuable." Copy, DLC-USG, V, 58. The date was not changed.

On April 4, Asst. Surgeon Samuel H. Hornor, Louisville, wrote a letter received at USG's hd. qrs. submitting his military history. DNA, RG 108, Register of Letters Received. On April 26, USG endorsed this letter. "Respy. referred to B. M. G. A. J. Smith, President Staff brevet board—Dr. Horner served under my command at Vicksburg and proves himself an energetic and efficient officer" Copy, *ibid.*

On March 31, Asst. Surgeon David L. Huntington, Philadelphia, wrote to USG. "In order to establish my record before the board now convened for the recommendation of Brevet Appointments, I would very respectfully ask if you would be willing to give me a brief endorsement of satisfactory service while under your command, during the Vicksburg campaign and up to the time of your assuming the command of the Mily. Div. of the Miss?" ALS, *ibid.*, RG 94, ACP, H1288 CB 1866. On May 3, USG endorsed this letter. "Asst Surgeon D. L. Huntington, U. S. A., was on duty as assistant to Surgeon Madison Mills, Medical Director of the Army of the Tennessee in the Vicksburg campaign and continued on same duty with Surg. John Moore, who relieved Surgeon Mills. In the discharge of his duties, which were principally in the field and on the march, he gave the most general satisfaction, and I may add that few officers, if any, of his corps in my command bro't to their aid a more intelligent and thorough knowledge of their profession and duties than did Asst. Surgeon Huntington. He is entitled to brevet promotion for the campaign of Vicksburg, and as he was continuously in the field to the close of the war, I have no doubt his subsequent services are entitled to like recognition." ES, *ibid.*

1. Joseph B. Brown of Mich., appointed asst. surgeon in 1849 and promoted to surgeon as of July 4, 1861.

2. Hornor of Pa., appointed asst. surgeon as of April 16, 1862.

3. Huntington, born in Mass. in 1834, who received medical training at the University of Pennsylvania, was appointed asst. surgeon as of July 11, 1862.

4. John W. Brewer of Md., appointed asst. surgeon as of Nov. 22, 1862. See *PUSG*, 9, 638.

To Edwin M. Stanton

Washington D. C. July 13th *1865*

HON. E. M. STANTON,
SEC. OF WAR.
SIR:

Mrs. Harris, the sister of Adm.l Porter and wife of T. Harris,[1] who is now confined in the penitentiary here, is in my office desirous of obtaining permission to visit her husband in his place of confinement. I would be pleased if you would give the necessary permission if not inconsistent with establishe[d] rules.

Very respectfully
your obt. svt.
U. S. GRANT
Lt. Gn.

ALS, DLC-Edwin M. Stanton. USG enclosed a letter of July 13, 1865, from Imogene Harris to Secretary of War Edwin M. Stanton requesting passes for herself, mother-in-law, and three attorneys to visit her husband in Old Capitol Prison, D. C. ALS, *ibid.* On the same day, Stanton wrote to USG. "The application of Mrs Harris to have an interview with her husband having been referred to the Bureau of Military Justice has just been reported against adversely   I am therefore compelled at present to deny the application" ALS, DNA, RG 108, Letters Received. Military prisoners against whom no charges had been pressed could not receive visitors. See *O.R.*, II, viii, 690.

1. Thomas A. Harris, born in 1826 in Warren County, Va., taken to Mo., withdrew from USMA after two years and practiced law in Hannibal, Mo. He married the sister of Real Admiral David D. Porter in 1856, served briefly as brig. gen. in the Mo. State Guard, and was elected to the C.S. Congress in 1861. He had been captured off the coast of Fla. in May, 1865, while attempting to reach Havana.

Endorsement

The Valley as far up as supplied from Harpers Ferry should be under the command of Gen. Hancock. It was so that I instructed Gn. Curtis. Staunton will be under the command of Gn. Terry ~~as~~ and is about the most Northern point, in the Valley he will be re-

quired to send troops to. The order ~~shoul~~ defining Depts. should be
so modified as to place Winchester & the counties bordering on the
Potomac in the Mid. Dept.

U. S. GRANT
Lt. Gn

July 13th/65

AES, DNA, RG 94, Letters Received, 739A 1865. Written on a telegram of
July 12, 1865, from Maj. Gen. Alfred H. Terry, Richmond, to Maj. Thomas M.
Vincent, AGO. "I have recd your telegram of this morning in reference to the
muster out of troops, I did not receive the telegram of like tenor sent on the
7th inst. I sent Genl Curtis Chf of Staff to Machester to make arrangements for
the disposition of the troops in the Valley, Was obliged to go by way of Washn,
While there he saw Lt Genl Grant who informed him that none of the troops
in the Valley of the shenandoah would be under my command but would remain
under Command of Genl Hancock He also informed him that the boundaries of
this Dept would be changed & that an order to that effect would be issued in a
few days. The Lt Genl at the same time sent me a verbal order by Genl Curtis
to relieve such of Genl Hancock troops as are at Staunton for this purpose troops
have been sent from here I have already caused to be mustered out of service
all vols Regt. batteries except two. †These two A & E first Penna L A I propose to
have mustered out this week, under instructions from the War Dept I have
ordered the 1st Conn H A & sixteenth N Y H A to Washn to report to Maj Genl
Augur & I have further instructions to send to Genl Augur such other Heavy
Arty as Can be spared I recd yesterday from Lt Gen Grant orders to send the
4th U S Infy to N Y. These orders will reduce my command by about three
thousand Under these Circumstances with the uncertainty as to the limits of
my territoral command with the understanding that none of Gen Hancocks
troops would be at my disposal for garrisoning such parts of the vally as would
be left in the Dept I have delayed taking action in regard to mustering out Infy
& Cavly for until the northern limits of the Dept are defined I am unable to determine whether any of these troops can be spared. Please inform me whether
after this explanation I am to obey the order contained in your telegram of this
morning & assume control of & order the muster out of troops in the Valley."
Telegram received (at 4:20 P.M.), *ibid*. On July 13, Vincent had endorsed this
telegram. "Respectfully submitted to Lt. Gen U. S. Grant Comdg Armies U S
for instructions. The order of yesterday (copy within) was given to Gen Terry,
as the Valley, by G. O. 118 C S, is within his Comd, The question is who shall
be charged with the Muster out of said Troops" AES, *ibid*.

On July 11, 2:00 P.M., USG telegraphed to Terry. "Send the 4th United
States Infantry to New York Harbor to report to the Commanding officer Dept.
of the East for duty." ALS (telegram sent), *ibid.*, RG 107, Telegrams Collected
(Bound); telegram sent, *ibid.*; copies, *ibid.*, RG 108, Letters Sent; DLC-USG,
V, 46, 109.

To Maj. Gen. Philip H. Sheridan

July 13th *1865* [*11:00* A.M.]

MAJ. GEN. P. H. SHERIDAN, NEW ORLEANS, LA.

I would like you to go to the Rio Grande in person for a few days and manage affairs there according to your judgement.[1] What you have done seems so well that I desire to change nothing.

Do you not think it advisable to relieve Granger from command in Texas? If so relieve him.[2]

U. S. GRANT
Lt. Gen.

ALS (telegram sent), DNA, RG 107, Telegrams Collected (Bound); telegram sent, *ibid.*; copies, *ibid.*, RG 108, Letters Sent; DLC-USG, V, 46, 109; (incomplete) USG 3. *O.R.*, I, xlviii, part 2, 1075.

On June 29, 1865, Maj. Gen. Philip H. Sheridan wrote to Brig. Gen. John A. Rawlins. "*Personal* . . . I have detained Bvt Brig. Genl Price of the Cavalry bureau longer perhaps than I should have done but his services were so important to me that I don't see how I could have done without him. the cavalry here was very much scattered and the regiments were unknown to me but by his admirable system of inspection I was at once enabled to select the best regiments and to collect together two of the handsomest columns of cavalry that have been organized during the present war, one under Genl Merritt which moves from Shreveport. the other under Genl Custer which moves from Alexandria La I have had many difficulties and delays in getting these cavalry columns together and in their magnificent trim but I am now out of the woods and only hope that I may have the pleasure of crossing the Rio Grande with them with our faces turned towards the city of Mexico. there is no use to beat around the bush in this mexican matter we should give a permanent government to that republic. our work in crushing the rebellion will not be done until this takes place. the advent of Maximilian was a portion of the rebellion and his fall should belong to its history. Juarez even if he was to be successful tomorrow could not give stability to a government there without our helping hand. most of the mexican soldiers of Maximilians army would throw down their arms the moment we crossed the Rio Grande. The french influence has governed by their impudence." LS, USG 3. Probably on July 12, USG endorsed this letter. "Respectfully forwarded to the President of the United States. Gen. Sheridan here expresses exactly the sentiments which I believe in, and have often expressed. Gen. Sheridan, however, will violate no instructions, and his instructions donot authorize him to cross the Rio Grande, unless aggressed upon by troops there." Copy (undated—marked as forwarded July 12), DNA, RG 108, Letters Received. On July 19, 2:30 P.M., Sheridan telegraphed to USG. "A report from the commander of Ringgold Barracks says Franco Mexico authorities stopped the importation of merchandize in the vicinity of Carmago before the evacuation, because they were not allowed to steal cotton I have therefore gradually limited the export of grain from New Orleans to Matamoris, and as they are pretty well starved out there according to all accounts it will cause much embarrassment It is possible that Mejia could be quietly carried out of Matamoris and turned over to Cortinas, This would complicate affairs very much, I have sent over to make a reconnoissance—" Telegram received (on July 21, 12:15 P.M.), *ibid.*, RG 107, Telegrams Collected (Bound); *ibid.*, RG 108, Telegrams Received; copies, DLC-USG, V, 54; DLC-Philip H. Sheridan; USG 3. *O.R.*, I, xlviii, part 2, 1092.

1. On July 18, 11:30 A.M., Sheridan telegraphed to USG. "I will get off from here on the 20th of this month for the Rio Grande—It was impossible for me to go at once after the receipt of your telegram—The latest news which I have from Franco-Mexico is the arrival of French & Austrian troops at Vera Cruz in considerable numbers and the report from there that another considerable body of troops is being organized in France & Austria for Mexico—This I give as reports from parties from Vera Cruz who came to Galveston Texas—The same parties report that the troops now debarking at Vera Cruz are to be sent to Matamoras in about two weeks" Telegram received (on July 19, 1:40 A.M.), DNA, RG 107, Telegrams Collected (Bound); *ibid.*, RG 108, Telegrams Received; copies, DLC-USG, V, 54; DLC-Philip H. Sheridan; USG 3. *O.R.*, I, xlviii, part 2, 1092. On Aug. 1, 9:30 A.M., Sheridan, New Orleans, telegraphed to USG. "I respectfully report my arrival here from the Rio Grande—The French and Austrian troops have been withdrawn from Matamoras, and the entire Rio Grande frontier is now in the possession of the Liberals except Matamoras; in fact Maximilian holds but little in Mexico except the towns occupied by Franco-Mexican troops and in some of these towns only the ground their troops are encamped upon—The necessity of troops along the Rio Grande has been very demoralizing to the Imperial cause and has withdrawn all Mexican support from it. All the troops France could send to Mexico will not restore the ground lost.— I am also happy to state that the rebels who went into Mexico have been defeated in their calculations and have been forced to join the losing side—In my previous visit and by the assistance of trusty scouts I posted the Liberals in what I believed to be their intentions which was to join them against Maximilian and when successful they would be able to control the new government; in fact take possession of it, and that the disaffected rebels from the south would flock to their standard in sufficient numbers to hold the government which would be one deadly hostile to the United States. There is no use disguising the fact that while the people of the south will obey the laws here, there is bitterness in their hearts. The result of this influence brought to bear on the Liberals turned them a[g]ainst the rebels, and the Governor of Nuevo a[r]rested Smith, Shelby & Company; disarmed them; rejected their overtures, but permitted them to go to *Molino Rey*. I saw Cortinas accidentally at Brownsville and found him in good spirits. He holds up to Matamoras and before I left stopped marketing from going into the city. Not a message is allowed to go into the interior and a state of great alarm exists at Matamoras; in fact if I was to say that the Government would give security and protection to this city I believe that it would declare for the Liberals without hesitation.—Shelby, finding his overtures to the Liberals rejected, has taken service with the Imperialists, in command of his battalion of four hundred Missourians with the rank of Lieut Col., and is t[o] operate against Cortinas along the Rio Grande It is reported that there are two more rebel regiments being organized at Monterey—What progress has been made in organising them I

donot yet know, but will soon. There is no doubt but that the Emperor has made an agreement with the rebels for the colonization of Tehuantepec and Chiapas. The government should look out for this. It may be what is called the Brazilian scheme.—The rebels in Matamoras are preparing to go to Tehuantepec and Chiapas under grants made by Maximilian and Gen. Slaughter has authority to colonize from the United States. Tehuantepec and Chiapas are held by the Liberals and are the richest provinces in Mexico, besides embracing the railroad route.—The Liberals are looking to the United States for support, and not only that but to give them a government—I think we ought to go after Shelby and his *command*. I feel certain that with six or eight thousand cavalry I can stir up the whole of Northern Mexico—The Liberals are suffeing for want of ammunition and Matamoras is vital to them on that account. Cortinas could take it with four hundred men if he only had the requisite grit. If I am not allowed to go after Shelby I believe that by going up to Eagle Pass and moving Merritts column to that point I could infuse much enthusiasm into the Liberals.—Negrete and Juarez have twelve thousand men—There are about Piedras Negras and San Fernando about one thousand men. I fear Juarez, if successful, would require the support of our Army for some time." Telegram received (on Aug. 2, 2:30 A.M.), DNA, RG 94, Letters Received, 1073G 1865; *ibid.*, RG 107, Telegrams Collected (Bound); *ibid.*, RG 108, Telegrams Received; copies (one sent by mail, misdated July 31), *ibid.*, Letters Received; (dated Aug. 1) DLC-USG, V, 54; DLC-Philip H. Sheridan; USG 3. *O.R.*, I, xlviii, part 2, 1147–48. On Aug. 2, Bvt. Col. Theodore S. Bowers endorsed this telegram. "Respectfully forwarded to the Hon. Secretary of War. . . . (In the absence of Gen. Grant)" AES, DNA, RG 94, Letters Received, 1073G 1865. At 1:00 P.M., Sheridan telegraphed to USG. "Since my telegram of this morning the following information has reached me from one of my scouts. He says there is no doubt about its truthfulness.—It is the list of prominent Confederates which have gone to Mexico through San Antonio— Governors Allen and Moore of Louisiana, Governor Edward Clarke and Murrah of Texas, Governor Harris of Tennessee, J. P. Benjamin, late Secretary of State, C S.—Breckenridge, Secretary of War C. S. Harrison, Jeff Davis' private secretary. Generals Smith, Magruder, Price, Shelby, Wilcox and Harris—Col Tyrell and Flononay, Walker, Col J. J. Hine. Major S. J. Davins, Green, Rains, Major Green, S. Macklin, Col. Elliott of Missouri Wm A Broadwell, Payne, Harrison and J. D. Elliott, Jackson, Miss. The whole number of pieces of artillery taken by these parties, was fourteen (14) which all fell into the hands of the Liberals. The Governor of Nuevo sent commissioner[s] to Brownsville to see me, but I did not see them. They came to ask protection from the United States I will send you a communication from the Governor by mail" Telegram received (at 10:55 P.M.), *ibid.*, RG 107, Telegrams Collected (Bound); *ibid.*, RG 108, Telegrams Received; copies (one sent by mail with variant text), *ibid.*, Letters Received; DLC-USG, V, 54; DLC-Philip H. Sheridan; USG 3. *O.R.*, I, xlviii, part 2, 1149. At 1:00 P.M., Sheridan also telegraphed to Rawlins. "I found the troops ~~the troops~~ from Brazos Santiago to Ringgold barracks in very good condition and very well contented. On the Indianola line much trouble has been encountered in landing animals and transportation. We had to lighter over the bar, then lighter by small schooners to shore. Every thing had been destroyed. On the Galveston line every thing was in fine condition. There is a brigade of colored cavalry attached to the 25th A C. I donot intend to mount it; it might be mustered out." Telegram received (at 10:45 P.M.), DNA, RG 107, Telegrams Collected (Bound); *ibid.*,

RG 108, Telegrams Received; copies (one sent by mail, misdated July 31), *ibid.*,
Letters Received; (dated Aug. 1) DLC-USG, V, 54; DLC-Philip H. Sheridan.
O.R., I, xlviii, part 2, 1149. Also on Aug. 1, Sheridan wrote to Bowers. "In compliance with my expressed intention in todays telegram to the Lieut General, I
enclose copy of a communication from Francisco DeLeon to Brig. Gen. E. B.
Brown" Copy, DNA, RG 108, Letters Received. The enclosure is *ibid*. See
letter to Maj. Gen. Philip H. Sheridan, Oct. 22, 1865.

    2. On July 14, Sheridan telegraphed to USG. "I regret that Texas and
Louisiana are united in one Dept—Either of these states is sufficient for a Military Dept at the present time—To have the Headquarters of the state of Texas in
New Orleans is inconvenient" Telegram received (on July 15, 1:35 A.M.),
DNA, RG 107, Telegrams Collected (Bound); *ibid.*, RG 108, Telegrams Received; copies, DLC-USG, V, 54; DLC-Philip H. Sheridan. *O.R.*, I, xlviii, part 2,
1077. On July 15, Sheridan telegraphed to USG. "I think it best that Genl
Granger should be relieved—He never would have been where he is had it not
been for Gen Canby & himself, who put his Corps en route in a great hurry before I reached New Orleans,—suspending the order for mustering out regiments
and sending them to Texas only to be immediately sent back—If he is relieved
it would be only to send him to the Rio Grand where I do not want him and
which would displace Genl Steele, who already feels sore about Genl Granger
being over him—I would suggest that he be ordered from Washington—I have
already re commended in a report to Gen Rawlins that the 13th Army corps be
consolidated into one division—" Telegram received (at 1:20 A.M.), DNA, RG
107, Telegrams Collected (Bound); *ibid.*, RG 108, Telegrams Received; copies,
DLC-USG, V, 54; DLC-Philip H. Sheridan. Printed as received at 1:20 P.M. in
O.R., I, xlviii, part 2, 1081. At 2:30 P.M., USG telegraphed to Sheridan. "Releive Gen. Granger and direct him to report to the A. G. for orders. Orders will
be made making Texas a seperate Dept. and breaking up Corps organizations of
the 13th & 16th Corps. You can have Wright for ~~Com~~ Command of Texas or any
officer now there." ALS (telegram sent), DNA, RG 107, Telegrams Collected
(Bound); telegram sent, *ibid.*; copies, *ibid.*, RG 108, Letters Sent; DLC-USG,
V, 46, 109. *O.R.*, I, xlviii, part 2, 1081. On July 17, 12:30 P.M., Sheridan telegraphed to USG. "Genl H. G. Wright will be entirely acceptable to me for
Texas—I would be very glad to have him—Genl D S Stanley who commands the
fourth Corps has some claims on account of rank—Either one will answer" Tele-
gram received (on July 19, 1:20 A.M.), DNA, RG 107, Telegrams Collected
(Bound); *ibid.*, RG 108, Telegrams Received; copies, DLC-USG, V, 54; DLC-
Philip H. Sheridan. *O.R.*, I, xlviii, part 2, 1086. On July 18, Sheridan telegraphed
to USG. "I respectfully recommend that Gen Steele be placed in command of the
Provisional 13th Corps when organized" Telegram received (marked as sent
July 16, received on July 19, 1:25 A.M.), DNA, RG 107, Telegrams Collected
(Bound); (dated July 18) *ibid.*, RG 108, Telegrams Received; copies, DLC-
USG, V, 54; DLC-Philip H. Sheridan. *O.R.*, I, xlviii, part 2, 1091. See *ibid.*,
p. 1094.

To Delphine P. Baker

Washington, D. C., July 14th, 1865.

Miss D. P. Baker:

I see no objection to the use of Point Lookout as a place for temporary use as a Home for disabled Soldiers. The number of public buildings already there, which are of no further use for the public service, makes it, I think, altogether peculiarly appropriate for that purpose.

The fact that Point Lookout was a watering place before the war, I should think sufficient reply to the suspicion of unhealthfulness.

Yours truly,
U. S. Grant,
Lieutenant-General.

Copy (printed), DNA, RG 107, Letters Received from Bureaus. The letter was endorsed by twenty prominent individuals. Delphine P. Baker, born in Grafton County, N. H., in 1828, traveled widely before the Civil War advocating better education for women. During the war, she published the *National Banner*, a monthly newspaper, using proceeds for the support of sick and wounded soldiers. She believed that the U.S. government had an obligation to provide life-long care for totally disabled soldiers and lobbied Congress to establish a National Military and Naval Asylum. The bill passed on March 3, 1865, with USG named as one of the incorporators. *U.S. Statutes at Large*, XIII, 509–10. See Linus P. Brockett and Mary C. Vaughan, *Woman's Work in the Civil War* (Boston, 1867), pp. 754–59.

Probably in Nov. or Dec., 1864, USG had signed a petition of prominent citizens requesting establishment of a "National Home for totally disabled Soldiers and Sailors of the Army and Navy of the United States." DS, DNA, RG 46, Senate 38A–H10.5, Petitions and Memorials, Military Affairs and the Militia. Printed in *SMD*, 38-2-3. On March 14 and May 11, 1865, USG *et al.* issued invitations to attend meetings of the incorporators on April 19 and June 7. D (printed), DNA, RG 46, Senate 39A–H10. There is no evidence that USG attended either meeting. He did, however, attend such a meeting on Oct. 18. *Cincinnati Enquirer*, Oct. 19, 1865; *Baltimore Sun*, Oct. 21, 1865.

On Oct. 16, USG wrote to Secretary of War Edwin M. Stanton. "I would respectfully ask that Genl Meigs be directed to withhold from sale all public buildings at Point Lookout until he recieves special directions from you for their disposal. That Point may be selected as a suitable one for a soldiers home, and if so it would be desirable to retain for such purpose all the buildings now there." Copies, DLC-USG, V, 46, 109; DNA, RG 108, Letters Sent. On Dec. 23, USG wrote to Stanton. "I would resspectfully recommend that the Govt. buildings at

Point Lookout, Md., be sold at as early a day as practicable. I would also recommend the same thing for the temporary structures at Ft. Monroe, Va., with the exception of such of them as may still be required for the public service. This I would recommend should be determined by a Board to consist of three officers, one of them the Commander of the post one an officer of the Freedmen's Bureau, and one an officer of the Medical Staff of the Army." Copies, *ibid.* See *HMD*, 40-1-45.

To Andrew Johnson

Washington D. C, July 15th *1865*

HIS EXCELLENCY, A. JOHNSON,
PRESIDENT OF THE UNITED STATES,
SIR:

Looking upon the French occupatio[n] of Mexico as part and parcel of the late rebellion in the United States, and a necessary part of it to suppress before entire peace can be assured, I would respectfully recommend that a leave of absence be given to one of our General officers for the purpose of going to Mexico to give direction to such emigration as may go to that country.

I would not advise that emigration be invited or that such officer should go under special instructions. He would probably take service under the Liberal Government of Mexico and by giving head and shape to the foreign and Native element already there would insure the restoration of the Liberal or Republican Government.

Mexico has men enough if she had Arms to defend herself. With the large surplus on hand I do not see why we should not sell her these. I presume there would be no objection raised to sell the English or French Government Arms. I do not see therefore why we should not be allowed to sell them to the only Government we recognize on Mexican soil.

I write this for instructions because I will not do or authorize anything not receiving the proper sanction. Of the sale of Arms I

have nothing to do. I speak therefore in reference to giving leaves of absence for the purpose stated.

I send this direct the Sec. of War being absent from his office to-day.

> Very respectfully
> your obt. svt.
> U. S. GRANT
> Lt. Gn

ALS, NHi. See letter to Maj. Gen. Philip H. Sheridan, July 25, 1865.

On June 16, 1865, 6:10 P.M., USG telegraphed to Maj. Gen. John M. Schofield. "When you can leave your Dept. I would like to see you in Washington for a few days." ALS (telegram sent), DNA, RG 107, Telegrams Collected (Bound); telegram sent, *ibid.*; telegram received (on June 17), DLC-John M. Schofield. *O.R.*, I, xlvii, part 3, 649. On June 17, Schofield, Raleigh, N. C., telegraphed to USG. "I have just completed a tour of inspection of my Department and will have every thing arranged in a few days, when I will start for Washington as you desire." ALS (telegram sent), DNA, RG 107, Telegrams Collected (Unbound); telegram received, *ibid.*; (on June 18, 12:15 A.M.) *ibid.*, Telegrams Collected (Bound); *ibid.*, RG 108, Telegrams Received. *O.R.*, I, xlvii, part 3, 650. Schofield arrived in Washington in late June or early July to discuss taking command of an army corps to be organized within Mexico, consulting with USG, President Andrew Johnson, Secretary of War Edwin M. Stanton, Secretary of State William H. Seward, and Matías Romero, Mexican minister. See Schofield, *Forty-six Years in the Army* (New York, 1897), pp. 379–80.

On July 24, Schofield, USMA, telegraphed to USG. "Will you be here soon or shall I meet you in Washington?" Telegram received (at 12:05 P.M.), DNA, RG 107, Telegrams Collected (Bound); *ibid.*, RG 108, Telegrams Received; copies, DLC-USG, V, 54; DLC-John M. Schofield. *O.R.*, I, xlvii, part 3, 678. At 1:40 P.M., USG telegraphed to Schofield. "I will be at West Point to-morrow." ALS (telegram sent), DNA, RG 107, Telegrams Collected (Bound); telegram sent, *ibid.*; telegram received, DLC-John M. Schofield. *O.R.*, I, xlvii, part 3, 678. On July 25, USG, USMA, wrote to Stanton. "I respectfully ask that leave of Absence for Twelve Months, with permission to leave the United States, be granted to Major General J. M. Schofield, leave to commence on the date of his departure from the territory of the United States." ALS, DNA, RG 94, Letters Received, 1394A 1865. *O.R.*, I, xlvii, part 3, 679. On July 28, Stanton drafted the orders requested. ADS, DNA, RG 94, Letters Received, 1394A 1865. Schofield, however, did not go to Mexico as originally discussed; he went to France instead. See letter to Maj. Gen. John M. Schofield, March 24, 1866.

To Brig. Gen. John A. Rawlins

———

Washington D. C, July 16th *1865*

DEAR RAWLINS,

I shall leave here to-morrow week, the 24th inst. for Galena. As I shall stop a few days each at West Point and Saratoga, and a week or more in Canada, I will not reach there before the middle of August. Before that time I presume you will return to Washington, I hope with health materially improved. I wish you would telegraph me, on receipt of this, about the time you expect to return.

I have finished my official report of ~~for~~ the last years operations. It has been very hastily drawn up, writing only of mornings before coming to the office, and without notes, and may when it comes to be copied require some changing and some additions. If such should prove the case I will return to Washington at any time and write up what ever may be required, sign the document, and go back.[1]

My family and the Staff are all well and join me in desiring to be remembered to Mrs. Rawlins and the children. Jess wants Jimmy to use his poney, either under the saddle or in harness, during his absence.

Remember me to the good people of Galena.

Yours Truly
U. S. GRANT

ALS, Ohioana Library, Columbus, Ohio.

1. See letter to Edwin M. Stanton, June 20, 1865

To Maj. Gen. George G. Meade

———

Washington D. C, July 17th/65 [*11:00* A.M.]

MAJ. GN. G. G. MEADE, PHILA PA:

Send Staff officers to each Va. N. C. & S. C.[1] and direct the musterout of all Cavalry that can be dispensed with and the sale of their horses when dismounted. When it is necessary to retain Cavalry for want of after troops dismount them and have their horses sold except the actual number of mounted men required. A few hundred mounted men in each state I would think the greatest abundance. Order also the musterout of all Cavalry possible to dispense with in the other Depts. of your Command the horses to be turned over to Quartermasters and reported to the Quartermaster General. Require Dept. Commanders to report the number of men and horses disposed of under this order.

U. S. Grant

Lt. Gen

ALS (telegram sent), DNA, RG 107, Telegrams Collected (Bound); telegram sent, *ibid.*; copies, *ibid.*, RG 108, Letters Sent; (2) *ibid.*, Letters Received; *ibid.*, RG 393, Dept. of Va. and N. C., Letters Received; DLC-USG, V, 46, 109. *O.R.*, III, v, 94. On July 17, 1865, Col. George D. Ruggles, adjt. for Maj. Gen. George G. Meade, telegraphed to USG. "Your dispatch of today recd and transmitted to General Meade at Boston. The orders will be promulgated at once on his acknowledgement" Telegram received (at 5:40 P.M.), DNA, RG 107, Telegrams Collected (Unbound); *ibid.*, RG 108, Telegrams Received; copies, *ibid.*, RG 393, Military Div. of the Atlantic, Letters Sent; DLC-USG, V, 54. On July 24, Ruggles telegraphed to Bvt. Col. Theodore S. Bowers. "In the absence of Maj Gen'l Meade the following dispatch is transmitted for the action of the Lieut General. . . . 'By Telegraph from Richmond Va July 23rd 1865. To Br Gen G D Ruggles A. A. G Phila The muster out of the cavalry in this Department renders it necessary to distribute all of the 24th A. C to the different geographical districts into which the department is divided. Under these circumstances is it intended to keep up the organization of the Corps? (signed) Alfred H. Terry Maj Gen' " Telegram received (at 11:45 A.M.), DNA, RG 94, Letters Received, 803A 1865; *ibid.*, RG 107, Telegrams Collected (Bound). On July 26, Meade endorsed three inspection reports. "Respectfully forwarded for the information of the Lieut General Comd'g. This inspection and report has been delayed by the failure of the War Department to issue the order organizing the Military Division of the Atlantic. Since the order requiring it to be made, various orders have been issued by the War Department mustering out some of the troops herein recommended to be mustered out. The recommendations of Bv't Major General Webb are approved, and I would respectfully apply for the 3d and 10th Regiments U. S. Infantry to be posted in the Department of the East to supply the places of some of the troops to be mustered out. This application is made in accordance with the notification from Head Quarters United States Army. that these two regiments were available." ES, *ibid.*, RG 108, Letters Received.

Also on July 17, 12:30 P.M., USG telegraphed to Meade. "Order the 194, 195 & 214 Pa Vols. and the 195 Ohio Vols. from Shenandoah valley to report to Gn. Augur in Washington." ALS (telegram sent), *ibid.*, RG 107, Telegrams Collected (Bound); telegram sent, *ibid.*; copies, *ibid.*, RG 108, Letters Sent;

DLC-USG, V, 46, 109. On July 20, Ruggles telegraphed to Bowers. "General Grant on 17th inst directed the 194th. Pa Vols sent from Shenandoah Valley to Washington. General Hancock telegraphs that the regiment is not in his command. Was not the 194th *Ohio* now at Martinsburg intended" Telegram received (at 4:30 P.M.), DNA, RG 107, Telegrams Collected (Bound); *ibid.*, RG 108, Telegrams Received; copies (dated July 18), *ibid.*, RG 393, Military Div. of the Atlantic, Letters Sent; (dated July 20) DLC-USG, V, 54.

1. On July 21, USG telegraphed to Bvt. Maj. Gen. Thomas H. Ruger. "Reduce the Cavalry in N. C. to one regiment of Maximum strength by mustering out of service the surplus." ALS (telegram sent), DNA, RG 94, Vol. Service Div., Letters Received, A1085 (VS) 1865. On the same day, USG telegraphed to Maj. Gen. Alfred H. Terry, then to Maj. Gen. Winfield S. Hancock. "Reduce the Cavalry force in your Command to two regiments by Musterout." "Reduce Cavalry in West Va. to one regiment mustering out remainder." ALS (telegrams sent), *ibid.* Also on July 21, Bowers wrote to Bvt. Brig. Gen. William Redwood Price, Cav. Bureau. "Orders have been issued this day to reduce the Cavalry force as follows, Department of North Carolina to one Maximum Regiment Department of Virginia to two Maximum Regiment[s] Department of West Virginia to one Maximum Regiment It is believed that Three Thousand Horses will be a sufficient number to be kept on hand at Giesboro Depot As soon as practicable a corresponding reduction in Cavalry will be ordered in the West." Copies (in tabular form), DLC-USG, V, 46, 109; DNA, RG 92, Letters Received through the Chief of Staff; *ibid.*, RG 108, Letters Sent. On July 28, Bvt. Col. James C. Biddle, aide to Meade, wrote to Bvt. Maj. Gen. Alexander S. Webb reporting on cav. in N. C. ALS, *ibid.*, Letters Received. On July 31, Meade endorsed this letter. "Respectfully forwarded to the Lieu't. Gen'l. with the remark that the instructions committed to me from Head Quarters, Armies of the United States, for mustering out of troops in Dept of North Carolina, were found by Col. Biddle, on his arrival at Raleigh, to have been executed under orders received direct from the War. Department." ES, *ibid.*

To Maj. Gen. George H. Thomas

Washington D. C, July 17th *1865* [*11:00* A.M.]
MAJ. GEN. G. H. THOMAS, NASHVILLE TENN.

Order the musterout of all Cavalry in your Division that cann be spared and the sale of their horses where they now are. Where it is necessary to retain Cavalry for want of other troops to do Garrison duty dismount them and sell their horses. A very limited number of mounted men in each state is all that is necessary. Report here the number mustered out and number of horses disposed of on this order.

U. S. GRANT
Lt. Gn.

ALS (telegram sent), DNA, RG 107, Telegrams Collected (Bound); telegram sent, *ibid.*; copies, *ibid.*, RG 108, Letters Sent; *ibid.*, RG 393, Military Div. of the Tenn., Telegrams Received; DLC-USG, V, 46, 109. *O.R.*, I, xlix, part 2, 1081. On July 26, 1865, Maj. Gen. George H. Thomas telegraphed to USG. "The 8th 11th & 12th Ky 14th 16th & 11th Illinois & 11th N. Y. Cavalry will be mustered out. I do not think it safe to muster out more until after the election on third of aAugust" ALS (telegram sent), DNA, RG 107, Telegrams Collected (Unbound); telegram received (on July 27, 9:00 A.M.), *ibid.*, Telegrams Collected (Bound); *ibid.*, RG 108, Telegrams Received. *O.R.*, I, xlix, part 2, 1091.

To Israel Washburn

Washington July 17th *1865*

HON. I WASHBURN
DEAR SIR:

Yours of the 15th is just received. I hope to get off from here the evening of the 24th inst. and will probably reach Portland on the 31st.

I would like to be as quiet as possible but of course cannot object to seeing the good people of your City. About the 2d of August I will avail myself of your kind offer of the use of the Revenue Cutter "Mahoning" to go to Halifax,[1] and will be most happy to have your company on that occation.

I shall not care to remain in Halifax more than one day. There will be with me Mrs. Grant, my four children, two staff officers and two servants, too large a family to intrud[e] upon the hospitalities of a private family.

Yours Truly
U. S. GRANT
Lt. Gn.

ALS, DLC-Israel Washburn. Israel Washburn, born in 1813, served as U.S. representative from Maine (1851–61) and governor of Maine (1861–63). President Abraham Lincoln appointed Washburn collector of customs at Portland, Maine, in 1863. On July 21, 1865, Israel's brother, U.S. Representative Elihu B. Washburne, Boston, wrote to Bvt. Col. Adam Badeau. "Please drop me a line before you leave Washington, addressed to me at Hallowell, Maine, telling me if you start according to the programme, and whether you will probably follow it out. I will want to know so that my brother, Gov. Washburn, may meet you in this city and make provision for your entertainment, and for your trip to Portland. It is necessary to know something definite of your movements. I shall leave here for the State of Maine in the morning. Dont fail to write." ALS, USG 3.

On July 22, 2:50 P.M., Saturday, USG telegraphed to John W. Garrett, president, Baltimore and Ohio Railroad. "I ~woul~ will be going to New York on the 7.30 p. m. train Monday with my family and four staff officers. Will you be kind enough to give me a special car?" ALS (telegram sent), DNA, RG 107, Telegrams Collected (Bound); telegram sent, *ibid*. USG left Washington on July 24 for an extended tour of the U.S. and Canada accompanied by Julia Dent Grant, their four children, Bvt. Cols. Orville E. Babcock, Adam Badeau, Ely S. Parker, and Horace Porter. See letter to Brig. Gen. John A. Rawlins, July 16, 1865. USG received numerous public ovations during the tour, widely reported in newspapers. He first visited USMA, arriving on July 25, and from there he traveled to Saratoga, N. Y., on July 27. In Saratoga, he was entertained by William W. Leland, a former staff officer (see *PUSG*, 3, 300, 331), leaving for Boston on July 29. *New York Times*, July 29–31, 1865.

On July 28, Governor John A. Andrew of Mass. wrote to USG. "I have the honor to introduce to you Brig. Genl Wm Schouler, Adjt. Genl of this Commonwealth whom I have directed to report to you at Albany, (and if you will permit it), to accompany you to Boston, if it should be your purpose to honor this capital by a visit, in the hope that by such attentions as he may be enabled to render, your journey may be facilitated and the trip more satisfactorily accomplished. I do not desire to interfere with any views which convenience or pleasure may dictate to yourself, and have instructed Genl Schouler to give no publicity to your movements, not distinctly authorized by ~yourself~. But I assure you General that it would confer great pleasure on the people of Massachusetts to accord to you some reception which might help to express their cordial sentiments of honor and gratitude for the services you have rendered your country. I beg to commend General Schouler to your regard, and I am with the highest respect faithfully . . ." LS, USG 3; (press) State Library of Massachusetts, Boston, Mass. On the same day, Andrew issued a Special Executive Order assigning William Schouler to escort USG. DS, USG 3. While in Boston (July 29–Aug. 1), USG attended a public reception at Faneuil Hall on July 31, and Mayor Frederick W. Lincoln, Jr., addressed the audience: "FELLOW-CITIZENS: We have assembled in Faneuil Hall to honor a distinguished guest, . . . I am desired by him to express his thanks to you for this demonstration, and to say that he is not in the habit of speaking and will not address this assembly. A portion of you, however, he will gladly take by the hand, but, as he is not a man of iron, it can hardly be expected that he will be able to greet all of you as you pay your respects to him." *New York Times*, Aug. 1, 1865. After shaking hands with approximately 800 people, USG reportedly stated: "LADIES AND GENTLEMEN: I would like to take you all by the hand, but I find that it will be impossible. I

thank you for this and for your kindness. I will bid you good afternoon." *Ibid.*
On July 31, Andrew issued Special Executive Order No. 2. "The Adjutant
General is ordered to report to Lieut-General Grant. U. S. A. and offer his own
services, in the name of the Governor, with such other Members of the General
Staff of Massachusetts as can be spared from duty, tomorrow, to accompany
the Lieut-General to Portland, in the State of Maine. The members of the
Governor's Staff, hereby detailed will consider themselves for the time being as
under the orders of Lieut-General Grant, for the purpose of rendering him and
his family and suite any aid in the further prosecution of their journey. And the
Adjutant General is directed to present the farewell compliments of the Governor
on the fulfilment of the duties prescribed in this order." DS, USG 3.

On Aug. 1, USG left for Portland, stopping briefly at Lawrence to visit the
Pacific Mills. *New York Times*, Aug. 1, 2, 1865. On Aug. 2, USG traveled to
Brunswick, Maine, to attend commencement ceremonies at Bowdoin College
during which he was presented an honorary degree by Bvt. Maj. Gen. Joshua L.
Chamberlain. A newspaper report stated: "Gen. GRANT really made a speech at
Bowdoin Commencement. As he had declined to speak Gen. CHAMBERLAIN said:
'I have tried to get Gen. GRANT to speak, but he say, "No," and when he says
that word, he means it. LEE knows it means something.' GRANT broke in, saying
'I continue to fight it out on that line.' " *Ibid.*, Aug. 6, 1865. USG returned to
Portland that evening, and spent Aug. 3 at Augusta, where he was honored at
the state capitol, again returning to Portland in the evening. *Ibid.*, Aug. 4, 1865.
USG left Portland on Aug. 4, spending the night at Gorham, N. H., and traveled
to Quebec, Canada, on Aug. 5. *Ibid.*, Aug. 5, 1865. See letter to Edwin M.
Stanton, Aug. 8, 1865.

1. On July 29, B. Hammatt Norton, U.S. consul, Pictou, Nova Scotia,
wrote to USG. "Noticing in the Public prints that you intend visiting Nova-
Scotia on your way to Canada, I take the liberty of expressing the gratification
it would afford me, if you would visit our little Port on your route." ALS, USG 3.
On July 31, Mayor Samuel H. Dale of Bangor, Maine, wrote to USG. "The
telegraph of to day gives our people the gratifying intelligence that you are to
visit our State on your way to Halifax NS—The good people of this City and the
Vally of our Penob. Scot., would be delighted in welcoming you, and will feel
disappointed Should they not have the pleasure of taking you by the hand—in
their behalf and in behalf of those of our vicinity who have So nobly Stood by
you, and their country in hours of terrible battle, and in behalf of this City
whom it is my pleasure to represent, I would cordially invite you, to visit us on
Such a day as will be most conveint for you and your family—Awaiting a favorable answer to the invitation . . ." ALS, *ibid.* USG did not go to Halifax as
originally planned. On Aug. 4, he toured the harbor at Portland aboard the
revenue cutter *Mahoning. New York Times*, Aug. 5, 1865.

To Edwin M. Stanton

Washington D. C, July 19th *1865*

HON. E. M. STANTON,
SEC. OF WAR,
SIR:

Since verbally approving the recommendation of Gen. Delafield for the assignment of the graduating class of this year from West Point I have seen a statement of the vacancies existing in the Army which entirely changes my views.

In the Infantry there are 3676 vacancies; in the Cavalry 60, Artillery 44, Engineers 16 and Ordnance 1. Gen. Delafields recommendation fills up the Engineer and Ordnance Corps, and that by taking graduates who were not recommended for the Engineers. He gives but eight to the Infantry.

I would recommend putting but five, the first five in the class, in the Engineers, ten in each the Cavalry and Artillery, and all the balance in the Infantry. In selecting those to go in the Artillery and Cavalry I would take the highest graduates making those corps their second choice until the above numbers are filled and then assign all the balance to the Infantry.

> Very respectfully
> your obt. svt.
> U. S. GRANT
> Lt. Gen.

ALS, DNA, RG 94, ACP, G332 CB 1865. On June 28, 1865, Brig. Gen. Richard Delafield, chief of engineers, had written to Secretary of War Edwin M. Stanton concerning assignments for the USMA class of 1865. LS, *ibid.* USG's list of the number of vacancies and Delafield's list of graduates are *ibid.*

On July 22, U.S. Senator Ira Harris of N. Y. wrote to USG. "My stepson Jared L. Rathbone graduated at the Military Academy in June last—I deemed it very important for his good that he should be *assigned to the Artillery*—When I had the pleasure of seeing you in Washington a few weeks since you mentioned that you had just seen the Secretary of War on the subject and that it had been determined that the recommendation of Gen. Delafield should be carried into effect—Of course I was satisfied for that would place my son in the Artillery where I desired he should be—But now I regret to learn that some change is contemplated which may have the effect of throwing him into the

Cavalry or Infantry—This, for reasons I need not state, I should greatly dep-
recate—I know very well that I have no right to interfere in the matter and
should apologize perhaps for saying as much as I have—I will only add that if it
is not too late when this reaches you and you should deem it consistent with
your own sense of public duty to place my young friend in the *Artillery* I should
regard it as a very great kindness, & one for which I should ever be grateful—"
ALS, USG 3. Docketing indicates that Harris was informed that no action could
be taken; 2nd Lt. Jared L. Rathbone was assigned to the 12th Inf.

To Maj. Gen. Alfred H. Terry

Washington July 19th 1865 [*12:40* P.M.]

MAJ. GN. A. H. TERRY, RICHMOND VA,

The force at Culpepper on account of claiming the right to be
mustered out of service are reported to be behaving very badly and
robing the people generally. I think it advisable for you to withdraw it and place there a small force of reliable men. It seems to me
from sixty to one hundred men will be sufficient for Culpepper.
The Cavalry formerly there are highly spoken of.

U. S. GRANT
Lt. Gn.

ALS (telegram sent), DNA, RG 107, Telegrams Collected (Bound); telegram
sent, *ibid.*; telegram received, *ibid.*, RG 393, Dept. of Va. and N. C., Hd. Qrs.
Telegrams Received. On July 19, 1865, Maj. Gen. Alfred H. Terry telegraphed
to USG. "Your despatch is recd. I have directed the troops at Culpepper to be
replaced by reliable men. An investigation to be had & the Commanding officer
if responsible for not controlling his men to be placed in arrest with charges. The
men heretofore there belong to a Regt now being mustered out." Telegram received (at 3:00 P.M.), *ibid.*, RG 107, Telegrams Collected (Bound); *ibid.*,
RG 108, Telegrams Received; copies, *ibid.*, RG 393, Dept. of Va. and N. C., 1st
Military District, Telegrams Sent; DLC-USG, V, 54. On July 21, Terry telegraphed to USG. "I received this morning the papers relative to the disorder at
Culpepper. The Statement of the force there is grossly exaggerated It is but
five cos of the 96th N Y The whole of which has but 518 officers & men present.
Genl Harris who commands the District between the North Anna & the Potomac
denies the truth of the report He says that with the exception of a slight disturbance at first the men have behaved in an ex[e]mplary manner. I am having
an investigation made & will report further." Telegram received (at 2:30 P.M.),
DNA, RG 107, Telegrams Collected (Bound); *ibid.*, RG 108, Telegrams Received; copies, *ibid.*, RG 393, Dept. of Va. and N. C., 1st Military District,
Telegrams Sent; DLC-USG, V, 54.

To William H. Seward

[*July 20, 1865*]

Respectfully refered to the Sec. of State. I have known Gen. Hovey well from the begining of the late rebellion. He is a man uniting good sense with great integrity. His course at the begining of the rebellion no doubt exercised a most salutary influance in bringing out early volunteers from the state of Indiana. He is a union man of the right stamp and I will guarantee would fill the position of Minister to Chili with great credit to himself and satisfaction to this country.

AE (undated), InU; copy (dated July 20, 1865), MH. On July 20, Bvt. Col. Adam Badeau wrote to Bvt. Maj. Gen. Alvin P. Hovey. "Lt. Gen. Grant directs me to acknowledge the receipt of your communication of July 18th, and to inform you that it has been forwarded to the Secretary of State, with an endorsement of which I enclose the draft." ALS, InU. On Aug. 3, Hovey telegraphed to Badeau. "Say to Lieut Genl [Grant] I will be pleased to accept [the] mission to Buenos Ayres as Envoy Extraordinary & Minister Plenipotentiary. A less grade would not pay expenses & enable me to sustain the position—" Telegram received (at 8:15 P.M.), DNA, RG 107, Telegrams Collected (Bound). Hovey was nominated as minister to Peru on Dec. 19, confirmed on Jan. 22, 1866, and served until 1870.

To Edwin M. Stanton

Washington D. C. July 20th *1865*

HON. E. M. STANTON,
SEC. OF WAR,
SIR:

As a matter of justice to Capt. Jas. H. Stokes, Chicago Board of Trade Battery, who was, as it would now appear, mustered out of service on entirely erroneous grounds by Spl. Orders No. 279 of August 20th 1864, I would now respectfully recommend the revocation of the above order.

As Capt. Stokes was appointed a Capt. & Asst. Adj. Gen. to rank from the same date, the difficulty of having two persons filling the same place is obviated.

Capt. Stokes was several times recommended for the appointment of Brigadier General. I know Gens. Crooke and Thomas so recommended him. As the order refered to has a tendency to effect Capt. Stokes prospects in civil life I would recommend his appointment now to the rank of Brigadier General to go out of service upon.

> Very respectfully
> your obt. svt.
> U. S. GRANT
> Lt. Gn.

ALS, DNA, RG 94, ACP, 496 1872. Secretary of War Edwin M. Stanton favorably endorsed this letter. AES, *ibid*. See telegrams to Secretary of War Edwin M. Stanton, Sept. 22, 1864, Jan. 31, 1865; letter to Brig. Gen. John A. Rawlins, Aug. 20, 1865.

On June 22, 1865, Maj. Robert Williams, AGO, prepared a memorandum for USG. "I have the honor respectfully to submit the following memorandum in the case of Capt. Jas. H. Stokes, A. A. G. of Vols. for instructions as to where this officer shall be ordered to report for assignment to duty. James H. Stokes, (whose appointment was ordered by the Secretary of War) has been confirmed by the Senate as Asst. Adjutant General of Volunteers, with the rank of Captain to date from August 22nd 1864, and his commission has been signed & is now ready for transmittal—but there are yet no orders for Capt. Stokes' assignment to duty. By S. O. 297, A. G. O., June 12th 1865, Capt. H. W. Bowers, A. A. G. of Vols. was ordered to report to the Comdg. General Dept. of Washington for assignment to duty with the 2nd Brig. 3rd Cavalry Division, the Commanding Officer of which had made application for an Asst. Adjt. General   June 19th 1865 the Secretary of War upon the recommendation of the Examining Board at Cincinnati, Ohio, ordered the honorable discharge of Capt. H. W. Bowers, A. A. G., from the Service of the U. S. on account of physical disability." DS, DNA, RG 94, Letters Received, 682A 1865. On June 23, Brig. Gen. John A. Rawlins favorably endorsed this memorandum. ES, *ibid*. On July 10, USG wrote to Maj. Gen. Christopher C. Augur. "Capt. J. H. Stokes is directed to report to you for duty. When he does so permit him to go to Baltimore, or elsewhere, to await the action of the War Dept. in a cash which he will have before the Dept." ALS, *ibid*., Staff Papers, Stokes. On Aug. 2, Brig. Gen. James H. Stokes, Baltimore, wrote to Brig. Gen. Lorenzo Thomas requesting back pay. ALS, *ibid*., ACP, 496 1872. On Aug. 7, Rawlins endorsed this letter. "It is respectfully recommended that Jas H Stokes be allowed pay as Lieut Col. and Quartermaster to the date of receipt of the order of muster out of same as such. Application for pay from that date as Captain and Asst Adjt Gen. to the date of his receipt of commission as such not approved." ES, *ibid*.

To Maj. Gen. William T. Sherman

Washington July 20th 1865 [*noon*]

MAJ. GEN. W. T. SHERMAN, ST. LOUIS MO.

Direct the discharge of all troops that can possibly be dispensed with in your Military Division and especially reduce the Cavalry force as much as possible. Now that we have so many General officers of known merrit I think it will be well to designate one to relieve Gen. Sully[1] in the Northwest.

U. S. GRANT
Lt. Gen.

ALS (telegram sent), DNA, RG 107, Telegrams Collected (Bound); telegram sent, *ibid.*; copies, *ibid.*, RG 108, Letters Sent; *ibid.*, RG 393, Dept. of the Mo., Letters Received; *ibid.*, Military Div. of the Miss., Telegrams Received; DLC-USG, V, 46, 109. *O.R.*, I, xlviii, part 2, 1108. On July 20, 1865, Maj. Gen. William T. Sherman telegraphed to USG. "Dispatch of twelfth [*twelve noon*] Received   will instruct Ord & Reynolds and will see Genl Pope regarding Sully today. Please assign to me such of the General officers of Logans army as you think will be retained giving me the names by telegraph   Dodge will go to Leavenworth to Command operating on the plains." Telegram received, DNA, RG 94, War Records Office, Dept. of the Cumberland; copies, *ibid.*, RG 393, Military Div. of the Miss., Telegrams Sent; DLC-USG, V, 54. *O.R.*, I, xlviii, part 2, 1108.

On July 21, 1:10 P.M., Bvt. Col. Theodore S. Bowers telegraphed to Sherman. "The following assignments are in tended. The order has not yet been promulgated, and change, may be made: Generals Logan, Cox, Leggett, McIntosh, Pitcher and Wilcox to Gen. Ord. Generals Dodge, Blair, Chapman, Wheaton, Upton, C. T. H. Smith, P E Conner, Sully, Walcutt and Elliott to General Pope. Generals T. J. Wood, H. J Hunt, E A Carr, C H Morgan and A S Williams to Gen Reynolds. By General Order No. 123, A. G. O., of date July 20 1865 Commanders of Military Divisions are authorized to assign General & Staff officers within their commands in such way as their services may be most required." LS (telegram sent), DNA, RG 107, Telegrams Collected (Bound); telegram sent, *ibid.*; copies, *ibid.*, RG 108, Letters Sent; *ibid.*, RG 393, Military Div. of the Miss., Telegrams Received; DLC-USG, V, 46, 109. *O.R.*, I, xlviii, part 2, 1111. On July 22, Sherman wrote to Bowers. "I had the honor last night to receive your despatch of 12 M giving a list of the Generals attached to the Departments Composing this Division. I notice only the omission of one who would do admirable service viz General J. M. Corse, & renew the expression of my wish that he be retained as long as possible even permanently in the Military Service. The process of discharging the Armies is progressing as fast as possible—and under the direction of Dept Commanders will go on to the end—All things seem to be moving harmoniously & well—Gen Dodge will go on Monday up to Leavenworth to superintend the only military movements now in progress within the limits of my command, and as they are in progress no officer could be better qualified than he to watch them to their conclusion. I propose to attend on the invitation of Governor Morton some Celebration at Indianapolis next Tuesday in honor of the Volunteers of that state, who have returned, and resumed so quietly and well their Civil duties. Thence I propose to return home to Lancaster where unless necessity calls me away I hope to spend the month of August, but I will leave here in St Louis my Adjt, Qr Master, and other officers to attend to all Routine business. All the Records are now here and it will take Col Sawyer a full month to transfer to the Books of the Division the matter contained in the Blotters that I carried with me to the Field. I beg you will continue to address me here as though present & send all orders as he will properly dispose of them, but anything needing speedy action, or calling for my personal action can be addressed to me at Lancaster Ohio. I will be Careful to keep you at all times advised of my whereabouts." ALS, DNA, RG 108, Letters Received. *O.R.*, I, xlviii, part 2, 1114.

1. Alfred Sully, born in Philadelphia, Pa., in 1821, USMA 1841, served in the Mexican War and on the frontier before the Civil War. Appointed col., 1st Minn., as of Feb. 22, 1862, he fought in the Peninsular campaign, and, after the battle of Antietam, was appointed brig. gen. as of Sept. 26. In the summer of 1863, he was ordered to the Northwest to command the District of Dakota. Some time before July 19, 1865, U.S. Delegate Walter A. Burleigh of Dakota Territory wrote to USG. "I have the honor to lay before you, herewith, a report which I made to the Com'r. of Indian Affairs on the 18th day of February 1865—with accompanying papers. A copy of this report was laid before Maj. Gen'l. Halleck, who after a careful examination of the same, assured me that the charges therein contained relating to the conduct of Brev. Maj. Gen'l. Sully, should be, thoroughly and impartially investigated, and that if found to be true, he should be removed from his present command. I believe this whole matter was referred to Maj. Gen'l. John Pope, who ordered Col. John N. Du Bois—a member of his Staff—, to inquire into the matter. These charges against Gen'l. Sully have not been investigated in the manner in which Gen'l. Halleck assured me they should be. The investigation ordered by Gen'l. Pope was not thorough, but extremely partial and imperfect,—and I have in my possession the means of showing that it was extremely unfair, if not fraudulent. I did not make these charges against Gen'l. Sully from any feelings of personal ill will, but simply because I knew that he had failed to discharge his duty as a commanding officer,— and I now reassert that the charges against this officer, contained in that report are strictly, true, and I can prove them to be so, whenever I can have a fair opportunity. I ask that this matter may receive at your hands, the attention which it deserves,—and that Gen'l. Sully be removed from his present command, and a suitable officer assigned thereto." ALS (dated July), DNA, RG 94, Letters Received, 145I 1865. On July 19, Bowers endorsed this letter. "Respectfully referred to Major General W T. Sherman, who will please direct an officer of his own selection to investigate thoroughly the charges herein contained, and after ascertaining the facts give such orders and direct such changes in commanding officers as he may deem necessary." ES, *ibid.* On July 9, U.S. Representative Asahel W. Hubbard of Iowa wrote to Secretary of the Interior James Harlan. "I have just been informed that Burleigh of Dokota (the delegate elect) is about visiting Washington for the purpose among other things of procuring an order for

the removal of the Military Post at Sioux City to some point in the Territory. This is a matter in which the citizens of north-west Iowa take a deep interest and they would very much dislike to see the Post removed, Burleigh upon this and other subjects will not hesitate to make any statement which he may think will further his interests, and he may misrepresent the facts to the Secy of War—If he should make the effort, and you can find it convenient to do so I wish you would say to the Secy, that Iowa wants to be heard upon this subject, before final action, is taken." ALS, *ibid.*, RG 108, Letters Received. On July 22, Maj. Thomas T. Eckert, act. asst. secretary of war, referred this letter to USG. ES, *ibid.* On July 25, Bowers endorsed this letter. "Respectfully referred to Maj. Gen. W. T. Sherman, Comdg. Mil. Div. Miss., for his action." ES, *ibid.* See following telegram.

To Maj. Gen. John Pope

Washington D. C, July 21st/65 [4:00 P.M.]

MAJ. GN. POPE, ST. LOUIS, MO,

I meant Sully in my dispatch to Sherman. The order for a change is not imperative but the complaints against Sully, and the management of the Quartermaster's Dept. in the Northwest are such that, whilst we have so many Generals of known ability, I think a change can do no harm and may do great good. No officer has a patent wright to a command until he is proven *incompetant*.

U. S. GRANT
Lt. Gn.

ALS (telegram sent—marked as sent on July 22, 1865, 11:10 A.M.), DNA, RG 107, Telegrams Collected (Bound); telegram sent, *ibid.*; telegram received (on July 22, 2:30 P.M.), *ibid.*, Telegrams Collected (Unbound); *ibid.*, RG 94, Generals' Papers and Books, Alfred Sully. *O.R.*, I, xlviii, part 2, 1111. On July 21, Maj. Gen. John Pope telegraphed to USG. "In your dispatch to Gen Sherman of today do you mean Gen Sibley or Gen Sully to be relieved in the north west?" Telegram received (at 12:40 P.M.), DNA, RG 108, Telegrams Received; copy, DLC-USG, V, 54. *O.R.*, I, xlviii, part 2, 1111. See preceding telegram.

On July 27, Pope wrote to USG. "I have the honor to acknowledge the receipt of your Telegram of the 21st inst., in relation to General Sully. When the dispatch to General Sherman was received, he showed it to me, and asked what it meant; I replied [remembering the conversation I had with you concerning Sibley,] that 'I presumed Sibley, and not Sully, was intended, as this confusion of names had frequently occurred in telegraphic dispatches concerning these officers.' At General Sherman's request I telegraphed you on the subject. Whilst [as you say,] 'no officer has a patent right to a command until he is proved incompetent,' yet Sully's case is peculiar, and I think should be dealt with, not so much with reference to his special qualifications for his command, as to the fact that he is complained of by persons whose personal views and objects he will not promote at the expense of the public interests. These persons have openly proclaimed that they will bring about his removal at any cost, and in any manner. They are persons holding official positions in the Indian Department, and traders and contractors connected with them. I have heard of no others who object to General Sully, though it is possible that other persons operated upon by these officials, may have done so without themselves possessing any personal knowledge of the charges or complaints against him. His removal from his command would simply be a triumph of these people, and a reproach upon General Sully's military and personal character, and would give little encouragement to any officer who should succeed him, to resist the like combinations of interested parties. I believe that General Sully has performed his duty with ability, fidelity and honesty, and I am therefore, disposed to sustain him though of course, if you desire his removal, I shall at once comply with your wishes. The same complaints against him, which were laid before you, were made to me. I ordered the Inspector General of this Department to proceed to Sully's Military District and make a careful inspection of it, and an examination of the charges against him. I directed him to call on the parties making the complaints, for their statements, and for the names of witnesses to substantiate them, directing him to examine the witnesses, and make full report to me. He reports that the principal complainant, Mr. Burleigh, late Indian Agent at Yanckton, Dakotah Territory, and now Delegate in Congress from that Territory, although notified that he was there to take testimony and requested to give it, carefully avoided him, and even left his home to avoid an interview. The report in question, I have the honor to transmit enclosed, and in justice to General Sully, and to the Military generally who have always been the subject of such attacks on the frontier, I request that this report be carefully examined. Whilst, under ordinary circumstances, no officer has the right to any command or any reason to complain if he is relieved from any duty to which he may have been assigned, yet when that removal is made upon charges which he has never seen, and has had no opportunity to reply to; but which seriously affect his official and personal character, the case becomes peculiar, and the act of removal is properly interpreted to be the officer's condemnation by his Government, on the charges against him. This is precisely General Sully's case, and I therefore, as his immediate military superior, consider it my duty to present the matter fully to the proper authorities in order that no injustice may be done to a faithful and meritorious officer. I have directed the Chief Quartermaster of this Department to examine into, and report upon, the condition and management of his Department, in General Sully's Military District—His report is enclosed. General Sully, being now far out on the Plains beyond communication, leading an expedition against the hostile Sioux, near Devil's Lake, cannot be relieved until his return. I will then replace him by some other officer according to your wishes, unless meantime, I receive other instructions." LS (brackets in original), DNA, RG 108, Letters Received. *O.R.*, I, xlviii, part 2, 1125–26. The enclosure is in DNA, RG 108, Letters Received. On Oct. 27, Maj. Gen. William T. Sherman, St. Louis, wrote to Brig. Gen. John A. Rawlins. "I had the honor to receive by due course of Mail the papers touching a controversy existing between Genl Sully Commanding the U. S. Forces in Dacotah Territory and the civil authorities there were, especially with W. A.

Burleigh, Delegate as contained in his communication of ___ July 1865 endorsed by order of Lt Genl Grant of date July 19, 1865, with orders for me to ascertain the facts and to make such changes as the case called for. I selected Bvt Maj Genl Chas. C. Walcutt well Known to me as an officer in whom I have often relied and imparted to him all information in my official possession, with orders to proceed to Dakotah and ascertain the truth. He has just returned and submits the enclosed Report which is full. It is utterly impossible that he should have any feeling or prejudice in the matter, so that I adopt his Report without a shadow of doubt, and do not think General Sully should be removed to give force to complaints idle, groundless & malicious. I think it is eminently our duty to support Officers enforcing a General or national policy against local pressure & clamor, and from Genl Walcutts observation I learn that the Inhabitants of Dahcotah, instead of sharing the feelings of their Delegate in this matter, manifest towards General Sully great official and personal respect." ALS, *ibid*. For the report of Bvt. Maj. Gen. Charles C. Walcutt exonerating Brig. Gen. Alfred Sully, see *ibid*., RG 94, Letters Received, 1451 1865.

To Maj. Gen. Philip H. Sheridan

Washington D. C. July 21st *1865* [*10:40* A.M.]
MAJ. GN. SHERIDAN, NEW ORLEANS, LA.

Direct commanding officer at Brasos to countermand order for purchase of Cavalry horses. At present Cavalry can be kept up in Texas by discharging Cavalry regiments and giving their horses to troops retained. The Q. M. Dept. has a large supply of horses too that can be shipped if required.

U. S. GRANT
Lt. Gen

ALS (telegram sent), DNA, RG 107, Telegrams Collected (Bound); telegram sent, *ibid*.; telegram received, *ibid*., Telegrams Collected (Unbound). *O.R.*, I, xlviii, part 2, 1110. On July 20, 1865, Bvt. Maj. Gen. Montgomery C. Meigs had written to USG. "I have the honor to enclose copy of Order of the Major General Commanding troops in Texas to purchase three hundred (300) Cavalry horses, with request that you countermand the Order by telegraph We are selling Cavalry horses at half the price he would be obliged to pay for them and had better ship the horses of some of the discharged Cavalry to Texas than have this purchase made." LS, DNA, RG 92, Miscellaneous Letters Sent (Press).

On Aug. 4, Maj. Gen. Philip H. Sheridan telegraphed to Brig. Gen. John A. Rawlins. "If the regular Cavalry regiments are sufficiently Strong they could be sent to Texas and take the ~~arms~~ Horses, arms & equipments of the volunteers now there who could be mustered out—This would Save much trouble and expense to the government as their transportation to the western frontier fully equipped would be expensive" Telegram received (on Aug. 5, 1:10 A.M.), *ibid.*, RG 107, Telegrams Collected (Bound); *ibid.*, RG 108, Telegrams Received; copies, DLC-USG, V, 54; DLC-Philip H. Sheridan. *O.R.*, I, xlviii, part 2, 1164.

To Maj. Gen. William T. Sherman

Washington July 22d 1865 [*7:30* P.M.]

MAJ GEN. W. T. SHERMAN, ST. LOUIS MO.

Capt. Potter[1] telegraphs from Ft. Leavenworth for authority to purchase horses for Cavalry purposes. Authority cannot be given but horses can be sent from ~~Leavenw~~ Louisville and elsewhere where Government has large surplus.

I wish you would look into this matter and see if the supply can not be kept equal to the requirements of the service by Mustering out troops and retaining their animals. There has been several thousand horses sent to Mo. since the surrender of the rebel Armies already.

U. S. GRANT
Lt. Gen.

ALS (telegram sent), DNA, RG 107, Telegrams Collected (Bound); telegram sent, *ibid.*; copies, *ibid.*, RG 108, Letters Sent; (misdated July 23, 1865) *ibid.*, RG 393, Military Div. of the Miss., Telegrams Received; DLC-USG, V, 46, 109. *O.R.*, I, xlviii, part 2, 1114. On July 23, Maj. Gen. William T. Sherman telegraphed to USG. "I will instruct Gen Easton my Chf Q. M. to look into the matter of horses for the Cavalry if any are needed it is for the Expedition for the plains." Telegram received (on July 24, 9:40 A.M.), DNA, RG 107, Telegrams Collected (Bound); *ibid.*, RG 108, Telegrams Received; copy, DLC-USG, V, 54. *O.R.*, I, xlviii, part 2, 1116.

1. Joseph A. Potter, born in Potter's Hollow, N. Y., in 1816, worked for the U.S. government as a civil engineer before the Civil War. He was appointed 1st lt., 15th Inf., as of Sept. 27, 1861, and also capt. and q. m. as of Sept. 27. Perhaps on July 25, 1865, Sherman telegraphed to USG. "Have Just seen General Pope about Captain Potter's Requisition for horses at Leavenworth.—He thinks no horses are needed. Much confusion results from Quartermasters being somewhat independent of Military Commanders—making Requisitions direct to Washington.—Give me orders and I will have my Quarter-master control all such matters: It seems to me economical not to sell good horses in Kentucky but to drive them slowly to Leavenworth or Arkansas where they can be herded and fed cheap, and will be needed next year." Copy (misdated July 15), DNA,

RG 393, Military Div. of the Miss., Letters Sent. This telegram may not have been seen by USG.

To Sgt. Thomas McGraw

————

Washington, July 22d *1865.*

SERGEANT THOMAS McGRAW
Co. "B" 23D ILLINOIS VOLS.

The sum of four hundred and sixty dollars was sent to me by patriotic citizens to be presented as a reward for gallantry to the soldier who should first raise our flag over Richmond.[1] As Richmond was not taken by assault, I have concluded that the donor's wishes will be best carried out by dividing the sum between the three soldiers most conspicuous for gallantry in the final and successful assault on Petersburg. You have been selected by Major General John Gibbon, Commanding 24th Army Corps, as entitled to this honor on behalf of that command; and I herewith present to you one hundred and fifty three dollars and thirty three cents, as one third of the original sum.

It affords me great satisfaction to receive from your Commanding General such unqualified testimony of your gallantry and heroism in battle; and to be the medium of transmitting to you this recognition of the worth of your services in defense of our common country

U. S. GRANT
Lieut. General

Copies, American Jewish Archives, Cincinnati, Ohio; DLC-USG, V, 46, 109; DNA, RG 108, Letters Sent. *O.R.,* I, xlvi, part 1, 1262–63. On July 22, 1865, USG wrote similar letters to Sgt. David W. Young, 139th Pa., 6th Army Corps, and to Corporal Jacob R. Tucker, 4th Md., 5th Army Corps. Copies, American Jewish Archives, Cincinnati, Ohio; DLC-USG, V, 46, 109; (Tucker) DLC-Grover Cleveland; DNA, RG 108, Letters Sent. *O.R.,* I, xlvi, part 1, 1262. Tucker and Sgt. Thomas McGraw, 23rd Ill., later received the Congressional Medal of Honor.

1. On Oct. 25, 1864, Secretary of War Edwin M. Stanton had written to USG. "I have the pleasure of transmitting herewith a copy of a communication received from the Secretary of State, and a letter to yourself from Thomas

Savage, Esquire, United States Vice Consul at Havana, who has directed to be deposited, to your order, in the City Bank of New York, the sum of $350 65/100, being the contribution of certain American citizens residing in Cuba who desire that the money shall be given by you to the first soldier of the Union Army who shall enter Richmond, should that city be taken by assault, or that it shall be applied to the relief of the wounded and bereaved, or disposed of as may seem best to you, in case of doubt as to who first entered or of the abandonment of the city without a struggle." LS, DNA, RG 108, Letters Received. Stanton enclosed a letter of Oct. 15 from Thomas Savage, vice consul gen., Havana, to USG. "I have directed to be deposited in the City Bank of New York, subject to your order, the sum of $351 65/100, the contribution of a few kindred spirits in this City, that fully appreciate the noble efforts of the brave army under your command, in upholding the cause of our country, which being the cause of humanity, of justice and universal freedom, they look upon as their own. By the request of these, our friends, I ask of you the favor to give the money to the non-commissioned officer or private, who may be the first to enter Richmond, should that City be taken by assault, and in the event of his being killed, to his legal heirs. In case of doubt as to who first entered, or of the abandonment of the City without a struggle by the enemy, you may then apply the donation to the relief of the wounded, widows or orphans, or in the manner which to your judgment may seem best. In carrying out the above request, I also comply with the pleasing duty of conveying to you, the anxious wish of the donors, that you may meet with the most perfect success in the great enterprise entrusted to your direction by the President, with the approbation and confidence of all the loyal and true of the country. Allow me, Sir, to express the sentiments of high respect and regard, with which I am, your grateful fellow citizen . . ." LS, *ibid.*

To Edwin M. Stanton

Washington D. C July 24th *1865*

Hon. E. M. Stanton
Sec. of War,
Sir:

In reply to J. S. Doolittle's dispatch of the 19th, refered to me, I have to state that Gen. Herron has ma[d]e a temporary treaty with all Indian tribes along, and South of, the Overland Mail route. This of course includes all the ¡Indians South of the Arkansas and stops hostilities until a regular treaty can be entered into.

The papers in this matter have been refered to your office approving Gen. Herron's action and recommending that Col. Parker

of my Staff be appointed one of the Commissioners to treat with the
Indians.[1]

> Very respectfully
> your obt. svt.
> U. S. GRANT
> Lt. Gn.

ALS, DNA, RG 108, Letters Received. On July 19, 1865, U.S. Senator James R.
Doolittle of Wis. had telegraphed to Secretary of State William H. Seward and
Secretary of War Edwin M. Stanton. "Met dispatches for Mr Foster at Taos,
We reach Denver to morrow morning He is well and homeward bound Does
any thing require him immediately? Kit Carson and Col Wm Bent say, if
authorized they can make peace with the Indians along and below the Arkansas,
Col Bent says he will guarantee it with his [head, but] upon c[on]dition no
hostile ~~caus~~ campaigns are made south of the Arkansas, until they make the
effort, Shall they attempt it, and will you direct the commanders not to make
such campaigns? Earnestly we advise it," Telegram received (on July 21, 9:00
A.M.), *ibid. O.R.*, I, xlviii, part 2, 1094. See *ibid.*, pp. 1117–18, 1122. Stanton
referred this telegram to USG some time between July 21 and 24. AES, DNA,
RG 108, Letters Received.

1. On July 9, Maj. Gen. Philip H. Sheridan, New Orleans, wrote to Brig.
Gen. John A. Rawlins. "On the 7th inst I forwarded to the Hd Qrs—Armies of
the U. S. the terms of an agreement entered into between the commissioners
Sent up to Council Grove, to obtain information of the condition of affairs in the
Indian country, and the Chief of the Choctaws. A grand council meets Septr 1st
1865 at Armstrongs Acadamy & I consider it important that the Indian Department have commissioners there as it is best to agree at once with these tribes
while they are somewhat alarmed. these people are numerous. Some four
thousand wild indians being near, Fort Arbuckle they have been fed for three
years by the rebel government of Texas to prevent depredations in that State,
notwithstanding which within a few days an agent has been here with claims
against the U S. Govt and I have no doubt but that he is rascal enough to present them to the Indian Department for payment," LS, *ibid.*, RG 107, Letters
Received from Bureaus. On July 20, USG endorsed this letter. "Respectfully
forwarded to the Secretary of War. The papers within referred to as having
been sent forward on the 7th inst., have not yet been received." ES, *ibid.* On
July 7, Sheridan had written to Bvt. Col. Theodore S. Bowers. "I have the honor
to enclose herewith for the information of the Lieut Genl Comd.g papers relating to the Indian tribes of Western Texas and vicinity, and would respectfully
request, that in pursuance of the agreement entered into by Lt. Col Mathews
and Genl Pritchlynn Chief of the Choctaws, commissioners be sent to Armstrongs
Acadamy Choctaw Nation to meet the various delegations from the Indian tribes
on the 1st of Septr 1865. for the purpose of entering into a treaty of peace between the U. S. Govt and the Indian tribes." LS, *ibid.*, RG 108, Letters Received. On July 20, USG endorsed this letter. "Respectfully forwarded to the
Secretary of War. The acts and proceedings of the Commissioners sent out by
Gen. Herron, are approved, and it is respectfully recommended that a commis-

sion be appointed to meet the Indians of the SouthWest, to enter into and negotiate a Treaty of Peace and Amity. I would respectfully suggest that the place
of holding the Grand Council be changed from Armstrongs Academy to the
vicinity of Fort Gibson. I would also respectfully suggest Col. E. S. Parker of
my staff as one of the Commission to attend said Council." ES, *ibid.* See *O.R.*,
I, xlviii, part 2, 1095–1107. On Aug. 8, 10:40 A.M., Rawlins telegraphed to
Bvt. Col. Ely S. Parker, "Care Lt. Gen. Grant Quebec." "You have been ordered
to report by the Secretary of War to report to the Secretary of the Interior for
duty: Order awaits you here." Telegrams sent (2), DNA, RG 107, Telegrams
Collected (Bound); copies, *ibid.*, RG 108, Letters Sent; DLC-USG, V, 46, 109.

To Maj. Gen. Philip H. Sheridan

West Point, N. Y. July 25th *1865*

MAJ. GN. P. H. SHERIDAN,
COMD.G MIL. DIV. OF THE GULF,
GENERAL,

Maj. General J. M. Schofield[1] goes to the Rio Grande on an
Inspection tour, carrying with him a leave of absence for one year,
with authority to leave the United States. If he avails himself of
this leave he will explain to you the object more fully than I could
do in the limits of a letter, and much more fully than I could do
now, under any circumstances, because much that will have to be
learned to fix his determination, whether to go or not, has yet to be
found out in Washington whilst I shall be away. This however I
can say. Gen. Schofields leave has been given with the concurrence
of the President, he having full knowlede of the object. I have both
written my views to the President and had conversations with him
on the subject. In all that relates to Mexican affairs he agrees in
the duty we owe to ourselves to maintain the Monroe doctrine, both
as a principle and as a security for our future peace.

On the Rio Grande, or in Texas convenient to get there, we
must have a large amount of surrendered Ordnance and Ordnance
stores, or such articles accumulating from discharging men who
leave these stores behind. Without special orders to do so send
none of these articles back but rather place them convenient to be
permitted to go into Mexico if they can be got into the hands of the

defenders of the only Government we recognize in that country. I hope Gen. Schofield may go with orders direct to receive these articles, but if he does not I know it will meet with general approbation to let him have them if contrary orders are not received.

It is a fixed determination on the part of the people of the United States, and I think myself safe in saying on the part of the President also, that an Empire shall not be established on this Continent by the aid of Foreign bayonettes. A War on the part of the United States is to be avoided, if possible, but it wil[l] be better to go to war now when but little aid given to the Mexicans will settle the question than to hav[e] in prospect a greater war, shure to come, if delayed until the Empire is established. We want then to aid the Mexicans without giving cause of War between the United States and France. Between the would be Empire of Maximilian and the United States all difficulty can easily be settled by observing the same sort of neutrality that has been observed towards us for the last four years.

This is a little indefinite as a letter of instructions to be governed by. I hope with this you may receive them, instructions, in much more positive terms. With a knowledge of the fact before you however that the greatest desire is felt to see the Liberal Government restored, in Mexico, and no doubts exists of the strict justice of our right to demand this, and enforce the demand, with the whole strength of the United States, and your own judgement, gives you a basis of action that will aid you.

I will recommend in a few days that you be directed to discharge all the men you think can be spared in from the Dept. of Texas, where they are, giving transportation to their homes to all who desire to return.—You are aware that existing orders permit discharged soldiers to retain their arms and accoutrements at low rates, fixed in orders?

> Very respectfully
> your obt. svt.
> U. S. GRANT
> Lt. Gen.

ALS, Barney Papers, CSmH. USG gave this letter to Maj. Gen. John M. Scho-field on July 26, 1865, at USMA to carry to Maj. Gen. Philip H. Sheridan. Schofield, however, did not go to Tex., and Sheridan probably did not see this letter until years later. See letter to Andrew Johnson, July 15, 1865; telegram to Maj. Gen. Philip H. Sheridan, Aug. 13, 1865; letter to Maj. Gen. Philip H. Sheridan, Oct. 22, 1865; letter to Maj. Gen. John M. Schofield, March 24, 1866.

1. On May 30, 1865, USG wrote to Schofield. "The bearer of this Sr. Y. Mariscal is attache[d] to the Mexican Legation in this City. Attention paid him will be appreciated by the Minister, Romero, as well as myself." ALS, DLC-John M. Schofield. On the same day, USG issued a pass for Ignacio Mariscal, secretary, Mexican legation, to Raleigh, N. C. Copy (printed in Spanish), Matías Romero, comp., *Correspondencia de la Legacion Mexicana en Washington durante la Intervencion Extranjera 1860–1868* (Mexico, 1870–92), V, 345. Mariscal offered Schofield command of Mexican troops to fight the French. See *ibid.*, pp. 343–45, 360–61, 374–77, 390–93.

To Maj. Gen. William T. Sherman

Saratoga, N. Y. July 28th *1865*

Maj. Gen. Sherman,
St. Louis, Mo.

The Quartermaster and Commissary Generals report requisitions of such magnitude as coming from Leavenworth as to alarm them. Look into them and stop all unnecessary expeditions and reduce all necessary ones to actual requirements. Returns show a Cavalry force in the Dept. of Mo. which it would seem might be materially reduced. Look into this matter also.

U. S. Grant
Lieut. Gen'l

Telegram, copies, DNA, RG 94, Letters Received, 858A 1865; *ibid.*, RG 108, Letters Sent; (dated July 29, 1865) *ibid.*, RG 393, Military Div. of the Miss., Telegrams Received; (dated July 29) *ibid.*, Dept. of the Mo., Telegrams Received; DLC-USG, V, 46, 109. *O.R.*, I, xlviii, part 1, 350; printed as addressed to Maj. Gen. John Pope, dated July 29, *ibid.*, p. 364; *ibid.*, I, xlviii, part 2, 1128. See *ibid.*, pp. 1149–59. Bvt. Col. Theodore S. Bowers endorsed this telegram. "Respectfully furnished for the information of Brig. Gen. E. D. Townsend, Asst. Adj. Gen." AES (undated), DNA, RG 94, Letters Received, 858A 1865. On July 28, 11:00 A.M., Secretary of War Edwin M. Stanton had telegraphed to USG, West Point, N. Y. "The Quarter Master General has made a report this morning of requisitions from the Department at Leavenworth indicating an expedition of such magnitude and expense beyond the capacity of the appropriations to meet. The transportation estimates alone are two millions per month exclus and this exclusive of the cost of materials &c The Commissary Department also ins in a state of alarm. I beg to direct your immediate attention to this subject as I am not advised of the extent or necessity of the proposed operations." ALS (telegram sent), *ibid.*, RG 107, Telegrams Collected (Bound); telegram received (at 4:00 P.M.), *ibid.*, RG 108, Telegrams Received. *O.R.*, I, xlviii, part 2, 1127. On the same day, USG, Saratoga, N. Y., telegraphed to Stanton. "I Know of no expedition or the necessity for one of the magnitude represented in your despatch—I will telegraph to Sherman to look into it & correct all extravagance" Telegram received (at 11:45 P.M.), DNA, RG 107, Telegrams Collected (Bound); copies, *ibid.*, RG 108, Letters Sent; DLC-USG, V, 46, 109. *O.R.*, I, xlviii, part 2, 1127. On Aug. 3, Pope wrote to Lt. Col. Roswell M. Sawyer, adjt. for Maj. Gen. William T. Sherman, reporting steps taken to reduce forces and expenditures. Copy, DNA, RG 94, Letters Received, 908A 1865. *O.R.*, I, xlviii, part 2, 1161. On Aug. 19, Brig. Gen. John A. Rawlins endorsed this letter. "Respectfully forwarded to the Secretary of War." ES, DNA, RG 94, Letters Received, 908A 1865.

On July 26, Bvt. Maj. Gen. Montgomery C. Meigs wrote to USG. "It has been deemed necessary to order to Fort Leavenworth, Kansas, the 1000 wagons and teams sent from this depôt, to Louisville in May last,—the demand at that Fort for means of transportation to supply troops on the plains being very urgent. In view of this transfer I have the honor to inquire whether the Lieut.-General commanding the Armies of the U. S. desires to have the transportation thus ordered away from Louisville replaced? We have it elsewhere—" LS, *ibid.*, RG 108, Letters Received. On Aug. 10, Rawlins wrote to Meigs. "In reply to your communication of date 26th ult., stating that the teams sent to Louisville, Ky., from this Depot in May last have been sent to the plains, and inquiring whether the transportation thus ordered away should be replaced, Lieut. Gen. Grant directs me to say that it is not necessary to send any more teams to Louisville, Ky." Copies, *ibid.*, Letters Sent; DLC-USG, V, 46, 109.

On July 29, Bowers directed the AGO to issue orders: "Brevet Brigadier General W. Redwood Price, Actg. Inspector General Cavalry Bureau, will proceed without delay via St Louis to Fort Leavenworth, Kansas, and such other places as he deems necessary, on business connected with the Cavalry Bureau On the completion of these duties he will return to his proper station." Copy, DNA, RG 94, Letters Received, 811A 1865. On Sept. 5, Bvt. Brig. Gen. William Redwood Price, Cav. Bureau, wrote to Bowers. ". . . I consider much of the abuse that has transpired in this section attributable to the want of an efficient commanding officer at Fort Leavenworth during the time these commands were being organized for the plains. In the first place such an one would not have counselled the sending such a large number of troops to fight Indians; these bodies, moving in columns of from 2000 to 5000 men, will not be likely to encounter any Indians. It is well known that previous to the outbreak of the rebellion, small expeditions of a few hundred men were more successful against the Indians than large ones; and I do not conceive that the Indians have so increased as to make it now necessary for expeditions of several thousand to be sent against them with such large waste of property as indicated above. Much dissatisfaction that might have been prevented by proper organization (and was prevented by similar columns raised in Texas), arose among the troops at being retained in service; the brigade organizations were not kept up and the commands were sent out by regiments as they were prepared for the field. A mutiny arose in one regiment, and a very demoralized spirit maintained in most of them. Under these circumstances I consider the present campaign a failure. General Pope furnished me a copy of a letter of instructions to General Dodge on the subject of reduction in his force, in which, however, he says: 'of course the expeditions against the Indians should not, and must not, be arrested.' As the expeditions against the Indians comprise almost the entire force, I see little chance of stopping this great useless expense to the government, under present instructions I would therefore respectfully recommend that General Pope be positively directed to muster out fifteen regiments of Cavalry of his command at once; and that they be ordered to Fort Leavenworth for the purpose of turning in their horses and arms. I would recommend that, if possible, one regiment of regular Cavalry be ordered to the plains, which will do more good against the Indians than all this force. . . ." LS, *ibid.*, RG 108, Letters Received. The enclosure is in *O.R.*, I, xlviii, part 2, 1154–55.

To Edwin M. Stanton

Boston Mass. July 30th *1865*

HON. E. M. STANTON,
SEC. OF WAR,
SIR:

In view of the Cavalry force now in Texas being beyond the wants of the service I would respectfully recommend that authority be sent to General Sheridan to muster out of service all he thinks can be dispensed with. I would also extend the authority to all other Arms of service as well as Cavalry.

As many troops may choose to remain in the South I would respectfully suggest that present orders for Muster out be changed so as to authorize all who wish to do so, to receive their discharges where they are.

> Very respectfully
> your obt. svt.
> U. S. GRANT
> Lt. Gen. U, S, A,

ALS, DNA, RG 94, Vol. Service Div., Letters Received, A1086 (VS) 1865. See telegram to Maj. Gen. Philip H. Sheridan, Aug. 13, 1865.

To Bvt. Col. Theodore S. Bowers

From Boston, 8 a m July 31st 1865

COL. T. S. BOWERS, AAG.

Gen. Gilmore can retain the number of white troops he proposes; let him muster out the colored troops raised in the north, and hold his surplus subject to orders. If Gen. Meade can dispense with white troops by having colored troops sent to him, then two regiments may be ordered from South Calolina—to him—

U S. GRANT.

Lt. Genl.

Telegram received (at 11:00 A.M.), DNA, RG 94, Vol. Service Div., Letters Received, W2191 (VS) 1865; *ibid.*, RG 107, Telegrams Collected (Bound); *ibid.*, RG 108, Telegrams Received; copies (dated July 30, 1865), *ibid.*, Letters Sent; DLC-USG, V, 46, (dated July 31) 54, 109. *O.R.*, I, xlvii, part 3, 681. On July 29, 3:30 P.M., Bvt. Col. Theodore S. Bowers had telegraphed to USG. "Gen. Gilmore's present force is thirteen thousand, two hundred and twenty seven (13227). He proposes to reduce it to five thousand, eight hundred and thirty nine (5839), *first* by mustering out two thousand, six hundred and fifty three (2653) white troops; second, by sparing six (6) regiments of colored troops, numbering four thousand, seven hundred and thirty five (4735) for which he has no use. Of the colored troops three (3) regiments were raised in the north. He thinks he can not get along without retaining two thousand, five hundred (2500) white troops. Do you approve this? There are a number of permanent forts in the Department of the East that require garrisons of twenty five (25) men each. Gen. Meade ~~recommends~~ ~~reports~~ recommends that as he has no troops to put in charge of them that the Engineer Department hire civilians to take care of them. Would it not be well to order a regiment or tw[o] of these colored troops to report to Gen. Mead[e] for this and other duty?" LS (telegram sent), DNA, RG 107, Telegrams Collected (Bound); telegram sent, *ibid.*; copies, *ibid.*, RG 108, Letters Sent; DLC-USG, V, 46, 109. *O.R.*, I, xlvii, part 3, 681. On Aug. 8, Maj. Gen. Quincy A. Gillmore, Hilton Head, S. C., twice wrote to USG. "I have the honor to transmit herewith, copies of Gen'l Orders, numbered 1. to 12, c. s. from these Headquarters, in compliance with your order of July 31st/65." "I have the honor to transmit herewith, copies of General Orders. numbered 20 to 112 inclusive, and Circulars 3. 4 & 5 c. s. from 'Headquarters Dept of the South' in compliance with your order of July 31st 1865." Copies, DNA, RG 393, Dept. of the South and S. C., Letters Sent.

On July 31, Bvt. Brig. Gen. Edward D. Townsend telegraphed to USG. "A. J. Smith, Steele, Stanley, Mower, Merritt, Custer, G. A Smith, Gibbs, Doolittle and T. W. Sherman, are designated for Department of Louisiana and Texas. Since division of the Department who of these shall go to Texas?" ALS (telegram sent), *ibid.*, RG 107, Telegrams Collected (Unbound); telegram received (at 11:00 P.M.), *ibid.*, RG 108, Telegrams Received. On Aug. 1, USG, Boston, telegraphed to Townsend. "Assign all officers enumerated in your despatch except Doolittle and W T [*T. W.*] Sherman to Texas." Telegram received (at 11:00 A.M.), *ibid.*, RG 94, Letters Received, 815A 1865; copies, *ibid.*, RG 108, Letters Sent; DLC-USG, V, 46, 109.

To Edwin M. Stanton

Montreal Canada Aug. 8th 1865

HON. E. M. STANTON,
SECRETARY OF WAR,
SIR:

Since my arrival here I have seen Mr. Potter,[1] our Consul and find that in his judgment after investigation that the charges made against Dr. Montrose Pollen[2] of trying to extort from a witness in the conspiracy trial a contradiction of his testimony in the case is probably without foundation. As amnesty had been extended to Dr. Pollen, and was revoked in consequence of the charge I would respectfully recommend that he be paroled to go to St. Louis, to await whatever action may be thought necessary in his case. I would also recommend that Mr. Potter our Consul be authorized to parole Gen'l D. M. Frost[3] to go to St. Louis to await action in his case: General Frost voluntarily went before the American Consul at Quebec and took the proper steps and Oath for making his application for Amnesty.

Very respectfully
Your obt. Servt
U. S. GRANT
Lieut Gen'l

Copies, DLC-USG, V, 46, 109; DNA, RG 108, Letters Sent. See letter to Edwin M. Stanton, Sept. 7, 1865. USG had been invited to tour eastern Canada by Maj. Gen. Charles Hastings Doyle. Born in Ireland in 1805, Doyle had been appointed to command British forces in Nova Scotia in 1861. He visited USG at City Point in Oct., 1864, and again in March, 1865. James Harrison Wilson, *The Life of John A. Rawlins* (New York, 1916), p. 265; George R. Agassiz, ed., *Meade's Headquarters, 1863–1865: Letters of Colonel Theodore Lyman* . . . (Boston, 1922), pp. 244–45; *O.R.*, I, xlvi, part 2, 915. Probably in late Feb. or early March, Doyle, "Wormleys Hotel," wrote an unaddressed letter, presumably to

Secretary of War Edwin M. Stanton. "I have just arrived at Washington, and am anxious to obtain at your hands a similar favour to that which you were kind enough to grant me some months ago, viz. permission to revisit General Grant at City Point—Having already enjoyed his Kindness and hospitality I had delicacy in applying to you for permission to go until I first ascertained from him that I should not inconvenience him by going to him just now and I accordingly, wrote to him from New York to enquire whether my presence at this moment would be inconvenient You will see, by the accompanying letter, he will be happy to receive me, so I trust there will be no objection on your part to my going to see him—" ALS (undated), DNA, RG 107, Letters Received, D828 1865. On April 25, Doyle, Halifax, Nova Scotia, wrote to USG. "I only returned yesterday, from the Island of Bermuda, a distant part of my Command, and heard, for the first time, on landing, of the glorious termination (for so it may now be safely called,) of your campaign against Rebeldom, and also the dreadful intelligence of the assassination of the President and attempt to murder both Mr Seward and his Son, which I heard with dismay & sorrow, each and all of them having treated me with so much kindness upon both occasions of my visiting Washington—There seems to me to be every probability of the recovery of the two latter, and I hope if their lives are spared, you will Kindly, when they are well enough to see you, express to them my very sincere condolences upon all the sufferings they have undergone but, the *chief cause* for my taking up my pen is, to offer you my very sincere congratulations upon your continuous and glorious successes. How much I should have liked to remain another fortnight with you to have been an eye witness of this wind up of your Campaign. You have gained imperishabl[e] honor and glory, and I hope you will live to enjoy them for many a long year to come—In conclusion I have only to remind you of your *promise* to pay me a visit, and to bring Mrs Grant with you, that I may have an opportunity of repaying, in part at any rate, the Kindness and hospitality you so obligingly bestowed upon me—I hope, the Campaign being now over, there can be no doubt of your being able to carry your promises into effect— When you are able to make up your mind upon the subject you must let me Know, that I may not be absent from home when you come—. . . Pray remremb[er] me most Kindly to Mrs Grant and all your Staff—" ALS, USG 3. On Aug. 5, Doyle, Quebec, wrote to USG. "I am on a visit to Lord Monck, the Governor General of Canada, who lives at 'Spencer Wood,' about 2: miles from Quebec, and came in hoping to be the first to greet you on your arrival here, but find the Train by which you are expected cannot arrive here before *8. P. M.* and as we dine at *7.30* I am obliged to run away without seeing you, but I will be here tomorrow immediately after Church, and fix upon a plan of operations, & if you do not object to do so on *Sunday* I would propose to escort you over the Citadel, and to take you to the opposite side of the River, where the New Works are to be erected, they will I dare say interest you—We have but two Regiments of the Line and a couple or three Batteries of Artillery here, if you would like to see them out *on Monday*, on which day the Governor General hopes you will all do him the favor to dine with him—On *Tuesday* the Function of opening the Houses of Parliament, by the Governor General, will take place, and as it may amuse you & Mrs Grant to see that *Melodramatic Scene* of *Monarchical Govermt*, I hope to induce you to be present at it. It is much the same *form* as that observed by the Queen of England when she opens or closes in Person our Houses of Parliament—On Wednesday it is proposed to have a Pic Nic to the

Falls of Montmorenci, which are certainly the thing best worth seeing of any thing in this neighbourhood However we will talk all this over tomorrow morning—I have transacted all the business, Military, & Civil, that brought me to this part of the World, and am consequently entirely at your Service so long as you remain in the British Provinces—I hope to accompany you to Montreal, and when you have seen all that is worthy of note there, you will not I am sure 'go back' from your original *promise*, to visit me on my *own Dunghill at Halifax* to which I am on my way back—and which is, I assure you, quite as well worth seeing as anything here. With Kind regards to Mrs Grant & Col. Badeau & any others of your Staff who happen to be with you . . ." ALS (dated only "Saturday"), *ibid*. USG arrived at Quebec during the evening of Aug. 5. *New York Times*, Aug. 6, 7, 1865. See letters to Israel Washburn, July 17, 1865; Brig. Gen. John A. Rawlins, Aug. 20, 1865.

On Nov. 9, 1868, Doyle, Halifax, wrote to USG. "The newspapers, which always speak the truth (?) say you generally receive a *thousand* letters a Day! I ought not, therefore, to inflict an additional one upon you, but I promise to be short—I wrote at the termination of the War with the South to congratulate you upon the great victory you had achieved, and I beg now to express the great gratification I have experienced in finding you have beaten your *civil* enemy as completely as you did your former one, and I congratulate you, with great sincerity, on having attained the highest honor your Country can bestow upon you, in being chosen as President—The only drawback, in my mind, is, that it will almost put it out of your power to pay me the long promised visit—I I sincerely wish you may live long to enjoy your well merited honors, and, with kind remembrances to Mrs Grant I remain . . ." ALS, USG 3. On Jan. 12, 1869, Doyle wrote to USG. "Will you allow me to introduce to your notice the Bearer of this, the Honorable Mr Joseph Howe, one of our most distinguished Colonial Statesmen, who is about to visit your country, and I shall feel grateful for any attention you may be Kind enough to shew him, as he is a personal friend of mine—You have too much on hand to care about a long letter from me I shall therefore beg you kindly to remember me to Mrs Grant, and with every wish for your success in the very arduous duties you will soon be called upon to perform, I remain . . ." ALS, CtY.

On Aug. 2, 1865, Charles E. Barrett, "Grand Trunk Railway Co. of Canada," Portland, Maine, wrote to USG. "I called at your lodgings soon after one this P. M., in behalf of Mr C. J. Brydges, Managing Director of the Grand Trunk Rway Co., to tender to you a special train for yourself, family & staff, over the Road of the Company. Finding that you haved left the City not to return till quite late this evening, I beg to hand you, herewith, a Copy of Mr Brydges telegram to me, & will do myself the honor to call on you in the morning, at as early an hour as may suit your convenience, to ascertain your wishes & communicate them to Mr Brydges at Montreal." ALS, USG 3. On Aug. 3, Barrett wrote to USG. "The train for your accommodation upon the Grand Trunk Railway has been arranged by Mr Brydges, as you suggested to me this morning—to start from the Portland Station at 2 P. M. tomorrow—friday, & from Gorham at 10 ocloc[k] Saturday morning & proceed thence direct to Quebec. I shall be happy to meet you at the Station and shew you your Car. If you desire to invite any of your friends to accompany you upon the train, I beg you will consider it at your disposal." ALS, *ibid*. On Aug. 5, Mayor John P. Stockwell of Danville, Canada, and Mayor John Greenshutes of Shipton, Canada, wrote to USG. "The undersigned in behalf, and by order of Citizens of Danville Canada East, Cherishing though we do, sentiments of Loyalty toward Her Majesty Queen Victoria and the goverment under which we live, Nevertheless do hereby tender you a welcome to Canadian Soil and Canadian atmosphere for the time. And we desire also to express our utmost appreciation of your able and successful service during the late sore Conflict in the United States. And we assure you that in common with the Citizens of that neighbor Country we, too, rejoice in the glorious Issue of that war of defence for the Constitution, The vindication of its principles of Human Rights and Liberties and the demolition of Slavery which had been the darkest blot on the page of the Country's history. In all this, we see the warrant to hope that Order shall there soon be restored and that Amity shall henceforth prevail between the two countries now shaking hands. Please accept our hearty Congratulations." LS, *ibid.* On the same day, H. Baily telegraphed to USG. "Mayor and corporations of Sherbrooke the first place of importance you strike in Canada are anxious to present an address. I would give no answer without your approval" Telegram received, *ibid.* On the same day, Mayor J. G. Robertson, Sherbrooke, Canada, addressed USG. "On behalf of the Corporation and Citizens I have much pleasure in tendering you a hearty welcome to the Town of Sherbrooke. Your career while in command of the United States Army is was well known to our people, who watched the progress of the great struggle in which you were engaged with little—if any—less interest than was felt by Citizens of the United States. You may rest assured that our people generally sympathized with the people of the Northern States in their efforts to maintain the unity of the Republic, and the propogation of the principles of freedom to all classes of Community in your Country. While as Citizens of a portion of the British Empire we possess attachment to our beloved Queen, and our connection with the Mother Country at the same time we feel and rejoice that the United States enjoys those great blessings of civil and religious liberty, alike common to both countries and characteristic of our common origin, and calculated to produce in the highest degree those blessings which flow from self government in a free and enlightened Community. We deeply deplore the loss of life and property consequent upon the unhappy rebellion, and especially the loss of your late beloved President, and hope that the sacrifices made so cheerfully by your Citizens in support of the constituted authorities will only endear their institutions to their hearts and tend to perpetuate them to future generations. We congratulate the United States most sincerely on the restoration of peace to that country, and have much pleasure in having the opportunity of adding our humble tribute of respect and congratulation to you, for your brilliant, persevering and successful efforts in bringing the affairs of your Country to such a successful issue. We sincerely wish you,—General—, happiness and prosperity, and pray that yourself and family may have a pleasant journey through this part of the Queen's dominions, & may be long spared to enjoy the gratitude and love of your admiring Country and the satisfaction of having faithfully performed your duty." ADS, *ibid.* USG responded: *"Mr. Mayor.*—It gives me great pleasure to meet you. I assure you, sir, that I have the kindest feelings, not only towards Canada, but all the British provinces." *Galena Gazette*, Aug. 16, 1865. On Aug. 7, Monday, C. J. Brydges telegraphed to Bvt. Col. Orville E. Babcock. "I am very sorry you left Quebec before I had an opportunity of Seeing Genl Grant I Have instructed The Supt of The Western District Mr Spicer to see you tomorrow tuesday morning & He will make all the arrangement necessary for The Genls

Journey to Toronto & Detroit   If he purpose going There I regret very much that busines Compels me to remain here for two 2 or Three 3 days or I should have done myself The pleasure of accompanying Genl Grant on his Journey to Toronto"   Telegram received, USG 3. USG traveled to Montreal on Aug. 7 by steamboat, departing for Toronto by train the evening of Aug. 8. He arrived at Toronto during the morning of Aug. 9 and immediately embarked on a steamboat for Detroit via Niagara Falls. *New York Times*, Aug. 8–10, 1865; *Montreal Gazette*, Aug. 8–10, 1865.

On Aug. 8, Mayor W. H. Herrick, Oswego, N. Y., telegraphed to USG. "In behalf of the people of Oswego I have the honor of tendering you the hospilaties of our city and earnestly request that you will favor us with a call during your trip up Lake Ontario"   Telegram received, USG 3.

1. John F. Potter, born in 1817 in Maine, educated at Phillips Exeter Academy, served three terms as a Republican U.S. representative (1857–63) from Wis. Defeated for reelection in 1862, he was appointed U.S. consul gen. at Montreal.

2. Montrose A. Pallen, born in 1836 in Vicksburg, taken to St. Louis when young, graduated from St. Louis University Medical College in 1856. He served the C.S.A. as a medical officer until early 1863, when he was sent to Montreal to investigate the condition of prisoners held in the U.S. See *O.R.*, II, vi, 718. Captured while attempting to return to Richmond in 1864, Pallen was on parole in New York City until the termination of the war. At the trial of the conspirators in the assassination of President Abraham Lincoln, Sanford Conover (an alias of a man later imprisoned for perjury) testified that Pallen had been involved in a plot to poison the reservoirs supplying water to New York City. Benn Pitman, ed., *The Assassination of President Lincoln and the Trial of the Conspirators* (Cincinnati and New York, 1865), pp. 30–31; Seymour J. Frank, "The Conspiracy to Implicate the Confederate Leaders in Lincoln's Assassination," *Mississippi Valley Historical Review*, XL, 4 (March, 1954), 629–56; Edwin P. Jordan, "Conspiracy and the American Medical Association," *The Virginia Medical Monthly*, 99 (June, 1972), 637–42. On June 19, 1865, Potter wrote to Secretary of State William H. Seward forwarding Pallen's oath of allegiance. ALS, DNA, RG 59, Dispatches from U.S. Consuls in Montreal. Pallen met with USG on Aug. 8 in Montreal. *Montreal Gazette*, Aug. 9, 1865.

3. Daniel M. Frost, a prewar friend of USG (see *PUSG*, 1, 349n, 359, 360n; *ibid.*, 2, 5n), resigned as C.S.A. brig. gen. in late 1863 to take his family to Montreal after his wife had been banished from St. Louis. J. Thomas Scharf, *History of Saint Louis City and County* . . . (Philadelphia, 1883), I, 504. On Aug. 7, 1865, Frost, Quebec, wrote to President Andrew Johnson applying for amnesty and enclosing an oath of allegiance. ALS and DS, DNA, RG 94, Amnesty Papers, Mo. Docketing indicates that Frost was pardoned as of Oct. 23. *Ibid.*

To Edwin M. Stanton

_____

Detroit Mich
Aug 12th 1865 [2:00 P.M.]

HON EDWIN M STANTON
SECY OF WAR

I have heard nothing from Gen Sherman in answer to my dispatch directing a reduction of forces in the North West and for him to look into the Indian Expeditions and curtail them. They have been planned under Gen Popes direction and I am not posted as to the necessity of them—

I will go to St Louis in a few days and look into the matter myself—In the meantime I think all extraordinary requisitions should be disapproved—

I shall not go back to Washington for some weeks—

U S GRANT
Lt Gen

Telegram received (at 3:00 P.M.), DNA, RG 107, Telegrams Collected (Bound); copies, *ibid.*, RG 108, Letters Sent; DLC-USG, V, 46, 109. *O.R.*, I, xlviii, part 2, 1178–79. On Aug. 12, 1865, 9:30 A.M., Secretary of War Edwin M. Stanton telegraphed to USG. "The President is much concerned about the Indian Expedition. The Secretary of the Treasury declares his inability to meet an expenditure so large and unexpected and not sanctioned by the Government. Have you any information to relieve the Presidents anxiety or to satisfy him as to the object and design of the expedition, who planned it, whether Sherman has reduced it any, a and its probable results. Please answer speedily and state when you expect to return to Washington" ALS (telegram sent), DNA, RG 107, Telegrams Collected (Bound); telegram received (at Detroit, noon), *ibid.*, RG 108, Telegrams Received. *O.R.*, I, xlviii, part 2, 1178. See telegram and letter to Maj. Gen. William T. Sherman, July 28, Aug. 21, 1865. On Aug. 11, Maj. Thomas T. Eckert, act. asst. secretary of war, had telegraphed to USG. "Please telegraph me where a telegram will meet you tomorrow." Telegram sent, DNA, RG 107, Telegrams Collected (Bound). At 11:05 P.M., Bvt. Col. Orville E. Babcock, Port Edward, Ontario, telegraphed to Eckert. "To Detroit Mich." Telegram received (press), *ibid.* On Aug. 12, Babcock telegraphed to Eckert. "Cipher recd all OK" Telegram received (at 3:00 P.M.), *ibid.*

On July 19, J. C. Whiting and Co., Detroit, had written to USG. "Understanding that you intend to visit Detroit Mich. during this month or next. we beg leave to offer and extend to you the hospitalities of our boats should you wish to make a visit to the Lake Superior Country. It is a new and wonderful country for one of so recent growth and the pure and invigorating air of the Lakes is extremely beneficial to persons seeking relaxation. We enclose circulars and a 'Free Pass' for yourself and Lady. Should you honor us with its acceptance please to inform us of the date you would like to leave Detroit or Cleveland. We will take pleasure in reserving for you accomodations" ALS, USG 3. Docketing indicates that an indefinite answer was sent on July 23. *Ibid.*

On July 25, Maj. Gen. Edward O. C. Ord, Detroit, telegraphed to USG. "do you expect to visit us soon; if so, when" ALS (telegram sent), Ord Papers, CU-B. On the same day, Babcock, West Point, N. Y., telegraphed to Ord. "Shall be with you in about two (2) weeks" Telegram received (at 4:45 P.M.), *ibid.* On Aug. 8, Ord telegraphed to Babcock. "When can I meet the General at Niagara.—" Telegram sent, *ibid.* On the same day, Tuesday, Babcock, Montreal, telegraphed to Ord. "Genl Grant will be in Detroit Friday" Telegram received (at 8:10 P.M.), *ibid.* On Aug. 11, Babcock, Sarnia, Ontario, telegraphed to Ord. "Gen Grant will leave here for Detroit by rail at nine (9) a m tomorrow Saturday" Telegram received, *ibid.* Ord noted on the telegram received: "recd 15th August" ANS, *ibid.*

On Aug. 11, S. Dow Elwood, president, Detroit City Council, wrote to USG, sending resolutions passed by the council welcoming him to Detroit. ADS, USG 3. On Aug. 12, Saturday, Elwood wrote to Bvt. Col. Adam Badeau. "Your favor acknowledging the receipt of the Resolutions of the Common Council of this City is at hand—The Common Council with the City officials will be pleased to Call upon Genl Grant at Monday Morning Next at 9½ o. c." ALS, *ibid.* USG arrived at Detroit during the morning of Aug. 12, staying at the Biddle House. During the evening, he appeared on the hotel balcony before a large crowd and, after a lengthy welcoming address by Theodore Romeyn, reportedly responded: "I bid you all good night." *New York Times*, Aug. 17, 1865. The crowd continued calling for a speech by USG, but he refused. An account of the reaction of his son, Jesse Root Grant, Jr., to USG's refusal to speak is in John Y. Simon, ed., *The Personal Memoirs of Julia Dent Grant* (New York, 1975), pp. 163–64. See also Silas Farmer, *History of Detroit and Wayne County and Early Michigan* (Detroit, 1890; reprinted, 1969), p. 106. On Aug. 14, C. N. LaCroix *et al.*, Association de Bienfaisance Lafayette, wrote to USG making him an honorary member. ADS (in French—thirteen signatures), USG 3. USG left Detroit on Aug. 15, 4:00 P.M., for Chicago on the Michigan Central Railroad, making brief stops at towns along the route where large crowds had gathered. At Kalamazoo, USG reportedly spoke: "I am not going to reply to the address, gentlemen: I could not do so, if I should try." *New York Times*, Aug. 20, 1865. USG arrived in Chicago during the morning of Aug. 16, taking rooms at the Tremont House, and dined at the home of J. Russell Jones that evening. See *Galena Gazette*, Aug. 17, 1865. USG left Chicago for Galena on Aug. 18. *Chicago Tribune*, Aug. 18, 1865.

On Aug. 19, James W. Romeyn *et al.* wrote to USG. "We have the honor to enclose to you the report of the 'Committee on Organization' of the 'Monument Association' of the State of Michigan. We have, also, the honor to inform you that at a meeting of the 'Board of Directors' of said Association held Aug 11th 1865. at the Governors room in this city, we were directed by a resolution passed unanimously, to invite you to be present at the inauguration ceremonies to take place at *Young Mens Hall* in this city Aug 31st 1865. Feeling assured of your sympathy in the purpose of our Association, we can only express, the

hope and our earnest desire, that you will notify us of your acceptance, and that
you will contribute by the inspiration of your presence to the successful issue
of an undertaking, second only to the *one* in which your powers of mind and
heart have for the last four years been engaged, a period the annals of which
you have been instrumental in rendering illustrious by glorious achievements."
ALS (three signatures), USG 3. See Farmer, *History of Detroit . . .* , pp.
311–12.

To Maj. Gen. Philip H. Sheridan

Detroit Mich. Aug. 13th 1865 [*10:00* P.M.]

MAJ. GEN. P. H. SHERIDAN
NEW ORLEANS, LA.

The order for muster out in your command was made with the
view of avoiding the necessity of sending Cavalry horses to you
and not with any idea that your force should be reduced to the
smallest wants for keeping Texas in the traces. The Imperial
troops in Mixico still require watching and before all the seed of
the rebellion can be regarded as crushed out they must go back to
their homes. We must hold ourselves ready to demand this.

U. S. GRANT
Lieut. Gen'l

Telegram, copies, DLC-USG, V, 46, 109; DNA, RG 108, Letters Sent; (in-
complete) USG 3. *O.R.*, I, xlviii, part 2, 1180. On Aug. 21, 1865, Monday, 1:00
P.M. and 1:30 P.M., Maj. Gen. Philip H. Sheridan twice telegraphed to Brig.
Gen. John A. Rawlins. "If the regular cavalry regements were ordered to Texas
I could mount and equip them from the Vol. cavalry now there & muster most of
it out—This would be a great saving to the Govt. & I strongly recommend it
The muster out of the armies of the Potomac & Tennessee has given the troops
such good grounds to ask for the same that it is astonishing how quietly they
have behaved—When I go to Texas I will at least muster out two regements of
cavalry & perhaps some of the fourth Corps—I do not intend to call on the Govt
for cavalry horses for the cavalry force in Texas" "I will leave here for Texas
on next Thursday. All telegrams or communications will be sent after me, or
telegrams can reach me at Galveston Via St Louis—" Telegrams received (the
first at 9:00 P.M., the second at 7:30 P.M.), DNA, RG 107, Telegrams Collected
(Bound); *ibid.*, RG 108, Telegrams Received; copies, DLC-USG, V, 54; DLC-
Philip H. Sheridan. *O.R.*, I, xlviii, part 2, 1198. On Aug. 22, 11:00 A.M., Secretary of War Edwin M. Stanton telegraphed to USG. "Sheridan asks all the
regular cavalry to be sent to him in order that he may muster out volunteer
cavalry. Is there any objection to this? Schofield is here. He is going to France

Paris." ALS (telegram sent), DNA, RG 107, Telegrams Collected (Bound); telegram received (at Galena), *ibid.*, RG 108, Telegrams Received. At 6:00 P.M., USG telegraphed to Stanton. "All regular cavalry not absolutely necessary where it now is might be sent to Genl Sheridan but I would not advise the interferences of any of it now in Genl Popes Dept" Telegram received (on Aug. 23, 1:35 A.M.), *ibid.*, RG 107, Telegrams Collected (Bound); copies, *ibid.*, RG 94, Letters Received, 650G 1865; (no addressee—marked as sent at 7:00 P.M.) *ibid.*, RG 108, Letters Sent; DLC-USG, V, 46, 109. *O.R.*, I, xlviii, part 2, 1200.

On Sept. 6, 9:00 A.M., USG, Galena, telegraphed to Sheridan. "Reduce the force in all your Division except Texas by mustering out troops as low as the service will bear." Telegram, copies, DLC-USG, V, 46, 109; DNA, RG 108, Letters Sent. *O.R.*, I, xlviii, part 2, 1223. On Sept. 20, Sheridan, New Orleans, telegraphed to Rawlins. "I have directed the muster out of three thousand men present for duty, or about forty five hundred, present and absent of the Fourth corps; also the muster out of three regiments of cavalry and the fourth and Seventh Massachusetts Batteries—All these troops are in Texas, but this will not effect the threatening force. The War Department has ordered the muster out of all colored troops enlisted at the north belonging to the Twenty fifth (25th) corps, and mustering officer has been sent to execute the order—I will direct Genl Canby to muster out two thousand white troops in his Department, and he can spare six thousand colored if authority is sent to me to muster them out. This will leave Gen Canby about two thousand white troops of all arms and about ten thousand colored troops, I have also directed Gen Foster to muster out the Second Maine Cavalry in the Department of Florida," Telegram received (on Sept. 21, 1:25 P.M.), DNA, RG 107, Telegrams Collected (Bound); *ibid.*, RG 108, Telegrams Received; copies, DLC-USG, V, 54; DLC-Philip H. Sheridan. *O.R.*, I, xlviii, part 2, 1235. On Oct. 7, Sheridan telegraphed to USG. "There is much dissatisfaction on the part of troops in Texas on account of muster out leading to a disposition to destroy or take but little care of public property. I can spare a large number of Infantry and Cavalry so soon as the Lieut Genl deems the necessity of a threatening force obviated. I have already mustered out of the present strength of the 4th Corps three thousand men and will muster out more as they are on an interior line unless ordered to the contrary I will muster out three Regts more of Cavalry as soon as the 4th U S gets here. The muster of the Colored regiments raised in the north is going on" Telegram received (on Oct. 8, 1:00 A.M.), DNA, RG 107, Telegrams Collected (Bound); (press) *ibid.*; *ibid.*, RG 108, Telegrams Received; copies, DLC-USG, V, 54; DLC-Philip H. Sheridan. *O.R.*, I, xlviii, part 2, 1237–38. See *ibid.*, p. 1244. On Oct. 13, 11:30 A.M., USG telegraphed to Sheridan. "You may go on with the muster out of Volunteers as proposed in your despatch of 7th The 6th Regular Cavalry is ordered to report to you and three or more Regular Infantry regiments will be sent, among them two, three battalion regiments." Telegram sent, DNA, RG 107, Telegrams Collected (Bound); copies, *ibid.*, RG 108, Letters Sent; DLC-USG, V, 46, 109. *O.R.*, I, xlviii, part 2, 1240. On Oct. 19, Sheridan telegraphed to Rawlins. "Since the receipt of the Telegram of the Lieut Gen of october thirteenth I have ordered the muster out of all, the regiments of the provisional divisions of the fourth army Corps except three also three reg'ts of Cavalry also one thousand men of the strength present for duty from the command of maj Gen Mower in the Eastern Dist of Texas I will continue the muster out gradually & in accordance with our ability to transport the troops back" Telegram received (on Oct. 21, 1:00 P.M.), DNA, RG 107, Telegrams Collected (Bound); *ibid.*, RG 108, Telegrams Received; copies, DLC-USG, V, 54; DLC-Philip H. Sheridan. *O.R.*, I, xlviii, part 2, 1242.

On Oct. 28, 1:35 P.M., USG telegraphed to Sheridan. "You may discontinue mustering out troops in Texas. Those who have been notified may go out but reduce no further." ALS (telegram sent), DNA, RG 107, Telegrams Collected (Bound); telegram sent, *ibid.*; copies, *ibid.*, RG 108, Letters Sent; DLC-USG, V, 46, 109. *O.R.*, I, xlviii, part 2, 1248. On Oct. 30, 11:00 A.M., Sheridan telegraphed to Rawlins. "The telegram from Lieut Genl Grant, discontinuing the muster out of troops in Texas has been received, and acted upon," Telegram received (on Nov. 1, 1:30 P.M.), DNA, RG 107, Telegrams Collected (Bound); *ibid.*, RG 108, Telegrams Received; copies, DLC-USG, V, 54; DLC-Philip H. Sheridan. *O.R.*, I, xlviii, part 2, 1249.

To Brig. Gen. John A. Rawlins

Galena Ill. August 20th 1865.

DEAR RAWLINS,

You will see from the papers how Galena spread herself [o]n Friday last in giving me a welcome home.[1] It was very flattering though some what embarrassing. The same might be said of the whole journey through Canada. You have, no doubt, seen reported what I said in Canada relative to affairs in Mexico![2] All officials in Canada, Civil and Military, called on me. They show by their questions and conversation that they feared a rupture between the United States and Great Britain, and that they would use all honorable means of averting such a calamity. What I am reported to have said is nearly true except I did not say how many troops we had on the Rio Grande, nor did I say what Government would do. I spoke freely, however, of my own feeling in the matter and what I believed to be the feeling of the American people.

Your letter enclosing one for me to sign recommending the assignment of Col. Morgan was received the evening of my arrival here. You will find it signed and enclosed herewith.

I regret that I did not write to you to remain here as long as you found your health benefited by the stay. If you think a winter of quiet, in this latitude, advantageous why not come here and spend the Fall and Winter? The house presented to me[3] by the kindness of the Citizens is entirely at your service if you choose to do so. You will find it very comfortable and containing everything necessary for housekeeping.

I shall not return to Washington before the 1st. of October unless called there.[4] I have had a severe cold and cough, with sore throat, almost ever since I left until the last two days. At Detroit begining to be alarmed about it I commenced taking medicine and care and I believe am getting well. I have gained in flesh until I now weigh 152 pounds, two pounds more than my highest ambition.

I enclose you with this a letter from J. H. Stokes which astonishes me.[5] I have never done him an unkindness that I am aware of. Burnside and Osborn former President of the Ill. C. R. R. made such a statement against him that, taking it for ~~granted~~ true, I recommended his muster out. After receiving his statement in the matter charged I bilived great injustice had been done him. I so wrote ~~to~~ and so stated in writing and in conversation with the Sec. of War. I recommended the revocation of the order mustering him out and I did all else that he asked me to do to rectify the injury so far as it could be done. The Sec. of War must have turned him off bluntly throwing all blame for what has been done on me. I wish you would see the Sec. and ask him for me to have Stokes placed as near right as ~~possible~~ law will allow. Stokes' letter is uncalled for and relieves me of all obligation to do anything to assist him. But beliving that he has suffered innocently, and not knowing but he may have heard something to lead him to think I may have acted insincerely, I want you to do for him what is just.

Remember me to all the Staff. When any of you write I should like to hear how my horses flourish.

Yours Truly
U. S. GRANT.
Lt. Gen.

Copy, Wy-Ar. On Aug. 14, 1865, Brig. Gen. John A. Rawlins wrote to USG. "Enclosed please find an application to have Col Morgan assigned to duty at Fort Leavenworth. This perfectly agreeable ~~to~~ to the Col. whether he gets the assignment with the rank of Col or only as Captain, but while others have the position of Colonel for the same services he woul[d] like it also. Morgan purpose is very commendable, & I think if some other staff officers in the country would seek duty in their respective corps it would greatly reduce the number on fancy duty. We are working away on the records to accompany your report and getting along quite well   I am as well as usual but yesterday had considerable bleeding of the throat   Docters in NewYork say my lungs are sound,   I work but about four hours a day and am taking things quite leisurely for me. We have ~~business~~ no business to speak of, in the office   every thing goes to the Adjt Genls Office There is nothing here specially to call you back, but as a matter of policy I think it would be well for you to come back for a few days, there seems from some cause or other to be a sort of an undersstanding that you will be back about the 25th inst but that you will return again   Every body here is well. Comstock is back. So is Williams & Dent, but Williams has gone we all suppose to get married. Mrs Rawlins & family are well   all send regards to yourself and family & the members of the staff with you   Please sign the recommendation if you approve of it & return it to me and I will hand it to the secretary   Genl. Eaton is very anxious for it." ALS, Morristown National Historical Park, Morristown, N. J. On Aug. 20, USG, Galena, wrote to Secretary of War Edwin M. Stanton. "I would respectfully recommend that Fort Leavenworth be made a principal subsistence depôt, and that Brevet Colonel M. R. Morgan, USA., now on duty as Inspector, Subsistence Department, be assigned to it with the rank of Colonel." LS, DNA, RG 94, Letters Received, 925A 1865.

1. USG left Chicago by train during the morning of Aug. 18 for Galena, making brief stops at Elgin, Marengo, Belvidere, Rockford, Freeport, and Warren to acknowledge large crowds. *Galena Gazette*, Aug. 19, 1865. Galena citizens had made extensive preparations to welcome USG home. *Ibid.*, July 27, 29, 31, Aug. 5, 7, 14, 1865. U.S. Representative Elihu B. Washburne delivered the welcoming address. *Ibid.*, Aug. 19, 1865. USG responded: "MY FRIENDS AND FELLOW CITIZENS OF THE CITY OF GALENA: I am truly glad to meet you at this time, and I have requested Mr. Vincent, who came with me on the train, to return to you my very sincere thanks for this demonstration." *Ibid.* John H. Vincent spoke in USG's behalf. See Leon H. Vincent, *John Heyl Vincent: A Biographical Sketch* (New York, 1925; reprinted, 1970), pp. 101–3; *PUSG*, 5, 133.

On Aug. 19, Mayor John Thompson, Dubuque, Iowa, wrote to Washburne extending an invitation for USG to attend a reception in his honor. ALS, DLC-Elihu B. Washburne. USG visited Dubuque on Aug. 23, and Bvt. Maj. Gen. William Vandever delivered the welcoming address. *Galena Weekly Gazette*, Aug. 29, 1865. USG responded: "LADIES AND GENTLEMEN:—I am glad to meet you. You all know I am not accustomed to making speeches, and if I were, I could not find words to express to you my thanks for this hearty welcome." *Ibid.* Washburne then addressed the audience, and USG returned to Galena shortly after 10:00 P.M. *Ibid.*

On Aug. 20, Washburne wrote to his brother, former Maj. Gen. Cadwallader C. Washburn. "Genl. Grant thinks of leaving on the 'Itaska' for Saint Pauls next Thursday. If he actually leave I will telegraph you. The boat might stop at La-Crosse for an hour, so that the people could see him if they wished. I will speak to the General about Whittlesey. He had a very fine reception on his return home. The Genl will return on same boat. All well." ALS, WHi. USG started for

St. Paul, Minn., aboard the *Itasca* on Thursday, Aug. 24, meeting Washburn near La Crosse, Wis., on Aug. 25. USG arrived at St. Paul during the morning of Aug. 26, and responded to a welcoming address. "Ladies and Gentleman: It is not my habit to make speeches but I thank you for this very cordial welcome which you have given me to St. Paul" *Galena Weekly Gazette*, Sept. 5, 1865. That evening, he responded to another address. "Gentlemen and Firemen of St. Paul. I am just about to leave, after a very pleasant visit to your city and State. I am much obliged to you for the cordial welcome I have received. Good night." *Ibid*. USG then left St. Paul, returning to Galena on Aug. 28. On the same day, USG, Julia Dent Grant, Jesse Root Grant *et al*., Dunleith, Ill., signed a testimonial. "The undersigned, passengers on board the North Western Packet Company's steamer 'Itasca,' on the trip from Dunleith to Saint Paul and return, just completed, before leaving the boat, beg leave to tender their most sincere thanks to Capt. N. F. Webb for his skill and promptness exhibited in the management of his boat, his polite and gentlemanly attentions and his considerate regard for our comfort and pleasure. . . ." Unidentified newspaper clipping, Babcock Papers, ICN.

Also on Aug. 28, USG as president, Jo Daviess Soldiers' Monument Association, signed an unknown number of membership certificates. Several examples are in ICHi.

During the evening of Sept. 3, USG traveled by train to Milwaukee, arriving on Sept. 4, 3:00 A.M. Former Wis. Governor Edward Salomon addressed USG at a late morning reception. *Galena Weekly Gazette*, Sept. 12, 1865. USG responded: "*Ladies and Gentlemen*: Senator Doolittle has kindly consented to speak in my behalf today, and to express to you the thanks which I would express for this very hearty welcome." *Ibid*. U.S. Senator James R. Doolittle of Wis. then addressed the audience, followed by brief remarks by Maj. Gen. John Pope. *Ibid*. USG left Milwaukee by train during the morning of Sept. 5, attended the Illinois State Fair in Chicago that afternoon, left Chicago at 10:00 P.M., and returned to Galena on Sept. 6, 7:00 A.M. On Aug. 17, John P. Reynolds, secretary, Illinois State Agricultural Society, Springfield, had written to USG. "Be kind enough to accept the enclosed Complimentary Ticket for the coming State Fair of Illinois & permit me to express the sincere hope that it will be your pleasure to attend. I beg to assure you, General, that this is not a deliberate attempt to increase the attractions of the Fair by placing a public favorite on Exhibition at the sacrifice of all pleasure to himself. This Fair will certainly be a very large & excellent Exhibition of the industry of the Northwest & as such will present subjects of much interest to one whose sympathy with that industry is so well understood as is yours—" ALS, USG 3. A complimentary ticket for USG is in Babcock Papers, ICN.

On Sept. 9, 11:00 A.M., USG traveled to Freeport by train, arriving at 1:00 P.M., to attend a reception in his honor, and was met at the depot by an estimated 10,000 people. Thomas J. Turner addressed USG. *Galena Weekly Gazette*, Sept. 12, 1865. USG responded: "Ladies and Gentlemen: I know that none of you will expect a speech from me. I thank you for this hearty welcome, and will leave speech making to those who will do it better than I can. Again I thank you." *Ibid*. Speeches followed by Washburne, Maj. Gen. John A. Logan, and Governor Richard J. Oglesby of Ill. *Ibid*.

On Aug. 17, Oglesby had telegraphed to USG. "Our people are anxious to see you. What day can you be in Springfield? You have not forgotten your promise to visit us in August, with your family" *Illinois State Journal*, Aug. 18, 1865. On the same day, Bvt. Col. Orville E. Babcock telegraphed to Oglesby. "General Grant directs me to say, that he intends to make his promise good, but cannot say the exact time now. Will give you notice." *Ibid*. On Aug. 23, John M. Douglas, president, Illinois Central Railroad, wrote to USG. "Having learned that you intend to visit St Louis at an early day, I have the honor to tender to yourself and friends the courtesies of the Road, and shall be happy to place at your disposal a special train to be run directly to St. Louis by way of Springfield or any other route you may elect. Hon. E. B. Washburne has been advised of our intentions in this matter, and himself and friends requested to accompany you. Please advise me of the time you intend to leave Galena that the necessary preparations may be made in due season." ALS, USG 3. On the same day, Douglas wrote a similar letter to Washburne. ALS, DLC-Elihu B. Washburne. On Sept. 7, Douglas wrote to Bvt. Col. Adam Badeau. "The special train that is to convey the Genl & party from Galena to Springfield will leave Galena on tuesday morning Sept 12th at 7 oclock promptly   Train will arrive in Springfield at four 4 oclock p. m" Copy, USG 3. USG ended his visit to Galena on Sept. 12, leaving by train at 7:00 A.M., stopping briefly at Bloomington (at 1:00 P.M.), and arriving in Springfield as scheduled. After a procession to the capitol, U.S. Representative Shelby M. Cullom of Ill. delivered the welcoming address. *Illinois State Journal*, Sept. 13, 1865. USG responded: *"Fellow Citizens, Ladies and Gentlemen:*—It has long been known to you all that I never make a speech, but I thank you for this gratifying reception. There are others here who will express the thanks I cannot utter." *Ibid*. Speeches followed by Logan and Oglesby. USG spent several hours that evening at a reception at the Governor's mansion. USG left Springfield during the morning of Sept. 13, arriving at St. Louis at 2:00 P.M.

2. While in Canada, USG had reportedly spoken "without reserve to several persons on the Mexican question. He said that he had placed one hundred thousand men on the Rio Grande, as an army of observation, and that the French would have to leave Mexico peaceably, if they chose, but forcibly if they refused. The situation of Mexico he looked upon as one which had been created by the rebellion, and the rebellion would really not be overcome until MAXIMILAN was compelled to depart, and the Mexican people allowed to organize a government without foreign interference. With regard to the relations between the United States and England he did not think the present friendly state would be disturbed, unless complications ensued by reason of England's mixing herself up with France in the Mexican question." *New York Times*, Aug. 10, 1865. See letter to Edwin M. Stanton, Aug. 8, 1865.

3. Washburne and other prominent Galena citizens purchased a furnished house and presented it to USG on Aug. 18. A deed had been recorded in USG's name on Aug. 15. USG 3. See John Y. Simon, ed., *The Personal Memoirs of Julia Dent Grant* (New York, 1975), p. 90; Thomas A. Campbell, Jr., "The U. S. Grant Home State Historic Site," *Historic Illinois*, I, 5 (Feb., 1979). Plans for the house are in Grant Family Papers, ICarbS.

4. On Aug. 23, 1:30 P.M., Bvt. Col. Theodore S. Bowers telegraphed to USG. "Do you intend to return to Washington for a few days. There are some matters here awaiting your action." ALS (telegram sent), DNA, RG 107, Telegrams Collected (Bound); telegram sent, *ibid*.; telegram received (at Galena), *ibid*., RG 108, Telegrams Received.

5. On June 24, James H. Stokes, Chicago, wrote to USG. "I have visited

Washington twice to see you, but finding you absent, saw Col Bowers A. A. G—
Col Bowers stated to me explicitly that on your return he would relate to you
the purpose of my visit and write me, but for some reason I have not heard from
him—For nearly Eleven months, I have been waiting the promised revocation of
this order mustering me out of service—During this time I have been withheld
from any business arrangements by the odium of this injustice, and in the constant expectation that notice of my restoration would be received—When last
in Washington May 1st. 65. I was told by the Secty of War, that finding the
revocation of the order which he had stated to M Washburne he had directed,
to be impracticable, that the President had nominated and that I had been
confirmed to a new commission, and that the commission had been made out,
signed and was then in the hands of the President waiting his signature—Ex
Senator Browning of Ill now writes of date June 21st that he went to the Adjt
Genls office and was told by him that the Commission was with the President
and that he then went to the President who told him that he had signed all the
Commissions and returned them to the War Dept—My purpose General is
simply to ask some definite official action—I do not expect justice, but I cannot
believe that the War Dept could degrade itself to an underground persecution,
and I therefore ask of you the simple act, to have me notified of its intentions—
There must be some mode of reaching this 'toss in the Blanket to which I am
subjected'—and if the purpose is to forbid my restoration by this 'cant File
system', it is a savage exercise of position, to frustrate by a continuance of this
odium over me, any effort to obtain civil employment—I have not had the means
General, even thus far to await this slow action of the War Dept—and to continue it in return for services, to render which I made great personal sacrifices,
is too base to be admitted—" ALS, *ibid.*, Letters Received. On Aug. 9, Stokes
wrote a letter received at USG's hd. qrs. acknowledging his promotion. *Ibid.*,
Register of Letters Received. On Aug. 23, Bowers wrote to the AG. "Please order
Brigadier General James H. Stokes, U S Vols., to proceed to his place of residence,
and from there report by letter to the Adjutant General of the Army for orders."
LS, *ibid.*, RG 94, Letters Received, 931A 1865. See letter to Edwin M. Stanton,
July 20, 1865.

To Maj. Gen. William T. Sherman

Galena, Ills., Aug 21st *1865*

MAJOR GENERAL W. T. SHERMAN
COMDG. MILITARY DIV. OF THE MISS.
GENERAL:

Dispatches from Washington, received whilst I was in Detroit,
express great alarm at the magnitude of requisitions coming in for
expeditions fitting out to go on Indian hunts. They also ask me if

they were fitted out under my orders and if there is a necessity for them

Now that the Indians cannot expect aid from the rebels by making us spend so much force in another direction, it looks to me as if the number of troops sent in each party might be materially reduced. The treaty which will soon be in progress at Fort Gibson, I. T., possibly renders some of the expeditions which Gen Pope contemplated sending out altogether unnecessary. I think also that Missouri, Arkansas and Kansas might now be stripped pretty bare of troops, and especially of cavalry. This at least would apply to Kansas and Missouri.

I wish you would give the subject of reducing the forces within your command attention, and let Gen Rawlins know what you think can be done.[1] I will be in St Louis about the 12th of next month.

Yours truly

[U. S. GRANT]

Lieutenant General.

Copies, DNA, RG 94, Vol. Service Div., Letters Received, W2191 (VS) 1865; *ibid.*, RG 108, Letters Sent; DLC-USG, V, 46, 109. *O.R.*, I, xlviii, part 2, 1199. On Aug. 19, 1865, USG, Galena, telegraphed to Secretary of War Edwin M. Stanton. "I have recd applications from several paroled prisoners of war for permission to leave the country I would recommend the publication of an order authorizing any paroled prisoner who chooses to leave the country not to return without authority" Telegram received (at 10:00 P.M.), DNA, RG 107, Telegrams Collected (Bound); copies, *ibid.*, RG 108, Letters Sent; DLC-USG, V, 46, 109. *O.R.*, II, viii, 719. On Aug. 21, 1:30 P.M., Stanton telegraphed to USG. "Your despatches concerning the further reduction of troops and leave o̶f̶ to paroled rebels to D̶e̶p̶a̶r̶t̶ leave the Country have been received. Orders have been given the Adjutant General to go on with the reduction of the force to such extent as may be deemed safe by the Commanding officers and I have reccommended the order to be made f̶o̶ in respect to paroled rebels. Nothing of importance has transpired since your departm̶e̶n̶ture. No satisfactory information has been received in respect to the Indian Expedition or the measures taken to reduce its dimensions and expense. This subject still occupies the anxious consideration of the President and of this Department. General Meade has been directed to visit the Southern portion of his Command in order to see to the discipline o̶f̶ ̶t̶h̶e̶ and administration of the Military and of the Freedman's bureau concerning which some complaint has been made." ALS (telegram sent), DNA, RG 107, Telegrams Collected (Bound); telegram received (at Galena, marked as sent at 1:00 P.M.), *ibid.*, RG 108, Telegrams Received. *O.R.*, I, xlviii, part 2, 1197–98. The telegram received included a postscript: "A rather

warm day." Telegram received, DNA, RG 108, Telegrams Received. At 7:00
p.m., USG telegraphed to Stanton. "Before receiving your dispatch I wrote to
Gen. Sherman on the subject of reduction of troops in the West, and for information concerning Indian Expeditions to be sent to Gen Rawlins [g]iving him at
the same time my views, Copies of my letters forwarded to Gen Rawlins today."
Telegram received (on Aug. 22, 1:20 p.m.), *ibid.*, RG 107, Telegrams Collected
(Bound); copies, *ibid.*, RG 108, Letters Sent; DLC-USG, V, 46, 109. *O.R.*, I,
xlviii, part 2, 1197. Bvt. Col. Theodore S. Bowers later wrote an undated memorandum for Maj. Thomas M. Vincent, AGO. "Upon inquiry I find that Gen.
Rawlins had reference in his conversation with you, to the general instructions
to Department Commanders to reduce, and the promise of Dodge to promptly
comply with them. Herewith I hand you copies of letters from Grant to Sherman
and Thomas on the subject of reduction—received this morning" ADS, DNA,
RG 94, Vol. Service Div., Letters Received, W2191 (VS) 1865. See following
letter.

1. On Aug. 22, Maj. Gen. William T. Sherman wrote a letter received at
USG's hd. qrs. reporting on "reduction of forces and expenses on the Plains,
advocates said reduction &c.," DNA, RG 108, Register of Letters Received.
On Sept. 7, Brig. Gen. John A. Rawlins endorsed this letter. "Respy. forwarded
to the Secty. of war." Copy, *ibid.* On Aug. 25, Maj. Gen. John Pope, St. Louis,
wrote a lengthy letter to Sherman answering USG's and Stanton's inquiries. LS,
ibid., RG 94, Letters Received, 1807M 1865. *O.R.*, I, xlviii, part 2, 1210–11.
On Aug. 28, Sherman endorsed this letter. "Respectfully forwarded to Genl
Rawlins Chief of Staff, and his attention invited to the Contents, also request
that it be laid before the Sec of War." AES, DNA, RG 94, Letters Received,
1807M 1865.

To Maj. Gen. George H. Thomas

Galena, Ills., Aug. 21st *1865*

Maj. Gen. G. H. Thomas
Comdg. Mil. Div.
Gen'l.

It is now the desire of Government to reduce the military force
of the Country and expenses of the Government, all that it is possible. Under the authority given you in orders you can muster out
of service any organization you may deem dispensable. My own
views are that two regiments of cavalry will be sufficient to retain
in service for the whole State of Tennessee, and one regiment for

each of the other States in your Militay Division, except Kentucky where I would keep none. I would also think five thousand infantry for Tennessee and three thousand for Kentucky—mostly colored—sufficient. The number of posts garrisoned ought to be reduced to three or four in each State from which troops can be sent to any post where they may be required either to suppress hostilities or to aid the civil laws. Give me information of what you are doing and think you can safely yet do in the way of reducing the force at your command.

I expect to visit Nashville before returning to Washington. Your answer to this letter will reach me here.

> Very Respectfully
> Your Obdt Servant
> [U. S. GRANT]
> Lieutenant General.

Copies, DNA, RG 94, Vol. Service Div., Letters Received, W2191 (VS) 1865; (misdated Aug. 26, 1865) *ibid.*, RG 108, Letters Sent; DLC-USG, V, 46, 109. Misdated Aug. 26 in *O.R.*, I, xlix, part 2, 1106. See preceding letter. On Aug. 14, 6:30 P.M., USG, Detroit, telegraphed to Secretary of War Edwin M. Stanton. "Now that the elections are over in Kentucky and Tennessee I think a large number of troops might be mustered out from those two States. I would recommend that General Thomas be directed to muster out all he can dispense with, especially of Cavalry" Telegram received (at 10:00 P.M.), DNA, RG 107, Telegrams Collected (Bound); copies, *ibid.*, RG 108, Letters Sent; DLC-USG, V, 46, 109. *O.R.*, I, xlix, part 2, 1100. On Aug. 15, Maj. Thomas M. Vincent, AGO, telegraphed to Maj. Gen. George H. Thomas transmitting USG's telegram to Stanton. ADfS (telegram sent), DNA, RG 94, Vol. Service Div., Letters Received, W2191 (VS) 1865; telegram sent, *ibid.*, RG 107, Telegrams Collected (Bound); copies, *ibid.*, RG 393, Military Div. of the Tenn., Telegrams Received; (sent by mail) *ibid.*, Dept. of the Tenn., Letters Received.

On Aug. 23, Thomas telegraphed to USG. "I have the honor to acknowledge the receipt this day of your letter of the 21st inst. Since the receipt by me of your telegram from Detroit to the Secretary of War, advising, that I be instructed to muster out of service all the white troops, that can be spared, I have directed Gen'l's Woods, Steedman and Stoneman to report the smallest number of white troops they can get along with. I have received Gen'l Stoneman's Report and have ordered him to muster out all white Volunteer troops in his Department, except the 1st Minn. Heavy Arty: the 12th Ohio Vol. Cav'y, the 8th and 11th Mich Cav'y. and the 6th Indiana. I shall to day order him to muster out the 1st Minn. Heavy Arty, the 8th Michigan and 6th Indiana Cavalry. He will then have under his Command the 16th U. S. Infantry, one Battery of U. S. Light Art'y. the 1st and 3d U. S. Cold Heavy Art'y and two Batteries of Light Art'y and the 3d U. S. Cold Cav'y at Memphis. One Battery of Light Arty, the 15th 17th and 101st

U. S. Cold Inft'y at Nashville The 12th 13th and 111th U. S. Cold Inft'y on North-Western Rail-Road. The 110th U S. Cold Inft'y at Gallatin. The 14th 16th and 18th U S. Cold Inft'y at Chattanooga and the 40th 42d & 44th U S. Cold Infty in East Tennessee. Major General Palmer has been this day ordered to muster out all Volunteer troops under his Command, except the Cold Organizations: General Woods has reduced his Command to seventeen thousand white and twenty five hundred Cold troops, Infty and Cav'y., which he thinks is as low, as his forces should be reduced for the present, or until the State of Alabama is reorganized. Of this force however there are eight Cav'y Regiments, which I would recommend to be reduced to three until the state is reorganized and then to be reduced to one. Stoneman can spare Woods five Regiments of Cold Inft'y and thus enable him to muster out an equal number of white Infantry. Gen'l Steedman has reduced his Command to twelve thousand five hundred and fifty white Volunteers present and absent, three thousand seven hundred and eighty five Cold Infantry present and absent, the 4th U. S. Cav'y—Seven hundred and fifty, present and absent, Company "I" 4th Art'y, sixty five present and absent and the Nineteenth U S Inft'y six hundred and fifty present and absent. I do not think it prudent to reduce that number until after the reorganization of the State of Georgia. If the Sixth U. S Infantry, taken away by Gen'l Gilmore from Savannah, as I think without authority; be sent back; the force in Georgia can be reduced after the reorganization to the two Infantry Regiments, the 4th U. S. Cav'y. Co. "I" 4th Art'y and the three Cold Infty Regiments with perfect safety. I shall be prepared to give you full information of the State of affairs in my Command, when you come to Nashville and hope you will consent to be my guest during your visit." LS (telegram sent—forwarded by mail to USG's hd. qrs., received on Sept. 7), *ibid.*, RG 94, Letters Received, 628T 1865; copies, *ibid.*, RG 393, Military Div. of the Tenn., Letters Sent; *ibid.*, Depts. of the Cumberland and Tenn., Letters Sent. On Sept. 7, Brig. Gen. John A. Rawlins endorsed this telegram. "Respectfully forwarded to the Secretary of War." ES, *ibid.*, RG 94, Letters Received, 628T 1865. On Sept. 11, Thomas twice telegraphed to USG. "All the white Vol troops in Ky and Ten. are being mustered out. have ordered the Black troops to be concentrated, at the most convenient points to meet emergencies, and ordered five Regiments of Blacks to Ala, thus inabling Genl Wood to muster out a like number of white Regts—It is my opinion that all the White Infty Regiments of ~~in~~ Vol in Ala & Georgia, can be safely mustered out as soon as those States are reorganised. The Forts on the Sea Coast should be garrisoned if possible by Regulars. that done it will only be necessary to retain in service a sufficient number of the Negro troops to guard the Depots of supplies—" ALS (telegram sent), MH; telegram received (on Sept. 13), DNA, RG 108, Letters Received. "Will you visit Nashville before the End of this month if Not I desire to go to N. York to bring my wife out to Nashville which will take 2 weeks" Telegram received, *ibid*. On Sept. 13, 10:00 A.M., USG, Springfield, Ill., telegraphed to Thomas. "Your telegrams have been received. The disposition of and order for muster out of troops is so satisfactory that it will not be neccessary for me to visit Nashville. You are authorized to go to New York at your pleasure" Copies, DLC-USG, V, 46, 109; DNA, RG 108, Letters Sent. *O.R.*, I, xlix, part 2, 1112.

To Edwin M. Stanton

Cipher   *Dated* Galena Ill 11 a m Aug. 30. [*28*] *1865.*
                                               For'd from Washn. Sept. 1.
                                    Rec'd, Sept. 2. *1865* 12 *o'clock,* — *min. M.*

To HON. EDWIN M. STANTON
SECY OF WAR,
HIGHLANDS N. J.

I would respectfully recommend the removal of Genl. Wilde[1] from the Freedman's Bureau in Georgia,   Men should be appointed who can act from facts and not always be guided by prejudice in favor of color.

I would further recommend that Gen. Comstock be ordered on an inspection tour into Georgia, Alabama & Mississippi to report upon the situation and management of the freedmen in those States, He would give facts as they exist and probably enable Gen. Howard to correct abuses if there are any.

                                    U. S. GRANT
                                    Lt. Genl.

Telegram received, DLC-Edwin M. Stanton; (marked as sent on Aug. 28, 1865, received on Aug. 29, 10:00 A.M.) DNA, RG 107, Telegrams Collected (Bound); copies (dated Aug. 28), *ibid.*, RG 108, Letters Sent; DLC-USG, V, 46, 109. On Sept. 4, 10:00 A.M., Maj. Thomas T. Eckert, act. asst. secretary of war, telegraphed to USG. "General Howard has been directed to relieve Wilder and the Adjutant General has been instructed to assign Comstock to the inspection duty you recommend." LS (telegram sent), DNA, RG 107, Telegrams Collected (Bound); telegram received (on Sept. 6, 3:00 P.M.), *ibid.*, RG 108, Letters Received.

1. Edward A. Wild, born in 1825 in Mass., graduated from Harvard (1844) and Jefferson Medical College (1846), served as a medical officer in the Turkish Army during the Crimean War, then practiced medicine in Mass. until the outbreak of the Civil War when he was appointed capt., 1st Mass. Appointed col., 35th Mass., as of July 24, 1862, and brig. gen. as of April 24, 1863, he served in the Army of the James during 1864–65. For Wild's activities in Ga., see George R. Bentley, *A History of the Freedmen's Bureau* (Philadelphia, 1955), pp. 68–69.

To Edwin M. Stanton

———

Galena Ill.
Aug. 31st 1865.

Hon. E. M. Stanton,
Sec. of War,
Sir:

I would respectfully recommend the appointment of Col. T. J. Cram,[1] U. S. Engineers to the rank of Bvt. Brig. Gen. in the Regular Army.

Gen. Rawlins, Chief of Staff, has been breveted a Maj. General of Volunteers. I would recommend that he now be breveted to the same grade in the Regular Army for distinguished and Meritorious Services.

> Very respectfully
> your obt. svt.
> U. S. Grant, Lt. Gn

ALS, DNA, RG 108, Miscellaneous Papers of Theodore S. Bowers.

1. Thomas J. Cram, USMA 1826, was promoted to col., U.S. Engineers, as of Nov. 23, 1865. Probably during the summer of 1865, an undated letter to Secretary of War Edwin M. Stanton had been prepared for USG's signature. "I would respectfully recommend the appointment of Colonel T. J. Cram, U. S. Engineers, to the rank of Brevet Brigadier General in the Regular Army." Copy (undated and unsigned), *ibid.* Bvt. Col. Ely S. Parker noted on the docket: "Genl. directs that the matter relating to Cram be delayed & held in abeyance—" AN, *ibid.*

To Brig. Gen. John A. Rawlins

———

Gen. J. A. Rawlins, Chief of Staff,
I wish you or Comstock would see the Adj. Gn. of the army and have the case of Lt. Wm Sims hunted up and settled as soon as possible. Sims died of disease contracted in the service when within forty miles of his home. He leaves a wife and four or five children in most destitute circumstances. They are now living in Hanover.

The pay due Sims would be of great service to his family and if they are entitled to a pension it might, to a great extent, prevent want.

U. S. Grant

Lt. Gn.

Aug. 31st/65

AES, DLC-Cyrus B. Comstock. Written on a letter of Aug., 1865, from Samuel W. Hemenway, former capt., 27th Iowa, Lansing, Iowa, to Orvil L. Grant, Galena. "I beg leave to submit the following as a correct abstract of the accounts and military history of 2nd Lt William S. Sims. Enlisted at Lansing Io. Aug. 8th 1862 by P. J. Harrington Period—3 Yrs, mustered in Oct. 3rd 1862 at Dubuque Io, by Capt. G. S. Pierce. Served as Private until July 15th 1863, when promoted to 1st Sergt. Promoted to, and Mustered in as 2nd Lt Aug. 3rd 63 at Little Rock Ark. by Lt Wilson Served as 2nd Lt from that date to Aug 3rd 65 date of his death, Pay due as 2nd Lt from Feb. 28th 1865 to time of death Last Paid by Maj. J. B. Young to Feb. 28th 65. Pay due for responsibility of Arms and Clothing (while commanding Co,) for months of March and April 1865 Twenty Dollars ($20 00) also 3 months Pay proper. Servant employed— 'Doc' (Colored) aged 14 years, 5 feet high Eyes—Black, Hair—Black, Complexion—Black. Miles from place of [en]listment to place of Discharge of Regt 190 Died of 'Remittent fever' (contracted in the line duty), at Clinton Iowa Aug 3rd 1865. Post Office address of attending Surgeons Dr. David C. Hastings Quasqueton Iowa and Dr. John E Sanborn Epworth Iowa. The above, I think comprises all the points, but if I have omitted any thing, a note to that effect to me here, will meet with prompt attention" ALS, *ibid.*

To Edwin M. Stanton

———

Dtd *From* Galena [*Sept.*] 1 *1865.*

Hon E M Stanton
Secy War

The Papers announce the Muster out of Gen J C Robinson[1] he was one of the officers specially assigned to duty in Previous orders & having lost a leg in service I think it unjust to him to Muster him out whilst others are retained it has probably been by Mistake if he was Mustered out & I would ask to have the order revoked in this case.

U. S Grant

Telegram received (at 5:25 P.M.), DNA, RG 107, Telegrams Collected (Bound); copies, *ibid.*, RG 108, Letters Sent; DLC-USG, V, 46, 109. On Aug. 27, 1865, Bvt. Maj. Gen. John C. Robinson, Lake George, N. Y., telegraphed to Brig. Gen. John A. Rawlins. "I see my name published in a list of Genls, mustered out of service—Mine is the only one of these lately assigned by Genl. Grant—Can this be correct—My services & sufferings entitle me to more consideration—Please send answer immediately to Albany" ALS (telegram sent), DNA, RG 107, Telegrams Collected (Unbound); telegram received (dated Aug. 28, received at 5:25 P.M.), *ibid.*, Telegrams Collected (Bound). On Aug. 28, Governor Reuben E. Fenton of N. Y. telegraphed to USG. "Is it true that Brevet Maj Gen Robinson in command of northern & western District N Y to which he was recently assigned is by order mustered out of service? I hope it is not so. We feel deeply interested in his behalf and anxious for his retention" Telegram received (at 9:50 P.M.), *ibid.* On Aug. 29, USG, Galena, telegraphed to Robinson, Astor House. "I do not think it possible you have been mustered out of service—certainly was not intended & I have seen no order indicating such a thing" Telegram received, *ibid.*, RG 94, Generals' Papers and Books, Robinson. On the same day, Robinson telegraphed USG's message to Bvt. Brig. Gen. Edward D. Townsend. Telegram received (press), *ibid.*, RG 107, Telegrams Collected (Bound). On Aug. 30, Townsend telegraphed to Robinson that his muster out had been an error. Telegram received (on Aug. 31), *ibid.*, RG 94, Generals' Papers and Books, Robinson.

1. Robinson, born in N. Y. in 1817, left USMA in his third year (1838) to study law, and was appointed 2nd lt., 5th Inf., as of Oct. 27, 1839. He served in the Mexican War and commanded Fort McHenry, Baltimore, at the outbreak of the Civil War. Appointed col., 1st Mich., as of Sept. 1, 1861, and brig. gen., as of April 28, 1862, he served with the Army of the Potomac until severely wounded during the battle of Spotsylvania while commanding the 2nd Div., 5th Army Corps.

To Edwin M. Stanton

Galena Ill. Sept. 6th *1865*

HON. E. M. STANTON,
SEC. OF WAR,
SIR:

Col. Frank Washburne, who fell mortally wounded at the battle of High Bridge Va. on the 6th of Apl. 1865, was recommended for a brevet Brigadier Generalcy, for gallant conduct on that occation, by Gen. Ord. I am not certain that the recommendation ever reached the War Dept. His friends now write that they are about erecting a monument to his memory and are anxious to know if he is to have the brevet appointment so as to get the inscription correct. I would respectfully recommend that the appointment be made and notice of it sent to Jno. D. Washburne Esq.[1] Worcester Mass.

> Very respectfully
> your obt. svt.
> U. S. GRANT
> Lt. Gn.

ALS, DNA, RG 94, ACP, G455 CB 1865.

On June 25, 1865, Lt. Col. Henry B. Scott, 4th Mass. Cav., "near Manchester Va," had written to USG. "Will you allow me to ask your attention to the meritorious services of some of the officers of this Regiment at High Bridge Va April 6th during the last campaign and their claims for Brevets. By some accident the recommendation then made was mislaid; The facts are briefly these—Colonel Washburn with 67 enlisted men and 12 officers including a Surgeon & Chaplain an aggregate of 80, was sent on the morning of the 6th April to destroy the High Bridge over the Appomattox on the South Side Rail Road—Two regiments of infantry were sent with him—Later instructions were sent not to destroy the bridge, but only one span of it—Almost immediately upon their arrival they were sharply attacked in the rear. The infantry were quickly driven back and it was evident would not fight   Colonel Washburn soon made up his mind that whatever was to be done must be done by the Cavalry. He accordingly formed in single rank, charged and broke the enemy's line, capturing more prisoners than he had men   Rallying and again forming he then charged again into the midst of all of Rosser's cavalry, consisting, as I was informed by Rosser himself of three Brigades. A sharp hand to hand sabre fight then ensued which only ended when two of the Captains and one Lieutenant were killed, both of the Field Officers wounded, one of whom, Col. Washburn, has since died and three other of the officers left for dead on the field. These last mentioned three being only severely wounded will probably live. The remaining officers were captured. The colors of the Regiment were burned. I beg permission to call your attention to the sharpness of the fight and it's important results. Gen. Rosser informed me that in the course of his experience he had never known such desperate fighting. A rebel Colonel who was captured at Farmville told one of our officers that he had heard of hand to hand fights but never seen one—until that day's, and that the fighting was of the most gallant description. The result was to give General Lee the impression that this force must have a large force in support and caused him to halt and give what Col. Peyton described to Gen. Ord as a stampeding order. This halt enabled Sheridan to come up with Ewell at Sailor's Creek and to gain the victory which was achieved there. And this delay also enabled Gen Ord so to close up with them as to cut them off at Appomattox on the 9th. This, at least, is the opinion of many rebel officers with whom I have talked on the subject, and it is plausible. I therefore ask that the following Brevets may be conferred for especial gallantry at High Bridge Va to date April 6th 1865   Col. Francis Washburn to be Brevet Brig. Genl. was severely wounded, has since died—Lieut Col. Horatio Jenkins Jr to be Brevet Colonel was severely wounded (alive)

Captain John D. Goddard to be Brevet Major. was killed by a sabresthrust
Captain Wm T. Hodges to be Brevet Major killed by a pistol shot & sabre cut
Captain John A. Caldwell to be Brevet Major severely wounded & crippled alive
1st Lieut Geo F. Davis to be Brevet Captain was killed on the field sabre cut &
pistol shot   1st Lieut Allen F. Belcher Regtl Commissary to be Brevet Captain
sabre thrust over eye, will probably lose it (alive)   2d Lieut Gilbert Thompson
to be Brevet First Lieutenant severely wounded and crippled (alive)   For the
opinion of Major General Ord as to the importance of the fight and the gallantry
of the officers engaged I beg to call your attention to his official report, to which
unfortunately I have not access. I have taken the liberty of writing this communication although not commanding the Regiment because the modesty of
Colonel Jenkins would prevent him from speaking of the fight as it deserves and
because it was the subject of a similar communication by me when in command
of the Regt in the absence of Col. Jenkins. That communication was mislaid—. . .
These Brevets can be forwarded to the friends of deceased officers through
Regimental Head Quarters" ALS, *ibid.* On July 5, USG endorsed this letter.
"Approved and respectfully forwarded to the Secretary of War." ES, *ibid.*

   1. John D. Washburn, born in Boston in 1833 (a cousin of Elihu B. Washburne), graduated from Harvard Law School (1856) and practiced law in
Worcester, Mass.

To Edwin M. Stanton

Galena Ills Sept 7th 1865

Hon E. M. Staunton
Secretary of War,
Sir:

   I wrote a letter from Montreal Canada which was mailed from
Niagara Falls, recommending that our consul in U. C. Mr Potter
be authorized to parole Dr Montrose Pollen and Mr. D. M. Frost
to go to St Louis Mo, to await the action of the government in their
cases. I now understand from Mrs. Frost that my letter was never
recieved by you and I therefore renew the recommendation.

   I am satisfied that both Frost and Pallen are entirely cured of
rebellion and secession. They are both wealthy through their wives
parents.

   Where their property cannot be reached for confiscation, and
I think it policy to have such people spend their means in the
United States, instead of abroad when no injury can result from it.

I respectfully renew the recommendation that Genl Frost and Dr Pallen be allowed to return to the United States to await action of Government,

U. S. GRANT, Lt-Genl

Copies, DLC-USG, V, 46, 109; DNA, RG 108, Letters Sent. See letter to Edwin M. Stanton, Aug. 8, 1865.

To Andrew Johnson

Galena Ill.
Sept. 8th 1865

HIS EXCELLENCY A. JOHNSON PRESIDENT,
SIR:

Seven weeks absence from Washington, and free intercourse with all parties and classes of people, has convinced me that there is but one opinion as to the duty of the United States towards Mexico, or rather the usurpers in that country. All agree that, besides a yealding of the long proclaimed Monroe doctrine, nonintervention in Mexican affairs will lead to an expensive and bloody war hereafter, or a yealding of territory now possessed by us.—To let the Empire of Maximilian be established on our frontier, is to permit an enemy to establish himself who will require a large standing army to watch. Military stations will be at points remote from supplies and therefore expensive to keep up. The trade of an Empire will be lost to our Commerce and Americans, instead of being the most favored people of the world, throughout the length and breadth of this Continent, will be scoffed and laughed at by their adjoining neighbors both North and South; the people of the British provinces and of Mexico.

Previous communications have given my views on our duty in the matter here spoken of so that it is not necessary that I should treat the subject at any length now. Conversations with you have convinced me that you think about it as I do, otherwise I should never have taken the liberty of writing in this manner. I have had the opportunity of mingling more intimately with all classes of community than the Executive can possibly have and my object is to give you the benefit of what I have heard expressed.

I would have no hesitation in recommending that notice be given the French that foreign troops must be withdrawn from this Continent and the people left free to govern themselves in their own way. I would openly sell, on credit, to the Government of Mexico all the arms, Munitions and clothing they want, and aid them with officers to command troops. In fine, I would take such measures as would secure the supremicy of the Republican Government in Mexico.

I hope you will excuse me for the free manner in which I address you. I but speak my honest convictions, and them with the full belief that a terrible strife in this country is only to be averted by prompt action in this matter with Mexico.

> I have the honor to be,
> Very respectfully
> your obt. svt.
> U. S. GRANT
> Lt. Gn.

ALS (marked as received on Sept. 11, 1865), DLC-Andrew Johnson; copies (misdated Sept. 1), DLC-USG, V, 46, 109; DNA, RG 108, Letters Sent. Dated Sept. 1 in *O.R.*, I, xlviii, part 2, 1221.

To Maj. Gen. William T. Sherman

Galena, Sept. 10th *1865*

DEAR GENERAL,

I shall be in St. Louis on the 13th inst. and shall prefer staying at the same house you do. Mrs. Grant and the children will be with me but will probably go to the country the day after our arrival in the city. I shall not remain in Mo. more than seven or eight days.

I dread going back to Washington and at the same time feel as if I should be there all the time. This feeling detracts largely from the enjoyment I should otherwise have at being released for a time from the close confinement of the last four years.

Give Mrs. Grant's and my kindest regards to Mrs. Sherman and the children and accept the same for yourself.

Yours Truly

U. S. GRANT

ALS, Amherst College, Amherst, Mass. On Sept. 11, 1865, Monday, Bvt. Col. Orville E. Babcock, Galena, telegraphed to Maj. Thomas T. Eckert, act. asst. secretary of war. "Lt Gen. Grant will start next tuesday 12th for St. [L]oui[s] where he will be about one week—Please notify Secretary of War and Gen Rawlins & oblige" Telegram received (at 4:00 P.M.), DNA, RG 107, Telegrams Collected (Bound); copies, *ibid.*, RG 108, Letters Sent; DLC-USG, V, 46, 109. USG arrived in St. Louis during the afternoon of Sept. 13, and departed the evening of Sept. 22 for Cincinnati. Newspaper reports blamed Maj. Gen. William T. Sherman for the failure of St. Louis to provide a proper welcome for USG. Unidentified newspaper clipping, Babcock Papers, ICN; *Galena Weekly Gazette*, Sept. 19, 1865; *Missouri Democrat*, Sept. 14, 1865; *Illinois State Journal*, Sept. 16, 1865.

On Sept. 13, Mayor James S. Thomas *et al.*, St. Louis, wrote to USG. "We the undersigned, members of the City Council and the Board of Managers of Lafayette Park, do most respectfully request that you and the members of your staff will be pleased to visit Lafayette Park, next Friday afternoon, Sept 15th and remain there from 3 until 6 o'clock. Please answer at your earliest convenience and oblige" ALS, USG 3. On the same day, Bvt. Col. Adam Badeau wrote to Thomas *et al.* "Lieutenant General Grant directs me to accept your polite invitation, for himself and the members of his staff, to visit Lafayette Park on Friday next, at 3 P. M." *Missouri Democrat*, Sept. 14, 1865. An estimated 10,000 people attended the reception at Lafayette Park during which Lt. Governor George Smith of Mo. addressed USG. "In the absence of the Governor, it is a source of great pleasure to me, to have the opportunity to unite with the Mayor, City Council, and Citizens of St Louis in their congratulations to you, upon this occasion. Permit me to say, General, that not only here in St Louis, is your perseverance, genius and valor appreciated; but I can assure you that there is no portion of our great State, where a love of the 'Stars & Stripes' exists, or loyalty prevails, but what you will receive a like kind reception and cordial greeting. I hope it may suit your convenience to extend your visit to the Northwest and other portions of our State, in order that our people may have an opportunity of giving to you an expression of their regards." AD, USG 3. USG responded: "GOVERNOR SMITH: It will be impossible for me to visit any other portion of the State, as I am called to Washington on Saturday week. At some other time I will be pleased to visit your section of the State." *Missouri Democrat*, Sept. 16, 1865. On Sept. 21, Babcock wrote to U.S. Representative Elihu B. Washburne. ". . . We have had a very stupid time here I think it all comes from Shermans wish *to save the Genl all annoyance* The City has done nothing—and I guess it will be all for the best. . . ." ALS, DLC-Elihu B. Washburne.

On Sept. 12, Barton Able and Joshua H. Alexander, Union Merchants' Exchange, St. Louis, wrote to USG. "The Committe of Arrangements appointed by the Exchange to entertain the party of English Capitalists now visiting our Country, respectfully invite you to accompany said party on an excursion on board of the Steamer 'Jennie Deans' from the Keokuk Packet Landing at 10 o clock a. m. thursday next, and on the evening of the Same day at 9 o clock to join them at dinn[er] at the Southern Hotel." ALS, USG 3. During the evening of Sept. 14, USG attended a banquet honoring a group of English railroad investors touring the U.S., and Sherman addressed the gathering praising USG. *New York Times*, Sept. 20, 1865; *Missouri Democrat*, Sept. 15, 1865.

On Sept. 17, USG, St. Louis, wrote to John H. Williams, Quincy, Ill. "It will be impossible for me to visit Quincy as I had hoped to do. I have Private business will take up several days of this week and on Saturday I must start East." ALS, OClWHi. On Sept. 19, Sherman wrote to Governor Richard J. Oglesby of Ill. "The Telegraph has served me so many shabby tricks of late that I prefer to trust to Old honest Ink, to unravel the mystery of the Past week. On the 9th inst you telegraphed me that General Grant would have a public reception at the Capitol of Illinois on the next Tuesday. Of Course I never got it or not till long after, Else would surely have come. On saturday last after my work I went to my dinner at the Lindell Hotel when either the office Clerk or the operator of the telegraph then handed me your despatch. I read it hastily supposing of course it referred to the next Tuesday, viz today, and made my answer on the spot, that if Gen Grant came up to Springfield I would come also. I got your telegraphic reply same day, that you would expect us. Genl Grant and family were then out at Mr Dents 11 miles in the Country, and as soon as he came yesterday I asked him if he were going to Springfield today, he said no, that he had been invited to Quincy but had declined. I went at once and got the despatch and lo it was dated the 9th and I saw I had been sold. Of course the mistake was mine jointly with whoever failed to deliver the despatch at the time of its receipt— The telegraph man charges the Hotel Clerk and the Clerk the Telegraph man, and the Supdt is now enquiring as to who is to blame. The moment I saw that your despatch referred to last Tuesday & not this I telegraphed the mistake to you, and soon after got yours of yesterday enquiring if Genl Grant & I were coming up. Of course the General cannot come, and it is no use in my coming without him and if you have been occasioned any trouble we must impose it on him who delivered me your despatch of the 9th on Saturday the 16th. Senator Yates was here last month and told me that after full Consultation it was resolved to postpone some grand Celebration for the returned volunteers in October, when I shall be most happy to visit you. In the mean time I must go to Lawrenceville Ind—Janesville Wisconsin, and Omaha Nebraska, but hope to be back by the middle or 20th of October. I regret exceedingly these mishaps lest you attribute them to a disinclination to come to Springfield. I do Confess that I am afraid of Celebrations because I am found to be rude in shutting my mouth, or by speaking give ground for a supposition that I seek notoriety which is my abhorrence. But to you personally & officially and to the brave and Glorious fellows whom Illinois Contributed to the War I want to do all possible honor. I therefore this explanation will prove satisfactory to you." ALS, IHi. For the confusion caused by Sherman's misunderstanding, see *Missouri Democrat*, Sept. 18, 19, 1865; *Illinois State Journal*, Sept. 19, 1865.

On Sept. 20, J. S. Andrews, gen. superintendent, St. Louis and Wisconsin River Lumber Co., wrote to USG. "Enclosed I hand you a certificate of Stock of $10.000, in the great Western Petroleum & Refing co. of Venango Co Pa. This

Cos. Works is located in the heart of the great Oil district of the world—I have the most Sanguin Expectation the Stock will be worth par, before Many Months—'please accept this as a token of my Esteem—" ALS, USG 3.

To Bvt. Maj. Gen. Montgomery C. Meigs

Bloomington Ill
Sept 12th 1865 [*1:00* P.M.]

BVT MAJ GEN M C MEIGS Q M G.

I am credibly informed that an effort is being made to secure the Government Rolling Mill and the scrap iron in and around Chattanooga and Nashville in such a way that it will not be sold to the highest bidder   Please postpone sale ten days until other bids can come in—

U S GRANT
Lt Genl

Telegram received (on Sept. 13, 1865, 12:20 A.M.), DNA, RG 107, Telegrams Collected (Unbound); copies, *ibid.*, RG 108, Letters Sent; DLC-USG, V, 46, 109. On Sept. 13, Bvt. Maj. Gen. Montgomery C. Meigs telegraphed to USG. "Dispatch received   Bids received till noon today will be opened according to advertisement   unless an advantageous offer is received no sale will be immediately concluded—Proposals to purchase the rolling mill were invited but sale was not promised absolutely—& will not be recommended by me unless clearly to the interest of the U. S. The bids will be laid before the war Department with report—I see no danger of any intrigue succeeding, though I also have been warned against such intrigues" ALS (telegram sent), DNA, RG 107, Telegrams Collected (Unbound); *ibid.*, RG 77, Miscellaneous Telegrams Sent (Press). On the same day, Bvt. Brig. Gen. Charles Thomas, asst. q. m. gen., wrote to USG, incorporating a copy of Meigs's telegram. LS, *ibid.*, RG 108, Letters Received.

On July 20, Bvt. Maj. Gen. Joseph D. Webster, Chattanooga, wrote to USG. "I am not informed what measures, if any, have been taken in reference to the disposal of the property pertaining to the Military RailRoads. That property is immense in amount, having been provided with the most lavish expense. It is too late to inquire whether any part of that expense might have been avoided. This property will not be needed much longer for use by the Government, and it is not too late to take care that no unnecessary loss be incurred in disposing of it. I deem it my duty to advise most earnestly that *none* of the material be *sold at auction*. Such a mode of disposing of it will be taken advantage of, by combinations of interested parties, and the interests of the government be sacrificed. The locomotives, cars, new material, and even the scrap iron, *will all be wanted, and,*—I am satisfied from the results of my 'inspection' thus far, will be *paid for at fair prices, if the sale is rightly managed.* This matter is of great importance, and *millions* may be lost to the government by injudicious or dishonest management. I think the government has already suffered great loss from the latter cause. You are well aware how ready many men are to cheat the government who might have some scruples in the case of individual citizens. The Rail road service as at present organized has some persons in it who would not be troubled with scruples even in the case of individuals. It is highly necessary that they be not suffered to reap a further harvest from the sales of the vast amount of property soon to be disposed of. It seems to me that any sales of scrap iron or other property ought to be stopped—a valuation be made by competent parties of all property to be sold, with strict reference to Eastern prices and cost of transportation, and the property held for sale at this valuation. I take the liberty to make these suggestions from a strong impression that efforts will be made, and indeed *are* made, to induce the adoption of a course which would result in serious loss to the government at a time when it is the duty of evry citizen to do his utmost to lessen the present and prospective burden pressing upon the people." ALS, *ibid.* E. G. Barney added an undated note to USG at the foot of this letter. "Having witnessed during the last three years something of the immense losses sustained by the government through the neglect, mismanagement or dishonesty of those having Govt property in charge, I am fully of the opinion that the suggestions made by Genl Webster in the above, are of the greatest importance. There are many millions of dollars worth of property now suffering from neglect and exposure and much of it liable to be spirited away, by dishonest parties." ANS, *ibid.* On July 23, Webster, Macon, Ga., wrote to USG. "I deem it my duty to earnestly recommend that the railroads now operated by the United States be turned over to their respective companies so soon as (1) those companies shall elect officers and directors who can be relied on as thoroughly loyal to the Government, and (2) the accounts between the railroads and the Government can be properly adjusted. Although, as I have heretofore said, the roads might be economically and advantageously operated by the Government, it is yet not likely that, as a matter of fact, they will be so operated, and consequently they should be given up at the earliest moment that the two above specified conditions can be fulfilled. In the meantime, the United States ought not to be at the expense of putting the roads in thorough repair merely for the benefit of the companies. All work on track or bridges beyond what is absolutely necessary for the safety of trains should be discontinued. All repairs to locomotives and cars to which the companies have any claim should be stopped at once, as should also the running of the rolling-mill at Chattanooga. The proper adjustment of accounts between the Government and the roads will require a good deal of consideration. Some of the roads have been put by the Government in a much better condition than they were before it took possession. It will not be right to give them, without pay, the advantage of thorough repairs, new iron, permanent bridges, &c. If they claim compensation for the use of their roads, it is sufficient to answer that in the early stages of the war they voluntarily and zealously aided the enemy, furnishing them not only with the great 'interior lines' of communication and supply, of which all have heard so much, but with knowing heads and ready hands to operate them. Their able railroad men were of more service to the rebels than many of their general officers. No claim of theirs for pay or damages should be entertained a moment. It is only necessary to find out how much they are fairly indebted to the United States. To do this, the disbursing officers should be called on for reports of expenditures for permanent improvements. Of course it will be necessary, previous to relinquishing the roads, to make agreements as to future transportation of troops and supplies, mails, and such other matters as the convenience of the Government may require. The points herein noticed may have been already fully considered and decided upon, but as they are included in the letter of my instructions for my present duty, I make the suggestions, with a strong impression of the importance of early action in the matter." *O.R.*, III, v, 102–3. See *ibid.*, 101–2. On Aug. 7, Brig. Gen. John A. Rawlins endorsed this letter. "Respy forw'd to the sec of War" Copy, DLC-USG, V, 49. On Sept. 11, Webster, Washington, D. C., wrote a letter received at USG's hd. qrs. reporting on railroads in the South. DNA, RG 108, Register of Letters Received. See *PUSG*, 9, 287n, 290n–92n; *O.R.*, I, xlvii, part 3, 661; *ibid.*, III, v, 59.

To Edwin M. Stanton

Respectfully refered to the Sec. of War. I was not aware that either Gn. Rucker or Gn. Donaldson had been Breveted to the rank of Maj. Gen. in the Regular Army. If they have been I certainly would recommend Gens. Allen & Ingalls for the same grade. They of all other Quartermasters have occupied the most important positions in the War just concluded and have performed their duties in the most satisfactory manner.

U. S. GRANT
Lt. Gn.

ST. LOUIS, MO.
SEPT. 18TH/65

AES, DNA, RG 94, ACP, 2163 1878. Written on a letter of Sept. 14, 1865, from Brig. Gen. Rufus Ingalls (bvt. maj. gen. of vols.) to USG. "I am informed that Generals' Donaldson & Rucker have both received brevets of Maj-Gen. in the *Regular* service, while Gen'l. Allen and myself have received only brevets of Major-General of *Volunteers*. I am quite sure that there is no intention on your part or that of the Hon. Secretary of War to place those Officers in a higher or more permanent grade than ourselves, and the object of this communication is mainly to cause attention to be attracted to the case. Having been in the *field* during the entire War as Chief Qr-Mr. of the first, if not the principal army of the Republic, and having had charge of many of the largest Depots, always to the expressed satisfaction of all the Commanding Generals, I had hoped, as a soldier has a *right* to do, that I might win some substantial rank. General Allen and myself are but Majors in the qr. Master's Dept., and cannot expect to retain our *volunteer* rank any great length of time. I had always claimed, and submit the point for your consideration, that the position I have held, and the duties I have actually performed during the entire Rebellion, entitle me to as much promotion, at least, as any one in my Dep't., and I have never for a moment doubted, and do not doubt now, that I shall receive what is right and proper." LS, *ibid.*

To C. F. Vent & Co.

St. Louis, Mo
Sept. 18th 1865

C. F. VENT & CO
SIRS;

Your letter of the 16th inst. stating that Gn. Smith, formerly "Chief of Cavy" with me claims exclusive ~~privilege~~ access to the material to write my biography, and that Coppée's[1] claims are false, is received.

Gen. Smith asked of me the privilege of writing the biography he speaks of and being an old friend was not refused. Prof. Coppée however had asked the privilege of writing the work he advertises long before General Smith said any thing to me about the work he now proposed and I promised him all the information from my office he might require that was not inconsistent to give. Prof. C. so far as I know, has been furnished with all he asked. I do not know what he has said in his book but without intending that exclusive privilege should be given to one author Prof. Coppée is the only one, up to this time, who has had access to any information from my HdQrs. for the purpose of writing a book and Gn. Smith is the only other who has had the promise of any thing of the kind. Their works are different, one being a biography the other a history of Campaigns in this War.

ADf, ICarbS. See letter to William Sooy Smith, Sept. 27, 1865.

1. Henry Coppée, USMA 1845, served in the Mexican War and as an instructor at USMA (1848–49, 1850–55). He resigned from the U.S. Army to accept a professorship at the University of Pennsylvania. As editor (1864–66) of the *United States Service Magazine*, published by Charles B. Richardson of N. Y., Coppée wrote two articles on USG: "Lieutenant-General Grant," *ibid.*, I, vi (June, 1864), 561–64; "Grant," *ibid.*, III, v (May, 1865), 401–3. Maj. Gen.

William T. Sherman wrote an undated letter to Coppée correcting errors made in the first article. Adam Badeau, *Military History of Ulysses S. Grant* (New York, 1868–81), I, 602–5. In 1864, Coppée wrote a ten-page pamphlet, *Sketch of the Life of Lieut.-Gen. U. S. Grant* (New York, 1864), "TO ACCOMPANY THE FINE STEEL PORTRAIT PUBLISHED BY C. B. RICHARDSON." *Ibid.* The pamphlet printed a letter of June 27 from Julia Dent Grant to Coppée. "I wish to express to you my thanks for the beautiful portrait of my husband which you have kindly sent to me. It seems to me perfect. I do not see how it can be improved; no picture that I have seen will compare with it in lifelike accuracy and artistic merit, in which unreserved commendation my family all unite." Richardson, in association with C. F. Vent & Co. of Cincinnati, published Coppée's *Grant and His Campaigns: A Military Biography* (New York, 1866). In the preface, Coppée wrote: "I must express my hearty thanks to General Grant for his kindness in sanctioning my attempt to portray his military career, and to Major-General Rawlins for his invaluable assistance in furnishing materials without which the work could not have been written." *Ibid.*, p. 4. Vent & Co. advertised for agents to sell Coppée's book by subscription, promising that Coppée had exclusive access to "official documents and private records" of USG. An example of the advertisement appeared in the *Illinois State Journal*, Sept. 13, 1865, during USG's visit to Springfield, Ill. A revised edition was entitled *Life and Services of Gen. U. S. Grant* (New York, 1868). The fly-leaf printed a letter of Aug. 8, 1865, from Brig. Gen. John A. Rawlins to Coppée. "With the especial approval of General Grant, I have the pleasure of sending you, herewith, such material as will be of service to you in the preparation of your History of 'Grant and his Campaigns,' and shall be happy to give you, at any time, any assistance in my power in securing accuracy and completeness in your work." On Nov. 20, Rawlins wrote to Coppée transmitting information and copies of documents. Copy, Hillyer Papers, ViU.

To Jesse Root Grant

St. Louis, Sept. 19th 1865

DEAR FATHER,

I shall leave here on Friday evening for Cincinnati and reach there probably about 10 a. m. Saturday. Gov. Morton of Ia. made me promise some time since to visit Indianapolis[1] before returning to Washington and I expected to have done so on my way to Cincinnati. But starting so late in the week I shall not be able to do so. It is likely however that I will return there either early next week or immediately on my return from Brown County.[2] Julia and the children are all well and enjoying themselves very much.

ULYSSES.

ALS, MoSHi. On Sept. 14, 1865, Benjamin J. Spooner, former col., 83rd Ind., *et al.*, Lawrenceburg, Ind., wrote to USG. "The Dearborn County Agricultural Fair, commences on monday Septr 25th Inst—And Maj. Genl. W. T. Sherman has given us a positive promise, that he will be here on Wednesday the 27th Inst—The Second Company mustered into the service of the U. S. in the State of Indiana under Pres Lincolns first Proclamation, was raised in this County, and in the immediate vicinity of this City—Old Dearborn, has been represented upon almost every battle field of this war—and her Soldiers, with all loyal *people*, love to honor their Generals—From the very hour of your promotion to the command of our great armies, the true friends of the Union everywhere—had the most implicit confidence in your patriotism and ability, and felt sure, that with you as our military leader, Victory would in due time, crown our arms—In this they have not been disappointed, and now that the bloody strife is over, Soldiers and citizens, desire to see you, grasp your hand, and hear you speak, though it be but a single word—We respectfully and earnestly invite you to visit this city on the 27th Inst (next Wednesday week), but if this time does not suit your convenience, say the 28th—and we trust that your engagements are such as will enable you to say, 'I will come'—You will remember that Lawrenceburgh is situate on the Ohio River, at a point some Twenty miles below Cincinnati, and is accessible by the O & M. and Ind & Cin Rail Road—May we hope for an early, and favorable answer—" ALS, USG 3. USG did not accompany Maj. Gen. William T. Sherman although he did pass through Lawrenceburg (see footnote 1). On Sept. 18, James M. True, former col., 62nd Ill., Mattoon, Ill., wrote to USG. "According to Arrangement made when I met you in Chicago on the 5th of this month I write to ask you what day you will be through this place? Please give the hour as well as the day if you can as the people are very anxious to see you as you pass through" ALS, *ibid.*

On Sept. 20, Bvt. Col. Orville E. Babcock, St. Louis, wrote to Mayor L. A. Harris, Cincinnati. "The Lieutenant-General desires me to acknowledge the receipt of your kind offer, tendering the hospitalities of your city, &c. He says he accepts the same with pleasure. Under present arrangements he will leave St. Louis on the regular evening train, Friday, September 22, over the Ohio and Mississippi Railroad, reaching Cincinnati Saturday morning. Should any other arrangements be made, will notify you." *Cincinnati Enquirer*, Sept. 21, 1865. USG arrived in Cincinnati during Saturday morning, Sept. 23, and attended a reception at Pike's Opera House. Harris addressed USG: "No official preparation has been made for your reception. This immense gathering of the people is spontaneous. They have assembled to testify, by their presence, the honor in which they hold you in their hearts, for the distinguished part you have taken in suppressing a wicked and causeless rebellion, and to assure you by the cordiality of your reception, if such a thing were nece[s]sary, how highly they esteem your services, and how heartily you are welcome to us all. This is the people's own welcome. It comes directly from them, it was inaugurated by and received its force and direction from them, and though the City Council of Cincinnati have, by their resolution, appointed their President, Mr. Weasner, and myself to extend the hospitalities of the city to you, we but give expression to the sentiment of the entire people, when we most cordially welcome you, and extend to you the hospitalities of the city. Ladies and gentlemen, I have the honor of presenting to you Lieutenant-General Grant." *Ibid.*, Sept. 25, 1865. USG responded: "MR. MAYOR, AND LADIES AND GENTLEMEN: I thank you for this very cordial welcome and reception. I say to you as I have said elsewhere, I do not receive these demonstrations as particularly intended for myself; but as showing the loyalty of the people to the cause we have been fighting for for the past four years. Again, I thank you." *Ibid.* On Sept. 25, USG addressed the Cincinnati Chamber of Commerce. "Mr President: I thank you, and through you the Cincinnati Chamber of Commerce, for their kind reception and welcome to-day, and am pleased to know them as my friends." *Ibid.*, Sept. 26, 1865. That afternoon, USG traveled to Covington, Ky., to visit his parents and attended a reception. Ky. AG John W. Finnell addressed USG: "We bid you welcome to Kentucky. In the earlier days of the rebellion, when those in authority in the South boastingly declared that the soil of Kentucky was necessary to the symmetry of the Southern Confederacy, and must be secured at whatever cost of blood and treasure; when Cumberland Gap and Bowling Green and Columbus, and with them nearly one-half the State, was in the hands of the enemies of the Union, and the whole State was threatened with subjugation, you, sir, came promptly and offered your life in our defense. Although, then, almost unknown to some, your manly bearing won for you the confidence and respect of our loyal people, and bound them to you by ties which can never be sundered. We have rejoiced continually in your promotion, step by step, to the exalted position you now occupy. The achievements of yourself and your brave comrades in arms electrified the civilized world and saved to us and to posterity the Union of these States, and to the oppressed of other lands the asylum promised to them by our fathers. Your victories, sir, are too numerous to be recounted on an occasion like the present. Of them it may be well said, as was written of the triumphs of a distinguished soldier of former times, 'None but the historian can paint his victories with truth and fidelity.' The nation delights to honor you. Your name is written on the hearts of the American people in characters that will not fade. Your modesty in the hour of triumph, your magnanimity and your generous forbearance toward a vanquished and fallen foe, challenge the admiration of true men every-where; and now, and in all time to come, will shed a halo round your fame that will be to your children and your children's children an inheritance beyond all price. Again, sir, in the name of all our people, I bid you a cordial and heartfelt welcome." *Ibid.* USG responded: "Ladies and Gentlemen: I will not attempt to reply to the complimentary remarks of your distinguished Adjutant-General. If I should, I know that it would end in failure. If my presence here to-day affords you any gratification, I am much pleased. I thank you for this cordial reception." *Ibid.* USG returned to Cincinnati that evening for a banquet at the Cincinnati Club, and again visited Covington briefly on Oct. 1, attending church with his parents. *Cincinnati Gazette*, Oct. 3, 1865. On Sept. 29, Harris wrote to USG. "If your engagements will permit I will call for you on Monday afternoon at 2 o'clock for a drive on the Avenue and a brief visit to the Ohio Military Academy: I am deeply interested in the success of the Academy, and it will afford the Directors and myself great pleasure to have you visit the institution. If your engagemen[ts] will not permit on Monday I will call any other time." ALS, USG 3. See *Cincinnati Enquirer*, Oct. 4, 1865.

On Oct. 3, Tuesday, Babcock, Cincinnati, wrote to Brig. Gen. John A. Rawlins. "I send you all the letters and telegrams on hand. We start 8 A. M to day for columbus and to night on to Pittsburg, and Wednesday night to Philadelphia, from which place the General will probably run on to Washington for a day, before bringing Mrs. Grant and the children. We have no new, all are well and send kind regards to all." Copies, DLC-USG, V, 46, 109; DNA, RG 108, Letters Sent. USG arrived at Columbus at 1:00 P.M. and went to the state capitol where Mayor James G. Bull delivered a welcoming address for which USG expressed his gratitude. *Ohio State Journal*, Oct. 4, 1865. At 4:00 P.M., USG attended a banquet at the Neil House where Ohio Governor Charles Anderson welcomed USG; USG responded: "I don't know that I can do better than to ask the Governor to reply to his own toast. He knows I never speak, and that I will not on this occasion. I thank you, however, for the manner in which the toast was received." *Ibid.*; *Cincinnati Gazette*, Oct. 4, 1865. Former Ohio Governor David Tod then spoke in USG's behalf. *Ibid.*

On Sept. 19, Mayor James Lowry, Pittsburgh, and nine others wrote to USG. "At a meeting of a large number of the most respected and influential citizens of Pittsburgh and Allegheny held in the 15th inst. the following Resolution was unanimously adopted: '*Resolved*, That an Executive Committee of thirteen citizens, the Chairman of this Meeting, and the Mayors and Presidents of the Councils of Pittsburgh and Allegheny, be appointed to extend to Lieutenant General Grant an invitation to visit Pittsburgh, and make the necessary arrangements to receive and welcome that distinguished soldier and patriot.' In the discharge of this most acceptable duty the Committee feel at some loss to find words wherein to convey the earnest solicitude of our whole population to enjoy the occasion of a personal greeting and heartfelt welcome in ou[r] midst: and whilst nothing shall be omitted to honor one so justly 'clothed with deeds of brave renown,' it may be truly said that the community we represent is given to the exhibition of no unmeaning display or empty parade. It will, therefore, be our effort to abstain from whatever might prove onerous or offensive to that estimable delicacy and reserve which mark your high career. To the people of these loyal cities you have hitherto been personally a stranger, but will permit us to say there does *exist some* affinities to which it may not be out of place to refer on the present occasion. The honored name which you bear, and to which your glorious achievements have given imperishable lustre, has been from the foundation of our city a 'household word.' A marked, and, as it came from the hand of the Great Architect of Nature, a beautiful elevation rising from the margin of our noble rivers, crowned with massive public buildings of the County: their spreading domes: and the graceful spires of Temples for the worship of the Most High, all in close proximity, are the first objects which attract attention on every approach to the City. This, dear General, is *Grant's Hill*, So named and baptised in the precious blood of our colonial ancestry in a sanguinary conflict with the French and their savage allies for the Command of the great Ohio, which has, as you know, *its source* in the confluence of the Allegheny and Monongahela rivers, which wash our borders on either side. And may we not, also, advert to the fact, that Pittsburgh, then an inconsiderable village was for years, the first abode, west of the mountains, of the maternal ancestors of your beloved children, Still remembered with most affectionate regard by some, yet living amongst us for their elevated Christian attainments, domestic virtues and social refinement. Surely these reminiscences will find a yielding place in your generous heart for the yearning of the loyal people we represent, to grasp, on some not distant day, that hand and arm which, for four years, have been wielded with such brilliant Success in defence of the laws, and the integrity of the United States, and covered our broad and now happy land with the wings of peace and reconciliation through all its borders, extending our proffered welcome to the gentlemen of your military family." LS, USG 3. USG arrived in Pittsburgh during the morning of Oct. 4, and after a reception, responded: "Ladies and Gentlemen: I heartily thank you for this very warm welcome. I am not in the habit of making speeches. I will, therefore, again thank you." *Cincinnati Gazette*, Oct. 6, 1865. The *Baltimore Sun* (Oct. 6, 1865) reported that a crowd of 100,000 met USG in Pittsburgh. USG left the city that evening, arriving in Harrisburg, Pa., on Oct. 5, 8:00 A.M., where he received another reception before traveling on at 1:30 P.M. *Philadelphia Inquirer*, Oct. 6, 1865. USG arrived in Washington, D. C., on Oct. 6.

1. On July 22, Governor Oliver P. Morton of Ind. had written to USG. "Knowing your disposition to shun rather than to court observation, I almost hesitate to request you to do that which may be personally distasteful, however gratifying it might be to your appreciative fellow citizens   Believing however, that public men owe it to their times to submit to some personal discomfort for the gratification of the popular desires, especially when those desires spring from patriotic impulses, I shall ask you to take the same view of the subject, and proceed with the request which I was about to make. By the choice of our late wise and good President, you occupied the grand central position in the mighty struggle which has so happily ended in the salvation of the nation, and by the logic of events as well as the verdict of your countrymen, you were the man for that position. Many of the brave officers and men from this State, who have fought the battles of the Republic under your direction as Commander in-Chief, have never had the good fortune to see you, and these, in common with their fellow citizens generally, are anxious that you should visit the Capital of the State, and give them an opportunity of testifying their admiration of your character and services   I respectfully request, General, that you will name a time when it will suit you to visit Indiana and be received as the guest of the State. Hoping that you will comply with this request, . . ." LS, USG 3. On Aug. 11, William H. Schlater, Indianapolis, wrote to USG. "By direction of Governor Morton, I have the honor to inclose a duplicate letter mailed to your address Washington City July 22d 1865, inviting you to visit Indiana, No answer having been received to the original this duplicate is forwarded fearing the first had failed to reach you." ALS, *ibid.* On Aug. 14, Bvt. Col. Adam Badeau, Detroit, wrote to Morton. "Lieut. Gen. Grant directs me to state that he has this day received your communication dated July 22d, and forwarded him from Washington D. C. He directs me to express his thanks for the invitation to visit Indiana and become the guest of the state, which you so kindly tender, and to say that he accepts the invitation, and will write to you in person indicating the time at which he will be able to be in Indiana, so soon as his arrangements are so far completed as to allow this." ALS, Morton Papers, In. On Sept. 19, Morton telegraphed to USG, St. Louis. "When may we expect you here. Please answer"   Copy, *ibid.* On Sept. 20, Babcock, St. Louis, telegraphed to Morton. "Genl. Grant directs me to telegraph you that he will visit Indianapolis from Cincinnati. He will be in Cincinnati Saturday morning and notify you from there what day he will be with you." Copy, *ibid.* On Sept. 24, Babcock, Cincinnati, wrote to Morton. "The Lieut General directs me to inform you that he will visit your city Tuesday next Sept 26th. Leaving this city in time to reach Indianapolis by 12 M. and will return from there late in the evening of the same day"   ALS, *ibid.* On Sept. 25, Morton telegraphed to USG. "Arrangements will be made

to receive you at noon to-morrow, Tuesday. It is hoped you will remain during the evening. If you will do so an extra train can return with you to-morrow night. Please answer." Copy, *ibid*. USG traveled to Indianapolis on Sept. 26, arriving at noon, and perhaps stopping briefly at Lawrenceburg en route. Morton introduced USG to a large crowd assembled at the capitol, and USG responded: "Ladies and Gentlemen: You are all aware that I am not in the habit of speaking, and would not have me make my first attempt before so large an audience as this. I therefore thank you for your attention, and will take my seat." *Indianapolis Journal*, Sept. 27, 1865; *Daily State Sentinel* (Indianapolis), Sept. 27, 1865. At 11:00 P.M., USG boarded a special train to return to Cincinnati; an attempted derailment is described in the *Cincinnati Gazette*, Sept. 28, 1865. In a later report printed on the same date, the newspaper stated that two sleeper cars of the train carrying Sherman to Lawrenceburg had been thrown from the track (rolling over) near Vincennes, Ind., around midnight, Tuesday, but that no one had been seriously injured.

2. On Sept. 12, George W. Hulick *et al.*, Batavia, Clermont County, Ohio, wrote to USG. "Learning that you will shortly be in Cincinnati O. we, in behalf of the soldiers and people of Clermont *your native County*, most cordially invite you to visit Batavia, to receive from the grateful people a warm welcome and a hearty reception. If it meets your approbation to accept the invitation, please notify us of the time." ALS, USG 3. Docketing indicates that an affirmative answer was sent on Sept. 16. On Sept. 26, Isaac Lynch, Connersville, Ind., wrote to Philip B. Swing, Batavia. "In looking over the Cin. Gazette of to-day my eye was arrested by the announcement that Lt. Gen. Grant would visit Batavia next Thursday, and that you, in behalf of the citizens, are to bid him welcome. Seeing your name and his together in this connection, created in my heart feelings and reflections which I am wholly unable to describe—for I remembered that in days long ago both of you had been my pupils, though not at the same time. In the year 1836 I taught a class of little girls and boys, in an old brick school house which stood on a bluff ridge in the outskirts of Georgetown Brown Co. Among the number, came daily a boy, whom I then particularly noticed, only, for his quiet demeanor, studious attention to his books, and remarkably good behavior That boy was Ulyssus S Grant—now the man whom the nation delights to honor. I have never met with him, since, but the image of his young face is indelibly fixed upon my memory. Although I exalt in the eminent distinction of one who was once my pupil it seems to me that I should feel more real pleasure in taking by the hand the *little boy* that I knew him to be—I should be awed at the majestic loftiness of the Lieut. General. . . ." ALS, *ibid*. USG drove a buggy to Batavia on Sept. 28, accompanied by Julia Dent Grant, his youngest son Jesse, and his father, Jesse Root Grant, arriving at noon. Swing delivered a lengthy welcoming address, and USG responded: "LADIES AND GENTLEMAN: You all know that I am not much of a speech-maker, and you will have to excuse me from making one upon this occasion. I am very glad to meet so many Clermonters here to-day, and recognize among them faces which I remember of having seen in my boyhood. I thank you very kindly." *Cincinnati Gazette*, Sept. 29, 1865. That afternoon, after a brief stop in Bethel, he went to Georgetown, Brown County, where he stayed with his cousin John Marshall. USG attended a reception in his honor at the Brown County Fairgrounds during the afternoon of Sept. 29, speaking to the crowd. "Ladies and gentlemen of Brown county: You are all aware that I am not in the habit of making speeches.

I am glad that I never learned to make speeches when I was young, and now that I am old, I have no desire to begin. I had rather start out in any thing else than in making a speech. And now, ladies and gentlemen, I can only say to you that it affords me very much pleasure to get back to Brown County where my boyhood was spent." *Ohio State Journal*, Oct. 3, 1865. Jesse Root Grant then delivered a lengthy speech. See *Indianapolis Journal*, Oct. 3, 1865; P. C. Headley, *The Life and Campaigns of General U. S. Grant . . .* (New York, 1869), pp. 562–63. USG returned to Cincinnati on Sept. 30, stopping on the way to dine with his uncle Samuel Simpson near Bethel. See Garland, pp. 338–41; Carl N. Thompson, ed., *Historical Collections of Brown County, Ohio* (Piqua, Ohio, 1969), p. 107.

To William Sooy Smith

Cincinnati Ohio
Sept 27th 1865

DEAR SMITH

Since receiving your letter asking from me a written Statement in regard to the extent of the authority I had given you to publish my Biography, I have received letters from two of the publishers of Profr Coppeé's book asking a similar statement in regard to the claims set forth by them for that work—Soon after the surrender of Gen. Lee Prof. Coppeé, an old West Point acquaintence of mine, called on me in Phila and stated that he wished to write up a history of my Campaigns and asked if I would authorize some member of my staff to furnish him from the records in my office such information as he could not obtain elsewhere, and as was not improper to give in advance of official reports. Knowing Coppeé as I did to be a man of ability, and believing that he would endeavor to give a correct history of what he wrote about I promised him all he asked. Since that time a similar request has been made by another party.

Although I did not promise exclusive privilege to one party, I informed the second applicant of the authority given to Prof. Coppeé and referred to him for such information as he might be willing to give to others engaged in a similar work.

Your request to me was for authority to publish my Biography.

Although much of the same matter will necessarily be embraced in such a work as is embraced in a history of the campaigns of the war just passed, yet they are different. I gave my free consent for the work proposed by you believing, and I still believe it does not conflict with any previous promise made. I now state that no other party has asked for information from me to enable them to write such a work as you propose, and should any do so in future, I will inform them of the promise made to you, and refer them to you for such aid as you may be willing to give.

Your friend
U. S. GRANT
Lt. Gen.

Copy, PPRF. See letter to C. F. Vent & Co., Sept. 18, 1865. On June 20, 1865, William Sooy Smith, Noyesville, Cook County, Ill., wrote to USG. "As I was quietly at work on my little farm this morning, I wondered whether there was any suitable person engaged writing your life. I would like to undertake it; and if my success Should not prove entirely satisfactory to you my attempt need never see the light. I am willing to devote to it what means I can Command, and my own best energies for such years of my own life as it may require. My health, impaired in the Service, will not bear me out in my efforts to earn my living by hard work. I know you will not attribute this request to any vain desire to be carried into notoriety by the skirts of your uniform—I can secure the assistance of the best literary talent of our Country so far as this may be needed, and I ask the privilege under the stimulus of my own necessities and the affection that I have always felt for you since our very first acquaintance. Please consider this note strictly confidential, and if you respond favorably I will be in Washington with my family just as soon as I can close up my little affairs here. We are all well—" ALS, MiU-C. On Sept. 15, Smith wrote to USG. "Will you have the kindness to put your permission to me to write your life, in writing. It will be of great value to me in my negociations with my publisher. If you can give me some such letter as the one enclosed from Genl. Sherman to Col. Bowman it will be worth a great deal to me. I regret to trouble you with this request; but I have staked so much on the work that I must strive to give it all the strength I can. . . . We would all be kindly remembered to Mrs. Grant & the children." ALS, *ibid.* Samuel M. Bowman, former col., 84th Pa., and Richard B. Irwin, former lt. col. and adjt. for Maj. Gen. Nathaniel P. Banks, wrote *Sherman and His Campaigns: A Military Biography* (New York, 1865). Charles B. Richardson of N. Y. published the book in association with C. F. Vent & Co. of Cincinnati. Vent & Co. advertised for agents to sell the book by subscription, printing a letter of July 31 from Maj. Gen. William T. Sherman to Richardson stating that Bowman had exclusive access "to read my secret thoughts and acts." *Illinois State Journal*, Sept. 6, 1865. See letter to Maj. Gen. William T. Sherman, Nov. 5, 1865.

To Elihu B. Washburne

Washington Oct. 8th *1865*

DEAR WASHBURNE,

I reached this city yesterday[1] and have been busy since in getting out orders I desire, and which I could get out in less than one tenth of the time if there was nothing between me and getting of them out, which will reduce expenses materially.—On arrival I found your letter relative to our Jay Cook[2] speculation. I saw Cook. He says that he took advantage of our confidance in him and changed our speculation so that we will make about $25.00[3] to close out now. I said close. Even would be a good thing and I guess the best we can do is to let Cook close up for us at once.

My whole trip has been condusive to health if one judges from corpulancy. I have got to be afraid to weigh almost. Mrs Grant and children keep pace with me, in enjoyment of travel, if one judges from the dificulty with which they are got up to time in starting from any point where we have spent a day.

Our kindest regards to Mrs. Washburne and children. Soon we will be fixed at housekeeping and will always have a spare room for you which we expect you to occupy when you are in Washington.—I left Mrs. Grant and children in Phila to do Fall shopping but will go after them this evening.

Yours Truly
U. S. GRANT

ALS, IHi.

1. USG arrived in Washington on Friday, Oct. 6, 1865.
2. Jay Cooke, born in 1821 in Sandusky, Ohio, became a prominent banker and financier in Philadelphia. In 1864, Jay Cooke & Co. subscribed $1,000 toward a house presented to USG in Philadelphia. See *PUSG*, 13, 234, 235n. USG met with Jay Cooke, Jr., at City Point in March, 1865. Ellis Paxson Oberholtzer, *Jay Cooke: Financier of the Civil War* (Philadelphia, 1907), I, 494–95.
3. See letter to Elihu B. Washburne, Oct. 25, 1865.

To Edwin M. Stanton

Washington Oct. 13th *1865*

HON. E. M. STANTON,
SEC. OF WAR,
SIR:

I would respectfully recommend that immediate orders be given for the removal or disposal of all public property, belonging to the Military branch of the public service, at Annapolis and to the abandoned forts around Washington. This would enable us to dispense with at least one regiment.

I would also suggest that the order require the immediate removal or disposal of all public property of forts hereafter abandoned.

Very respectfully
your obt. svt.
U. S. GRANT
Lt. Gn.

ALS, DNA, RG 94, Letters Received, 1107A 1865.

To Maj. Gen. Philip H. Sheridan

Washington Oct. 13th *1865*

MAJ. GEN. P. H. SHERIDAN,
COMD.G MIL. DIV. OF THE GULF,
GENERAL,

Herewith I enclose to you statement of J. Riggin Jr. and orders from Gen. Canby, touching action that has been had relative to the Merchant's Bank, and the Bank of New Orleans. At this distance I cannot presume to act in matters which, except in a state of War, belong purely to the Civil Authorities. As a rule I am opposed to the Military taking the law into their own hands. In this case Gen. Canby seems to have done so and it may be justly. I refer the mat-

ter to you however for such action as you may deem proper, either
to revoke all Gen. Canbys orders and leave the matter where Civil
Authority had placed it; to sustain his orders, or if improper legal
proceeding had been gone through in the first instance to give the
case back to Civil Courts.

> Very respectfully
> your obt. svt.
> U. S. GRANT
> Lt. Gen.

ALS, DNA, RG 393, Dept. of the Gulf and La., Miscellaneous Records. In
Aug., 1865, John Riggin, Jr., New Orleans, wrote to USG. "The undersigned
respectfully asks that you will read the following statement of facts, and take
such action in the matter as your good sense of justice and law shall dictate. If
the statement, and accompanying papers should seem long, the fact that it is
no fault of mine and the great importance of the subj[e]ct is my apology—
Immediately after resigning my position of Col. and A. D. C. on your staff, I
became a merchant and resident of New Orleans—Being a large creditor (over
$47.000) of the 'Bank of New Orleans' and the 'Merchants Bank' of N. O. and
finding it impossible to get any payment or settlement of my notes from said
banks, I applied to Maj. Genl Hurlbut, then commanding the Dept of the Gulf,
for such relief in the matter as the General might deem proper. Maj. Genl
Hurlbut would not interfere in the matter, deeming it one in which recourse
should be had to the Civil Courts. I then waited during the tedious Session of
the late Legislature of Louisiana hoping that the Legislat[ure] might pass an
act which might affect the liquidation of these Banks; but owing to peculiar influences brought to bear upon this peculiar assembly, the Legislature adjourned,
having done nothing. I then waited about two months hoping that the Officers
of the Banks might do something for their creditors, when finally I felt forced, to
protect myself, to sue these Banks, asking the court to put them into Liquidation
according to law. In the latter part of may 1865, the third District Court of
New Orleans, at the instance of the Attorney General of the State, as the law
directs, ordered these Banks to go into liquidation, and appointed three reliable
and competent citizens as Liquidators in each case; requiring good and approved
bonds for One hundred thousand Dollars from each of the Liquidators of the
'Bank of New Orleans' and Thirty thousand Dollars from each of the Liquidators
of the 'Merchants Bank'. At the time that these Banks were put in liquidation
their affairs were in a most deplorable and perishing state; suits having been
commenced against them, judgments in some cases rendered, and their property
siezed and advertised for sale by the Sheriff and the U, S, Marshal, and it was
only by the timely intervention of these Liquidators that great sacrifices of the
Banks property were prevented. At the time of these Liquidators taking charge
and management of the affairs of these Banks, the notes of the Bank of New
Orleans were selling at thirty two (32) cents on the dollar, and the notes of
the Merchants Bank at twenty five (25) cents on the dollar—In a few weeks,
under the management of these Liquidators, the bills of these Banks advanced to
eighty (80) cents on the dollar for Bank of New-Orleans, and seventy (70)

cents on the dollar for Merchants Bank notes. When on June 22nd, to the great surprise and injury of the creditors of these Banks, Genl Canby, Commdg Dept of the Gulf published orders 'annulling and setting aside' the appointment of Liquidators for these Banks by the civil courts, (copies of which orders, and other contradictory orders are herewith enclosed) and appointing as Liquidator[s] in the case of the Bank of New Orleans, the former officers or Directors of said Bank; notwithstanding the fact that this Bank went int[o] liquidation at the request of this same Directory—see copy from minutes of the Board hereto attached—and the further fact that it wa[s] under the old management of the Bank that it was brought to th[e] condition in which we found it, by their squandering Eight hundred and twenty thousand five hundred Dollars of the Banks money to assist the 'Confederate Government'. In the case of the Merchants Bank, Maj. Genl. Butler, when in command here, directed its affairs to be liquidated, and appointed the former direction or officers of the Bank to liquidate them; but instead of accepting the trust, the President went through our lines to Mobile, Ala, with nearly all of the most valuable assets of the Bank. The Cashier was imprisoned by Genl B., at Fort Jackson, and nearly all the Directors left for 'Confederate Territory': whereupon Genl Butler verbally appointed three persons to take charge of, and dispose of certain assets of the Bank, to pay certain claims against the Bank; which charge being fulfilled, their authority ceased. Now, when the Liquidators appointed according to law began their duties, they found the assets and property of this Bank scattered, and perishing. Troops had been quartered in their Banking house, and the books, seals and other property of the Bank left unprotected, being found as a pile of rubbish. The notes and papers of the Bank were found, part in New Orleans and part in Mobile, where what had not been disposed of were left, and, as before stated, the Banks were in ~~imminent danger of losing~~ imminent danger of losing their property through suits against, and seizures made of the same—In place of the legally appointed Liquidators of the Merchants Bank, Genl Canby appointed three others, one of whom is the Administrator of the estate of the late President of the Bank, who took out of our lines over $160.000. of the coin of the Bank, beside Bonds and papers to a large amount; none of which have ever been accounted for—Now General, it is true that the legally appointed Liquidators are not the relatives and intimate friends of the former managers of these Banks, nor of the friends and relatives who borrowed, and have been using for several years the money of these Banks, and for which the Banks now hold their paper (the larger portion of which is worthless), and it is true that, had they not been interfered with, they might have made some of these parties pay up, in order that the long suffering and outraged creditors of these Banks might have been releived; and it is also true that the affairs of these Banks are now suffering greatly because the legal Liquidators are deterred from acting. The Banking-house of the Merchants Bank was sacrificed at Marshals sale a few days ago, and the cotton of the Bank of New Orleans is being stolen in large quantities daily, because of the inability of irregularly appointed persons to protect their interests. In conclusion, General, I beg that the extraordinary proceedings in these cases may be immediately stopped by reinstating the Liquidators appointed by the Civil Courts, who alone can legally administer the affairs of these banks and protect the interests of all parties concerned." LS, *ibid.* The enclosures are *ibid.*

On Jan. 26, 1866, 12:30 P.M., USG telegraphed to Maj. Gen. Philip H. Sheridan. "Please forward to these Headquarters an official report of your action

and that of Gen Canby in the matter of the statement of John Riggin Jr relating
to the incorporated banks of New Orleans, referred to you October 13th 1865"
Telegram sent, *ibid.*, RG 107, Telegrams Collected (Bound); copies, *ibid.*, RG
108, Letters Sent; DLC-USG, V, 47, 109. On Jan. 31, Sheridan wrote to Brig.
Gen. John A. Rawlins. "In compliance with telegraphic instructions from the
Lieut General dated War Department January 26th I have the honor to make the
following report of the action taken, by Genl Canby and myself, on an application from a Mr John Riggin Jr to remove the military control from certain
chartered banks in the city of New Orleans   Mr Riggin presented a letter to me
from Lieut Genl Grant, a copy of which is herewith enclosed, marked A. On
the receipt of this letter I sent my Judge Advocate to Genl Canby's office to get
the necessary data about the banks. He returned reporting he was not well received   I then gave the order marked "B" which after considerable delay brought
me sufficient data to conclude, after close investigation, that the military control
of these banks was unnecessary and I gave the letter of directions marked "C"—
Acting under this letter Genl Canby came to me with the manuscript of his order
marked "D"—. To this order I saw no objection except to Paragraph VII. which
I intended to rescind as soon as I was notified that the bonds in Washington
would be returned. I see no objection to this method of removing military control
over these banks, which in my judgement should never have been assumed. Mr
Riggin wanted me to act in this matter so that he would be again restored as a
liquidator. That would have been very satisfactory for his side, but there were
other interests in these banks besides his, and I saw no objection to the appointment of directors" LS, DNA, RG 108, Letters Received. The enclosures are *ibid.*
On Jan. 5, Maj. Gen. Edward R. S. Canby had issued General Orders No. 2,
Dept. of La.; paragraph VII stated: "The liquidation will continue under the
Directors; and the civil courts of the State are prohibited from interfering with
it in any manner, until after the expiration of thirty days from such time as the
National Government may return to the State Auditor the bonds and securities
deposited to secure the circulation, and now held by the Federal authorities as
captured." Copies (2—one printed), *ibid.*

On July 12, 1865, Sheridan had telegraphed to Bvt. Col. Theodore S. Bowers.
"Probably about four and a half millions of Bank securities all worth their face
found in the hands of rebels at Shreveport—They were Louisiana State securities—If the Government has no claims on them I propose to turn them over to
the State auditor—Please inform me" Telegram received (on July 13, 2:40 A.M.),
ibid., RG 107, Telegrams Collected (Bound); *ibid.*, RG 108, Telegrams Received; copies, DLC-USG, V, 54; DLC-Philip H. Sheridan. *O.R.*, I, xlviii, part 2,
1073. On July 13, USG endorsed this telegram. "~~Secretary of War. I think they~~
~~should be held by the United States at least until title to them is vested in other~~
~~parties b~~ . . . Respectfully refered to the Sec. of War. I think Govt. should hold
these securities at least until the President decides otherwise." AES, DNA, RG
108, Telegrams Received. *O.R.*, I, xlviii, part 2, 1073. At 11:00 A.M., USG
telegraphed to Sheridan. "Send the Bank securities captured at Schrivesport to
the Adj. Gen. at Washington. They will be held here for future decission." ALS
(telegram sent), DNA, RG 107, Telegrams Collected (Bound); telegram sent,
ibid.; copies, *ibid.*, RG 108, Letters Sent; DLC-USG, V, 46, 109. *O.R.*, I, xlviii,
part 2, 1075. On July 25, Julian Neville, La. state auditor, New Orleans, wrote
to USG. "Inclosed please find a copy of a letter received by me from Maj Gen.
Sheridan, commanding this Department. The Bonds referred to, were deposited

by the Banks with the State Auditor, in accordance with the Law of this State, to secure the redemption of their circulating notes. They are consequently the property of the State, till the Banks shall have redeemed their notes & returned them to the Auditor for cancellation. I earnestly solicit your investigation of the subject as early as possible, & hope that you may see proper to order the return of the Bonds. Their seizure by the Military Authorities has caused a great depreciation of the value of the notes, and if we could be assured of their return, it would create a renewal of confidence in the Banks that would secure the bill holders from further loss." LS, DNA, RG 108, Letters Received. The enclosure is *ibid.*

On Jan. 5, 1866, Sheridan telegraphed to USG. "I have directed Gen Canby to relinquish Military control of the City of New Orleans & respectfully [*request*] that the bonds sent to the Adjutant Generals Office by your order be released so that they can go on with their liquidation. All but two of the Banks can redeem their circulation & pay their depositors & from fifty to ninety per cent on the stock" Telegram received (at 6:15 P.M.), *ibid.*, RG 94, Letters Received, 743G 1865; *ibid.*, RG 107, Telegrams Collected (Bound); *ibid.*, RG 108, Telegrams Received; copies, DLC-USG, V, 54; DLC-Philip H. Sheridan. On Jan. 6, USG endorsed this telegram. "Respectfully forwarded to the Secretary of War, with the recommendation that the bonds referred to be released." ES, DNA, RG 94, Letters Received, 743G 1865. Also in Jan., Sheridan wrote a letter received at USG's hd. qrs. "Matter of 'Merchants Bank in New Orleans, La.' in case of John Riggins and Geo. B. Fields." *Ibid.*, RG 108, Register of Letters Received. On March 15, USG endorsed this letter. "Respy forwarded to the Sec of war with renewal of a previous recommendation that the bonds referred to in Par 7. Sp order No. 2 Department of Louisiana, be returned to the auditor of the state of Louisiana, and that, whether said bonds are returned or not, the control of the banks mentioned in said order be remitted to those entitled to it under the laws of that state, and that the military authorities cease all further control of them" Copy, DLC-USG, V, 58. On April 18, Secretary of the Treasury Hugh McCulloch telegraphed to Governor J. Madison Wells of La. that the sequestered bonds would be returned. *Bankers' Magazine*, XV, 12 (June, 1866), 987. La.'s banking system before the Civil War required banks to deposit bonds with the state in order to protect depositors. See Stephen A. Caldwell, *A Banking History of Louisiana* (Baton Rouge, La., 1935).

To Maj. Gen. John Pope

Washington, D. C. Oct 14 1865. [*1:15* P.M.]

MAJ GEN POPE
ST LOUIS MO

I will send you four regiments of colored Infantry, or more if they can be used to advantage, to take the place of white Volunteers on the plains. Send them as far out as you can this Fall. In the spring I think these troops can be used to advantage guarding the highways through Indian Territory and in New Mexico. Let me know if you think more than four regiments of these troops can be used to advantage

U. S. GRANT
Lt Gen

Telegram sent, DNA, RG 107, Telegrams Collected (Bound); copies, *ibid.*, RG 108, Letters Sent; DLC-USG, V, 46, 109. *O.R.*, I, xlviii, part 2, 1240. See letter to Maj. Gen. William T. Sherman, Oct. 31, 1865. On Oct. 10, 1865, Maj. Gen. John Pope had telegraphed to USG. "I wrote you through Gen. Sherman, about ten days since, requesting authority to consolidate into one Regt. and reenlist for one year, the second (2) & third U. S. Vols. whose term of service expires this month. All the vol. Regts on the plains are dissatisfied and mutinous, &, are even now rapidly deserting. Unless other troops which are reliable can be had to replace them, I very much fear that, before winter sets in, they will abandon the posts & stores on the Plains. It is now too late in the season to send Regular Regts., to the remote points & I wish to reorganize the two Regts (second & third U S. Vols.) so as to keep them where they are. They are good soldiers, in good discipline, &, unless I can reorganize them at once, I fear we shall have great difficulty on the plains. Please answer." Telegram received (at 4:15 P.M.), DNA, RG 107, Telegrams Collected (Bound); *ibid.*, RG 108, Telegrams Received; copy, DLC-USG, V, 54. *O.R.*, I, xlviii, part 2, 1239–40. On Oct. 16, Pope telegraphed to USG. "It is too late in the season to get troops out farther than Fort Kearney two regiments colored troops can be used this winter West of Leavenworth to replace two white regiments two more could probably be used for the same purpose in New Mexico They could be sent in the winter Via Texas in the spring all troops needed in Minn ~~an~~ the upper Moon the platte & In Utah & New Mexico might be colored troops two regts colored can be used west of Leavenworth this winter" Telegram received (at 8:00 P.M.), DNA, RG 107, Telegrams Collected (Bound); (at 7:55 P.M.) *ibid.*, RG 108, Telegrams Received; copy, DLC-USG, V, 54. *O.R.*, I, xlviii, part 2, 1240–41. On Oct. 28, 2:30 P.M., Pope telegraphed to USG. "The tenth U S Infantry has reported two hundred & fifty 250 men aggregate the third U S Infantry arrives today having only ninety men eighty of whom will be discharged this winter. I cannot relieve many volunteer regiments with these two 2 regular regiments when I telegraphed you I supposed them to be at least two thirds full." Telegram received (at 3:35 P.M.), DNA, RG 107, Telegrams Collected (Bound); *ibid.*, RG 108, Telegrams Received; copy, DLC-USG, V, 54. *O.R.*, I, xlviii, part 2, 1245.

On Oct. 19, 11:20 A.M., USG telegraphed to Maj. Gen. George H. Thomas and to Maj. Gen. Philip H. Sheridan. "Send the 100th Colored regement at once to report to Gen. Pope." "I am ordering some Colored troops to Gen. Pope to take the place of White Volunteers. He reports that some might be sent from Texas to New Mexico during the Winter season. Answer if you concur in this view." ALS (telegrams sent), DNA, RG 107, Telegrams Collected (Bound); telegrams sent, *ibid.*; copies, *ibid.*, RG 108, Letters Sent; DLC-USG, V, 46, 109. The second is in *O.R.*, I, xlviii, part 2, 1241. On Oct. 21, Sheridan, New Orleans, telegraphed to USG. "The difficulty of sending Colored troops from

Texas to New Mexico would be very great ~~at~~ almost an impossibility in the winter season   I am not well acquainted with the line from Leavenworth but my judgment is against the movement   I think Colored troops if well Officered would do well in New Mexico"   Telegram received (on Oct. 23, 9:10 P.M.), DNA, RG 107, Telegrams Collected (Bound); *ibid.*, RG 108, Telegrams Received; copies, DLC-USG, V, 54; DLC-Philip H. Sheridan. *O.R.*, I, xlviii, part 2, 1242.

On Oct. 19, Secretary of the Interior James Harlan wrote to Secretary of War Edwin M. Stanton enclosing a request for an escort for Cheyenne and Arapaho Indians returning to their tribes. ALS, DNA, RG 94, Letters Received, 147I 1865. The enclosure is *ibid.* On Oct. 20, Stanton referred this request to USG. AES, *ibid.* On the same day, USG endorsed the request. "Respectfully returned to the Secretary of War. A small escort can be put at the disposal of the Secty of the Interior for the purpose within named. If you desire, Iwill order Genl Pope to furnish the same." ES, *ibid.* On the same day, Bvt. Brig. Gen. Edward D. Townsend wrote to USG. "The Secretary of War requests that you will please issue orders for such an escort as you deem proper, to be put at the disposal of the Secretary of the Interior, for the purpose of bringing safely to their tribes, the Arrapaho and Cheyenne Indians who are now north of the Platte and desire to return to their homes, in compliance with request contained in the telegram from Bvt. Major General J. B. Sanborn, to the Hon. Secretary of the Interior which was referred for your consideration this morning." ADfS, *ibid.*; LS, *ibid.*, RG 108, Letters Received. On Oct. 21, 3:30 P.M., USG telegraphed to Pope. "You will place at the disposal of the Secretary of the Interior such escort as may be deemed necessary to bring safely to their tribes the Arrapaho & Cheyenne Indians, now north of the Platte river." Telegrams sent (2), *ibid.*, RG 107, Telegrams Collected (Bound); copies, *ibid.*, RG 75, Colo., 1865 A984—1867 C288; *ibid.*, RG 108, Letters Sent; DLC-USG, V, 46, (2) 109. On Oct. 23, Pope telegraphed to USG. "I have directed an Escort to be furnished subject to the order of the Secy of the interior at Kearney Cottonwood Julesburg or Laramie as he may deem most Convenient" Telegram received (at 6:00 P.M.), DNA, RG 107, Telegrams Collected (Bound); *ibid.*, RG 108, Telegrams Received; copy, DLC-USG, V, 54. On Nov. 23, Harlan again wrote to Stanton requesting an escort for Cheyenne and Arapaho Indians. LS, DNA, RG 107, Letters Received from Bureaus. Enclosures are *ibid.* On Nov. 30, Bvt. Col. Theodore S. Bowers endorsed this letter. "Respectfully returned and attention invited to the enclosed copies of endorsements and orders, by which it will be seen that Gen. Pope was directed on the 21st October to place at the disposal of the Secretary of the Interior such military escort as he might call for for the purpose indicated. The present application differs from the previous one only in requesting that Major Wyncoop be placed in command of the escort. This request it may not be practicable to comply with by reason of his probable muster out." ES, *ibid.* On Dec. 1, Maj. Thomas T. Eckert, act. asst. secretary of war, wrote to Harlan enclosing a copy of Bowers's endorsement. LS, *ibid.*, RG 75, Colo., 1865 A984—1867 C288.

On Oct. 24, Pope telegraphed to USG. "Is it expected that the U. S. furnish mounted escorts for the overland stages? Such service is enormously expensive as it kills up both horses & men at a fearful rate, & requires very large force, more than the gov't is willing to allow. With the Sums appropriated to carry the mail, the Company ought to be and I think is able to furnish enough men itself to accompany the coaches. If the military are to furnish mounted escort they had best carry the mails themselves. With one fifth the amount paid to the mail company the mil'y in this Dept. can carry the mails regularly without additional expence to the gov't. I would be glad to be informed whether I am required to furnish mounted escorts to the coaches, if so it will need more troops than I have specified & a constant supply of horses. The stage Company threatens to draw off their coaches & stock & stop carrying the mail unless I furnish the mounted escorts" Telegram received (at 12:10 P.M.), *ibid.*, RG 107, Telegrams Collected (Bound); (marked as received at 12:10 A.M.) *ibid.*, RG 108, Telegrams Received; *ibid.*, Letters Received; copy, DLC-USG, V, 54. *O.R.*, I, xlviii, part 2, 1243. On the same day, USG endorsed this telegram. "Before answeri[n]g this dispatch I would like the views of the Sec. of War. I do not know what the contract is with the Mail Company. If Govt. is not pledged to furnish the escort called for I would not favor giving it. The whole Cavalry force of the Army would be required to give the Aid asked and it would be kept up at a very great expense." AES, DNA, RG 108, Letters Received. On Oct. 25, Stanton wrote to USG. "In reply to an inquiry of this Department, the Postmaster General states that there is no stipulation, on the part of the Government, in the contracts with the Overland Mail Company, to furnish mounted escorts, or military escort of any description. With this information, I refer back to you the telegram of Major General Pope, dated October 24, for such action as you may deem proper. The communication of the Postmaster General is also herewith enclosed." LS, *ibid.* At 12:40 P.M., USG telegraphed to Pope. "You need not furnish escorts to the overland stages except where it can be done without much inconvenience or expense. The route should be as well protected as practicable with the means at your disposal and when troops are moving over it they might move with the stages. With the Colored and regular troops sent to you can you not now muster-out of service all the volunteers remaining?" ALS (telegram sent), *ibid.*, RG 107, Telegrams Collected (Bound); telegram sent, *ibid.*; copies, *ibid.*, RG 108, Letters Sent; DLC-USG, V, 46, 109. *O.R.*, I, xlviii, part 2, 1244. On Oct. 26, Pope telegraphed to USG. "In answer to your dispatch of yesterday, I have to say that the four 4 Colored & four 4 regular Infantry reg'ts which I understood are assigned to this Dept would give me all the inf'y force I need if it were possible to get them on the Plains this winter november is the worst month in the year for heavy snow storms on the Plains I can however use the troops being sent to relieve all volunteer troops East of and including Fort Lyon on the upper arkansas & Fort Kearney on the Platte. I have altogether of Inf'y & Cavalry Seven thousand two hundred 7200 men west & south of the Missouri River Including everything as far west as Oregon & California of this force I can relieve about two thousand 2000 as Soon as the regular regiments arrive. It would not be possible to relieve troops further west than Kearney & Lyon without ernormous cost for forage & other trains & great suffering to men it is probably practicable to send troops to New Mexico ŧ via Texas this winter but even that would be very difficult & expensive. I see no way to relieve troops west of the posts named this winter. All Volunteers in Minnesota will be at once mustered out & replaced by tenth U S Infy" Telegram received (at 6:10 P.M.), DNA, RG 107, Telegrams Collected (Bound); *ibid.*, RG 108, Telegrams Received; copy, DLC-USG, V, 54. On Dec. 4, William K. Lothrop, secretary, Manhattan Gold Mining Company of Colo., New York, wrote to Postmaster Gen. William Dennison requesting escorts for gold shipments in Colo. ALS, DNA, RG 108, Letters Received. On Dec. 5, Dennison referred this letter to Stanton. AES, *ibid.*

On Dec. 11, USG endorsed this letter and a copy of Stanton's letter of Oct. 25 to USG. "Respectfully returned to the Secretary of War, attention being invited to the accompanying copies of communications, by which it appears that the request of 'Manhattan Gold Company' cannot be complied with." ES, *ibid.*, RG 107, Letters Received, Irregular Series.

Also on Oct. 25, Stanton wrote to USG. "The accompanying application of the Secretary of the Interior, for an escort for certain trains about to start from Kansas City, Missouri, for New Mexico, is referred to you, for report, and to issue such orders in relation thereto as the condition of the service will admit without prejudice to the public interests." LS, *ibid.*, Letters Received from Bureaus. The enclosure is *ibid.* On the same day, USG endorsed this letter. "Respectfully returned to the Secretary of War. As a general rule I am opposed to furnishing Escorts for the purpose named, but, in this case, the application is approved, and the necessary orders for an escort have been sent to Gen. Pope." ES, *ibid.* At 2:30 P.M., USG telegraphed to Pope. "You will please place at the disposal of the Secretary of the Interior an escort sufficient to guard a train of Indian goods from Kansas City to the Navajoes, in New Mexico, if the same can be done without prejudice to the public service." LS (telegram sent), *ibid.*, Telegrams Collected (Bound); telegram sent, *ibid.*; copies, *ibid.*, RG 108, Letters Sent; DLC-USG, V, 46, 109. On Oct. 26, 11:00 A.M., Pope telegraphed to USG. "I can escort train of Indian supplies for Navajoes to New Mexico from post to post on the route but it is much too late in the season to send trains across the plains & it should be perfectly understood in advance that no forage can be supplied to the train proposed to be sent by any of the military posts. I do not believe it possible to get a train across the plains without full supply of forage & a wagon loaded with forage coul[d] not haul enough for the mules that pull it. No forage for such a train can be supplied by the military posts which have only enough for their own use. it is very unwise to say the least to think of sending a train across the Plains at this time of year" Telegram received (at 6:15 P.M.), DNA, RG 75, Bureau of Indian Affairs, Central Office, Letters Received, Miscellaneous; *ibid.*, RG 107, Telegrams Collected (Bound); *ibid.*, RG 108, Telegrams Received; copy, DLC-USG, V, 54. On Oct. 27, USG endorsed this telegram. "Respectfully submitted to the Secretary of War, with the request that the substance of this dispatch be communicated to the Hon. Secretary of the Interior, and the parties interested in the transportation of the goods to the Navajoes." ES, DNA, RG 75, Bureau of Indian Affairs, Central Office, Letters Received, Miscellaneous.

To Hugh McCulloch

Respectfully referred to the Hon. Secretary of the Treasury.

During the months of January, February and March 1863 whilst the army under my command was laying in Louisiana, near Vicksburg, Miss., it was to a great extent fed from the plantations on the river above the city. Forage for all public animals was exclusively, or nearly so, procured from them. The horses and mules from accessible plantations were many, or all, taken for public use. All required for the army were retained and many sent north to the Quarter masters Dept. for issue elsewhere.

Several thousand bales of cotton were also taken and shipped to the Quartermaster in Memphis, Capt. A. R. Eddy, and sold for the benefit of Government. I cannot answer as to the particular plantations of Mrs Bass—what was on them or what was taken away, but every plantation from the Arkansas river to Vicksburg, probably without a single exception, was visited for the purpose of gathering beef and other provisions, and forage   what there was on Mrs Bass' plantations in this way must necessarily have been taken. I donot doubt the testimony here given as to the property taken, Mrs. Bass (now Madame Bartinetti) having never been within the rebel lines during the rebellion, and never having aided it nor abetted it in any way, so far as I know; and having expressed herself in favor of the Union during the rebellion and as far back as the first time I ever saw her (in the summer of 1863) I think she is entitled to remuneration for all the property taken and used by the Gov't., that is, pay for horses [and] mules at the rate th[e Gov't.] was paying at that time, and apply the same rule to other provisions. For the cotton I would fix the price at what Captain Eddy received for such as he sold in March or April 1863, transportation and Gov't taxes off.

U. S. GRANT
Lieut General.

HEADQRS. A U S
OCT. 16. '65

ES, DNA, RG 94, Amnesty Papers, Miss. See *ibid.*, RG 277, Southern Claims Commission, Approved Claims, Washington County, Miss., 154. Written on the report of a board of investigation convened at Vicksburg by the post commander on July 7, 1865, to examine claims of Mrs. Eugenia P. Bass for cotton and supplies taken by U.S. forces from her plantations in Miss. in early 1863. DS, *ibid.*, RG 94, Amnesty Papers, Miss. Mrs. Bass, widow of a wealthy planter, took the oath of allegiance on May 22. DS, *ibid.* On Sept. 6, 1865, Mrs. Bass married Count Joseph Bertinatti, Italian minister to the U.S. See Walter T. Durham, "Tennessee Countess," *Tennessee Historical Quarterly*, XXXIX, 3

(Fall, 1980), 323–40. On Oct. 13, USG wrote to Madame Bertinatti, Georgetown, D. C. "I will be in my office daily from 10 a. m. until 4th p. m. and will see you with pleasure on any day between those hours on business. From 7 in the evening I will generally be at my house in Georgetown and will see you there if preferable to you." ALS (facsimile), *Confederate Veteran*, XII, 4 (April, 1904), 158.

On Sept. 18, 1863, after Mrs. Bass had met USG at Vicksburg, Brig. Gen. John A. Rawlins issued a permit. "Special permission is hereby granted Mrs. Eugenia Bass, of Skipwith landing Miss. to ship all the cotton she now has of her own production to Memphis, for sale, and any Steamer is authorized to land at Skipwith landing, for the purpose of receiving the same under the protection of the Gunboats." Copies (2), DNA, RG 107, Letters Received from Bureaus; *ibid.*, Letters Received, H169¾ 1864. On the same day, Rawlins issued a safeguard for Mrs. Bass's property near Princeton, Miss. *HRC*, 43-1-262, p. 30. See John Y. Simon, ed., *The Personal Memoirs of Julia Dent Grant* (New York, 1975), pp. 121–22. On Nov. 22, Lewis Dent, Goodrich's Landing, La., wrote to "General." "Permit me to introduce to you Mrs. Bass and her daughter-in-law, Mrs James Bass. These ladies go to you to obtain from you a candid and impartial investigation of a charge made against a son and husband, by name of James Bass, recently tried before a Court of Military Commission at this place, Col. Young, presdt. The facts are briefly these. Mr James Bass, the prisoner, is charged with breaking the house and assaulting the person of one Hays, at night. The witnesses, declare that he was present aiding and abetting the act. ☞ Evidence of prosecution Mr Hays, swears to his voice, Mrs Hays swears to his person, one negress, swears to his person and *declares herself to be the slave* of Mrs Hays. Evidence for defence Col. Woods, makes oath that Mrs Hays, in lodging the complaint, declared in reply to his repeated inquiries, that she did *not see James Bass, but that the negroes did*, contradicting her evidence on the prosecution. The negress *declaring herself to be the property* of Mrs Hays, *is disqualified as a witness* ~~because~~ *in any case in which her owner is conserned.* There are three witnesses unimpeached who declare James Bass, to have been, at his own house on the night charged (22nd Oct) one, inferentially, two directly, and declare on oath that he could not have been absent from his house without their knowledge, on that night. In a court of law this evidence would acquit him. Mr Bass was sent yesterday hand-cuffed to Vicksburgh. The evidence taken by the Commission accompanies him. His mother and Wife go to day to bespeak the interposition of your justice and clemency. May I introduce these ladies as the unfortunate victims of Civil War reduced from affluence to poverty, and now asking *justice only* from the conqueror to save them from Shame & disgrace. I acted as counsel in the case and am the friend of these unfortunate ladies, and well knowing Genl McPherson's reputation for justice and his qualities as a soldier and a gentlemen I confidently introduce them." ALS, DNA, RG 109, Union Provost Marshals' File of Papers Relating to Individual Civilians. On Nov. 23, Maj. Gen. James B. McPherson endorsed this letter. "Lt. Col. Clark you will have Capt Pullen obtain the record in this case, and review the proceedings Mr Dent is the Brother in law of Genl. Grant" AES, *ibid.* On Jan. 7, 1864, Mrs. Eugenia Bass wrote to Secretary of State William H. Seward seeking the release from prison of C.S.A. Maj. Henry C. Bate, her brother, and asking that Seward intercede with President Abraham Lincoln to secure compensation for her losses. ALS, DLC-Robert T. Lincoln. Misdated Jan. 15 in Lincoln,

Works, VII, 131*n*–32*n*. On Jan. 12, Judge James Hughes, U.S. Court of Claims, wrote to Secretary of War Edwin M. Stanton. "I am advised by a letter received from Mrs. Eugenia Bass, that Adjutant General Thomas has ordered her plantations near Vicksburgh Mississippi, to be siezed in the name of the Government of the United States, and leased, and that this has been done under the impression that Mrs. B. is disloyal and has *a son* in the rebel army. The facts are, that Mrs. Bass is not disloyal, that she took the oath of allegiance in May 1863, that she has but one son, a lad about 15 years old, who is not, and never has been in the rebel army, and that her plantations were leased by her last fall, to a loyal Union citizen named Fuller, who was recommended to her by Gen. A. P. Hovey; the contract, which I have seen, is in General Hovey's handwriting, and Mr. James Casey, brother of the late M. C. from Kentucky informed me that he, (Casey) was interested with Fuller. The effect of Gen. Thomas' order will be, not only to ruin Mrs. Bass, but also Mr. Fuller, who has invested his means to stock the plantations. I am under the impression, also, that Gen. Grant has allowed a written safeguard for the property of Mrs. Bass. The action of the Adjutant General having evidently been founded on a misapprehension of facts, it is respectfully submitted, that his order ought to be rescinded, and on behalf of Mrs. Bass, I make that request." ALS, DNA, RG 107, Letters Received, H169¾ 1864. Mrs. Bass's son later joined the C.S. Army. Durham, "Tennessee Countess," p. 327. On Jan. 15, Lincoln wrote to Brig. Gen. Lorenzo Thomas concerning the leasing of Mrs. Bass's plantations. Lincoln, *Works*, VII, 131. On Feb. 8, Bvt. Maj. Gen. Alvin P. Hovey, Indianapolis, wrote to USG. "You will no doubt remember Mrs Bass who was presented to you last August by myself at Vicksburgh—The President has given an order which she will send you for the purpose of having a Board organized to adjust her claims—I have no doubt of her loyalty and the justness of her claims and trust you will make the order liberal enough to enable her to receive payment without again passing through the circumlocution officers at Washington . . . You will confer a favor by sending the papers to me by Leut Walker who will hand this to you—" ALS, DNA, RG 393, Military Div. of the Miss., Letters Received. On the same day, Mrs. Bass, Indianapolis, wrote to USG. "You may remember me by having formerly done me a favor—You gave me permission last September to ship a few bales—of cotton from my plantation in Mississippi—to Memphis—It has been my misfortune to suffer severely by both Armies—The rebels—burned over 2.000—bales of cotton for me—and the Officers of the United States took for the use of the Army—All my Mules—cattle—bacon—and other property—that could be used to supply their wants—I was not at home at the time—and consequently received neither pay, nor vouchers.—The President has kindly given me the enclosed order—which I hope you will have immediately enforced I have always been in favor of the Union—and have long since taken the oath of allegiance—May I hope General, that you will give me such an order—(My loyalty being established) as will do me justice without a second trip to Washington You will perceive the President's order will permit payment if the board investigating it so decree—Have the kindness to send the papers—to Gen Hovey at Indianapolis by Lt—Walker as I fear I might lose them if sent by mail—Gen Hovey has promised to transmit them to me—or I—will wait at Indianapolis for the papers—" ALS, *ibid*. The enclosed order stated: "General Grant will cause an inquiry to be made into the claims of Mrs. E. P. Bass of Mississippi, for Quartermasters, Commissaries and Hospital Stores, Supplies and Property, alledged to have been taken from her plantations in Mississippi, by the United States forces, for the public service, and not receipted for; and have proper compensation made for any just demands she may have, if it further appears that she is loyal to the United States." Copy, *ibid.*, RG 109, Union Provost Marshals' File of Papers Relating to Individual Civilians. On Jan. 25, Lincoln had endorsed this order. "I have declined to sign the within; and yet I do desire that an examination of Mrs Bass' losses may be made by those having the means of doing so, and that she be paid, or her account forwarded to the War Department, in due form, accordingly as the rules of the service may apply to her case." AES (facsimile), American Art Association, Anderson Galleries, Sale No. 3823, Feb. 25–26, 1930, no. 240. Lincoln, *Works*, VII, 149. On Feb. 9, Lt. Col. Theodore S. Bowers endorsed this order. "Respectfully referred to the Commanding Officer at Vicksburg Miss., who will immediately appoint a Board of three officers, one of whom shall be an Asst Quartermaster and one a Commissary of Subsistence, for the purpose of ascertaining and reporting the amount and value of Quartermasters and Commissary Stores and other property alledged to have been taken by United States forces from Mrs Bass' plantations situated in the State of Mississippi. This paper will be returned to these Headquarters with the report of the Board." ES, DNA, RG 109, Union Provost Marshals' File of Papers Relating to Individual Civilians. On June 10, 1865, USG and President Andrew Johnson endorsed this order. "The endorsement hereon will be executed by the present commander of Vicksburg." "The endorsement of Gen'l Grant hereon is approved, and will be carried into execution." AES (facsimiles), American Art Association, Anderson Galleries, Sale No. 3823, Feb. 25–26, 1930, no. 240. Lincoln, *Works*, VII, 149. On June 19, Bowers wrote to the commanding officer, Vicksburg. "You will please cause to be delivered from the Quartermaster's Department to Mrs. E. P Burtinatti, ten serviceable mules, in lieu of mules taken from her plantation near Vicksburg for the use of Government. A similar order was issued soon after the fall of Vicksburg, but it now appears it was never complied with" Copies, DLC-USG, V, 46, 109; DNA, RG 108, Letters Sent. On June 20, Rawlins wrote a similar letter to Bvt. Maj. Gen. Montgomery C. Meigs. Copies, *ibid.*

On June 5, 1866, the cabinet discussed the claims of Madame Bertinatti. Howard K. Beale, ed., *Diary of Gideon Welles* (New York, 1960), II, 522. See *ibid.*, p. 526. On June 8, Johnson endorsed a letter of the same day from Stanton. "Approved & referred to the Secretary of the Treasury to pay to Madam Bertinatti the awarded value of the cotton within mentioned to wit $16,200.—" Copy, DNA, RG 366, Records Relating to Captured and Abandoned Property, 1866–73, Letters Sent. The Stanton letter is *ibid.* See *HMD*, 42-2-21, p. 3; *HED*, 39-2-114, p. 7; *ibid.*, 44-1-189, p. 3. On April 8, 1870, Count Bertinatti, Turin, wrote to USG urging settlement of the remainder of his wife's claim. Copy (in French), Seward Papers, NRU. In 1873, the Southern Claims Commission allowed an additional payment of $11,860 for other losses, after Madame Bertinatti claimed that she did not know that her agent had invested in C.S.A. bonds, an issue that had stopped an identical award in 1871. *HMD*, 42-2-16, p. 9; *ibid.*, 42-2-21; *ibid.*, 43-1-23, p. 15; Frank W. Klingberg, *The Southern Claims Commission* (Berkeley and Los Angeles, 1955), p. 97.

To Maj. Gen. Joseph J. Reynolds

Washington Oct. 16th 1865 [*6:00* P.M.]

MAJ. GN. REYNOLDS LITTLE ROCK,

Mrs. S. A. Douglas[1] has in Lafayette Hempstead & Columbia Counties Ark. a number of hundred bales of cotton. Please authorize such Govt. transportation as can be spared without detriment to the public service to move it this to Little Rock or Schrieveport. Please direct the Comd.g officer at Schrieveport to render the same aid.

U. S. GRANT
Lt. Gn.

ALS (telegram sent), DLC-Thomas Ewing Family Papers; telegram sent, DNA, RG 107, Telegrams Collected (Bound); copies, *ibid.*, RG 108, Letters Sent; *ibid.*, RG 393, Dept. of the Gulf, District of La., Letters Received; DLC-USG, V, 46, 109. On Oct. 19, 1865, Lt. Col. John Levering, Little Rock, Ark., adjt. to Maj. Gen. Joseph J. Reynolds, wrote to USG. "Your personal telegram of yesterday, to Maj. Genl. Reynolds. directing that transportation be furnished. to move certain cotton, owned by Mrs. S. A. Douglass, in Lafayette, Hempstead and Columbia Counties in this state, to this place, or Shreveport La. has been received. In the temporary absence of Genl. R. permit me to ackknowledge receipt, and to remark:—From the tenor of your dispatch, we anticipate a call, from an agent sent by Mrs. D. who will point out the places, at which this produce may be found, and superintend the shipment? The counties designated, are in the south west corner of the state, and near to Shreveport. The delivery would be convenient, at that point. We have two companies of troops at Washington, Hempstead Co. and one company at Lewisville, Lafayette Co. one Co. at Paraclifta, Sevier Co. They have supplies for more than two months, but a trains may be sent from here, with further supplies, which can return with cotton. Every facility will be rendered." ALS, DNA, RG 108, Letters Received. On Nov. 2, noon, USG telegraphed to Maj. Gen. William T. Sherman. "Authority was sent Gn Reynolds to use public transportation in getting Cotton purchased in Ark by Mrs Douglas to Little Rock. Inform him that that authority is now revoked." ALS (telegram sent), *ibid.*, RG 107, Telegrams Collected (Bound); telegram sent, *ibid.*; copies, *ibid.*, RG 108, Letters Sent; *ibid.*, RG 393, Military Div. of the Miss., Telegrams Received; DLC-USG, V, 46, 109. At noon, USG also telegraphed to Maj. Gen. Philip H. Sheridan. "Authority was sent for the use of govt. teams in transporting private Cotton from the interior to the Red River. That authority is now revoked." ALS (telegram sent), DNA, RG 107, Telegrams Collected (Bound); telegram sent, *ibid.*; copies, *ibid.*, RG 108, Letters Sent; DLC-USG, V, 46, 109. On Nov. 3, Sherman telegraphed to USG. "Despatch concerning Mrs Douglass cotton rec'd & shall have immediate attention" Telegram received (at 1:00 P.M.), DNA, RG 107, Telegrams Collected (Bound); *ibid.*, RG 108, Telegrams Received; copies, *ibid.*, RG 393, Military Div. of the Miss., Letters Sent; DLC-USG, V, 54.

1. USG purchased a home in Washington in late Oct. two doors from the former home of Senator Stephen A. Douglas. See letter to Charles W. Ford, Oct. 28, 1865; Bvt. Col. Adam Badeau to Elihu B. Washburne, Nov. 9, 1865, DLC-Elihu B. Washburne. On Jan. 23, 1866, USG attended the wedding of Adèle C. Douglas, widow of Douglas, and Maj. Robert Williams. *Galena Weekly Gazette*, Jan. 30, 1866.

To Edmund Kirby Smith

Washington D. C.
October 16th 1865.

E KIRBY SMITH
LATE GENL SOUTHERN ARMY.

Your letter dated Havana July 31st 1865 reached me but a day or two since, as I have been absent from this City since the middle of July.

After consultation with the President of the United States I am of the opinion that you had better return to the United States, take the amnesty oath and put yourself on the same footing with other paroled prisoners, I am authorized to say that you will be treated with exactly as if you had surrendered in Texas and been there paroled

Yours &c.
U. S. GRANT
Lt. Gn.

LS, Edmund Kirby Smith Papers, Southern Historical Collection, University of North Carolina, Chapel Hill, N. C. On July 31, 1865, Edmund Kirby Smith, former C.S.A. gen., Havana, had written to USG. "Relying upon the friendship of past years, I unhesitatingly write you, and ask not only your advice but your good services. I arrived here day before yesterday from Vera Cruz, having been frightened away from Texas by the reported indictment of Gen Lee, and the Amnesty proclamation of the President—I understood that if I gave my parole I would not be permitted to leave the country, and would be liable to indictment for treason—on the urgent entreaty of my friends I left Texas untill the Government should have clearly determined upon the policy to be pursued towards the south. I am now abroad with not more than sufficient means to subsist upon for ten or twelve months—I am seperated from my family who are dependent upon my exertions for their support—I must go to work and do not wish to live under a foreign government or to seek employment in a foreign land—Will you write to me and candidly advise me what to do—I do not think I am asking anything that conflicts with your duty—I wish to return home, will give my parole, take the oath of allegiance and quietly and peaceably settle down at some occupation by which I can make a support—Write to me under cover to C. L. Beissner & Co Havana—I may go to Merida Yucatan where I understand I can live economically. My letters will be forwarded by Mr Beissner—" ALS, CSmH. On Oct. 24, Alexander N. Zevely, third asst. postmaster gen., wrote to USG. "I have the honor to return to you, as the Writer, the enclosed letter, addressed C. L. Bussner & Co. Havana, Cuba, the same having been sent to the Dead Letter Office, for want of full prepayment of postage, its weight exceeding that covered by single rate postage." LS, Smith Papers.

On March 15, 1866, Smith, Lynchburg, Va., wrote to USG. "In your official report, as published in the journals, the charge of bad faith is made against me in the following extract Viz 'Genl Kirby Smith surrendered his entire command to Maj Genl Canby. The surrender did not take place however, until after the capture of the rebel President and Vice President; and the *bad faith* was exhibited of first disbanding his army, and permitting an indiscriminate plunder of property' I trust, General, the examination of the enclosed documents, will entirely remove the impression of bad faith on my part, which I am satisfied was made in your mind, by a misapprehension of the events preceeding the surrender of the Troops in my Department. About the middle of May 1865, I received & positively declined the only proposition made me for the surrender of the Troops under my command (*No 1. No 2*). I retained Col John S Sprauge, the U. S. Commissioner, until the meeting of the Trans Miss Governors, which had been convened by me at Marshal Texas, hoping that negotiations might then be opened upon a basis that would result in a convention to which I could honorably subscribe. Col Sprague left Shreveport on the 19th of May, 1865. On the morning of the 20th, I departed, in advance of my staff, for Houston Texas—Depots had been established, and the main body of the army concentrated in that vicinity—Orders were issued for the transfer of Dept Hed Qrs to Houston. I reached Crocket on the 21st where, by telegram I learned that the Infty of Genl Walkers Corps had that morning disbanded at Hempstead Texas. The Telegraphic lines were cut, and from that time all communication ceased with Shreveport, and the District was soon filled with disorganized and disorderly soldiery, suspending travel and making life and property insecure. I arrived at Hempstead on the morning of the 25th, having been compelled to remain 36 hours in Huntsville to escape the mob of disorderly soldiery thronging the roads. At Hempstead, I found a despatch from Genl Magruder announcing the disbandment of all the Troops in his district. (*No 3*) is my letter calling upon Genl Magruder for explanation of the causes which produced this disorganization. (No 4) proceedings of a Court of Inquiry convened by me to examine into those causes. (*No 5*) Report of Maj Genl Walker, Commanding Corps Texas Troops. In Houston I issued an address to the Troops (*No 6*), which was copied in the

Texas papers and which placed the responsibility where it justly belonged, and urged obedience to the laws, and a quiet return to the avocations of peace. Finding I was powerless myself, I called upon Governor Murrah of Texas to employ the State Troops, still under his control, in collecting and preserving public property (*No 7*). By despatch from Galveston of the 31st May, I received notice of the arrival at that Port, from New Orleans, of Brig Genl Davis U S A and Capt Meem my aide de Camp. In Galveston, June 1st, I learned through Capt Meem, for the first time, that Lt Genl Buckner my chief of staff, had, after my departure from Shreveport, proceeded to New Orleans and in my name opened negotiations with Maj Genl Canby for the surrender of the Trans Miss Dept. The disbandment of the army in Texas, and the disorganized condition of the Troops remaining in Louisiana, had determined Genl Buckner in this course. The breaking of the Telegraphic [l]ines, and the occupation of the roads and country by disorderly bands of soldiery had interrupted all communication with Shreveport. I signed the articles of surrender off Galveston Bay on the 2nd of June—In my interview with Brig Genl Davis, I stated that the Troops in Texas had disbanded and gone to their homes. (*No 8. No 9. & No 10*) evidence that the necessary orders were issued, and measures taken to insure the execution of the terms of the surrender, as far as remained within my power. (*No 11*) charges the commander of the Dist of Texas &c with the general superintendence of the surrender within the limits of his District. Lt Genl Buckner, chief of Staff, superintended the surrender in the District north of Texas—he at the time commanded the District of Ark & W La. (*No 12 & No 13*) assign Brig Genl P A Hebert to the command of the Dist of Texas &c after the departure of Genl Magruder and provide for the execution of the terms of surrender in that District. The above documents clearly demonstrate, *1st* That I was, in no way, responsible for the disbandment of the Troops within my Departmt or for their seizure of the public property. *2nd* That those acts were previous to any negotiations having been opened for the surrender of the Department. *3rd* That I made every exertion to remedy the evil, and to collect the abandoned and stolen property, even before I was apprised that Lt Genl Buckner had initiated steps for the surrender. *4th* That I conscientiously endeavored to secure the proper execution of the terms of the surrender. In conclusion General I request that these documents may be filed with my letter in the War Department; and I appeal to you as a soldier jealous of your own high reputation, to remove the imputation of bad faith undeservedly made against me a brother officer, whose only legacy the wars and misfortunes of his country have left him, is the consciousness of having honestly and faithfully discharged his duties and obligations." Copy, Smith Papers. Some of the enclosures are *ibid.* See letter to Edwin M. Stanton, June 20, 1865.

On June 15, 1866, Smith, Washington, D. C., wrote to USG. "My signature ratifying the articles of Convention surrendering the Troops under my Command in the Trans. Miss. Dept. to Maj Gen Canby has always been regarded by me as a parole, and has honestly and conscienciously been observed as such. In November of 1865 I took the amnesty oath; the Provost Martial declining to take my parole, declaring, after the above circumstances were stated by me, that the parole was not required and would be superfluous. The same view was taken by U. S. Officers whom I consulted, in which number was Maj Gen Hitchcock. As

I desire to go to Kentucky and Tennessee & engage in business, and lest I might there be placed in a false position, I would again most respectfully express my readiness to sign a parole of the same form and nature as that required of the Officers surrendering under my command—and request that this document be placed on record as evidence of a desire, on my part, to comply fully with all that could be required of me under the terms of surrender." ALS, NHi; ADfS, Smith Papers. *O.R.*, I, xlviii, part 2, 602. See *ibid.*, pp. 600–2; Joseph Howard Parks, *General Edmund Kirby Smith, C.S.A.* (Baton Rouge, 1954), pp. 483, 491–95.

To Edwin M. Stanton

Washington D. C, Oct. 17th *1865*

HON. E. M. STANTON
SEC. OF WAR,
SIR:

I would respectfully recommend that all Volunteer General officers now in service, except Department Commanders and those disabled by wounds received in service, be granted thirty days leave of absence and at the end of that time be mustered out of service or returned to their positions in the regular service.

A sufficient number of the Brevet Brigadier and Major Generals could then be assigned to duty according to their Brevet rank for all the requirements of the public service.

This proposition or one that all Volunteer General officers should be mustered out, honorably, and Brevets assigned I would approve. The latter proposition however would leave Generals in command with the pay only of inferior grades and would take out of service the wounded class who in justice it would seem should be provided for at least for a time.

Very respectfully
your obt. svt.
U. S. GRANT
Lt. Gn.

ALS, DLC-Edwin M. Stanton.

To Edwin M. Stanton

Washington Oct. 18th 18665.

HON. E. M. STANTON
SECRETARY OF WAR,
SIR:

I would respectfully recommend that the Veteran Reserve Corps of the Army be mustered out of service.

Applications from nearly all the enlisted men are coming in for their discharge. The services of the corps are by no means commensurate with the expense of keeping it up. The majority of the officers of the corps have no claim upon the Government beyond what all officers and men who served faithfully during the rebellion, and it will be much more for the public good to provide other assistance to those few who have such claims

> Very respy.
> Your obt. servt.
> U. S. GRANT
> Lt. Gen'l

Copies, DLC-USG, V, 46, 109; DNA, RG 108, Letters Sent. On Oct. 4, 1865, Private Caleb Mott *et al.*, 3rd Veteran, New Haven, Conn., petitioned USG. "We the undersigned in behalf of forty six of fifty one members of Co "A" 3d Regt Vet Res Corps, have the honor respectfully to make the following statement We are aware of our presumption and the delicate position we assume, and know that to address an Officer of your rank is predjudicial to good disciplin, But Sir, you are the only one we have to look too, Our Officers misrepresent our feelings, and the press of the Country, do us the injustice by insinuateing, that it is for our interest for the Goverment to keep us in Service. Sir patience has ceased to be a virtue, and we take this as the last resort, trusting that you will respond to our plea now as we responded to yours at Donelson, Vicksburg, and the bloody fields of the Wilderness, feeling to day as proud of our scars, and worthy the name of a 'American Soldiers as ever. Though the press, and our Officer, classes us as Invalids, and almost beggars, by saying we cannot earn our liveing, out of the service, we therefore respectfully ask your honor to discharge us from the military Service of the United States, for the following reasons Viz: We were among the first Volunteers, and when we asked the privledge of Veterans were refused, and had to join the Vet Res Corps, or have Copperheads call us cowards, and ask us if we had got enough, we swore by the eternal no, and again took up the musket, and said we would not lay it down while our flag had an enemy, we received no Goverment bounty, nor State aid as did the Veterans, We succumbed willingly to all this, Always performing our duty creditably, not only

to our Country, but ourselves. Sir look at Sixteen Dollars per month, Our Wives
and Children looking two months for our thirty-two dollars, to pay for rent,
procure food, fuel, and clothing, and will your honor blame us who knows the
feelings of a husband and father, to cease to respect our Officers, when they tell
us and Maliciously represent us as being better off in the service than out. Sir
though Soldiers of four Years service, We love our little ones, and would like
to be with them, and who can do up an old Wound with more satisfaction than
can our Wives. Sir some of our families are really suffering for the necessaries
of life, and as the Goverment dont want us now, only as a favor towards us, we
ask to be discharged, that we may be with them to provide for, and comfort
them, as we were 'wont to do before the Goverment asked our services. Sir in
'God's name thwart the design of those Officers, who would hold us in service, and
leave our families to suffer for their own personal interests. May we hear favorably
from your Honor soon, and live long to respect the name of U. S. Grant. General
pardon us if we have done wrong, for we look to you as our only friend." DS
(six signatures), *ibid.*, Letters Received. Five additional petitions (one undated)
to USG of Sept. 23, Oct. 4, 5, and 10 from different Veteran regts. are *ibid.*
On Oct. 13, Private David Fisher *et al.*, Springfield, Ill., petitioned USG. "You
will, we feel confident, pardon this obtrusion upon your notice, when the object
which prompts it is considered. The gigantic civil war which has reigned over
our land—such as no nation ever withstood, and which has deluged our country
in blood, and distributed mourning broad cast throughout the land, has ceased
to be; at last the din of battle is hushed, and the 'Angel of peace smiles o'er
Victory's way.' Officers and Men have done their duty, and done it well,—and
amid the crumbling of the *Southern Confederacy* is heard the death-wail of dying
secession. All feel that their task is accomplished, and desire to return to their
homes and families. We, your petitioners, members of the 4th and 15th Vet.
Res. Corps desire to be discharged, and that those of our Corps who may wish
to remain in the service may be retained. The monthly pay is not sufficient to
support our families. We have done the Government some service, and we feel
that our next duty is due our families. Hoping, General, you will favorably consider this appeal," DS (eighty-five signatures), *ibid.*

On Oct. 20, USG wrote to Secretary of War Edwin M. Stanton. "In view of
the charge of injustice to a class of men who deserve well of their country, that
might be raised if the Veteran Reserve Corps are all mustered out of service, I
will change my recommendation on this subject to an order mustering out all
who desire it. When the effect of such an order is seen, further directions can be
given for what remains. I do not know but it would be well to embrace in the
musterout order all officers of the corps who have not been disabled by wounds
recieved in battle." Copies, DLC-USG, V, 46, 109; DNA, RG 108, Letters Sent.

To Thomas E. Bramlette

Washington D. C. Oct. 18th 1865.

HIS EXCELLENCY T. E. BRAMLETTE,
GOVERNOR OF KY.
DEAR SIR:

Many complaints have been made to Washington, through unofficial sources of the situation of affairs in Ky. and particularly of
the difficulties that have beset Union men for their observance of
an order published by Gen'l Palmer prior to your late election. I
do not know that I ever saw the order referred to nor whether it
was one that I would have sanctioned. But it does seem that all persons who have got themselves into complications with the civil
authority of the state by their observance of this order should, in
some manner, be protected by the General Government. At the
time of the promulgation of Gen'l Palmer's order the State of Ky.
was under Martial law and I do not see how her citizens could
avoid the observance of even an improper order. The question now
is to determine how the necessary protection can be given. To
ascertain all the, and to advise what is the real situation, and especially in the case of those Kentuckians who have been indicted
because of their observance of a military order. I send Col. O. E
Babcock of my Staff, the bearer of this, to make an inspection.
Before going further he will first consult with you, and, if deemed
necessary with Gen'l Palmer,   It is highly desirable that all matters should be settled by civil authorities if they can. If the Military
must come in to settle any question it is then desirable that it
should be as little offensive to the civil as circumstances will admit
of. For this reason I want to know exactly what the difficulties are
before acting and want also to consult you as the head of the State
Government. If the matter of indictments stand as I am told they
do, I think the Courts that granted them should dismiss them so as
to avoid conflict. If asked, as a measure to preserve quiet in the
State, to do so might they not accede to the proposition? Col. Bab-

cock has no special instructions further than are contained in this
letter.

> I have the honor to be
> Very respectfully
> Your obt. Servt.
> U. S. GRANT
> Lieut. Gen'l

Copies, DLC USG, V, 46, 109; DNA, RG 108, Letters Sent.

To John Tucker

———

> Washington D. C.
> October 18th 1865

DEAR SIR:

On my return to Washington from my late visit to Phila I
found so many papers awaiting my action, and received so many
calls from parties having business to transact with Army Head
Quarters, that I have not until now found time to empty my
pockets of letters stored in them. Yours of the 7th to me, asking
for a written statement of the late Maj. Gen. Chas. F. Smith's services, such as you had heard me verbally express, was among a
pocketfull of letters so stored, and, I regret to say forgotten.

If anything I can say of the merits and services of that gallant
old soldier can benefit his widow and orphan children I will be but
too happy to say it. He was among the best known officers in the
old Army, among Army officers, for his Military bearing and fa-
miliarity with all the duties of a soldier. In time of peace he was
regarded as about the best if not the very best soldier in the Army.
In war he sustained the reputation made in time of peace.

It was my fortune to know Gen. Smith well. Most of my
Cadetship at West Point was under him as Commandant. I served
with him again in the Mexican War. In this war most of his ser-

vices were subordinate to me. At Fort Donelson he shone out conspicuously among, and above, all other officers present. At the time I accorded him the credit of having led, not ordered, the assaulting column which carried the enemy's fortifications and forced their surrender. For this service he was promoted to the rank of Major General.

Gen. Smith ended a career of usefulness at Savannah, Ten. in hearing of the guns of Shiloh. I saw some time before that he could not recover from the illness which confined him and urged upon the necessity of his leaving the field. But his sense of duty to his country would not permit of his doing so whilst a battle seemed to be pending. A lingering hope seemed to pervade him that, in such an event, he might in some way be useful. After the battle he consented to go but it was then too late.

I sincerely hope your efforts in behalf of Mrs. Smith and her children may prove successful. The family of such a man have a claim upon the gratitude of their country.

> Very Truly
> your obt. svt.
> U. S. GRANT
> Lt. Gn.

To HON. JOHN TUCKER
PHILA PA

ALS, ICarbS. See letter to Miss Smith, July 21, 1866; *SRC*, 41-2-44.

On Jan. 3, 1877, USG wrote to James Pollock, director, Mint of the United States. "Miss H. L. Smith, the daughter of Maj: Gen. C. F. Smith, one of our most gallant Generals in the rebellion: Commandant of Cadets, at West Point when I entered the Academy, and who died under me at Pittsburg Landing, Tenn., in 1862,—has applied to me to aid her in procuring a position in the Phila. Mint. There is nothing that I would not do to aid the children of my once old chief and afterwards subordinate in their life struggles. I sincerely hope you will find it convenient to aid Miss Smith." Copy, Schoff Collection, MiU-C.

To Brig. Gen. George P. Este

Head Quarters Armies of the United States
October 19th 1865.

SIR:

In reply to your inquiries concerning my knowledge of William H. Harris[1] of Carroll Parish, State of Louisiana, I would state: That shortly after my arrival at Young Point in the Spring of 1863, Mr. Harris called upon me at my quarters. I understood that he was then residing upon his plantation a few miles above, engaged in its cultivation; that he remained at home and during the Spring or Summer took into partnership a Northern man by the name of Dunham. From all I learned afterward I have no doubt that Dunham and other Northern Cotton Speculators treated Harris badly, and finally compelled him to leave his home. I gave him permission to go into Mississippi and return. This I understood was used against him by charging him with communicating with the enemy. He was frequently at my Quarters and I regarded him as a peaceable well-disposed and harmless citizen.

U. S. GRANT
Lt. Genl

TO GEN. GEO. P. ESTE

Copy, DNA, RG 393, 5th Military District, La., Miscellaneous Records. George P. Este, born in N. H. in 1829, educated at Dartmouth College, practiced law in Toledo, Ohio. He was appointed col., 14th Ohio, as of Nov. 20, 1862, and brig. gen. as of June 26, 1865. On June 22, USG had written to Secretary of War Edwin M. Stanton. "I would respectfully recommend that Col Geo P. Este, 14th Regt Ohio Vols Infantry, and Brevet Brigadier General of Volunteers, be appointed a full Brigadeir General of Volunteers. I make this recommendation in view of the fact that he has been strongly recommended for the position by his immediate Commanding officers for his ability and gallantry in the field. He is now about to retire from the service and I think it would be a just recognition of his services to afford him the opportunity of resigning from a brigadier generalcy." LS, *ibid.*, RG 94, ACP, E143 CB 1865. He resigned as of Dec. 4.

1. William Hawes Harris, born in Va., owned two plantations in Carroll Parish, La., with 166 slaves in 1860. Joseph Karl Menn, *The Large Slaveholders of Louisiana—1860* (New Orleans, 1964), pp. 177–78. After the Civil War, Harris was awarded substantial claims for cotton "Erroneously seized as abandoned"; Este was his attorney. *HED*, 39-1-114, p. 8; *ibid.*, 44-1-189, p. 5;

HMD, 46-2-30, p. 5. On March 1, 1872, Harris, Vicksburg, wrote to USG. "There is a bill before Congress and I learn it has passed establing the Northern District of Louisiana as a Judicial District of the United States A judge of that District will be appointed and I must ask the favor that you will give me the High position as Judge of that District I will discharge it duties with fidelity to the Goverment and to the best of My Capacity I *am and have ever felte* the deepest obligations of gratitude to you for your Confidence and Kindness while you were In Command at Millkens Bend &c and this favor would place me under renewed obligations I must beg that you will pardon the liberty and trouble that I make on your time" ALS, DNA, RG 60, Appointment Records.

To Edwin M. Stanton

Washington, Oct. 20th *1865*

HON E. M. STANTON,
SECRETARY OF WAR.
SIR:

I have the honor to submit the following report of the reduction of the army, and to make some suggestions for the reorganization of the regular army. The surrender of the rebel armies and the collapse of the rebellion rendered a large part of our military force unnecessary, and immediate steps were taken to reduce it, by stopping enlistments, discharging non-effectives, and the muster-out of men and regiments whose terms of service expired before given dates.

By the 1st of July 1865 the spirit in which the results of the war were accepted by the south was known; already two months had passed without a collision of any importance between the soldiers of the rebel army returned to their homes, and our troops; every where submission was perfect, and all that was asked by them was permission to resume the ordinary pursuits of civil life. The reduction of the army was now made by organizations, and during the month of July, the two most important armies in the country—that of the Potomac and of the Tennessee—returned to the people from whom they had come four years before. Since that time the reduction of troops left in the southern states to secure order and protect the freedmen in the liberty conferred on them, has been gradually going on, in proportion as continued quiet and good order have justified it.

On the 1st of May, 1865, the aggregate of the military force of the United States was one million, five hundred and sixteen (1,000,516) men. On October 20th this had been reduced, as is estimated, to two hundred and ten thousand (210,000), and further reductions are still being made.

These musters-out were admirably conducted, eight hundred thousand men passing from the army to civil life so quietly that it was scarcely known, save by the welcomes to their homes, received by them.

The ordinary process was to muster out the regiments in the field or wherever they might be, transport them as organizations to the States from which they came, and there pay them off and discharge them from service.

The apprehensions felt by some of disturbance and disorder at so vast a force being suddenly thrown upon the country to resume the occupations of civil life after having been so long absent from them, proved entirely unfounded, the soldiers showing by their conduct, that devotion to their country in the field is no disqualification for devotion to it at home.

At the beginning of the war our small regular army was barely adequate to protect our overland routes and our Indian frontier, and garrison our seacoast works; at its close we practically had no Indian frontier as the mines of the Rocky Mountains had scattered settlements at numerous points along their slopes, and the force employed in protecting these settlements and the overland routes, was double that of the whole regular army at the beginning of the war.

In view of the vast extent of our country, the recent hostile condition of a portion of it, with the possibility of future local disturbances arising from ill feeling left by the war or the unsettled questions between the white and black races at the south, I am of opinion that a regular army of eighty thousand men is needed; and would recommend the following legislation:

1. Two additional regiments of cavalry, to be added to those now in the regular service.

2. Each of the battalions of the nine regiments of infantry added to the regular army in 1861, to have two companies added to it, and to be made into a regiment.—

3. All companies of artillery, infantry and cavalry to have a maximum strength of 100 enlisted men.

4. The additional regiments necessary to make the force eighty thousand men, to be of infantry.

5. The Quartermasters, Commissary's, Medical and Adjutant Generals Departments to be increased commensurately with the increase of the army.

6. The Corps of Engineers and Ordnance to remain as at present, notwithstanding the 12th section of the act of March 3d 1865, merging the Corps of Engineers and Topographical Engineers.

7. The five regiments of artillery to have a uniform organisation, that of the 5th artillery.

8. Two-thirds of the original vacancies created, to be filled by officers of volunteers who have served at least two years during the war, or have left the service on account of disabling wounds, and one third by officers of the regular army.

9. President to be authorized to retain or raise if he deems necessary, an additional force of colored troops, not to exceed twenty thousand men; to officer the same and to disband it when no longer needed.

I would further recommend that on the reorganization of the army the President designate companies or regiments of the regular army into which men disabled in the war be allowed to enlist for garrison duty under such regulations as shall be deemed proper.

There is in my opinion further legislation needed for the regular army, but I deem that suggested the most important and first to be obtained.

> Very respectfully
> Your obt. servant
> U. S. GRANT
> Lieut-Gen'l.

LS, DNA, RG 94, Letters Received, 1232A 1865. Incomplete in *O.R.*, III, v, 126–27. See letter to Edwin M. Stanton, Nov. 3, 1865; letter to Henry Wilson, Jan. 12, 1866. On Oct. 1, 1865, Bvt. Brig. Gen. William Redwood Price, chief, Cav. Bureau, wrote to Brig. Gen. John A. Rawlins concerning cav. reorganization. LS, DNA, RG 94, Letters Received, 1232A 1865; (dated Sept. 1) Bender Collection, Wy-Ar. On Nov. 23, USG endorsed this letter. "Respectfully forwarded to the Secretary of War. The general plan of the reorganization of the cavalry is approved, except in the number of regiments, which should be twelve. This would require a corresponding reduction of the infantry force heretofore recommended." ES, DNA, RG 94, Letters Received, 1232A 1865. On the same day, USG wrote an identical endorsement on papers supporting cav. reorganization submitted by Price. ES, *ibid.*

To Edwin M. Stanton

Respy. forwarded to the sec of war with the recommendation that the Q M Gen. be ordered to settle for the services of the steamer "Dictator" in accordance with the charter made by Gen Ingalls. The services of this boat were necessary at the time the charter was made by the Government and it was by my authority. If the Q M G. will take the pains to look, I think he will find he had no cheaper transportation in service than the "Dictator", and that the money returned to his Department by the boat would pay the greater part of the charter money. I had supposed this matter settled long ago. Certainly the acts of a bonded officer binds the Government in a case like this, and if it is wrong, recourse must be had upon the officer himself & the Army Commander, who approved his action

U. S. GRANT
Lieutenant General

HEAD QRS A U S.
OCTOBER 20, 1865.

Copy, DLC-USG, V, 58. Written on a letter of Oct. 11, 1865, from Brig. Gen. Rufus Ingalls received at USG's hd. qrs. "Calls the attention of Lieut Genl Grant, to fact, of no settlement being yet effected with Q. M. Genl. for charter of the 'Steamer Dictator' plying as mail boat during siege of Petersburg, Va., between Washg & City Point, Va., notwithstandig he (Gen Ingalls) called Lt.

Genls attention to the matter on 3d of June 1865." DNA, RG 108, Register of Letters Received. On June 3, Ingalls had written a letter received at USG's hd. qrs. concerning the *Dictator*. DLC-USG, V, 58. On June 3 and 15, USG endorsed this letter. "Respy referred to the Q M G. who will make settlement for the services of this boat upon terms agreed upon by General Ingalls" "Respy. forwarded to the Sec of War with request that the Qr Mr. General be directed to settle for the services of this boat upon the terms agreed upon & recommended by General Ingalls" Copies, *ibid.*

To Charles W. Ford

Washington D. C. Oct. 21st *1865*

DEAR FORD,

We got back here all safe and had a very pleasant trip of it too after leaving you. I expected to remit you $698 30, the amount of my indebtedness, immediately on my return but did not find it convenient to do so. Will send it however next week and a few hundred besides which I wish you would give to S. Sappington on demand.

I enclose with this a letter to S. Sappington who lives in the stone house near Dr. Barretts opposite Mr. Dent. I want to get Sappington to attend to the payment of the taxes on land which Mr. Dent owns in Jefferson County and which will be sold on the 1st of next month if not paid before. The mails to Sappington P. O. only go once a week, on Teusdays, and if I trust to the mails it will be too late. Will you do me the favor to send some one with this letter to Sappington and send with it $400 00. As I say I will send the money next week.

I have so much to do you must excuse me from writing a long letter. If you can ever get to Washington come immediately to my house to stop.

Yours Truly
U. S. GRANT.

ALS, USG 3. See letter to Charles W. Ford, Oct. 28, 1865.

To Maj. Gen. Philip H. Sheridan

Confidential   Washington D. C. Oct. 22d *1865*
DEAR GENERAL,

You are probably aware that I have been absent from Washington for eleven weeks. During that time your dispatches touching Mexican affairs were received at the office but none of them forwarded to me. I only read them two days ago for the first time. This will answer a seeming negligence in my not replying to you.

Immediately on my return from my Western tour I had a long conversation with the President on Mexican affairs. On that subject he feels just as I do, in fact as the whole country does irrespective of parties. Before I left Washington I procured a leave of absence for Schofield for the purpose of allowing him to go to Mexico to take service there. I think Mr. Seward has been the stumblingblock in the way of his starting. Some correspondence it is said is going on with the French Government in relation to the withdrawel of French troops from Mexico which it is necessary to get a reply to before action. The President however told me that arrangements were made to supply the Liberal Government with arms without regard to their having means to pay for them. There is also I believe a project on foot to supply Schofield, or who ever goes, there with emigrants who will enlist after they reach Mexican soil. Of this however the Government knows nothing and I only learned it from the fact that enquiries have been made of me how far emigration will be prevented. I have no hesitation in saying that I would like to see any amount of assistance given to the Liberals and if I had my way I would use United States forces to give to them the Rio Grande country as a base to start from. That is I would clear out the south bank for them. This hower is not permitted.

I believe, as is indicated in some of your dispatches, that the Mexicans have no great leader capable of using even the resources at their disposal. It will take some man from the United States to fill the place. Schofield, if he can get the start, is fully equal to the task.

When Congress meets I have but little doubt but the Mexican question will be taken up and the withdrawel of all foreign troops insisted upon. If so this will settle the whole question. In the mean time all you can do is to encourage the Liberals to use their greatest exertions until they do get aid. If they give up themselves and, like MacKauber wait for something to turn up, they may loose every thing.

Some of your letters received in my absence I have furnished copies of to the President. Your course, and views, are heartily concured in by me and I am satisfied they are also by the President and Sec. of War. Mr. Sec. of State I fear is working against the Liberal cause in Mex. I hope I do him injustice in this matter.

Yours Truly
U. S. GRANT
Lt. Gn

TO MAJ. GN. P. H. SHERIDAN
COMD. MIL. DIV. OF THE GULF.

ALS, DLC-Philip H. Sheridan. *O.R.*, I, xlviii, part 2, 1242–43. See letter and telegram to Maj. Gen. Philip H. Sheridan, July 25, Aug. 13, 1865; letter to Maj. Gen. John M. Schofield, March 24, 1866. On Nov. 5, 1865, Maj. Gen. Philip H. Sheridan, New Orleans, wrote to USG. "I am in receipt of your communication of the 22nd ultimo, and am glad you wrote me as I must confess that for three or four weeks past I did not exactly understand on which side the land lay. What I have written in reference to the feeling in Mexico against Maxamillian is correct; nine and one half tenths of the people are against him. He cannot collect taxes, and what money he gets in Mexico is from forced contributions on the merchants of the towns he happens to hold, and these towns may be considered in a state of seige, all communications with them being interrupted or entirely cut off by the Liberals. Substantially he has no Government, and no party to support him. In reference to american Emigrants to help the Liberals, some care and judgement must be exercised. The Rio Grande frontier is nearly a desert, and soldiers and emigrants will find it hard to live on Frejolis and Torteas, which is all the country can afford, and these not in abundance; in fact those who come should bring everything with them, and indeed there are many difficulties to be surmounted until Metamoras is captured, in which event a port of entry is opened which cannot be blockaded, as Brazos Santiago can supply via Bagdad or Brownsville. My own idea is that if our Government means to take the contract, only six thousand cavalry is required, and a demand for the surrender of Metamoras which would be given up. This Cavalry could be started into the country from Fort Duncan, and the whole of Northern Mexico would rise with it: Monterey, Paris, and all towns could be taken with their small garrisons. The French cannot concentrate in this part of Mexico against a cavalry force, on account of supplies. The supplies are not abundant in the country, and the lines to the valley of Mexico are difficult and long. The Rio Grande frontier is very bad for Infantry operations on account of the great distances. If Schofield comes he will have to depend mainly on the native population. I will help him with my whole heart, but would advise the main reliance to be put on the Liberals instead of imigrants; all that is required is a good leader. Our soldiers cannot live as the Mexican soldier does, and most of their force is mounted. I am very familiar with that country and could give Schofield much information about it should it be prudent for him to call to see me. I make the foregoing remarks on emigrants in anticipation of the disgust that would naturally seize them on first entering a country which will not come up to their expectations in the way of supplies and general character. I sometimes think there is still an understanding between the rebellious of the Southern States and Louis Napoleon. That such an understanding did exist before the surrender of Lee there is no doubt. The contest in this country for the last four years was the old contest between Absolute-ism and Liberalism, and Lous Napoleon saw it and acted on it, but waited too long: had he anticipated the rapidity with which the bottom fell out of the Rebellion, we would have had much work on our hands, therefore let us not imitate his example and wait too long in this Mexican affair lest we make a mistake" LS, DNA, RG 108, Letters Received; ADf, DLC-Philip H. Sheridan. *O.R.*, I, xlviii, part 2, 1252–53. A notation on the letter reads: "Duplicate: Original by Mail Nov 6th 1865" AN, DNA, RG 108, Letters Received. On Nov. 23, USG endorsed this letter. "Respectfully forwarded to His Excellency the President for perusal, with the request that this letter be returned when read." *O.R.*, I, xlviii, part 2, 1253.

On Aug. 5, Sheridan had telegraphed to USG. "I am now very well Satisfied that the removal of the French & Austrian troops from Matamoras was caused by the fear that the City might be captured and the French Govt did not wish the complications which would arise" Telegram received (on Aug. 7, 1:00 A.M.), DNA, RG 107, Telegrams Collected (Bound); *ibid.*, RG 108, Telegrams Received; copies, DLC-USG, V, 54; DLC-Philip H. Sheridan. *O.R.*, I, xlviii, part 2, 1165. Also on Aug. 5, Sheridan telegraphed to Brig. Gen. John A. Rawlins. "I directed the railroad from Brazos in the direction of Rocho Chica to the Rio Grande at Whites Ranch to be builded when I first came to this command— This involved only the expense of cross ties as we have everything else—The contract for these ties has been disapproved on the strength of an order obtained from the Secretary of War for the continuance of this road to Brownsville from Whites Ranch—The Short road from Brazos for which these ties were gotten out and delivered long ago is So necessary that it seems like a want of reflection or a suggestion on the part of some old man who was in the Mexican War, when we got along without it—The sooner these people die off the better it will be for the public economy" Telegram received (on Aug. 7, 1:40 A.M.), DNA, RG 107, Telegrams Collected (Bound); *ibid.*, RG 108, Telegrams Received; copies, DLC-USG, V, 54; DLC-Philip H. Sheridan. *O.R.*, I, xlviii, part 2, 1165.

On Aug. 9, Sheridan telegraphed to USG. "Another band of between six and seven hundred armed confederate soldiers under command of Col Terry crossed the upper Rio Grande a short time ago. They were captured by Cortinas and disarmed, and their transportation taken, It is alleged that they were on their way to Sonora, but when disarmed they made their way to Monterey" Telegram received (on Aug. 10, 12:45 P.M.), DNA, RG 94, Letters Received, 869A 1865; *ibid.*, RG 107, Telegrams Collected (Bound); *ibid.*, RG 108, Telegrams Received; copies, DLC-USG, V, 54; DLC-Philip H. Sheridan; USG 3. *O.R.*, I, xlviii, part 2, 1174. On Aug. 10, Bvt. Col. Theodore S. Bowers endorsed this telegram. "Respectfully forwarded to the Hon. Secretary of War." AES, DNA, RG 94, Letters Received, 869A 1865.

On Aug. 18, 1:30 P.M. and 2:00 P.M., Sheridan twice telegraphed to USG. "Scouts and an Agent from Cortinas have arrived here from the Rio Grande, There is no great change in the condition of affairs there since my last telegram, The Franco-Mexico Rebels hold Matamoras and Monterey, The Liberals all the balance of the country, The Imperialists are getting shaky about their connection with the Rebels. Juarez is stupid—He does not Know what he has in his hands, I will be obliged to go to San Antonia next week to fix up the cavalry columns and move some to Levado [*Laredo*] and Fort Duncan if possible, I will go as far as Fort Duncan, and will possibly sec Juarez, The Col Terry whom I reported in a previous dispatch as having crossed the Rio Grande and being disarmed, was Judge Terry of California notoriety—" "It is more than probable that E Kirby Smith came to this city on last thursday sub-rosa, On friday afternoon I learned of his arrival—On saturday morning I found Beauregard came up nearly sub rosa—Sunday night there was assembled a few indiveduals at Beauregards house—Monday night I had his house searched, but did not find Smith, There has been quite a collection of Rebel Generals here in the last two weeks, some sub rosa, some by authority—I feel quite certain that the burden of their mission here, was the Mexican colonization scheme There appears to be a free masonry among all rebels in New Orleans An offer of ten thousand men was made not long ago to Maximellian through Mejia, There is but little doubt of this, but Mejia is getting shaky, and it is said rejected the offer, The Maxemillian Government in Mexico is a farce. He holds only a few cities and towns, and cannot collect revenue except on the line from Vera Crux to the city of Mexico, If our government does not watch these rebels closely, there will be a Franco-Mexico Rebel League, If France means to support Maximillian she will do it with rebels if possible—" Telegrams received (on Aug. 19, the first at 2:00 P.M., the second at 1:45 P.M.), *ibid.*, RG 107, Telegrams Collected (Bound); *ibid.*, RG 108, Telegrams Received; copies, DLC-USG, V, 54; DLC-Philip H. Sheridan. *O.R.*, I, xlviii, part 2, 1192.

On Sept. 21, 2:30 P.M., Sheridan telegraphed to USG. "I have just returned from an extended trip in Texas going from Galveston to San Antonia—thence to the Rio Grande & Fort Duncan & returning via Austin City. I find the condition of affairs in Texas very good Some depredations by small bands of the Kickapoo Indians in Western Texas These Indians are located at Santa Rosa in Mexico—I have decided not to establish any permanent posts with volunteer troops. It would be an enormous expense to the Government and no econemy could be expected from Officers or men. The Indian difficulties are trifling and I can control them by sending small cavalry expeditions from San Antonia, out west, as far as the Rio Grande, to stay out fifteen or twenty days, their return alternating with other detachments or regiments, Northern Texas will be controlled in the same way from Austin City, This method will be more effective than permanent posts with dissatisfied troops—The troops in Texas are very anxious to be mustered out, and as the War Dept has thrown all the responsibility on me, I am annoyed by Governors of States and friends of the soldiers at home— I wish regular troops could be sent to replace ~~these~~ these men or new organizations raised for a limited time. I could spare more troops were it not for ~~the~~ the threatening force required on account of the troublesome state of affairs in Mexico, I am pretty well posted on the condition of things there and will communicate by letter to you—" Telegram received (on Sept. 22, 10:00 A.M.), DNA, RG 107, Telegrams Collected (Bound); *ibid.*, RG 108, Telegrams Received; copies (one sent by mail), *ibid.*, Letters Received; DLC-USG, V, 54; DLC-Philip H. Sheridan. *O.R.*, I, xlviii, part 2, 1235–36. On Sept. 22, Sheridan wrote to USG. "While visiting in Texas, in order to determine about the establishment of a few permanent Military Posts on the Northern frontier and in Western Texas I extended my trip to Fort Duncan to ascertain correctly how much dependence could be placed on Mexico in supplying forage. I learned the following in regard to the condition of affairs in that country On the 5th of August Juarez evacuated his Capitol, the city of Chihuahua, falling back to Conception with about (3400) Thirty four hundred of all arms and abandoning Eighteen pieces of artillery On the 10th fifteen hundred (1500), French troops his only enemy entered Chihuahua having marched from Durango shortly after the occupation of the city by the French troops The Liberals rose in their rear at the town of Parral and captured the French garrison left there to protect their line of communication and isolated this command from Durango and the Liberals say it shall never get back: so much for the condition of affairs in the state of Chihuahua—which is all Liberal—as well as every other portion of Northern and Eastern Mexico except in the individual cases of French, English, or rebel merchants While this affair was going on in Chihuahua Cortinos, and other Liberal leaders held the country and interrupt all communications between the cities held by the French in the states of Tamaulipass Nuevo Leon and Coahuila. The Liberals at a little place called China attacked a train which was being ~~which was being~~ sent from Monterey to Matamoras Esscorted by about (900) nine hundred men captured between four and (500) five hundred and drove the rest back to Monterey All the parties in Nuevo Leon Coahuila and Tamaulipas were uniting at Lampessias between Monclova and Monterey, I have sought to unite these parties and in fact General nearly everything which has been done west of the Rio Grande has been under my influence or direction but in such a way as not to compromise the Government Much more could have been done had it not been for General Steele who has done everything he could to annoy me, and counteract what I wished to do and what I thought you wished in your conversation with me and in your telegrams since and he has done it understandingly Shortly after the success in Chiahuahua more and important successes attended the Liberals in the Valley of Mexico I met at Fort Duncan a Colonel direct from Juarez and Negrete, the latter is at El Paso this officer went to Lampissas The whole country General is Liberal and on the Rio Grande wherever I found a rebel I found an Imperialist and where I found a liberal I found a Union man The parties are as distinct as they were in our own country I privately and unofficially gave the liberals as much back bone as I could and particularly advised offensive operations as defensive in a country which is to be conquered would not soon win I sent a Pontoon train to Brownsvill about the time I reviewed the Cavalry at San Antonio and asked General Merritt to accompany me to the Rio Grande it had a good effect. I also while at Fort Duncan made enquiry as to the quantity of forage that could be obtained out in the direction of Monterey and Monclova with the view of supplying the Posts on the Rio Grande from this point This enquiry may have been misconstrued but it was a proper and legitimate one" LS, DNA, RG 108, Letters Received. On Oct. 6, 2:00 P.M., USG telegraphed to Sheridan. "Relieve Gen Steele from duty with thirty days leave to report by letter to the Adjt General for orders at the expiration" Telegram sent, *ibid.*, RG 107, Telegrams Collected (Bound); copies, *ibid.*, RG 108, Letters Sent; DLC-USG, V, 46, 107. *O.R.*, I, xlviii, part 2, 1237. On Oct. 8, 10:30 A.M., Sheridan telegraphed to Rawlins. "I have the honor to acknowledge the receipt of telegram directing me to relieve Gen Steele" Telegram received (at 12:00 P.M.), DNA, RG 107, Telegrams Collected (Bound); *ibid.*, RG 108, Telegrams Received; copies, DLC-USG, V, 54; DLC-Philip H. Sheridan. *O.R.*, I, xlviii, part 2, 1239.

On Oct. 13, USG wrote to President Andrew Johnson. "The enclosed copy of a letter just received from Gen. Sheridan is respectfully forwarded for your information." ALS, DLC-Andrew Johnson. USG enclosed a letter of Sept. 26 from Sheridan to USG. "PRIVATE! . . . I see it reported in the newspapers that the U. S. Government will probably recognize Maximilian. I wish to say that at the present time I consider the Liberal cause as in better condition than at any other period since the advent of Maximilian. I further say that nearly the whole of Mexico is against Maximilian in feeling and that if the government recognizes the Empire it recognizes the power of Louis Napoleon and not the will of the Mexican people. Maximilian has for his friends in Mexico only the french, English and rebel merchants. Fifteen hundred french captured Chihuahua: they were indiscreet to have ventured even that small number of men so high up when they are meeting with reverses in the valley of Mexico, and evry city out of the valley occupied by the french may be considered in state of seige. The object of the advance into Chihuahua was for effect with the outside world, not for any effect it will have in Mexico. to day I learn of the advance from Lampissas against Monterey by the Liberals who are reported strong. The Government need not be afraid that I will compromise it." LS, DNA, RG 108, Letters Received; copy (misdated Sept. 28), DLC-Andrew Johnson. On Sept. 28, Sheridan wrote to USG. "*Private* . . . The Government should be very careful about recognizing Maximilian: the liberal cause is now in better condition than it ever has been. Eight thousand liberals marched from Lampissas on Monterey and when last heard from were about thirty five (35.) miles from the city; the whole country is represented as turning against Maximilian. he has not even a party to back him and must leave the country The liberals are anxious that the United States Government refuse to recognize the Empire; they are now beginning to realize that they can accomplish the work themselves. The appearance of our large force in Texas has dispelled their despondency now they know we are strong and think our people sympathise with them, The rebels had made them believe our government weak and our numerous failures in the Trans Mississippi Department went to confirm it." LS, DNA, RG 108, Letters Received. USG endorsed this letter. "Respectfully refered to 'The President' for perusal with the request that this letter be returned" AES (undated), *ibid.*

On Oct. 25, Sheridan telegraphed to USG. "I respectfully forward the following information, The Liberals under Escabino and Cortinas I think, attacked Matamoras on the Nineteenth or twentieth instant, with every prospect of success, unless the eight or nine hundred rebel soldiers in the city join with the Imperialists, in the defence of the place, My information goes to show that they will not, Should the Liberals get Matamoras, northern and eastern Mexico, will pass into the hands of the Liberals" Telegram received (on Oct. 26, 10:50 A.M.), *ibid.*, RG 107, Telegrams Collected (Bound); *ibid.*, RG 108, Telegrams Received; copies, DLC-USG, V, 54; DLC-Philip H. Sheridan. *O.R.*, I, xlviii, part 2, 1244. On Oct. 30, 3:00 P.M., Sheridan telegraphed to USG. "There has been severe fighting between the Liberals and Imperialists in & about Matamoras with no decisive results up to the evening of the 25th One small fort was captured by the Liberals and recaptured by the Imperialists—On the 26th there was another engagement according to reports—results not known Up to the 25th the information is reliable" Telegram received (at 11:00 P.M.), DNA, RG 107, Telegrams Collected (Bound); *ibid.*, RG 108, Telegrams Received; copies, DLC-USG, V, 54; DLC-Philip H. Sheridan. *O.R.*, I, xlviii, part 2, 1249.

To Edwin M. Stanton

Washington October 25th 1865

HON. E. M. STANTON
SEC. OF WAR
SIR:

I have an application for Mrs. Lubbock of Texas to visit her husband, Ex Governor Lubbock, who is confined in Ft. Deleware. I do not know anything of the circumstances of his arrest or the charges against him and therefore only submit whether the permission should be granted—

Mrs. L. is represented as an old lady, in feeble health and in great anguish to see her husband once more.

Very respectfully
Your obt. servt.
U. S. GRANT
Lieut. Genl

Copies, DLC-USG, V, 46, 109; DNA, RG 108, Letters Sent. Francis R. Lubbock, born in S. C. in 1815, moved to Tex. in 1836, and served as governor (1861–63). Appointed col. and aide to C.S.A. President Jefferson Davis as of June 14, 1864, he was captured with Davis during the flight from Richmond. On Oct. 24, 1865, Mary R. Rhodes, "Church Home," Baltimore, had written to USG in behalf of Lubbock's wife, Adele. "I have very much mistaken your character if any apology is necessary for approaching you in the interests of humanity—The wife of Ex. Gov. Lubbock of Texas is a friend of mine of more than 20 years standing. She is in feeble health, distracted with anxiety about her husband who has been for many months a prisoner at Fort Delaware—She implores me, in the most touching manner to try & get permission for her to go to Fort Delaware where if she 'can only see him in his daily walk & know that he is well, she will be satisfied—' She is willing, General, to take the journey from Texas here, in *very* feeble health, too *see* her husband only—For thirty three years she has been an devoted wife & whatever Mr. Lubbocks political errors have been, all who know him can certify to his loving care of a feeble woman who, childless, as she has been, has been wrapt up in her husband—She asks but little—God grant that the heart of Mr. Stanton may be for once softened that he may grant her prayer—I have, with other old friends of Mr. Lubbock petitioned in vain to see him in the presence of the Commanding officer at Fort Delaware who knows me well, & that tho' active in the interests of humanity I have rigidly adhered to the line of *my* duty to the Government & asked no favor of him inconsistent with *his*—I implore of you, General, to use your influence with the War Department to grant permission to Mrs. Lubbock to *see* & if *possible speak* to her husband—They are no longer young—Life is fast fading away from both—Surely it is a small boon to grant or to be granted by a Govt as powerful as ours—A feeble heart broken wife pleads to see her husband—Shall it be in vain?—" ALS, USG 3. Docketing indicates that Secretary of War Edwin M. Stanton granted permission on Oct. 25. *Ibid.* See *O.R.*, II, viii, 816–17.

To Elihu B. Washburne

Oct. 265th *1865*

DEAR WASHBURNE,

It is seldom I get time to write and now have nothing special I wish to say.—I have received all the letters you have written to me but in the matter of discharges have attended to none of them for the reason that Pope said he would have all his Infantry but four Regiments mustered out by the 1st of this month. I have sent him regulars and colored troops enough to take all them out. On accoun[t] of the inaccessability of some of his troops, and the nervousness of our frontier settlers this busine[ss] has gone on slower than I expected. But all will be mustered out soon I hope.

I have not seen Cook this week but when I saw him last sSaturday he told me that he had closed out $75000 00 of our compound interest notes and directed the closing out of the balance that day. He said our gains would pay $1100 lost on the 10 x 40s and give us between $2500 & $2700 clear gain.

Mrs. Grant and the children are well. Give our kindest regards to Mrs. Washburne and family

> yours Truly
> U. S. GRANT

ALS, IHi. See letter to Elihu B. Washburne, Oct. 8, 1865. On Nov. 6, 1865, Bvt. Col. Orville E. Babcock wrote to U.S. Representative Elihu B. Washburne. "The Genl requests me to say that there is $1312 50/100 at Jay Cooke and Company to your credit—result of your investment—. . ." ALS, DLC-Elihu B. Washburne.

To Bvt. Maj. Gen. Montgomery C. Meigs

> Washington D, C,
> October 28th 1865

MAJ. GEN. M. C. MEIGS,
QR. MR. GEN. U, S, A,
GENERAL;

Bvt. Maj. Webster, A. Q. M. of Volunteers is an applicant for the same rank and position in the regular Army. I will freely sign his recommendation but prefer having the endorsement of the Chief of the Dept. before doing so. Maj. Webster has been on duty at Hd Qrs. for the past year and was with the Army of the Potomac through all the campaign of last year. He has given entire satisfaction and I think is well qualified for the duties of Capt. & a, q, m.

> Very respectfully
> your obt. svt.
> U. S. GRANT
> Lt. Gn.

ALS, DNA, RG 94, ACP, W80 CB 1869. See *PUSG*, 12, 460. On Oct. 19, 1865, Maj. Gen. Joseph Hooker wrote to Secretary of War Edwin M. Stanton recommending Capt. and Bvt. Maj. Amos Webster, q. m., for appointment in the U.S. Army. LS, DNA, RG 94, ACP, W80 CB 1869. On Nov. 1, USG endorsed this letter. "Approved and respectfully forwarded. Major Webster has proven himself an efficient quartermaster in the field, and I am in favor of giving present vacancies, and any new ones that may be created by legislation this coming winter, in any of the staff corps, to officers who have filled faithfully and efficiently such offices during the rebellion. Major Webster is an officer of this class." ES, *ibid*. On Dec. 4, Webster, Washington, D. C., wrote to USG. "I have the honor to apply for a commission in the Regular Army of the United States in such branch of the service as may be determined by the Board appointed for examining such applications & recommendations for appointments in said service. I have had over four years experience in the field, entering the Volunteer service as private in the 1st Mass Vol Infy." ALS, *ibid*. On Dec. 5, Brig. Gen. John A. Rawlins endorsed this letter. "Respectfully forwarded to the Secretary of War—approved.—The within applicant enlisted as a private soldier in the 1st Regt Mass. In. Vols. May 24 1861. He was in the Peninsular Campaign and was promoted to a 2d Lieut'cy in his reg't by the Governor of Massachusetts. At Harrisons Landing he was assigned to duty on the staff of Maj. Gen. Hooker, commanding a division in the 3d Army Corps, as chief ambulance officer of that command, and continued to fill the same position during the several administrations of the Corps. During this time he also performed the duties of acting Assistant Q. M. Upon being relieved from the 3d Corps staff he was ordered to report to Brig. Gen. R. Ingalls, Chief Q. M. of that Army, for duty in his Dept., and was assigned as Aide de Camp. Oct 1 '64 he received the appointment of Captain and Aqm of Vols. and was ordered to report to Lieut Gen Grant for duty. He has participated in all the engagements of the Army of the Potomac from July 17 '61 to the surrender of the Army of Northern Virginia, April 9th 1865." ES, *ibid*.

On Oct. 24, 1866, USG wrote to Stanton. "I have the honor to recommend Bvt. Maj. Amos Webster, A. Q. M. of Volunteers to be appointed Capt. & Asst. Qr. Mr. Regular Army, Vice A. C. Gillem promoted Col. of Infantry." ALS, *ibid*. On Feb. 2, 1867, USG wrote to Stanton. "I have the honor to recommend the appointment of Capt. Lewis Cass Forsythe, and Capt. Amos Webster, Assistant QuarterMasters, to the Regular Army to fill two of the three vacancies now existing in the Quartermaster's Dept. under the Act of the 28th of July 1866. Both these officers have received the recommendation of the Quarter-Master General." ALS, *ibid*., G39 CB 1867. On March 9, USG wrote to President Andrew Johnson. "I have the honor to renew special recommendation, previously made by me, for the appointment of Capt. L. Cass Forsythe, and Capt. Amos Webster, Volunteer Quartermasters, for the same appointment in the regular Army. Both these officers were recommended by the Q. M. Gen." ALS, *ibid*., G161 CB 1867. Lewis C. Forsyth was appointed capt. and q. m. as of March 11. On April 11, USG wrote to Stanton. "I have the honor to recommend Maj. Amos Webster, Volunteer Quartermaster, for the appointment of 2d Lt. 5th U. S. Cavalry. There are now seven vacancies in thatis regiment." ALS, *ibid*., W80 CB 1869. Webster was appointed 2nd lt., 5th Cav., as of March 7, while remaining on USG's staff. On Aug. 5, Bvt. Maj. Gen. Rufus Ingalls wrote to Rawlins recommending Webster for bvt. promotion. LS, *ibid*. On Aug. 9, USG endorsed this letter. "Approved for Brevet Lieut-Colonel of Vols." ES, *ibid*.

On April 8, 1869, USG nominated Webster as register of wills for D. C.; Webster resigned from the U.S. Army as of April 15.

To Charles W. Ford

————

Washington D. C.
October 28th 1865.

DEAR FORD,

Enclosed please find draft for $1098 30 payable to your order. This will pay the $500 00 which I borrowed from you when last in St. Louis, the $198 30 taxes which you were kind enough to pay for me and the $400 00 which I asked you to give to Sappington. No doubt Sappington will call on you for more still. If he does please let him have it and notify me and I will pay up promptly.

I have not heard the result of the last trial for possession with White.

All are well in my family. I have bought a house[1] in the City for $30000 00 which, with the expense of furnishing will keep me in debt for ten years, just the credit I get on the place. I suppose a man out of debt would be unhappy. I never tried the experiment myself however.

Yours Truly
U. S. GRANT
Lt. Gn.

ALS, USG 3. Probably on Nov. 3 (dated Nov. 8), 1865, 10:30 A.M., USG telegraphed to Charles W. Ford. "Did you receive two letters from me one containing draft?" ALS (telegram sent), DNA, RG 107, Telegrams Collected (Bound); telegram sent, *ibid.* On Nov. 4, Ford, St. Louis, wrote to USG. "Your letter of the 21st Oct as also, the one of the 28th enclosing Dft. fr $1098 30 are both duly recd   On the receipt of the first—having no better man than myself to do the errant down to Sappingtons—I orderd the Colts—and on as bright a morning as I ever saw, took our Buffalo friend, Mr Kip, and down to the Gravois went we. I found Mr Sappington had come up to town—but I left your letter, with a request that he would call & see me. From there we went over to Mr Dents place—It was a most beautiful day—and the county looked splendid. We found no one at home but the Judge, Mrs Dent & Mrs Casey—(the latter not over well) were over at Mrs Sharps—spending the day. After a pleasant hour with the Judge—we came home, both *indebted* to you for an excuse to get away from business and have a nice ride into the Country. To come back to Sappington—he never called upon me, until day before yesterday, but he gave a good account of himself when he did come—It appears—he wrote to Jeff Co. and ascertained the Amt of money he would require—and showed me the answer—in Amt $470— & some cents. He said he would have to pay for the making out of some papers—

he did not know how much—So I added $10. to it—and herewith enclose you his receipt for $480—I told him I hoped your interests had not suffered by the delay. He said they had not—and he would take good care that whatever you had entrusted him with, should not be neglected. Your suit with White has not come off yet. It will come on about the 23d inst—Your Atty is a clever fellow, but he cant keep a hotel, I wish some old & more experienced lawyer had the Case in hand—No news here; every thing quiet & orderly—and our town doing a fair business—You tell me you have bought a new house & put yourself in debt for ten years to come. Thats bad: Suppose you were to write a nice note to the donors of the Phila house—setting forth—that your duties require your presence in Washington & you must have your family with you—As the house was donated to you with the expectation you would reside in it, and it being demonstrated that you cannot, and there is but one way to dispose of it—towit, to return it to the original donors—What would they do? Take it back? Not a bit of it. They would authorize you to sell it, (with many regrets that you could not occupy it) and appropriate it the proceeds as you thought proper—Try it & see if I am not right—They would look well doing any thing else. If they would be mean enough to keep it—under such circumstances—*Our* Petroleum Co. will soon give you a lift. We are getting on splendidly—& by the 1st Dec. hope to strike—'Ile' I hope. Pardon this long letter. Remember me to Mrs Grant & family . . ." ALS, USG 3. See letter to Charles W. Ford, Oct. 21, 1865.

On Nov. 2, Sebastian Sappington signed a receipt: "Recd of Genl Grant per C W Ford Four Hundred & Eighty Dollars to pay taxes &c." ADS, USG 3. On Nov. 5, Sappington wrote to USG. "I received yours note and the monney you sent to mee to pay taxes in Jefferson County I went down 3 inst and found the taxes on Mr Dent land with out the 160 acres you spoke about to bee $160 90 and your tax on your 600 acres was $49 45 and my expence for going dow and back was $5 60 and I will have to carge ten-dollars for attend to the business, and I made enquireys about your property and I find by several of the eighbors that the best of the wood have bin cut off but they no the land to sell all in one boddy can be sold for ten or twelve dollars per acre but to cut it up in small tract it will bring more if you think best to sell write to mee what to do, and I, will the first time I goe to the cty I will have a dee wrote for Mr Dent land and send it to you suit with Mr White will be set on the tweth of this month for trial when it comes off I will in form you how it is desided." ALS, *ibid.*

1. See letter to Elihu B. Washburne, Nov. 9, 1865.

To Edwin M. Stanton

Respectfully returned to the Secretary of War. I know of no way in which aid can be rendered to the Planters of Louisiana in repairing the Mississippi levees unless under an act of Congress Because a large portion of the levees were destroyed by the U S

Military authorities is no reason why the Government should re-place them.

The release of the cotton mentioned as having been seized by order of Gen. Canby as captured property is a question controlled by the Hon. Secretary of the Treasury.

U. S. GRANT
Lieut Gen

HEADQRS A U S
OCT. 30. '65.

ES, DNA, RG 107, Letters Received from Bureaus. Written on a letter of Oct. 9, 1865, from Governor J. Madison Wells of La. to President Andrew Johnson enclosing a printed memorial requesting that war-damaged levees in La. be repaired by the U.S. ALS, *ibid.* On the same day, Wells wrote to USG. "I take the liberty to enclose you printed copy of a Memorial addressed to Major Genl Canby, commanding this Department, through me as the Governor of the State, on a subject of vital importance to our people, involing the material prosperity, if not the very existence of the state and one in which I am sure you must feel a deep concern, although we have not the honor of claiming you as a citizen of Louisiana. Owing to the Bankrupt condition of the state and the impossibility of raising means to rebuild the vast extent of Levee destroyed, I addressed Major Gen'l Canby Commd'g this Dep't, on the 1st of August last, earnestly invoking the aid and assistance of the United States government through him, in the construction of the Levees. I assumed the ground that a large portion of the Levees had been destroyed by the United States Military forces and that it was but just that the Gen'l Government should at least replace those Levees. In reply to my communication, the General stated that he had no authority to divert the funds under his control for that purpose, but that he would apply to the War Department, for the necessary funds to restore the Levees to the extent they had been destroyed by the military forces of the United States. Nothing further hav-ing been heard in the matter, and as the season was far advanced in which the work was to be done, a large number of the planters interested, felt it to be their duty to meet together, with the view of taking action in the premises. The result of their deliberations is the memorial enclosed, which was presented to Gen'l Canby by the Committee in person, and on which occasion, I had the honor to be present. On the next day, the memorial was returned through me with the fol-lowing endorsement—towit. 'H'd Quarters Dept of La N Orls Oct 6/1865 By direction of the Major Gen'l Commd'g the Division of the Gulf, this memorial is returned to the memorialists. I Send it through His Excellency the Governor as the readiest means of reaching its destination very respectfully Signed ED R S. CANBY M. G. C As the memorial is entirely respectful and courteous, and con-tains nothing whatever, as far as I am able to judge, that can be construed as disrespectful towards the United States, or the Major Gen'l's Commd'g this Division or Dep't, I am at a loss to imagine the cause of its summary rejection. My chief concern however is, on account of the Levees, and the effect this action of Gen'l's Sheridan & Canby may have, in witholding the assistance, we so confidently expected from the U. S. to build them. In this extremity of our Stateituation Gen'l, I have made so bold to appeal to you, if it is in your power to do anything for us. You have a thorough Knowledge of our Levees at least in the Parishes of Madison and Carroll—the destruction and devastation caused by the overflow in those Parishes and I am sure your sympathizes will be enlisted in our favor and that you will use your influence with the War Department to place the necessary funds at Gen'l Canby's disposal to rebuild the Levees destroyed by the United States forces." ALS, *ibid.*, RG 108, Letters Received.

On Nov. 8, B. Desha Harman, Memphis, wrote to John T. Pickett or E. Parkman concerning the use of U.S. Colored Troops to repair the levee at Lake Providence, La. ALS, IHi. On Nov. 10, USG endorsed this letter. "Respectfully returned to the President of the United States. I deem the cutting of the Canal in question a legitimate act, demanded by the necessities of the case, and for which there is no legitimate claim against the United States for damages. It would undoubtedly be an advantage to the United States, as advancing the general property of the Country if this Canal were closed; but I do not think that it should be undertaken by U. S. troops without special legislative authority" ES, *ibid.*

On Feb. 16, 1866, Maj. Gen. George H. Thomas, Nashville, telegraphed to USG. "The following telegram just rec'd is forwarded for the information of the Secy. of War. 'By Telegraph from Vicksburg, Feby. 14th 1866, To BRIG. GEN. WHIPPLE Chf of Staff   The order for furnishing the Seven (7) Regts to work on the Levee has been suspended by the Secy. of War through Gen. Canby, has any thing further been heard from it? Something should be done with these troops. (Signed) T. J. WOOD Maj Gen'l'   The seven (7) Regts referred to were ordered by me to be mustered out on the 8th Jany. The order was countermanded by the Secy. of War. The troops to be put at work on Levee. aAre these troops to be mustered out, retained in service, or put to work on Levee." Telegram received (at 2:15 P.M.), DNA, RG 107, Telegrams Collected (Bound); *ibid.*, RG 108, Telegrams Received; copies, *ibid.*, Letters Received; (dated Feb. 15) *ibid.*, RG 393, Dept. of the Tenn., Telegrams Sent; DLC-USG, V, 54. On the same day, USG endorsed this telegram. "Respectfully forwarded to the Hon. Secretary of War. No reply has been made to this dispatch from these Hd Qrs. The troops refered to can be mustered out of service unless they are needed to work on the levees." AES (first sentence in hand of Bvt. Col. Theodore S. Bowers), DNA, RG 108, Letters Received. On Feb. 17, Maj. Thomas M. Vincent, AGO, endorsed this telegram. "Respectfully returned to Lieutenant General Grant, Commanding Armies of the United States. In reply to the within, Major General Thomas, by telegram of this date, has been instructed as follows, viz:—'The seven (7) regiments of Colored troops intended for work on the Levees, and referred to in your telegram of yesterday to Lieut. General Grant will be mustered out provided their services are not required by Major General Canby at whose request their muster out was suspended.' " ES, *ibid.*

On Feb. 2, Richard L. Shelley, *New York Tribune* correspondent, New Orleans, wrote to U.S. Senator Henry Wilson of Mass. "Permit me to call your attention to the fact that several regiments of Colored troops are being mustered out in this Department conditional to their accepting employment on the Public levees at one dollar per day, a sum totally inadequate for their support, and much below the average price of labor in this market—One company for refusing to submit to this arbitary decree, was disarmed, and sent to Fort Jackson to keep company with Dr Gwin and other Rebels. I have mentioned this fact in my public correspondence" ALS, *ibid.*, RG 94, Letters Received, 172G 1866. On Feb. 13, Secretary of War Edwin M. Stanton endorsed this letter. "Referred to Lieutenant General Grant for investigation & report" AES, *ibid.* On Feb. 28, Maj. Gen. Edward R. S. Canby endorsed this letter. "Respectfully returned. January 4th 1866 I ordered the muster out of the 96th U S C T (S. O. No. 3 par 1., C S. enclosed.) January 11th I received instructions from the Secretary of War, to proceed immediately to repair the Levees, on the Mississippi River, and 'to furnish for this purpose such details for labor as might be necessary.' January 13th under these instructions, I suspended the order for the muster out of the 96th (S. O. No. 11 par 2. C. S. enclosed.) See also telegraphic instructions from Sec'y War of Jan 17th copy enclosed. Subsequently, upon the representation of the Commanding Officer of the Regiment, that many of the men had made contracts for labor upon plantations, and elsewhere, after the order for the muster out was issued, and that it was important to their interests to execute these contracts, I decided to permit the muster out to proceed, provided that a sufficient number of the men would contract for one months labor upon the levees, at one dollar a day, rations, and Shelter. About two thirds of each company agreed to the condition, and the muster out was effected. Co "H" refused to work upon the 'levees.' I therefore decided to keep them in the Service until the contract of the other men of the Reg't. had expired, and ordered them to Fort Jackson; not *disarmed*, but as part of the Garrison of that post (S. O. No. 17 par. 5. C. S) Subsequently, upon receiving instructions from the Sec'y of War to suspend work upon the levees, I cancelled the contract with the discharged men of the 96th, and at the same time ordered the muster out of Co "H" (S. O. No. 44 par 1. C. S enclosed) It is only necessary to add, that in August last I arrested the writer of this letter, for false pretences, in passing himself off as a Commissioned officer, and drawing his pay as such, when he was none, and in making use of my name to further a fraud upon a Paymaster." ES, *ibid.*

On July 18, Bvt. Col. Adam Badeau wrote to U.S. Representative Benjamin Eggleston of Ohio. "Lt. Gen. Grant directs me to acknowledge the receipt of your note of the 16th inst, ~~with its enclosures~~, asking his opinion as to the propriety of Congress making an appropriation of $1,500,000 for the purpose of reconstructing and repairing the levees on the Mississippi river, in the States of Louisiana, Missississippi & Arkansas. ~~Gen. Grant~~ He considers that the rebuilding of those levees is a work of great importance, not only to the region itself, but to the whole country; involving as it does the cotton interest, and affording also employment to many of the freedmen in the states mentioned who will not otherwise be likely soon to obtain occupation. Gen Grant is familiar with the lands alluded to, and knows them to be of immense value, and that unless reclaimed in the manner indicated they will be worthless. About three and a half millions of acres are in this condition. For these reasons ~~Gen Grant therefore~~ For these reasons he regards the prosecution of the works as eminently desirable; but ~~as to~~ whether Congress should vote away the public money at this juncture, for this purpose, is a question upon which he ~~desires~~ prefers to express no opinion, regarding it as entirely beyond his province to do so." ADfS, USG 3.

To Maj. Gen. William T. Sherman

Washington Oct. 31st 1865

MAJ. GEN. W. T. SHERMAN
COM'D'G MIL. DIV. OF THE MO.
GENERAL:

Your letter to General Rawlins, referring to the progress of the two Pacific railroads has been received.[1] I immediately saw the Secy. of War and had a conversation with him on the subject of urging that Government Aid be given to both enterprises. He informed me that both roads had been accepted by the Government and were now in a fair way to be pushed forward

The subject of stationing troops to give the best protection to the overland lines of travel, and frontier and mountain settlements, will have to occupy your attention. In making orders or in recommending them to the President, I shall rely almost entirely upon your suggestions so far as the territory embraced in your command is concerned   In view of the rapid progress that is now being made by the two roads pushing West, and the settlements which have sprung up in the last four years, I do not think it advisable to establish many permanent posts or to expend more money than is absolutely necessary to preserve the health of the men. I sent four regiments of Colored Troops to Pope with the view of having them sent as far West as possible. If more can be used to advantage, I will send them. I believe these troops will do very well on the Plains, much better than dissatisfied Volunteers, and it may also furnish labor hereafter for our railroads and mining interests. Let me know if you can use more of these troops now. I telegraphed to Sheridan to know if troops could not be sent from the Rio Grande to New Mexico at this season of the year. He replied they could not without very great expense and loss of life. Do you not thing it practicable to discharge Volunteers from the Dept. of Arkansas? In discharging troops give the preference to Illinois and Indiana troops when you can. About two thirds of all the Volunteers retained in service are from the States of Ohio Ia. & Ills., and more from the two latter States than from Ohio.

Recruits will be sent to you rapidly to fill up the Regular organizations you now have. In view of Winter being now near at hand can you not anticipate this increase, and discharge Volunteers accordingly.

> Very respectfully
> Your obt servt.
> U. S. GRANT
> Lieut. Genl

Copies, DLC-USG, V, 46, 109; DNA, RG 108, Letters Sent. *O.R.*, I, xlviii, part 2, 1250. On Nov. 6, 1865, Maj. Gen. William T. Sherman, St. Louis, wrote to USG. "I have yours of the 31st of October. I will continue to give the Subjects pointed out my whole attention. At present Ord has in his Dept. only the 4 cos. 4th Inf. one of Regular Artillery, and a scattered set of Veteran Reserves. These will nearly all go out by voluntary discharge under the recent orders of the War Dept—and I take it for granted if all the privates elect to be discharged, the officers will not be retained. By the assignt to Pope of the 3rd, 10th and 18th Inf. he will muster out the Volunteers in Minnesota—Missouri, Kansas and Nebraska, all he can reach this winter. This will leave him only the few Volunteers up the Missouri—in Utah & New Mexico, who are beyond our reach until Spring, but by that time the Regulars will be recruited up and evry volunteer shall be mustered out as soon as we can send relief. He has his very best officers distributed judiciously and economically—Corse in Minnesota, Sully up the Missouri—Dodge & Elliott at Leavenworth, Wheaton at Laramie, Upton at Denver, Conner at Salt Lake, and Carleton in New Mexico. You know that the Regular Regts are mere squads, that they came to us late, indeed the 18th is not yet come, but they have been pushed out as far on the Plains as the Season will justify this Winter. In Arkansas Reynolds has retained more volunteers than in any other part of my command. I did intend to go there this month But Reynolds came north in my absence and I expect him daily back from Indiana en route for Arkansas, and I will see him an[d] order the discharge of all the Indiana, Illinois & Ohio Regts in his dept. and substitute the four negro Regts still at Louisville waiting orders. I urged on Pope to use these Regts, but he says truly that it is too late for them this year to reach the remote Posts, but I think Reynolds can use them and spare an equal if not greater number of white volunteers that ought to be discharged. In the Spring if matters justify it I can order them to march from Arkansas to the Upper Arkansas, and New Mexico to relieve any troops there. New Mexico has so recently been added to Genl Popes Command, that he is not yet in possession of Genl Carletons Reports. Touching the future of the Plains Genl Pope has made & sent you some detailed Reports which are worthy your study. You know that the Indians are under the General supervision of the Dept of the Interior and I am not even advised of the treaties which must of course be respected by us. There have been and must continue to be conflicts between Commanding officers of Posts, and of Expeditions and Indian Agents, traders &c. If the whole managemt of the Indians, their treaties annuities, and traders could be transferred back to the War Dept, it would much simplify our work. But if there be good reasons why the Dept of the Interior should keep this branch of public service out of our hands, we should have at least copies of the Treaties that we might know their terms and Conditions. I think with the Regular Regiments now assigned me, when approximately full, I will have enough troops to maintain a general state of quiet on the Plains, bu[t] if our Emigrants and wanderers will go in small parties through the Indian Reservations & hunting grounds we must not be astonished if some of them lose their horses, cattle and scalps. I have given Ord one of the Batteries of artillery, to Pope two, and to Reynolds one, and I will have them equipped and put in apple pie order. In like manner I will aim to get the 2nd Cavalry, now at & beyond Fort Riley—and the 3rd Cavalry now in Arkansas thoroughly mounted & equipped by or before next May so that they can make a tour of the entire Plains next summer. As soon as the Indians see that we have Regular Cavalry among them they will realize that we are in condition to punish them for any murders or robberies, and then the legitimate travel across the Plains will cease. Even this year there has been less of Indian disturbance than we had reason to apprehend. I will send a copy of your letter to Genl Pope, and furnish one to General Reynolds when he comes, and will continue to study the whole subject so as to be ready for action on the opening of Spring." ALS, DLC-William T. Sherman.

On Sept. 23, Sherman had written to Brig. Gen. John A. Rawlins. "I have the honor to report every thing within the Area of this command in quiet and good order. In order to be prepared for future Contingencies I propose in person to visit certain localities with which I am not already familiar and propose to start next Tuesday, Sept 26, to make a tour looking to the future Base and lines leading thereto, viz will go to Chicago, thence straight by Rail to Omaha, via Desmoines. There I will endeavor to meet Gen Dodge, or other officers now out on the Plains towards Montana, and acquaint myself with the new Routes and circumstances grown up since I was on that Frontier From Omaha, I will go to Leavenworth & Riley and return to St Louis by way of the new Pacific Railroad, which is just completed to Kansas City, and is represented as being rapidly in progress to Fort Riley. I will leave a good staff officer at these Head Qrs. to give Despatch to all papers passing through this office, and to report to Dept Commanders all official matter Coming from the War Dept, or the Head Quarters of the Army. Should anything arise calling for my personal action it can reach me by telegraph, but as All the Dept Commanders are Present I apprehend no necessity for my actual presence in St Louis the coming month, the only matters of interest transpiring being on the plains towards which I will be. General Grant left here Eastward yesterday at 3. P M." ALS, DNA, RG 94, Letters Received, 2022M 1865. On Sept. 29, Rawlins referred this letter to Secretary of War Edwin M. Stanton. ES, *ibid.* On Oct. 16, Sherman, Fort Leavenworth, telegraphed to USG. "Arrived at Leavenworth from Omaha yesterday expect Genl Dodge in from the Plains since the enlargement of Popes Dept Wisconsin should be added to Ord's even then there is no necessity of more than a few of Companies of Artillery at the Old Lake Posts & all other troops in the Dept of the Ohio might be discharged we need more Regulars out on the Plains Vols. are all discontented & unreliable I will be back to St Louis early next week." Telegram received (at 4:00 P.M.), *ibid.*, RG 107, Telegrams Collected (Bound); *ibid.*, RG 108, Telegrams Received; copies, *ibid.*, RG 393,

Military Div. of the Miss., Letters Sent; DLC-USG, V, 54. *O.R.*, I, xlviii, part 2, 1240. On Oct. 28, Sherman, St. Louis, telegraphed to Rawlins. "I have assigned to Gen Pope the Second 2 Cavalry & third & tenth Infantry with orders to muster out an equal or greater number of Volunteers. In like manner the battalion of eighteenth infantry & one battery of artillery is given to Gen Ord, who undertakes to dispense with all other troops in his Department with Wisconsin added. I renew my recommendation that Wisconsin be transferred to the Department of the Ohio. I think with one good regiment of regular infantry & one of cavalry we ought to muster out everything in arkansas" Telegram received (at 3:30 P.M.), DNA, RG 107, Telegrams Collected (Bound); *ibid.*, RG 108, Telegrams Received; copy, DLC-USG, V, 54. *O.R.*, I, xlviii, part 2, 1245. See *ibid.*, p. 1249.

On Nov. 7, 1:40 P.M., USG telegraphed to Sherman. "You may suspend Gen. Popes order for reducing the force in New Mexico until other troops can be got there to take their place." ALS (telegram sent), DNA, RG 107, Telegrams Collected (Bound); telegram sent, *ibid.*; copies, *ibid.*, RG 108, Letters Sent; *ibid.*, RG 393, Military Div. of the Miss., Telegrams Received; *ibid.*, Letters Sent; DLC-USG, V, 46, 109. On Nov. 8, Sherman twice telegraphed to USG. "Dispatch to suspend General Popes order relative to the discharge of troops in New Mexico is received & orders made accordingly." "Gen Reynolds is here & agrees to discharge every vols in his Dep't on receiving the nineteenth Infantry. I will give him three (3) of the kentucky Regts & instruct him to muster out all Vols & to have the third Cavy & nineteenth Regulars out on the frontier by spring ready for New Mexico or wherever else required." Telegrams received (the first at 1:10 P.M., the second at 4:20 P.M.), DNA, RG 107, Telegrams Collected (Bound); *ibid.*, RG 108, Telegrams Received; copies, *ibid.*, RG 393, Military Div. of the Miss., Letters Sent; DLC-USG, V, 54. *O.R.*, I, xlviii, part 2, 1255. See *ibid.*, p. 1248.

1. On Oct. 23, Sherman wrote to Rawlins. "I returned on Saturday night from a rather extended trip through the settled part of the North West chiefly to see for myself the changes and progress of settlement and improvement since I had last seen this part of our Country. I need not say that I was more than Convinced that in the fertile lands of the North West we have a future of the most flattering kind, and that its development will give our poeple plenty of honest work for a long time to come. But I wish now to write of two things that will be the topics of Controversy and Contention in which spite of our wishes General Grant and I will be drawn in, viz the two Pacific Roads I gave both a close and critical examination not officially by any means, but because I see that each will soon enter largely into our Military Calculations. The 1st. begins at Omaha, not far from the Old Council Bluffs, and is designed to run substantially up the Valley of the Platte. Until the Railroads East of Omaha Connect with our markets on the Mississipi and Chicago, this Road will not be of material help to us. at present there is a break of 150 miles from BoonesBoro on the Des Moines River to Omaha, and I could not make up a proximate calculation as to the time when this break will be filled, but surely not in 1866. In the Spring of the Year when the Missouri River is full stores could go up to Omaha, and thence be carried Westward by this Road, but this will hardly be economical till the Road is finished out to within one days haul of Fort Kearney. At present 14½ miles of Rail are laid over which I passed, and I found a heavy force laying

track at the rate of ½ mile per day. The road bed is good, and the parties are using good materials all save the ties which are in great part of Cotton wood, a
poor quality of timber but the best that is within reach. The ties are being
steeped in a solution of the Sulphate of Zinc, or 'Chloride' which it is claimed
will preserve the wood, in the same way as the old mode of Kyanising. This
company is evidently working in good faith and with large Capital as is illustrated by the character and amount of work already done and in progress. I saw
on the ground enough iron for 60 miles of road, vast amounts of Cross ties and
Bridge timber, and several large brick buildings were in course of rapid construction for machine shops, Car houses &c &c. After next year this Road will be
of vast use to us, especially if a connection east from Omaha by Rail is made,
for it will practically throw our frontier out to Fort Kearney, and enable us to
supply amply a cavalry force well out on the Plains, whence it can subdue and
control absolutely the bands of Indians who come down from the north, and
break up the Stage and other lines East and West. On tha[t] Line Fort Kearney
will become the Great Depot and Center of operations, and it should be kept up
and enlarged, whilst all posts & establishmts this side should be allowed to go
into disuse. The other or second Line of Railroad West is that which begins
at the mouth of the Kansas or Kaw at Kansas City or Wyandotte, two towns at
its mouth on the Missouri River. I learn that there has been much controversy abut
this Road, with which I have nothing to do. I went over it in company with Mr
Shoemaker Contractor for finishing the Road, as far as Fort Riley. The road is
located in the bottom of the valley near the River on its north bank, 40 miles
to a point opposite the thriving town of Lawrence, and thence in the bottom for
ten miles in the direction of Riley. I found a heavy working force laying road
at the rate of from ½ to ¾ of a mile per day, using excellent iron and oak cross
ties. The road bed seems to have been made too low, and the heavy freshets of
the past summer covered some parts of the road and damaged materially its cuts,
embankments and bridges. All of these have been repaired since the subsidence
of the waters, except a part of the Bridge across the Kansas near its mouth, but
the Cars now run daily from the bank of the Missouri River at the town of
Wyandotte to Lawrence at the rate of 20 miles per hour, and appears to be doing
a most prosperous business. Mr Shoemaker assured me that if the present most
favorable weather lasted he would have the road in running order out as far as
Topeka 26 miles west of Lawrence or 66 miles out from the Missouri River in
30 days. I regard the Road as the most important element now in progress to
facilitate the military ~~progress~~ interests of our Frontier. It has connection with
all the Railroads of our Country East by & through the Missouri Pacific Railroad
now well finished from St Louis to Kansas City so that troops with military
stores may be sent by Continuous Rail from any Point East of the Mississipi
to its terminus. I hope the General Governmt will not delay or hinder the Construction of this Road one hour, for evry mile added to it may be of infinite use.
I am well acquainted with most of the parties interested in this Road and its
Connections. Within a month the little break now in Kansas City will be ~~done~~
repaired, and also connections will be made to Fort Leavenworth by next June
by a short Road from Kansas City to Leavenworth and from Leavenworth to
Lawrence a kind of triangle that will bring Fort Leavenworth in communication
with the Roads East and West. The Main Line up the Kansas Valley will hardly
be of use to us until it is completed to Fort Riley, when it will be of immense
saving. Fort Riley is a well built post with ample quarters stables and store-

houses, and from that point radiate Roads to Kearney, Denver and New Mexico, and the moment stores can be delivered there by Rail it will become the Grand Depot of the Frontier. It so happens also that the Fertile Lands and bad Roads there terminate and Sterile land and good Roads begin. I therefore repeat that the Govt will save a vast amount in money, and will increase the efficiency of the Army on the Frontier by facilitating by all means in its power the Construction of the Pacific Railroad to that point. It is a physical impossibility to complete it by this season, but during next year it ought to be done in the most perfect manner. The present road is all that could be asked as to iron, ties and equipment, and the interest of the Company will make them make the roadbed higher above the natural lay of the valley. The new part West of Lawrence is being prepared right, and that completed from Kansas City up to Lawrence is being repaired as fast as labor can be had. I have seen General Dodge and many others who have Spent the Summer and fall out on the plains, and will write you on these Subjects when the occasion arises, and need only say that matters on and beyond the Frontier seem as regular, and well arranged as Could be expected under the Circumstances." ALS, DNA, RG 94, Letters Received, M2603 1865. On Oct. 27, USG endorsed this letter. "Respectfully forwarded to the Secretary of War for his information." ES, *ibid.* On Oct. 24, Sherman wrote to USG. "*Unofficial* . . . I telegraphed you from Leavenworth and wrote to Gen Rawlings yesterday about Railroad matters. There is some rivalry and seeming hostility between the two Railroads now building westward from Omaha and Kansas City, dependent somewhat on Governmt Aid. The truth is this rivalry and hostility are foolish for the roads are 300 miles apart and there is work enough for both. By Law they are designed to come together at some point on the 100th Parallel west of Fort Kearney, but I dont believe they will ever come together. One will naturally follow the Platte and the other will follow the Kansas and should not come together at all unless forced to do so, by the nature of the ground. I hope the Govt will favor both Roads out as far as Kearney on the one and Riley on the other. This will save an immense amount in hauling and will put forage out far enough so that Cavalry can reach & punish the Indians any where on the Plains. A good deal of feeling is manifested by reason of the joint control of Indian affairs by the Interior & War Depts. I remember when the Indian tribes were put under the jurisdiction & control of the Interior Dept, and think it was a mistake. Indians always look to the man or men who have soldiers, and the Sooner we regain absolute & unqualified Control of the Indians and all who travel & deal with them the Sooner can we get them under Control. Still I do not wish to commit myself too far, as all I know on the Subject comes from Conversations with officers & men who are prejudiced. Generals Pope & Dodge have just left me, and the latter will make an official report of certain facts that fall under his own observation that will enable you to make up your mind if you propose to take any steps in the matter. I will give to Pope the Regulars ordered to me that he may push them out along the lines of travel as far as possible before Winter Closes in. I had a very pleasant trip and saw much that may be of use to me hereafter. The whole Country west & north appears prosperous and yet there is room enough for all the world that wants to plow and reap. Since the first order dividing up the Country into Departments, Colorado, Utah & New Mexico have been ordered into Popes Dept, so that he has now an immense territorial command. This mostly lies West of the Mississipi, but Wisconsin is embraced in his Dept. This state bordering the Northern Lakes naturally belongs to the Dept of the Ohio: and I recommend it be so added. There is in fact no use of having any soldiers North of the Ohio & East of the Mississipi, & a few Companies to garrison the Lake Frontier will answer evry purpose—West of the Mississipi we will need for a long time just as many troops of the Regular Army as you can spare and therefore whenever you have a skeleton of an old Regular Regimt for which you have no other use, send it to me and I will give it a Recruiting District and push its organized part out on some one of the Lines West, to replace volunteers that ought to be discharged for their own good, and for the interest of the United States. I want before Winter Comes to visit Arkansas and see its frontier, and will probably go there in All November, not to make any changes but to observe & study the Country prepared for the Future. I am now in my new House, and most comfortably situated, but Cannot promise to be as quiet as I ought to be but like the Irish man will promise to be as Aisy as I can. To you I wish all honor, peace & comfort, and if ever you want me to do any thing, let me know beforehand, and it shall be done if in my power." ALS, USG 3.

Testimonial

Washington D. C. Oct. 31st *1865*

During the time that Hd Qrs. of the Dept. of the Tenn. was at Jackson Tenn. I became acquainted with Mr. E. Parkman. All his talk and professions indicated loyalty to the government and he was at all time ready to communicate any information he was able to collect from conversation with the disloyal of that locality. Sometimes this information was of importance and was communicated voluntarily. I believe the first information I had of the intention of Van Dorn to attack Corinth was communicated by Mr. Parkman *unsolicited*. I have no doubt about the loyalty of Mr. Parkman.

U. S. Grant
Lt. Gen.

ADS, DNA, RG 108, Letters Received. Additional letters attesting to the loyalty of Edward Parkman are *ibid.* On Feb. 3, 1866, Parkman wrote a letter received at USG's hd. qrs. enclosing testimonials to his loyalty. *Ibid.*, Register of Letters Received.

On July 25, 1862, Brig. Gen. John A. Logan, Jackson, Tenn., wrote to USG. "Mr. E. Parkman the barer of this is a citizen of this place, who has at all times so far as I can learn been a quiet man, and certainly has sympathy with the Govt. being origanaly a northern man, his statements may be relied on to the fullest extent, and in view of the many depredations that have been committed in the Vicinity of Trenton & Humbolt, I do think it would be well to cause an assessment to be made on the Regts who have been so wilful, as an example to others. Complaints are daily made from that quarter. Some that probably do not reach you, and were never forgot while the 7th Kansas were there." ALS, *ibid.*, RG 107, Letters Received, 394P 1869. On Aug. 1, Parkman, Jackson, wrote to USG, Corinth. "In Consequence of Sickness in my family I am unable to present my claim personally as was my intention The bearer Mr Saml C. Beman is in my employ and will present you the papers, and is herby authorized as my lawful attorney for me and in my name to adjust the claim." ALS, *ibid.* On May 26, 1869, Parkman wrote to Secretary of War John A. Rawlins. "While Genl Grant had his Hd Quarters at Jackson, Tenn. the 7th Kansas Cavalry came from Columbus, Ky. via:—Trenton, and Jackson, Tenn. to their destination at Corinth Miss. At Trenton, they broke open the depot, and took therefrom belonging to me a large quantity of sugar, and Tobacco. Trenton was the most accessable point on the Rail Road for me to ship to and from my Tobacco-Manufactory at Dresden, Weakly County, Tenn. distant 28 miles from Trenton. The sugar was in transitu to, and the Tobacco from my factory, I submitted to Genl Grant, the evidence in the case, including the affadavits of the Commander of the post, and provost marshal at Trenton, on which evidence, Genl Grant ordered Genl Rosecrance then in command at Corinth Miss to assess, collect from their next pay the amount of the property taken at Trenton belonging to me, and to pay the same to me. I sent an order for the amount to Genl Rosecrance some two weeks after the paymaster had made his circuit at Corinth, (which was delayed some two months from the time he was expected) Genl Rosecrance informed my agent that he had assessed, and collected the amount, and it had been sent to Gen Grants head Qrs at Jackson, Tenn. I called on you in person at your office in Jackson, you enquired of one of your associates who after looking over his books replied, that the amount had been received at your Hd Qrs and sent to Washington, you said you would have it looked up, and attended to. Soon after the army moved down the Miss Central R. Road to make an attack on Vicksburg. I did not see you again until you returned from that expedition, and your office was in Planters Bank building in Memphis, where you again assured me you would endeavor to give the matter your attention. I met you once while the army was at Millikins Bend, and again called your attention to the matter, receiving the same assurance of your attention as before. The subsequent activity of the army, your removal to the Potomac, and the incidents attendant upon the successfull termination of the War, have so engrossed your attention, that I have never alluded to the subject but once, and that was to Genl Logan two years since who promised to see you on the subject, but I presume that the political duties pressing upon him caused it to pass from his mind, as I never heard from him on the subject. The amount of my bill ordered assessed by Gen Grant was about two thousand eight hundred Dollars (2800) as near as my recollection serves me. The records will, in your office will show, or should. As you may, or may not remember, I am a resident of Jackson, Tenn. and of my loyalty have letters from many offices of the Army including Gen Grant, and also of the Navy, you may possibly remember my position. I will not allude to or rehears my pecuniay condition, or necessities. Should this plain statement of facts, find you with leisure enough to direct the matter looked into, and my equitable rights secured, I have no question but that it will be done.

I am obliged to leave in the morning, and leave this with my friend Frank. W. Brooks Esq who will present it and if allowed I will give him the necessary pwr-Atty to adjust it. . . . The evidence on which Genl Grants order was based were left in your office in Jackson   My impression is that one Regiment of Infantry was implicated with the 7th Kansas Cavalry. Whether the order for assessment applied to both regiments I do not remember but the order will show"   ALS, *ibid*. Additional papers concerning the 7th Kan. Cav. are *ibid*. See *PUSG*, 5, 260–61; *ibid*., 6, 153.

To Edwin M. Stanton

———

Washington, Nov. 1st *1865*

HON. E. M. STANTON
SECRETARY OF WAR.
SIR:

I would respectfully suggest that brevets for services in the field should in all cases where record of such service exists in the Adjutant Generals Office be given ~~be given~~ for actions in which the officer was present. This alone gives value to brevets as rewards for gallant service, and benefits the army by giving a spur to officers who care for reputation.

I enclose a list of actions for which officers already brevetted should receive their brevets (the brevets being changed) and wish it could be extended so as to give all officers who have earned them brevets for actions, instead of "for faithful and meritorious services during the war."

Very respy, Your ob't. servant
U. S. GRANT
Lieut. General.

LS, DLC-Edwin M. Stanton.
On Oct. 6, 1865, USG wrote to Bvt. Brig. Gen. Edward D. Townsend. "Please send me a list of all brevets in the regular army which have been given since the adjounment of Congress & for what given, and a list of all recommendations since the beginning of the war for such brevets, received at the War Dept, the list stating by whom the recommendation was given, for what; and by whom approved while being forwarded." LS, DNA, RG 94, ACP, G504 CB 1865. On Nov. 3, USG wrote to Secretary of War Edwin M. Stanton. "I have the honor to forward a list of recommendations for brevets in the regular army. In

case any of the officers have already been brevetted to the rank recommended, such action renders the recommendations in those cases unnecessary." LS, *ibid.*, G594 CB 1865. The list is *ibid.*

To Maj. Gen. Quincy A. Gillmore

Washington Nov. 1st 1865

MAJ. GEN. GILMORE, CHARLESTON S. C.

See that your quartermaster carries out existing orders for the reduction of government or chartered transports. No more steamers should be retained than is absolutely necessary for the Government service. The Inspector General reports two as sufficient. Should not Hilton Head be broken up and Charleston made the Depot.

U. S. GRANT
Lt. Gen.

ALS (telegram sent), DNA, RG 107, Telegrams Collected (Bound); telegram sent, *ibid.*; telegram received, *ibid.*, Telegrams Collected (Unbound). On Nov. 3, 1865, Maj. Gen. Quincy A. Gillmore, Hilton Head, S. C., wrote to USG, telegraphing the same message on Nov. 4. "Your despatch of Nov first is received—On the 14th ultimo I telegraphed for permission to move Head quarters to Charleston. I also recommended that the large Steamers between this place and New York be replaced by small Propellors.—I shall not Keep more than two chartered transports in this Department—I will report by letter in regard to transferring Depot from Hilton Head to Charleston.—" LS, *ibid.*, RG 108, Letters Received; telegram received (on Nov. 5, 9:20 A.M.), *ibid.*, RG 107, Telegrams Collected (Bound); *ibid.*, Telegrams Collected (Unbound); *ibid.*, RG 108, Telegrams Received; copy, DLC-USG, V, 54. On Oct. 28, Gillmore had written to Col. George D. Ruggles, adjt. for Maj. Gen. George G. Meade, concerning moving his hd. qrs. to Charleston, and also stating: ". . . I invite special attention to the remarks of Brvt Brig General Bennett in reference to the School Houses in the City of Charleston. ‡There would seem to be neither reason nor justice in the Freedmens Bureau retaining possession of all these houses, or in forcing the white and colored children to be mixed together in the same rooms, to the annoyance and mortification of both races.—. . ." LS, DNA, RG 108, Letters Received. On Nov. 10, USG endorsed this letter. "Respectfully forwarded to the Sec. of War—the recommendations of Gens Bennett and Gillmore in relation to the public schools of Charleston is approved. The proposed change of Dept. Hdqrs. from Hilton Head to Charleston and the reduction of the forces at Hilton Head, except a necessary guard for the public property there, is also, approved." ES, *ibid.* On Dec. 2, USG, Charleston, telegraphed to Secretary of War Edwin M. Stanton. "I would recommend that the ordinace Dept be ordered to remove all the powder from Hilton Head & Send an Officer to Separate the Serviceable ordnance Stores from the unservicable and Sell off all the latter The Stores Can be taken Care of then without the use of Troops all buildings put up at Hilton Head Can then be sold." Telegram received (on Dec. 3, 3:40 P.M.), *ibid.*, RG 107, Telegrams Collected (Bound); copies, *ibid.*, RG 108, Letters Sent; DLC-USG, V, 46, 109.

To Edwin M. Stanton

Washington D. C. Nov. 3d *1865*

HON. E. M. STANTON,
SEC. OF WAR,
SIR:

I have the honor to recommend a change in my report recommending Congressional legislation for increase of the regular army as follows; towit: Instead of all the regiment having ten companies each I would leave the Cavalry and Artillery, as now, with twelve companies each. This gives three battallions of four companies each to each regiment, quite as large a force as is likely ever to be thrown together of either of these arms of public service.

On the basis of One hundred men to each company this would give, if my recommendation is adopted, Eighty two thousand six hundred men as a full compliment. Instead of One hundred to each company I would recommend that but sixty-four be allowed for the peace establishment. This would make a standing army of Fifty-two thousand eight hundred & seventy men.

Very respectfully
your obt. svt.
U. S. GRANT
Lt. Gn.

P. S. As all the companies of an army will never be full at the same time and as no one company can go beyond the number of men fixed by law in making estimates for the army it will be safe to fix the number estimated for at fifty thousand men.

U. S. G.

ALS, DNA, RG 94, Letters Received, 1232A 1865. See letter to Edwin M. Stanton, Oct. 20, 1865. On Nov. 2, 1865, Secretary of War Edwin M. Stanton wrote to USG. "Please inform me, at your earliest convenience, what number of troops will be required for the peace establishment of the United States, reducing it to the lowest amount which you deem compatible with the public safety." LS, DNA, RG 108, Letters Received; copy (dated Nov. 1), DLC-Edwin M. Stanton.

To William Coffin

Washington D. C. Nov. 3d *1865*

MR. WM COFFIN, ESQ.
DEAR SIR:

Your letter of the 1st is received. The arrangement you have made for renting the Phila house is perfectly satisfactory to me. I will write to ~~Mr.~~ Capt. Janes immediately to have the furniture packed and removed at once. It may be the 1st of Jan.y before I will be able to get into the house which I have taken in this city. But Capt. Janes will be able to store my furniture until it can be received here and give possession next week.

With the exception of the glasses between the parlor windows I would prefer bringing them all away. I feel much indebted to you for the trouble you have taken for me and hope in some way to be able to show my appreciation of it.

As I have said I hope to be in my new place by the 1st of Jan.y. I will then have abundance of room for my family and always a few extra rooms for friends. I shall hope to see you and family then and take occation now to say that yourself or daughters must not come to this City without coming directly to my house.

Yours Truly
U. S. GRANT

ALS, Free Library of Philadelphia, Philadelphia, Pa. William Coffin had subscribed $1,000 toward the purchase of a house for USG at 2009 Chestnut Street, Philadelphia. See *PUSG*, 13, 235n. On July 14, 1865, USG wrote to Coffin, 2007 Chestnut Street, Philadelphia. "Please let the bearer, Hon. E. B. Washburn, have the keys of my house, and oblige . . ." ALS, DLC-Edward McPherson. On Nov. 9, Coffin wrote to USG. "Your favors of 3d and 8th inst are at hand contents noted. Enclosed please find two leases executed by Mr S. Baugh, please execute them, retain the one that is signed first by Mr Baugh and forward the other to me that I may hand it over to him. You will notice the rent commences on the First day of December, I let the rent commence at this date by way of compromise with Mr B. (as he expected the use of Mirrors and some other matters) which I trust will meet with your approval. In regard to your favor of 8th inst, I called on Messrs H. B Blanchard & Co N. E corner 13th & Chesnut Streets this morning. They will take charge of the Carpets, and with my assistance will match them if possible and make them up in accordance with your draft of the different rooms. Do not pay any Bills until I have examined them and marked them as correct. Be under no hesitation in asking me to attend to any business for you here for I assure you it affords me great pleasure at any and all times to be of service to you and while on this subject I beg to proffer my services in collecting the Rent, payment of Taxes, Water Rent &c, if you accept them please advise me. Be good enough to say to Mrs Grant that the Butter she ordered will be here within two weeks from this time and that I will forward it immediately upon its receipt. With sincere wishes for your good health and comfort in your new quarters I remain . . ." ALS, USG 3.

On Jan. 26, 1867, USG wrote to Edward C. Knight, Philadelphia. "I have the honor to acknowledge receipt of the Policies of insurance on my Phil. house which you have been kind enough to present me with. The kindness of the Philadelphia public as well as the individual kindness of the Insurance Companies represented by you, will be ever remembered by me most gratefully. Please present my thanks to the Pennsylvania, Delaware Mutual and North American Insurance Companies for their favor." Union League, Philadelphia, *Banquet in Commemoration of the Seventieth Anniversary of the Birthday of Ulysses S. Grant* (Philadelphia, 1892), p. 59.

On Dec. 7, 1871, USG wrote to Louis D. Baugh. "I have duly received your favor of the 5th. instant, with enclosed check for five hundred dollars ($500.) for rent of house No 2009 Chesnut St., due on the 1st inst." Copy, DLC-USG, II. On Dec. 13, 1873, Levi P. Luckey wrote to Baugh. "The President requests me to write you and call your attention to the fact that the verbal lease of the house in Philadelphia for five years expired on the 1st inst. He does not know whether you desire to keep it longer or not. He is perfectly willing you should do so for another year or until the usual time of the year for moving. The President wishes me to request your desires in the matter because he has received application for the house and if you did not intend remaining in it he should not like to lose an opportunity of securing a good tenant. He also said to mention incidentally in my letter that he had not received the last quarter's rent." Copy, *ibid.* Copies of sixteen letters dated between June 2, 1869, and Dec. 4, 1875, from presidential secretaries to Baugh concerning receipt of rent are *ibid.* Repair and rent receipts (the last dated Dec. 29, 1880) are in USG 3.

To Maj. Gen. George H. Thomas

Washington D. C. Nov. 4th 1865 [*1:00* P.M.]
MAJ. GN. G. H. THOMAS, NASHVILLE TENN.

~~The~~ Can you not now so dispose the regular troops in your command as to discharge all or nearly all the White Volunteers. Colored troops can garrison the sea coast entirely and the number of interior posts may be reduced as low as you deem expedient.

U. S. GRANT
Lt. Gen.

ALS (telegram sent), DNA, RG 107, Telegrams Collected (Bound); telegram sent, *ibid.*; copies, *ibid.*, RG 108, Letters Sent; DLC-USG, V, 46, 109. On Nov. 5, 1865, Maj. Gen. George H. Thomas telegraphed to USG. "I have been considering the disposition of the Regular troops in my Command to effect what you ask in your telegram of yesterday, and think I can materially reduce the number of White Vol. very shortly. The peaceful condition of the Country is very encouraging—and I am in hopes that in a few weeks I can dispense with nearly all White Volunteers." ALS (telegram sent), MH; telegram received (at 1:00 P.M.), DNA, RG 107, Telegrams Collected (Bound); *ibid.*, RG 108, Telegrams Received. On Nov. 8, Thomas wrote to USG. "In accordance with General Sherman's request I have issued orders to troops in Kentucky as follows. 125th Regt. U. S. Colored Inf.y. to report by letter to Maj. Gen. Ord at Detroit for orders. The 5th & 6th Colored Cavly and 4th Colored Artillery (Heavy) to proceed by steamer to Helena Arkansas and report to Maj. Gen. Reynolds at Little Rock. Gen Sherman also says that he is desirous of having the 19th Infy sent to Genl Reynolds as soon as I can spare it as when it arrives Gen. Reynolds will discharge every volunteer in his command. I cannot spare the 19th Infy until another battalion of the 16th Infy is sent to me which can take the place of the 19th at Augusta." LS, *ibid.*, Letters Received. On Nov. 21, Maj. Robert Williams, AGO, endorsed this letter. "Respectfully returned to Lieut.-Gen. U. S. Grant, Commanding Army of the United States with the following information: . . . The companies of the 16th Infantry are being organized as rapidly as possible, and as each one is completed it will be sent immediately to General Thomas. That officer has been furnished with the above information" ES (tabular material omitted), *ibid.* On Nov. 14, Thomas telegraphed to USG. "The following is the number of Regts now in West Tennessee. 1 Regt Cavalry, 1 Regt Heavy-Artillery, 3 Regts Infantry, 2 Light Batteries, they are colored troops, the 10th Michigan Cavly is mustered out and embarked on the 11th inst. One Regt is all that is required there. I would recommend the 3rd U. S. Heavy Art be filled up by consolidating one of the other Regts with it, & the ballance of the troops be mustered out and that they should not be permitted to purchase their Arms—" Telegram received (at 7:30 P.M.), *ibid.*, RG 107, Telegrams Collected (Bound);

ibid., RG 108, Telegrams Received; copies, *ibid.*, RG 393, Military Div. of the Tenn., Telegrams Sent; DLC-USG, V, 54.

On Nov. 24, 3:00 P.M., USG telegraphed to Thomas. "If possible muster out the 12th Iowa the first among those going from Alabama." ALS (telegram sent), DNA, RG 107, Telegrams Collected (Bound); telegram sent, *ibid.*; copies, *ibid.*, RG 108, Letters Sent; *ibid.*, RG 393, Military Div. of the Tenn., Telegrams Received; DLC-USG, V, 46, 109. On Dec. 8, Thomas telegraphed to USG. "Yours of the twenty fifth ult just received today in consequence of my absence I have ordered the twelfth Iowa to be mustered out of service as soon as possible." Telegram received (at 7:15 P.M.), DNA, RG 107, Telegrams Collected (Bound); *ibid.*, RG 108, Telegrams Received; copy, DLC-USG, V, 54. On Jan. 9, 1866, 11:00 A.M., USG telegraphed to Thomas. "If possible discharge the 12th Iowa Vols. That regiment have been in service since 1861." ALS (telegram sent), DNA, RG 107, Telegrams Collected (Bound); telegram sent, *ibid.*; copies, *ibid.*, RG 108, Letters Sent; *ibid.*, RG 393, Dept. of the Cumberland, Telegrams Received; DLC-USG, V, 47, 109. On the same day, Thomas telegraphed to USG. "The order for the muster out of the 12th Iowa Infy was issued yesterday" Telegram received (on Jan. 10, 9:00 A.M.), DNA, RG 108, Telegrams Received; copies, *ibid.*, RG 393, Dept. of the Cumberland, Telegrams Sent; DLC-USG, V, 54.

On Dec. 4, 1865, USG, Savannah, Ga., telegraphed to Thomas. "Why are the 147th & 151 Ills. Vols. whose times expire in Feby., retained in service and the 12th Maine & 90th New York with long terms to serve ordered mustered out? Answer at Augusta" Copies, *ibid.*, V, 46, 109; DNA, RG 108, Letters Sent. On Dec. 7, Thomas telegraphed to USG, Augusta, Ga. "The selection of troops to be mustered out, has been left to Department Commanders. I can therefore only refer you to Gen. Steedman. Yours of Dec 4th just received" Copy, *ibid.*, RG 393, Military Div. of the Tenn., Telegrams Sent.

On Dec. 11, 3:00 P.M., Bvt. Brig. Gen. Cyrus B. Comstock telegraphed to Thomas. "There having been some conflict of orders in reference to the muster out of troops in the Dept of Tennessee, Lt. Gen. Grant desires that you make in the Depts of Kentucky and Tennessee the reductions you proposed, and that you reduce the aggregate white force in the Depts of Georgia Alabama and Mississippi to seven thousand (7000) men, regulars included." ALS (telegram sent), *ibid.*, RG 107, Telegrams Collected (Bound); telegram sent, *ibid.*; copies, *ibid.*, RG 94, Vol. Service Div., Letters Received, W2191 (VS) 1865; *ibid.*, RG 108, Letters Sent; DLC-USG, V, 46, 109. On Dec. 12, Thomas telegraphed to Comstock. "Your Telegrams of yesterday just recd. The instructions of the Lieut General in reference to The muster out of the Troops in the Departments of Kentucky & Tenn and of the reduction of the white Troops in the Departments of Georgia ~~and~~ Alabama & Mississippi will be Carried out as soon as the necessary orders Can be given" Telegrams received (2—at 8:40 P.M.), DNA, RG 107, Telegrams Collected (Bound); *ibid.*, RG 108, Telegrams Received; copy, DLC-USG, V, 54. On Dec. 30, 3:30 P.M., USG telegraphed to Thomas. "Muster-out of service all troops in your Division whose time expires in Feb.y 1866. Reduce the force in Tenn. to 4.000 men." ALS (telegram sent), DNA, RG 107, Telegrams Collected (Bound); telegram sent, *ibid.*; copies, *ibid.*, RG 94, Colored Troops Div., Letters Received, 400A 1866; *ibid.*, RG 108, Letters Sent; DLC-

USG, V, 46, 109. On Dec. 31, Thomas telegraphed to USG. "In reducing the force in the Departments of Georgia Alabama & Mississippi included all organizations whose terms expired in February 1866.—I have ordered all volunteer organizations now serving in Tennessee to be mustered out of service except the 14th. U. S. C. I. four hundred & twenty seven (427) Strong:—Sixteenth 16th U. S. C. I. five hundred & five 505 strong: first (1st) U. S. C. I. artillery, heavy, six hundred & twenty nine (629) strong, fifteenth (15th) U. S. C. I. two hundred seventy six 276 strong Seventeenth 17th U. S. C. I. three hundred & seventy seven (377) strong one hundred & eleventh 111th U. S. C. I. five hundred & thirty two (532) strong & the third (3d) U. S. C. artillery heavy seven hundred (700) strong." Telegram received (on Jan. 1, 1866, 1:00 P.M.), DNA, RG 108, Telegrams Received; copy, DLC-USG, V, 54. On Jan. 0, Thomas telegraphed to USG. "I have this day ordered Bvt. Maj. Gen'l C. R. Woods to muster out of service the eighteenth (18th) Forty second (42d) & one hundred & tenth (110th) U. S. C. infantry now serving in his Dept. also Maj. Gen'l T. K. Wood to muster out of service seven reg'ts of colored troops in the Dept. of Miss.—This will be an additional reduction to that ordered by you by telegraph Dec. 11th, 1865.—" Telegram received (at 5:45 P.M.), DNA, RG 107, Telegrams Collected (Bound); *ibid.*, RG 108, Telegrams Received; copies, *ibid.*, RG 393, Dept. of the Cumberland, Telegrams Sent; DLC-USG, V, 54.

On Dec. 19, 1865, Thomas telegraphed to USG. "General orders number one sixty nine 169 from the War Dep't has been received. It is impossible to carry out its provisions in this Military Division as there are not soldiers enough to guard the property & do the necessary work in the Q m Dept at the same time" Telegram received (at 3:15 P.M.), DNA, RG 107, Telegrams Collected (Bound); *ibid.*, RG 108, Telegrams Received; copies (dated Dec. 18), *ibid.*, RG 393, Military Div. of the Tenn., Telegrams Sent; (dated Dec. 19) DLC-USG, V, 54. On Dec. 20, 2:20 P.M., USG telegraphed to Thomas. "If general order No. 169 cannot be carried out in full execute it as far as possible. The object of the order is to secure economy. and in every way this can be secured it is desirable that it should" ALS (telegram sent), DNA, RG 107, Telegrams Collected (Bound); telegram sent, *ibid.*; copies, *ibid.*, RG 108, Letters Sent; DLC-USG, V, 46, 109. On Dec. 21, Thomas telegraphed to USG. "Your telegram of this date recieved   Measures have already been taken to retrench in the disbursing departments and to economize throughout my command as much as possible" Telegram received (at 11:00 P.M.), DNA, RG 107, Telegrams Collected (Bound); *ibid.*, RG 108, Telegrams Received; copies, *ibid.*, RG 393, Military Div. of the Tenn., Telegrams Sent; DLC-USG, V, 54. On Jan. 6, 1866, Thomas telegraphed to USG. "All quarter master Employees except a limited number of clerks have been discharged at all the depots in Georgia Ala. & Miss. & at this place place, Chattanooga Louisville Lexington & Camp Nelson   They have been reduced as much as possible until authority is rec'd from the Qr. Mr. Generals either to remove the large amt. of stores principally at this place Chattanooga & Louisville or dispose of them by sale." Telegram received (at 7:30 P.M.), DNA, RG 107, Telegrams Collected (Bound); *ibid.*, RG 108, Telegrams Received; copies, *ibid.*, RG 393, Dept. of the Cumberland, Telegrams Sent; DLC-USG, V, 54.

To Maj. Gen. William T. Sherman

———

Washington D. C.
Nov. 5th 1865

Dear Sherman,

Your two *private* letters, the first speaking of errors perpetuated and others ~~committed~~ originated in "Sherman's March to the Sea," and the other recommending Allen for Q. M. Gen. in case of a change, is received. I have not yet had time to look over the book refered to. I can assure you however that I shall not be disturbed by any errors committed in hastily prepared books when the errors are directed to the credit of any other officer than myself. I have seen ~~too~~ many of these things slipped into the loose writings of newspaper scribblers in praise of me, when I knew I had no direct or indirect agency in putting them there, ever to suppose others, who I knew as well as I do you, to possess the weakness to do such things. Rest assured that whatever the book contains I shall have no suspicion that you even knew of it before publication.

I do not think there is any change of Q. M. Gn. contemplated. Should there be Allen would be my first choice. Allen ought to feel this because whilst he has been distant from Washington, (whilst I was away also) and, therefore neglected when brevet promotions were given to officers of his department, as soon as I have heard of them I have written in his behalf and secured his promotion and asked to have his appointments dated back so that no junior of his should be placed above him.

I have purchased a fine house in the City on a ten years credit. It will be ready for occupation probably by Christmass. If you or any of your family come to the City after I get in it I shal[l] expect you to stay with me.

Yours Truly
U. S. Grant

To Maj. Gn. Sherman.

ALS, DLC-William T. Sherman. On Oct. 30, 1865, Maj. Gen. William T. Sherman, St. Louis, wrote to USG. "I have just been looking over a Book entitled Sherman & his Campaigns—one whose publicatin I have long dreaded, but could not avoid. I had no hand in its compilation or publication and only assented to it to enable to make money to support his family. I find it contains mistakes, perpetrating other mistakes which I have tried again & again to stop, but *once* in print it seems impossible to stop them. There is on in particular that I have Corrected in Nichols Book, and every where I have seen it in print, but this Book contains the same error, viz in my letter from Raleigh, when I write I think the General Govt of the U. S. has made a mistake—it is printed 'I think Genl Grant of the U. S. Army has made a mistake.' I hope you will be as little annoyed at this as is possible for I assure you it has annoyed me beyond measure, and I envy you your calm stoicism which places you above all such petty annoyances, but I will try and correct this error. I have had no agency in this publication and charged Bowman specially to publish no original matter that had not already been published by or through the War Dept or Congress. All well here, and I am glad to hear through Genl Hancock that you are about to procure in Washington a house & property suited to your Office & station. Mine suits admirably"   ALS, USMA.

To Edwin M. Stanton

Washington, Nov. 6th *1865*

Hon. E. M. Stanton
Secretary of War
Sir:

A copy of complaints as to the manner in which neutrality is observed by United States forces on the Rio Grande, made by the Legation of France, is now before me. The first complaint is that the "dissenting forces of Cortinas are recruiting many colored persons; and that this partizan chief passes the Texan frontiers whenever he pleases, going to Brownsville (Texas) to get whatever he needs." On this subject I am not informed. No instructions have been given by me to the commander in Texas which would touch this matter either way. My instructions were to preserve the same neutrality that had been observed towards us by the French, or Imperialists, when Brownsville and most of the Rio Grande was held by the rebels. If it was found that rebels had been able to "cross and recross the Mexican frontier at will, and go into Matamoras and get whatever they needed," then existing instructions might authorize a corresponding course on our part towards the Liberals. In fact I do not suppose there is any regulation which prevents either Imperialist or Liberal from crossing the Texas frontier or going into Brownsville to make purchases. If recruiting has been allowed by officers in command it has been without authority, but American emigration has been invited to Mexico by the Imperialists, and I am not aware of any law or order preventing it. As the Liberal Government of Mexico is acknowledged by the United States, no objection can be urged to as many of our citizens as choose going to that country and taking whichever side they like. Whilst the United States hold their present attitude towards Mexican affairs, however, military commanders should not allow either party to recruit soldiers upon our territory. I will give instructions in accordance with these views, if approved of.

The second complaint is that "about the end of July last Cortinas attacked the steamer "Señorita" on the river, loaded with cotton taken on board at Camargo, and destined for Matamoros. The attack occurred on Texas ground, and the captured vessel was made fast to the Texan shore, where she has remained in possession of the dissenters since the 27th of July." In the course of the same month a convoy of goods was to start for Monterey; Cortinas, who was in Brownsville, heard of it and enlisted men openly to attack it. His armed troops crossed the river, &c"

If this was allowed, it was entirely inexcusable on the part of the commander at Brownsville.—The whole of these complaints will be referred to Maj. Gen Sheridan, commanding Military Division of the Gulf, with suitable instructions, and directions to report the facts as to what has previously passed.—I will state, however, that we have a long frontier upon the Rio Grande where no United States troops are stationed. Either of the belligerents might easily make war upon the other from United States soil without it being known to United States authority in time to prevent it

I would, beg leave to differ with M. de Monthelon when he says "it would be difficult for neutrality to be more openly violated, &c." In my opinion, he would not have to go off the Rio Grande, nor beyond the events of the last two years to find instances of more flagrant violations of neutrality, and where material aid has been given to the rebellion and against the United States

Very respectfully

Your obdt servant

U. S. GRANT

Lieut General

LS, DNA, RG 107, Letters Received from Bureaus. *O.R.*, I, xlviii, part 2, 1253–54. On Oct. 31, 1865, Secretary of State William H. Seward had written to Secretary of War Edwin M. Stanton enclosing a protest from the French minister. ALS, DNA, RG 107, Letters Received from Bureaus. See *O.R.*, I, xlviii, part 2, 1241; *HED*, 39-1-1, part 3, pp. 443–48.

On Nov. 7, USG wrote to Maj. Gen. Philip H. Sheridan. "Enclosed I send you copy of protest sent by M. Montholon, French Minister, against alleged violations of Neutrality on the Rio Grande and my endorsement thereon. I wish you would have this matter investigated and report how far these statements are true and at the same time report such violations of Neutrality on the part of French troops as can be substantiated. In this part of the investigation you can go back as far as you please." Copies, DLC-USG, V, 46, 109; DNA, RG 108, Letters Sent; USG 3. *O.R.*, I, xlviii, part 2, 1254. On Nov. 23, Sheridan drafted a letter to USG which may not have been sent. ADf (incomplete), DLC-Philip H. Sheridan. On Dec. 23, Sheridan, New Orleans, wrote to USG. "Immediately on the receipt of your communication of Novr 7th enclosing a copy of the French Ministers communication to Mr Secretary Seward containing complaints of alleged violations of Neutrality on the Rio Grande frontier, I ordered Bvt Lt Col Parsons one of my Inspectors to proceed to Brownsville Texas, and thoroughly investigate the matter and I herewith forward you his report showing the complaints to be groundless. The Rio Grande frontier is one where although the utmost vigilance is used on our part still there might be, unknown to us, a violation of Neutrality, this however does not at present and for some time past hold good against the Franco Mexican authorities occupying the cities of Mata-moros and Bagdad, who could, on account of their circumscribed limits easily control their people, still they have annoyed me and excited our troops to such an extent that I have of late frequently reiterated my orders to prevent violations of neutrality; thinking their acts might provoke some overt act on the part of our troops. The constant violations of neutrality on the part of the Franco Mexican Government during our late troubles with with the rebellious States by a whole-sale supply of subsistence, clothing arms and munitions of war to not only the rebels in arms in the Trans Mississippi Department, but for the hostile inhabitants of that extensive territory calls loudly for an explanation on the part of the Franco Imperial Govt of Mexico. When last in Texas I found that on the line from Pieadras Negras to San-Antonio hundreds of wagons had been employed hauling supplies for the rebel army and disloyal inhabitants of Texas during the war, the same was also true of the lines from San Antonio to Laredo, and from Brownsville to Gonzales and on Eastwardly from that point. I found at Piedras Negras 50.000 pounds of lead which was caught there en route upon the Surrender of the rebel Commander Genl E. Kirby Smith. Large quantities of Confederate Cotton which legitimately belonged to the United States Government was run into Mexico at the points on the Rio Grande frontier which were held by the Franco Mexican authorities; horses and cattle of all descriptions belonging to the loyal citizens of the United States resident in Texas were run across the Rio Grande and no redress could be obtained; this however the Franco Mexican Officers do not seem to have considered any violation of neutrality; or the French either, You will also recollect that a Battery of Artillery was sold to the Imperial Govt of Mexico at Brownsville and was only given up on demand, That the steamer Lucy Gwin was run out of the Port of Indianola and taken to Matamoros and finally given up after threatening correspondence; that a rebel newspaper 'The Ranchero' was established and is yet continued in Matamoros which is hostile to our Govt and the President, calling him the murderer of Mrs Surratt and other abusive names; that the Contra-geurilla regiment of Matamoros was to a great extent recruited by desertions from our troops; these and other annoyances I have borne with patience and this, when I had forces in Brownsville and vicinity strong enough to have left their arms on the American side of the river and booted the Franco Mexico troops out of the city so comparatively insignificant were they. More recently the Imperial forces have induced men of my command to desert by offering extraordinary pay and bounties and have on the most frivolous pretences impressed some of our soldiers and put them to work on the fortifications around Matamoros until demands were made for their release. The French Officers on that line have addressed impertinent and insulting letters to our officers and the Steamer 'Eugenia' an American craft was without changing her Nationality and while her papers were still in the possession of the Acting U. S. Consul of Matamoros (and against his emphatic protest,) converted into a Gun Boat and used against the forces of the Republic of Mexico, while we were at the same time holding a legitimate prize of the Republican forces to prevent her being converted into a Gun Boat in order that we might avoid even the appearance of breaking the laws of Neutrality" LS, DNA, RG 107, Letters Received from Bureaus. The enclosures are *ibid*. On Jan. 11, 1866, USG endorsed this letter. "Respectfully returned to the Secretary of War, and attention invited to the accompanying report of Maj. Gen. P H. Sheridan, Comdg Mil Div. of the Gulf." ES, *ibid*.

To Edwin M. Stanton

Washington D. C. Nov. 6th *1865*.

HON. E. M. STANTON,
SEC. OF WAR,
SIR:

Enclosed I send you a letter from A. L. Gusman who is now confined in Fort Lafayette. If he is simply held as a refractory prisoner of War who has declined to take the oath of allegiance to the United States I would respectfully recommend that the opportunity be again held out to him of obtaining his release by now taking it.

> Very respectfully
> your obt. svt.
> U. S. GRANT
> Lt. Gn.

P. S. A similar communication was submitted to these Headquarters, Oct 31st upon which the following endorsement was made.—

"Respectfully returned to the *Secretary* of *War*, with the recommendation that *Mr. Gusman* be released upon taking the neutrality oath, and giving his pledge to go abroad and not to return, without permission of the *President* of the U. S.

> (sgd.) U. S. GRANT,
> Lieut Genl.

Hd Qrs AUS, Oct 31, 65.

If the recommendation of the endorsement has been carried into effect no further action would seem necessary

> U. S. G.

ALS (postscript not in USG's hand), DNA, RG 94, Letters Received, 1378A 1865. The enclosed unaddressed letter of Oct. 26, 1865, from Anthony L. Gusman, former capt., 8th La., Fort Lafayette, N. Y., is *ibid.* USG's endorsement of Oct. 31 is written on a letter of Oct. 20 from Gusman to Maj. Gen. Joseph Hooker. ES and ALS, *ibid.*, 875G 1865. On Nov. 6, Maj. Thomas T. Eckert, act. asst. secretary of war, endorsed this letter. "Referred to the Adjt Genl. Gusman will be discharged without any oath on condition that he leaves the United States not to return without permission of the President" ES, *ibid.*

To Maj. Gen. George G. Meade

———

Washington D. C. Nov. 6th *1865*

MAJ. GEN. G. G. MEADE,
COMD.G MIL. DIV. OF THE ATLANTIC,
GEN.

In view of the peaceful condition of the South I think now the number of interior posts held may be materially reduced in num-

bers and where regular troops are used they can generally be one
and two company posts. In this way you may be enabled to discharge from service most of the White Volunteers still remaining
within your command.

I wish you would send one or more of your staff officers through
the Southern states of the command with full instructions to designate the posts to be held, the garrisons to be put in in them &c.
Let all surplus troops then be mustered out of service. Instruct
your Inspectors to see that all previous orders for the reduction of
transportation and expenses in every way are being carried out.
Let them also report all public property which in their judgement
may be removed or sold with advantage to the public service.

Property is many times so scattered as to make a large force
necessary for performing guard duty alone, where, but for the
public property to be cared for, but few troops would be necessary.
Let this subject receive attention also.

> Very respectfully
> your obt. svt.
> U. S. GRANT
> Lt. Gn.

ALS, DNA, RG 393, Military Div. of the Atlantic, Hd. Qrs. Letters Received.
O.R., III, v, 212. On Nov. 8, 1865, Maj. Gen. George G. Meade, Philadelphia,
wrote to USG. "In compliance with your instructions of the 6th inst, I have
ordered Bvt Brig Genl. Ruggles A. A. G. to the Department of So Ca. and Brvt
Maj- Genl Webb to the Depts of Va & No Ca, with instructions to confer with
Department Commanders and execute your orders as far as practicable—These
officers are directed to report to these Hd Qrs as soon as possible the number of
regiments in each Department whose services can be dispensed with.—I forward
herewith an abstract of the last returns made to these Hd Qrs showing the number of troops on duty in each Department—From it you will percieve the regular
force is very small there being in So Ca only one regiment, in No Ca none, and
in Virginia Two regiments of Infantry and 4 cos of Artillery—It will not therefore be practicable to reduce the volunteer force on the ground of supplying their
places with regulars—The reduction must be made on the ground alone that
troops are not required any longer in the states lately in insurrection.—Upon this
point I beg leave to refer to a report made by me on the 20th of Septr last, on
completing an inspection of the states of So Ca No Ca & Virginia. I therein
stated that so far as any danger to the stability of the Government was concerned, I did not deem the presence of a soldier necessary in these states—but the
absence of civil law, the disorganisation of labor, resulting from the destruction
of slavery, and the necessity of the Govt protecting the Freedmen in the rights
which had been guaranteed to them all combined to render necessary a military

surveillance in each of these states, and the exercise of certain power over them, until by the restoration of civil law, and the passage of such laws by the respective states as would guarantee to Freedmen the essential civil rights—would render un-necessary the presence of any armed force. It was the decided opinion of each of the Department Commanders, at the time I refer to, that the withdrawal of all military force would very likely be followed by a war of races, and circumstances of recent occurrence in So Ca would seem to confirm this view—Brig. Genl Bennett in a recent communication reports 'I do not believe the negroes would permit a white man to live on the plantations on the Ashepoo & Edisto rivers were the military withdrawn   one of my officers Lt. Col. Pope 54th Massts—whilst on a tour of inspection to the "Barrows" was hooted at & threatened with violent expulsion from the plantation, if he did not instantly leave, he being told that they wanted nothing to do with white men.'—Under these circumstances, and for the foregoing reasons, I have instructed Genls Webb & Ruggles to report the largest reduction of the present force, consistent with the existing condition of affairs in the several states they visit. In all these states, the greater portion of the agents of the Freedmen's Bureau are commissioned officers, indeed most all the operations of this Bureau are conducted by the military—so intimate is this connection that I recommended in the report already alluded to, that the Asst Commissioners of the Bureau, should be made subordinate to the Department Commanders—The evils of the independance now existing, will be set forth in a report from Maj Genl. Gillmore recently recieved, which I am about transmitting to you. I also transmit herewith copies of reports made by Maj- Genl. Gillmore & Brvt Maj. Genl. Ruger of the number of colored troops required to carry out the provisions of Par VI—Gen. orders No 144 War Dept—Their reports were made to me at my special request the order only requiring reports to be made to the Adjutant General.—It will be seen both Gens. Gillmore & Ruger construe sea-coast defences to mean works erected by the rebels during the war—whereas my construction would limit these works to the permanent fortifications erected by the Engineer Department before the war—Under this last construction—the works at Port Royal, ~~Va~~ So Ca Fort Hatteras, Fort Fisher & Smithville Battery in No Ca would not be included, and I should deem one strong regiment in each state sufficient to garrison its sea coast defences   This matter is however merely mentioned that your attention may be called to it.—" ALS, DNA, RG 108, Letters Received. The enclosures are *ibid.* On Nov. 9, Bvt. Brig. Gen. Cyrus B. Comstock wrote to Meade. "The Lt. Gen. Com'd'g directs me to acknowledge the receipt of your letter of the 8th inst. and to say that the intention ~~of~~ is to garrison such points of the sea coast as it is necessary to hold against a naval enemy, whether works have been erected at those points by the rebels or ourselves. Of those mentioned in your letter, the Lieut. Gen'l deems it necessary to hold Port Royal and Fort Fisher, but not necessary to hold Ft. Hatteras and Smithville battery, unless there are special reasons aside from the question of seacoast defense which make it advisable. You are therefore authorized to break up those posts if you deem it best." Copies, *ibid.*, Letters Sent; DLC-USG, V, 46, 109.

On Nov. 20, Meade wrote to Brig. Gen. John A. Rawlins. "In compliance with the instructions of the Lt. Genl Comdr dated the 6th inst—I despatched Brv. Maj- Genl. Webb—A. I. Genl—to the departments of Virginia & North Carolina, with orders to report what reduction of the forces in those departments was practicable under the existing condition of affairs. I enclose herewith the report of Maj- Genl Webb, and have to ask that the necessary orders be issued by competent authority for the muster out in Virginia of the following organisations . . . A reference to the reports of Genl. Webb will show how the remaining troops in each of these Departments will be posted.—In connection with the recommendation that the three colored organisations in North Carolina be mustered out—it is proper to advise you, that under G. O. No 130 War Dept these regiments were declared surplus, but have not been mustered ~~owing~~ out, owing to a tegraphic order sent to Brvt Maj- Genl. Ruger a copy of which is herewith enclosed.—" ALS (tabular material omitted), DNA, RG 94, Vol. Service Div., Letters Received, W2191 (VS) 1865. On Nov. 23, Meade wrote to Rawlins. "I enclose for the information of the Lt. Genl-Comdr the report of Brvt. Brig Genl Geo. D. Ruggles, sent by me to the Dept. of So Ca to execute the orders of the Lt. Genl—of Nov. 7th inst.—I am of the opinion three can be spared at once & have therefore to ask the necessary order for muster out may be issued the following regiments—*54th N. Yk Vols—47. Pa Vols.*—& The *28th 33d* & *35th U. S. Colored Troops* This will leave in the Department 2314 enlisted men of white troops & 1510 enlisted men of colored troops or an aggregate of 3824 enlisted men—The attention of the Lt. Genl is called to the enormous amount of ordnance stores which have been accumulated at Hilton Head, the preservation & care of which seem to require an un-necessary large force at that point.—" ALS, *ibid*. On Nov. 25, USG endorsed this letter. "The within recommendation of Gen. Meade's is approved with the request that the Adjutant General issue the necessary orders for the immediate muster out of the regiments named." ES, *ibid*. See *ibid*., Letters Received, 934R 1865.

To Andrew Johnson

Washington D. C. Nov. 7th *1865*

His Excellency, A. Johnson President,

Sir:

Knowing that Gen. Longstreet, late of the Army which was in rebellion against the Authority of the United States, is in the City, and presuming that he intends asking Executive clemency before leaving, I beg to say a word in his favor.

Gen. Longstreet comes under the 3d 5th & 8th exceptions made in your Proclamation of the 29th of May 1865. I believe I can safely say that there is no where among the exceptions a more honorable class of men than those embraced in the 5th & 8th of these, ~~exceptions~~ nor a class who will more faithfully observe any obligation which they make take upon themselves. General Longstreet in my opinion stands high among this class. I have known him well for more than twenty-six years; first as a Cadet at West Point, and afterwards as an officer of the Army. For five years from my graduation we served together, a portion of the time in the same regiment. I speak of him therefore from actual personal acquaintance.

In the late rebellion I think not one single charge was ever brought against Gen. Longstreet for persecution of prisoners of War or of persons for their political opinions. If such charges were ever made I never heard them. I have no hesitation therefore in recommending Gn. Longstreet to your Excellency for Pardon. I will further state that my opinion of him is such that I shall feel it as a personal favor to myself if this pardon is granted.

> Very respectfully
> your obt. svt.
> U. S. GRANT
> Lt. Gen.

ALS, DNA, RG 94, Amnesty Papers, Ala. On Nov. 7, 1865, James Longstreet, former C.S.A. lt. gen., wrote to President Andrew Johnson requesting a pardon. LS, *ibid.* On Dec. 12, Longstreet, New Orleans, wrote to USG. "I presume that you are aware that I did not succeed in procuring my Amnesty whilst I was in Washington inconsequence of an indisposition on the part of the Administration to act upon such cases at that time. But as the President and the Secy of War gave me assurances that they had no personal objections to doing so I write now to ask your further aid in my case. The objection to my case was that it would, in all, probability, prejudice the interests of other cases when Congress met, *to grant it just at that time.* I suppose that that objection may not exist, to such an extent, at this time, as to make it necessary to withhold my pardon, any longer, and your great kindness, has encouraged me to hope that will interest yourself further in my behalf. Secy Stanton also expressed great kindness of feeling, and some interest in my case, and will without doubt readily second any efforts on your part. If however it is still thought inexpedient I hope that you will do me the favor to give me some authority which will enable me to proceed in any business that I may find myself best fitted for—. . . I hope that you will excuse this note as I cannot use a pen with any facility with my left hand" ALS, USG 3. On Dec. 26, Bvt. Col. Adam Badeau wrote to Longstreet. "Lt. Gen. Grant directs me to acknowledge the receipt of your communication of the 12th inst. and to say that although he is not officially authorized to make any statement in your case, he yet feels warranted in informing you, after conversation with the President, that you can engage in any business without fear of molestation, just as if you had received amnesty, and as faor as the amnesty itself, you need have no concern but that it will eventually be granted" Copies, DLC-USG, V, 46, 109; DNA, RG 108, Letters Sent. Longstreet was pardoned as of June 17, 1867.

To Elihu B. Washburne

—————

Washington D. C.
November 9th 1865.

DEAR WASHBURNE,

Enclosed I send you a check for $100 00 to give to the woman in charge of my Galena house to keep her along until more is due. Mrs. Grant has been scolding me for some time for neglecting this.

I will be in my new house by Christmass. Without furnishing the 4th story I will have abundance of room for myself and friends. If Mrs Washburne comes on to visit Washington this Winter bring her to our house.

I shall visit New York City[1] a few days next week to fix up the papers on my house purchase and when I return go South on an inspection tour. Once back from that I shall square down for hard work as long as Congress is in session.

All are well and desire to be remembered to yourself and family.

Yours Truly
U. S. GRANT

P. S. I have seen the Asst. Sec. on the subject of Richardsons[2] appointment and will write again as soon as I learn what can be done.

U. S. G.

ALS, IHi. On Oct. 25, 1865, U.S. Representative Elihu B. Washburne, Galena, wrote to Bvt. Col. Adam Badeau. ". . . I must say I am sorry that the General is going to N. Y. If every body knew him as you and I do, it would be different, but as they do not, they attribute to him motives that we know never entered his head. Copperheads will invite him to a reception and make a great ado over him and then turn round and abuse him, saying that he is making a 'show' of himself and trying to make political capital. As unjust and outrageous as all this is, it is calculated to weaken the hold which he has upon the people.—The great Napoleon, (not greater than Grant) understood all this thing. Returning to Paris after his campaigns, he kept himself shut up, and never exhibited himself to the people. And another consideration. The President and the Lieut. General seem now to be in perfect accord and it is vastly important to the country it should continue so.—I do not know what Mr. Johnson's views and wishes are touching a re-election. Should he have an eye that way, it would be inevitable that he would become jealous of every public moment of the Lt. General, and the ordinary feelings would, of course, follow. *We* know how the people will settle this Presidential question in 1868, but perhaps Mr. Johnson may not know, and we are not bound to proclaim it to him. All this does not apply to a trip through the South, at the *request of the President*, to see into the actual situation of matters. These considerations have not only occurred to me, but they have occurred to other, more influential and distinguished, but not more sincere friends to the General than myself. . . ." ALS, *ibid.* On Nov. 9, Badeau wrote to Washburne. "Your kind letter came duly to hand. I showed it to the General, as the best way of letting him know your views. He said he knew your sincerity and how much interest you felt in him, but he meant to go to New York. . . ." ALS, DLC-Elihu B. Washburne. On Nov. 23, Badeau wrote to Washburne. ". . . The New York trip was more brilliant than any thing that preceded it. We were there ten days, and the General received every imaginable civility from any body of any consequence in New York. The grand reception transcended the great ball given to the Prince of Wales, in which I had a great deal to do, so that I know what I am talking of. . . ." ALS, *ibid.*

1. On Nov. 11, 8:00 P.M., USG telegraphed to John W. Garrett, president, Baltimore and Ohio Railroad, Baltimore. "I will take the 11 15 train. Will it be necessary for me to telegraph to secure a special car from Philadelphia?" ALS (telegram sent), DNA, RG 107, Telegrams Collected (Bound); telegram sent, *ibid.* On the same day, Garrett had telegraphed to USG. "I have just received Col Badeau's note of yesterday in order to go through to New York by daylight by Regular Train without Change of cars at Philada it will be necessary to take the 7.35 A. M. train—The trains leaving washington at 11.15 transfers passengers through the center of Philada upon which will you prefer to go? A special car will be attached to the train you may select." Telegram received, *ibid.* USG arrived in New York City, Monday evening, Nov. 13, and left the city during the evening of Nov. 21 to return to Washington, D. C. USG's stay in New York City received widespread newspaper coverage.

On Nov. 12, James H. Hackett telegraphed to USG. "Will it be agreeable & convenient any one or two evenings while here to witness my Faltaff of either Henry Fourth or Merry wives of Windsor or both. . . . Please Ans. tonight" Telegram received, USG 3. On Nov. 20, Hackett wrote to USG. "By a note recd. from Judge Daly last evening, I learned—much to my chagrin—that my inquiry by telegram to you at Washington Sunday evng. 12th insts had been promptly & gracefully answered in the affirmative by a letter through your Private Secry; which, however, was not before heard of, nor has yet been received—On Tuesday last I called at your hotel to pay my respects; but learning you had 'just gone out!' I left my card—I would have called again, but was apprehensive that, in my ambition to gratify a desire wh you had so complimentarily expressed in a note to me at 'Cairo, Ill, Oct. 1863,' I might seem importunate & prove troublesome—of late years, I have appeared upon the stage of this—my native city very rarely and irregularly; &, through previous arrangements at our theatres with other objects last week presented certain obstacles, an evening for a representation of Shakespeare's King Henry IV might have been secured,—had I received your polite reply prior to even Wednesday last—Nonetheless, I will cherish the hope of finding some opportunity—mutually convenient here or elsewhere—for acting Falstaff for your special pleasure; & expect to have the honor with Mrs Hackett of offering—en passant with the crowd of our citizenry—our respects to yourself & Mrs Grant, at the public Reception arranged for this evening at the Fifth Avenue Hotel—" ALS, *ibid.*

On Nov. 14, George Wilkes, "Wilkes' Spirit of the Times," wrote to USG.

"I find it will be most convenient for the owners of the great horses you wish to see, to accept of Thursday next as the time when they will be happy to perform them in your presence. I have there fore named 3 o'clock P. M, of that day for them to have their horses at Dubois' private Association track, on the Bloomingdale road, this city. If this is agreeable to you, Mr Bonner and I will call for you, on Thursday at from 2 to 2½ P. M. with the ele celebrated *Ledger* team, of which you no doubt have heard, to drive you to the course." ALS, *ibid.* See *New York Times*, Nov. 17, 1865.

On Nov. 14, Alexander T. Stewart *et al.*, Fifth Avenue Hotel, issued an invitation to USG. "The people of this Commercial Metropolis are deeply sensibl[e] of their obligations for the signal services you have rendered to the Cause of the Union. They desire to offer you in person an expression of their regard for your character as a Citizen and their admiration of your brilliant career as a Soldier. With these views, they respectfully ask that you will permit them to receive Mrs Grant and yourself, with the members of your family at present in this City, at this Hotel, on such evening during your stay, as may be most consistent with your convenience." ALS, USG 3. Stewart presented this invitation to USG. "We present ourselves before you as a Committee on the part of the Citizens of New York to request that you will honor them with the presence of yourself, your family, and suite, at a public reception to be given at the 5th Avenue Hotel on Monday evening next at 8 O'Clock.—Our Citizens desire to express their deep sense of gratitude to the Soldier, who, after conducting the Country safely and honorably through the perils of an unexampled war, has been not less successful by his wise and dignified forbearance in promoting harmony and good will, and restoring to us the blessings of peace and prosperity. To Mrs Grant the ladies of New York desire to testify their respect on the same occasion, and we request that this privilege and pleasure may be afforded them." AD, *ibid.*; *Philadelphia Inquirer*, Nov. 20, 1865. On Nov. 16, William B. Astor, chairman, Committee of Invitations, and twenty-two others issued approximately 1500 invitations to a reception in USG's honor to be held at the Fifth Avenue Hotel on Nov. 20. On Nov. 17, Stewart wrote to Badeau. "I take pleasure in enclosing you a copy of the Invitation to Lieut General Grant, with the names appended up to the present time, but to which many more will be added. Please call the General's attention, and request if convenient a response during the day, adding, that the original will be given him on Monday." ALS, USG 3. On the same day, USG, Metropolitan Hotel, wrote to "Committee of Citizens of New York." "Your polite note, of ot-day, inviting my family and staff and myself to a public reception of the citizens of this city, to be given at the Fifth Avenue Hotel, on Monday evening next, is received. It affords me great pleasure to accept this invitation, and, in doing so, allow me to express the great gratification I feel, in receiving such an invitation from the citizens of the metropolis of our country, and, twenty years hence, of the world." *Philadelphia Inquirer*, Nov. 20, 1865. For the reception, see *New York Times*, Nov. 20, 21, 1865; Harold Earl Hammond, ed., *Diary of a Union Lady, 1861–1865* (New York, 1962), pp. 371–78; Allan Nevins and Milton Halsey Thomas, eds., *The Diary of George Templeton Strong* (New York, 1952), IV, 50–52. On Nov. 22, Henry M. Taber wrote to USG. "I have in my possession the letter addressed to you by the Citizens of New York asking the favor of a reception to Mrs Grant & yourself at the Fifth Avenue Hotel, which letter was retained here in order to obtain the additional signatures of those who had not had an opportunity of signing it, previous to your leaving the city. Those signatures having now been obtained, I write to ask (as Secretary of the Committee) that you will instruct me if I shall send this letter to you by mail, or what other disposition I shall make of it." ALS, USG 3. On Nov. 24, Taber wrote to USG. "I have the pleasure to own rect from Colo Badeau, of his note of yest.y containing your instructions to send the letter of invitation from the Citizens of New York—(to which my note of the 22d inst, to you, alluded—) to your (or his) address, & in compliance therewith hand you the same herein: I learn further from Colo Badeau, & with much pleasure that I will be favored with the acknowledgement of its receipt from *you.* Awaiting which & wishing you a pleasant trip to the South . . ." ALS, *ibid.*

On Nov. 15, A. L. Robertson wrote to USG. "I have the honor to inform you that on the 2nd Aug 1865 you were unanimously elected a life member of the Union Club Enclosed I beg to hand you a copy of the constitution &c" ALS, *ibid.* For the Union Club, founded in 1836, see James Grant Wilson, ed., *The Memorial History of the City of New-York* (New York, 1893), IV, 234–36. On the same day, 10:30 P.M., USG attended a reception in his honor at the Union League Club, founded in 1863 (*ibid.*, IV, 251–52), and Benjamin F. Beekman addressed USG. "We bid you welcome here not for the first time. You have honored us as your friends with your presence when you came here fresh from your victories. We thank you now for the victories of peace—for the wonderful and rapid return to the workshop and the farm of your soldiers, who without tumult or insubordination have fallen into their old places at home as promptly and quietly as you taught them while soldiers to form in time of war in line of battle. They have but imitated their great captain, who knew how to refrain from seeing the capital he had conquered, and has never yet entered Richmond since its surrender. The rebellion you have crushed had for its object the establishment of an empire. It was the foe of republican institutions, though disguised in republican form. Grasping at the hopeful opening made by the temporary success of these conspirators, European ambition has striven to establish another empire over a sister Republic. MAXIMILLIAN, by stranger arms, has been forced upon her brave and unwilling people. Fouler wrong never outraged human annals than the present occupation of Mexico by the French. We sympathize with our sister Republic in her day of adversity, and firmly believe in her coming deliverance. A Mexican GRANT will yet restore his country, as you have saved your own. . . ." *New York Times,* Nov. 16, 1865. USG responded: "I hope you will excuse me from thanking you at any great length. But there is one sentiment uttered in your address, which is mine also. It is the one touching the future of Mexico." *Ibid.*

On Nov. 17, James I. Ruggles, secretary, New York Club, wrote to USG. *"The Directors have the honour to inform you that, at the request of Mr* Sherwood, *your name has been placed on the list of visitors admitted to the privileges of the Club for two weeks."* LS, USG 3. John D. Sherwood helped organize the Nov. 20 reception for USG. Also on Nov. 17, Col. Lloyd Aspinwall, 22nd N. Y. National Guard, wrote to USG. "I have the honor to tender you an invitation to be present at a presentation of eight *medals* of *'Military Merit'*—to a like number of men, comd. officers or private of the 22d National Guard S. N. Y. I need not add Gen, how very highly, your presence, would be appreciated by the Regiment, or how gratifying it would be to myself as a token of your approval, of the rewards, at that time to be given to deserving soldiers, The National Guard have proved their usefulness and patriotism on the battle field, and in other ways during the past four years, and your presence on an occasion of this kind, would be looked upon, as a recognition of the services rendered—Trusting your engagements will permit you to attend, at the 22d Regiment Armory, in 14th street on Tuesday evening at 8 o'clock—" ALS, *ibid.*

On Nov. 18, James Kelly, postmaster, New York City, wrote to USG. "When I had the pleasure of seeing you this morning you kindly Consented to call at the Post office on Monday next, and give our clerks (many of whom were soldiers during the late war & served under you) an opportunity, which, owing to their onerou[s] duties they could not otherwise ha[ve] looking upon & greeting the man whom all consider as being entitled (under Providence) to the name of Saviour of his Country—If convenient to yourself I should be pleased t[o] see you here at any time on Monday from 11 to 2 ocl'k—or on Tuesday, if that would suit you better—A line from you, stating what day and hour would be preferable, would greatly oblige, . . ." ALS, *ibid.* USG, accompanied by William S. Hillyer, visited the post office on Nov. 21. *New York Times*, Nov. 22, 1865. On the same day, USG visited the Mercantile Library to view "Grant and his Generals," a painting by Ole Peter Hansen Balling, and signed the register. "Visited Mr. Ballings excellent composition this date." ANS, National Portrait Gallery, Washington, D. C. See *New York Herald*, Nov. 22, 1865. On Sept. 23, 1864, President Abraham Lincoln had issued a pass. "Allow the bearer, Mr H. Balling to pass to Gen. Grant, to whom he is hereby introduced" ANS, National Portrait Gallery, Washington, D. C. Also on Nov. 21, 1865, USG visited the studio of Mathew B. Brady to provide materials for James McHenry of London, who was preparing a life-size portrait of USG, and signed Brady's register. DS, Mathew B. Brady register, vol. 2, 1864–65, NN; *New York Times*, Nov. 22, 23, 1865.

On Nov. 18, Harvey P. Peet, principal, Institution for the Deaf and Dumb, wrote to USG. "In behalf of one of the most humane and benevolent institutions of the day, I beg leave to tender to you a sincere and cordial invitation to visit it on Monday or Tuesday next, at any hour that may suit your convenience. Though our pupils are unable to express their loyalty in loud demonstration, their patriotism is not the less deep and ardent though uttered in the silence of gestures. They are familiar with your brilliant exploits, and nothing could give them greater pleasure than to welcome to their Alma Mater the man whose name is but the synonym of heroic achievement. My friend Mr Fuller who will place this in your hands, will confer with you as to the time and manner of your visit." ALS, USG 3. On the same day, Samuel S. Randall, superintendent, Department of Public Instruction, wrote to USG. "If Mrs. Grant and yourself would like to look in upon a few of our Public Schools, previous to your departure from the City, it would afford me very great pleasure to wait upon you at any time you may please to indicate. I need not say that the honor of such a visit would be a high gratification to the officers, pupils & teachers of these Institutions." ALS, *ibid.* The *New York Times* (Nov. 15, 1865) had reported that USG "will visit several of our public schools, and probably the Deaf and Dumb Institution." Also on Nov. 18, Mayor Alfred M. Wood of Brooklyn wrote to USG. "At the solicitation of a large number of my fellow citizens, permit me to invite you to visit Brooklyn and thus afford our people the opportunity which they so earnestly desire, formally to pay their respects to you. There are three hundred thousand of us here, general, who would be gratified to look upon, (if nothing more,) the distinguished soldier, whom they regard as the main instrument, in the hands of Divine Providence in suppressing the wicked rebellion which so recently threatened the integrity of the Republic. Will not your engagements, ere you leave New York permit you to gratify us? Please inform me" ALS, *ibid*. Docketing indicates that Badeau answered Wood after USG had left N. Y. *Ibid*.

2. On Oct. 20, Badeau wrote to Washburne. "The General wishes me to inform you that immediately on his return here, he saw the Sec of the Treasury about Hon Daniel Richards, and was told that the appointment you had solicited for him had already been made in favor of another applicant that very day. Mr. Richards's rival had seen the President in person and procured the appointment. Some other place however could be given to Mr. R., if it should be particularly desirable. . . ." ALS, DLC-Elihu B. Washburne. Daniel Richards was nominated as direct tax commissioner for the District of Fla. on Dec. 19 and confirmed on Feb. 2, 1866. On April 12, Richards, Fernandina, Fla., wrote to USG. "Reports anticipated difficulties arising between former property holders and loyal citizens in his district in state of Florida." DNA, RG 107, Letters Received from Bureaus. On April 27, USG endorsed this letter. "Respectfully referred to Maj. Gen. Foster, Comdg. Florida Dept., who is directed to see that all titles to land and other property obtained from the United States authorities, are respected until decisions are given against them by the United States Courts." Copy, *ibid*. On May 7, Maj. Gen. John G. Foster, Tallahassee, Fla., wrote to Maj. George K. Leet. "I have the honor to acknowledge the receipt of a communication from D. Richards, Tax Commissioner for Florida, addressed to Lieut. Genl Grant, which you have referred to me. I desire to state, that Mr Richards has no just grounds for apprehension that the U. S. forces in this Command will be used in any other way, than in support of U. S. laws and its officers, or that any failure will exist in so using them.—I enclose a copy of my last letter upon the subject to Colonel Sprague.—I beg leave in this connexion to explain that all the trouble at Fernandina has arisen from the tax sales, of the course pursued by the Tax Commissioners.—It is asserted that some of the property was sold twice; that the sales were sometimes irregular, and at others did not conform to the requirements of the law.—Judge L. D. Stickney, one of the Tax Commissioners, declares that they ought to be made null and void, and that such must be the final decision of the Courts.—Under these circumstances I have tried to keep out of the processes as far as possible, always, however, supporting the titles received from the Tax Commissioners, when it became necessary to do so.—At present the trouble arises mainly from the adverse claims of the original owners, who have redeemed their property and received certificates of redemption from the Commissioner, on the one part, and the purchasers on the other part.—According to law the for[mer] cannot obtain possession until the Certificates of Purchase, held by the latter, are surrendered to them; and the Purchaser cannot be required to yield his Certificates until the purchase money is refunded to him.—But by Law and Regulations of the Treasury Department, the purchase money is not to be refunded until the action of the Commissioners, in granting the redemption, receives the approval of the Secretary of the Treasury, when a Check for the purchase money is to be issued by him in favor of the purchaser.—The great delay arising from this procedure, causes great dissatisfaction, and in some cases suits at law, and is the origin of much bitter feeling.—If possible this should be corrected.—The remedy properly lies with the Treasury Department and the Tax Commissioners." LS, *ibid*. On May 21, USG endorsed this letter. "Respectfully forwarded to Secretary of War, for his information." ES, *ibid*. On May 12, Foster wrote to

Brig. Gen. Lorenzo Thomas forwarding papers concerning the situation in Fernandina. On May 29, USG endorsed this letter. "Respectfully forwarded to the Secretary of War, for his action, in connection with papers on same subject forwarded 21 inst" ES, *ibid.* On May 14, Richards wrote to Washburne. "Enclosed please find resolution of thanks to Gen. Grant which you will hand to him, and give him my special regards besides. Some of our friends here think it may subserve a good purpose in having the resolution published, and I do not see any harm in doing so. But perhaps you or the General may, and we leave that to your own discretion." ALS, DLC-Elihu B. Washburne. On May 31, forty-three residents of Fernandina petitioned USG. "A communication addressed to you on the 12th Inst. by D. Richards Esq., Tax Commissioner for Florida, grossly misrepresents our people, and if his position is sustained by military authority the result will be ruinous to them. Mr Richards had been in Florida but a single week when he wrote this Communication, he was in ill health, and had made the acquaintance of no former owner of property whom he could truthfully call disloyal. All the former owners who had redeemed their property from the Direct Tax Sale are embraced in two classes—minor children, or persons under legal disability; second, loyal persons who had proved to the satisfaction of the Board of Tax Commissioners that they had not aided or abetted the insurgents in the late rebellion against the Government of the United States, nor given them aid or comfort. Surely, such persons could not have left this town to join the rebel forces, as Mr Richards charges. Having redeemed their property from Tax Sale, and paid the amount required by law, thus divesting the purchaser of all right and title, they seek through the civil courts possession thereof. Again, there are former owners who believe the sale of their property by the Direct Tax Commissioners is void. For example; the Direct Tax Act provides that property of the value of five hundred dollars or less, belonging to individuals, shall be exempt from taxation, and yet in many instances such property was sold for the Tax. Now the poor owner, whom Congress intended to protect from even the burden of a tax, is stripped of his whole property, if denied the legal remedy guarantied to every Citizen by the Constitution. Proceedings are instituted in the State Courts of general jurisdiction, not of present organization and made up for the express purpose of throwing out holders of tax titles, as Mr Richards alledges, but dateing from the establishment of our State Government in 1846, because there is no other having jurisdiction. Citizens of Florida Cannot be plantiff and defendant, within the state where the suit is brought, in the Federal Courts, therefore to compel them to wait the decisions of the United States Courts is simply a denial of justice. If Mr Richards intended to convey to you the impression that the former owners expected to obtain from Major General Foster any order which was not strictly proper, he does both them and that gallant officer great injustice. The fact is Mr Richards lent a too credulous ear to another Tax Commissioner, Austin Smith, whose son Robert M. Smith was a large purchaser of these Tax sales, and the father invokes your authority to perpetuate titles so tainted with fraud no court would sustain them. Mr Smith officially heard and decided cases of redemption from his son's tax title, (his decisions being for his son against the ruling of his associates) and this is the loyal man who cannot under the present organization of the State Governmt and the Courts, retain possession of his property. We, like yourself, general, are Citizens of a Common Country, loyal to its Constitution and laws, and, ready at its call to defend against all its enemies, that flag you triumphantly bore on so many battle fields." DS,

DNA, RG 108, Letters Received. On June 30, William Mason, New York, wrote to USG. "The people of Fernandina and St Augustine complain, that your Order No   which limits proceedings to recover possession of lands sold for taxes and redeemed under the act of Congress, to the courts of the United States and excludes the jurisdiction of the state courts, operates to deprive them of all remedy in as much as it is believed, that by the law the United States courts have no jurisdiction of suits of ejectment or other suits involving the question of titles to lands or their possessions where the parties to the suit *reside in the same state*, but the state courts only—The suit in many cases would be commenced in the state court and may be carried by appeal or writ of error to the Supreme court of the United States—Judge Long who will hand you this will explain further—It appears to me the state courts of Florida ought to be left free to execute the laws, particularly in all matters of civil right" ALS, *ibid.*, RG 107, Letters Received from Bureaus. On July 2, USG endorsed this letter. "Respectfully forwarded to the Hon. Secretary of War, with the request that the opinion of the Attorney General be had upon the legality of the enclosed endorsement made April 27th 1866, upon a communication from D. Richards, Tax Commissioner at Fernandina, Fla. Other papers relating to the tax difficulties in Florida were submitted to the War Dept. May 7th and May 29th 1866." ES, *ibid.* On Aug. 18, USG telegraphed to Maj. Gen. Philip H. Sheridan. "Instructions to Gen Foster given some months ago prevent citizens of Florida appealing to other than United States courts for recovery of property sold for taxes. Those instructions will be now annulled and purchasers will look to civil courts and the Civil Rights Bill for their protection" Telegram sent, *ibid.*, Telegrams Collected (Bound); copies, *ibid.*, RG 108, Letters Sent; DLC-USG, V, 47, 60.

On Jan. 12, 1867, Col. John T. Sprague, 7th Inf., Tallahassee, wrote to USG. "To day his Excellency Gov Walker had an interview with myself in regard to affairs at Fernandina. He says he is unable to execute the laws of the State at that point without the aid of the military, and makes a request accordingly. The difficulty arises out of the property held and purchased under Tax-titles. The sheriff attempted to execute a writ under the authority of the State. It was successfully resisted. A Committee have waited upon Gov. Walker representing the matter and asking the execution of the writ: The Governor declines for the reason that he has not the Militia force under his control. He sends by mail to night full particulars to his Excellency the President of the United States. I have seen them and am satisfied that the state of affairs at Fernandina is critical. The large number of freedmen there armed, and instigated by bad men, and vague stories, render the necessity of prompt and vigorous measures. Temporary expedients will be of little avail, the whites as well as the freedmen require the strong arm of power: a bad example there may have its influence throughout the State. If Martial law could be considered as existing over Amelia Island until further orders, it would control the city of Fernandina and the freedmen. All parties are now awaiting the action of the Executive and the Military, in answer to his Excellencies application for Military assistance to execute the Civil-law. The instructions to Maj. Gen. Foster of October 22nd 1866, from the Secretary of War, by telegram, and the letter to Major Gen. P. H. Sheridan, dated Hd. Qrs. Armies of the United States, Washington Nov 1st 1866., are decided, clear, and conclusive, by which I am at present governed. Enclosed are copies of the communication from his Excely. Gov. Walker and my reply, also the latest and only reports received from the officer temporarily in command at

Fernandina. I have directed that Capt. A. A. Cole, 7th Infty, Bvt. Major U. S. A., be relieved from his present duty on Gen. C. M. and immediately return and resume command of Fernandina." Copy, DNA, RG 393, Dept. and District of Fla., Letters Sent. On Jan. 25, 2:00 P.M., USG telegraphed to Sprague. "If military aid is required to execute laws of the State you will notify the Dep't commander who will judge of the propriety of furnishing such aid" Telegram sent, *ibid.*, RG 107, Telegrams Collected (Bound); copies, *ibid.*, RG 108, Telegrams Sent; DLC-USG, V, 56. At the same time, USG telegraphed to Sheridan transmitting a copy of the telegram to Sprague. Telegram sent, DNA, RG 107, Telegrams Collected (Bound); telegram received, *ibid.*, RG 393, Dept. of the Gulf, Telegrams Received. On Jan. 26, Sprague, Tallahassee, wrote to USG. "I have the honor to enclose a copy of a letter, the latest information received from Lieut W. S. Dodge, 7th U. S. Infty, Commdg at Fernandina, Fla. Unofficial information has reached me this morning that Capt and Brvt Major Cole, 7th U. S. Infty, has returned and assumed command of the Post, and that the City was quiet. At the present time there is an apprehension of difficulties: the commotion arises from the dissatisfaction of parties who have acquired property under Tax-sales, and assumes the character of personal encounters and recrimination often ending in curses and blows. There are excited parties who appeal to the Governor for the execution of laws, and this is to gratify personal revenge and pecuniary interests. The material is bad in that community, and the officer is required to protect the lives of the citizens and property, and to abstain from interfering in the execution of State laws. The presence of a U. S. District Judge is greatly needed. The peace of the Country and the rights of citizens demand it, and I would most respectfully and urgently request that a U. S. District Court be opened at St. Augustine as soon as possible. My communication of the 12th inst. with enclosures, I presume has been received." Copy, *ibid.*, Dept. and District of Fla., Letters Sent. On Jan. 30, Sprague, Fernandina, wrote to USG. "I have the honor to report; that I arrived in this City, accompanied by His Excellency Governor Walker, on the 28th instant. The excitement had [s]ubsided in anticipation of his arrival. After meeting, and talking with all parties, the people have settled down into quietness, and no further commotion is apprehended at the present time. There, however, remains enough of ill feeling in regard to Tax-sales and the possession of property, to excite, at any moment, a spirit of lawlessness and retaliation. The opening of a United States Court would bring these irritating questions to adjustment. I would repeat what I have before said, that the presence of a United States Judge is necessary for the peace and security of this portion of the State. To hold the Freedmen in check, and to put down the councils and influences of bad men, I have placed a company of U. S. Troops in this City to insure peace, security, and good order. The order, ~~copy~~ duplicate is herewith enclosed: also the reports of Liutent Wm S. Dodge U. S. A (copies) who was in command during the absence of Bvt Major Cole. I return to Tallahassee tomorrow, or as circumstances will permit." ALS, *ibid.*, RG 94, Letters Received, 95S 1867. On Jan. 31, Richards wrote to USG. "Governor Walker and Col. Sprague are here to try and learn the truth about the difficulties in this place between the late rebels and the union men. Col. Sprague desired to maintain with the military, a strict neutrality between the parties, but as the Governor persists in his determinatn to execute these writs of possession issued by two *justices of the Peace*, and dispossess parties of their property, and learning that stern resistance would be shown, and most certainly lead to bloodshed, the Col. has deemed it prudent to station a small military force in our town to maintain peace and good order and protect the lives and property of our citizens. All the property in dispute, and for the possession of which these writs are issued, are cases that have been properly appealed to the U States Courts and there await adjudication. But these former owners are unwillng to await the action of these tribunals, or they are not satisfied to trust them, and proceed by this summary mode, to take possession of this property. The Governor claims that an appeal with proper bonds filed does not stay all proceedings, and says that notwithstanding the appeal, when a redemption is completed, the redemptor is entitled to possession. On the contrary, the parties in possession claim, that any appeal with proper bonds filed, from an inferior tribunal, but continues if the case in court, and the rights of parties are to remain the same, until a final judgment, from the higher tribunal. I learn that Governor Walker is not well pleased with the action of Col. Sprague and ~~goes to~~ starts for Washingtn by next boat, probably to have Sprage removed from Command in this state, and that is why I trouble you General with this Communicatn. I assure you General, that Col Sprague's action in this case, and his administratn in this state thus far, meets the warm approval of the Union men, and *that*, you know is the best complimt any good officers can earn in this country." ALS, *ibid.*, RG 108, Letters Received. On Feb. 8, Leet endorsed Sprague's letter and a copy of Richards's letter. "Respectfully referred to Major Gen'l P H Sheridan, Comdg. Dept. of the Gulf, for such action as he deems necessary, and report." AES, *ibid.*, RG 94, Letters Received, 95S 1867. Additional papers are *ibid.* See Jerrell H. Shofner, *Nor Is It Over Yet: Florida in the Era of Reconstruction, 1863–1877* (Gainesville, Fla., 1974), pp. 99–101, 168–69.

To William H. Seward

Washington, Nov. 10th *1865*

HON. WM H. SEWARD,
SEC. OF STATE,
SIR:

In case it is determined by the United States Government to make a survey of the Isthmus of Darien for the purpose of determining the practicability of constructing a Ship Canal by that route, I have the honor to state that, in my opinion, the survey can be made without any special appropriation for the purpose. By making it a joint duty of the Army and Navy a suitable officer of each branch of the service could be selected to make the surveys. The Navy Dept. could furnish a vessel, or more if necessary, for guarding the Coast and furnishing details of men to do the work upon the

Bays and streams in the interior. Colored troops could be sent in sufficient numbers to guard the surveying party against hostile Indians and to do all the labor upon land.

The importance of the work contemplated I need not dwell upon, nor the importance of keeping it out of the hands of any other first class power than our own, for I presume that has fully attracted your attention.

> Very respectfully
> your obt. svt.
> U. S. GRANT
> Lt Gn

P. S. This is written without consultation with the Sec. of War whos approval would be necessary in case any such use was made of the Military forces of the country as are here mentioned and is therefore a private note in answer to your request of this morning.
U. S. G.

ALS, Seward Papers, NRU. On Nov. 14, 1865, Secretary of State William H. Seward wrote to USG. "Your letter of the 10th instant giving me your views upon the importance and practicability of cutting a ship canal through the isthmus of Darien, has been received, and will engage my attentive consideration." LS (press), *ibid.*

Also on Nov. 10, USG wrote to Seward. "In compliance with your request I have the honor to state that the aggregate strength of the army is at present 182.784. men; and that including Louisiana 81.256. of these men are West of the Mississippi river. I case of emergency 50.000 additional men could be made disposible east of the Mississippi" Copies, DLC-USG, V, 46, 109; DNA, RG 108, Letters Sent.

To Lyman Abbott

Washington D. C. Nov. 10th *1865*

REV. LYMAN ABBOTT,
GEN. SEC. AMERICAN UNION COMMISSION,
SIR:

I have received your invitation to be present at the meeting of the "Union Commission" in the City of New York on the 13th inst.

At the time of receiving this invitation I did not know but it would be possible for me to attend. I now find that it will not be possible. It affords me great pleasure however to see so respectable an organization as yours interested in so deserving a cause. However we may have differed from our Southern brethren in the events of the last four years we have now become again one people and with but one interest. The war has worked such ruin upon much of the South that without some aid from those who can give it there must be much suffering the coming Winter. The work of your Commission while it will give present aid where it is so much needed will also serve to heal old wounds.

Whatever is calculated to increase the friendship and brotherly feeling betwen the two sections of our Country I heartily approve of.

> Very respectfully
> your obt. svt.
> U. S. GRANT
> Lt. Gn.

ALS, Abbott Memorial Collection, MeB. Lyman Abbott, born in Mass. in 1835, graduated from New York University and practiced law. In 1860, he became a Congregationalist minister serving in Terre Haute, Ind., until 1865, when he became corresponding secretary, American Union Commission, in New York City. On Nov. 2, Joseph P. Thompson, George W. Lane, and Abbott had written to USG. "We respectfully invite you to attend a public meeting, to be held in the City of New York on the 13th. inst. at Cooper Institute, for the purpose of setting before the people the wants of the suffering masses in the South, and arousing a public interest in measures for their relief, and especially for the restoration of industrial and educational systems. His Excellency, the President of the United States, Major. Gens. Sherman, Meade, Howard, Hon. W. H. Seward, Hon. E. M. Stanton, Hon James Pollock, Hon. Jno. A. Andrew, Hon S. P. Chase, Hon. George Bancroft, Wm. C. Bryant, Esqr. & others have been invited to attend and participate in this meeting—Believing that you recognise the importance of the objects to which we desire to call the attention of the public, and that you sympathise in our endeavor thus to assist in the restoration of the Union by promoting that general good feeling & popular intelligence which must underlie it, . . ." LS, USG 3. See *New York Times*, Nov. 14, 1865.

To Edwin M. Stanton

———

Washington Nov. 13th 1865

HON. E. M. STANTON
SECY OF WAR.
SIR

In view of the fact that the Senate of the United States at its last session failed to confirm the present Paymaster General, I would respectfully recommend Maj. Gen. Hunter for that post if a change is made. General Hunter has served longer as Paymaster I believe than any other officer in the Department. No officer has conducted the duties more faithfully or efficiently than he has. In the rebellion Gen. Hunter has alwawys been ready to take duty when offered and to retire, when in the judgment of those whose duty it was to select commanders, it was thought best. In his campaign against Lynchburg he rendered important service, and I believe prevented the reinforcement of Johnson's army.

Before the death of our late President, he spoke to me on the subject of restoring Gen. Hunter to the Pay Dept. and asked me if I thought well of it: saying at the same time that he thought Gen. H. desired it, and he, the President, was anxious to accommodate him, as an officer would scarcely resigin a Colonelcy in the line for a Majority in the Staff.

I would not be understood as urging anything against Gen. Brice,—I recognize the fact that he has filled the post of Paymaster General with distinguished ability, through the most trying times ever known in the country. The only question is, should another name be selected after the rejection of the one first offered, I would recommend that that name be Gen. Hunters.

Very respectfully
Your obt. Servt
U. S. GRANT
Lt. Gen'l

Copies, DLC-USG, V, 46, 109; DNA, RG 108, Letters Sent.

To Maj. Gen. Henry W. Halleck

————

                            Head Quarters Armies of the United States
                                    Washington D. C Nov. 13th 1865.

MAJ GEN H. W. HALLECK
COMDG. MIL DIV OF THE PACIFIC
GENERAL:

The New York Herald of the 11th contains the enclosed order No. 17[1] Oct 11th 1865, purporting to have been issued by Maj Gen McDowell,   If such an order has been issued it should be revoked at once,   France has taken no steps to prevent rebels purchasing and receiving whatever they could pay for, and it should not be our policy to prevent the liberals of Mexico from getting all they need from us.

We do not want to give a more liberal construction of the meaning of neutrality than was given by the French Government when we were in trouble.

                            Very Respectfully
                            Your obt. svt.
                            U. S. GRANT
                            Lt. Gen.

Copies, DNA, RG 94, Letters Received, 1768P 1865; *ibid.*, RG 108, Letters Sent; DLC-USG, V, 46, 109. On Dec. 8, 1865, Maj. Gen. Henry W. Halleck, San Francisco, wrote to USG. "In accordance with your instructions of November 13th Major General McDowell has been directed to revoke his General Orders No. 17, of October 11th 1865. I understand that these orders were issued, not with reference to the conduct of France or England during the recent war of rebellion, and of which our government has so frequently complained, but in strict accordance with our own statute laws, which it was his duty to enforce until they were repealed, or orders given by superior authority to disregard them. It is believed that the revocation of these orders will be of greater advantage to the French than to the Mexicans, as the facilities of the former for obtaining arms and munitions of war in California are much greater than those of the latter. I presume it was not your intention to have these orders revoked in regard to one belligerent and not the other. If the Mexican authorities have asked this suspension of our neutrality laws on this coast, they have I think adopted an ill-advised ~~course~~ policy which will operate to their own injury—But on this point opinions may differ. In connection with this matter I respectfully call your attention to the correspondence of General McDowell, copies of which are herewith enclosed." LS, DNA, RG 108, Letters Received. The enclosures are *ibid.* On Dec. 11, Halleck telegraphed to Brig. Gen. Lorenzo Thomas that General Orders No. 17 had been revoked. Telegram received (on Dec. 12, 9:30 A.M.), *ibid.*, RG 94, Letters Received, 1724P 1865. On Dec. 12, USG endorsed this telegram. "Respectfully returned with copy of letter to Maj. Gen. Halleck." ES, *ibid.* On July 18, 1866, Maj. Gen. Irvin McDowell wrote to Lt. Col. Robert N. Scott, adjt. for Halleck, concerning a French protest about a shipload of men possibly heading for Mexico. LS, *ibid.*, 430P 1866. On Aug. 24, Bvt. Maj. Gen. Edward D. Townsend endorsed this letter. "Respectfully submitted to General Grant. Major General McDowell reports to the Hd. Qrs Mily Div of the Pacific and Genl Halleck forwards the same, that he has received a communication from the French Consul through Division Hd Qrs. alleging that the Ship 'Keoka' has sailed from San Francisco with a body of men *nominally* for Color[a]do, but *really* for the service of the Mexican Government, and asking that such proceedings be stopped. He informs Genl Halleck that the order previously issued by him in reference to the observance of neutrality had been revoked and he supposed it was the intention of the Government that the military should not act in the matter—He should therefore refer the French Consuls letter to the U. S. Dist. Attorney." ES, *ibid.*

1. On Oct. 11, 1865, Lt. Col. Richard C. Drum, adjt. for McDowell, issued General Orders No. 17. "It is made the duty of the officers commanding the Districts of Arizona and southern California—whilst keeping in view the recent orders allowing the exportation of arms and munitions of war,—to instruct the commanders on the southern frontiers, within this Department, to take the necessary measures to preserve the neutrality of the United States with respect to the parties engaged in the existing war in Mexico, and to suffer no armed parties to pass the frontier from the United States, or suffer any arms, or munitions of war, to be sent over the frontier to either belligerent. This not to prevent individuals from passing with arms for their personal protection." Copies (printed), *ibid.*; *ibid.*, RG 108, Letters Received. See *SED*, 39-1-40.

To Edwin M. Stanton

Respectfully forwarded to the Secretary of War. The appointee to the sutlership at Fort Riley being a clerk in the Quartermaster Department at that post, I would recommend that his appointment be not confirmed for the present. There has been much complaint about the management of the Quartermaster Department in Kansas during the war, and as much at Ft Riley as at any other place. I would not therefore recommend favors to any one connected with it in that State without first knowing their record.

Mr. H. F. Mayer I know nothing of personally. He is hower,

the present sutler of Fort Riley, and Gen. Sanborn speaks well of him.

U. S. GRANT
Lieut Gen.

HDQRS. A U S
Nov. 23. '65

ES, DNA, RG 94, ACP, M1690 CB 1865. Written on a letter of Nov. 18, 1865, from Henry F. Mayer, New York City, to USG. "On 25th July 1863 I was appointed Sutler to Fort Riley, Kansas, I forwarded my appointmt for a Warrant, the Asst Adjt Genl wrote me they were not issuing Warrants for Posts that would be garrisoned by Regular Troops after the War; I then wrote, it would be too uncertain to invest 20.000$ subject to the caprice of a few officers at the Post: he replied, that if I had a Warrant I could be removed for a cause, & in either case I could only be removd on cause. I then made the investmnt and have always conducted the business with an obliging and accommodating spirit and strictly according to Regulations—A few weeks since the Post was garrisoned by Regulars of 5 companies with 4 commissioned officers; a council of Admintration was called and a clerk in the Quartermaster's office was appointed: altho the office before the election, told me they had nothing against me, that I had treated them with kindness. By being suddenly compelled to give up my business, and very likely not be able to make a sale of my effects to the one appointed, I may sustain a very heavy loss, without a cause and without any benifit to the Public Service. I therefore respectfully ask you, General, to see me righted, and will recommend what you may deem just." ALS, *ibid.* Mayer enclosed a letter of Nov. 1 from Bvt. Maj. Gen. John B. Sanborn, Fort Riley, to Secretary of War Edwin M. Stanton recommending Mayer. ALS, *ibid.* See *ibid.*, 1157M CB 1865.

On Jan. 13, 1868, R. McBratney, attorney for Mayer, Washington, D. C., wrote to USG discussing at great length Mayer's efforts to reclaim his position or receive compensation for his property. LS, *ibid.*, Letters Received, 165D 1865. Additional papers are *ibid.*

To Townsend Harris

Washington D. C. Nov. 23d *1865*

HON. TOWNSEND HARRIS,
DEAR SIR:

I have received the *Sabre d'honneur* presented to you by His Majesty, the Tycoon of Japan, together with your note of the 15th inst. accompanying it. This present under ordinary circumstances would be highly appreciated; but coming with the assurances it

does, not only of the intense loyalty of one of our Country's foreign Ministers, during the darkest days ever any Country passed
through, but with the complement to myself paid in that note it
will not only be appreciated by myself but will be handed down to
my children and their children with the note itself.

I am not vain enough to assume that you have selected the right
person to become the recipient of this gift, or token, but feel complimented to know that you should think so.

With assurances of my best wishes for your future welfare permit me to sign myself,

> Very truly & respectfully
> your obt. svt.
> U. S. GRANT
> Lt. Gn.

ALS, Townsend Harris Collection, City College, City University of New York,
New York City, N. Y. On Nov. 15, 1865, Townsend Harris, Union Club, New
York City, had written to USG. "On the occasion of my audience of leave, his
Majesty the Tycoon of Japan presented me with a sabre d'honneur, which gift
President Lincoln kindly permitted me to retain. It is my desire to transfer it to
one of the bravest and worthiest of my countrymen, and the united voice of the
whole world unmistakbly points to you as the man I seek. I pray you, sir, to
accept this sword as a small mark of my deep sense of the great debt of gratitude
which I (in common with all my countryme[n)] owe to you for your eminent
service in saving my beloved country from the ruin that threatened [her.]" Copy,
USGA.

To Andrew Johnson

———

> Washington D. C.
> Nov. 26th 1865

HIS EXCELLENCY, A. JOHNSON, PRESIDENT &c.
SIR:

As it has been my habit heretofore to intercede for the release
of all prisoners who I thought could be safely left at large, either
on parole or by Amnesty, I now respectfully recommend the release
of Mr. C. C. Clay.

The manner of Mr. Clay's surrender I think is a full guarantee that if released on parole to appear when called for, either for trial or otherwise, that he will be forthcoming.

Argument I know is not necessary in this or like cases so I will simply say that I respectfully recommend that C. C. Clay, now a state prisoner, be released on parole not to leave the limits of his state without your permission and to surrender himself to the civil authorities for trial whenever called on to do so.

I do not know that I would make a special point of fixing the limits to a state only that at any future time the limits could be extended to the whole United States as well as if those limits were given at once.

> I have the honor to be
> Very respectfully
> your obt. svt.
> U. S. GRANT
> Lt. Gn.

ALS, DLC-Andrew Johnson. See Virginia Clay-Clopton, *A Belle of the Fifties* ... (New York, 1905), pp. 315–18. Clement C. Clay, Jr., imprisoned at Fort Monroe, was released as of April 17, 1866. *O.R.*, II, viii, 899. Almost immediately afterward, Mrs. Clay, Virginia C. Clay, drafted a letter to USG begging kinder treatment for Jefferson Davis, also imprisoned at Fort Monroe. ADf (incomplete and undated), Clay Papers, Duke University, Durham, N. C.

To Maj. Gen. Edward O. C. Ord

Washington D. C. Nov. 26th *1865*

MAJ GEN E. O. C. ORD
COMD'G. DEPT. OF THE OHIO—
GENERAL,

Your letter of the 14th inst. to the Adjt. Genl of the Army stating that large Fenian organizations exists all along the Canadian frontier, and asking instructions in case they attempt to invade Canada, is referred to me.

Whilst the United States and Great Brittain are at peace, it is clearly our duty to prevent war being made upon her territory by citizens of the States and also to prevent the fitting out and departure from our territory of hostile bodies of men of whatever nationality they may be. Great Britain or British officials, have not observed this rule very closely towards us during the existence of the late rebellion.

But their wrong doing is no justification for our following their example. You will therefore prevent all armed and equipped Military organizations going from the United States into Canada when you can. It will not be necessary even for you to know that they are going for the purpose of making war upon a country with which we are at peace. It is sufficient to know that, without the invitation of the Canadian authorities, no organized military companies have a right to enter their country—

You must understand however that the force at your command is not to be used as a police force to discover the designs of the so called Fenians. The power of raising and organizing military companies exists all over the country. Militia or independent companies are being drilled every day   The scare got up about Fenians need not attract our attention in the least. It is only when they or any militia or other body of armed men attempt to go into another country, or out of ours, that you need interfere.

I am General
Very Respectfully
Your Obt. Svt.
U. S. GRANT
Lieut Genl

LS, DNA, RG 94, Letters Received, O311 1865. On Nov. 26, 1865, USG wrote to Secretary of War Edwin M. Stanton. "Enclosed I send you a letter from Gen. Ord with my instructions to him in reply for your approval or disapproval." ALS, *ibid.* On Nov. 14, Maj. Gen. Edward O. C. Ord, Detroit, had written to Bvt. Brig. Gen. Edward D. Townsend requesting instructions from USG on how to handle Fenian threats to invade Canada. LS, *ibid.* USG's letter to Ord may not have been sent. Stanton referred USG's letter to Secretary of State William H. Seward for comment. On Nov. 27, Seward wrote to Stanton enclosing a new draft. ALS and ADf, *ibid.* Stanton made additional changes in this draft and on the same day Townsend wrote to Ord incorporating the changes. "Your letter of the 14th instant, to the Adjutant General of the Army, stating that large Fenian organizations exist all along the Canadian frontier, and asking instructions in case they attempt to invade Canada, has been received and in answer thereto the

Secretary of War gives you the following instructions   Whilst the United States and Great Britain are at peace, it is clearly our duty to prevent war being made upon her territory by citizens of the states, and also to prevent the fitting out and departure from our territory of hostile bodies of men of whatever nationality they may be. It may be alleged by way of excuse by movers of such expeditions that Great Britain or British officials have not observed this rule very closely towards us during the existence of the late rebellion. But that is a consideration which belongs to the government of the United States and is not a question for individual citizens much less for military bodies to act upon. You will therefore prevent all armed and equipped military organizations going from the United States into Canada. It will not be necessary even for you to know that they are going for the purpose of making war upon a country with which we are at peace. It is sufficient to know that without the invitation of the authorities of Great Britain no organized military companies have a right to enter their country or their provinces. You must understand however that the force at your command is not to be used as a police or detective force for civil and political purposes. The power of raising and organizing military companies exists, under the laws of the states, all over the country. Militia or independent companies are being drilled every day. The excitement got up by or about Fenians need not attract the attention of the army of the United States in the least. It is only when they or any militia, or other body of armed men attempt to go into another country or out of ours, that you need interfere. You will please report to this Department any action you may take under these instructions." LS, *ibid.*

To Julia Dent Grant

Richmond, Va., Nov. 28th *1865.*

DEAR JULIA,

I arrived here at ½ past two this afternoon. The run from Washington is a very pleasant one except for the getting up so early in the morning. Dr. Sharp, Nelly and the children are all well. I spent part of the evening with them and the Dr. spent the remainder here with me. I find the Citizens of Richmond have been expecting me for some time and now would like to have me remain over. As I am anxious to be back soon after the meeting of Congress I cannot remain however. I shall go to Raleigh leaving here at Six in the morning. I will write to you again from there. But as I am traveling away from home letters written but one day apart will be two days separated.

You and your father will find it a very easy trip coming here to visit Nelly. The rail-road part of your journey only takes four hours. Be sure to go to Philadelphia this week.[1] I will be back next week and by the week after we will be able to move into our new house.

Love and kisses to you and the children. Good night.

ULYS.

ALS (written on Spotswood Hotel stationery), DLC-USG. See letter to Andrew Johnson, Dec. 18, 1865.

1. On Nov. 29, 1865, Capt. William M. Dunn, Jr., twice telegraphed to William Coffin, Philadelphia. "Mrs. Grant leaves for philadelphia, Pa. at 11.15 to day." "Mrs Grant will not leave for Philadelphia to day" ALS (telegrams sent—at 10:45 A.M. and 12:30 P.M.), DNA, RG 107, Telegrams Collected (Unbound). Probably on the same day, Julia Dent Grant, "Georgetown Hights," wrote to Mrs. William S. Hillyer, New York City. "I started this morning for Philedelphia, but got there just in time to see the cars moove off. . . ." ALS (dated "November late"), Robert C. W. Hillyer, San José, Costa Rica.

*

To Julia Dent Grant

Raleigh N. C.
Nov. 29th 1865

DEAR JULIA,

We arrived here last night and this morning have been waited on by Committees of both Houses of the Legislature with invitations to visit those bodies. As soon as this is written I shall go.[1] There seems to be the best of feeling existing and nothing but the greatest desire expressed, by both original Secessionests and Unionests, to act in such a way as to secure admittence back and to please the general Government.

I leave here this evening for Charleston[2] where I will remain one or two days and then either return immediately home or go to New Orleans. On account of affairs on the Rio Grande it seems almost absolutely essential that I should see Gen. Sheridan. On account of the early meeting of Congress however I do not feel that I should be so long away from Washington. I do not know yet what

I shall do but will write again from Charleston unless I come immediately back.

Love and kisses to you and the children.

ULYS.

ALS, DLC-USG. See preceding letter.

1. On Nov. 29, 1865, Samuel F. Phillips, speaker of the house, N. C. legislature, addressed USG. "In the name of the People of North Carolina, I welcome you to a seat upon this floor. It is a matter of ~~pleasure~~ personal gratification to me that it has fallen to my part to perform this duty. After having been, in the hand of God, the chief instrument in restoring our country to its proper territorial proportions, it is your singular good fortune to be universally regarded as being qualified to play a great part in re-establishing those other bonds which are essential to the full re-organization of ~~our~~ a free society. In your ability and disposition to advance this prime object we entertain great confidence, and hope for you therein a success not less than that which has attended your deeds in arms. Accept, Gen. Grant, our best wishes for your personal welfare and happiness." ADS, USG 3.

2. On the same day, USG telegraphed to Secretary of War Edwin M. Stanton. "Will leave for Washn [*Charleston*] Via Wilmington this evening" Telegram received (on Dec. 1, 3:45 P.M.), DNA, RG 107, Telegrams Collected (Bound); copies, *ibid.*, RG 108, Letters Sent; DLC-USG, V, (misdated Nov. 28) 46, 109.

To Maj. Gen. Philip H. Sheridan

———

Charleston S. C. Dec. 1st *1865* [2:00 P.M.]

MAJ. GEN. P. H. SHERIDAN
N. ORLEANS,

In view of probable action by Congress on Mexican affairs do all you can to preserve strict neutrality pending such action

U. S. GRANT
Lieut. Gen'l

Telegram received (on Dec. 2, 1865, 2:00 P.M.—faded), DNA, RG 107, Telegrams Collected (Bound); copies, *ibid.*, Letters Received from Bureaus; *ibid.*, RG 108, Letters Sent; DLC-USG, V, 46, 109. *O.R.*, I, xlviii, part 2, 1258.

On Nov. 14, Maj. Gen. Philip H. Sheridan telegraphed to Brig. Gen. John A. Rawlins. "On the Second inst the 4th U. S cavalry left here fully equipped for San Antonia and the 6th U S Cavy left fully equipped for Austin on eleventh inst. ~~B~~both Regts to be mounted at these places respectively with horses turned in by Volunteer Regts mustered out" Telegram received (on Nov. 15, 6:45

P.M.), DNA, RG 107, Telegrams Collected (Bound); *ibid.*, RG 108, Telegrams Received; copies, DLC-USG, V, 54; DLC-Philip H. Sheridan. *O.R.*, I, xlviii, part 2, 1256. On Nov. 15, Sheridan telegraphed to USG. "Escabado, Cortinas, Canates, Mendo, are still closely investing Matamoras" Telegram received (on Nov. 17, 1:50 P.M.), DNA, RG 107, Telegrams Collected (Bound); (at 1:30 P.M.) *ibid.*, RG 108, Telegrams Received; copies (one sent by mail), *ibid.*, Letters Received; DLC-USG, V, 54; DLC-Philip H. Sheridan. *O.R.*, I, xlviii, part 2, 1257. On the same day, Sheridan telegraphed to Rawlins. "The telegraph Communication from here to Galveston Austin & San Antonio, is complete & in good working order" Telegram received (on Nov. 17, 1:30 P.M.), DNA, RG 107, Telegrams Collected (Bound); *ibid.*, RG 108, Telegrams Received; copies (one sent by mail), *ibid.*, Letters Received; DLC-USG, V, 54; DLC-Philip H. Sheridan. *O.R.*, I, xlviii, part 2, 1257.

On Nov. 20, 1:30 A.M., Sheridan telegraphed to USG. "The Liberal force withdrew about six miles from Matamoras on the Seventh 7th inst. but I have reason to believe that they have again attacked the place—We have been subjected to the most violent abuse by the Imperial newspaper in Matamoras. It constantly calls the President the Murderer of Mrs Surratt—Some of our soldiers who were visiting Matamoras were arrested and put to work upon their fortifications, and our Officers and men fired upon by their gunboats. The most insulting letters from French Officials have been addressed to Gen Weitzel, and other officers, and all this by a small force, which our troops could drive out of Matamoras by firing over their boats. The consequence is, much excitement on the part of our soldiers, and a great desire on the part of the colored to troops to go to that country if discharged. The commandant of the Imperial troops in Matamoras, is always ready with an apology, I have given notice that hereafter apologies for these insults will not be received" Telegram received (on Nov. 22, 9:00 A.M.), DNA, RG 107, Telegrams Collected (Bound); *ibid.*, RG 108, Telegrams Received; copies (one sent by mail), *ibid.*, Letters Received; DLC-USG, V, 54; DLC-Philip H. Sheridan; USG 3. *O.R.*, I, xlviii, part 2, 1257. See *ibid.*, p. 1258. At 5:30 P.M., Sheridan telegraphed to USG. "My telegram of to day about affairs on the Rio Grande need not give you any alarm. Everything is well in hand there, and well understood." Telegram received (on Nov. 22, 12:30 A.M.), DNA, RG 107, Telegrams Collected (Bound); *ibid.*, RG 108, Telegrams Received; copies (one sent by mail), *ibid.*, Letters Received; (marked as received at 2:30 A.M.) DLC-USG, V, 54; (marked as sent at 5:20 P.M.) DLC-Philip H. Sheridan. *O.R.*, I, xlviii, part 2, 1257.

On Nov. 26, 1:00 P.M., Sheridan telegraphed to USG. "I respectfully forward the following facts for your consideration. The scheme for emigration to Mexico is now fully organized in the City of Mexico, with Capt Maury, Sterling Price and Genl J. B. Magruder as the prominent men. They hold titles and honors, from Maximillian, and are now officers of His Majesties Government, Commissioners have been appointed for all the Southern States, and I think the commissions forwarded. I caught the commissioner for the state of Louisiana, and his commission is en route, and will be received by me. This emigration scheme is not confined to emigrants from the Southern states, but extends to Europe, and was without doubt hatched by Louis Napoleon. This information is without question, and is a premonitory symptom of what I have for some time believed; that we can never can have a fully restored Union, and give a total and final blow to all malcontents, until the French leave Mexico." Telegram received (on

Nov. 27, 2:35 P.M.), DNA, RG 107, Telegrams Collected (Bound); *ibid.*,
Letters Received from Bureaus; *ibid.*, RG 108, Telegrams Received; copies (one
sent by mail), *ibid.*, Letters Received; DLC-USG, V, 54; DLC-Philip H. Sheridan;
USG 3. *O.R.*, I, xlviii, part 2, 1258. On Nov. 27, Bvt. Col. Ely S. Parker endorsed this telegram. "Respectfully forwarded to the Secretary of War." AES,
DNA, RG 107, Letters Received from Bureaus. On Dec. 28, Sheridan wrote to
Rawlins. "On the 26th of Nov. I telegraphed to the Lieutenant General about
the emigration scheme of Louis Napoleon in Mexico, at the head of which was
Captain Maury, Sterling Price and General John B Magruder; that I had the
commissioner for the State of Louisiana, and that I would forward his commission, which was then en route to him. I have since received said commission
and respectfully forward it with accompanying papers for the information of the
Government. I have notified Mr Dennis, the commissioner, that I will not
permit him to act under this commission, and respectfully request an approval
or disapproval of this action as I feel convinced that I may at any time be subjected to the test of practically preventing emigrants from going to the Valley
of Mexico in the interests of a power not friendly to our country" Copies (2),
ibid., RG 108, Letters Received. During Jan., 1866, Bvt. Col. Theodore S.
Bowers wrote to Sheridan. "I am directed by Lieutenant General Grant to acknowledge the receipt of your communication of date December 28th 1865, in
relation to the Franco-Mexican Emigration Scheme; and to say to you in reply
that your orders in the matter meet his approval, and that you are authorized
and directed to execute your suggestions respecting emigrants by force of arms
if necessary." Copies (dated only Jan.), DLC-USG, V, 47, 109; DNA, RG 108,
Letters Sent; *ibid.*, Letters Received. On Jan. 29, Sheridan wrote to Rawlins. "I
have the honor to enclose herewith, a scrap taken from the 'Louisville Courier'
of the 15th instant; bearing on the Emigration scheme of Maury, Price, Magruder,
Louis Napoleon & Co   To day I overhauled a party under a gentleman from
South Carolina, as they were about embarking for Vera Cruz. I see that old Jubal
Early has gone there too, and I can assure you that many more Ex-Rebel Generals
will yet go, and with no good in their hearts for the United States Government."
LS, *ibid.*, RG 94, Letters Received, 909A 1866; *ibid.*, RG 108, Letters Received. On Feb. 7, Sheridan wrote to USG. "As I had anticipated in my com-
munication of Dec 28th to you, on the subject of Emigration to the Valley of
Mexico. I am now called upon to practically put a stop to it. I find throughout
most of the Southern States a intention on the part of a large class, to go to the
Valley of Mexico. Some have already arrived at New Orleans, and I hear of a
great deal of excitement throughout the South on the subject. Under your
letter of January 10th I have stopped those who have already arrived here.
They are all very bitter against the Government, and say that they will not live
under our flag &c   Unless the Government is firm on this question, there will
be a large party to back Maximilian in Mexico in the course of a year from this
time, and if the scheme is not broken up, every act of our Government which is
distasteful to these people, will cause a fresh exodus to Mexico   This Rebel
Emigration scheme looks to me as if it was conceived by Louis Napoleon. Only
a few days ago I received a letter from the city of Mexico stating the hostility
of all classes to Maximilian, and their sympathy with people from the United
States." LS, *ibid.* On Feb. 16, USG endorsed this letter. "Respectfully forwarded
to the Hon. Secretary of War, for his information" ES, *ibid.* On April 16,
Sheridan wrote to USG. "I see it reported in the public press, that the emigration

scheme of Maury, Price Louis Napoleon and company, is a failure. I have no good reason to believe this to be the case; on the contrary a large number of emigrants, or adventurers; are going to the Valley of Mexico. Some few have gone from this port by evading the surveillance which I established here, and it was only last week that Mr Courtenay, a steamship agent, who was about to establish a line to Vera Cruz, informed me that there was then about (3,000) three thousand who desired to go there. These adventurers are mostly young men, not of industrious habits, and it is certain that if they cannot earn their living by honest labor here, they cannot in Mexico, so that it may be considered a certainty that they will enter the army of the so-called Emperor. I enclose you copies of communications addressed by me to the British Consul and Mr Courtenay, from which you can judge of the system adopted to break up this indirect violation of neutrality. I have not interfered with the clearance of vessels, but prevent the emigrants from going on board, so that no question has arisen with foreign consuls. How ever, it is hard to maintain this surveillance here, when there is perfect liberty for those men to sail from New York or other ports, for Vera Cruz." LS, *ibid.*, RG 94, Letters Received, 252G 1866. On April 27, USG endorsed this letter. "Respectfully forwarded to the Hon. Secretary of War, for his information." ES, *ibid.*

On Nov. 27, 1865, 3:00 P.M., Sheridan telegraphed to USG. "There is on his way to Mexico a General R. Clay Crawford, who says he goes to take command of the Liberal forces on the Rio Grande. Do you know anything about him and what countenance is he to have from me?" Telegram received (at 10:30 P.M.), *ibid.*, RG 107, Telegrams Collected (Bound); *ibid.*, RG 108, Telegrams Received; copies, DLC-USG, V, 54; DLC-Philip H. Sheridan. On Nov. 28, 10:00 P.M., USG, Raleigh, N. C., telegraphed to Sheridan. "I do not know R. clay crawford. I presume there is no objec[tio]ns to his going to mexico if he wishes, but I can give no directions in his case." Telegram sent (encoded version in hand of Bvt. Col. Orville E. Babcock), DNA, RG 107, Telegrams Collected (Unbound); copies, *ibid.*, RG 108, Letters Sent; DLC-USG, V, 46, 109. On the same day, Parker telegraphed to Sheridan. "Mr Crawford's enterprise in going to Mexico is purely of a private character and need not engage your attention—" ALS (telegram sent), DNA, RG 107, Telegrams Collected (Bound); telegram sent, *ibid.*; copies, *ibid.*, RG 108, Letters Sent; DLC-USG, V, 46, 109. See telegram to Maj. Gen. Philip H. Sheridan, Jan. 25, 1866; letter to Edwin M. Stanton, Feb. 16, 1866; Matías Romero, comp., *Correspondencia de la Legacion Mexicana en Washington durante la Intervencion Extranjera 1860–1868* (Mexico City, 1870–92), V, 833–34.

To Julia Dent Grant

———

Chaleston S. C.
December 1st 1865

DEAR JULIA,

We have just arrived at this place and will remain until Sunday morning. I shall then go to Savannah and possibly to New

Orleans. Should I not go to N. Orleans will be at home about Friday next. The rail-roads in the south are in such wretched condition, and bridges gone, that travel by them is but little faster than old time travel by stage coach.

I have no special news to write. Have only just reached the city and do not know what it looks like yet.

Love and kisses to you and the children

ULYS.

ALS, DLC-USG. On Dec. 1, 1865, Mayor Peter C. Gaillard of Charleston wrote to USG. "On behalf of the City Council of Charleston, I would respectfully ask that you would name a time and place, at which we may call upon you, and pay our respects—" ALS, USG 3. On the same day, T. D. Wagner and seven others wrote to USG. "The undersigned Merchants and Citizens of Charleston desire the pleasure of your Company at dinner at the Charleston Hotel at such time during your visit to the City as will be most Convenient to yourself. Trusting that your engagements will enable you to accept this invitation, . . ." ALS, *ibid*. See *New York Times*, Dec. 11, 1865.

On Dec. 2, Bvt. Brig. Gen. Cyrus B. Comstock, Charleston, wrote to Maj. Gen. Daniel E. Sickles. "The Lieut. Gen'l Com'd'g desires, in case the plantation on Edisto Island belonging to Gov. Aiken can be restored to him without prejudice to the freedmen now on it by authority of the United States, that it be restored He wishes you to send an officer to the plantation to ascertain the facts in the case previous to action" Copies, DLC-USG, V, 46, 109; DNA, RG 108, Letters Sent. See letter to Maj. Gen. Daniel E. Sickles, Jan. 26, 1866.

To Julia Dent Grant

Augusta [*Savannah*] Ga.
December 4th 1865

DEAR JULIA;

Arrived here this morning. The weather is beautiful but too warm for thick clothing. I shall start in the morning for Augusta, the Head Qrs. of the Dept. where I shall spend one day and start home. It will probably be Saturday[1] evening when I get there. As from this out I will be traveling towards home as fast as mails will go it will not be necessary for me to write any more letters to you.

I have no news to write. People all seem pleasant and at least towards me, to and I thinks towards the Government, to enter faithfully upon a course to restore harmony between the sections.

Love and kisses to you and the children. Saturday evening if nothing happens I think you may look for me home.

ɄLYS.

ALS, DLC-USG. On Dec. 4, 1865, Mayor Richard D. Arnold, Savannah, Ga., wrote to USG. "Will you do me the favour to name an hour at which the Mayor and Aldermen of the City of Savannah could pay their respects to you in person" ALS, USG 3. A note is appended. "The Mayor and Aldermen of the City of Savannah will wait upon Lt General Grant at *nine* ock this evening precisely" AN, *ibid.* See *New York Times,* Dec. 11, 1865.

1. USG returned to Washington, D. C., on Monday, Dec. 11, traveling via Augusta, Atlanta, Knoxville, and Lynchburg. See letter to Andrew Johnson, Dec. 18, 1865. Perhaps on Dec. 5 or 6, USG, Augusta, telegraphed to G. G. Herd, N. Y. "Yes will be there" Telegram received (dated only "26"), DNA, RG 107, Telegrams Collected (Unbound).

To Edwin M. Stanton

Washington, December 14 *1865*

HON E. M. STANTON
SECRETARY OF WAR.
SIR:

In reply to your letter of the 13th inst. in reference to desertions, I would make the following remarks.

I donot think the present plan of recruiting as carried out sufficent to fill up the regular army to the force required, or to keep it full when once filled.

The duty is an important one and demands I think the exclusive attention of an officer of the War Department, aided by a well organized system extending over the country. I think the officer best fitted for that position by his experience during the present war, is General Fry, and would recommend that the whole subject of recruiting be put in his hands, and all officers now on recruiting duty be directed to report to him.

He should also have charge of the apprehension of deserters, should be authorized to offer such rewards as will secure their apprehension; when caught they should be tried and the sentences rigidly carried into effect. This would soon stop the present enormous amount of desertion.

I would recommend that the duties heretofore performed by provostmarshals be hereafter performed by officers detailed for recruiting duty.

> Very respectfully
> Your obt Servant
> U. S. GRANT
> Lieutenant General.

LS, DNA, RG 94, Letters Received, 806A 1866. On Dec. 13, 1865, Secretary of War Edwin M. Stanton had written to USG. "Your attention is invited to the accompanying report of the Provost Marshal General upon recent desertions from the regular army, to wit: for the months of August, September and October, 1865. You will please give the subject your immediate attention, and recommend such measures as in your opinion will be most efficient to prevent the enormous desertion which seems now to be prevalent." LS, *ibid.*, RG 108, Letters Received. The enclosure is *ibid.* On Jan. 24, 1866, Brig. Gen. James B. Fry, provost marshal gen., forwarded papers received at USG's hd. qrs. concerning desertions from the commands of Bvt. Lt. Col. Thomas M. Anderson and Bvt. Col. John Hamilton. *Ibid.*, Register of Letters Received. On Jan. 26, USG endorsed these papers. "Respy forwarded to the sec of war. I would respectfully renew my suggestions of December 14, as to the managemt of the Recruiting Service and the necessity of a thorough organized system for the apprehension of deserters. I do not understand that there is at present any effective system for the detection & arrest of deserters, and as a consequence soldiers feel that if they desert there is comparatively little danger of their being hunted up and brought to punishment. When they are made to realize that organized & continuous effort are made to discover their where abouts, and that the nearest Recruiting officer, or officer in command of troops will be sent to arrest them & that punishment is certain to follow, desertion will be attended with more danger & will become less frequent. If a change is not authorized in the present system, I would recommend that the AG. be directed to detach an officer in each specil case where it is reported a deserter may be found to hunt him up & make the arrest. Unless some efficient measures are adopted to prevent the fearful number of desertions now occurring the army will become seriously demoralized in consequence" Copy, DLC-USG, V, 58.

On Feb. 20, USG endorsed a letter of Feb. 2 from Private Charles E. Cowan, 12th Inf., Fort Monroe, concerning desertion. "Respy. returned to Hon Henry. Wilson, U. S. Senate, with the opinion that the statements of this man are in the main untrue, and arises from some personal feeling. The subject of desertion and the cause have been carefully looked into, and the subject of feeding recruits, and their treatmt receives particular attention. If such causes exist, it is my opinion the instructions now given will correct the error" Copy, *ibid.*; DNA, RG 108, Register of Letters Received.

To Maj. Gen. Philip H. Sheridan

Washington Dec. 14th *1865* [*11:30* A.M.]

MAJ. GN. SHERIDAN, NEW ORLEANS LA,

There is great complaint of cruelty against Gen. Custer. If there are grounds for these complaints relieve him from duty.

U. S. GRANT

Lt. Gn.

ALS (telegram sent), DNA, RG 107, Telegrams Collected (Bound); telegram sent, *ibid.*; copies, *ibid.*, RG 108, Letters Sent; DLC-USG, V, 46, 109. On Dec. 15, 1865, Maj. Gen. Philip H. Sheridan, New Orleans, telegraphed to USG. "There is no foundation for complaint against Gen Custar for at the time he had very hard work to maintain discipline—His troops were determined to be mustered out and were instigated to insubordination by their friends at home— This has all been remedied except in the case of the first Iowa Cavalry and I can spare that regement and in fact two other Cavalry regts and recommend muster out but have been restrained by your instructions of October 28 1865—See communication sent by Custar to the Secy of War giving an account of the difficulties he had to overcome—I have given my personal attention to the matter and know that the troops are not subjected to any unusual hardship or discipline & Custar has not done anything that was not fully warranted by the insubordination of his command—If anything he has been too lenient" Telegram received (at noon), DNA, RG 107, Telegrams Collected (Bound); *ibid.*, RG 108, Telegrams Received; copies, DLC-USG, V, 54; DLC-Philip H. Sheridan.

On Oct. 5, Horton J. Howard, Mount Pleasant, Iowa, had written to Secretary of the Interior James Harlan complaining about Maj. Gen. George A. Custer's treatment of vols. in La. and Tex. ALS, DNA, RG 108, Letters Received. On Oct. 11, Harlan wrote a letter received at USG's hd. qrs. concerning Custer's treatment of the 1st Iowa Cav. *Ibid.*, Register of Letters Received. On Oct. 19, William J. Cochran, New Boston, Iowa, wrote to Secretary of War Edwin M. Stanton on the same subject, enclosing a newspaper clipping. ALS, *ibid.*, Letters Received. On Oct. 18, Governor James T. Lewis of Wis. wrote a letter received at USG's hd. qrs. complaining about Custer's mistreatment of the 2nd Wis. Cav. and 4th Wis. Cav. *Ibid.*, Register of Letters Received. On Oct. 20, Bvt. Col. Ely S. Parker endorsed this letter. "Respectfully referred to Maj Gen P. H. Sheridan, Comdg Mil. Div. of the Gulf for such action as the facts of the case will warrant." Copy, *ibid.*

On Oct. 17, Cadwallader C. Washburn, La Crosse, Wis., wrote to USG. "Accounts that Come up from Texas, from the troops under the Command of Gen. Custar are not to the credit of that officer. Copies of his orders have been sent to me, by officers & men shewing that the most brutal & unusual punishments, are habitually inflicted upon the men for trifling offences. From one of his orders I extract the following Viz, 'Owing to the delays of Courts Martial, and their impracticability when the Command is unsettled, it is hereby orderd, that any enlisted men of this Command, violating the above order, or

Committing depredations on the persons or property of citizens will have his head shaved and in addition will receive twenty five lashes upon his back, well laid on.' Punishments as discussed in said order are frequent, tho, none have ever been inflicted upon the Regt I formerly Commanded, ~~which is~~ the 2nd Wis, that I am aware of, which Regt is with Custar—If this Regt the 2nd Wis. Cav. Can be musterd out of the Service without detriment, I wish it might be—It is a veteran Regt & most of the men have been in for four years—They feel that their services are useless where they are, and they utterly despise the upstart brute who Commands them." ALS, *ibid.*, Letters Received. On Nov. 20, Sheridan endorsed this letter. *"Respectfully* returned to Hd, Qr's. Army of U. S. with the information that the 2nd Wis'. Cav. has been ordered to be mustered out." ES, *ibid.* On Oct. 23, U.S. Representative Elihu B. Washburne, Galena, had written to USG. "Maj. Genl Washburn sends me these papers at the request of Genl. Morgan. In his letter to me Genl Washburn says: 'I have heard a good deal about Custar's treatment of his men. My old regiment (the 2d Wis. Cav.) is with him. He had a Sergeant, one of the best men of the regiment, tried and sentenced to be shot for having signed a petition asking the Lt. Col. of the regiment to resign. *The man was blindfolded and sat upon the coffin with a file of men drawn up to shoot him, when, graciously, Custar reprieved him and Commuted his sentence to ten years at Dry Tortugas, where he is now serving, and his family are now objects of public charity at Eau Claire.'* I do not know but it is necessary for Custar to do all these inhuman and barbarous thing to maintain discipline, but I have observed that it was not necessary for *you* to do such things in any Command *you* ever had." ALS, USG 3. On Oct. 26, Bvt. Col. Adam Badeau wrote to Washburne. "Gen. Grant directs me to say in reply to your note with its enclosure, relating to Gen. Custar, that similar complaints have been previously forwarded him, which he referred immediately to Gen. Sheridan, with directions to investigate them, and act accordingly. The General however is of opinion, from what he has already learned, that Custar has really *modified* some harsh sentences of courts-martial, passed on mutinous soldiers. This will be ascertained definitely. . . ." ALS, DLC-Elihu B. Washburne. See John M. Carroll, *Custer in Texas: An Interrupted Narrative* (New York, 1975).

To Julia Dent Grant

Dec. 14th *1865*

DEAR JULIA,

Gens. Oglesby and Logan[1] will dine with us at 5 p. m. Tell Fler to be at the office with the carriage at ½ past 4 to take Col. Badeau after them. Gen. Comstock, Col. Badeau and Col. Babcock will also dine with us.

Send word to the orderly to bring the buggy, not the horse and saddle, for me at ½ past 3.

ULYS.

ALS, DLC-USG.

1. On Nov. 23, 1865, USG telegraphed to John A. Logan. "I learn your Commissio[n] to Mexico has gone to you by mail. I think it will be pleasant to Mr. Seward if you do not decide upon the non acceptance of it until you see him. If you accept well enough." ALS (telegram sent), DNA, RG 107, Telegrams Collected (Bound); telegram sent, *ibid.*; copies, *ibid.*, RG 108, Letters Sent; DLC-USG, V, 46, 109; DLC-Logan Family Papers. On Nov. 23, Logan, Carbondale, Ill., telegraphed to USG. "Yours received. I will be in Washington as soon after first of December as I am able, I am now quite unwell. Will postpone my defenite action in the Mexican mission, if not required by the Secretary of State sooner" Telegram received (on Nov. 24, 11:40 A.M.), DNA, RG 107, Telegrams Collected (Bound). Logan declined the appointment. See James P. Jones, *"Black Jack:" John A. Logan and Southern Illinois in the Civil War Era* (Tallahassee, 1967), pp. 270–71.

To Maj. Gen. Philip H. Sheridan

Washington Dec 16th 1865

MAJ. GEN. P. H. SHERIDAN
COM'D'G MIL. DIV &c
GEN'L:

This will introduce to you Mr. J. P. Tweed of New York formerly of Cincinnati Ohio. Mr. Tweed is one of the first business men of the North, a man of wealth and standing. I have known him from boyhood and take great pleasure in introducing him to you.

Mr. Tweed informs me that he goes to Texas on some business matters. In this connection I commend him as of a class entirely different from those we have been accustomed to see whilst the war was in progress who were willing to embarass military movements if they could make anything out of it. Attention shown Mr. Tweed will be duly appreciated by him and myself

Yours Truly
U. S. GRANT
Lt Gen'l

Copies, DLC-USG, V, 46, 109; DNA, RG 108, Letters Sent. See *PUSG*, 5, 124*n*; *ibid.*, 10, 134*n*.

To Andrew Johnson

Washington D. C. Dec. 18th 1865

His Excellency A. Johnson
President of, the United States
Sir:

In reply to your note of the 16th inst., requesting a report from me giving such information as I may be possessed of coming within the scope of the enquiries made by the Senate of the United States, in their resolution of the 12th inst., I have the honor to submit the following:

With your approval and also that of the Hon. Sec. of War, I left Washington City on the 27th of last month for the purpose of making a tour of inspection through some of the Southern states, or states lately in rebellion, and to see what changes were necessary to be made in the disposition of the Military forces of the Country, how these forces could be reduced and expenses curtailed. &c. and to learn as far as possible the feelings and intentions of the citizens of these states towards the General Government

The State of Virginia[1] being so accessible to Washington City, information from this quarter therefore being readily obtained, I hastened through the state without conversing or meeting with any of its citizens. In Raleigh N. C. I spent one day, in Charleston, S. C., two days, Savannah and Augusta, Ga. each one day. Both in travelling and whilst stopping I saw much and conversed freely with the Citizens of these states, as well as with officers of the army who have been stationed among them. The following are the conclusions come to by me:

I am satisfied that the mass of thinking men of the South accept the present situation of affairs in good faith. The questions which have heretofore divided the sentiment of the people of the two sections, Slavery and States Rights, or the right of a State to secede from the Union, they regard as having been settled forever, by the highest tribunal, arms, that man can resort to. I was pleased to learn from the leading men whom I met that they not only accepted the decision arrived at as final but that now that the smoke of battle has cleared away and time has been given for reflection that this decision has been a fortunate one for the whole country, they receiving like benefits from it with those who opposed them on the field and in council.

Four years of War during which law was executed only at the point of the bayonet, throughout the states in rebellion, has left the people possibly in a condition not to yield that ready obedience to civil authority the American people have generally been in the habit of yielding. This would render the presence of small garrisons throughout the states necessary until such time as labor returns to its proper channel and civil authority is fully established. I did not meet any one, either those holding place under the Government or citizens of the Southern States who think it practicable to withdraw the Military force from the South at present. The white and the black mutually require the protection of the General Government.

There is such a universal acquiescence in the authority of the General Government, throughout the portions of the country visited by me, that the mere presence of a Military force, without regard to numbers, is sufficient to maintain order. The good of the country, and economy, requires that the force kept in the interior where there are many freedmen (elsewhere in the Southern States than at forts upon the Sea coast no force is necessary) should all be White troops. The reasons for this are obvious without mentioning many of them. The presence of Black troops, lately slaves, demoralizes labor both by their advice and furnishing in their camps a resort for the Freedmen for long distances around. White troops generally excited no opposition and therefore a small number of them can maintain order in a given district. Colored troops must be kept in sufficient bodies to defend themselves. It is not the thinking man who would use violence towards any class of troops, sent among them by the General Government, but the ignorant in some places might, and the late slave seems to be imbued with the idea that the property of his late master should by right belong to him, or at least should have no protection from the colored soldier. There is danger of collisions being brought on by such causes.

My observations lead me to the conclusion that the citizens of the Southern states are anxious to return to self government, within the Union, as soon as possible: that whilst reconstructing they want and require protection from the Government: that they are in earnest in wishing to do what they think is required by the Government, and not humiliating to them as citizens, and that if such a course was pointed out they would pursue it in good faith. It is to be regretted that there cannot be a greater commingling at this time between the citizens of the two sections and particularly of those entrusted with the law-making power.

I did not give the operations of the Freedman's Bureau that attention I would have done if more time had been at my disposal.[2] Conversations on the subject however with officers connected with the Bureau, with Military Commanders and with citizens lead me to think that in some of the States its affairs have not been conducted with good judgment or economy, and that the belief widely spread among the freed men of the Southern states, that the lands of their former owners will at least in part be divided among them has come from the Agents of this bureau. This belief is seriously interfering with the willingness of the freedmen to make contracts for the coming year. In some form the Freedman's Bureau is an absolute necessity until civil law is established and enforced securing to the freedmen their rights and full protection. At present however it is independent of the Military establishment of the country and seems to be operated by the different agents of the bureau according to their individual notions. Everywhere Gen. Howard the able head of the bureau, made friends by the just and fair instructions and advice he gave: but the complaint in South Carolina was, that when he left, things went as before. Many, perhaps the majority of the Agts. of the Freedman's Bureau, advise the Freedmen that by their own industry they must expect to live. To this end they endeavor to secure employment for them and to see that both contracting parties comply with their engagements. In some instances I am sorry to say the freedman's mind does not seem to be disabused of the idea that a freedman has the right to live without the care or provision for the future. The effect of the belief in division of lands is idleness and accumulation in camps, towns and cities. In such cases I think it will be found that vice and disease will tend to their extermination, or great reduction of the colored race. It cannot be expected that the opinions held by men at the South for years can be changed in a day, and therefore the freedmen require for a few years not only laws to protect them, but the fostering care of those who will give them good counsel and in whom they rely.

The Freedmen's Bureau being seperated from the military establishment of the country, requires all the expense of a seperate organization. One does not necessarily know what the other is doing, or what orders they are acting under. It seems to me that this could be corrected by regarding every officer on duty with troops in the Southern States as agents of the Freedmen's Bureau, and then have all orders from t[he] head of the Bureau sent through Department commanders. This would create a responsibility that would secure uniformity of action throughout the South: would insure the orders and instructions from the head of the bureau being carried out, and would relieve from duty and pay a large number of employees of the Government

> I have the honor to be
> Very respectfully
> Your obt. Servt
> U. S. GRANT
> Lt. Gen'l.

Copies, DLC-USG, V, 46, 109; DNA, RG 108, Letters Sent. On Dec. 16, 1865, President Andrew Johnson had written to USG. "Forwards certain enquiries made by the Senate of U. S. concerning those states of the U. S. lately in rebellion against the National Government—asks for all information touching same in Headquarters, A U S." *Ibid.*, Register of Letters Received. USG had already discussed his trip through the South with Johnson. Accompanied by Bvt. Cols. Adam Badeau and Orville E. Babcock and Bvt. Brig. Gen. Cyrus B. Comstock, USG had left Washington on Nov. 27 making stops at Richmond, Raleigh, Wilmington, Charleston, Hilton Head, Savannah, Augusta, and Atlanta. He returned to Washington on Dec. 11, traveling via Knoxville and Lynchburg. See letter to Elihu B. Washburne, Nov. 9, 1865; letters to Julia Dent Grant, Nov. 28, 29, Dec. 1, 4, 1865; Comstock diary, DLC-Cyrus B. Comstock; Garland, pp. 344–46; James Harrison Wilson, *Under the Old Flag* (New York and London, 1912), II, 377–79; Howard K. Beale, ed., *Diary of Gideon Welles* (New York, 1960), II, 396–97, 400; *New York Times*, Dec. 11, 1865.

On Dec. 18, Johnson wrote to the U.S. Senate transmitting USG's letter and Carl Schurz's more extensive report on conditions in the South which had already been requested by the Senate. *SED*, 39-1-2.

1. On Nov. 27, 11:30 P.M., Bvt. Brig. Gen. John E. Mulford, Richmond, wrote to Badeau. "I am extremely sorry that I have not had an opportunity to talk with you tonight, but I was so long with our mutual idol that I thought best to defer my interview until you come again, which I learn from the Genl will be soon. I am delighted that I have had an opportunity to give the Genl a better insight into the *real sentiment* of the Southn people, and their high regard and *preference for him & & &* When you ascertain at what time you are to be in Richmd, just send me an unofficial (or *official*, as you please) telegram saying John Jack (or anybody else) will be here; or leave here; at the time you are to arrive, I desire this information for a specific purpose which *you* will approve" ALS, USG 3.

2. On Dec. 22, Maj. Gen. Oliver O. Howard, Bureau of Refugees, Freedmen, and Abandoned Lands, issued Circular No. 22. "The attention of Assistant Commissioners is called to the Report of the Lieut General dated Dec 18th 1865. The most thorough inspection will at once be made, and the evils complained of corrected. No order from the War Department makes the 'Bureau' independent of the 'Military Establishment' and agents should be furnished with complete instructions according to the Orders and Circulars issued from this branch of the War Department. Any agent or officer who presumes to act contrary to such instructions will be forthwith removed or reported to the Department Commander for trial by Court Martial. In all matters of a military character, the officers and agents within a military department, are under the directions of the Department Commander, in the same manner as an officer of Engineers building a fort in the same Department, who reports directly the Chief Engineer. Every Asst Commissioner will constantly seek cooperation with the Department Commander, and must keep him furnished with all information in his possession. His formal approval must be secured when possible, to all orders and Circulars issued Asst Commissioners." Copy, DNA, RG 108, Letters Received. On Jan. 23, 1866, Howard endorsed a copy of this circular to USG. ES, *ibid*. Accompanying papers are *ibid*.

To Edwin M. Stanton

Washington Dec. 18th *1865*

HON. E. M. STANTON,
SEC. OF WAR,
SIR:

Capt. Michael V. Sheridan, the brother of Gen. Sheridan and now an officer on his Staff, is an applicant for a Lieutenancy in the regular Cavalry. A few days since I wrote a letter to the Board now engaged in examining applications for appointments in the regular army requesting them to take up Capt. Sheridans recommendation and give it a favorable consideration. They have since informed me that they do not find his papers before them.

Capt. Sheridan has filled all the requirements necessary to qualify him for one of the appointments to be given. He was in the battle of Stone River in 1863 and has served continuously ever since.

I would now respectfully request that Capt. Sheridan be appointed Lieutenant of Regular Cavalry.

> Very respectfully
> your obt. svt.
> U. S. GRANT
> Lt. Gen

ALS, DNA, RG 94, ACP, 4432 1878. On Dec. 4, 1865, Capt. and Bvt. Maj. Michael V. Sheridan, New Orleans, wrote to Secretary of War Edwin M. Stanton requesting an appointment in the U.S. Army. ALS, *ibid.* On Dec. 11, USG endorsed this letter. "Respectfully forwarded to the Secretary of War, earnestly recommended." ES, *ibid.* On Dec. 14, USG wrote to Col. Henry K. Craig. "I wish to call special attention of the examining board to the case of Capt. M. V. Sheridan A. d. C., to Maj. Gen. Sheridan, now an applicant for promotion in the Regular army." Copies, DLC-USG, V, 46, 109; DNA, RG 108, Letters Sent. Sheridan was appointed 2nd lt., 5th Cav., as of Feb. 23, 1866.

To Maj. Gen. Philip H. Sheridan

Washington D. C. Dec. 19th *1865*

MAJ. GEN. P. H. SHERIDAN,
DEAR GENERAL;

After my dispatch to you of the 16th[1] inst. I saw the President and shew him yours to which mine was an answer. I can say this after consultation. The President, as well as the whole country, is interested in the sucsess of the liberal cause in Mexico. It cannot, the way relations now stand, be given as a direct order that commanders on the Rio Grande shall take part either in battles or in agreements between belligerents as to what protection or guarantee

the gGovernment will give to either in any case. But there are no
extradition treaties existing between the United States and any
other govt. which requires the giving up of belligerents to their
enemies.

Officers of the Army on the Rio Grande should, officially, be
neutral in the same sense that the belligerents on the other side of
the river have been when we were in trouble. Their sympathies are
their own and they alone are responsible for them.

Many rebels are supposed to have crossed the Rio Grande to
join their fortunes with those of the Empire. It cannot be expected
of us that we will keep up a police force on that river to prevent
persons who may possibly take up the opposite side from crossing.

I think a visit from you to the Rio Grande at this time will do
good. If you go let me hear from you on your return the situation.

It is not improbable that Congress will, before the end of the
session, take decided measures on our affairs in Mexico and demand the withdrawel of all foreign troops from her soil. I hope so
at least.

> Very respectfully
> Your obt. svt.
> U. S. GRANT
> Lt. Gn.

ALS, DLC-Philip H. Sheridan. *O.R.*, I, xlviii, part 2, 1260. Also on Dec. 19,
1865, 11:30 A.M., USG telegraphed to Maj. Gen. Philip H. Sheridan. "Instruct
the commander on the Rio Grande that he can make no agreement with Imperial
or Liberal commanders. If either belligerent lays down their Arms and cross over
to the United States they will not be given up to their enemies but will be protected from theirm enemy on the other side" ALS (telegram sent), DNA, RG
107, Telegrams Collected (Bound); telegram sent, *ibid.*; copies, *ibid.*, RG 108,
Letters Sent; DLC-USG, V, 46, 109; USG 3. On Dec. 16, 4:00 P.M., Matías
Romero, Mexican minister, had telegraphed to Col. Enrique A. Mejía, Mexican
Army, New Orleans. "Your despatch received. Gen. Sheridan will soon receivee
full instructions from Lieut. Gen. Grant. Act in concert with him and do whatever he may desire you. Inform me of further develops: I can send no funds.
Raise them at Matamoras if possible." ALS (telegram sent), DNA, RG 107,
Telegrams Collected (Bound); telegram sent, *ibid.* USG noted on the ALS:
"Cipher) . . . Care Gen Sheridan N. Orleans." AN, *ibid.* On Dec. 21, Mejía
telegraphed to Romero. "I can get no decision from Gen Sheridan. He can give
none—What we want is, that Matamoras be secured by Gen Weitzel, as the
inhabitants fear being sacked if our enemies take the City" Telegram received
(at 3:40 P.M.), *ibid.*, RG 108, Telegrams Received; copy, DLC-USG, V, 54. On

Dec. 22, Maj. Robert Morrow, adjt. for President Andrew Johnson, endorsed this telegram. "Respectfully referred to Lieut. General Grant, Commanding Armies of the United States." AES, DNA, RG 108, Telegrams Received. On the same day, Romero telegraphed to Mejía. "Your telegraph received. Do the best you can without committing any officer in the U. S. service." ALS (telegram sent), *ibid.*, RG 107, Telegrams Collected (Bound); telegram sent, *ibid.* USG endorsed the ALS: "Approved" AES, *ibid.*

On Dec. 14, Bvt. Col. Theodore S. Bowers wrote to Bvt. Brig. Gen. Edward D. Townsend. "Lieut. Gen. Grant desires that you order the 1st Regiment U. S. Cavalry, now serving with Gen. Sheridan, to proceed by vessel to California and report to Gen. Halleck,—leaving their horses at New Orleans." ALS, *ibid.*, RG 94, Letters Received, 1317A 1865. On Dec. 18, Sheridan, New Orleans, telegraphed to USG. "The 1st Cavy will sail from here on the 26th inst I will have their Horses some 700 Very fine animals. do you intend to send me a Regt to replace the first Cavy and take these horses There is no Cavy left in this Dept except a Colored Regt which Is not of much service and will be musterd out soon" Telegram received (on Dec. 21, 3:00 P.M.), *ibid.*, RG 107, Telegrams Collected (Bound); *ibid.*, RG 108, Telegrams Received; copies, DLC-USG, V, 54; DLC-Philip H. Sheridan. On Dec. 22, 3:00 P.M., USG telegraphed to Sheridan. "The regular Cavalry is all disposed of so no more can be sent to you. All surplus horses can be turned in to the Qr. Mr." ALS (telegram sent), DNA, RG 107, Telegrams Collected (Bound); telegram sent, *ibid.*; copies, *ibid.*, RG 108, Letters Sent; DLC-USG, V, 46, 109. On Dec. 28, Sheridan telegraphed to USG. "As the fifth Cavalry is very much separated can you give me for orderly duty one squadron of it. I do not like to break into the two regts in Texas I have horses to mount the sqadron." Telegram received (on Dec. 30, 11:00 P.M.), DNA, RG 107, Telegrams Collected (Bound); *ibid.*, RG 108, Telegrams Received; copies, DLC-USG, V, 54; DLC-Philip H. Sheridan. On Dec. 30, Sheridan telegraphed to USG. "The first cavalry sailed this morning for Aspinwall. They were delayed three days on account of the nonarrival of the steamer McClellan from Keywest aggregate present twenty 20 officers six hundred & twenty one 621 enlisted men." Telegram received (on Dec. 31, 4:40 P.M.), DNA, RG 108, Telegrams Received; copy, DLC-USG, V, 54. On Dec. 27, 12:40 P.M., USG telegraphed to Sheridan. "Give Capt. Trimble 1st Cavalry four months leave with permission to visit Washington." ALS (telegram sent), DNA, RG 107, Telegrams Collected (Bound); telegram sent, *ibid.*; copies, *ibid.*, RG 108, Letters Sent; DLC-USG, V, 46, 109. On Dec. 31, Sheridan telegraphed to USG. "Lieut Tremble of the 1st. Cavalry declined to take the leave you authorized me to give him, & sailed with his regiment.—" Telegram received (on Jan. 1, 1866, noon), DNA, RG 108, Telegrams Received; copy, DLC-USG, V, 54. On Jan. 19, Sheridan telegraphed to USG. "The Steamer which took the 1st Cavalry has returned. She made connection with the Steamer to SanFrancisco—The regiment sailed for Panama on the 8th of January all well" Telegram received (on Jan. 23, 10:10 P.M.), DNA, RG 107, Telegrams Collected (Bound); *ibid.*, RG 108, Telegrams Received; copies, *ibid.*, RG 393, Military Div. of the Southwest and Dept. of the Gulf, Telegrams Sent; DLC-USG, V, 54; DLC-Philip H. Sheridan.

1. On Dec. 16, 1865, 4:00 P.M., USG telegraphed to Sheridan. "I will see the President and give you a full answer to your dispatch relating to affairs on the Rio Grande as soon as I can." ALS (telegram sent), DNA, RG 107, Tele-

grams Collected (Bound); telegram sent, *ibid.*; copies, *ibid.*, RG 108, Letters Sent; DLC-USG, V, 46, 109. *O.R.*, I, xlviii, part 2, 1259. On Dec. 15, Sheridan had telegraphed to USG. "Brig Gen W F Clark accompanied by Col Mejia of the liberal army has just arrived from the Rio Grande—They report as follows— Gen Mejia made a propositions to Gen Weitzel to turn over Matamoras for the sum of two hundred thousand dollars & a guarantee of protection to the city when occupied by the liberal forces This money was about to be raised & the city turned over to Col Mejia of the liberal army but it appears that Gen H Clay Crawford arrived and learning the condition of things offered Gen Mejia a greater sum & broke off the whole affair & has put things in a regular mess He then started for Gen Escabados camp but couriers from Gen Mejia at Brownsville preceeded him to warn Gen Escabado to have nothing to do with him I think that Gen Mejia will give up Matamoras if the thing is well managed & Gen Clark and Col Mejia say that Gen Mejia is only waiting their return from New Orleans The presence of Crawford & his assertions that he is acting under the authority of the President embarrasses me much Can you give me any instructions? I think it best to make a short trip over to the Rio Grande if you do not object 280 Austrians have arrived at Rio Grande that is all answer quick please" Telegram received (at 12:00 P.M.), DNA, RG 107, Telegrams Collected (Bound); *ibid.*, RG 108, Telegrams Received; copies (one sent by mail), *ibid.*, Letters Received; DLC-USG, V, 54; DLC-Philip H. Sheridan. *O.R.*, I, xlviii, part 2, 1259. On Dec. 16, 12:00 P.M., Sheridan telegraphed to USG. "Subsequent information from the Rio Grande brought by Major Parsons, my Inspector, makes me believe that the report given me by Genl Clark & sent to you yesterday may be a little Colored and excited—I have again notified Genl Weitzel to preserve strict neutrality & have nothing to do with the transaction spoken of in my telegram yesterday" Telegram received (at 8:00 P.M.), DNA, RG 107, Telegrams Collected (Bound); *ibid.*, RG 108, Telegrams Received; copies, DLC-USG, V, 54; DLC-Philip H. Sheridan. *O.R.*, I, xlviii, part 2, 1259.

To Andrew Johnson

Washington D. C. Dec. 21st *1865*

HIS EXCELLENCY, A. JOHNSON,
PRESIDENT OF THE U. STATES
SIR:

I would respectfully recommend the release from further punishment the Rev. F. Brown,[1] of Arkansas.

Mr. Brown was tried by Court Martial for the offence of slling a negro and has already undergone more than one years punishment in penitentiary for the offence. I think I am right in saying more than one year though am not positive as to the time. He has at all events been severely punished by a Military Court and now as a rule I would generally recommend that sentences so given whilst the war was in progress be remitted.

> I have the honor to be
> Very respectfully
> your obt. svt.
> U. S. GRANT
> Lt. Gn.

ALS, DNA, RG 94, Letters Received, 1753B 1865. On Dec. 11, 1865, Isaac N. Morris, "Steamer Commercial Fifty miles below Memphis," wrote to USG. "This will be handed to you by Judge Backster, one of the Senators elect from the State of Arkansas, whom I beg to introduce to your favorable acquaintance. Having been on a business tour to his State I first made his acquaintance there, and have had the pleasure of travelling several days with him on a Boat. You will find him an able, honest, sincere and patriotic gentleman, and any attention you may Show him he will greatly receive and it will add to my already numerous obligations The Judge is very desireous of obtaining your co.operation in an effort which he designs to make to procure the release of the Rev Mr Brown, who was sentenced to the Penetintiary from Arkansas, by a Courts Marshal, for the alleged offince of selling a negro after the Proclamation was issued and took effect, and will lay before you all the facts of the case, which I learned from other parties, and which I deem of such a character as to require Mr Brown's immediate discharge. I think he was a victim of conspiracy and never deserved the punishment inflicted upon him, but even if he did he has, in all conscience, been punished enough already. To continue his punishment longer would, in my judgement, be unjust on the part of the Government, and therefore I do hope you will find it consistent with your sense of duty to aid Judge Backster in his humane and worthy object. I feel—I know you will regard it right to do it if you can see the case as I do, and I hope hope and trust you will. Let me add General that I have been travelling somewhat through Arkansas, and have had the satisfaction of making the acquaintance of many of her citizens, and find them well disposed towards the Government. They are frank to acknowledge the entire overthrow of the so called Southern Confedracy and cheerfully acquisce in the termination of Slavery, but do desire a speedy restoration of their civil and political rights. These, I think, they should have, for the reason I do not believe they would abuse them, and because it is neither wise or politic to trample on a fallen foe The sooner we are one people—one brotherhood and one Government again the better for all. and the way to bring this speedily about is to be just, liberal and magnanimous. At the risk of being adjudged unwise in giving utterance to the expression, I will say that I do not believe there is any more necessity for an army in ArKansas than in Illinois to day." ALS, *ibid.*

1. For Fountain Brown, see Lincoln, *Works*, VII, 357n; *O.R.*, II, vii, 159–62, 1151–52; *ibid.*, II, viii, 837.

To James Speed

Washington D. C.
Dec. 21st 1865

HON. JAS. SPEED
ATTY. GN. OF THE U. STATES
SIR;

This will introduce to you the Rev. Mr. Brand,[1] brother-in-law of General Barnard of the Eng. Corps U. S. army.

Mr. Brand calls in behalf of Col. Harrison, now a state prisoners at Ft. Delaware. I do not know the special charges against Harrison and therefore abstain from making recommendation in his behalf. Generally however I am in favor of releasing from prison all who are not to be tried and such of them who are as can be paroled with a fare prospect of their appearing when called on for trial.

Very respectfully
your obt. svt.
U. S. GRANT
Lt. Gn

ALS, DNA, RG 94, Letters Received, 2598M 1865. On Dec. 16, 1865, Bvt. Maj. Gen. John G. Barnard had written to USG. "Burton N. Harrison at one time private Secretary to Jefferson Davis, and now a prisoner at Fort Delaware, is a nephew of my first wife and a protege of mine, having been educated by me at Yale College, and was at the Commencement of the rebellion, an Assistant to my brother Dr F. A. P. Barnard, then Chancellor of the University of Mississippi. His Southern birth and connections carried him into the tide of Secession, but in Everything that concerns him as a gentleman and man of honor, I have seldom met one who was more highly endorsed. If I am not mistaken, he alone (besides Davis himself) is the only remaining political prisoner. It is generally understood and believed, that he is retained only as a witness in the trial of his former Chief. I write this to ask if it would be possible to have him, like Stephens, Reagan and others, paroled. So far as he is concerned, I would guarantee his remaining wherever ordered, and appearing when called for: and written bonds of influential men in Maryland (where his more youthful days were spent, though he is a native of Louisiana) could likewise be furnished. Should you think an arrangement of this kind could be made; I should deem it a great favor if you would use your influence to carry the same into Effect— Submitting, if you see fit, this letter to the Hon. Secretary of War." ALS, *ibid.* On Dec. 18, USG endorsed this letter. "Respectfully forwarded to the Secretary of War." ES, *ibid.* Additional papers are *ibid.*

1. William F. Brand, born in 1814, uncle of Burton N. Harrison, served as rector of St. Mary's Church, Emmorton, Md. See Mrs. Burton Harrison, *Recollections Grave and Gay* (New York, 1911), pp. 69–70.

To Andrew Johnson

Washington D. C. Dec. 28th *1865*

HIS EXCELLENCY, A. JOHNSON,
PRESIDENT OF THE U STATES,
SIR:

Application having been made to me for an extension of the limits to which Mrs. Jefferson Davis is now confined so as to permit her to go where she pleases in the United States, or Canada, without forfeiting her present privilege of corresponding with her husband, I would respectfully recommend the following; that Mrs. Davis, and her family, be put precisely on the same footing as the families of other State prisoners only excluding her from visiting this Capital, or her husband, except with special permission.

I have the honor to be
Very respectfully
your obt. svt.
U. S. GRANT
Lt. Gen.

ALS, DNA, RG 94, Record & Pension Office, 52183. *O.R.*, II, viii, 840–41. On Dec. 18, 1865, Mrs. Varina Davis, Mill View, Ga., wrote to USG. "To you as the head of the army, and the highest military authority, I appeal for redress— I know when you contemplate my forlorn, sorrowing and barren life you will stir up your strength to help me—My Husband is getting old, is not strong, and has been subjected to a very rigorous imprisonment—which has racked his frame greatly—but a kind hearted sensitive gentleman in command of his place of incarceration would greatly modify the pains inseparable from such a condition of things—I am satisfied that he is tormented by a series of petty tyrannies exercised over him by the man now in command. Witness the anecdote of his hair being cut—which is now going the rounds of the newspapers—and the other more offensive one that Genl Miles lady friends were posted by the Genl Miles where they would meet him on his walk—and that my poor Husband not wishing to be made a spectacle turned to go to his quarters when his the females pursued him, and he took out a cigar and lit it—which being found offensive by the audience—Genl Miles forbade him cigars for the future—could any thing be more—well I will not characterise it—Unless Genl Miles has leisure to walk— Mr Davis does not go—and Mr Davis is not permitted to write except when Genl Miles chooses to send him paper—he then reads all Mr Davis' letters notwithstanding that the Atty Genl does so too—and returns them to him if he does not approve the contents. Some time since I wrote to know about his room—and to beg a description of it, and if the Sentinels were in his room night and day because I like to imagine to myself how he sits, and [w]here he is— and becaus[e] the sentinels in his room disturbed [h]im [v]ery much—he wrote to me the description, and Genl Miles required him to rewrite the letter leaving that out—he wrote two letters before they suited the General—Please Genl go down to Fortress Monroe, and see Mr Davis—and will you not change Genl Miles for an older, and a kinder man—will you not do away with the constant light in his room it is destroying his eye sight, and if he be not spared to me I have no hope of keeping the wolf from my children's door—You know that all we had is lost, that labor is all to which we can look forward but this will be a happy future for me if my Husband is but spared—If he is done to death by petty tyranny, it matters little to me if I lose him how this great affliction comes—I do not beleive I shall plead in vain to you—Genl Miles may be all the world says he is, but he is not kind, he is not refined Unfortunately for me I saw him at Hampton Roads, and he drove the barb as deep into my heart as strange hands could send it—You must be too great a man to sympathise with one who would tyrannise like this one—I feel sure that you will not permit it—Accused of no crime I am ke[p]t in the State of Georgia seperated from my children who are all small—but who are old e[n]ough to remember the vile, and degrading accusations of assassination and theft against their Father and therefore were sent out of the country—My Mother is old, and as I hear from a letter to night, in bad health and she is their only guardian—Restore to me the right to go where I please, to join them in Canada and to return when I desire to do so without forfeiting my privilege of correspondence with my Husband, and I will teach those children to pray that God may abundantly bless you and yours—My kind friend Col Barnard induced me to hope for your sympathy in my cumulative afflictions, and I throw myself upon your mercy I really have suffered until I am scarcely responsible for my words or thoughts—nearly seven months in one long agony of dreads and doubts—Little hope has lighted me through the valley of the shadow of death into which I seem to have walked—You will probably receive this in the season of your family re[joicing] and good cheer contrast your lot with ours—a[nd your] Servant promises to remember at the last day that I was in prison [an]d ye visited me—sick and ye [mini]stered unto me—for as much [as y]e did it unto one of these—ye [did] it unto me—Do it unto us [and I] will know you ever as good as well as great—merciful as well as brave— Place your own Wife in my condition—poor and and among strangers, deprived of every earthly tie—and imagine yourself tyrannised over by a young pitiless man, and you will realise how wretched are we—*Will you* write to me—tell me that you grant my requests—I pray God you may—and will you keep this letter confidential between *us for obvious reasons*—and make me ever you[r] most respectful friend . . . My address is to the care of Mr George Schley, Augusta Ga—" ALS, Dearborn Collection, MH. On Dec. 30, USG wrote to President Andrew Johnson. "Herewith I have the honor of forwarding direct to you Copy of a recommendation which I forwarded through the Sec. of War on the 28th inst. and to which no reply has as yet been made. I would respectfully ask a reply that I may answer the applicant whether or not the request asked can be granted." ALS, DLC-Andrew Johnson. USG enclosed a copy of his letter of Dec. 28.

To Don Carlos Buell

Washington D. C. Dec. 29th *1865*.

GENERAL:

Your letter of the 27th inst calling my attention to a letter which you wrote me in August last is received. The letter referred to reached my office in my absence from the City and was placed in a private desk and never came to my attention until it was handed to me by a Staff officer on the cars whilst on my way to New York City early in November last. I put the letter in my pocket expecting to answer it while in New York. Not finding time there however the letter remained pocketed, and has either been mislaid or lost.—I will answer the letter, from memory, as far as possible.

I have no recollection of any conversation in Springfield, Mass, or elsewhere during last summer in which your name was mentioned. I am often questioned however about this officer and that one and in such cases endeavor not to do them injustice. Conversations are rarely quoted correctly and in the case referred to by you I know mine could not have been, for I am made to say things which I never believed. For instance in regard to your want of ability to command in the presence of an enemy or in battle.

I have always thought, and frequently expressed the opinion, that in that precise case you would do as well as almost any General that could be selected.

I did receive a telegraphic dispatch from Gen. Halleck dated more than two weeks before the attack at Pittsburg Landing, Tenn, from which or from the courier bringing it I gathered the idea saying that you were within four days march of Savannah, and would be up in that time. That dispatch was telegraphed to your care, if I remember rightly, and sent by you to me by courier. At all events, the dispatch came by way of Nashville to the Army commanded by you and thence to me by courier. This fact I may have mentioned and drawn the conclusion that if you had been up in the time mentioned, or double the time, that instead of being attacked I would have taken the initiative. On the subject of your heart never having been in the cause I must certainly have been entirely misunderstood. I supposed you to be as earnest at the beginning of the war and whilst in command as any other officer engaged in it in the maintainance of the Government. Your own letters published since have rather given the idea that you wanted the Union saved in a particular way, and that way different from the one which was being pursued. I drew such a conclusion from them and state so frankly. although I have no recollection of ever having mentioned the fact in such a way as to have my opinion get into print. But if I did, what I may have said was based upon your own writing, or what purported to be, and which the whole community had access to.

I do not remember any of the other points alluded to in the Newspaper article which you sent.

I have in the course of the war been the subject of very severe Newspaper criticisms and never appealed to the press for vindication and now very much dislike to be called on to deny, or affirm, the statements of some irresponsible reporter without the slightest idea of who he is. But I shall always be much more ready to correct an injustice done another than if I were the injured party.

Very respectfully
U. S. GRANT

Copies, Munson-Williams-Proctor Institute, Utica, N. Y.; DLC-USG, V, 46, 109; DNA, RG 108, Letters Sent. One of USG's letterbooks contains a cancelled postscript. "P. S. Since writing the foregoing I have examined the record to find the dispatch from Gen Halleck referred to. My recollection is distinct as to the time I expected you at Savannah and of a conversation with Sherman at the time on the subject. But I fail to find any dispatch which gives the time when you would arrive and conclude therefore that this must have been fixed in my mind by the statements of the courier who brought the dispatch" Copy, DLC-USG, V, 109. On Aug. 5, 1865, Don Carlos Buell, Richfield Springs, N. Y., had written to USG. "My attention has been directed to a paragraph affecting me in the enclosed slip cut from the New York Herald of the 3rd instant, under the head of 'Personal intelligence.' It purports to give your comments at Springfield, Mass.

upon my conduct during the war. Coming in the particular form that it does, and from a Journal especially friendly to you, you will not think it strange that I bestow more consideration upon it than such paragraphs are usually entitled to; and if I am not mistaken you will not hesitate to avow or disavow the remarks imputed to you, nor be surprised that I request you to do so. As I do not know how else to direct this so that it may surely and speedily find you, I will send it to the care of the Adjutant General at Washington to be forwarded. I will thank you to direct your reply to the city of New York, New York Hotel, though I shall probably be at Niagara Falls from the 15th instant until the 1st of September." ALS, USG 3. The enclosed clipping is *ibid*. "General Grant while at Springfield, Mass., conversed very freely upon topics of general interest connected with the army. He said that General Buell was thoroughly versed in the theory of war, but knew nothing about handling men in an emergency, and that his heart was never in the war from the first. He said that Buell might have reached Pittsburg Landing several days earlier than he did, in which cas[e] General Grant would have been the attacking party. [In] speaking of the cruel treatment of our prisoner[s,] General Grant said he did not think General Lee was especially to blame about it, but that Davis and Benjamin were the ones who were responsible for it. In regard to Mexico, he expressed [t]he opinion that unless the French gave up the armed protection of Maximilian there would be war between the United States and France in less than five years. Mrs. Grant also talked freely, and whenever she spoke of her husband it was as 'Mr. Grant.' It does not seem natural to her to call him General." On Dec. 27, Buell, New York Hotel, wrote to USG. "In August last I brought to your notice certain remarks concerning me which you were reported, in the New York Herald, as having made at Springfield, Mass., during your tour through that state last summer. As my letter was sent to the care of the Adjutant General, it must probably have reached you. I need not, therefore, repeat the remarks alluded to, and I confine myself in this note simply to inviting your attention to my previous letter." ALS, USG 3. On April 3, 1866, Buell wrote to USG at length defending his movements before the battle of Shiloh. *New York World*, April 6, 1866. See *PUSG*, 5, 17; *Memoirs*, I, 358–59.

To Maj. Gen. George G. Meade

Washington Dec. 30th 1865 [*3:30* P.M.]

MAJ. GN. MEADE, PHILA PA

Musterout ~~any~~ all volunteers you may have in Ea[s]tern Dept. reduce the number in Middle Dept. to 1.500 men, Va to 2.500 and musterout one white regiment in North Carolina.

U. S. GRANT
Lt. Gn.

ALS (telegram sent), DNA, RG 107, Telegrams Collected (Bound); telegram sent, *ibid.*; telegram received, *ibid.*, RG 393, Military Div. of the Atlantic, Telegrams Received. On Dec. 30, 1865, Maj. Gen. George G. Meade telegraphed to USG. "Telegram in reference to reduction and Muster out of Volunteer Troops received" Telegram received (at 6:40 P.M.), *ibid.*, RG 107, Telegrams Collected (Bound); *ibid.*, RG 108, Telegrams Received; copy, *ibid.*, RG 393, Military Div. of the Atlantic, Letters Sent.

On Jan. 3, 1866, Meade telegraphed to USG. "Does your telegraphic order of Dec 30th directing muster out of all Volunteers in Eastern Dept include officers & men of Veteran Reserve corps who have elected to remain in service and does it include the 1st Army Corps Veterans. (Hancocks Corps) also in the numbers you require the troops reduced to, do you mean aggregate present & absent, or only the present for duty" Telegram received (at 2:05 P.M.), *ibid.*, RG 107, Telegrams Collected (Bound); (misdated Jan. 4, received at 2:05 A.M.) *ibid.*, RG 108, Telegrams Received; copies, *ibid.*, RG 393, Military Div. of the Atlantic, Letters Sent; DLC-USG, V, 54.

On Jan. 8, Meade telegraphed to USG. "In the number of twenty five hundred to which you have ordered department of Virginia to be reduced, do you include both volunteers and regulars, or is this the minimum of volunteers exclusive of regulars?—There are now in Dept. present & absent forty five hundred and fifty five volunteers, & twenty six hundred & nine regulars.—" Telegram received (at 4:50 P.M.), DNA, RG 94, Vol. Service Div., Letters Received, W2191 (VS) 1865; *ibid.*, RG 108, Telegrams Received; copies, *ibid.*, RG 393, Military Div. of the Atlantic, Letters Sent; DLC-USG, V, 54. On Jan. 9, 11:00 A.M., USG telegraphed to Meade. "Twentyfive hundred (2500) was intended as the aggregate force of regulars & Volunteers, present and absent to be retained in Virginia. Under the circumstances all the volunteers should be mustered out." LS (telegram sent), DNA, RG 107, Telegrams Collected (Bound); telegram sent, *ibid.*; telegram received (at 11:00 A.M.), *ibid.*, RG 393, Military Div. of the Atlantic, Telegrams Received.

To Maj. Gen. Philip H. Sheridan

Washington, D. C. Dec 30th *1865.* [*3:30* P.M.]

MAJ GEN SHERIDAN
NEW ORLEANS LA

If practicable reduce by muster out the white troops in your Division to ten thousand white and ten thousand colored troops If this reduction cannot be safely reached approach it as near as possible

U. S. GRANT
Lieut Gen

Telegram sent, DNA, RG 107, Telegrams Collected (Bound); copies, *ibid.*, RG 108, Letters Sent; DLC-USG, V, 46, 109. *O.R.*, I, xlviii, part 2, 1260. On Jan. 3, 1866, Maj. Gen. Philip H. Sheridan telegraphed to USG. "Your telegram of December Thirtieth (30th) is received, I will go on with the muster out, leaving approximately one thousand (1.000) and ten thousand (10.000) colored, The exact numbers remaining will be reported as soon as possible" Telegram received (on Jan. 4, 12:40 P.M.), DNA, RG 108, Telegrams Received; copies (one sent by mail), *ibid.*, Letters Received; *ibid.*, RG 393, Military Div. of the Southwest and Dept. of the Gulf, Telegrams Sent; DLC-USG, V, 54. The cipher clerk added a note to the telegram received. "Have repeated Gen Grants telegram of Dec 30th to Gen Sheridan, and asked to have correct answer," ANS, DNA, RG 108, Telegrams Received. On Jan. 6, 10:30 A.M., Sheridan telegraphed to USG. "Your telegram of the 30th ult. read thousand 1.000 white and ten thousand 10.000 Colored troops, and the order for muster out was given accordingly, but will be changed so as to retain ten thousand 10.000 white and ten thousand 10.000 Colored troops, as per your telegram of the 5th No white troops will go out under this order as I have not ten thousand 10.000 white troops in my Division." Telegram received (at 7:00 P.M.), *ibid.*, RG 107, Telegrams Collected (Bound); *ibid.*, RG 108, Telegrams Received; copies (one sent by mail), *ibid.*, Letters Received; *ibid.*, RG 393, Military Div. of the Southwest and Dept. of the Gulf, Telegrams Sent; DLC-USG, V, 54; DLC-Philip H. Sheridan. On Jan. 7, 1:00 P.M., Sheridan telegraphed to USG. "I have the honor to report that there are present in this Division of Volunteers Six thousand five hundred & fifty white and nineteen thousand Seven hundred & sixty eight colored troops—The aggregate present & absent is nine thousand one hundred and twenty eight white & twenty five thousand two hundred & eighteen colored—Under your telegraphic instructions of the fifth there are about nine thousand five hundred colored troops mustered" Telegram received (at 4:30 P.M.), DNA, RG 107, Telegrams Collected (Bound); *ibid.*, RG 108, Telegrams Received; copies, *ibid.*, RG 393, Military Div. of the Southwest and Dept. of the Gulf, Telegrams Sent; DLC-USG, V, 54; DLC-Philip H. Sheridan.

Calendar

1865, MAY 1, 10:50 P.M. To Brig. Gen. John D. Stevenson, Harpers Ferry. "You may permit the soldier living in Memphis to go home through the North. The two officers belonging in S. C. may be passed through the Provost Marshal in Baltimore to City Point on their way home. Free transportation is only given on boats and roads run by Govt."—ALS (telegram sent), DNA, RG 107, Telegrams Collected (Bound); telegram sent, *ibid.*; copies, *ibid.*, RG 108, Letters Sent; DLC-USG, V, 46, 76, 108.

1865, MAY 1, 11:40 P.M. To commanding officer, Fort Monroe. "Direct a Staff officer to visit the Mail boat which left here to-day on her arrival at the Fort and notify Gen. Humphries to return to Washington. Should the Mailboat leave for City Point before you receive this forward the dispatch after Gen. Humphries."—ALS (telegram sent), DNA, RG 107, Telegrams Collected (Bound); telegram sent, *ibid.*; telegram received (press), *ibid.* On May 2, Col. Joseph Roberts, 3rd Pa. Heavy Art., Fort Monroe, telegraphed to USG. "Telegram received, and contents made known to General Humphreys at 7½ oclock this morning at the Steamboat Wharf."—ALS (telegram sent), *ibid.*, Telegrams Collected (Unbound); telegram received (at 10:00 A.M.), *ibid.*, Telegrams Collected (Bound); (at 9:40 A.M.) *ibid.*, RG 108, Telegrams Received.

1865, MAY 1. Maj. Gen. Winfield S. Hancock to Bvt. Col. Theodore S. Bowers. "I am informed that 39 Officers and about 600 men of Echols command surrendered and were paroled yesterday at Lewisburg West Va A Company of the 18th Va Cavalry numbering 56 men also surrendered to Genl Emory on Saturday—All the forces in the Valley seem to be coming in—Concurrent reports leave little room for doubt that Genl Early died of congestive fever near Salem last week—"—LS, DNA, RG 108, Letters Received. *O.R.*, I, xlvi, part 3, 1065. Jubal A. Early died in 1894.

1865, MAY 1. Bvt. Col. Theodore S. Bowers to U.S. Treasury Agent William P. Mellen. "Herewith I return the papers you left with me, signed by the General. He directs me to say to you that after preparing his order he discovered that the Secretary of War had issued an order on the subject, and in order to avoid confusion he has submitted his order to the Secretary. Its publication has therefore been delayed, and he is unable to furnish you a copy. His leading idea is to give the largest possible freedom to trade consistant with the interests of the country"—ALS, DNA, RG 366, 1st Special Agency, Miscellaneous Papers. On the same day, Bvt. Col. Adam Badeau wrote to "All Military Commanders East of the Mississippi River." "Lieut. Gen. Grant directs me to state that Mr. W. W. Mellen, Special Agent of the Treasury Department, is about to visit the military posts of the seaboard in the states hitherto in insurrection, for the purpose of reopening trade under the regulations adopted by the Treasury Department. Military commanders are informed that the armed forces of the Rebellion East of the Mississippi having been overthrown, it is now the policy of the

government to facilitate and protect internal trade and commerce, and they
are directed to conform their action to this policy. They will therefore
afford Mr. W. W. Mellen every assistance and facility in their power,
while engaged in the duty above indicated."—ALS, *ibid.* On the same day,
Bowers drafted general orders. "1. . The following Executive order is published for the information and guidance of all concerned, viz. 2. . For the
purposes mentioned in the foregoing order, the States of Tennessee, Virginia, North Carolina and South Carolina, are declared to be within the
lines of national military occupation, and such portions of Georgia, Florida,
Alabama, Mississippi and Louisiana, will in like manner be regarded as
within the limits of military occupation as the Commanders of the Departments in which those States are embraced, may consider can have the trade
facilities allowed by the Executive order extended to them consistently
with the public interests. 3d. The trade herein provided for will be restricted to persons who take an oath insuring their future allegiance to the
Government, and will be carried on in the manner prescribed by law, and
the regulations that may be established by the Treasury Department.
4. For the present trade will be permitted at all ports and places, within
the States named, now occupied by the military forces, and at such other
places in the interior as may be authorized by Department Commanders.
5. The amount of goods which may be allowed to be sold at any one place
will be limited only by the amount applied for. 6. The object of this order
is to restore to the States specified free trade, as far as the public interests
will admit, and the laws authorize, and Department Commanders will be
governed accordingly."—ADf, DLC-Edwin M. Stanton.

1865, MAY 2.   USG endorsement. "Respy. referred to BMG. M. C. Meigs
Q. M G. for any information he may have on the subject within referred
to. The boat was seizd and sunk by my orders and the claim should be paid
at the earliest possible moment"—Copy, DLC-USG, V, 58. On May 5,
Bvt. Maj. Gen. Montgomery C. Meigs wrote to USG. "I have the honor to
acknowledge the receipt of the communication of Wm A. Wright, Esq. of
the 1st inst. with enclosures, relative to his claim against the Government
for the Schooner 'Gen. Armstrong' sunk as an obstruction in the James
River—which has been referred to the Quartermaster General for any information he may have on the subject. A claim for this vessel, amounting
to $22,779.63, was, ~~was~~ received on the 9th of February 1865, from Brig.
Genl Ingalls, Chf. Q. M. of the Armies operating against Richmond, and
on the 13th of the same month all the papers in the case were transmitted
to the Third Auditor of the Treasury. Inasmuch as the payment of the value
of vessels lost should be made to the legal owners, and as the title is required to be proven by evidence which is more properly decided upon by
the Accounting officers of the Treasury, it has been the practice of this Department to refer all such cases to the Third Auditor for his examination
and final action."—LS, DNA, RG 108, Letters Received.

1865, MAY 2.   Brig. Gen. Frederick T. Dent, Richmond, to USG. "There is a starving multitude here—we are feeding them—Some have money to purchase—but no provisions are for sale—the Port was opend for domestic Comerce—but the Treasury regulations will not allow Clearances (except on Trade Store permits—issued by agents of Tres Dept) to goods or provisions—to come to Richmd   in the mean time the Government is feeding those who could feed themselves were the provisions here for sale   cannot this be remidied"—ALS (telegram sent), CSmH; telegram received (at 4:00 P.M.), DNA, RG 107, Telegrams Collected (Bound); *ibid.*, Telegrams Collected (Unbound); *ibid.*, RG 108, Telegrams Received. *O.R.*, I, xlvi, part 3, 1069. At 8:30 P.M., Bvt. Col. Theodore S. Bowers telegraphed to Maj. Joseph B. Collins, City Point. "Report with your Command to Brig Gen. F. T. Dent. at Richmond for duty, until further orders."—ALS (telegram sent), DNA, RG 107, Telegrams Collected (Bound); telegram sent, *ibid.*; copies, *ibid.*, RG 108, Letters Sent; DLC-USG, V, 46, 76, 108. *O.R.*, I, xlvi, part 3, 1066.

1865, MAY 3.   Brig. Gen. John A. Rawlins to Maj. Gen. Henry W. Halleck. "Gen, Grant directs that as soon as the Army of the Potomac is well under way, you will please relieve Brig, Gen, Rufus Ingalls, Quartermaster, from duty at City Point and order him to report to him in person at Washington D. C."—Copies, DLC-USG, V, 46, 76, 108; DNA, RG 108, Letters Sent. *O.R.*, I, xlvi, part 3, 1074. On May 8 or 9, probably the former, Brig. Gen. Rufus Ingalls telegraphed to Bvt. Col. Theodore S. Bowers. "Gen. Halleck has just telegraphed an order for me to report in person to, the Lieut-Gen'l. I shall leave at once and will report Wednesday morning. Every thing is arranged here. My reports are all rendered to Generals Halleck and Meigs. Copies will be sent to your office."—ALS (telegram sent, dated May 8), DNA, RG 107, Telegrams Collected (Unbound); telegram received (marked as sent on May 9, received at 11:35 A.M.), *ibid.*, Telegrams Collected (Bound); *ibid.*, RG 108, Telegrams Received. Printed as sent on May 9 in *O.R.*, I, xlvi, part 3, 1118. See *ibid.*, pp. 1124–27.

1865, MAY 4.   Bvt. Brig. Gen. Cyrus B. Comstock to Brig. Gen. Patrick E. Connor, Denver. "A. copy of your report of Apr. 6/.65 has been forward to the Lt. Gen. Comdg. and he desires me to express his appreciation of your efforts. It is not believed that an institution like Mormanism can exist permanently, in free & close communication with the civilized world. Our efforts should therefore aim to make such communication safe, by thorough protection of 'Gentiles' against Mormons, whether as transient visitors or permanent settlers, and trust mainly to the ordinary laws which govern civilization for the gradual removal of what is believed to be in opposition to those laws & which can derive vitality only from persecution."—Copies, DLC-USG, V, 46, 76, 108; DNA, RG 108, Letters Sent; Dodge Papers, IaHA. *O.R.*, I, l, part 2, 1221. See *ibid.*, pp. 1184–86.

1865, MAY 4.   Bvt. Col. Theodore S. Bowers to Maj. Gen. John M. Scho-field. "You will please clear out the Hospital building at Morehead City with as little delay as possible and turn the same over to the Medical De-partment"—Copies, DLC-USG, V, 46, 76, 108; DNA, RG 108, Letters Sent. *O.R.*, I, xlvii, part 3, 392.

1865, MAY 5.   USG endorsement. "Respectfully submitted to the Secre-tary of War with the recommendation that the order of the War Dept. with-in referred to be recinded."—ES, DNA, RG 94, Letters Received, 934M 1865. Written on a telegram of May 2, 2:20 P.M., from Maj. Gen. John Pope, St. Louis, to USG. "I request respectfully that War Dept order no one eighty eight (188) Par 2 assigning Lieut Col Setgreaves as Chief Engineer of this Div be revoked   Capt Wheeler Engineer Corps already occupies that position & having served a long time in Dept of Arkansas is perfectly familiar with the whole Country to be covered with military opera-tions   I greatly prefer to retain him. Please answer by telegraph"—Tele-gram received (at 5:00 P.M.), *ibid.*; *ibid.*, RG 107, Telegrams Collected (Bound); copy, *ibid.*, RG 393, Military Div. of the Mo., Telegrams Sent. *O.R.*, I, xlviii, part 2, 292.

1865, MAY 5.   To commanding officer, Camp Chase, Ohio. "You may release Philip Griffin on his taking the oath of allegiance,   he is confined in Prison two (2) Barracks Six (6) Camp Chase, O,"—Telegram received, DNA, RG 109, Unfiled Slips and Abstracts, Philip Griffin; copies, *ibid.*, RG 108, Letters Sent; DLC-USG, V, 46, 76, 108. On May 6, Bvt. Brig. Gen. William P. Richardson, Camp Chase, telegraphed to USG. "Phillip Griffin was released this day"—Telegram received (at 4:40 P.M.), DNA, RG 107, Telegrams Collected (Bound); *ibid.*, RG 108, Telegrams Received; copy, DLC-USG, V, 54.

1865, MAY 5.   USG endorsement. "I would advise as a cheap way to get clear of guerillas that a certain time be given for them to come in—say the 20th of this month, up to which time their paroles will be recieved, but after which time they will be proceeded against as outlaws."—Copy, DLC-USG, V, 58. *O.R.*, I, xlix, part 2, 419. Written on a letter of April 20 from Col. Arthur A. Smith, 83rd Ill., Clarksville, Tenn., to Maj. Burr H. Polk, adjt. for Maj. Gen. Lovell H. Rousseau. "Application has been made to me, through citizens, by guerrillas in this district to know upon what terms they could lay down their arms and become peaceable citizens. As a de-cision in one case might form a precedent for others, I respectfully refer the question to district headquarters for decision."—*Ibid.*, p. 418.
On May 11, Bvt. Col. Theodore S. Bowers wrote to Bvt. Brig. Gen. Edward D. Townsend. "Please publish the accompanying General Order." —ALS, DNA, RG 94, Letters Received, 493A 1865. Bowers enclosed an unnumbered general order. "All the forces of the enemy east of the Missis-sippi river having been duly surrendered by their proper commanding offi-

cers to the Armies of the United States under agreements of parole and disbandment, and there being now no authorized troops of the enemy east of the Mississippi river, it is—Ordered, That from and after ~~this date any~~ the first day of June, 1865, any and all persons found in arms against the United States, or who may commit acts of hostility against it east of the Mississippi river will be regarded as Guerrillas and punished with death. The strict enforcement and execution of this order is especially enjoined upon the commanding officers of all United States forces within the territorial limits to which it applies."—ADf, *ibid.* Printed as AGO General Orders No. 90 in *O.R.*, I, xlvi, part 3, 1134.

1865, MAY 5. Maj. Gen. Winfield S. Hancock to Bvt. Col. Theodore S. Bowers. "I have the honor to report that General Torbert Comdg Army of the Shenandoah reports to me by telegram of this date, that the Cavalry force under Col Reed of the 22d N. Y. Cavalry has returned from Staunton having paroled about 750 men, in addition to those heretofore reported— Generals Rosser and Lilly left Staunton the day before Col. Reed arrived there, having been engaged without success in endeavoring to raise men to go South—General Torbert expects to receive on Monday the surrender of the remnant of Deerings old Brigade—The people are reported as well disposed—Guerrillas are reported as troublesome in the vicinity of Mount Jackson—I have directed a force to be sent against them—and no quarter to be shown . . . The return of Col Reed does not intefere with the movement of the force of Infantry and Cavaly now enroute for Staunton, which left Winchester yesterday morning—The number previously reported as paroled in the valley is about 2300"—ALS, DNA, RG 108, Letters Received. *O.R.*, I, xlvi, part 3, 1095.

1865, MAY 6. USG endorsement. "Respy. forwarded to the sec of war and earnestly recommended. Of the many Commissaries of subsistence it has been my fortune to meet with, Capt D. D Wiley, C. S. of Vols is one of the most efficient. He is thorough in the knowledge of his duties and courteous & prompt in their discharge, and is a gentleman of the highest integrity of character"—Copy, DLC-USG, V, 58. Written on a letter of Bvt. Col. Thomas Wilson, chief commissary, Army of the Potomac, recommending Bvt. Maj. Daniel D. Wiley for appointment in the U.S. Army. —*Ibid.*

1865, MAY 6. To commanding officer, Johnson's Island, Ohio. "Upon receipt of this you will release Lieut Robt. Bolling 9th Va., a Confederate prisoner of war, upon his taking the oath of allegiance—"—Telegrams sent (2), DNA, RG 107, Telegrams Collected (Bound); copies, *ibid.*, RG 108, Letters Sent; *ibid.*, RG 249, Letters Received; DLC-USG, V, 46, 76, 108. On May 9, Col. Charles W. Hill, Johnson's Island, telegraphed to USG. "Robert Bowling Lt Ninth 9 Va has been released ~~upon~~ taking oath amnesty pursuant to your telegram recd this day."—Telegram received (at 6:40

P.M.), DNA, RG 107, Telegrams Collected (Bound); *ibid.*, RG 108, Telegrams Received; copy, DLC-USG, V, 54.

1865, MAY 6. USG endorsement. "All paroled prisoners of war, including those of lees and Johnsons armies, not excepted from the benefits of the Presidents Proclamation, by taking the oath prescribed in that Proclamation should be permitted to return to their homes in the states that have not been in rebellion. They cannot be considered deserters, nor recieve the benefits provided in any order relating to deserters"—Copy, DLC-USG, V, 58. Written on a letter of Capt. Edward W. Andrews, provost marshal, Harpers Ferry, concerning paroled prisoners.—*Ibid.*

1865, MAY 6. USG endorsement. "Respectfully returned. In the present condition of affairs I deem the within proposition impracticable as well as impolitic. I do not therefore approve it."—ES, DNA, RG 107, Letters Received, S1321 1865. Written on a petition of April 5 of Jonathan Strine, Martinsburg, West Va., and others asking that disloyal persons be taxed to provide compensation for loyal persons whose property was damaged during the war.—DS, *ibid.*

1865, MAY 6, 1:23 P.M. Brig. Gen. John A. Rawlins to Maj. Gen. Edward R. S. Canby. "The Chief Engineer deems it indispensable that Capt. McFarland should return to Key West to take charge of the operations there. If he can be spared please direct him to do so."—LS (telegram sent), DNA, RG 107, Telegrams Collected (Bound); telegram sent, *ibid.*; copies, *ibid.*, RG 108, Letters Sent; DLC-USG, V, 46, 76, 108. *O.R.*, I, xlviii, part 2, 329; *ibid.*, I, xlix, part 2, 642. On May 13, Canby telegraphed to Rawlins. "Your despatch of the sixth (6) inst has been recd and Capt McFarland has been ordered to return to his station at Key West"—Telegram received (on May 18), DNA, RG 107, Telegrams Collected (Bound); (on May 18, 3:55 P.M.) *ibid.*, RG 108, Telegrams Received; copy, DLC-USG, V, 54. *O.R.*, I, xlviii, part 2, 425; *ibid.*, I, xlix, part 2, 755.

1865, MAY 6. Bvt. Col. Theodore S. Bowers to Maj. Gen. John A. Logan. "The Lieutenant General congratulates your command on the extraordinary march it has made from Raleigh. He directs that you rests your men, provide yourself with supplies, and await Maj. Gen. Sherman's arrival."—ALS (telegram sent), DNA, RG 107, Telegrams Collected (Bound); telegram sent, *ibid.*; telegram received, *ibid.*, Telegrams Collected (Unbound). *O.R.*, I, xlvii, part 3, 413. At 2:30 P.M., Logan, Petersburg, had telegraphed to Bowers. "My Command is encamped six miles from this City. We commenced the march from Neuse river near Raleigh, at 5, A. M. the first instant, troops in good condition."—ALS (telegram sent), DNA, RG 107, Telegrams Collected (Unbound); telegram received (at 8:20 P.M.), *ibid.*; (at 8:00 P.M.) *ibid.*, Telegrams Collected (Bound); (at 8:05 P.M.) *ibid.*, RG 108, Telegrams Received. *O.R.*, I, xlvii, part 3, 413.

1865, MAY 7. Bvt. Col. Theodore S. Bowers to Capt. Paul A. Oliver. "Your telegram in relation to Lt Col. F. W Roberts has been referred to Maj Gen. Sheridan, who makes the following endorsement on it. Lt. Col. Roberts makes an untruthful statement, and I believe him to be ~~an~~ a suspicious character.—Last winter he was at Martinsburg and I gave him a pass to visit me at Winchester. He attempted to go south on the pass and was arrested in passing my lines, but was released on his representing that he was [o]n his way to Winchester. He afterwards passed the lines [a]t some other point. I sent parties after him but he [es]caped and went south. (Signed) P. H. SHERIDAN. Arrest Roberts and send him here under guard [wi]th statement of all the facts you have."—ALS (telegram sent), DNA, RG 107, Telegrams Collected (Bound); telegram sent, *ibid.*; telegram received, *ibid.*, Telegrams Collected (Unbound); *ibid.*, RG 108, Letters Received. Other documents concerning this man, whose name is also given as Frank W. Robarts, are *ibid.*

1865, MAY 8. Bvt. Col. Theodore S. Bowers to Maj. Gen. Christopher C. Augur. "Please send all paroled prisoners of the late Rebel Armies now confined or detained at Alexandria Va, to their homes, Those whose homes were at the time of joining those Armies in States that have never been in rebellion and who desire to return to them, will be required to take the oath prescribed in the Presidents Amnesty Proclamation, provided they are not excepted from its benefits. If so excepted they will be detained Those living in Texas will be sent in charge of an officer, and will be landed on the westbank of the Mississippi, about the mouth of Red River."—Copies, DLC-USG, V, 46, 76, 108; DNA, RG 107, Letters Received, H1364 1865; *ibid.*, RG 108, Letters Sent. *O.R.*, I, xlvi, part 3, 1116. See *ibid.*, p. 1112; *ibid.*, II, viii, 539.

1865, MAY 8. Maj. Gen. John Pope to USG. "I have the honor to transmit enclosed copy of an order from General Palmer Commanding Department of Kentucky to Bvt Brig Genl Hammond, directing the latter to report to me for duty. I do not know by what authority General Palmer issued this order, but as Genl Hammond has reported here in compliance with it, I have assigned him to temporary duty until your decission in the matter is received. General Hammond you doubdtless remember as an Officer on Genl Sherman's Staff. His health is bad and he desires service in Kansas or Nebraska in the hope of re-establishing it. He expects I believe to be mustered out of service when the Army is disbanded and desires if possible to settle in Kansas. As you know him and his merits and claims better than myself I submit the matter for your action. He is ordered to Nebraska where an Officer is needed for the present."—Copy, DNA, RG 393, Military Div. of the Mo., Letters Sent.

1865, MAY 8. Mrs. M. C. Roby, Baltimore, to USG. "I appeal to you to allow my son Harry Roby to return to his home in Baltimore He is a paroled prisoners under the terms of Genl Lee's surrender & has taken the oath in Virginia—in defiance of your authority this is not permitted. He is under age & I pledge myself that he will fully honor the obligations of his oath."—Telegram received (at 12:20 P.M.), DNA, RG 107, Telegrams Collected (Bound); *ibid.*, RG 108, Telegrams Received; copy, DLC-USG, V, 54.

1865, MAY 9. To Secretary of War Edwin M. Stanton. "I have the honor to make requisition for, Five thousand dollars ($5000—) of the appropriation, 'for expenses of Commanding General's Office', and request that it may be drawn in favor of Major Geo, K, Leet A, A, G, of my Staff, for the use of my Office"—Copies, DLC-USG, V, 46, 76, 108; DNA, RG 108, Letters Sent.

1865, MAY 9. USG endorsement. "Respectfully forwarded to the Secretary of War, with the recommendation that Brig Gen N. M. Curtis, for gallant and meritorious conduct in the field, especially in the assault on Fort Fisher Jany. 15th 1865, be appointed a Maj. Genl. by Brevet of Vols. He was appointed a full Brig. Genl. for that action, but his great services there would receive no more recognition than they deserve by his further promotion—"—ES, John H. Atwood, Houston, Tex. Written on a letter of May 6 from Maj. Gen. Edward O. C. Ord to Secretary of War Edwin M. Stanton. "It is not necessary to call your attention to the gallant part Genl Curtis took in the capture of Fort Fisher—I can however speak of the part he would have taken had he and his Brigade have had the opportunity requested by them at the first landing of our troops there—I believe it was mainly due to Genl Curtis statement that the second and successful attempt was made—wherein he was wounded *four* times and he has only had one promotion—besides what he has done, he possess the rarer merit of being able to perform well all the duties of the grade next above the one he now holds—"—ALS, *ibid.*

1865, MAY 9. Col. William Norris, C.S.A. commissioner of exchange, Raleigh, to USG. "I came here a Commissioner of Exchange, under a flag of truce, and with many prisoners of war, to confer with the U. S. Commissioner. I have important matters to adjust with him; the execution of the cartel; the delivery of Federal prisoners in the Trans-Mississippi department and elsewhere, not subject to the convention of April 26th with Genl. J. E. Johnston; the reception of Confederate prisoners from your lines; and the settlement of accounts of money belonging to Federal prisoners. Having stated the object of my coming to Major Genl. Schofield, he invited me to remain here until my application could be referred to you. I have since been arrested, and forced to give my parole not to leave here, against which violation of my rights as Commissioner under a flag of truce I again earnestly protest. If the Cartel is to be continued, which my appointment and special instructions from the Secretary of War show a desire on our part should be done, I must confer with Genl. Mulford and Colonel Ould; and for that purpose I renew my application for a safe conduct for myself and officers to Richmond. If this be refused and an interview with Genl Mulford, within your lines or ours, be impossible, I respectfully demand that our parole be cancelled and that we be returned to our lines. By no interpretation am I subject to the convention with Genl Johnston as seems to be the theory of my arrest; I had nothing whatever to do with him, reporting to the Secretary of War alone; whilst the prisoners brought here I turned back, when actually on their way South under a guard over which General Johnston had no control."—ALS, DNA, RG 108, Letters Received. Other papers concerning Norris are *ibid.*; see also *O.R.*, II, viii, 643, 652. On Nov. 17, Norris, New York, wrote to Joseph E. Johnston at length, seeking his assistance in vindicating Norris's conduct in May, and on Feb. 10, 1866, Johnston endorsed this letter. "This letter was not received in New York a[s] the writer intended. I respectfully ask Lt Genl Grant to consider this case. I can vouch for the fact that the writer was regarded as Comr for exchange of prisoners in april last—& for the further fact that he was not under my Command—but belonged to that of the Sec: of War of the Southern States, who was then known to be within the geographical limits of my command—& of course was not, nor his party, included in the terms of the convention."—ALS and AES, NHi.

1865, MAY 9, 12:35 P.M.   To commanding officer, Palmyra, N. Y. "Send Thos. Ballentyne Co. "I" 1st Veteran Reserve Corps to Washington on Special detail at the White House."—ALS (telegram sent), DNA, RG 107, Telegrams Collected (Bound); telegram sent (at 1:30 P.M.), *ibid.*

1865, MAY 10.   USG endorsement. "Respectfully forwarded to the Secretary of War, and favorable consideration recommended"—ES, DNA, RG 105, Letters Received. Written on a letter of April 14 from Col. Samuel Thomas, Vicksburg, to Brig. Gen. John A. Rawlins. "I am presuming upon your acquaintance with Col John Eaton Jr in sending you the enclosed papers. I feel that no man in the nation is so well qualified to fill the position of Commissioner at the head of Freedmen affairs (as authorized by the last Congress) as Col Eaton. If you can give him any assistance or influence the President in his choice of a man to fill the place I would be glad to have you forward the enclosed papers. The President has received many petitions both Military and civil for the same. They have been forwarded through other channels. I feel that it is for the good of the country that a good man is placed in the position"—ALS, *ibid.* On May 17, Maj. Gen. Oliver O. Howard wrote to Bvt. Col. Theodore S. Bowers. "I have the honor to request the temporary detail of Col. John Eaton Jr Comdg U S. Col. Regt. for duty with this Bureau."—ALS, *ibid.*, RG 94, Letters Received, 314F 1865. On the same day, USG endorsed this letter. "Respectfully referred to the Adjutant General of the Army who will make the special order within requested, and who will order Col. Eaton to Washington by telegraph"—ES, *ibid*. Also on the same day, Col. William A. Nichols, AGO, telegraphed to the commanding gen., Memphis. "Lieutenant General Grant directs that Colonel John Eaton, Junior, Sixty third U. S. Colored Troops, repair to this city, and report to Major General O. O. Howard Commissioner Bureau of Freedmen—"—LS (telegram sent), *ibid*., RG 107, Telegrams Collected (Unbound); copy, *ibid*., RG 94, Letters Sent. On May 20, Col. John Eaton, Jr., Memphis, telegraphed to USG. "Your telegrams just recd. Will start at once."—Telegram received (on May 23, 10:45 P.M.), *ibid*., RG 107, Telegrams Collected (Bound); *ibid*., RG 108, Telegrams Received; copy, DLC-USG, V, 54.

On Oct. 16, USG wrote to Secretary of War Edwin M. Stanton. "I understand that Col. J. Eaton Jr. of the Freedman's Bureau will be leaving the service soon. As a recognition of his valuable services during the war, and particularly for the zeal and efficiency shewn by him in the management of Freedman affairs, before the extablishment of the bureau for their management, indeed before any law had passed Congress for the establishment of it, I would recommend that the rank of Brevet Brigadier General be confered on him."—ALS, DNA, RG 94, ACP, G525 CB 1865.

1865, MAY 10.   USG endorsement. "Respectfully returned to the Secretary of War. The recommendations of the Chief Engineer as to works in the defensive line around Washington and Alexandria, to be dismantled, and the manner of doing it, are approved. It is not practicable as yet to fix definitely the permanent garrisons for cities referred to in the rebellious States."—Copy (unsigned), DNA, RG 108, Letters Received; (dated May 11) DLC-USG, V, 58. *O.R.*, I, xlvi, part 3, 1101. Written on a letter of May 6 from Brig. Gen. Richard Delafield to Secretary of War Edwin M. Stanton recommending the reduction of the seventy-four forts and batteries around Washington, D. C., to twenty-three, and discussing garrisons in the South.—Copy, DNA, RG 108, Letters Received. *O.R.*, I, xlvi, part 3, 1099–1100.

1865, MAY 10.   USG endorsement. "Brevet Major General M. C. Meigs, ~~Chief~~ Quarter Master General of the Army, will please order, Captain C. A. Reynolds, Assistant Quarter Master U. S. A. to report to Gen. Dent. for duty at Richmond."—ES, DNA, RG 107, Letters Received from Bureaus. Written on a telegram of April 23 from Brig. Gen. Rufus Ingalls to Bvt. Maj. Gen. Montgomery C. Meigs reporting the request of Brig. Gen. Frederick T. Dent that Capt. Charles A. Reynolds be assigned as q. m. at Richmond.—Copy, *ibid*. On May 15, Reynolds, Washington, D. C., wrote to USG. "I ask your indulgence, for thus trespassing on your time and attention, by presenting a statement of my military service, to you, with a view to enlist your influence for my promotion to a Colonelcy. . . ."—ALS, *ibid*., RG 94, ACP, 1172 1875. On the same day, Reynolds wrote to Brig. Gen. John A. Rawlins enclosing the letter above and asking his assistance in gaining promotion.—ALS, *ibid*. No promotion followed. On April 24, 1866,

Reynolds, Nashville, wrote a letter discussing his services to a board considering applications for bvts.—ALS, *ibid.* On May 25, USG endorsed this letter. "I have personal knowledge of Captain Reynolds' long and faithful Services in the field, during the late rebellion, and where officers are being brevetted for 'faithful and meritorious Service' his claims would, in my opinion, entitle him to the brevet of Lieutenant Colonel. I respectfully recommend his promotion by brevet to that grade."—ES, *ibid.* On July 19, President Andrew Johnson nominated Reynolds as bvt. maj. and lt. col. to date from March 13, 1865.

1865, MAY 10.   To David B. Parker, special agent, Post Office Dept., City Point. "If the P. M. Gen. makes application for Proudfit he can get him. Not without."—ALS (telegram sent), DNA, RG 107, Telegrams Collected (Bound); telegram sent, *ibid.*; copies, *ibid.*, RG 108, Letters Sent; DLC-USG, V, 46, 76, 108.

1865, MAY 10.   Maj. Gen. Philip H. Sheridan to Brig. Gen. John A. Rawlins. "Miss Irene Orndorff and Misses M. and Kate Godwin now living in Richmond Va. desire to take the oath of allegiance & go to Baltimore Md to reside; these ladies were Secessionists & Genl Wallace while in command of the Middle Department Sent them South. I am acquainted with Miss Orndorff & I think that by this time She is convinced of the fallacy of Secession. They returned from Richmond on a permit from Genl Weitzel and were again ordered by Genl Wallace out of his Department.   their willingness to take the oath and their great distress & want of means induces me to make this application for them to return."—LS, DNA, RG 108, Letters Received.

1865, MAY 10, noon.   Maj. Gen. George H. Thomas to USG. "Many officers & soldiers of Johnston's army—who were absent on detached duty, on furloughs & in Hospitals at the time of his surrender, claim the right of parole under the terms of said surrender. Shall I parole them, or require them to take the oath of allegiance, or send them north as prisoners of war?"—Telegram received (at 4:30 P.M.), DNA, RG 107, Telegrams Collected (Bound); *ibid.*, RG 108, Telegrams Received; copies, *ibid.*, RG 393, Dept. of the Cumberland, Telegrams Sent; DLC-USG, V, 54. *O.R.*, I, xlix, part 2, 698. On May 11, 3:20 P.M., Brig. Gen. John A. Rawlins telegraphed to Thomas. "Allow the officers and soldiers of Johnstons Army referred to in your dispatch of 12 m. yesterday, the right of parole under the terms of the surrender. Those whose homes are in Tennessee, or were at the time of their enlistment in States which have not been in rebellion, and who are not excepted from the benefits of the Presidents Amnesty Proclamation, will be allowed to return to those States, on taking the oath prescribed therein. Otherwise they will not."—LS (telegram sent), DNA, RG 107, Telegrams Collected (Bound); telegram sent, *ibid.*; copies, *ibid.*, RG 108, Letters Sent; *ibid.*, RG 393, Dept. of the Cumberland, Telegrams Received;

DLC-USG, V, 46, 76, 108. Printed as received at 4:10 P.M. in *O.R.*, I, xlix, part 2, 718.

1865, MAY 11. USG endorsement. "Respy. returned to the Secretary of War. After an examination of this report and testimony having reference to Gen Hurlbut & Col Robinson I am of the opinion that the public interests will be as well subserved by the immediate trial of Col Robinson as by the arrest, imprisonment and trial of General Hurlbut against whom no formal charges have yet been preferred, and against whom these papers do not furnish a basis for formal charges. Developments may occur in the trial of Robinson that may place Gen Hurlbuts guilt and complicity in a clearer light than is shown by the papers submitted, and be of material service against General Hurlbut should he be tried"—Copy, DLC-USG, V, 58. Written on a letter of April 26 from Maj. Gen. William F. Smith and James T. Brady, New Orleans, concerning Maj. Gen. Stephen A. Hurlbut and Col. Harai Robinson, provost marshal, Dept. of the Gulf.—*Ibid.* See Jeffrey N. Lash, "Stephen Augustus Hurlbut: A Military and Diplomatic Politician, 1815–1882," Ph.D. dissertation, Kent State University, 1980, chapter V.

On May 1, Maj. Gen. Edward R. S. Canby wrote to Secretary of War Edwin M. Stanton. "I have the honor to report, that, upon the application of the Special Commission, of which Major General W. F. Smith is President, I have directed the arrest of Major General S. A. Hurlbut, with a view to his trial upon the charges preferred by that Commission. I have not had time until today to examine the voluminous papers that relate to this subject; and, while they satisfy me of the necessity of this action, they do not, in my judgment, warrant a resort to the extreme measures recommended by the Commission, and which will be resorted to, only, when I am satisfied of a disposition on the part of General Hurlbut to evade an investigation. In view of the gravity of these charges, the rank of the officer implicated, and the important bearing which the investigation will have upon the service in the South West, I have the honor to recommend that the Court may be appointed by the highest authority, and be composed of officers of as high rank and experience as can be spared, and that it may be assembled at as early a period as possible."—ALS, George Cotkin, Brooklyn, N. Y. On May 18, USG endorsed this letter. "Respectfully returned to the Secretary of War. The recommendation of Maj. Gen. Canby in this case is approved." —ES, *ibid.* On the same day, USG wrote to Stanton. "The enclosed dispatches addressed to you I return with answers which I would respectfully recommend the adoption of."—ALS, Straus Collection, NjP. This communication may not refer to the Hurlbut case, but the date and mysterious tone suggest that it does.

On May 27, Hurlbut wrote to Lt. Col. Christian T. Christensen, adjt. for Canby, tendering his resignation.—ALS, DNA, RG 94, ACP, H427 CB 1865. On May 30, Canby endorsed this letter. "Respectf[u]lly forwarded. As Genl Hurlbut is now subject to the action of the War Department upon charges prefered by the Commission of which Major Genl W. F. Smith is President I recomended that ~~the~~ a court be convened for the trial of the charges as soon as possible"—AES, *ibid.* On June 19, USG endorsed this letter. "Believing it inadvisable to have Courts I would advise that Gen. Hurlbut and his staff be mustered out of service at his own request."—AES, *ibid.*

On July 5, Hurlbut, Belvidere, Ill., wrote to Brig. Gen. John A. Rawlins. "I respectfully ask of the Lieut Genl an order to report at Washington about the last of this month. I have secret service accounts which I wish to settle with the Adjutant Genl and am desirous to compel if possible either a public trial on charges hitherto preferred by Maj Genl Smith, or a full retraction before I leave the service. This I think is due to my position and my services without any Egotism on my part I cannot consent to go out of service with any imputation on my good fame, and as a Soldier and a gentleman I urgently request the interposition of the Chief of our Armies who ought to know me if any man does."—ALS, *ibid.*, Letters Received, 991H 1865. On July 10, USG endorsed this letter. "Respectfully refered to, the Sec. of War. I was under the impression that Gn. Hurlbut had been mustered out of service, at his own request. If he has, no order is necessary to enable him to come to Washington. If he has not been mustered out it will probably be well to bring him before a Court Martial."—AES, *ibid.*

On July 6, Hurlbut wrote to Brig. Gen. Lorenzo Thomas. "In obedience to Special order herewith enclosed I report myself at this place waiting orders. I decline to resign and protest against being mustered out until full investigation of the Charges preferred at the instigation of Maj Genl. W. F. Smith, holding myself responsible to military jurisdiction and challenging trial"—ALS, *ibid.*, 931A 1865. On July 19, USG endorsed this letter. "As I understand Gn. Hurlbut was mustered out of service at his own request. It may however save future trouble to give him a trial on charges prefered by Gn. W. F. Smith."—AES, *ibid.*

1865, MAY 11. USG endorsement. "I recommend that this request of this officer be granted, and that it also be extended to his Aid-de-Camp."—ES, DNA, RG 94, Letters Received, 676P 1865. Written on a letter of April 25 from Brig. Gen. William H. F. Payne, Johnson's Island, Ohio, to Maj. Gen. Winfield S. Hancock asking his release by explaining that he had just emerged from hiding to arrange to send his parole to U.S. authorities through his aide when he was captured at 3:00 A.M., April 15.—ALS, *ibid.* See *O.R.*, II, viii, 567–68.

1865, MAY 11. USG endorsement. "There is no duty in the East to which Gen. Buford can be assigned, nor are his services in the field likely to be soon required."—ES, DNA, RG 94, ACP, B46 CB 1863. Written on a letter of March 20 from Brig. Gen. Napoleon B. Buford, St. Louis, to Bvt. Brig. Gen. Edward D. Townsend. "It is quite important to me that the enclosed letter should be placed in the hands of the secretary of War. May I beg of you the favor to place it in his hands? I am on my way to Rock Island Ills where I am ordered to report—As my house is rented for the War, I have no home there at present—I desire to be ordered to Washington, or some place in the East. In my present state of health it would be well for me to have a month of other duties before taking the field—Please write to me at Rock Island—"—ALS, *ibid.*

1865, MAY 11. USG endorsement. "Plan and suggestions within approved."—*O.R.*, III, v, 3. Written on a memorandum of May 1, prepared by Maj. Thomas M. Vincent, AGO, concerning the muster out of vols. —*Ibid.*, pp. 1–3.

1865, MAY 11. USG endorsement. ". . . that immediate action may be had in favor of the very deserving officers named . . ."—Kenneth W. Rendell, Inc., Catalogue 85 [1973], no. 74. Written on a letter of Brig. Gen. Rufus Ingalls.

1865, MAY 11. USG pass. "Lt. Col. O. Latrobe, a paroled prisoner of War, has permission to pass to Canada for the purpose of taking passage to Europe."—ANS (facsimile), *Gary Hendershott Sale 36*, June, 1986, no. 82. Bvt. Brig. Gen. Cyrus B. Comstock added an undated endorsement. "The above named paroled prisoner of war has permission to stay one day at the home of his father J H B Latrobe at the Relay House Md."—ANS (facsimile), *ibid.*

1865, MAY 11. Bvt. Col. Theodore S. Bowers to Maj. Gen. Philip H. Sheridan. "In view of the General Order of the War Department calling for a reduction of the Cavalry force, the Lieutenant General Commanding desires that you will at once order all Officers and men of Cavalry on duty with your Command that belong to Regiments serving elsewhere to join their respective Regiments Maj. Gen, Hancock will be directed to send to your Command all Officers and men that belong to it, and that are now serving in the Middle Military Division"—Copies, DLC-USG, V, 46, 76, 108; DNA, RG 108, Letters Sent. *O.R.*, I, xlvi, part 3, 1136–37.

1865, MAY 11, 8:30 A.M. Maj. Gen. George G. Meade, Fairfax Station, Va., to USG. "I have to report my arrival at this point. The fifth & Second Corps will reach the Occoquan to night. Have you any place Selected for us to camp in? I propose to camp in the Vicinity of Arlington mills unless you desire other wise. I shall await here your reply."—Telegram received (at 9:30 A.M.), DNA, RG 107, Telegrams Collected (Bound); *ibid.*, RG 108, Telegrams Received; copy, DLC-USG, V, 54. Printed as sent at 8:45 A.M. in *O.R.*, I, xlvi, part 3, 1134. On the same day, Bvt. Brig. Gen. Cyrus B. Comstock wrote to Maj. Gen. Christopher C. Augur. "General Meade is now at Fairfax Station and thinks of going into Camp at Arlington Mills, Lt, Gen, Grant desires that you inform him what steps you have taken It will be for him to decide on the position"—Copies, DLC-USG, V, 46, 76, 108; DNA, RG 108, Letters Sent. *O.R.*, I, xlvi, part 3, 1138. At 10:50 A.M. (sent at 11:15 A.M.), Comstock telegraphed to Meade. "Lt. Gen. Grant desires you to use your discretion as to the position of your camp. Gen. Augur had been directed to look out for a position for you to facilitate matters on your arrival & ~~may~~ will be able give you information as to what he has done."—ALS (telegram sent), DNA, RG 107, Telegrams Collected (Bound); telegram sent, *ibid.*; copies, *ibid.*, RG 108, Letters Sent; DLC-USG, V, 46, 76, 108. *O.R.*, I, xlvi, part 3, 1134.

1865, MAY 11.   Maj. Gen. John Pope to USG. "I have the honor to transmit enclosed a letter to the Secretary of War on business of much importance to this State. May I request that you deliver it into his hands for such action as he deems judicious."—Copy, DNA, RG 393, Military Div. of the Mo., Letters Sent. *O.R.*, I, xlviii, part 2, 395. The enclosure, opposing the assessment of disloyal citizens in north Mo. to reimburse loyal citizens for property destroyed, is *ibid.*, pp. 395–97.

1865, MAY 11.   John Eddy and David Wilber, hop merchants, Milford, N. Y., to USG. "We have a Lawsuit pending growing out of our Cotton operations in West Tennessee. The Suit involves a large amount of Money and on the trial it will be important for us to Show in evidence Your order issued about the last of July 1862 prohibiting the payment of Gold for Cotton. If You Could furnish us a Certified Copy of Said order You would greatly oblige . . ."—AL, DNA, RG 108, Letters Received.

1865, MAY 12.   USG endorsement. "Respy, returned. It is inconsistent with the good of the service at the present time to grant Courts Martial or Courts of Inquiry when not possitively demanded by the serious nature of charges made against officers. In the present instance I do not think the necessity exists. I do not think that a single member of the Court of Inquiry on the causes of the failure of the 31st July 1864 thought of casting censure on Gen. Wilcox to the extent of effecting his standing as a General officer. It had not the effect to weaken my confidence in him one iota, and if the present military establishment was to be kept up, I would renew my recommendation formerly made for his promotion to the full rank of Major General"—Copy, DLC-USG, V, 58. Written on a letter of Brig. Gen. Orlando B. Willcox requesting a court-martial.—*Ibid.*

1865, MAY 13.   To Secretary of War Edwin M. Stanton. "I have the honor to acknowledge the receipt of your communication of the 11th inst., enclosing telegram from Major General Halleck, relative to rebel officers at Ft Monroe, and proposition of the Commander of the French Corvette 'Phagelon' to take said officers from that place, and directing me to forward a report of my action in the case. Enclosed herewith please find a copy of telegram on this subject which was sent to General Halleck on the 11th

inst., prior to receipt of your communication."—LS, DNA, RG 94, Letters
Received, 517A 1865. On May 11, Stanton wrote to USG. "I enclose to
you a telegram from Major General Halleck, dated the 10th instant, in relation to some rebel officers at Fortress Monroe proposed to be taken from that
place by the commander of the French corvette 'Phagelon'. You will please
issue to Genl. Halleck such order as you deem proper to meet the case. You
will please report your action to this Department—"—LS, *ibid.*, RG 108,
Letters Received. The enclosure is in *O.R.*, I, xlvi, part 3, 1123. On the
same day, USG telegraphed to Maj. Gen. Henry W. Halleck. "You may
order transportation for all rebel paroled prisoners now at Fort Monroe to
their homes   I would not let French vessels take them"—Telegram sent,
DNA, RG 107, Telegrams Collected (Bound); telegram received, *ibid.*,
Telegrams Collected (Unbound). Printed as sent at 12:30 P.M. in *O.R.*,
I, xlvi, part 3, 1133.

1865, MAY 13.   Secretary of War Edwin M. Stanton to USG. "In order
that provision may be made, without delay, for the payment of troops ordered to Washington, you will please issue instructions (as much in detail
as possible) to the Paymaster General, specifying what troops are to be discharged and what troops will be retained here, with such other information
as may be necessary to enable him to provide for prompt payment."—LS,
DNA, RG 108, Letters Received. On May 19, Brig. Gen. John A. Rawlins
wrote to Bvt. Brig. Gen. Benjamin W. Brice, paymaster gen. "The lieutenant-general desires to know about what time the troops in and around Richmond, and the armies commanded respectively by Generals Sherman and
Meade, and now in the vicinity of Washington, will be paid. Will you please
furnish the desired information?"—*O.R.*, III, v, 28. On May 20, Brice wrote
to Rawlins. "Yours of yesterday this moment received, and I have the honor
to reply: All the efforts of the Treasury have been directed, for the past two
weeks, to the means necessary for the final payment of troops ordered to be
mustered out, amounting, according to the Adjutant General's lists, to about
123.000 men, all told. The payment of these with the large arrears due,
the large bounties due, and the three months extra to officers, will require
about $50.000.000. These payments will be met promptly and without
peradventure, the Treasury having very nearly, if not quite, met the emergency. It will depend upon the ability of the Treasury entirely as to the time
when the payments about which you inquire can be made. I will have an
early conference with the officers of that Department and endeavour to give
you an early response. In addition to the forces named, I regret to say that
Genl Thomas' command, in the West, is yet unpaid since August 31 last.
The Army of the Potomac and troops about Richmond have been paid to
December 31. Therefore after Sherman's Army, paid to August 31, Thomas'
should be next paid. All these payments you will readily perceive will require a very large sum of money to be yet provided."—LS, DNA, RG 108,
Letters Received. *O.R.*, I, xlvi, part 3, 1180; *ibid.*, III, v, 28.

1865, MAY 13.   Maj. Gen. Henry W. Halleck to USG. "Nothing yet heard of the party sent to Lynchburg. There is no telegraph line to that place." —ALS (telegram sent), DNA, RG 107, Telegrams Collected (Unbound); telegram received (at 11:00 A.M.), *ibid.*, Telegrams Collected (Bound); *ibid.*, RG 108, Telegrams Received. *O.R.*, I, xlvi, part 3, 1142. At 11:00 A.M., Halleck telegraphed to USG. "Have just learned that the Sanders papers and books of Orange R. R. company have been secured & are on the way in. Boulware has been captured & will be immediately sent to Washington."—ALS (telegram sent), DNA, RG 107, Telegrams Collected (Unbound); telegram received, *ibid.*

1865, MAY 17.   USG endorsement. "Respectfully returned to his Excellency the President I think this request as to all of the State of Arkansas north of the Arkansas river might with great propriety be complied with, but as to that part of the State south of the Arkansas, I donot think it advisable to comply with it at present"—ES, DNA, RG 56, Div. of Captured and Abandoned Property, Letters Received. Written on a letter of May 6 from William M. Fishback, Carrollton, Ill., to President Andrew Johnson. "You will probably remember my name as the Senator elect from Ark. Having noticed in your proclamation removing the restrictions upon trade in certain Rebellious States that Ark. is omitted, I take the Liberty of calling your attention to certain considerations which I could hope would induce you to open to unrestricted trade all that portion of Ark. lying north of the Arkansas River and including the post of Ft. Smith. As you will remember the State of Ark. has never Seceded by a vote of her people and the convention, after voting down the ordinance, finally voted for Secession only at the point of the bayonett. This should entitle them to favorable consideration at least. In the city of Ft Smith and the northwestern portion of the State where the loyalty has always approached unanimity (being a mountainous region composed mostly of East Tennesseeans) the Armies of the Union remote from any base of supplies were compelled for a long time to subsist on the people consuming their all before the River rose so that supplies could be furnished from elsewhere—Since the rise of the River the trade regulations have still kept back supplies and thus those who have not been compelled to emigrate are left in an absolutely suffering condition. The River will be down in a few weeks so that no more provisions can be carried up. Hence the need of immediate relief and Hence this appeal for which under the circumstance I may be pardoned—"—ALS, *ibid.*

1865, MAY 17.   To Secretary of War Edwin M. Stanton. "In Feby last a letter of recommendation for the promotion of Col Chas. J. Powers 108 N. Y. Infy. to a Brevet Brig. Generalcy, was transmitted to the War. Dept. for its consideration and action. This recommendation, I am assured was strongly endorsed by Brig Genls. T. A. Smythe, S. S. Carroll and Maj Gen. Hancock. It appears that no action has yet been taken by the War Dept.

upon the recommendations submitted. I would therefore respectfully ask that this case receive your favorable consideration at the earliest moment practicable."—LS, DNA, RG 94, ACP, 65P CB 1865.

1865, MAY 17.   USG endorsement. "Respectfully submitted to the Secretary of War with the recommendation that the boat be discharged, and that Gen. L. Thomas be directed to call on the Quartermaster for transportation as he may desire it from time to time."—ES, DNA, RG 94, Letters Received, 320T 1865. Written on a letter of March 17 from Lt. Col. William H. Thurston, New Orleans, to Bvt. Col. Theodore S. Bowers. "In compliance with Special Order No 39. Ex 1. H'Qtrs Armies in the Field 25'th Feby 1865 I have the honor to report that Brig Genl Lorenzo Thomas Adjutant General U. S. A. & his Staff are now using the Steam Boat Rocket for Officers Quaters, while laying at the landing at New Orleans La."—ALS, *ibid.* On March 20, Brig. Gen. Lorenzo Thomas, New Orleans, wrote to Bowers. "I have received an extract from the Department of the Gulf, an extract of Special Orders No 39, dated Head Quarters Army of the United States, City Point, Va., February 25, 1865, prohibiting the use of water transportation of any kind for officers' quarters, or for Head Quarters of Commanding Officers, except when their commands are afloat or in transit by water. It is nearly two years since I received instructions to proceed to the Mississippi river, for the special purpose of taking charge of the large amount of negroes thrown suddenly on our hands, and to organize the able-bodied men into Regiments—It was absolutely necessary that I should have a small steam boat, under my own control, to proceed from point to point on the river, and on which I could transact my business, which, as time went on, rapidly increased, until it assumed vast proportions—As my duties extend from Kentucky to New Orleans and Pensacola, as long as I am on the duty on the river, I do not see how I can dispense with a small steamboat. At first I had such a boat assigned to me, the stern wheel boat 'Rocket', which I have used ever since. Some months since when in Washington, the 'Rocket', having been discharged, I represented the case to the Quartermaster General, who directed the re-charter of the boat for my purposes. And she is now in service under such charter. Under these circumstances I have supposed that the Order was not intended to apply to my case, but, if wrong in this view, I request to be so informed. The Lieutenant General is fully aware of the nature of my duties, and can readily decide the case. As soon as I have an interview with Major General Canby in the Bay of Mobile, I shall ascend the Mississippi, and an answer to this communication will reach me at Memphis."—LS, *ibid.*; (duplicate) *ibid.*, 338A 1865.

1865, MAY 17.   USG endorsement. "Respy. forwarded to the secretary of war. In cases like this, in my opinion it would be well to treat the applicants as sincerely and in good faith desirous of returning to their true allegiance, and to encourage them in so doing by extending to them the full benefits of the Presidents amnesty Proclamation, except where some objection, special to the applicants exists, other than the general ones for which they now stand excepted from its benefits"—Copy, DLC-USG, V, 58. Written on a letter of May 1 of C.S.A. Lt. Col. Thomas G. Williams, Richmond, a paroled prisoner, asking about his status after taking the oath of allegiance. —*Ibid.*

1865, MAY 17.   USG endorsement. "Respy. forwarded to the Sec of War with the recommendation that this request be granted, except in the cases of those committed for investigation, or charged with being guerillas or blockade runners"—Copy, DLC-USG, V, 58. Written on a list of prisoners at the Old Capitol Prison, Washington, D. C., requesting permission to take an oath of allegiance.—*Ibid.*

1865, MAY 17.   USG endorsement. "Respectfully returned to the Secretary of War, disapproved, with the recommendation of the Chief Engineer approved."—ES, DNA, RG 94, Letters Received, 411R 1865. Written on a letter of Dec. 13, 1864, from Chaplain Edward P. Roe, U.S. General Hospital, Fort Monroe, to Secretary of War Edwin M. Stanton asking if a private group could erect a temporary chapel and reading room for the use of soldiers at the hospital.—ALS, *ibid.* On May 11, 1865, Brig. Gen. Richard Delafield endorsed this letter. "Respectfully returned to the Head Quarters of the Army. This Chapel will not only interfere with the defenses of Fort Monroe, but will be an addition to the number of temporary wooden structures already existing outside the fort and constituting a most serious and dangerous evil which should be removed rather than added to"—ES, *ibid.*

1865, MAY 17.   Bvt. Col. Theodore S. Bowers to Maj. Gen. Quincy A. Gillmore. "Your communication of the 29th ult, relating to the north end of Hilton Head Island is recieved,   All the lands on the north end of Hilton Head Island bordering upon Port Royal Harbor S, C, and now reserved for Military purposes will be permanently occupied by the Government for such purposes until further orders"—Copies, DLC-USG, V, 46, 76, 108; DNA, RG 108, Letters Sent. *O.R.,* I, xlvii, part 3, 524. See *ibid.,* p. 351.

1865, MAY 17.   Bvt. Col. Theodore S. Bowers endorsement. "Respy. referred to Maj Gen John Pope, Commanding Military Division of the Missouri who will take such action in this matter as he may deem most expedient"—Copy, DLC-USG, V, 58. *O.R.,* I, xlviii, part 1, 1081. Written on a letter of Col. Charles A. R. Dimon, 1st Vol. Inf., Fort Rice, Dakota Territory, to Maj. De Witt C. Cram, adjt. for Brig. Gen. Alfred Sully, requesting cav.—*Ibid.,* p. 1080.

1865, MAY 18, 4:30 P.M.   To Maj. Gen. Grenville M. Dodge. "The course proposed in your dispatch of 15th towards Indian prisoners in your hands approved."—ALS (telegram sent), DNA, RG 107, Telegrams Collected (Bound); telegram sent, *ibid.*; copies, *ibid.*, RG 108, Letters Sent; DLC-USG, V, 46, 76, 108.

1865, MAY 18. USG endorsement. "No interferance with the execution of the within contract will be caused by the Military Authorities of the United States, but, on the contrary, every facility will be given by them to carry out the contract in good faith."—AES (facsimile), DLC-Miscellaneous Manuscripts. Written on documents of President Abraham Lincoln, March 7, and President Andrew Johnson, May 18, giving permission to James Andrews of Pittsburgh to sell "products of the insurrectionary States" that he claimed "to own or control."—DS, *ibid.* Lincoln, *Works,* VIII, 339–40. A copy of these documents bears an endorsement of Oct. 1 of Brig. Gen. Hugh Ewing stating that the permits were given "for the benefit of the Douglass family."—AES, DLC-Charles Ewing. Using the permits, Andrews bought cotton in Ark. When U.S. authorities seized the cotton, Andrews's claim was disallowed because he had not owned or controlled the cotton.—*HRC,* 46-2-618.

1865, MAY 18. USG endorsement. "Respectfully forwarded, and acceptance of the resignation recommended."—ES, DNA, RG 94, Vol. Service Div., Letters Received, C1400 (VS) 1865. Written on a letter of May 8 from Maj. William C. Carroll, Washington, D. C., to the AG submitting his resignation.—ALS, *ibid.* On June 6, Carroll wrote to the AG. "I have the honor to represent, that in November last, I was tried before a Court Martial at Pine Bluff, Arkansas, and sentenced 'to be cashiered' as promulgated in General Court Martial Orders No 90, Head Quarters Department of Arkansas, Little Rock Arkansas, December 29th 1864. That believing, upon good grounds, this act to have been but a matured conspiracy on the part of certain Officers, whose misdeeds I undertook, and did expose to the Lieutenant General, through his chief of Staff, and that the act of my cashiering was one of wanton injustice I made application to the late President, Mr Lincoln, to have my case referred to the Judge Advocate General for review and report, which was granted, and resulted in the disapproval of the findings and sentence, of said Court Martial, and my restoration to duty, 'by order of the President of the United States, as per enclosed copy of Orders No 235 from your Office. It was believed and understood, by myself, as well as by many prominent Officers serving with the Lieut General, that this order, carried full pay from the date of Cashiering, but after having tendered my resignation, which was accepted at your Office, (Special Orders Nos 254 and 265) I found my construction of the intention of the Order differed from that of the Pay Department. I would now state that I came directly from my Regiment to this City, where I have remained up to the present time, engaged entirely in efforts to obtain the disapproval of the injustice inflicted upon me. That by the delays consequent, and my journey to this place, my expenses have been fully equal to the pay I would draw, in case I am awarded that claimed, also that in consequence of wrong information received at Head Quarters Department of Arkansas, I received pay *only* up to date of Orders Cashiering me, instead of the date of *receipt of* said orders, being one month subsequent, and I am now without any means whatever. I therefore most respectfully ask that an order be issued in my case granting me pay from the 29th day of December 1864, to the date of my honorable discharge from the service"—ALS, *ibid.* On the same day, USG endorsed this letter. "Respectfully forwarded to the Adjutant General of the Army with the recommendation that an order be issued authorizing Major W C Carroll, 13th Ills. Cav., to receive pay from the 29th day of December to the date of his honorable discharge"—ES, *ibid.* See "William C. Carroll in the Civil War," *USGA Newsletter*, X, 2 (Jan. 1973), 7–16.

1865, MAY 18. Bvt. Maj. Gen. Montgomery C. Meigs to USG. "The Potomac at the Aqueduct Bridge, Georgetown, is narrow, and if the armies, after passing in review, are to return to the South Bank of the Potomac, I advise that, to prevent all possibility of accident to the Aqueduct Bridge, a Ponton Bridge be laid to Mason's Island from the docks of Georgetown, and that they return by this route. It is impossible to know the precise condition of every stick of timber in the Aqueduct Bridge, which is old and has frequently been repaired. Its worn timbers are concealed by [sheathing]"— LS, DNA, RG 92, Miscellaneous Letters Sent (Press). *O.R.*, I, xlvi, part 3, 1169. On the same day, Bvt. Col. Theodore S. Bowers endorsed this letter. "Respectfully referred to Maj. Gen. C. C. Augur, commanding Department of Washington."—*Ibid.* See *ibid.*, p. 1170.

1865, MAY 18. Maj. Gen. Henry W. Halleck to USG. "To avoid any misunderstanding among district & local commanders, I suggest that an order be issued that 'the Dept of Virginia will include so much of that state as lies west of the Chesapeake bay & south of the Rappahannock River & of the counties of Fauquier, Warren & Shenandoah'."—ALS (telegram sent), DNA, RG 107, Telegrams Collected (Unbound); telegram received (at 11:00 A.M.), *ibid.*; *ibid.*, RG 94, Letters Received, 230J 1865; *ibid.*, RG 108, Telegrams Received. *O.R.*, I, xlvi, part 3, 1167. On the same day, USG endorsed a telegram received. "Respectfully submitted to the Secretary of War with the recommendation that an order be issued in accordance with the suggestions of Gen Halleck"—ES, DNA, RG 94, Letters Received, 230J 1865. At noon, Brig. Gen. John A. Rawlins telegraphed to Halleck. "All the of City Point, Virginia, and the lands between the James and Appomattox rivers, within and to include the outer line of the defences of City Point will be reserved for military purposes until further orders."—Telegrams sent (2), *ibid.*, RG 107, Telegrams Collected (Bound); copies, *ibid.*, RG 94, War Records Office, Dept. of Va. and N. C.; *ibid.*, RG 108, Letters Sent; DLC-USG, V, 46, 76, 108. Also on May 18, Halleck telegraphed to USG. "I find that staff officers here recieve orders from Washington which often conflict with orders given here, and also lead to movements & operations of which I have no knowledge. This necessarily leads to confusion & delays. Such orders should be sent through me, or at least copies should be sent to me."—ALS (telegram sent), DNA, RG 107, Telegrams Collected (Unbound); telegram received (at 3:40 P.M.), *ibid.*, Telegrams Collected (Bound); (at 3:45 P.M.) *ibid.*, RG 108, Telegrams Received. *O.R.*, I, xlvi, part 3, 1168.

1865, MAY 18.   Maj. Gen. Henry W. Slocum, Alexandria, to Brig. Gen. John A. Rawlins. "I arrived at Alexandria this morning and have taken up my HeadQrs. two miles from Alexandria on the road leading to Washington [I] expect the troops of my command to arrive this evening—Gen Sherman will probably arrive this evening"—Telegram received (at 1:15 P.M.), DNA, RG 107, Telegrams Collected (Bound). Printed as sent at 1:15 P.M., received at 1:20 P.M., in *O.R.*, I, xlvii, part 3, 528.

1865, MAY 18.   Charles Labarthe, Geneva, Switzerland, to USG asking for information of the whereabouts of his son, 1st Lt. Charles Labarthe, 2nd Colored Cav.—ALS (in French), USG 3.

1865, MAY 19.   USG endorsement. "Respectfully forwarded to the Secretary of War. I trust this may meet with favorable consideration and that the necessary orders may be immediately issued appointing the officers to the commands for which they are recommended. No officer in the service has more justly entitled himself ~~more justly~~ to such a recognition of eminent services as this would be, than Major General Jno A Logan."—ES, DNA, RG 94, Letters Received, 1015M 1865. Written on a letter of May 19 from Maj. Gen. William T. Sherman, Alexandria, to Brig. Gen. John A. Rawlins. "I have the honor to apply for the appointment of Major Genl. John A. Logan U. S. V. to the command of the Army of the Tennessee, vice Major Genl. O. O. Howard assigned to duty in the War Department. Also for the appointment of Major Genl. J. B. Hazen U. S. V. to the command of the 15th Corps in the event of the transfer of General Logan."—LS, *ibid. O.R.*, I, xlvii, part 3, 532.

1865, MAY 19, 8:15 P.M.   Brig. Gen. John A. Rawlins to Maj. Gen. Henry W. Halleck. "Lieutenant General Grant desires that you will order all officers and men at the dismounted cavalry camp near City Point belonging to the cavalry commanded by Mjr General Sheridan, now near this city, to ~~report with~~ join their respective regiments with as little delay as practicable."—LS (telegram sent), DNA, RG 107, Telegrams Collected (Bound); telegram sent (at 8:25 P.M.), *ibid.*; telegram received, *ibid.*, Telegrams Collected (Unbound). *O.R.*, I, xlvi, part 3, 1175.

1865, MAY 19.   Bvt. Col. Orville E. Babcock to Maj. Gen. George Crook. "The Lieut, Genl, Comdg directs me to instruct you to report to Maj, Gen, Geo. G. Meade Comdg Army of the Potomac with your Command for the review to take place on the 23rd inst.,"—Copies, DLC-USG, V, 46, 76, 108; DNA, RG 108, Letters Sent. *O.R.*, I, xlvi, part 3, 1177.

1865, MAY 19. Bvt. Col. Theodore S. Bowers to Maj. Gen. Wesley Merritt. "The Lieutenant General Commanding directs that the troops under your Command move with as little delay as practicable from the Camp they now occupy to grounds in the vicinity of Bladensburg, which will be indicated by Col, W, R, Price Asst, Insp- Genl Cavalry Bureau, and also that you report for instructions regarding the review appointed to take place on Tuesday next [*May 23*] to Major General Meade Commanding the Army of the Potomac, under whose orders the Cavalry have been placed for that occasion. The Brigade of Horse Artillery Commanded by Captain Robinson has been directed to report to you for the purpose of moving with the Cavalry at the review on Tuesday"—Copies, DLC-USG, V, 46, 76, 108; DNA, RG 108, Letters Sent. *O.R.*, I, xlvi, part 3, 1177.

1865, MAY 19. Secretary of War Edwin M. Stanton to USG. "I refer to you certain papers herewith, from which it appears that a Provost Court established by Major General Schofield is exercising jurisdiction over civil matters, and other subjects not pertaining to military operations. You are aware that the jurisdiction and authority of such courts have been investigated and reported upon by the Judge Advocate General, and that it has been held that all such jurisdictions are void, unauthorized by any law, and tend greatly to oppression, and the demoralization of the army. You will please issue orders to Genl Schofield that will put a stop to these abuses of authority by Provost Courts, or any military tribunals."—LS, DNA, RG 108, Letters Received. On May 20, 4:30 P.M., Brig. Gen. John A. Rawlins telegraphed to Maj. Gen. John M. Schofield. "Stop all proceedings in the cases before the Provost Court at Newberne. N. C. in which Augustus Johnson and William Behr are defæendants, and in all other cases relating to civil matters pending before such Courts and military tribunals for they are wholly unauthorized by law. Further instructions are on the way to you by mail."—Telegrams sent (2), DNA, RG 107, Telegrams Collected (Bound); telegram received, *ibid.*, Telegrams Collected (Unbound); *ibid.*, RG 109, Union Provost Marshals' Files of Papers Relating to Two or More Citizens. *O.R.*, I, xlvii, part 3, 541. On the same day, Bvt. Col. Theodore S. Bowers wrote to Schofield. "Certain papers of Messrs Johnson and Behr have been referred to these HeadQuarters by the Secretary of War, from which it appears that a Provost Court, established by your orders is exercising jurisdiction over civil matters and other subjects not pertaining to military operations, The jurisdiction and authority of such Courts have been investigated and reported upon by the Judge Advocate General and held by him to be void and unauthorized by any law, You will therefore issue orders immediately upon receipt of this, revoking all orders empowering Provost Courts or any other Military tribunals, to adjudge or in any manner pass upon cases of purely a Civil character that may have been issued by you or that may be in existence in your Department and correcting as far as possible any abuses of authority that may have been had, by such Courts and un-authorized Military tribunals"—Copies, DLC-USG, V, 46, 76, 108; DNA, RG 108, Letters Sent. *O.R.*, I, xlvii, part 3, 542.

1865, MAY 19. Maj. Gen. Henry W. Halleck to USG. "I am informed that the following troops of the twenty fifth (25) Corps are absent from the Department of Virginia, viz: The twenty ninth (29) Conn and de-tachments of the tenth (10) and twenty eighth (28) U S Regiments are at Point Lookout, and the twenty second (22) U S Regiment at Port To-bacco, Md."—Telegram received (at 10:40 A.M.), DNA, RG 107, Tele-grams Collected (Bound); (at 11:40 A.M.) *ibid.*, RG 108, Telegrams Re-ceived; *ibid.*, RG 393, Middle Military Div., Telegrams Received; copy, DLC-USG, V, 54. Printed as sent at noon in *O.R.*, I, xlvi, part 3, 1174. On the same day, Bvt. Col. Theodore S. Bowers endorsed this telegram. "Re-spectfully referred to Maj Gen W. S. Hancock Comd'g Mid. Mil. Div. who will releive all the troops within named with the least possible delay, and order them to join their Corps, which is under orders to move at once to the south—He will also direct the Commanding Officers of each organiza-tion to report by telegraph immediately on being releived to Maj Gen Halleck, Richmond for orders—He will also provide necessary transporta-tion from their present stations to City Point, unless otherwise ordered by Gen Halleck—"—ES, DNA, RG 393, Middle Military Div., Telegrams Received.

1865, MAY 19. Vladislav, Chevalier de Zieliński, Poland, to [USG] re-questing information concerning his brother, Jaroslav Jacob, Chevalier de Zieliński, 4th Mass. Cav.—ALS (in French), USG 3. On June 19, Bvt. Col. Adam Badeau wrote to Maj. Gen. Alfred H. Terry requesting this in-formation, and endorsements indicate that Zieliński was serving as private, Co. G, 4th Mass. Cav.—ALS and ES, *ibid.* See Stanley Sadie, ed., *The New Grove Dictionary of Music and Musicians* (London, 1980), 20, 681.

1865, MAY 20, 2:00 P.M. To Maj. Gen. George G. Meade. "I have no objection whatever to the cadence step being used from the capitol to the Presidents House, but only require it for the distance indicated in the order for the review."—Telegrams sent (2), DNA, RG 107, Telegrams Col-lected (Bound); copies, *ibid.*, RG 108, Letters Sent; DLC-USG, V, 46, 76, 108. At 10:30 A.M., Meade telegraphed to USG. "Have you any ob-jection to the cadence step being taken from the Capitol to the Presidents house—I think both officers & men desire it—"—ALS (telegram sent), DNA, RG 393, Army of the Potomac, Miscellaneous Letters Received; telegram received (at 12:35 P.M.), *ibid.*, RG 107, Telegrams Collected (Bound); *ibid.*, RG 108, Telegrams Received.

1865, MAY 20.   USG endorsement. "Respectfully returned—There is such an apparant want of sympathy between our Armies and the French Armiesy in the support of Maximillian in Mexico that I cannot recommend compliance with this request."—ES, DNA, RG 107, Miscellaneous Letters Received. Written on a letter of May 19 from Act. Secretary of State William Hunter to Secretary of War Edwin M. Stanton. "The Minister of France has presented at this Department Messrs M. M Wolf Legoune, Viellaume, and Claudel officers of the staff and of the line of the French army in Mexico who are understood to be on their way to their own country, and has asked for them passes to visit the hospitals, arsenals, quarter masters offices, and other places in this vicinity interesting to members of the profession. I will thank you to cause the request to be complied with."—LS, *ibid.*

1865, MAY 20.   USG endorsement concerning retaining a good paymaster in service.—Forest H. Sweet, List No. 105, item 91.

1865, MAY 21.   To Capt. William M. Dunn, Jr., Philadelphia. "I will see that Mrs. Southwicks father has quarters provided for him in Washington."—ALS (telegram sent), DNA, RG 107, Telegrams Collected (Bound). On May 20, USG had telegraphed to Mrs. Southwick, Philadelphia, "stating he could not secure the rooms at Willard's for her father." —Parke-Bernet Galleries Sale No. 1744, March 26, 1957, p. 46. On May 27, Dunn, Washington, D. C., telegraphed to Mr. Southwick, Philadelphia. "Mrs Southwick left for home on 11.15 train."—ALS (telegram sent), DNA, RG 107, Telegrams Collected (Bound).

1865, MAY 22, 11:25 A.M.   Maj. Gen. John Pope to USG. "Can permission now be obtained from English minister to pursue hostile Indians into British uninhabited Territory   I wish to send a Cavalry force to Devils Lake against some bands of hostile Indians but it will be useless to do so unless we can obtain this permission as Indians are only a few miles South of British Line & can retreat into British Territory as soon as troops get near them   We cannot have entire peace on Minnesota frontier unless we can pursue hostile indians into British Territory & the English will prevent British subjects from furnishing hostile indians with means to Commit hostilities"—Telegram received (at 12:40 P.M.), DNA, RG 107, Telegrams Collected (Bound); (at 1:00 P.M.) *ibid.*, RG 108, Telegrams Received; copies, *ibid.*, RG 393, Military Div. of the Mo., Telegrams Sent; DLC-USG, V, 54. *O.R.*, I, xlviii, part 2, 539–40.

1865, MAY 22.   Maj. Gen. John Pope to USG. "I have the honor to transmit enclosed copies of despatches received from Generals Dodge and Reynolds. The Bushwhackers and Guerrillas in AMissouri and Arkansas are rapidly coming in and surrendering. There will be peace and quiet in Missouri and Northern Arkansas I think very shortly provided the people do not persecute and maltreat those who have been in the Rebel Army and the Bush, but who have surrendered and are coming in to surrender. I will endeavor to keep down any such exhibition of hostility. Since I last wrote you three of the Mail Stations on the Overland Route have been attacked but the assailants were repulsed. These stations are this side of Fort Kearney and actually within the White settlements where no danger was apprehended. There are some singular circumstances connected with these attacks which render it considerably more than doubtful whether Indians had anything to do with them. The settlers had no knowledge that there were any hostile Indians in the Country. Nothing was known of the matter until the attacks were made and it is very singular that none of the white settlements or settlers were molested. I need not tell you that there are a great many lawless rascals roaming about the Country particularly is this the case along the Kansas border. Thousands of disloyal men have left Missouri for the Idaho and Colorado mines are now scattered about the frontier. I have little doubt that if a good opportunity presented these roving reckless men would attack a train or Mail Coach and Station. I am investigating these last attacks and I very much incline to the belief that they will be found to have been made by white men or half breeds. General Dodge anticipating no danger this side of Fort Kearney had ordered all trains to be organized at that Post and escorted beyond. There has been no trouble whatever either on the Salt Lake or Santa Fe routes except these last attacks *within* the settlements—These will be attended to."—LS, DNA, RG 108, Letters Received. *O.R.*, I, xlviii, part 2, 540–41. The enclosures are *ibid.*, pp. 466, 472, 509, 512, 523–24, 528, 545, 549.

1865, MAY 22.   U.S. Senator Benjamin F. Wade of Ohio to USG. "The Committee on the Conduct of the War have hitherto found themselves unable to take testimony in regard to the many campaigns in which you have been engaged since the commencement of the rebellion. They desire to place upon their record some reliable account of those campaigns, and as the most ready way of doing so, they have directed me to forward to you the enclosed interrogatories, and to request you to prepare answers to them, & to forward the same to the Chairman at any time prior to the commencement of the next session of Congress for publication. The Committee desire that you will make your statement as full & detailed as may be necessary to a clear understanding of the subject of enquiry. And for that purpose they would like for you to submit such interrogatories as may suggest themselves to you, to those of your subordinates whom you may deem best qualified to give information; their answers to be forwarded with your own."—LS, DNA, RG 108, Letters Received. The enclosure: "Q—Please state what positions you have held & what commands you have exercised since then commencement of the rebellion, giving the periods during which those respective commands have been exercised by you. Q—Please state such particulars as you may deem necessary to a proper understanding of the several campaigns in which you have been engaged: setting forth the orders & instructions under which those campaigns were conducted, and the principal orders and instructions given by you: with such incidents & circumstances as you consider will be of interest to the public: appending to your statement copies of your, reports & those of your principal subordinates keeping the account of each campaign by itsself as far as convenient"—*Ibid.* USG did not respond. Reports of commanders who answered these questions were printed in supplementary volumes of the 1865 report of the Joint Committee on the Conduct of the War.

1865, MAY 23. Maj. Gen. John Pope to USG. "Following dispatch from Gen Dodge just received. Gen Connor who Commands Colorado & nebraska & has charge of overland routes is the very best and most active officer I have & can be thoroughly trusted Brigade of Cavalry here not yet mounted We have no other to send . . . Genl Connor reports that five hundred 500 Indians attacked three 3 Crossings on Sweetwater & torn down Telegh wire He says the Indians are coming down from north in large bodies & threaten the line all way to Salt Lake & that he will need considerable more Cav'y I think we better get a few regts at Ft Leavenworth besides those here If I have to throw in more troops on the South Pass line it will take some three 3 Regts more. Signed. G M DODGE Maj Gen"—Telegram received (at 12:40 P.M.), DNA, RG 107, Telegrams Collected (Bound); *ibid.*, RG 108, Telegrams Received; copies, *ibid.*, RG 393, Military Div. of the Mo., Telegrams Sent; DLC-USG, V, 54. *O.R.*, I, xlviii, part 2, 544, 565.

1865, MAY 23. Maj. Gen. John Pope to USG. "I have the honor to transmit enclosed a copy of a letter from General Curtis in relation to a late Indian Raid in Minnesota. That you may fully understand the situation there it will be proper for me to make the following statement. Up to the time of the Massacres in Minnesota in 1862, several tribes of Sioux Indians now hostile occupied the upper Minnesota river and were in immediate contact with the White settlements. The usual difficulties resulting from this close contact of Whites and Indians broke out and culminated in the dreadful atrocities of the Indian massacres of the summer of 1862. I arrived in Minnesota about the last of September of that year. Colonel (now Brig Genl) Sibley had been sent to the frontier by the Governor of the State with all the troops that could be collected. The Indians in force were devastating the entire border settlements and had destroyed at least one considerable town. Large numbers of people estimated by persons of standing in Saint Paul at 50.000 had abandoned their farms and villages and were crowding into the large towns on the Mississippi river. Every where I found consternation and dismay. Sibley was successful in beating the Indians (who fought him boldly in large force). An expedition under Sibley was sent against the Indians in 1863 and a cooperating force under Sully sent up the Missouri river in the same Summer. Both expeditions met and defeated the Indians. In 1864 Sully again marched against them from the upper Missouri and defeated

them in several severe fights. The results are, that the Sioux Indians have
been entirely driven from Minnesota. There is no large body of these Indians
who are hostile, nearer to the settlements of Minnesota than Devils Lake
in Dakotah Territory a distance of over three hundred miles. The late excitement in Minnesota was caused by what is said to be a raiding party of
sixteen Indians on foot who came from Devil's Lake passed the outer line
of Military posts without being discovered and were first heard of near
Mankato on the Minnesota River. The fact that this party was headed by
one Carpenter a half-breed who had enlisted in our Army, had served in
Tennessee, was then tried for robbery, escaped and came back to Minnesota
renders it doubtful whether the party were really not men like himself and
not Indians. There are in Minnesota eighteen Companies of Cavalry four
Companies of Infantry and one Company of Artillery. The District of Minnesota in which these troops are is Commanded by General Sibley one of
the earliest citizens of the State and a man of character and standing. He has
lived twenty five years or more in that section of Country and is thoroughly
familiar with it and with the tribes of Sioux Indians concerned. It would
seem then that with a force of more than twenty three hundred men according to General Sibley's last return and those mostly Cavalry Commanded
by an Officer who has always lived in the state and knows the Country and
the Indians well, Minnesota has been furnished by the General Government with every means for protection against Indians. Surely if this large
force of Cavalry cannot protect the settlements against sixteen Indians on
foot who are obliged to traverse a distance of over three hundred miles and
pass a line of Military Posts before they can reach any of the frontier settlements, it would be difficult to say how many troops would be necessary.
This is all that has occasioned the stampede in Minnesota, and it seems
strange that such a raid of a few Indians on foot should have been made
undiscovered over such a great distance and permitted to reach the frontier.
Of course if this party really came all the way from Devil's Lake it was due
to carelessness and want of vigilence of the troops. In addition to the troops
mentioned however there is a considerable number of half breeds and Indian
Scouts who are occupied in watching the country beyond the posts. Through
these scouts also, this small party of Indians on foot must have passed. The
hostile Sioux driven from Minnesota and the southern portions of Dakotah
Territory have made a temporary rendezvous at Devil's Lake in the northern part of Dakotah. This great lake is near the British Line and whenever
the Indians are pressed they take refuge in the British possessions. By
British subjects these Indians are supplied with arms, amunition and all
other articles they need and are encouraged and incited to keep up hostilities. So long as these Indians are at war with the people of the United States
the British Settlements monopolise the trade with them. Again and again
their unfriendly acts, to call them no worse, have been brought to the notice
of British Officials, without eliciting any satisfactory results. Permission
has been asked to pursue these hostile Indians who have murdered women
and children into the uninhabited portions of the British possessions but

permission has been refused by the English Government which will neither protect our frontier from hostile savages harboring in British Territory nor permit the United States Government to do so in the only manner possible. I shall send a force to Devils Lake, but the Indians will only retreat a few miles across the British Line where they will be safe. We are compelled in fact to occupy a line of frontier posts in Minnesota to protect the settlements against small raiding bands of these Indians. There is not and cannot be any thing like an Indian War. There seems to me to be troops enough in Minnesota with ordinary care for complete security. The fact is, in relation to the Indian Tribes on the Plains, that we are now reaping the harvest of the bad management and bad policy which have characterized our Indian system for so many years. The Indians are every day in the hope that a treaty of peace such as has hitherto been made, will be offered them, thus securing them immunity for what they have done and supplies of goods, and money and arrangements for yearly annuities of both. They keep up hostilities in this view and in the light of their past experience they are doubtless right enough. It has long been a saying of the Sioux Indians along the Platte river that whenever they were poor and needed blankets and powder and lead they had only to go down on the overland routes and kill a few White men, and so bring about a 'treaty' which would supply their wants for a time. The effects of this system we are now enjoying. There is however another and a wider view of our present relation with the Indians of the Plains and of the Rocky Mountains which should engage serious attention and enlist an earnest effort to arrive at some definite and permanent policy. The great development of mining regions in Colorado, Montana and Idaho has attracted enormous numbers of Emigrants who are crowding over the plains in every direction and on every route. The Indian Country is penetrated every where, highways are made through it and the game driven off or killed. The Indians are therefore crowded more and more into narrow limits where they are less able every day to subsist themselves by hunting. Of course they are becoming exasperated and desperate and avail themselves of every opportunity to rid their Country of the Whites. The opportunities are numerous enough owing to the carelessness and eagerness to reach the mines, of the White Emmigrants. They have been in the habit of travelling without precaution in the smallest parties and striving with each other to arrive first in the Mining regions. The Indians always watchful and alert lose no opportunity of attacking them. We can by sending troops enough beat these Indians whereever they appear but what is to become of them? Every day is reducing them more and more to actual suffering for food and with this rush of Emigrants continued for a few years their game will become so scarce that they cannot live at all. Of course we fight them to protect our people. They keep up hostilities in the expectation every day of making treaties which will supply their necessities for a time and as these necessities will grow greater every day and the supplies will last for a less and less time we seem likely to have an endless Indian War under the present system. If we now make one of the usual treaties with

them it will only encourage them to another outbreak as soon as the supplies given them under such a treaty are exausted. I still think that the
plan proposed in my letter to the Secretary of War referred to in previous
letters to you is the best both for the sake of the Government and of the
Indian. Wisdom and humanity alike seem to demand some policy which
shall save the Indian from complete and violent extinction. This question
is now directly and barely presented. Either the extermination of the Indian
tribes by force or some policy of supporting them by the General Government at places where deprived of Arms and of the power to do injury or
indulge their wandering habits, they can be subsisted and protected and
subjected under the most favorable circumstances to all the influences of
education and Christianity. This generation of Indians might not profit
by such a system but the next would and even this generation could be
made harmless members of a community under charge of the General Government. This subject demands and should recieve serious attention. Your
own experience on the frontier and in Indian service makes you as familiar
as I am with this whole matter. You know the means which Indian Agents,
Indian Traders and other unscrupulous white men more or less directly engaged in Indian trade, will resort to in the Newspapers or otherwise to
thwart any effort to change the present deplorable condition of affairs. You
know how Officers exposing these abuses and seeking to bring about needed
reforms, will be abused and denounced, and how every sort of effort will
be made to depreciate them and secure their removal from Command. With
all such proceedings your experience has made you familiar and you know
very well that in these Indian affairs no man can make a movement towards reform without paying the penalty in abuse and Misrepresentation.
How much influence with the authorities such attacks on an Officer thus
seeking honestly to inform his Government and reform abuses, has had
or is likely to have it would be difficult to say but I trust that the report of
the Congressional Committee lately sent out to examine into the abuses of
the present Indian System and the conduct of Indian Officials will go far to
enlighten the public mind and destroy the effect of malicious abuse. I care
little for such attacks coming from such people except as they affect the
Authorities at Washington and through them the best intersests of the
public service."—LS, DNA, RG 108, Letters Received. *O.R.*, I, xlviii, part
2, 565–68. The enclosure is *ibid.*, pp. 412–13.

1865, MAY 24, 10:10 P.M.   To Maj. Gen. John M. Palmer. "If Mar-
quette is not a Paroled prisoner of War arrest and confine him. His being a
French subject gives him no privileges whatever but aggrevates his of-
fence."—ALS (telegram sent), DNA, RG 107, Telegrams Collected
(Bound); telegram sent, *ibid.*; telegram received, *ibid.*, RG 109, Union
Provost Marshals' File of Papers Relating to Individual Civilians.

1865, MAY 24, 4:00 P.M.   Maj. Gen. John Pope to USG. "The following
despatch from Gen Dodge just received. We have not at present troops

enough to furnish escorts to all these parties but hope soon to clear the region of Indians—We will certainly do so as soon as I can get the brigade of Cavalry, now here, mounted—Fort Leavenworth may twenty fourth (24) Sixty five (65) MAJ GEN POPE I find on arrival here some five (5) surveying parties under General Contract, Two (2) Indian Agents, one wagon road company & others all asking for Escorts—The Country they operate in is entirely unsafe & it will take at least Regt part Infantry & part Cavalry to supply the demand This is getting to be a serious question & I would like your advice If I give escorts I will have to bring the troops here to do it—The parties seems to have proper claims on the Govt The freight contractors to Utah & New Mexico have to be guarded and the number of trains leaving on Govt account will use up a Small army The Indian Agents have goods but Col Livingston got after their Indians & used them up I think all the band that was engaged in robberies this side of Kearney were killed Signed G M DODGE M G"—Telegram received (at 6:00 P.M.), DNA, RG 107, Telegrams Collected (Bound); *ibid.*, RG 108, Telegrams Received; copies, *ibid.*, RG 393, Military Div. of the Mo., Telegrams Sent; DLC-USG, V, 54. *O.R.*, I, xlviii, part 2, 583.

1865, MAY 24. Brig. Gen. Rufus Ingalls to Brig. Gen. John A. Rawlins. "I have the honor to inform you, that the Master of Transportation of the Baltimore & Ohio R. R. reports that there can be transported over that road on thirty six hours notice, 'from Washington to the West via Relay House five thousand men or more daily, and six thousand others daily from Washington to Baltimore at the same time, making eleven thousand men daily from fWashington to the West and North' I have also just been informed, that the Michigan Cavalry, ~~will~~ would commence loading at 10 A. M. to day."—LS, DNA, RG 108, Letters Received. *O.R.*, I, xlvi, part 3, 1203.

1865, MAY 24. Silas F. Miller, Burnet House, Cincinnati, to USG. "I write you this to ask your interposition, in behalf of one of the oppressed residents of Vicksburg, to explain the matter still further, I will give you a short history of his action in the commencement of the rebellion, I allu[de] to the Hon Thomas A Marshall a lawyer of Vicksburg, and one who had attained considerable eminence in his profession, When the election for Members of the Mississippi convention was ordered he was elected as a cooperationist, which if you remember was the mildest name they dare assume who professed Union sentiments, as such he was elected from Warren Co to the convention, and opposed the ordnance of secession in the ablest speech of his life, the ordnance of secession as you well Know was passed, he refused to sign it, and when compelled to do so, did it under protest, and has never had any thing to do with the War; but has resided at Newton station ever since Farragut first passed Vicksburg with his fleet, having been ordered away by the so called confederate authorities, When he left Vicksburg with his family he left a Mr Muir, in posession of his dwelling and the same person has occupied it ever since, or a small portion of it, the Treasury agents however I believe now claim it as abandoned property, and a Mr Montague resides in it with the exception of one or two rooms, which Mr Muir still occupies, I have just received a letter from Mr T A Marshall, who is my brother in law, asking to be put in posession of his property in Vicksburg and Warren Co. Miss, of which he owns a considerable amont, He has a large family some ten children and this is his all, he wishes to return to Vicksburg in the fall with his family and without this property he and his wife with their large family are penniless The question is whether these Treasury agents of whose conduct generally you are as well aware as I am can tell you, are to despoil a man of his property, who dared to stand by the Union, when secession was rampant, or whether our govenment is going to see that all citizens have their rights who have thus acted. I Know and feel that your orders in regard to this matter will be respected by all officers Civil as well as Military, I therefore ask of you to send to my address here an order for any one having possession of Thomas A Marshalls property to give up the same to him or his agents, With a thousand thanks for your effective measures in putting down this rebellion . . ." —ALS, DNA, RG 108, Letters Received. On May 31, Bvt. Col. Theodore S. Bowers endorsed this letter. "Respectfully referred to the commanding General Department of Mississippi, who will order the restoration to Mr. Marshal of all property belonging to him where it can be restored; and where it can not, by reason of previous action by the Treasury agents, report the facts in full to these Headquarters."—ES, *ibid.*

1865, MAY 25. To Secretary of War Edwin M. Stanton. "I would respectfully recommend the appointment of Brig. Gen. J. D. Webster, Chief of Staff to General Sherman, to the rank of Major General by brevet. Gen. Webster has served from the begining of the rebellion to the present time most faithfully and has well earned this mark of recognition. As Gen. Webster may be leaving the city within a few days I would be pleased if this appointment could be given without delay."—ALS, DNA, RG 94, ACP, W1016 CB 1865.

1865, MAY 25. USG endorsement. "Respectfully fo[r]warded to the Secretary of War. I approve of Maj Gen Pope's orders and instructions touching the treatment of Indians and the management of Indian affairs on our frontiers, and earnestly recommend their approval by Government. If we can keep white men, Indian Agents, and traders except those under proper military control from among the Indians, I believe we can have quiet on the frontiers. Immediate action is most respectfully asked in this matter."—ES, DNA, RG 94, Letters Received, 1390A 1865. Written on a letter of May 18 from Maj. Gen. John Pope to USG. "General Conner reports from Denver City the surrender of two thousand, Sioux and Arapahoes and that he expects the surrender of three thousand more in a short time. General Sully reports that runners have come in to Fort Rice on the Upper Missouri announcing the approach of three thousand lodges (about seven thousand warriors) to that post to see him and beg for peace. In order to avoid the certain results of the present system of treaty making by Indian Agents, involving the expenditure of much money and the presenting of large quantities of goods to Indians but recently hostile who regard such gifts as bribes dictated by fear, I have instructed the Commanding Officers on the frontier, that Indians in actual hostility must be dealt with by the Military alone and that all Indians who have been recently in arms against the whites, and who are now coming in to beg for peace, are considered prisoners of War under the exclusive control of the Military authorities. No presents are to be given to them and no Treaties made beyond the mere understanding to be had with them by the Military Authorities, that so long as the Indians keep the peace they will not be molested by the U. S. Troops. That if they continue to be hostile the troops will continue to pursue and kill them and will continue to establish new Military Posts in their country and drive off or destroy all their game. The troops also guarantee the Indians against outrages by the whites and will assist all who come in and surrender to defend themselves against other hostile Tribes. The Indians perfectly understand such a Treaty as this and will keep it much better than such treaties as have hitherto been made. I have directed Commanding Officers on the frontier not to permit any Treaties to be made with Indians other than such as are herein specified. Of course the Indian Dept will object strenuously to this course. There are large sums appropriated by Congress at its last session to make Treaties with Indians. It is simply a waste of money, and will only lead to renewed breaches of peace in order that new Treaties may be made and more money expended. I need not tell you that the present system of Indian management is bad. Your experience on the frontier has long since made this very clear I do not doubt. I send you the paper of Hon I. K. Brown of Minnesota on this subject which was inadvertently left out of my last letter to you on this subject. It is full of wisdom, and I think expresses the experience of every honest man who has lived on the frontier and knows the history of Indian management. The Cheyennes will probably be the only tribe on the Plains, west of the Missouri, which will remain hostile this summer; with them we can easily deal. The overland routes are secure and will I think remain so. Some plan for the disposition and management of the large numbers of Indians coming in to surrender ought to be adopted. It is certain that they ought not to be rewarded by presents and by arrangements to pay them regular annuities of money and goods, for the outrages they have committed. The practice seems to be to reward *hostile* Indians but not peaceful Indians. It seems to me best to keep all these Indians under Military control according to the orders I have made on the subject, copies of which were forwarded to you a short time since. My letter to the Secretary of War published in the Official Army and Navy Gazette of April 26th 1864. I think covers this whole subject and I trust it will be sustained by the Government, as it promises peace at a small cost of money or life. I transmit enclosed a letter just received from General Curtis. I do not attach much importance to the 'stampede' they seem to be getting up in Minnesota. It has been of yearly occurrence ever since I have been in this region. Small raids are to be expected; but eighteen Companies of Cavalry and four of Infantry seem to me enough to protect the settlements. I do not see what could be done with more. A campaign against Indians at Devil Lake would be enormously expensive and would lead to no good results so long as the Indians can find refuge in British Territory only a few miles north of Devils Lake. We cannot cross the British Line to pursue them, permission having been refused by the British Government. There are only a part of the Indians in that region who are hostile. I will endeavor soon to go up to Minnesota myself. I have had so much of the same kind of exaggerated reports from that quarter for the past two years that I do not attach any great consequence to General Curtis's letter. He has not had the same experience of the 'specu-lative' character of these alarms and calls for Troops, that I have had. If I find that more troops are really needed in Minnesota, I will advise you."— LS, *ibid. O.R.*, I, xlviii, part 2, 492–94. The enclosed letter of Maj. Gen. Samuel R. Curtis is *ibid.*, pp. 412–13. Also on May 18, Pope had tele-graphed to USG. "I have eighteen (18) companies of Cavalry & four (4) of Infantry in Minnesota. I consider this force able if properly disposed and handled. I do not anticipate any serious Indian disturbances in that State. There will probably be occasional small raids to steal horses. Have written you fully today concerning Indian affairs"—Telegram received (at 2:55 P.M.), DNA, RG 107, Telegrams Collected (Bound); *ibid.*, RG 108, Tele-grams Received; copies, *ibid.*, RG 393, Military Div. of the Mo., Telegrams Sent; DLC-USG, V, 54. *O.R.*, I, xlviii, part 2, 492. On May 26, Pope endorsed a letter of Curtis. "This letter of Genl. Curtis is respectfully for-warded for the information of the Genl. in Chief. It contains substantially the same view of the Indian 'Stampede' in Minnesota hitherto sent."— Copy, DNA, RG 393, Military Div. of the Mo., Register of Letters Re-ceived. *O.R.*, I, xlviii, part 2, 474. The Curtis letter is *ibid.*

1865, MAY 25. USG endorsement. "Respectfully refered to the Sec. of War with recommendation that Col. Myers be appointed a Brig. Gn. by Bvt."—AES, David R. Smith, Burbank, Calif. Written on a letter of May 21 from Brig. Gen. Robert Allen, Louisville, to USG. "I find that L. B. Parsons has just been made a Brigadier General, and that Col. W. Myers is still passed over Knowing how faithfully and efficiently Col. M. has performed his duties, and seeing that many of his juniors are promoted over him, I venture again to ask your kind offices in his behalf. Of course Brigadier Generals commissions will be no longer granted to Staff Officers, but there is room for brevets, and this is all that I ask for him"—ALS, *ibid.*

1865, MAY 25. Brig. Gen. John A. Rawlins to Maj. Gen. Winfield S. Hancock. "You will please relieve by other troops all your West Virginia and Maryland troops now on duty guarding Rail roads, and report them through these Head Quarters to the Secretary of War, for musterout of the service"—Copies, DLC-USG, V, 46, 76, 108; DNA, RG 108, Letters Sent.

O.R., I, xlvi, part 3, 1216. On the same day, Bvt. Col. Theodore S. Bowers wrote to Hancock. "Please send immediately one large regiment, or two smaller ones, of good reliable troops to Fort Delaware to relieve the 11th Maryland regiment now on duty there, As soon as the Maryland regiment is relieved order it to Baltimore and report it for musterout, The regiments sent forward should leave behind, all men whose term of service will expire under existing orders."—Copies, DLC-USG, V, 46, 76, 108; DNA, RG 108, Letters Sent. *O.R.*, I, xlvi, part 3, 1216.

1865, MAY 25. Bvt. Col. Theodore S. Bowers to Bvt. Brig. Gen. Henry E. Davies. "To the end that the Cavalry force under your Command may be supplied with as much economy as possible, The Lieutenant General Commanding directs that it be moved from its present position to Camps to be selected by you in the rear of Alexandria, along the line of the Orange and Alexandria Rail road, the situation of the new Camp, you are desired to see that the Citizens are put by the presence of your troops, to the least inconvenience practicable, and it is especially enjoined upon you to issue the most stringent orders to prevent any unnecessary depredations upon private property"—Copies, DLC-USG, V, 46, 76, 108; DNA, RG 108, Letters Sent. *O.R.*, I, xlvi, part 3, 1212. On May 26, Bowers wrote to Maj. Gen. Christopher C. Augur. "The order will be issued to day assigning the Cavalry force at present Commanded by Brig, Gen, H, E, Davies to your Command, This Cavalry is now encamped near Bladensburg, but instructions were issued yesterday for it to move to the rear of Alexandria and establish Camp along the line of the Orange and Alexandria R, R,"—Copies, DLC-USG, V, 46, 76, 108; DNA, RG 108, Letters Sent. On the same day, Brig. Gen. John A. Rawlins wrote to the AG. "The Lieutenant General. commanding desires that an order be issued, and sent out to day, assigning the Cavalry force, at present commanded by Brigadier General H. E. Davies, to duty in the Department of Washington; and directing that it be reported accordingly to Major General Augur, the Department commander."—LS, *ibid.*, RG 94, Letters Received, 545A 1865. See *O.R.*, I, xlvi, part 3, 1218.

1865, MAY 25. Bvt. Col. Theodore S. Bowers endorsement. "Respectfully referred to Maj. Gen. J. M. Schofield, Com'd'g Department of North Carolina for investigation and report."—AES, DNA, RG 108, Letters Received. *O.R.*, I, xlvii, part 3, 431. Written on a letter of May 7 from Capt. Henry Brown, Co. H, 10th Ohio Cav., to "Chief of Police." "On the fourth of May/65 Companies B. & K. of the 10th Ohio Vols Cav at the rail Road Companies Shops of the North Carolina Rail Road between Hillsboro & Greensboro N. C. found between $80.000 & $100.000 in Gold burried, in boxes and sacks, and Marked Commercial Bank of New Berrne N. C. the Money has been devided Amongst the finders and Officers of the command, There is to be An investigation of the Matter by Division Officers but of course that will not Amount to Any thing, I understand some of the Officers concerned Are About resigning with their Booty in their pockets, I should have sent information through the proper Military chanel but have no ideas that such a comunication would reach the proper source, If Any Action is taken in the Matter it Should be at Once"—ALS, DNA, RG 108, Letters Received. *O.R.*, I, xlvii, part 3, 431. On June 6, Maj. Gen. John M. Schofield endorsed this letter. "Respectfully returned. My attention was called to this matter some two weeks ago and steps were immediately taken to recover the money. Several thousand dollars have been recovered and I hope to get much more, but it will take time, as the most of it was secreted by the men who found it. I will make a full report as soon as practicable."—AES, DNA, RG 108, Letters Received. *O.R.*, I, xlvii, part 3, 431. See *ibid.*, pp. 512, 522, 632.

1865, MAY 25. Maj. Thomas T. Eckert to USG. "By direction of the Secy of War I send you herewith copy of a cipher telegram found on the person of Genl Wheeler of the Rebel Army & forwarded to this Dep't by Br Genl Schoepf Com'd'g at Fort Delaware—"—ALS, DNA, RG 108, Letters Received. *O.R.*, I, xlviii, part 2, 591. The enclosed telegram of March 7 from Gen. Edmund Kirby Smith to C.S.A. President Jefferson Davis is *ibid.*, I, xlviii, part 1, 1411–12.

1865, MAY 25. Brig. Gen. John D. Stevenson to Brig. Gen. John A. Rawlins. "~~Trussell~~ Trestle at Harpers Ferry completed so as to pass trains. let General Know the fact—"—Telegram received (at 7:30 P.M.), DNA, RG 107, Telegrams Collected (Bound); *ibid.*, RG 108, Telegrams Received; copy, DLC-USG, V, 54. *O.R.*, I, xlvi, part 3, 1217.

1865, MAY 25. Jane M. (Mrs. Wilson M.) Cary, Baltimore, to USG. "In view of past kindness I am encouraged to appeal to you for justice. By yr permission I last winter visited Richmond—by yr permission I returned to my home. I have never in any way since the commencement of the war, given offence to, or incurred the censure of our authorities here. Altho' known to them as a Southern sympathiser I have never violated any order, or been called before them on any charge whatever. On my return to Balt: it was therefore incredible to me that I could be in any danger, having acted throughout under your supervision; but my confidence yeilded to the fears of my family & I went to Washington to apply to you for fuller protection than (as it appeared) your pass-port gave me. I recd it—returned home— was immediately arrested, & when I showed yr protection was told 'you did not mean what you said.' I was kept under guard for 24 hours & then brought before Maj: Weigel whose violent & brutal manner, was so entirely unlike what I was accustomed to in the Federal authorities in Richmond, that it positively frightened me & almost deprived me of all self control. On my accepting the parole he offered—with great violence & temper he said we should swear to it. As he was administering this oath he said I smiled, & angrily ordered that we sd be taken back to imprisonment. I *did not* smile, & told him so, he appealed to an officer present, who said he had not seen it, but some person out of uniform declared I *had*, & again we were detained in custody for 24 hours. No charge was brought against me—my only offence was having gone to Richmond, but I have you full permission for doing so, sent me thro' Genl: Barnard—then have I not a *right* to claim yr protection Genl, & to feel assured that I shall receive it when the case is placed before you? I ask for justice at *yr* hands, for I have received none here,—& I believe firmly you will accord it. No *man* could have witnessed Maj: Weigel's brutal manner to my daughter Mrs Pegram, & not have felt the blood boil in his veins. Genl: I know you have a heart—a brave soldiers heart—my poor child is a brave soldiers widow; a man noble among the noblest, educated in yr own military school—I well know that *you* feel no wish to crush one so bowed down already by the greatest of all earthly sorrows, weak, sick, broken hearted—with true manly instinct you have mercifully extended your protection to her—but *that* has been cruelly set aside, & she refused permission to go to Washington to appeal to you in person, is obliged sick or well every other day to report to Maj: Weigel, the very sound of whose voice throws her into such a state of agitation & tremulousness that she can scarcely stand for hours after. Many charges *may* have been brought against her by enemies, I do not know, but *most truly* she was innocent of all, save going to Va,—& once returning on a visit to us of a week unknown to the authorities here, but she brought nothing & took nothing back with her. She is feeble in health, & sorrow stricken, & desires & needs country air, & retirement, but altho you have positively accorded it to her, she is as positively forbidden to avail herself of yr intended kindness. She never goes to report that she does not expect imprisonment. I implore you Genl: to relieve her from this painful position by enforcing yr order that she shall be placed on the same footing 'as other residents of Baltimore'. Thinking it probable you may have forgotten the wording of yr order, I beg permission to append it to this petition. I am truly sorry to intrude upon yr time but it is my only hope of escape from the petty tyranny to wh I am unjustly subjected; O I appeal to you boldly Genl: I have been told by those had a right to know you, that you had a heart to feel for private sorrows even engrossed as you are with affairs of weight."—ALS, DNA, RG 108, Letters Received. On the same day, Bvt. Col. Theodore S. Bowers wrote to Maj. Gen. Lewis Wallace. "The Lieutenant General Commanding directs that Mrs Jane M. Cary, and her daughter Mrs Pegram, who are understood to be now in Baltimore, be allowed to remain in that City, or permitted to go elsewhere should they desire to, exempt from any restraint from the military authorities until they commit some act requiring their arrest; and in that event the cause of arrest will be reported to these Headquarters."—LS, *ibid.*, RG 109, Union Provost Marshals' File of Papers Relating to Two or More Civilians. See telegram to Maj. Gen. Lewis Wallace, April 21, 1865.

1865, MAY 25.   Michael [Rowoninout], Fall River, to USG. "Send order on First National Bank Fall River for my money"—Telegram received (at noon), DNA, RG 107, Telegrams Collected (Bound).

1865, MAY 26.   To Secretary of War Edwin M. Stanton. "I would respectfully request the appointment of Brig. Gen. Hugh Ewing as Maj. Gen. by brevet. General Ewing has been actively employed, in the field, from the begining of the war until within a few months and now, before leaving the service I think this recognition due."—ALS, Mrs. Walter Love, Flint, Mich.

1865, MAY 26, 10:00 A.M.   To Maj. Gen. John Pope. "The necessary provisions for supplying the starving people about Fort Gibson will be left entirely to your action."—ALS (telegram sent), DNA, RG 107, Telegrams Collected (Bound); telegram sent (at 10:05 A.M.), *ibid.*; telegram received (at 11:20 A.M.), *ibid.*, Telegrams Collected (Unbound). *O.R.*, I, xlviii, part 2, 608.

1865, MAY 26.   Bvt. Col. Theodore S. Bowers to Maj. Gen. Winfield S. Hancock. "You will please send immediately to the Coal Regions of Schuylkill County Pennsylvania a small regiments of Infantry under Command of a competent and discreet Officer with instructions to maintain order among the operatives and miners in the Coaleries of the New York and Schuylkill Coal Company and all other Coaleries there furnishing Coal for the supply of Government and protect the persons and property of all persons working or willing to work in their Coaleries"—Copies, DLC-USG, V, 46, 76, 108; DNA, RG 108, Letters Sent. On May 20, Bvt. Maj. Gen. Montgomery C. Meigs wrote to Secretary of War Edwin M. Stanton. "I have the honor to forward papers in relation to the interruption of coal mining in Schuylkill County, Pennsylvania. The contractors for supply of coal to the Quartermaster's Department state that men willing to work are prevented by violence and threats of the workmen who are on a strike. I respectfully recommend that a small force of troops, either State or National, be ordered into the disturbed districts, with instructions to afford efficient protection to all miners and other operatives willing to work in the colleries from which the contractors draw their supplies of coal for the United States."—LS, *ibid.*, Letters Received. On May 26, Stanton endorsed this letter and its enclosures to USG. "Approved and referred to Lt General Grant to issue such orders in respect to the troops to be assigned as may meet the emergency & to give the officers in command the requisite instructions"—AES, *ibid.* See *O.R.*, I, xlvi, part 3, 1220, 1226–27; *New York Times*, May 8, June 3, 12, 1865.

1865, MAY 26.   Maj. Gen. Edward R. S. Canby to Brig. Gen. John A. Rawlins. "The marshall warehouse at Mobile used as a temporary Ordnance Depot was blown up yesterday afternoon causing a considerable loss of life & property The cause of this Explosion is not yet known but as it occurred when a train of captured Ordnance Stores from Meredian was being brought out it is probably due to the explosion of a percussion shell, aA Court of Inquiry will investigate the circumstances the losses are not reported"—Telegram received (at 5:20 P.M.), DNA, RG 107, Telegrams Collected (Bound); *ibid.*, RG 108, Telegrams Received; copy, DLC-USG, V, 54. *O.R.*, I, xlix, part 2, 911–12. See *ibid.*, I, xlix, part 1, 566–67.

1865, MAY 27.   USG endorsement. "Respectfully forwarded to Secretary of War. The papers of Mr. W Alvin Loyd have been [exa]mined, and satis-factorily [prov]ed that he has been a prisoner in southern prisons over two years: Also that he has a pass from President Lincoln [o]n special business. Mr Loyd desires payment for services [in] accordance with verbal [a]gree-ment with Mr Lincoln."—ES, DNA, RG 94, Letters Received, 640L 1865. Written on papers concerning William Alvin Lloyd, publisher of a steam-boat and railroad guide, who claimed to have served in the U.S. secret service during the Civil War.—*Ibid.* See also *O.R.*, II, ii, 1408–9.

1865, MAY 27.   USG endorsement. "Respectfully returned to the Secre-tary of War. I recommend that the leave of absence be granted."—ES, DNA, RG 94, Letters Received, 425R 1865. Written on a letter of May 24 from Maj. Gen. William S. Rosecrans to President Andrew Johnson. "Unofficial . . . In pursuance of the ideas I mentioned to you at in my inter-view with you about three weeks since I wish to visit the Pacific Coast to examine its mining and other resources and to see what openings they pre-sent for the satisfactory and successful employment of many of our soldiers. I think if some one of experience who can survey the field and consider the matter with a view of so combining, the interests of capital and labor as to provide fields of successful enterprize for many of our young officers and solders who cannot command the capital and means to help themselves it will be a great benefit to them and to the country. I propose on this account as well as for the purpose of looking to civil life myself to go to the Pacific Coast, And if your Excellency considers my proposed examinations a mat-ter of sufficient public interest would like an order 'to proceed there on special duty under your instructions' which will be to examine and report to you on the mining resources and interests of the pPacific Coast and their political and eCommercial relations with sister states. If not in your judge-ment a matter of such public interest, then I wish to go and examine for rea-sons stated and request your orders that I may have leave tfor six months with permission to go out of the U. S."—ALS, *ibid.* On May 25, Johnson endorsed this letter. "Respectfully referred to the Hon: Secretary of War, with the request that the leave of absence &c applied for within be granted, if there is no particular reason for denying it."—AES, *ibid.*

1865, MAY 27.   USG endorsement. "Respy. returned I do not advise that Captain Semple be placed on a different footing than other Prisoners of

war"—Copy, DLC-USG, V, 58. Written on a statement of Capt. Maurice
W. Wall, 69th N. Y., concerning harsh treatment he received while a pris-
oner at Columbia, S. C., from C.S.A. Capt. Semple, provost marshal. Bvt.
Brig. Gen. William Hoffman endorsed this statement recommending soli-
tary confinement on bread and water for Semple; Maj. Gen. Ethan A.
Hitchcock disapproved this recommendation.—*Ibid.*

1865, MAY 27, 11:10 A.M.   Maj. Gen. John Pope to USG. "Following
dispatch from Gen Dodge just recd   Ft Leavenworth May 26th   To MAJ
GEN JNO POPE   Everything appears to be working well   I am pushing
Everything out on to the overland route & will stay until we are all right   All
the mounted men are on move with Conner & with Ford & are doing good
service   Trains are going out daily with stores for all points on the plains &
none as yet have been successfully interfered with   We have got back
most of stage stock   I feel considerable anxiety about these indians west
of mountains & watch closely for further developements   Stages run regularly   signed G M DODGE M G"—Telegram received (at 12:40 P.M.),
DNA, RG 107, Telegrams Collected (Bound); *ibid.*, RG 108, Telegrams
Received; copies, *ibid.*, RG 393, Military Div. of the Mo., Telegrams Sent;
DLC-USG, V, 54. Incomplete in *O.R.*, I, xlviii, part 2, 612–13.

1865, MAY 28, 1:15 P.M.   To Maj. Gen. Edward O. C. Ord. "You may
authorize Gn. Longstreet to visit Washington."—ALS (telegram sent),
DNA, RG 107, Telegrams Collected (Bound); telegram sent, *ibid.*; telegram received (marked as sent at 1:30 P.M.), Ord Papers, CU-B. *O.R.*, I,
xlvi, part 3, 1230. On May 26, Ord had telegraphed to Brig. Gen. Lorenzo
Thomas. "The following telegram forwarded by Gen Gregg Commanding
at Lynchburg Va was recd yesterday and is transmitted for the action of
the [Li]eutenant-general-Commanding . . . To BRIG GENL THOMAS Adjt
Gen Washington   I respectfully ask permission to visit Washington on
important private [bu]siness   (signed) LONGSTREET"—Telegram received
(at 2:10 P.M.), DNA, RG 107, Telegrams Collected (Bound). *O.R.*, I,
xlvi, part 3, 1218. On the same day, USG endorsed this telegram. "I do
not approve of Gen Longstreet coming to Washington to attend to private
business, but I am satisfied his business here is principally to move with his
family to Texas, passing through the northern states for convenience. I
recommend that authority be given him to do so. Longstreet is really on of
the least objectionable officers lately engaged in rebellion & would no doubt
be willing himself to return to citizen ship"—Copy, DLC-USG, V, 58.
On May 27, Ord telegraphed to Bvt. Col. Theodore S. Bowers. "The following telegram & its [a]nswer are forwarded for the information of the
Lieut General Commanding—also Genls R W Johnson, Walker, Clarke
and since others rebel Generals have taken the oath or applied for its privileges. . . . Lynchburg 26th   BR GEN CURTIS. The assistant Provost Marshal of Campbell County on yesterday administered the amnesty oath to
Gen Longstreet. He being excepted by the Presidents proclamation. What

are the instructions in his case & others of Similar character which may present themselves? (Signed). J. I. GREGG Bt Br Gen Vols'. 'Richmond May 27. To BT BR GEN GREGG. Lynchburg Va. The instructions in the case of Genl Longstreet are the same as of all others who have taken the oath & are excluded from the benefits of the Amnesty proclamation. All persons are permitted to take the oath but receive none of the benefits until Specially authorized by the President. They can make application for the benefits of the proclamation and they will be forwarded through the military channels. By order of Maj Gen Ord"—Telegram received (at 4:00 P.M.), DNA, RG 107, Telegrams Collected (Bound); *ibid.*, RG 108, Telegrams Received; copy, DLC-USG, V, 54. *O.R.*, I, xlvi, part 3, 1224.

1865, MAY 28. Maj. Gen. John M. Schofield to USG. "Gen Kilpatricks troops have not been paid for nine months and the families of the officers & men are suffering for the necessaries of life—Cannot a paymaster be sent to pay them at once"—Telegram received (at 5:00 P.M.), DNA, RG 107, Telegrams Collected (Bound); *ibid.*, Telegrams Collected (Unbound); copies (dated May 29), *ibid.*, RG 393, Army of the Ohio and Dept. of N. C., Telegrams Sent; DLC-John M. Schofield. Printed as received on May 29, 5:00 P.M., in *O.R.*, I, xlvii, part 3, 585.

1865, MAY 29. USG endorsement. "Respectfully forwarded to the Secretary of War."—ES, DNA, RG 94, ACP, G173 CB 1865. Written on a petition of officers of the 5th Cav. inquiring about Sgt. Maj. Alfred Guiton, 5th Cav., whose nomination for appointment as 2nd lt. had been withdrawn because of rumors that he had deserted the British Army.—DS, *ibid.* See *ibid.*, L316 CB 1865.

1865, MAY 29. USG endorsement. "Disapproved for the present"—ES, DNA, RG 94, Letters Received, 776B 1865. Written on a letter of May 6 from Col. Robert C. Buchanan, New Orleans, to Maj. Wickham Hoffman, adjt. for Bvt. Maj. Gen. Thomas W. Sherman. "I have the honor to recommend that the 1st Regiment of Infantry be ordered to the North in order that it may be filled up to the proper strength and that the Officers and men may enjoy the benefits of a more bracing climate during the time necessary for that purpose—The present strength of the Regiment gives a total of *283*, of which number *6* are to be discharged by the 26th inst—There are 2 Field and 11—Company Officers present for duty—There are *33* enlisted men permanently detached at the various General Head Quarters, and *13* absent in confinement at Tortugas and elsewhere—The daily details for Regimental and other guards require *53* men, and for the last month the average number of sick has been 16, per day—The average of men confined for various offences for the last month was *21*—The number therefore actually available for all the various calls to which the Regiment is liable is *147*—As this number comprises non. Com. Officers as well as Privates, it is manifestly too small for the duties required of it—I have no desire to change the station of the Regiment for the sake of change, but am simply anxious to take all steps in my power to increase its strength and improve its efficiency—I hope therefore that my application will meet the approval of the several commanders through whom it must pass on its way to the Adjutant General of the Army—"—ALS, *ibid.*

1865, MAY 29.   USG endorsement. "Respectfully approved. The age of Sixteen is a mere matter of regulation and not law for Cadets entering West Point. Almost ever year Cadets are allowed to enter younger by special authority."—AES, DNA, RG 107, Letters Received, A682 1865. Written on a letter of the same day from Maj. Gen. Christopher C. Augur to Secretary of War Edwin M. Stanton. "I have the honor to request that my son just appointed a Cadet 'at large,' and who under existing regulations cannot enter until August, on account of his age, may be authorized to enter in June. I desire particularly that he may have the advantage of the summer encampment."—ALS, *ibid.*

1865, MAY 29.   Bvt. Col. Theodore S. Bowers to Bvt. Maj. Gen. Marsena R. Patrick. "Permit me to introduce Brig Gen. R. B. Hayes, member of Congress elect from Cincinnati. He visits Richmond for the purpose of seeing objects rendered interesting by the late Campaign. Any courtesey you may be able to extend him will be greatfully appreciated, and will oblige"—ALS, ICHi.

1865, MAY 29.   Maj. Gen. Edward O. C. Ord to USG. "Existing regulations requiring no passes from Civillians leaving the Dept. open the door to desertion and in one instance 12 men have deserted from a single Company   Shall I require passes from Civillians Coming here ~~from~~ via City Point so as to show they have a right to go back and Visa them on their entering the Steamer to go north"—ALS (telegram sent), Ord Papers, CU-B; telegram received (at 2:30 P.M.), DNA, RG 107, Telegrams Collected (Bound); *ibid.*, RG 108, Telegrams Received.

1865, MAY 29.   Maj. Gen. John Pope to USG. "I have the honor to transmit enclosed telegrams just received from Genl Reynolds at Little Rock & Genl Dodge at Ft Leavenworth—They are only important as showing that all Guerillas & Bushwhackers who have disturbed the peace in Arkansas & Missouri are rapidly surrendering—I hope that entire quiet will soon be restored in Arkansas & Missouri and in that view I would be glad to know whether my suggestions for the restoration of Civil Law & Administration in Arkansas, submitted in my letter to the President are approved—I think some steps toward that end should be adopted as soon as possible"—LS, DNA, RG 108, Letters Received. *O.R.*, I, xlviii, part 2, 657. The enclosures are *ibid.*, pp. 583, 632, 665. Also on May 29, 5:00 P.M., Maj. Gen. Joseph J. Reynolds, Little Rock, telegraphed to USG. "Gen'l Dockery of the late C. S. A. has come in to Pine Bluff to surrender the Confederate forces in

South Arkansas—Four captains of independent companies also in today— This I believe includes about all of the rebel forces in this state—Papers giving result of an informal interview with prominent citizens from Washington Ark are enroute to War Department by mail, will probably reach Washington about the 8th June, also referring to state of civil affairs in Arkansas"—Telegram received (on May 30, 4:00 P.M.), DNA, RG 107, Telegrams Collected (Bound); *ibid.*, RG 108, Telegrams Received; copies, *ibid.*, RG 393, Dept. of Ark. and 7th Army Corps, Letters Sent; DLC-USG, V, 54. *O.R.*, I, xlviii, part 2, 658.

1865, MAY 29. Maj. Gen. Lewis Wallace, Baltimore, to USG. "I have the honor to acknowledge the receipt of your order dated May 27th, 1865, directing the release of George C. Irwin and to report that the order was promptly executed. In explanation of the arrest of Irwin, I would respectfully state, that it was made, not only at the instigation of many prominent citizens, who felt themselves aggrieved, at his presence here, but to protect him from violence. Your attention is respectfully invited to a correspondence with the Hon. Secretary of War, and to a considerable number of papers called for by the Secretary, making a complete history of Irwin's case. Instructions were asked for, as to disposition to be made of Irwin, but, up to the receipt of your order, none had been received."—LS, DNA, RG 108, Letters Received.

1865, MAY 30. USG endorsement. "Respectfully forwarded to the Secretary of War, and recommended."—ES, DNA, RG 94, ACP, 1646S CB 1865. Written on two letters of May 30 from Maj. Gen. William T. Sherman to Bvt. Col. Theodore S. Bowers. "I have this day recommended for Brevet the officers of my personal staff including Col O. M. Poe of the Engineers. You will remember that Col Poe was at one time appointed by President Lincoln a Brig Genl, and actually exercised the Command, but by reason of the number of appointmts exceeding the Law some were not confirmed among the number Col Poe. This Reason together with the more important one of services of the highest value, induces me to write this special letter again recommending that Col Poe be brevetted as Brigadier General. U. S. A." "I have the honor to ask that the officers attached to my official and personal Staff be advanced one degree or step by Brevet for services rendered the Governmt, during the recent Campaigns of Atlanta, Savannah, and the Carolinas. I herewith subjoin a List."—ALS, *ibid.* The first is printed in *O.R.*, I, xlvii, part 3, 598.

1865, MAY 30. Brig. Gen. John A. Rawlins to Maj. Gen. Winfield S. Hancock. "Orders have been issued for the movement of all troops of Maj, Gen, Shermans Command belonging in the West and now here to Louisville, The movement is to commence at once Please order all places where Liquor is Kept along the line of the Baltimore and Ohio Rail Road closed until the movement is Completed"—Copies, DLC-USG, V, 46, 76, 108; DNA, RG

108, Letters Sent. *O.R.*, I, xlvi, part 3, 1239. On June 20, Collector of Internal Revenue George W. Land, Ellicott's Mills, Md., wrote to USG. "Enclosed you will find a petition from Our Citizens which I think ought be allowed, as they have really suffered needless losses, No Soldiers having stopped here since the issue of the Order forbidding the sale of Liquors. As these Citizens pay their taxes (federal) to me, they naturally expect me to do what I can to protect them from unnecessary losses."—ALS, DNA, RG 393, Middle Military Div., Letters Received. The petition is *ibid.* On June 22, Bvt. Col. Theodore S. Bowers endorsed this petition. "Respectfully referred to Major General W S Hancock Comdg Middle Military Div. The necessity for the ~~issu~~ order prohibiting the sale of liquors along the line of the railroad having passed, the order may now be revoked."—ES, *ibid.*

On June 2, 10:30 A.M., USG telegraphed to Maj. Gens. John A. Dix, George Cadwalader, and Joseph Hooker. "Suppress all sale of liquor on the lines traveled by troops returning to be mustered out and at rendezvous for discharge until troops are all dispersed. ~~This order need not apply to large Cities~~"—ALS (telegram sent), *ibid.*, RG 107, Telegrams Collected (Bound); telegram sent, *ibid.*; telegram received (at noon), *ibid.*, RG 393, Army of the Ohio, Northern Dept., Telegrams Received. On July 10, Surgeon St. John W. Mintzer, York, Pa., wrote to Bvt. Lt. Col. John S. Schultze, adjt. for Cadwalader. "I have the honor to report that I was arrested by the Sheriff of York County at 3 oclock today on a 'Capias' issued at the instance of one Seechrist a citizen, the complainant charges me with trespass in enforcing General Orders No 68 of Dep't H'd Q'rs. I declined to enter Bail until I should receive instructions from Head Quarters, as I claimed that I acted in good faith in the discharge of my duty, that I committed no offence, and being an Officer in Commission and on duty in the service of the United States, I could not be removed by Civil Authorities without full and sufficient cause, and that I believed it to be my duty to resist imprisonment: under these circumstances, the Prosecuting Attorney, granted me time to receive necessary instructions. Seechrist is the Keeper of a low Tavern in the rear of this Hospital, adjoining two noted low holes of prostitution, Known as the 'Snuff Boxes', They all sell liquor, and have been nuisances and a source of trouble, frequently drunken Soldiers are arrested there by the Patrol. On Saturday last on Inspection I found a number of the windows of the 7th Ward broken, and Bricks and Stones on the floor, the attending Ass't Surgeon informed me that they were thrown by the Soldiers made drunk while at these Houses opposite—I ordered the Guard to bring in all enlisted men found there, and empty on the ground all liquor on the premises. If you desire me to give bail I will forward charges and Specifications against Sechrist for your approval, as I must sustain my position, otherwise my authority will be brought into contempt, and open the door for further trouble. The number of cases of Shooting and Stabbing that have occurred here within the last two months, has compelled me to take decided measures for the protection of the men under my Charge. . . . P. S. Mr. Henry Kraber a worthy Union Citizen addressed me a note requesting an interview to day.—He informs me that Seechrist had no License and applied for one to day—and that he has been urged on by his political advisers—Hospital Steward Chas Weimich was held to Bail for assisting in arresting a man that shot a soldier with attempt to Kill. It is my desire to be as Kind and conciliatory with the Civil Authorities, and especially at this time, and I have every reason to believe that they Know I am actuated by these feelings, but how far they can invade my rights as an officer, in the discharge of my duty or those under my command I desire to determine, and accept this case as a precedent."—ALS, *ibid.*, RG 94, Letters Received, 1392M 1865. USG added an undated endorsement. "Surgeon Mintzer seems to have acted in accordance with orders and should be protected. If it becomes necessary to employ council the expense should not be borne by him. Respectfully refered to the Sec. of War."—AES, *ibid.*

1865, MAY 30. Maj. Gen. Henry W. Halleck endorsement. "Respectfully referred to Lt. Genl. Grant. It is said that Genl. B. R. Johnson violated his parole given to Genl. Grant in person at Fort Donelson. If so, I am not disposed to extend him any favors."—Richard J. Frajola, Inc., *Manuscripts, Free Franks and Confederate Postal History*, Catalogue, July 10, 1982, p. 26. Written on a letter of May 10 from C.S.A. Maj. Gen. Bushrod R. Johnson to Col. John C. Kelton asking to take an oath of allegiance, then go to Ill. to "abide in retirement, in peace, and in solitude . . ."—*Ibid.*

1865, MAY 31. To Secretary of War Edwin M. Stanton. "I see by the papers that enlistments of Colored troops is going on briskly in Ky. I would recommend that all enlistments of Colored troops throughout the United States be discontinued and that orders to that effect be telegraphed." —Copies, DLC-USG, V, 46, 76, 108; DNA, RG 108, Letters Sent; *ibid.*, RG 393, Military Div. of the Miss., Cav. Corps, Letters Received.

1865, MAY 31. USG endorsement. "Respectfully forwarded to the Secretary of War and the promotion of Brig. Generals Long and McCook to be MajorGenerals by brevet recommended. The promotion of Gen Upton to a full MajorGeneral is not recommended."—ES, DNA, RG 94, ACP, 393W CB 1865. Written on a letter of April 23 from Bvt. Maj. Gen. James H. Wilson to Bvt. Brig. Gen. Edward D. Townsend. "I have the honor to recommend the following promotions: Bvt Maj Genl E. Upton, U. S. V. to be Major General of Volunteers to date from April 1st for personal gallantry and good management in the engagement at Ebenezer Station, Alabama, also at Columbus Georgia, where by a night attack with three hundred men, he carried the rebel works, captured the bridges over the Chattahoochie river, took (1200) twelve hundred prisoners, and fifty two (52) guns. Throughout the entire campaign Genl Upton has exhibited the highest qualities of a general officer, and demonstrated his fitness for advancement. Brig. Genl Eli Long, U. S. V. to be Brevet Major General of Volunteers, for personal gallantry and good management in the command of his division in the assault of the fortifications of Selma, resulting in the capture of the place, (2700) twentyseven hundred prisoners, (32) thirty two guns in position—April 2nd 1865. Brig. Genl E. M. McCook, to be Brevet Maj. General, for uniform good conduct throughout the expedition." —ALS, *ibid.*

1865, MAY 31. William Johnson, Norfolk, to USG. "I write at the instance of the aged parents and afflicted sister of Frederick M Peed, late 2d Lieut Huger Battery under Lee, now a prisoner at Johnsons Island and willing to take the oath and become hereafter a good loyal subject of the U S. May I beg that you will exert your influence in his behalf to the end that he may be speedily released?—He may never see his sister again if his imprisonment continues long   Your attention will oblige his parents and . . ."—ALS, DNA, RG 109, Unfiled Papers and Slips. On June 9, Ann A. Peed, Norfolk, wrote to USG. "Will You be so Kinde to release My son Who is A Prisoner at Johnsons, Island—Lt. Fred- M- Peed—it Would—be Such—A Gratfication to his Father, as We—are both Veay old—And—depening on him—for A support   he belong to Gen Lee—army—Was taken at the Surrender—oh—General—release my Son—for his Poor—Mother Sake—"—ALS, *ibid.*

1865, MAY 31. Nathan Sargent, Washington County, D. C., to USG. "At the interview which the Committee representing the County of Washington, D. C. had with you on Monday last in regard to the destruction of property of the citizens of said county by the troops constituting the army of the West, in speaking of the mode of assessing those damages and obtaining remuneration therefore, the Committee understood you to say, or assent to the proposition, that Commissioners should be appointed to assess whatever damages have been committed; and also to say that the matter had better be postponed until the troops had gone. It was suggested at the same time by some one, that the damages ought to be deducted from the pay of those who had done the wrong. If the latter was to be done, it would seem to be necessary that the damages should be assessed before the troops are paid off. At any rate, the subject was left in so indefinite a shape that Maj. Burr and myself, acting for the Committee, deemed it our duty to call, and did call on you this morning, with a view to be better informed as to what course should be pursued by those citizens who have suffered, not being ourselves able to inform them, or even to assure them that they will be remunerated at all. We were not so fortunate, however, as to obtain an interview with you, and are therefore in the dark on the subject. As quartermasters refuse to sign requisitions to cover what has been destroyed, our people have no remedy known to them, and must bear their losses as best they may unless some mode of giving them relief be devised by those in authority. Not wishing to draw you into correspondence on the subject I submit this letter asking no written reply, but only requesting that a remedy may be devised, if possible, whereby they may be remunerated at least in part. . . . Post Script. June 2d. 1865. Since writing the above I have passed through various parts of the county, and while some few have suffered badly by depredations, I am most happy to say that the citizens generally have suffered comparatively little:—not as much as I had been led to suppose."—LS, DNA, RG 108, Letters Received.

1865, [MAY?]. USG signature printed with a "Testimonial for George F. Robinson." "The friends of George F. Robinson, the brave soldier who saved the life of Mr. Seward, when attacked by a powerful and determined assassin, have obtained his consent to have his photograph sold for his benefit. The undersigned refer to the following letter from distinguished gentlemen of New York, to show the estimation in which his heroic conduct is held, and to the reply of Mr. Robinson, as evidence of his modesty and patrotism in harmony with his noble action. We believe that a very large number of persons will be glad to obtain photographs of Mr. Robinson, (the copyright of which has been secured for him,) and, at the same time, know that they are contributing to place in an independent position one who. by the blessing of God, has endeared himself to the people in saving from the relentless hands of the most cruel assassin the world has ever known a life, the value of which is universally acknowledged by a grateful nation, but which posterity only can fully appreciate. The sale of the photographs has been placed in the hands of P. M. Clark, of Washington, D. C., to whom all communications respecting it should be addressed. We commend the subject to the hearts of the people."—DLC-Clay Family Papers. Other documents printed in this folder included a letter of May 5 from New York merchants to Private George F. Robinson, Co. E, 8th Maine, forwarding $1,612, a letter of May 11 from Robinson, Douglas Hospital, Washington, D. C., acknowledging the gift, and a letter of July from P. M. Clark offering signed photographs for sale.—*Ibid.*

1865, JUNE 1. USG endorsement. "Respectfully refered to the Sec. of War with the recommendation that Jefferson Barracks, with the public grounds attached, be *loaned* as a home for disabled soldiers & Sailors until such time a permanent place is secured."—AES, DNA, RG 108, Letters Received. Written on a letter of June 1 from William G. Eliot to USG. "On behalf of the Western Sanitary Commission (of St Louis Mo) and by its direction, I respectfully suggest that 'Jefferson Barracks' be set apart and used for the purposes of a Home for Invalid & Disabled Soldiers, under such regulations as may hereafter be determined. It has all the requisite buildings & conveniences for immediate occupation, with Seventeen Hundred Acres of land. So far as the whole Western Army is concerned no location coud be more favorable, as a permanent Institution, I take the liberty of adding that the above named Commission, of with whose labors during the past four years you are familiar, would gladly render all service in its power, to aid whatever officers might be placed in charge, & would appropriate not less than Twenty five Thousand Dollars to meet the first wants of such an establishment. A much larger sum can be guaranteed, by an appeal to the public, if necessary, for permanent support, for the general feeling at the West is that our Western Soldiers should be provided for, at some proper place on their own side of the mountains, and I believe that a half million of Dollars could readily be obtained."—ALS, *ibid.* On June 10, Bvt. Maj. Gen. Montgomery C. Meigs wrote to Secretary of War Edwin M. Stanton opposing any use of Jefferson Barracks for disabled soldiers.— LS, *ibid.*

On July 8, Maj. Gen. William T. Sherman, Cincinnati, telegraphed to Bvt. Brig. Gen. Edward D. Townsend requesting that the 1st Battalion, 13th Inf., be ordered to Jefferson Barracks.—Telegram received (at 1:20 P.M.), *ibid.*, RG 94, Letters Received, 1336M 1865. On July 12, Maj. Robert Williams, AGO, endorsed this telegram. "Respectfully submitted to Lt Genl Grant Com'dg Armies U. S. Jefferson Barracks, Mo: is now used as a General Hospital but as it is believed that it will be very much needed for the use of troops, it is respectfully recommended that as soon as the exigencies of the service shall no longer require it to be used for hospital purposes, it be turned over to, and for occupiedation by troops"—ES, *ibid.* On July 20, USG endorsed this telegram. "Approved, with request that the Medical Department be directed to turn over Jefferson Barracks for occupation by troops as soon as the exigencies of the service shall no longer require it for hospital purposes."—ES, *ibid.*

1865, June 1.   USG endorsement. "Respectfully returned to the Secretary of War with the recommendation that the Secretary of the Interior be requested to furnish the surveyor asked for, and if he is unable to do so Gen Carlton be directed to detail one of his own officers for the duty, applying to the engineer department for the necessary instruments."—ES, DNA, RG 393, Dept. of New Mexico, Letters Received. Written on a letter of April 24 from Brig. Gen. James H. Carleton, Santa Fé, New Mexico Territory, to the AG requesting surveyors to assist in the organization of Indian lands. —LS, *ibid.*

1865, June 1, 10:30 A.M.   To Maj. Gen. Edward R. S. Canby. "You will see by recent orders Miss. is no longer a Department. You can assign any officer ~~within your command to the~~ under you to the command of that Destrict."—ALS (telegram sent), DNA, RG 107, Telegrams Collected (Bound); telegram sent, *ibid.*; telegram received, *ibid.*, RG 94, War Records Office, Dept. of the Gulf; (3) *ibid.*, RG 107, Telegrams Collected (Bound). *O.R.*, I, xlviii, part 2, 714. See *ibid.*, pp. 475, 746. On May 29, Canby had telegraphed to Brig. Gen. John A. Rawlins. "Should the resignation of Maj Gen Warnerren be accepted I recommend Maj Gen P. J. Osterhaus be assigned to the Dept of Miss."—Telegram received (on June 1, 9:45 A.M.), DNA, RG 107, Telegrams Collected (Bound); (3) *ibid.*, Telegrams Collected (Unbound); (on June 1, 9:25 A.M.) *ibid.*, RG 108,

Telegrams Received; copy, DLC-USG, V, 54. Printed as sent on May 28 in *O.R.*, I, xlviii, part 2, 640. See *ibid.*, pp. 519–20, 622, 779.

1865, JUNE 1.   USG endorsement. "I would respectfully recommend that Private Robert Blackburn now in confinement on charge of desertion recieve full pardon. He is quite young & served one enlistment faithfully— and has now been confined many months to this offense. If authorized so to do, I will telegraph to Lexington, Ky, for the immediate release of this prisoner"—Copy, DLC-USG, V, 58. Written on a letter from Mrs. J. F. Weed asking for the release from prison of her son.—*Ibid.* On June 1, 2:20 P.M., USG telegraphed to Maj. Gen. John M. Palmer, Louisville. "Have private Robt. Blackburn, now in prison No. 3 Lexington Ky. on the charge of desertion taken to Louisville to await orders."—ALS (telegram sent), DNA, RG 107, Telegrams Collected (Bound); telegram sent, *ibid.*; copies, *ibid.*, RG 108, Letters Sent; *ibid.*, RG 393, Dept. of Ky., Telegrams Received; DLC-USG, V, 46, 76, 108. On June 22, 3:40 P.M., USG telegraphed to Palmer. "Please telegraph if Robert Blackburn has been ~~relieved~~ released from prison in Nashville."—ALS (telegram sent), DNA, RG 107, Telegrams Collected (Bound); telegram sent, *ibid.*; telegram received, *ibid.*, RG 109, Union Provost Marshals' File of Papers Relating to Individual Civilians. On June 23, Brig. Gen. Edward H. Hobson, Louisville, telegraphed to Bvt. Col. Theodore S. Bowers. "Robert Blackburn was released on the 19th Inst"—ALS (telegram sent), *ibid.*; telegram received (at 12:50 P.M.), *ibid.*, RG 107, Telegrams Collected (Bound).

1865, JUNE 1, 12:55 P.M.   To William Scott, New York City. "It will be impossible for me to accept your invitation for Friday evening"—Telegrams sent (2), DNA, RG 107, Telegrams Collected (Bound).

1865, JUNE 1.   Maj. Thomas M. Vincent, AGO, to USG. "Official Copy resply furnished for the information of Lt. Gen U. S. Grant Comd'g Armies U. S. This is in answer to the telegram directing all vol. white troops, whose terms expire prior to Oct 1st to be mustered out."—AES, DNA, RG 108, Letters Received. *O.R.*, I, xlix, part 2, 928. Written on a telegram of May 29 from Bvt. Maj. Gen. James H. Wilson to Vincent stating that there would be sufficient forces left in Ga. after compliance with orders.—Copy, DNA, RG 108, Letters Received. *O.R.*, I, xlix, part 2, 928.

1865, JUNE 1.   William W. Matthews, 15th S. C., Fort Delaware, to USG. "Allow me to present to you my case, And ask your assistence in procureing me a Release from prison, where I Have been since the battle of gettysburg, at which time I became convinced that I was in the wrong place and voluntarily surrendered myself to the union forces, With a view of Returning to my former allegiance as soon as I was permitted to Return to my home and parents, my father is a verry poor man and took No part in the Rebellion whatever, he is well stricken in years a large Family to surport and no one to assist him, I have made frequent Applications to the War department for my Release but could get no Hearing, having no one to entercede for me I have to depend Entirely upon my own feeble exertions. I hope *Gen*, you will Condesend to give this your attention, and give me a Hearing as soon as conveniet with you, if the situation of My fathers family was not such a destitute one I would await The discretion of the *president*, as Regards my Release, but feeling It my duty to seek pardon, and be come once more a Respectable Citizen of U. S, I appeal to you *Gen*, to aid me, What I have Above stated is correct and I hope it will meet your approbation, It is just my feelings and has been for some time My confament I think has paid the penalty of which I have Repented, as I never fired a gun in the Cause, Please honor me with a hearing as soon as practicable"—ALS, DNA, RG 109, Unfiled Papers and Slips.

1865, JUNE 2. USG endorsement. "Respectfully refered to the President. The writer is an old West Point and Army acquaintance of mine and I can vouch for his statements."—AES, DNA, RG 94, Amnesty Papers, Ga. Written on a letter of June 1 from Charles T. Baker, Madison, N. J., USMA 1842, to USG. "This will be handed to you by Mr Frank Lathrop, who goes to Washington to seek from the President pardon for his brother-in-law Mr Wm H. Gibbons of Georgia Who comes under the head of those worth more than twenty thousand dollars of taxable property—Mr Gibbons is a cousin of mine, and I have known him all his life—He has never mingled in politics, either before or since the rebellion, was always opposed to secession, has been fined, and imprisoned by the Rebel Authorities for refusing to furnish his negroes to work upon their fortifications,—and finally, when compelled to enter the Rebel service sought and obtained some position in the Quarter-Master or Commissary Department, in order to avoid more active service against the Government. Mr Lathrop takes with him to lay before the President substantialy the facts herein stated, and the object of this letter (Mr Lathrop being a stranger to the President) is, that some one near the Government may be able to vouch for the respectability of the source from which they come, and believing that you will have confidence in the statement of an old fellow-soldier, who desires nothing but that justice may be meted to all, but who believes that Mr Gibbons case will be one of the most favorable presented for Executive clemency, and who doubts not but that the President will be pleased to grant him a full pardon when made cognisant of all the facts in his case, I have thought I could with propriety, fall back upon our old acquaintance, and ask the favor of you, to speak a kind word for one I believe deserving of it—Congratulating you upon your successes & advancement—"—ALS, *ibid.* On June 2, President Andrew Johnson endorsed this letter. "REFERRED TO the Hon: Attorney General, with whom I desire to have a conference before any pardons of this character are granted."—ES, *ibid.* A notation indicates that William H. Gibbons was pardoned on July 6.—AN, *ibid.*

1865, JUNE 2. USG endorsement. "Respy returned to the Sec of War. Mil Division & Departmet Commanders should be allowed to publish orders in newspapers immediatly affecting citizens in rebellious states, and no one of a less command than a Division or Dept (Military) should be allowed so to do. The publication in newspapers of orders relating to our effective troops only should be prohibited in all cases, except where especially authorized by the War Dept."—Copy, DLC-USG, V, 58. Written on a letter of May 19 from Brig. Gen. George H. Gordon, Norfolk, "relative to the publication of military orders in the 'Norfolk old Dominion' "—*Ibid.*

1865, JUNE 2. USG endorsement. "Respectfully forwarded and approved for promotion in the volunteer service by brevet"—ES, DNA, RG 94, ACP, S1624 CB 1865. Written on a letter of May 29 from Maj. Gen. John Pope, St. Louis, to USG. "I have the honor to request that the following officers of my Staff be Brevetted for service set opposite their names respectively— As the Staff Officers of Maj Gen Curtis & other Generals serving in this Military Division have been thus honored for services in my judgment neither so important nor so conspicuous it seems only fair that the officers on my Staff be also promoted—1st Lt Col. Fred. Myers. A A D. C & Chief Quartermaster Military Division of the Missouri to be Bvt Brig Genl. for distinguished services in the Campaign of the Army of Virginia & for highly meritorious service as Chief Quartermaster Dept of the North West. & of Military Division of the Missouri—2nd Capt J. McC. Bell A. A G to be Lt Col by Brevet for distinguished services in the Campaign of the Army of Virginia & since in the Dept of the North West & the Military Division of the Missouri—3rd Capt D Pope, A A D. C. for distinguished services in the Campaign of the 'Army of Virginia' & since in the Dept of the North West and Military Division of the Missouri—None of these Officers have received any promotion whatever for these services"—ALS, *ibid. O.R.,* I, xlviii, part 2, 657.

1865, JUNE 2. USG endorsement. "Respectfully recommended that the printing asked for be authorized at the Govt. Printing office The object be-ingg a charitable one, to look up and ascertain the fate of officers and soldiers who have fallen into the hands of the enemy and have never been restered to their families and friends, is one which the Government can well aid"— Copy, DLC-Clara Barton. Written on a letter of May 31 from Clara Barton to President Andrew Johnson.—*Ibid.* On June 2, Bvt. Col. Theodore S. Bowers issued a pass. "Miss Clara Barton, engaged in making inquiries for soldiers reported as missing in action, will be allowed, until further orders, with her assistants, not to exceed two in number, free transportation on all Government railroads and transports."—DS, *ibid.* On June 16, Bvt. Brig. Gen. William Hoffman wrote an endorsement. "Resptflly submitted to Lt. Genl. Grant. The work in which Miss Barton is engaged is one of very general interest and is attended with much labor which she generously performs without pecuniary compensation, and it is respectfully suggested that there is no one laboring for the good of the Soldiers & their friends who better deserves any public assistance that can properly be extended to her."—Copy, DNA, RG 249, Letters Sent.

1865, JUNE 2. Bvt. Col. Theodore S. Bowers endorsement. "Respectfully referred to Maj Gen Wallace Comd'g Mid. Dept,"—AES, DNA, RG 108, Letters Received. Written on a letter of May 31 from C. C. Shriver, Baltimore, to USG. "In Danville Va on the 5th of May 1865 I was paroled by Lt Col Fletcher 1st Maine Vet Vols as a Sergeant in Co "I" 3rd Regt Va Inft. and was given a pass to return to my home in this State and to remain here unmolested. Upon my arrival in Richmond I was detained some weeks: and prevented from returning by the authorities in Balto: A recent order issued by you promised protection to the Soldiers from this State, who had served in the Southern Army, upon their taking the amnesty oath prescribed by President Lincoln, dated 8th Dec 1863. This oath was administered to me, on the 24th of May 1865—by Lt Col Chas Warren 11th Conn: Vols, at Exchange Hotel Richmond. I reached Balto, on my way to my home, at Macon Mills, Carroll, Co. Md last week but have feared to go further as I have been informed that I have been indicted for treason in Carroll Co and that my oath of amnesty would not secure me from imprisonment and trial. I left my home before I had attained my majority, and have never Exercised the right of Suffrage in the United States. I appeal to you that I may obtain such papers as will secure me from molestation. My address is 209 Franklin St Baltimore."—ALS, *ibid.* On June 7, Lt. Col. John Woolley, provost marshal, endorsed the letter. *"Respectfully returned to* Lt. Col. Lawrence A. A. G. with information that under the new constitution and laws of the State the man is liable to indictment and imprisonment on a charge of treason. I am not aware that the Military authorities intend or even desire to interfere in cases of this kind. Mr. Shriver is in Baltimore and no one molests him. If he cannot go to his former home on account of a criminal indictment pending there, I do not see how the Military authorities can interfere" —AES, *ibid.* On June 1, W. F. Holmes, 4th Tenn. Cav., and J. Y. Gooch, 32nd Tenn., Baltimore, wrote to USG. "With a due sense of my presumption in adressing You, can only offer as apology my present unfortunate condition. Am a paroled prisoner of War from Army of Genl Johnson, being in Hospital at Charlotte N. C. having one leg Amputated from which am still Suffering, was sent by provost Marshal of Charlotte by this route to my home in Tennessee, but on arrival at this place Provost Marshal says cannot go any further Am a stranger without means or friends am not capable of seeking employment and if at home could obtain attention which cannot expect at The hands of strangers. Your sympathy for poor friendless Soldiers induces me to apply for some means of reaching my home, which am not able to obtain for myself I am staying at soldiers Rest in this place a partner of mine from same state who has come with me from N. C. and assisted me hitherto also Paroled prisoner unable to go further begs your Kind and generous consideration in our difficulties. with due defer-ence to Your decision am Your very humble petitioners"—ALS, *ibid.* On June 2, Bowers endorsed the letter. "Respectfully referred to Maj Gen Wallace Comd'g Mid, Dept,"—AES, *ibid.* On June 7, Woolley endorsed the letter. "*Respectfully returned to* Lt. Col. Lawrence A. A. G. with remark that these men are at Soldiers Rest the one legged man is in a bad condition. I have no orders to furnish transportation, hence these men are compelled to remain where they are and trust to luck for means to get to their homes."—AES, *ibid.* On June 8, Maj. Gen. Lewis Wallace endorsed both letters. "*Respectfully returned to* Lieut: Col: T—S. Bowers A. A. G, whose attention is invited to the endorsement of Lt. Col. Woolley Pro: Mar: 8th A. C. in each case. In the cases of *Gooch* and *Holmes* now at soldiers rest, no authority is known for furnishing transportation to their homes."—ES, *ibid.*

1865, JUNE 2, 11:40 A.M. Maj. Gen. George G. Meade to Brig. Gen. John A. Rawlins. "The 6th corps reached here this morning & is now going into camp on 4 mile run between Hall's hill & Balls X roads—Hd Qrs near Balls X roads—The regiments & men belonging to this corps included in existing orders will be mustered out without delay."—ALS (telegram sent), DNA, RG 94, War Records Office, Army of the Potomac; telegram received (at 11:45 A.M.), *ibid.*, RG 107, Telegrams Collected (Bound); *ibid.*, RG 108, Telegrams Received. *O.R.*, I, xlvi, part 3, 1247.

1865, JUNE 2. Maj. Gen. John Pope to USG. "The following despatch just received & forwarded for your information—Fort Leavenworth Kan June 1st 1865—MAJ GEN JNO POPE. Lt Col Davis reports by letter dated Helena Ark May twentieth 20 that he has got through at Wittsburg on St Francis River and is on way to Jacksonport. he paroled at Wittsburg two thousand one hundred men & officers & Gen Thompson says there will be three times as many at Jacksonport. Everything went off satisfactory, but little public property turned over (signed)—G M DODGE. M G C."—Telegram received (at 2:40 P.M.), DNA, RG 107, Telegrams Collected (Bound); *ibid.*, RG 108, Telegrams Received; copies (sent at 11:30 A.M.), *ibid.*, RG 393, Dept. of Mo., Telegrams Sent; DLC-USG, V, 54. Incomplete in *O.R.*, I, xlviii, part 2, 722.

1865, JUNE 2. John F. Guthrie, 1st lt., 61st N. C., to USG. "Having been confined at this post for several months as a Prisoner of War—And being extremely Anxious to return My Allegiance to the U S. And return to my home, I address this note to you with an earnest request that you will obtain My discharge from custody. My home is in No. Carolina And I have no friends in the North who have influence sufficient to obtain from the War Department An order for my release, And Knowing your generosity to the vanquished I am induced to address this petition to you with an earnest hope that you will interest yourself in my behalf, A word from you in My favor will restore Me to My home And family And will Make me sincerely grate-

ful to you for your Kindness"—ALS, DNA, RG 109, Unfiled Papers and
Slips, Guthrie, John F.

1865, JUNE 3. To Secretary of War Edwin M. Stanton. "I would respectfully recommend that Col. W. H. Morgan, 3d Regt U S Veterans, of
the 1st Army Corps be appointed a Brigadier General by brevet and assigned to duty with such brevet rank for gallant and meritorious services."
—LS, DNA, RG 94, ACP, S1624 CB 1865.

1865, JUNE 3. USG endorsement. "Respectfully forwarded to the Secretary of War for instructions. I am of the opinion that General Pope's views
and action are correct."—ES, DNA, RG 108, Letters Received. Written on
a letter of May 30 from Maj. Gen. John Pope, St. Louis, to USG. "A very
singular question has arisen in this State to which I desire to invite the attention of the Government. An Ordinance of the late Constitutional State
Convention of Missouri, vacated all the civil offices in the State and conferred
upon the Governor the power to fill them by his own appointment. In accordance with this Ordinance, he has by original appointments, and by re-
appointments, filled all the offices thus vacated. In some cases the present in-
cumbents, having been elected at the last general election, assert that the
Vacating Ordinance is unconstitutional, and therefore, refuse to surrender
their offices or their records to the new appointees. If the Supreme Court of
the State were intact, there would be no doubt as to the legal mode of procedure in these cases, but unfortunately the offices of the Supreme Judges
were also vacated by this Ordinance, and there seems to be no judicial
tribunal to which the decision on these cases can be referred. The Governor
of the State is therefore left to enforce this Ordinance and to install his new
appointees into office in the manner which seems to him most judicious. He
has called on the Military Commanders of United States Troops in Missouri to send a force under his direction to dispossess the old State Officers,
and install the new. I have thus far declined to furnish this force. First:
Because I do not think it necessary to do so in a State like Missouri, which
has a loyal State Executive, and a majority of over Forty Thousand loyal
voters. Second: Because I do not feel authorized to furnish United States
Troops for such a purpose until the 'civil Posse' and the Militia of the State
have been called out and have proved unable to execute these ~~orders.~~ processes Third: Because, where a state is in the condition of Missouri with a
loyal Executive, a large and organized Militia Force, and a very large majority of office holders, loyal men, it is abundantly able to enforce its own
laws and ordinances, and has no right to call upon United States Troops
before using its own civil and Military power. Neither do I think it well for
the United States Authorities to interfere in any manner in questions of this
kind arising in a state like Missouri, and confined entirely to citizens of the
State. For the good of the people of the State, and to secure confidence on
their part that they will hereafter, as heretofore,—before the War—be left
to settle all questions of a civil character arising among themselves, unmo-

lested by the United States Government, or by outside force or influence, I recommend that no orders be sent me which will require me to change or modify the policy of non-interference in civil matters in this State, which I have pursued with such satisfactory results since I have been in command here. In states differently situated intervention, on the part of the Government, might and probably would be necessary. In Missouri, having a loyal State Executive and a majority of over forty thousand loyal voters and all the machinery of Civil Administration in operation, sustained by an organized and armed militia force under the command of the State Executive, such intervention could not fail in my judgement to be attended with injurious consequences to the people. I ask respectfully therefore, that my course in this matter be sustained. I have the honor to transmit enclosed copy of a letter to the Governor of Missouri on this subject, and request that I be notified by Telegraph of the decision of the Government on the course I have decided to pursue."—LS, *ibid. O.R.*, I, xlviii, part 2, 682–83. The enclosure is *ibid.*, pp. 685–86. See *ibid.*, p. 797. On June 5, Secretary of War Edwin M. Stanton wrote to Pope. "Your communication of the 30th ultimo, addressed to Lieut. General Grant, in reference to the difficulty existing between the Governor of Missouri and certain persons holding civil offices in that State, was referred to the President, who has approved the course you have pursued in the matter, and expressed the opinion that no further action is at present necessary."—LS, DNA, RG 393, Dept. of Mo., Letters Received.

1865, JUNE 3, 10:40 A.M.   To Brig. Gen. George W. Cullum. "I will be at West-Point Teusday morning."—ALS (telegram sent), DNA, RG 107, Telegrams Collected (Bound); telegram sent, *ibid. O.R.*, I, xlvi, part 3, 1250. On Sunday, June 4, 6:10 P.M., Bvt. Col. Orville E. Babcock telegraphed to Cullum. "Genl Grant will not be at West Point until Thursday morning instead of Tuesday."—ALS (telegram sent), DNA, RG 107, Telegrams Collected (Bound); telegram sent, *ibid. O.R.*, I, xlvi, part 3, 1252. On June 8, USG, West Point, wrote to Hamilton Fish. "My stay at West Point being limited to a few hours, myself and Staff will be unable to accept your kind invitation for Friday afternoon."—Typescript, DLC-Hamilton Fish.

1865, JUNE 3.   Brig. Gen. John A. Rawlins endorsement. "Adjutant General will please issue the within order"—ES, DNA, RG 94, Letters Received, 580A 1865. Written on Special Orders No. 276. "Major General Geo. G. Meade, Command'g Army of the Potomac will send all western troops, including those from the State of Ohio, now serving in the Army of the Potomac and that are not to be discharged under existing orders, to Louisville, Kentucky, to report to Major General Jno A Logan, Commanding Army of the Tennessee. The Quartermasters Department will furnish necessary transportation."—Copy, *ibid. O.R.*, I, xlvi, part 3, 1250. See *ibid.*, p. 1255.

1865, JUNE 3. Bvt. Col. Theodore S. Bowers endorsement. "Respectfully referred to Maj. Gen. Jno. A Logan, Comdg Army of the Tenn., who will take immediate steps to carry out the recommendation of the Quartermaster General of the Army."—AES, DNA, RG 393, Dept. of the Tenn., Unbound Materials, Letters Received. Written on a letter of June 2 from Bvt. Maj. Gen. Montgomery C. Meigs to USG. "A citizen residing in the neighborhood of this city informs me that he has been offered a mule or mules by soldiers of the 16th army corps apparently for thirty dollars—That the mules are not branded & that they are being sold at such prices—I presume that they must be captured mules which in the haste of Shermans march have not been branded & which replace mules abandoned during the march or which have been brought in by soldiers & not turned in to the Quarter masters Department To secure this property to the UStates I respectfully recommend that the special attention of army corps commanders be called to the subject & that they be instructed to cause all such mules to be turned in to the Chief Quartermaster of the Depot of Washgtn immediately. All that are allowed to remain in the camps should be branded as required by the regulations of the army"—ALS, *ibid.*, RG 108, Letters Received. A notation on the letter received indicates that Bowers also referred Meigs's letter to Maj. Gen. Henry W. Slocum.—Copy, *ibid.*

1865, JUNE 3. Bvt. Maj. Gen. Montgomery C. Meigs to USG. "Respectfully submitted to Lt General Grant—Shall these horses be forwarded to City Point I understood that the Artillery would be much reduced. There ought to be mules enough on about Richmond for all purposes—It is reported that mules & horses have been given away there by order of the military commanders—"—AES, DNA, RG 92, Miscellaneous Letters Sent (Press). Written on a letter of June 3 from Brig. Gen. Rufus Ingalls. On the same day, Brig. Gen. John A. Rawlins endorsed the request. "Respectfully returned to the Quartermaster General. This requisition need not be filled at present."—Copy, *ibid.*, Supplies and Purchases, Public Animals, Letters Received.

1865, JUNE 3, 6:00 P.M. Maj. Gen. John Pope, St. Louis, to USG. "Gen Reynolds asks for authority to fill up the 3rd U. S. Regular Cavalry now at Little Rock with recruits from discharged volunteer Regts—I have authorised him to do so. He asks also that a field officer of the Regt. be sent him, which I respectfully ask may be done."—Telegram received (at 7:45 P.M.), DNA, RG 107, Telegrams Collected (Bound); *ibid.*, RG 108, Telegrams Received; copies, *ibid.*, RG 393, Military Div. of the Mo., Telegrams Sent; DLC-USG, V, 54. *O.R.*, I, xlviii, part 2, 750. See *ibid.*, p. 752.

1865, JUNE 3. G. M. Hart, Kent County, Md., to USG. "I hope you will pardon me for taking the liberty of writing you a few lines I feel asshured from your magnimity that you will not only pardon me but that you will appeciate the feelings that promt me to do so. I have a son Lieut., William

E Hart., a prisner of war at fort Delaware ~~that~~ that your victorious armies captured last may one year ago at Spotsilvania in Virginia. he sir is a citizen of Virginia and was practng law in King Wm County when this Rebelion broke out he has a famly still Residng there when capturd on the 12 of may 64 he was held as a pisner on fort delawer untill august of 64 he was then Removed down on Morris Iland undr fire of Confederate Batters for Several months then he contractd Scurvy and desintery and was confined in the hospittal for long time Sent Back to fort delawar wheere he has Recovered his Helht ~~in~~ he belong to Lees army had he not bin a prisner at the time Genl lee was capturd he would have bin at liberty with the Rest of the army now as the war is over and he tells me has filed application at washington for to take the oath and be discharged and as the author[ities] there have delayed for weeks to notice it—he asks your Excelency please Give an order to the Commander at the fort for his discharge he is willing and has bin for mont[hs] to comply with all the Requiremnts of Goverment and Many officers have bin discharge from there. I undrstoo[d] by your Kindness oh General if you will only please to notic this feeble Request Sattisfactory you will confer a great Blessing on aged parents and an Erring Son for wich we pray that Heavens choise Blessings May Ever Rest on you and yours"—ALS, DNA, RG 109, Unfiled Papers and Slips, Hart, William E.

1865, JUNE 4, 10:50 A.M. To Maj. Gen. John M. Schofield. "Order the Signal Corps to Washington."—ALS (telegram sent), DNA, RG 107, Telegrams Collected (Bound); telegram sent (marked as sent at 11:05 A.M.), *ibid.*; telegrams received (3), *ibid.*, Telegrams Collected (Unbound). *O.R.*, I, xlvii, part 3, 621. On June 3, 10:10 A.M., Schofield, Raleigh, had telegraphed to USG. "The Signal Corps is no longer of any service in this Department. What shall be done with it?"—ALS (telegram sent), DNA, RG 107, Telegrams Collected (Unbound); telegrams received (4—at 6:00 P.M.), *ibid.*; *ibid.*, Telegrams Collected (Bound); *ibid.*, RG 108, Telegrams Received. *O.R.*, I, xlvii, part 3, 618.

1865, JUNE 4, 11:05 A.M. To Maj. Gen. George H. Thomas. "Send one of your pontoon bridges from the Tenn. river to Gn. Pope if it can be spared. If it can not be sent advise me."—ALS (telegram sent), DNA, RG 107, Telegrams Collected (Bound); telegram sent, *ibid.*; copies, *ibid.*, RG 108, Letters Sent; DLC-USG, V, 46, 76, 108. On June 2, Maj. Gen. Grenville M. Dodge, Fort Leavenworth, had telegraphed to USG. "The trip north of Platte River is very much delayed by the crossing of Loup Fork at Columbus and the Platte River at Kearney. If one of the pontoon bridges across the Tenn River in Dept of Cumberland could be sent me it would be taken out from Omaha & placed across these streams & be a great benefit to Govt as well as the emergency & we could use it for several years. Think I could get it transported ~~to~~ from Omaha free of cost to Govt. It could be sent from Nashville to Omaha by boat. The bridge I built at Decatur,

French batteaux would be the best. Can it be had"—Telegram received (at
11:40 P.M.), DNA, RG 107, Telegrams Collected (Bound); *ibid.*, RG
108, Telegrams Received; copies, *ibid.*, RG 393, Dept. of Kan., Telegrams
Sent; (misdated June 3) DLC-USG, V, 54. *O.R.*, I, xlviii, part 2, 734.
See *ibid.*, p. 755. On June 4, Brig. Gen. William D. Whipple, chief of staff
for Thomas, Nashville, twice telegraphed to USG. "Shall pontoon train
be sent with 4th Corps?" "Can ship a train of 40 boats from this point [to]
Genl Pope in 3 days. The 4th Corps has 60 or 70 more. Do not know exactly what there is in Tennessee river."—Telegrams received (the first at
3:40 P.M., the second at 4:10 P.M.), DNA, RG 107, Telegrams Collected
(Bound); *ibid.*, DNA, RG 108, Telegrams Received; copies (the first
dated June 3), *ibid.*, RG 393, Dept. of the Cumberland, Telegrams Sent;
DLC-USG, V, 54. On June 6, 11:00 A.M., USG telegraphed to Thomas.
"You need not send pontoon with 4th Corps. Send Gen. Pope a Pontoon train."—ALS (telegram sent), DNA, RG 107, Telegrams Collected
(Bound); telegram sent, *ibid.*; copies, *ibid.*, RG 108, Letters Sent; *ibid.*,
RG 393, Dept. of the Cumberland, Telegrams Received; DLC-USG, V,
46, 109. *O.R.*, I, xlix, part 2, 961. On June 6, 11:30 A.M., Bvt. Brig.
Gen. Cyrus B. Comstock telegraphed to Maj. Gen. Philip H. Sheridan. "Can
you get all the ponton equipage you want at New Orleans? If not how
much do you want and of what kind?"—ALS (telegram sent), DNA, RG
107, Telegrams Collected (Bound); telegram sent, *ibid.*; telegram received, *ibid.*, Telegrams Collected (Unbound). *O.R.*, I, xlviii, part 2, 790.
On June 9, 10:35 A.M., Sheridan, New Orleans, telegraphed to Comstock.
"I find here all the Pontoon Equipment I shall want"—Telegram received
(on June 10, 3:00 P.M.), DNA, RG 107, Telegrams Collected (Bound);
ibid., RG 108, Telegrams Received; copies, DLC-USG, V, 54; (2) DLC-
Philip H. Sheridan. *O.R.*, I, xlviii, part 2, 827.

On June 20, Dodge wrote to Maj. Gen. John Pope requesting a different
type of pontoon bridge than the one sent from Nashville.—Copy, DNA,
RG 108, Letters Received. *O.R.*, I, xlviii, part 2, 947–48. On June 21, Pope
endorsed this letter. "Respectfully forwarded to the Genl in Chief of the
Army with the recommendation that the request of Genl Dodge be com-
plied with—The Batteaux afford the cheapest & speediest method of bridg-
ing the Platte river over which every thing now is ferried—"—AES, DNA,
RG 108, Letters Received. *O.R.*, I, xlviii, part 2, 948. On June 26, Brig.
Gen. John A. Rawlins endorsed this letter. "Respectfully referred to the
Chief Engineer of the Army who will please furnish the bridge within
required, if there is one to spare from those here tofore in use"—ES, DNA,
RG 108, Letters Received. *O.R.*, I, xlviii, part 2, 948. On June 27, Dodge
telegraphed to Capt. Joseph M. Bell, adjt. for Pope, on the same matter.—
Telegram received (at 9:00 A.M.), DNA, RG 108, Letters Received.
O.R., I, xlviii, part 2, 1008. On the same day, Pope endorsed this telegram
to USG.—AES, DNA, RG 108, Letters Received. At 11:45 A.M., Bvt.
Col. Theodore S. Bowers telegraphed to Pope. "How many feet in length
of Wooden pontoon bridge does Gen Dodge need."—ALS (telegram sent),

ibid., RG 107, Telegrams Collected (Bound); telegram sent, *ibid.*; telegram received (at 2:00 P.M.), *ibid.*, Telegrams Collected (Unbound). On June 28, Pope telegraphed to USG. "General Dodge reports that he needs 2000. feet of bridge to supply all necessary points—If that length cannot be supplied he can trestle out"—Telegram received (at 4:20 P.M.), *ibid.*; *ibid.*, Telegrams Collected (Bound). See *O.R.*, I, xlviii, part 2, 1032, 1046.

1865, JUNE 4.   Maj. Gen. John M. Schofield, Raleigh, to USG. "I respectfully request leave of absence for thirty days, with the privelege of applying for an extension, to take effect as soon as I get the affairs of my Department in such shape that I can leave it temporarily without detriment to the service. The condition of this state is so perfectly quiet that the presence of troops seems almost unnecessary, and the appointment of a Provisional Governor will relieve me from the most important and difficult duties heretofore devolved upon me. The muster out of troops, reduction of expenditures and similar matters will require my attention for a short time. Genl Cox will of course leave the service with the majority of his troops which are to be mustered out as soon as possible. Genl Terry will return from leave of absence by the 15th of this month. He is fully qualified to command the Department either temporarily or permanently. I have been called upon by the Congressional Committee on the Conduct of the War to answer certain questions, which will amount to giving a history of all the campaigns I have been engaged in during the rebellion. To do this will consume considerable time and render it necessary for me to visit Louisville and St. Louis where I can have access to official records   The above facts, in addition to my desire to visit my family and enjoy a short rest after four years of constant hard work, are my reasons for asking a leave of absence."—ALS, DNA, RG 108, Letters Received. *O.R.*, I, xlvii, part 3, 621.

1865, JUNE 4.   Maj. Gen. William T. Sherman, West Point, N. Y., to USG.—*The Collector*, March, 1953, B264.

1865, JUNE 4.   Lavinia Butt, Norfolk, to USG. "I take the liberty of addressing you, in behalf of my Son George W. Butt, who was a private in the Huger Battery 'of Genl Lees Army,' and was captured in front of Petersburg about the 21st of April and sent to Point Lookout. The last information I received from him, he was in the Hospital at that place; he has expressed a desire to take the 'Oath of Allegiance' to the United States, and return to his home,   I hope he may be allowed to do so, as his father & myself are both advanced in years, with a large family dependant on us for support,   independent of the Solicitude that we have as parents, we require the Services of our Son George, (who is now twenty two years of age) to support his Sisters and ourselves. I do most humbly pray that you will grant this petition as my Son has always been a good and dutiful boy, and you will be doing an act of Charity towards his parents."—ALS, DNA, RG 109, Unfiled Papers and Slips, Butt, George W.

1865, JUNE 4.   John R. Joynes, "Near Norfolk," to USG. "I am an invalid (with a Wife & four Small children) and have been for two years and cant be of much assistance to my family only at intervals   I lost evry thing I had at the burning of Hampton   My house and furniture   did not Save the first article that was in it   I am in my fifty Sixth year   I have two Sons grown, Prisoners at Point Lookout   Captured Sunday the 2nd day of April before Petersburg   They were Members of the N L A Blues Capt Grandy and have been at Point lookout Since the 5th of April   They might and would be a great help to me and my family were they released as they are ready & willing to take the Oath of Alegiance to the U N States   Would you be so kind as to give have them released forthwith   As under in my present state of health I may go to that Bourne whence no Traveler ever yet returned and they not See me   I assure you it would be confering a great favour on me as well as a blessing to my family for you to have them released   in So doing you will much Oblige . . . Their names Are Solon H Joynes & William A Joynes Now in Co B 9th division care of Major A G Brady Camp of Prisioners"—ALS, DNA, RG 109, Unfiled Papers and Slips, Jones, John R.

1865, JUNE 5.   To Secretary of War Edwin M. Stanton. "I would respectfully recommend the muster out of the 15th & 50th N. Y. Vol. Eng. troops, Also now with the Army of the Potomac, and of the 1st N. Y. Vol. Eng.s with the Army of the James,"—ALS, DNA, RG 94, Vol. Service Div., Letters Received, A1078 (VS) 1865. On the same day, Stanton endorsed the letter. "Approved, and referred to Col. Vincent to issue order." —ES, *ibid.*

1865, JUNE 5.   To Secretary of War Edwin M. Stanton. "I have the honor to request, that Lieut, Col, M, R, Morgan Commissary of Subsistence U. S. Vols. and Brevet Col, U. S. A, be transferred from the 25th Army Corps and assigned to duty at these Head Quarters as Inspector of the Subsistence Department, with his Brevet rank"—Copies, DLC-USG, V, 46, 76, 108; DNA, RG 108, Letters Sent. *O.R.*, I, xlvi, part 3, 1254.

1865, JUNE 5, 2:00 P.M.   To Maj. Gen. George Cadwalader. "You may direct the reissue of Arms to returned troops until after the parde in the City."—ALS (telegram sent), DNA, RG 107, Telegrams Collected (Bound); telegram sent, *ibid.*; copies, *ibid.*, RG 108, Letters Sent; *ibid.*, RG 393, Depts. of the Susquehanna and Pa., Register of Letters Received; DLC-USG, V, 46, 76, 108.

1865, JUNE 5, 11:50 A.M.   To Maj. Gen. John A. Dix. "I will order the 1st Vt. Cav.y to report to you to relieve the Frontier regt. They will be sent without horses and will be mounted on the horses turned over by the regiment you disband."—ALS (telegram sent), DNA, RG 107, Telegrams

Collected (Bound); telegram sent, *ibid.*; copies, *ibid.*, RG 108, Letters Sent; DLC-USG, V, 46, 76, 108.

1865, June 5.   B. F. Allen, Point Lookout, Md., to USG. "I was formerly a member of the Army of Nothern Virginia; and taken prisoner on the 6th of April. I write to solicit at your hands my release. I have a family dependent upon me for support, and who have been since my capture, in a destitute condition. I do not write from any sense of personal merit, nor do I make the application as a demand for justice; for such claims would be absurd in the highest degree; since I have been arrayed in arms against you and your government (which I hope soon to claim as mine): but lay siege to your charity, for the sake of the loved ones at home who are suffering through my actions, for the sake of those who may now be even suffering the pangs of hunger, do I humbly solicit your influence in my behalf. Hoping that I may not be disappointed in my expectations of a speedy release."—ALS, DNA, RG 109, Unfiled Abstracts, Allen, B. F.

1865, June 5.   F. J. Cassidy, 11th S. C., Fort Delaware, to USG. "I respectfully apply to you for my release.—I have an old Father and Mother, brothers and sisters, depending on me as the oldest member of the family for support.—My parents are both poor and in needy circumstances.—I am anxious to procure some good situation which would be preferable to remaining in prison, where I could be of more advantage to parents and country than I am in Fort Delaware.—Hoping you will order my release immediately, . . ."—ALS, DNA, RG 109, Unfiled Papers and Slips, Cassidy, F. J.

1865, June 5.   William G. Taylor, Richmond, to USG. "I have the honor to make an application for the release from prison my two brothers in law Capt. H G Richardson Co G 44th Va Infantry captured at spottsylvania C. H. on the 12th of may 1864 now confined at Fort Delaware, and private E A Richardson of Co. B. 18th Va infantry Picketts Divn. but designated in the prison as C.o A 5th Division at Point Lookout. Capt. Richardson has been in confinement for more than a year and is willing and desirous of taking the oath of allegiance to the U. S Government and has expressed his willingness to do so many months ago; he is most anxious as you may suppose to be released from confinement which has resulted in detriment to his health and return to the peaceful persuits of life. He entered the southern army as he beleived from a sence of duty and as the rebellion is now overthrown he will be as devoted in his loyalty as any citizen of the Country. E A Richardson is only a youth of 18 years of age   was conscribed and put in the army last winter   he is anxious to take the oath of allegiance and be released from prison—I have writen to you because of your well deserved reputation for humanity and generous magnaminity to your oppressed and erring countrymen and especially as longer confinement of these young men can serve no purpose of public policy either civil or military, I therefore appeal to you as the great military chieftain of our country whose only purpose is to promote the common good of all & with the least oppression to any to release the young men upon their taking the required oath that they may return to their homes ~~and engage~~ and contribute in their humbled way to the general prosperity of the country—I refer you to Mess Lewis Johnson &C Washington, J S Benner &C Baltimore or Judge Gholson of Cincinatti Ohio."—ALS, DNA, RG 109, Unfiled Papers and Slips, Taylor, William G.

1865, JUNE 6. To Secretary of War Edwin M. Stanton. "I would recommend that all enlistments for the Veteran Reserve Corps, be discontinued. Transfers from the Volunteer Service, of men desiring to go into that Corps, and who are unfit for active service, should be the only increase allowed in my judgment."—Copies, DLC-USG, V, 46, 109; DNA, RG 108, Letters Sent; *ibid.*, RG 110, Veteran Reserve Corps, Letters Received, G266 (VRC) 1865. *O.R.*, I, xlvi, part 3, 1257.

1865, JUNE 6, 11:30 A.M. To Maj. Gen. Henry W. Halleck. "Please send permit to Wm H. Tompkin Salem Va. to return to Maryland. He has taken the Amnesty oath."—ALS (telegram sent), DNA, RG 107, Telegrams Collected (Bound); telegram sent, *ibid.*; copies, *ibid.*, RG 108, Letters Sent; DLC-USG, V, 46. USG's Aunt Rachel had a son named William H. Tompkins who served with C.S.A. forces. See letter to Mary Grant, April 29, 1861; Arthur Hastings Grant, *The Grant Family* (Poughkeepsie, N. Y., 1898), p. 144.

1865, JUNE 6, 11:10 A.M. To Mayor John L. Chapman, Baltimore. "Previous engagements will prevent me accepting your invitation for today."—ALS (telegram sent), DNA, RG 107, Telegrams Collected (Bound); telegram sent, *ibid.*

1865, JUNE 6, 11:48 A.M. To William S. Hillyer, New York City. "I will be in New York only for the day. Will leave at 12 O'clock at night. Have ~~mad~~ arranged to stay at the Astor-House while there."—ALS (telegram sent), DNA, RG 107, Telegrams Collected (Bound).

1865, JUNE 6. To C. T. Jones and four others, Philadelphia. ". . . The achievements of our volunteers for the last four years entitles them to the lastin[g] gratitude of all loyal people and I therefore rejoice at the enthusiastic reception which they ar[e] everywhere receiving.—It is not likely that I will be present at any of these receptions but I know the men will do me the justice to believe that all my sympathies are with them."—ALS (incomplete facsimile), Sotheby Parke-Bernet Sale, Dec. 17, 1975, no. 798. On June 1, William S. Stokely, Philadelphia, had telegraphed to USG. "A committee from City [Councils] will await upon the Secretary of War to-

morrow to urge the importance of [*coming*—] for a few days [to] Philadelphia organizations so that we can receive [*them*] in a body with such a welcome as their achievements have earned. We earnestly urge your assistance
in this matter, satisfied [t]hat a word from you will secure this"—Telegram
received (at 3:30 P.M.), DNA, RG 107, Telegrams Collected (Bound).

1865, JUNE 6, 12:40 P.M. Maj. Gen. John Pope, St. Louis, to USG.
"Please instruct me how [to] answer following telegram. You will see the
necessity of an answer being given today—."—Telegram received (at 4:45
P.M.), DNA, RG 107, Telegrams Collected (Bound); copy, *ibid.*, RG
393, Military Div. of the Mo., Telegrams Sent. *O.R.*, I, xlviii, part 2, 793.
On June 5, Maj. Gen. Grenville M. Dodge had requested instructions from
Pope regarding orders from Secretary of War Edwin M. Stanton to eject
squatters from the Delaware Indian Reservation. U.S. District Judge David
J. Brewer threatened to arrest Dodge for carrying out Stanton's instructions.—*Ibid.*, p. 784. See *ibid.*, pp. 795, 806. On June 12, Pope endorsed
a communication from Dodge. "Respectfully referred to the Genl. in Chief of
the Army for any further instructions which may be thought necessary. Both
Courts and people in that region are all on the side of squatters and unless
the U. S. Courts act in the matter without prejudice or feeling, then it is
wrong to keep off these squatters except by posting a military force and
keeping them off by violent measures. This process will subject the soldiers
and officers to constant conflicts with the civil courts, which I am unwilling
to begin without the approval of the Government."—Copy, DNA, RG 393,
Military Div. of the Mo., Register of Letters Received.

1865, JUNE 6 or 7. Bvt. Maj. Gen. James H. Wilson, Macon, Ga., to
Brig. Gen. John A. Rawlins. "The muster out is depriving me of best officers Every recommendation & effort having failed to procure the promotion
of Col LeGrange of the 1st Wis Cav he will be lost to the service unless I
can get appointed a Major in the R I. G Dept which I have recommended
him. Please do what you Can for him for I am sure there's no better officer
in the service. If Gen Thomas is in town show this telegh ask him to put
upon it his endorsement as the interest of the service requires."—Telegram
received (marked as sent on June 7, received on June 9, noon), DNA, RG
107, Telegrams Collected (Bound); *ibid.*, RG 108, Telegrams Received;
copies (dated June 6), *ibid.*, RG 393, Cav. Corps, Military Div. of the
Miss., Telegrams Sent; (dated June 7) DLC-USG, V, 54. Dated June 7
in *O.R.*, I, xlix, part 2, 967. See *ibid.*, p. 1078.

1865, JUNE 6. Thomas F. Blakemore, Philadelphia, to USG. "I have a
nephew at Fort Delaware. he is ill.—to spare his life. I make to you this
appeal. to ask at your hands, or of you influence the discharge of *Private.
Marcus M Bayly. Co. H. 13 Rg. Va Infy.*—I have no words to say how
deeply. eternally grateful I shall be for this exercise of your generous.
goodness towards this poor boy.—and. so, confiding in your proverbial mag-

nanimity. I add only. my apologies for trespassing upon time so valuable."
—ALS, DNA, RG 109, Unfiled Papers and Slips, Bayly, Marcus M.

1865, JUNE 6. Thomas Dunn, Portsmouth, Va., to USG. "I would beg
of you, that you use your influence in causing the release of my Son William
H. Dunn, who is at present a prisoner of war at Point-Lookout. He was captured some time before the fall of Richmond, and has been in the above
named prison since his capture. He has expressed a desire to take the oath
of allegiance to the United States Government, and return to his home, there
to remain a peaceful citizen. I write to you, general, for I know that it requires but a word from you, to ensure his release; and if you would lend
your influence in his favor, you will make a lasting debtor of . . ."—ALS,
DNA, RG 109, Unfiled Papers and Slips, Dunn, William H. On the same
day, U.S. District Attorney Lucius H. Chandler, Norfolk, endorsed the letter. "Believing the above named Wm H. Dun will be faithful to the obligations he may assume upon taking the 'Oath of alegiance, I hope he may be
released—"—AES, *ibid.*

1865, JUNE 6. William T. Joynes, Petersburg, to USG. "On behalf of
Mr Thomas C. Christian, an old and very worthy citizen of this place, I
beg to call your attention to the case of his son, Capt: Emmet B. Christian,
now a prisoner at Fort Delaware, and respectfully to ask his release from
prison. Capt: Christian commanded Company C 41st Virginia Regiment,
Genl Weisiger' Brigade, Genl Mahone' Divisn, Genl Hill' Corps, Army of
Northern Virginia, and was captured on the 19th day of August 1864, in
one of the engagements on the Weldon Rail Road. Capt: Christian is a
young man of respectable character, and of very moderate circumstances.
He had been married only a few weeks at the time of his capture. He entered
the army as a private in 1861, and had been promoted to a Captaincy but a
short time before the engagement in which he was taken prisoner—His
father is a poor but most worthy man, who never held an office or involved
in any way in politics or public affairs—"—ALS, DNA, RG 109, Unfiled
Papers and Slips, Christian, Emet B.

1865, JUNE 6. 1st Lt. William C. Keith, 1st S. C. Rifles, and 2nd Lt.
Thomas J. Hall, 1st S. C. Rifles, Johnson's Island, Ohio, to USG. "We trust
you will pardon this trespass on your valuable time, when we plead in
excuse the condition of our families and their want of our presence and assistance. We have been prisoners of war for Some time; Applied for the
oath immediately after notice of its tender, was published to the inmates of
this prison, and have seen many, who held back for days after us, released
through the mediation of influential friends and relatives, while we are
Still retained without any such hope or prospect. Being unpretending citizens of upper South Carolina, we have no Such outside influence in our
favor and apply to you, as *To the Soldiers friend*, believing you will assist
us, as readily as the wealthiest & most honored. If released, We not only

promise a willing compliance with the requirements of the oath, but also to use our influence to preserve order and restore harmony in our Sections. We sincerely hope our petition will meet with your favorable consideration and an order for our release will be obtained & forwarded & we will be permitted to return to our families, under obligations to So worthy a man"— ALS, DNA, RG 109, Records Relating to Prisoners, Oaths and Paroles, Johnson's Island, Ohio.

1865, JUNE 6. William Pearson, Norfolk, to USG. "Excuse the liberty I take in addressing you, as the end will justify the motive I am a Northern man from Brooklyn, N. Y.—reference the Rev Newton Heston, of Brooklyn—I came here two weeks ago, for a mercantile purpose I have come across a good many cases of suffering arising out of the course our erring fellow citizens have taken in the terrible war which you have so nobly helped to subdue,—among others that of Thomas E. Elliott, Co. B., Norfolk Art. Blues, 9th Division, Army of Virginia, under Gen R. E. Lee, taken prisoner at Petersburgh, Ap 2, 1865, and now confined at Point Look Out. His family here consistes of of a wife and 2 children; in a suffering condition. He writes home that he now sees the folly of the cause he espoused, and is willing to take the oath and become a good and loyal citizen of these United States. There is a situation open for him here, where he can earn a good living for his family and restore them to comparative happiness. I ask of you as a favor to grant his discharge,—if at all compatible with your sense of duty. You know the teaching of our Lord and master—it is human to err, but Divine to forgive Returning this man to the bosom of his family will be an act that will not only ameliorate their condition, but tend to bring him under an act of gratitude to you and the cause of which I consider you now the foremost military champion. I hope and trust it will be be said of you, as of the immortal Washington—'the first in war, the first in peace, and the first in the hearts of his countrymen!' I have seen enough to satisfy me. that the Rebellion is completely quelled, and before a great space of time Virginia will be one of the most loyal States of our glorious Union. My heart is full of gratitude to God, for his wisdom in giving us the right men in the right place. I know you will feel like the good Samaritan of old—to do a good deed creates a pleasant reflection that be can derived from no other source. .... P. S. This man writes to his family that the confederate prisoner are dying at the rate of from ten to twenty every day. I hope and trust the Prison at Point LookOut will not prove to the Confederates what Anderonville proved to be to our Union boys"—ALS, DNA, RG 109, Unfiled Papers and Slips, Pearson, William.

1865, JUNE 7. USG endorsement. "Approved and respectfully forwarded to the Secretary of War."—ES, DNA, RG 94, ACP, S1624 CB 1865. Written on a letter of June 6 from Maj. Gen. George G. Meade to Bvt. Col. Theodore S. Bowers recommending ten officers for bvt. promotion.— LS, *ibid. O.R.,* I, xlvi, part 3, 1259.

1865, JUNE 7. USG endorsement. "Respectfully forwarded to the Secretary of War—approved."—ES, DNA, RG 94, ACP, S1624 CB 1865. Written on a letter of June 6 from Bvt. Maj. Gen. Joseph D. Webster to USG. "I beg leave to bring to your notice the claims of Captain W. L. B. Jenney, Additional Aide de Camp to an advancement of rank by Brevet. I have had opportunity since an early period of the war, to know of the great intelligence and assiduity with which Captain J. has discharged his duties (in the Engineer Department) and am strongly of opinion that he has well earned the recognition of his merits herein suggested. His name has stood for a good while at the head of the list of Additional Aids of the grade of Captain and it would seem that *two* grades higher would not be in advance of his just claims."—LS, *ibid.*

1865, JUNE 7. Maj. Gen. John M. Schofield, Raleigh, to USG. "I respectfully request that Col. Willard Warner, 180th Ohio Volunteers may be appointed Brevet Brigadier General for gallant and meritorious services in the Georgia Tenn. & North Carolina campaigns. He is a most deserving officer and is highly recommended by all his commanders. I will forward recommendations by mail, but Col. Warner will be mustered out of service before they can be acted upon. Hence this request by telegraph."—ALS (telegram sent), DNA, RG 107, Telegrams Collected (Unbound); telegram received (at 6:30 P.M.), *ibid.*, Telegrams Collected (Bound); (at 5:40 P.M.) *ibid.*, RG 94, ACP, W1408 CB 1865. *O.R.*, I, xlvii, part 3, 638. On June 9, Brig. Gen. John A. Rawlins endorsed this telegram. "Respectfully forwarded to the Secretary of War"—ES, DNA, RG 94, ACP, S1624 CB 1865. On June 16, USG endorsed this telegram. "Approved and respectfully forwarded to the Secretary of War."—ES, *ibid.*, W1408 CB 1865. Docketing indicates that the appointment had already been made.—*Ibid.* On June 6, Maj. Gen. Jacob D. Cox had written to Lt. Col. John A. Campbell, adjt. for Schofield, recommending Col. Willard Warner for promotion to bvt. brig. gen.—LS, *ibid.*, C540 CB 1865. On June 13, Schofield endorsed this letter. "Respectfully forwarded to the Adjutant General of the Army earnestly recommended. Request was forwarded by telegraph on the 7th inst to Lieut General Grant."—ES, *ibid.* On June 24, USG endorsed this letter. "Approved"—ES, *ibid.*

1865, JUNE 7. Mary F. Stanworth, Norfolk, to USG. "I would respectfully beg your intercession for the release of my brother Jas. H. Conner held as a prisoner of war at Point Lookout Co "I" 9th Div. Trusting my petition will meet with your favorable consideration . . ."—ALS, DNA, RG 109, Unfiled Papers and Slips, Stanworth, Mary F.

1865, JUNE 7. A. C. Stewart, Danville, Mo., to USG. "I have a Son, Charles Stewart who has been in the U. S. Service for the last three years and a half in the Commissary Dept. Eight months Since he was appointed by the President to position as commissary with the rank of captain, and is now on duty as Such at Fayetteville Ark. He is finely educated, and pronounced by the examining Board as proficient in the duties of his Office. He is delighted with the Service and desires a place in the 'Regular Army' At the Suggestion of my wife (formerly Sarah Johnson of Georgetown Ohio. an old School mate of yours.) I make the request of you to give him Some position in the Regular Army if possible. He is a young man of Steady habits, well qualified for any position you may please to confer upon him, and I think will not disgrace any position you may be pleased to give him. Col. Haines, Chief Com of this Dept. will give all necessary recomendations as to his efficiency morals &c. And if necessary I will Send you the recommendation of Gov. Fletcher, Judge Lovelace of the Supreme Court, Senators Henderson and Brown, representatives Rollins and Anderson, and others. I have been litterally torn up by the rebels and Bushwhackers—My Store robbed three times, and finally bursted up, our Town Burned and depopulated, and the citizens made beggars. I well know you are over run with like requests, but Still I thought you might have a place for my Son. Will you be kind enough Genl. to answer this letter? I called to See you when you were last in St. Louis, but you were in the country."—ALS, USG 3.

1865, JUNE 7. Susan Wilkins, Norfolk, to USG. "I have the honor to address you relative to the release of my son now a prisoner of war at Point Lookout Md: 9th Division Co. "B"—He has been a prisoner for many months & by being released would render much comfort & aid to a widowed mother—His name is Wm. P. Wilkins—"—ALS, DNA, RG 109, Unfiled Papers and Slips, Wilkins, Susan.

1865, JUNE 7. "A friend of the Prisoner," Norfolk, to USG. "Having just learned that my Young friend Leroy M. Lee of Norfolk light artilery Blues is a prisoner at Point Lookout Md, I take this method of appealing to your Sympathy for his release I know that your Kind heart can feel for a poor misguided youth. and will do all that is necessary for His immediate relief."—AL, DNA, RG 109, Unfiled Papers and Slips.

1865, JUNE 8. Peter M. Dox, Huntsville, Ala., to USG. "*Private.* . . . Immediately after the organization of the late rebellion, and when the purpose of it's originators was evidenced by the assault on Fort Sumpter, I, with my wife, left the South, and crossing the Ohio River about the 25th April 1861, we remained away from our home in Alabama (a portion of the time in Western New-York, and for a year in St Louis) until March 1864 when we again returned to Huntsville then in possession of the United States military authorities. In Huntsville we remained until the place was evacuated by our forces in December last, on which occasion I again left for Nashville, and remained in that City until after the rebel army under General Hood was defeated, and driven back across the Tennessee River. On the re-occupation of Huntsville by our forces, I again returned to my home, where I have since remained, with the exception of a few days absence on business at Nashville within the past few weeks. Having opposed Secession in it's inception, I refused, in any form, at all times, during the existence of the rebellion, to recognize—either negatively, or otherwise, by implication or actual assent—voluntarily or by compulsion, the authority of the confederate Government. At all times, and on every occasion, I have denounced the rebellion as treason—it's authors as traitors, and it's results, whatever the issue of the struggle might be, as disastrous in the extreme to the Southern people; and I even persistently refused to remain in any place in the South, where the authority of the Government was not recognized and respected, and the Union flag did not wave. When the rebellion commenced, we were in comfortable circumstances, having enough to satisfy our moderate wants for life—At it's end, we find ourselves stripped of every thing, and I am compelled to begin life anew, relying for a support upon the earnings of my daily labor. How long, even this reliance can be depended on, God alone knows; but I am sometimes apprehensive, that it cannot last long. But that consideration would not affect me, were it's consequences to be confined to myself alone: my wife, in the event of my death, would be left dependent. Her devotion to the Union has seconded and sustained me in all that I have done from love of Country in the last four years of trial; And it is to provide for her comfort and independence, that I venture to address you, as her and my personal friend, and to ask whether, in your opinion, it will be possible for us to obtain from the Government compensation for our losses, or any part of them? If we had remained in the South, as other loyal persons (so called) have done during the rebellion, I should expect to suffer without much hope of remuneration—tho. even then, that would be hard to bear, and seem any thing but just. But I venture to say, that there cannot be found, in the insurrectionary States, a parallel to our case, even among the loyal, however *large* in numbers that class may now claim to be. Even with that class, residence under rebel authority, or submission and acquiescence, for the time, to rebel military power, or in some other way by implication at least, are most persons involved in the consequences pursuing a people in revolt. If there be any other case than my own to which these conditions, or some of them, cannot be imputed, I have yet to be informed of it. When you have time to think of this matter, General, if you can discover any way in which I may seek, with some hope of success, to obtain from the Government some compensation for our losses, I hope you will let me know it, and thereby add to the large debt of gratitude I already owe you. I trust you will excuse this personal appeal. You may, perhaps, be the more inclined to do so, when you remember, that hitherto I have, almost always, addressed you in behalf of others rather than myself. The politicians from this, and other States, have so occupied the time of the President, of late, that I would not venture to go to Washington. I should have done so, however, had I supposed that by my presence there, the business of reconstruction could have been promoted. But provisional Governors having been appointed for all the States which needed such an officer, I trust it may not be regarded premature to submit my personal wants to your friendly consideration. Mrs. Dox joins me in regards to Mrs Grant and yourself."—ALS, USG 3. On May 12, Dox had written to USG congratulating him on his victories.—ALS, *ibid.* On May 26, Dox had written to USG to secure the release of John P. Spence, 7th Ala. Cav., from Fort Delaware.—ALS, DNA, RG 109, Unfiled Papers and Slips, John P. Spence.

1865, JUNE 8. James Longstreet, former C.S.A. lt. gen., Lynchburg, Va., to USG. "I address you this communication at the earnest solicitation of a friend who has some relatives confined as prisoners of war and who is very anxious for their release—These young men were captured a few miles from the High bridge, on Thursday the 6th day of April last—Their names are Capt Hugh Nelson Co F 28th Regt Va Vols—at Johnsons Island   Lieut C R Nelson Co F 28th Regt Va Vols—at ~~Point Lookout~~ Johnsons Island   Lieut Robt Camm of late C—S—Navy. Johnsons Island   Private Wm S. Nelson Co H 11th Va regt—(22d Co. 1st Divn Newport News Va—As I understand they signify a perfect willingness to take the Amnesty Oath as a condition precedent to their release. My impression has been Genl. that there was a verbal agreement that the prisoners who had been captured on Genl Lee's retreat, previous to the surrender were also to be paroled. I of course am not aware what motives may influence the Government, in longer retaining prisoners, now that the war is at an end: but it seems to me that their release and their presence at home, would do much good ~~in~~ toward restoring order & tranquility in the Country, besides bringing joy to many households—Why too need they longer languish in prison? I most earnestly solicit your influence to the end, that all prisoners of war be released, and permitted to return to their homes friends, and to the pursuit of peaceful avocations. If however this be not the policy of the Govt at present, I ask that you please procure the release of the four above mentioned young men and much oblige . . . P. S. These young men are the sons of widows who very much need their services at home. Besides taking the oath they are willing to give any other assurances that may be required of them for ~~their~~ any course of conduct—"—ALS, IC.

1865, JUNE 9, 3:00 P.M. Brig. Gen. John A. Rawlins to Maj. Gen. George H. Thomas. "Please send foward without delay to Shreveport, La., to report to Maj. Gen. Sheridan, the following regiments of Cavalry now serving near Memphis, Tenn., if their services can possibly be spared from present duty. If ~~all cannot be spared send such of them as can be~~—Fifth (5th) & Twelfth (12th) Illinois Seventh (7th) Indiana First (1st) Iowa and Second (2d) Wisconsin. If all cannot be spared send such of them as can be"—Telegrams sent (2), DNA, RG 107, Telegrams Collected

(Bound); copies, *ibid.*, RG 108, Letters Sent; DLC-USG, V, 46, 109.
O.R., I, xlix, part 2, 972–73. See *ibid.*, p. 997; *ibid.*, I, xlviii, part 2, 814,
840, 908.

1865, JUNE 9. Philip H. Bush, Covington, Ky., to USG. "I have been
personally acquainted with J Douglas Bruce for many Years, I know him
to be a highly educated Gentleman and a man of great personal integrity I
do beleive that he will faithfully discharge all obligations he may become
responsible for or promise to do—and will honorable adhere to any oath
he may take and would be greatly pleased to see him discharged in conformity to his request and the rules of your department . . . J Douglas
Bruce is the son of John Bruce of Winchester Va who emigrated from
Scotland some fifty Years since, and married a highly respectable Lady of
that place—"—ALS, DNA, RG 249, Letters Received. U.S. Representative
Green Clay Smith of Ky. endorsed this letter. "I am personally unacquainted
with J. Douglas Bruce but am well acquainted with the writer of the
above—His statement is true, and from his representations I have no doubt
Mr J. D. Bruce will strictly conform to whatever oath he may subscribe—
Mr P. S. Bush is one of oldest and most respectful citizens—I trust you
will grant his request—"—AES, *ibid.* On June 5, C.S.A. Lt. Col. J. Douglas Bruce, 47th Va., Johnson's Island, Ohio, had written to Bush for assistance.—ALS, *ibid.* Docketing indicates that Jesse Root Grant also wrote
in behalf of Bruce, and that military authorities ordered the release of
Bruce on June 17.—*Ibid.*

1865, JUNE 9. U.S. Representative Green Clay Smith of Ky., Covington,
to USG. "The order for release of L't Frank Riggs Johnsons Island not
obeyed. Will you telegraph Col Hills"—Telegram received (at 11:30
A.M.), DNA, RG 107, Telegrams Collected (Bound); (at 11:20 A.M.)
ibid., RG 108, Letters Received. On the same day, Brig. Gen. John A.
Rawlins endorsed this telegram. "Respectfully referred to Gen. Hoffman,
Comsy. Gen. of Prisoners."—ES, *ibid.* On June 10, Bvt. Brig. Gen. William
Hoffman endorsed this telegram. "Respectfully returned to Lieut Gen'l U. S.
Grant, Comd'g U. S. A. The Hon G. Clay Smith is under a mistake. The
order was issued on the 2nd inst, the day it was received in this Office."
—AES, *ibid.*

1865, JUNE 9. J. T. Thomas, Philadelphia, to USG. "May I ask of you
to secure the release of Lt, James A Hardin, now a prisoner at Fort Delaware—He is suffering both in mind and body as I am informed—having
been in prison a long time. I would respectfully ask an investigation of his
case—I am told he was at one time, insubordinate—but the punishment he
has undergone has fully subdued him—And he is now desirous of taking
the oath of allegiance."—ALS, DNA, RG 109, Unfiled Papers and Slips,
Hardin, James A.

1865, JUNE 10. USG endorsement. "Respectfully forwarded to the Secretary of War and attention invited to the endorsement of Gen. Pope hereon."—ES, DNA, RG 94, Letters Received, 1235M 1865; copy (dated June 15), DLC-USG, V, 58. The latter date suggests that a staff officer prepared the endorsement for USG's signature on June 10, and USG signed on June 15 after returning from a trip to Chicago. Other endorsements were probably handled in a similar manner during USG's absence (June 8–14). USG's endorsement is written on a letter of May 15 from Col. William A. Phillips, 3rd Indian Home Guards, to Asst. Secretary of War Charles A. Dana complaining that a recent order of Maj. Gen. John Pope restoring southern Kan. to control of the Dept. of Ark. would again allow corrupt parties into the area and cause serious problems with Indians.—ALS, DNA, RG 94, Letters Received, 1235M 1865. On May 30, Dana referred this letter to USG.—ES, *ibid.* On June 1, Bvt. Col. Theodore S. Bowers endorsed this letter. "Respectfully referred to Major General John Pope, Commanding Military Division of the Missouri, for report."—ES, *ibid.* On June 6, Pope endorsed this letter. "respectfully returned to the Genl in Chief of the Army—The District of South Kansas was extended south to include Indian Country west of Arkansas (except Ft Smith) & at the same time all the northern part of that Dist with all the military posts and troops in it was cut off from it & left in Dept of Missouri—The only object was to assembly a cavalry force at F Gibson for a raid into Northern Texas in conjunction with the proposed movement against Kirby Smith from Arkansas river—It was necessary to have a part of South Kansas in this Dist in order to frustrate any movement of the enemy into that Section of Kansas by the force at Ft Gibson—The evils complained of in this letter can be & I do not doubt have been corrected or prevented by Genl Reynolds. I invite the attention of the Genl in Chief to the fact that this letter is addressed & sent direct to the Asst Sec of War by one of my subordinate officers in violation of of Regulations & official propriety—As it has been received and acted on by the Asst Secty of War I cannot now hold the officer in question accountable for his breach of Military propriety but I trust that the Genl in chief will take such action upon the matter as may be necessary to correct such irregularity."—AES, *ibid.*

1865, JUNE 11. James Nicholson, "Lingun," Cape Breton Island, to [USG]. "I am proud in Your victorious Which you have geaned Greate pleasure to them that was in fighting for ther Rights for all My Son is from me and dont no wher he is Which I hope that you will Let me no all About him when you will Receve my hande wrighting Der Sir he Inlisted at Portland Maine U S A and his Name is William S Nicholson Born on the Island of C B and Left two years a go or abouts and very atendive in wrighting till the Last Cruell Battles that was foght in your victorious his Commanders I dont no But he Inlisted 1st Maine Cavlry Company K 2nd Div 2nd Bragede and he was very big for his Eage he was 6 feet about and his

Eage was about 19 years so I hope you will Answer my Request so I pray to you that you will feavour me so mutch as to trep him up so I will come to a Close hoping you my Long Live to potect your Contry and allways in staf office General Grant . . . exques my hand wrighting Sir"—ALS, USG 3. On June 29, Bvt. Col. Adam Badeau wrote to Maj. Gen. Alfred H. Terry requesting information about Private William S. Nicholson, Co. K, 1st Maine Cav.—ALS, *ibid.* Endorsements indicate that Nicholson was present for duty, and docketing indicates that Badeau sent the information to Nicholson's father on July 19.—*Ibid.*

1865, JUNE 12.   USG endorsement. "Respy. forwarded to the secretary of war, and attention invited to that part of Gen Schofields' endorsement in which he speaks of the importance of compliance with orders to stop seizures of private property, and requests that such orders may be sent to the Naval Commanders on the coast of North Carolina"—Copy, DLC-USG, V, 58. *O.R.* (Navy), I, xii, 159. Written on a letter of May 19 of Col. Jones Frankle, 2nd Mass. Art., concerning the seizure of private property after the cessation of hostilities, endorsed by Maj. Gen. John M. Schofield on June 2. —*Ibid.*, p. 158. See *ibid.*, p. 163.

1865, JUNE 12.   Col. John C. Kelton to Bvt. Col. Theodore S. Bowers. "I send by Ad[am]s Express to you today the original letters of general officers withdrawn from the files of the Head Quarters of the Army for the purpose of making copies for Maj Genl Halleck. The enclosed list shows the letters retained by him, either because they were of a private nature, or for the reason that copies are in the possession of the War Dept. with the files of Lt Genl Grant's papers, or have been printed with the proceedings of the milty comtt on the conduct of the War"—ALS, DNA, RG 108, Letters Received. The material retained by Maj. Gen. Henry W. Halleck included original letters of USG and others. Many of the USG letters later appeared on the autograph market although some exist only in letterbook copies. For an exception, see *PUSG*, 6, 87.

1865, JUNE 13, 7:40 P.M.   Maj. Gen. John Pope, St. Louis, to USG, Chicago. "I think the time has come when I can properly issue an order revoking Martial Law in Missouri—With your assent I will by the concurrence of the Governor of the State issue the necessary order—Please advise me if you approve—"—Telegram, copy, DNA, RG 393, Military Div. of the Mo., Telegrams Sent. *O.R.*, I, xlviii, part 2, 870. On the same day, Pope instructed his chief of staff, Col. John T. Sprague. "You will proceed to Chicago, Ill. without delay, and submit the enclosed communication to Lieut Genl Grant and give him such verbal information upon the subject as he may require. Upon concluding your business, return to these Head Quarters."—Copy, DNA, RG 393, Military Div. of the Mo., Letters Sent. USG did not leave Chicago until Tuesday morning, June 14, but there is no evidence that he received Pope's telegram or spoke with Sprague. On June 14, at 3:40 P.M., Pope telegraphed to USG. "I have mailed a letter to you expressing my own wishes and views about new arrangements of Commands—I trust that if consistent with public interests any orders establishing new commands may not be issued until my letter is received"—Telegram received (at 4:40 P.M.), *ibid.*, RG 107, Telegrams Collected (Bound); *ibid.*, RG 108, Telegrams Received; copies, *ibid.*, RG 393, Military Div. of the Mo., Telegrams Sent; DLC-USG, V, 54. *O.R.*, I, xlviii, part 2, 879.

1865, JUNE 15. USG endorsement. "Respy. forwarded to the Secretary of war with the recommendation that all rebel officers who were paroled for the purpose of distributing supplies to Confederate prisoners be permitted to go to their homes on parole"—Copy, DLC-USG, V, 58. *O.R.*, II, viii, 649. Written on a letter of June 10 from C.S.A. Col. Milton D. Barber *et al.*, Camp Douglas, Ill., to USG. "We, the undersigned, (late) officers in the Confederate Army, do respectfully represent to you that, under an agreement made between yourself and General Lee for the supply of prisoners of war, we were ordered on our parole from Johnson's Island in the month of February last, for the purpose of distributing the proceeds of cotton sold in New York to prisoners of war confined at Camp Douglas. We respectfully represent that our mission has terminated some time ago, and we have made an application, through these headquarters and approved by the commanding general of this post, either to be paroled upon the terms granted by yourself to our respective commands, or that we may be allowed to return to our families (from whom we have been absent during the progress of the war) upon taking the oath of allegiance. These applications were made shortly after the surrender of General Lee's army to you at Appomattox Court-House, and prior to the late proclamation of amnesty by the President, and as they have not been acted upon, we are induced to renew our most earnest application to you, either to extend the limits of our parole, that we may be allowed to return to the bosom of our families, or upon taking the oath of allegiance we may be released from imprisonment. Hoping, general, that you will fully appreciate our present anomalous position as prisoners of war in peace times, and will so act as to secure our release, . . ."—*Ibid.*, pp. 648–49.

1865, JUNE 15. Bvt. Col. Theodore S. Bowers to Maj. Gen. Winfield S. Hancock. "From the Cavalry of your Mil. Division, including the Cavalry Corps, you will select the force you actually require and have it posted according to the requirements of your command. Such of it as is not required for duty in your Mil. Div. order to report without delay to Maj. Gen'l Crook, Com'd'g Cavalry Corps, who will immediately consolidate and muster out of the service such of them as come within orders already issued or that may be issued for the consolidation and muster out of Cavalry."—Copies, DLC-USG, V, 46, 109; DNA, RG 108, Letters Sent. *O.R.*, I, xlvi, part 3, 1281. On June 8, Bvt. Lt. Col. Elmer Otis, Cav. Bureau, had written to Brig. Gen. Charles H. Morgan, chief of staff for Hancock, about 1500 cav. horses available for use in the Middle Military Div.—LS, DNA, RG 108, Letters Received. On June 10, Hancock endorsed this letter. "As I am not aware that the Government require any more Cavalry mounted—. Before taking action in this matter I respectfully refer it to the Lieut General—Commanding the Armies for advice."—ES, *ibid.*

1865, JUNE 15. Bvt. Brig. Gen. William Hoffman, commissary gen. of prisoners, to USG. "Resptflly submitted to Lt. Genl. Grant. comd'g U S. Army From the within report it appears that the paroled prisoners heretofore reported by this Office as having arrived at Annapolis from Jacksonville Fla, were taken charge of at Jacksonville Fla by Maj. Thompson Pro. Mar. Genl. Dept. of the South, that most of them were forwarded by him to Annapolis and that he permitted some of them, though on parole, to join his Regiment. Maj. Thompson has up to this time, furnished no roll of the prisoners received by him, nor has he made any report of the disposition which he made of them. He seems to have been aware of the order regarding paroled prisoners to be sent to Annapolis, but notwithstanding allowed some of them, in violation of that order, to join their regiments. It is impossible that this Office can account properly for paroled troops, if Officers who receive them are so negligent in the performance of their duties as Maj. Thompson has been in this case. Other reports received in this Office show, that there were 50 to 60 of these prisoners, then remaining at Jacksonville. Fla. Maj. Genl. Gilmore, comdg Dept of the South has been requested to order the paroled men who joined their Regts. to be sent to Camp Parole near Annapolis Md"—Copy, DNA, RG 249, Letters Sent. *O.R.*, II, viii, 635. Written on a letter of June 2 from Bvt. Brig. Gen. Benjamin C. Tilghman, Tallahassee, Fla., to Hoffman.—*Ibid.*, pp. 634–35.

1865, JUNE 16. USG endorsement. "Approved and respectfully forwarded to the Secretary of War. I think Gen Kilpatrick has fully entitled himself by his services to this promotion."—ES, DNA, RG 94, ACP, K427 CB 1866. Written on a letter of June 6 from Maj. Gen. John M. Schofield, Raleigh, to Secretary of War Edwin M. Stanton recommending Brig. Gen. Judson Kilpatrick for promotion to maj. gen.—ALS, *ibid.* On Dec. 30, USG favorably endorsed a letter of Dec. 21 from Kilpatrick to Brig. Gen. Lorenzo Thomas tendering his resignation as maj. gen. of vols.—ES and ALS, *ibid.* On Oct. 15, 1867, USG favorably endorsed a letter of Aug. 10 from Kilpatrick, U.S. legation, Santiago, Chile, to Stanton tendering his resignation as capt., 1st Art.—ES and LS, *ibid.* On Dec. 1, Kilpatrick wrote to USG, secretary of war *ad interim.* "I have to request that the acceptance of my resignation be dated back to take effect Dec. 1st 1865 the date of my acceptance of the Chilian Mission—this I ask in justice to Capt. G. V. Henry and others who have been kept back from promotion—in consequence of the tardy acceptance of my resignation."—ALS, *ibid.* Kilpatrick resigned as of Dec. 1, 1865.

1865, JUNE 16, 2:40 P.M.   To Maj. Gen. Quincy A. Gillmore. "You may send the whole of the 144 N. Y. regiment North for musterout. I understand nearly the entire regiment goes out under existing orders."—ALS (telegram sent), DNA, RG 107, Telegrams Collected (Bound); telegram sent, *ibid.*; telegram received, *ibid.*, Telegrams Collected (Unbound). *O.R.*, I, xlvii, part 3, 649. On the same day, Governor Reuben E. Fenton of N. Y. had telegraphed to USG. "Owing to the want of discriptive lists a portion of one hundred forty fourth 144th N. Y. Regiment cannot return without Special order   I understand all this Regiment come within provisions of General Orders of muster-out. I request that Entire Regiment may be ordered home discriptive lists to be furnished after reaching state rendezvous. Telegraph order to Hilton Head if granted before twentieth (20th) inst."—Telegram received (at 11:25 A.M.), DNA, RG 107, Telegrams Collected (Bound); *ibid.*, RG 108, Telegrams Received; copy, DLC-USG, V, 54.

1865, JUNE 16.   To George H. Stuart. "I will spend the latter part of next week in Phila. when it will be convenient for me to meet the Citizens of that City, or the members of the Union League in any way agreeable to them . . . it will be equally convenient for me to be present any day you may designate . . ."—Joseph Rubinfine, List 88 [1987], no. 3. On June 20, Tuesday, 9:40 P.M., USG telegraphed to Stuart. "Friday and saturday will be convenient days for me to be in Phila."—ALS (telegram sent), DNA, RG 107, Telegrams Collected (Bound); telegram sent (on June 21, 12:45 A.M.), *ibid.* On June 21, 4:00 P.M. and 9:20 P.M., USG telegraphed to Stuart. "I will leave here in the 11 a. m. train but will go to Burling to see my children and spend to-morrow night." "I will not be able to leave here until 7.30 p. m. to-morrow evening."—ALS (telegrams sent), *ibid.*; telegrams sent, *ibid.* At 7:05 P.M. and 8:20 P.M., USG telegraphed to John W. Garrett, president, Baltimore and Ohio Railroad. "I would like to go to Phila in the 11 a m train to-morrow with my family." "I will not be able to leave here in the 11 a. m. train to-morrow"—ALS (telegrams sent), *ibid.*; telegrams sent, *ibid.* On June 22, 12:55 P.M., USG telegraphed to Stuart. "I will leave at 7.30 this evening and will go to the Continental for the night."—ALS (telegram sent), *ibid.* At 1:15 P.M., USG telegraphed to Garrett. "I will leave for Phila in the 7.30 train this evening. Can I be put off there? I will have only two or three Staff officers with me and do not care for an extra car."—ALS (telegram sent), *ibid.* During USG's stay in Philadelphia (June 23–25), he attended various functions including a reception at the Union League House. On Sunday, June 25, USG attended services at Spring Garden Street Methodist Episcopal Church and reportedly donated $500 in his name and $100 in Julia Dent Grant's name to the church. Later that day, church members reportedly raised an additional $1,000 to dedicate a pew to the exclusive use of the Grant family.—See Philadelphia *Daily Evening Bulletin*, June 24, 26, 1865; *Philadelphia Inquirer*, June 26, 1865.

1865, JUNE 16.   Bvt. Brig. Gen. William Hoffman, commissary gen. of prisoners, to USG. "I have the honor to enclose herewith lists of citizen prisoners in confinement at various military prisons, without charges, or not under Sentence. Some at Nashville are awaiting Sentence. I respectfully suggest that all who are not charged with any offence and those against whom there are no Serious charges, upon which they may be immediately tried, be at once released on their taking the Oath of allegiance."—LS, DNA, RG 249, Letters Received. *O.R.,* II, viii, 654–55. On the same day, Brig. Gen. John A. Rawlins endorsed this letter. "The within recommendations of Gen. Hoffman approved, and all proper cases of citizen prisoners will be at once released."—ES, DNA, RG 249, Letters Received.

1865, JUNE 16.   Henry Chittenden, London, to USG. "In July 1864 you did me the very great favor to reply by the hands of your Aide-de-Camp Lieut Col. O. E. Babcock to a communication made by me on behalf of a widowed lady whose Son had enlisted in the name of A. S. Vermont in the Federal Services, in the 8th Regt Conn a u s Legion on 2d. Nov. 1862, and was promoted to a Sergeant. At the time the last letter was received from him (about Jan/64 he had joined 69th Regt. N. Y. S. N. G and when Col. Babcock by your instructions replied to my letter he was supposed to be a Federal 'Prisoner of War'. The object of my present communication is to ask if any thing has been heard of him since, and of hearing how he may be communicated with, also that he may be informed his Mother replied to each of his letters, telling him that all which might trouble his mind had from the first been forgiven and forgotten. Permit me, Sir to take this opportunity of most sincerely thanking you for the great Kindness, and promptitude with which you caused my previous letter to be replied to, and to assure you of the deepest gratitude of his anxious mother for the same" —ALS, USG 3.

1865, JUNE 17.   To Secretary of War Edwin M. Stanton. "I would respectfully recommend the muster out of the following Cavalry regiments: to wit: 1st Mass. 2d N. Y. 8th N. Y. 1st N. Y. Dragoons, 1st N. Y. Lincoln Cav.y, 1st Va. 2d Va. & 3d Va."—ALS, DNA, RG 94, Vol. Service Div., Letters Received, W2191 (VS) 1865. At 10:40 P.M., USG telegraphed to the commanding officer, Parkersburg, West Va. "The 1st, 2nd and 3rd Regts West Virginia Cavalry left Washington this afternoon for the West. Stop them at Parkersburg, and put them into camp there until further orders."—Telegrams sent (2), *ibid.,* RG 107, Telegrams Collected (Bound); copies, *ibid.,* RG 108, Letters Sent; DLC-USG, V, 46, 109. *O.R.,* I, xlvi, part 3, 1285. On June 18, Maj. Thomas M. Vincent, AGO, telegraphed instructions to Capt. Edward P. Hudson, Veteran Reserve Corps, chief mustering officer, Wheeling, West Va., to muster out the three West Va. cav. regts.—Copy, DNA, RG 108, Letters Received. On June 19, Vincent endorsed this telegram. "Respectfully furnished for the information of Lt. Gen U S Grant Comdg Armies of the U. S."—AES, *ibid.* On the same day, Vincent wrote an identical endorsement on a telegram of June 19 to Hudson giving additional instructions.—AES, *ibid.*

1865, JUNE 17.   To Secretary of War Edwin M. Stanton. "I would respectfully request that Brevet Major General J. G Barnard be relieved from all other duty and assigned to the special duty referred to in the enclosed memorandum."—LS, DNA, RG 94, Letters Received, 1392A 1865. On June 12, Bvt. Maj. Gen. John G. Barnard, Washington, D. C., had written to Brig. Gen. John A. Rawlins. "By special orders No 288 (W. D. A. G. O.) I am directed to report for duty to the Chief Engineer U. S. A. Under actual orders from the Lieut General I am actually engaged in superintending surveys of the defences of Richmond & Petersburg and of the battle fields connected therewith   This duty will not be completed for several weeks. Before leaving for the West the Lieut. General left a memorandum for orders to be issued to me on my return from Richmond to report on the organization, equipment &c of Engineer troops for service in this country—upon the most suitable kinds, forms & construction of Engineer material, and upon the use of field fortifications, as the experience of the war has taught. This report adequately executed will require at least 6 months of hard labor and in an Engineering point of view—or in its relations to the general military service hereafter is second in importance to no Engineering duty that could be assigned me."—ALS, *ibid.*, RG 108, Letters Received. *O.R.,* I, xlvi, part 3, 1272–73. See *ibid.*, pp. 719, 1143–44, 1222.

1865, JUNE 17.   Maj. Gen. John Pope, St. Louis, to USG. "I have the honor to transmit enclosed list of General Officers serving in the Department of Arkansas who desire to remain in the service, with the remarks of Major General Reynolds in the case of each.—those about whom no remarks are made, it is believed that Genl: Reynolds does not consider suitable persons to remain in the service.—His remarks and recommendations are approved and confirmed by me and are respectfully forwarded for such action as may be thought judicious—If the War Department considers it well to have the Officers recommended by General Reynolds examined, it can be done, though time will be consumed thereby, but I should esteem the opinion of such an Officer as General Reynolds much more valuable concerning those who have been so long under his immediate command than the report of any Examining Board—Boards for the examination of Officers below the rank of Brigadier General are in session under the Orders of Department Commanders and their reports will be forwarded as fast as possible—the list of General Officers recommended or otherwise reported on by Genls: Dodge and Curtis will be also forwarded as soon as recieved"—LS, DNA, RG 108, Letters Received. The enclosure is *ibid.* On the same day, Pope wrote to USG. "I have the honor to transmit enclosed a list of Officers serving at these Head quarters, who desire to remain in service with my recommendations and remarks in each case—They can be examined by a Board if it is thought judicious, but as those mentioned have been almost continuously on duty with me for several years, the opportunities of any Board of Officers to ascertain their qualifications cannot in the nature of things, be as good as my own have been. I do not suppose that the reports of such a Board would add any weight to my recommendations"—LS, *ibid.* The enclosure is *ibid.*

1865, JUNE 17.   Col. Benjamin F. Fisher, chief signal officer, to USG. "In as much as a number of Signal Officers are unassigned at present, I have the honor to submit for your consideration, a proposition that one Signal Officer with a Detachment of Enlisted men, be assigned as a part of the permanent garrison in each of the principal fortifications in the several harbors along the coast, and at such fortifications in the interior, as may be important strategic points. Prudence, with the light of Experience, would seem to dictate such a disposition of a portion of the Corps. Had a Signal Detachment been with the forces at Harpers Ferry in the fall of '62, communication might have been opened with the advance of the Army under General McClellan, which would have without doubt, saved the Garrison with the immense stores thus captured by the enemy. The presence of a Detachment in Fort Sumpter in the spring of '61, would have also enabled our Fleet to communicate with its Garrison. In support of this assertion, I will instance one of the occurrences of this kind on record. I give it in the language of General Sherman, viz: 'When the enemy had cut our wires, and actually made a lodgement on our Rail Road about Big Shanty, the Signal Officers on Vining's Hill, Kenesaw, and Allatoona, sent my orders to General Corse, at Rome, whereby General Corse was enabled to reach Allatoona just in time to defend it. Had it not been for the services of this Corps, (Signal Corps), on that occasion, I am satisfied we should have lost the Garrison at Allatoona, and a most valuable depository of provisions there, which was worth to us, and the country, more than the aggregate expense of the whole Signal Corps, for one year' The officers and men of these several Detachments should be considered a part of the permanent Garrison, and when not performing Signal duty, should be required to do stated garrison duty the same as the other troops, Except in the place of drilling with muskets flag practice should be substituted, in connection with the Cavalry drill of the dismounted trooper."—LS, DNA, RG 108, Letters Received.

1865, JUNE 19.   To Secretary of War Edwin M. Stanton. "I respectfully recommend the promotion of Col. W. H. Noble, 17th Conn. Vol. Infantry to the rank of Brig. Gn. by brevet. He has recommendations from Gn. Ames and other General officers under whom he has served. As Col. Noble will be mustered out of service within a few days I would ask early action on this recommendation."—ALS, deCoppet Collection, NjP.

1865, JUNE 19.   To Secretary of War Edwin M. Stanton. "I have the honor to respectfully recommend that the notification from the Adjutant Generals Office honorably discharging Major M. B Brown, Add. Paymaster, on the 15th inst. be revoked and that Major Brown be restored to duty. This will enable him after filing his bond and qualifying for the office to resign, if his services are no longer required. I am particularly anxious that this should be done."—LS, ICarbS. Stanton noted on this letter: "(Suspended)"—AN (undated), *ibid.*

1865, JUNE 19. USG endorsement. "Respectfully returned with the information that the application of Captain Speed for a Court of Inquiry in his case was recieved, and that I returned the same disapproved. I have not, and donot at present recommend the dismissal of Capt. Speed. The report of the officer who investigated the causes of the disaster on the Sultana was forwarded to the War Dept on the 2d day of June 1865."—ES, DNA, RG 94, Letters Received, 1119P 1865. Written on letters of May 26 and June 5 from Capt. Frederic Speed, adjt. for Maj. Gen. Gouverneur K. Warren, Vicksburg, to U.S. Senator Jacob M. Howard of Mich., and from Howard to President Andrew Johnson requesting a court of inquiry in the *Sultana* disaster.—ALS, *ibid.* On June 17, Asst. Secretary of War Charles A. Dana had referred these letters to USG.—ES, *ibid.* On June 2 and 15, USG forwarded reports to Secretary of War Edwin M. Stanton concerning the *Sultana.*—DLC-USG, V, 49. On June 8, Dana had forwarded to USG a request by Speed for a court of inquiry.—*Ibid.* On June 16, USG endorsed this request. "Disapproved"—Copy, *ibid.*

On May 1, Bvt. Col. Theodore S. Bowers had issued Special Orders No. 79. "Brevet Colonel Adam Badeau, Military Secretary, will proceed without delay to the Department of the Mississippi, and make a full investigation of all the facts and circumstances connected with the loss of life of released Federal prisoners by the recent explosion of the steamboat Sultana on the Mississippi river. All officers of the military service are required to afford Colonel Badeau all necessary facilities to enable him to comply fully with his instructions."—Copies, *ibid.*, V, 57, 65. See *O.R.*, I, xlviii, part 1, 210–20. On May 9, Bvt. Col. Adam Badeau, Memphis, telegraphed to USG. "F. Delgado late clerk of the Pauline Carroll tried to get some of the troops put on her which were given to the Sultana He is in New York City about leaving for France His testimony would be important. If you determine to have him stopped dDuncan S Carter Secy of Atlantic & Miss Steamship Co St Louis Knows his address"—Telegram received (on May 10, 10:00 A.M.), DNA, RG 107, Telegrams Collected (Unbound); *ibid.*, RG 108, Telegrams Received; copy, DLC-USG, V, 54.

On Aug. 26, Brig. Gen. John A. Rawlins forwarded to Stanton the proceedings of an investigation of the *Sultana.*—Copy, DNA, RG 108, Register of Letters Received.

1865, JUNE 19. Brig. Gen. John A. Rawlins endorsement. "Respectfully referred to Major General O O Howard, Commissioner, Bureau of Refugees, Freedmen and Abandoned Lands, and his attention called to that part of the communication especially referring to freedmen"—ES, DNA, RG 105, Bureau of Refugees, Freedmen, and Abandoned Lands, Letters Received. Written on a letter of June 11 from Bvt. Maj. Gen. John E. Smith to Bvt. Col. Theodore S. Bowers.—Copy, *ibid.* Dated June 12 in *O.R.*, II, viii, 651. On June 26, Bowers endorsed this letter. "Respy returned. So much of this communication as relates to freedmen has been referred to General Howard Com of Bureau of Freedmen &c. &c. Under the arrangement made by Gen Canby, paroled prisoners of war are entitled to transportation to the nearest practicable points to their homes; and you are authorized and directed to furnish them transportation accordingly"—Copy, DLC-USG, V, 58. *O.R.*, II, viii, 651.

1865, JUNE 19. Bvt. Col. Theodore S. Bowers to Maj. Gen. John G. Parke. "H. S. Burnett, member of the late Rebel Congress is in this city, and is supposed to be stopping at the Metropolitan Hotel. In pursuance of directions from the Secretary of War you will immediately arrest him, and forward him under guard to Maj. Gen. John M. Palmer, Commanding Department of Kentucky. Select for the execution of this order a discreet officer—one who will keep the matter secret until Burnett is secured. Report your action to these Headquarters."—ALS, DNA, RG 108, Letters Received. On June 22, Parke returned this letter indicating that the instructions had been carried out.—ES, *ibid.* On June 23, Brig. Gen. Edward H. Hobson, Louisville, Ky., telegraphed to Bowers. "M H C Burnett recd what disposition is to be made of him"—Telegram received (12:50 P.M.), *ibid.*, RG 107, Telegrams Collected (Bound); *ibid.*, RG 108, Telegrams Received; copy, DLC-USG, V, 54. On the same day, Brig. Gen. John A. Rawlins wrote to Secretary of War Edwin M. Stanton. "I have the honor to inform you that H. C. Burnett, member of the late Rebel Congress was arrested in this city on the evening of the 20th inst, and that he was forwarded in charge of Lieutenant Hamilton, 9th Regt. Vet Res. Corps, to Maj. Gen. J. M. Palmer, Commanding Department of Kentucky."—LS, DNA, RG 108, Letters Received. On June 24, Bvt. Brig. Gen. James A. Hardie endorsed this letter. "Respectfully returned to Head-Qrs Armies. U. S. with instructions to direct Brig—Genl. Hobson to parole H. C. Burnett to repair to his home in Kentucky and remain there—"—ES, *ibid.* At 2:00 P.M., Rawlins telegraphed to Hobson. "In pursuance of instructions from the Secretary of War you will ~~parole H C~~ release H. C. Burnett upon parole to repair to his home in Kentucky, there to remain."—Telegrams sent (2), *ibid.*, RG 107, Telegrams Collected (Bound); telegram received, *ibid.*, RG 109, Union Provost Marshals' File of Papers Relating to Individual Civilians. On the same day, Hobson telegraphed to Bowers. "A demand has been made for Henry C. Burnett by U S Marshal to answer an indictment for treason found by U S circuit court in this City   Please answer with instructions"—Telegram sent, *ibid.*; telegram received (at 1:35 P.M.), *ibid.*, RG 107, Telegrams Collected (Bound); *ibid.*, RG 108, Telegrams Received. At 3:20 P.M., Bowers telegraphed to Hobson. "Your dispatch of 1:35 P. M is received. Instructions have been sent you."—ALS (telegram sent), *ibid.*, RG 107, Telegrams Collected (Bound); telegram sent, *ibid.*; copies, *ibid.*, RG 108, Letters Sent; DLC-USG, V, 46, 109. See *Calendar*, Jan. 12, 1866.

1865, JUNE 19. James C. Moodey, St. Louis, to USG. "I sent you today by mail two nos of the Mo Republican containing my decision on the strange action of the late Convention and the proceedings of an immense meeting of the people of this city on the late *Lawless* acts of our Governor—By reading them, with your previous knowledge of our condition here, you will at once see the state of affairs in Missouri—A few men, whose loyalty was at least very doubtful in '61 & '62, got the control of the late Convention, & after the war was over instituted a new social one that threatens every day to involve us in a hand to hand fight—They represent, or rather control, about ¼ of the people—Of their number is our New Governor—He has no sense nor discretion—He seems to think he is not only the Executive but also the Legislature & Judiciary—and he acts accordingly—While the whole country is rejoicing in the prospect of *peace*—these men who were for *peace* in '61 & 62 are determined we shall have no peace *now*—Governor Fletcher is their stupid tool—He has grossly outraged the Constitutional rights of the people; and now patrols the streets with negro soldiers (caught and pressed into *his* service last week) to protect his excellency from imaginary dangers which he apprehends at the hands of men whose loyalty never was questioned—'The wicked flee when no man pursueth—' In my judgment the quiet administration of the civil law can not be restored in Missouri with Gov Fletcher as Executive—I hear good men every day express the wish that he were deposed and a Military Governor placed temporarily in his place—If such should be the case pray God it may be a Soldier, educated as such—not a deputy clerk promoted to be a militia colonel—Proper orders to Genl Pope might relieve us—No fault is found, so far as I know, with him—"—ALS, DNA, RG 108, Letters Received.

1865, JUNE 20. To Secretary of War Edwin M. Stanton. "On the recommendation of Gen. Pope I would respectfully ask that an order be made assigning Brevet Brig. Gn. C. W. Blair, Col. 14th Kansas Cavalry to duty with his Brevet rank."—ALS, DNA, RG 94, ACP, B568 CB 1865. On June 10, Maj. Gen. John Pope had written to Brig. Gen. John A. Rawlins. "In consequence of relieving many General Officers from duty in this Division and directing them to repair to their homes & report by letter to the Adjt Genl. of the Army, in compliance with the order of the Genl-in-chief I find myself—very short of General Officers—I have the honor therefore to request that Bvt Brig Genl Blair 14th Kansas Cavalry be assigned to duty according to his Brevet rank—He is now serving in this Command"—ALS, *ibid.*, P296 CB 1865. An enclosed list of fourteen gen. and staff officers relieved from duty is *ibid.* On June 14, Rawlins endorsed this letter. "Approved"—ES, *ibid.*

1865, JUNE 20. USG endorsement. "Respectfully refered to the sec. of War with recommendation that authority be telegraphed for Mr. Walker to visit Washington. I know Mr Dox who asks this. He is a loyal Alabaman who has been a refugee from his home until the Federal lines were extended to take in his home."—AES (undated), DNA, RG 94, Letters Received, 1398A 1865; copy (dated June 20), DLC-USG, V, 58. Written on a telegram of June 19, 4:30 P.M., from Peter M. Dox, Nashville, to USG. "I respectfully ask for permission and a passport to L P Walker Esq of this place to visit Washn   Genl Granger says that neither he nor Gen Thomas has the power to give such permission, I therefore appeal to you for the passport and recommend that it be given to Mr Walker,"—Telegram received (on June 20, 9:00 A.M.), DNA, RG 94, Letters Received, 1398A 1865; *ibid.*, RG 107, Telegrams Collected (Bound).

1865, JUNE 20. Maj. Gen. Grenville M. Dodge, St. Louis, to USG. "While the reorganization of the Army is progressing I desire to call your attention to two Officers in this Department—Col T. J. Haines. A. A. D C & C. S. and Col Wm Myers. A. A. D. C. & Chief Q. M.   You are familiar with their services during the entire war. That they have performed their duties fully, all must admit, and that they have stood up here manfully for the Government and protected it against all who desired either to defraud it or speculate upon it, *I* Know. It has been no fault of theirs that they have not taken part in the active campaigns; their labors have been none the less because they have not. Both of them are as competent, reliable & efficient Officers in their Departments as I have ever met—both of excellent habits & strict integrity. In my position I have had excellent opportunities to observe their conduct & judge of their capacitys. I most earnestly recommend that they be retained in the Regular Army with present rank and duty—and I further recommend that they be made Brigadier Generals of Vols. I write this without their knowledge and what I ask is what I consider due them for their past services"—LS, DNA, RG 108, Letters Received.

1865, JUNE 20. Jacob Ammen, Lockland, Ohio, to USG. "Presuming upon former acquaintance I take the liberty of forwarding through you the application of my son Capt. W. P. Ammen, for an appointment as an Infantry officer in the regular service. He entered the service at the commencement of the war in the 7th Ind. V. I., served three months, was mustered out,—Volunteered again in an Indiana battery, was in Missouri, Arkansas, &c—until March 1863, when he was promoted to the rank of Capt. & A. A. Gen., on the recommendation of the officers under whom he had served. From that time to the present, he served on my staff, and with Maj. Gen. Stoneman. When he resigned he did not expect to request an appointment in the regular service, and therefore made no application to Gen. Stoneman for a recommendation as to his qualifications— He has just written to Gen. Stoneman, and will forward his recommendation as soon as received—He is well educated, moral, temperate, in good health, and capable of active service—I found him attentive to his duties, competent, prompt, efficient, and well informed—The order of Gen. Stoneman, will in the absence of his recommendation, give an idea of his opinion of him as an officer—I would not forward his application, if not satisfied that he will make a good officer, and that his long and faithful military service during the rebellion, give him some claim to the position to which he aspires—Please present his application to the proper authority with such recommendation as you may feel at liberty to make, and I will feel under additional obligations to you for your kindness—"—ALS, DNA, RG 94, ACP, A666 CB 1865. On Nov. 6, Bvt. Col. Ely S. Parker endorsed this letter. "Respectfully forwarded"—AES, *ibid.*

1865, JUNE 21, 4:00 P.M. Brig. Gen. John A. Rawlins to Maj. Gen. John Pope. "The whole of the State of Arkansas [yo]u will regard as under your command so far as [i]t may be necessary for the military authorities to aid the civil authorities in establishing civil government, and all questions appertaining thereto Gen Reynolds will report to you. There will be orders issued in a few days settling all questions of divided jurisdiction in Arkansas."—LS (telegram sent), DNA, RG 107, Telegrams Collected (Bound); telegram sent, *ibid.*; telegram received (on June 22, 9:00 A.M.), *ibid.*, Telegrams Collected (Unbound). *O.R.*, I, xlviii, part 2, 958. On June 20, 10:40 A.M., Pope, St. Louis, had telegraphed to USG. "The divided jurisdiction in Arkansas is occasioning some inconvenience. The End of the war in that state leads to the necessity of reestablishing as far as possible civil jurisdiction to preserve peace & quiet in local communities & re establishing civil courts & civil officers in Northern Ark; but that portion of the state lying south of Ark river having been put into Genl Sheridans Command, it is necessary in any arrangements in that part of the state to refer to him. This makes a divided & very inconvenient jurisdiction in that state both civil & Mily. That part of Reynolds troops north of Ark river he is responsible for to me, that part south he is responsible for to Sheridan. His position & duties therefore are anomalous & confusing, aAs no military operations are longer necessary, Iit is altogether advisable to put the whole state into one (1) jurisdiction. you will Easily understand the necessity of this and the condition of things in that state requires as speedy action as possible"—Telegram received (at 6:00 P.M.), DNA, RG 107, Telegrams Collected (Bound); *ibid.*, RG 108, Telegrams Received; copies, *ibid.*, RG 393, Military Div. of the Mo., Telegrams Sent; DLC-USG, V, 54. *O.R.*, I, xlviii, part 2, 947.

1865, JUNE 21. Maj. Thomas M. Vincent, AGO, to USG. "Respectfully submitted to Lt. Gen U S Grant Comd'g Armies of the U. S. The objection within in regard to the order mustering out of all dismounted volunteer Cavalry was brought to the notice of the Dept, thro Maj. Gen Hancock, concing the Cavalry of his Command some days ago, and the

Secretary of War directed the suspension of the order so far as the Mid. Mil Div was concerned, until the return of the Lieut General then absent. The papers were sent to the Hd. Qrs. of the Armies, but, have not been recd back, and the action if any, taken thereon is not known to this office."—AES, DNA, RG 94, Vol. Service Div., Letters Received, W2191 (VS) 1865. Written on a telegram of June 17 from Maj. Gen. Philip H. Sheridan to Vincent protesting an order to muster out all dismounted cav. because men would kill their horses to get out of the service.—Telegram received (on June 19, 7:25 P.M.), *ibid.* On June 21, Brig. Gen. John A. Rawlins endorsed this telegram. "Respectfully returned, with the recommendation that, instead of mustering out all dismounted cavalry-men, the Cavalry regiments having the shortest time to serve be dismounted and mustered out by entire organizations, and their horses transferred to the regiments having the longest time to serve until a sufficient number of horses are thus accumulated to mount the dismounted men of the latter regiments.—"—ES, *ibid.* On June 7, Bvt. Maj. Gen. Henry E. Davies had written to Brig. Gen. Charles H. Morgan, chief of staff for Maj. Gen. Winfield S. Hancock, requesting modifications of the order mustering out dismounted cav. for the same reason.—LS, *ibid.* On the same day, Rawlins endorsed this letter. "Respectfully forwarded to the Secretary of War"— ES, *ibid.* See *O.R.*, I, xlviii, part 2, 1001–2.

1865, JUNE 22. USG endorsement. "Respectfully forwarded to the Secretary of War."—ES, DNA, RG 94, Amnesty Papers, Mo. Written on a letter of June 17 from Maj. Gen. John Pope, St. Louis, to USG. "I send enclosed an application from Dr McPheeters of this city whom you no doubt will remember, for a pardon under the President's Amnesty Proclamation—Dr M. is an old citizen of this city and a man who has long enjoyed the respect and regard of his neighbors here. He is very anxious naturally to return to such a condition as will enable him to be free from civil prosecution & I trust you will do me the kindness to have his application acted on as soon as convenient—Will you please have the reply sent to me—"—ALS, *ibid.* The enclosure is *ibid.*

1865, JUNE 22. USG endorsement. "Respectfully forwarded to the Secretary of War with the recommendation that the order mustering Surgeon E McDonnell, U S Vols., out of service be revoked; and that before commissioned surgeons of volunteers are mustered out of the Service, all contract surgeons be discharged. If the final order of muster out in this case has not been issued it is recommended that Surgeon McDonnell be assigned to duty"—ES, DNA, RG 107, Letters Received from Bureaus. Written on a letter of June 16 from Surgeon Edward McDonnell to Bvt. Col. Theodore S. Bowers requesting that the order mustering him out of service be revoked.—ALS, *ibid.* On June 19, Brig. Gen. John A. Rawlins had endorsed this letter. "Respectfully referred to Brig Gen Barnes, Surgeon General of the Army, for remarks. As far as the Lieutenant General is personally acquainted with this officer his services have been faithful and satisfactory"—ES, *ibid*. On June 20, Brig. Gen. Joseph K. Barnes, surgeon gen., endorsed this letter. "Respectfully returned to the Lieutenant General Commanding the Armies of the United States. Under instructions from the Hon: Secretary of War, several Surgeons and Assistant Surgeons of Volunteers have been mustered out of service, this Department reporting from time to time, those whose services can be dispensed with. The application of these instructions is general and a majority of the officers of the Volunteer Medical Staff will be reported as supernumerary and mustered out before the meeting of Congress, the War Department having decided that an Act of Congress is not necessary to disband the Corps. The only safe redress in this instance would be the revocation of the General Order as exceptions cannot be made without injustice to others."—ES, *ibid*. On July 17, McDonnell, National Hotel, Washington, D. C., wrote to USG. "I have the honor respectfully to request a position in the Medical Staff of the regular Army—I herewith submit my military history and Testimonials—. . ."—ALS, *ibid*., RG 94, ACP, M419 CB 1865.

1865, JUNE 22.   To S. Bishop and Co. acknowledging a gift of a portrait of George Washington created by arranging the words of the Declaration of Independence. ". . . I will prize this very highly and will have it framed to hand down to my children . . ."—Ben Bloomfield, List JH, 38.

1865, JUNE 22.   Brig. Gen. John A. Rawlins to Maj. Gen. George H. Thomas. "If the 4th Army Corps has not yet sailed, please transfer from it all Kentucky Regiments and fill their places in it with other Regiments."—Telegrams sent (2), DNA, RG 107, Telegrams Collected (Bound); copies, *ibid*., RG 108, Letters Sent; DLC-USG, V, 46, 109. *O.R.*, I, xlix, part 2, 1023. On June 20, W. G. Goodloe, Lexington, Ky., probably William C. Goodloe, had telegraphed to USG. "Will you order the Kentucky troops in the 4th Corps to Kentucky to remain until after the August election?"—Telegram received (at 6:00 P.M.), DNA, RG 107, Telegrams Collected (Bound); *ibid*., RG 108, Telegrams Received; copy, DLC-USG, V, 54. On June 23, Thomas telegraphed to Rawlins. "The fourth 4 Corps left Several days since—"—Telegram received (at 5:35 P.M.), DNA, RG 108, Telegrams Received; copy, DLC-USG, V, 54.

1865, JUNE 22.   Bvt. Col. Theodore S. Bowers endorsement. "Respectfully referred to Major General. P. H. Sheridan for compliance with orders of the Secretary of War herein endorsed."—Copy, DNA, RG 109, Union Provost Marshals' File of Papers Relating to Two or More Civilians. Written on a letter of June 19 from Secretary of State William H. Seward to Secretary of War Edwin M. Stanton requesting that Maj. Gen. Philip H. Sheridan be ordered to watch for certain C.S.A. sympathizers reported en route to Tex. from Europe.—Copy, *ibid.* On June 20, Asst. Secretary of War Charles A. Dana had endorsed this letter. "Respectfully referred to Lt Genl Grant with directions to give the orders requested by the Secretary of State"—Copy, *ibid.*

1865, JUNE 22.   J. A. Rowland, private secretary for Attorney Gen. James Speed, to USG. "The Attorney General desires to have a pardon issued to A. P. Merrill, Jr. whose application you have endorsed, but the applicant's residence is not given in his petition. The Attorney General will thank you, if you can furnish this office with his place of residence, so that it may be inserted in the recital of the Warrant."—ALS, USG 3. See *PUSG*, 9, 216–17.

1865, JUNE 23.   Mrs. Ann Hoult, Leicestershire, Great Britain, to USG. "You will excuse an anxious Mother troubling you but as I have had a Son serving in your Army from whom I have heard nothing since the 3rd of January 1865, I have taken the liberty of writing to you humbly requesting that you will favour me with information respecting him, or direct me how I may ascertain whether he is still living and where. When I last heard from him his address was John Trigg First New York Mounted Rifles Troop,   up to that time although he had been in many Engagements he was unhurt. I trust he is still living but as it is much longer than usual since I heard from him I often fear. I shall feel unspeakably thankful to you General if you will favour me with a letter to the following address —. . ."—ALS, USG 3. On July 12, Bvt. Col. Adam Badeau wrote to Maj. Gen. Alfred H. Terry requesting information about Private John Trigg, 1st N. Y. Mounted Rifles.—ALS, *ibid.* Endorsements indicate that Trigg was on duty with his co. and that Mrs. Hoult was so informed on Oct. 18.—*Ibid.*

1865, JUNE 24.   Maj. Gen. Quincy A. Gillmore, Hilton Head, to USG. "The Battalion of New York Volunteer Engineers is ready to go to Richmond but have no transportation for them. The 'Fulton' & 'Arago' will both be required to transport regiments which are to be mustered out, for some time to come. A transport had better be sent here."—Telegram received (on June 28, 10:45 A.M.), DNA, RG 107, Telegrams Collected (Bound); *ibid.*, Telegrams Collected (Unbound); copy, *ibid.*, RG 393, Dept. of the South and S. C., Letters Sent. See *O.R.*, I, xlvii, part 3, 640.

1865, JUNE 26.   To Secretary of War Edwin M. Stanton. "I have the honor respectfully to request that Brevet Brigadier General Loren Kent, (Colonel commanding 29th Regiment Illinois Infantry Volunteers) be assigned to duty with his brevet rank. Colonel Kent is now, and has been for a year, commanding a brigade, and it is desirable that he be assigned as above requested."—LS, DNA, RG 94, ACP, K182 CB 1865. *O.R.*, I, xlvii, part 3, 664.

1865, JUNE 26. USG endorsement. "Respectfully returned. The Army of the Potomac should be regarded as in the field, and the allowance of hard bread issued should be for the present one pound per day."—ES, DNA, RG 192, Letters Received by Referral. Written on a letter of Bvt. Col. Joseph S. Smith, chief commissary, 2nd Army Corps, to Bvt. Col. Thomas Wilson, chief commissary, Army of the Potomac.—ALS, *ibid.*

1865, JUNE 26. Secretary of War Edwin M. Stanton endorsement. "Referred to the Lt General with instructions to issue orders to Military Commanders in conformity with the Presidents directions"—AES, DNA, RG 108, Letters Received. Written on a letter of June 22 from Secretary of the Interior James Harlan to Stanton. "By direction of the President, as contained in his order of this date, herewith enclosed, I have the honor to transmit a copy of the instructions, this day delivered to the Hon Wm P. Dole, Commissioner of Indian Affairs, to visit, and treat with, the various Indian tribes in the territories of Dakota, Idaho, Montana and Colorado."— LS, *ibid.* On the same day, President Andrew Johnson had instructed Harlan. "It having been deemed expedient to send the Hon: William P. Dole, Commissioner of Indian Affairs, to visit and treat with the Indian tribes in the territories of Dakota, Idaho, Montana and Colorado, with a view, if possible, to terminate hostilities, and to secure a more cordial and lasting peace with them, the Secretary of the Interior, is hereby directed to furnish to the Secretary of War a copy of the instructions he has this day given to Mr Dole, and the Secretary of War will, immediately, communicate them to the Commanders of the proper Military Departments, and require them to coöperate and assist the Commissioner in the discharge of the duties, which have been devolved upon him."—DS, *ibid.* A copy of Harlan's instructions of the same day to Commissioner of Indian Affairs William P. Dole is *ibid.* Johnson endorsed these instructions. "Approved"— AES (undated), *ibid.*

1865, JUNE 26. W. M. Clark, cashier, First National Bank, Norfolk, to USG. "This will be handed you by Mrs E. Dye of Norfolk, Va. an intimate personal friend of mine, who visits Washington for the purpose of procuring the release of her Son James Dye a prisoner of War at Point Lookout Md. if you can assist her in this her object, I shall feel under great obligations."—ALS, DNA, RG 109, Unfiled Papers and Slips, Dye, James.

1865, JUNE 26. Egbert Decker, Jr., New London, Conn., to USG. "I have the honor to make application to you for an appointment to the Military School at West Point. I have been a private of the 9th New York Cavalry, detailed at Hart Island N. Y. H. as clerk to A. A. Surg. Edward S. Brown U. S. A. and discharged by reason of G. O. No 77. War Dep't A. G. O. (C S). I am 20 years of age, Sound and healthy in every particular. I have received a good academical education, and would now like to acquire the knowledge that would enable me to perform the duties, and assume the responsibilities of a Soldier. And to serve the Nation to the best of my ability. I feel that I am capable of sustaining such a position, with credit to myself and the Country."—ALS, DNA, RG 94, Cadet Applications. USG endorsed this letter. "Respectfully forwarded to the Sec. of War."—AES (undated), *ibid.*

1865, June 27. To Secretary of War Edwin M. Stanton. "I would respectfully recommend that Capt. Geo. W. Campbell C. S. be appointed Col. in his Dept. and assigned to duty at Chicago. This appointment would come under the provisions of an Act of the last Congress giving the rank of Colonel to officers of the Subsistence Department when on duty as Chief to an Army, Dept. or at a Depot."—ALS, DNA, RG 94, ACP, C713 CB 1865.

1865, June 27. USG endorsement. "Approved and respectfully forwarded."—Parke-Bernet Sale No. 2205, Sept. 24, 1963, no. 201. Written on a letter of June 26 from Maj. Gen. John M. Schofield to USG recommending three staff officers for promotion.—*Ibid.*

1865, June 28. To Secretary of War Edwin M. Stanton. "I would respectfully recommend that the resignation of Maj. Phillip Van Renssleaer, 2nd N. J. Cavalry be accepted. If his resignation cannot be found on file in the Adjt. Gen's office I would then ask that he be honorably mustered out of service"—Copies, DLC-USG, V, 46, 109; DNA, RG 108, Letters Sent. On June 27, Henry C. Carey, Philadelphia, wrote to Bvt. Col. Adam Badeau. "I wrote to my friends at Burlington yesterday, requesting them to telegraph to you the facts in regard to Major Van Rensselaer, and so they have probably done. This evening's mail has brought me a letter that seems to have been written before the receipt of mine, and which is here enclosed. Do me the favor to read it, and to do what may be needed for speeding to his home the subject of it."—ALS, USG 3. Carey enclosed a letter of June 26 from Edward B. Hodge, Burlington, N. J., to Carey requesting that he use his influence to have the resignation of Maj. Philip Van Rensselaer, 2nd N. J. Cav., accepted because of the illness of Van Rensselaer's mother. —ALS, *ibid.*

1865, June 28. USG endorsement. "Brig. Gen. L. Thomas' statement shows that Capt. Thomas has been performing the duty of a mounted officer, and that he was on duty as such at the time of his detail. Under such circumstances the law, I think, gives him cavalry-pay"—ES, DNA, RG 94, ACP, T41 CB 1866. Written on a letter of June 20 from Capt. Lorenzo Thomas, Jr., 1st Art., to his father Brig. Gen. Lorenzo Thomas requesting back pay for services while on his father's staff.—ALS, *ibid.* On Sept. 29, Thomas, Jr., Boston, wrote to USG. "I have the honor to apply for four or six months leave of absence as I have private business which I have neglected since the war began   My record shows but one leave of

absence and I would especially request that my request be granted."—
ALS, *ibid.*, Letters Received, 713T 1865. On Oct. 3, Thomas, Sr., endorsed this letter. "I know very well that Bvt Major Thomas' private affairs
have suffered that he requires some little time to attend to his business;
and I hope may receive a reasonable extension of his twenty days leave of
absence   Respectfully referred to Lieut General U. S. Grant Comdr in
Chief"—AES, *ibid.* On Jan. 30, 1866, USG favorably endorsed a letter
of Jan. 8 from Thomas, Jr., New Orleans, to his father tendering his resignation.—AES, *ibid.*, ACP, T41 CB 1866. On Nov. 14, 1873, Thomas,
Jr., Washington, D. C., wrote to USG. "I respectfully make application
for a Commission in the Pay Department, as Major, to fill one of the
vacancies which now exist. I served during the entire rebellion as an Officer of the 1st Artillery, with I beleive credit to myself and honor to my
country, and now being without employment, I feel that I can reasonably
ask for the position, feeling fully competent to fulfill the duties of the
Office."—ALS, *ibid.* On the same day, Thomas, Sr., wrote to USG. "My
son Bvt. Major Lorenzo Thomas Jr being now out of employment, is
desirous of re-entering the Army, and has applied for the position of Paymaster, for which I think his early training as a merchant, and his varied
services during the whole rebellion fit him for the appointment he requests.
I have given three members of my family to the service of my country, who
have laid down their lives in battle, son in law, son and cousin all of whom
were appointed at my request, and I hope your Excellency will accede to
his request."—ALS, *ibid.* On March 11, 1875, Thomas, 2nd Auditor's
Office, Treasury Dept., wrote to USG. "The death of my Father incurs
additional expense on me, and I would ask you if you could not give me an
appointment more lucrative, whether at home or abroad. I was in hopes of
being appointed a Paymaster as my papers were in but was sadly disappointed. Should there be any vacancies in the Q M. D I would like very
much to be appointed. The bill reducing this office 24 clerks will throw
me out of work here unless I could get into some other Dept. There are
vacancies in the Interior but I have no influence   I dislike to trouble you,
especially at such a time when you are so very busy but necessity knows
no law   Please think of this matter and I will be under the deepest obligations."—ALS, *ibid.* On March 16 and June 11, Thomas wrote to USG
requesting an appointment as paymaster.—ALS, *ibid.* No appointment
followed.

1865, JUNE 28.   Bvt. Col. Theodore S. Bowers endorsement. "The Adjutant General will please issue the within Special Order immediately, and
telegraph the same to Gen Meade at his Headqrs with the Army of the
Potomac"—AES, DNA, RG 94, Letters Received, 684A 1865. Bowers
enclosed his draft of Special Orders No. 339. "Upon the execution of existing orders for the muster out of troops in the Army of the Potomac, Maj.
Gen. G. G. Meade will consolidate each of the existing corps into a division,
and organize from these divisions a Provisional Corps, ~~and~~ assigning Maj.

Gen. H. G. Wright to the Command of the same. All officers relieved under this order will proceed to their places of residence and report by letter to the Adjutant General of the Army for orders. On the organization of the Provisional Corps, Maj. Gen. Wright will march it to some point on the Baltimore and Ohio Railroad, west of the Monocacy, to be selected by him for healthfulness of location and convenience to supplies"—ADf, *ibid.* *O.R.*, I, xlvi, part 3, 1301.

1865, JUNE 28.   Bvt. Col. Horace Porter to Maj. Gen. William B. Franklin. "General Grant directs me to say to you, in reply to your letter of yesterday, that he has never, at any time, been opposed to giving you an active command in the field, and that, although he cannot, at present, promise you more active duty than that of serving upon boards and courts, you will not, by any action or recommendation of his, be mustered out of Service as long the Volunteer Generals are retained."—ALS, DLC-William B. Franklin.

1865, JUNE 29.   USG endorsement. "Approved and respectfully forwarded to the Secretary of War."—ES, DNA, RG 94, ACP, 1883 1875. Written on a telegram of June 27 from Maj. Gen. Edward R. S. Canby, New Orleans, to USG. "Gen Hawkins has been recommended for the brevet of Major Genl and I have the honor to recommend if it be conferred that he be assigned to duty according to that brevet. This with a view to his assignment to the command of west La. Gen sheridan also wishes the assignment to that Dist."—Telegram received (on June 28, 9:00 A.M.), *ibid.*; *ibid.*, RG 107, Telegrams Collected (Bound); copy, *ibid.*, RG 393, Dept. of the Gulf and La., Letters Sent. *O.R.*, I, xlviii, part 2, 1002. See *ibid.*, p. 1095.

1865, JUNE 29.   Stephen Duncan, New York City, to USG. "Do not I pray you, think me disposed to trespass too far on your very great kindness. I trust this will be my last appeal to you for aid, to myself or others. My son in law J. J. Pringle, of parish of Point Coupee Louisiana (the husband of a dearly loved Daughter), desires the exercise of the Executive clemency in granting to him such amnesty, under his proclamation of 29th May. I can & will vouch for Mr Pringles loyalty. He has been a true & consistant loyal man throughout—from the inauguration to the termination of the war. In fact I know no man in the South who has been more pesistently true to the cause of the Union—or whose whole conduct—is more free from the taint of disloyalty, or more exempt from all suspicion. Though a citizen of Louisiana—he holds property in right of his wife, in the State of Missississi, and in order to protect & shield his rights in both states, he applies for a pardon—or such other act of the Executive, as will effectually shield him & his property. . . . My Son Stephen Duncan Junr who you will probably remember, as a resident of Issaquena County Miss;—is also an applicant for ~~Congressional~~ Executive clemency. If you can commend him to those present, you will oblige him as well as myself. I thinke, you may have seen my son, in the neighborhood of Vicksburg. I consider him among the most loyal men of the South. He has been a citizen of this city, for near two years—having taken the oath of Allegiance in 1862."—ALS, USG 3. On the same day, Duncan wrote to Bvt. Col. Adam Badeau. "I have just recd your most kind note of yesterday. I am sorry I cannot fully express—the sense of obligation I owe to Genl Grant & yourself, for the manifestation of your kindness in offering to serve me. But I fear, you will find in me a demonstration of the old adage—of 'waking up to 'whip the willing horse.' I rely however, on your frankness, to disregard my applications, when they become onerous. I enclose another letter, for the Genl which when you have read, please place before him."—ALS, *ibid.* On June 23, Duncan had written to Badeau. "I take the liberty of enclosing for Genl Grant a letter addressed to me, and a letter addressed to president Johnston you will do me a favor by placing both, in the hands of Genl Grant—and if you can aid, in forwarding my wishes, you will confer a favor on me, which will be cherished. If I have obtruded on Genl Grants time, by inviting the favor of his attention to my wants—please say to him, that I may have been inclined, by his former kind attention to my requests, to ask more than I had any just claims to. The Genl however—is well informed; of my true status —by his residence in Vicksburg & his visit to Natchez in the summer of 1863."—ALS, *ibid.* On June 26, Duncan wrote to Badeau. "I take leave to introduce the bearer, my son, Saml P. Duncan. He visits Washington for the purpose of laying before the President a full history of his life, for the past three years—with a view to to elict such relief, under the amnesty proclamation, as the executive clemency may warrant. I, of course, feel much interest in his success, & if you can aid him—please do so. If opportunity offers, please introduce him to Genl Grant—provided you can do so, without interfering with the Generals occupations."—ALS, DNA, RG 94, Amnesty Papers, La. On July 5, Samuel P. Duncan, New York, wrote to President Andrew Johnson. "Having been an officer of the Confederate Army I have the the honour to submit for your Excellency's consideration the following brief statement of my status, and respectfully ask, to receive the pardon offered in your Proclamation of May 29th 1865. When the Rebellion was inaugurated I was in N. Orleans and a Capt of a Fire Co— when the city was threatened with invasion the Fire companies were organized into a Battalion of which I was elected the Major. When the city surrendered in 1862 I immediately returned to my father's residence near Natchez Miss. Soon after reaching there I was conscripted, and furnished a substitute, who was regularly mustered into service. Under subsequent legislative action of the State in which I then was I became a second time liable to military duty, when I applied for and received the position of volunteer aid on the staff of Brig Genl Slaughter. This position being afterwards abolished by the Confederate authorities at Richmond I applied for and received a commission as Captain and A. A. Genl which I held until the close of the war, being at that time on the staff of Lt Genl Taylor. On the surrender of Genl Taylor I came here at the solicitation of my father, Dr Stephen Duncan formerly of Natchez Miss, now, & for two years past, a resident of the city of New York. And I now respectfully appeal to your clemency for exemption from the penalties of the 13th clause of the Amnesty Proclamation, having as will be shown by the accompanying oath evinced my desire to return to my rightful allegiance. Prior to the 'Emancipation Proclamation' my property was worth over $20,000—What it is now worth, or would now bring, I have not the means of knowing. Should this application receive your favourable consideration I respectfully ask that the necessary papers be sent to my father's residence, No 12 Washington Square New York."—ALS, *ibid.* The two letters were forwarded to Attorney Gen. James Speed in an envelope addressed in USG's hand.—D, *ibid.* Docketing indicates that USG favorably endorsed Samuel P. Duncan's application and that Duncan was pardoned as of July 11.—*Ibid.* On July 7, Stephen Duncan wrote to Badeau. "Accompanying this, you will receive the applications, & the statements of my Son Stephen Duncan Jun.r. & my son in law J. J. Pringle. My Son Saml P. Duncan, is now in Washington, on some business. Had I know of his intention to leave on Wednesday, I would have given him a letter to you—for the purpose of having you introduce him to your chief. I think Genl Grant is already acquainted with my Son Stephen Duncan. I do hope, all these applications may prove successful.—I feel deeply interested, in the success of the parties. Please examine the statements of my son & son in law—enclosed in the letter addressed to Atty Genl Speed: & ask Genl Grant to do me countless kindness, by reading these statements"—ALS, USG 3. On July 5, John J. Pringle, New York, wrote to Johnson applying for amnesty.—ALS, DNA, RG 94, Amnesty Papers, La. On July 8, USG endorsed this letter. "Respectfully refered to the Atty. Gn. of the United States. Amnesty recommended as no offence has been committed by applicant."—AES, *ibid.* Johnson also endorsed this letter. "Let a pardon be filled up in this Case—"—AES (undated), *ibid.* Docketing indicates that Pringle was pardoned as of July 11.—*Ibid.* It is probable that the applications for amnesty of Stephen Duncan, Stephen Duncan, Jr., Samuel P. Duncan, and Pringle were forwarded by USG at the same time but separated by a clerk. On July 12, 14, Sept. 13, Oct. 16, and Nov. 4, Stephen Duncan wrote to Badeau. "Your kind note of 10th Inst was recd yesterday. I dont know how I can sufficiently thank you—for your many favors. I can only assure you, they will be gratefully remembered—My son Saml can give me no information in regard to Genl Grants opinion of the necessity or propriety of my taking the amnesty oath of President Johnson. He seems to have confounded, the *Oath*—with the *application for Pardon.* I have resolved, however, to take the oath, as soon as my health will admit of my getting upstairs to the office of Genl Dix. This may be some days however, unless intelligence from you, should in the mean time urge *immediate* compliance. Mr Surget & my son, will give you the earliest information of the rect of their pardon, should they come direct to them. Your friend: (our onetime neighbor) Mr

Mac Gregor—has been very ill, but is reported better today." "Enclosed you will find my amesty oath, taken before Major C. O Johns—who very politely & kindly, called on me, for the purpose. I hope now there will be no difficulty in the way of obtaing my pardon I see it has been suggested, that the Pardon only exempts me from prosecution for the crime of treason; but does not shield my property from the operations of the confiscation act. I cannot think, this construction is correct. A pardon exempts from all the penalties for the crimes of Treason—& if so must protect my property against all acts confiscating my property for the guilt of Treason." "I wrote to you some weeks since, expecting you would have returned to Washington city, by 1st Sept.: I now learn, it may be, 18th Oct.r before you will reach your head quarters. I write now, to say,—that my son Sam.l P. Duncan—has recently returned from Washington, & brought with him the Presidents Pardon. He informs me,—he found his application with mine & my son S. Duncan Jun.r. & my son in law: J. J. Pringle's—in a package (I think) in the Attorney Gen.ls office;—with-drew his own—& presented it in person, to the President,—who received him courteously & very soon complied with his request. He further says, he presented my application,— to the President—who replied 'I cannot see why your Father should be an applicant for Pardon,—for he has been Loyal all his life' My application then, rests in statu quo. I dont know,—but there may be more necessity *now* than ever,—for my pardon: for the fact of my having applied for it, & not obtained it—may be assumed as proof, that I was deemed inworthy of it. But I confess, I am now indifferent about obtaining it—than I was at first. I believe there will a general, if not universal amnesty granted, ere long. Excuse this hand scrawl, writing has become very irksome to me—of late." "Your favor of 14th has just been recd. No apology from you,—was needed or expected. as I was fully aware of your long absence, I could not but expect a considerable accumulation of business as a necessary consequence. I think, the cause of the delay,—is attributable altogether, to the Atty Genl, who is universally spoken of, as most inefficient in the discharge of his duties,—& most negligent & careless with all papers entrusted to him. Donot put yourself out of the way,—to attend to this pardon business. On my *own* acct I can well have it postponed still longer, & on acct of my son S. Duncan Jun.r & my son in law J. J Pringle, I wd be pleased, if their pardons are passed, *before the meeting of congress.*" "I have recd through the office of the Sec.y of State my Pardon from the Prest of the U. S. dated 3d July 1865 I presume the pardon of my Son in Law J. J. Pringle, has been forwarded to Gov.r Wells of Louisiana, & Mr. P. will receive it there. I acknowledge myself—your debtor for the many favors conferred—by you Please present me respectfully to your chief.—"—ALS, USG 3.

On July 12, Eustace Surget wrote to Badeau. "Your message through Dr Duncan has been delivered to me, and while I regret to say that I have heard nothing whatever from my application for Executive clemency, permit me to tender you my best thanks for the attention you have so kindly bestowed upon the matter. May I venture to trespass further and ask that you will at some leisure moment see Col Browning, the Presidents private secretary, upon the subject. He has I believe been written to by Genl. Rozencrans about the matter and perhaps a copy of my Application furnished him. My case in all it's bearings is one of unusual urgency, and I therefore feel the greater anxiety to get it acted upon as speedily as possible."—ALS, *ibid.* On June 20, Surget, Washington, had written to Johnson requesting amnesty.—ALS, DNA, RG 94, Amnesty Papers, La. On the same day, USG endorsed this letter. "Respectfully forwarded with recommendation that the benefits of Amnesty be extended to E. Surget. But for the possibility of the remaining portion of his estate being worth more than $20.000 he would come within the range of the Amnesty Proclamation without special application."—AES, *ibid.* Docketing indicates that Surget was pardoned as of July 11.

1865, JUNE 30.   To Secretary of War Edwin M. Stanton. "After carrying out existing orders for Musterout and distribution of Cavalry there will still be left about Washington the 1st Provisional N. Y. 1st Provisional Pa 9th N. Y. and 1st N. H. Cavalry, numbering in the whole over 3000 men. These troops are not likely to be required and I recommend their Musterout of service."—ALS, DNA, RG 94, Vol. Service Div., Letters Received, A1081 (VS) 1865. Probably on the same day, Bvt. Col. Theodore S. Bowers wrote to the AG. "Lieutenant General Grant desires the following order in substance to be carried into effect: Order: Department Commanders except in the Departments of Louisiana and Texas, will immediately reduce their commands to the minimum requirements of the service, by mustering out all surplus troops. In executing this order whole organizations will be mustered out, giving the preferance to Veteran Regiments having the shortest period to serve. This order will not apply to the Provisional Corps of the Army of the Potomac, the Army of the Tennessee, or the 1st Army Corps."—ALS (undated), *ibid.*, A1077 (VS) 1865. See *O.R.*, III, v, 65–66.

1865, JUNE 30.   To Secretary of War Edwin M. Stanton. "I respectfully recommend that Private Joseph W. M. Shaw. Co "F," 9th Regt. Vet. Res. Corps, now on duty in the vicinity of Washington be honorably discharged the service"—Copies, DLC-USG, V, 46, 109; DNA, RG 108, Letters Sent.

1865, JUNE 30.   USG endorsement. "Respectfully forwarded to the Secretary of War."—*O.R.*, I, xlvi, part 1, 606. Written on a letter of June 29 from Maj. Gen. George G. Meade to Bvt. Col. Theodore S. Bowers enclosing a map of operations of the Army of the Potomac from March 29–April 9.—*Ibid.* Also on June 29, Meade wrote to Bowers. "I understand it is the design of the Lt. Genl Comdg to present to the War Dept the names of regular officers, who have served with distinction in the volunteer service for promotion by brevet in the regular service—I consider this most eminently just & proper, and beg leave therefore to submit the names of these officers, who have served under my command, giving their regular & volunteer rank—I have not made, any recommendation for the rank to be given these officers, leaving this to be settled by the Lt. Genl on general principles governing other cases of the same character.—"—ALS, DNA, RG 108, Letters Received. The enclosed list is *ibid.*

1865, JUNE 30, 11:00 A.M. To Maj. Gen. Philip H. Sheridan. "Muster out all the Volunteer Light Artillery in La. Fla. & Miss."—ALS (telegram sent), DNA, RG 107, Telegrams Collected (Bound); telegram sent, *ibid.*; telegram received (dated "30"), *ibid.*, Telegrams Collected (Unbound). *O.R.*, I, xlviii, part 2, 1031. On July 1, Brig. Gen. James W. Forsyth, chief of staff for Sheridan, New Orleans, wrote to Maj. Gen. Edward R. S. Canby. "I am instructed by Genl. Sheridan to enclose you the within copy of telegram just recd from Lieut: Genl. Grant. The General thinks that it was sent to him by mistake—"—ALS, DNA, RG 94, War Records Office, Dept. of the Gulf. *O.R.*, I, xlviii, part 2, 1036. On July 11, Maj. Gen. Peter J. Osterhaus telegraphed to Brig. Gen. John A. Rawlins. "By copy of telegraph from Lt Genl Grant to maj Gen Sheridan, it appears that the Volunteer Light Artillery in Mississippi is ordered to be immediately mustered out. In the absence of a department commander, I ask instructions."—Telegram received (at 8:00 P.M.), DNA, RG 94, Vol. Service Div., Letters Received, A971 (VS) 1865; *ibid.*, RG 107, Telegrams Collected (Bound). On July 13, Bvt. Col. Theodore S. Bowers endorsed this telegram. "Respectfully referred to Col. Thos H. Vincent, Asst Adjt Genl with the request that instructions be sent Gen. Osterhaus to have the troops mustered out as heretofore directed."—ES, *ibid.*, RG 94, Vol. Service Div., Letters Received, A971 (VS) 1865. On June 22, Forsyth had written to Rawlins. "I have the honor to enclose you the following papers &c &c, for the information of the Lieutenant General Commanding. Reports of Artillery (Light and Heavy) in the Trans Mississippi Department June 1st Assistant Chief of Ordnance report of condition of affairs at Mound Prairie. Letter of J J. Williamson on condition of Ordnance &c at Shreveport. Letter of Genl Heron with report of condition of affairs at the C. S. Government Works, Mound Prairie Texas."—LS, *ibid.*, RG 108, Letters Received. *O.R.*, I, xlviii, part 2, 962. The enclosures are *ibid.*, pp. 963–67.

On June 30, 11:00 A.M., USG also telegraphed to Maj. Gen. George H. Thomas. "Muster out of service all the Vol. Light Artillery in your Mil. Div. If Artillery is required to replace any of it Companies of regulars can be sent to supply the place."—ALS (telegram sent), DNA, RG 107, Telegrams Collected (Bound); telegram sent, *ibid.*; copies, *ibid.*, RG 108, Letters Sent; *ibid.*, RG 393, Dept. of the Cumberland, Telegrams Received; *ibid.*, Military Div. of the Tenn., Telegrams Received; DLC-USG, V, 46, 109. *O.R.*, I, xlix, part 2, 1053. On the same day, Thomas, Nashville, telegraphed to USG. "Orders sending all Volunteer artillery to states for muster out have been in operation in this Military Division for the last ten days. Most of the Batteries have gone."—Telegram received (on July 1, 2:30

P.M.), DNA, RG 107, Telegrams Collected (Bound); *ibid.*, RG 108, Telegrams Received; copy, DLC-USG, V, 54.

On June 29, Bowers wrote to Maj. Gen. George G. Meade. "You will please cause an inspection to be made of the Middle and Eastern Departments of your Division, with a view of determining what regiments in those Departments can be mustered out. There are two regular regiments available that can be furnished you upon application, for duty in those Departments. You will also cause all volunteer light artillery within your Military Division to be mustered out of service. If you need other light artillery to replace it you will report the fact to these Headquarters, when it will be sent from here."—LS, DNA, RG 393, Military Div. of the Atlantic, Letters Received.

1865, [JULY?].   USG endorsement. "Now when so many General officers, many of them of great merit, must necessarily leave the service because of the great reduction of the force ~~retained~~ heretofore in service I do not think it justice to them to promote officers for the purpose of keeping them in. It would simply lead to mustering out one of this class of officers to retain another. Being in service will give Gn. Avery no additional claim for an appoint. in the regular service when such appointments come to be made." —AES (undated), DNA, RG 94, ACP, A651 CB 1865. Written on a letter of July 5 from Governor Reuben E. Fenton of N. Y. to Secretary of War Edwin M. Stanton recommending Bvt. Brig. Gen. Matthew H. Avery, col., 1st N. Y. Provisional Cav., for an appointment in the U.S. Army.— Copy, *ibid.* USG probably wrote his endorsement in early July because Avery was mustered out as of July 19.

1865, JULY 1.   To Secretary of War Edwin M. Stanton. "From present indications I think it is perfectly safe to Musterout of service the remaining Veteran regiments of the Army of the Potomac and of the Army of the Tenn. I would therefore respectfully recommend that orders be issued for such musterout."—ALS, DNA, RG 94, Vol. Service Div., Letters Received, A1082 (VS) 1865. *O.R.*, III, v, 65.

1865, JULY 1.   To Secretary of War Edwin M. Stanton. "I would respectfully recommend the discharge of the 54th & 55th Mass Vols. These are colored regiments raised in the North."—Copies, DLC-USG, V, 46, 109; DNA, RG 108, Letters Sent.

1865, JULY 1, 3:55 P.M.   To Maj. Gen. George H. Thomas. "Relieve Gen. B. S. Roberts from duty and direct him to report to the A. G. by letter." —ALS (telegram sent), DNA, RG 107, Telegrams Collected (Bound); telegram sent, *ibid.*; telegrams received (2), *ibid.*, Telegrams Collected (Unbound). On June 24, Brig. Gen. Benjamin S. Roberts, Memphis, had telegraphed to Bvt. Col. Theodore S. Bowers requesting permission to retain two staff officers.—Telegram received (at 5:20 P.M.), *ibid.*, Telegrams

Collected (Bound); *ibid.*, RG 108, Telegrams Received; copy, DLC-USG, V, 54. On June 25, 10:25 A.M., Bowers telegraphed to Roberts. "No exception can be made in [t]he case of the Officers referred to in your dispatch. They must join their Regiments. Officers of the Staff Corps will be furnished you on application"—ALS (telegram sent), DNA, RG 107, Telegrams Collected (Bound); telegram sent, *ibid.*; copies, *ibid.*, RG 108, Letters Sent; DLC-USG, V, 46, 109. On June 30, Roberts telegraphed to Bowers the message of June 24 with approval of Thomas added.—Telegram received (on July 1, 4:00 A.M.), DNA, RG 107, Telegrams Collected (Bound); *ibid.*, RG 108, Telegrams Received; copy, DLC-USG, V, 54. On July 3, 11:30 A.M., Bowers telegraphed to Thomas. "The application of Gen Roberts [to] retain on his Staff Lt. Col. McQueen and Lt S. S Craig, 1st Iowa Cavalry, is I not approved. These officers must join their regiment" —ALS (telegram sent), DNA, RG 107, Telegrams Collected (Bound); telegram sent, *ibid.*; telegram received, *ibid.*, Telegrams Collected (Unbound).

On May 26 and 31, Roberts had written to USG. "It may not add to your satisfaction, that an old army officer who has made so small a figure in this unexampled war, sends you congratulation on the final triumph and success of your Arms. Your campaigns and combinations stand in conspicuous prominence, quite above the plans and conceptions, on whatever scale, of any of the great Captains of history, modern or ancient. Their Execution, through sacifices, toil, perils marches, combats, battles and sieges, displaying tenacity of purpose and unalterable resolves to conquer, have culminated in successes that are without parallel in the annals of war, and vindicates the enormous cost of life and treasure to the country. General, I ask to send you my congratulations and to salute you as the Captain of the age, without a Peer. May the Divine Goodness that has led you safely and successfully to this happy consummation, vouchsafe to you many days and years in the satisfaction and repose of the peace you have restored to the country. Yours will be that unalloyed enjoyment of mind conscious of rectitude and duty well and faithfully done. The sentiment of gratitude, a grateful people feel for the heroic loyalty of your army & your personal sacrifices, will find expression in the care they will take that the country shall fittingly bestow upon you rewards and honor. As a West Pointer, I must add, that your unostentatious and modest bearing, adds genuine lustre to honors and fame, none can wear gracefully but the truly great, unconscious of their greatness."—ALS, USG 3. "*Private & personal* . . . I have addressed to Genl Rawlins an official communication relating to my embarrassment here, in consequence of the assignment of Brevet Major General J. E. Smith, my junior in rank as Brigadier General, to the command of the District of Memphis, while I his *senior* am on duty in the same District. My letter was written under the conviction, that you were ignorant of the fact that I was here on duty and had previously exercised the command of this District under special assignment by Genl Canby, and that you would not knowingly bring on an officer of my *thirty* years service, the mortification and

reproach of supercedure by an Officer junior to me, whose term of service
is only *four* years. I write now General with great hesitation and reluctance,
not wishing to trouble you with my personal grievances. But I feel assured
that you, an old army Officer, will not strike me down when I have grown
grey in service, or subvert ~~the~~ my good record of *thirty years* of hard, un-
requited army toil. My reputation I desire to transmit unimpaired to my
children, and I beg you now after my hard labours, sacrifices and devotion
to my profession in this and other wars, not to exhibit me to the army, as
unfit to command this District, by the assignment of a Junior officer over
me. In the name of God do not subject me to this mortification I do not
believe these things were known to you or intended. Permit me to express to
you the sense of injustice and wrong, never before expressed, that the services
I rendered in New Mexico, on Popes campaign, at Harpers Ferry, in Western Va, in the Department of the NorthWest, in Louisiana and Texas, have
not long since been acknowledged. I beg to refer you to the reports of
Generals Pope and Canby, and the special urgency of their recommendations
for my promotion for Distinguished conduct in the field. But these were all
overlooked or rather kept from the knowledge of the Secretary of war &
President, & I have remained in the rank of a Brigadier. I had inexorable
enemies at Washington, and too old to to supplicate political influence, I
was ignored there, and I feel that injustice and wrong amounting to crime,
has been done me. You General, I am sure will not add to this chapter of
wrongs. I am too old to begin life anew and too poor to resign, and I am
unconvinced that you or the Government will coerce an old officer to such
an alternative. I appeal to your sense of justice and acknowledged magnanimity, and ask your careful reconsideration of the assignment of Genl
Smith to the command of this District over me his Senior. It would not
operate unjustly to Genl Smith to assign him to the command of the Post
& Defenses of Memphis and to put me his Senior officer in command of this
District. As one of your friends who has sustained and vindicated you from
the beginning, I ask this simple act of justice at your hands. . . . N. B.
Since writing the above, I have seen Genl Smith, and learned from him that
he has been assigned to duty with his Brevet rank of Major General. *This
fact* places him properly over me in rank & leaves me no cause of complaint,
if in fact, I had any in supercedure by a junior. I therefore desire to express
my entire willingness to remain with my present command, that greatly
needs reorganization and instruction."—ALS, PHi. The second letter,
marked "filed," had been received by USG on June 21.—DLC-USG, V, 49.
The present location of the letter indicates that someone later removed it
from the files.

On Jan. 16, 1866, Roberts, Washington, D. C., wrote to USG. "On 7th
May 1861. Lt Col: Geo B. Crittenden of the Regiment of Mounted Riflemen deserted from his Post at Fort Stanton N. M. He proceeded to Texas
and was commissioned a Brigadier General in the confederate army. See
monthly return of Fort Stanton for May 1861, and Regimental Report of
Regt Mounted Riflemen. At that date, reference to the old army Register

shows, that the Field officers of that Regiment in the order of rank stood as follows, Loring Colonel. Geo. B. Crittenden Lt Col: Simonson & Ruff, Majors. On 13th May Loring resigned, and *Major* Simonson was appointed *Colonel* in his place. On *10th June* special orders of the War Department announced the *risignation* of Lt Col Geo. B. Crittenden, to take effect on that day. It is clear that if *Lt Col* Geo. B. Crittenden had been in service on *13th May*, when Col Loring resigned, that Lt Col Crittenden would have been promoted to the Colonelcy of the Regiment, and not *Major Simonson*, his *junior* officer. I was the *senior* captain of the Regiment of Mounted Riflemen on 7th May 1861, and by a law of Congress and the Regulations of the army, regulating promotion, I was entitled to promotion to a *Majority* on that date; when Lt Col Geo. B. Crittenden abandoned his Post and command and deserted to the enemy; going out of New Mexico by the way of Texas and entering the Confederate Army. *I know* that Lt Col Crittenden deserted, for he left the Post where I was serving under him, and had previously declared to me his intention to do so and to take the Regiment with him to Texas; and he had urgcd to me to join, in this attrocious treason and treachery to his Government while yet in its pay. I am *informed* and have reason to believe, that Lt Col Geo. B. Crittenden never tendered any resignation; but that in consideration of the pride and grief of his venerable Father, the war Department, dropped him from the army rolls, by announcing a resignation. If Lt Col Crittenden ever tendered a resignation, it certainly was after he had deserted, and had joined the confederate army. I have the honor to ask that you refer this matter to some officer expert in the laws of the army and its regulations governing promotion, or to a Board of Officers, for a report of the facts and an opinion, as to my lawful right to promotion as a Major of Mounted Riflemen on 7th May, and to subsequent promotion in the Regiments of Cavalry, according to date of that Majority; with a view of refering the question to the Attorney General for his judicial opinion on the case. I now go back to my Regiment as a Major of Cavalry, after nearly 31 years service, 20 of which have been on the frontiers and in the field; and the correction of this error will place me high on the list of Lieut Colonels."—ALS, DNA, RG 94, ACP, R576 CB 1863. On Jan. 17, USG endorsed this letter. "Respectfully forwarded to the Secretary of War."—ES, *ibid*. Roberts was promoted to lt. col., 3rd Cav., as of July 28.

1865, JULY 2. USG endorsement. "Respectfully refered to the Atty. Gn. of the United States. I know the writer of this letter well and believe he is perfectly sincere in all his statements. Without recommending too much haste in in receiving back to full citizenship those who have been conspicuous in the rebellion against the Govt. I do recommend Gn. Steele as one of the earlyest to receive the benefits of amnesty."—AES, DNA, RG 94, Amnesty Papers, Tex. Written on a letter of June 6 from former C.S.A. Brig. Gen. William Steele, Austin, Tex., to USG. "The uniform courtesy with which you have treated Confederate Officers and the relations which once existed between us as Officers induces me to ask your influence in my behalf   In 1861 I resigned without intending to take up arms in the Confederate cause though believing in the justice of that cause. Circumstances afterwards induced me enter the service contrary to my first intentions, I have served it to the best of my ability and oppertunities but having failed to establish a seperate nationality, I yield to the logic of events which has decided that we are in the wrong and am now disposed to become a peacable citizen obeying the laws and discouraging any further resistance. I can give no better garante[e] of my future conduct than to assert my firm conviction that the war which has just closed has been inagerated under more favourable circumstances than will ever again present themselves and the consequent belief that any attempt to overturn the U. S. authority will be not only foolish in the extreme, but morally wrong. Such being my opinions you may rest assured that I shall take no part in plots against the govt I have now a way open to leave this country. I am in no duress. therefore this is only the result of a wish to remain in this country. Your own knowledge of my character will enable you to place a proper value upon the statemets I have made. Should you think proper to exert your influence in my behalf you can do so without fear of favouring one who has persecuted others. I have when in power kindly treated those who differed with me in opinion & have exercised severity only upon those who taking advantage of the absence of civil law have murdered or plundered unoffending citizens."—ALS, *ibid.*

1865, JULY 3. To Secretary of War Edwin M. Stanton. "I would respectfully recommend Lt. Col. Henry F. Clarke C. S. for the brevet of Colonel and of Brig. Gen. in the regular army"—Copies, DLC-USG, V, 46, 109; DNA, RG 108, Letters Sent. Lt. Col. Henry F. Clarke had been a classmate of USG at USMA.

1865, JULY 3, 1:00 P.M. Maj. Gen. Alfred Pleasonton, St. Louis, to USG. "To mount dismounted Cavalry necessary for service on the plains fifteen hundred 1500 horses will be needed. There are no horses being purchased by branch of Cavalry Bureau here & there seems no prospect of mounting the required number of Cavalry unless horses be sent from the East. Cannot the requisitione number be ordered sent here for immediate use."—Telegram received (at 4:10 P.M.), DNA, RG 107, Telegrams Collected (Bound); *ibid.*, RG 108, Telegrams Received; copies, *ibid.*, RG 393, Military Div. of the Mo., Telegrams Sent; DLC-USG, V, 54. *O.R.*, I, xlviii, part 2, 1043.

1865, JULY 5, 6:30 P.M. To Maj. Gen. Alfred H. Terry. "It is not necessary to keep up the fortifications about Norfolk and Portsmouth. All public property however must be guarded and preserved."—ALS (telegram sent), DNA, RG 107, Telegrams Collected (Bound); telegram sent, *ibid.*; copies (dated July 6), *ibid.*, RG 108, Letters Sent; DLC-USG, V, 46, 109. On June 21, Terry had telegraphed to Brig. Gen. John A. Rawlins. "Are any of the works at City Point and around Portsmouth & Norfolk to be kept up or ~~should~~ should they all be dismantled & the guns &c. shipped"—ALS (undated telegram sent), DNA, RG 107, Telegrams Collected (Unbound); telegram received (at 1:35 P.M.), *ibid.*, Telegrams Collected (Bound); *ibid.*, RG 108, Telegrams Received. On July 3, Terry again telegraphed to Rawlins. "Is it desireable to keep up the fortifications around Norfolk and Portsmouth. The Ordnance and Ordnance stores in ~~them~~ works require considerable details, for guard duty   if the artillery is taken out smaller garrisons will ~~be required~~ suffice in those Cities."—ALS (telegram sent), *ibid.*, RG 107, Telegrams Collected (Unbound); telegram received (at 2:40 P.M.), *ibid.*, RG 108, Telegrams Received.

1865, JULY 5. Maj. Gen. Edward O. C. Ord, Detroit, to USG. "I notified Genl Hooker from Baltimore that I was ordered here to take Command of the Department of the Ohio   today I received the following telegram from him. Cincinnati July. fourth Eighteen hundred sixty five 1865 MAJ GEN ORD. Your telegram today to Col Hoyt has been referred to me   as I have no orders to turn over this command to any one you know that I cannot do it   have been looking for orders ever since the receipt of your telegram from Balto   (Sigd) MAJ GEN HOOKER—"—Telegram received (at 12:45 P.M.), DNA, RG 107, Telegrams Collected (Bound); *ibid.*, RG 108, Telegrams Received; copy, DLC-USG, V, 54. *O.R.*, I, xlix, part 2, 1067.

1865, JULY 5. Jesse Root Grant, Covington, Ky., to USG. "I have a note before me from Philip B. Swing of Batavia recommending the bearer Col John Henry of the 5th Ohio Cavalry for assignment to some favorable post—I can say that I saw and became acquainted with Col then Capt Henry at Lagrange in June 63—He is the man that reenforced Col Morgan with fifty men in Davis mills when Van Dorn was so disastrously routed—Besides this any recommendation made by P. B. Swing you may rely upon with the greatest safety—He is *the* man of Clermont County, & you will recollect the son-in-law of Judge Fishback"—ALS, DNA, RG 59, Applications and Recommendations, Lincoln and Johnson. The enclosure is *ibid.*

1865, JULY 6. USG endorsement. "Respectfully returned to the Secretary of War, and attention invited to the accompanying reports."—ES, DNA, RG 94, Letters Received, 340K 1865. Written on a petition of May 27 from Martin Kenosskey, Memphis, to Secretary of War Edwin M. Stanton requesting the return of gold taken from him by military authorities at Memphis on March 24, 1864, while returning to his home in Grenada, Miss.— DS, *ibid.* On June 5, 1865, Asst. Secretary of War Charles A. Dana endorsed this petition. "Referred to Lieutenant General Grant to require of Major General Hurlbut an explanation upon this subject, and a statement of the present whereabouts of the gold."—ES, *ibid.* On June 7, Brig. Gen. John A. Rawlins endorsed this petition. "Respectfully referred to Major General Canby, Commanding Department of the Gulf, who will require of

Major General S A Hurlbut a full compliance with endorsed order of the
Secretary [o]f War hereon; and forward without delay, through these Headquarters, Gen Hurlbuts [e]xplanation and statement in the case."—ES, *ibid.*
On June 22, Maj. Gen. Stephen A. Hurlbut, New Orleans, submitted an
explanation. "I have the honor to report on the within case principally from
memory as the records of the 16th Corps are not accessible to me. Some time
in March 1864 a Jew, Cotton & Gold Dealer and smuggler was arrested by
the Prov. Marshal's force at Memphis in the act of passing the lines South
with a quantity of Gold. This was contrary to Treasury Regulations, the
orders of Genl Grant and my own orders. The case was reported to me by
Capt George A Williams 1st U. S. Infantry, then Provost Marshal at Memphis; I directed the man to be imprisoned & tried and ordered the Gold to be
confiscated to the use of the United States all which appears upon the Records of the 16th Army Corps. The Gold the amount of which I cannot now
give, was sent under my direction by Capt. Williams to St Louis or Chicago,
and converted into paper currency at the proper premium. My Head Quarters were removed to Cairo; at that place the messenger in charge reported
to me the amount of U. S. Notes the produce of the Exchange.—$8861—
This amount was taken up by me and has been lawfully used in the Secret
Service of the United States for which I am at all times ready to account &
display proper vouchers   The annexed account will shew the statement
of this particular fund up to 4th May 1865̶4̶ when I ceased to command the
16th army Corps. The amount of $5001. charged to Lt. Col. W. H. Thurs-
ton ass. Insp Genl 16th A. Corps—was left with him for the use of my
successor in Command of the Corps. No successor was appointed & that
sum was paid back to me by him & expended in the Department of the Gulf.
I am satisfied this man has no claim on the United States but request that a
report be required from Capt George A Williams 1st U S. Infantry as to his
merits"—ADS, *ibid.* On July 13, Maj. Thomas T. Eckert, act. asst. secretary of war, endorsed this report. "Returned to Major General Hurlbut with
directions to furnish this Department with the accounts of the disposition
made of this money."—ES, *ibid.* On Oct. 15, Hurlbut, Washington, wrote
to Rawlins. "I have the honor to return through you to the War Department
the Enclosed Communication from the Secretary of War of date July 6.
1865 together with this Report and the Accounts & vouchers following.
The delay in answering has been caused by mistake in the Express Companies in forwarding my papers from New Orleans. The Accounts lettered
"A" to "F" inclusive, the Book of Consolidated Accounts & the original
vouchers with letter of Major D. J. Benner my Senior Aide are also transmitted for Examination   There are some few items Expended by myself
individually for which no vouchers appear. As to these I certify on honor
that they were expended for the public service under circumstances which
prevented the taking of vouchers. During my Command at Memphis I determined to make the crime of the Country support the secret service. At
New Orleans the money was drawn from the Pro Marshal. Major Benner

had charge of the funds and now resides in Gettysburgh Penna The Character of expenditures was governed by my own discretion and was I believe judiciously Exercised. If any further Explanations are required I am ready to give them. These papers are originals & the only ones I have, as this account was not kept or the vouchers taken in duplicates"—ALS, *ibid.* On Oct. 16, USG endorsed this letter. "Respectfully forwarded to the Secretary of War."—ES, *ibid.*

1865, July 6. Joseph E. Segar, Richmond, to USG. "Mr. H. H. Selden, late a quarter Master Confederate Army, is desirous to be released from Johnson's Island, where he is now a prisoner of war. He is entirely willing to take Oath of allegiance: He is the son of a most worthy citizen of my state, whose solicitude is, most naturally, much excited for the discharge of his son. Please allow me to say that his release will be to me a personal Kindness."—ALS, USG 3. On July 7, Henry Heth, former C.S.A. maj. gen., wrote to USG. "You will confer a personal favour by releasing from Confinement my brother-in-law, and Cousin, Major H. H. Selden, formerly a QrMaster in the C. S. Army. Major S. was captured at, or, near Sailors Creek in Apl: last. and is now in confinement at Johnson's Island,"—ALS, PHi.

1865, July 7. To Secretary of War Edwin M. Stanton. "I have been looking up the law creating the 'Signal Corps' of the Army and find nothing which requires its continuance in service. I would give it as my opinion that it is no longer of service commensurate with the expense of keeping it up and do therefore recommend that all officers and men connected with it be ordered to their regiments or corps where the same are retained in the service, and where they are not, that the officers and men be honorably discharged."—Copies, DLC-USG, V, 46, 109; DNA, RG 108, Letters Sent. On July 2, Bvt. Brig. Gen. James A. Hardie had forwarded to USG several communications from Col. Benjamin F. Fisher, chief signal officer, concerning duty assignments for officers of the U.S. Signal Corps.—AES, *ibid.,* Letters Received. The enclosures are *ibid.* On July 10, Maj. Gen. Winfield S. Hancock wrote to Brig. Gen. Lorenzo Thomas reporting that a Signal Corps detachment was unnecessary in the Shenandoah Valley.—LS, *ibid.,* RG 94, ACP, S1030 CB 1865. On July 13, Maj. Thomas M. Vincent, AGO, endorsed this letter. "Respectfully referred to the Chief Signal Officer of the Army, for remark, and also for information as to the number of men belonging to the Signal Corps whose services can be dispensed with. This to be returned."—ES, *ibid.* On July 17, Fisher wrote to Vincent reporting how he believed Signal Corps detachments should be distributed.—LS, *ibid.* On July 21, USG endorsed this letter. "I would recommend that all officers and men of the signal Corps, as organized by Act of Congress for the War, now east of the Mississippi river, be mustered out, their services in my judgment being no longer necessary"—ES, *ibid.*

1865, JULY 7, 9:40 A.M.   To Maj. Gen. Thomas H. Ruger, Raleigh. "To guard against disease give the most stringent orders for the police of New Berne & Wilmington. Should the yellow fever break out at either place move the garrisons to the pine woods away from the Cities leaving no more than what is necessary to guard public property."—ALS (telegram sent), DNA, RG 107, Telegrams Collected (Bound); telegram sent, *ibid.*; telegram received, *ibid.*, RG 393, Army of the Ohio and Dept. of N. C., Telegrams Received. *O.R.*, I, xlvii, part 3, 675–76.

1865, JULY 7.   Maj. Gen. John Pope, Washington, D. C., endorsement. "The enclosed despatches just received from Genls. Dodge & Conner in relation to the condition of Indian affairs on the 'Plains' are respectfully transmitted for the information of the Genl in Chief of the Army"—AES, DNA, RG 108, Telegrams Received. *O.R.*, I, xlviii, part 2, 1059. Written on a telegram of July 6 from Maj. Gen. Grenville M. Dodge, St. Louis, to Pope. "Care Lieut Gen Grant—When will you return and what disposition has been made of commands   Camanches & Kioways sue for peace   have left southern route gone south.   will have interviews with them in few days   Cheynees & Araphoes are for fight. aAll indians in Gen Connors Command defy us and attack on opportunity—we have had several fights since you left & indians on southern route have been severely punished   Genl Connor sends following dispatch fFort Laramie   July 6th [5] to MAJ GEN DODGE—I understand by telegraphic reports that Efforts will be made to make treaties with the hostile indians   I have the honor to represent that any treaty made with the hostile in this district prior to their thorough Chastisement will not be observed by for six months & will only result in injury to them & the settlers & traders in this district & a continual Expense to the Govt   unacquainted as they are with the power of the Goverment overtures of peace would be look upon by them as a weakness on our part and a treaty would only be observed as long as they recd presents   they now boast that one (1) Indian Can whip five (5) Soldiers   they have Certainly been sucessful against our troops in the last year & until they are taught a lesson treaties would prove unmerciful   (signed) P. E. CONNOR Brig Gen Comdg—"—Telegram received (misdated June 6, received at 7:00 P.M.), DNA, RG 107, Telegrams Collected (Bound); (dated July 6) *ibid.*, RG 108, Telegrams Received; copy, DLC-USG, V, 54. *O.R.*, I, xlviii, part 2, 1051–52, 1058.

1865, JULY 7.   Maj. Gen. John E. Wool, Troy, N. Y., to USG. "It is rumored through the press that Major General Dix is soon to be relieved from the Command of the Department of the East. In such a case, I would ask to be restored to that Command for the following reasons, which I have already transmitted to the Hon. Edwin M. Stanton, Secretary of War. . . ."—LS, DNA, RG 108, Letters Received. On July 10, Wool wrote to USG again discussing his war record at length.—LS, *ibid.*

1865, JULY 7. Susan Capens, "Burnt hills," Saratoga County, N. Y., to [USG]. "i have sat Done With a soraful hart to pen afew lines to you to lett you no that i have gott a sone in the arme By the name george W gray he Went out West october last on the Way some Wone got hime to inlist the Curnell Pay hime thold hime to pute his name Done 21 years old he sueposed it Was all rite he seid he Wood give hime three hundrd dollers he Was taken sick as soone as he get his $125 Done then some of the Boys stold $1 Dollers frome hime $1 Dollers he hant got of his Bounty money he is onely 16 years old october 21 last he in listed in ontario oswego County november lat he Did inlist Without my Consent he is not able to Do mileyterey Duty he Was no able to Do much Wor[k] of iney kind he is very nerves and got the Certare in his head he is now sick he ses he cant lid long if he Cant Come home he is Just as poore as he Cane bee Indead it is hard to have a child suffer so have rote tree letter to hime But hant got no ancer so i cant tell how he is now they all say heare that you Will Dizscharge hime & i thought i Wood rit to you to see Wat you Wood say or Wat you Wood Do about it i Coud git hime home By law if i had money to spare But i ame poore he is my onely Chile i Can prove his age an prove that he Did in list un nowen to me he Did in list in the 16 U S infr C F regular [. . . . .] Brigade [. . . . .] looke Mountain Tenscc you no all aboot this Bigment i subspose please tell me how long he has got to stay if he shoud live please tell me Wat you Can do fore hime if you Will have the goodness to give hime ordes fore a furlaw fore a few Days par haps it Wood Do hime good ore if you Wood give me a pase so i cod goan see himme i Dont feale able to pay my fare out thare how Cane i bare to have Die so he Dont no Enuff to take Care of hime self We have sent hime some things he Dont git them rite as soone as you gitt this you Will bee rememer fore ever an Will never fore get you Do all you Can for the Boy"—ALS, USG 3. On July 20, Bvt. Col. Adam Badeau wrote to Maj. Gen. George H. Thomas requesting information about Private George W. Gray, 16th Inf.—ALS, *ibid.* Accompanying reports and endorsements show that Gray's co. commander had recommended his discharge for being underage. Docketing indicates that Badeau so informed Capens on Oct. 16.—*Ibid.*

1865, JULY 8. Bvt. Maj. Gen. George H. Gordon, Framingham, Mass., to USG. "*Personal* . . . I have written the following letter to the Secy of War for the purposes, which the letter, best reveals—'HON E. M. STANTON SECY OF WAR Framingham Mass July 8 1865 I see by the papers—it may be true or false—that "one hundred and fifty Major & Brigr Generals who have not been in active service for a year or two past" are to be mustered out of service. I am here—having reported by letter to the Adjt Genl—by an order from the War Dept I trust the Honble Seceretary will not allow my name to appear on the list of the "One hundred and fifty." as he will undoubtedly remember that I was retained by his personal order at Norfolk—As I was about leaving under Gen Grants order to take an active part in the last campaign—upon the ground that I was doing more good there than if in command of a corps in the field—I trust I need not say that I always made evy effort for fighting service, and never had any other save when compelled by sickness, which was *never* when my command was engaged in ~~bat~~ in action—I have not written this letter to beg to be retained in the service if the Gvt has no further need for my labor—I shall cheerfully acquisce in its orders— . . .' May I intrude, in this private way, for the purposes indicated in my letter to the Secy—I am afraid I did not make friends with the cotton men at Norfolk—They would gladly present facts to my disadvantage."—ALS, USG 3. Gordon was mustered out as of Aug. 24.

1865, JULY 10.   Maj. Gen. John A. Logan, Louisville, to USG. "I desire to call your attention to the following brief statement of services rendered the government, by Brigadier General E. W. Rice during the war just ended. General Rice entered the service early in the spring of 61, as Major of the 7th Iowa Volunteers. He participated in the Battle of Belmont, where he was severely wounded, while bringing his regiment off the field, and although unable to walk without a cane, was with his regiment at Forts Henry, and Donalsen, At the latter place his regiment supported the 2nd Iowa, in the charge that carried the enemies line of works on the left. He was engaged, with his regiment both days at Shiloh, and was elected Colonel, by the unanimous choice of its officers, He participated in the Seige of Corinth, Battle of Iuka, and Battle of Corinth, where he led the last charge on the enemies line in front of that place, Since the 3d of March 1863, he has commanded a Brigade or Post. He was on the Atlanta campaign, and at the crossing of the Ostanaula River below Resacca, the command of the Division, was turned over to him by General Sweeny, He effected the crossing, laid the pontoon, fought Walkers Division, whipped and drove him away. He was promoted to the rank of Brigadier General for meritorious Conduct in front of Atlanta. He was on the Savanah and Carolina campaigns, where he showed himself the thorough soldier, patient, industrious, and skillful, always enjoying the confidence of his superior Officers, never asking for orders or promotion, but cheerfully and faithfully performing every duty. I consider him eminently deserving some mark of appreciation from the government, and therefore respectfully recommend that he be promoted to the rank of Major General of Volunteers by Brevet." —LS, DNA, RG 94, ACP, R254 CB 1863. On Sept. 1, Brig. Gen. John A. Rawlins endorsed this letter. "Approved."—ES, *ibid.* On July 25, 1863, President Abraham Lincoln had endorsed an earlier recommendation for the appointment as brig. gen. of Col. Elliott W. Rice, 7th Iowa. "Without if or and appoint Elliott W. Rice a Brigadier General."—AES, *ibid.* Misdated [c. June 6, 1864?] in Lincoln, *Works,* VII, 379. Rice was not appointed brig. gen. until June 20, 1864, because his brother, Col. Samuel A. Rice, 33rd Iowa, had been appointed brig. gen. by mistake as of Aug. 4, 1863. See *PUSG,* 9, 594–95.

1865, JULY 11. To Secretary of War Edwin M. Stanton. "I would respectfully recommend that Col. Danl McCauly, 11th Ia Vol. Inf.y be appointed Bvt. Brig. Gen. for gallant services at the battle of Cedar Creek, October 19th 1864. Col. McCauly commanded a Brigade in that battle, was wounded and was recommended by Gen. Sheridan for a brevet."—ALS, DNA, RG 94, ACP, M666 CB 1865. On May 12, Col. Daniel Macauley, 11th Ind., Fort McHenry, Baltimore, wrote to USG. "I forward enclosed a letter from Gen. Emory which I respectfully ask your attention to. I have been an officer in my Regiment four years last month as Adjutant, Major, Lt. Col. and Colonel. I have held the latter rank and performed the duties since March 10th 1863, over two years. Have participated in a number of battles, among them Fort Donelson, Shiloh, Port Gibson Champion Hills, and those of Sheridan's Shenandoah Campaign last summer. Have commanded brigades over one year. I have good reason to believe I can procure letters of like character from Major General's Weitzel, Ord and Grover. Am an applicant for position in permanent service—Field position if possible. Feel qualified and might not stand a foot office on acct of last wound—the ball still remaining in the hip. Have a family to support, no money but my salary and having worked hard four years in the field for my country would respectfully ask it to do something of the nature I propose for me."—ALS, *ibid.*, M789 CB 1866. On Nov. 6, Bvt. Col. Ely S. Parker endorsed this letter. "Respectfully forwarded."—AES, *ibid.* No appointment followed. On Sept. 5, Macauley, Indianapolis, wrote to Bvt. Brig. Gen. James A. Hardie asking about the status of his bvt. rank of brig. gen. as he had been mustered out for twenty-four hours before accepting the appointment as col., 9th Veteran.—ALS, *ibid.* On Oct. 16, USG endorsed this letter. "The brevet rank undoubtedly ceased when the officer was mustered out."—ES, *ibid.*

1865, JULY 11, 2:30 P.M. To Maj. Gen. John A. Logan. "Appoint a Board of Officers [to] assess damages, and forward their report for the action of the Secretary of War"—Telegrams sent (2), DNA, RG 107, Telegrams Collected (Bound); telegram received, *ibid.*, RG 393, Dept. of the Tenn., Unbound Materials, Letters Received. On the same day, Logan, Louisville, had telegraphed to USG. "Shall I order the Payment by the Qr Mrs dept of damages done to premises of Liber & Co by reason of encamping troops there-on, after Proper assessments, by board of Competent officers, or shall they be referred to board of Claims at Wash.n? Damages have not been very extensive for number of troops"—Telegram received (at 1:40 P.M.), *ibid.*, RG 107, Telegrams Collected (Bound); *ibid.*, RG 108, Telegrams Received; copies, *ibid.*, RG 393, Dept. of the Tenn., Letters Sent; DLC-USG, V, 54.

1865, JULY 11, 2:00 P.M. To Bvt. Maj. Gen. James H. Wilson, Macon, Ga. "Discharge Edward Hughes Compy "D" 4th Ky. Mounted Infantry." —ALS (telegram sent), DNA, RG 107, Telegrams Collected (Bound);

telegram sent, *ibid.*; telegram received (dated "11"), *ibid.*, RG 94, War Records Office, Miscellaneous War Records.

1865, JULY 11.   To John Logan. "It affords me pleasure to bear evidence to the faithful services rendered by you in the early part of the War whilst in command of the above numbered Ill. regiment. My own knowledge of these services cover the period in which the battles of Fort Henry, Fort Donelson and Shiloh were fought, in all of which the 32d Illinois Inf.y participated, under your command, and in the last of which you were wounded."—ALS, DNA, RG 60, Records Relating to the Appointment of Federal Judges, Marshals, and Attorneys. Logan, born in Hamilton County, Ohio, in 1809, was taken to Mo. when six years old, and eventually to Jackson County, Ill. After serving in the Black Hawk War, he studied medicine in St. Louis and established a practice in Carlinville, Ill., in 1853. Appointed col., 32nd Ill., as of Dec. 30, 1861, and mustered out in 1864 as a bvt. brig. gen., he was appointed U.S. marshal for the Southern District of Ill. in 1866. On March 5, 1869, Logan, Springfield, wrote to USG. "I most respectfully request a reappointment to the office of U. S. Marshal for the Southern District of Illinois which position I now fill. I would respectfully refer to Hon Richard Yates U. S. Senate   Hon S. M. Cullom M. C. 8th District   Hon I. H. Moore M. C. 7th District   Hon John B. Hay M. C. 12th District and Hon John A. Logan M. C. State at large"—LS, *ibid.* Seven letters from prominent Illinoisans to USG supporting Logan's reappointment are *ibid.* A petition of March 22 from four residents of Macoupin County, Ill., opposing reappointment is also *ibid.*

1865, JULY 11, 2:50 P.M.   To John O'Fallon. "I have no power to releive prisoners."—ALS (telegram sent), DNA, RG 107, Telegrams Collected (Bound); telegram sent, *ibid.*; copies, *ibid.*, RG 108, Letters Sent; DLC-USG, V, 46, 109. On July 10, O'Fallon, St. Louis, had telegraphed to USG. "Can you have merriweather Lewis Clarke released or paroled   Answer" —Telegram received (on July 11, 12:55 A.M.), DNA, RG 107, Telegrams Collected (Bound); *ibid.*, RG 108, Telegrams Received; copy, DLC-USG, V, 54.

1865, JULY 13.   USG note. "The Adjutant General of the Army will make the following orders and assignments:"—Copy, DNA, RG 94, Letters Received, 812A 1865. The enclosed list of duty assignments for gen. officers, issued as General Orders No. 130, July 28, is in *O.R.*, I, xlvii, part 3, 679–80.

1865, JULY 13.   To Maj. Gen. Alfred H. Terry. "This will introduce to you Mr. N. Corwith a particular friend of mine from Galena, Ill. Mr. Corwith visits Richmond for the purpose of seeing some relations of his who reside near there. Attentions shown Mr. Corwith will be appreciated by him and will be regarded as a favor to me."—ALS, The British Museum, London, England.

1865, July 13, 3:00 p.m. To Maj. Gen. George H. Thomas. "Dismount all the Mounted Infantry in your Command and have their horses turned in to the Quartermaster. If the Cavalry sent from the East to report to Gen. Logan is not required have that, or their equivalent in other troops, mustered out also."—ALS (telegram sent), DNA, RG 107, Telegrams Collected (Bound); telegram sent, *ibid.*; copies, *ibid.*, RG 108, Letters Sent; *ibid.*, RG 393, Military Div. of the Tenn., Telegrams Received; DLC-USG, V, 46, 109. *O.R.*, I, xlix, part 2, 1078–79. On July 14, Thomas, Nashville, telegraphed to USG. "Your telegram relating to the dismounting of mounted Infantry rec'd. Orders have been issued."—Telegram received (at 7:10 p.m.), DNA, RG 107, Telegrams Collected (Bound); *ibid.*, Telegrams Collected (Unbound); *ibid.*, RG 108, Telegrams Received; copies, *ibid.*, RG 393, Dept. of the Tenn., Telegrams Sent; DLC-USG, V, 54. *O.R.*, I, xlix, part 2, 1079.

1865, July 13. To Governor William A. Buckingham of Conn. "Your invitation of the 7th inst. for me to be present at a 'Festival of the friends of Yale College' on the 26th inst. is just received. It would afford me great pleasure to comply with this invitation but as I am very desirous of getting through with public business so as to enable me to visit friends who I have not seen since the commencement of the rebellion which has so distracted the country for the last four years, and hope to get off about the time of your festival, I will be impossible for me to attend."—ALS, Connecticut State Library, Hartford, Conn.

1865, July 13. Maj. Gen. John A. Logan, Louisville, to USG. "K Co. 10th Ills Cava[lry la]te "K" Co. 15th Ills Cavalry on duty at these Head Quarters [has] always been considered as [part] of this Army. The regimen[t] is supposed to be in Arkansas Shall this company be mustered out under orders mustering out this Army?"—Telegram received (at 4:00 p.m.), DNA, RG 107, Telegrams Collected (Bound); copy, *ibid.*, RG 393, Dept. of the Tenn., Letters Sent.

1865, July 14. To Secretary of War Edwin M. Stanton. "I would respectfully recommend the promotion of Col. J. Stewart, 9th N. J. ~~Cavalry~~ Vols to the rank of Brig. Gn. by brevet. The Col. has done good service and I believe is now about being mustered out of service."—ALS, DNA, RG 94, ACP, S648 CB 1865. On July 12, Daniel Dougherty, Philadelphia, had written to Bvt. Col. Adam Badeau. "I have received your kind favor of 10th for which accept my thanks. I heard this morning that all the troops in the Division (3rd Division 23rd Corps) in which Col Stewart is, are to be mustered out. I am afraid therefore before the recommendations from his Superiors reaches Head Quarters that he will have returned to private life. His friends tell me the difficulty is that he has been changed about from one department to another. He has been with Burnside, Foster, Hunter Butler—(wounded at Fort Darling)—then four months before Petersburg and now in North Carolina. I do not know whether it is customary to give a Brevet after an officer has been mustered out. I suppose it is now too late for him to receive the Brevet. I however take pleasure in thanking you for your attention. I will always look back with real delight to the Evening I had the honor of spending with the General and Mrs Grant—thanks to your courtesy"—ALS, USG 3. On June 10, Governor Joel Parker of N. J. had written to Dougherty requesting assistance in securing an appointment of bvt. brig. gen. for Col. James Stewart, Jr., 9th N. J.—ALS, *ibid.*

1865, JULY 15.   To President Andrew Johnson. "Mrs. M. C. Bledsoe has called on me for a free pass to Millikin's Bend La. and return on the ground of loyalty and having lost all available means by the War. My authority does not extend to giving passes except to persons traveling in the service of the United States. I write this note because Mrs. Bledsoe has been refered to me for the purpose of giving her the pass and she desires my statement in writing disclaiming the authority to grant her request."—ALS, DNA, RG 107, Letters Received from Bureaus.

1865, JULY 15.   James L. Bates *et al.*, Columbus, Ohio, petition to USG. "We the undersigned citizens of the city of Columbus, and state of ohio, respectfully represent: That our city, and vicinity, is infected by a large number of men, whose business seems to be, to cheat the discharged soldier, out of his money: By means of *Museums, 'Snake Shows' Gift Enterprises*, and *gambling devices of all Kinds*, they aim to entice the soldier, who has just received his hard earned pay, into their dens, and by fraud, or force, swindle or rob him of it all. We have reason to believe that such institutions, have robed their unsuspecting victims of at least one hundred thousand dollars, within the past two years. By the prompt action of the military authoritis, they have been made to disgorge their illgotten gains, in many cases, but the efforts to suppress the evil have so far been thwarted by writs of *'habeus corpus'* and other interference by the civil authorities and we therefore ask for the sake of the returned Soldier, that an order may be issued directing the closeing of such places, and the placeing of them under guard, until the discharge of soldiers, at this point ceases."—DS (thirty-five signatures), DNA, RG 393, Military Div. of the Miss., Letters Received. On July 21, Maj. and Bvt. Col. John W. Skiles, 88th Ohio, draft rendezvous, Columbus, wrote to USG. "I have the honor to transmit the enclosed Petition and to very Respectfully, call your attention to the characters of those who have signed. Judge Bates of the court of common pleas, Judge Swan, Adjutant General Cowen, in fact all who have signed are the responsible men of this community. The statements as to the robbery of soldiers by these museum. and snake show men, is substantially correct. It has been in my line of duty often to arrest. and force them to return the money taken from the Soldiers."—LS, *ibid.* On July 24, Bvt. Col. Theodore S. Bowers endorsed these communications. "Respectfully referred to Maj. Gen. W. T. Sherman, Com'd'g Military Division of the Missouri."—AES, *ibid.*

1865, JULY 17. To Secretary of War Edwin M. Stanton. "I would respectfully recommend the brevet promotion of Brigadier General in the Volunteer service of Col. Wm Bartlett; 2nd N. C., Mounted Infantry."— Copies, DLC-USG, V, 46, 109; DNA, RG 108, Letters Sent.

1865, JULY 17. To Secretary of War Edwin M. Stanton. "I would respectfully recommend the promotion of Capt. J. P. Martin, 7th U. S. Infantry, Cavy. Bureau for the brevet rank of Lieut. Col. in the Regular Army." —Copies, DLC-USG, V, 46, 109; DNA, RG 108, Letters Sent.

1865, JULY 17. Maj. Gen. John A. Logan, Louisville, to USG. "Brev Brig Genl A S. Williams who has been in the service for four years is about being ordered home to report by letter to the War Department. I desire especially to call your attention to him. he has commanded with much ability, alternately, his Division, and the Corps, with which he served for a greater portion of the time since appointed a Brig. General. I became well acquainted with him during the several campaigns that the combined Armies made under Genl. Sherman, and freely bear testimony to his untiring energy and ability as an Officer and Soldier. I would be glad to see him retained in the service. he would fill any position assigned him, I am sure to the satisfaction of his superiors. I hope that you will favorably consider the matter, and reward a Veteran Soldier."—Copy, DNA, RG 393, Dept. of the Tenn., Letters Sent. *O.R.,* I, xlix, part 2, 1083.

1865, JULY 18. To Secretary of War Edwin M. Stanton. "I would respectfully recommend the full appointment of Maj. General for Bvt. Maj. Gen. J. W. Geary, who has frequently been recommended for this promotion, before going out of service. General Geary has numerous testimonials from officers under whom he has served, which are now on file in the A. G's. office, in the shape of recommendations for promotions."—Copies, DLC-USG, V, 46, 109; DNA, RG 108, Letters Sent. *O.R.,* I, xlvii, part 3, 678. No appointment followed.

1865, [JULY 18–21]. USG endorsement. "Respectfully refered to the Sec. of War. I know of no authority to retain a Colonel after his regiment is mustered out but feel inclined to favor Gen. Sheridn's recommendation. U. Unless it is by giving full promotion I see no way of doing so."—AES (undated), DNA, RG 94, ACP, S640 CB 1865. Written on a letter of July 4 from Maj. Gen. Philip H. Sheridan to Secretary of War Edwin M. Stanton requesting that Col. and Bvt. Brig. Gen. Francis T. Sherman, 88th Ill., be appointed brig. gen.—LS, *ibid.* On July 17, Sheridan telegraphed to Bvt. Col. Theodore S. Bowers. "The Regiment of which Brevet Brig Genl F. T. Sherman was Col is mustered out—He [i]s my Provost Marshall I want him as my Chief of Staff—I have applied for his full promition—Please help me in this matter or at least have him put on duty according to Brevet rank" —Telegram received (on July 18, 4:40 A.M.), *ibid.*, RG 107, Telegrams Collected (Bound); copy, DLC-Philip H. Sheridan. Sherman was appointed brig. gen. as of July 21.

1865, JULY 18. USG endorsement. "This is respectfully forwarded to be put on file as a recommendation for Lt. Col. Saml. K. Schwenck for appointment in the Regular Army under the provisions of Gn. Order No. 86 of May 9th 1865. . . . This is a copy of original papers left with Gen O. O. Howard of the Freedmans Beaurea."—AES, DNA, RG 94, ACP, 2263 1874. Written on a letter of June 10 from Col. William H. Telford, 50th Pa., to Secretary of War Edwin M. Stanton recommending Lt. Col. Samuel K. Schwenk, 50th Pa., either for assignment to duty in the Freedmen's Bureau or an appointment in the U.S. Army on account of a severe wound received at the battle of Cold Harbor.—ALS, *ibid.* On July 24, USG wrote to Stanton. "I would respectfully recommend that Lt. Col. Saml. Schwenck, 15th Pa. Vols be appointed a Bvt. Brig. Gen. to be mustered out of service upon."—ALS, *ibid.* On July 12, 1866, U.S. Representative Myer Strouse of Pa. *et al.* wrote to President Andrew Johnson recommending Schwenk for appointment in the U.S. Army.—ALS (thirteen additional signatures), *ibid.* On Aug. 3, USG endorsed this letter. "The Military recommendations of Gen. Schwenck for appointment in the regular Army are on file in the A. G.s Office and are from the highest officers under whom he has served." —AES, *ibid.* On Sept. 10, Schwenk wrote to Stanton requesting appointment in the U.S. Army.—ALS, *ibid.* On Sept. 17, USG endorsed this letter. "Refered to Gn. Comstock to be considered in making recommendations for appointments in the regular Army."—AES, *ibid.* Schwenk was appointed 1st lt., 41st Inf., as of July 28.

1865, JULY 18, 3:00 P.M. To Maj. Gen. Philip H. Sheridan. "You may direct the discharge of all cavalry you can dispense with and the sale by the Quartermasters Dept of the horses where they are. In Louisiana Mississippi and Florida dismount such cavalry as you may think necessary to retain for garrison duty, and keep the minimum number of mounted men required for the services to be performed."—Telegram sent, DNA, RG 107, Telegrams Collected (Bound); telegram received, *ibid.*, Telegrams Collected (Unbound). *O.R.*, I, xlviii, part 2, 1091–92. Misdated June 18 in DLC-USG, V, 46.

1865, JULY 18. USG endorsement. "M. Grarvin of the 69th N. Y. Vols. who lost a leg at the battle of Malvern Hill is deserving of the sympathy of all loyal men and should have the preference over any sound man for such employment as he is capable of, in Government service, and is recommended to the sympathy of citizens who may have light employment to give."—AES, DNA, RG 94, ACP, G401 CB 1867. Written on a letter of Feb. 15, 1864, from Capt. John C. Phillips, 2nd Ill. Art., to U.S. Representative Isaac N. Arnold of Ill. recommending Michael Garvin, former private, 69th N. Y., for employment.—ALS, *ibid.* On Aug. 6, 1867, USG appointed Garvin superintendent of the National Cemetery at Seven Pines, Va.—DS, *ibid.*, G679 CB 1867. On Nov. 14, Garvin wrote to Bvt. Maj. Gen. Edward D. Townsend declining the appointment on account of poor health.—ALS, *ibid.*

1865, JULY 19.   Peter Conrad, 91st N. Y., to USG. "How much is my transportation to New orleans? I was with you in All your campaigns I want to get home immediately   Have been sick"—Telegram received (at 5:40 P.M.), DNA, RG 107, Telegrams Collected (Bound); *ibid.*, RG 108, Telegrams Received. The 91st N. Y. had been mustered out as of July 3.

1865, JULY 20.   USG endorsement. "Respectfully forwarded to the Sec. of War with the recommendation that Capt. A. F. Garrison C. S. be released from arrest and ordered to report in person to the Com.y Gen. when such action can be taken as he may deem necessary."—AES, DNA, RG 107, Letters Received from Bureaus. Written on a letter of June 26 from Capt. Amos F. Garrison, Fort Union, New Mexico Territory, to Brig. Gen. Amos B. Eaton, commissary gen., reporting that he had been in arrest for over seven months.—ALS, *ibid.* On Dec. 26, Eaton wrote to the AG recommending that Garrison be released from arrest and mustered out of service.—LS, *ibid.*, RG 94, ACP, S2080 CB 1865. On Jan. 6, 1866, USG favorably endorsed this letter.—ES, *ibid.* A report on the charges against Garrison is *ibid.*

1865, JULY 20.   USG endorsement. "Respectfully returned. Maj. Gen. A. H Terry has been directed to cause an immediate reduction of the expenses of the Govt. Printing Office at Norfolk, Va., to the lowest limit of consistent with the interests of the service. The proceedings of the Court of Inquiry, of which Brig Gen. Gordon was Presid't, forwarded to the War Dep't, gives a full statement of Gen. Butlers printing operations, and without knowing what action has been taken on it, I refrain from any recommendations on so much of that subject as is presented in the within report."—ES, DNA, RG 107, Letters Received, L938 1865. Written on an inspection report of June 28 from Maj. Elisha H. Ludington to Bvt. Brig. Gen. James A. Hardie.—ALS, *ibid.* On June 29, Asst. Secretary of War Charles A. Dana referred this report to USG.—ES, *ibid.* On July 20, Bvt. Col. Theodore S. Bowers wrote to Maj. Gen. Alfred H. Terry. "It appears from the report of a special Inspector sent by the Inspector General of the Army to investigate certain matters relating to public printing at Norfolk, Va that much unauthorized and unecessary printing is being done at that place. You will therefore issue instructions for the immediate reduction of expenses &c, in the Government Printing Offices at Norfolk, Va., to the lowest limit consistent with the interests of the service"—Copies, DLC-USG, V, 46, 109; DNA, RG 108, Letters Sent.

1865, JULY 20.   USG endorsement. "Respy. returned. It is impracticible to grant the Court requested. I share in Gen Meades regret that the order prepared by him under a misapprehension of the facts, should have reached several newspapers. It was unjust to the to the troops and their Comdg officers; but General Meade has done all in his power to counteract any unfavorable influance created in the public mind by it. I have full confidence in General McLaughlin as a brave, gallant and competent officer"—Copy, DLC-USG, V, 58. Written on an application of Bvt. Brig. Gen. Napoleon B. McLaughlen requesting either a court of inquiry or a court-martial to investigate the behavior of his command during the battle of Fort Stedman, Va., March 25.—*Ibid.* See *O.R.,* I, xlvi, part 3, 174, 206, 232.

1865, JULY 21.   To Secretary of War Edwin M. Stanton. "I would respectfully recommend that Col. & Bvt. Brig. Gn. Beckwith, of the Subsistence Dept. be ordered to report to Maj. Gen. G. H. Thomas for duty. As assignments of Chief Comy. now stand, Beckwith, and Haines, are both in the same Military Division, on account of late changes in Division limits and commanders, Beckwith following his Division Commander."—ALS, DNA, RG 94, Letters Received, 1379A 1865. On Aug. 11, Col. Alexander E. Shiras wrote to Maj. Gen. William T. Sherman that Bvt. Brig. Gen. Amos Beckwith's reassignment had not been caused by interference by Secretary of War Edwin M. Stanton; USG and Brig. Gen. Amos B. Eaton had made the decision because two commissary officers of the same rank and outstanding ability were stationed at St. Louis.—ALS, DLC-William T. Sherman. On Aug. 15, Sherman wrote a letter received at USG's hd. qrs. requesting revocation of orders transferring Beckwith.—DNA, RG 108, Register of Letters Received. On Aug. 17, USG, Chicago, endorsed this letter. "There is no objection to Bt. Brig Gen. A A Beckwith, C. S., being relieved from the operations of that Special Orders No 407 which requires him to report to Major General Thomas for duty. I request this change to be made, and General Beckwith be left for future assignment"—Copy, *ibid.*

1865, JULY 21.   To Secretary of War Edwin M. Stanton. "Will you please have the name of Col. John Bedell 3d New Hampshire Vols. placed on the list of Colonels to be breveted Brigadier Generals of Volunteers before going out of service?"—ALS, DNA, RG 94, ACP, B824 CB 1865. On July 14, U.S. Representative Gilman Marston of N. H. had written to Stanton recommending Col. John Bedel, 3rd N. H., for appointment as bvt. brig. gen.—ALS, *ibid.* On July 20, USG endorsed this letter. "Not approved"—ES, *ibid.*

1865, JULY 21.   Bvt. Col. Adam Badeau to George H. Stuart, Philadelphia. "Lieut. Gen. Grant directs me to acknowledge the receipt of your communication of the 20th inst., and to state that he is perfectly willing for the cabin in which he lived at City Point to be placed wherever you or the citizens of Philadelphia may prefer. He also directs me to state, in reply to your request for a history of the cabin, and especially to your reference to a supposed council of war between President Lincoln, Gen Sherman and himself, that he held no council of war at City Point or any other place, at any time; that the interviews between Mr. Lincoln, Gen Sherman and himself to which you allude, were rather insignificant than 'momentous,' and that the only conversation of any importance which did occur between them took place on a steamboat; it consisted of Gen. Grants announcement that he intended to move out against Gen Lee at a certain time, with his directions to Gen. Sherman to cooperate in North Carolina. The cabin, however, you will permit me to say, has an interest beyond that to which in Gen. Grant's eyes, it seems entitled. It was built ~~late~~ in November 1864, so that the last four months of the Rebellion, immediately prior to the great movements which resulted in its overthrow, were passed by him within its walls. There he received the reports of his great subordinates almost daily, and sent them each their orders and their rewards. There he watched Sherman's route as he came across the continent to the sea, and afterwards along his memorable march through the Carolinas; from here he dispatched his instructions to Thomas, which resulted in the battle of Nashville and the discomfiture of Hood, so that a concentration of any great force in front of Sherman was impossible. From here he directed Terry in the operations which culminated in the fall of Fort Fisher. From here he directed Sherman and Schofield, ~~sending~~ bringing one Northward through the Carolinas and the other Eastward in dead winter across the North, and then sending him by sea to meet his great captain at Goldsboro, the cooperation being so complete that the two armies arrived one from Nashville and the other from Savannah, on the same day. Here he received the Rebel commissioners on their way to meet President Lincoln; here he ordered Sheridan's glorious movements, whose importance in producing the last great result can hardly be over estimated; from here he directed Canby in the campaign whose conclusion was the fall of Mobile; from here he despatched Wilson and Stoneman on their final raids. Here he received the President, Gen. Sherman, Gen. Sheridan, Gen Meade and Admiral Porter in an interview interesting beyond comparison in the meeting at one time and place of so many men of such importance by their talents and their position; and here the lamented Lincoln passed many of the latest hours of his life before its crowning success had been achieved. Here the last orders for all these generals were penned before the commencement of the great campaign which terminated the war These are reminiscences which I have ventured to recall, conscious that they must always be of transcendent interest to the patriot and the historical student, although to the appreciation of my chief they seem, as he directs me to style them—insignificant."—LS, DLC-George H. Stuart. The cabin occupied by USG at City Point, purchased by Stuart, was moved to Philadelphia, arriving on July 14. See *Philadelphia Daily Evening Bulletin*, July 15, 22, Aug. 4, 1865.

1865, JULY 22.   Mrs. Joseph B. Plummer, Washington, D. C., to USG. "When I called with my Son upon you at your Office. I inferred from what you said that you would put him in the Cavalry agreeable to his request. He much prefers that arm of service to the Infantry and will be greatly disappointed if he is not assigned to it. My friend Mr Washburne promised to speak to you upon the subject and I hoped the matter was settled satisfactory until some one intimated to my Son that he might be assigned to the Infantry and must not set his heart upon the Cavalry for fear of disappointment. This remark coming from an officer who would be posted on the subject, I sent my Son to see you to learn the truth of the matter,   as you were not in the office at the time he called, I take the liberty of addressing this note to you, hoping you will pardon me for troubling you & relieve me from suspense, even tho' you cannot gratify our desire."—ALS, USG 3. Satterlee C. Plummer, USMA 1865, was appointed 1st lt., 17th Inf., as of June 23.

1865, JULY 24, 10:40 A.M.   To Bvt. Maj. Gen. Thomas H. Ruger, Raleigh. "Send the 150 pound Armstrong gun captured at Fort Fisher to West Point."—ALS (telegram sent), DNA, RG 107, Telegrams Collected (Bound); telegram sent, *ibid.*; telegram received, *ibid.*, RG 393, Army of the Ohio and Dept. of N. C., Telegrams Received. See *PUSG*, 13, 277*n*–78*n*.

1865, JULY 24.   Secretary of State William H. Seward to USG. "Friends of Captain J. W. Adams, late of the army, have asked me to recommend him for a diplomatic or consular office. Before deciding upon the subject I will thank you for your opinion of his professional and other merits. . . . A Memorandum on the subject is enclosed, ~~with~~ which I will thank you to return"—LS, DNA, RG 59, Applications and Recommendations, Lincoln and Johnson. The enclosure is *ibid.* On Aug. 8, Bvt. Col. Theodore S. Bowers endorsed this letter. "Respectfully referred to Maj. Gen. G. G. Meade, Commanding Military Division of the Atlantic, for remarks."—AES, *ibid.* Additional endorsements reflected favorably upon Julius W. Adams, USMA 1861, former capt., 4th Inf.—*Ibid.* On Nov. 1, USG endorsed this letter. "Respectfully returned to Hon. W H Seward, Secretary of State."—ES, *ibid.* Adams died on Nov. 15.

1865, JULY 24.   Maj. John C. McFerran, q. m., to Bvt. Col. Theodore S. Bowers. "I arrived here this morning from Head Quarters, Department of New Mexico as General James H Carleton's Chief of Staff, charged by him with important verbal communications which I was ordered to deliver to the General in chief, in person. I called at the office, three times to comply, with my instructions, but found on each occasion, the General in Chief too much occupied to see me, and that he would leave the city at 6 o'clock, this P. M. As it is important that he should be informed of a part, at least, of my instructions, before he leaves, I beg that you will, if possible, lay this informal letter before him. I. I am instructed to say that the Comanche and Kiowa tribes of Indians, are hostile, and disposed to give the people of New Mexico much trouble, and to attack trains transporting supplies and merchandise to New Mexico. The Utah tribe also, show a like disposition, The large portion of the Navajo tribe, some nine thousand, who, last year, surrendered themselves, and were placed upon a reservation, are restless; and try daily to escape to their old haunts; to renew their depredations upon the people. Besides these troubles, present and anticipated, many restless and lawless characters, who are unable to live in the East, are flocking to New Mexico, and can only be governed and Kept in order by a military police. The force at the disposal of the Department Commander, being only some three thousand men of all arms, is entirely inadequate to Keep all these restless spirits in subjection. An increase is considered absolutely essential, both for the safety of life and property. The General Comdg the Department, desired me to say that two more full regiments of efficient troops—one to be Cavalry—could accomplish that end. If two regiments cannot be furnished him, he would ask that one of Cavalry be sent from the East—and that recruits be sent out at once, to fill up the U. S. 5th Infy to its full standard. If this can be done at an early day, much good will result, and many lives be saved. I have just learned, by private letters, that the Navajo Indians are leaving the reservation, in *very* large numbers; and that Capt Gorman and ten men of his compy of California Cavalry, were Killed in trying to bring some of them back. The Dept Commander is concentrating all the force he can, around the reservation, to try to prevent this escape of the Indians, but will, if he abandon all his Posts, be then outnumbered three to one by the Indians. I could give many other details and reasons why the force in New Mexico should be largely increased—but fearing that the General in Chief would not have time to hear them, I submit the above."—ALS, DNA, RG 108, Letters Received.

1865, JULY 25. George B. Carhart, New York and New Haven Railroad, New York City, to USG. "I understand you have in contemplation, at an Early day, a trip to the White Mountains, if we are correctly informed, we should be much pleased to have you accept the compliment of a special car for the use of yr self, family & such friends, as may be of the party, by the route, on our road & its connections, If this, therefore, meets with yr approval please let me know the same in good time that the car may be in readiness—"—ALS, USG 3. On July 26, James H. Hoyt, superintendent, New York and New Haven Railroad, wrote to USG. "Understanding from an article in the N. Y. Express newspaper, that you purpose visiting Newport, R. I. during the early part of next month, I take much pleasure in offering to you the courtesies of this Road, & would be happy to place at your disposal a special car for the accommodation of yourself, family and friends, at such time as may meet your convenience—"—Copy (by G. M. Willson), *ibid.* On Aug. 4, George W. Fellows wrote to USG. "I am requested by the Presidents & Directors of the Boston & Providence, Providence and New London, New London & New Haven, New Haven & New York, Railroads To tender you the cortesies of their roads on your return trip to New York. They will be happy to place at your disposal a special train for the accommodation of yourself, family and friends, at such times as may meet your convienance,   With the compliments of myself and associates . . ."—ALS, *ibid.* Docketing indicates that the invitation was declined on Sept. 21.—*Ibid.*

1865, JULY 25.   Allen Thomas, former C.S.A. brig. gen., Washington, D. C., to USG. "I have the honor to represent—that I was one of the Vicksburg capture of the 4th of July 1863—at which time I was comdg a Brig in the C. S. A. After the capitulation I was deprived by the national troops of two horses used by me for field purposes—. Upon representing these facts to Major Gen McPherson he gave me an order, & furnished me with a guard, to take the Horses wherever found.   failing to recover them—he gave me an order to select in their stead from the horses belonging to the U S Government then at Vicksburg.—Among these there was none suitable for field purposes. I was then directed by Gen McPherson to leave a description of the horses.—And was assured by him that in the event of their recovery they should be returned to me.—Shortly after my departure from Vicksburg One of them a Dapple Gray was recovered. & is now in the possession of Capt Curtis Provost Marshall at Vicksburg.—After repeated efforts I have failed to recover this horse—And if have been advised by my brother officers of the C. S. A to lay the matter before you. Knowing that you will see justice done in the matter.—Having ridden this horse in many engagements I am much attached to him—And I would further add that Gen McPherson informed a citizen of Vicksburg when the horse was found that he intended to restore him to me—Trusting General that you will excuse my thus trespassing upon your valuable time . . ."—ALS, PHi.

1865, JULY 26.   To Secretary of War Edwin M. Stanton from West Point. "I would respectfully recommend orders be immediately made declaring who of the cadets found deficient shall be turned back and who discharged so that new appointments can be made for september to fill vacancies. I would recommend that Harris be retained."—Telegram received (at 4:30 P.M.), DNA, RG 107, Telegrams Collected (Bound); copies, *ibid.*, RG 108, Letters Sent; DLC-USG, V, 46, 109. On July 27, USG, West Point, telegraphed to Stanton. "Please give authority by telegraph for second 2 class detained from furloughs all to go together   some few by

~~constitution~~ construction given to regulations have to be detained here a few days longer than the majority"—Telegram received (at 2:10 P.M.), DNA, RG 107, Telegrams Collected (Bound); copies, *ibid.*, RG 108, Letters Sent; DLC-USG, V, 46, 109.

1865, JULY 26.   Maj. Gen. John Pope, St. Louis, to USG. "The Territory of Utah having been taken from this Department, and attached to that of California, it is proper that I should suggest to you that the condition of affairs in that Territory needs immediate attention. The relations between the Mormons, and other citizens of the United States not belonging to the Mormon Church, are critical, and unless attended to at once, are likely to break out in very serious disturbance, which will be difficult to subdue. The Mormons, in all difficulties with other citizens of the United States, at once resort to the Indians, and stir up hostilities to break up mail routes and obstruct or put an end to emigration. There is little doubt that they are now engaged in this manner, and it will be wise to invite the immediate attention of the proper Department Commander to the subject—The fact is, that, for a time, some military officer, with troops at his command, should be Governor of Utah."—LS, DNA, RG 393, Military Div. of the Miss., Letters Received. *O.R.*, I, xlviii, part 2, 1123. See *ibid.*, p. 1004. This letter may not have been sent to USG because on July 27 Capt. Joseph M. Bell, adjt. for Pope, issued orders restoring Utah Territory to the Dept. of the Mo.— *Ibid.*, p. 1126.

1865, JULY 26.   Col. Robert C. Wood, asst. surgeon gen., Louisville, to USG. "It is with some reluctance I write you on a case of personal import., but I think I may safely rely on your justice and military sense of right. Without my Knowledge, my friends in the West have applied to the proper authorities with great unanimity, for a brevet for my services—for this I am grateful; though I again reiterate without any *Knowledge* or consent on my part, until within a few days.—I learn it has met with unexpected opposition. I need not assure you, General, that after having served with credit in Florida and Mexico, as Medical Director, and in the present War received the approbation, and endorsement of such distinguished soldiers as yourself, Generals Sherman, and Thomas, it does not inflict much mortification, nor is it becoming in me, other than to advert to it.—The circumstances which induce me now to address you, are these,—Within a few days, two brevets of Lieut. Colonel & Colonel have been sent to my Assistant in the Office for the last three years—I do not deny these brevets are worthily bestowed, but they are given to my subordinate,—the instrument of carrying out my orders and instructions—for services, where—in my Office—rewarding the subordinate, and passing by the principal.—I will venture to say it can have no precedent in military annals. You can appreciate it, and as Chief of our noble Army, and as a representative, and protector of its rights, I have to ask that I may be presented to the President, not as a personal applicant

for honors, but as sensitive on points involving my future reputation.—"
—ALS, USG 3. On Aug. 20, Bvt. Col. Adam Badeau noted on this letter.
"Answered (affirmatively)"—AN, *ibid.*

1865, JULY 28. William C. Church, editor, *Army and Navy Journal,* to
USG. "I am anxious to procure regularly for the Army & Navy Journal such
orders & circulars from the Head Quarters of the Army & the War Department, as are proper for publication, as well as full lists of appointments,
promotions & dismissals, & the changes in the Regular Army & in the various Staff Corps & Departments of the Service In short, whatever is necessary to enable me to publish a full Gazette of the Army, such as is published
in every other country maintaining an Army. As the Army & Navy Journal
is now the only military paper published in this country, in making this request I interfere with no one & ask only what it would seem to be for the
interest of the Service that I should have If it is desirable that we should
have a Military Journal in the United States the A & N. Journal would certainly seem to be entitled to that place; established as it is firmly in the confidence of the army by two years of trial & success. If it is thought necessary
in order to make it more complete that it should be issued from Washington
I am ready to publish it here instead of in NewYork. I am aware that it is
necessary that I should go to the War Department for what I ask but, before
laying the matter before the Secretary, I venture to ask that you will favor
me me with your approval of my request."—ALS, USG 3. Docketing indicates that Church was sent an affirmative answer on Oct. 17 subject to the
approval of Secretary of War Edwin M. Stanton.—*Ibid.* See Donald Nevius
Bigelow, *William Conant Church & The Army and Navy Journal* (New
York, 1952), pp. 105–6, 129–30.

1865, JULY 28. George Gilbert, Union College, Schenectady, N. Y., to
USG. "I have the honor of informing you. that the Board of Trustees of
Union College, at the Commencement Exercises held Thursday, July 27th
1865. conferred upon you the Honorary Degree of 'Doctor of Laws'—In
testimony of which the Official seal of said Trustees is hereunto affixed—"
—ALS, USG 3.

1865, JULY 28. William S. Hillyer, New York City, to USG. "I have received two letters from Senor Romero lately with regard to a demonstration
in NewYork on the Mexican question—This matter we are now maturing
and we will have an immense meeting. Almost every body here is *sound* on
the question—What is needed is concentration—Although a political it is
not a party question—Men of all shades of politics concur on this subject.—
Senor R. is very anxious that your views on this question should be made
public and writes to me that he thinks you are willing—He desired me to
see you and ascertain if you would write a letter expressing your views in
response to an invitation to attend this meeting or in any other manner you

thought best. I intended to have seen you on the subject as you passed
through the city but had no opportunity—I should have gone up to West-
point for this purpose but could not leave the city. I think I know your views
on this subject. The question is, should you receive a letter of invitation
from a committee composed of such men as Gen Dix, Jno VanBuren, Moses
Taylor &c would you be willing to respond to it expressing your opinions—
I have thought this matter over and can see no reason why you might not
with propriety as it is no sense a party question—I have always to the extent
of my ability labored to shield you from the charges of being a political
General, which every body now knows you are not. I certainly would not ask
you to do anything which would make you the subject of partizan attacks—
But in a great question. like the Monroe Doctrine and its application to the
present status of Mexico, when the honor of the nation as well as the liberties
of a sister Republic are at stake, it seems to me eminently proper that soldiers as well as citizens should avow their opinions to the world. I do not presume to advise you on this subject but make these statements to explain
my own motives—I hope you will answer this immediately. Your reply will
be regarded confidential unless you desire it otherwise—."—ALS, USG 3.
On Aug. 3, Bvt. Col. Adam Badeau, Portland, Maine, wrote to Hillyer.
"Gen Grant directs desires me to reply to your ~~letter~~ note to him of July 28
in which you ask if he is willing to write a letter for publication expressing
his views on the Mexican question,   When this subject was originally
broached to him, he did intend to write a letter airing the opinions entertained by him in regard to the Monroe Doctrine and its application to Mexico: But ~~he has decided~~ as it is now apparent to him that the matter is destined to become one of the great political issues of the day, ~~and~~ on which
perhaps ~~public~~ policy will be formed ~~and~~ he is ~~therefore~~ compelled in his
position to decline giving any publicity to his ~~views~~ sentiments on the matter, or doing anything calculated to ~~give~~ attach a political character to his
actions,   At the same time he entertains the fullest sympathy with the
movement in favor of enforcing the Monroe doctrine in Mexico and hopes
speedily to see the overthrow of the imperial rule ~~in that republic~~ established
by European bayonets"—ADf, *ibid.* On Aug. 24, Matías Romero, Mexican
minister, New York City, wrote to USG. "I beg leave to call your attention
to the enclosed slip from to day's New York 'times' containing some important Mexican news. I have often written to you through Gen. Rawlings and
Col. Bowers   I suppose you have received all my letters, regularly. Gen. S.
has accepted the mission to France and is only waiting his instructions to
sail. He expects them early on next week. When I hear that you are coming
to Washington, I will go there to meet you. Please present my kindest regards to Mrs. Grant, . . ."—ALS, MH. On Sept. 17, Cayetano Romero
wrote to Badeau. "I have the honor to acknowledge the receipt of your
favor of the 13th instant, which was delivered to me this morning. I thank
you very sincerely for the information you are kind enough to communicate
to me and which will be transmitted to my brother by first opportunity,

taking care to follow the instructions it contains. Please present my kindest regards to the General & Mrs. Grant and family, and receive for yourself the assurance of my consideration."—ALS, USG 3.

1865, AUG. 4, 5:00 P.M. Maj. Gen. George H. Thomas, Nashville, to USG. "Is it intended to muster out immediately all the White Volunteers or are the one year troops to be retained till the expiration of their term."—ALS (telegram sent), DNA, RG 107, Telegrams Collected (Unbound); telegram received (dated Aug. 5, received on Aug. 6, noon), *ibid.*, Telegrams Collected (Bound); *ibid.*, RG 108, Telegrams Received.

1865, AUG. 7. Maj. Gen. Philip H. Sheridan, New Orleans, to Brig. Gen. John A. Rawlins. "There is great difficulty about getting cotton from the Red River country on account of some confederate cotton being at numerous points in that section I would recommend to the Govt. to relinquish its claims and ~~tax~~ let the collector of customs levy a tax on all cotton It will be satisfactory to the people and will be for the benefit of the Govt This would simplify affairs very much and would defeat all rascals now engaged in keeping it out of market"—Telegram received (on Aug. 8, 5:00 A.M), DNA, RG 107, Telegrams Collected (Bound); *ibid.*, RG 108, Telegrams Received; copies, DLC-USG, V, 54; DLC-Philip H. Sheridan. *O.R.*, I, xlviii, part 2, 1168.

1865, AUG. 15. Charles Randolph, president, Board of Trade, Chicago, to USG. "This Board intend to occupy their new Hall on the 30th inst, and they take advantage of the occasion to invite to Chicago representations from the different Commercial organizations throughout this Country and the Canadas, to participate in the Inaugural cerimonies. In the name of the Board I tender you an invitation to be present, and sincerely hope you will do so."—LS, USG 3. Docketing indicates that the invitation was declined. —*Ibid.*

1865, AUG. 16. Maj. Gen. William T. Sherman, St. Louis, endorsement. "Respectfully referred to the General in Chief. I do not profess to know much of matters out on the Plains but Gn Popes recommendation appears wise. No troops can be relied on Except Regulars, or troops enlisted since the War is closed."—AES, DNA, RG 108, Letters Received. Written on a letter of Aug. 15 from Maj. Gen. John Pope to Sherman discussing the insubordination and unreliability of vol. regts. and the need to replace them with U.S. Army regts.—LS, *ibid. O.R.*, I, xlviii, part 2, 1183–84. On Aug. 5, Pope had written a similar letter to Lt. Col. Roswell M. Sawyer, adjt. for Sherman.—LS, DNA, RG 108, Letters Received. *O.R.*, I, xlviii, part 2, 1165–66. On Aug. 23, Sherman endorsed this letter. "Respectfully referred to the Commr in chief, in connection with Genl Popes letter of 15th inst herewith enclosed"—AES, DNA, RG 108, Letters Received.

1865, AUG. 17.   C. E. Hill, Grand Rapids, Mich., to USG. "The citizens of Grand Rapids tender to you the hospitalities of the city and hope you may, at some future day, honor them with a visit."—ALS, USG 3.

[1865, AUG. 17?].   USG letter regarding the establishment of a soldiers' college.—B Altman & Co. advertisement, *New York Times*, May 7, 1972.

1865, AUG. 21.   Maj. Gen. John Pope, St. Louis, to USG. "I do not know whether it is the purpose of General Order No 130, to relieve Major General Alfred Pleasanton from duty in this Department, or to muster him out of service, as Major General of Volunteers. I trust that neither will be done. I very much need officers of the old Army, with rank and experience enough to reduce troops and expenditures on the Plains, to something like the standard which obtained before the Rebellion began. No one who does not know by experience the condition of military affairs on the Plains before the War, and the strict economy then enforced, can possibly realize the necessities of the present situation. Volunteer Officers of whatever merit, have had no experience of Military life, except in the great operations of the late War, when every whim, on however large a scale, however costly or difficult, was gratified, without a moments Consideration of the expense. Such officers I find it almost impossible to impress with the absolute necessity of coming down to the strictest economy. They have no knowledge of what obtained before the War, and could not, if they would, restore the simple and economical arrangements on the Plains, to which old Army officers have always been accustomed. I need old regular officers to perform this duty, and can illy spare such an officer as General Pleasanton. I trust therefore, and respectfully ask, that he be retained as Major General of Volunteers, and left on duty in this Department. I could use several other officers of the old Army, having the same character and experience to great advantage, to travel over the various routes across the Plains as Inspectors, with authority from me to reduce the number of troops and of posts, and to arrange their stations to the best advantage. Such officers are greatly needed to bring down expenses to the scale which seems to be expected, and demanded, by the Government."—LS, DNA, RG 108, Letters Received. On Aug. 22, Maj. Gen. William T. Sherman endorsed this letter. "Respectfully forwarded."—AES, *ibid.*

1865, AUG. 29.   USG, Galena, endorsement. "Respectfully forwarded to the Sec of War"—AES, DNA, RG 94, Letters Received, 1799M 1865. Written on a petition of Aug. 22 from W. J. McNemar and forty-one others, Luney's Creek, West Va., to USG. "The under-Signed, formerly soldiers in the Confederate Army, beg leave, to make the following Statement to you, and entreat your interposition on our behalf, We were privates belonging to diffirent Commands in the regular service of the Confederate Government, and Continued in that service till the surrender of Genl Lee,

We were afterwards paroled, and Subsequently took the oath of Amnesty, But since our return home many of us have been served with writs issued under the Government of West Va in which the most exhorbitant damages are claimed by union men for property which in many instances was never taken, and which in some instances was taken by some of us, but by order of our Commanding Officers, For instance some of us have been served with writs claiming damages for Seven thousand Eight hundred dollars (7800) when said property was only worth by *bill* $500 North Carolina Money, We never in any instance took horses or any other property from union men unless ordered to do so by our Commanding Officers, We returned home at the close of the War with the Conviction that we were fairly beaten—And with the determination in good faith to be true to the United States, This has been, and is, our purpose, we desire by honest effort to repair the desolation of our homes, and to Contribute our part,—as far as in us lies—towards the re-union—in heart and feeling—of the North & South, But we return home only to find ourselves weighed down by unjust and oppressive Suits—Not to be tried in our own County—but some Sixty miles distant—instituted by men who were never in the regular service of the United States—who under the assumed name of States troops or Home Guards received their pay in Safety—Whose military Career Consisted in plundering the defenceless:—men without Charactor or Conscience, and who would sell the Union for fifty dollars a man, On the ground therefore that we were privates in the regular service of the Confederate Army—, that we were paroled—that we took no property unless ordered to do so by our Commanding Officers—and very seldom, and to a very limited Extent were such Commands issued to us, on the ground that we were recognized as belliggerants—On the ground that we took the Oath of Amnesty in good faith or as many of us—as have had opportunity and desire to do all we Can towards the restoration of of a real Union—On the ground that by the express terms of the surrender we were to be allowed to return to our homes and remain there *unmolested*—above all on the ground of your known humanity and love of justice as a Soldier and a man we appeal to you and entreat you to see to it that these oppressive Suits shall be Stopped, and we fairly permitted to become true citizens of the United States. We entreat your interposition at an early time, as the suits are to be tried on the 14th prox, and from what we know of the Charactor of the Courts of West Va. only one result Can be anticipated, We desire to discharge our whole duty to the union and we are *now* truer union men, than the men who under the form of law seek to plunder and oppress us: but in order to this we ask fair play, and that these unjust and appressive suits which so much discourage us, and paralize our energies shall be stopped, Only *permit* us to be loyal, and it will soon be manifest where we stand, and your memorialists will ever pray &c"—ADS, *ibid.*

1865, AUG. 29. Mrs. Virginia I. Mosby, "Idle Wilde," to USG. "Circumstances have occured which induces me to write and state as briefly as possible the case of my Son. On the 21st of this month, Genl Curtis commanding the Post at Lynchburg had my son arrested, it was a very cool morning & he walked to the Depot *on our own land*, a few hundred yds from our house with a uniform coat on, he had never had the coat on since the order not to wear military buttons had been isued, & would not have worn it at all *from home*, he had purchased a suit of light summer clothes on account of the order, he has been under guard ever since, & Genl Curtis has to day gone on with him to Richmond to have him court marshaled. I wrote a most respectfull letter to him asking to use his influence on a speedy release, his answer was 'I have no authority or inclination to use my influence to release your Son'. It needs no comment from me, the spirit it breathes shows his feeling, & the respect due a lady from a gentleman you percieve is lacking. I presumed from his high position he wd at least have treated me politely. My husband called on Genl Curtis to enquire if there was no other offence but the buttons, he sd 'There was not,' the thing I complain of is this, the order is continually disobeyed, & other young men are arrested & taken to an Officer & the offending buttons removed, not one case of imprisonment has followed, and I can assure you my son has manifested no spirit of rebellion, but has in every thing been prudent & cautious not to disobey any order, & wd not have used the coat but on account of the cool early morning about 6. Oc, Genl Curtis & others had seen him frequently in his summer clothes in Lynchburg. I deem it a case of palpable persecution I have no idea of the motive Gen Curtis can have in being so anxious to have my son punished, he has taken the oath, & the other Genls at this Post told my husband they did not see why our son sd not be immediately released. The young men as far as I have any knowledge are all using every effort to restore order & good will it is much desired by the South, and I think the course Genl Curtis is pursuing is not one to conciliate, but to engender ill feeling. I write to you because the South respects you & have confidence in your ability & good will towards us, the truly great are allways magnanimous, they have a fame not founded on petty persecution but built on a foundation of great deeds. I thought I would write to the President, but concluded you were the right man, altho the President is the cherished friend of some members of my family. I know you have the power, and I most respectfully ask you to have my Son released, Genl Curtis passed here on his way to Richmond to day, I heard he sd the case wd not come off, for some weeks, I presume he well knew that the offense would not be seriously punished & he will have it delayed as long as possible to gratify some pique that no one but himself has any idea off. I assure you again we as a people desire peace & the cessation of all this petty strife, We are all submitting with a commendable grace to the powers that be, The South has the highest respect for you & our President, we desire friendship & good will, & only hope we may be bound together by the strong Ties that are only formed by act of kindness & good will. I feel that I can come to you with a confidence that I shall not be rudely turned away, the truly great are humble & not puffed up by Office & the flattery of Men, I have sd all I can on the subject, you well know better than any one else how to act—Hoping I have not called upon you in vain. . . . I will on this page write personally of my Son, William H. Mosby, he was Adjutant to the 43d Battalion Mosby's Command. He is nineteen years old. My address is Mc-Ivors Station. Amherst Co Va. O & A. R. R. Care of Provost Marshal Lynchburg Virginia. Our mails not being established we recieve our letters at the different Stations & Depot, sent out by the order of the Provost Marshal. . . . I refer you most respectfully to Genl Briscoe, at his Post in Lynchburg & Capt Burger at Amherst C H, under whose charge my Son has been since arrested by the order of Genl Curtis, he can testify to the uniform good conduct of my Son & his bearing since arrested, they all speak in the highest terms of my Son."—ALS, DNA, RG 108, Letters Received. On Sept. 1, Bvt. Col. Theodore S. Bowers endorsed this letter. "Respectfully referred to Major General A. H. Terry, Command'g Department Virginia." —AES, *ibid.* On Sept. 20, Maj. Gen. George G. Meade returned this letter. "Returns com'n. of Virginia J. Mosby concg. release of her son Wm H. Mosby. Gen Meade refers to endorsement of Gen A. H. Terry Comdg. Virginia Department, by which it will be observed the said W. H. Mosby was released upon his taking the Oath of allegiance."—*Ibid.*, Register of Letters Received. William H. Mosby was the younger brother of John S. Mosby.

1865, AUG. 31.   E. Elderkin, "Elk Horn Walworth Co. Wis.," to USG. "You are to be at Milwaukie next Monday and Tuesday at Chicago, as I see by the papers of yesterday, and I am instructed by the Prest & Ex. Com. of our County Agl Society to invite you to be present at our Co. Fair, to be he[l]d here on the 12. 13 & 14th days of Sept. 1865. [We] should be extremely glad to see you here on the last two days or either of them and I am instructed to offer you $200.00 if you will favor us with your presence on either of those days, and notify me of the fact at once so that I may publish it to our people and the surrounding country. Now, Genl, if you can make it possible for you, I beg you to accept this call upon you. I do not offer the $200.00 as any compensation but only for the purpose of showing you the earnest desire of our people to see you."—ALS, USG 3.

1865, SEPT. 2.   H. J. Turney, Columbus, Ohio, to USG. "The Board of Agriculture of your native State will hold their annual exhibition at Columbus on the 12th to the 15th of September instant, and cordially invite you, if consistent with your other engagements to be present with them & be their guest on that occasion. We hardly need suggest to you General, how much pleasure it would afford the many thousands of the people of Ohio in attendance at our State Fair to have the opportunity of manifesting their approbation of your brilliant & successful achievements in defence of the Republic Should you do us and your native State the honor of accepting this invitation, we will endeavor so to arrange matters that you shall enjoy the visit in your own way."—ALS, USG 3.

1865, SEPT. 4.   Brig. Gen. Lorenzo Thomas, Washington, D. C., to USG. "I have recently relieved Captan Philip R Forney 13th Infantry from my staff. His Father John W Forney Esq is very desirous, for special reasons, that his son should receive a leave of absence for four months to accompany an exploreing expedition to the Territory of Colorado, for the purpose of developing the mineral resources of a portion of that country. I beg to recommend that the leave of absence be granted."—ALS, DNA, RG 94, Letters Received, 981A 1865. On the same day, Brig. Gen. John A. Rawlins favorably endorsed this letter.—ES, *ibid.*

1865, SEPT. 6, 9:00 A.M.   To Secretary of War Edwin M. Stanton from Galena. "I would recommend that Genl Augur be directed to reduce the forces in his Department to six thousand: Also that all colored troops enlisted from the northern states be mustered out. If any plan can be devised for reducing the forces of colored troops throughout the country to one half the present numbers without leaving the men a burthen upon the Government, I would recommend it"—Telegram received (at West Point, N. Y., 5:00 P.M.), DLC-Edwin M. Stanton; (at 3:00 P.M.) DNA, RG 94, Vol. Service Div., Letters Received, W2191 (VS) 1865; *ibid.*, RG 107, Telegrams Collected (Bound); copies, *ibid.*, RG 108, Letters Sent; DLC-USG, V, 46, 109. On Sept. 8, Bvt. Col. Theodore S. Bowers telegraphed to USG. "In your order for the muster out of colored troops raised in the Northern States, did you intend to include those raised in the States of Missouri and Kentucky or only those raised in the free states?"—Telegram sent, DNA, RG 107, Telegrams Collected (Bound). At 6:00 P.M., USG telegraphed to Bowers. "I intended only those colored troops who were free prior to the Emancipation Proclamation, but would like to have the colored troops further reduced in any other way practicable,"—Telegram received (on Sept. 9, 11:00 A.M.), *ibid.*; *ibid.*, RG 94, Vol. Service Div., Letters Received, W2191 (VS) 1865.

1865, SEPT. 6.   To Secretary of War Edwin M. Stanton from Galena. "I would respectfully recommend that the following Brevets be given Major Franklin D. Callender, Ordnance Department to wit: Brv't. Lieut Colonel, for faithful and meritorious services in the Siege of Corinth, to rank from the 20th of May, 1862. Brv't. Colonel, for faithful and meritorious services in his Department of St. Louis, Mo., to rank as such from March 1st, 1864. Brv't. Brig. General, for faithful and meritorious services in his Department, to rank as such from April 9th, 1865."—Copies, DNA, RG 108, Letters Received; *ibid.*, Letters Sent; DLC-USG, V, 46, 109. On Sept. 18, U.S. Senator B. Gratz Brown of Mo., St. Louis, wrote to Stanton recommending Maj. Franklin D. Callender, Ordnance Dept., for appointment as bvt. brig. gen., enclosing a copy of USG's letter.—ALS, DNA, RG 108, Letters Received.

1865, SEPT. 6.   Act. Secretary of the Navy Gustavus V. Fox to USG. "Your letter of the 2nd inst, recommending H. W. Schaefer for appointment to the Naval Academy has been received. In reply I have to state that the President has filled all his appointments, at large for this year, and as you are aware, Congress has forbidden the appointment of Midshipmen from any district not represented in Congress. I may remark that Hon. E. B Washburne has made two successive nominations this year, to fill a vacancy in his district, and the latter Candidate,—Jos. H. Utley—has not yet been examined, but is to be between the 20th and 30th inst. As there is a possibility of this Candidates failure, if Hon Mr Washburne will fill up the enclosed blank in favor of Mr Schaefer, and return it to the Department, and will arrange to have his Candidate, Utley—report for examination on the 20th inst. or within a day or two thereafter, there will be time to get young Schaefer to Annapolis before the examination closes in case Utley should fail to pass."—Copy, DNA, RG 45, Miscellaneous Letters Sent. On Feb. 16, 1866, Secretary of the Navy Gideon Welles wrote to USG. "The letter of H. H. Houghton, in favor of the appointment of Henry Schaefer to the Naval Academy, transmitted with an endorsement by you to the Department on the 10th inst. is received. In reply I would state that Hon E. B. Washburne, who provisionally nominated the lad last year, and if he chooses to renew the nomination on or after the 5th proxo, a permit for examination will be issued."—Copy, *ibid.* Henry W. Schaefer graduated from the U.S. Naval Academy in 1870.

1865, SEPT. 6.   Henry A. Wise, former C.S.A. maj. gen. and Va. governor, to USG. ". . . If General Terry was governed by earnest and honest convictions of duty, of right and authority in all he did, so was I. If he was a patriot, so was I. If he gave proof of his devotion, so did I. If he thought he had the shield of constitutional law and political sovereignty to protect him against the charge of rebellion and treason, so I thought I had. If he loved and cherished the Union of these States, I loved and cherished it so cordially that I never from choice would have seceded from it, but prepared to fight 'in the Union:' and if he wonders how I now can truly declare these sentiments, after voting for Secession and taking up arms against the acts of the Federal Executive and Congress, I must beg him to remember that he and I have been taught in different schools of politics, and that will account for our differences of opinion, and ought to allow a large margin for charity at least, if not toleration. If he was trained in the school of Hamilton and the elder Adams, I was in that of Jefferson and Madison; and he would boldly expose himself to the charge of bigotry and presumption who would charge either school with teaching rebellion and treason. It is dangerous to either to adopt the dogmas of treason and rebellion against the other, alternating in domination as they have done so often already in our history. Each might shoot and hang the other by turns in the course of half a century. If General Terry believed in consolidation, I believed in States' rights and powers. If he believed that the Federal Executive and Congress, and the judiciary possessed absolute, I believed they had only relative and delegated sovereignty. If he believed that they were unchecked and unbalanced by other powers, I believed that the whole system of the United States, State and Federal, was composed of reciprocal checks and balances, and that the sovereign States were the basis, checks and balances of the Federal Government. I was taught that the States were not *unum*, but *e pluribus unum*, and this *many in one, one in many*. When called a Rebel I shall point to the _____ of Virginia's buckler and claim that my sovereign State is sole sponsor for the acts of her own citizens and subjects. I am no Rebel or traitor, and never was, and my State cannot be either. She has still a sovereignty by the Constitution of the United States, and by the original authority before it ever existed, unless she is now utterly demolished by subjugation, and unless that is destroyed by any force which has demolished her. These are still the tenets of my faith, and I believe these truths will perpetually revive and prevail to preserve the republican freedom of the people of the United States. When the civil liberty for which I devoutly pray really comes again, I can, without hindrance, fall on the bosom of my country and weep with her 'for any wrongs we have done.' I am now a prisoner on parole. I dare not *now* ask of her any favor, *great* or *small*. I claim only of her good faith, the precious privilege, promised me by her highest agents, to go to my home and be at peace. . . . So far from my being opposed to the name 'freedmen,' as indicating the condition of slaves freed by the war, *the chief consolation I have in the result of the war is that slavery is forever abolished, that not only the slaves are in fact, at last freed from bondage, but that I am freed from them.* Long before the war indeed, I had definitely made up my mind actively to advocate emancipation throughout the South. I had determined, if I could help it, my descendants should never be subject to the humiliation I have been subject to by the weakness if not the wickedness of slavery; and while I cannot recognize as lawful and humane the violent and shocking mode in which it has been abolished, yet I accept the fact most heartily as an accomplished one, and am determined not only to abide by it and acquiesce in it, but to strive by all the means in my power to make it beneficent to both races and a blessing especially to our country. I unfeignedly rejoice at the fact, and am reconciled to many of the worst calamities of the war, because I am now convinced that the war was a special providence of God, unavoidable by the nations at either extreme, to tear loose from us a black idol from which we could never have been separated by any other means than those of fire and blood, sword and sacrifice. . . ."—(incomplete) *Philadelphia Inquirer*, Sept. 8, 1865. The *Philadelphia Inquirer* later reported: "The War Department has returned to General Terry, commanding the District of Virginia, an application made by Henry A. Wise to General Grant for the restoration of his landed property, now occupied by freedmen. General Terry's course in refusing to give up the property was approved, so Wise gained nothing by the application to Grant."—*Ibid.*, Oct. 25, 1865.

1865, SEPT. 10.   USG, Galena, endorsement. "If any inconvenience to the
service is going to occur from the transfers and changes here approved
they need not be ordered. The four regular regiments now with Gn. Thomas
may be needed until the two authorized to remain with him are filled up.
When filled up however I think two regiments of White troops will be
sufficient for his entire Mil. Div. and will enable him to muster out all
volunteers except the colored troops. . . . Relieve all staff officers with Generals not on duty and send them to their regiments or Corps where such are
still in service. All others muster out of service."—AES, DNA, RG 94, Letters Received, 1383B 1865. Written on a letter of Sept. 7 from Bvt. Brig.
Gen. Edward D. Townsend to USG. "If you will please give me your views
on the points presented below, it will enable me to issue orders in your name
which I think should go out as soon as possible. I have written each proposition so that you can mark it approved, or disapproved, or indicate your
wishes, and then, if you see fit, return this paper without further trouble.
1. . . . Some commanders of artillery regts. have designated the old companies mounted before the war, to retain their batteries, and one or two have
designated different companies—There is considerable feeling among the
artillery officers in favor of retaining the old batteries, and I think it will
be best to announce them in orders. If a captain does not prove well suited
for an Instructor, or is permanently absent, another can be transferred to
the Battery—Under the old Regulation a vacancy in the captaincy of a
Battery was filled by selection. [Approved] 2—There are many officers like
Casey, Heintzelman and others, now mustered out of volunteer commissions
and reporting for orders—should they not be ordered to join their regiments? [Approved] 3 . . . As a rule, all regimental officers of the Regular
Army should be relieved as fast as possible from staff and detached duty,
to aid in recruiting and disciplining their regts. There is much difficulty
in getting them to this duty. They want leaves of absence, and to be put on
the staff of Generals. Except where the law allows a General of the *Regular*
Army to appoint a Regular officer his aide, no one should at this time be
allowed to fill that place—Please see the enclosed table showing 429 officers
absent from regiments, of whom 45 are aides or staff officers. Also please
see memorandum embracing a recommendation in special cases. [Approved]
4. . . . There are now a number of assistant adjutant Generals of volunteers
thrown out of place by muster out of their commands—should they not be
mustered out as fast as their services are no longer required? [Muster out
all unemployed Staff officers in Volunteer service.] 5. . . . All *Additional*
Aides-de-camp who are not on duty should be mustered out. And all officers,
such as Cram, Engrs, Ruggles A. A. Genl, &c. who are doing duty in their
own Corps but not as aides—[Muster out all Additional Aides now unemployed but not those doing duty even when it is in their own Corps.] 6. There
is another class of aides who should be mustered out immediately—They
were commissioned and confirmed by the Senate under the special act allowing three aides to Generals commanding Army Corps—Several of those
Generals are now out of service—their aides still continue, some of them

serving with other Generals—Their commissions really expired by limitation when their Generals were relieved from command of an Army Corps or from a higher command—Capt. Schuyler Crosby was so appointed for Genl Banks, now mustered out. He has just been ordered to Genl Sheridan, but he should go as Lieutenant of Artillery—Genl Sickles has applied to have two aides who were appointed for him as an Army Corps commander, ordered to him now as a District Commander—One is a Major, the other a captain—They are with other Generals—I think they should be discharged as above. [Approved.] 7—The question of staff for the Generals who have been retained and assigned to commands, needs consideration. Every *District* commander expects a full and complete staff, whether he has a company of troops in his District or not—The allowance of staff officers should be brought down to near what it was before the war. [Reduce staff of General officers except Mil. Div. Comdrs to peace establishment allowance.] No General officer (except by brevet) should be on the staff of Division or other Generals—[Approved except for Commanders of Mil. Div's] Chiefs of artillery are no longer needed—[Approved] chiefs of cavalry are no longer needed—[Approved] No officers of the Regular corps of Engineers should be on the personal staff of Generals. They should all be brought under the orders of the Chief Engineer who needs their services—Capt. McAlester, on Genl Canby's staff is applied for now by Genl Delafield. [Disapproved] A Judge advocate is not needed at Hd. Qrs. of Military Divisions because Department commanders have all the legal control over the subject of Courts Martial—[Approved] A chief Quartermaster chief commissary medical Director not needed at Division Head Quarters. [Approved] Quartermasters, Commissaries and Medical officers should not be a part of the staff of District commanders, but should be assigned for duty at such stations as the Department commander thinks proper. [Approved] If military Provost marshals are needed, they can be detailed from officers of a commands but should not be announced as part of a staff. [Approved] The following allowance of staff officers is suggested for your consideration: *For a Mily Geol Division Commander*—1 assistant adjutant General—1 assistant Inspector General—Three aides-de-camp. [For the present disapproved] *For a Mily Geol Department commander*—1 asst. adjutant General—1 asst. Inspector General—1 chief Quartermaster—1 chief Commissary—1 medical Director—1 Judge advocate—2 aides-de-camp—[Approved] *For Generals Commanding Districts*—2 aides-de-camp—Perhaps an asst. Adjt. Genl may be necessary in the Southern District commands. [One Aid can Act as Act. Asst. A. G. Approved] General officers should be required to relieve immediately all officers heretofore announced on their staff & not allowed in the foregoing lists, if the same are approved—The enclosed orders issued by certain Generals will show the extent to which their staff is carried—[Approved.] 8—If it is intended to garrison forts on the seaboard by artillery companies, I propose to order the companies now here doing nothing, to relieve Infantry and volunteers, and to assign the regiments to certain districts along the coast according to their former service—Below is a list of

Forts, and the proposed number of companies is placed opposite such as it seems most proper to occupy—The Light batteries are not included in this calculation. . . . [Order all forts on Southern seaboard to be garrisoned by Colored troops and all on Northern seaboard by the regular Artillery and volunteers relieved to be mustered out of service.] The 2d U. S. artillery has gone to the Pacific Division. [Send] If it is intended to garrison posts along the Northern Lake Frontier, I should think one regiment of the Old Regular Infantry would be sufficient, distributed as follows—Fort Mackinaw, Michn—Sault St Marie—2 cos. Fort Wayne, Detroit—2 cos. Fort Porter, Buffalo, N. Y. Hd. Qrs, & 2 cos. [Hd Qrs. Sackets Harbor N. Y] Fort Niagara, Youngstown—1 co. Fort Ontario, Oswego, N. Y,—1 co. Fort Montgomery, Rouses Point, N. Y.—2 cos.—10 comps [Approved send 4th Inf.y and 2d to Texas as soon as filled up.] Either the 2d or the 4th Infantry might be assigned to those posts—These regiments are about equal in strength, say 500 men each, and are not at any post where they are needed— . . . Genl Steedman complains that Genl Gillmore ordered the 6th U. S. Infy from Savannah to Dept. So. Ca. & wishes it returned for a Provost Guard—If the 4th is ordered to the Northern Lakes, the 2d might go to Savannah. [Make no change of 6th Inf.y at present.] General Carleton wishes 1000 Infantry sent to New Mexico, but no Cavalry—I doubt whether one of the three Battalion Infantry regts. can be recruited in time to get it over the Plains this Fall—I would designate either the 11th Colonel Ketchum, or the 17th Colonel Heintzelman—[Designate 11th] 11th Infantry —Colo. Ketchum, Lieut. Col. R. S. Granger 1st Battln & 1 compy organized in in Dept. of Virginia 2d & 3d Battlns not organized—The two unorganized Battalions of the 12th should when recruited join the 1st Battalion and relieve the 11th—at Richmond. Va. [Approved] 17th Infantry—Colo. Heintzelman No companies of the regt. yet complete. The whole of the 13th—(3 Battln) Infantry, should be sent to Sherman's Division as fast as organized. He specially asked for the 1st Battn which is to be stationed at Jefferson Bks. There are also 3 organized companies beside at St Louis. [Approved.] . . . [Order 18th & 19th to Sherman as soon as they can be spared from where they are.] The 3d and 10th old Infy regts. are in Washington, much reduced in strength—The 8th is at Baltimore—I think these regts—had better stay where they are as long as troops are needed there— *3d Inf.* Col. Wm Hoffman, Major C. Grover.—10th *Infy* Colo. E. B. Alexander, Lt. Col. Sidell—[Approved] . . . General Sheridan has telegraphed that if regular cavalry regiments are sent him without horses he will mount them, and muster out Volunteer Cavalry—[Send them.] General Price, Inspector of Cavalry, reports the Cavalry in Dept. of Missouri as in a most deplorable condition, and he recommends its muster out. [Approved.] The following is the present distribution of the Regular Cavalry: 1st cavalry—Division of the Gulf—Col. Blake. 2d cavalry—numbering only about 400, is on the Baltimore & Ohio Rail-road—Col. T. J. Wood Capt. C. E. Norris, Comdg. [Send to Sheridan Sherman] 3d Cavalry, in Dept. of Arkansas, Col. M. S. Howe 4th Cavalry in Division of the Tennessee, Col. L. P.

Graham Maj. Chambers, Comdg [Send to Sheridan] 5th Cavalry—6 companies are at Cumberland, Md. 5 comps. in Washington, escort to the Lieut. General. 1 comp. not organized—Col. W. H. Emory. Capt. Leib, Comdg. [S̶e̶n̶d̶ t̶o̶ S̶h̶e̶r̶m̶a̶n̶] 6th Cavalry—lately recruited to full strength, awaiting assignment—Col. Hunter Major R. M. Morris Comdg. [Send to S̶h̶e̶r̶m̶a̶n̶ Sheridan]"—ALS (some in tabular form) and AN (bracketed material in USG's hand), *ibid.* On Sept. 11, Bvt. Col. Orville E. Babcock wrote to Townsend. "The Lieut Genl directs me to transmit your communication with his views and instructions noted thereon He desires you to have a copy made at once with his remarks and sent to Maj Genl Rawlins Chief of Staff for record in his office."—ALS, *ibid.* On Oct. 6, USG wrote a memorandum. "Order four regiments of Colored troops from N. C. to Dept. of Washington Direct all Seacoast Garrisons south of Ft. Monroe, exce[pt] Ft. Taylor and Dry Tortugas, to be garrisoned by colored troops. All c̶o̶l̶-̶ o̶r̶e̶d̶ t̶r̶o̶o̶ other colored troops to be mustered out of service as fast as they can be dispensed with. Order the Musterout of all Volunteer Cavalry East of the Mississippi. Order four companies of 5th Art.y to Ft. Monroe and six companies to Dry Tortugas and Ft Taylor, Hd Qrs. of Regt. Ft Monroe. Order discharge of Heavy Arty. regt. at Ft Monroe as soon as relieved by other troops. Order 2d Cav.y to Gn. Sherman 6th to Gn. Sheridan."—AD, *ibid.*, 1087A 1865. USG's instructions of Sept. 10 were partially combined with the memorandum of Oct. 6 and issued by Townsend on Oct. 9 as General Orders No. 144.—(Printed) *ibid.*

1865, SEPT. 11. Maj. Gen. Henry W. Halleck, San Francisco, to Secretary of War Edwin M. Stanton and USG. "I recommend Maj Gen A. J. Smith G Crook C C. Augur or F Steele to command Dept of the Columbia." —Telegram received (on Sept. 15, 9:40 A.M.), DNA, RG 107, Telegrams Collected (Bound); *ibid.*, RG 108, Letters Received.

On Nov. 8, Maj. Gen. Frederick Steele, St. Louis, telegraphed to USG. "I am on my way to Fort Vancover like the command wish permission to visit Washington asked the adjutant General but received no answer"— Telegram received (at 1:15 P.M.), *ibid.*, RG 107, Telegrams Collected (Bound); *ibid.*, RG 108, Telegrams Received; copy, DLC-USG, V, 54. On Dec. 21, Steele, New York City, telegraphed to USG. "My Baggage has not arrived. Can I delay Sailing until next Steamer? Please reply to Metropolitan Hotel"—Telegram received (at 1:47 P.M.), DNA, RG 108, Telegrams Received; copy (misdated Dec. 26), DLC-USG, V, 54. At 2:40 P.M., USG telegraphed to Steele. "You are authorized to remain over one Steamer."—Telegram sent, DNA, RG 107, Telegrams Collected (Bound).

1865, SEPT. 12. Brig. Gen. Richard Delafield, chief of engineers, to USG. "I transmit herewith for your use ten copies of the Map of Central Virginia shewing your Campaigns & the Marches of the Armies under your command, made in this Department, having all the recent additions & corrections on them."—Copy, DNA, RG 77, Letters Sent. On Aug. 4, Delafield had written to Brig. Gen. John A. Rawlins transmitting "sketches of Forts Henry and Donelson, of the works in their vicinity, and the roads connecting the two places,"—Copy, *ibid.*, Miscellaneous Letters Sent.

1865, SEPT. 14.   John T. Peirce, Hampshire County, West Va., to USG. "There is at present a state of things existing in the State of West Virginia, a farce being enacted which it seems to me are in direct violation of the terms of Gen. Lees surrender to which I desire to call your attention   I together with many others belonging to Gen. T L Rossers command have returned to our homes in this & the adjoining counties with the understanding as we supposed & as set forth in our paroles that our persons & property were to be unmolested   We however no sooner arrive home than we are sued by private citizens who do not even claim that the Damage which they sustained was inflicted by us but because they were injured by that portion of the Confederate States Army to which we belonged & in which we were acting simply as soldiers   There is a law here in West Virginia authorizing all Loyal Citizens who have lost property or sustained damage by the war to institute suit & recover damages from any one who has aided abeted or sympathised with the rebellion   Under this law I presume there have been at least forty suits instituted against persons living in Hampshire Co. Most of these suits were instituted in the Circuit Court of Preston Co under a special act of the Legislature, many of them by publication & attachment before the termination of the war; the consequence is that judgment was rendered in many cases before the parties knew they had been sued & my property is now avertised for sale part on the 23rd inst before the Courthouse in Romney & part at my home on the 30th inst to satisfy Executions amounting to about $6000.—& there are still pending against me suits the plaintiffs in which claim damages to the amt. of between $50.000.—& 60.000. —Regarding this war as having established the fact that the laws of the United States are the supreme laws of the land I can but look upon these suits as the most palpable violation of the paroles which the soldiers of Gen Lees Army took upon his surrender. If we are to be thus plundered by a set of modern Shilocks under laws which have not a parrelel in history, our paroles are utterly worthless and the war which has terminated between organised Armies is to be carried on indefinately between private citizens   I simply desire to call your attention to these facts hoping that you may be able to provide or find a remedy for these evils   I should be glad to receive an answer to this directed to Ridgeville Hampshire Co W. Va." —ALS, DNA, RG 108, Letters Received. Bvt. Brig. Gen. Cyrus B. Comstock noted on the docket of this letter: "The military authorities have no power in civil suits. Protection in cases like this lies in the civil courts and authorities alone."—AN, *ibid.* Cancellation marks through Comstock's note suggest that Peirce's complaint was not answered.

1865, SEPT. 16.   Alexander H. Stephens, "Fort Warren B. H. Mass," to USG. "All the apology I have to offer for this letter as well as its explanation are to be found in the facts herein presented—I am now in confinement in this place as you are probably aware—I have been here since the 25th of May last—I am exceedingly anxious to be paroled as a great Many others have been who [w]ere arrested as I was—I think I am as justly intitled to discharge on parole as many of those to whom I allude. No man in the Southern States I thinke exerted his powers to a greater extent than I did to avert the late lamentable troubles of our country ~~than I~~ did no man Strove harder to bring about ~~prevent~~ the evils of war nor and no man can be more anxious now than myself to see Peace order ~~and~~ harmony and prosperity speedily restored than myself—You know my feelings on this subject when we met at city Point—They were correctly set forth in your telegram to Secr of War—upon that the Hamtons Road con[ference was] granted— When I parted with you I assured you that while nothing definite had been accom[p]lished that I was hopeful that [good would result.] In that hope I was disappointed—No one could have been more pained mortified and chagrined than I was at the result—I refer to this because you were then fully assured of my views—and I now drop you this line simply to ask if you feel at liberty to do so to lend the great weight of your name & influence with the President, Sec. of War & State for my release on parole—I have applied for Pardon & Amnesty but if the President for any reasons feels disposed to post pone the decision of that matter I am perfectly content—what I desire mainly is a release from imprisonm[ent] either on parole as others or on bail if it shod be required—In no event would I attempt to avoid a prosecution or trial if it should be thought proper for any considerations to adopt such a course towards—I wish release both in consequence of my health and private affairs—My case and request are briefly submitted to you. Act in the premises as your sense of duty shall directly—"—ADf, Emory University, Atlanta, Ga. The letter received is printed in Adam Badeau, *Grant in Peace* (Hartford, Conn., 1887), pp. 28–29. In Oct., Bvt. Brig. Gen. Cyrus B. Comstock wrote to Stephens. "Lieut.-Gen. Grant desires me to say in reply to your note of Sept. 16, that he has already spoken once or twice to the President in reference to your case, and will do so again."—Printed as received on Oct. 9 in Myrta Lockett Avary, ed., *Recollections of Alexander H. Stephens* ... (New York, 1910), p. 527. See *O.R.*, II, viii, 763–64.

1865, SEPT. 18. USG, St. Louis, endorsement. "In the reorganization of the Army, in case of an increase, I would most heartily recommend Gen. Grierson for the appointment of Colonel of Cavalry in the Regular Army. Gen. Grierson has rendered efficient service throughout the Rebellion, without failure at any time. He was the first officer to set the example of what might be done ~~for~~ in the interior of the enemy's country, without a base from which to draw supplies."—AES, DNA, RG 94, ACP, G553 CB 1865. Written on a letter of Sept. 10 from Maj. Gen. William T. Sherman to the AG recommending Bvt. Maj. Gen. Benjamin H. Grierson for appointment in the U.S. Army.—ALS, *ibid.* On March 9, 13, 18, 1866, Grierson wrote to his wife about his appointment as maj. gen. of vols.—ALS, IHi. On March 23, Grierson wrote to Secretary of War Edwin M. Stanton. "I have received my Commission as Major General of Volunteers and accepted the Appointment which dates from May 27, 1865. I respectfully ask your approval to this, my application for the balance of pay which may be due me as Major General from that date."—LS, *ibid.* On March 24, USG endorsed this letter. "Approved and respectfully recommended."—AES, *ibid.* On March 28, USG wrote a memorandum. "I hereby certify that General Grierson was appointed a full Major General to enable him to draw pay of that grade from May 27th 1865, the date from which he ranks as such, and recommend that he receive the full pay and allowances of a Major General from that date."—Copy, *ibid.* Grierson was appointed col., 10th Cav., as of July 28.

1865, SEPT. 20. Maj. Gen. Edward O. C. Ord, Detroit, to USG. "Special letter from Asst. Adjt Gen'l. R Williams of Washington orders Lieut C. B. Atchison to join his company. Can I retain him and send Capt. Thos G. Welles, A d C., to report to Gen Sully? This will suit all parties."—Telegram received (at 11:45 A.M.), DNA, RG 108, Telegrams Received; copy, DLC-USG, V, 54. On the same day, Bvt. Col. Orville E. Babcock, St. Louis, telegraphed to Ord. "Gen Grant directs me to inform you that you can apply to Washington in Maj Achisons case with his approval of your request"—Telegram received (at 10:00 P.M.), Ord Papers, CU-B; copies, DLC-USG, V, 46, 109; DNA, RG 108, Letters Sent.

1865, SEPT. 20. J. D. Osborne, Newark, N. J., to USG. "While in the 'Wildernes' May 7th 1864 you were making for yourself an imperishable name & gaining for our Country glory happiness & prosperity, a boy was born to us.—our first born. A few days later while with you as Surgeon of the 4th Regt N. J. Vols I recieved the information of the fact, & in my reply proposed to [my wife] that his name should be 'Grant.' Knowing that you will appreciate the only motive we coul[d] have in giving him your name I beg leave to send you his Carte de Visite—taken, when he was sixteen months old & hope you will be pleased with it. Could you spare the time from your many duties to send your own to your namesake. I have now doubt should he live to be a man he will take great pride & satisfaction in knowing it came from one whom he will be taught to love & revere—His mother heartily joining me in the wish to give him your name also joins me in this"—ALS, USG 3.

1865, SEPT. 22. Maj. Gen. Philip H. Sheridan to USG. "Should Slocums resignation be accepted I want a good commander for the Department of Mississippi and would respectfully suggest Genl Getty or Gibbons—I have great confidence in Getty and would prefer him, but would be satisfied with Gibbons"—Telegram received (on Sept. 23, 4:30 P.M.), DNA, RG

107, Telegrams Collected (Bound); copy, DLC-Philip H. Sheridan. *O.R.*, I, xlviii, part 2, 1236. See *ibid.*, p. 1234.

1865, SEPT. 28.   William Böttner, New Orleans, to USG. "On the 4th of July 1862 the respectfully undersigned had the honor to receive the officers & the Staff of Lieut: Gen: U. Grant and other Generals at his establishment in Memphis Ten: & a dinner has been ordered by Gen: Terry & others, by which occasion Gen: Grant were presiding, for which I have not been paid since. My bill amounting the sum of $385. had been delivered and approved by Lieut: Gen: Grant also by Colonel Bowerson, who was the recipient of the necessary documents. The latter declared positively, that Lieut: Gen: Grant were well recollecting the whole affaire & promising to pay the amount due to the undersigned with interests.—Since I left Memphis I took sick and could not attend to my business personally, therefore Mrs: Böttner traveled three times to Washington for the purpose of collecting the money, upon which occasion Col: Bowerson repeatedly assured, that the amount kindly requested should be paid in a short time. Arrived in the City of New-Orleans I been suffering upon the necessaries—of live, wherefore I very seriously pray, that my request should be granted and the money be paid to the undersigned. Hoping, that Lieut. Gen: Grant will have the kindness—to order the bill to be setteled immediately, I take the liberty to remain . . ."—ALS, DNA, RG 108, Letters Received. On July 4, 1862, Brig. Gen. John M. Thayer and officers of the 1st Neb. gave a dinner in USG's honor at Memphis. See *Memphis Bulletin*, July 6, 1862; Richardson, pp. 261–62.

1865, SEPT. 29.   Bvt. Col. Theodore S. Bowers endorsement. "Respectfully referred to Major General G. H. Thomas, Commanding Military Division of the Tennessee, for his action."—ES, DNA, RG 94, Letters Received, 873T 1865. Written on a letter of Sept. 28 from W. F. Taylor, Washington, D. C., to USG. "I respectfully send herewith copies of notes from Alabama, & ask orders may be given to stop the outrages, & thieving complained of, Mr Holcroft lives on my land three miles north of Uniontown. Mr Ramey also lives on my land six miles west of Uniontown, being in Perry & Marengo Counties, Alabama. I left Alabama in July, with my nephew for my agent during my absence, to whom the notes were written, who sent them on to me. Colo Britton with a Regt. of Illinois Volunteers were at Uniontown—(the first troops stationed there) when I left Alabama. If any more evidence is required I can introduce to your department, Mr Jamieson, Mr Walthall, Mr Fitts & others of the most respectable Citizens of Ala now in Washington. I refer you to General Ramsey U. S. A. for my position, not having the honor of your acquaintance"—ALS, *ibid.* The enclosures are *ibid.*

1865, OCT. 1.   To Maj. Gen. John M. Palmer, Louisville, from Cincinnati. "Release L D. Huston Who was arrested on yesterday In Newport   if there are charges against Him Leave the Civil Courts to take Cognizance"—Telegram received (on Oct. 3), DNA, RG 109, Union Provost Marshals' File of Papers Relating to Individual Civilians; copies, *ibid.*, RG 108, Letters Sent; (misdated Oct. 3) *ibid.*, RG 393, Dept. of Ky., Telegrams Received; DLC-USG, V, 46, 109. On the same day, 1st Lt. and Asst. Provost Marshal Nathan S. Wheeler, 125th Colored, Louisville, wrote to Brig. Gen. Louis D. Watkins directing that Lorenzo D. Huston be banished to Tenn.—ALS, DNA, RG 109, Union Provost Marshals' File of Papers Relating to Individual Civilians. Probably on the same day, a group of prominent individuals had approached USG concerning Huston's arrest. —*Missouri Republican*, Jan. 23, 1868. On Oct. 2, USG responded to a question concerning Huston: "I have already ordered his unconditional release. *It is time that military arrests and military commissions were at an end.* We are now at peace, and if any citizen commits any political offence he should be *taken before th civil courts and there tried for his crime.*"— *Ibid.* On Oct. 5, Thomas W. Bartley, Cincinnati, telegraphed to USG. "Dr. Huston has not been discharged but was started from Louisville to Nashville yesterday tuesday morning as I learn   Please require obedience to your orders"—Telegram received (at 4:30 P.M.), DNA, RG 107, Telegrams Collected (Bound); *ibid.*, RG 108, Telegrams Received; copy, DLC-USG, V, 54. On Oct. 6, 1:00 P.M., USG telegraphed to the commanding officer, Nashville. "Release Rev Dr Huston who was arrested in Newport Ky. one week ago. Leave his case to civil laws"—Telegram sent, DNA, RG 107, Telegrams Collected (Bound); copies, *ibid.*, RG 108, Letters Sent; DLC-USG, V, 46, 109. See E. Merton Coulter, *The Civil War and Readjustment in Kentucky* (Chapel Hill, 1926), p. 399.

1865, Oct. 2.   To Secretary of War Edwin M. Stanton from Cincinnati. "I would respectfully recommend the transfer of Capt. W. W. Van Ness, A. Q. M. from the Volunteer to the regular service to fill any vacancy that may now exist, or ~~to~~ in case there is no vacancy to take the first that may occur. Capt. Van Ness has been in the Volunteer service from the breaking out of the war to the present time and has the highest testimonials from all officers under whom or with whom he has served."—ALS, DNA, RG 94, ACP, V35 CB 1866. No appointment followed.

1865, Oct. 6.   Col. Sidney Burbank, 2nd Inf., Newport Barracks, Ky., to USG. "As Suggested by you I telegraphed to enquire as to the movement of Second Infantry"—Telegram received (at 2:10 P.M.), DNA, RG 107, Telegrams Collected (Bound); *ibid.*, RG 108, Telegrams Received; copy, DLC-USG, V, 54.

1865, Oct. 7.   USG endorsement. "Notify Genl Halleck of number of regular troops ordered to the Pacific, and direct him to muster out all Volunteers on the Pacific coast—as many as possible immediately—and the balance of them on the arrival of the last of the troops sent   Orders have been given today to attach New Mexico to Genl Pope's Dept. Direct Genl Pope to take immediate steps to relieve all Volunteers with one ~~year~~ old regiment or one battalion (new regiment) of regular Infantry and as much Cavalry as he may deem necessary,—not to exceed however four full companies. The Volunteers will all be mustered out on the arrival of these regular troops, and one regiment of them immediately on the receipt of this order. Order all regiments of California Vols, serving in New Mexico, to proceed at once to California there to be mustered out"—Copy, DLC-USG, V, 41. Written on a telegram of Sept. 17 from Maj. Gen. Henry W. Halleck and other papers indicating 12,020 troops in the Military Div. of the Pacific.—*Ibid.* On Oct. 16, Halleck, San Francisco, telegraphed to Secretary of War Edwin M. Stanton and USG. "We Cannot musterout the California Cavy till mounted Troops are sent to relieve them"—Telegram received (on Oct. 20, 9:00 A.M.), DNA, RG 107, Telegrams Collected (Bound); *ibid.,* RG 108, Telegrams Received; copies, *ibid.,* Letters Received; DLC-USG, V, 54.

1865, OCT. 7. USG endorsement. "Respectfully returned with the information that I have this day asked for the muster out of all Cavalry east of the Mississippi River, and that transportation be reduced to one four-mule team for two Companies. In addition to this, the Infantry force will be materially reduced without delay. From these facts it will be seen that these estimates are unnecessarily large."—Copies (2), DNA, RG 92, Supplies and Purchases, Public Animals, Letters Received; *ibid.,* RG 108, Letters Received; *ibid.,* Register of Letters Received. Written on a letter of Sept. 21 from Bvt. Maj. Gen. Montgomery C. Meigs to Secretary of War Edwin M. Stanton estimating the amount of forage needed for the Military Div. of the Tenn.—Copy, *ibid.,* Letters Received.

1865, OCT. 7. Maj. Gen. Philip H. Sheridan, New Orleans, to Brig. Gen. John A. Rawlins. "I see it published in the papers that a delegation from Louisianna represented great difficulties between the Military & civil powers in this state. There is no great trouble here, politicians purposely get up difficulties with the Pro Marshal in the Freedmans Bureau in order to get persecuted if possible. In the three, four instances they have accomplished their purpose on account of bad management on the part of the Pro Marshalls and have magnified a mole hill into a mountain in order to be elected to the next Legislature or to Congress or to some other fate office I have advised Dept Commanders to look out for the Legitimate rights of the Govt for the military statutes, former injustice against Freeman and to give away to civil authority when their rights were not effected for it is hard to enforce martial law after war has ceased and a form even of civil Govt is in existence. The Govt should not allow itself to be deceived by Ex partee representations"—Telegram received (on Oct. 8, 1:00 A.M.), DNA, RG 94, Letters Received, 2277W 1865; *ibid.,* RG 107, Telegrams Collected (Bound); (press) *ibid.; ibid.,* RG 108, Telegrams Received; copies, *ibid.,*

RG 94, Letters Received, 2277W 1865; DLC-USG, V, 54; DLC-Philip
H. Sheridan. *O.R.*, I, xlviii, part 2, 1238. On Oct. 9, Bvt. Col. Theodore
S. Bowers endorsed this telegram. "Respectfully forwarded to the Hon. the
Secretary of War."—ES, DNA, RG 94, Letters Received, 2277W 1865.
On the same day, President Andrew Johnson endorsed this telegram. "Re-
ferred to the Sec of War—In structions will be given confining the Military
within proper limits and prohibiting all interference with the civil authority
whatever; but required to give all assistenc practicable in the restoration of
of Civil Govmt—I hope the Sec will attend to this at once"—AES, *ibid.* On
Oct. 9, Secretary of War Edwin M. Stanton telegraphed to Sheridan transmitting Johnson's instructions.—ALS (telegram sent), *ibid.*, RG 107,
Telegrams Collected (Unbound).

1865, OCT. 8.   USG endorsement. "Respectfully refered to the Atty. Gen.
with the recommendation that this pardon be speedily granted. I think it is
now time when some pardons should be extended to officers who left the old
Army. As a rule they are a class who will keep any obligation, and are so recognized."—AES, DNA, RG 94, Amnesty Papers, Ala. Written on a letter of
Oct. 6 from Turner Reavis (of Gainesville, Ala.), Washington, D. C., to
President Andrew Johnson requesting a pardon for his son-in-law, Thomas
K. Jackson, USMA 1848, who had resigned from the U.S. Army as of April
1, 1861.—ALS, *ibid.* Reavis (who had been pardoned as of Sept. 9, 1865,
ibid.), enclosed a letter of Aug. 30 from James Longstreet, Macon, Miss.,
to USG. "I take the liberty of addressing you in behalf of Major T. K.
Jackson of the late Confederate Army. He, like most of the Army officers
from the Southern States, resigned at the begining of the war and returned
to his State. This step was taken under the conviction that his services and
allegiance, were due to his native State. I think I can safely assure you,
that he was always a national, rather than a sectional man, and had he been
in a position to do so, would have made any sacrifice for the safety and
honor of the country. If he has been misguided, he has committed an error
that was common to one half of the world, and those who were called upon
to act under it, have already greviously answered it. Before I left the old
Army, I asked some officers from the Northern States, who advised me not
to resign, whether they would resign if their States had done as mine had
done. They invariably admitted that they would return to their States. Yet
all of these officers have served in your Army during the war, and some of
them, with considerable distinction, and are accepted as the truest and bravest in your great Army. Let me appeal to you then to determine, whether
there is justice or honor in pursuing a fallen foe, whose only crime is error
of judgement, and who now sues for pardon. Besides, it is my humble opinion that the terms granted by you at the surrender of Gen'l Lee, extended
to all of us the benefit of the Amnesty Proclamation of President Lincoln of
1863. These terms were approved by President Lincoln, and are, therefore,
irrevocable."—ALS, *ibid.* No action followed.

1865, OCT. 9. Abraham C. Myers, USMA 1833, Paris, to USG. "You will excuse me I trust for writing to you upon a purely personal matter, but it has occurred to me that from our service together in Mexico you will feel inclined, if it is not inconsistent with rules you have prescibed to yourself in similar cases, to lend me your aid and influence—At the time of the surrender of the Confederate armies to you I was in Texas and had not been connected with the military service since August 1863 when Mr Davis deprived of the position of Quarter Master General. I came to Europe in July last and on the 24th of the month took the oath of allegiance to the United States before Mr Bigclow the U. S. Minister to France, and sent my application for pardon through him to the President. I have not heard any thing of it—In anticipation of a general Amnesty, my friend Genl W. T. Sherman writes me to return to america, which I purpose doing in a few days.—but I cannot do business as Executor of an Estate in which my wife and minor children are alone interested until I am pardoned—Do me the Kindness to look at my application to the President, and procure his action upon it. Mr James Hewitt writes me from Liverpool that he is on his way to Washington to get his pardon—Will you please inform him about my case, and let me hear from you in reply to this note directing your letter to me at the New York Hotel New York City."—ALS, USG 3. Docketing indicates that this letter was unanswered.—*Ibid.*

1865, OCT. 13. USG endorsement. "Respectfully forwarded to the Secretary of War. I would respectfully recommend that General Meigs be directed to furnish the vessels herein named (the crew and coal only to be supplied by Government) without further bonds than the personal obligations of A. S. Mercer, that they shall be delivered to the Qr. Mr. in San Francisco. It should be the duty of the Qr Masters Dept. to see that the vessels go under proper commanders and crew, and that there can be no danger of the loss of them, further than the ordinary dangers of navigation."—Copy, DNA, RG 108, Register of Letters Received. Written on a communication of Oct. from Asa S. Mercer, agent, Washington Territory. "Presents com'ns from Adjutant General and Quartermaster General in relation to furnishing transportation for seven hundred females, mostly widows & orphans of soldiers killed in the service, from New York to San-Francisco."—*Ibid.* On Oct. 16, USG endorsed a communication from Bvt. Maj. Gen. Montgomery C. Meigs on the subject. "After hearing the further objection of the Quartermaster General to furnishing Complete transportation to the Pacific for female emigrants I would modify my recommendation to Conform to that of the Qr. Mr. Gen. except in the matter of bonds to be given for the delivery of the Vessel to named parties in San Francisco. In that respect I would recommend that the individual bonds of Mr Mercer for the value of the Vessel be all that is required; and that an Agent of the Quarter Masters Department be sent with the vessel, to see to her proper delivery."—Copy, DLC-USG, V, 41.

On July 17, Governor William W. Pickering of Washington Territory, Washington, D. C., had written to Maj. Gen. Oliver O. Howard, Bureau of Refugees, Freedmen, and Abandoned Lands, in support of Mercer's project, and Howard favorably endorsed this letter to USG.—ALS and AES, DNA, RG 108, Letters Received. Through his acquaintance with Bvt. Col. Theodore S. Bowers, Mercer met USG in July.—*New York Times*, Sept. 30, 1865. On July 18, Brig. Gen. Rufus Ingalls wrote to Bvt. Brig. Gen. Stewart Van Vliet, New York City. "The Lieut-Genl Comd'g the Armies of the United States desires to aid Mr A. S. Mercer, Emigrant Agent for Washington Territory, in the Speedy transportation of Emigrants, not to Exceed Seven hundred, Such as he may present, from Newyork City to Aspinwall, or via Cape Horn to San Francisco. If you have any Government vessels bound to Either of the places above named,—the latter preferably— it is the order of the Lieut.-General that you give the required transportation. —If no Government vessel is available, you can probably assist Mr. Mercer in making a Satisfactory arrangement with the Panama Line for the Transportation of his Emigrants to San Francisco or Washington Territory, without incurring a greater Expense to the Government than would be engendered by the use a Steamer in the Service of the Qr. Masters Department, on a voyage to Aspinwall."—Copy, DNA, RG 94, Letters Received, 1657M 1865. See D. Alexander Brown, "Brides by the Boatload," *American History Illustrated*, I, 1 (April, 1966), 40–46; Nard Jones, *Seattle* (Garden City, N. Y., 1972), pp. 83–93; Mercer, *Washington Territory . . .* (Utica, N. Y., 1865; reprinted, 1971).

1865, OCT. 13. USG endorsement. "I would respectfully recommend that the order for the musterout of Gn. A. Shimmelfining be revoked to give his family the benefit of pay to the day of the Gns. death, and also to give them whatever avantage may arise from such a course in securing a pension." —AES, DNA, RG 94, ACP, S1396 CB 1863. Written on papers concerning the death of Brig. Gen. Alexander Schimmelfennig. Included was a letter of Sept. 7 from John Hill Martin, Bethlehem, Pa., to USG. "Permit an old classmate at West Point to congratulate you upon your success in life and the inestimable benefit your services have been to our beloved country. And to present a petition on behalf of the family of gallant soldier and noble gentleman, Brig Gen: Alex: Schimmelfennig died yesterday of disease contracted during the seize of Charleston and leaves behind him, a wife and three little children penniless in a strange country. Cannot the Order mustering him out of service be *rescinded* so that his wife can get a pension?"—ALS, *ibid.* Martin, a nongraduate of USMA (1838–41), became a Pa. lawyer in 1844.

1865, OCT. 13, Friday. Mrs. Mary C. Walling, Parker House, Boston, to USG. "I Sincerely desire your presence at my lecture Sunday or Monday evening—Shall be most happy if you can favor us and will make the announcement"—Telegram received (at 5:00 P.M.), DNA, RG 107, Telegrams Collected (Bound). Mary Cole, born in Pa. in 1838, married C. A. Walling of Tex. Although her husband served with C.S.A. forces, she was forced to leave Tex. in 1863 because of her Unionist views. She became a well-known lecturer and was granted the use of the U.S. Senate chamber to speak on Reconstruction on the evening of May 10, 1866. See *Senate Journal,* 39-1, pp. 326, 331, 333, 392–93, 410; *Courier-Journal* (Louisville), June 14, 1925.

1865, OCT. 14. To Secretary of War Edwin M. Stanton. "I would respectfully recommend the appointment of Col. René E. De Russy, Eng. Corps, to the rank of Brevet Brigadier General in the Regular Army for long and faithful services."—ALS, DNA, RG 94, ACP, D661 CB 1865. Col. René E. de Russy, USMA 1812, in charge of fortifications at San Francisco during the Civil War, died on Nov. 23. On March 12, 1866, Maj. Gen. Henry W. Halleck forwarded communications received at USG's hd. qrs. recommending René E. De Russy, Jr., former 2nd lt., 4th N. Y. Heavy Art., for appointment in the U.S. Army.—*Ibid.,* RG 108, Register of Letters Received. On April 20, USG endorsed this letter. "Respy. forwarded and the appointment of R. E. De Russey to one of the vacancies existing in the regular Army recommended."—Copy, *ibid.* On March 3, 1875, De Russy, Raleigh, petitioned USG for reappointment to the U.S. Army, asserting that his offense concerning duplicate pay vouchers, for which he had submitted a forced resignation, was technical.—DS, *ibid.,* RG 94, ACP, 728 1872. On April 9, De Russy wrote to USG asking that his petition be granted or that he be appointed to a "civil position under Government."—ALS, *ibid.* Other letters to USG supporting De Russy are *ibid.* No appointment followed.

On March 6, 1874, Helen A. de Russy, San Francisco, had written to USG concerning her pension. "I am the widow of General R. E. de Russy late Colonel Corps of Engineers whose family have already been the recipients of so many kind acts from you that nothing but necessity would induce me to trouble you further. . . ."—ALS, *ibid.,* RG 48, Miscellaneous Div., Letters Received.

1865, OCT. 14. To Maj. Gen. Henry W. Halleck, San Francisco. "Capt. Hodges, A. Q. M. has been ordered to the Pacific to report to the Chief Quarter Master there. I procured this order with the express purpose of having him go to Oregon and will be pleased if you can have him sent there." —ALS, DNA, RG 393, Military Div. of the Pacific, Letters Received. Capt. Henry C. Hodges, q. m., USMA 1851, had crossed the Isthmus of Panama with USG in 1852.

1865, OCT. 14. USG endorsement. "I would not approve the revocation of the order accepting the resignation of Gen. Milroy. We have now many more Gen. Officers than the service requires. There are no appointments outside the Army in which I am interested and therefore can make no rec-

ommendation."—Typescript, Atwood Collection, InU. Written on a letter
of Aug. 23 from Robert H. Milroy, former maj. gen., Rensselaer, Ind., to
President Andrew Johnson. ". . . To avoid being thus kicked out of service
by West Pointers, I sent to you my resignation, smarting under the forgoing
and former wrongs from West Pointers. Since the acceptence of my resignation, I have seen a general order assigning generals to duty, and all not
thereby assigned to duty were given three months leave of absence before
being mustered out. I therefore respectfully ask that my resignation by recalled and I be granted three months leave of absence or assigned to duty
as may be thought best. . . ."—Typescript, *ibid.* On Aug. 29, Johnson endorsed this letter. "Respectfully referred to the Hon. Secretary of War, with
the hope that Gen. Milroy's request can be complied with."—Typescript,
ibid.

1865, OCT. 16.   USG endorsement. "Respectfully refered to the Sec. of
the Treasury with the recommendation that Mrs. Biggs be put in immediate
possession of her plantation known as the Hesperia plantation, about five
miles below Vicksburg in Louisiana. The place is now leased I believe under Treasury regulations. Mrs. Biggs will show exibit papers to show loyalty now and that she has been always loyal."—AES, DNA, RG 107, Letters Received, B2695 1865. Written on a letter of Sept. from Maj. Gen.
Henry W. Slocum to Maj. Gen. Oliver O. Howard. "Mrs. S. A. Biggs proposes to visit Washington for the purpose of presenting a claim for the restoration of her property now held by the Governmt and certain claims for
damages—I am satisfied Mrs Biggs has sympathised with the Governmt in
this War—and has done nothing to our injury—She has suffered heavy
losses—I hope anything that can be done for her consistent with law and
existing orders, will be done—"—ALS, *ibid.* On Nov. 4, Flora F. Kelley
wrote to USG. "As I cannot get a verbal hearing excuse my placing before
you a few notes to enlighten your views in my Aunts case. In 1850, her husband became involved, and it was with remarkable energy and exertion that
she paid the debts and saved my Grand fathers lagacy which consisted of
the negros belonging to the plantation now in controversy, the plantation
had just been relieved of its insolvency and was in a prosperous condition
when the war commenced. She is now again bereft of every thing by the
fortunes of war, her life indeed has been checkered, her husband having
been lamed, afflicted, and a care to her since 1850."—ALS, *ibid.*, Letters
Received from Bureaus. On the same day, Mrs. Susan A. Biggs wrote to
USG. "You know the situation of the country between Vicksburg and Monroe La. It is that portion of the country, that I have to transport my family
across, befor the rising of the waters in the swamps, which is now near at
hand. it always commences with the Fall rains. It is this emergency that
urges me to place before you my situation, and if I do not find a friend in
you Genl, then, I have none in Washington, unless I yet make one in the
President. May I ask the favor of you to look over my petition and affidavits
now in the hands of the Secy of War, and use your influence with him, to

accord justice to me. aAs all law is based upon justice I do not understand, what law could keep my home in the possession of another, without an indemnity to me, for its use and damages when I have brought proofs of the facts, that neither myself or family, have taken any part in the rebellion, eithe[r] in the field, council, office or acts of any kind. we passed our time quietly in the back parishes of La. General, I have an only son, with a laudable desire to educate him and cultivate his mind to be useful to his country. It is an exceeding trial to me to be bereft of all recources to procure the means to send him to school. General, I will be under obligations to you for life, if you will use your influence to relieve my situation. I saw Mr Stanton yesterday and he informed me he could do nothing for me until he heard farther information from the South respecting my affairs, if you and the Secy doubt my affidavits, if you think it best, I will return home and bring Millitary information as well as from my own family servants who are known to the facts I have asserted. Excuse the liberty I take in subscribing myself your petitioner"—ALS, *ibid.* On the same day, USG endorsed these letters. "Respectfully forwarded to the Secretary of War."—ES, *ibid.* On Nov. 21, Biggs wrote to USG discussing her claim in detail.—ALS, *ibid.*, RG 108, Letters Received. Additional papers are *ibid.* Biggs's claim for $78,884.50 for damages to her plantation was disallowed.—*HMD*, 46-2-10, p. 18.

1865, OCT. 16.   USG endorsement. "Approved and respectfully forwarded to the Secretary of War."—ES, PHi. Written on a letter of Oct. 7 from Mansfield Lovell, former C.S.A. maj. gen., New York City, to USG. "I am very anxious to go over to England (to return in a few weeks) to attend to some private pecuniary matters of great importance to myself & family— I hear that permission to do so is required, but do not know whether this be so. I have taken the oath of allegiance to the U. S: although among those excluded in the amnesty proclamation—If permission to visit England & return be required, will you be kind enough to send me the necessary authority, addressed to 'Mansfield Lovell—New York Hotel New York. I do not know whom to address in the matter, which must be my excuse for troubling even an old friend."—ALS, *ibid.* See *PUSG*, 6, 117*n.*

1865, OCT. 17.   USG endorsement. "Respectfully returned to the Secretary of War—disapproved for the reason that Mr. Munford was allowed to leave the country and escape trial on a capital charge on condition of not returning, as a special clemency."—ES, DNA, RG 94, Letters Received, 2066M 1865. Written on a letter of Oct. 5 from William E. Munford, former C.S.A. 1st lt., 14th Tenn., Windsor, Canada, to Maj. Gen. Edward O. C. Ord requesting permission to return to the U.S.—ALS, *ibid.* See letter to Edwin M. Stanton, July 12, 1865.

1865, OCT. 17, 4:00 P.M.   To William Prescott Smith, Baltimore and Ohio Railroad. "I would like to accompany the excursion to Harpers Ferry tomorrow, and would but there is a meeting of the corporators of the Soldiers and Sailors Home tomorrow of which I am one and must be present." —Telegram sent, DNA, RG 107, Telegrams Collected (Bound); copies, *ibid.*, RG 108, Letters Sent; DLC-USG, V, 46, 109. See letter to Delphine P. Baker, July 14, 1865. On the same day, Smith, Baltimore, had telegraphed to USG. "I visited Washington to see you last night but did not find your whereabouts until too late an hour to disturb you, Mr Garrett and our directors wish you to join us in complimentary observation trip to Harpers Ferry to morrow Wednesday, You would leave Washington in a special car on the 7 30 A M train, join us at Relay, reach Harpers Ferry at 12 noon, leave about 2 P M & reach Washn again before 8 P M, Can you do this. We are all very anxious There will be no ceremony, but you will meet interesting people of our own, as well as the visitors—"—Telegram received (at 1:50 P.M.), DNA, RG 107, Telegrams Collected (Bound).

1865, OCT. 18. Anonymous, Washington, D. C., to Bvt. Col. Theodore S. Bowers. "There have recently been several instances of injury done to colored persons, by the soldiers from the encampment on 20th St at the Cor of N. St, which we understand are a detachment of the 5th U. S. Cavalry. On Friday evening the 13th inst Lewis Medley—a young colored man— was assaulted not far from the encampment & severely bruised on his face. The next Saturday afternoon a colored woman was passing by the encampment on the opposite side of the St when some of the soldiers threw stones at her whereupon in self-defense she threw *one* back: several then came over to where she was, and were in the act of beating her when a gentleman whom she thinks was an officer ordered them to desist. The same evening a colored man of peaceable character while coming up 20th St was without provocation fired upon twice by a person whom he identified as a soldier; the last shot took effect but did not instantly kill him; he has since, after much suffering, died from the effects of the wound. The surgeon who extracted the ball said that it was one of the kind used by the Cavalry. The next Sunday, not far from the same place, a colored man was severely beaten, and much bruised and cut about his face by the soldiers, who to use their own expressions said they would 'kill every d——d nigger' they met. There are reports that some others have been injured but these cases have come directly to our knowledge; we having in three several instances received the information directly from the injured parties. Threats made by the soldiers of killing and injuring the the negroes so often come to their knowledge, as to intimidate them about going in that locality after dark We are very sure that in not one of these cases has there been just cause or provocation for the injuries inflicted."—AL, DNA, RG 108, Letters Received. On Oct. 20, Capt. Julius W. Mason, 5th Cav., commanding USG's escort, endorsed this letter. "Respectfully returned with the following report. The only troubles that have come to my knowledge are, 1st a Gun shot was fired from a wooden building near my stables occupied by negroes, on some of the men of my command, which was followed by a throwing of stones, in retaliation, which was immediately stopped by myself. 2nd on the evening of the 13th Oct a Corporal and Private of my command were 'put upon' by a number of negroes, near corner of 20th and M Street, the Corporel being badly and perhaps fatally stabbed, and the private badly wounded, this without provocation   There seems to be much doubt about the within named negros being shot by a man in the 5th U. S. Cavy. There is a current story that he was shot by a colored gentleman, who was jealous of him." —AES, *ibid.*

1865, OCT. 19.   To Secretary of War Edwin M. Stanton. "I would respectfully recommend Bvt. Col. D. S. Walker, A. A. G. for the Brevet of Brigadier General of Volunteers. This officers has been been highly recommended by Gens Sheridan, Hancock, and others under whom he has served, for gallantry in battle."—ALS, DNA, RG 94, ACP, G544 CB 1865. On May 10, Brig. Gen. John A. Rawlins favorably endorsed a letter of resignation of May 6 from Lt. Col. Duncan S. Walker to Brig. Gen. Lorenzo Thomas.—ES and ALS, *ibid.*, W284 CB 1865. On Aug. 11, Bvt. Maj. Gen. William H. Emory, Cumberland, Md., wrote to Thomas recommending Walker for appointment as bvt. brig. gen. and Maj. Peter French, 46th N. Y., for bvt. promotion.—LS, *ibid.*, E202 CB 1865. On Oct. 28, Bvt. Col. Ely S. Parker favorably endorsed this letter.—AES, *ibid.* On Oct. 19, Robert J. Walker, former U.S. financial agent and former governor of Kansas Territory, wrote a memorandum calling attention to his son's services.—ADS, *ibid.*, W1027 CB 1865. On Oct. 30, USG endorsed this memorandum. "Respectfully forwarded to the Secretary of War. Recommendation for brevet promotion approved."—ES, *ibid.*

1865, OCT. 20.   To Secretary of War Edwin M. Stanton. "I would respectfully recommend that 1st Lieut. James Duncan Graham, 13th United States Infantry, be transferred to the 4th U. S. Cavalry. This young officer graduated this year and made application for the regiment above named because his father is Colonel of it. He has been raised with Cavalry troops and I think it likely he will be of more service with that arm than any other."—ALS, DNA, RG 108, Letters Received. Endorsements on the docket indicating that no vacancy existed are *ibid.* On April 30, 1866, 1st Lt. James D. Graham, 13th Inf., Fort Leavenworth, wrote to USG. "I have the honor to Apply to be transferred to a Cavalry Regiment, in the event of the regular Army being increased by new Regiments of Cavalry."—ALS, *ibid.* Later, Graham and 1st Lt. Patrick W. Horrigan, 2nd Cav., requested permission to exchange regts.—DS (undated), *ibid.*, RG 94, ACP, H90 CB 1867. On Feb. 9, 1867, USG endorsed this request. "Approved and recommended that the order of transfer be made."—AES, *ibid.*

1865, OCT. 20.   USG endorsement. "Respectfully returned to the Secretary of War, with the information that the necessary orders have been sent to Maj Genl. Halleck, to comply with the within request, if called upon, by

Agent Davidson."—ES, DNA, RG 107, Letters Received from Bureaus. Written on a letter of Sept. 30 from Special Indian Agent M. O. Davidson to Act. Commissioner of Indian Affairs Robert B. Van Valkenburg requesting an escort for supplies going from Calif. to Arizona Territory.—Copy, *ibid.* On Oct. 21, 2:10 P.M., USG telegraphed and wrote to Maj. Gen. Henry W. Halleck. "You will furnish transportation for M. O. Davidson, Special Indian Agent, and the goods in his charge, either from Drum Barracks or Fort Yuma, to the Indian Agency near Tubac, if called upon by Mr. Davidson for that purpose."—LS (telegram sent), *ibid.*, Telegrams Collected (Bound); telegram sent, *ibid.*; LS (sent by mail), *ibid.*, RG 393, Military Div. of the Pacific, Letters Received.

1865, OCT. 20. USG endorsement. "Approved and respectfully forwarded to the Secretary of War."—ES, DNA, RG 94, ACP, F16 CB 1865. Written on a letter of the same day from Asst. Secretary of the Navy Gustavus V. Fox to USG. "Young Foote, son of your old comrade the Admiral is a waif without Father or Mother or near relation and asks only that you will retain him in the Vol. force as long as possible. I don't know as this is the verry best for him as he is young enough to start on some secure path, nevertheless I have the honor to urge his request."—ALS, *ibid.* Augustus R. S. Foote, son of Rear Admiral Andrew H. Foote, appointed midshipman as of Oct. 1, 1863, resigned as of Feb. 14, 1865, and was appointed capt. and adjt. as of March 22. On Dec. 14, Foote wrote to the AGO requesting assignment to duty.—ALS, *ibid.* On Dec. 21, Bvt. Brig. Gen. Edward D. Townsend endorsed this letter. "Respectfully submitted to Lieutenant General Grant, Commanding the Army of the U. S. By Special Orders No 287, Headqrs. Department of Virginia, October 30th, 1865, Captain A. R. S. Foote, Assistant Adjutant General of Volunteers, was relieved from duty in that Department, and ordered to repair to his home and report thence by letter to the Adjutant General of the Army. The services of Captain Foote being no longer needed, it is respectfully recommended that he be honorably mustered out of service, under the provisions of General Orders Number 79, May 1st, 1865, from this office."—ES, *ibid.* On Dec. 23, Bvt. Col. Theodore S. Bowers approved Townsend's endorsement and Foote was mustered out as of Jan. 12, 1866.—AES, *ibid.* On March 3, 1869, Foote wrote to Secretary of War John M. Schofield requesting the return of a letter written by USG in his behalf around Feb. 14, 1865.—ALS, *ibid.* Docketing indicates that USG's letter was returned to Foote.—*Ibid.*

1865, OCT. 21. To Secretary of War Edwin M. Stanton. "I respectfully recommend that E. Szabad, Capt. and A. D. C., be mustered out, his services being no longer required."—LS, DNA, RG 94, ACP, G554 CB 1865. Éméric Szabad, born in Hungary in 1822, came to the U.S. to fight in the Civil War, and was appointed capt. and aide as of June 16, 1862. Szabad later wrote "Le Général Grant," *Spectateur Militaire; Recueil de Science D'Art et D'Histoire Militaires*, series 3, X, 8–9 (15 Nov.–15 Dec., 1867),

258–75, 430–48, and a pamphlet entitled: *Le Général Grant: Président de la République Américaine* (Paris, 1868). On June 8, 1869, Szabad wrote to Secretary of War John A. Rawlins requesting permission to use War Dept. files to prepare a history of the war.—ALS, DNA, RG 94, Letters Received, 764S 1869. Permission was refused; on July 23, U.S. Senator Henry Wilson of Mass. wrote to Rawlins enclosing a letter of July 3 from Szabad to Wilson on the same subject.—ALS, *ibid.* The enclosure is *ibid.*

1865, OCT. 21. USG endorsement. "Respectfully returned to the Secretary of War. I believe that an officer can perform no better service to the Govt, if properly performed, than that proposed to be done by General McCook on the Overland Dispatch route & therefore approve his application for leave of absence."—ES, DNA, RG 94, Letters Received, 2129M 1865. Written on a letter of Oct. 20 from Maj. Gen. Alexander M. McCook, capt., 3rd Inf., to Secretary of War Edwin M. Stanton requesting a one-year leave of absence to provide security against Indians for the "Butterfields Overland Despatch Co."—LS, *ibid.* On Oct. 21, Stanton approved USG's endorsement and McCook resigned as maj. gen. as of the same day.—*Ibid.*

1865, OCT. 21, 3:00 P.M. To Maj. Gen. George G. Meade. "Adml. Farragut is not in town. I will go to Phila on Monday, and make my own arrangements for getting there. The President thinks he will not be able to go."—ALS (telegram sent), DNA, RG 107, Telegrams Collected (Bound); telegram sent, *ibid.*; copies, *ibid.*, RG 108, Letters Sent; DLC-USG, V, 46, 109. On the same day, Meade had telegraphed to USG. "I have told the managers of the Fair for disabled soldiers & sailors that you and Admiral Farragut would attend the opening of the Fair on Monday evening next, and we rely on your coming, Will you make in Washington the arrangements for a special train, or shall we do it here, & will you communicate with the Admiral at Willards? Please ~~answer reply~~ reply"—Telegram received (at 11:40 A.M.), DNA, RG 107, Telegrams Collected (Bound). On Oct. 23, Monday, USG attended the opening of the Philadelphia Fair held on behalf of soldiers and sailors. After addressing a large audience, Meade introduced USG. In response to calls for a speech, USG bowed several times, evidently having been promised that he would not be called upon to speak. William D. Lewis stated: "General Grant has held the committee strictly to their promise. He means that we should keep it."—*Philadelphia Inquirer*, Oct. 24, 1865. One item sold at the fair was a bronze medallion of USG modeled from life by Franklin Simmons.—*Ibid.*, Oct. 28, 1865.

1865, OCT. 21. S. Herbert Lancey, United Service Club, Boston, to USG. "The United Service Club of Massachusetts, an association of officers late in the Army and Navy of the United States, have already made quite a collection of books, reports, maps, charts, portraits, &c. which have reference to the late Rebellion. They now propose to organize a library association for the purpose of making it a National affair, and to place it under the same roof with 'The National Gallery of Fallen Heroes' which is now being established in this City by the munificence of Count Schwabe, a German nobleman of large fortune and generous impulses. It is proposed to secure for this Library one copy of every volume, of whatever character, all reports, pamphlets, maps, charts, engravings, portraits &c. which have any thing to do with the late struggle, whether directly or indirectly; thus bringing together, in official reports and personal observations and research, a full and reliable history of the [lat]e matter. The following name has been selected for the organization, and the following persons proposed for its officers —'THE UNITED SERVICE NATIONAL LIBRARY ASSOCIATION': President, Lt. Gen. U. S. Grant; 1st Vice Prest. Vice Admiral D. G. Farragut; 2nd Maj. Gen. Wm T: Sherman; 3d Rear Admiral D. D. Porter; 4th Maj. Gen. Phil. Sheridan; 5th Rear Admiral J. A. Dahlgren; 6th Maj. Gen. Geo. G. Meade; 7th Rear Admiral C. H. Davis; 8th Maj. Gen. O. O. Howard. Will Lt: Gen. Grant permit the use of his name in connection with this noble enterprise,— one that will constitute, when completed, a most magnificent and enduring memorial of his own successful efforts in crushing out a powerful and relentless armed Rebellion. With assurances of high regard, and with best wishes for the health, happiness and prosperity of yourself and family,"— ALS, USG 3. On Dec. 28, Lancey wrote to Bvt. Maj. Gen. Montgomery C. Meigs seeking copies of documents.—ALS, DNA, RG 92, Consolidated Correspondence, United Service National Library Association. Lancey wrote on printed stationery that listed Bvt. Lt. Gen. Winfield Scott as president, USG as a vice president, excluded Maj. Gens. George G. Meade and Oliver O. Howard, and included Maj. Gen. George H. Thomas.—*Ibid.*

1865, OCT. 24. USG endorsement. "I do not doubt that during the heat of the War much has been done under excitement, that would not otherwise have occurred I deem it advisable to clear our prisons so far as possible of prisoners for mil offences, and if deemed advisable would recommend executive clemency in this case."—Copy, DNA, RG 108, Register of Letters Received. Written on a letter of Oct. 20 from Samuel M. Bowman, former col., 84th Pa., to President Andrew Johnson concerning the case of John W. McCue.—*Ibid.* On July 20, Mrs. S. C. E. McCue, Nelson County, Va., had written to USG. "Your proverbial kindness and humanity to the soldiers of the late Confederate States, and great liberality to all, whether citizens or soldiers, recently arrayed in hostility to the government encourage me to appeal to you, and thru you to the President in a matter involving the liberty of a noble and beloved son, and my happiness for life. In June '64 my son, John Willis McCue, just after attaining the age of eighteen years, was *conscripted* into the service of the Confederate States, and shortly there after became a member of Mosby's command. On the 29th of March last, he, together with four others of the same command, in obedience to orders from their commanding Officer, proceeded, on a raid into Maryland, And at a place called Crosse in Prince George County, they, (two of the party having deserted) in an effort to get possession of the U States Post Office on the night of the 3rd of April, came in contact with four armed Detectives of that Gov'nt and the Post Master; At the first volley from the Detectives two others of my son's comrades fled leaving him alone to fight against fearful odds for his life. In the Uneaqual rencounter one of his antagonists was killed and another wounded, but he was overpowered and taken to Baltimore where on the 12th May was arraigned and tried before a military commission as a Guerrilla on the charge of Murder and sentenced to imprisonment for life in the Clinton Penetentiary N York. Now General, that the angel of Peace is again nestling her wings over our county, that for four years has been drenched in fraternal blood, and under the benign influence of the President, the prison doors are being thrown open, and the captives set free all over the land, May I not hope, that thru your instrumentality, my beloved and noble son may like wise have his shackles broken, and permitted once more to enjoy the blessings of liberty—'lie down under his own vine ang fig tree and none to make him afraid' and return to the bosom of an almost crushed and heart broken mother, whose sacred honor is pledged that henceforth he shall be an upright and law abiding citizen."—ALS, *ibid.*, Letters Received.

1865, OCT. 24. USG endorsement. "Respy. forwarded to the Secty of War with the recommendation that G. T. Beauregard be permitted to leave the United States, provided he do so within one month from the date of the permission. That the private clothing and that of his sons be returned to him, but that the tone of his application is not such as to give him a claim to the return of the semi official papers asked"—Copy, DNA, RG 108, Register of Letters Received. Written on a letter of Aug. 12 from Pierre G. T. Beauregard, New Orleans, received at USG's hd. qrs. "Incloses copies of two letters addressed on July 8, 1865 to Secty of War and Maj Gen Sherman, relative to seizure of the baggage & private papers of the said Beauregard near Athens, Ga. in May 1865 in direct opposition to terms of Military Convention of April 26, 1865. Mr. Beauregard feeling no longer secure in his property asks for permission to leave the U States."—*Ibid.* The letters of July 8 from Beauregard to Secretary of War Edwin M. Stanton and Maj. Gen. William T. Sherman (ALS and copy) are *ibid.*, RG 107, Letters Received, B2644 1865. On Oct. 15, 1866, Beauregard, Washington, D. C., wrote to USG. "On the 13th inst, I had the honor of submitting to you, verbally, my application for the return of my baggage & papers, taken possession of by a part of Genl Wilson's Cavalry, near Athens, Ga., in May 1865, after the surrender of Genl Johnston & myself at Greensboro N. C. to Genl Sherman. I beg now to submit the same statement in writing for your favorable endorsement—to be then laid before his Excellency President Johnson for his consideration & action. In April 1864, being ordered from Charleston to Virginia—I sent my two sons baggage, my own & my papers to Macon Ga. for safe keeping. After the surrender at Greensboro N. C. I ordered those effects to be sent to meet me at Atlanta or Montgomery, on my way to New Orleans—they were unfortunately met, *in transitu,* by a small force of Wilson's Cavalry, who seized them & sent them to Augusta, Ga., where they arrived after I had left that City on my return home—One of my relatives residing at Augusta, claimed them, but was referred by Brig. Genl Molineux—Comdg—to Genl Sherman. Before he could be heard from, however, a telegram was received from the Hon: Secretary of War—Mr Stanton—ordering those effects to this City, where they are still, I believe in the Bureau of Captured Archives. I have the honor respectfully to submit, that being private property accidently captured after the surrender, it should be returned to me. Among those papers, are my office copies & vouchers, letters, reports &c sent to the War Department at Richmond, & relating to my Military Department of South Carolina, Georgia & Florida—the originals were surrendered, I understand, with the other C. S. Government papers by Genl Johnston at Charlotte N. C. I do not suppose that my office copies can be claimed with any Justice by the War Department, for they fell accidently into its hands after the surrender, and they are of the same kind as Genls. Lee, Johnston, Bragg, Kirby Smith, Hood &c, &c, have been allowed to keep since their surrender. Should the Government desire, however, copies of those office papers of mine, they could be sent to Genl Sheridan at New Orleans, to be copied & then returned to me."—Copies, *ibid.*, RG 94, Letters Received, 1521S 1865; (2—one marked "Null") DLC-Pierre G. T. Beauregard. On Nov. 14, Maj. Gen. Philip H. Sheridan wrote to Bvt. Brig. Gen. Edward D. Townsend stating that he had returned to Beauregard his personal baggage forwarded by the War Dept.—LS, DNA, RG 94, Letters Received, 1521S 1865. Beauregard's papers, however, were not returned.—*Ibid.* In 1867, Beauregard renewed efforts to reclaim his papers, but on Dec. 3, Townsend informed him that USG, secretary of war *ad interim*, declined to reverse an earlier decision of Oct. 22 not to return the papers.—ADfS, *ibid.* See T. Harry Williams, *P. G. T. Beauregard: Napoleon in Gray* (Baton Rouge, 1955), p. 259.

1865, OCT. 24.   Maj. Gen. John Pope, St. Louis, to USG. "Gen Curtiss of the Indian Commission telegraphs from Fort Sully as follows,   Chief of Minneconygrs Sioux for themselves & ten others tribes met us here on fifth   they want peace & sign articles for themselves & take copy for other tribes including Cheynnes & Arapas to Sign. The Sioux & several other tribes have also come in. They all complain of our encroachments on their hunting grounds & our lines of emigration through their buffalo grounds but they want peace. They say it is difficult however to restrain their young men & our troops must therefore continue on the Plains & be on the alert but please notice any efforts of Chiefs to present these papers if they emanate from this Commission   Signed S R CURTIS,   The young men of the Cheynnes are committing some depredations on the ꝑPlatte route on their way south."—Telegram received (at 7:35 P.M.), DNA, RG 107, Telegrams Collected (Bound); *ibid.*, RG 108, Telegrams Received; copy, DLC-USG, V, 54. *O.R.*, I, xlviii, part 2, 1243.

1865, OCT. 25. To Secretary of War Edwin M. Stanton. "I would respectfully recommend that so much of General Orders, No 135, as musters-out of the Volunteer Service, Brev't Maj. General Cuvier Grover, be revoked, and that his name be put upon the next list for muster out."—LS, DNA, RG 94, ACP, 448 1871. On Sept. 9, Maj. Cuvier Grover, 3rd Inf., Washington, D. C., had written to Bvt. Col. Theodore S. Bowers protesting his muster out as brig. gen. and bvt. maj. gen. of vols. as of Aug. 24 because officers of lesser distinction had been retained in rank.—ALS, *ibid.* No action followed.

1865, OCT. 25, 12:50 P.M. To Maj. Gen. George H. Thomas. "If you can spare them I wish you would discharge the 33d & 47th Ill. regiments. The proportion of volunteers from Ill. is much larger than from any other state."—ALS (telegram sent), DNA, RG 107, Telegrams Collected (Bound); telegram sent, *ibid.*; copies, *ibid.*, RG 108, Letters Sent; *ibid.*, RG 393, Military Div. of the Tenn., Telegrams Received; DLC-USG, V, 46, 109. On Nov. 1, 3:50 P.M., USG telegraphed to Thomas. "Can you not give up Cumberland Gap as a Military post and thereby break up the great expense of transportation from Camp Nelson. The latter place could then be abandoned or turned over to the Freedman's Bureau."—ALS (telegram sent), DNA, RG 107, Telegrams Collected (Bound); telegram sent, *ibid.*; copies, *ibid.*, RG 108, Letters Sent; (misdated Oct. 31) *ibid.*, RG 393, Military Div. of the Tenn., Telegrams Received; DLC-USG, V, 46, 109. On Nov. 2, Thomas, Nashville, telegraphed to USG. "I had given the order to break up Cumberland Gap before I went North and reitereted the order on the thirtieth (30) at ‡Louisville also to reduce Camp Nelson to a mere Garrison. I will take measure to have it transferred to the freedmens Bureau will order forty seventh Ill Vols mustered out The thirty third is not in my command unless on duty in Mississippi from which department I have not yet received any returns"—Telegram received (at 7:00 P.M.), DNA, RG 107, Telegrams Collected (Bound); *ibid.*, RG 108, Telegrams Received; copies, *ibid.*, RG 393, Military Div. of the Tenn., Telegrams Sent; DLC-USG, V, 54.

1865, OCT. 25. USG endorsement. "With reference to claim of Wm. J. Morris for services rendered as scout states that Morris was employed by him as a scout in 1863 for which services he was paid, since which time he knows nothing of him"—DNA, RG 94, Register of Letters Received. On Dec. 11, 1876, W. J. Morris, Pocahontas, Ill., wrote to USG. "I will inform you that there are guns and amunition being shiped to South Carelina That I suppose you alredy Know But there are somthing you donot Kow or at least evry precaution is taken to Keep you in the dark There are to assemble in Washington D. C. a sufficient mumber of men to forcably Inaugrate sam Tilden They are to come a few at a time and as far as you or any one [c]an see unarmed the arms are to be near by and ready for use when the time comes Now for the reasons that I know the above to be true I heard it fully arranged by men who semed to fully understand what they sed when at Washington a few days ago. you may say that if it was to be a secret how was it that I was made acquainted with the facts you Know that during the war I was a spy and as the Signs and pass words of the Nights of the Golden Circle was indespenciple to me I acquired them from a friend and as the present organisation of the White liners are substantially the same and as I was in the South when it was organised and wishing to Know whether it was all rite or not I made myself acquainted with it and that is the reason I can inform you of the facts and the same reason and the same Sign will allow me to enter the Gallery of the House when I failed without on the first day of the session When the Democracy first gained a majority in the house in 64. It was strongly talked by the White Liners, to assasinate you and all that saved it was the Senat being in the way. act as you please but I would be in danger if this was Known and as I am a pore man I donot want to be assasinated and leave my helpless family"—ALS, *ibid.*, RG 60, Letters from the President.

1865, OCT. 27. USG endorsement. "Respectfully returned to the Secretary of War, with the report that I have no distinct recollection or knowledge of the within case. If Colonel Jefferson forced the bank guard and entered it, the fact was not reported to me at the time—else I should have have the matter investigated and proper record made of the same. The bank was not entered by my knowledge or order, but if Col. Jefferson has properly turned over the assets of the bank to the U S Treasury, the Gov't. would be responsible for it to the claimants, otherwise it seems to me that the parties must have recourse for remedy against Col. Jefferson."—ES, DNA, RG 94, Letters Received, 1891G 1865. Written on a letter of Oct. 10 from Joshua and Thomas Green, Jackson, Miss., to Secretary of War Edwin M. Stanton requesting the restoration of assets taken from their bank by USG's forces during the occupation of Jackson, May 14–16, 1863.—LS, *ibid.* On Jan. 30, 1866, John W. Jefferson, former col., 8th Wis., endorsed this letter. "Respectfully returned, allegations set forth in the Greens' letter, resolutly *denied*—so far as relates to forcing the Guard &c. The Guard was placed there, as well as elsewhere about the city, by my orders, I presume that Genl Grant knew nothing about Greens' Bank or its rebel deposits. More important matters occupied his Mind, I acted in this matter under Orders from my immediate superior, Brigr Genl Mower—Mily Govr & Com'd'r of the city & he recd his Orders—he informed me—from Maj Genl Sherman, I am pleased to learn of the Ever loyalty of the Greens'. It seems strange however, that it was necessary for them to take the Oath of allegience, & be *Pardoned* (for What? Loyalty?) by his Excellency President Johnson, It Pains me to know that the Greens' large 'Cotton Goods Manufactory' valued at from Two Hundred to 200 Hundred & fifty thousand Dollars, was destroyed thro' my Orders, by orders recd from Staff Officers Rawlins, & Willson—*now* Majr Genls,—in consequence of its continued use for Manufactoring Goods for Rebels in Arms against the Govt, together with Eleven Million Dolls worth of like property, of other parties, for like offences, destroyed during the Two & half days I was Prov Mar at Jackson Miss. Attention is respectfully called to my return of date June 30th 1863, addressed & mailed to Q- M- Genl, Maj Genl Meigs Washington D- C, Enclosing my *Voucher*, Signed by Lt Col J. Condit Smith, chief Q- M. 15th A- C. dated at Walnut Hills Miss June 9th 1863, for sunds turned over to him by me, Among which there were, One, One thousand Dollar U, S, Texas Bond & Coupons; Twenty nine Dolls in old & odd Gold & Silver coins; (Valuables) & from One Hundred & fifty to Two Hundred thousand Dolls in, the so-called confederate Bonds, certificates for Bonds, Brand new confe'd, Bank Bills, cut Bank Bills &c (Worthless) Request that the Lt General be shown this, paper."—AES, *ibid.* On May 3, USG again endorsed this letter. "Respectfully returned to the Secretary of War. I have no doubt of the entire correctness of Col. Jefferson's endorsement of his action while provost marshal of the city of Jackson, including that in the matter of this bank and disposition of its assets. While I stated in my endorsement hereon of date Oct. 27. 65 'I have no distinct recollection or knowledge of the within case' I should have added, and do so now with pleasure, that so far as I had knowledge of Lt Col. Jefferson's acts as provost marshal of Jackson, Miss., they had my approval, and the orderly and efficient manner in which he executed his orders merits special commendation."—ES, *ibid.* The Greens later made a substantial claim for the destruction of their cottonmill at Jackson as well as the assets seized from the bank which was disallowed. See *HRC*, 43-1-376; *ibid.*, 43-2-5; *Memoirs*, I, 507; *O.R.*, I, xxiv, part 1, 754.

1865, OCT. 28. Maj. Gen. John Pope (with Maj. Gen. William T. Sherman's approval), St. Louis, to USG. "An experienced & active quartermaster is greatly needed at Fort Leavenworth to take charge of the quartermasters Department at that place—Col Potter though a good & faithful officer I do not think has experience enough of Service on the plains & of the management of such a Depot with economy & efficiency. Col & Bvt Brig General Wm Myers is admirably qualified & I request that in view the great public interests Confcentrated at Leavenworth He be placed in charge of that Depot. I have no doubt that Greater economy & more efficiency would follow the depot at St Louis is less difficult to manage & is really much less important as it can constantly be overlooked to by Chief q m of the Dep't. & some other officer can be placed in charge of it."—Telegram received (at 3:20 P.M.), DNA, RG 107, Telegrams Collected (Bound); *ibid.*, RG 108, Telegrams Received; *ibid.*, Letters Received; copies, *ibid.*, RG 92, Letters Received from Hd. Qrs.; DLC-USG, V, 54. On Nov. 6, Bvt. Maj. Gen. Montgomery C. Meigs endorsed this telegram. "Respectfully returned to the Lieutenant General, Commanding, Armies of the United States. Colonel Joseph A. Potter has rendered faithful and efficient services as Depot Quartermaster at Chicago and at Fort Leavenworth. At the time he went to Fort Leavenworth, he was without experience in the business of the Plains and the Quartermaster General would not have ordered him there. He was assigned to duty as Depot Quartermaster at Fort Leavenworth by the express order of the late President Lincoln, himself, who made the selection and gave the order that Capt Hodges should be relieved and Colonel. Potter assigned to duty in his place He has since that time gained experience and knowledge which are especially valuable at that post. I cannot recommend a change at present."—ES, DNA, RG 108, Letters Received; *ibid.*, RG 92, Miscellaneous Letters Sent (Press).

1865, OCT. 30.   Petition of Thomas G. Foster, collector of customs, and sixty-nine others, St. Augustine, Fla., to USG. "The Under signed Citizens of the United States and inhabitants of St Augustine, have heard with profound regret that the Companies of the 7th U. S. Infantry at present in Garrison at this Post, are to be withdrawn and two companies of Colored troops are to replace them. We beg leave respectfully to represent that this change and Substitution of Colored troops for white, will exert a most baleful effect upon the prospects of our Town—We are poor and without any resources except what are found among ourselves, occasionaly encreased and aided by the coming among us of Strangers from the North, in Search of the renovation of health, and to escape the rigour of a northern winter. This source will be entirely cut off by the establishment of a negro Garrison in our midst.—We say in our midst, for Fort ~~Moultrie~~ Marion and St Frances Barracks are situated in the heart of our Town, and the troops garrisoning those positions, are necessarily, and must be (no matter under what discipline,) continually among its inhabitants. A very large portion of our white inhabitants are women and children—we have an unusually large negro population, with a constantly encreasing influx of colored people among us, and the presence of a negro garrison will aid in calling together an added supply of these people. We will not speak of the encrease of crime and immorality which may be thus introduced. It is useless to pretend to conceal it, but negroes will be negroes. With the expression of our conviction, that the multitude of people from the northern States who have already made arrangements to make St Augustine their winter residence, and many others who might be attracted hitherward, will be almost totally kept away by the substitution of a negro for a white garrison of this Post, we beg leave to enclose you copy of a letter addressed to General Gillmore from citizens of this place on the 22d of May ~~last~~ 1864. The reasons therein against the occupancy of the Town by negro troops, remain yet in equal force."—DS, DNA, RG 108, Letters Received; (no signatures) *ibid.*, RG 393, Dept. of Fla., Letters Received.

1865, OCT. 30.   Isaac F. Quinby, Rochester, N. Y., to USG. "In reply to my letter of the 30th of September last Colonel Badeau writes by your direction that if possible you will place Col Gardner, my father-in-law on duty. I now write to say that the state of Colonel G's health is such that he feels it necessary to pass the winter months in a more southern latitude than this and he proposes to leave Rochester in a few days for Tarrytown on the Hudson River to leave from there for a point Still further South Should the rigor of the winter there prove too severe for him. He and I would feel under great obligation to you could you find a place in which his services would be of value to the Govt and where the climate would not be too severe for him, but if this prove impracticable during the winter I trust that you may be able to gratify him next Spring— . . . P. S. My Colleague Dr Cutting informs me that he wrote you in my behalf a few days since and begs that you will not consider him presumptuous in so doing"—ALS, PHi. On Nov. 4, Bvt. Col. Ely S. Parker wrote to Bvt. Brig. Gen. Edward D. Townsend. "Please issue an order that Colonel John L. Gardner, 2d U S Artillery (a retired officer) report to the Comdg. Officer, Dept. of South Carolina, with instructions that he be assigned to the command of one of the permanent forts in that Department. It is respectfully suggested that many, if not all, of the retired officers, on account of their large experience in the service, would be excellent men to put in command of the permanent fortifications at the south, the recommendation is therefore made that they be ordered to such duty when deemed necessary."—ALS, DNA, RG 94, Letters Received, 1190A 1865.

1865, Oct. 31. Lt. Commander James W. Shirk, Philadelphia, to USG. "The copies of two letters enclosed will explain themselves, Since mine was written I have heard that the persons who signed the one to which mine is an answer, intend to make a request direct to you, for a favorable consideration of their claim for extra pay or compensation for work done by them on the disabled transports, I suspect that some land-shark of a claim agent is inciting them to this proceeding, and if they do write you, I want you to know that I have had no hand in it. The work was not voluntary on their part but they did the work under orders from me, instructed by Rear Admiral Porter, and was as much in their line of duty as if they had been repairing the vessel to which they belonged, of which, they had enough to do after the fight at Grand Gulf, as you yourself can bear witness. I must do Mr Hartuper the justice to say that *he* will not make any claim, as he has informed me that the letter purporting to have been signed by him was written while he was absent from home."—ALS, USG 3. The enclosures are *ibid.*

1865, Nov. 1. To Secretary of State William H. Seward. "I have the honor to forward for your perusal the Prospectus of the Mexican Express Co. forming in New York City for the undoubted purpose of aiding the Imperial Government of that Country and also ~~send~~ some slips taken from the New York papers throwing some light upon the subject. Your particular attention is respectfully called to the article taken from the New York Courier des Etats Unis."—Copies, DLC-USG, V, 46, 109; DNA, RG 108, Letters Sent. On the same day, Seward wrote to USG. "I have the honor to acknowledge the receipt of your letter of this date, enclosing for my perusal the Prospectus of the Mexican Express Company forming in NewYork City, and the three slips taken from NewYork papers, throwing some light upon the operations of that Company with the view of aiding the, so-called, imperial government of Mexico. In reply, I have the honor to state that the proper measures have been adopted by this Department to prevent a violation of the laws of the United States and the existing treaty stipulations, between the United States and the Mexican Republic. In this connection, I transmit, for your information, a copy of my note to Señor Romero, of this date, upon the same subject, a copy of which has also been forwarded to C. A. Seward, Esqre, of NewYork. You will be pleased to accept my thanks for the information communicated by you to this Department."—LS, USG 3. See *HED*, 39-1-1, part 3, pp. 570–73; *ibid.*, 39-1-38.

1865, Nov. 1. USG endorsement. "Respectfully returned to the Secretary of War, with the request that the following endorsement be submitted to the Secretary of the Treasury.—Mrs Ann Lum was throughout the war an eminently loyal woman. Her house, which was a very fine one, was torn down and the grounds around it destroyed, it being in the new lines of fortifications constructed by our engineers. It is therefore respectfully recommended that the money paid by Mrs. Lum for rent be refunded to her, and that the Treasury Agent at Vicksburg be instructed that hereafter she is allowed to occupy her house free of rent."—ES, DNA, RG 56, Div. of Captured and Abandoned Property, Letters Received. Written on a letter of June 28 from Mrs. Ann Lum, Vicksburg, to Maj. Gen. Peter J. Osterhaus calling attention to safeguards from USG and Maj. Gen. James B. McPherson and stating ". . . In Consequence as aforesaid of the necessity of her residence being torn down and in Conformity with the Assignment she did move into and take the peaceable possession of the Residence so Assigned to her until about the first of October 1864, when She was notified by T. C. Callecott Asst spcl Agent of the Treasury Dept that the property occupied by her was abandoned property and She would have to pay rent therefore at the rate of Forty Dollars per month or vacate the House. And notwithstanding she exhibited the safe Guard given her by Genrl Grant and the Assignment Free of rent by Order of General McPherson, and insisted that they should be respected, as she was not recieving any remuneration whatever from the Government for the destruction of her late residence or the ground on which it had stood Still he insisted and Compeled her to take out a lease for said property at the rate of Forty Dollars per Month which Sum she has been Compeled to pay monthly ever Since, excepting for the present month (June), she was charged thirty Dollars which she has paid, making the Total paid for rent up to this time, three Hundred and fifty ($350 00) Dollars The reciepts for which she now holds in her possession in addition to which she has been Compeled to pay as a street Gas Tax the Sum of Seventy four & 25/100 Dollars. She therefore earnestly asks and prays you to interfere in her behalf that as she is not recieving any rent from the Government for the property of her late residence, that an order may be issued & executed releasing her from having to pay rent for the property where she now lives. Also that the amounts which she has already paid may be paid back to her and such other & further relief may be extended to her as in justice and the facts in the case may seem proper and equitable"—LS, *ibid.* See *PUSG*, 9, 77*n*–78*n*; *ibid.*, 13, 499.

1865, Nov. 1. USG endorsement. "Approved for brevet lieutenant-colonel for faithful and meritorious services during the war."—ES, DNA, RG 94, ACP, 1047 1877. Written on a letter of Sept. 3 from Maj. Gen. William T. Sherman, St. Louis, to Secretary of War Edwin M. Stanton recommending Capt. Asher R. Eddy, q. m., for bvt. promotion.—Copy, *ibid.* On Dec. 16, U.S. Representative John W. Leftwich of Tenn. wrote to President Andrew Johnson stating that Eddy had been unfairly treated in his bvt. promotion.—ALS, *ibid.* On Jan. 9, 1866, Bvt. Maj. Gen. Montgomery C. Meigs endorsed this letter. "Respectfully returned to the Lieutenant General Commanding Armies U. S. The Quartermaster-General has not recommended the brevet promotion of Capt. A. R. Eddy, A. Q M."—ES, *ibid.* On Jan. 12, USG endorsed this letter. "No further action recommended."—ES, *ibid.* On March 21, USG wrote to Stanton. "I would respectfully recommend that Capt. and Bvt. Lt. Col. A. R. Eddy, A. Q. M. be Breveted to the rank of Colonel in the Regular Army."—ALS, *ibid.*, G97 CB 1866.

1865, Nov. 1. Bvt. Brig. Gen. Cyrus B. Comstock to Maj. Gen. Henry W. Halleck. "The Lieutenant General requests that you will forward to these Headquarters as soon as practicable maps showing the position of all military posts in each of your Depts. which it is proposed to retain for the present, and that hereafter any changes which occur be reported at the time"—Copies, DLC-USG, V, 46, 109; DNA, RG 108, Letters Sent. On Dec. 8, Halleck wrote to USG providing a long narrative report concerning posts in his dept.—LS, *ibid.*, Letters Received. *O.R.*, I, l, part 2, 1290–93. On Jan. 13, 1866, USG endorsed an extract from the first portion of this letter recommending that a U.S. Navy steamship patrol Puget Sound. "Respectfully forwarded to the Secrety of War, with the recommendation that it be brought to the attention of the Navy Department."—ES, DNA, RG 108, Letters Received.

On Jan. 15, Brig. Gen. Richard Delafield wrote to USG. "I have the honor to acknowledge the reference, for remarks, from the Headquarters Armies U. S., of an extract from a communication of Maj-General Halleck, Com'd'g Mil. Div. of the Pacific, Dec. 8, 1865, suggesting a Board of Engineers to select sites for permanent fortifications on the Pacific Coast. On the 7th Sept. '65, the Engineer Department selected many sites in Washington Territory that the President was requested to have reserved from sale by the Land Office. On the 5th Dec. 65, I requested that Bvt. Lieut. Colonel Williamson, then assigned to duty on the staff of General Mc-

Dowell, should report to me, and that Lieut. Wm H. Heuer, just then transferred to the Corps of Engineers, should report to Colonel Williamson, in
order that I might assign the latter to making surveys of the several designated sites, that the proper ones be permanently reserved, and others restored for sale by the Land Office. The Department regrets not being enabled to command the services of Colonel Williamson or other officers to
put on this duty. There are several points about the city of San Francisco
that must be surveyed to establish their fitness for military purposes, for
which duty I have no officer whose services can be commanded. To succeed
to the superintendence and responsibilities lately in charge of General De
Russy, another officer is necessary. His death, and that of Colonels Graham
and Bowman, the resignation of Majors Palfrey and Turnbull, and the absence on detached duty of four Lieut. Colonels, six Majors, and eight Captains, render it impracticable for this Department to cause the public interest and welfare to be properly cared for,—one particular being the service
referred to by General Halleck. This Department will not lose sight of the
defenses of the Pacific Coast, and will give it all the attention in its power.
In relation to the three sites referred to by General Halleck as expedient to
abandon at this time, I would request that military possession be held until
surveys can be made and a selection made of the most advantageous sites
for *military purposes*."—ALS, *ibid.*

1865, Nov. 1.   Miss Flora F. Kelley, Washington, D. C., to USG. "I am
truly grateful to you for your kindness in the *past* to me, and the kind consideration you treated my Uncles claim two days since. May I ask the favor
of you to treat my Mothers claim likewise, so far as the Quartermasters
and Commissary Stores are conserned. I will send South for farther proof
respecting the quantity of Cotton my Mother had when your army came in,
as there is evidently an error in the opinion of your informer, or myself,
respecting the quantity she had. When we were bereft of every thing even
to the sustinance of life, our family prostrated with illness, it was then I
petitioned to Genl Sherman for help, he promised me 10 bales of Cotton,
Genl. Sherman's Quartermaster told me to go to you, and ask you for 53
bales, which I did, I was afraid to ask for more, for fear I would not get
any. You gave me the order for 53 bales, I received 44—The ballance of
the 80 bales, is yet due my Mother, It was taken as I am informed to
build brest works at Big Black Bridge, but I will send and get farther proofs
of the quantity. I put the full 80 bales, in the petition, my Mother has when
your army came in, not knowing whether it would be your pleasure to have
the 53 bales, you gave me an order for, deducted, from this amount my
Mother had, or whether it was a present to me from you of captured Cotton
It is for you to decide   Remember Genl, this Cotton and the few Quarter
master & commissary Stores is all that stands between my Mother and
want, with all its accompaning sorrows, and deprivations, we have no
land, our negros being freed by the Gov, we are left with nothing, except
what your sense of justice see's proper to allow us in these claims. This a full

explanation of the Cotton; You will please excuse me for begging your perusal of it, as when I am in your presence I cannot command language to express myself, your time is generally so limited."—ALS, DNA, RG 108, Letters Received. Miss Kelley enclosed a list of damages to Mrs. Elmira J. Kelley's plantation in Warren County, Miss., near the Big Black River Bridge, endorsed on Sept. 23 by Maj. Gen. William T. Sherman, St. Louis. "Respectfully referred to the Congress of the United States that alone has power to appropriate money for such purposes. I know of my own Knowledge nothing of the merits of this Claim and simply refer it to the proper authorities"—AES, *ibid.* On Jan. 11, Miss Kelley, Evanston, Ill., had written to President Abraham Lincoln stating that USG and Sherman had given her and her mother a pass to go north, that her mother had returned to Miss. to protect her property, and she requested a pass to rejoin her mother. —ALS, *ibid.*, RG 109, Union Provost Marshals' File of Papers Relating to Individual Citizens. Mrs. Kelley's claim of $8,090 in damages to her plantation was disallowed.—*HMD*, 44-1-30, p. 22.

1865, Nov. 2.   USG endorsement. "Respectfully forwarded to Secretary of War. In my opinion in receiving the paroles of the officers and soldiers of the rebel armies, the United States guaranteed them on condition of surrender and return to their homes freedom from molestation by the United States for all previous warlike acts of theirs not in violation of the laws of war, until exchanged. I would accordingly recommend the publication of an order announcing this so as to relieve paroled prisoners from annoyance by local U. S. authorities."—ES, DNA, RG 107, Letters Received from Bureaus. Written on a letter of Oct. 30 from Alfred E. Jackson, former C.S.A. brig. gen., Washington Springs, Va., to USG. "I would respectfully represent that I held the rank of Brigr General in the Provisional Army of the Confederate States, and by assignment, belonged to the Army of Tennessee, commanded by Genl Jos E. Johnston, but for some time prior to the surrender of the Confederate forces, in consequence of physical disability, had been doing light duty in the Departments of S. W. Va & E Tenne then commanded by Brigr Genl John Echols. Upon the disbanding of his command, which occured immediately after the surrender of Genl Lees Army, I returned to this place where my family had been temporarily sojourning for some months—After quietly remaining here for some time I went to Lynchburg Va then the most accessable Military Post for the purpose of surrendering myself as a prisoner of War (being without any organised Command)—On the 1st June I was paroled & took the Amnesty Oath prescribed by Presdent Lincoln in proclamation of Decr 8th 1863— By the terms of this parole I was permitted to return to my home in Jonesboro E Tenn. there to remain undisturbed but before I could arrange for the return of my family, I learned I had been indicted in the Federal Court held at Knoxville Tenne on a Charge of Treason and by order of one high in authority in Tenne with very many others, had been indicted for Treason against the State in the State Courts—These Indictments added to the bitter

& vindictive spirit prevailing in East Tenn against all Rebels have prevented my return.—~~Shortly af~~ On the 25th June I transmitted to President Joh[n]son a certified copy of the Oath I had taken and asked to be specially pardoned but up to this time am not advised of any action having been taken upon My application My purpose General in addressing you & thus detailing my participation in the late Rebellion and my subsequent Action is to ascertain if the parole given me by one of your subordinate Officers does not secure me against arrest & trial for Treason in any of the U. States Courts—and if so respectfully to ask that you will cause such orders to issue as will protect me against molestation by any U. S. authorities (Civil or Military) on account of my participation in the rebellion—at least pending the action by the President on my application for special pardon—and that you will direct protection papers to be forwarded to me at the earliest practicable Moment Hoping that this Communication suggested by Genl. Jos. E. Johnson may receive your early attention"—ALS, *ibid.* On Nov. 2, Bvt. Brig. Gen. Cyrus B. Comstock wrote to Jackson. "Lieut. Gen. Grant desires me to say that your letter has been forwarded to the Sec. of War with the recommendation that an order be issued announcing that paroled prisoners of War under the terms of Lee's surrender are not liable to molestation from U. S. Authorities for acts previous to their paroles, not in violation of the laws of war."—Copies, DLC-USG, V, 46, 109; DNA, RG 108, Letters Sent.

1865, Nov. 2. To Virginia Paine Grant, New York. "I shall not go to New York this week. What hour will you reach Washington?"—ALS (telegram sent), DNA, RG 107, Telegrams Collected (Unbound).

1865, Nov. 3. USG endorsement. "Respectfully referred to the Secy of War.—I know nothing of the circumstances under which Lt. K. D. Taggard, 2d N. Y. M't'd Rifles was dismissed the service. The war being ended, however, I would recommend the revocation of par. 23, S. O. 344, dismissing him; and that he be honorably discharged from the same date if there were not circumstances attending his case making such a course entirely inadmissible. I make this recommendation on the same principle that I now recommend pardon to all who can properly receive it, and especially to those who have fought on the side of the Union."—ES, DNA, RG 94, Vol. Service Div., Letters Received, T793 (VS) 1865. Written on a letter of Aug. 3 from five officers, 2nd N. Y. Mounted Rifles, to Maj. Thomas M. Vincent, AGO, requesting the reinstatement of 1st Lt. Kleber D. Taggard, 2nd N. Y. Mounted Rifles, who had been dismissed as of June 30 for drunkenness. —ALS, *ibid.*

1865, Nov. 3, 10:10 A.M. To Maj. Gen. John Pope, St. Louis. "You can detail such officers from your command as are necessary for Staff duty in excess of what is allowed by orders. Inspectors appointed in each district can report to the Inspector retained at your Hd Qrs."—ALS (telegram sent),

DNA, RG 107, Telegrams Collected (Bound); telegram sent, *ibid.*; copies
(dated Nov. 5), *ibid.*, RG 108, Letters Sent; DLC-USG, V, 46, 109. On
Oct. 18, Pope had written to USG. "I have the honor to state that Order No.
141. designating the Staff Officers for Department Commanders does not
leave me officers enough to do the business at these Head Quarters, nor elsewhere in the Department. It is to be remarked that this Department is more
than eight times as large as most other Departments and much more than
twice as large as the largest; that it embraces the whole theatre of all active
Military operations west of the Mississippi, except Texas, and includes as
Districts what were several Military Departments in time of peace before
the War. In addition there are, at these Head Quarters the Records of thirty
years. The Records of all the regimental organizations in the West for
nearly four years past are here; Rolls, Discharges, and letters on every di-
scription of the immense business transacted here for the last four years. I
could not answer the calls for information made on me from Washington
alone with the Staff Officers allowed me in the Order referred to. An Inspector General travelling without intermission an entire year could not in
that time visit all the Military posts in the Department—scarcely, indeed,
the Head Quarters of Districts. New Mexico, just added to the Department
as a District, has always been a Military Department—Utah, the same.
Under present orders, the requisitions for each separate post in all this vast
region must be sent to the Chief Quartermaster here direct for revision. It
is impossible that he can decide upon the necessity of requisitions. In fact, it
would be difficult for him to consolidate them without other business. The
same may be said of the Chief commissary and Medical Director. I trust that
you will make an exception of this Department in the Order in question. I
need at least three Officers of the Adjutant General's Department; at least
two Asst. Inspectors General; and, at least, three other officers on duty in
the various offices here. I also need a Quartermaster and Commissary in
most of the Districts to act as Chief Q. M. or C. S. of the District, and in
addition, take charge of any Depôt in his District. Such officers especially
are needed in New Mexico, Utah and Minnesota. I hope you will leave to
my discretion the number of officers to be kept on duty at these Head Quarters, being assured that I will not keep a man I can dispense with. I have
three Aides; but, they are in charge of branches of the office here, and perform no duties of Aides. An officer of Rank in the Adjutant General's Department ought to be here.—I suggest Colonel and Bvt. Brigadier General
Kelton. St. Louis is the Head Quarters of nearly the entire business of the
Army in the West—the Depot of nearly all the Records. There is as much
army business here probably as in nearly all the other Departments combined. I have the honor, therefore, to ask respectfully that Order No. 141.
be suspended as far as this Department is concerned, at least for the present."—LS, DNA, RG 108. Letters Received. On Nov. 1, Pope telegraphed
to USG. "will you please inform me what action if any has been taken on
my letter of eighteenth (18) ulto in relation in to staff officers? It is really
not possible for me to do business of such a Dept as this with the staff pre-

scribed in Gen order no one forty one"—Telegram received (at 4:35 P.M.), *ibid.*, RG 107, Telegrams Collected (Bound); *ibid.*, RG 108, Telegrams Received; copy, DLC-USG, V, 54.

On Dec. 12, Pope wrote to USG. "I learn by orders, received here, that Major Sherburne, Assist. Adjt. Genl. has been ordered to report to me for duty. I respectfully ask, that Order No 141, fixing the Staff of Department and District Commanders, be modified in the case of this Department.—It now embraces what were three military Departments before the War and involves a quantity and variety of business, unknown to any other Department. I cannot detail Officers of regiments, serving in the Department, for duty at these Head Quarters, 1st because of the regular troops, sent here, there is only one Officer to a Company,—2nd that I cannot take Captains from their Companies, without leaving Companies in Command of boys without military education or experience and I cannot detail Lieutenants for important Staff duties because of this very fact. I really need here not less than three Officers of the Adjutant Generals Department, one Inspector, one Engineer Officer, to Compile maps and keep the official maps constantly up to the reports and sketches of the Country every day sent in from the Plains,—to the Government and the Country as well as to the military authorities, these services of an Engineer Officer are invaluable. I have now but one Assist. Adjt. Genl. and I really find it impracticable to do the business of this Dept. with only one. I would respectfully ask also for one Adjutant General for each of the following Districts, the Head Quarters of Genl. Dodge, for the District of New Mexico, for the District of Nebraska, and for the District of the Upper Missouri. I think you know General, that I would not ask for these Officers, unless their services were actually necessary and I trust you will accept my view of the necessity. I send this letter direct as General Sherman is in Arkansas and expects to be absent two or three weeks."—Copies, DNA, RG 393, Dept. of the Mo., Letters Sent; *ibid.*, Military Div. of the Miss., Letters Received. Maj. Gen. William T. Sherman endorsed this letter. "read & approved"—AES (undated), *ibid.* On Dec. 18, Bvt. Col. Theodore S. Bowers endorsed this letter. "The A G. will please notify General Pope Comdg. Departmt of Missouri that he is specially authorized to retain Brevet Col Bell and Maj Swain A A G. for the present; and that the other recommendations in this communication are disapproved"—Copy, DLC-USG, V, 58. On the same day, Bvt. Col. Horace Porter wrote to U.S. Representative James A. Garfield of Ohio. "I laid the case, we were speaking of this morning, before the General, and he has consented to make this an exception to his order, and arrange it so that Swain can be retained on Gen. Pope's Staff."—ALS, Merlin E. Sumner, Schaumburg, Ill. On Nov. 24, Pope had written to Bvt. Brig. Gen. Edward D. Townsend concerning retention of staff officers.—LS, DNA, RG 94, ACP, P688 CB 1865. On Dec. 22, USG endorsed this letter. "On the 12th inst. a similar application from Gen Pope was sent to the A G O. from these Headquarters, with directions to notify Gen. Pope that he would be allowed to retain Bvt Col. Bell and Major Swaim, Asst Adjt Genls of Volunteers for the present; and to inform him further that his request that Asst Adjutant Generals be assigned to the several districts in his command was disapproved."—ES, *ibid.*

1865, Nov. 4. To Secretary of War Edwin M. Stanton. "I respectfully request that the name of Bvt Maj. Kilbourn Knox 13th Infy may be added to the list of recommendations for brevets sent in to you a day or two ago, for a brevet Lt. Colonelcy for the war."—LS, DLC-Edwin M. Stanton.

1865, Nov. 4. [USG] endorsement. "Respectfully forwarded to Secretary of War, and recommended."—ES (unsigned), DNA, RG 94, ACP, 5556 1875; copy (marked "not forwd, held back for the present."), *ibid.*, RG 108, Register of Letters Received. Written on a letter of Sept. 8 from Bvt. Maj. Gen. Edward Hatch, Knoxville, Tenn., to USG. "I Wish to enter the Regular, or standing Army of the United States. From inclination, Study and four years active service, believe I am qualified, having served in every capacity up to the present grade, beginning with a musket, have never had evidence of disapprobation from my commanding officers, on the contrary have been repeatedly mentioned in general orders Should you think me worthy of some position, and can recommend to one for which I am capable, you will greatly oblige . . ."—ALS, *ibid.*, RG 94, ACP, 5556 1875. On Jan. 10, 1866, U.S. Representative Hiram Price of Iowa and three others wrote to Secretary of War Edwin M. Stanton recommending Hatch for an appointment in the U.S. Army.—ALS, *ibid.* On Jan. 16, USG endorsed this letter. "Col. Hatch has been one of the most active and efficient Cavalry Officers in service. I most heartily recommend him for a Field Officer of Cavalry on the reorganization of the Army."—AES, *ibid.* Hatch was appointed col., 9th Cav., as of July 28.

1865, Nov. 6. Bvt. Maj. Gen. Montgomery C. Meigs endorsement. "Respectfully forwd to Lt Gen Grant for his information I fear that this command is in danger of great suffering. Capt Turnley is an experienced officer & will do what is possible"—AES, DNA, RG 92, Miscellaneous Letters Sent (Press). Written on a letter of Oct. 17 from Capt. Parmenas T. Turnley, q. m., stating that 900 cav. en route to Utah had been improperly supplied. —*Ibid.* On Oct. 23, Turnley, Denver, Colorado Territory, wrote to Meigs stating that Brig. Gen. Patrick E. Connor had mismanaged the campaign against Indians.—Copy, *ibid.*, RG 108, Letters Received. On Nov. 13, Meigs endorsed this letter. "This copy of a letter from Capt Turnley asst Qurmaster is respectfully forwarded to the Lieutenant General"—AES, *ibid.* On Nov. 20, Bvt. Col. Theodore S. Bowers forwarded this letter to Maj. Gen. William T. Sherman.—*Ibid.*, Register of Letters Received.

1865, Nov. 8. To Secretary of War Edwin M. Stanton. "In the appointments about being made in the regular army I would respectfully request that Walter Comstock of West Wrentham, Mass. be appointed a second lieutenant for faithful and meritorious service during the war."—ALS, DNA, RG 94, ACP, G590 CB 1865. On Nov. 24, USG endorsed this letter. "The within applicant has served two years during the war"—ES, *ibid.* On Nov. 3, Bvt. Col. Ely S. Parker had written to Bvt. Brig. Gen. Edward D. Townsend. "In the recommendations for appointments in the regular army, it is particularly desirable that the following appointments be made on account of faithful and meritorious services during the war. William Mc-Kee Dunn, Jr., to be placed at the head of the list of new appointments. George Griffith, Bethel, Clermont Co. Ohio. C. H. Graves, at present Major and A. A. G. of Vols. with Gen. Terry."—ALS, *ibid.*, G747 CB 1865. On Nov. 24, USG wrote to "The Board examining applications and recommendations for appointments in the Regular Army." "I have the honor to request that the cases of the following named applicants for commissions in the Regular Army be examined at your earliest convenience, and reported to the Secretary of War for such commissions as you may find them entitled to Wm McKee Dunn, Jr. Geo. Meade Geo. Griffith C. H. Graves Walter Comstock W. A. Cameron."—Copies, DLC-USG, V, 46, 109; DNA, RG 108, Letters Sent. All received appointments in the U.S. Army as of Nov. 29. At 2:20 P.M., USG telegraphed to Maj. Gen. George G. Meade. "Has your son preference as to what arm of service to be commissioned in."— Telegrams sent (2), *ibid.*, RG 107, Telegrams Collected (Bound); copies, *ibid.*, RG 108, Letters Sent; DLC-USG, V, 46, 109. On the same day, Meade, Philadelphia, telegraphed to USG. "My Son prefers the Artillery or Infantry to the Cavalry—Between the Artillery & Infantry would be governed by chance of promotion"—Telegram received (at 7:00 P.M.), DNA, RG 107, Telegrams Collected (Bound). On Oct. 15, Capt. and Aide George Meade had written to Townsend requesting an appointment in the U.S. Army.—ALS, *ibid.*, RG 94, ACP, 3819 1874. On Nov. 24, USG endorsed this letter. "The within applicant has served two years during the war."—ES, *ibid.*

On Oct. 31, Maj. Gen. Alfred H. Terry, Richmond, wrote a letter received at USG's hd. qrs. recommending Maj. Charles H. Graves, adjt. for Terry, for appointment in the U.S. Army.—*Ibid.*, RG 108, Register of Letters Received. On Nov. 2, USG endorsed this letter. "Respy. forwarded to the Secty of war, appd, and recommended strongly"—Copy, *ibid.* On Nov. 13, William A. Cameron, former capt., 16th N. Y. Cav., wrote to Bvt. Col. Theodore S. Bowers requesting an appointment in the U.S. Army.—ALS, *ibid.*, C325 CB 1870. Parker endorsed this letter. "Approved and respectfully forwarded to the Secretary of War."—AES (undated), *ibid.* On Oct. 3, 1870, Mrs. N. K. Bishop, Charlestown, Mass., wrote to USG. "I see the name of Lt. Cameron on the unassigned list. I think there must be some mistake about it, as he was such a gallant soldier & officer during our late war and firm patriot, [and] since that time has served in important positions faithfully & well, he is a strong upholder of this Goverment & ready at any moment to risk his life for his Country   He is engaged to my daughter and the wedding day has for some time been fixed for the 7th of Nov. and I feel therefore doubly anxious that no disgrace should attach to his name. My brother in law Genl Burnside is in Europe or he would use his influenc[e] with you to restore him to his regiment. O do not refuse my request, put your self in my place, with but my two daughters left [o]ut of six & they father-less, & your sympathies as a Father & soldier will cause you to grant it   Wm. Camerons War Record is remarkably fine & the disgrace would be terribly hard for him to bear. Pardon me for troubling you in the matter, but the subject is of the most vital importance, & I think some enemy who has tried his best at other times to injure him must have been at work."—ALS, *ibid.*

1865, Nov. 8.   USG endorsement. "Respectfully forwarded to Secretary of War with recommendation that this be considered with the other applica-tions."—ES, DNA, RG 94, Cadet Applications. Written on a letter of Nov. 4 from John F. Richards, Milwaukee, Wis., to USG. "I take the liberty of addressng you a few lines on a Subject which I hope you will not consider out of Place   I See from a Card from the United States Military Academy at West Point that appointments at large not to exceed Ten are annually in the Months of February and March Made by the President   the applica-tions are to be placed in the register of the office of the Chief Engineer   My Son Lafayette Richards being of Propper age together with the necessary health and other requirements for his Admission into that institution whether you could consistently with with Position and so if so whether you would do me the Personal *kindness* of giving me the benefit of your Personal influance in Secureing my Sons Admission into that instution   I can not succeed through the Congressional Dist. on acct of advance promeses but *General Paine* our member Elect from this Dist. has kindly promesed me all he can do in the matter but thought if I could Secure your influence that I would Succeed   any thing you can Consistently do for me or that you might feel Disposed to do will be more than appreciated   My Son went into the Mili-tary Service before he was Eighteen years old went into the 39th Regiment United States Wisconsin Volunteers Served the time for which he Volun-teered with credit to to himself which was fully responded to by his Capt. he is Very anxious for a Military education   under these circumstances if you feel Disposed to do any thing for an old friend and acquaintance your Kindness will be more than appreciated   hoping you will bestow sufficient attention on the above Communication to Answer me all for which I shall feel very grateful . . ."—ALS, *ibid.*

1865, Nov. 9.   To Bvt. Maj. Gen. Montgomery C. Meigs. "I understand that in the settlement of Mr. James Cameron's accounts (Cameron of Chat-tanooga) a positive statement as to his loyalty is required. I have no hesita-tion in saying that I do not believe any more loyal persons live than Mr. and Mrs Cameron, or than they have been throughout the rebellion"—Copies,

DLC-USG, V, 46, 109; DNA, RG 108, Letters Sent. See *PUSG*, 9, 576, 577*n*; *ibid.*, 11, 390–91.

1865, Nov. 10. USG pass. "Pass General Ortega through states and Territories of the United States by whatever route or routes he may select to travel. Favors shown Gen Ortega will be duly appreciated."—ADS, CU-B. On Nov. 9, Matías Romero, Mexican minister, New York City, had written to USG. "Gen. Ortega is going to Mexico and as there is some danger in the rout he has to take, he would like to have a pass from you or a letter for the commanders of the different forts from Kansass City to Franklin, N. M. Territory. I have heard that you are coming to this city. If that is so, I will remain here until your arrival."—ALS, USG 3.

1865, Nov. 11. USG endorsement. "Respy. forwarded to the Secretary of War, and attention called to the recommendation for the transfer of the control of Indian Affairs from the Department of the Interior to the War Department, which is entirely concurred in, and, also, to the remarks of Carson and Bent on Indian Reservation and on issuing rations to Indian scouts"—Copy, DNA, RG 108, Register of Letters Received. Written on a letter of Oct. 27 from Col. Christopher Carson, 1st N. M. Cav., and William W. Bent, St. Louis, to Maj. Gen. John Pope.—Copy, *ibid.*, Letters Received. On Nov. 6, Pope endorsed this letter. "Respectfully referred to Maj Genl Sherman comd'g Mil Div of the Miss for his information, with the request that as the statement of Kit Carson & W. M. Bent have an important bearing on the question of Legislation hoped for this winter on the subject of Indian affairs, it may be forwarded to the Genl in Chief of the Army that copies may be furnished to the committee on Indian affairs—It is unessesary to say that eCarson & Bent are men of standing and reliability, thoroughly acquainted with Indians and Indian management by the experience of their whole lives & that what they have herein stated may be entirely relied on in any measures adopted by congress. Their Statements simply reiterate with uncommon forbearance, the experience & opinions of all honest persons in the Army or out of it, who have ever served on the frontier. It is sufficiently desireable that copies of their statements be furnished to the congressional committee on Indian Affairs"—Copy, *ibid.* On Sept. 11, Carson, Fort Riley, Kan., had written to Capt. Benjamin C. Cutler, adjt. for Brig. Gen. James H. Carleton, concerning the location of Indian reservations and treatment of dissident Indians.—Copy, *ibid.* On Nov. 13, Col. William A. Nichols, AGO, forwarded this letter to USG.—AES, *ibid.* On Dec. 9, Pope also forwarded a copy of this letter to USG.—ES, *ibid.*

On Oct. 23, Pope wrote a letter received at USG's hd. qrs. concerning Indian affairs.—*Ibid.*, Register of Letters Received; DLC-USG, V, 58. On Nov. 22, USG endorsed this letter. "I entirely concur in the views expressed of the necessity of Indian affairs being under control of the War Dept., but am not prepared at present to recommend the guarding of but one route across the Plains"—Copy, *ibid.*

On Jan. 31, 1866, Pope telegraphed to Maj. Gen. William T. Sherman, Washington, D. C. "I wish you would press matters in the proper quarter in relation to transfer of Indian affairs to War Dept. Our Indians affairs on the plains are now in favorable condition for final and general pacification provided the Military authorities are authorized to control them and regulate the treaties. The Indians insist on treating with the Military and avow their determination to put no trust in Indian agents whether they are right or wrong. The interests of the Govt requires that their wishes should be consulted. unless they are our Indian affairs are likely at any time to be generally disturbed. This matter ought to be pushed and fully explained" —Telegram received (at 9:00 P.M.), DNA, RG 107, Telegrams Collected (Bound). On Feb. 2, USG endorsed this telegram. "Respectfully forwarded to the Secretary of War."—Copy, *ibid.*, RG 108, Register of Letters Received.

1865, Nov. 23, 10:00 A.M. To Maj. Gen. John Pope. "I shall be absent from Washington for some weeks hence could not see Maj. Davis if he were to come on."—ALS (telegram sent), DNA, RG 107, Telegrams Collected (Bound); telegram sent, *ibid.*; copies, *ibid.*, RG 108, Letters Sent; DLC-USG, V, 46, 109. On Nov. 21, Pope, St. Louis, had telegraphed to USG. "Col N H Davis asst Inspector Gen U S A has just arrived here sent by Gen Carleton to give me information about affairs in New Mexico. I wish him to explain to you personally as he can do with knowledge & intelligence & ask authority to order him to report to you in Washington for that purpose"—Telegram received (at 7:30 P.M.), DNA, RG 107, Telegrams Collected (Bound); *ibid.*, RG 108, Telegrams Received; copy, DLC-USG, V, 54.

On Dec. 20, Maj. and Asst. Inspector Gen. Nelson H. Davis, St. Louis, wrote to USG. "I have the honor to enclose you a memorial to the U. S. Senate, which explains the claim I make, and the grounds therefore—Believing you will do what may be in your power to give and old army officer his *legal* and *just rights*, I do most respectfully but urgently request that you will use your influence and give your active support to secure my rights—I might add, that so far as I have heard, all of the old army officers who are acquainted with my case, acknowledge my *right* to the promotion as Ins. Genl. vice Col. Van Rensselaer deceased—You will percieve this case involves a principal regulating promotions in the Army, dear and sacred to every officer—If I could be ordered to Washington for a short time, I should like it—"—ALS, DNA, RG 108, Letters Received. The enclosure is *ibid.* On Jan. 1, 1866, noon, USG telegraphed to Pope. "Detain Maj. N. H. Davis in St. Louis until further orders from Washington."—ALS (telegram sent), *ibid.*, RG 107, Telegrams Collected (Bound); telegram sent, *ibid.*; copies, *ibid.*, RG 108, Letters Sent; DLC-USG, V, 47, 109. On Jan. 11, noon, Bvt. Col. Theodore S. Bowers telegraphed to Pope. "Major N. H. Davis. Assistant Inspector General U. S. A. is to return at once to New Mexico."— ALS (telegram sent), DNA, RG 107, Telegrams Collected (Bound); tele-

gram sent, *ibid.*; copies, *ibid.*, RG 108, Letters Sent; DLC-USG, V, 47,
109.

1865, Nov. 23.   To Maj. Gen. Philip H. Sheridan. "Your communica-
tion of Nov. 3rd 1865, is at hand. You will place, as you suggest, the
Cavalry in such position as you can best forage them, and make such ar-
rangements for posts in the Spring as you think best."—LS, DNA, RG 393,
Military Div. of the Gulf, Letters Received. *O.R.*, I, xlviii, part 2, 1258. On
Nov. 3, Sheridan, New Orleans, had written to USG. "The Fourth (4th)
U. S. Cavalry left here this morning for Indianola to proceed to San Antonio
Texas. It is well equipped in clothing and camp and garrison equipage. I
directed it to report to Genl Merritt to be mounted. I have telegraphed to
Genl Merritt to know if he preferred to come here as chief of cavalry or to
take command of a District in North Eastern Texas. I will dispose of the
cavalry as soon as I get his reply, transferring it to you. The 6th U. S. Cavalry is now here and I propose sending it to Austin where it, I think, should
winter. I intend to let you fix these matters yourself however, It is too late
to occupy frontier posts this winter still I would like to have your views. I
send Bvt Brig Gen G. A. Forsyth to Brazos to day and will ask him to see
Genl Weitzel and to impress on him the necessity of but little intercourse
with Matamoros."—LS, DNA, RG 108, Letters Received.

1865, Nov. 23.   USG endorsement. "Whilst the war was going on—I frequently heard of the case of Mrs Allen who was said to be in prison in Richmond, Va. on the charge of treason to the so called Southern Confederacy.
Her sufferings were said to be very great, and caused solely because of her
love to the Union. The accompanying affidavits would show conclusively
that some of her property has been taken and used by the United States
Government in prosecuting the war against Rebellion. It would seem she
should be as much entitled to compensation for such property as the loyal
northern man who sold his property to an Agent of the Governmt—I would
recommend that if the amount here presented can be paid—that it be so
paid"—Copy, DLC-USG, V, 58. Written on papers submitted by Bvt. Maj.
Gen. Montgomery C. Meigs concerning the claim of Mrs. Mary C. Allan,
Goochland County, Va., for horses and mules taken by U.S. forces.—*Ibid.*
See Mary Elizabeth Massey, *Bonnet Brigades* (New York, 1966), p. 101;
Clifford Dowdey, *Experiment in Rebellion* (Garden City, N. Y., 1946), pp.
302–3.

1865, Nov. 24.   To Mrs. William Fisher. "I have just been informed by
Col. Badeau of my staff that you never received my acknowledgement of
the beautiful Afghan which you were kind enough to send me last June."—
Anderson Galleries, Sale No. 4158, 1935.

1865, Nov. 27.   Brig. Gen. John A. Rawlins endorsement. "Respectfully
referred to Commanding General Department Mississippi, with instructions

to have Mr. Burwells house turned over to him, provided he has been pardoned or comes within the provisions of the amnesty"—ES, DNA, RG 108, Letters Received. Written on papers concerning a claim of Armistead Burwell.—*Ibid.* On Sept. 18, Burwell had written a letter received at USG's hd. qrs. "Claims possession of 'Manlove house' at Vicksburg (taken from Mr. C. A. Manlove by Gen. J. W. Davidson) as per agreement with (late Gen) H. W. Slocum."—*Ibid.*, Register of Letters Received. On Dec. 13, Maj. Gen. Thomas J. Wood, Vicksburg, endorsed the papers in the case. "Respectfully returned to Brevet Major General John A. Rawlins chief of Staff, with the following statement for the information of the Commander-in-chief: 1st The records of the Provost Marshals Office and the records of the civil functionaries authorized to administer the oath of amnesty, though both have been examined, fail to disclose the fact that Mr A. Burwell has taken the Amnesty oath, or has received a pardon. the most reliable information goes to show he has never applied for a pardon. 2nd Without being able to obtain perfectly indisputable evidence, the information obtained goes to show that Mr Burwell comes within the $20,000 exception appended to the Presidents Amnesty proclamation, therefore requires a special pardon before he can be restored to his civil rights. The attention of the Commander-in-chief is respectfully invited to the report of Major General Osterhaus dated Dec 10th 1865. It is proper to observe that the records of this office contain no evidence of any correspondence between General Slocum and Mr Burwell. With this state of facts, taken in connection with the conditional instructions of the Commander-in-chief, endorsed on Mr Burwells application, I deem it proper not to turn the house over to him, but to submit the case for further instructions. That the Commander-in-chief may have a full understanding of the case I think it proper to append this further statement. During the past Autumn Mr Manlove (who it appears took the oath of amnesty in May last, but who has not yet been pardoned,) and who is also a claimant to have the same house turned over to him, made an application therefor, through Govenor Humphreys to the President—this application was referred, by order of the Secretary of War, to these Headquarters for report—said application, with the report of B'v't Brig Gen'l H. M. Whittelsey, chief Quartermaster of the Dep't, and my endorsement, has been returned to the War Department—copies of General Whittelsey's report and my endorsement on Mr Manlove's application are herewith respectfully submitted for the information of the Commander-in-chief."—ES, *ibid.*, Letters Received. On Dec. 28, Bvt. Col. Theodore S. Bowers wrote to Wood. "Lieutenant General Grant directs me to acknowledge the receipt of your report in the 'Burwell house' case, referred to you on the 27th of November, and to say that your action is satisfactory."—ALS, *ibid.*, RG 393, Dept. and District of Miss., Letters Received. On Dec. 5, 1866, Burwell wrote to USG. "In the winter of 1863–4—property belonging to me in Vicksburg was destroyed for the purposes of our Goverment—In July 1863 this property known as 'the Castle' was taken possession of and used as quarters by your order; and soon after the house was destroyed and fort Castle erected on the scite. The ground (16 84/100 acres) now turned back to me, is in such condition, that it will cost me more than I am able to expend to put it in order for building upon it. I respectfully ask you. 1st. To cause the ground to be restored as near as can be done to to the condition it was in, when taken by our forces. Allow me to suggest that this work might be done without great expense to the Government, by directing the employment of labourers on it, who will apply for and draw rations for their support. 2nd I also respectfully ask you to direct a board of Officers to inquire and report the Damage done to my property by the destruction of the House and other improvements. There is a board here composed of Brvet Brig: Genl Dudley and Capts Scully & Valentine, which has reported in a somewhat similar case—as I am informed. I ask that the same Board be directed to report in mine embracing the question of rent as well as of Damage."—ALS, *ibid.*, RG 77, Accounts, Property Returns, and Claims, Letters Received. On the same day, Wood endorsed this letter. "Respectfully forwarded, through the Dept. Commander. approving both requests made in this communication. Mr Burwell was a thoroughly loyal, devoted union man from the first to the last of the war. He resisted secession when it was being debated, and he resisted it when it sought to accomplish its fell purpose by force of arms. He has suffered much and heavily in person and property for his devotion to the Union and the Government, and I know no citizen who has stronger claims on the Government, to be remunerated for his losses. If it be determined that the fortifications, on his property ought to be leveled by the Government, I respectfully request authority to hire citizen labor to do the work, as the experiment now being made of leveling the fortifications on Mrs Lum's property, by soldier's labor, with the number of soldiers available for the work, shows it will be a long and tedious operation. It is hardly necessary to remark, that soldiers employed so long as laborers, suffer much in discipline, instruction and efficiency."—ES, *ibid.* On Jan. 12, 1867, USG endorsed this letter. "Respectfully forwarded to the Secretary of War, without recommendation."—ES, *ibid.* Additional papers are *ibid.* See *PUSG*, 9, 419–21.

1865, DEC. 2. Maj. Gen. Philip H. Sheridan, New Orleans, to USG. "In the Sale of Means of Transportation I have directed the chief quarter masters to retain three hundred and twenty (320) very fine mule teams The work now being done by these teams could be done by contract at a little less expense but in my opinion that number of Teams should be kept as aviable Teams in this Depot please give me your Judgement on this subject"—Telegram received (on Dec. 3, 5:30 P.M.), DNA, RG 107, Telegrams Collected (Bound); (at 5:20 P.M.) *ibid.*, RG 108, Letters Received; copies (one sent by mail), *ibid.*; DLC-Philip H. Sheridan.

1865, DEC. 11, 10:10 A.M. To Maj. Gen. Philip H. Sheridan. "If possible muster out the 46th Ill. regiment and relieve ~~them~~ it with two or more companies from some other parts of the command."—ALS (telegram sent),

DNA, RG 107, Telegrams Collected (Bound); telegram sent, *ibid.*; copies, *ibid.*, RG 108, Letters Sent; DLC-USG, V, 46, 109. On Dec. 14, Sheridan, New Orleans, telegraphed to USG. "Your dispatch of the Twelfth (12th) received and will muster-out the forty Sixth (46) Illinois"—Telegram received (at 8:00 P.M.), DNA, RG 107, Telegrams Collected (Bound); *ibid.*, RG 108, Telegrams Received; copies, DLC-USG, V, 54; DLC-Philip H. Sheridan.

1865, Dec. 11. Maj. Gen. George Stoneman, Knoxville, to USG. "I have ordered my Inspector General to make a thorough inspection of the Post of Nashville and will give the results in a few days"—Telegram received (at 4:00 P.M.), DNA, RG 107, Telegrams Collected (Bound); *ibid.*, RG 108, Telegrams Received; copies, *ibid.*, RG 393, Dept. of Tenn., Telegrams Sent; DLC-USG, V, 54. USG had stopped briefly in Knoxville on Dec. 9.

1865, Dec. 13. To Brig. Gen. Joseph K. Barnes. "Dr. Woods of your Corps is very anxious to be stationed at New Pork Bks. Ky. The Dr. is now growing old in service, and has served faithfully, and I would therefore recommend that he be assigned according to this reques[t] if compattible with the interests of the service."—ALS, DNA, RG 94, Medical Officers and Physicians, Personal Papers, Wood. On Dec. 15, Maj. Robert C. Wood wrote a letter received at USG's hd. qrs. requesting assignment to Fort Delaware and on Dec. 18, USG endorsed this letter. "Respy forwarded to the Sec of War. I would be gratified if Surgeon Woods request could be granted. His faithful & valuable services in the West as Asst Surg General entitle him to consideration. Unless there are objections of which I am not aware—I would recommend his assignmt as within requested"—Copy, DLC-USG, V, 58.

1865, Dec. 14. To Secretary of War Edwin M. Stanton. "I would respectfully recommend that Maj. & Brevet Lt. Col. Henry H. Humphreys, son of Maj. Gen Humphreys, name be ~~placed~~ sent specially before the Board now in session for the purpose of making selections to fill vacancies in the regular army. Col. Humphreys has served throughout most if not all the war, and a braver soldier cannot be found."—Copies, DLC-USG, V, 46, 109; DNA, RG 108, Letters Sent. On Oct. 16, Maj. Gen. Andrew A. Humphreys, Philadelphia, had written a letter received at USG's hd. qrs. recommending Maj. Henry H. Humphreys for appointment in the U.S. Army.—*Ibid.*, Register of Letters Received. On Oct. 18, USG endorsed this letter. "Respectfully forwarded to the Secretary of War with the recommendation that whenever transfers from the Volunteers to the Regular Army are made, or whenever selections are made for officers in the Regular Army from men who have served in the Volunteer force, during the war, that the case of Major Humphreys be favourably considered."—Copy, *ibid.* Humphreys was appointed 1st lt., 17th Inf., as of Feb. 23, 1866.

1865, DEC. 14.   To Secretary of War Edwin M. Stanton. "I have the honor to recommend that the following General Officers of Volunteers be mustered out of the service of the U S to date from Jan. 15 1866. . . ."— LS, DNA, RG 94, ACP, C61 CB 1864. USG added a tabular list of 17 maj. gens. and 126 brig. gens., some of whom had already resigned. On Dec. 28, President Andrew Johnson approved the list.—AES, *ibid.*

1865, DEC. 14.   Lewis Wallace, Indianapolis, Ind., to USG. "After working in New York in behalf of the Mexican Loan until I became satisfied that it was for the present hopeless in that section, I came West: now, after a pretty thorough trial, I have concluded, greatly against my wishes, that the enterprise is equally desperate here. With all the influences at my command, backed by a confidential report of an interview had with the President by Hon. Robert Dale Owen, in which the former almost directly requests capitalists to interest themselves, I cannot get respectable bankers to do so much as undertake the sale of the bonds. In Gen. Schofield's absence, I have thought it best to inform you of the failure, that you may understand the true cause of the delay in our movement, and be able to submit the matter to the President, and devise, if you consider it best, some remedial action. Every where I find sympathy with the cause. I will even go so far as to say, that I have not met one intelligent man, East or West, who does not assert that the government should take positive and immediate action to relieve Mexico ~~of her so called empire~~. Unfortunately, this opinion is the very cause of the failure of the loan. People whom I address on the subject say, with a unanimity really astonishing, 'Why should we take a Mexican bond? We doubt the Mexican faith; we have no assurance that if Maximilian was driven away, the Mexicans could manage their resources so as to meet promptly the interest or principal due on their bonds. The inducements offered don't compensate for the risk.' 'But,' I reply 'our government is friendly to this loan. It would like to see our citizens take every dollar of it.' 'Then let the government say so publicly. Let it assure us that we will be indemnified.' In short, the invariably conclusion is that it is the duty of the Government to give instant notice to Maximilian to get out, and if he declines, to drive him by force of arms. And every body believes that it will do so before the winter is over. Inquire the reason of this faith, and the reply is, 'Grant is in favor of that course, and he wouldn't say so, unless the President agreed with him.' One of the consequences, therefore, is, that unless the President or Congress will do something more explicit toward the relief of Juarez, we can do nothing ~~toward th~~ further in raising the necessary funds ~~so necessary to initiate a movement toward~~ from our citizens. In my last interview with Mr. Romero, I urged him to let me the use the bonds for the purpose of contracting for material, and transportation, and in the way of bounties and monthly pay. This he declined, on the ground that it would ruin the loan. And now I find myself at my 'wits end,' ~~except the~~ compelled to turn to you or the President. Is it not possible to effect something through a secret fund? Or, cannot a secret loan treaty be made with Mexico? I know Mr. Romero has full authoritys from his government, while the confirmation of ~~the~~ our Senate can be had in executive session. Or, cannot there be a private transfer of the other essential materials along with the arms now in Washington? Please consider these suggestions, and see if something cannot be done to enable me to at least begin the expected operation. I grow more and more impatient every day. I feel that Matamoras, as a base, ought to be in Liberal hands before Gen. Schofield returns from France. Help us if you can, . . ."—ADfS, InHi.

1865, DEC. 15. To Secretary of State William H. Seward. "Permit me to recommend to you the Galena Gazette as one of the most loyal and true supporters of the Administration throughout the rebellion, and one entitled in the highest degree to the support of the Government. I would respectfully recommend therefore that it be given the publication of the laws of Congress, a patronage heretofore had, I believe, by this paper."—ALS, DNA, RG 59, Correspondence Regarding Publication of Laws.

1865, DEC. 16. USG endorsement. "Respy referred to the President of the United States. Judge Moodys letter fully explains what he wants, and what he is politically. I know Judge Moody well. Prior to the war he called himself a radical abolitionist, since slavery has been practically abolished he is a conservative union man, opposing some of the extreme measures pursued in Missouri. He is a man of great ability and high legal attainment." —Copy, DLC-USG, V, 58. Written on a letter of Dec. 1 from James C. Moodey, St. Louis, to USG. "Presents his case to the Lieut General, and says he intends running for circuit court Judge of U. S. in Missouri— wishes the Lieut Generals influance."—DNA, RG 108, Register of Letters Received. On Feb. 9, 1866, Moodey wrote to USG. "There is something to me inexplicable about the fate of papers sent by me to the President—The enclosed papers will shew the mystery but do not furnish any explanation— I do not wish to trouble you about this matter—But as you have kindly taken some interest in it I feel it my duty to let you know 'the situation'—I wrote you sometime ago remonstrating against the removal of Howard & Foy— presently McNeil has been appointed surveyor of the Port vice Howard removed—This is a bad damper upon the friends of the President—It is a lift to Fremontism, Cleaveland Conventionism & Lawlessness generally—How *could* it have been accomplished?"—ALS, USG 3. Enclosed was a letter of Jan. 22 from Moodey to James P. Justin listing papers that had been forwarded to President Andrew Johnson, including Moodey's letter to USG and USG's endorsement.—ALS, *ibid.* On Jan. 31, J. Hubley Ashton, attorney general's office, wrote to Justin that the letters had not reached his office. —ALS, *ibid.* Moodey endorsed this letter. "Mr Justin writes me that the letters having the pencil check in the list are in the hands of the President— Where can the others be?"—AE (undated), *ibid.* USG's endorsement was among the missing papers.

1865, DEC. 16. Arizona Territory Concurrent Resolution "Regarding National Affairs" expressing appreciation to USG *et al.*—AD, USG 3.

1865, DEC. 17. Raphael Semmes, "Steamer Louise *en route* from Mobile to New Orleans," to USG. "I enclose a copy of a Protest, which will explain itself. This protest was handed by me to General Woods, commanding at Mobile, on the 16th Inst, upon my leaving that city for Washington—As Commander-in-Chief (under the President) of the Armies of the United States, and the Commanding General under whose orders and authority General Sherman acted, I respectfully request that you will make known to the President of the United States, the facts stated in the protest, and ask to have my arrest, in violation of a solemn military capitulation, annulled. I need not say to you, that by the terms of the Capitulation, I am to be un-molested in person, for any act of War, committed anterior to the date there-of. In other words, Genl Sherman stipulated, with your consent and appro-bation, that so far as the molestation of person was concerned, there was to be an oblivion of all past acts of War. I have been arrested for my escape off Cherbourg, after my ship sunk from under me, and I was forced to leap into the sea for the preservation of life, and this escape, which I claim to have been legitimate, is charged against me as a violation of the usages of War—If it were such violation, it was known to the Government nearly a a year before the capitulation and was condoned by the capitulation itself. If the Government designed to proceed against me on this charge, it should have refused to have regarded me as a prisoner of War, and should have withheld from me the benefit of General Sherman's convention. Having permitted me to participate in that convention, with full knowledge of the facts, it is estopped from 'molesting' me—Reposing entire faith and con-fidence in the Government, I have been peaceably residing at my home for the space of seven months since the capitulation, and now I find myself ar-rested by military authority, in violation of its solemn compact."—Copy, Museum of the City of Mobile, Mobile, Ala. *O.R.*, II, viii, 836. The en-closure is *ibid.*, pp. 836–37.

On Dec. 27, Joseph E. Johnston wrote to Maj. Gen. William T. Sher-man. "I have just received information from Capt. Raphael Semmes, late Commander of the Confederate vessel Alabama, that he was arrested on the 15th instant, by order of the Secretary of the Navy, on the charge of vio-lating the usages of war by his escape off Cherbourg. This Confederate officer belonged to My command at the time of our convention on the 26th of last April—assumed the required obligation, & received the correspond-ing guarantee of protection. I respectfully submit that immunity was thus granted for all acts of his then known to the government—& that the act in question was as well known then as now. Under these circumstances, I earnestly ask the interposition of your influence for the protection of one of those who laid down their arms in the full Confidence of receiving that protection at your hands."—ALS, DNA, RG 108, Letters Received. On Jan. 2, 1866, Sherman endorsed this letter. "Respectfully forwarded to the

Lt Genl Comdg. with the mere remark, that the Govt of the U. S. will of course keep its pledged faith, when that is legally ascertained, no matter how it results"—AES, *ibid.*

1865, Dec. 18.   Bvt. Col. Theodore S. Bowers endorsement. "Respectfully referred to Maj. Gen. M. C. Meigs, Q. M. General of the Army, for remark."—ES, DNA, RG 92, Letters Received from Hd. Qrs. Written on a letter of Dec. 14 from Maj. Gen. John Pope, St. Louis, to USG. "I have the honor to state, that orders have been given by the Quartermaster General of the Army to the Chief Quartermaster of this Department, requiring, that all disbursements or payment of vouchers in the Department with a few unimportant exceptions, be made in St. Louis by the Chief Quartermaster of the Department.—Such I understand to be the substance of the order, but no copy of it has been furnished to me. I am sure, it is unnecessary to point out to you or to any one else, familiar with the business or necessities of such a Department as this, that such an order will work incalculable hardship to individuals, having contracts or furnishing supplies in New-Mexico, Utah, Colorado, Dacotah, Nebraska, Minnesota and indeed everywhere else in this Department outside of this city.— . . ."—LS, *ibid.*

On Jan. 12, 1866, Bvt. Maj. Gen. Montgomery C. Meigs wrote to USG. "I have the honor to enclose an abstract of a report from the Chief Quartermaster of the Military Division of the Mississippi, in regard to reduction in expenditure in that Military Division by the Qr. Mr. Department. It appears from that report, that there were on 1st Nov. in the Department of Missouri alone, about 18.700 troops. The estimated expenditure of the Qr. Mr. Dept. in the Department of Missouri, for December, is stated at $950,000.—This is at the rate of $50. per month for every soldier in that Department, or at the rate of $600. per annum, and is exclusive of the cost of clothing and equipage and other supplies delivered to the troops from accumulated stores. It is also exclusive of the expenses of the other Departments,—Subsistence, Ordnance, Medical &c. At this rate the appropriation for next year, if based upon the estimates submitted to Congress will be consumed in the Department of Missouri alone, unless great reduction can be effected in the number of troops, and the cost of their maintenance. I had understood, that in October the number of troops on the Plains would be reduced by muster out below ten thousand. This report shows on 1st Nov. 18.700 in the Department of Missouri which includes New Mexico. . . ." —LS, *ibid.*, RG 393, Military Div. of the Mo., Letters Received.

1865, Dec. 18.   George W. Dent, St. Charles Hotel, New Orleans, to USG. "Get McCulloch to appoint me Treasury Agent for Texas. Dennisons resignation occurs Second January."—Telegram received (on Dec. 22, 7:15 P.M.), DNA, RG 107, Telegrams Collected (Bound). On Dec. 25, 4:40 P.M., Secretary of the Treasury Hugh McCulloch telegraphed to Dent. "You will be appointed to succeed Dennison. Report immediately to Wm P. Mellen and look carefully into Dennison's operations."—ALS (telegram sent), *ibid.*, Telegrams Collected (Unbound). On May 26, 1866, Dent, Galveston, Tex., wrote a letter received at USG's hd. qrs. "Appointment as Collector of Internal Revenue in Texas District on removal of Mr. Milton Stapp, present Collector there."—*Ibid.*, RG 108, Register of Letters Received. On June 27, USG endorsed this letter. "Respy. submitted to the Secretary of the Treasury."—Copy, *ibid.*

1865, DEC. 19. To Secretary of War Edwin M. Stanton. "I have the honor to recommend that Bvt. Col. George Sykes, U. S. A., be brevetted Brig. Gen'l U. S. A."—Copies, DLC-USG, V, 46, 109; DNA, RG 108, Letters Sent.

1865, DEC. 19. Brig. Gen. Orlando B. Willcox, Detroit, to USG. "I respectfully enclose to you recommendations from the Governor of Mich, State Officers, & the whole Legislature, together with that of the Corps Division brigade & regimental Commanders of the 9th Corps for my promotion as Maj Gen of Volunteers. These papers were signed without my solicitation & sent to me last March, but I made no use of them. I desire now to employ them for whatever they may [*be wor*]th towards securing an appointment as a Brigadier General in the regular army. I have been recommended for M. G. by yourself & Genls Meade Burnside & McClellan, & my name was once sent to the Senate by President Lincoln, though unfortunately it was about the time when all the names were sent back because of a surplus. I have served throughout the war without any attempt whatever at personal aggrandizement—three years as Division Commander & several times as Corps Commander. My battles fights & skirmishes number some thirty-~~five~~. I gave up everything to the war in the way of business My law practice & most of of the legal knowledge is gone & I have not yet been able to see an opening into civil life. My family is so large that I feel it my duty towards them not to throw myself back upon the bare possibilities of civil employment withou[t] an effort to obtain such a position as ~~my~~ the war & my military education may fairly entitle me to with due reference to the claims of others. The senators from this state have expressed themselves willing to do all in their power."—ALS, DNA, RG 94, ACP, W1376 CB 1865. Willcox was appointed col., 29th Inf., as of July 28, 1866.

1865, DEC. 20. To Bvt. Brig. Gen. Edward D. Townsend. "Many cases come to these Head Quarters of persons who have enlisted in the regular army for the purpose of obtaining immediate promotion. Please have an order published that hereafter any person must have served at least two years in the regular army before his application for examination and promotion will be considered."—LS, DNA, RG 94, Letters Received, 1326A 1865.

1865, DEC. 20. Jacob De Witt, Montreal, Canada, to USG. "I have the honor to inform you that at the Annual Meeting of the Members of the New

England Society of Montreal, you were unanimously elected an Honorary Member of the Society—On behalf of our Society I beg to convey our warm thanks and deep sense of appreciation of the noble and soldierly qualities you have displayed in the suppression of the late dreadful and bloody rebellion—Our Society consists of Americans and descendants of Americans residing in this vicinity without reference to the States whence they came, our only bond being that we owe our Origin to that Great Republic to which we ever look with pride and joy Some of our number had the pleasure of meeting you when you visited our city last summer, but that occasion afforded no opportunity for exchanging congratulations on the downfall of the civil war, and the restoration of peace throughout our beloved Native Land —We trust that the time may be far distant when Columbia shall again call her sons to the field, but feel confident that should that time come, they will be ready—In requesting your acceptance may I be allowed to express our high esteem for you personally, and to pray that the Great Giver of all Good may ever hold you in his keeping"—ALS, USG 3.

1865, DEC. 21. USG endorsement. "In the absence of the Sec. of War, respectfully refered to the President of the United States. In my opinion the Paroles given to the surrendered armies lately in rebellion against the Government should be held inviolate unless in cases where all rules of civilized Warfare have been violated and in case of such charges an immediate trial should be had. I would respectfully recommend therefore that Capt. Winder either have an immediate trial or that he be released on bonds for his appearance when called on for trial."—AES, DNA, RG 108, Letters Received. *O.R.*, II, viii, 815. Written on a letter of Nov. 23 from Joseph E. Johnston, New York City, to USG. "I respectfully Submit the accompanying Statement—in the full belief that the writer is entitled to protection under the convention between Major Genl Sherman & myself,—approved by you. As you understand better than I, the value of the promise of protection given in this case by the authorized agent of the government, I will trouble you with no attempt at argument. But ask the interposition of your great influence & authority in favour of Mr R. B. Winder—"—ALS, DNA, RG 108, Letters Received. *O.R.*, II, viii, 814–15. On March 23, 1866, W. H. Winder, New York Hotel, New York City, wrote to USG. "Some months since I enclosed, to C. H. Winder Esq of Washington, a letter, to you from Genl. Joseph E. Johnston in which your attention was called to the long imprisonment of Capt R. B. Winder who had been surrendered under the convention entered into between Genls Sherman & Johnston, confirmed and sanctioned by yourself. Capt Winder was duly paroled & had reported himself to the provost marshal at his residence. Copy of his parole & statement of his case by himself were enclosed with Gen Johnston's letter. Genl Johnston invoked the influence of your name and great authority for the release of Capt Winder whose imprisonment was a clear violation of the Federal faith so sacredly pledged in that Convention. Mr Winder presented to you that letter and sought your aid to free Capt Winder To accomplish that result you endorsed on Genl Johnston's letter your declaration that the Convention did guarantee immunity to Capt Winder against any disturbance, & that he ought to be liberated, unless guilty of violation of the laws of War, th[a]t if there were any such charges, he was entitled to an immediate trial or release on bonds to appear if wanted for trial. It will, doubtless, surprise you, General, to learn, that, notwithstanding this emphatic announcement of your judgment, Capt Winder is still confined in prison in violation of the Convention, without trial & so far as can be ascertained without charges Had it been Genl Lee who had been imprisoned, your attention would have been so importunately called to any neglect or delay to your demand for his release, that little time would have elapsed before you would have forced a respect to the faith of the Government which you had plighted. I beg leave, General, to assert that where the arrest of Genl Lee would be a more conspicuous violation of the Convention, it could not be a more flagrant one, & although, officially, on a lower sphere, Capt Winder was equally incapable of violating the Laws of War & of honor. But I apprehend you will find in this case cause stronger than any personal appeal, to induce your prompt & efficient action: it is that the Sanction of your high authority pledging the Federal honor, gave confidence to the Confederates & brought Capt Winder within reach of arrest. The simple statement of the case is strongest, & I trust, that not even the multitudinous & onerous duties of your office can divert you from such action as shall insure the release of Capt Winder"—LS, DNA, RG 94, Letters Received, 249W 1866. On March 24, USG endorsed this letter. "Respectfully forwarded to the Hon. Secretary of War, with the recommendation that Capt Winder be released if there are no charges against him of violation of the laws of war; and if there are such charges that he have an immediate trial, unless inconsistent with the public interest."—ES, *ibid.* On April 6, Judge Advocate Gen. Joseph Holt endorsed this letter. "Respectfully returned. Mr Ambrose Spencer has not yet furnished this Bureau with such details of the criminality of R. B. Winder, as are required before formal charges & specifications can be preferred against him. It is now believed that he will not do so, for reasons connected with his personal safety, in view of the intolerant & proscriptive rebel spirit prevailing in Georgia where he resides. Under these circumstances, I am without the testimony necessary to proceed further in the contemplated prosecution of the case. For this reason & not for any thing alleged in the within insolent letter I find no ground for opposing the recommendation of Lt Gen Grant—"—AES, *ibid.*

1865, Dec. 22. Maj. Gen. William T. Sherman, St. Louis, to USG. "I got back from Arkansas yesterday. I did not go to Fort Smith but limited my visit to General Carr at Helena, Genl Morgan at Duvalls Bluff and Genl Reynolds at Little Rock. I found all things satisfactory & write so to Genl Rawlings today. In returning via Memphis I met in succession the Presidents Message—Report of the Sec of War, Yours, & yesterday the shorter message of the President & your letter referring to your visit South, all of which I need not say gave me unqualified pleasure. I must congratulate you on the skilful and admirable manner in which you grouped the events of 1865. So far as my own part is concerned I am more than satisfied and further say that in apportioning the values attached to the shares of each of your subordinates I believe you have done ample justice. Of course I could not but be amused at your illustrating a Great Military Principle by the simile of a 'balky team', a figure of speech that would shock somewhat the English Brain and the Still more striking one of the tightly corked bottle in which you put Butler. Of course your Report will be printed in Book form, and if you have one bound in convenient shape for preservation do not fail to send it to me. My own observations South confirm yours literally. I talked freely with whites & Blacks of all classes, and I know all will be satisfied with yours and President Johnsons action in the premises. A few of the Blacks will need some help this winter, but by February and March I think every one will be lucratively employed at labor to which they are accustomed and will receive wages with which to clothe and provide for the old and young, the feeble & helpless. On my return I happened to fall in with General Jos. E. Johnston at Memphis, and we were together until we parted at Oden Illinois he going east & I west. We talked over all matters of the Past, and I infer he now has far more respect for the Govt of the United States than he ever had, and I honestly believe he will labor as faithfully as possible to execute your wishes & those of President Johnson as if he were bound by an oath of office. I hope you will if convenient resume your tour of Inspection South, as far as Texas, looking to Alabama & Mississipi which seem to me to need attention. As to Arkansas the only slave State in my Command, I have no hesitation in saying that Reynolds has all things as well in hand as you could ask. He has more troops than are needed, but will continue to reduce as fast as possible. Present to Mrs Grant & the children my Christmas compliments & believe me as ever your friend."—ALS, USG 3. See letter to Edwin M. Stanton, June 20, 1865; letter to Andrew Johnson, Dec. 18, 1865. On the same day, Sherman wrote a lengthy report to Brig. Gen. John A. Rawlins.—ALS, OFH. Printed as *SED*, 39-1-20.

1865, DEC. 23, 10:30 A.M. To Reverend John B. Gibson, Burlington College, Burlington, N. J. "Please inform me the hour my boys left for home."—ALS (telegram sent), DNA, RG 107, Telegrams Collected (Unbound). See John Y. Simon, ed., *The Personal Memoirs of Julia Dent Grant* (New York, 1975), p. 132.

1865, DEC. 26. USG endorsement. "Respectfully refered to the Sec. of War with recommendation that in this case as in all other like cases that occupants of abandoned property be forbidden from injuring their value further than natura[l] wear by occupation until the question of restoration is entirely settled. In the matter of ~~pardon~~ amnesty in this case I have no special recommendation to make."—AES, DNA, RG 105, Land Div., Letters Received, C117. On Dec. 24, William I. Walker, Passenger Dept.,

Baltimore and Ohio Railroad, Washington, D. C., had written to USG. "This will introduce my friend Mr. J. W. Cooke, the gentleman in whose behalf I spoke to you yesterday at Willards Hotel. Mr. Cooke, as I informed you, General, was formerly a Lieut in the U. S. Navy. At the commencement of our late difficulties, he, like many others, tendered his resignation; and, said resignation, was *accepted.* During the War, his property, sixty (60) acres, in Fairfax Co. Va was taken possession of by the Goverment. Mr. Cooke is now *repentent,* and as such, is an applicant for *pardon* at the hands of our magnanimous and kind-hearted President. The position which Mr. Cooke held, brings him, of course, under the head of 'exceptional cases,' and, for that reason, I most earnestly solicit your speedy intervention, which you have kindly promised me in his behalf. The property of Mr. Cooke is now occupied by Freedmen, and he informs me that the beautiful grove surrounding the House, is being cut-down by said occupants. I most earnestly appeal to you to arrest this wanton destruction. Relying upon your kindness and magnamity, I am confident my appeal will not be in vain."— ALS, *ibid.* James W. Cooke resigned from the U.S. Navy as of May 2, 1861, and served in the C.S. Navy during the Civil War. He was pardoned as of Aug. 13, 1866. See *ibid.*, RG 94, Amnesty Papers, Va.

1865, DEC. 29.   To John E. Fehr. "Herewith find a letter for Mr. Vogelsandt . . . and a check for $340, payable to your order and for the benefit of Mr. Vogelsandt. If you will convert the check into a European draft and send it to Vogelsandt and send me a receipt for it you will much oblige me." —Kenneth W. Rendell, Inc., *Autographs and Manuscripts: The American Civil War*, Catalogue No. 98, 1974, p. 44.

1865, DEC. 30.   To Bvt. Brig. Gen. William E. Strong congratulating him on his successes during "the great struggle for National existence."— Richard C. Frajola, Inc., *Manuscripts, Free Franks and Confederate Postal History*, Catalogue, July 10, 1982. On July 20, 1864, Brig. Gen. Walter Q. Gresham, near Decatur, Ga., had written to USG recommending Strong for promotion.—*Ibid.*

[*1865*?].   To Julia Dent Grant. "Please have dinner at 3 p. m. so that I can take ½ past 4 p. m. train and thus get to Phila shortly after dark instead of at midnight. I have got the money for your father."—ALS, DLC-USG.

[*1865–1869, March 3*?].   To Julia Dent Grant. "Gen. Blair, an old Georgetown school mate of mine, will go home with me to dine. It will be half past four before we get there so that five or half past five will be early enough for dinner."—ALS (undated), DLC-USG.

[*1865*?].   Addressee unknown. "I regret that I shall be unable to be present at the meeting of Officers of the Army & Navy, called for the purpose of considering the best means of procuring employment for disabled Soldiers & Sailors &c. I need hardly say that I heartily approve of its object and trust that you will succeed in devising some plan by which work may be provided for all the brave and unfortunate defenders of our country. . . ."—Diana J. Rendell, Inc., Catalogue 3, May 15, 1985, p. 16.

[*1865*?].   President Andrew Johnson note. "If not inconvienent I would be pleased to see Genl Grant a few minutes this morning."—ANS, DLC-Cyrus B. Comstock.

Index

All letters written by USG of which the text was available for use in this volume are indexed under the names of the recipients. The dates of these letters are included in the index as an indication of the existence of text. Abbreviations used in the index are explained on pp. xvi–xx. Individual regts. are indexed under the names of the states in which they originated.